NOTE TO READER

As this book came off the press, we were advised by the printer that 30 percent of the book was printed on paper from a different dye lot. We considered reprinting the book but concluded that the environmentally responsible decision was to use the book as printed. Our apologies for the slight discolouration of the last 30 percent of the book.

Emond Montgomery Publications

The Civil Litigation Process
Cases and Materials

Fifth Edition

Garry D. Watson
Osgoode Hall Law School
York University

Janet E. Mosher
Faculty of Law
University of Toronto

W.A. Bogart
Faculty of Law
University of Windsor

Tim Pinos
Cassels Brock & Blackwell
Toronto

Allan C. Hutchinson
Osgoode Hall Law School
York University

Janet Walker
Osgoode Hall Law School
York University

1999
EMOND MONTGOMERY PUBLICATIONS LIMITED
TORONTO, CANADA

Printed in Canada.

Edited, designed, and typeset by WordsWorth Communications, Toronto.

Canadian Cataloguing in Publication Data

Main entry under title:

The civil litigation process : cases and materials

5th ed.
Fourth ed. published under title: Civil litigation, cases and materials.
Earlier eds. published under title: Canadian civil procedure.
Includes bibliographical references.
ISBN 0-920722-95-4

1. Civil procedure — Canada — Cases. 2. Actions and defenses — Canada — Cases. I. Watson, Garry D. II. Title: Civil litigation, cases and materials.

KE8348.5.W38 1999   347.71′05   C99-931785-7
KF8839.ZA2C58 1999

Acknowledgments

This book, like others of its nature, contains extracts from published materials. We have attempted to request permission from and to acknowledge in the text all sources of such material. We wish to make specific reference here to the authors, publishers, journals, and institutions that have been generous in giving their permission to reproduce works in this text. If we have inadvertently overlooked any acknowledgment, we offer our sincere apologies and undertake to rectify the omission in any further editions.

Alberta Law Review	L. Chartrand, "The Appropriateness of Lawyer as Advocate in Contemporary Aboriginal Justice Initiatives" (1995), XXXIII *Alberta Law Review* 874-81.
Bancroft-Whitney Company	Louisell and Wally, *Modern California Discovery*, 2d ed. (San Francisco: Bancroft-Whitney, 1972).
Andrew Brockett	"New Initiatives in Legal Ethics" (1993), 6(1) *Westminster Affairs* 16.
Canada Law Book	D. Paul Emond, "Alternative Dispute Resolution: A Conceptual Overview," in D. Paul Emond, ed., *Commercial Dispute Resolution: Alternatives to Litigation* (Aurora, ON: Canada Law Book, 1989).
Canadian Bar Review	Garry D. Watson, "Duplicative Litigation: Issue Estoppel, Abuse of Process, and the Death of Mutuality" (1990), 69 *Canadian Bar Review* 623.
Carswell	Garry D. Watson, "Ontario's New Class Proceedings Legislation—An Analysis," in Watson and McGowan, *Ontario Civil Practice 1999* (Toronto: Carswell, 1999).
	Garry D. Watson and Craig Perkins, Holmested and Watson, *Ontario Civil Procedure* (Toronto: Carswell, 1984) (looseleaf).

iii

N. Duclos   "Passion for Justice in a Multicultural Canada"
                                   (unpublished, 1990).

Dana Easthope   "The New Wave of Civil Justice Reform: Efficiency
                                   and Effectiveness" (unpublished, 1997).

Owen M. Fiss   "Against Settlement" (1984), 93 *Yale Law Journal*
                                   1073.

                                   "A Solution in Search of a Problem," in Ontario Law
                                   Reform Commission, *Study Paper on Prospects for
                                   Civil Justice* (Toronto: Ontario Law Reform
                                   Commission, 1995).

Georgetown Journal of Legal   A. Smiley, "Professional Codes and Neutral
    Ethics   Lawyering" (1993), 7 *Georgetown Journal of
                                   Legal Ethics* 213.

The Globe and Mail   Thomas Claridge and Andre Picard, "Tainted-Blood
                                   Suits Settled Out of Court," November 15, 1997.

Harvard Law Review   Abram Chayes, "The Role of the Judge in Public
                                   Law Litigation" (1976), 89 *Harvard Law Review*
                                   1281.

Peter W. Hogg   Peter W. Hogg, *Constitutional Law*, 4th ed. (Toronto:
                                   Carswell, 1997).

Jossey-Bass Inc.   Jay Folberg and Alison Taylor, *Mediation: A
                                   Comprehensive Guide to Resolving Conflicts Without
                                   Litigation* (San Francisco: Jossey-Bass, 1984), 1-15.
                                   Used with permission of publisher
                                   and authors.

Journal of Law and Social   R. Carey, "Useless" (UOSLAS) v. The Bar: The
    Policy   Struggles of the Ottawa Student Clinic To Represent
                                   Battered Women" (1992), 8 *Journal of Law and
                                   Social Policy* 55.

                                   A. Zuckerman, "A Reform of Civil Procedure—
                                   Rationing Procedure Rather Than Access to Justice"
                                   (1955), 22 *Journal of Law and Society*.

Law and Philosophy   Michael Bayles, "Principles for Legal Procedure"
                                   (1986), 5 *Law and Philosophy* 33.

Law and Society Review

William L.F. Felstiner et al., "The Emergence and Transformation of Disputes: Naming, Blaming, Claiming ..." (1980-81), 15 *Law and Society Review* 631.

D. Lepofsky

"Equal Access to Canada's Judicial System for Persons with Disabilities: A Time for Reform" (unpublished, 1995).

Ontario Civil Justice Review

Civil Justice Review, *First Report* (Toronto: Ontario Civil Justice Review, March 1995).

Ontario Law Reform Commission

Ian Morrison and Janet Mosher, "Barriers to Access to Civil Justice for Disadvantaged Groups," in Ontario Law Reform Commission, *Rethinking Civil Justice: Research Studies for the Civil Justice Review* (Toronto: Ontario Law Reform Commission, 1996).

Osgoode Hall Law School

Neil Brooks, "The Judge and the Adversary System," in A. Linden, ed., *The Canadian Judiciary* (Toronto: Osgoode Hall Law School, 1976).

Zemans and Monahan, *From Crisis to Reform: A New Legal Aid Plan for Ontario* (Toronto: Osgoode Hall Law School, 1996).

Oxford University Press

Excerpts from *Courts and Country: The Limits of Litigation and the Social and Political Life of Canada* by W.A. Bogart. Copyright © Oxford University Press Canada 1994. Reprinted by permission of Oxford University Press Canada.

S. Prichard

J. Robert and S. Prichard, "A Systemic Approach to Comparative Law: The Effect of Cost, Fee, and Financing Rules on the Development of the Substantive Law" (1988), 17 *Journal of Legal Studies* 451.

Queen's Printer

Canada, Report on the Royal Commission on Aboriginal Peoples, "Governance," in *Restructuring the Relationship*, vol. 2 (Ottawa: Queen's Printer, 1996).

Queen's Printer

"Public Inquiry into the Administration of Justice and Aboriginal People," in *The Justice System and Aboriginal People*, vol. 1 (Winnipeg: Queen's Printer, 1991).

Report of the Ontario Legal Aid Review, "A Blueprint for Publicly Funded Legal Services" (Toronto: Queen's Printer, 1997).

J. Robert

J. Robert and S. Prichard, "A Systemic Approach to Comparative Law: The Effect of Cost, Fee, and Financing Rules on the Development of the Substantive Law" (1988), 17 *Journal of Legal Studies* 451.

Russell Sage Foundation

M. Galanter, "Adjudication, Litigation and Related Phenomena," in Leon Lipson and Stanton Wheeler, eds., *Law and Social Sciences* (New York: Russell Sage Foundation, 1986), 152, at 152-60.

Texas Technical Law Review

D. Kennedy, "The Responsibility of Lawyers for the Justice of Their Causes" (1987), 18 *Texas Technical Law Review* 1157-63.

Thomson Canada Limited

Peter W. Hogg, *Constitutional Law*, 4th ed. (Toronto: Carswell, 1997). Reprinted by permission of Carswell, a division of Thomson Canada Limited.

Marvin A. Zuker, *Ontario Small Claims Court Practice* (Toronto: Carswell, 1991). Reprinted by permission of Carswell, a division of Thomson Canada Limited.

M. Trebilcock

"The Case for Contingent Fees: The Ontario Legal Profession Rethinks Its Position" (1989), 15 *Canadian Business Law Journal* 360-68.

UCLA Law Review

C. Menkel-Meadow, "For and Against Settlement: Uses and Abuses of the Mandatory Settlement Conference" (1985), 33 *UCLA Law Review* 485.

University of Chicago Law Review

J.H. Langbein, "The German Advantage in Civil Procedure" (1985), 52 *University of Chicago Law Review* 823-66.

University of Toronto Press

Kent Roach, "Teaching Procedures: The Fiss/ Weinrib Debate in Practice" (1991), 41 *University of Toronto Law Journal* 247.

Martha Shaffer, "Divorce Mediation: A Feminist Perspective" (1988), 46 *University of Toronto Faculty Law Review* 349.

Ernest Weinrib, "Adjudication and Public Values: Fiss's Critique of Corrective Justice" (1989), 39 *University of Toronto Law Journal* 1, 1-18. Reprinted by permission of University of Toronto Press Incorporated.

Virginia Law Review

S. Ellman, "Client-Centredness Multiplied" (1992), 78 *Virginia Law Review* 1103.

Garry D. Watson

"The New Wave of Civil Justice Reform: Efficiency and Effectiveness" (unpublished, 1997).

Windsor Yearbook of Access to Justice

Rod MacDonald, "Access to Justice and Law Reform" (1990), 10 *Windsor Yearbook of Access to Justice* 287.

Wydrzynski, Hildebrandt, and Blonde, "The CAW Prepaid Legal Services Plan: A Case Study of an Alternative Funding and Delivery Method for Legal Services" (1991), 10 *Windsor Yearbook of Access to Justice* 22-78.

Wisconsin Law Review

William Simon, "The Ideology of Advocacy: Procedural Justice and Professional Ethics" (1978), *Wisconsin Law Review* 29.

The Women's Press

Lorenne Clark and Debra Lewis, *Rape: The Price of Coercive Sexuality* (Toronto: The Women's Press, 1977).

The Yale Law Journal

Rob Atkinson, "How the Butler Was Made To Do It: The Perverted Professionalism of *The Remains of the Day*." Reprinted by permission of The Yale Law Journal Company and Fred B. Rothman & Company from *The Yale Law Journal*, vol. 105, pages 177-220.

The Yale Law Journal   Owen M. Fiss, "Against Settlement." Reprinted by
                              permission of The Yale Law Journal Company and
                              Fred B. Rothman & Company from *The Yale Law
                              Journal*, vol. 93, pages 1075-90.

                              Charles Fried, "The Lawyer as Friend: The Moral
                              Foundations in the Lawyer–Client Relation."
                              Reprinted by permission of The Yale Law Journal
                              Company and Fred B. Rothman & Company from
                              The Yale Law Journal, vol. 85, pages 1060-89.

Yale University Press   T. Tyler, *Why People Obey the Law* (New Haven,
                              CT: Yale University Press, 1990).

Summary Table of Contents

Detailed Table of Contents

Preface to the Fifth Edition

This casebook is the long-awaited revision of Watson, Bogart, Hutchinson, Mosher, and Roach, *Civil Litigation: Cases and Materials*, 4th edition, published in 1991. The departure of Kent Roach from the authorship team and the arrival of Janet Walker and Tim Pinos did not so much signal a change in direction for the book as it did the continuing expansion and increasing complexity of the subject.

Building on themes and issues presented in the 4th edition, we have endeavoured to keep pace with current developments in both the litigation process itself and the critical appreciation of it that has fuelled the movement to alternative forms of dispute resolution and other significant initiatives. As well as a burgeoning literature, a great deal has happened since the release of the 4th edition—new rules have been promulgated, such as those in Ontario dealing with deemed undertakings, mandatory mediation, case management, and simplified procedure; class proceedings have been established by legislation in Ontario and British Columbia; and legal aid has been significantly reformed. As a result, the revisions to the 4th edition have necessarily been substantial in technical detail and structural organization. Nevertheless, the basic approach of the book remains constant—to offer a contextual and critical account of the various processes by which civil disputes are resolved, with especial emphasis on litigation.

In presenting the traditional concerns of litigation and the recent developments, we have tried to strike a balance between the practical and theoretical dimensions of the subject. Accordingly, we have sought to consider the current issues in sufficient detail to address the real-life concerns of litigators and to explore the underlying principles in sufficient depth to permit meaningful reflection on the critical fundamentals of dispute resolution. Further, in pursuing this ambitious project, we have been mindful of the fact that this casebook is intended to provide materials that are manageable in scope for use in an LLB course on this subject, in many cases a first-year required course. With this in mind, we have struggled to confine this edition to the length of the previous edition through rigorous application of the rule that for every page of material sought to be added the remaining work had to be reduced by a page. As can be imagined, this provided many an occasion for lively debate among the authors. On this note, we pride ourselves on representing a diverse range of approaches to the subject and hope that this will prompt useful and challenging readings for professors and their students alike. Also, we have tried to design the book so that individual teachers might still be able to take up the material in whatever order best suits their own teaching commitments and approaches.

We are profoundly grateful to a number of people in the completion of this book—previous co-authors whose influence and work remains influential; the editors and staff at Emond Montgomery for their forbearance in the lengthy period during which this work was produced and their expert handling of the first digital manuscript of this work; and the many students who worked on the preparation of this and earlier editions.

G.D.W.
W.A.B.
A.C.H.
J.E.M.
T.P.
J.W.

July1999

Table of Cases

A page number in bold-face type indicates that the text of the case or a portion thereof is reproduced. A page number in light-face type indicates that the case is quoted briefly, referred to, or mentioned.

PART I

Overview

Introduction to Civil Actions
and Courts

I. INTRODUCTION

Chapter 1 introduces some of the fundamentals of civil litigation. This basic information will ground students in the essentials of civil procedure and the courts. In addition, it provides a useful overview for the theoretical and policy issues raised in part 2, Theory and Context of Civil Procedure.

The chapter begins with 3 narratives—stories based on actual cases. The narratives provide concrete examples of human conflict that can ripen into litigation; they also raise many issues that will be examined in detail in later chapters. They ask overarching questions about procedure that are revisited, at appropriate places. Subsequent chapters will refer to the narratives to illustrate issues that the chapters raise.

The next section describes briefly and simply the main stages of a civil action, first, by means of a concise overview, and second, by charting those main stages. Obviously, many important details are ignored and will be pursued in following chapters. However, this section provides a concise account of the main elements of civil litigation so that students can acquire a good sense of the "forest" before labouring to master the intricacies of the "trees." In addition, the section provides an important context to equip students to respond to the more abstract discussions pursued in part 2.

The final section provides a brief description of the origins and the functions of Canadian courts. Again, the purpose is to provide important basic information to ground discussion of specific issues regarding the role of civil courts that will be pursued at many points later in the casebook.

II. THREE NARRATIVES

A problem that we have encountered in teaching an introductory course on civil litigation is that students (and sometimes teachers) with little or no practical experience in litigation often have a difficult time relating to the diverse and human side of dispute resolution and litigation. What follows are three narratives based on actual cases. They tell the stories of people involved in very different kinds of disputes. At this stage, try to understand the nature of their disputes and develop a sense of the dispute resolution options open to them. Questions throughout the book will refer back to the problems raised by these three narratives.

Later, you will encounter many of the intricate questions these people would face were they to have their dispute litigated in court. Appendix I contains various litigation material developed with regard to the protagonist of the first narrative, Albert Starr.

A. Albert Starr

Albert Starr is 32 years old and married, with one child, 4 years old. He has grade-12 education and, at the time of this incident, had been a salesman for three years. Before that, he was a bookkeeper in the same company. He lives near Belleville, Ontario where he was born and raised.

He is intelligent—perhaps more intelligent than his grade-12 education and job would suggest. He is of a serious nature and has always been considered by his friends and family as somewhat withdrawn and lethargic. His job as a salesman requires him to travel, to meet people, and to do a certain amount of entertaining. Because of his withdrawn and reserved nature, the job doesn't really suit him, but he doesn't know what else to do. He is well liked by his employer who recognizes, however, that it might have been a mistake to put him in a position where he had a higher profile with the public. In other words, Albert Starr was a competent bookkeeper, perhaps too bright for the position; as a salesman, he was somewhat over his head—not for lack of wit or intelligence, but because he finds personal contact somewhat difficult. For some time before the incident, he had been considering a change of job, but had been unable to find alternate employment.

On the evening of January 18, 1995, Starr drove to the Richardson House, approximately half a mile from his home. The Richardson House is in the country, approximately two miles from the Belleville city limits. It is accessible only by car. It is primarily a beer parlour, although it offers a few hotel rooms.

Starr had been a regular customer at the Richardson House for the last two or three years. He was well known to the manager, George Richardson, who came on duty on the evening of January 18 as manager and tap man at approximately 7 o'clock in the evening. Starr sat by himself at a table approximately 20 feet from Richardson, behind the bar, where Richardson could observe him at all times. Starr came to the hotel at approximately 7:30 p.m. and left at approximately 10:30 p.m., during which period he was served at least 10 beers, possibly as many as 16, by two waiters.

On a previous occasion, about six months before this incident, Richardson had asked Starr to leave the hotel because he had become intoxicated and somewhat abusive to other patrons. On the evening of January 18, at approximately 10:25, Richardson became aware that Starr had consumed to excess and that he was becoming abusive to several patrons. In particular, he had been troubling a group of younger customers, two men and two women, who were taking exception to some of the remarks he was making to them.

At about 10:25, Richardson went over to Starr and told him to leave. Starr stood up, obviously unsteady, and indicated that he was not ready to go, that he wanted to sit for a while "to steady down." Richardson took him by the arm and escorted him from the beverage room to the door leading out to the parking lot. Richardson asked Starr how he planned to get home; Starr mumbled that since he was too drunk to walk he would have to drive, and that he had no money for a taxi. Richardson waited at the door while Starr struggled to his car. Richardson could see that Starr was intoxicated and that he was having difficulty walking to the car, finding his keys, and getting the car started. Richardson says that the reason he waited until Starr got into the car was to make sure that he would not try to come back into the beverage room. Starr managed to get the car going and drive out of the hotel parking lot, but, within a few hundred yards, the car went off the road and struck a tree. Starr has no recollection of anything that happened after he got into his car.

In the collision with the tree, Starr sustained a broken wrist that has adequately healed. He also struck his head on the windshield and suffered a minor concussion. He had not been wearing a seatbelt. He was found, unconscious, shortly after the impact and taken to Belleville General Hospital where he was examined, treated, and discharged within two days, his wrist in a cast and apparently recovered from the bump on his head. Starr was convicted in criminal court of impaired driving as a result of the accident.

Starr returned to work within one week of the incident, but experienced great difficulty in accomplishing his normal work. He was unable to perform his salesman's functions and began to suffer from severe headaches approximately two weeks after the incident. He describes the headaches as involving his whole head and a feeling of pressure, as if his head were in a vice. The headaches made it impossible for him to continue working and after approximately two-and-a-half weeks of trying to work, he stayed at home, receiving disability benefits for the period allowed by his insurance. He is still experiencing severe headaches although they have become less frequent. However, he is entirely unable to function and has not returned to work. He has no interest in returning to work or in finding another job. At present, his wife, who was not engaged in paid employment before the accident, is working and supporting the family. Starr stays at home looking after their child and is extremely withdrawn and lethargic. He is unwilling to see friends and shows very little interest in life. He finds it difficult to concentrate on any task he undertakes, is irritable, depressed, and weeps easily. He often feels faint, spends prolonged periods in bed, suffers from excessive sweating, and says that he has recurring dreams of being in a car accident.

Starr's general practitioner referred him to a psychiatrist. The psychiatrist examined him on two occasions and concluded that Starr is suffering from a neurosis brought on by the trauma of the accident on January 18, 1995. The psychiatrist stated that the neurosis was triggered by the accident, but was not solely caused by the accident. According to the psychiatrist, Starr had definite emotional and psychological problems before the incident, but had been coping with these problems. The psychiatrist stated that, as a result of the trauma of the collision, Starr is now entirely unable to cope.

Starr has refused to undergo a course of treatment recommended by the psychiatrist because he is convinced that his problem is of a purely physical nature.

NOTES AND QUESTIONS

1. Litigation arising out of motor vehicle accidents has long constituted a significant component of Canadian court dockets. In recent years, however, this has begun to change as various provinces have introduced "no-fault" auto insurance schemes that limit or preclude access to the courts. In Ontario, for example, before 1990, not-at-fault victims of auto accidents had full access to the courts to sue for damages and a modest scheme of no-fault benefits supplemented this unrestricted tort access. However, legislative changes introduced in 1990 marked a shift away from tort and toward no-fault benefits as the primary mechanism for compensating auto accident victims. The right to sue was greatly restricted. Indeed, it has been estimated that only 6 percent of accident victims met the legislative threshold to pursue a tort claim. Since 1990, the no-fault and tort mix has twice been changed and, at present, there exists a rather complex relationship between the two with a range of limitations on the right to sue. A separate dispute resolution scheme to address disputes over no-fault benefits between insured persons and their insurers was created in 1990 and modified slightly in 1996. The scheme includes many of the dispute resolution processes we examine in chapter 4, "Challenges to the Traditional Model"—mediation, arbitration, and neutral evalutaion. The legislation also creates specific procedures governing tort claims arising from auto accidents.

The debates over no-fault versus tort engage questions central to much of the material found in chapters 2 to 4—what are the goals of dispute resolution (compensation, deterrence, or corrective justice) and what are the best vehicles for achieving those goals?

2. The court file for the Albert Starr case is contained in Appendix I. The Albert Starr narrative is loosely based on the facts of a case that was litigated to the Supreme Court of Canada: *Menow v. Jordan House Hotel Ltd.*, [1974] SCR 239.

3. Assuming you were retained by Albert Starr, what advice would you give him? Assuming the decision is made to make a claim against Richardson House, and a letter is sent informing Richardson House of the claim, what advice would you give Richardson House if you were retained by them?

4. What if the facts are changed slightly? Assume that after he drove out of the hotel parking lot, Starr was involved in a head-on collision with another car that had suddenly swerved to miss a poorly lit road repair obstruction put there by the local Township. This other vehicle was driven by Mike Sandelli, who was also seriously injured in the collision. Given these facts, would your advice to Starr be any different? (What if Mike was an under-age driver who was joy riding in his parents' car without their consent?) If you were acting for Richardson House what advice would you give it?

5. Note that either version of the Starr facts represents a civil dispute in which it is likely that Starr will seek a transfer of funds from somebody else to him as compensation for his injuries. But, as we will see, a claimant will not always seek a transfer of funds.

6. Legally, is Starr's claim against Richardson House an "easy" or "difficult" one? Is it "innovative" or "ordinary"? What, if any, social benefits could arise from a successful claim by Starr against Richardson House? Is such a lawsuit a good way to provide compensation to Starr and his family? Is it a good way to prevent such injuries in the future?

B. Jane Doe

Jane Doe comes to you for legal advice in July 1997. She describes herself as 35 years old, frightened, depressed, and extremely angry. She tells you that she has worked for a number of years as a free-lance still photographer in the film industry in Toronto. She goes on to recount the horrific events of August 24, 1996.

In the summer of 1996, Jane was living alone in an apartment on the second floor of an apartment building in the downtown neighbourhood of Church and Wellesley streets in the city of Toronto. She had lived there for two years, had spent a lot of time and energy fixing up the place, and had come to feel at home and safe in her surroundings. One of the most attractive features of the apartment was a balcony—it was a fabulous place to relax in the evenings, a space to enjoy the evening air. Access to the balcony was by way of a door from Jane's living room, a door that she always locked securely before going to bed or before leaving her apartment.

On the night of August 24, 1996, Jane was sexually assaulted in her apartment by a man who entered her home by climbing up the outside of the building and forcibly entering through the locked balcony door. He wore a mask, held a knife to her throat, and threatened to kill her. He covered her head and sexually assaulted her. He then escaped through the front door. Jane immediately called the police, who shortly thereafter arrived at her apartment, questioned her, and then took her to Women's College Hospital.

On October 3, 1996, Harrison Smith was arrested by the police and charged with the sexual assault of Jane Doe. Jane was called by the Crown to give evidence at the preliminary hearing of the charges against Smith; at this time, she learned that Smith had also been charged with several other counts of sexual assault. Each of these other counts had occurred within a year before the assault on Jane Doe and in her immediate neighbourhood. In each and every case the attacker had entered through a balcony door, on the second or third floor of an apartment building in the Church and Wellesley area. In every case it was a woman living alone who was the victim of the attack. The attacker wore a mask on every occasion, threatened the life of each woman while holding a knife to her throat and covered her head while assaulting her. As Jane heard this account of horror, described time and time again during the course of the preliminary hearing—each time the same account with the only significant change being the name of the victim—she became increasingly infuriated with the conduct of the police. If the police had known all of this information, had known in effect that she was a very likely victim for attack, why had no one warned her?

Smith entered a plea of guilty to all of the counts against him shortly after the completion of the preliminary hearing. The police, content that they "had their man," and believing that the matter was thus at an end, closed their file on Jane Doe. But Jane is not at all content. Of course, the assault itself is something that Jane will never lay to rest—indeed, she describes to you in vivid detail the horrible nightmares that frequently interrupt her sleep, the bouts of anxiety and depression from which she suffers, and the never-ending sense of vulnerability that she feels. But Jane is also deeply disturbed by the manner in which the police conducted the case and strongly believes that the police file must be reopened and subject to public scrutiny. Had they only warned her of the threat lurking in her neighbourhood, she believed that the events of August 24 would probably never have happened.

You take on the case for Jane and discover in the course of your inquiries that two members of the Metropolitan Toronto police force, Constables Jones and MacKay, undertook an investigation in early August 1996, before the assault on Jane. As a result of this investigation, they identified those apartments that would be the likely targets of the "serial" rapist. The description of the likely targets reads like an account of Jane's home—second- and third-floor apartments with balcony access occupied by single women in the Church-Wellesley area. Indeed, assume the police had prepared a list of likely victims and Jane's name was included in this list.

When you question Constable Jones about the apparent failure of the police to provide any kind of warning to the women most at risk, he concedes that Jane and other women similarly situated to her were likely targets and that none of them was given a warning nor provided with any information regarding the circumstances of the attacks in their neighbourhood. When you press him for an explanation he suggests that "warning the women would cause hysteria on the part of the women and alert the suspect to flee and not engage in further criminal activity."

NOTES AND QUESTIONS

1. This narrative is loosely based on a case that was litigated in the Ontario courts and the facts of which occurred in 1986. In the actual litigation, the case proceeded under the name of "Jane Doe" in order to protect the identity of the plaintiff. In the narrative, the names of the other individuals involved have been altered.

A preliminary procedure (a motion) challenging the basis of Doe's action against the police was resolved in her favor: *Jane Doe v. Bd. of Comm. of Police for the Municipality of Metro. Toronto* (1990), 74 OR (2d) 225 (motion for leave to appeal denied, (1991), 1 OR (3d) 416 (CA)). The court held that the novelty of the cause of action should not prevent it from going forward. The case went to trial and resulted in a decision for the plaintiff in July 1998; see *Doe v. Metropolitan Toronto (Municipality)*

Commissioners of Police (1998), 39 OR (3d) 487; 160 DLR (4th) 697 (Gen. Div.) and K. Honey, "Police Failed Rape Victim, Judge Rules," *The Globe and Mail*, July 4, 1998. The plaintiff received $220,000, including $175,000 for breach of other Charter rights.

2. What advice will you give Jane Doe? Is what she "wants" similar to, or different from, what Albert Starr wants? If it is different, how and why is it different and is there a broader or narrower range of alternative strategies available to you than in Starr's case? In chapter 4, "Challenges to the Traditional Model," some of the alternative strategies open to Jane Doe, such as making a complaint to a police complaints agency or a human rights commission, will be examined.

3. Jane Doe's suit may be viewed as being quite innovative and closely related to recent societal changes, such as increased concerns about violence toward women and society's increased willingness to concern itself with how the police operate. But recall that 20 years ago, when the case on which the Albert Starr narrative is based was litigated, the imposition of civil liability on a publican whose customer got drunk and then injured himself was considered quite novel.

C. Harriette Nandise

Harriette Nandise is a 22-year-old computer programmer who four years ago bought a GM Milano car. This was Nandise's first car and she had gathered a lot of information about the available choices within her price range. She was attracted to the Milano because of its price and because General Motors (GM), in its advertising campaign, constantly promoted its reliability and care-free maintenance.

Harriette purchased the Milano from Hanks Autos in Windsor for $13,000. Unfortunately, trouble started almost as soon as she bought it. Basically, the car never operated satisfactorily. There was nearly always something wrong with it and she took it back repeatedly to Hanks. At first, Hanks obliged and did repairs without charge. However, after a year, Hanks told Ms Nandise that it would no longer do repairs free of charge because the warranty had expired. In any event, Hanks went bankrupt shortly thereafter.

Things went on this way until about a year ago when Harriette became so exasperated that she decided to trade the Milano. She took it to several car dealers handling a variety of makes of cars. Their reactions varied, except in one respect—they all commented on the fact that Milanos now had a notorious reputation, and they would not be able to give much for a trade-in because Milanos were very, very difficult to sell as used cars. She then tried to sell it privately, and after several months she finally sold it for $3,000. This struck her as shockingly low for a three-and-a-half year old car.

She mentioned all this to an acquaintance, Shiranda Singh. Dr. Singh is dean of arts at the University of Windsor and is also vice-president of the Consumers Association of Canada (CAC). CAC had been monitoring the experience with Milanos ever since it started receiving numerous complaints about their chronic unreliability and their depressed resale value.

Shiranda put Harriette in touch with Jean-Paul Tousignant, a lawyer in Windsor who has worked with CAC in the past. Jean-Paul told Harriette when they met that he believed her claim would be worth at least $2,000, reflecting the depressed resale value, and assuming GM's liability could be established. However, he said that there were approximately 5,000 Milanos sold in Canada before GM stopped making them two years ago, and he wanted to see whether it might be possible to get a large group of people to sue and share the considerable legal fees the suit would entail. He promised he would get back to her once he had more information. In the meantime, he secured her consent to discuss and publicize her experience in order to create public interest and support for claims for compensation against GM.

Three weeks ago, Harriette received a visit from Pauline Blott-Turner, who introduced herself as a claims adjuster from GM. The result of the meeting was that Blott-Turner offered Harriette a settlement of $1,500 in return for Nandise agreeing not to discuss her complaint, or the terms of settlement, with any third party. Blott-Turner said that if this settlement was not acceptable GM would consider taking legal action against Nandise and her agents for defaming GM and disrupting its competitiveness in the market due to the publicizing of the allegations surrounding Nandise's purchase and resale of her Milano.

NOTES AND QUESTIONS

1. This narrative is loosely based on a case previously litigated to the Supreme Court of Canada on preliminary issues: *Naken v. General Motors of Canada Ltd.* (1983), 144 DLR 385.

2. As Tousignant, what advice are you going to give Harriette? In view of the events that have taken place, are you still in a position to advise Harriette?

3. What if the offer made by Blott-Turner were different? If it were made to you and Nandise and were to the effect that GM would pay Nandise $2,500 and you $5,000 for your costs to date, in return for an agreement that (1) she would not discuss her complaint or the terms of the settlement with any third party, and (2) that you would agree not to act for any other person seeking compensation against GM in respect of Milano automobiles?

4. Is Harriette's claim an individual or a group claim? Is it really an individual claim that the lawyer Tousignant seeks to "transform" into a group claim? Does it make any difference if it is an individual or group claim? Either way is the claim still one merely seeking a "transfer of funds or compensation?"

5. Does it become more of a "group" claim if GM is still selling the car through an advertising campaign that promotes its reliability and care-free maintenance, and what is sought is to stop GM making such claims? What steps could be taken to stop GM in these circumstances? Is civil litigation the best option? If resort is to be had to a civil action does there need to be a group of plaintiffs, or can Harriette (or Tousignant) sue alone?

III. THE STRUCTURE OF A CIVIL ACTION

This section sets out the main stages of a civil action. It is a brief and simple overview. Many important details and issues will be covered in subsequent chapters. The goal is to provide an overall account of a civil action in order to orient students in terms of the more detailed and specific treatment of issues that follow in other sections of the casebook.

The overview is provided in two ways: first, by means of a concise description, and second, by setting out the main stages in a chart. However, before contemplating litigation there are important preliminary considerations.

A. Considerations Before Commencing Litigation

When a client comes to a lawyer with a potentially litigious problem, the prudent lawyer will not immediately and automatically commence an action on behalf of his or her client. Litigation is expensive, time-consuming, and, when contested, its outcome is usually uncertain. Before resorting to litigation, the responsible lawyer will explore alternatives and give close consideration to a number of matters.

A lawyer will usually advise his or her client to explore the possibility of settlement before bringing an action. Often a client will have attempted to reach a private settlement before he or she consults a lawyer. No doubt, he or she appreciates and wants to avoid the expenses and risks of litigation. Indeed, many disputes of the kind that courts entertain never reach a lawyer's office—they are disposed of by agreement between the parties themselves. Most complaints are legitimate, and many prospective defendants, realizing that they will probably not defeat an action brought against them, capitulate or offer terms that the prospective plaintiff finds acceptable. Whether or not the client has attempted a compromise for his or her claim, a lawyer who is asked to act in the dispute will normally canvass the possibility of settlement before bringing an action. At the very least, he or she will take the step of sending a letter of demand on behalf of the client. Commencing an action is usually a measure of final resort, taken after other efforts to persuade the defendant to remedy the plaintiff's grievance have failed.

The decision to sue is influenced by a variety of factors and a lawyer should give these careful consideration before advising his or her client to institute proceedings. The lawyer will first need to satisfy himself or herself that the client has a reasonable prospect of winning the action. This involves a determination that on the facts as the client has stated them there is a complaint for which the law gives a remedy. This is a question for the substantive law. Next, if the defendant will dispute the facts at trial, the lawyer will have to conclude that the probabilities favour the court accepting the client's version of the facts. (Of course, it should be kept in mind that there is always the possibility that the defendant will not defend the action, which means that the plaintiff can obtain judgment without a trial. Also, often the mere commencement of proceedings will suffice to persuade a recalcitrant defendant to settle the claim.)

Second, the client should understand the financial consequences not only of losing but also of winning the action; there still may be considerable expenses to pay. The lawyer has a responsibility to explain these consequences (which will be examined in chapter 2, "The Value of Procedure") to the client before he embarks on litigation.

Finally, it must be remembered that success in an action is one thing, recovering on a favourable judgment another. Success will be illusory if defendants cannot satisfy the judgment and there is no prospect of them ever doing so. Consequently, before commencing an action and incurring the expenses involved in litigation, it will be prudent to make some enquiry as to the ability of the defendant to satisfy a judgment. There will usually be no problem if the plaintiff seeks an order from the court directing the defendant to perform some act or to refrain from committing some act. The failure or refusal of a party to obey such an order amounts to a contempt and the court has ample power to compel compliance by fine or imprisonment. However, it is not a contempt of court to fail to satisfy a judgment for a money sum. The defendant can only be compelled to obey such a judgment if he or she has sufficient assets within the jurisdiction. The law provides a party who has a money judgment in his or her favour with a variety of methods of execution for reaching the assets of the other party within the jurisdiction.

The ability of the defendant to satisfy a judgment is therefore an essential matter to be considered by a plaintiff in deciding whether to commence or continue an action. And the client has to remember that he or she will be liable for his or her own lawyers' fees in any event; failure to recover from the defendant does not excuse payment of these costs. In many tort situations, typically the automobile accident case, the prospective defendant will be insured against liability. In such circumstances the extent of the personal assets of the defendant will not be material for the insurer will satisfy the amount of any judgment against its insured to the extent of the policy limits.

Once a litigant and his or her legal advisor arrive at the decision to sue, steps must be taken to commence the legal proceedings.

B. Concise Description of the Main Stages of a Civil Action

1. Deciding To Sue

What steps must be followed to initiate a lawsuit and properly guide its journey to the courtroom?

All plaintiffs must first determine whether or not they have a good *cause of action*—that is, a claim that will be recognized in the substantive law. In reality, this and most subsequent steps are carried out by their lawyers and the plaintiffs' ultimate decision to sue depends heavily on their lawyers' advice.

In determining whether plaintiffs have a valid cause of action, their lawyers will assume for the moment that they will be able to prove, through evidence that is admissible under the laws of evidence, the facts on which their complaints are based. Thus, in the Albert Starr narrative, it will be assumed that Albert can prove that Richardson was aware that he had consumed alcohol to excess and was going to drive and that Albert had asked to stay before he was ejected from Richardson House. Similarly, Jane Doe and her lawyers would assume that they could prove that the police had developed a profile of the targets of the rapist that included women in Jane's circumstances and that they did not warn these women because of a fear of hysteria. The lawyers must then determine, given these facts, whether the law will recognize that a legal wrong has been done and afford their clients some form of relief, often, but not always, by way of damages. If so, they have a good cause of action.

It must be noted that in cases raising innovative legal claims, lawyers cannot be certain that they have a good cause of action. Albert Starr's claim about the publican's liability for his own drunken driving was innovative when it was first asserted. It is now established law, but the liability of social hosts who allow the guests to drink and drive is still an open question. In the 1990s, Jane Doe's claims to equal and non-discriminatory protection from the police are innovative. When a client pursues an innovative claim, we will see that the defendant has an option at a preliminary stage of the litigation to ask the court to strike out the claim as disclosing "no reasonable cause of action"—that is, no cause of action known in law.

2. Selecting the Appropriate Court

All plaintiffs, in most provinces, must decide in which court they will commence their lawsuit. The choice is relatively simple in Ontario. There is now a court of general civil jurisdiction, the Superior Court of Ontario. This court has a branch known as the Small Claims Court. Its monetary jurisdiction is prescribed by regulation but presently its limits are $6,000. There are also other courts with civil jurisdiction in Ontario, but they hear only family law matters. In a few other provinces there are still two levels of court with general civil jurisdiction. The lower level (usually called the County or District Court) usually has a limited monetary jurisdiction while the higher (usually called the Supreme or Superior Court) has no such limit.

Two basic factors will determine in which court the action is brought. The first is that the court have jurisdiction over the subject matter of the case. The Superior Court of Ontario has all the power and authority exercised historically by courts of common law and equity in Ontario and England. The plaintiffs would only be concerned with subject matter jurisdiction in limited circumstances. They might have to bring certain claims involving federal subject matter in the Federal Court of Canada and some family law disputes in a specialized family law court.

Second, the plaintiffs would be concerned with any limits on the jurisdiction of the courts to award remedies such as damages. The plaintiffs in the Harriet Nandise case could potentially bring their claims in the Small Claims division of the Superior Court of Ontario if they claimed relatively modest amounts. Both Albert Starr and Jane Doe, however, would sue in the Superior Court of Ontario because their claims involve damages over the Small Claims Court's monetary jurisdiction. If Jane Doe sought relief other than damages—for example, an injunction requiring the police to issue warnings—she would also have to go to the Superior Court of Ontario, which as a court of equity has the power to issue such orders.

3. Commencing the Proceeding

a. *Actions*

Until January 1985, plaintiffs commenced their action by means of a document known as a writ of summons. Using a standard form, they prepared the writ of summons (usually referred to as the "writ"), and then attended at the court office where a clerk issued the writ. To do so, the clerk collected a fee from them, affixed a seal to the original writ, assigned a number to it, dated it, and signed the name of the registrar of the court on the writ. The clerk retained a copy of the writ for the court files and returned the original to them.

The writ of summons has been abolished in Ontario, as it has been in many other jurisdictions. Actions are now commenced by statement of claim, issued by the clerk in the same manner as described. In case of urgency, an action may be commenced by notice of action, to be followed shortly by a statement of claim.

The statement of claim will contain a description of the parties to the action—the plaintiff and the defendant. For example, Albert Starr will be the plaintiff and Richardson House and George Richardson the defendant. The action will be known as *Albert Starr v. Richardson House and George Richardson*. This description of the parties to the action is called the "title of proceeding," formerly "style of cause."

Starr must now serve a copy of the claim on Richardson by means of personal service. To do this, somebody will have to locate Richardson and hand him a copy of the claim. Because the co-defendant, Richardson House, is a corporation, it will only be necessary to leave the statement of claim with an officer, director, or agent of the corporation, or with a person at their place of business who appears to be in control or management. If Jane Doe sues a municipality, a board, or commission, personal service may involve leaving a copy of the statement of claim with a person in authority.

Usually, the plaintiff will engage the service of the sheriff's office or employ a private process server to carry out service. However, Starr's lawyer may attend to the service of the claim. The rules also provide for certain alternatives to personal service (by mail or by leaving a copy at defendant's residence). Should Starr be unable to locate Richardson for the purpose of serving him in the manner required, or if it appears that Richardson is purposely evading service, Starr can ask the court to grant permission to allow him to effect substituted service. In this way, the court will permit service in a manner other than by personal service, perhaps by an advertisement in a newspaper.

The statement of claim will contain a formal notice to the defendant that, if no steps are taken to defend, judgment may be given by default.

b. *Simplified Procedures in an Action*

Some superior courts have rules that attempt to simplify procedures where comparatively small amounts of money are involved—for example, in Ontario $25,000 or less. Details vary with different courts that use this device. However, generally these procedures attempt to reduce costs and time associated with discovery (see below). The procedures also attempt to eliminate the need for a trial altogether—for example, by encouraging the use of summary judgment (see below). In addition, if a trial is required, the rights of parties may be circumscribed—for example, regarding cross-examination of witnesses in order to save time and to minimize costs.

c. *Applications*

The plaintiffs may also have the option of starting proceedings by way of an application rather than an action. Applications are generally used with respect to matters where it is unlikely that there will be any material fact in dispute (that would require oral evidence for its determination). As will be examined, they differ from actions by their use of written evidence known as affidavits. Thus, most stages of an action do not apply to application. For example, there are no pleadings nor is there a trial in application. Given the factually contentious nature of their claims and the need for oral evidence, all plaintiffs in the narratives would likely commence proceedings by way of an action.

4. Asserting Claims and Defences: Pleadings

How detailed should the statement of claim be? Obviously, the degree of detail could vary from a very simple allegation to a detailed and complex narrative of what the plaintiff alleges took place. Thus, Albert Starr may state, "Richardson injured me and owes $50,000." On the other hand, he might give a complete account of the accident itself and elaborate in detail the evidence by which he intends to prove this account. Under our system of civil procedure, he should adopt neither of these alternatives. Rather, his statement of claim must contain only a statement in a summary form of the facts on which he relies in support of his case and a statement of the relief sought. Thus, the statement of claim will contain Starr's allegation of the bare facts constituting the cause of action, but not the evidence by which he expects to be able to prove those facts. Through the vehicle of the statement of claim, Starr will notify Richardson of the basis of his complaint.

Another purpose served by the statement of claim is to permit the court to determine at an early stage whether the plaintiff has a good cause of action. If the facts alleged in the statement of claim do not disclose a cause of action, the defendant is entitled to ask the court to dismiss the action. The rationale for this is that even given that Starr may be able to prove each and every fact alleged in the statement of claim, if those facts do not constitute a cause of action, the court will not grant him relief. Consequently, it would be unreasonable to require the defendant to incur the expense and inconvenience of a trial in which he is bound to succeed.

After Starr has delivered his statement of claim, Richardson, if he wishes to avoid default judgment, must file his own pleading, which is known as a *statement of defence*. What must it contain? Like Starr, Richardson must allege the facts on which he relies in support of his defence. In addition, defendants must also indicate which of the allegations in the statement of claim are in dispute.

After Richardson has served his statement of defence, Starr, if he wishes to respond, may deliver a further pleading known as a *reply*.

There are other pleadings that may be available to a defendant in some cases. If a defendant has sustained some damage as a result of a plaintiff's conduct, then he or she may assert a *counterclaim* against the plaintiff. This document, like the statement of claim, will allege the facts relied on; must be served on the plaintiff; and may be subject to a reply and a defence by the plaintiff in the main action. If the defendant wishes to make a related claim against a co-defendant or a person not yet party to the proceeding, or wishes to allege that he or she is responsible for the plaintiff's damages, the defendant may bring a *crossclaim* or *third-party claim*.

In addition to their notice-giving function, the pleadings also serve to define the issues in the case. For instance, if Richardson denies that Albert Starr was drunk, then that fact becomes an issue at trial that Albert must prove. However, if Richardson admits serving Albert and that Albert was drunk, then these are no longer issues between them.

There is a further aspect to the issue-defining function of pleadings. When the action reaches trial, the plaintiff and the defendant are permitted to produce evidence only with regard to the allegations set forth in the pleadings. If either seeks to prove a fact that is not alleged in the pleadings, a *variance* is said to occur. The proof offered by a party must conform to the issues raised in the pleadings. At trial, parties may request permission from the judge to *amend* their pleadings to raise matters not already pleaded. Whether such permission will be granted will depend on the circumstances of the cases.

5. Obtaining Information Before Trial: Discovery

The pleadings are not the only device available to plaintiff and defendant for the development of the issues in their case. Our procedural system is premised on the philosophy that each party is entitled to go to trial knowing the case that must be met. Pleadings go only part way to achieving this goal. Various *discovery* devices provide the means by which a party is able to obtain more information about the opponent's case. Also, these devices permit parties to gather facts or information to support or prove their own case.

Harriet Nandise can obtain *discovery of documents* by requiring GM to disclose under oath, by means of an *affidavit* of documents, all documents now, or previously, in its possession pertaining to the action.

Nandise will also have the right to conduct an *oral examination for discovery* of a representative of GM. Our procedural system permits the parties to an action to examine one another under oath, before trial, concerning the issues in the action. On such an examination Nandise will be able to ask a GM official to disclose the facts on which GM relies in support of its case. The questions and answers will be transcribed and made available to the parties for use at trial. If the answers given by the official at trial differ from those that he or she gave on examination for discovery, the examination may be used for the purposes of impeaching credibility. Also, Nandise may use any admissions that the official makes on his or her examination for discovery at trial to prove her case.

Various discovery devices, such as orders to inspect property and orders requiring parties claiming personal injuries to submit to medical examinations to determine the validity and extent of injuries, are available to both plaintiffs and defendants. If parties intend to introduce medical or other expert evidence at trial, they must make a version of such evidence available to their opponent before trial.

6. Disposition Without Trial

Do the parties have any alternative methods of resolving their dispute in order to avoid the time, expense, and delay involved in taking the case all the way through to trial? Our system provides a number of formal devices that may lead to disposition without trial. There is the possibility of a *settlement* of a dispute before trial. In this regard, the Ontario Rules of Civil Procedure create incentives (through potential adverse costs awards) to settle matters. Usually, prospects of settlement are best after discovery when, for the first time, each party knows the facts on which the opposite party relies. With this information at their disposal, parties are in a good position to negotiate a settlement.

What are the formal devices provided for disposing of a case short of trial? We have already mentioned one of them in the context of the failure of the statement of claim to state a reasonable cause of action. In such a situation, the defendant can ask the court to dismiss the action. Similarly, if the statement of defence fails to raise any matter that could in law amount to a defence, the plaintiff can apply for judgment. In circumstances where the parties agree about the facts and the only issue between them is the applicable law, parties can agree to proceed by placing a question of law before the court. By this procedure, the parties set forth their agreed statement of facts (thereby avoiding the necessity of bringing witnesses before the court), and the court decides which legal principles apply and renders judgment in the action. In other circumstances, if a party has made admissions in pleadings or on discovery that clearly entitle the opposing party to succeed in the action, that party may move for judgment.

While the above devices are infrequently invoked, many actions are disposed of without trial on grounds that there really can be no doubt on the facts that one side or the other will prevail in the end. Most of these cases are simple "collection" matters where the plaintiff sues to collect the price of goods sold, services provided, or money lent. The Rules of Civil Procedure make provision for *summary judgment* in cases where one party can demonstrate that there is no triable issue in the case.

Of course, in cases where the defendant fails to deliver a statement of defence, the plaintiff may obtain *default judgment*. Similarly, if the plaintiff fails to proceed with the action, the defendant may have the action dismissed for want of prosecution.

7. Case Management and Alternative Forms of Dispute Resolution

There are two comparatively recent innovations in the resolution of disputes and the conduct of litigation that can alter substantially the way parties dispose of claims—case management and alternative forms of dispute resolution (ADR).

a. *Case Management*

Canadian courts have moved toward a more activist role in controlling the preliminary stages of litigation. These alterations, particularly in the role played by the judiciary, are said to be motivated by the rising costs of litigation and delays in bringing proceedings to some resolution. Essentially, case management shifts much more responsibility for the pace of litigation to the court. Such supervision depends on establishing reasonable but firm time limits for various procedures and on the court policing these limits to ensure compliance by the parties.

This management can be effected in a variety of ways. One means, particularly when the litigation is complex, is through the use of case-management conferences where, in appropriate circumstances, the court, after receiving representation from the parties, basically sets a schedule for the various pre-trial stages of the litigation. The court then monitors the proceeding to ensure compliance with the schedule and to achieve other efficiencies regarding the conduct of the litigation.

b. *Alternative Forms of Dispute Resolution*

Alternative Forms of Dispute Resolution (ADR)—for example, mediation, arbitration, and conciliation—have existed for a long time, but increasing attention is being paid to ADR as a way of curtailing costs and delay and giving more control to the parties. If

ADR as an independent means of resolution is selected—for example, arbitration—the parties may bypass the courts altogether.

However, ADR (particularly mediation) is also increasingly used in litigation in court—that is, court-annexed ADR. This form of ADR is used to enhance the possibility of resolving litigation without the expense, delay, formality, and limited terms of disposition of trial. In most instances, court-annexed ADR is an option that all parties must agree to try in an attempt to settle their differences. However, some courts are experimenting with mandatory court-annexed ADR: see Ontario r. 24.1. Such experiments have generated controversy.

8. Setting the Case Down for Trial

After the pleadings are completed and the plaintiff has conducted pre-trial discovery and has brought interlocutory motions such as he or she deems appropriate—for example, to amend the statement of claim—he or she puts the case on the list for trial, and the parties then wait until their case is called by the court.

Increasingly, courts are concerned about caseload management, as indicated above, and they may require litigants to explain delays in getting a case to trial.

9. Mode of Trial

Our legal system provides for two methods of trial—by a judge alone and by a judge sitting with a jury. In trials before a judge alone, the judge decides all matters, both of law and fact. In jury trials, these functions are divided, with the jury deciding questions of fact and the judge deciding questions of law.

In most actions, either party is entitled to have the case tried by a *jury*. However, there are some cases that, for historical reasons, cannot be tried by a jury.

At the commencement of the trial, the parties must select the members of the jury. In Ontario, there are 6 persons in the civil jury. (A jury in a criminal case has 12 members.) A large number of persons, selected in an impartial manner from the municipal assessment rolls, will have been ordered to report to the court house for jury duty. If it is known to Starr's counsel, for example, that one of the persons called is a personal friend of Richardson, there probably will be a successful *challenge for cause* by Starr's counsel. However, suppose that the defendant is a physician and his counsel learns that one of the panel has recently had an unfortunate experience with a doctor. This will likely be insufficient to result in a successful challenge for cause. However, concerned that the juror may be prejudiced against his client, the defendants' lawyer will probably exercise one of his or her four *peremptory challenges* for which no reason need be given. Ultimately, the panel of six jurors will be chosen.

In Ontario, while most civil actions are tried by a judge alone, we will assume that, in our cases, one of the parties has elected a trial by jury. Although the discussion that follows relates to a jury trial, many of its aspects are common to a non-jury trial.

10. The Trial

At the trial, the plaintiff's lawyer, after the jury has been selected, makes an *opening statement*. For the benefit of the judge and jury, the nature of the case is outlined, as are the facts intended to be proved through the evidence of witnesses. The lawyer presents evidence by asking questions of each of the witnesses for the plaintiff and obtaining their answers on oath. The examination of witnesses by the lawyer for the party calling them is known as *examination-in-chief*. After the plaintiff's lawyer has examined a witness in-chief, the defendant's lawyer has the opportunity to *cross-examine* that witness. The main purposes of cross-examination are to test the veracity of the witness and to obtain answers which assist the case of the cross-examining party. Following the cross-examination, should there be any point that the plaintiff's lawyer wishes to clarify, the witness may be *re-examined*. This procedure continues until the plaintiff has called all of his or her witnesses. The questions put to the parties and other witnesses, and their answers, are transcribed either by a shorthand reporter or by some mechanical means.

Strict *rules of evidence* apply with regard to the testimony that is permitted at trial. These rules are complex and their study forms the basis of an entire course at law school. However, at the very least, to be admissible, evidence must be relevant to the issues that the parties have raised in their pleadings. It is for the trial judge to make rulings throughout the trial with regard to the admissibility of evidence. If, for example, a lawyer is of the opinion that evidence is inadmissible, he or she must *object* to that evidence and ask the trial judge to make a ruling.

After the plaintiff's lawyer has called all of the witnesses, the case for the plaintiff is closed. At this point in the trial, the defendant's lawyer may wish to contend that the plaintiff has failed to adduce sufficient evidence to establish his or her case. In other words, there may be an application for a *non-suit*, asking the judge to dismiss the action. The trial judge will not rule on this motion unless the defendant's lawyer elects not to call any evidence. If he or she indicates an intention to call witnesses, the trial judge will reserve his or her decision on the motion until all of the evidence in the case has been completed. On the other hand, if the defendant's lawyer elects to call no evidence, the trial judge may rule on the motion for non-suit at once. However, because this is a jury trial, the judge will only rule on the motion after the jury has had the opportunity to consider the evidence and reach its decision.

Where the defendant's lawyer does not move for a non-suit, or has moved for a non-suit and elects to call evidence, the defendant then presents his or her case. He or she does so in exactly the same manner as the plaintiff, by calling witnesses who are examined-in-chief, cross-examined, and re-examined. After the defendant has concluded his case, the plaintiff is allowed to meet any issues raised by defence evidence by calling evidence in reply. However, the plaintiff cannot use the right to call reply evidence for the purpose of introducing evidence that he or she should have introduced initially but that, for some reason, he or she overlooked. The right of reply is restricted to meeting new issues raised by the defendant.

After all evidence has been concluded, counsel for the parties have the opportunity to *address the jury*. In a jury trial, the jury has the duty of finding the facts; the judge has the duty of making all decisions with regard to the law. At trial, the jury must accept the directions of the judge about the law that they are to apply to the facts as they find them.

In addressing the jury, the plaintiff's lawyer will attempt to convince members that the plaintiff has discharged those *burdens* that rest on him or her. The plaintiff has the *burden of persuading* the members of the jury that they should accept the version of the event given in evidence by the plaintiff's witnesses and the plaintiff, and that the conduct of the defendant amounted to negligence or a violation of some other legal standard. Thus, the plaintiff's lawyer will summarize the evidence and base argument on it in urging the jury to find for the plaintiff. In addressing the jury, it is improper for the lawyers to rely on anything other than what the witnesses have said. The defendant's lawyer will have the opportunity to address the jury after the plaintiff's lawyer has done so. He or she, too, will summarize the evidence, but will attempt to convince the members of the jury that the plaintiff has not proved his or her case.

After counsel have addressed the jury, it is the function of the trial judge to deliver his or her *charge*. The judge will also summarize the evidence in the case but, unlike the lawyers, is permitted to express an opinion with regard to what evidence is believable and what evidence is not. However, the judge must caution the jury that members are to keep an open mind and that they can accept or reject the judge's comments with regard to the credibility of the witnesses according to their own view of the evidence. The judge's major function is to instruct the jury on the law that they must apply to the facts as they find them. After concluding the charge, the jury will retire to consider the case.

After the trial judge has charged the jury, if one or more of the parties disagrees with anything that the judge has said, they may *object* to the charge. If the judge sustains the objection, the jury will be recalled and recharged on the point to which objection was made.

Although other methods of obtaining the decision of the jury are available, the most common method employed in Ontario is to require the jury to answer a series of questions. The trial judge will usually render judgment in conformity with the jury's answers to the questions. However, the judge is not obliged to do so and may, at the request of one of the parties to the action, give judgment *notwithstanding the verdict of the jury*—that is, judgment not for the party in whose favour the jury found, but for the opposite party. The judge will only do this where he or she is of the opinion that there was no evidence on which the jury, acting reasonably, could have reached its verdict.

Where a judge hears the trial without a jury the procedures are simpler. The judge hears the evidence and submissions of the parties. He or she then renders oral judgment immediately or in writing after further consideration of the evidence and submissions.

11. The Judgment, Its Enforcement, and Its Effect

The *judgment* of the court is the final determination of the lawsuit, subject to any appeal. In many cases, the judgment will be in the form of an award of money that the defendant is required to pay. However, a money award represents only one type of judgment that may be given by the court. In an appropriate case, the court may make a declaration of rights between the parties, order the specific recovery of property, or make an order requiring or prohibiting some future activity. For example, Jane Doe might ask for a declaration that her Charter rights had been violated or even for a mandatory order of the court (an injunction). An injunction, for example, could require the police to warn potential targets of known rapists.

The fact that the plaintiff has been awarded damages against a defendant is of little significance unless the plaintiff can collect the amount of the damages. The burden lies on the plaintiff to take the appropriate procedure to collect his or her money. *Execution* is the common method of forcing the losing party to satisfy a money judgment in situations where he or she does not voluntarily do so. The plaintiff will obtain a *writ of execution* from the court commanding one of its officers, usually the sheriff, to seize the defendant's property and, if necessary, to sell it at a public sale and use the proceeds to satisfy the plaintiff's judgment. In a case where the plaintiff's recovery takes the form of an order (an injunction) requiring the defendant to do something, or to stop doing something, known as an *injunction,* the judgment is said to operate against the defendant's person. If the defendant fails to obey, the plaintiff may apply to have the defendant found in *contempt of court*, and, if so found, the defendant may be punished by a fine or imprisonment.

Costs, as provided by the tariffs contained in the rules, are usually awarded to the successful party and are included in the judgment of the court. Usually these costs represent only some of the fees (about 50 to 65 percent) that the successful party is required to pay to the lawyer plus those disbursements contained in the tariff and incurred by the lawyer. The successful party prepares a *bill of costs*. If the unsuccessful party does not agree to the amount of the bill, the other party is required to have the bill assessed before a judicial officer. If the costs are not paid voluntarily after assessment, they can be recovered by execution in the same way as a money judgment.

Subject to the right of appeal, the judgment rendered in an action is final and binding on the parties and may not be challenged in any subsequent proceeding. Their dispute is said to be *res judicata, a thing decided*, and cannot be relitigated.

12. The Right of Appeal and Motions

a. *Appeals*

The judicial system in Ontario, as in other jurisdictions, provides a right of appeal in almost every case. In Ontario, this right of appeal is, depending on the amount at issue or whether the decision finally disposes of the rights of the parties in the action, either to the Divisional Court or to the Court of Appeal. (In the following paragraphs, "Court of Appeal" includes Divisional Court.) A party exercises this right by filing a notice of appeal which sets forth the ground of appeal. If the defendant is the unsuccessful party and elects to appeal, he will be known as the appellant. The plaintiff will be known as the respondent. The appellant is required to file with the court a statement of fact and law that sets out the facts of the case and a brief resume of the points of law on which he or she relies. Similarly, the respondent is given the opportunity to file a statement of fact and law in reply to that of the appellant.

The powers of the Court of Appeal are very broad. It may affirm the decision appealed from, reverse it, or vary it. In appropriate cases, if the appeal is allowed, it may substitute for the decision of the trial judge the decision that ought to have been reached. In other cases, however, it may be necessary to direct that there be a new trial. While the powers of the Court of Appeal are broad, there are certain limitations. The major limitation is in relation to the findings of fact made at trial. Even though the Court of Appeal would have come to a different finding of fact if it had been the initial tribunal, it will not substitute its own finding for that reached at trial, if there was evidence on which the trial judge or jury could reasonably have found the facts as it did. Therefore, relatively few cases are successfully appealed on the ground that the finding of fact at trial was in error.

Rather, most appeals are based on errors of law—for example, if the trial judge incorrectly instructed the jury with regard to the applicable law. In such a case, if the trial judge was clearly wrong and thereby occasioned a miscarriage of justice, the case will likely be sent back for a new trial. However, in a non-jury case, if the trial judge misapplied the law to the facts, or applied an incorrect principle of law, the Court of Appeal will be able to apply the law correctly and substitute its own decision for that of the trial judge.

Another ground of appeal relates to the admissibility or inadmissibility of evidence. In such circumstances, where the trial judge's error with regard to the admissibility of evidence has resulted in a miscarriage of justice, the Court of Appeal will order a new trial so that the proper evidence can be considered by a new trial judge or jury.

Appeals are usually argued on the basis of a transcript of the evidence of the witnesses taken at trial. Counsel will present their oral arguments before the Court of Appeal and no witnesses are called. There is a limited right of appeal from a decision of the Divisional Court to the Court of Appeal and limited rights of appeal to the Supreme Court of Canada.

b. *Motions*

In discussing appeals, it is necessary to mention one area of procedure that has been referred to only briefly. These are motions, which are made to the court by a party to an action before the trial itself. (There may also be certain kinds of motions in applications. Applications were described above under section III.B.3., "Commencing the Proceeding." Such motions frequently relate to the pleadings or to discovery. They are usually made to a judicial officer known as the master, but certain motions must be made to a judge. As mentioned previously, parties may frequently seek to amend their pleadings to include, for example, facts of which they were unaware at the time the pleadings were initially prepared and that may have subsequently been obtained, perhaps as a result of discovery. In such circumstances, the party will apply to the master for leave to amend the pleadings. Another common example of a motion results from the refusal of a party to answer certain questions on examination for discovery. In order to compel an answer, the opposite party must bring a motion before the master for that purpose and the master will decide whether the witness must answer the questions. There is a limitation with regard to the appealability or reviewability of orders. The right of appeal from such orders is restricted. If it were not, actions could be delayed by an inordinate number of motions followed by a series of appeals.

C. Flowchart of an Action Under the Ontario Rules of Civil Procedure

This flowchart on pages 24-25 depicts the steps that are or may be taken in an action under the Ontario Rules of Civil Procedure. The dark line and boxes indicate the steps that will occur in every action (that proceeds that far). The light boxes indicate motions that *may be* made, or steps that *may be* taken, but which will not necessarily occur in every case. (The actual stage at which such motions or steps may be taken can vary and in this regard the chart location merely represents what will happen in most cases.)

An asterisk (*) indicates that an interlocutory appeal under rule 62, Appeals from Interlocutory Orders, may be possible (for an illustration see the arrows leading out of box A).

Of course an action may be settled at any time, discontinued, or the defence withdrawn (rule 23, Discontinuance and Withdrawal), in which case judgment will usually be entered under rule 59, Orders (see box 7). When a motion is decided this will result in an order that will be entered under rule 59.

D. The Structure and Purpose of Civil Procedure

The term "civil procedure" is typically used to refer to the rules that have to be followed in the conduct of a particular type of dispute resolution—that is, adjudication in the courts. (Obviously there are other methods of dispute resolution—for example, negotiation and mediation—and there are also other forms of adjudication—for example, arbitration that takes place outside of court and before somebody who is not usually a judge.)

Described generally, adjudication by a judge normally involves (1) the judge hearing the evidence put forward by the parties; (2) the making of findings of fact by the judge; and (3) the judge applying the law to those facts to reach a decision. (Where the trial is by a judge and jury, the jury will make the factual findings and will apply the law, as announced by the judge, to arrive at its verdict.)

Most of the cases that you read in law school courses are appellate cases that are concerned with resolving competing arguments about what law is applicable in a particular case. However, at the trial court level, generally the fact-finding process dominates—whether it be a three-hour or three-week trial, most of the time will be taken up by the parties adducing their evidence. Typically a small percentage of the time is spent arguing about the law. Indeed, there may be little dispute between the parties about what law is applicable. Often, what divides parties is the differing view of the facts. At the trial court level, the majority of decisions turn on the facts, not on the law.

I would like to consider two different ways of viewing or explaining civil procedure. Both approaches are essentially functional—that is, designed to explore the function or purpose of civil procedure. The first is a quasi-historical perspective that argues that by adopting a particular form of adjudication—a fact-finding trial that comes at the end of the process—we have more or less conditioned what had to come earlier in the process. The second approach, a due process perspective, is more abstract and poses the question what characteristics the civil procedure process should possess in order to be "fair."

1. Historical Perspective

I suggest that to understand the structure of our civil procedure one has to understand its historical genesis, because one particular characteristic of the civil procedure process conditioned its overall basic structure. If one goes back into the 19th century, at common law all civil actions were tried by a jury, and trials had a particular character—they were

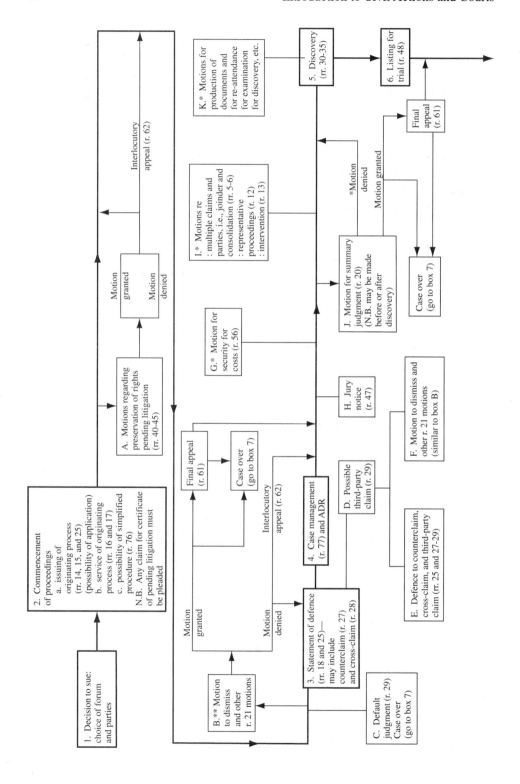

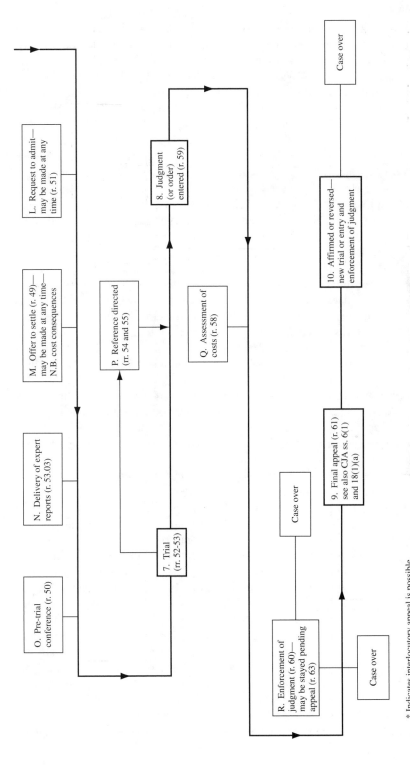

L. Request to admit—may be made at any time (r. 51)

M. Offer to settle (r. 49)—may be made at any time—N.B. cost consequences

N. Delivery of expert reports (r. 53.03)

O. Pre-trial conference (r. 50)

P. Reference directed (rr. 54 and 55)

Q. Assessment of costs (r. 58)

7. Trial (rr. 52-53)

8. Judgment (or order) entered (r. 59)

R. Enforcement of judgment (r. 60)—may be stayed pending appeal (r. 63)

Case over

Case over

9. Final appeal (r. 61) see also CJA ss. 6(1) and 18(1)(a)

10. Affirmed or reversed—new trial or entry and enforcement of judgment

Case over

* Indicates interlocutory appeal is possible.
** Depending on its nature, a rule 21 motion may be made before or after the delivery of a statement of defence. If brought before a statement of defence is delivered and the motion is denied (either at first instance or on appeal), the defendant must then deliver a statement of defence.

"oral, continuous trials" (and this is still largely true today). They were "oral" in the sense that witnesses attended in person, were sworn, and gave their evidence orally, although documents might be proven by oral evidence and thus received into evidence. By contrast, in equity (the judicial system that competed with the common law) the fact-finder was confronted not with live, oral evidence, but with evidence that had been reduced into writing in the form of affidavits or written transcripts of examinations. This orality ("oralness") has both a purpose and a consequence. The purpose is to better enable the fact-finder to evaluate the evidence—to make a determination about the credibility of the witnesses—by being able to observe the manner in which the evidence is presented and in particular the demeanour of the witness. But an important conse-quence of this process (from the lawyer's perspective) is its *immediacy*. The production of the evidence and its receipt by the trier of fact takes place simultaneously, unlike the situation where, for example, evidence is being adduced by affidavit. If I am adducing a witness's evidence by affidavit, I will know what the witness's evidence is when the affidavit is sworn, which will usually be well in advance of when it is presented to the judge. More important, you (as opposing counsel) will typically see that affidavit before the hearing and before the judge hears (or sees) the evidence. Hence you know in advance of the hearing what my evidence will be (indeed, exactly what my evidence will be, assuming that I have to serve you with my affidavits before the hearing). By con-trast, at an oral trial, you (as my adversary) hear my witness's actual evidence at the very same time as it is heard and received by the judge.

This brings us to the second aspect of the oral, continuous trial. At common law, trial by jury was always continuous. If you, as my adversary, were taken by surprise by the evidence you heard for the first time when my witnesses testified orally, there was no question of relieving against this surprise by granting you an adjournment—that is, stopping the trial for some days or weeks while you developed a response to the unan-ticipated evidence that you had just heard for the first time. The jury, a group of stran-gers brought together for the purpose of trying the case, could not be sent away (it was felt) and told to come back on another day to hear further evidence. So as not to inconvenience the jury, there could be no adjournments.

Although today trial by jury in civil cases is the exception rather than the rule and it is much easier for a judge sitting alone to grant an adjournment, our modern-day civil procedure continues to be shaped by the notion of the oral, continuous trial. We want the process to be fair (more of this later under due process); if there is to be an oral, continuous trial, in order for the process to be fair, the parties need to know in advance what evidence is going to be adduced at trial. Otherwise, parties can be faced with what is often referred to as "genuine surprise." By this term we usually mean that parties are confronted at trial with evidence that, had they known in advance that such evidence was going to be adduced, they would have been able to contradict by marshalling and producing evidence. We thus have developed pre-trial procedures that are designed, *inter alia*, to avoid surprise at trial by (in a sense) "scripting in advance" what will happen at the trial. We do this principally through various forms of notice giving. The issues to be litigated are defined in advance through the exchange of written allegations and responses referred to as *pleadings*—the plaintiff sets forth what he or she alleges the defendant did, and the defendant responds in writing stating whether he or she agrees with this statement or how he or she otherwise responds to these allegations. However, in developing our pre-trial procedure (at least in North America), we have gone beyond merely requiring the parties to articulate their allegations and responses well in advance of the trial. We also require parties to go a long way in terms of disclosing, before the trial, the facts and evidence they will adduce at the hearing. This process of fact disclosure is generically referred to as discovery and encompasses both the disclosure of documents and the disclosure of facts and evidence through the process of pre-trial examination for discovery (and to a lesser extent through such other discovery devices as medical examinations and orders for the inspection of property). It is now well recognized that the major objective of "discovery" is to avoid surprise at trial—that is, situations where a party is confronted with evidence for the first time at the oral hearing, which does not give the party a fair opportunity to respond to the evidence.

If you think about it, there are other ways to deal with this problem of surprise, at least if you are not wedded to the concept of an oral, continuous trial. One obvious way to deal with it would be to abandon the concept of a continuous hearing and simply adopt a rule that if a party is genuinely surprised by evidence that is adduced at trial then we will grant an adjournment—that is, sufficient time for the surprised party to marshall evidence in response to the surprising evidence. Indeed, today in cases of genuine surprise this is how the court will often react (at least if it is a trial by judge alone; in jury trials, a court is still loath to grant adjournments). However, such an approach can be inefficient and lead to increased costs that will have to be borne by somebody. Continental procedure never found itself in this "bind" of how to deal with surprise, because it never adopted the idea of an oral, continuous trial. Typically, in continental procedure, the hearing wasn't continuous but rather a series of partitive hearings with the court, for example, sitting for a day or two to take evidence and then reconvening, perhaps a month later, to hear some more evidence. This vehicle of partitive hearings allowed the parties to deal with any problem of surprise by turning up at the next hearing date prepared to counteract evidence that may have been heard at an earlier hearing date. But this was not the style of the common law. At least in conception, the trial is viewed much like a theatrical play, oral and continuous, which starts and continues until it is finished. And just like a play, the common law concluded that the trial must be scripted in advance through the devices of pleading and discovery.

So, I have argued, the oral, continuous trial necessitates the procedural notice-giving devices of pleadings and discovery. But the analysis does not stop there. Other characteristics of the trial have also conditioned or structured our civil procedure.

Provisional remedies. The common law assigns fact finding to the trial—a culminating event that comes at the end of the process and that nearly always takes a considerable time to reach (at least, in part, because the pleading and discovery phases take time). Because of this, the common law has had to allow for *provisional remedies* (for example, for interim injunctions to restrain allegedly injurious activity) before trial and before the court has an opportunity to finally rule on whether the alleged injurious activities are in fact illegal. (Such remedies, and indeed any relief that a party wishes to seek before the trial, are obtained by making a *motion* to a non-trial court. This is typically done by a document called a *notice of motion*, if necessary supported by affidavit evidence.)

If there are no facts in dispute, we do not need a trial. The trial is a forum for resolving disputed issues of fact. As explained earlier, that is why the hearing is oral—so that the fact-finder (judge or jury) can hear and see the witnesses and make findings as to their credibility. It follows logically from this proposition that if there are no genuine issues of fact to be resolved, we do not need a trial. This is the role of a *motion for summary judgment*. If one party can show early in the litigation and long before trial (despite what is said by the parties in their paper allegations—that is, the pleadings) that there is no genuine issue or dispute with regard to the facts, the court will rule that a trial is unnecessary. If the dispute between the parties is simply about applicable law, a trial is unnecessary, because the purpose of the trial is to hear oral evidence and resolve disputes about the facts. If no facts are in dispute, a non-trial court (for example, the court hearing the motion for summary judgment) is in as good a position to enunciate and apply the law as any trial court would be, and it will do so and grant a final judgment.

If a claim or defence is legally invalid, we do not need a trial. Similarly, a trial is unnecessary if a party's claim or defence is untenable or *invalid in law*. In such cases we do not need a trial (or any of the procedures that are designed to aid *factual* develop-ment—that is, discovery). Typically, in the pleading, the plaintiff will frame his or her case as broadly as possible (alleging multiple grounds of liability or multiple causes of action). If the defendant can convince the court that if the plaintiff proves everything that is set out in his or her statement of claim, he or she will lose at trial because of the applicable law, a non-trial court can dismiss the action as "failing to state a reasonable cause of action" without allowing the case to proceed to trial. Similarly, if the defence pleaded by the defendant is not a valid defence in law, it can be struck out in advance of the trial by a non-trial court.

2. Due Process Perspective

Let us now view civil procedure from a different, but still functional, perspective—that is, due process. What do we mean by this term? In certain contexts, this term has developed a technical meaning, but here it simply embodies the idea that the process of adjudication (that is, the rules for the conduct of the adjudicative process) should be "fair" to both parties. In this context, due process or fairness is simply a basic element of what we understand to be justice. If the process of adjudication is to determine the rights of the parties, we hope that the final decision will be accurate (that is, correct), but in any event the losing party should not be able to complain that the process by which the decision was arrived at was unfair.

What characteristics must the court's procedure have to satisfy this notion of fair-ness? Here we run into what may be considered an enigma. There is no body of *case law* that tells us what are the criteria or indicia of fairness in court proceedings. This is because we have typically addressed the issues of fairness *legislatively*, embodying our notions of fairness in the rules that have been enacted for the conduct of litigation (the rules of civil procedure). This matter rarely falls to be determined by the court in case-by-case decisions, because fairness of the procedure has been earlier addressed by the bodies that draft and enact the rules of civil procedure. Moreover, there is no constitu-tional or common law doctrine that *says* the procedure in court proceedings must be fair.

(This is true in the Canadian context, but it is not the case in the United States. The 14th amendment to the US constitution forbids governments to deprive individuals of "life, liberty or *property*" without due process of law. Since rules of civil procedure are clearly governmental or state action, and since civil proceedings are usually about "property," in the United States ultimately all rules of civil procedure are subject to scrutiny as to whether or not they afforded the parties "due process." In Canada, as a consequence of the deliberate decision to exclude "property" from the Charter's s. 7 guarantee of funda-mental justice, civil procedure is not subject to the same constitutional scrutiny as in the United States.) Of course, courts are called upon all the time to interpret these written procedural rules and what is "fair" will play an important part in that process.

In Canada, the context in which we find the courts articulating notions of funda-mental justice, due process, or natural justice is in the context of administrative law. One of the basic tenets of administrative law is that the procedure followed by the govern-mental decision makers must be "fair." It falls to the courts (through the process known as "judicial review of administrative action") to review administrative procedures for fairness and to articulate—for administrative tribunals and decision makers—what types of procedures are fair. If the procedures followed were not fair, the proceedings under review may be invalidated or set aside. (In fact, in recent years in some jurisdictions, the minimum standards of fairness to be followed by administrative tribunals have been spelled out legislatively.)

However, as already mentioned, the procedures to be followed by courts in their adjudicative process are spelled out by subordinate legislation (that is, the Rules of Civil Procedure) that typically goes beyond the minimal levels of due process or natural justice that the courts require administrative tribunals or decision makers to follow.

What, then, are the ingredients of fairness within the court-based adjudicative proc-ess? What do you think they should be? Are the following what most people would consider to be the basic elements of procedural due process?

- *notice*—that there is a proceeding and the nature of the allegations made by the adversary;
- the concept of notice incorporates the further concept that the notice must be in writing and brought to the attention of the opposing party—that is, that the opposing party was *served* with the documents setting out the adversary's contentions;
- *the right to be heard*—the right to participate in the adjudicative process through the adduction of evidence as to what are the relevant facts and to make submissions as to what is the relevant law;
- the decision maker (the judge) will be *impartial* and not biased;
- a party will receive not only notice of the institution of the proceedings against him or her but also timely notice of any relevant step in the proceeding;
- the right not to be bound by any decision except one in which a party has an opportunity to participate through the adduction of evidence and the making of argu-ment (third-party proceedings and issue estoppel);
- the right to a reasoned decision and to reasons for the decision;
- the right to appeal an initial adverse decision (to keep the initial decision maker "honest"); and

- the right not to be dragged through discovery and trial where there is no genuine issue for trial (summary judgment) or where the adversary's pleadings fail to start a reasonable cause of action or defence.

We can see that these "statements of rights" are becoming more tenuous or less compelling as *basic* rights than the rights initially articulated. However, one of the characteristics of civil procedure, certainly in higher courts, is that (unlike administrative law) it provides not minimal fairness, but "maximal" fairness.

IV. THE HISTORY AND ORGANIZATION OF THE COURTS

A. The History of Courts and Their Procedure

Here we present, in broad outline, a history of courts and their procedure. A major purpose in so doing is to indicate the general similarity between 19th century developments in Ontario and in England and the United States. More detailed historical accounts appear in 1 Williston & Rolls, *The Law of Civil Procedure* (1970), at 41-59 (on which our description is based); in Riddell, *The Bar and Courts of the Province of Upper Canada* (1928); and in McRuer, *Royal Commission Inquiry Into Civil Rights*, Report No. 1 (1968), at 865-91.

Though courts existed in Canada, and in part of what was later to become Ontario, before 1791, our account begins by looking at the situation at that time. The Constitutional Act of 1791 led to the division of the province of Quebec into Upper Canada and Lower Canada. At the time of that division, or shortly thereafter, there were several courts in Upper Canada.

The *Court of King's Bench* was a court of original jurisdiction possessing all "such powers and authorities as by the law of England are incident to a Superior Court of criminal and civil jurisdiction." In essence, this means that the court was one of unlimited jurisdiction. But this court was a court of law only and consequently it had no jurisdiction to administer the principles of equity developed in England by the Court of Chancery. In the Court of King's Bench all issues of fact were determined by a jury, not by a judge. It seems reasonable to assume that the procedure followed in this court was that prevailing in the English common law courts at this time (c. 1795). As in England, this court went on circuit to try cases in the various district towns.

The *Court of Requests* is said to have originated because of the prevailing general rule that every issue of fact was required to be tried by a jury. This mandatory jury trial made the trial of small actions inconvenient and expensive. Consequently, provision was made for the Court of Requests in which judges sitting alone had full power to give judgment in cases of claims not exceeding 40 shillings. Each district was divided into divisions, and each division had a Court of Requests. It was the early analogue of the modern Small Claims Court.

District Courts existed in each district for the "cognizance of small causes." These courts had jurisdiction in actions of contract for sums above 40 shillings and not exceeding £15.

At this time, no general appellate court, as such, existed within Upper Canada. Appeals from the Court of King's Bench, if the matter in controversy exceeded £100, were taken to the governor and the Executive Council. Where the matter in controversy exceeded £500, a further appeal lay to the Privy Council in England.

One matter that should be quite obvious, and rather surprising, from the foregoing description, is that there was no court that exercised equitable jurisdiction—that is, there was no Court of Chancery. However, from time to time, after 1795, there was agitation for the creation of a court that could exercise jurisdiction based on equitable rather than legal principles. Eventually, the judges of Upper Canada advised the British Parliament that all of the judges of the King's Bench should be given equitable jurisdiction "with competent authority to one or more of them to hold a Court of Equity ... at certain periods distinct from the existing law Terms."

One pamphlet by John Godfrey Spragge, later a Chancellor of Upper Canada, argued for the need for a court of equity as follows:

> The common law was never meant, nor is it calculated, by itself to form the jurisprudence of a country. Without being tempered by equity law, it would often work injustice, and in its actual operation the application of its rules did work injustice, until a language began to be used in our Court of King's Bench which would have sounded strangely in the ear of a common lawyer in England. What was called the equitable jurisdiction of the court was not unfrequently appealed to as absolutely necessary, in the absence of a Court of Equity, to correct the rigour of the common law; a more dangerous doctrine could scarcely be broached, or one more calculated to subvert the common law itself. There are judges whose *bent* of mind would incline them to strain the common law rather than that a flagrant injustice should be committed, by applying its rules in their integrity to the case before them—"to do a great good, do a little wrong." The temptation to do so flowing from a love of justice and a hatred of wrong, thus, by degrees the common law would cease to be what it is and ought to be—a system of law built up on precedent and authority—so that a man may, with reasonable certainty, know what the law is, and govern himself accordingly; but it would degenerate into an uncertain hybrid system, neither common law nor equity, but an incongruous compound of both, so that no man could tell what his rights were, inasmuch as they would, in so great a measure, depend on the half-legal half-equitable view which the judge or judges might take of them.
>
>   The law would soon deserve a reproach such as Selden applied to the Court of Chancery in his time: "In law we have a measure, and know what to trust to. Equity is according to the conscience of him that is Chancellor; and as that is larger or narrower so is equity. 'Tis all one, as if they should take the standard for the measure, the Chancellor's foot. What an uncertain measure this would be! One Chancellor has a long foot, another a short foot, a third an indifferent foot. It is the same thing with the Chancellor's conscience." For the word equity, substitute slaw, and for the word Cancellor, substitute judges, and you have a quaint but forcible and true description of what our law would become.

This proposal met with serious opposition on the ground that equity could never be administered in a court of law. The outcome was the establishment, in 1837, of a separate Court of Chancery. Falconbridge, "Law and Equity in Upper Canada" (1914), 63 *University of Pennsylvania Law Review* 1, provides an account of the "equityless" period and of the establishment of the Court of Chancery. Almost from the outset, however, jealousy and discord existed between the Courts of Queen's Bench and Chancery in what seemed to be a repetition of the historic conflict seen in England more than two centuries before. At various times proposals were made for the creation of a single court to administer both law and equity, but such a radical departure from tradition was viewed with alarm and it drew strong opposition. It was not accomplished until 1881 when Ontario adopted the English Judicature Act reforms of 1873. (However, in 1853, the District Courts, which had in 1849 been renamed County Courts, were given equitable jurisdiction.)

The Court of Chancery was not the only new court to be established in this period. Another court with an English analogue was also created. In 1849 the *Court of Common Pleas* with the same jurisdiction, practice, and course of proceeding as the Court of Queen's Bench was established. The result of this rather bizarre step was "two common law courts of equal and concurrent jurisdiction and dignity, identical in practice and differing only in name, and the plaintiff could select the court in which he wished to bring his action."

As already mentioned, at the time of the creation of the province of Upper Canada, appeals were not to a court as such, but to the governor and Executive Council, though there was provision for the chief justice to sit with this body. It appears that while appeals could be brought in this way they were not common and very seldom succeeded. In 1849 a general appellate court, known as the *Court of Appeal*, was established. Though it subsequently underwent several changes in name and structure, this court is the precursor of our modern Ontario Court of Appeal.

The remaining major developments in the structure and procedure of the Ontario courts in the 19th century parallel the English reforms of that period.

In 1837, the judges of the courts of King's Bench were authorized to "make rules in respect of pleading and practice generally." The statute authorizing this step directed the judges to bring such rules before the legislature within five days of the beginning of the session. But even at that time the courts moved slowly, and it was not until 1842 that the judges presented the rules. This was the first step toward the development of a written code of procedure.

As the courts developed and the province increased in size, the administration of justice became the subject of increasing criticism. The practice and procedure of the courts was neither efficient nor satisfactory and it became apparent that the practice had to be consolidated. To this end, the Common Law Procedure Act of 1856 was passed. This Act introduced the procedure that governed until the Judicature Act of 1881.

In the following decade two reforms took place that instituted practices still with us today. As previously stated, at the time of the creation of Upper Canada, it was provided that the trial of every issue of fact be by a jury (with the exception of trials in the Court of Requests). In 1868, it was enacted that, in general, all issues of fact and every assessment of damages in the superior courts of law and in the County Courts should be tried by a judge, unless either party served a notice requiring a jury. In certain classes of cases a jury trial was *prima facie* mandatory, but even in such cases the parties might at trial dispense with the jury on consent. This is essentially the system that prevails today.

In 1869, judges were authorized to make rules for enabling a clerk of the Court of Queen's Bench to exercise the jurisdiction of a judge in chambers. This was a significant change and it is the origin of the jurisdiction today exercised by masters.

The culmination of the 19th century reform movement did not come in Ontario until 1881. However, significant changes were made by the Administration of Justice Act of 1873. Three reforms wrought by that Act were particularly important. First, it provided that the courts of law and equity should "be as far as possible auxiliary to one another … for the more speedy, convenient and inexpensive administration of justice in every case." To this end, equitable pleas were permitted to be set up in an action at law in the common law courts and the action could be transferred to the Court of Chancery if it appeared that justice would be better attained thereby. The process of amalgamating the administration of law and equity in the superior courts was thus under way.

Second, the shrouds of secrecy that had previously surrounded the pretrial stages of an action were swept away by granting to any party the right to obtain an order for oral examination of his or her opponent touching the matters in question in the action. By this provision the basis was laid for our modern system of discovery.

Third, the Act of 1873 provided that "no proceeding either at law or in equity shall be defeated by any formal objection." This laid the foundation for the liberal power of amendment to cure errors in procedure that plays such a major and pervasive role in procedure today.

The Benthamite reform movement of the 19th century culminated in Ontario in the Judicature Act of 1881. This legislation was to Ontario, and its courts and procedure, what the Judicature Act of 1873 was to England and the Field Code of 1848 was to the United States. By this Act, all of the superior courts—Queen's Bench, Common Pleas, Chancery, and Appeal—were united and consolidated together to constitute "one Supreme Court of Judicature for Ontario." The new court was to consist of two divisions— one to be called The High Court of Justice for Ontario and the other, The Court of Appeal for Ontario. (In truth, the courts were not at this stage completely amalgamated. "Divisions" within the High Court, approximating the old courts, were maintained. It was not until 1913 that these divisions were abolished and one High Court established. The Act of 1881 also created another institution known as "Divisional Courts of the High Court." These were something different from the divisions of the High Court. They were courts with a specified appellate jurisdiction and were subsequently abolished in 1913.)

The new Supreme Court of Judicature was given all the jurisdiction formerly exercised by the courts of common law and equity. Thus was the administration of law and equity finally amalgamated, and it was provided that in any matter in which there was a conflict or variance between the rules of equity and those of the common law, the rules of equity were to prevail.

The Judicature Act of 1881 went part way, though not all of the way, toward establishing a unified and codified procedure for the new Supreme Court. Elaborate rules were annexed to the statute and power was given to make any further and additional rules of court for carrying the Act into effect. Mr. Justice Middleton (in a preface to Lennox, *The Guide to Ontario Practice* (1938)) described the extent to which the rules of 1881 achieved the object of codification and the extent to which this had to await later developments:

The history of the Rules of Practice is not without interest. Before 1881 we had Common Law Courts, governed by the Administration of Justice Act and the Common

Law Procedure Act, and the Court of Chancery established and governed by the Chancery Act. The Common Law Courts had their Rules of Court. The Court of Chancery had its general orders. Behind both was the practice of the corresponding English Courts, which governed in many matters not provided for by the rules.

In 1873 the great reform embodied in The Judicature Act was introduced in England. There was to be one Court by which all justice was to be administered. This was brought about gradually, and the reforms were made step by step. In Ontario we followed not far behind. Our Judicature Act of 1881 was a great reform, but partial only. The Courts were not completely amalgamated. "Divisions" were maintained, and it was not until 1913 we attained the ideal of a united Supreme Court of Judicature.

At the time of the Judicature Act of 1881 there were introduced some 500 Rules of Court founded on the English Act. There were also many of the Rules of Court and general orders still in force. The "most convenient" practice was to be followed. The result, chaos prevailed. In 1888 the Judges endeavoured to secure order once more by the Consolidated Rules of Practice. These repealed all existing rules and enacted 1264 new rules mostly based on pre-existing rules. Some were chosen from the Common Law, some from Chancery and some from The Judicature Act. It was provided that these should form a complete code of practice. It was further provided "as to all matters not provided for in these rules the practice, as far as may be, is to be regulated by analogy thereto" and that "all practice inconsistent therewith is superseded." This was a marked advance but resulted in many amendments before conflicting provisions could be reconciled, and in 1897 the Rules of Practice were again consolidated.

In 1913 I undertook for the Government to make a thorough revision of the rules and did so, resulting in the Rules of Practice of that year. The number of rules was reduced to 772. Included in these were a large number of practice provisions previously found scattered throughout the statutes, and there were also included definite provisions for many things theretofore not dealt with.

In summary, generally, the history of civil procedure in Ontario followed lines similar to those in England. Until the passage of 19th-century statutory reforms, Ontario had suffered under a system of multiple courts, a division in the administration of law and equity, and different procedures at law and in chancery. The Judicature Act unified the administration of law and equity in one court, the Supreme Court of Ontario, and the rules consolidation of 1888 finally brought about the replacement of common law and chancery procedure with a written code of rules, the Rules of Practice of the Supreme Court. These rules, frequently amended, though never radically changed, remained in force until the introduction of the current rules in 1985.

The history of procedure in England, Ontario, and the United States can be divided into analogous periods. All three jurisdictions experienced a period in which law and equity were administered by separate courts and procedure was largely governed by non-statutory rules developed by the judges on a case-by-case basis, the period of "common law pleading and procedure." In essence, this was the pre-Judicature Act period in Ontario and England, and the pre-Field Code period in the United States.

Following the reforms of the middle or late 19th century, all three jurisdictions entered a period of "code-pleading and procedure"—a period in which the rules of procedure were set out in a statutory or written form. The common aim and achievement in each country was to codify rules for the conduct of litigation that were considerably less technical and formal than the common law rules. In basic philosophy and approach, though not in details, the procedural codes in the three jurisdictions were similar.

In 1938, US procedure was radically altered. By contrast, major procedural reform did not take place in England, Ontario, and the other Canadian common law provinces until the onset of a reform movement spanning the period 1965-85, and which has stopped short of embracing the most radical changes in procedural philosophy that have occurred in the United States. However, it is not to be assumed that English and Canadian procedure is identical. In particular, they differ with regard to the important matter of the availability of pre-trial discovery. The English rules make no provision for the oral examination for discovery of parties, whereas this procedure is universal in Canada. Instead, discovery in England is limited to discovery of documents and, with leave of the court, the administration of interrogatories (written questions to be answered on oath in writing by the opposing party). (These procedures are changing with the introduction of witnesses' statements to be made available before trial).

The basic principles of procedure are similar throughout the common law provinces of Canada and in the period 1965-1997 the provinces (and the Federal Court of Canada) have rewritten (and sometimes rewritten again) their rules. These revisions have drawn on each other, on the English rules of 1965, and, to a certain extent, on the US Federal Rules of Civil Procedure.

With the passage of the US Federal Rules of Civil Procedure in 1938, procedure in the United States moved into a third period—one into which the courts in Canada and England, generally, have not yet entered. The Federal Rules represent a radical revision of the former US code procedure and have been so well received in the United States that they have been adopted by, or have influenced subsequent revisions in, most of the states of the Union. The chief reform occasioned by the Federal Rules of 1938 was to de-emphasize and simplify pleadings and to place a much greater emphasis on pre-trial discovery and the pre-trial conference as devices for defining the issues in an action. A major feature of the Federal Rules is that the scope of pre-trial discovery is broad and extends not only to the examination of the parties, but also to non-party witnesses.

While the US Federal Rules had a substantial impact on recent Canadian procedural reforms, those reforms stopped short of adopting the most radical aspects of US procedure. Typically, in Canada, only parties may be orally examined for discovery as a right, and, typically, non-parties can only be examined with leave of the court. Also, Canadian procedure still places more emphasis on the pleadings than does US procedure, and the very liberal class action rules available in the United States have been adopted in Canada in only a few provinces—that is, Quebec, Ontario, and British Columbia. However, several features of the US Federal Rules—for example, broad summary judgments procedures and pre-trial conferences—have generally been adopted in Canada.

NOTES AND QUESTIONS

1. What are the differences between equity and common law? Can one exist without the other? Note that Ontario and some US states had an "equitless" period, but also

note Spragge's criticisms of what this did to the common law. As will be examined in chapter 7, "The Size and Scope of Litigation," some now believe that we have gone too far and that contemporary procedure is all based on the exercise of equitable discretion. These critics claim that there are no rules—for example, any party or claim can be joined in an action, there are no limits to discovery, and judges face no constraints in the exercise of their remedial discretion.

2. Is it fair to say that equity and common law are truly merged? Note that many equitable subjects such as trusts, specific performance, and injunctions are still taught separately.

B. The Organization of the Courts

Any discussion of the organization of the courts in Canada must begin with an examination of the Constitution Act, 1867. That Act provided for the federal union of several former British colonies into the Dominion of Canada and divided legislative power between the Parliament of Canada, on the one hand, and the provincial legislatures, on the other. For our purposes several provisions of the Constitution Act are important. By section 92(14) exclusive legislative competence was conferred on provincial legislatures with respect to "the administration of justice in the Province, including the constitution, maintenance and organization of provincial courts both of civil and criminal jurisdiction and including procedure in civil matters in these courts."

At Confederation, provinces generally had three levels of trial courts: (1) a superior court with unlimited jurisdiction; (2) "county" or "district" courts with jurisdiction limited by territory and subject matter (including the amount claimed in civil cases); and (3) "inferior" courts often staffed by lay magistrates and justices of the peace to hear "minor" criminal and civil cases.

Section 96 of the Constitution Act, 1867 requires that judges of the superior, district and county courts in each province be appointed by the governor-general. Generally speaking, the salaries, allowances, and pensions of these judges are fixed and provided by Parliament. The provinces appoint and pay the judges of the "inferior" courts, now called provincial courts. Of course, by virtue of s. 92(14), the provinces are responsible for the administration of superior, county or district, and provincial courts.

Finally, by s. 101 of the Act, power is conferred on the Dominion Parliament to provide for the constitution, maintenance and organization of a general court of appeal for Canada and for the establishment of any additional courts for the better administration of the laws of Canada. The general Court of Appeal is the Supreme Court of Canada, established in 1875 and empowered to hear appeals on matters of constitutional, federal, and provincial law. In the case of civil cases, leave to appeal must be obtained based on a showing that the case raises issues of national importance. Before the Supreme Court of Canada hears appeals, there has been an appeal to an intermediate appellate court, usually known as the provincial Court of Appeal. Its judges are appointed by the federal government but the court is administered by the province.

The establishment of the Federal Court of Canada, under s. 101, as an additional court for the better administration of the laws of Canada marks a departure from the unitary court structure described above. The Supreme Court of Canada, the provincial courts of appeal, the superior courts, the county or district courts, and, in certain instances, the provincial courts, can all decide matters involving federal or provincial law. In contrast, as will be seen, the Federal Court, created under s. 101, can only determine matters involving federal law.

The general structure of the courts has not changed much from Confederation until the 1970s. Starting then, most provinces merged their superior and county or district courts into one larger superior court.

Below, we examine the court structure in Ontario, established by the Courts of Justice Act as amended by the Courts Improvement Act, SO 1996, c. 25 (in force April 1999). In the other common law provinces, the court structure is similar. Generally the court structure in the common law provinces of Canada can be represented diagrammatically as shown below.

C. Courts with Civil Jurisdiction in Ontario

As a result of the 1990 court reforms, and subsequent changes to the names of the courts taking effect in April 1999, there now exist in Ontario the following courts.

• The Court of Appeal for Ontario, a separate court and the highest court in the province.

• The Court of Ontario (formerly the Ontario Court of Justice), consisting of two divisions—the Superior Court of Ontario (formerly the Ontario Court (General Division)) and the Ontario Court of Justice (formerly the Ontario Court (Provincial Division)). The Superior Court of Ontario is a trial court of general jurisdiction in criminal and civil matters (including divorce). In addition, it contains two branches—the Divisional Court and the Small Claims Court.

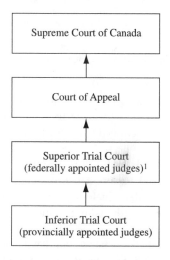

[1] In Nova Scotia there is still a trial court (the County Court) with federally appointed judges that is not, however, a superior court.

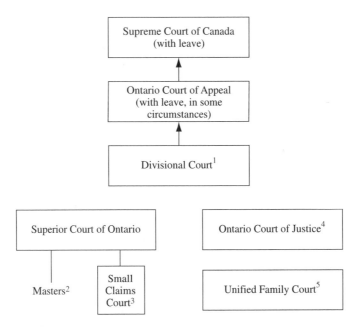

[1] The Divisional Court is in fact a branch of the Superior Court of Ontario. It is located in the diagram above the Superior Court because it exercises appellate jurisdiction over decisions made by the Superior Court. (See the Courts of Justice Act, s. 17, et seq.)

[2] Masters are officers of the Superior Court—that is, they are not federally appointed judges (as are the judges of the Superior Court) but are appointed by the province. However, they play an important role in the area of procedure hearing interlocutory proceedings, principally in Toronto (although there are also masters in Ottawa and Windsor).

[3] This is also, in fact, a branch of the Superior Court; see the Courts of Justice Act, s. 21, et seq. Every judge of the Superior Court is also a judge of the Small Claims Court, but in practice Small Claims Court proceedings are heard either by provincially appointed Small Claims Court judges (in some large metropolitan areas) or by deputy judges (lawyers appointed on a part-time basis).

[4] The judges of the Ontario Court of Justice are appointed by the province, not by the federal government. The court hears criminal and non-divorce family law matters. See generally the Courts of Justice Act, s. 33, et seq.

[5] The Unified Family Court exists only in some parts of the province. The judges are federally appointed and they have jurisdiction in all family law matters, including divorce.

• The Ontario Court (Provincial Division), now renamed the Ontario Court of Justice, was the result of the 1990 merger of the former Provincial Court (Criminal Division) and the Provincial Court (Family Division). Its jurisdiction is limited to criminal and (non-divorce) family law.

• Finally, there is the United Family Court (UFC), a superior court that exists only in specified areas (in southern and eastern Ontario, though not in Toronto), which has jurisdiction in all family law matters, including divorce. (This court started some years ago as a "pilot project" in unifying the administration of all family law in one superior court. The experiment was a success and the UFC is now being gradually "rolled out" across the province. Because it is a superior court with federally appointed (and paid) judges, the rollout requires federal–provincial cooperation. (The UFC has not yet spread to northern areas because of lack of population density.)

The present structure of the Ontario Court system can be represented diagramatically, as shown on page 38.

1. Small Claims Court

The jurisdiction of this court is presently limited to claims for $6,000 *10,* or less. All the judges of the Superior Court can sit as small claims court judges but the Courts of Justice Act also provides for the appointment of deputy judges for a three-year term by regional senior judges of the Superior Court. The Small Claims Court has its own set of rules. They resemble the rules applicable to the Superior Court but are intended to be more informal.

Marvin A. Zuker, *Small Claims Court Practice*
(Toronto: Carswell, 1998), 2-3, 6, 20-21

Small Claims Courts originated in response to a perception that the complex and technical regular civil procedure made it virtually impossible for wage earners and small businessmen to use the court system to collect wages or accounts which they were owed. The basic problem was perceived to be caused by cumbersome formal civil court procedures that resulted in unreasonable delay and expense, since a lawyer was a virtual necessity to enable litigants to find their way through the complex procedural requirements. The primary aim was to reduce delay by simplifying the court process by reducing the need for litigants to be represented by a lawyer.

While the adversary process was retained, in the sense that each side to a dispute was responsible for presenting the arguments and facts in its favour, it was envisioned that the judge in a small claims proceeding would play an active role at trial—assisting litigants in bringing out relevant facts and clarifying the legal issues involved. Trial procedures and rules of evidence were to be "informal" and were left largely to the discretion of the trial judge. Generally, a small claims judgment was still required to accord to the rules of substantive law, although in some jurisdictions the small claims judge was directed, in addition, to do "substantial justice" between the parties.

The crux of the small claims procedure is informality and simplicity, in the sense that little paperwork is required beyond a brief initial claim commencing the action. Formal rules of trial procedure and rules of evidence are often waived. In some jurisdictions, no formal answer is required of the defendant beyond appearing in court on the trial date to explain his or her side of the case. ...

Over the years, a number of goals have been identified for the small claims process. Early reformers emphasized providing accessibility to the machinery of law for all classes—specifically, working and tradespeople. Since the primary problem with existing civil procedure was seen to be its complexity with resulting delay and expense, early goals were simplicity, speed and low cost. By simplifying the process of adjudication, early reformers also hoped to maximize self-representation by litigants. Small claims decisions were intended to be "fair," in that judges were required to arrive at even-handed decisions by applying the regular substantive law to the facts of a case.

Generally, all Small Claims Courts share the basic characteristics of informal adjudication set out in the proceeding section: most procedural steps and paperwork are eliminated, and informal rules of procedure and informal rules of evidence are often used at trial. Small claims jurisdiction is almost always limited to a specified monetary range of civil claims that can be satisfied in money damages. Beyond these common features, however, several other procedural features have evolved as different paths of moving closer to the goals of the small claims process. ...

An important development in the small claims process is using Small Claims Court clerks to assist litigants in filing (such as filling out a claim form) and to provide information on what types of proof will be needed at trial, or when supporting witnesses may be required and how to subpoena them. Some courts presently permit court clerks to give quasi-legal advice to litigants, such as how to determine the correct defendant, how to sue business defendants, and so on.

Small Claims Courts are organized administratively around the small claims clerk's office. ...

The most common types of claims are actions for debt recovery or damages. A debt is a sum of money due by certain and expressed agreement where the amount is fixed and specified and does not depend on any subsequent valuation by the court to settle it. Examples of debt actions include those for services rendered, goods sold and delivered, promissory notes or dishonoured cheques. Damage claims are those for loss, injury or deterioration caused by the negligence, design or accident of one person to another, the amount claimed being a sum which must be evaluated by the court. ...

In order to simplify and speed up the process of getting to trial, the focusing and clarification of issues is often left to the trial. This requires a more judicially active role at trial. Even in courts which permit lawyers, in a significant number of cases the judge will still have to assist the parties without a lawyer to explain their side of the controversy and to identify the relevant facts in a case.

The inquisitorial trial procedure used in a small claims court is much more efficient than rigid formal trial procedure in getting quickly to the heart of a dispute, since the judge has more control over the trial and can question litigants and witnesses to draw out relevant facts and clarify conflicting testimony.

Typically, small claims trials are conducted as follows. The judge summarizes the small claims complaint in his or her case file, identifying the plaintiff and defendant and describing the alleged cause of action and the amount claimed as damages. The plaintiff is then asked if this is correct in order to verify the claim. The plaintiff is then sworn in and told to tell his story in his own words. Testifying parties are directed to sit in a witness chair in front of the judge's bench or to stand in front of the bench. Generally, judges do not permit any interruptions or questions by the other side or by a solicitor while a litigant is testifying; also, judges assist the testifying party in laying out the facts and examining receipts or other documents which the plaintiff has brought to court. If the plaintiff has brought any witnesses, these witnesses are then sworn in and testify after the plaintiff. Finally, the defendant tells his story and presents witnesses, if any. Judges then permit the plaintiff and defendant to cross-examine each other, or their witnesses.

The degree of judicial activism observed in small claims trials is usually reflected in the extent to which judges "control" the trial process. More active judges, many "inquisitorial" or "investigatory," move from a brief review of the case to questioning the plaintiff to establish the necessary cause of action and proof of damages. They then shift to questioning the defendant to clarify his side of the case to bring out any defences or any facts by the plaintiff. After an opportunity for questions by the litigants, the judge announces a decision, explaining how he arrived at the dollar amount of the award. Judges who use this inquisitorial approach justify it on the grounds that it speeds up trials, enabling the judge to skip over or to cut short rambling or extraneous testimony and take the burden off inexperienced litigants.

NOTES AND QUESTIONS

1. For a recent and thorough review of the literature on and issues facing small claims court, see I. Ramsay, "Small Claims Courts: A Review," in Ontario Law Reform Commission, *Rethinking Civil Justice Research Studies for the Civil Justice Review* (Toronto: Ministry of the Attorney General, 1996).

2. Should lawyers be banned from small claims courts? One study suggests that fewer than 25 percent of small claims court litigants use lawyers and that they do not fare better than other litigants. See K. Hildebrandt, B. McNeely, and P. Mercer, "The Windsor Small Claims Court: An Empirical Study of Plaintiffs and Their Attitudes" (1982), *Windsor Yearbook of Access to Justice* 86.

3. Another alternative is to make better use of mediation in the small claims context. While there is no formal mediation process attached to the Small Claims Court, the court does make extensive use of pre-trial conferences where the parties meet together with a court officer in an attempt to settle the case or narrow the issues for trial. During these meetings the court officer often acts as a facilitator of the discussions between the parties. At times, they apply considerable pressures on the parties to settle. Further, at the date scheduled for trial, it is not uncommon for the judge to summons the parties into his or her chambers and attempt to settle the case there. What are the advantages and disadvantages of such procedures? Could they be improved and, if so, how? At least one law school is experimenting with mediation of Small Claims Court actions as part of a course and program in mediation: see The University of Windsor Mediation Service, *Annual Report 1996/97*.

2. Superior Court of Ontario (formerly Ontario Court (General Division))

This court is the result of the 1990 merger of the former Supreme Court (also called the High Court) and the District Court (previously known as the County Court). These two levels of trial courts formerly had similar procedures except that the County or District Courts were limited to claims of $25,000 or under. The Supreme Court was considered a more elite institution with approximately 50 members, while the District Court had over 200 judges. Members of both courts were appointed by the federal government but only those appointed to the Supreme Court were Superior Court judges. Under s. 99 of the Constitution Act, 1867, judges of Superior Courts hold office during good behaviour and are subject to removal only by the Governor-General on Address of the Senate and the House of Commons. With the creation of a unified trial court of civil jurisdiction in

1990, Ontario has followed the path set by all provinces except Nova Scotia. Until 1999, this unified trial court was known as the Ontario Court (General Division). In that year, it was given its present name—the Superior Court of Ontario.

The Superior Court of Ontario has no monetary limit. Appeals can be taken to either the Divisional Court or the Ontario Court of Appeal depending on the amount in issue or whether the decision is final or interlocutory. All of the Superior Court's judges are appointed by the federal government and are designated as judges of a Superior Court.

Unlike the old Supreme Court, which used to be based in Toronto, with judges spending some weeks in each year "riding circuit" in other areas of the province, and the District Court, with a courthouse in each county, the Superior Court of Ontario is arranged around eight regions in Ontario. Each region has a senior judge who manages judicial resources subject to direction from the Chief Justice of the Court of Ontario who presides over the General Division.

3. Ontario Court of Justice (formerly Ontario Court (Provincial Division))

Unlike the Superior Court, the judges of this court are appointed by the provincial government but, like the Superior Court, this court is also administered on a regional basis. The court has criminal and family divisions. Although most criminal trials are heard in the Ontario Court, judges of that court cannot hear cases with juries and they serve as judges in preliminary inquiries before crimes are tried in the Superior Court of Ontario. Similarly, judges of the Ontario Court cannot grant divorces, although they do have jurisdiction to decide all other family law matters including custody and support.

Although the judges of the Superior Court of Ontario are appointed by the federal government, the administration of justice is, under s. 92(14) of the Constitution Act, 1867, a matter of provincial jurisdiction. The numerous administrative officials who make sure that both the Superior and the Ontario Courts can function are provincial civil servants. These include court registrars and clerks who prepare trial lists, record judgments, and have other duties. Sheriffs deliver summonses to witnesses and other court documents, execute judgments (sometimes by seizing property), and help in jury selection. The provincial government is also responsible for providing courts with their annual budgets and building and maintaining their facilities.

4. The Divisional Court of the Superior Court of Ontario

Created in 1972, the Divisional Court is a branch of what is now the Superior Court of Ontario. It consists of the chief justice of the Court of Ontario, who is president of the court, and those judges of the Court of Ontario who may be designated by him or her, from time to time, as judges of the Divisional Court. A panel of three judges is required to hear most matters before this court which sits continuously in Toronto. Provision is made for sitting elsewhere in the province. The jurisdiction of the Divisional Court is defined by s. 18 of the Courts of Justice Act and includes appeals from judgment at trial for amounts less than $25,000, final judgment, or orders of masters and, with leave, from interlocutory judgments or orders of a judge of the Superior Court. It also has jurisdiction to hear applications for judicial review under the Judicial Review Procedure Act, SO 1971, c. 48.

The expression "judicial review" deserves some explanation. Broadly speaking, an application under the Act for judicial review is an application to the court to review the decision of an administrative board or tribunal established under a provincial statute—for example, the Municipal Board or the Human Rights Commission. The common law courts traditionally exercised a supervisory function in relation to proceedings before inferior tribunals with the prerogative writs of *mandamus*, *prohibition*, and *certiorari*. As a rule, the courts would not review the decision of such a tribunal merely on the ground that it had reached the wrong conclusion on the facts, but it would intervene if the tribunal had acted without jurisdiction. The body would lack jurisdiction, for instance, if it had not conducted the proceedings according to the principles of natural justice—for example, by failing to notify parties of the case against them or to allow them to be heard, or, if in reaching its decision, it had acted unlawfully either by taking into account some extraneous factor or by ignoring matters it was required by statute to consider. In these circumstances, a common law court would quash the tribunal's decision by issuing either a writ of *prohibition* or a writ of *certiorari*. If the complaint was not that the decision was wrong, but that the body had failed or refused to exercise the jurisdiction it was required by law to exercise, the court would issue a writ of *mandamus* commanding it to hear and determine the matter.

But the prerogative writ procedure was cumbersome and highly technical, and often applicants with a meritorious grievance would fail because they had applied for the wrong form of writ. This was an understandable mistake as the line between the writs of prohibition and *certiorari* was sometimes difficult to draw. Also, applicants sometimes had to show that the error of which they complained was apparent on the face of the record of the tribunal, and what constituted the record was defined very narrowly. It meant just the formal written order of the tribunal, and did not include the evidence on which its decision was based.

The Judicial Review Procedure Act abolished the old prerogative writ practice and substituted a single and uniform procedure of review. Now, an application that was formerly made for *mandamus*, *prohibition*, or *certiorari* is to be "made, treated and disposed of as if it were an application for judicial review" (s. 7).

5. The Court of Appeal for Ontario

This court is the highest appeal court in the province. It consists of a chief justice (the chief justice of Ontario) who acts as president, an associate chief justice, and other justices of appeal. All appeals are heard in the city of Toronto. This court obtains its jurisdiction from the Courts of Justice Act and exercises a general jurisdiction in appeals from judgments of the Ontario Court.

It should, however, be noted that the Court of Appeal is not the sole appellate tribunal in the province. For example, the Divisional Court has a very broad appellate jurisdiction as discussed in the previous section.

6. The Supreme Court of Canada

The Supreme Court of Canada was established in 1875 by the Dominion Parliament as a court with general appellate jurisdiction. It has been said that this court was created "to speak with authority for the Dominion as a whole and, as far as possible, to establish a uniform jurisprudence especially within matters falling within s. 91 [of the Constitution Act, 1867] where legislation is for the Dominion as a whole (such as with respect to criminal law) or, ... where purely provincial legislation may be of general interest throughout the Dominion." However, it should be noted that on appeals from provincial courts of civil or criminal jurisdiction, the court sits as a court of appeal for that province and not as a federal court. This is crucial, for example, in appeals from the courts of Quebec. In these appeals, the civil as opposed to the common law governs. Before 1933 in the case of criminal appeals and before 1949 in the case of civil appeals, a further appeal could be taken from an order of the Supreme Court of Canada to the Judicial Committee of the Privy Council in England. However, since these dates, the Supreme Court of Canada has acted as the final court of appeal for Canada.

The Supreme Court hears appeals from the courts of appeal of the provinces and from the Appeal Division of the Federal Court of Canada. The jurisdiction and procedure of the court are regulated by the Supreme Court Act, RSC 1970, c. S-19, as amended, and regulations made thereunder. The court is composed of the chief justice of Canada and eight puisne judges. The Supreme Court Act requires that three of the judges should be appointed from Quebec, and by convention the court includes three appointees from Ontario, two from the maritime provinces, and two from western Canada. Sittings of the court are held in Ottawa from October to June.

Except in certain criminal cases an appeal does not lie as of right from the court of appeal of a province to the Supreme Court of Canada. The criminal law exceptions arise under the Criminal Code when the appeal raises a question of law alone and in certain cases when the attorney general is the appellant. In all other criminal cases and in all civil cases leave to appeal is necessary. Leave may be obtained from the provincial court of appeal or from the Supreme Court of Canada itself.

A provincial court of appeal may grant leave from a final judgment of that court where in its opinion the question involved in the appeal is one that ought to be submitted to the Supreme Court for decision. The Supreme Court of Canada may grant leave to appeal, whether or not leave has been granted by any other court, where the court is of the opinion that the question involved is, by reason of its public importance or the importance of any issue of law or any issue of mixed law and fact involved in such question, one that ought to be decided by the Supreme Court or is, for any other reason, of such a nature of significance as to warrant decision by it. This has been the situation since the Supreme Court Act was amended in 1974. Before then an appeal in civil cases lay as of right if the amount or value of the matter in controversy exceeded $10,000. Leave had to be obtained if the amount or value in question was less than that sum. Practice before this court is governed by a separate body of rules, promulgated by the judges of the court pursuant to s. 97 of the Supreme Court Act.

7. The Federal Court of Canada

The Federal Court of Canada is divided into two divisions: (1) the Federal Court—Trial Division, and (2) the Federal Court—Appeal Division. The seat of the court is in Ottawa, but each division of the court can sit at any place in Canada "to suit, as nearly as may be, the convenience of the parties." The procedure of the court is regulated by the General Rules and Orders of the Federal Court of Canada, 1971.

The jurisdiction of the Federal Court is of two kinds—exclusive jurisdiction and concurrent jurisdiction—that is, concurrent with the provincial superior courts. Speaking broadly (until recently) the court had *exclusive* jurisdiction with respect to actions *against* the Crown, administrative appeals, and judicial review of the decisions of federal agencies and officials. The court has *concurrent* jurisdiction with respect to action *by* the Crown, intellectual property claims (copyright, trademarks, and patents), and admiralty claims. (An appeal lies to the Supreme Court of Canada from a final judgment or determination of the Appeal Division of the Federal Court, with the leave of that court or of the Supreme Court.)

Section 101 of the Constitution Act, 1967 confers on the federal Parliament the power to establish "any additional courts for the better administration of the laws of Canada" and thus authorizes Parliament to establish a system of federal courts to determine cases arising under federal laws. Generally the federal Parliament has been content to leave the provincial courts with jurisdiction to determine federal as well as provincial issues. Until 1875, there were no federal courts at all. When the federal Parliament established the Exchequer Court of Canada in 1875, it gave it a very limited jurisdiction over cases involving the revenue and the Crown in the Right of Canada. Over time this jurisdiction was gradually increased to cover intellectual property, admiralty, tax, citizenship, and a few other matters regulated by federal laws. When the Exchequer Court was replaced by the Federal Court of Canada in 1971, the new court inherited the jurisdiction of its predecessor, but was also given additional jurisdiction, including the power to review the decisions of federal agencies and officials. The establishment of the Federal Court, with its broader jurisdiction and more elaborate structure—that is, a trial division and an appeal division—represents a step in the direction of the dual court system in the United States, a system which leads to multiple litigation and complex jurisdictional disputes. See, generally, P. Hogg, *Constitutional Law of Canada*, 4th ed. (Toronto: Carswell, 1996), chapter 7.

The jurisdiction of the Federal Court has been surrounded in controversy that has been compounded by a series of court decisions over the past 15 years. The federal Parliament's power to establish courts is limited by the terms of s. 101 of the Constitution Act, 1867, which does not authorize the establishment of courts of general jurisdiction akin to provincial courts. It authorizes only courts "for the better administration of the laws of Canada," which means that the Federal Court can be given jurisdiction over only subject matters governed by "the laws of Canada."

In a series of restrictive decisions, the Supreme Court of Canada has given the phrase "the laws of Canada," and hence the jurisdiction of the federal court, an extremely narrow interpretation. Beginning in 1976, the court rejected the view that a federal court could be given jurisdiction over any matter in relation to which the federal Parliament had legislative competence, even if that matter was not in fact regulated by federal statute law. (On this view, the "laws of Canada" could include a rule of provincial statute law or a rule of the common law if its subject matter was such that the law could have been enacted or adopted by the federal Parliament.) The Supreme Court of Canada held that the federal court could not constitutionally assume jurisdiction over a case unless the case was governed by "applicable and existing federal law."

This doctrine adopted by the Supreme Court created difficult questions surrounding the federal court's jurisdiction. Moreover, the situation was complicated by the court's refusal to adopt techniques developed in the United States to prevent the fragmentation of jurisdiction between two court systems and to avoid a multiplicity of litigation by allowing a federal court to settle matters of "state" law presented in one functional dispute. In the following extract, Peter Hogg critically analyzes the court's approach to these issues. He notes that the problem has now been largely ameliorated by amendments to the Federal Court Act in 1990, making the jurisdiction over proceedings against the Crown *concurrent*, rather than exclusive. He also offers his views about whether Canada really needs a federal court.

P. Hogg, *Constitutional Law of Canada*
4th ed. (Toronto: Carswell, 1996), chapter 7 (footnotes omitted)

The decisions in *Quebec North Shore* [1977], 2 SCR 1054 and *McNamara Construction* [1977], 2 SCR 655 [restricting the jurisdiction of the Federal Court] are, in my view, open to serious criticism. First, it seems to me that the test of federal legislative competence, which was well established before 1976, is a perfectly defensible definition of "laws of Canada" in s. 101. Any laws within federal legislative competence could easily be converted into federal laws by the enactment of a federal statute incorporating them by reference (or adopting them) as federal statute law. Since this can be so easily done, it seems to me that laws within federal legislative competence should be regarded as laws of Canada without requiring the referential incorporation.

Secondly, even if one accepts the requirement of "applicable and existing federal law," I can see no reason why the rules of the common law in a field of federal legislative competence should not qualify as "laws of Canada." Indeed, it seems almost unarguable that "because the common law is potentially subject to overriding legislative power, there is federal common or decisional law and provincial common or decisional law according to the matters respectively distributed to each legislature by the BNA Act." But that is not what the Supreme Court of Canada has decided. According to the Court, the contracts in *Quebec North Shore* and *McNamara Construction*, although subject to overriding federal legislative power, were, as a matter of constitutional law, beyond the jurisdiction of the Federal Court. The same result has been reached with respect to a dispute over a contract to build a federal office building. It is implicit in these decisions that there is no such thing as federal common law. And yet the Supreme Court has from time to time made obscure reference to the existence of federal common law, and has actually held that some parts of the common law do qualify as federal law. One of these is the contractual liability of the federal Crown, which has the curious consequence that a federal government contract is within Federal Court jurisdiction if the federal Crown is the defendant, but not if the federal Crown is the plaintiff. Although the Court has never offered any criteria for the identification of these little enclaves of federal common law, it may be that the Court has in mind those few common law doctrines that cannot be altered by the provincial Legislatures.

A third criticism of the requirement of "applicable and existing federal law" is that it is exceedingly difficult to apply, often requiring litigation to determine the appropriate forum for cases in which the applicable laws come from a variety of sources. Where a single cause of action is governed partly by federal law and partly by common law, the Supreme Court has in two cases been willing to concede federal jurisdiction. In *Roberts v. Canada* (1989), however, the Court disapproved of a dictum that it is sufficient "if the rights and obligations of the parties are to be determined to some material extent by federal law." In that case, the Court also rejected the doctrine of "pendent jurisdiction," which has been developed by the federal courts of the United States to reduce the fragmentation of litigation between the federal and state court systems. Under the doctrine of pendent jurisdiction, where a federal court has jurisdiction over a particular case, then the court has jurisdiction to determine all of the issues that are derived from the "common nucleus of operative fact," including "state" issues over which the federal court would have no independent jurisdiction. Why this sensible doctrine would be unacceptable to the Supreme Court of Canada is a mystery. It means that there is no clear rule to deal with a cause of action governed by both federal and provincial law. And it means that where there are two causes of action against the same defendant, arising out of the same facts, only the cause of action based on federal law can be tried in the Federal Court; if the second cause of action is based on provincial law, a second proceeding must be brought in a provincial court.

A fourth criticism of the requirement of "applicable and existing federal law" is that the Federal Court cannot dispose of the whole of a controversy when some issues are governed by federal law and some are not. We have noticed that proceedings against a single defendant may have to be split where there is more than one cause of action. Where there is more than one defendant, or a third party, or a counterclaim, it is common to find that the liability of some parties is governed by federal law, and that of others is not. This situation is illustrated by *R v. Thomas Fuller Construction*, [1980] 1 SCR 6. In that case, an action was brought against the federal Crown by a contractor (Foundation) who was constructing a building for the federal government. This action was brought in the Federal Court, and it satisfied the requirements stipulated by the previous cases. The Federal Court Act granted jurisdiction over the cause of action. The Constitution Act, 1867, by s. 91(1A), conferred federal legislative competence over the liability of the federal Crown and over federal public property. And, in this case, the liability of the federal Crown was assumed to be governed by "applicable and existing federal law." The principal action was therefore properly brought in the Federal Court and could in fact be brought in no other court, because federal-court jurisdiction over suits against the federal Crown was exclusive. However, the federal Crown issued a third-party notice against a contractor (Fuller) (also working on the same building), in which the Crown claimed indemnity against or contribution towards the Crown's liability to the plaintiff (Foundation). The problem was that the liability of the third party (Fuller) was not based on federal law, but on either (a) the contract between the federal Crown and the third party (Fuller), or (b) Ontario's Negligence Act providing for contribution between joint and concurrent tortfeasors. The Supreme Court of Canada, in a majority opinion written by Pigeon J, held, therefore, that the requirement of "applicable and existing federal law" was not satisfied, and the Federal Court was prohibited by the Constitution from taking jurisdiction over the third-party proceeding. The decision in *Fuller Construction* meant that the federal Crown would have to bring a separate action in the Ontario courts in order to recover indemnity or contribution against the third party. A minimum of two lawsuits, and perhaps as many as four lawsuits, would be necessary to settle the rights and liabilities of the three parties.

Fuller Construction is not an unusual case. Multi-party litigation in the Federal Court often has to be fragmented into federal and provincial components. Recognizing this problem, Reed J of the Federal Court, Trial Division, has held that parties can be joined in the Federal Court when the two claims are "so intertwined that findings of fact with respect to one defendant are intimately bound up with those that would have to be made with respect to the other." This doctrine of intertwining has been rejected by the Federal Court of Appeal, but given cautious approval in an obiter dictum of the Supreme Court of Canada. The doctrine of intertwining, if it becomes established, would be a long step in the direction of the American doctrine of "ancillary jurisdiction," which permits a federal court in the United States, when it has jurisdiction over a particular proceeding, to take jurisdiction over an "ancillary" proceeding of which it could not take cognizance if it were independently presented. Like the doctrine of pendent jurisdiction, mentioned above, the doctrine of ancillary jurisdiction rests on the reasonable assumption that a federal court should have the power to resolve a case in its entirety.

Fuller Construction illustrates the deficiencies of the Supreme Court of Canada's rigid approach to the requirement of "existing and applicable federal law." It also illustrates a deficiency in the Federal Court Act that has now, fortunately, been corrected. Until 1990, the Federal Court Act conferred on the Federal Court *exclusive* jurisdiction over proceedings against the federal Crown. This meant, obviously, that a plaintiff with a cause of action against the federal Crown had no choice but to sue in the Federal Court. However, the Federal Court would normally have no jurisdiction over federal Crown servants, or federal Crown agents, who might also be involved in the dispute; and the Court would normally have no jurisdiction over other co-defendants, third parties, or counterclaims by the Crown. In 1990, the Federal Court Act was amended to make the jurisdiction over proceedings against the Crown concurrent rather than exclusive. Since this amendment, proceedings against the federal Crown can be brought in the appropriate provincial court, which is likely to have jurisdiction over all the other parties as well. If the plaintiff chooses the provincial forum, split proceedings can be avoided.

The 1990 amendment to the Federal Court Act invites the question whether there is any reason to preserve even concurrent Federal Court jurisdiction over proceedings against the federal Crown. The same question could be posed with respect to other parts of the Federal Court's jurisdiction. As noted earlier in this chapter, Canada does not need a dual court system. The provincial courts have general jurisdiction over all causes of action; the judges of the higher courts are federally appointed; and consistency of decisions is guaranteed by the appeal to the Supreme Court of Canada. The existence of a parallel hierarchy of federal courts cannot fail to give rise to wasteful jurisdictional disputes and multiple proceedings. I accordingly regret the expansion of the federal-court system which has occurred in Canada since 1875. But it cannot be denied that the Constitution Act, 1867, by s. 101, authorizes the federal Parliament to create a federal-court system, and that the federal Parliament has deliberately chosen to do so. In these circumstances, it seems to me that the Supreme Court of Canada should develop rules which will enable the parallel jurisdictions to operate as smoothly as possible. It must be remembered that the burden of inadequate rules is borne not by governments but by individual litigants who have no means of escape from the uncertainties, expenses, delays, inconsistencies and injustices which are inherent in multiple lawsuits. The Supreme Court of Canada's rejection of the rule of legislative competence as the definition of "laws of Canada," and the Court's refusal to develop rules of ancillary and pendent jurisdictions, have exacerbated the problems of a dual court system.

NOTES AND QUESTIONS

1. For a more detailed criticism of the doctrinal developments referred to by Hogg, see Hogg, "Comment" (1977), 55 *Canadian Bar Review* 550; Hogg, "Federalism and the Jurisdiction of Canadian Courts (1981), 30 *University of New Brunswick Law Journal* 9; Laskin and Sharpe, "Constricting Federal Court Jurisdiction" (1980), 30 *University of Toronto Law Journal* 283; Evans, "Comment" (1981), 59 *Canadian Bar Review* 124; Scott, "Canadian Federal Courts and the Constitutional Limits of Their Jurisdiction" (1982), 27 *McGill Law Journal* 137; and Evans and Slattery, "Comment" (1989), 68 *Canadian Bar Review* 817.

2. *Pacific Western Airlines Limited et al. v. The Queen*, [1979] 2 FC 476 graphically demonstrates the problems caused by the granting of exclusive jurisdiction to the Federal Court in actions against the Crown in the Right of Canada. This involved the crash of a PWA Boeing 737 at the Cranbrook (BC) airport killing 43 people. The action was brought in the Federal Court because the Crown was a major defendant, being the operator of the airport. In all there were 43 defendants, including the City of Cranbrook, Boeing, and the manufacturer of the plane's thrust reverser. Applying the doctrine developed by the Supreme Court of Canada and described by Hogg, Collier J held that the Federal Court had exclusive jurisdiction in respect of the claims advanced against the Crown, but it did not have jurisdiction in respect of the claims advanced against any of the other defendants. He observed as follows:

> That conclusion creates an undesirable situation. The plaintiffs, if they wish to continue against all defendants, must pursue their remedy in more than one Court. Multiplication of proceedings raises the spectre of different results in different Courts. The plaintiffs then face the question, in respect of the defendants, other than the Crown: the Court of which province, or perhaps more than one province? Some of the Crown servants reside in Ontario and performed their duties there; others reside in Edmonton, Vancouver, Calgary and Cranbrook, and performed their duties in those cities. The Cranbrook group resided, and committed their alleged defaults, in British Columbia. Can the American groups be impeded, or a remedy obtained, in the Courts of any particular province? There may well be other jurisdictional questions. I do not know the solutions to any of them. Nor do I venture any opinions or suggestions.
>
> The situation is lamentable. There are probably many other persons who have claims arising out of this air disaster. The jurisdictional perils must be, to all those potential litigants, mystifying and frightening.
>
> But all these undesirable consequences may be a fact of life in a federal system, such as we have in Canada, with the division of legislative powers as set out in the British North America Act, 1867.

Subsequent to the passage of the 1990 amendments to the Federal Court Act—giving concurrent jurisdiction to the provincial courts over claims against the federal Crown—litigation such as the *PWA* case may now be brought in a provincial court.

Under the doctrine developed by the Supreme Court, if a plaintiff sues the Crown in the Federal Court in a situation where the Crown wishes to institute a counterclaim or third-party proceeding, the jurisdictional problem surfaces again. To resolve this problem the 1990 Federal Court Act amendments provide such a situation, the action in the Federal Court shall be stayed and the plaintiff given a respite of 100 days from the operation of limitation periods in which to commence proceedings in an appropriate provincial court (which has jurisdiction to consider the counterclaim or third-party proceeding).

Theory and Context of Civil Procedure

Part II places civil litigation in the larger context of dispute resolution. It does so in two ways. First, chapter 2, "The Value of Procedure," examines the reliance that our society places on procedure to legitimate decision making. It discusses the relationship between procedure and the legitimacy of decision-making processes, the impact of procedure on substantive outcomes, and the theoretical underpinnings of procedure.

Second, the section examines a number of models of decision making for non-criminal disputes. Throughout the section we also discuss the roles of lawyers and legal ethics in the various models. The central point regarding these models is that the courts have generated a "traditional" model that has long dominated civil conflict resolution. However, that model has competed with a number of other models within and outside civil courts. This competition has become particularly accentuated in the last decades and continues at an intense level in the late 1990s. Because the examination of these models is an intricate and challenging exercise, at this point it is useful to provide a brief overview of the models and their contribution to a theoretical framework for civil procedure.

We begin in chapter 3, "The Core Features and Values of the Traditional Model," by looking at the traditional model fashioned by the courts. The *traditional* model focuses on the lawsuit as a mode of dispute resolution centred on the determination of interests and remedies on an individual basis. In many ways it remains the most dominant model. Indeed, a common characteristic of the other models we examine is that they are all, in various ways, a reaction to attributes of the traditional model.

In chapter 4, "Challenges to the Traditional Model," we examine these other models. Their various challenges have resulted in reforms to court-based litigation itself and to the development of alternative models of dispute resolution, many of which are outside the courts. At the outset of chapter 4, we provide an overview of the current major challenges and reforms. We will see that these challenges and reforms are propelled by a number of competing values and by changing ideas regarding the roles of judges and lawyers.

In concluding this overview, we note that the models are used to organize and present a complex and changeable reality. We do not claim that the "real world" corresponds to these models in a neat and precise fashion. In the day-to-day justice system, these models interact, collide, and overlap. Thus, for example, it is possible to see strands of the traditional model and the public law model in the same lawsuit. Similarly, adjudication as a method of dispute resolution will be discussed in chapter 3. In its purest form, adjudication is most closely identified with the traditional model. At the same time, adjudication, at times modified in critical ways, is certainly present in other models—for example, in the administrative state model for some human rights determinations. Some judges engaged in case management seem, at times, to be making only incremental adjustments to the traditional model while others enthusiastically embrace ADR in their role as mediator of conflicts.

Part II seeks to present an organized way of thinking about these variations and nuances. Its goal is to provide a theoretical framework for civil procedure that also reflects an intricate and varying landscape of disputing.

The Value of Procedure

I. INTRODUCTION

Chapter 2 explores the fundamental question of why we value procedure so highly. Throughout the course there will be much discussion about which procedures are appropriate at particular stages of the decision-making process. Chapters 3 and 4 look at various models of disputing. Some of those models maintain that other methods of dispute resolution besides litigation in court ought to be invoked to resolve differences.

Throughout the debates on these many issues regarding procedure there is an underlying acceptance of the necessity of procedure to legitimately decide issues. Moreover, you will examine the pervasiveness of procedural issues in the determination of outcomes in other courses such as criminal, administrative, and family law. The importance of procedure scarcely begins or ends with a law school curriculum. In many ways, the very legitimacy of democracy rests on questions of procedure. A critical claim of governments to authority rests not on the basis of agreement with the government's policies but, rather, on the basis that the government exercises power as the result of acceptable procedures—free and fair elections. We thus need to look at the fundamental question why we value procedure so highly.

Under the heading "Procedure and Legitimacy," we look at the ways that procedures used to make decisions are linked to the acceptance of those decisions by those affected by them. We begin by presenting a fanciful excerpt from Rabelais that raises a serious question. Overwhelmingly, we recoil from the suggestion that a roll of the dice or a flip of the coin should be the "procedure" to determine outcomes. But why is that exactly? After all, coin tossing has many attributes of procedure that are very attractive—for example, low cost, accessibility, neutrality, and speed.

The excerpt by Tyler presents a dramatically different significance for procedure than one envisaged by coin flipping. He argues, based on empirical evidence, that procedures affect the legitimacy of a decision regardless of its outcome—that is, whether an individual wins or loses.

Throughout the casebook we discuss ways that procedural determinations can affect substantive outcomes. Under the heading "The Impact of Procedure," we take an initial look at the link between procedure and substantive outcomes by examining a dramatic (and exceptional) instance. Because of the particular circumstances in *Murphy v. Dodd*, insufficient notice of a proceeding ultimately results in the determination of the substantive question at issue in the action.

Finally, under the heading "Theoretical Underpinnings of Procedure," the materials raise issues about how various aspects of procedure are determined and implemented. In other words, procedure may be important but, more precisely, how do we decide what ought to be the specifics of procedures used to resolve conflicts?

The Bayles excerpt attempts to provide a framework for determining the goals to be achieved by procedure and for making the necessary trade-offs among those goals to the extent that they conflict. For example, we want procedures that result in accurate determination of contested facts while, at the same time, we need procedures to be affordable and speedy. Yet accuracy, on the one hand, and affordability and speed, on the other, may conflict in basic ways. To the extent that there are such conflicts, how is a balance to be struck?

The Simon article raises a far-ranging challenge. Procedures may indeed be critical. However, does their importance result in justice or injustice for most members of society? Do procedures that seem neutral on their face in fact promote a set of underlying values that can be at odds with other important ends for a society truly interested in justice for all? More specifically, what are the consequences of promoting such underlying values in terms of even handed access to legal services and of assertion of claims and defences in litigation?

II. PROCEDURE AND LEGITIMACY

The following iconoclastic piece written by Rabelais in 1532, in its own idiosyncratic and satirical manner, emphasizes the (mythic?) weight we place on the existence and efficacy of procedure.

François Rabelais, *Gargantua and Pantagruel*
trans. J. Le Clercq (New York: The Modern Library, 1944), chapters 39-40

Next day, at the appointed hour, Pantagruel reached Miralingua. The president, senators and counsellors invited them to attend the hearing; Judge Bridlegoose was to defend and justify the sentence he had pronounced against Touchcircle, a tax-assessor. To the court of the hundred judges, this decision of Bridlegoose's had not seemed at all equitable. Pantagruel accepted their invitation, and, going in, found Bridlegoose seated in the middle of the enclosure.

As the case progressed, Bridlegoose, for all argument, replied only that he was getting old, and that his sight was failing; he cited, into the bargain, various other vexations and calamities brought on by senescence. ...

Unable to read the dice as clearly as in the past, Bridlegoose compared himself to Isaac, who, being old and dimsighted, mistook Jacob for Esau. Thus, having to decide the case in question, he had doubtless taken a four for a five; he begged to assure the learned judges that he had used a very small pair of dice. ...

"Now, my friend," said Trinquamelle, or Blusterer, the Lord High President of the court, "what dice are you speaking of?" ...

"You, too, gentlemen, employ these dice in your sovereign court, as do all other judges when sitting upon a case. ... [F]ate or hazard is a worthy, honest, useful and necessary element in the decision of differences and lawsuits." ...

"And how do you judge, my friend?" Blusterer inquired.

"I shall answer you briefly," said Bridlegoose. ... "Well then, gentlemen, I judge just as you yourselves do, according to the custom of the judicatory office, which our law commands us always to observe. ...

"First, I view and review, read and re-read, ponder, weigh, thumb and digest the bills of complaint, subpoenas, appearance by proxy, reports of hearings, investigations, instruments of deposition, petitions, articles of evidence, allegations, rejoinders, rebuttals, requests, inquests, surrejoinders, surrebuttals, confirmation of former testimony, acts, writs, bulls, exceptions taken, grievances, objections, counter-objections ... confrontation of witnesses and accused; confrontation of the various co-accused ... certificates, libels and apostoles requesting the judge to refer the case to another court ... letters of attorney; royal letters; instruments of compulsion, forcing a clerk to produce a document ... declinatories, questioning the court's competence ... anticipatories, arguing the opponent's probable plea ... references to other jurisdictions ... returns of cases to the judges that had referred them ... conclusions, accessory contestations, appointments, appeals, confessions, notifications or executions of sentence ... and all other such spiceries and sweetmeats. ..." ...

"On the end of the table in my chambers, I place all the bags containing the defendant's plea, and I allow him the first hazard of the dice, just as you gentlemen do. ...

"This done—just like yourselves, gentlemen—I place the plaintiff's dossier at the other end of the table ... . Then I throw the dice for the plaintiff, too."

"But, my friend," Blusterer asked, "how do you determine the obscurity of arguments offered by the litigants?"

"Exactly as you, gentlemen," Bridlegoose replied. "When there are many bags on either end of the table, I use my small dice, just as you do, gentlemen, in accordance with the law. ...

"Of course I have other large, handsome and most suitable dice, which I use—like you gentlemen—when the matter is more liquid, that is to say, when the bags bearing the pleas are lighter."

"But when you had done all this," Blusterer insisted, "how did you pass sentence, my friend?"

"Just like yourselves, gentlemen," said Bridlegoose. "I decided in favor of the party who won at the judiciary, tribonian and praetorial throw of dice." ...

"Very well, my friend," said Blusterer, "but, since you pass sentence by the throw and hazard of dice, why do you not settle the matter then and there, the very same day and hour the litigants appear before you? Of what use are the papers and writs in the litigants' bags?"

"I find these documents as useful as you, gentlemen, find like documents, in similar instances. They are helpful in three exquisite, requisite and authentic manners: first, for formality; secondly, as physical exercies; thirdly, from considerations of time."

Bridlegoose then went on to explain.

(1) To begin with, form must be observed. If not, whatever a judge decided was valueless ... . Besides, the gentlemen of the court knew only too well that, in judicial proceedings, formalities destroyed the materiality and substance of the cases. ...

(2) Next, all these documents served Bridlegoose, as they served his honorable judges, here assembled, in the way of honest and healthful exercise. ...

(3) Bridlegoose's last reason for studying the documents involved a question of time. Like the gentlemen now sitting in judgment upon him, he realized that time brought all things to maturity. Time made everything clear; time was the father of truth. ...

"Accordingly, like yourselves, gentlemen, I put off, delay and postpone my definitive sentence, so that the suit, having been thoroughly sifted, winnowed and thrashed out, may, in process of time, attain its full maturity. Thus, when the fatal throw of the dice takes place, the condemned party will bear its misfortune more cheerfully. ...

"On the contrary, sentence passed when the suit is crude, unripe, and in its earliest stages, would cause the same discomfort as, according to the physicains, prematurely lancing an abscess, or purging the human body of a peccant humor before its digestion."

NOTES AND QUESTIONS

1. What exactly is wrong with using the process of dice-throwing to decide substantive issues? Does it not promote impartiality and objectivity? For an interesting discussion, see H. Greely, "The Equality of Allocation by Lot" (1977), 12 *Harvard CR-CLL Review* 113 and G. Calabresi and P. Bobbit, *Tragic Choices* (New York: W.W. Norton and Co., Inc., 1978), 41-44.

2. What is the relation between substantive and procedural justice? Does a particular procedure affect the range of likely outcomes?

In the following excerpt, Tyler argues on the basis of empirical evidence that procedures influence individuals' views about the legitimacy of the processes that affect them and that these views exist independently of how the individuals fare in terms of outcomes. How persuasive is the evidence that Tyler presents?

T. Tyler, *Why People Obey the Law*
(New Haven, CT: Yale University Press, 1990),
at 4-5, 6-7, 162-65 (footnotes omitted)

In this book I examine the extent to which normative factors influence compliance with the law independently of deterrence judgments. Data collected in a longitudinal study of randomly selected citizens in Chicago are used to examine the role of normative factors. In the first wave of the study 1,575 citizens were interviewed about their normative and instrumental views concerning the law, as well as their behavior toward the law. A subset of 804 respondents were reinterviewed about the same topics one year later (this procedure is the basic characteristic of a panel study). ...

The Meaning of Procedural Justice

The final goal of this book is to explore the meaning of procedural justice by contrasting the normative and instrumental approaches. The instrumental view of procedural justice contained in the control theory of Thibaut and Walker ... suggests that people do not focus directly on the favorability of the outcomes they receive from third parties. Instead, they focus on the degree to which they are able to exert influence over third-party decisions. People recognize that to the extent they have it, control over decisions leads to favorable outcomes. This control therefore represents indirect control over the favorability of outcomes. Thibaut and Walker suggest that people react to their experiences in terms of the favorability of outcomes, which is the key characteristic of an instrumental model. ...

The instrumental perspective on procedure suggests that assessments of procedural fairness are based on the favorability of the outcomes received: where people feel that they have control over decisions they believe that the procedure is fair; where they feel they lack control they believe it is unfair. If judgments about procedural fairness do simply reflect the favorability of outcomes, then aspects of procedure not linked to outcomes will contribute little to an understanding of whether people feel fairly treated, beyond what would already be learned by knowing the degree to which they control decisions.

The normative perspective on procedural justice views people as being concerned with aspects of their experience not linked only to outcomes. Normative aspects of experience include neutrality, lack of bias, honesty, efforts to be fair, politeness, and respect for citizens' rights. All these potential features of a procedure are conceptually distinct from its outcome and therefore represent values that may be used to define procedural fairness in terms not related to outcome. The extent to which people define the fairness of a procedure by using aspects of the procedure that are related and unrelated to its outcome reflects the influence of instrumental and normative aspects of experience on their judgments of whether they have received a fair procedure.

The meaning of procedural justice is examined in the same interviews about recent personal experience that are used to explore the impact of experience on legitimacy. Those interviewed were asked a series of questions about different aspects of their experience. These aspects of experience corresponded to elements of procedural justice related and unrelated to outcome. ...

If one accepts the image of the person that is put forth by the Chicago study, one will look in a new way at how people react to decisions in political, legal, and work organizations. In the legal arena citizens will be seen as reacting to the procedures through which court decisions are made, as well as to the decisions themselves. In politics people will react to policies and politicians on procedural grounds. And in the workplace they will be concerned with how decisions are made about pay and promotions. Therefore, decision makers can gain public acceptance for their decisions and rules by making and implementing them in ways that the public thinks is fair.

One clear implication is that authorities are freer than they commonly believe to follow painful policies that are sound in the long term. Authorities often feel that their legitimacy is linked to their ability to deliver tangible positive outcomes to self-interested citizens. They reflect the assumptions of the economic model, and think that people affected by their decisions will react to the decisions based on the extent of their personal gain or loss. That people attend to matters of procedure gives authorities latitude to pursue long-term policies by stressing the fairness of the procedures through which they came about. ...

Given the importance of procedural justice to legitimacy, it is crucial to understand how people define fair procedures. Again, an instrumental perspective contrasts with a normative one. According to the instrumental perspective of Thibaut and Walker ... , people define fairness primarily by the extent to which they are able to influence the decisions made by the third party. According to a normative perspective, there are many other aspects to the fairness of a procedure, which have little or nothing to do with outcomes or the control of outcomes. The Chicago study reinforces the normative perspective on the meaning of fair process. Judgments of procedural justice are found to be multi-dimensional. They involve many issues besides favorability of outcome and control of outcome. In fact, the criterion of fair procedure most closely related to outcomes (that is, consistency) is found to be of minor importance. In contrast, judgments about the social dimensions of the experience, such as ethicality, weigh very heavily in assessment of procedural justice. In the context of people's experiences with police officers and judges, the Chicago study found that seven different aspects of procedure independently influenced judgments about whether the procedure was fair.

One important element in feeling that procedures are fair is a belief on the part of those involved that they had an opportunity to take part in the decision-making process. This includes having an opportunity to present their arguments, being listened to, and having their views considered by the authorities. Those who feel that they have had a hand in the decision are typically much more accepting of its outcome, irrespective of what the outcome is. An additional advantage of procedures that allow both sides to state their arguments is that each side is exposed to the other. Because a party to a dispute is often unaware of the feelings and concerns of the other party, this exposure is very important. ...

Judgments of procedural fairness are also linked to judgments about the neutrality of the decision-making process. People believe that decision makers should be neutral and unbiased. They also expect decision makers to be honest and to reach their decisions based on objective information about the case. As is true of questions of participation, these issues are linked to settling the dispute or policy issue involved. Procedural fairness is also related to interpersonal aspects of the decision-making procedure. People place great weight on being treated politely and having respect shown for their rights and for themselves as people. The way people are dealt with by legal and political authorities has implications for their connection with the social group and their position in the community. It therefore has important implications for self-esteem ... and group identification ... . People are unlikely to feel attached to groups led by authorities who treat them rudely or ignore their rights. The treatment accorded by public officials is also an indication of the likelihood that people will receive help if they have problems in the future, and so has important implications for feelings of security. People will not feel identified with officials whom they regard as unresponsive to their problems and unwilling to help and protect them.

The importance that people attach to their relationship to authorities is reflected in the importance of another criterion of procedural justice: inferences about the motives of the authorities. The way people assess procedural fairness is strongly linked to their judgments of whether the authority they are dealing with is motivated to be fair. Because motivational inferences require considerably more cognitive effort then assessments of such surface features as honesty and bias, one might expect them to be avoided. Why are they instead central to assessments of procedural fairness? One advantage of inferences of motive or intention is that they reflect dispositional characteristics, that is, features of the person that are likely to predict their future behavior ... . The centrality of such inferences to issues of procedural justice reflects people's concern with knowing how authorities will act toward them in the future.

Finally, the fairness of procedures is linked to whether the procedures produce fair outcomes. Procedural issues are not independent of questions of outcome. Fair outcomes are one thing that people expect from a fair procedure, and a procedure that consistently produces unfair outcomes will eventually be viewed as unfair itself.

Although the factors outlined typically emerge as central to judgments about procedural justice, it is also important that the same issues are not used to judge the fairness of procedures with regard to all issues. In different situations people evaluate the fairness of procedures against different criteria of procedural justice: there is no universally fair procedure that can be used to resolve all types of problems and disputes. At the same time, different types of people do not evaluate the fairness of procedures against different criteria. Within the context of a particular type of problem or dispute, different types of people generally agree about the criteria that should be used to judge the fairness of the procedure. This finding is consistent with other recent evidence that there is a substantial consensus among Americans about what is fair.

III. THE IMPACT OF PROCEDURE

In the following case was lack of proper procedures the only issue? Does confining the ambit of the problem to procedural questions mask an even more difficult issue?

Murphy v. Dodd
(1989), 63 DLR (4th) 515 (Ont. HC)

[Gregory Murphy, who alleged he was the father of the fetus that Barbara Dodd was carrying, obtained an injunction restraining Dodd from having an abortion. On the initial hearing of the motion for this injunction, before O'Driscoll J, Dodd did not appear and was not represented by counsel. The matter had proceeded swiftly—the papers had been

served Friday, June 30th and the motion was heard on Tuesday, July 4th. Shortly thereafter, Dodd moved before Gray J to set aside the order granting the injunction. Motion
based on rules 38.12(1) and 59.06(2) to set aside an order of O'Driscoll J enjoining the
respondent from having an abortion.]

GRAY J (orally): In the Supreme Court of Ontario, Court File No. 1566/89 between
Gregory Murphy, applicant, and Barbara Dodd, Women's College Hospital, John Doe,
Jane Doe and other persons unknown, respondents.

In these reasons for judgment I will refer to Gregory Murphy as the applicant and
Barbara Dodd as the respondent because that was their status on the proceeding before
O'Driscoll J, on July 4, 1989. In the present motion before me the respondent Barbara
Dodd seeks leave to bring this motion on short notice and seeks an order setting aside
the order of O'Driscoll J, dated July 4, 1989. After hearing submissions I granted leave
to her to bring this motion on short notice. The disposition of her motion to set aside the
order aforesaid will be dealt with later.

The Canadian Hearing Society sought an order permitting it to intervene, pursuant
to rule 13.02 of the Rules of Civil Procedure in the present motion. It also sought leave
to bring its motion on short notice together with an order permitting the filing of the
affidavits of Joseph Regan and Denis Morrice as evidence in the respondent's motion.
After hearing submissions I granted leave to bring its motion on short notice and I make
an order permitting the Canadian Hearing Society to intervene and I made a further
order permitting the filing of the affidavits of Joseph Regan and Denis Morrice.

Rule 13.02 reads thus:

> Any person may, with leave of a judge or at the invitation of the presiding judge or
> Master, and without becoming a party to the proceeding, intervene as a friend of the
> court for the purpose of rendering assistance to the court by way of argument.

It is to be noted that the leave to intervene as a friend of the court would be granted
for the purpose of rendering assistance to the court by way of argument. The Canadian
Hearing Society takes no position with respect to the principal argument between the
parties and limited its submissions to a consideration of the applicability of rule 38.12(1)
in the present motion between the parties. I made the order permitting the society to
intervene because I was convinced that the society as a friend of the court could render
assistance to the court by way of argument.

The next matter I mention is of great importance. Notwithstanding certain publicity
which has been given to this motion, I must make it very clear that this motion is not an
appeal from the order of O'Driscoll J. This motion is expressed in the notice of motion
as a motion to set aside the said order. The two rules upon which the motion is based are
rules 38.12(1) and 59.06(2)(a). For the sake of completeness, I will set forth rule[s]
38.12(1) and (3) and 59.06(2)(a):

> 38.12(1) A person who is affected by a judgment on an application made without
> notice or *who fails to appear at the hearing of an application through accident, mistake*
> *or insufficient notice* may move to set aside or vary the judgment, by a notice of motion
> that is served forthwith after the judgment comes to the person's attention and names the

first available hearing date that is at least three days after service of the notice of motion. [Emphasis added.] ...

(3) On a motion under subrule (1), the judgment may be set aside or varied on such terms as are just. ...

59.06(2) A party who seeks to,

(a) have an order set aside or varied on the ground of fraud or of facts arising or discovered after it was made; ...

[m]ay make a motion in the proceeding for the relief claimed.

To fit within rule 38.12(1) the respondent must prove that she failed to appear on July 4, 1989, "through accident, mistake or insufficient notice," and to fit within rule 59.06(2) the respondent must prove the ground of fraud or facts arising or discovered after the order was made on July 4, 1989.

This is the endorsement made by O'Driscoll J, on July 4, 1989.

The time is 10:40 a.m.; counsel for the Applicant advises me that she has had indirect communication with the Respondent Dodd; neither Respondent appears nor does Dodd intend to appear by counsel. No-one is here to represent the hospital.

Order to go as requested in paragraphs 1(a), (b), (c) and (d) of the within Notice of Motion.

Counsel for the Applicant asks that I state that the order is granted on the grounds set out in para. 2(a) to (e) inclusive of the Notice of Motion. Assuming that I did agree with some or all of the said grounds, I do not find it necessary to volunteer opinion or obiter dicta on matters not necessary for the granting of injunctive relief.

No order as to costs. July 4/89, J O'Driscoll J.

This is the order of Mr. Justice O'Driscoll of that date, or I should say this is the substance of part of the order:

1. THIS COURT ORDERS that the Applicant is hereby granted leave to bring this application on short notice.

2. THIS COURT ORDERS that the Respondents, their servants, or agents are hereby restrained from taking the life of the infant Dodd-Murphy, either by performing or undergoing an abortion or a Caesarean operation or otherwise and from committing a trespass to the person of the infant Dodd-Murphy by assault or battery or otherwise.

3. THIS COURT DECLARES that the said infant Dodd-Murphy en ventre sa mere is under the protection of this honourable Court.

4. THIS COURT ORDERS THAT THERE BE NO ORDER AS TO COSTS.

I feel that O'Driscoll J was in a very, very difficult position. This is quite apparent from the wording of the endorsement and the short time which elapsed between the opening of weekly court and the time of 10:40 a.m.

I turn now to rule 38.12(1) and observe its wording. If the respondent is to succeed, she must convince me that she failed to appear through accident, mistake or insufficient notice. It would seem to me that the important words in this regard are the words "insufficient notice." Those words permit me to take into account all the circumstances surrounding the service. It is true that the parties were together for some considerable period of time on June 29, 1989, in the circumstances set forth in para. 29 of the applicant's most recent affidavit, together with the further facts set forth in paras. 30 and 31 thereof. The respondent's version is best understood by paras. 25 to 27 of her affidavit which reads thus:

25. On Thursday, June 29th, 1989, Greg came to me at Filmore's where I was working. I asked him to leave because he had made such a big scene at Elaina's recently. He made it clear that his family did not like the idea of my having an abortion and that he wanted me to go see a Father Lombardi who would try to persuade me to go through with the pregnancy. He also showed me what looked to me to be legal papers, the same legal papers.

26. Greg said to me on Thursday night at Filmore's, "I can spend thousands of dollars a day to prevent you having an abortion." This was the first time Greg actually stated to me that he opposed my abortion.

27. That on Friday, June 20, 1989, I was downstairs in my own home when Angela Costigan knocked at the door. I answered the door and she presented to me some papers and I asked her what are these. She answered me by speaking to me but she did not use the sign language of the deaf. I tried to follow her words and she said that it was something about the abortion. She did not explain to me anything about the proceeding, that I had to appear in Court, and I took the papers and glanced at them feeling very upset and shut the door. Over that weekend I had an opportunity to read the documents and understood that they were about trying to stop me from having an abortion. I was confused and afraid when I read these documents. I do not know any lawyers and I did not speak with members of my family nor did I have anyone to give me any advice. My abortion was scheduled for Tuesday July 4, 1989 and now the court date was also scheduled for the same time. I was torn between these two events and did not know what to do. At no time did I appreciate the significance of this court hearing and that it could affect my own choice to end my pregnancy. I was too frightened and confused and alone to appreciate this fact. If I had understood this fact, I would have spoken to my family and retained the services of counsel immediately to defend this injunction. To add to this problem, I felt that it was the long weekend and I could not get an interpreter or a lawyer to go to court with me. It was all muddled in my mind.

I accept that the respondent has some knowledge of courts from her earlier experiences in the Provincial Court (Criminal Division) and in matrimonial matters. The facts surrounding the service, however, are that the applicant's counsel served her on Friday, June 30, at 12:25 p.m., with the notice of application which in part reads thus (quoting from a portion of the printed form of the notice of application, there are three paragraphs to this):

IF YOU WISH TO OPPOSE THIS APPLICATION, you or an Ontario lawyer acting for you must forthwith prepare a Notice of Appearance in Form 38C prescribed by the Rules of Civil Procedure, serve it on the Applicant(s) lawyer(s) or, where the Applicant(s) do(es) not have a lawyer, serve it on the Applicant(s), and file it, with proof of service, in this court office, and you or your lawyer(s) must appear at the hearing. IF YOU WISH TO PRESENT AFFIDAVIT OR OTHER DOCUMENTARY EVIDENCE TO THE COURT OR TO EXAMINE OR CROSS-EXAMINE WITNESSES ON THE APPLICATION, you or your lawyer(s) must, in addition to serving your Notice of

Appearance, serve a copy of the evidence on the Applicant(s) lawyer(s) or, where the applicant(s) do(es) not have a lawyer, serve it on the applicant(s), and file it, with proof of service, in the court office where the application is to be heard as soon as possible, but not later than 2:00 p.m. on the day before the hearing.

IF YOU FAIL TO APPEAR AT THE HEARING, JUDGMENT MAY BE GIVEN IN YOUR ABSENCE AND WITHOUT FURTHER NOTICE TO YOU. IF YOU WISH TO OPPOSE THIS APPLICATION BUT ARE UNABLE TO PAY LEGAL FEES, LEGAL AID MAY BE AVAILABLE TO YOU BY CONTACTING A LOCAL LEGAL AID OFFICE.

I also accept that the respondent is an intelligent person and that there are no special rules in the Rules of Civil Procedure covering service of documents on deaf persons. I do not intend to establish any special procedure in that regard because that is a matter for the legislature or the rules committee. The fact that the respondent has a hearing deficiency or is almost totally deaf, in itself, does not assist. This notice was served on Friday at 12:25 p.m., and the respondent required to take action not later than 2:00 p.m. on the same day. The Monday following was a statutory holiday and the application came on in weekly court at 10:00 a.m. on Tuesday, July 4, 1989. I ask myself whether the respondent would understand the significance of such things as an injunction, an interim injunction, a declaration or leave to bring the application on short notice.

I am not prepared to hold that the respondent is a person lost in the justice system, but in all of the circumstances on the special facts of this case, it is my view that the notice in this case is an insufficient notice under rule 38.12(1). I emphasize the special facts of this case as to the matters referred to in the Regan affidavits, the time factors, the nature of the application and all the surrounding circumstances.

I turn now to rule 59.06(2). The position of the respondent is that O'Driscoll J would not have made the injunction order if there had not been what is called a fraud so far as the court was concerned. It is urged that the applicant misled the court by leaving the impression that he is the father of the fetus in question. He described the fetus as "our child" and "my child" throughout and spoke of "the infant Dodd-Murphy." Counsel for the applicant stresses the fact that on this branch the applicant cannot be accused of any fraud on the court by stating matters which he believes to be true or by stating matters which are the opinions of medical experts. The applicant's affidavit clearly left the impression that he is the father. He did not allow O'Driscoll J to have the knowledge that another man might be responsible for the paternity of the fetus in question.

Another factor concerns "danger to the respondent." There is a direct conflict in the evidence of Doctor Morad Sarref and the applicant, and there is good reason to believe that the order of O'Driscoll J would not have been made if this evidence of "danger to the respondent" had been put forward in Doctor Sarref's words. I cannot be expected in oral reasons for judgment to summarize all of the affidavit evidence, but there is considerable evidence to support the allegations concerning Doctor Sarref's position, he, being the respondent's gynecologist.

The respondent's position on para. 15 of her factum reads thus:

It is respectfully submitted that had the Honourable Mr. Justice O'Driscoll been aware that the hearsay assertion respecting medical advice that the Respondent's life was at "serious risk" by the prospective abortion was a bold-faced lie, he would never have acted upon the request for an injunction.

I have reached the conclusion that there was a fraud on the court within rule 59.06(2) within the learning set forth in *100 Main Street West v. Sakas* (1975), 8 OR (2d) 385 at p. 389, 58 DLR (3d) 161 at p. 165 (CA), and that the fraud related to issues that were material as that word was considered by Osborne J, in *International Corona Resources Ltd. v. LAC Minerals Ltd.* (1988), 66 OR (2d) 610 at pp. 622-3, 54 DLR (4th) 647 at pp. 658-9 (HCJ).

For these reasons, an order will issue setting aside the order of O'Driscoll J dated July 4, 1989.

As I stated in open court, I am obliged to counsel for their assistance in this matter, which was brought on with great expedition and is a credit to the administration of justice in Ontario.

I do not choose to deal with the subject of motive or the questions concerning injunctive relief, namely (1) whether standing should be granted to the applicant; (2) the status of the fetus on the present applicable law; and (3) whether injunctive relief to prevent abortion is to be granted in Ontario following the recent leading cases. Nor do I get into the classic learning concerning the granting of injunctions generally. I have been advised that until a few days ago, no injunction has been granted against a woman to prevent abortion, except the case at bar.

It may be that the matters with which we are concerned are matters for Parliament. In the result, therefore, as stated earlier, an order will issue setting aside the order herein of O'Driscoll J dated July 4, 1989.

I was going to ask counsel if they have any submissions with respect to the question of costs. I should say at the outset while my mind is open, I, at the present time, would not be inclined to do anything with respect to the order of costs made by Mr. Justice O'Driscoll which was, no order as to costs.

[Submissions re costs.]

The disposition with respect to costs in civil matters ... is that costs normally follow the event and normally follow the event on a party-and-party basis. However, since the new rules have come into effect, there was a great deal of learning that decided in certain instances, if there were unusual situations of some misconduct, solicitor-and-client costs can be ordered. I am relatively experienced in the question of costs. This is a matter on which there should not be costs on a solicitor-and-client basis and the question I put to myself is whether there should be no order as to costs for one or two reasons. One, because it is as a matrimonial matter, although strictly speaking not a matrimonial matter. ... Secondly, it is a rather unique case, which is difficult. No one knows more than I do since I started it yesterday morning. In the circumstances, it is my view that there should be no order as to costs.

NOTES AND QUESTIONS

1. In this case, Dodd asked to have the judgment set aside on the basis of rule 38.12. Did she succeed in this ground? Gray J stated that "[t]he fact that the respondent

has a hearing deficiency or is almost totally deaf, in itself, does not assist … but in view of all of the circumstances on the special facts of this case, it is my view that the notice in this case is an insufficient notice under rule 38.12(1)." Was Dodd's hearing loss a consideration that weighed in the result? Ought it to be a consideration?

Observe that the court expressly said that it is up to the Rules Committee to determine whether there should be special rules covering the service of documents on deaf persons. But if the court considers one's hearing capacity as a relevant consideration in assessing the sufficiency of notice, is the court not in fact creating rules with respect to service on deaf persons? The subject of service is dealt with in a subsequent chapter.

2. Dodd also asked to have the judgment set aside in the ground of rule 59.06(2). Did she succeed in this ground? What was Gray J's reasoning on this issue?

3. Although not contained in the report, immediately after Gray J gave his decision, counsel for Murphy requested a stay of Gray J's order (which would have had the effect of temporarily leaving in place O'Driscoll J's order) so that Murphy could appeal Gray J's order. Gray J refused the stay and Dodd proceeded immediately to have an abortion. She subsequently indicated to the press her regret that she had had the abortion: see *Toronto Star*, July 19, 1989, "Dodd now 'regrets' having abortion—'I wished I had more time to think.'"

4. The court permitted the Canadian Hearing Society to intervene to assist it through argument on the issue as to whether Dodd had received sufficient notice. In what ways might the Canadian Hearing Society have assisted the court? By allowing "interest groups" such as the Canadian Hearing Society to participate does the court process start to resemble a legislative process? Intervention as a device to expand the range of issues in litigation is dealt with in detail in a subsequent chapter.

5. Gray J noted that the case involved a number of issues that he chose not to decide—for example, whether standing should be granted in these proceedings to Murphy, and whether injunctive relief to prevent an abortion was an appropriate remedy to be granted. (Do you understand what is meant by "standing" in this context? Issues of standing are discussed in detail in a subsequent chapter.)

Subsequently, the Supreme Court of Canada addressed these more substantive issues. In *Daigle v. Tremblay*, [1989] 2 SCR 536, a trial judge had issued an injunction prohibiting a pregnant woman, Chantal Daigle, from obtaining an abortion. The plaintiff was her ex-boyfriend, Jean Guy Tremblay. The Quebec Court of Appeal in a 3-2 decision upheld the injunction and the Supreme Court of Canada reversed in an unanimous decision.

The Supreme Court heard the appeal in a special session during the summer recess. At that time, Chantal Daigle was 21 weeks pregnant and medical evidence indicated that no hospital in Quebec would perform an abortion after 20 weeks. During argument, the court was informed by counsel for Ms Daigle that she had obtained an abortion in the United States. Notwithstanding this fact, the court continued to hear the appeal because of its public importance and decided there was no legal basis for either foetal or father's rights under the Quebec Charter of Rights and Freedoms.

6. In deciding abortion cases do you think judges are influenced by their own views and attitudes toward abortion? If you were a judge would your decision be influenced by your views on the issue? If judges are so influenced is this proper or improper? What would it mean to decide this issue without reference to your own views?

IV. THEORETICAL UNDERPINNINGS OF PROCEDURE

The study of procedural rights involves two interdependent questions: when is there a right to any procedure and what procedures are appropriate? The answer to these questions will vary depending on the context and circumstances. For instance, what is an appropriate procedure, if any, for a disciplinary hearing *might* depend on whether it involves a professional, a student, or a prisoner. Further, it might be relevant whether the decision is about whether to grant someone a right or to take one away. An informed answer to these questions demands an understanding of the justifications, values, and objectives that underlie procedural systems. The central concern throughout must be why do we use particular procedures in particular situations? Procedural law is a cultural and social institution. As such, it takes its shape and colour from the larger social and political context within which it operates. No less than the substantive law, it reflects and embodies cultural values. Although often implicit, every judgment speaks to the crucial issue of what are the necessary and sufficient features of any procedural system or practice to warrant being termed "fair" or "just."

This issue is particularly pertinent in systemic terms. A particular rule may appear unjust in isolation, but may be justified in the context of the overall process. A whole set of prescriptive legal norms regulate and constitute the procedural system. These questions raise problems that go to the heart of the legal enterprise. In recent years, legal theorists and courts have begun to take procedure much more seriously.

The following extract summarizes and critiques some of the most prominent approaches to analyzing procedural values that have been advanced in the last several years.

Michael Bayles, "Principles for Legal Procedure"
(1986), 5 *Law and Philosophy* 33 (footnotes omitted)

The central normative question is: What principles would rational persons accept courts using to decide cases in a society in which they expected to live? As acceptable principles could and should vary with the type of society, the society is assumed to be an industrialized Western one with a common-law system. The crucial concepts to clarify are those of rational persons and principles. ...

Dispute Resolution and Truth

Two general purposes are inherent in the ... concept of adjudication—resolving disputes and finding the "truth." That courts render decisions in cases and controversies implies that one purpose is the resolution of disputes. If judicial decisions were not intended to resolve disputes but, say, only to indicate support for one side or the other, there would be little reason to litigate. One must be clear about the sense in which a dispute is resolved. Even after final judgment, losing parties can still think that they were right, and enmity can still exist between the parties. Courts do not necessarily resolve disputes at the psychological level, only at the practical level, and even there they are not always successful. If Abramowitz claims Baxter owes her $5439 and the court finds for her, then she is entitled to use state power to collect. Usually, but not always, Baxter will pay. The difficulty ex-spouses have in collecting spousal and child support indicates that court decisions do not always result in a practical settlement.

The purpose of ascertaining truth is less obviously inherent in the concept of adjudication. Adjudicators are to decide disputes by the application of rules and principles. Even assuming that the substantive rules and principles are correct, a dispute will not be properly decided in accordance with them unless the "truth" or correct facts are determined. The truth needs to be found not for its own sake but to apply the rules and principles to the dispute correctly. The particular aims of the substantive rules and principles—justice, economic efficiency, public policy—make no difference. If the situation is not accurately understood and described, then the aims cannot be rationally served by the decision either as a resolution of the particular case or as a guide in others. To the extent courts formulate rules for practical guidance, they need to be based on accurate information about the situations to which they are to apply, otherwise they might prescribe impractical and even harmful conduct.

Of course, judicial decision making is not a simple application of rules and principles to facts. First, finding facts is not a straightforward descriptive process. Facts must be classified for the application of rules and do not come neatly labeled. Second, many so-called factual questions are matters of evaluation. Determining whether someone was negligent, reasonable, or insane requires judgment and evaluation. Third, even when the facts are clear, it is not always clear what the rules and principles imply. Is a child on a railroad tie extending over a public river on railroad property or not? Nonetheless, there are core factual matters that one needs to get correct—that the child was on the tie, that the tie was fastened to railroad property, and so on.

The purposes of dispute resolution and ascertainment of the truth do not provide usable criteria for evaluating legal procedure; they are too general. Dispute resolution is the purpose of the whole of law, substantive as well as procedural. Unlike pure science, the law does not aim at the truth, the whole truth, and nothing but the truth. That would be too expensive and often irrelevant to the purpose of dispute resolution. Yet, disputes could be resolved without any concern for the truth. Arbitrary fiats or flips of a coin could be used practically to resolve many disputes. Consequently, more specific aims are needed to evaluate legal procedures.

Economic Costs

Although this section focuses on economic analysis of procedure, it is merely a specific instance of "single value instrumentalism." That is, the underlying concept is to design legal procedures as a means to maximize a single value or end. The economic approach seeks to maximize wealth or economic efficiency. Like any other instrument, legal procedure is viewed as an expense incurred in achieving an end, so the aim is to minimize the expense. The costs of incorrect decisions are called error costs, and those of making the decisions direct costs. The short statement of the aim is to minimize the sum of error and direct costs [Richard A. Posner, "An Economic Approach to Legal Procedure and Judicial Administration" (1973), 2 *Journal of Legal Studies*, at 399-400; Richard A. Posner, *Economic Analysis of Law*, 2d ed. (Boston: Little, Brown and Co., 1977), 429; and

Gordon Tullock, *Trials on Trial* (New York: Columbia University Press, 1980), at 5-6.] If
"EC" stands for error costs and "DC" for direct costs, it can be written as follows:

Minimize Sum (EC + DC)

One does not aim to minimize either cost alone but the sum of the two. If one tried to
minimize only direct costs, error costs might become exorbitant. Similarly, at some
point the increase in direct costs to achieve accuracy is greater than the savings in
reduced error costs.

A homey analogy might help one understand the view. In grocery shopping, one
aims to achieve the most value for the least expense. An error cost occurs when one
purchases an item at one store, say, a can of beans, when it could have been purchased
for less at another. The direct costs are those of obtaining information about prices at
various grocery stores and of transportation to and from them. One could drive from
store to store with one's shopping list and price the various items, and then return to the
stores buying the items at the lowest price. However, the investment of time and automobile expenses would probably make the total cost greater than simply purchasing all
the items at one store. Many shoppers take an intermediate approach. They determine
which store generally has the lowest prices for frequently bought staples. They also
subscribe to the local newspaper and read the food advertisements for specials. When
they go shopping, they do most of their shopping at the low priced store but stop at
others nearby to purchase specials. Although some items purchased could have been
obtained for less elsewhere, the combined cost of groceries, transportation, and newspaper is less than on any alternative. The economic approach recommends the same general method for evaluating legal procedure.

Legal error costs arise when an incorrect decision is made. The defendant is in fact
either guilty or innocent. (Criminal terminology is used for ease of expression; for civil
cases one can substitute "liable" and "not liable" for "guilty" and "innocent.") There are
thus four possible outcomes. The court can convict a guilty person (CG), convict an
innocent person (CI), not convict a guilty person (~CG), or not convict an innocent
person (~CI). Two of these decisions—CI and ~CG—are incorrect, and two—CG and
~CI—are correct. If the aim of the substantive law is economic efficiency, then each
incorrect decision results in an inefficient use of resources and is an inappropriate
expense. For example, if a tortfeasor is mistakenly found not liable, then economic
deterrence will not be achieved; insufficient resources will be spent on safety and the
cost of accidents will increase. Moreover, because courts might make such incorrect
decisions, some potential defendants will fail to invest in safety equipment, and some
potential plaintiffs with good cases will not bother to sue. A very rough estimate is that
US courts make incorrect decisions in about one-eighth of cases. In criminal cases,
conviction of innocent persons is probably much lower, but still significant—from 1 to 5
percent of cases. The error of false convictions are likely balanced by many more errors
of false acquittals.

Direct costs are those of running the legal system. These include the public costs for
judges' salaries, juries, courthouses, and so on, and the private costs of the parties in
hiring lawyers, obtaining expert testimony, and so forth. In general, as private costs
increase fewer cases are taken to court and public costs decrease, although many other

factors influence decisions to go to trial, such as the amount at stake and the estimated chances of winning. The direct costs of settling out of court or plea bargaining are significantly less than trials. Consequently, an increase in settlements decreases direct costs. Most economic analysts assume that increased settlements increase error costs. This assumption appears well founded, because a settlement of a civil case is usually incorrect. Suppose the total damages in a tort case are $10,000. A settlement will almost always be between zero and the maximum a losing defendant can expect to pay. However, either the defendant should pay $10,000 or nothing, so the settlement involves the defendant paying less or more than he or she ought. (This argument does not apply under contributory negligence if the plaintiff's negligence is in dispute, for then the defendant's proper liability might be near the settlement.) ...

Two objections are commonly made against the economic approach. First, many people claim that one cannot place a dollar value on the concerns of plaintiffs. The loss of life or limb, it is said, cannot be adequately valued in monetary terms. However, this objection goes as much to substantive law as to procedural law. It applies more to the calculation of monetary damages for tort losses than it does to procedural law. Criminal cases might be a better basis for the objection. Nonetheless, an economic analyst can reply that crime costs money. It can be given a monetary value by considering its actual costs (for example, amount stolen) and the costs of deterring it. Even those plaintiffs in defamation actions who want vindication more than damages indicate how much vindication is worth to them by how much they are willing to spend to obtain it.

The second objection is that the economic approach or any other single value analysis omits important values. One can reasonably be concerned about the fairness as well as total cost of legal procedures. A process might be less expensive than another but unacceptable because distinctly less fair. Other suggested values that might be omitted from an economic analysis are dignity and participation. However, an economic analyst can reply that, as in the case of vindication in defamation cases, one need only place a dollar value on concerns for equality or dignity and the theory can accommodate them. Here, however, the response is not adequate. In the previous objection, the concern was with outcomes. The economic approach is concerned only with the costs of outcomes—producing them and their being incorrect. Concerns for fairness and dignity are not necessarily aspects of outcomes (error costs) or costs of the procedure (direct costs). Fairness is not necessarily the same as the minimization of error. This issue is considered further in the section on process benefits.

The economic approach does at least indicate one important factor to be taken into account in evaluating legal procedure. One has no reason to increase economic costs without good reasons. In short, all else being equal, anyone concerned with wealth has a good reason to prefer lower to higher economic costs, whether they be direct or error costs. *(1) The principle of economic costs: One should minimize the economic costs of legal procedures.*

Moral Costs

Another approach to legal procedure emphasizes that values other than economic costs are involved in evaluating outcomes. The moral cost approach of Ronald Dworkin

[Ronald Dworkin, "Principle, Policy, Procedure," in C.F.H. Tapper, ed., *Crime, Proof and Punishment* (London: Butterworths, 1981), at 193-225] is an instance of "multivalue instrumentalism," that is, an approach that evaluates procedures by seeking to maximize several values of outcomes. Dworkin contends that utilitarian (including economic) approaches to procedure ignore rights. He focuses on criminal cases in which he claims there is a right not to be punished if innocent. A utilitarian single value instrumentalism looks at what Dworkin calls the "bare harm" inflicted by mistaken decisions; it considers how much suffering actually results from mistaken decisions. Dworkin contends that convicted innocent persons might not suffer any more bare harm than results from failing to convict guilty persons. Consequently, there need be no greater reason to avoid convicting the innocent than to avoid not convicting the guilty. This gives inadequate weight to a right not to be convicted if innocent.

Economic analysts do argue that there is a greater cost in convicting innocent persons than in failing to convict guilty ones. This then supports the higher burden of proof required for criminal than civil liability. One reason for lower error costs for failing to convict the guilty than for convicting the innocent is that failure to convict one guilty person will probably not have much of an effect on the law's deterrence, and an increased crime rate is the chief error cost. Nonetheless, the fewer guilty persons convicted, the greater the punishment has to be to maintain an effective deterrent. Thus, as the burden of proof requirement is raised, the amount of punishment also needs to be raised to maintain an equal deterrence. It is not clear that innocent persons benefit from a lower chance of a greater punishment.

The moral cost approach implies that there are at least two types of error costs. Consider the two possible mistaken decisions, convicting the innocent (CI) and not convicting the guilty (~CG). The first is worse than the second, regardless of the bare or economic harm involved in the two, because it infringes the right not to be convicted if innocent. Such violations of rights are moral harms or costs. Moral harm can also occur in civil cases. If one party has a right that might be infringed by an incorrect decision and the other party does not, then procedures should be biased against infringing that right and causing moral harm. Often in civil cases a mistake in either direction involves equal moral harm. For example, whether a deserving tort plaintiff is denied recovery or an "innocent" tort defendant is made to pay damages, moral harm is involved. But in some civil cases, moral harm is perhaps greater on one side than another, for example, suffering an uncompensated defamation rather than paying damages for a truthful libel.

The moral cost approach adds another determinant to the economic approach's analysis of error costs. Besides the economic or bare harm costs of error, there are also moral costs. Thus, the aim of legal procedure can be stated as minimizing the sum of the economic and moral error costs and the direct costs. If "EC" here stands for the economic or bare harm error costs and "MC" for the moral error costs, then the moral harm view merely adds another term to the economic approach's formula:

$$\text{Minimize Sum (EC + MC + DC)}$$

Moreover, according to Dworkin, moral cost is an objective and constant factor across cases of the same type. That is, moral harm is the same whenever the same right is infringed, so moral costs are a constant factor for each type of cases. ...

One has good reason to add moral costs to economic costs if one has good reason to prefer one type of error over another. To do so, one need not accept Dworkin's notion of rights being involved. One might arrive at the same position as Dworkin regarding the aim of avoiding punishment of innocent persons without invoking rights. So long as CI is a less desirable outcome than ~CG, there is a reason to prefer ~CG errors to CI errors. The same result occurs whenever a principle of substantive law is based on something other than economic efficiency. Moral costs are simply the costs of failure to achieve aims other than economic efficiency, such as not enforcing unconscionable contract terms or providing compensation in tort. *(2) The principle of moral costs: One should minimize the moral costs of legal procedures.*

The moral cost approach does not differ from the economic approach as significantly as might appear. First, some economic analysts have recognized that the substantive law might have aims other than economic efficiency. If the failure to achieve a substantive aim can be evaluated in monetary terms, the same cost minimizing approach can be used. Second, one cannot plausibly maintain that no monetary value can be placed on moral costs, because the moral cost approach requires balancing monetary error and direct costs with moral costs. Even if a price cannot be directly placed on moral costs, an indirect pricing occurs. One need only consider how much one is willing to pay in economic costs to avoid moral costs. That amount is the price of the moral costs. For example, the cost of increased crime and punishment resulting from placing the burden of proof on the prosecution is the price of the moral harm in punishing the innocent. Third, the moral cost approach is still an instrumentalist one. Legal procedure is simply a means to achieving proper outcomes. ...

The instrumentalism of the economic and moral cost approaches has a significant implication for legal procedure. One can evaluate procedures as leading to correct and incorrect outcomes (consider error costs) only if outcomes are either correct or incorrect. The economic approach is assured of outcomes being correct or incorrect, if the aim of substantive law is economic efficiency. An outcome either is or is not economically efficient. Similarly, one of Dworkin's major theses is that legal cases always have a right answer. But if they are wrong and there are no correct answers, there are no error costs. If there are no error costs, both the economic and moral cost approaches prescribe minimizing direct costs. Consequently, one should not have a hearing with the presentation of information but merely flip a coin or otherwise inexpensively render a decision to settle the dispute.

One must distinguish some or a few cases not having a correct answer from there never being correct answers for certain types of cases. The dire implications above result only if cases of a certain type never, or almost never, have correct answers. If only a few cases of some type fail to have correct answers, then one might design legal procedures on instrumental grounds for the usual cases with correct answers. Nonetheless, the amount of direct costs one should rationally bear to avoid error costs should be reduced by some amount to account for cases without correct answers.

Another implication of instrumentalist approaches and our first two principles deserve notice. Substance and procedure are closely related. The more significant the substantive issues, whether economically or morally, the greater the error costs. A mistaken judgment in a case involving $500 does not impose the error costs a similar mistake in a case involving $500,000 does. Similarly, moral costs vary with the substantive principle involved or the amount of moral harm (different amounts of punishment). Contrary to Dworkin, the moral harm of imprisoning an innocent person for five years is greater than that of imprisoning an innocent person for five months. The moral harm is greater the greater the violation of a right. Consequently, fewer direct costs are justified in cases involving less significant substantive matters. This reasoning supports less expensive and less elaborate procedures for smaller matters—small claims courts, traffic violations, and so on.

Because they are instrumentalist approaches concerned with the costs of avoiding errors, the economic and moral cost approaches focus on truth finding. If there is no truth to be found, there is no reason for legal procedure. They are concerned with dispute resolution only in that decisions give correct answers to disputes. One can view the next approach as adding a concern with resolving disputes, at the psychological as well as practical level.

Process Benefits

Another approach to legal procedure is to consider values or benefits of procedures independent of their effect on the accuracy of outcomes. [See Robert S. Summers, "Evaluating and Improving Legal Processes—A Plea for 'Process Values,'" (1974), 60 *Cornell Law Review*, at 1-52, and Jerry L. Mashaw, "Administrative Due Process: The Quest for a Dignitary Theory," (1981), 61 *Boston University Law Review*, at 885-931.] There might be values such as dignity, fairness, and participation served by legal procedures even though they do not increase the accuracy of decisions. One might describe this approach as an "inherent process value" approach. However, the concept of inherent value can be misleading. It might suggest that the values are independent of the effects of a process. This is not the case, or at least, need not be the case. The moral and economic error costs are the result of incorrect decisions. The inherent values served are simply independent of decision outcomes. Put another way, the causal chain from procedure to economic and moral error costs goes through the decision rendered, while the causal chain from procedures to process values or benefits does not go through the decision. Process values are logically in the position of direct costs, which are also independent of the decision. They are satisfactions derived from the process itself.

The process values served by legal procedure can be viewed as benefits corresponding to direct costs. Both the economic and moral cost approaches view legal procedures as expenses to be borne only if they contribute to reducing error costs. However, one might prefer one procedure to another even if both have the same direct costs and are equally effective in producing a desired outcome, have the same error costs. An analogy illustrates the point. Suppose one wants to lose ten pounds. Further suppose one can do so equally well by a daily exercise program of either calisthenics or tennis. One might prefer tennis to calisthenics, even if tennis costs more. One might consider tennis to have other benefits than mere weight loss. Similarly, one might prefer one type of legal procedure to another, even though they are equally accurate. ...

The argument so far shows that one might perceive benefits or values in legal procedures independent of outcomes. Moreover, these benefits should be kept distinct from direct costs. Consequently, the formula for evaluating legal procedures needs to have another term added to indicate process benefits. If "PB" stands for process benefits, the formula can be represented as follows:

$$\text{Minimize Sum } (EC + MC + DC - PB)$$

Process benefits are subtracted rather than added, because the other terms are costs.

This approach avoids one possible problem of instrumentalism, namely, the implication that if there is no correct outcome, then the least expensive procedure should be used. Process benefits might offset significant direct costs, so a fairly complex and expensive procedure might still be justified. Of course, if "least expensive" is confusingly taken to mean "the net of direct costs and process benefits," then one should use the least expensive procedure ($S-1$ being less expensive than S). The process benefits approach retains the instrumentalist implication that substance can affect procedure, because error costs are still relevant whenever they exist.

The argument has not yet established that there are any process values or the basis on which they can be determined, only that if there are such values, evaluation of legal procedure should explicitly take them into account. A basis for process values exists in the inherent purpose of dispute resolution. Instrumentalist approaches focus on truth finding, ignoring dispute resolution except as it results from correct decisions. Process benefits contribute to both psychological and practical dispute resolution. Features of legal procedure can contribute to dispute resolution without contributing to accuracy. Without claiming completeness, a number of process benefits and principles can be identified on these grounds.

(3) *The principle of peacefulness: Procedures should be peaceful.* This principle is one of the foundations of a legal system. Without legal procedures for resolving disputes, they are likely to result in violence and blood feuds. For the same reasons people rationally desire the criminal law, they also want peaceful procedures. This principle is especially important in limiting self-help.

(4) *The principle of voluntariness: People should be able voluntarily to have their disputes legally resolved.* This principle must be carefully restricted. It states that one should be able, if one chooses, to have disputes legally settled. It does not imply that if one party does not want a legal resolution, that party can veto such a procedure. Instead, the principle applies primarily to plaintiffs in civil cases. Defendants, whether civil or criminal, should not be able to block legal proceedings by enabling aggrieved parties to obtain an authoritative settlement. It thus also contributes to peace. An alternative would be to have state agents bring all cases. This would involve great public expense or else many disputes that could be legally resolved would not be. Not all disputes are open to legal resolution. For a variety of reasons, such as the trivial nature of the matter, courts should not undertake to resolve some disputes. Many of these limitations are part of the substantive law, for example, not usually allowing tort recovery for pure economic loss and not enforcing unrelied on and unwritten gratuitous promises.

(5) *The principle of participation: Parties should be able to participate meaningfully in the legal resolution of disputes.* This principle is evidenced in the common notion of having one's day in court. If one cannot participate, then one is denied one's day in court. The principle contributes to dispute resolution, because parties that have been able

to participate are more likely to accept a decision; although they might not agree with the decision, they are more likely to comply with it. Trials *in absentia* and *ex parte* hearings violate this principle and are used sparingly. One value underlying the principle is participation in decisions that significantly affect one's life. One reasonably desires to at least be heard, to have one's say, before decisions affecting one are made. Being permitted to participate also evidences others' respect, that one is to be considered seriously.

(6) The principle of fairness: Procedures should be fair—treat the parties equally. Fairness here essentially means equality of treatment in the procedures. Given an equal chance of being plaintiff or defendant, one would not want the procedures biased toward one side or another, except as that can be justified by considerations acceptable from both perspectives. For example, in the previous section it was noted that the burden of proof can justifiably be weighted due to substantive aims. Parties are less likely to accept decisions as resolving their dispute, either psychologically or practically, if they think the procedures used to arrive at them were unfair. Several subprinciples help spell out fairness. (1) The dispute settler should be neutral. People should not be judges in their own cases; a judge or jury should not be biased. (2) At the hearing, the information of both sides should be presented. (3) Each party should at least be aware of the information presented by the other and have an opportunity to respond to it. The principle of fairness only specifies that the parties have an equal opportunity to participate; the principle of participation provides a reason for significant participation.

(7) The principle of intelligibility: Procedures should be intelligible to the parties. Generally, rationality increases intelligibility. Consequently, the more rational the procedures for ascertaining the truth and arriving at decisions, the more rational parties will assent to the outcomes. That is, if people can understand the process and the reasons for a decision, they are more likely to accept it as settling their dispute. It follows that decisions should be articulated in terms of rational rules and principles and information developed at a hearing or trial.

(8) The principle of timeliness: Procedures should provide timely decisions. Timeliness is a mean between the extremes of haste and dilatoriness. Persons do not rationally want decisions made without adequate time to gather information and reflect on its significance. In part, this concern pertains to outcomes; hasty decisions are more likely to be incorrect. However, the concern the other way, to avoid dilatoriness, is not. People do not want to wait longer than necessary for resolutions of their disputes. Delay in dispute resolution is likely to encourage people to take matters into their own hands. The saying that "[j]ustice delayed is justice denied" is not correct substantively, for a delayed decision can be substantively correct. Nonetheless, delay prevents people planning and living their lives. An instrumentalist approach to delay is likely to ignore this aspect, concentrating only on its effects on settlements and economic costs.

(9) The principle of repose: A final resolution of a dispute should be made. Disputes are not resolved if they can be reopened. If appeals are always possible, if the same issues can be raised in another case, then the dispute is not settled. If people invoke legal procedures to settle disputes, then there must be a point at which they are finally settled, otherwise there is no point in invoking legal procedures.

The inherent purposes of legal procedure are truth finding and dispute resolution. Obviously, people want to achieve these purposes at as little cost as possible. The purpose of truth finding primarily involves the avoidance of economic and moral error costs. The purpose of dispute resolution involves process benefits making a practical resolution more likely. These elements must be considered in a framework of trying to keep the direct costs of legal procedure as low as reasonably possible. The general normative aim, then, is to minimize the sum of economic and moral error costs and direct costs less process benefits.

Finally, one important aspect of legal cases should be noted, namely, they are minus sum interactions. This point is implicit in the assumption that error and direct costs are greater than process benefits. Although individual plaintiffs can gain from legal cases by obtaining damages and other remedies, overall, legal cases are a net loss. Consequently, from a social perspective or that of potentially being either plaintiff or defendant, lawsuits are to be avoided. The justification of a legal system and procedures must be one of lesser evils, that legal resolution of disputes is preferable to blood feuds, rampant crime and violence, and so on.

QUESTIONS

Are you convinced by Bayles' conclusion that "the general normative aim is to minimize the sum of economic and moral error costs and direct costs less process benefits"? Is this aim capable of having any operative effect?

The following article provides criticisms of many of the assumptions of procedural justice, including those contained in Bayles.

William Simon, "The Ideology of Advocacy"
(1978), *Wisconsin Law Review* 29, at 39-52 (footnotes omitted)

In the Positivist view, society is an aggregate of egoistic individuals each pursuing his own ends. Government is an artificial creation, the basic function of which is to remedy the disorder which would result if the natural centrifugal tendencies of society went unchecked. Disorder is undesirable for two reasons. First, it makes for uncertainty, a constant fear about the future and an inability to plan one's activities so as to best attain one's ends. Second, it makes for oppression, the necessity of subordinating one's own ends to those of whomever is strongest at the moment. Since the need for order is the most basic of social needs and is shared by all men, a government which secures order has a claim to the loyalty of all its citizens.

Ends are natural, individual, subjective, and arbitrary. Social norms result from the random convergence of individual ends. By contrast, it is possible to construct a system of rules which is artificial, impersonal, objective, and rational. The best way to provide order is to create a sovereign (e.g., monarch, legislature, party) which is neutral toward the various ends of the citizens and which acts through rules. Rules will give a regularity to social life and thus eliminate uncertainty. Oppression will be eliminated once power is concentrated in the hands of a neutral ruler. An obstacle remains. The legitimacy of the sovereign rests solely on the unique end of order which all share. Yet, from the point of view of each citizen, this end extends only to the orderly behavior of the others. People will constantly be tempted to violate the rules in order to pursue their own individual ends. No one will be willing to pay the price of resisting such temptation without some assurance that the others will also obey. The solution is to have the rules provide for the administration of rewards and punishments in a manner calculated to insure general obedience.

The rules will define for each citizen a private sphere of autonomy. Within this sphere, he need not account to anyone for his actions. So long as he remains within his sphere, he need not fear coercion by the sovereign. The sovereign's enforcement of the rules against the other citizens will insure that they do not trespass within his sphere. Where disputes arise, they must be resolved in accordance with the rules. Since the sovereign cannot itself apply the rules to every particular dispute, it must appoint judges to act on its behalf. It is important that the judges apply the rules with impersonal regularity. They must not refer to their own personal ends. Otherwise, they would create uncertainty, and their decisions would be oppressive. The rules cannot specify a specific result for each situation to which they apply, but the judge will be able to determine the proper result in any given situation because the rules have a systematic quality. The system may involve formal logic, linguistic analysis, empirical observation, or some combination of these methods. The system enables the judge to reason from the general prescriptions of the rules of particular results. The judge applies the rules to the factual premises of the given situation. The disposition of the case is dictated by the system. The judge has no discretion; he is bound by the system. ...

The Procedural Problems

Procedure comes as something of an afterthought in Positivism, and the problems it creates are never fully acknowledged. Two procedural problems in particular—the problems of enforcement and access—represent serious dangers of uncertainty and oppression for which Positivism makes no adequate provision.

Positivist discussions of procedure begin with a belated recognition of a basic contradiction: in the Positivist system, the sovereign is both the only guarantee of order and the greatest threat to it. Since obedience to the rules does not come naturally, the sovereign must be charged with the power and duty to enforce them. But this task poses a terrifying prospect. The only effective means of enforcement involve torture, deprivation of liberty, invasion of privacy, or confiscation of property. These means are necessary both to get the information needed to determine that the rules have been violated and to deter future violations. Fact-finding holds the further danger that the sovereign will constantly be finding new evidence or revising his reasoning so as to upset previous determinations on which people have relied. Moreover, once the facts have been determined, there remains the further problem that the sovereign and its agents are likely to act inconsistently in applying the rules to different situations. No matter how elaborately the legal system is constructed, ambiguities will remain, and in choosing among alternative interpretations, the judges will act inconsistently, and will thus produce unpredictable results. ...

To meet this problem, Positivism proposes a second body of rules which limit the enforcement powers of the sovereign. As the purpose of the first set of rules is to impose regularity on conduct in the social world, the purpose of the second is to impose regularity on the actions of the sovereign. The first kind of rule is called substantive, and the second kind procedural. The procedural rules require that certain evidence be produced before the sovereign may act on the premise that a substantive rule has been violated. They limit the ways in which the sovereign can procure evidence and prescribe the manner in which it can be presented. They limit the authority of the sovereign to make and revise findings of fact and interpretations of rules. And they specify the sanctions which the sovereign may apply upon finding that the rules have been broken.

The establishment of this second body of rules has a curious consequence. The substantive rules reflect the basic purpose of the system, the securing of order in the social world. The procedural rules are designed to deal with a technical problem. Once the system is set into motion, however, the procedural rules play the more fundamental role. Order depends on the citizens' compliance with the substantive rules, and compliance depends on the application of sanctions by the sovereign. The application of sanctions is governed by the procedural rules. The key to the system is the operation of the sovereign, and the ultimate test of the legitimacy of any of the sovereign's acts is procedural. For the citizen, this means that compliance with the substantive law does not guarantee immunity from state sanctions. Nor does liability necessarily follow from violations of the substantive rules. The procedural rules legitimate results which may be substantively wrong. Having repudiated personal notions of justice at the outset of its system, Positivism ends by refusing to guarantee the citizen even the legal justice defined by the substantive law. All the citizen can count on is a day in court.

The citizen's bewilderment may be a matter of indifference to the Positivist, but it is not so easy for him to shrug off another difficulty. The second body of rules has not solved the problem of disorder. The risk of disorder from the sovereign has been diminished only by impairing the efficiency of the sovereign's enforcement powers and hence by increasing the risk of disorder from the citizens. The procedural rules give the citizens a broad range of discretion. The existence of this discretion undermines the Positivist claim to secure order through the delegation of power to a neutral sovereign who exercises it through a system of rules. The citizens can use their procedural discretion to thwart the enforcement of the substantive rules and to affect the exercise of state power in accordance with their individual ends. Once the existence of this discretion is recognized, the actions of the sovereign appear to result, not from the neutral, systematic application of rules to given factual premises, but from the strategic exercise of procedural discretion by private parties.

For instance, the procedural rules which require that evidence be produced before sanctions can be applied and which limit the ways in which evidence can be obtained enable people to conceal violations of the substantive rules by not leaving evidence or by withholding or destroying it. The rules which govern evidence at trial enable people to thwart the enforcement of the substantive law by excluding or discrediting probative evidence or by introducing misleading evidence. Procedural rules permit people whose claims have no substantive validity to put others to the risk of proof. They enable people to frustrate enforcement by delaying and by imposing expenses on their adversaries.

They permit people to influence enforcement by strategic choices as to whether to initiate proceedings, when to do so, and before which tribunal to do so. They make it possible for some to influence rule interpretation by framing legal issues for decision in factual contexts favorable to the interpretation which suits their ends. ...

Although the point is clearest in large-scale contests involving great interests, in fact almost all litigation has this instrumental, discretionary, *disorderly* character. In the vast majority of cases which are settled, there is not even a pretense that the result has been determined by the application of a system of substantive rules to given factual premises. The sovereign merely ratifies a result which the parties have negotiated by each giving up procedural discretion to injure the interests of the other. Even when there is a contested judgment it will rarely appear as a mechanical vindication of substantive commands. More often, it will seem a consequence of a party's exercise of discretion, for instance, to plead not guilty, or to choose a favorable forum, or to appeal to the prejudices of the jury. On Positivist premises, given the existence of such discretion, every lawsuit is likely to be a form of "legalized blackmail."

In creating a critical role for private discretion, procedure undermines the basic Positivist guarantee of order. Uncertainty becomes inevitable because the actions of the sovereign cannot be reliably predicted. The sovereign's actions are determined by procedural discretion. This discretion is not exercised by the citizens in any systematic fashion, but rather it is exercised instrumentally in the pursuit of their individual, subjective, and arbitrary ends. The problem is not just that procedure complicates the analysis. More importantly, the procedural rules create a situation in which outcomes depend on contingencies which are not susceptible to legal analysis. They depend on private decisions which are not controlled by the rules. Moreover, oppression still threatens. Positivism's claim to eliminate oppression is plausible only to the extent that people see state intervention as governed by a neutral system of rules. The system as a whole can be shown to be just vis-à-vis all the citizens, but no particular outcome can be shown to be just except by tracing it to the system. However, once the role of procedural discretion is recognized, the actions of the sovereign appear to be determined by private power. As such, they constitute oppression.

Thus, to the extent that procedure checks public anarchy, it unleashes private anarchy. ...

The second procedural dilemma of Positivism arises from the question of access to the legal system. Positivism recognizes that the strangeness and complexity of the law creates a new danger of oppression. The danger is that some will be able to anticipate state intervention better than others and that they will use their knowledge to the disadvantage of the less informed. Positivism's basic response to this danger is a promise to make counsel available to people regardless of their ends. Availability can mean either access for those who can pay, or some guaranteed level of access regardless of wealth. But neither approach is adequate.

Availability means merely formal access when Positivist legal theory is linked to the theory of the self-regulating market. ... According to this theory, each individual should be left to choose for himself which goods and services he will receive from the rest of society, but only within the limits of his wealth. The limits of his wealth should be determined by a series of bargains in which he sells his labor or whatever else he has for the best price he can get for it. In this view, legal services are merely another commodity which the individual can purchase or not according to his own schedule of satisfactions. Formal availability is the opportunity to use the proceeds of the sale of one's own labor to purchase legal services at the going rate. ...

This situation involves the citizen in a vicious circle. Because the process of economic bargaining is defined and regulated by the law, a person needs to know the law in order to understand his position and his options. In order to make the best bargains, he needs legal advice. Yet, in order to get legal advice, he needs to make good enough bargains to provide himself with the means to hire a lawyer. Contrary to the assumptions of those who advocate formal availability, legal services are not just another commodity, but rather a prerequisite to participation in the system. Where legal services are only formally available, the poor, who are unable to purchase legal services, may remain poor for precisely that reason. Their ignorance of the law puts them in an inferior bargaining position which will prevent them from realizing the full value of their labor in the market.

The profession's more recent response to the problem of access is to acknowledge some responsibility for making legal services available to those who cannot pay for them. Yet, in terms of Positivist theory, this solution is little more plausible than the formal one. There is no practical way of equalizing access to legal services sufficiently to preclude oppression. The society is not prepared to make the enormous expenditures necessary to provide everyone with substantial access to legal assistance. ...

Thus, knowledge of the rules will necessarily be unequally distributed, and as a practical matter large numbers of people will be denied any substantial access to the legal system. Those who can afford a large amount of legal services will be able to use their superior knowledge to maneuver others into situations where the sovereign's interventions will benefit them at the expense of the others. It may turn out that the sovereign's interventions routinely serve the ends of those with superior knowledge of the rules.

The problem of access is aggravated by the problem of enforcement. The citizen needs legal services not only to learn his rights, but also to enforce them against the trespasses of others. The advantaged can make far better use of their procedural discretion than the disadvantaged. They can engage in far more elaborate and sophisticated procedural strategies. They can use the procedural rules to increase the expenses of the disadvantaged in asserting their claims so that the latter must give up or compromise before their claims have been determined.

At the same time, any attempt to alleviate the problem of access by increasing the availability of legal services will only aggravate the problem of enforcement. The expansion of legal services multiplies the number of people able to exploit their procedural rights so as to thwart the commands of the substantive law and escalates their ability to do so.

QUESTIONS

Reread Bayles. Compare his analysis with Simon's. Do any of Bayles's positions hold up under Simon's criticism? Do you agree with Simon? To what extent is he proposing a solution?

CHAPTER THREE

The Core Features and Values of the Traditional Model

I. INTRODUCTION

With this chapter we begin a detailed discussion of the models for decision making for non-criminal disputes and their significance to a theoretical understanding of civil procedure. We will examine the following models: traditional, inquisitorial adjudication, case management, public law, ADR, administrative state, and dispute resolution in aboriginal societies.

This chapter discusses the traditional model in detail. We first analyze its structure and underlying values, and second look at the implications of this model for lawyering and legal ethics.

Regarding the first point, in crafting the traditional model, the common law focused on the lawsuit as a mode of dispute resolution centred on the determination of interests and remedies on an individual basis. The traditional model emphasized protection of proprietary or economic entitlement. In this depiction, a lawsuit is a claim on the part of a plaintiff and an assertion of a defence heard by an aloof, passive judge (or jury) finding relevant facts and applying the applicable law. If the plaintiff prevails, the remedy is simple and straightforward, usually a monetary payment or sometimes a directive to return something or to do a clearly defined act. If the plaintiff loses, he or she is heard from no more (other than by way of appeal). In either case, the court's involvement is contained and minimal and the lawsuit is perceived as a sealed, episodic event. The central focus of the model is vindication of interests; any policy making is incidental to that pivotal task.

Some commentators contend that the reasons for this structure are clear. In their view, Canadian courts have long been dominated in many areas (there are important exceptions) by classic liberal ideology. Such an organizing set of ideas places great emphasis on individual rights, autonomous and private ordering, and minimal state involvement.

Whatever its strengths and weaknesses, the traditional model, however modified, continues to dominate much civil litigation in Canada. Nevertheless, there have been strong reactions to this model. Such reactions will be apparent in the other models we examine in chapter 4, "Challenges to the Traditional Model."

We begin with the structure dictated by the traditional model. Here we reproduce an excerpt from a leading article that discusses adjudication. Adjudication takes many forms and is applied in many contexts. At its most basic, it refers to a decision-making process wherein a third party (an outsider to the dispute), after hearing proofs and arguments presented by the disputants, renders a decision binding on the parties to the dispute. In its purest form it is most closely linked to the traditional model in which the judge is cast in an aloof and passive role.

Under the heading "Values Underlying the Structure of the Traditional Model," we include part of an article by Brooks. For Brooks, the traditional model reflects the political and economic ideology of classic liberal individualism. The active parties, the passive judge, restrictive rules concerning standing and intervention, and a costs regime that rewards winning litigants by making losers pay costs have helped to reinforce his beliefs. (Standing, intervention, and costs are discussed in detail in later chapters.)

Under the heading "Illustration of the Structure and Values of the Traditional Model," we include two cases that exemplify the way the traditional model dictates specific roles for counsel, judges, and parties. These cases address the limited role of trial judges in that model, particularly concerning what they may do with regard to unsatisfactory presentation of evidence by the parties.

The section "Implications for Lawyering" analyzes the role of lawyers in the traditional model. The role of lawyers is similar in many of the models that we discuss. However, the lawyer as "zealous partisan" is most closely associated with the traditional model. The lawyer as zealous partisan is both defended and criticized in this last section of the chapter.

II. THE STRUCTURE DICTATED BY THE TRADITIONAL MODEL

A. Adjudication and Litigation

The following excerpt by Galanter discusses adjudication and its relationship to litigation. As indicated in the introduction to this chapter, adjudication is by no means limited to the traditional model. However, in its purest form, adjudication, with its emphasis on party control and a passive court rendering the narrowest decision possible given the issues in the case, is most closely associated with the traditional model. Such characteristics of adjudication and their claim to primacy in decision making are challenged, in various ways, by the other models we examine subsequently; square brackets in text appear in the original.

Marc Galanter, "Adjudication, Litigation, and Related Phenomena"
in Leon Lipson and Stanton Wheeler, eds., *Law and Social Sciences*
(New York: Russell Sage Foundation, 1986), 152, at 152-60 (footnotes omitted)

[The table on the following page] distinguishes several prominent varieties of third-party dispute processing.

... *adjudication* [is] a kind of third-party processing of disputes, in which disputants or their representatives present proofs and arguments to an impartial authoritative decision-maker who gives a binding decision, conferring a remedy or award on the basis of a preexisting general rule.

... *arbitration* refers to a family of processes that share such features as an impartial decision-maker, who enters a binding final award on the basis of proofs and arguments presented by the disputants (or their representatives). It commonly departs from adjudication in that the forum is selected by the parties (either ad hoc, by contractual undertaking, or by adhesion to a standing procedure) and that the forum is nongovernmental. There is also variation as to whether the arbitrator is constrained to decide in accordance with a prefixed body of norms and whether the norms applied are public ones or indigenous to a particular setting. Arbitration may be present in an attenuated form of *fact-finding* in which the parties accept the decisional implications of a finding on the facts and delegate the latter to an agreed upon third party—such as the lumber grader or the patent office. (Fact-finding may have important effects on negotiating positions even where parties have *not* agreed to accept its decisional implications.)

Many kinds and styles of arbitration can exist within a single society. Among the common varieties in the United States are labor arbitration, in which the "law of the shop" is applied; commercial arbitration in the standing bodies of self-contained trade associations applying norms of the trade; commercial arbitration by ad hoc arbitrators applying some version of governmental law; and the arbitration of tort cases or small claims under the auspices of a court that urges or requires that such cases be diverted to arbitration.

Mediation refers to a contrasting cluster of dispute processes in which the forum, rather than imposing a binding solution on the parties, arranges a settlement that is agreeable to them. Mediators range from the mere go-between carrying messages, to one who actively devises a solution and persuades the parties to accept it. The mediator may be a specialized standing body or a notable mobilized ad hoc for the purpose. Mediators may be reactive, or they may be proactive like the mediators in pre-Communist China and Communist China. Judges or arbitrators often seek to mediate a dispute, holding in reserve their power of binding decision. Although this mixed form ("med-arb") has been attacked as compromising the integrity of each process, it is strikingly prevalent in American dispute processing in settings as varied as labor arbitration, arrangement of consent orders by administrative agencies, plea bargaining in criminal cases, and judicial arrangement of settlements in civil suits.

A Taxonomy of Modes of Dispute Processing	
Three Parties	Adjudication
	Arbitration
	Fact-Finding
	Mediation
	Therapy
	Administrative Decision-Making
	Political Decision-Making
Immediate Forms	Champion (e.g., ombudsman)
	Parental Dyad (i.e., one party decides)
Two Parties	Bargaining/Negotiation
	Under threat of resort to third party
	In presence of group norms
	Under threat of exit, or other unilateral action
One Party	Exit
	Avoidance
	Self-help
	Resignation ("lumping it")
No Parties	Failure to Apprehend Remedy
	Claim
	Violation

NOTE: Arranged by the number of principal persons/roles involved in the process of seeking a remedy or resolution. This classification omits various support roles (informer, adviser, advocate, ally, and surrogate) described by Black and Baumgartner 1983.

Mediation shades off into _therapy_—that is, modes of dispute processing that aim not to secure agreement from parties as they are, but to change the parties by giving them insight into their situation or themselves. therapy, too, may be mixed with other forms, as in counseling under court auspices.

Like mediation and therapy, _administrative decision-making_ is prospective. But the administrator (for example, the school principal or welfare official) exercises control over the subject matter or parties that extends beyond the immediate dispute; he is responsible for fulfilling the goals of his organization; his aims are not confined to the universe of claims posed by the parties. His inquiry is not restricted by limiting rules of relevance and admissibility; his decision need not apply preexisting general standards. Of course, agencies with administrative responsibilities may commit themselves to abide by adjudicatory forms.

With _political decision-making_ we move away from the impartial and independent decision-maker to one who can be recruited as an ally. The permissible devices of persuasion are enlarged to include exchanges with the decision-maker (support, fealty) as well as proofs and arguments. We move away from the bi-polar case to the polycentric dispute and away from the obligation to decide by reference to a closed stock of preexisting rules to forthright fashioning of new rules—or away from general rules to individual ad hoc decisions. The same subject matters (divorce, incorporation, franchise, territorial dispute) may be handled by political, administrative, or adjudicative decision. Political decision-makers will often act as if they are subject to the constraints of an adjudicator and will engage in mock-adjudicative forms and justifications.

Although the most prestigious and visible third-party processes are governmental in location, sponsorship, personnel, norms, and sanctions, modern societies are honey-combed with third-party processes that are nongovernmental. These range from forums that are relatively independent in all of these respects (for example, religious courts) to those that are closely appended to governmental processes, dependent on them for norms and sanctions. These appended processes include private forums established to forestall governmental intervention in a trade as well as systems of negotiation or me-diation that flourish in the anterooms and hallways of official adjudicatory or adminis-trative decision-makers.

Dispute forums may be separate institutions (a court, the American Arbitration Association, or the like) or embedded within the social setting (workplace, school, church, and so forth) where a dispute occurs. Embedded forums range from those barely distinguishable from the everyday decision-making within the institution to those such as grievance hearings specifically constituted to handle disputes that cannot be resolved by everyday processes.

These three-party processes stand in contrast to *bargaining* or *negotiation* between two disputing parties. Negotiation ranges from that which is indistinguishable from the everyday adjustments that constitute the relationship between the parties to that which is "bracketed" as an emergency or a dsiruption of that relationship. Negotiations among businessmen, between injury victims and insurers, among parties to an uncontested divorce, or in (some styles of) plea bargaining of criminal charges are alike in that no third party is present; but the course of the negotiations is importantly affected by the kind, feasibility, and cost of potential third-party intervention. The ability to invoke a third party of a particular sort may be a crucial element in the bargaining, but such a threat may be insignificant compared with (usually tacit) threats to withdraw from beneficial relations or to cause reputational damage by circulating information to other interested parties. The bargaining parties may themselves have internalized the normative idiom of the third party.

The constrast between two- and three-party modes is further blurred by the presence of intermediate forms. The *champion*—neither an arbiter with authority to render a binding decision or a mere representative of one party—combines advocacy on behalf of one disputant with an element of investigative judging. The champion is familiar to us in his recent incarnation as the (government) ombudsman; and in the media ombudsman such as "action line" columns, the complaint bureau, the Better Business Bureau, and the elected official who intervenes on behalf of constituents.

The champion is a third party who is something less than a decision-maker. In another intermediate form which I call the *parental dyad* one of the two parties serves as decision-maker as well as disputant. Thus, insurance companies decide the complaints of aggrieved policy holders; automobile manufacturers decide the warranty claims of car buyers; architects serve as both arbitrators and owners' representatives in disputes between owners and building contractors. Such decision-makers may be obligated to observe some or many of the requirements ordinarily incumbent on an adjudicator—such as hearing arguments or deciding according to preexisting rules. When we recall administrators disposing of subordinates' complaints and parents deciding (their) disputes with their children, it is evident that the parental dyad is one of the most frequent dispute configurations.

So far I have been discussing modes of disputing that are discursive. But there are also unilateral—hence, nondiscursive—modes of processing disputes. These include *exit*—that is, withdrawal from a situation or relationship by moving, resigning, or severing relations, as well as various lesser forms that might better be termed *avoidance*.

Exit and avoidance may be the goal, as well as the sanction, in the dispute process. A disputant may threaten resort to a court in order to effectuate a desired exit. On the other hand, the presence of exit as a credible sanction may be important to the working of other remedies; that is, the threat of resort to exit may create a "bargaining endowment" just as does the threat of resort to adjudication. A remedy for one party may be a sanction to the other, and the threat of sanction may induce remedial action. Exit options are not inherently incompatible with the pursuit of other remedies. The rights-assertion dimension may be usefully distinguished from the exit-versus-remain dimension: an aggrieved party can remain and acquiesce (lump it) or remain and assert his claim; similarly, he may simply leave or he may leave and assert his claim as well.

Exit and avoidance do not exhaust the possibilities of unilateral dispute processing. *Self-help* includes various forms of direct action—taking or retaining possession of property as well as physical retaliation, overt or covert. Direct physical violence may be the most prominent element in a system of disputing or it may play an interstitial role.

Disputants may decline to pursue any of these options and may resign themselves to an unfavorable situation: gains of the available dispute options may appear too low or the cost too high (including opportunity costs, the psychic costs, and physical risks of disputing). Such *resignation* ("lumping it") behavior may be a matter of allowing a single incursion to pass without protest or it may involve acquiescence in continuing predation.

Resignation—"lumping it"—shades off into *failure to apprehend* a violation or grievance (or underestimation of its seriousness) or the possibility of remedy. Vast numbers of warranty violations, exposures to dangerous substances and conditions, acts of malpractice, and so forth remain undetected. With these cognitive barriers we eliminate the last of the parties and with it the dispute. ...

Adjudication is a blurred concept. Not surprisingly, for it invokes a cultural ideal which exists in several overlapping versions; it also points to a set of behaviors referring to and sometimes approximating this ideal. Ideal and behavior are components of larger systems of regulation and disputing. Much adjudication activity takes place in courts, although these institutions do other things as well. All of this is reflected in the experience and beliefs of varied participants and of wider audiences, popular and elite. This whole configuration of ideals, behavior, institutions, and experience is changing through time. ...

The terms "adjudication" and "litigation" overlap in their reference. Both refer to the encounter of "cases" with "courts." But each emphasizes different aspects of the process. Adjudication refers to something the court does—to the process of judging. It conjures up the ceremonious, stately, dignified, solemn, deliberative, authoritative. Litigation, on the other hand, refers to what the adversaries do: their activity may be noble or vindictive or frivolous. Litigation entails the possibility of adjudication, but they may become disassociated, so that there can be litigation without adjudication. They are fused, but the relationship is not invariate. They are two sides of a process, like education and school; they each drain meaning from the other. Hence, we can't understand that complex unless we look at both.

Adjudication refers to one of the core phenomena of the legal process. Though not one of the most frequent, it is important not only when it does occur, but also

1. as a potential recourse—a threat or escape;
2. hence, as a source of counters that can be used for bargaining or regulation in other settings;
3. as a model for other processes;
4. as a symbol exemplifying shared or dominant values and hence as a source of legitimacy for norms, offices, acts and so forth. (This aspect is compounded in common-law systems, where adjudication is the primary focus of legal scholarship and holds sway over legal thought vastly disproportionate to its prominence as a source of rules.)

Much of the meaning of other activities in the legal process is expressed in terms of this adjudication core. The making of claims, the arrangement of settlements, the assessment of official action—all these frequently involve reference to adjudication—to actual adjudication or to some imaginary adjudication that could take place.

The Adjudication Matrix

I began by viewing adjudication as a kind of third-party processing of disputes, in which disputants or their representatives present proofs and arguments to an impartial authoritative decision-maker who gives a binding decision, conferring a remedy or award on the basis of a preexisting general rule. I use this not as a set of essential qualities that define adjudication, but because it serves to plunge us in the midst of the set of phenomena to be examined. There is not a single discrete process which can be identified as adjudication. Instead we are addressing a family or cluster of processes that resemble one another and approximate this model in varying ways. ...

To identify the structural features and cultural commitments that we regard as adjudication and to understand the affinities and contrasts between different kinds of adjudicative processes, I suggest a series of contrasts or polarities. (These are not meant to indicate dichotomies; rather, they represent points on a set of continua.) In each, the first term is taken as a characteristic of adjudication (or at least of one type) as opposed to other dispute processes. These form a matrix of expectations that I find helpful to describe and explain adjudication and related phenomena.

The matrix is useful because there is a significant clustering among features on the left-hand side of Table 1, but not all these features are present in all real-world instances that we would call adjudication. Indeed, it is unlikely that they would be, in the light of the tensions between some of the characteristics associated with litigation. For example, adjudication involves a simultaneous commitment to decide according to general rules and to handle each case on its individual merits. This suggests that our list (and our commitments) embraces multiple and perhaps conflicting notions of adjudication. (I

Table 1   Some Elements of the Adjudication Prototype

	Elements	Departures
Intake	Individuated	Routine, Random
	Case-by-Case	Programmatic
	Reactive	Proactive
Process	Participative	Nonparticipative
	Forum governance	Disputant Control
	Narrow Relevance	Wide Relevance
Basis of Decision	Formalistic	Result-Oriented
	General Rules	Particularism
	Preexisting Rules	Rule-Making
Decision	Arbitral	Mediative
	Award or Remedy	Therapeutic Reintegration
	All or None	Compromise
	Binding	Advisory
	Final	Continuing Readjustment
Differentiation	Remote	Accessible
	Professional	Lay
	Mediated	Direct Participation
	Recondite	Common Understanding
	Impermeable	Permeable
Connection to Power	Impartial	Allied
	Independent	Dependent
	Governmental	Private
	Coercive	Voluntary

would expect even less clustering among the features represented by the right-hand end of each of these dimensions because deviations from adjudication may lie in very different directions. There are more than two kinds of things in the world.)

The items in the left-hand column reflect my sense of the "classical" picture of adjudication in the mid-twentieth century United States imparted to me in my legal education and embellished by subsequent reading and reflection. That this picture fuses descriptive and prescriptive elements is not without advantages. For the matrix enables us to locate competing visions of adjudication as an ideal. Certain of the features listed in the left-hand column are often taken as crucial elements of adjudication, and others as necessary means to achieve them. (Of course, there may be disagreement about which are ends and which are means.) Other observers commend departures from features listed on the left, on the ground that adjudication would be improved by a greater admixture of result orientation, rule-making, wide relevance, mediation, and so forth. Prescriptive visions of adjudication need not be projected to the end points of our continua.

For convenience, I sometimes refer to the locations where adjudication is found as *courts* and the presiding personnel as *judges*, although adjudication takes place at other institutional locations and under the auspices of persons without that title. And, of course, courts and judges in the narrow sense do many other things besides adjudication.

Table 1 lists the dimensions discussed below. To portray the variation along these continua, I give a brief sketch of each of the elements of the prototype. ...

Individuated, Case-by-Case Treatment

In the adjudication process the units of action are discrete *cases.* The forum addresses delimited controversies between identified persons (or corporate entities) rather than general situations, patterns, problems, or policies. It is obligated to give individuated treatment to each case, not treating cases en masse or on a random or probabilistic basis, but deciding each according to its own merits or qualities.

A case is typically bi-polar. There is a complaining party and one who is the subject of the complaint. Both sides may complain against each other, and each side may be a composite, with disputes among its members. Courts vary in the extent to which they permit a cluster of disputes to be treated as a single case. They also vary in the extent to which they permit whole classes of controversies to be aggregated or decided vicariously and the extent to which general problems may be deliberately packaged in the form of a case in order to address a general condition or to elicit a generalized pronouncement from the forum (for example, the "test case"). And while adhering to bi-polar forms, courts may address complex polycentric disputes in which a variety of contenders are arrayed around an issue. ...

Reactive Mobilization of Cases

The adjudicative forum is reactive in the mobilization of its agenda of cases. The cases are brought to the forum by the initiative of the parties (including institutionalized public accusers); the forum does not reach out proactively to bring cases into itself. ...

Participation

The disputants participate by presenting proofs and arguments. Often this participation is through expert intermediaries. Participation may be attenuated as, for example, where the forum undertakes responsibility for investigation and proof as is done by the Swedish Public Complaint Board, or it may approach management of the case by the disputants. ...

Forum Governance

Once initiated, the case proceeds under the control of the forum, according to procedures prescribed by the forum. The forum cannot be dismissed by the parties—as can an arbitrator—nor can they amend its procedures. ...

Narrow Scope of Relevance

The case is defined by claims that specific events, transactions, or relations should be measured by application of some delimited conceptual categories. The forum will hear only matters that are relevant to application of those categories. Frequently its willingness to admit proof and arguments is limited further by other policies—such as those crystallized in rules of evidence, and *res judicata*. Here the forum contrasts with other remedy agents like mediators and counselors who are open to a wide range of matters underlying and connected to the immediate dispute. ...

Formal Rationality

The discourse that goes on in connection with adjudication is not open and unbounded. There is a repertoire of legal concepts that is less inclusive than the whole universe of moral discourse or the whole array of sanctioned social norms. The claims of parties are assessed in the light of some bounded body of preexisting authoritative normative learning, to which the forum is committed in advance. Typically, the forum renders a decision by judging the conformance of the parties' claims to established general categories or classificatory concepts. Application of these general standards precludes response to the unique particularity of the situation or to the external consequences of the decision and proceeds without a fresh assessment of the wider consequences of the general norm that is being applied. Thus, adjudication approximates to "logically formal rationality" as postulated by Weber.

[In fact, courts depart from this model of austere formalism in various ways. Appellate judges frame general rules in the hope of producing optimum results. Judges at all levels are imbued with a sense that it is their mission to facilitate governmental policies of minimizing drunk driving, prostitution, or pollution. Or—in the style that Weber called "khadi justice"—judges feel impelled to respond to the particular circumstances rather than subsuming cases under general rules.

The inherent ambivalence of general standards requires that judges choose among alternative specifications of norms. In complex legal systems, choice is amplified by the inevitable conflicts and overlaps within a body of norms and among competing bodies—as, for example, in situations of "legal pluralism," where more than one system of legal concepts may be present and available to the disputants and the forum.

At least some adjudication involves parts of the law that are "open-textured," and judges have to choose among variant readings of the existing body of normative learning. Such open-ended rule-making authority may be acknowledged and cultivated or covert and confined. There may be more or less emphasis on the obligation to apply concepts consistently with earlier applications. One dramatic sort of unacknowledged change is the presence of legal fictions, in which fictitious recitals are employed to trigger a desired result without departing from the constraints of authoritative conceptual categories.]

Decision and Remedy

Rendering of some authoritative disposition is mandatory: the adjudicator, with her agenda assembled by the parties, is obliged to hear all those cases properly before her.

She cannot (as can, for example, the legislature or executive) decline to render a decision. The judge renders her decision on the merits (ascertained in terms of the authoritative learning) rather than arranging an agreement acceptable to the parties. The forum renders an award or remedy to one party rather than engaging in therapeutic reintegration of the parties. The decision is all or none: the forum grants or denies the claim of one party. Indeed, there may be norms against compromise. The decision is binding rather than advisory. The decision is final. Although there are procedures for trying to reopen it, there are also norms that render readjudication difficult. Typically, the forum cuts its links with the dispute and closes the case rather than undertaking a course of continuing supervision or readjustment of its decree. ...

Differentiation

Adjudication is differentiated from other activities. Typically, adjudication involves special locations, persons, roles, language, postures, costumes, and furniture. Often it involves moving to unfamiliar places and settings, movement that may represent substantial cost or an insurmountable barrier. Many reform schemes aim to dispel this remoteness and lower this cost.

Adjudication is, typically, conducted by professional specialists who have recourse to special forms of knowledge, discontinuous with everyday understandings, and not expressed in everyday language. This specialized learning may be generated in the adjudicative institutions themselves—as in common-law systems where the higher strata of judges produce the doctrinal literature—or there may be, as in contemporary Europe (continuing the Roman tradition), a division between the judge who decides the cases and the legal expert who cultivates and transmits doctrine.

Participation is, typically, indirect and through specialist intermediaries who are attached to the forum or have a monopoly on such intermediation. Enforcement, too, is entrusted to specialized functionaries (bailiffs, jailers) rather than carried out by the parties, their allies, or the community through ostracism or direct physical imposition.

The whole process is insulated from general knowledge about persons and their histories and statutes. Justice is blind; the decision-maker excludes the perceptions and commitments of everyday life to render a decision based solely on those aspects identified as salient by applicable legal categories. ...

Impartiality and Independence

The forum is impartial. It is not predisposed toward any party. The decision-maker is not an ally of either (set of) disputant(s), but is poised evenly between (or above) them. Unlike the manager or administrator, the adjudicator has nothing of her own at stake in the controversy. Nor is the judge an agent of any entity outside the forum, with responsibility to forward policies other than those crystallized in the applicable legal learning. Impartiality and independence are institutionalized in restrictions on contact with disputants and such devices as tenure and fixed pay to protect the judges against "command influence" and retaliation.

[Eagerness to preserve a visibly independent judiciary may induce regimes to remove from regular courts classes of cases thought to require politically responsive judging]. ...

Connection to Organized Power

The prototypical adjudicative institution is an organ of government: it is located in a public building, it is staffed by state officers who apply public norms, and its sanctions are imposed by the compulsory powers of the state.

[Historically, the notion that adjudication is a state monopoly is a relatively recent one. In practice, there is an immense amount of adjudication in the private sector—in tribunals embedded in various institutions (churches, universities, labor unions, exchanges, trade associations, and so forth) as well as specialized institutions for arbitration. The line between public and private is not a sharp one. Public norms may be applied in private tribunals and enforced by private sanctions; conversely, public tribunals, officials, and sanctions may be utilized to enforce private norms.]

Courts are coercive rather than voluntary. They impose outcomes regardless of the assent of the parties. But, in fact, their decrees are often unenforced. The coercive powers of courts are important even when they are not utilized, for the threat of their use induces settlements between the parties—often, capitulation by one party. The degree of compliance with settlements is higher than with verdicts.

NOTES AND QUESTIONS

1. Reread the Nandise narrative in chapter 1, "Introduction to Civil Actions and Courts." Could the prototypical model described by Galanter accommodate a "collective" complaint brought by all of the individuals affected? In general, what would the procedures look like? How would issues particular to individuals be addressed? How would the complaint of GM raised at the end of the narrative be responded to?

2. The prototypical model of adjudication presented by Galanter suggests that our courts are primarily designed to resolve disputes concerning the private grievances of individual citizens. Are the courts able to respond to the "public interest" nature of Jane Doe's claim?

B. Values Underlying the Structure of the Traditional Model

Adjudication in the North American context is invariably associated with an adversarial system of presentation. The following article by Neil Brooks details the features of an adversary system. At the most general level, an adversary system contemplates extensive participation of the disputants in (1) the definition of the issues, and (2) the presentation of facts and argument to the decision maker. Moreover, it contemplates that this presentation will be adversarial—that the parties are engaged in a contest, and each will seek to win a favourable judgment by presenting its case in its best light and attempting to cast the case of the opponent in the worst possible light.

In describing and critiquing the assumptions underlying an adversarial system of adjudication, Brooks challenges one aspect of the prototypical model of adjudication—that the judge must remain passive. He also suggests that the adversarial model closely reflects the characteristics of traditional liberal ideology. How appropriate is it to speak in terms of ideology in decision making? In any event what is wrong with liberalism as a model for decision making?

Neil Brooks, "The Judge and the Adversary System"
in A. Linden, ed., *The Canadian Judiciary* (Toronto: Osgoode Hall Law School, York University, 1976), at 90-116 (footnotes omitted)

The adversary system, as that term is used by many proceduralists and as it will be used in this paper, embodies two distinct principles. The issues resolved by these two principles raise the two most basic questions that confront any adjudicative procedural system. The first issue is what should the respective functions of the parties and the judge be with reference to the initiation and content of the adjudication. The adversary system rests on the principle of party-autonomy. That is to say, that the parties have the right to pursue or dispose of their legal rights and remedies as they wish. The second issue is what should the respective functions of the parties and the judge be with reference to the progress of a dispute through the procedural system once initiated and defined. The adversary system rests on the principle of party prosecution. This principle holds that the parties have the primary responsibility to choose without interference from the judge the manner in which they go forward with their case and the proofs they will present for the judge's consideration in adjudicating the dispute.

A. Party-Autonomy

The principle of party-autonomy has two aspects. First, it limits the judge's function to disputes which have been presented to him. A judge plays a role only when a conflict has arisen between two or more parties, and at least one of them seeks the assistance of the judge in resolving the dispute. John Chipman Gray, in defining a judge, summarized this principle: "A judge of an organized body is a man appointed by that body to determine duties and the corresponding rights upon the application of persons claiming those rights." The authors of a casebook on civil procedure described the principle more prosaically: "Courts ought not to function as self-propelled vehicles of justice and right like King Arthur's knights in Good Humor trucks." Lon Fuller quotes a socialist critic of bourgeois law who caricatured this premise of the adversary system by asserting that courts in such a system "are like defective clocks; they have to be shaken to set them going." Fuller noted that, "[h]e of course added the point that the shaking costs money."

The second aspect of party-autonomy is that the parties have the sole responsibility for defining the dispute that they would like adjudicated. Thus, if the parties want the judge to decide one dispute, he will not insist on resolving another even though he perceives that other issue to be the real cause of the conflict between the parties.

Both aspects of party-autonomy are subject to qualifications. While the judge cannot initiate proceedings, he can prevent the parties from initiating certain proceedings.

The courts have an important social function to perform by resolving disputes. Thus the judge can prevent parties from using the litigation process to resolve hypothetical or moot problems. He can judicially notice all facts he considers beyond reasonable dispute and thus prevent the parties from consuming the time of the court by presenting evidence on clear factual issues. He can also prevent misuse of the process by a judicial screening of cases, he can give judgment on the pleadings or give a summary judgment. Indeed he is assisted in controlling the use of the court's process by counsel for the parties. Lawyers have a professional responsibility to ensure that the claims and defences they put forward have merit and are related to a real conflict.

The limits of the principle of party-autonomy can, of course, only be defined by reference to the reasons why it is regarded as being an essential principle of the Anglo-American procedural system. Two justifications sometimes put forward fail to appreciate that party-autonomy is only a principle which defines the respective roles of the parties and the judge. In civil cases, it has been said that the principle of party-autonomy—that the judge only operates when the parties present him with a dispute to resolve—rests on the judgment that "the social interest in securing general observance of the rules of private law is sufficiently served by leaving their enforcement to the self-interest of the parties more or less directly affected." However, while this reason might explain why the state need not become involved in the enforcement of the civil law, it does not go directly to the issue of the roles of the parties and the judge in initiating actions. In many areas where there is an important public interest in the enforcement of the civil law, as in the enforcement of the criminal law, the state, through an administrative agency, might initiate actions enforcing the law. And yet, since it is not the judge who initiates such actions, the principle of party-autonomy would be satisfied.

Others have suggested that the principle of party-autonomy reflects a political ideology. Thurman Arnold asserted, "... the civil trial dramatizes the moral beauty of the noninterference of government in private affairs. ... The whole ideology, and procedural organization of the civil trial is designed to insulate the court and the government from taking the initiative in enforcing or even protecting the civil rights of individuals." Thurman Arnold was at the time decrying the resistance to the New Deal and exploring its causes. He went on, "[t]his role of the civil trial as a symbol of individual freedom from active interference by the government makes it a most important factor in preserving conservative traditions in the face of new legislation." While party-autonomy may reflect a laissez-faire philosophy, Arnold's point goes to the role of the government generally in the enforcement of the civil law.

Both of the above reasons given for the principle of party-autonomy stem from the misconception of what the principle demands. The principle does not require that the state refrain from initiating civil actions. It merely requires that the judge not initiate them. Fleming James more correctly stated the rationale when he noted, "... the adversary system and party-(autonomy) may well exist in areas extensively regulated by government in what is deemed to be the public interest. Their existence stems not from laissez-faire or a philosophy of individualism but rather from a notion of the proper allocation of function between the parties to a dispute (one of whom may be the government) and the tribunal which is to decide it, under any economic or social order, at least in a free society." Professor Lon Fuller also argued that the principle that an arbiter should not act on his own motion in initiating a case rests not on a political philosophy, but on a judgment that it increased the effectiveness of adjudication: "... it is generally impossible to keep even the bare initiation of proceedings untainted by preconceptions about what happened and what its consequences should be. In this sense, initiation of the proceedings by the arbiter impairs the integrity of adjudication by reducing the effectiveness of the litigant's participation through proofs and arguments."

B. Party-Prosecution

This principle holds that the parties have the right and the responsibility to choose the manner in which they will go forward with their case and the proof they will present to support it. The judge's role is to passively evaluate the merits of the case as and when it is presented to him.

In the remainder of this paper I will explore the reasons why the principle of party-prosecution is adhered to at trial, and offer some general comments on the parameters that these reasons place upon the judge's intervention in the conduct of the case. The conclusion that I reach is that viewed in this way the adversary system does not impose as severe restraints on the judge's intervention as is often assumed, and that in appropriate cases the judge should, if he deems it necessary, play a much larger role in the conduct of the case. My argument will be a plea for more judicial activism in controlling the conduct of the trial.

The principle of party-prosecution at trial rests, in the main, upon two broad empirical assumptions. Firstly, that the legitimacy of adjudication as a means of social ordering is enhanced if it is conducted according to an adversarial presentation. Secondly, that more accurate fact-finding is likely to result if parties motivated by self-interest are given the responsibilities of investigating facts and presenting arguments, and if the decision-maker remains passive.

2. The Adversary System Increases the Acceptability of Adjudication

Every means of social ordering used by the state must be acceptable not only to those immediately affected by its particular sanctions but also to all those governed by the state. This need for legitimacy is particularly paramount in a free society with respect to adjudication since a judge's decision might be perceived, in some sense at least, to be undemocratic.

Legitimacy or acceptability is a derivative value. That is to say, a decision-making process will be acceptable to the extent that it meets all the criteria that people expect of that decision-making process. With respect to adjudication these expectations undoubtedly include such considerations as expediency, finality, inexpensiveness, and the operation of privacy and other social values. To the extent that the adversary system furthers these values it will render the adjudicative process more acceptable than would some other procedural device for finding the facts. But aside from these considerations, which are necessary attributes of any acceptable adjudicative proceeding, it is often argued that the adversary system has unique characteristics which render it in judicial trials a more acceptable procedure in our society than other methods of fact-finding. The reasons for the acceptability of the adversary system, if indeed it is more acceptable than other methods of fact-finding, must rest ultimately upon complex questions of political theory and psychology. I can only be suggestive here, in part repeating what others have speculated. Four reasons might be given as to why the adversary system is a more acceptable method of fact-finding in judicial trials than any other method.

A. Relationship to the Prevalent Political and Economic Theory

The adversary system yields greater satisfaction to the litigants and others because it is a procedure that is consistent with the prevalent social and political ideology of western society. An assertion made in the editorial page of a bar association journal illustrates this argument: "If you believe in the Anglo-Saxon common law tradition, that the individual is the important unit of our society, and the state exists to serve him, then it seems that the adversary system is preferable. If you hold a corporate view of society, that is to say, that the community is the important unit, and that the citizen must be primarily considered as a part of the corporate unit, then it seems you should champion the inquisitorial system. ..."

Jerome Frank is well known for linking the adversary system with economic theory. In his writings he repeatedly associated it with classic, laissez-faire, economic theory and unbridled individualism. Surprisingly, however, only recently has scholarship emerged in the English language which attempts to seriously study the influence of political and economic theory on judicial procedure. Naively, perhaps, the assumption has been made that procedure is value-free. Scholars who have turned their attention to this question in recent years seem to agree that at least at a very general and theoretical level there are connections between ideology and procedural choices. The connection may not be direct, nor empirically demonstrable. However, at least arguably, the adversary system can be seen as reflecting the political and economic ideology of classic English liberalism in three ways: by its emphasis upon self-interest and individual initiative; by its apparent distrust of the state; and, by the significance it attaches to the participation of the parties.

The adversary system legitimizes, indeed necessitates, a self-interest role for the parties. Thus one of its premises would appear to be consistent with the premise of the capitalist system of economic organization that if each individual strives to promote his self-interest an optimum allocation of resources will result. As Professors Neef and Nagel note, "... at the base of the adversary proceeding we encounter the old laissez-faire notion that each party will (or indeed can) bring out all the evidence favorable to his own side, and that if the accused is innocent (if his is the best case) he can act to 'out-produce' the presentation made by his competitors." With this competitive individualism at its base, if the party with the better case—that is the case that is correct on the facts—were to lose, that result would be satisfactory in an adversary system because he, not the system, would be the author of his defeat. Initiative is rightly rewarded, laziness or ignorance penalized. This justification for the adversary system is illustrated in a statement made in a commentary on the Japan Code of Civil Procedure that was enacted after World War II when Japan adopted the adversary system:

> [S]ince civil litigation is essentially a dispute concerning private rights, as a matter of
> course, the responsibility and duty to present proof rests with the parties; it is neither the

responsibility nor the duty of the court. ... When the necessary facts to maintain the allegation of a party cannot be proven, the disadvantage should be borne by such party, and it is sufficient grounds for the court to issue him an unfavorable determination. The disadvantage is a consequence invited by the party himself, over and beyond which the court should neither assist a party on one side nor interfere.

If this is one of the justifications for the adversary system then not many people today would likely perceive of it as placing very serious constraints on the judge's intervention in the trial. Laissez-faire theory is no longer taken as being determinative in the economic and social fields. It would be incongruous if its basic postulate was still the premise used to define the respective roles of the parties and the judge in a judicial trial.

A basic socialist value is a strong emphasis on collectivism. The interests of the state and the individual are assumed to coincide, state power is not distrusted. On the other hand, liberal political philosophy is premised on a distrust of the state and public officials. The adversary system can thus be viewed in a liberal state as a means of decentralizing power, and as an attempt to prevent abuses of political power. This view finds some support in the fact that the genesis of at least some rules of procedure and evidence can also be explained on the basis of a felt concern to decentralize power. Professor Friedman in his recent text, a *History of American Law*, notes that the law of evidence "... was founded in a world of mistrust and suspicion of institutions; it liked nothing better than constant checks and balances. ..." This concern in an adversary system to decentralize power was illustrated during the period of Jacksonian democracy in the United States when a serious effect was initiated to take many rights from the judge including not only the right to comment upon the evidence but also the right to summarize the evidence to the jury.

Again, assuming this to be a premise of the adversary system, it would not appear to require that the judge be totally passive in the conduct of the trial. Indeed since in most cases he has the responsibility for the ultimate disposition of the case it would be incongruous to attempt to prohibit him from intervening in the proof-taking under the belief that his power was being constrained. This premise of the adversary system might have more relevance in defining the limits of party-autonomy.

Finally, the adversary system can be seen as being consistent with our prevalent political philosophy because it affords the parties the opportunity to participate in the making of decisions that affect their interests. Both psychological and theoretical literature in political philosophy support the view that the most acceptable type of decision in a democracy is personal choice. However, since it is clearly impossible to realize personal choice in many situations the best alternative is a system that assures to those affected by the decision some participation in the decisional process. A procedural system in which the judge assumes the primary responsibility for eliciting the proof, but permits the parties to assist in the proof-taking, would provide the parties a measure of participation in the decision-making process. However, Fuller argues that the adversary system "heightens the significance of ... participation" and thus "lifts adjudication toward its optimum expression." For this reason, he concludes that the adversary system is an essential characteristic of the adjudicative process.

The extent to which the judge's intervention in the trial, either in clarifying evidence or in calling for new evidence, impairs the parties' sense of participation is obviously an extremely complex question that cannot be explored in any detail here. In some instances, however, it might clearly be a consideration that leads the judge to the conclusion that he should not intervene. But in other situations his intervention in the form of asking questions might actually increase the meaningfulness of the parties' participation. Everyone has different cognitive needs and if the judge makes these needs known to the parties then it will make their participation more meaningful—obviously their participation will be meaningless unless the judge's understanding of the case is the meaning that they are attempting to convey to him. Also, even if the judge were to call additional proof, so long as he gives the parties the opportunity to test such proof and call rebutting proof their participation in the decision-making process would appear to remain meaningful.

B. Cathartic Effect

Particularly in civil suits the adversary system might be a more acceptable procedure for fact-finding than the inquisitorial system because it satisfies the psychology of the litigants by legitimizing a courtroom duel which is a sublimation of more direct forms of hostile aggression. It has been suggested that there are psychological benefits in the "battle atmosphere" of adversary litigation. Charles Curtis in his book *It's Your Law* summarized this argument. He said:

> The law takes the position that we ought to be satisfied if the parties are; and it believes that the best way to get this done is to encourage them to fight it out, and dissolve their differences in dissention. We are still a combative people not yet so civilized and sophisticated as to forget that combat is one way to justice.

The use of the adversary system to satisfy the primeval competitive urges of the litigants might be suggested by its genealogy. The ancestry of the trial is of course the blood feud, trial by battle and individual or class acts of revenge. This justification for the adversary system is also apparent in the frequent analogy of the judicial trial to a sporting event. It leads lawyers to talk of tactics and strategy and to refer to the judge as an umpire. This view of the adversary process is most clearly perceived if the trial is regarded as a "game," using that word in the sense that it is used by game theorists. The "sporting theory of justice" describes the rules of the game. There has been a social disturbance and the game is played only to gain some relief or satisfaction.

The adversary system viewed as part of a game perhaps explains the system's acceptance of the result when a party loses on a technicality, even if his loss was due to a violation of one of the technical rules of evidence or procedure which regulate the game. If justice is equated to the satisfaction of the litigants then the adversary system, which is directly responsible for this satisfaction, becomes an end in itself. The true facts of the case are less important than how well the parties play the game. Reasoning from this premise, Charles Curtis concluded:

> Justice is something larger and more initimate than truth. Truth is only one of the ingredients of justice. Its whole is the satisfaction of those concerned. ... The administration of justice is no more designed to elicit the truth than the scientific approach is designed to extract justice from the atom.

If this justification for the adversary system is correct then the judge's role in the trial would be a limited one. However, the basic premise of the argument is disputable. As one author posed the question: "Is the battle atmosphere of trial proceedings truly cathartic, in the sense of relieving tensions and aggressions that would otherwise find more destructive outlets, or does it instill an aggressive approach to problems that is incompatible with the need to compromise and co-operate in the vast majority of inter-personal contacts?" Unfortunately, no serious effort has been made to resolve this question by asking the ultimate consumers of the system—the litigants. Basing a judgment on common experience, however, most people would probably agree with Professor Garlan who wrote at the height of the legal realist movement, referring to the jurispru-dential theory of what he called "sporting fairness":

> The game has become too brutal, too destructive of human life, too exhaustive to those who win, and too fatal for those who lose. Living begins to look more like a struggle, than a game. The participant's sense of humor and sense of balance are worn, and the sporting morale is breaking up into a fighting morale. The sides are too unequal for successful competition, and, in the eyes of the defeated, the game looks more like exploitation than competition.

While we know very little about the psychology of litigants, I suspect that most of them do not view social conflicts as social events. They come to court expecting justice, and unless the rules of substantive law are perverse, that means they expect their dispute to be resolved according to the law. A theory about the judge's role that begins by assuming that rules of evidence and procedure are simply rules of competition is therefore deficient.

C. Role of Counsel

A third aspect of the adversary system that might render it more acceptable than the inquisitorial system is the role played by counsel. It has been hypothesized that "[i]f parties perceive their adversary attorneys as having interests convergent with their own, they may begin to experience the comforting strength of belonging to a coalition the total purpose of which is to gain a favorable verdict at the expense of the opposing party." Also the lawyer will be a person who, in some sense, shares in the litigant's defeat. Certain institutional characteristics of the adversary system encourage this coali-tion and the apparent identity of interest between the adversary lawyer and his client. However, assuming this to be true, intervention in the trial proceedings by the trial judge is unlikely to destroy in any way this coalition or this sense of shared purpose.

D. Appearance of Impartiality

Finally, the adversary system might be more acceptable than an inquisitorial system because it gives the tribunal the appearance of impartiality. Proponents of the Anglo-American procedural system attach great importance to the appearance of impartiality. While its importance cannot be denied, the intelligent control of the conduct of the trial need not leave a judge open to the charge of partiality. The possible appearance of impartiality is a matter a judge should consider when intervening, and to that extent it limits his intervention. For instance, if a judge calls a witness he must ensure that the parties have an opportunity to test the testimony of the witness and to call rebutting evidence or he might be open to the charge that he is shaping the record. If a witness is evasive in answering questions the judge must ensure that he does not appear hostile towards the witness. However, if the judge intervenes in a fair and dispassionate manner this consideration should not seriously impair his ability to intervene when he thinks it is necessary.

3. The Adversary System Increases the Accuracy of Fact-Finding

A second justification given for the adversary system [in addition to increasing the acceptability of adjudication] is that it is a better fact-finding mechanism than the inquisitorial system. That is to say, given all the interests that must be balanced in a procedural system, more accurate factual judgments about past events are likely to be achieved using the adversary system than using some other system. This justification rests, in turn, upon two premises. The first premise is that the adversary system will result in a more thorough investigation of the facts than the inquisitorial system. The second premise is that under the adversarial system the trier of fact is more likely to reach the correct decision because during the proceedings he will not acquire a bias towards one conclusion or the other. He will be able to remain completely disinterested in the outcome until all the proof has been elicited and the arguments made. In order to define the role of the judge in the adversary system these two premises must be explored in detail.

A. Parties Motivated by Self-Interest Are Likely To Be Most Diligent in Presenting and Critically Evaluating All the Evidence

The first premise of this justification for the adversary system is that in an adversary proceeding the judge will, when he makes his decision, be more informed as to the facts than a similarly situated judge in an inquisitorial system. This is so, it is argued, because parties who are given a free hand in pursuing their perceived self-interest are more likely than an official motivated only by official duty to transmit to the judge all evidence favourable to their case and to critically test all unfavourable evidence presented to him. Empirical studies have attempted to test whether this premise is correct. However, for purposes of defining the judge's role in the adversary system the premise must be accepted as true.

The parties do not have complete control over the presentation and testing of proof and this premise of the adversary system does not require them to have such control. Control is given to the parties to promote accurate fact-finding and to further achieve this end the parties are constrained in the conduct of their case by rules of procedure and evidence. The need for these rules arises because if this premise of the adversary system is to achieve its objective a number of factors must be present in the litigation of particular disputes. The rules are intended, in part, to ensure that these factors are present. If these factors are not present in a particular case the adversary system will not achieve its goal of accurate fact-finding; or if it is to achieve this end in their absence the judge may have to regulate his conduct accordingly. Thus the judge, in defining his role, must be sensitive to the presence or absence of these factors. For purposes of clarity I will discuss these factors as assumptions of the premise that the adversary system is an accurate fact-finding mechanism because parties motivated by self-interest will present and critically test all relevant evidence.

Assumption 1: The Parties Are Initially Motivated

The first assumption that this premise of the adversary system makes is that the parties are initially motivated to seek out all the evidence favorable to their case. This obviously depends upon both parties being equally interested in the outcome of the case, that is, equally interested in pursuing their respective rights and remedies and in opposing the rights of the other party. If this is not the case, if one of the parties is not motivated to oppose the other party's case, the requisite factual investigation and presentation of proof will not take place.

Assumption 2: The Parties Will Sustain Their Motivation

A second assumption of this premise of the adversary system is that throughout the proceedings both parties will sustain their motivation to present all the evidence. A number of rules of evidence have been developed to encourage parties to diligently pursue all the evidence favorable to their side; at least these rules can, in part, be understood by reference to this need. The privilege against self-incrimination, for instance, is sometimes justified on this basis. By denying the police the right to compel the accused to incriminate himself the rule forces them to seek more reliable evidence. In the same way rules requiring the corroboration of certain witnesses who are generally assumed to be unreliable might be justified on the basis that they compel the Crown to search for additional independent evidence. It is interesting to note that these rules apply in the main against the prosecution in criminal cases—they encourage the police to seek additional evidence. Perhaps this is so because there is a fear that, at least in some cases, the prosecution, motivated only by official duty, may not otherwise display diligence in pursuing evidence that the adversary system demands.

A further rule of evidence that has the effect of encouraging the parties to independently investigate all evidence in their favour is the solicitor–client privilege—at least that part of it that the Americans call the work product rule. This rule, in general, prevents one lawyer or litigant from demanding disclosure, particularly before trial, of the other litigant's trial briefs, witness statements and related materials prepared or collected for use in the litigation. If a litigant could compel such disclosure there would be a great temptation for each litigant to rely on the other to do the investigations and to gather the necessary information. Eventually, litigants would become more and more reluctant to make an independent effort to collect information and to prepare arguments for trial. Thus, the rule contributes to the efficiency of the adversary scheme of litigation. Professor Maguire observed, "so long as we depend upon thorough advanced preparation by opposing trial counsel to accumulate the necessary information about law, fact and evidence, we must not let the drones sponge upon the busy bees. Otherwise it would not be long before all lawyers become drones."

As well as forming the basis of a number of rules of evidence and procedure this assumption of party-prosecution has a more direct implication in defining the judge's role. In a system that relies on party prosecution the judge cannot intervene to such an extent in the trial that the parties begin to rely upon him to search out all the facts favourable to their case and thus become less diligent themselves in seeking out the facts. There is some evidence that this attitude on the part of the litigants results when the court assumes a large responsibility for proof-taking. At least it is a concern that has been expressed in countries in which the judge assumes such a role. For example, in Japan, when the adversarial system was adopted in 1948 the commentators on the new Code of Civil Procedure noted that, "[e]xcessive interference by the Court dampens the zeal of the parties and instead—it being entirely impossible under the present trial system for the court completely to gather all evidence *ex officio*—produces a result which is accidental in nature. This is the reason why we thoroughly follow the doctrine of party presentation under the new constitution, in which the freedom and responsibility of the individual is made a fundamental principle." ...

Assumption 3: The Parties Have Equal Capacity, Skill and Resources

Party-prosecution, as a principle of the adversary system, rests on a third assumption: that each party has the ability, skill, and resources to search out the evidence favorable to his or her case and to present it to the court. Do the parties always have the capacity or ability to obtain access to all facts favorable to their case? The adversary system encourages parties to assume a self-interested role. While casting the parties into this role it ensures that they will be diligent in presenting evidence favorable to their cause, it also legitimizes or at least would appear to sanction their suppressing evidence that is unfavorable to their case. This temptation laid before the parties is regarded by many as the greatest obstacle to accurate fact-finding in the adversary system. Professor Brett argued that because "... neither of the rival theorists ... [is] bound to put forward all the data in his possession—indeed ... each ... regard[s] it as proper to suppress any 'inconvenient' or inconsistent observations of whose existence he ... [knows,] 'the adversary system' must be regarded as basically unscientific in approach, and unsound." He further asserted that Macaulay's justification of the adversary system that "we obtain the fairest decision when two men argue, as unfairly as possible, on opposite sides, for then it is certain that no important consideration will altogether escape notice," confuses an incentive to obtain contradictory evidence with the capacity or ability to obtain it. Jerome Frank also noted, in supporting his contention that the "fight" theory of litigation does not coincide with the "truth" theory, that "frequently the partisanship of the opposing lawyers blocks the uncovering of vital evidence or leads to a presentation of vital testimony in a way that distorts it." There is little a judge in any system can do to prevent the parties from suppressing or falsifying evidence. A number of rules of evidence and procedure, however, attempt to provide both parties with access to as much evidence as possible. While these rules do not bear directly on the judge's role they are important in increasing our understanding of the adversary system and thus at least indirectly the judge's role in it.

First, rules of pre-trial discovery assist the parties in obtaining evidence. In civil cases, these rules generally permit a party to question the other prior to the trial about his knowledge of the facts in the case. It has been argued that pre-trial discovery is inconsistent with the adversary system. However, this argument confuses means with ends. If one begins the analysis by looking for reasons for the adversary system, the better view would appear to be that of Professor Goldstein who concluded that discovery "has as its object the harnessing of the full creative potential of the adversary process, bringing each party to trial as aware of what he must meet as his finances and his lawyer's energy and intelligence permit." ...

Finally, to ensure that the party's strong sense of self-interest and stake in the trial does not result in the degeneration of the trial into fraud and deceit, interposed between the litigant and the process is a lawyer; a person who will, to a large extent, conduct the proceedings and who has a responsibility not only to the litigant, his client, but also to the process. While the exact nature of the lawyer's responsibility to the process is the subject of dispute, there is agreement that he has a responsibility in most cases to protect the process from evidence he knows to be falsified.

For this assumption of the adversary system to be operative both parties must also have equal resources to investigate and collect facts favorable to their case, and both must be of equal skill in presenting these facts and in testing the facts presented that are unfavorable to their case. If the adversaries do not have equal representation—if for instance the accused in a criminal trial is unable to avail himself of effective counsel—this premise, upon which the adversary system rests, will be impaired. But even when both parties are represented by counsel, the quality of the representation will obviously seldom be equal. What is the role of the judge if one party is not represented or if her representation is inadequate? In such a situation the adversary system will fail to achieve its objective. The judge should not hesitate to intervene. Whatever dangers arise when a judge intervenes in such a situation, they are outweighed by the serious danger that is present if he does not intervene.

A final aspect of this assumption of the adversary system is the necessity that both parties have the resources to carry out a thorough investigation of the facts. This, of course, is seldom the case. Jerome Frank suggested that in all cases there should be some kind of government intervention to help an impecunious litigant obtain evidence. In criminal cases the state's facilities for investigation are obviously far superior to those of the ordinary defendant's. It might be possible to reduce this disparity by providing legal aid programs with the resources necessary to locate and investigate evidence favorable to the accused. A more efficient remedy, since it does not involve the costly duplication of investigation efforts, would be to place the results of government investigations in the hands of the defence. In the United States a rule of procedure that will have this result is emerging. Clearly if we do not wish to be accused of continuing to tolerate a system whose operations negate the reasons for having it we will have to continue to move in this direction. ...

Assumption 4: The Parties Will Be Given the Opportunity To Test Adverse Evidence

Party-prosecution assumes that each party will have the opportunity and the ability to thoroughly test the evidence unfavorable to his case. It assumes, also, that this testing of adverse evidence must be done by an adversary cross-examination as opposed to a dispassionate inquisitorial examination. Opinions on the utility of cross-examination are sharply divided. ...

Assumption 5: All Interests Affected Are Represented

Finally, the principle of party-prosecution assumes that all interests affected by the adjudication are represented by the parties. The adversary system depends upon the parties to bring forward the information upon which the judge will rely in reaching his decision. In reaching a decision the judge must reconcile all the competing interests affected by his decision. If he does not receive information about some of these interests because they are interests of no immediate concern to the parties before him the adversary system will be a defective method of fact-finding for that decision. ...

Another area in which the adversaries will not represent all the interests might be described broadly, if not with some circularity, as being the area of public interest law, such as environmental, consumer protection law. Again, in these areas, the wise judge might well call upon the intervention of third parties to represent those interests not represented by the immediate parties to the particular dispute. At the appellant level this is commonly done by means of asking for or inviting *amicus curiae* factums. ...

4. The Adversary System Counteracts Bias in Decision-Making

The second reason often given as to why the adversary system leads to more accurate fact-finding than an inquisitorial system is that the adversary system permits the judge to remain unbiased as between the parties throughout the proceedings. Bias is a word used in a wide variety of senses, many of which shade into each other. In this context, where important consequences are being drawn from the concept, it is particularly important to be clear about its meaning.

Bias in this context does not mean, as it commonly means in other contexts, a preconceived point of view about issues of law or policy, a personal prejudice against certain types of parties, or bias in the sense of being personally interested in the outcome of the case. No fact-finding mechanism can remove these types of biases. It refers to a bias or prejudgment that is acquired by a decision-maker because of the mechanism of fact-finding used. If the judge takes an active part in proof-taking, it could be argued he might acquire a bias towards one party or the other for one of the following reasons:

1. If the judge questions a witness and the witness is evasive, disrespectful, hostile, or in some way does not live up to the expectations of the judge, the judge may become antagonistic towards that witness and therefore tend to discredit his testimony.

2. If the judge in proof-taking is responsible for having some important evidence revealed, he may tend to give too much weight to that evidence, either because he is overly impressed with the skilful manner in which the evidence was presented, or because it is important to him that his intervention is seen to have served a useful purpose.

3. The judge may, in his investigation, become so concerned about a detail of the case that the balance of the evidence will escape his careful attention. This is perhaps the kind of consideration that judges are concerned about when they assert that their ability

to evaluate the credibility of a witness is impaired if they themselves become too involved in examining a witness. That is to say, as an investigator preoccupied with his own line of thought, the judge may unconsciously fail to explore important points, may amass so much detail that obvious truths are obscured, or may not carefully observe all of the diverse matters, such as demeanor evidence, that he should take into consideration in evaluating the probative value of testimonial proof.

4. A fourth source of bias that is not present in the adversary system, but which one might argue is present in the inquisitorial system, is the bias that is acquired when the judge is presented with a file of the evidence before the case is heard by him. In an inquisitorial system the judge will of course have had to study the documents contained in the file with some care if he is to be efficient in carrying out the proof-taking at trial. There is an obvious danger that the information supplied in the file will bias the judge towards one side or the other. As Glanville Williams noted, "Our reaction to the French system is that it creates a danger that the point of view of the prosecution will communicate itself to the judge before the case has been heard."

5. Finally, it has been contended that the adversary system is an unbiasing fact-finding technique because it counteracts what psychologists call decision-maker bias. Decision-maker bias is acquired when a decision-maker himself investigates the facts upon which he is to rest his judgment. It arises because of the need when one begins to investigate facts to form certain tentative hypotheses about the reality that one is called upon to reconstruct. More or less imperceptibly, these preconceptions influence the course of the investigation. As well, facts which confirm the original hypothesis will make a strong imprint upon the mind, while facts that run counter to it are received with diverted attention. This bias, which arises from the process of fact-finding, is avoided in the adversary system, it is argued. It is avoided because, in the advery system, the judge, since he is not responsible for the investigation, is able to avoid any judgment of the case until he has heard all the evidence.

While all of these kinds of bias may be present in an adversary proceeding, none of them should limit to any great extent, within the framework of our present trial, the judge's intelligent intervention in the case. A recognition of their presence should permit the judge to conduct the proceedings in a fashion that minimizes the dangers that might arise.

NOTES AND QUESTIONS

1. The Ontario Rules of Professional Conduct describe the lawyer's role as advocate as "openly and necessarily partisan. Accordingly the lawyer is not obliged ... to assist an adversary or advance matters derogatory to the client's case." See rule 10, commentary 13. What are the implications of this for a quest to ascertain the "truth"?

2. The adversarial approach to adjudication can be contrasted with an inquisitorial approach. An inquisitorial system of adjudication places the responsibility for the development of the factual and legal issues of the case largely on the court, rather than on the parties. So, for instance, the court will assume the main responsibility for gathering information relevant to the case. It is the judge who will interrogate witnesses and make the determination of what, if any, further information need be sought in the case. The implications that the inquisitorial system has for the contours of civil procedure is

canvassed in an article by John H. Langbein, "The German Advantage in Civil Procedure" (1986), 52 *University of Chicago Law Review* 823, to be discussed in chapter 4,
"Challenges to the Traditional Model."

C. Illustration of the Structure and Values of the Traditional Model

In reading the two cases that follow consider what arguments might be advanced to
justify the interventions of the respective judges. Would such arguments necessarily be
at odds with the tenets of the traditional model?

Fowler v. Fowler and Jackson
[1949] OWN 244 (Ont. CA)

An appeal by the plaintiff from the judgment of Treleaven J, dismissing an undefended
action by a husband for divorce.

At the trial the plaintiff and another witness gave evidence which, if believed, would
have supported an inference of adultery on two specific occasions. There was also
evidence that the defendant wife was living in the male defendant's house, and that the
defendants had been seen together on numerous occasions. At the close of the plaintiff's
case the trial judge said: "I want more than that. First of all, the defendants are here, I
understand, in court; that is what I am told." He then proceeded to call both the defendants, and proceeded to examine them at some length. During the course of these examinations by the trial judge, both defendants positively denied the commission of adultery,
although they admitted some of the other incidents. Counsel for the plaintiff neither
consented nor objected to the calling of these witnesses by the trial judge, and cross-
examined them both. Judgment was reserved, and the following reasons were later
delivered for dismissing the action:

> When the evidence of the plaintiff and Cecil Fowler, nephew of the plaintiff, was given
> as to the alleged adultery of the defendants, I was very skeptical of its truth. Neither of
> the witnesses impressed me and their evidence did not ring true. When the two
> defendants both absolutely denied adultery, I was more than ever convinced that the
> evidence for the plaintiff was untrue. It is true the defendants are living in the same
> house. I accept their evidence that they are not occupying the same bedroom, and that
> the defendant spouse is in the house as housekeeper, being paid regularly, and having
> under her care three small children—one of her own and two of her co-defendant's.
> Rejecting, as I do, the evidence of the plaintiff as to adultery, the case for the plaintiff
> rests entirely on suspicion and I accept the evidence of the defendants that they have not
> been guilty of adultery.

On the appeal counsel argued only the ground that the trial judge had no right to call
the defendants as witnesses without the consent of the plaintiff, that he had thereby
deprived himself of jurisdiction, and that the position was not affected by the fact that
the plaintiff's counsel had cross-examined the witnesses, since he was confronted with a
situation that he could not have foreseen.

At the conclusion of the argument on this one ground, the Court delivered judgment orally, allowing the appeal and ordering a new trial. Robertson CJO pointed out that the trial judge had assumed the functions of counsel rather than of judge, and that the case was somewhat analogous to a case where an arbitrator had acted in a similar manner. Since counsel had participated to the extent of cross-examining the witnesses, there should be no costs of the appeal.

New trial ordered.

NOTES AND QUESTIONS

1. Following the appeal in *Fowler*, a new trial was held at which the trial judge accepted the uncontradicted evidence of the plaintiff and granted the divorce: see S. Schiff, *Evidence in the Litigation Process*, 2d ed. (Toronto: Carswell, 1983), 62. Do you agree with the result? Are there other reasons that might be advanced?

2. Should the trier of fact be permitted to take into account information obtained outside the formal trial process? Consider the following situation that arose in *R v. Pallet*, [1970] 2 OR 222 (Ont. CA):

> The appellant was convicted on a charge of possession of marijuana and was given a suspended sentence. The ground of appeal is that the learned trial Judge made improper use of information that he himself personally obtained and that the information was not in evidence.
>
> It appears from the transcript that some time during the course of the trial the defendant had given evidence as to the temperature on the date of the alleged offence, claiming that it was somewhere between 65 and 70 degrees. The trial Judge had a constable telephone the Meteorological Branch at Ottawa and obtain information from them as to what the temperature was on that day. The constable then, without giving evidence, relayed the information to the trial Judge, apparently privately, and the trial Judge in giving his judgment, in which he said he disbelieved the evidence of the appellant, said this:
>
>> But I am not satisfied and I don't accept his evidence. One of the prime examples was the question about the weather on March 15th. He said it was a hot day, too hot to walk around, yet, of course, I had a check made with the weather office or the meteorological branch, and I find that on March 15th of this year there was a high of 38 and a low of 28.

What should the Court of Appeal do?

Phillips et al. v. Ford Motor Co. of Canada Ltd. et al.
[1971] 2 OR 637 (CA)

Plaintiffs brought this action for personal injuries and damages sustained by them when their motor vehicle collided with a public utility pole in the City of Toronto. No other vehicle was involved in the accident, and plaintiffs alleged that the cause of the accident was a defective braking system. The suit was framed in contract and alternatively in tort, and both the dealer selling the car and the manufacturer were named as defendants. At trial, plaintiffs succeeded, and were awarded damages. Defendants appealed.

Our mode of trial procedure is based upon the adversary system in which the contestants seek to establish through relevant supporting evidence, before an impartial trier of facts, those events or happenings which form the bases of their allegations. This procedure assumes that the litigants, assisted by their counsel, will fully and diligently present all the material facts which have evidentiary value in support of their respective positions and that these disputed facts will receive from a trial judge a dispassionate and impartial consideration in order to arrive at the truth of the matters in controversy. A trial is not intended to be a scientific exploration with the presiding judge assuming the role of a research director; it is a forum established for the purpose of providing justice for the litigants. Undoubtedly a court must be concerned with truth, in the sense that it accepts as true certain sworn evidence and rejects other testimony as unworthy of belief, but it cannot embark upon a quest for the "scientific" or "technological" truth when such an adventure does violence to the primary function of the court, which has always been to do justice, according to law. While I recognize that the adversary system has been subjected to criticism on the ground that its procedures may on occasions inhibit the search for ultimate truth, I believe it to be a workable system which has proved satisfactory over a long period, and I am not prepared to abandon it in favour of the presumed, but undemonstrable, advantages of a clinical, scientific approach to the adjudication of legal disputes.

The two fundamental errors which caused a completely unsatisfactory trial resulted from the almost constant intervention of the trial judge in his attempt to direct an inquiry instead of a trial, and in the assumption by Mr. McCaffrey, whom the trial judge appointed as an assessor ... to assist the court, of a function and authority to which he is not entitled under our procedure. In the instant case either defect was of such a serious nature as to warrant a new trial, unless one could say with conviction that, despite such defects, the result would have been the same or that, alternatively, the evidence properly adduced on behalf of the plaintiffs was of such a tenuous nature that, disregarding the defects, this court should set aside the trial judgment and dismiss the plaintiffs' action. I do not hold either of such convictions and expressly dissent from my brothers who are of the view that the plaintiffs' action must be dismissed. In my view the trial was conducted in a manner so far removed from that norm which we consider satisfactory that it amounted to a mistrial. The fact that on many occasions counsel for the plaintiffs adopted the suggestions of the trial judge and introduced evidence in an attempt to support the theories advanced by the court, coupled with the fact that he did not object to what I consider the unacceptable assumption of a partial position by Mr. McCaffrey, do not preclude the plaintiffs from their day in court. I believe that they can be adequately penalized in costs for their failure to object to the procedures adopted. ...

There is another matter upon which I wish to comment and that is right of the expert to participate in the examination of witnesses. I am unaware of any binding authority which gives him that right and I strongly deprecate such practice as it introduces into our judicial system a stranger to the action and clothes him with at least a *quasi*-judicial role. Clearly such expert was never intended to act as an advocate on behalf of a litigant and, since the court must adopt an impartial position, it has no need of an advocate. In my view it is highly preferable that the questioning of witnesses be left to counsel and, when necessary for clarification, to the trial judge. I concede that there may be rare occasions when a trial judge may permit an expert to put questions to witnesses, other than through the trial judge, but even in those unusual circumstances the trial judge must adopt those questions as his own and take responsibility for them. ...

Brooke and Kelly JJA concurred with Evans JA; Schroeder and MacKay JJA dissented.

NOTES AND QUESTIONS

1. To what extent is it feasible or desirable for judges to assume the passive posture the Court of Appeal requires in *Phillips*? How should judges react in cases where one side has much more information and resources to assemble and present its case? Is a lack of intervention neutral or impartial in such circumstances? Curtailment of legal aid is an important cause of the increase in unrepresented parties in court: see "The Legal Needs of Law—Ontarians," Report of the Ontario Legal Aid Review, *A Blueprint for Publicly Funded Legal Services*, vol. 1, c. 4 (Toronto: Ontario Legal Aid Review, 1997), 53.

2. Starting in the 1960s, many commentators such as Ralph Nader believed that the most scientific way to reduce injuries and deaths in traffic accidents was to have the government require auto manufacturers to install safety devices, such as air bags, in all their cars. Is *Phillips* an example of this enthusiasm to regulate traffic safety through control of auto manufacturers? If so, are the courts an appropriate institution for such a task?

3. The Ontario Rules of Civil Procedure contain the following rule on court appointed experts which was drafted with the experience of the *Phillips* case directly in mind. Does this rule adequately respond to the issues raised in the *Phillips* case? What conception of the procedural system appears to have motivated the rules committee in drafting this rule? In this context reconsider Brooks's discussion of the adversary system.

Court Appointed Experts

Appointment by Judge

52.03(1) On motion by a party or on his or her own initiative, a judge may, at any time, appoint one or more independent experts to inquire into and report on any question of fact or opinion relevant to an issue in the action.

(2) The expert shall be named by the judge and, where possible, shall be an expert agreed on by the parties.

Contents of Order Appointing Expert

(3) The order shall contain the instructions to be given to the expert and the judge may make such further orders as he or she considers necessary to enable the expert to carry out the instructions, including, on motion by a party, an order for,

(a) inspection of property under Rule 32; or

(b) the physical or mental examination of a party under section 105 of the *Courts of Justice Act, 1984.*

Remuneration of Expert

(4) The remuneration of an expert shall be fixed by the judge who appoints the expert, and shall include a fee for the expert's report and an appropriate sum for each day that attendance at the trial is required.

(5) The responsibility of the parties for payment of the remuneration of an expert shall be determined in the first instance by the judge.

(6) Where a motion by a party for the appointment of an expert is opposed, the judge may, as a condition of making the appointment, require the party seeking the appointment to give such security for the remuneration of the expert as is just.

Report

(7) The expert shall prepare a report and send it to the registrar and the registrar shall send a copy of the report to every party.

(8) The report shall be filed as evidence at the trial of the action unless the trial judge orders otherwise.

(9) The judge may direct the expert to make a further or supplementary report, and subrules (7) and (8) apply to that report.

Cross-examination of Expert

(10) Any party may cross-examine the expert at the trial.

Liability of Parties for Remuneration of Expert

(11) The liability of the parties for payment of the remuneration of the expert shall be determined by the trial judge at the end of the trial, and a party who has paid the expert in accordance with a determination under subrule (5), if not the party determined to be liable for payment under this subrule, shall be indemnified by the party determined to be liable.

How should this rule be used? What should the respective role of judges and counsel be under this rule?

III. IMPLICATIONS FOR LAWYERING

A. Introduction

Before embarking upon a discussion of the ethical norms governing lawyers within the traditional model of litigation, it will be useful to first review some of the basic features of the legal profession. The regulation of the practice of law is a matter within provincial jurisdiction, and, as is the case for many professions, the provinces have delegated to the legal profession the power to determine, and to enforce, standards for admission to the practice of law and standards of practice for the profession. These governance functions are carried out by the "benchers" of the provincial law society, who are elected by the members of the profession.

As such, we might think of the legal profession as having two central features—self-regulation (through its admission of members and enforcement of standards of conduct) and (near) monopoly (the legal profession is based on a licensure regime in which only those granted a license, having satisfied the criteria established by the profession, are entitled to practice law). As we will learn, in most circumstances it is a provincial offence for a person to engage in the unauthorized practice of law—that is, to practice as a barrister or solicitor without a license.

Each provincial and territorial law society has developed its own code of conduct for practising lawyers. Most of these codes have been modelled very closely after the Model Code of Professional Conduct prepared by the Canadian Bar Association (CBA). There are, however, many important differences between the codes of various jurisdictions, particularly in their treatment of the issue of confidentiality and its limitations. The preface to the CBA code notes that

> [t]he pertinent laws in Canada use various terms to describe conduct that subjects the lawyer to discipline, for example "professional misconduct," "conduct unbecoming," and "acts derogatory to the honour or dignity of the bar.

Codes do not attempt to define these terms; rather, they serve only as guides. As a former chair of the discipline committee of the Law Society of Upper Canada recently noted, not every breach of a rule contained in the applicable code will constitute professional misconduct, and, similarly, following each rule will not ensure that one has not engaged in professional misconduct. (See Marc Somerville, "Applying Ethical Standards to Lawyers" (1993), 6:1 *Westminster Affairs* 11.) Examine any code closely and you will find many inconsistencies, ambiguities, conflicts, and gaps; the rules do not always speak clearly and unequivocally, a point to which we will return in the discussion of *Meek v. Fleming*, below. If a lawyer is found guilty of conduct subject to discipline, that discipline may range from a reprimand to disbarment.

Much of the literature addressing the ethical norms that ought to govern a lawyer's conduct, and much in the model code, problematically presupposes that lawyers are acting within a traditional adversarial paradigm when the reality is that a significant portion of the profession does not do so. For example, corporate lawyers frequently complain that the model code, as well as the applicable codes of various jurisdictions, fail to address the practice of corporate law and hence on many issues provide little useful guidance. Moreover, as noted at the outset of this chapter, the traditional model of litigation has increasingly come under challenge and, in response to these challenges, has been modified in many ways. These modifications also invite questions as to whether the role of lawyers has, or ought to, change, and, accompanying that change of role, whether the ethical norms that ought to guide lawyers' conduct should similarly change. As we review some of the many challenges and modifications to the traditional model, we will come back to the discussion of the lawyer's role and the appropriate ethical underpinnings.

With respect to the role of lawyers within the context of traditional adversarial adjudication, the Atkinson article below notes two broad approaches—neutral partisanship (which might fairly be called the predominant approach) and moral activism. Neutral partisanship has two components, which David Luban labels "the principle of partisanship" and "the principle of non-accountability." (See David Luban, *Lawyers and Justice* (New Jersey: Princeton University Press, 1988).) The principle of partisanship postulates that it is the lawyer's role to be a zealous, partisan advocate for the interests of his or her client. In the writings of some proponents of this principle, there is no duty but to the client. However, it should be noted that the codes of conduct make it quite clear that the lawyer also owes a duty to the court; the precise scope of this duty and how that duty is to be reconciled in situations of conflict with the duty to the client is unclear. Indeed, in *Meek v. Fleming*, below, experienced counsel misjudged the extent of the duty owed to each. The principle of non-accountability postulates that the lawyer is in no manner morally implicated in the harms that his or her zealous advocacy on a client's behalf may work (on an adversary, a third party, or the community).

Two forms of justification are commonly offered for this vision of the lawyer's role. One common justification is that zealous partisanship by lawyers is absolutely essential to the performance of an adversarial system of justice. Of course, for this to work as a moral justification, one must be persuaded that the legal system is itself morally justifiable, that the role (of a neutral, zealous partisan) is essential to the legal system, that certain behaviour is required by the role, and that the act in question is an instance of the behaviour required by the role. The basic argument here is that an adversarial system is a just system of legal disputing (because it best approximates the truth and/or because one is persuaded that truth is only one component of justice and that being able to participate actively in the process is another) and, for it to work effectively, lawyers must be zealous partisans for their client's interests. As you will read below, Deborah Rhode offers many critiques of this argument. Like Neil Brooks, above, Rhode reminds us of the many assumptions underlying the adversarial system that do not hold in the real world. As such, arguments that the legal system is a just system can succeed only if assessed in a social and economic vacuum. In addition, her critique makes clear that many of the behaviours in which some lawyers engage—for example, attempting to confuse a witness on cross-examination or engaging in delay tactics—are not behaviours required for the performance of the role. Rather, the adversary system is used as a convenient and unconvincing excuse.

The second form of justification is fully developed by Charles Fried. He argues that the zealous advocacy of client interests, irrespective of any harm caused to others, is a moral good in itself. He argues that to seek for a client all that the law will give him or her is to maximize that person's autonomy, and he takes autonomy to be the central ethical value. Hence, the protection and enlargement of client autonomy is, of itself, a moral good. His argument resonates in many ways with the assumed purpose underlying the traditional model of litigation—the vindication of private interests. Rhode and Atkinson both offer several critiques of this form of justification, focusing in particular on why autonomy ought to be regarded as paramount and why the autonomy of clients ought to count for more than the autonomy interests of non-clients.

The second broad approach is that of "moral activism." As Atkinson notes, this approach is distinguished from that of neutral partisanship in that here service provided by the lawyer is limited by more than the client's will and by the outer bounds of the law. There are many different views within this broad approach but each sees lawyers as playing a more active moral role in the lawyer–client relationship. Some argue that "common morality" (including protecting innocent persons from harm) places bounds on what the lawyer ought to do. Others suggest that lawyers ought also to be constrained in their pursuit of client interests by the ideals of justice and concern for the interests of others. This approach, then, still acknowledges a heightened responsibility to client interests, but factors in other interests. As Atkinson notes, even some neutral partisans urge a responsibility on the part of lawyers to engage in dialogue with their clients about the moral consequences of their actions. The divide, however, is really over what is to be done in circumstances where client and lawyer fail to agree. Neutral partisans would argue that it is the lawyer's duty to proceed zealously to advance the client's interests. Moral activists, by contrast, give greater weight to the lawyer's moral concerns, suggesting that withdrawal and sometimes disclosure (breaching confidentiality) are appropriate. Do moral activists presuppose that lawyers are better moral agents than their clients? Is this appropriate? Do they have an adequate account of the ways in which power may operate within the context of a lawyer–client relationship?

As discussed above, the rules contained in the codes of conduct often do not speak clearly to a given situation, or different rules will point to conflicting courses of action. The preface to the CBA model code notes that the code

> is to be understood and applied in the light of its primary concern for the protection of the public interest. This principle is implicit in the legislative grants of self-government referred to above. Inevitably, the practical application of the Code to the diverse situations that confront an active profession in a changing society will reveal gaps, ambiguities and apparent inconsistencies. In such cases, the principle of protection of the public interest will serve to guide the practitioner to the applicable principles of ethical conduct and the true intent of the Code.

Is the view expressed here more compatible with that of neutral partisanship or moral activism? What is the "public interest"? When you read the Fried excerpt, think about what Fried's conception of the public interest might be?

B. Two Models

Rob Atkinson, "How the Butler Was Made To Do It: The Perverted Professionalism of *The Remains of the Day*"
(1995), 105 *Yale Law Journal* 177, at 181-94 (footnotes omitted)

The larger story is about an English butler looking back over his career in one of the great English country houses. The butler's name is Stevens, and he has been in service for most of his professional life to the fictitious but typical Lord Darlington. His retrospective is set in 1956, when the great era of the country house is over, and with it the age of the classic English butler. The Labor Government's wealth transfer taxes have begun to break up the ancestral estates of people like Lord Darlington. Members of the aristocracy are now opening their houses to throngs of tourists or, worse still, conveying them to the National Trust or, worst of all, selling them to foreign, even American, millionaires. This last indignity has befallen Lord Darlington's house.

Even for those with the money, like Darlington Hall's new owner, things are not what they were. In Stevens's words, "finding [staff] recruits of a satisfactory standard is no easy task nowadays." Even in the old days, as Stevens frequently laments, the less ambitious often opted out of domestic service to marry and raise families of their own. Stevens himself, however, has no children; he has never been married. For that matter, he has never taken a vacation.

When Stevens's new American employer learns of this, he insists that Stevens take the estate's Ford out for a week's holiday in the late summer when he is himself away in the United States. Stevens eventually assents, but only when he is able to convince himself that the trip has a professional purpose. He has just received the first letter in a long while from a former head housekeeper at the Hall, Miss Kenton, and he interprets this to mean that she may be ready, after twenty years of married life, to leave her husband and return to domestic service. He recalls "her great affection for this house, ... her exemplary professionalism." His taking a trip to her home in the West Country, he persuades himself, may convince her to return in her former professional capacity. But we begin to suspect that he has been interested in more than her exemplary professionalism, and that her affection was not always limited to the house.

In the course of his trip, Stevens reflects that social life in the country house is not all that has suffered since the war; the personal reputation of the recently deceased Lord Darlington is at a low ebb as well. In the mid-thirties, he had hosted several "unofficial" meetings between the British Foreign Secretary and German Ambassador von Ribbentrop, in an effort, as we would now say, to reanchor Germany in the West. In recognition of his good offices, he had been rather graciously received in the reconstituted Reich. Stevens is at pains to point out that many entirely loyal English aristocrats were initially inclined to trust the new German leadership, and that Lord Darlington was not the last to realize the true nature of Nazism. More ominously, Stevens admits, Darlington had flirted, intellectually and otherwise, with a female member of the British Union of Fascists and had entertained that organization's leader, Sir Oswald Mosley, at the Hall. But Stevens tries to minimize Darlington's association with the Black Shirts, reducing it to a very few incidents over a very brief time. It is on one of those incidents that I want to focus.

B. What the Butler Did

One summer afternoon Lord Darlington calls Stevens into the study, and, after the usual pleasantries, asks whether there are any Jews on the house staff. When informed that there are two Jewish housemaids, Lord Darlington tells Stevens, "Of course, you'll have to let them go." Apparently prompted by Stevens's barely perceptible surprise, Lord Darlington explains: "It's regrettable, Stevens, but we have no choice. There's the safety and well-being of my guests to consider. Let me assure you, I've looked into this matter and thought it through thoroughly. It's in all our best interests."

Because the two maids are under Miss Kenton's direct supervision as housekeeper, Stevens thinks it appropriate to inform her of their dismissal. He brings the matter up that very night at their routine meeting for cocoa in her parlor. Stevens offers Miss Kenton the opportunity to speak with the maids herself before sending them along to his pantry for their dismissal the next morning. Miss Kenton expresses outrage and warns Stevens that if the maids are dismissed, she will leave as well. But Stevens carries out the order, and Miss Kenton does not leave.

Before examining the incident in more detail, I want briefly to reassure the skittish, those who are beginning to wonder how this tale can possibly relate to the practice of law other than perhaps to imply a deprecating comparison between lawyers and domestic servants. Thus, for those of you who think the assertedly parallel lines are diverging, let me offer a brief aside. Suppose Lord Darlington, punctilious in all his affairs, had called his London solicitors to confirm that his firing of the maids was legally proper. He might have asked for a written opinion on the subject and for carefully drafted dismissal papers to effect their discharge. Predictably, Lord Darlington would have rung up a senior member of the firm, and that member might well have assigned the research and drafting to a junior associate. The subordinate would have discovered that, under traditional common law notions of employment, the Jewish maids could be dismissed for even immoral reasons. I suspect, however, that both he and his senior would have been troubled by the prospect of playing a part in that morally sordid but perfectly legal action. It thus takes no great stretch of the imagination to see the dilemma of the butler and the maid played out in perfectly parallel fashion in a law firm of their day—or of ours.

As the next part shows, the responses of Stevens and Kenton are typical of two competing approaches open to contemporary American lawyers in such a situation. Either answer, standing alone, is inadequate, and the story itself presents a more satisfactory, but by no means perfect, response. The medium in which Stevens and Kenton give their answers—a story—reveals not only the relative merits of the alternative answer, but also why Stevens and Kenton failed to choose that alternative, and at what cost. The factors influencing their choices operate on us as well, and we are at risk of incurring similar costs. To shift from the terminology of economics to the language of literature, we are in danger of suffering the same fate.

II. Perverted Professionalism

Whenever someone serves another, that service poses a question: Should the service be limited by anything other than the principal's will? Modern society imposes one obvious set of constraints: the outer bounds of the state's positive law. But are there other limits? That is a fundamental question of professional ethics: Should a professional always do all that the law allows, or should the professional recognize other constraints, particularly concerns for the welfare of third parties? This question divides scholars of legal ethics and thoughtful practitioners into two schools: those who recognize constraints other than law's outer limit, and those who do not. Mr. Stevens and Miss Kenton, in their treatment of the maids and in their professional lives generally, fall on opposite sides of this divide. The course of their lives suggests not so much that one answer is wrong and the other right, but that each poses distinct dangers to moral integrity and that each is the beginning, rather than the end, of moral analysis.

A. Mr. Stevens's Neutral Partisanship

Stevens's position closely parallels what students of the legal profession call "neutral partisanship." The second of these two correlated principles, partisanship, entails advancing client ends through all legal means, and with a maximum of personal determination, as long as the ends are within the letter of the law. The first principle, neutrality, lets the professional claim personal disinterest in, or even antipathy toward, client ends and moral nonaccountability for helping to advance them. So it was with Stevens's firing of the Jewish maids. Looking back on the incident, he sees it this way:

> [M]y every instinct opposed the idea of their dismissal. Nevertheless, my duty in this instance was quite clear, and as I saw it, there was nothing to be gained at all in irresponsibly displaying such personal doubts. It was a difficult task, but as such, one that demanded to be carried out with dignity.

When Miss Kenton expresses her outrage, he reminds her that "our professional duty is not to our own foibles and sentiments, but to the wishes of our employer."

For Stevens and the neutral partisans, the ultimate decision, in matters of morality and public policy, is the client's to make. Furthermore, this has an important corollary: The professional's job is essentially technical. In the words of a prominent academic proponent of neutral partisanship, the client is like an "individual facing and needing to use a very large and very complicated machine (with lots of whirring gears and spinning data tapes) that he can't get to work." In Stevens's words, "Let us establish this quite clearly: a butler's duty is to provide good service. It is not to meddle in the great affairs of the nation." Neutral partisanship tends to reduce the human dimensions of one's professional life, to deal with its unpleasantries in abstract and impersonal terms. Thus, for example, Stevens speaks of the "particular contracts to be discontinued," and refers to the maids as "the two employees concerned." And as neutral partisanship reduces professional service to technical assistance, so it tends to reduce moral concerns to matters of individual taste, if not idiosyncrasy. We have already heard Stevens dismiss his moral qualms as "foibles and sentiments."

This is not to say, however, that Stevens's position is totally divorced from morality, any more than is the contemporary justification of neutral partisanship as practiced by lawyers. Rather, Stevens firmly grounds his position in morality, in very much the same way today's neutral partisan lawyers do. Stevens insists that the moral dimension of one's professional role as a butler derives from the moral standing of one's employer:

> [T]he question was not simply one of how well one practised one's skills, but *to what end* one did so; each of us harboured the desire to make our own small contribution to the creation of a better world, and saw that, as professionals, the surest means of doing so would be to serve the great gentlemen of our times in whose hands civilization had been entrusted. ...
>
> A "great" butler can only be, surely, one who can point to his years of service and say that he has applied his talents to serving a great gentleman—and through the latter, to serving humanity.

• • •

Defenders of neutral partisan lawyering are also at pains to show how the professional role they prescribe serves the public good. In contrast to Stevens, they do not focus on the humanitarian impulses, or even on the moral status, of the client. Rather, the reverse is true: They are at pains to show that whenever the lawyer helps a client exercise legal rights, even in an immoral way, the lawyer has acted well as a professional. Yet this professional probity, like Stevens's, is grounded in an ethical good. In the case of neutral partisan lawyers, that ethical good is the client's exercise of moral autonomy as authorized by the law. Society recognizes individual autonomy as a good of the highest order, so the argument runs, and carves out a sphere in which individuals can exercise that autonomy without interference. By helping lay folk operate within that envelope—sometimes even by pressing its edge—the lawyer is accomplishing a moral and social, not just professional, good. When, accordingly, proponents of neutral partisanship describe their model as amoral, they are not referring to its ultimate grounding, which is emphatically moral. They are referring, rather, to the lawyer's immunity from the task of scrutinizing the morality of particular client acts. Theirs is morality at the wholesale but not the retail level; a morality of the long run, not the particular case; a morality of fidelity to role obligations, not attention to particular acts. ...

The skepticism at the root of neutral partisanship in lawyering generally takes a less personal, and more radical, form. It has been traced to the Hobbesian, positivist notion that "[e]nds are natural, individual, subjective, and arbitrary." On that view, the only ends individuals share are the desire to be free to pursue their private ends and the corollary desire for security in that pursuit. The legitimate function of law is to define limits within which individuals can exercise autonomy without impinging upon each other. The lawyer's job is to advise the client, faced with a bafflingly complex legal order, about where the outer edge of this sphere of autonomy lies. Not to assist the client in exercising autonomy up to the very margin allowed by law would be to usurp the role not just of judge and jury, but of the legislature as well. Ultimately, it would undermine the legitimacy of government itself. Thus, though the moral skepticism of neutral partisan lawyers is more global and less self-effacing than that of Stevens, it produces the same result: deferring to clients on moral judgments within the letter of the law. Thus, moral skepticism, somewhat paradoxically, is the foundation of Stevens's and the neutral partisan lawyers' faith in the rightness of fidelity to clients' ends.

B. Miss Kenton's Moral Activism

Miss Kenton's reaction to the firing of the maids offers a striking contrast to Mr. Stevens's response, and it implies a vision of professionalism quite different from neutral partisanship. She recoils from the technocratic, antiseptic attitude of Stevens, his treatment of the dismissals "as though [he] were discussing orders for the larder." In contrast to his references to "contracts" and "employees," she persistently refers to the maids by their first names, Ruth and Sarah, and invokes her long, personal relationship with them. And she does not dismiss deeply held personal aversions as "foibles and sentiments." She says she's outraged, and she puts her position in unmistakably moral terms: "Does it not occur to you, Mr Stevens, that to dismiss Ruth and Sarah on these grounds would be simply—*wrong*? I will not stand for such things." A bit later, she refers to the dismissals as "a sin as any sin ever was one." Most significantly, she takes direct moral responsibility for the immediate consequences of her actions, rather than insulating herself within her role. She will not be a partisan for what she believes to be a moral wrong, because she cannot be neutral professionally toward what she opposes personally.

In all of these respects, and most fundamentally in the last, Miss Kenton implicitly anticipates the growing ranks of scholarly critics of neutral partisanship in the legal profession. Although they differ on details, these critics all agree that, with narrow exceptions like criminal defense work and other David-versus-Goliath analogues, lawyers cannot claim moral absolution for unquestioningly assisting their clients in unjust acts, however legally proper. In their view, lawyers should not merely decline to assist in such acts; they should also act affirmatively to promote justice in their representation of private clients. Accordingly, following one of its chief proponents, I will call this position "moral activism."

Defenders of moral activism in the legal profession look to several sources outside the letter of the law for additional limits on what lawyers may properly do for clients, and these sources support Miss Kenton's position. Some moral activists factor ordinary morality, the shared moral norms of society—in particular, our common obligation not to harm the innocent—directly into the professional's ethical calculus. On that view, because the function of the professional role itself is to advance ordinary moral values, such as the discovery of truth and the protection of individual rights, any departure that the professional role requires from ordinary morality must be strongly justified in terms of ordinary morality itself. Ordinary morality is the most obvious source of Miss Kenton's resistance, sounded in her objection that "to dismiss Ruth and Sarah on these grounds would be simply—*wrong*." And moral objections can be grounded in religious as well as secular ethics; lawyers, like Miss Kenton, can conclude that complying with their employers' wishes would be "a sin as any sin ever was one."

Other moral activists, anticipating Stevens's dismissal of moral limits as subjective or idiosyncratic, find limits to the law's letter in its spirit. At the most basic level, they point out, lawyers justify their role in service to the law as "officers of the court," and the purpose of the law itself is to promote justice. Thus, when lawyers invoke particular laws on behalf of clients in ways that threaten to subvert justice, they undercut the very basis of their professional status. ...

Finally, some moral activists, skeptical of finding general agreement on either ordinary moral norms or professional values, look for the limits of professional conduct in the fundamental beliefs of smaller communities united in a common faith. Such faiths need not be conventionally religious and need not rest on anything beyond their adherents' personal commitments. Miss Kenton, echoing the prototypical Protestant, sounds this theme as well, albeit in a minor key: "I will not stand for such things."

C. Stevens and Kenton's Common Ground: Moral Isolationism

Stevens's vision of professionalism, like that of the neutral partisan lawyer, leaves the ultimate moral judgment to the client; Kenton, like neutral partisanship's critics, reserves that judgment for herself. It is important to note at this point, however, that it is the *ultimate* decision on which neutral partisans and their critics divide. More subtle proponents of neutral partisanship agree with their detractors on one critical point: the appropriateness of raising moral concerns with a client in an effort to discourage the client from committing what the professional believes to be a moral wrong.

On this point, both schools of lawyering would fault Stevens *and* Kenton—Stevens, for going along without remonstrating; Kenton, for believing that she should resign without remonstrating. Moreover, the official codes of legal ethics stand squarely behind the united front of neutral partisans and their critics on the point of giving moral advice to clients. The codes and virtually all commentators agree that, having determined that a client is about to do something legal but morally reprehensible, lawyers have an option before they reach the decision that divides neutral partisans from moral activists. Before deciding to assist in the wrong or terminate the representation, the lawyer may—in some views, should—try to persuade the client to do the morally right thing. Curiously, both Miss Kenton and Mr. Stevens skipped this step; in fact, this step does not seem to have occurred to either of them as a live option.

There was, in addition, another element of moral isolationism in Stevens and Kenton's story. They failed not only to talk with Lord Darlington, but also to talk in any meaningful way with each other. The importance of this second dialogue, a dialogue among professionals themselves or between professionals and their personal friends, is not well reflected either in codes of legal ethics or in academic treatments of lawyer professionalism.

C. The Defence of Neutral Partisanship

C. Fried, "The Lawyer as Friend: The Moral Foundations of the Lawyer–Client Relation"
(1976), 85 *Yale Law Journal*, at 1060-67 and 1076-87

Can a good lawyer be a good person? The question troubles lawyers and law students alike. They are troubled by the demands of loyalty to one's client and by the fact that one can win approval as a good, maybe even great, lawyer even though that loyalty is engrossed by over-privileged or positively distasteful clients. How, they ask, is such loyalty compatible with that devotion to the common good characteristic of high moral principles? And whatever their views of the common good, they are troubled because the willingness of lawyers to help their clients use the law to the prejudice of the weak or the innocent seems morally corrupt. The lawyer is conventionally seen as a professional devoted to his client's interests and as authorized, if not in fact required, to do some things (though not anything) for that client which he would not do for himself. In this essay I consider the compatibility between this traditional conception of the lawyer's role and the ideal of moral purity—the ideal that one's life should be lived in fulfillment of the most demanding moral principles, and not just barely within the law. So I shall not be particularly concerned with the precise limits imposed on the lawyer's conduct by positive rules of law and by the American Bar Association's *Code of Professional Responsibility* except as these provide a background. I assume that the lawyer observes these scrupulously. My inquiry is one of morals: Does the lawyer whose conduct and choices are governed only by the traditional conception of the lawyer's role, which these positive rules reflect, lead a professional life worthy of moral approbation, worthy of respect—ours and his own? ...

Two frequent criticisms of the traditional conception of the lawyer's role attack both its ends and its means. First, it is said that the ideal of professional loyalty to one's client permits, even demands, an allocation of the lawyer's time, passion, and resources in ways that are not always maximally conducive to the greatest good of the greatest number. Interestingly, this criticism is leveled increasingly against doctors as well as lawyers. Both professions affirm the principle that the professional's primary loyalty is to his client, his patient. A "good" lawyer will lavish energy and resources on his existing client, even if it can be shown that others could derive greater benefit from them. The professional ideal authorizes a care for the client and the patient which exceeds what the efficient distribution of a scarce social resource (the professional's time) would dictate.

That same professional ideal has little or nothing to say about the initial choice of clients or patients. Certainly it is laudable if the doctor and lawyer choose their clients among the poorest or sickest or most dramatically threatened, but the professional ideal does not require this kind of choice in any systematic way—the choice of client remains largely a matter of fortuity or arbitrary choice. But once the client has been chosen, the professional ideal requires primary loyalty to the client whatever his need or situation. Critics contend that it is wasteful and immoral that some of the finest talent in the legal profession is devoted to the intricacies of, say, corporate finance or elaborate estate plans, while important public and private needs for legal services go unmet. The immorality of this waste is seen to be compounded when the clients who are the beneficiaries of this lavish attention use it to avoid their obligations in justice (if not in law) to society and to perpetuate their (legal) domination of the very groups whose greater needs these lawyers should be meeting.

The second criticism applies particularly to the lawyer. It addresses not the misallocation of scarce resources, which the lawyer's exclusive concern with his client's interests permits, but the means which this loyalty appears to authorize, tactics which procure advantages for the client at the direct expense of some identified opposing party. Examples are discrediting a nervous but probably truthful complaining witness or taking advantage of the need or ignorance of an adversary in a negotiation. This second criticism is, of course, related to the first, but there is a difference. The first criticism focuses on a social harm: the waste of scarce resources implicit in a doctor caring for the hearts of the sedentary managerial classes or a lawyer tending to the estates and marital difficulties of the rich. The professional is accused of failing to confer benefits wisely and efficiently. By the second criticism the lawyer is accused not of failing to benefit the appropriate, though usually unidentified, persons, but of harming his identified adversary. ...

In this essay I will consider the moral status of the traditional conception of the professional. The two criticisms of this traditional conception, if left unanswered, will not put the lawyer in jail, but they will leave him without a moral basis for his acts. The real question is whether, in the face of these two criticisms, a decent and morally sensitive person can conduct himself according to the traditional conception of professional loyalty and still believe that what he is doing is morally worthwhile.

It might be said that anyone whose conscience is so tender that he cannot fulfill the prescribed obligations of a professional should not undertake those obligations. He should not allow his moral scruples to operate as a trap for those who are told by the law that they may expect something more. But of course this suggestion merely pushes the inquiry back a step. We must ask then not how a decent lawyer may behave, but whether a decent, ethical person can ever be a lawyer. Are the assurances implicit in assuming the role of lawyer such that an honorable person would not give them and thus would not enter the profession? And, indeed, this is a general point about an argument from obligation: It may be that the internal logic of a particular obligation demands certain forms of conduct (*e.g.*, honor among thieves), but the question remains whether it is just and moral to contract such obligations.

I will argue in this essay that it is not only legally but also morally right that a lawyer adopt as his dominant purpose the furthering of his client's interests—that it is right that a professional put the interests of his client above some idea, however valid, of the collective interest. I maintain that the traditional conception of the professional role expresses a morally valid conception of human conduct and human relationships, that one who acts according to that conception is to that extent a good person. Indeed, it is my view that, far from being a mere creature of positive law, the traditional conception is so far mandated by moral right that any advanced legal system which did not sanction this conception would be unjust.

The general problem raised by the two criticisms is this: How can it be that it is not only permissible, but indeed morally right, to favor the interests of a particular person in a way which we can be fairly sure is either harmful to another particular individual or not maximally conducive to the welfare of society as a whole?

The resolution of this problem is aided, I think, if set in a larger perspective. Charles Curtis made the perspicacious remark that a lawyer may be privileged to lie for his client in a way that one might lie to save one's friends or close relatives. I do not want to underwrite the notion that it is justifiable to lie even in those situations, but there is a great deal to the point that in those relations—friendship, kinship—we recognize an authorization to take the interest of particular concrete persons more seriously and to give them priority over the interests of the wider collectivity. One who provides an expensive education for his own children surely cannot be blamed because he does not use these resources to alleviate famine or to save lives in some distant land. Nor does he blame himself. Indeed, our intuition that an individual is authorized to prefer identified persons standing close to him over the abstract interests of humanity finds its sharpest expression in our sense that an individual is entitled to act with something less than impartiality to that person who stands closest to him—the person that he is. There is such a thing as selfishness to be sure, yet no reasonable morality asks us to look upon ourselves as merely plausible candidates for the distribution of the attention and resources which we command, plausible candidates whose entitlement to our own concern is no greater in principle than that of any other human being. Such a doctrine may seem edifying, but on reflection it strikes us as merely fanatical.

This suggests an interesting way to look at the situation of the lawyer. As a professional person one has a special care for the interests of those accepted as clients, just as his friends, his family, and he himself have a very general claim to his special concern.

But I concede this does no more than widen the problem. It merely shows that in claiming this authorization to have a special care for my clients I am doing something which I do in other contexts as well.

A. *The Choice of Clients: The Question of Distribution*

It is time to apply the concept of legal friendship to the first of the two criticisms with which this essay began: that the lawyer's ethic of loyalty to his client and his willingness to pick clients for any and every reason (usually, however, for money) result in a maldistribution of a scarce resource, the aid of counsel. It is this criticism which the lawyer shares with the doctor. The preceding sections demonstrated at least this much: that legal counsel—like medical care—must be considered a good, and that he who provides it does a useful thing. But this first criticism in no way questions that conclusion. On the contrary, precisely because medical care and legal counsel are benefits to those who receive them, the critic blames the individual doctor or lawyer for not bestowing his skills in the way which best meets the social need. The notion of legal friendship helps us respond to this criticism.

The lawyer–client relation is a personal relation, and legal counsel is a personal service. This explains directly why, *once the relation has been contracted*, considerations of efficiency or fair distribution cannot be allowed to weaken it. The relation itself is not a creature of social expediency (though social circumstances provide the occasion for it); it is the creature of moral right, and therefore expediency may not compromise the nature of the relation. This is true in medicine because the human need creates a relation of dependence which it would be a betrayal to compromise. In the lawyer–client relation, the argument is more complex but supports the same conclusion. The relation must exist in order to realize the client's rights against society, to preserve that measure of autonomy which social regulation must allow the individual. But to allow social considerations—even social regulations—to limit and compromise what by hypothesis is an entailment of the original grant of right to the individual is to take away with the left hand what was given with the right. Once the relation has been taken up, it is the client's needs which hold the reins—legally and morally.

If I have a client with legal needs, then neither another person with greater needs nor a court should be able to compel or morally oblige me to compromise my care for those needs. To hold differently would apply the concept of battlefield emergency care (*triage*) to the area of regular legal service. But doctors do not operate that way and neither should lawyers. For it is just the point about emergencies and wars that they create special, brutal, and depersonalized relations which civilization, by its very essence, must keep from becoming the general rule of social life.

So much for the integrity of the relation once it has taken hold. But what of the initial choice of client? Must we not give some thought to efficiency and relative need at least at the outset, and does this not run counter to the picture of purely discretionary choice implicit in the notion of friendship? The question is difficult, but before considering its difficulties we should note that the preceding argumentation has surely limited its impact. We can now affirm that whatever the answer to this question, the individual lawyer does a morally worthy thing whomever he serves and, moreover, is bound to follow through once he has begun to serve. In this he is like the doctor. So if there is fault here it is a limited fault. What would be required for a lawyer to immunize himself more fully from criticism that he is unjust in his allocation of care? Each lawyer would have to consider at the outset of his career and during that career where the greatest need for his particular legal talents lies. He would then have to allocate himself to that area of greatest need. Surely there is nothing wrong in doing this (so long as loyalty to relations already undertaken is not compromised); but is a lawyer morally at fault if he does not lead his life in this way? It is at this point too that the metaphor of friendship and the concept of self as developed above suggest the response. But this time they will be viewed from another perspective—the lawyer's as opposed to the client's rights and liberties.

Must the lawyer expend his efforts where they will do the most good, rather than where they will draw the largest fee, provide the most excitement, prove most flattering to his vanity, whatever? Why must he? If the answer is that he must because it will produce the most good, then we are saying to the lawyer that he is merely a scarce resource. But a person is not a resource. He is not bound to lead his life as if he were managing a business on behalf of an impersonal body of stockholders called human society. It is this monstrous conception against which I argued earlier. Justice is not all; we are entitled to reserve a portion of our concern and bestow it where we will. We may bestow it entirely at our discretion as in the case of friendship, or we may bestow it at what I would call "constrained discretion" in the choice and exercise of a profession. That every exercise of the profession is morally worthwhile is already a great deal to the lawyer's credit. Just as the principle of liberty leaves one morally free to choose a profession according to inclination, so within the profession it leaves one free to organize his life according to inclination. The lawyer's liberty—moral liberty—to take up what kind of practice he chooses and to take up or decline what clients he will is an aspect of the moral liberty of self to enter into personal relations freely.

I would not carry this idea through to the bitter end. It has always been accepted, for instance, that a court may appoint an available lawyer to represent a criminal defendant who cannot otherwise find counsel. Indeed, I would be happy to acknowledge the existence of some moral duty to represent any client whose needs fit one's particular capacities and who cannot otherwise find counsel. This is not a large qualification to the general liberty I proclaim. The obligation is, and must remain, exceptional; it cannot become a kind of general conscription of the particular lawyer involved. And the obligation cannot compromise duties to existing clients. Furthermore, I would argue that this kind of representation should always be compensated—the duty to the client who cannot afford representation is initially a duty of society, not of the individual lawyer. I go this far for a number of reasons. If the representation is properly compensated, then the very need to appoint a lawyer will be exceptional, an anomaly arising in one of two ways: a fortuitous perturbation in the law of supply and demand or a general, if not concerted, professional boycott of this particular client. If the first is the reason, then the lifetime imposition on any one lawyer will be slight indeed. If it is the second, then the assertion of a duty, oddly enough, serves to express and strengthen the principle of the lawyer's independence. For the moral position of the lawyer rests on the claim that he takes up his client's interests irrespective of their merits. By accepting from time to time the duty to represent the undesirable, he affirms this independence.

But surely I must admit that the need for legal representation far exceeds what such an unstructured, largely individualistic system could supply. Are there not vast numbers of needy people with a variety of legal problems who will never seek us out, but must be sought out? And what of the general responsibility that just laws be passed and justly administered? These are the obligations which the traditional conception of the lawyer, with his overriding loyalty to the paying client, is thought to leave unmet. At this point I yield no further. If the lawyer is really to be impressed to serve these admitted social needs, then his independence and discretion disappear, and he does indeed become a public resource cut up and disposed of by the public's needs. There would be no justice to such a conception. If there are really not enough lawyers to care for the needs of the poor, then it is grossly unfair to conscript the legal profession to fill those needs. If the obligation is one of justice, it is an obligation of society as a whole. It is cheap and hypocritical for society to be unwilling to pay the necessary lawyers from the tax revenues of all, and then to claim that individual lawyers are morally at fault for not choosing to work for free. In fact, as provision of legal services has come to be seen as necessary to ensure justice, society has indeed hired lawyers in an effort to meet that need.

Finally, I agree that the lawyer has a moral obligation to work for the establishment of just institutions generally, but entirely the wrong kind of conclusions have been drawn from this. Some of the more ecstatic critics have put forward the lawyer as some kind of anointed priest of justice—a high priest whose cleaving to the traditional conception of the lawyer's role opens him to the charge of apostasy. But this is wrong. In a democratic society, justice has no anointed priests. Every citizen has the same duty to work for the establishment of just institutions, and the lawyer has no special moral responsibilities in that regard. To be sure, the lawyer like any citizen must use all his knowledge and talent to fulfill that general duty of citizenship, and this may mean that there are special perspectives and opportunities for him.

B. The Choice of Means

More difficult problems are posed by the conflict between the interests of the client and the interests of some other concrete and specified person to whom the client stands in opposition. How does my friendship analogy help to resolve the conflict which a lawyer must feel if his client asks him to lie, to oppress, or to conceal—to do something which is either illegal or felt by the lawyer to be immoral?

1. Staying Within the Law

I have defined the lawyer as a client's legal friend, as the person whose role it is to insure the client's autonomy within the law. Although I have indicated that the exercise of the autonomy is not always consonant with the public interest, it does not at all follow that the exercise of that autonomy, therefore, must also violate the law. If the legal system is itself sensitive to moral claims, sensitive to the rights of individuals, it must at times allow that autonomy to be exercised in ways that do not further the public interest. Thus, the principle that the lawyer must scrupulously contain his assistance and advocacy within the dictates of the law seems to me perfectly consistent with my view of the lawyer as the client's friend, who maintains the client's interests even against the interests of society.

To be sure, there may have been and may still be situations where the law grossly violates what morality defines as individual rights; and there have been lawyers who have stood ready to defy such laws in order to further their client's rights—the rights which the law should, but did not, recognize. Whatever might be said about those cases, the lawyer's conduct in them travels outside the bounds of legal friendship and becomes political friendship, political agitation, or friendship *tout court*. But that is not the case I am examining. The moral claims which a client has on his lawyer can be fully exhausted though that lawyer contains his advocacy strictly within the limits of the law.

A critic who fails to see the importance of the lawyer's moral status in assisting the autonomy of his client, may also be inclined to complain that the constraints of the law restrain his advocacy of truly just causes too much. Such a critic has things wrong at both ends. Just as it is false to argue that the lawyer is morally reprehensible if he furthers the interests of some clients and not others or some purposes and not others, so it is false to assume that the lawyer fails to have the proper zeal if he does for his client only what the law allows. The distinction between the role of the lawyer as a personal advisor and that of the lawyer as a citizen and member of the community should be quite clear. It is by controlling what the law is and by varying the interests that clients may lawfully pursue that social policy would be effectuated; it is not by deforming the role of the lawyer as the client's legal friend and asking him to curb his advocacy in that relationship.

This explains why in a reasonably just system which properly commands the lawyer's loyalty, he must confine his advocacy to what the rules of advocacy permit. He may not counsel his client to commit a crime, nor to destroy evidence, nor to perjure himself on the witness stand. Of course, here as elsewhere there will be borderline problems. It may not be a crime to lie to the judge who has asked the improper and prejudicial question of the defense attorney, but the implicit or quasi-official rules defining the limits of the lawyer's advocacy may nonetheless forbid this. Nothing in my model should discourage the lawyer from observing such limits scrupulously.

A very difficult question would arise if the law imposed upon the lawyer an obligation first to seek and then to betray his client's trust, an obligation to do that which seems outrageous and unjust. I do not mean to say that the resolution of this question would be easy, but my analysis at least clearly locates the area in which a resolution should be sought. For such laws, it they are to be opposed, ought to be opposed as are other unjust laws, and not because the lawyer is in general entitled to travel outside the constraints of the law in protecting his client's interests. Maybe in such a dilemma a conscientious lawyer would keep his client's confidence as would a priest or a natural friend; but if conscientiousness requires this, it requires it as an act of disobedience and resistance to an unjust law, rather than as a necessary entailment of some extreme view of the lawyer's general role.

2. *Immoral Means*

I come to what seems to me one of the most difficult dilemmas of the lawyer's role. It is illustrated by the lawyer who is asked to press the unfair claim, to humiliate a witness, to participate in a distasteful or dishonorable scheme. I am assuming that in none of these situations does the lawyer do anything which is illegal or which violates the ethical canons of his profession; the dilemma arises if he acts in a way which seems to him personally dishonorable, but there are no sanctions—legal or professional—which he need fear.

This set of issues is difficult because it calls on the same principles which provide the justification for the lawyer's or the friend's exertions on behalf of the person with whom he maintains a personal relation. Only now the personal relation is one not of benefit but of harm. In meeting the first criticism, I was able to insist on the right of the lawyer as friend to give this extra weight to the interests of his client when the only competing claims were the general claims of the abstract collectivity. But here we have a specific victim as well as a specific beneficiary. The relation to the person whom we deceive or abuse is just as concrete and human, just as personal, as to the friend whom we help.

It is not open to us to justify this kind of harm by claiming that personal relations must be chosen, not thrust upon us. Personal relations are indeed typically chosen. If mere proximity could place on us the obligations of friendship, then there would soon be nothing left of our freedom to bestow an extra measure of care over and above what humanity can justly claim. But there is a personal relation when we inflict intentional harm; the fact that it is intentional reaches out and particularizes the victim. "Who is my neighbour?" is a legitimate question when affirmative aid is in question; it is quite out of order in respect to the injunction "Do not harm your neighbor." Lying, stealing, degrading, inflicting pain and injury are personal relations too. They are not like failing to benefit, and for that reason they are laid under a correspondingly stricter regime than abstract harms to the collectivity. If I claim respect for my own concrete particularity, I must accord that respect to others. Therefore, what pinches here is the fact that the lawyer's personal engagement with the client is urging him to do that to his adversary which the very principles of personal engagement urge that he not do to anyone.

It is not wrong but somewhat lame to argue that the lawyer like the client has autonomy. From this argument it follows that the lawyer who is asked to do something personally distasteful or immoral (though perfectly legal) should be free either to decline to enter into the relationship of "legal friendship" or to terminate it. And if the client can find a lawyer to do the morally nasty but legally permissible thing for him, then all is well—the complexities of the law have not succeeded in thwarting an exercise of autonomy which the law was not entitled to thwart. So long as the first lawyer is reasonably convinced that another lawyer can be found, I cannot see why he is less free to decline the morally repugnant case than he is the boring or poorly paid case. True, but lame, for one wants to know not whether one *may* refuse to do the dirty deed, but whether one is morally *bound* to refuse—bound to refuse even if he is the last lawyer in town and no one else will bail him out of his moral conundrum.

If personal integrity lies at the foundation of the lawyer's right to treat his client as a friend, then surely consideration for personal integrity—his own and others'—must limit what he can do in friendship. Consideration for personal integrity forbids me to lie, cheat, or humiliate, whether in my own interests or those of a friend, so surely they prohibit such conduct on behalf of a client, one's legal friend. This is the general truth, but it must be made more particular if it is to do service here. For there is an opposing consideration. Remember, the lawyer's special kind of friendship is occasioned by the right of the client to exercise his full measure of autonomy within the law. This suggests that one must not transfer uncritically the whole range of personal moral scruples into the arena of legal friendship. After all, not only would I not lie or steal for myself or my friends, I probably also would not pursue socially noxious schemes, foreclose on widows or orphans, or assist in the avoidance of just punishment. So we must be careful lest the whole argument unravel on us at this point.

Balance and structure are restored if we distinguish between kinds of moral scruples. Think of the soldier. If he is a citizen of a just state, where foreign policy decisions are made in a democratic way, he may well believe that it is not up to him to question whether the war he fights is a just war. But he is personally bound not to fire dum-dum bullets, not to inflict intentional injury on civilians, and not to abuse prisoners. These are personal wrongs, wrongs done by his person to the person of the victim. So also, the lawyer must distinguish between wrongs that a reasonably just legal system permits to be worked by its rules and wrongs which the lawyer personally commits. Now I do not offer this as a rule which is tight enough to resolve all borderline questions of judgment. We must recognize that the border is precisely the place of friction between competing moral principles. Indeed, it is unreasonable to expect moral arguments to dispense wholly with the need for prudence and judgment.

Consider the difference between humiliating a witness or lying to the judge on one hand, and, on the other hand, asserting the statute of limitations or the lack of a written memorandum to defeat what you know to be a just claim against your client. In the latter case, if an injustice is worked, it is worked because the legal system not only permits it, but also defines the terms and modes of operation. Legal institutions have created the occasion for your act. What you do is not personal; it is a formal, legally-defined act. But the moral quality of lying or abuse obtains both without and within the context of the law. Therefore, my general notion is that a lawyer is morally entitled to act in this formal, representative way even if the result is an injustice, because the legal system which authorizes both the injustice (*e.g.*, the result following the plea of the statute of limitations) and the formal gesture for working it insulates him from personal moral responsibility. I would distinguish between the lawyer's own wrong and the wrong of the system used to advantage by the client.

The clearest case is a lawyer who calls to the attention of the court a controlling legal precedent or statute which establishes his client's position even though that position is an unjust one. (I assume throughout, however, that this unjust law is part of a generally just and decent system. I am not considering at all the moral dilemmas of a lawyer in Nazi Germany or Soviet Russia.) Why are we inclined to absolve him of personal moral responsibility for the result he accomplishes? I assert it is because the wrong is wholly institutional; it is a wrong which does not exist and has no meaining outside the legal framework. The only thing preventing the client from doing this for himself is his lack of knowledge of the law or his lack of authority to operate the levers of the law in official proceedings. It is to supply that lack of knowledge or of formal capacity that the lawyer is in general authorized to act; and the levers he pulls are all legal levers.

Now contrast this to the lawyer who lies to an opposing party in a negoitation. I assume that (except in extreme cases akin to self-defense) an important lie with harmful consequences is an offense to the victim's integrity as a rational moral being, and thus the liar affirms a principle which denigrates his own moral status. Every speech act invites belief, and so every lie is a betrayal. However, may a lawyer lie in his representative capacity? It is precisely my point that a man cannot lie just in his representative capacity; it is like stabbing someone in the back "just" in a representative capacity. The injury and betrayal are not worked by the legal process, but by an act which is generally harmful quite apart from the legal context in which it occurs.

There is an important class of cases which might be termed "lying in a representative capacity." An example is the lawyer presenting to the court a statement by another that he knows to be a lie, as when he puts a perjurious client-defendant on the stand. There is dispute as to whether and when the positive law of professional responsibility permits this, but clearly in such instances it is not the lawyer who is lying. He is like a letter carrier who delivers the falsehood. Whether he is free to do that is more a matter of legal than personal ethics.

A test that might make the distinction I offer more palpable is this: How would it be if it were known in advance that lawyers would balk at the practice under consideration? Would it not be intolerable if it were known that lawyers would not plead the defense of the Statute of Frauds or of the statute of limitations? And would it not be quite all right if it were known in advance that you cannot get a lawyer to lie for you, though he may perhaps put you on the stand to lie in your own defense?

A more difficult case to locate in the moral landscape is abusive and demeaning cross-examination of a complaining witness. Presumably, positive law and the canons of ethics restrict this type of conduct, but enforcement may be lax or interpretation by a trial judge permissive. So the question arises: What is the lawyer *morally* free to do? Here again I urge the distinction between exposing a witness to the skepticism and scrutiny envisaged by the law and engaging in a personal attack on the witness. The latter is a harm which the lawyer happens to inflict in court, but it is a harm quite apart from the institutional legal context. It is perhaps just a matter of style or tone, but the crucial point is that the probing must not imply that the lawyer believes the witness is unworthy of respect.

The lawyer is not morally entitled, therefore, to engage his own person in doing personal harm to another, though he may exploit the system for his client even if the system consequently works injustice. He may, but must he? This is the final issue to confront. Since he may, he also need not if there is anyone else who will do it. Only if there is no one else does the agony become acute. If there is an obligation in that case, it is an institutional obligation that has developed upon him to take up a case, to make arguments when it is morally permissible but personally repugnant to him to do so. Once again, the inquiry is moral, for if the law enjoins an obligation against conscience, a lawyer, like any conscientious person, must refuse and pay the price.

The obligation of an available lawyer to accept appointment to defend an accused is clear. Any moral scruples about the proposition that no man should be accused and punished without counsel are not morally well-founded. The proposition is intended to enhance the autonomy of individuals within the law. But if you are the last lawyer in town, is there a moral obligation to help the finance company foreclose on the widow's refrigerator? If the client pursues the foreclosure in order to establish a legal right of some significance, I do not flinch from the conclusion that the lawyer is bound to urge this right. So also if the finance company cannot foreclose because of an ideological boycott by the local bar. But if all the other lawyers happen to be on vacation and the case means no more to the finance company than the resale value of one more used refrigerator, common sense says the lawyer can say no. One should be able to distinguish between establishing a legal right and being a cog in a routine, repetitive business operation, part of which just happens to play itself out in court.

Meek v. Fleming
[1961] 2 QB 366 (CA)

Appeal from Streatfeild J and a jury.

Motion for leave to adduce fresh evidence.

Alan Sidney Charles Meek, a press photographer, the plaintiff in an action for damages for alleged assault and wrongful imprisonment against Richard Fleming as a chief inspector of the Metropolitan Police, appealed from a judgment entered for the defendant on the verdict of a jury and asked for a new trial on the grounds, inter alia, of misdirection by the judge and that the verdict was against the weight of the evidence. Paragraph (6) of his notice of appeal was as follows: "That at the trial the rank and status of the defendant was by implication represented to be that of a chief inspector when in fact between the date of the matters complained of in the action and the date of the trial he had been reduced to the rank of a station sergeant by reason of misconduct and that the credit of the parties was a crucial issue at the trial."

By a further notice of motion for leave to adduce fresh evidence it was alleged that on the question of credit the defendant deceived or misled the court, and thereby occasioned a miscarriage of justice.

Victor Durand QC and W.W. Stabb for the defendant. The position of the defendant in relation to his demotion was carefully considered by leading counsel before the trial, with full knowledge of the facts. The considerations applied to the problem were: First, the facts relating to the cause of action could be prepared accurately in accordance with the proofs of the defendant and his witnesses, and they were so prepared. The emphasis on "facts" is important, for in the authorities relied on by the plaintiff a distinction was made between fresh evidence as to facts raising an issue in the case and evidence as to the credibility of a witness speaking to the primary facts. The evidence as to the night of November 5, 1958, was spoken to and tested throughout the trial, and there was a distinct variation on every aspect of that evidence between the case for the defendant and for the plaintiff.

Secondly, on the question of the character of the defendant the view was taken that a matter of discredit affecting the character of a party should not be disclosed to the court unless there were direct questions on it at the trial, in which case the defendant was instructed that he must answer frankly if he were asked about his present position.

Thirdly, the decision not to make known the present position of the defendant was not taken lightly, but was considered anxiously in the light of the counsel's duty to the court, his client and his opponent; and the decision was taken in the light of the guidance given on the duties of counsel in Boulton's Conduct and Etiquette at the Bar (2d ed., p. 67), that any deception of the court must be avoided but that counsel is under no duty to disclose facts known to him about his client's character or antecedent history, nor to correct information which may be given to the court by the prosecution if the correction would be detrimental to the client.

[PEARSON LJ: Is not that referring to criminal cases?]

It is reinforced by Denning LJ's observations in *Tombling's* case on the duty of counsel. This defendant was only one of eight witnesses who gave evidence as to the whole of the events on November 5, 1958. The jury had the unsupported evidence of the plaintiff on one side as to most material events, and on the other the word in most cases of four witnesses on the middle period, the defendant alone for a second or two, and then four different witnesses speaking against the version pleaded and spoken to by the plaintiff. The question whether the impact of a revelation as to the defendant's previous disciplinary conviction would have been so devastating as is claimed on behalf of the plaintiff must thus be judged on an analysis of the evidence as a whole on which the jury returned the verdict.

[HOLROYD PEARCE LJ: The clearest evidence that it would have had an impact is the trouble that was taken to conceal it.]

There is no duty to disclose the defendant's character or rank and no rule concerning his dress in a civil court. There is a rule that in a criminal court a police officer must appear in uniform, but it is not always obeyed. In the civil court he is sued as a person and his rank and character are quite irrelevant. To address a police officer as "Mr." is common practice among advocates. Even if the court had assumed that the defendant was of the highest character and had acted on that assumption, it is not the duty of counsel to correct that assumption. The belief that he was a chief inspector was irrelevant at the trial, and at no stage was the evidence weighted in favour of the defendant's behaviour by reason of his accepted rank.

HOLROYD PEARCE LJ: The plaintiff appeals from the judgment of Streatfeild J sitting with a jury given on October 21, 1960, after a trial lasting five days. The jury, after an absence of four hours, gave answers to certain questions on which the judge dismissed the action and entered judgment for the defendant. The plaintiff by his notice of appeal complains that the verdict was against the weight of evidence, and makes certain unsubstantial criticisms of the summing-up. These have not been stressed, and in my judgment no criticism can be made of the conduct of the judge or the verdict of the jury on the evidence before them. The real ground of this appeal is stated in the notice of appeal as follows: "(6) That at the trial the rank and status of the defendant was by implication represented to be that of a chief inspector when in fact between the date of the matters complained of in the action and the date of the trial he had been reduced to the rank of a station sergeant by reasons of misconduct and that the credit of the parties was a crucial issue at the trial." A further notice of motion for leave to give fresh evidence alleges that on the question of credit the defendant deceived or misled the court, and thereby occasioned a miscarriage of justice.

The plaintiff was claiming damages for assault and wrongful imprisonment in respect of an incident that happened on Guy Fawkes night, November 5, 1958. There was a disorderly crowd in Trafalgar Square, and many police officers had been detailed to deal with it. They made a number of arrests that night, and removed the arrested persons in a police tender to Cannon Row police station where they charged them and then, as a rule, released them. The defendant was the chief inspector at Cannon Row police station, and was actively engaged in helping to control the disorder in Trafalgar Square. The plaintiff, a press photographer with a good record, was there with his camera for the purpose of taking photographs. At about 9:40 p.m. the defendant arrested him on a charge of obstructing the police, and took him in a tender to Cannon Row police station where he was kept in a cell until 1:30 a.m.

If the plaintiff's story was correct, the defendant arrested him without proper cause, used considerable violence to him which caused physical injury, and without justification locked him up for some hours instead of charging him straight away and releasing him. If the defendant's story was correct, he acted with propriety; he was justified in arresting the plaintiff, and the subsequent violence (which was far less than the plaintiff alleged) was wholly occasioned by the plaintiff's own violence and resistance.

On November 17, 1958, the plaintiff issued the writ in this action. On December 17 he appeared at the magistrates' court and was convicted of obstructing the police and fined £5. Another charge was dismissed.

On December 16, 1959, while this action was pending, certain events occurred which at the trial were unknown to the plaintiff's advisers, and which they had no reason to know or to suspect. These events were deliberately concealed at the trial by the defendant and his legal advisers. It is on this concealment that the plaintiff relies in this appeal. He asks for a new trial in order that these facts may be proved by fresh evidence.

The facts have been agreed between the parties for the purpose of this appeal in the following terms: "(1) At the date when the defendant gave evidence at the trial of the action, his true rank in the Metropolitan Police Force was station sergeant. (2) The defendant was reduced from rank of chief inspector to station sergeant on December 16, 1959. (3) On December 16, 1959, the defendant appeared before a disciplinary board on the following charges: (i) Acting in a manner prejudicial to discipline by being a party to an arrangement with a police constable, whereby that officer purported to have arrested a street bookmaker on October 26, 1959, when in fact you were the officer who made the arrest. (ii) Without good and sufficient cause did omit promptly and diligently to attend to a matter which was your duty as a constable, that is to say having arrested ... for street betting on October 26, 1959, you did not attend the hearing of the case against him at Thames Metropolitan Magistrates' Court on October 27, 1959."

The defendant was reduced in rank to station sergeant on each charge, but on appeal to the commissioner on December 30, the punishment on the second charge was reduced to a reprimand, but there was no variation in the first punishment.

It is conceded that those facts were known to the defendant's legal advisers and his counsel, and that as a matter of deliberate policy they were not put before the court. A letter written by the defendant's solicitor on November 21, 1960, pending the appeal, says: "The learned Queen's Counsel instructed by me was throughout, as I believe you are aware, in full possession of all the facts relating to my client's past and present status and the reasons for his reduction in rank, and conducted the case in full knowledge of these facts in the manner he felt was consistent with his duty to his client and the court, and he is fully prepared to defend and justify his handling of the case at the proper time if called upon to do so."

It having been decided not to reveal these facts, the following things occurred at the trial. The defendant attended the trial not in uniform, but in plain clothes, whereas all the other police witnesses were in uniform. Thus there was no visible sign of the defendant's altered status. He was constantly addressed by his counsel as "Mr." and not by his rank of sergeant. Counsel tells us that he would so address a sergeant in the normal case. When the defendant entered the witness-box, he was not asked his name and rank in the usual manner. No suspicions were aroused since no one had any reason to suspect. The plaintiff's counsel, however, and the judge frequently addressed the defendant, or referred to him, as "inspector" or "chief inspector," and nothing was done to disabuse them.

The defendant started his evidence with a brief summary of his career up to the time when he was chief inspector at Cannon Row police station, but no reference was made to his reduction in rank. In cross-examination he was asked: "You are a chief inspector, and you have been in the force, you told us, since 1938? (A) Yes, that is true." That answer was a lie. Later: "(Q) You realise, as chief inspector, the importance of the note being accurate? (A) The importance of it conveying to me what I want to give in evidence." He was asked further: "Let us understand this. You are a chief inspector. How old are you? (A) I am forty-six years of age." And again: "(Q) I am not asking you whether you took part in the inquiries, but whether you as a responsible and senior adult man—never mind about your being a chief inspector—had no anxiety about this case, no concern or interest? (A) No. I can only repeat I have nothing to fear."

The judge referred to the defendant as "inspector" or "chief inspector Fleming" many times in his summing-up to the jury. It is clear that he reasonably considered that the defendant's rank and status were relevant on credibility in a case where there was oath against oath, and where there was a question of the defendant's conduct in the course of his duty. No doubt he felt what Singleton LJ expressed in *Mohahir Ali v. Ellmore*, [1953] 1 WLR 1300, when, in dealing with a matter concerning evidence, he said: "It appears to me that that evidence was irrelevant and unnecessary. The fact that a witness who is also a defendant is a superintendent of Leeds City Policy shows that he is of good standing, and that he has the confidence of his superior officers."

Nor was the defendant's counsel prepared to forgo the advantage to be derived from the status in the police force of his witnesses in general. The parties have, fortunately, in the interests of economy been able to use the reports of the case in "The Times" newspaper. These show that in his opening speech for the defence, counsel stated that the jury had not yet had an opportunity of listening to persons against whom it was at times fashionable to make wild hysterical allegations, but who could not have reached their positions unless they had shown to those who controlled the Metropolitan Police a substantial degree of responsibility. They were not concerned here with some newcomer to the force who had only just finished his course, and was out on the street full of enthusiasm to arrest the first person he could.

"The Times" report of the final speech of defendant's counsel shows that he said in reference to the allegations of the plaintiff: "That was un-English, and not what the jury would expect of any police officer who had passed through the sieve, been trained and risen to any rank in the Metropolitan Police." He then went on to contrast unfavourably the plaintiff's background in Fleet Street where "words come out in very large letters, and the range of adjectives and description is so wide as to make us callous." I accept from counsel that he was intending to refer to the generality of his seven or eight witnesses, all of whom had attained some rank above that of constable. Nevertheless, such references must inevitably have connoted in the minds of judge and jury a reference to the status of the defendant, who was the leading person in the case, and held (in their erroneous belief) the highest rank of all the witnesses.

The fact that the defendant's advisers were prepared to act as they did showed the great importance which they attached to the facts concealed. If one leaves aside for the moment any question of ethics, the hazards of such a course were extremely great. With so many police witnesses who might well know the truth (since the defendant's demotion was circulated in police orders) the chance of somebody in cross-examination referring to the defendant by his present rank of sergeant, or letting the truth out in some other way, was not negligible. Had that occurred, or had the plaintiff's counsel known the facts, and elicited them in cross-examination, it seems very unlikely that the jury would accept the defendant's case when they found how they had been deceived. Even without knowing the facts, the jury took four hours for their deliberations; and since the plaintiff's evidence was, broadly speaking, that of one against so many, one must, I think, conclude that he did well in the witness-box.

How then does the matter stand now that the turth has come out? This court is rightly loth to order a new trial on the ground of fresh evidence. Interest reipublicae ut sit finis litium. The cases show that this court has given great weight to that maxim. There would be a constant succession of retrials if judgments were to be set aside merely because something fresh that might have been material has come to light. In the case of fresh evidence relating to an issue in the case, the court will not order a new trial unless such evidence would probably have an important influence on the result of the case, though such evidence need not be decisive: *Rex v. Copestake, Ex parte Wilkinson*, [1927] 1 KB 468, 477 (CA) *per* Scrutton LJ, and *Ladd v. Marshall*, [1954] 1 WLR 1489 (CA). Such evidence must also, of course, be apparently credible and such that it could not have been obtained with due diligence, [1954] 1 WLR 1489, 1491. But in the present case the fresh evidence is agreed, and it could not have been found out with due diligence since there was no reason to suspect it. In the present case, therefore, these two latter considerations are not in issue.

Where, however, the fresh evidence does not relate directly to an issue, but is merely evidence as to the credibility of an important witness, this court applies a stricter test. It will only allow its admission (if ever) where "the evidence is of such a nature and the circumstances of the case are such that no reasonable jury could be expected to act upon the evidence of the witness whose character had been called in question" (*per* Tucker LJ in *Braddock v. Tillotson's Newspapers Ltd.*, [1950] 1 KB 47, 53) or "where the court is satisfied that the additional evidence *must* have led a reasonable jury to a different conclusion from that actually arrived at in the case": *per* Cohen LJ. Mr. Neville Faulks claims that the fresh evidence in the present case satisfies even that strict test. But whether that be so, it is not necessary for us to decide.

Where the judge and jury have been misled, another principle makes itself felt. Lord Esher MR in *Praed v. Graham* (1889), 24 QBD 53, 55, said: "If the court can see that the jury in assessing damages have been guilty of misconduct, or made some gross blunder, or have been misled by the speeches of the counsel, those are undoubtedly sufficient grounds for interfering with the verdict."

In *Tombling v. Universal Bulb Co. Ltd.*, [1951] WN 247 it was sought to adduce fresh evidence on the ground that there had not been revealed to the judge the fact that a highly material witness was at the time of the trial serving a prison sentence for a motoring offence. Counsel had allowed him to give in evidence a residential address which was his normal home, and asked him questions which indicated that he had in the past held a responsible position. The appeal was dismissed; but Singleton LJ described the case as "near the line." Denning LJ there said: "This raises an important question of professional duty. I do not doubt that, if a favourable decision has been obtained by any improper conduct of the successful party, this court will always be ready to grant a new trial. The duty of counsel to his client in a civil case—or in defending an accused person—is to make every honest endeavour to succeed. He must not, of course, knowingly mislead the court, either on the facts or on the law, but, short of that, he may put such matters … as in his discretion he thinks will be most to the advantage of his client." I respectfully agree with those words. He then discussed the facts of that case, and came to the conclusion that there had been nothing improper in the conduct of the case for the plaintiffs. In that case the failure to reveal was not a premeditated line of conduct. Nor was conviction for a motoring offence so relevant in credibility as the demotion of a chief inspector (who is a party to the case) for an offence which consisted in deceiving a court of law as to the accurate facts relating to an arrest. There is no authority where the facts have been at all similar to those of the present case, but in my judgment the principles on which we should act are clear.

Where a party deliberately misleads the court in a material matter, and that deception has probably tipped the scale in his favour (or even, as I think, where it may reasonably have done so), it would be wrong to allow him to retain the judgment thus unfairly procured. Finis litium is a desirable object, but it must not be sought by so great a sacrifice of justice, which is and must remain the supreme object. Moreover, to allow the victor to keep the spoils so unworthily obtained would be an encouragement to such behaviour, and do even greater harm than the multiplication of trials.

In every case it must be a question of degree, weighing one principle against the other. In this case it is clear that the judge and jury were misled on an important matter. I appreciate that it is very hard at times for the advocate to see his path clearly between failure in his duty to the court, and failure in his duty to his client. I accept that in the present case the decision to conceal the facts was not made lightly, but after anxious consideration. But in my judgment the duty to the court was here unwarrantably subordinated to the duty to the client. It is no less surprising that this should be done when the defendant is a member of the Metropolitan Police Force on whose integrity the public are accustomed to rely.

It was argued that there were several other police witnesses against the plaintiff's story; that although part of the issue depended on the evidence of the parties alone, the greater part of the defence depended on other witnesses than the defendant, and that therefore the concealment did not have any substantial result. But since the defendant and his advisers thought fit to take so serious a step, they must, in the light of their own intimate knowledge of their case, have regarded the concealment as being of overwhelming importance to their success. Therefore I am not prepared to countenance their present argument that it may have made no difference to the result.

It was argued that the defendant was justified in that a party need not reveal something to his discredit; but that does not mean that he can by implication falsely pretend (where it is a material matter) to a rank and status that are not his, and, when he knows that the court is so deluded, foster and confirm that delusion by answers such as the defendant gave. Suggestio falsi went hand in hand with suppressio veri. It may well be that it was not so clear in prospect as it is in retrospect how wide the web of deceit would be woven before the verdict came to be given. But in the event it spread over all the evidence of the defendant. It affected the summing-up of the judge, and it must have affected the deliberations of the jury. The defendant and his legal advisers, and probably some at least of his witnesses, on the one hand, were aware of the facts, and intent not to reveal them, in order that on the other hand the plaintiff and his counsel and the jury and the judge might remain in ignorance, and that the defendant might be thereby enabled to masquerade as a chief inspector of unblemished reputation enjoying such advantage as that status and character would give him at the trial. It would be an intolerable infraction of the principles of justice to allow the defendant to retain a verdict thus obtained. I would, accordingly, allow the appeal with costs, and order a new trial.

WILLMER LJ: In the present case there is no doubt that the course taken, which had the effect of deceiving the court, was taken deliberately. Counsel for the defendant has so informed us with complete candour. I accept his assurance that the decision was proper in all the circumstances. But for my part I am in no doubt that it was not taken lightly, but after careful consideration, and in the belief that the course taken was a wrong decision. I would venture to follow the example of Singleton LJ in *Tombling's* case in quoting from Lord Macmillan on "The Ethics of Advocacy." This is what Lord Macmillan said: "In the discharge of his office the advocate has a duty to his client, a duty to his opponent, a duty to the court, a duty to the State and a duty to himself." It seems to me that the decision which was taken involved insufficient regard being paid to the duty owed to the court and to the plaintiff and his advisers.

The result of the decision that was taken was that the trial proceeded in a way that it should not have done. Where the court has been thus deceived in relation to what I conceive to be a matter of vital significance, I think it would be a miscarriage of justice to allow a verdict obtained in this way to stand. For these additional reasons, as well as for the reasons already stated by my Lord, I agree that this appeal must be allowed.

PEARSON LJ: It was decided, after very careful consideration, that the defendant's case should be conducted in such a way as not to reveal to the judge and jury the fact that the defendant had been demoted from the rank of chief inspector to the rank of station sergeant. Well-devised and effective steps were taken to carry out the decision, with the consequences that the defendant appeared to the judge and jury throughout the trial as a person still holding the rank of chief inspector, and therefore as a highly credit-worthy person, whereas in fact he had been demoted for an offence involving deception of a court. Whatever erroneous analogies may have prompted the decision, which was well intentioned, it was, in my view, utterly wrong, and it had deplorable results. There was, in the result, at the trial of this action a deception of the court, and the defendant in cross-examination was giving uncandid (and at one point false) evidence in order to preserve the concealment of the truth.

Having regard to the deception of the court and the materiality of the fresh evidence, I agree that the appeal should be allowed with costs, and that there should be an order for a new trial.

DURAND QC: I indicated last week in the course of my argument before your Lordships that I took responsibility for the decision; I hope that the words I used then left the court under no misunderstanding as to my personal responsibility. It is right that I should say as emphatically and clearly as I can that the decision not to make disclosure of the defendant's change of status was mine, and mine alone. Having come to the conclusion that this course was justifiable, I determined and dictated the policy which was thereafter followed during the course of the trial. Neither my learned junior counsel, Mr. Stabb, nor my instructing solicitor was responsible for initiating or pursuing that policy, and indeed they expressed their disapproval of it. I thought it right, having regard to the observations made last week, to make that statement before your Lordships in open court, and I am very grateful to your Lordships for allowing me to make it.

NOTES AND QUESTIONS

1. Durand QC was disciplined and received a three-year suspension that on appeal was reduced to one year.

2. Examine rule 4.01 and the accompanying commentaries of the proposed draft rules of professional conduct in appendix II. If you were defending Durand in the disciplinary proceeding, what arguments might you make based on rule 4.01? What are Durand's obligations to the court; to his client? How do you resolve the apparent conflict between the two? What does it mean to treat the court with "candour" when one is "not obliged ... to assist an adversary or advance matters derogatory to the client's case"?

3. You act for a plaintiff in a civil matter. At the examination for discovery, your client gives evidence that does not correspond with what he had told you previously. Following the discovery, your client tells you that the version he gave under oath on the discovery was false. What do you do? Assume that you only learn of the lie after trial and after judgment has been entered awarding your client substantial damages. What should you do?

4. Do similar considerations apply to negotiations outside the court with other lawyers? See, generally, Rubin, "A Causerie on Lawyers Ethics in Negotiation" (1975), 35 *Louisiana Law Review* 577. Consider the following problems:

a) You represent a plaintiff in a personal injury action. There have been active settlement discussions with the defendant's lawyer. You have obtained a written medical report from your client's doctor stating that it is unlikely that your client can return to her former employment. The report has been furnished to the defendant's lawyer. You subsequently learn from your client that another physician has prescribed a new medication that has been completely effective but your client doesn't want to return to work until after the case is settled or tried. You receive a call from the defendant's lawyer who wants to engage in further settlement discussions. What is your duty in the circumstances?

b) You are representing your client in negotiations with a businessperson, represented by counsel, who wants to buy your client's business. Financial statements prepared one month ago have been supplied to the other side. As the deal is being finalized, but before it has been concluded, your client tells you that there has been a dramatic decline in sales during the last month. What is your obligation with respect to this information?

c) You are authorized by your clients to settle the case for $20,000, but they want you to get more if you can. Is it proper for you to say to defendant's counsel "My client will take $25,000 and not one penny less"?

5. A related and contested question is the ethics of cross-examination. Should a lawyer cross-examine a witness who is testifying accurately and truthfully in order to make the witness appear that he or she is mistaken, unreliable, or lying? Do you think that the English bar's statement of principles below strikes the correct balance? Is Fried's position different from that of the English bar?

(i) Questions which affect the credibility of a witness by attacking his character, but are not otherwise relevant to the actual inquiry, ought not to be asked unless the cross-examiner has reasonable grounds for thinking that the imputation conveyed by the question is well-founded or true.

(ii) A barrister who is instructed by a solicitor that in his opinion the imputation is well-founded or true, and is not merely instructed to put the question, is entitled *prima facie* to regard such instructions as reasonable grounds for so thinking and to put the questions accordingly.

(iii) A barrister should not accept as conclusive the statement of any person other than the solicitor instructing him that the imputation is well-founded or true, without ascertaining, so far as is practicable in the circumstances, that such person can give satisfactory reasons for his statement.

(iv) Such questions, whether or not the imputations they convey are well-founded, should only be put if, in the opinion of the cross-examiner, the answers would or might materially affect the credibility of the witness: and if the imputation conveyed by the question relates to matters so remote in time or of such a character that it would not affect or would not materially affect the credibility of the witness, the question should not be put.

(v) In all cases it is the duty of the barrister to guard against being made the channel for questions which are only intended to insult or annoy either the witness or any other person, and to exercise his own judgment both as to the substance and the form of the question put.

D. Challenging Neutral Partisanship

William H. Simon, "The Ideology of Advocacy: Procedural Justice and Professional Ethics"
(1978) *Wisconsin Law Review* 29

D. *The Finale: The Friendship Analogy*

In a recent article, Charles Fried has defended legal ethics in terms of ... friendship. Unlike drama, ritual, and game, friendship is an analogy, not for the legal system, but for the lawyer–client relation itself. It is interesting because it illustrates a tendency to think of the lawyer–client relation as having a value apart from and even antagonistic to the legal system as a whole. ...

Fried's principal purpose is to defend lawyer–client relations as "good in themselves." Fried is concerned with the embodiment of ideals such as "the ideal of personal relations of trust and personal care." But now the relevant ideals are embodied, not in the legal system as a whole, but in the attorney–client relationship itself. This relation is seen less as a component of a larger structure and more as an independent entity.

Fried attempts to rationalize legal ethics by emphasizing the personal worth of the relations defined by the professional norms of partisanship and neutrality. Fried suggests that partisanship is like friendship in that it involves "an authorization to take the interests of particular concrete persons more seriously and to give them priority over the interests of the wider collectivity." At the same time the lawyer's neutrality bespeaks a deference to the "concrete individuality" of the client which is similar to the deference one friend would show to another. The fact that the lawyer's concern is not reciprocated in kind by the client does not differentiate the relation from friendship. On the contrary, it exemplifies the lawyer's freedom to bestow and the client's "freedom to receive an extra measure of care" which also exists in friendship. Fried argues that, after one has recognized in the lawyer–client relation the qualities generally valued in friendship, one should accept the lawyer–client relation as good in itself. ...

Fried writes: "[L]ike a friend [the lawyer] acts in your interests, not his own; or rather he adopts your interests as his own. I would call that the classical definition of friendship." Now this is clearly an error. The classical definition of friendship emphasizes, not the adoption by one person of another's ends, but rather the sharing by two people of common ends. Moreover, the classical notion of friendship includes a number of other qualities foreign to the relation Fried describes. The missing qualities include affection, admiration, intimacy, and vulnerability. On the other hand, if Fried's definition is amplified to reflect the qualification, which Fried repeatedly acknowledges, that the lawyer adopts the client's interest *for money*, it becomes apparent that Fried has described the classical notion, not of friendship, but of prostitution.

The conflation of the ideas of friendship and prostitution is typical of the moral obfuscation which pervades the article. For Fried, the problem of a doctor who must decide what to do for "a severely deformed baby who can be kept alive only through extraordinarily expensive means" is "analogous" to the problem of a lawyer who must decide what to do for a client who wants "to avoid the effects of a tax or a form of regulation." The task of helping a "disagreeable dowager" tyrannize her relatives deserves the same intensity of commitment as the task of "defending the civil liberties case of the century."

Fried's lawyer is a friend in the same sense that your Sunoco dealer is "very friendly" or that Canada Dry Ginger Ale "tastes like love." The friendship analogy is one of those "self-validating, analytical propositions" which Marcuse describes as typical of "the closing of the universe of discourse":

> The unification of opposites which characterizes the commercial and political style is one of the many ways in which discourse and communication make themselves immune against the expression of protest and refusal. How can such protest and refusal find the

right word when the organs of the established order admit and advertise that peace is really the brink of war, that the ultimate weapons carry their profitable price tags, and that the bomb shelter may spell coziness? In exhibiting its contradictions as the token of its truth, this universe of discourse closes itself against any other discourse which is not on its own terms.

For Fried, the legal system is a condition of the value of the lawyer–client relation, but it is not the source of this value. Legal friendship arises from the fact that the client has a special need for help in order to exercise the autonomy which the legal system guarantees. The fact that this autonomy is a moral value legitimates certain of the lawyer's anti-social conduct, but it does not give it the special pathos and dignity celebrated by the friendship analogy. These qualities arise, not from the specifically legal character of the client's need, but from the fact that the need is integrally related to the integrity of the person, that it is "implicated in crises going to one's concreteness and individuality." Although Fried argues, somewhat half-heartedly, that the need is a special one which is different from needs for non-professional services, he expressly indicates that the need for legal help is similar to the need for other professional services, particularly medical help.

Of course, the legal system defines the patterns and boundaries of the relation, but these patterns and boundaries seem to limit, more than to promote, the qualities emphasized by the friendship analogy. Fried does not contemplate that the lawyer do many things which friends might be expected to do for each other, such as to destroy evidence, lie to the court, or do anything else which would violate the law or the *Code of Professional Responsibility*. After first extolling friendship in glowing and unqualified terms, Fried breaks the bad news that the lawyer is only a "special-purpose friend." Although the lawyer–client relation has value apart from considerations of fairness and efficiency, that value must yield in some situations to the need to maintain the integrity of the legal system. The legal system thus appears as a threat to the lawyer–client friendship. ...

If the Ideology of Advocacy is a rationalization of the ethical orientation of lawyers, then the friendship analogy seems both its culmination and its finish. The lawyer's distinctive identity has emerged from behind the facade of the legal system and is now openly celebrated as an end in itself. The irony of this development is that at the same time that it celebrates the legal profession more openly than previous defenses, the friendship analogy also comes closer than previous defenses to acknowledging the failure of the legal profession to accomplish the task for which the lawyer's role was created in the first place, the reconcilation of public and private ends. Previously, the lawyer justified his role in terms of the resolution of individual differences through order, justice, welfare, or ceremony. Yet, in fact, to the extent that he was sensitive to outcomes at all, he experienced them not as resolutions, but as arbitrary concessions to one of two opposing spheres. In emphasizing the remoteness and coolness of public ends, the friendship analogy admits that the magic with which the lawyer once claimed he could resolve the clash of individual wills is a fraud.

Yet, the admission is only implicit. The friendship analogy diverts attention from failure by conflating the lawyer with a less problematical social role. The same effect occurs in the familiar comparison of the legal role with that of doctors (also used by

Fried) or clergymen. Such comparisons emphasize the commitment of all three professionals to individual clients, patients, or penitents against the claims of the collectivity,
as illustrated particularly by the norms of confidentiality to which all three adhere. Yet,
they gloss over a critical difference. The insistence of the doctor and the clergyman on
maintaining the confidence of those they serve represents a commitment to the values
with which their professional activities are concerned above competing social values.
On the other hand, the lawyer's insistence on confidentiality represents a compromise
among the values with which he is professionally concerned, or perhaps even a sacrifice
of these values to extrinsic values. The doctor and the clergyman insist that for them
health and salvation must take precedence over justice. The lawyer asserts that his
relationship with his client must take precedence over justice, but in doing so he forgets
that his relationship was originally defined and rationalized in terms of justice.

In the friendship analogy, the plaintive tone of Ritualism reaches its highest pitch.
The lawyer tacitly concedes his failure, but rather than apologize for it, urges the society
to lower its expectations. Unable to justify his role in terms of public means and ends, he
urges that it be accepted as an end in itself. ...

VI. Conclusion: Non-Professional Advocacy

Showing that the Ideology of Advocacy is incoherent in theory and destructive in practice is not the same thing as showing that it should be abandoned. It remains to be shown
that there is a more satisfactory alternative. The alternative can be called "non-professional advocacy." ... The choice between the Ideology of Advocacy and non-professional advocacy rests on one's view of the relative priorities of individuality and
stability, and of the prospects of reconciling the tension between them.

Non-professional advocacy is difficult to describe with precision, but it is not at all
mysterious. On the contrary, it relies on a style of thought and conduct with which
everyone has at least some familiarity. The foundation principle of non-professional
advocacy is that the problems of advocacy be treated as a matter of *personal* ethics. As
the notion is generally understood, personal ethics presupposes two ideas diametrically
opposed to the foundation principles of the Ideology of Advocacy. First, personal ethics
apply to people merely by virtue of the fact that they are human individuals. The
obligations involved may depend on particular circumstances or personalities, but they
do not follow from social role or station. Personal ethics are at once more particular and
more general than professional ethics. On the one hand, they require that every moral
decision be made by the individual himself; no institution can define his obligations in
advance. On the other hand, the individual may be called upon to answer for his decisions by any other individual who is affected by them. No specialized group has a
monopoly which disqualifies outsiders from criticizing the behavior of its members.
Second, personal ethics require that individuals take responsibility for the consequences
of their decisions. They cannot defer to institutions with autonomous ethical momentum.

Personal ethics involve both a concern for one's own integrity and respect for the
concrete individuality of others. The non-professional advocate presents himself to a
prospective client as someone with special talents and knowledge, but also with personal
ends to which he is strongly committed. The client should expect someone generally

disposed to help him advance his ends, but also prepared to oppose him when the ends of advocate and client conflict. If the two sets of ends coincide, then a strong alliance on behalf of these ends is possible. If the two sets of ends are irreconcilably opposed, then no relationship will be possible. It is essential that neither advocate nor client feel strong pressure to accept the other. Between the extremes of an alliance on behalf of entirely shared ends and a situation in which no relationship is possible, there is a broad category where one party will be able to win over the other to his position or where the parties will work out a compromise.

Non-professional advocacy does not preclude conflict. Conflict is possible both inside and outside of the relationship. Where the ends are opposed, the advocate may engage in conflict with the client (although obviously any large measure of conflict will end the relationship). Where their ends are shared, advocate and client may join together to engage outsiders in conflict. On the other hand, non-professional advocacy does not presuppose conflict any more than it presupposes the stylized aggression of the Ideology of Advocacy. The advocate may lead the client to modify or abandon a collision course so as to make voluntary, informal resolution possible. Indeed, one of the most important effects of non-professional advocacy should be to increase the client's concern for the impact of his conduct on others, and to enlarge the minimal role which norms such as reciprocity and community now play in attorney–client decisions.

If the major foundation principle of non-professional advocacy is that advocacy be deemed a matter of personal ethics, the major principle of conduct is this: advocate and client must each justify himself to the other. This justification need not embrace the person's entire life, but merely those aspects of it which bear on the dispute. Each must justify the goals he would pursue and the way he would pursue them. In this manner, the advocate–client relation is reconstructed in each instance by the participants themselves. It is not set in advance by formal roles. Such relationships will sometimes arise spontaneously, but they will often arise only after patient, step-by-step efforts. Advocate and client may become friends, not in Fried's sense, but in the more familiar sense of an intimacy made possible by shared ends and experience. Yet, friendship is not necessary to the relationship. The basic requirement is that each have respect for the other as a concrete individual. In addition, some sharing of ends will be necessary, but this sharing need not approach a complete coincidence of ends.

Trust is an important value in non-professional advocacy. But it is not a formal, definitional property of the advocate–client relation. It is a quality which the parties must create or fail to create in each instance. When confidentiality may be important to the client, advocate and client should arrive at some understanding at the outset concerning this issue. The scope of confidentiality need not be defined for the entire relation at the outset. It can be defined in stages as lawyer and client gain greater understanding of each other. The client's claim to assurances of confidentiality is a strong one, and once assurances have been made, his claim that they be honored is much stronger still. Yet, these claims must be viewed in the context of other, potentially conflicting values. They must be considered in the context of the specific ends which the client seeks to further. The claim of a client who seeks legal services to exploit or oppress another cannot have the same priority as the claim of one who seeks to escape exploitation and oppression. This approach to the problem of confidentiality means that the client must take a risk in seeking an advocate, and that the advocate–client relation will sometimes end in betrayal. This element of risk is inherent in any effort by lawyer and client to come to terms with each other as concrete individuals. It is in part because of this risk that trust, when it is created, can be a vital and concrete psychological reality rather than an empty, formal claim. …

This brief suggestion of the nature of non-professional advocacy leaves many problems to be worked out in theory and in practice. For the present, it will be sufficient to anticipate two of the more prominent objections with which the basic proposal will be met.

First, it will be argued that non-professional advocacy will make it more difficult or impossible for many to secure an advocate. Lawyers will decline to represent at least some people whose values they do not share. Those with unpopular views may thus find themselves without representation. Moreover, people will be unwilling to consult lawyers or to confide in them for fear of oppression or betrayal. Contentions such as these are among the oldest and most common arguments on behalf of professional ethics. One answer to them is that they are beside the point. Since the principal thrust of the critique of the Ideology of Advocacy is to show the destructiveness of legal services as they are now rendered, the possibility that reform might diminish the availability of legal services is hardly a disadvantage. Even if it were a disadvantage, it would seem plausible that it would be outweighed by the qualitative improvement which non-professional advocacy would bring.

There is a further answer to these contentions. The parade of horribles which they put forth as the hypothetical outcome of hypothetical reform is in fact precisely the situation which obtains *now* and which has obtained for the past century under the hegemony of the Ideology of Advocacy. There is now a wealth of empirical studies which confirm what most laymen have always known: only a tiny minority, composed almost entirely of the wealthy and the powerful, is assured or ever has been assured substantial access to legal services. The majority of the public distrusts and dislikes lawyers and seeks their help, if at all, only in connection with a few types of routine transactions or in desperate situations as a last resort. This distrust is well grounded; lawyers commonly pursue self-interest at the expense of their clients' interests. The history of the profession mocks the contention that there is any connection between the Ideology of Advocacy and the adequate provision of legal services. In this dismal situation, the risks of reform are slight. At best, the abandonment of professional ethics, by broadening the lawyer's ethical perspective, will lead to a more equitable distribution of services than now exists. At worst, it is difficult to see how it could produce a less satisfactory situation than now exists.

Second, it will be objected that non-professional advocacy puts an unrealistically large moral and psychological burden on the lawyer. The constant responsibility for the consequences of his efforts on behalf of so many others with varying ends will generate a "role strain" which will make non-professional advocacy intolerable for lawyers. The often voiced premise of this criticism—that the lawyer's conditions of work involve greater responsibility or ethical pressure than others—seems wrong. Most occupations involve, directly or indirectly, constant, and often intimate and confidential, dealings with strangers which implicate moral responsibilities. The real difference between the position of the lawyer and that of, for instance, the corporate bureaucrat lies not in the greater pressure on the lawyer, but in his greater freedom. The autonomy of the lawyer should not be exaggerated. Most lawyers work under conditions of bureaucratic routine. Nevertheless, compared with most other occupations, lawyers have achieved a remarkable measure of autonomy in their conditions of work. Not every lawyer has the opportunity to act like Brandeis, but some do, and many have more latitude in defining the nature of their work than the most powerful corporate executives. The strain which the lawyer feels results less from the weight of his responsibilities than from the weight of his freedom. The corporate executive sacrifices his personal values more easily because he perceives his choices as more limited. The lawyer must undertake more strenuous efforts to rationalize his compromises because the pressures on him to compromise are weaker. Non-professional advocacy merely asks the lawyer to make the most of the freedom he has.

The proposal to abolish legal professionalism will strike most lawyers as radical and unrealistic. But at least in some respects this impression is wrong. After all, it has become commonplace to speculate on the "death of law." It should not be surprising that such discussions rarely embrace the death of the legal profession; or indeed, that they often take place within the bastions of professional privilege and power. For legal professionalism thrives on contempt for the ideal of law. Yet, the ideal of law and the values of individuality have been a potent historical alliance, and they may well prove more tenacious than the most entrenched contemporary institutions. In this light, the death of the legal profession may be a more conservative and more practical alternative to the death of law.

D.L. Rhode, "Ethical Perspectives on Legal Practice"
(1985), 37 *Stanford Law Review* 589, at 595-66 (footnotes omitted)

A. Formalism: The Adversary System's Invisible Hand

Although most legal practice occurs outside any formal adversarial framework, justifications of partisanship often lean heavily on that paradigm. Underlying those justifications is a mixed formalist and free market conception of adjudicative processes. The bar seeks to resolve the contradiction between fidelity to a particular client and to the legal system as a whole by reference to a combative scheme of social ordering. The premise is that "truth" or the "right" result is attainable through competitive presentations of relevant factual and legal considerations. Paralleling Karl Popper's concept of scientific rationality, the theory assumes that knowledge will emerge through a dialectic of conjecture and refutation. ...

The most obvious difficulty with this premise is that it is neither self-evident nor supported by any empirical evidence. As Geoffrey Hazard, Reporter for the Model Rules Commission, candidly acknowledges, we have "no proof that the adversary system of trial yields truth more often than other systems of trial." Neither is it intuitively obvious that truth is more often revealed by self-interested, rather than disinterested, exploration. The virtues of private initiative and judicial passivity come at a cost. Lawyers are concerned with the production of belief, not of knowledge. Why assume, to paraphrase Macaulay, that the fairest results will emerge from two advocates arguing as unfairly as possible on opposite sides? That is not the way most countries adjudicate controversies, nor the way the bar itself seeks truth in any setting outside the courtroom. In preparing for trial, for example, lawyers do not typically hire competitive investigators.

To retain plausibility, this defense of adversarial processes must proceed in a social and economic vacuum. The conventional paradigm presupposes combatants with roughly equal incentives, resources, and capabilities. How frequently those suppositions hold is open to question in a social order that tolerates vast disparities in wealth, renders most litigation enormously expensive, and allocates civil legal assistance almost entirely through market mechanisms. Under these circumstances, one would expect that the "haves" generally come out ahead. Commonplace as this point must be to any practicing attorney, it is conspicuous only by absence in most official explications of adversarial premises. Only one submission to the Model Rules Commission questioned adversarial processes on grounds of unequal access to legal talent.

The disparities in representation ignored by conventional paradigms are readily amplified under current practices. The adversary system's extensive procedural protections generate frequent opportunities for evasion, harassment, and delay. In large-scale litigation, principal pathologies include endless wrangling over peripheral issues, as well as over- and under-production of discoverable material. Pretrial proceedings too often give rise to casuistic constructions of discovery requests, disingenuous assertions of the attorney–client privilege, or "Hiroshima" responses to document demands (with any damaging items buried in a mass of trivia). Although the bar's conventional response to such problems has been that they "should be left to the procedural rules and sanctions of the court involved," these correctives have repeatedly proven inadequate. Sanctions are expensive to seek and administer, and judicial responses to adversarial imbalance or pretrial pugnacity are constrained by time, information, and perception of role. Although recent amendments to the Federal Rules encourage greater use of discovery sanctions, such formal mandates are likely to have limited effect on the incentive and information structures that impede judicial oversight.

These constraints on judicial governance are readily exploited by resourceful counsel. Many of the nation's most eminent law firms are noted for their skill in genteel procrastination. Among the most celebrated examples are Covington & Burling's 12-year delay of regulations governing peanut butter content, and Cravath, Swaine & Moore's 14-year defense of an antitrust case that, according to its chief litigator, involved thousands of exhibits, a 50,000-page record, and no real dispute about the facts. Nor is delay the only pretrial pathology. The adversarial framework has often generated an ethos in which truth becomes more an obstacle than an objective. In a national survey of 1500 large firm litigators, half of those responding believed that unfair and inadequate disclosure of material information prior to trial was a "regular or frequent" problem. Similarly, 69% of surveyed antitrust attorneys had encountered unethical practices in complex cases; the most frequently cited abuses were tampering with witnesses' responses and destroying evidence.

As in Norman trial by combat, the prime objective in much contemporary litigation is to force the adversary to "cry craven" well before discovery of critical facts or adjudication by a neutral decisionmaker. The objective is frequently achieved. According to a survey of Chicago litigators, one in three cases was concluded without at least one party having discovered potentially significant information. Since close to 90% of all civil cases are settled prior to trial, and relatively little of lawyers' advocacy occurs in the presence of impartial adjudicators, the adversary paradigm offers an inadequate foundation for the partisanship role.

Even in full-dress hearings, it is questionable how often the invisible hand asserts itself. Bar ideology assumes that responsibility for ferreting out false testimony or for insuring "fair treatment" of unrepresented and inadequately represented opponents rests elsewhere. If an unmeritorious claim prevails, the fault lies with the judge, the jury, or the litigant who failed to secure adequate counsel. Yet such deflections of blame elide the inherent inadequacies of adversarial frameworks. Not all individuals have the information or resources to ensure an even contest, and neither the judge nor the jury may be well-situated to make appropriate adjustments. Carefully scripted court performances often bear limited resemblance to the actual facts triggering dispute. And conventional techniques of witness selection and preparation can easily yield guided tours down memory lane with predetermined destinations clearly in view. ...

Fundamental difficulties remain in adversarial premises as well as practices. Under conventional formalist accounts, just results emerge through the rational application of law to fact in the course of competitive presentations. Thus, the preamble to the *Model Rules* submits: "[W]hen an opposing party is well represented, a lawyer can be a zealous advocate on behalf of a client and at the same time assume that justice is being done." In effect, this perspective conflates substantive and procedural justice. Thus conceived, the perspective is vulnerable to all the critiques of formalism that have become standard fare in modern jurisprudential analysis.

Bar ideology makes no adjustment for the possibility that formalist application of legal rules may work injustice that other branches of government fail to redress. A recurring theme in bar rhetoric is that problems such as corporate immorality or adversarial imbalances are the responsibility of legislators, not lawyers. Ad hoc attorney paternalism is considered an inappropriate response to systemic failures. Publicly accountable officials, not privately appointed Platonic guardians, should determine the appropriate corrective. If counsel's zealous representation impedes the control of hazardous products or toxic substances, the fault rests not with the attorney but with those who failed to pass the requisite standards or to appropriate sufficient funds for enforcement.

Such genuflections to legislative process, however rhetorically reassuring, remain morally unpersuasive. Presumably, few lawyers are unaware of the inherent limitations in democratic procedures and regulatory solutions. Time lags in acquiring information and designing appropriate correctives are inevitable, and attorneys with access to confidential studies may often be more knowledgeable about injurious conduct far sooner than politicians or administrative officials. Even where problems are apparent, the costs of regulation may seem excessive, or interest group pressures and inadequate enforcement resources may prevent socially optimal resolutions. As long as disparities of wealth, knowledge, and power affect both the agenda and outcome of political debate, statutory solutions will imperfectly reflect societal values. Any legislative or administrative body may, as Duncan Kennedy notes, prove too "anaesthetized or simply overworked" to remedy obvious deficiencies in legal standards. Nonetheless, the bar's adversarial premise equates justice with the mechanical application of these standards.

This constricted view of legal processes yields a correspondingly myopic perception of professional responsibilities. Within this framework, counsel need not contemplate any broader notion of justice than that defined by existing legal norms. Ironically enough, contemporary bar discourse depicts a far more circumscribed moral universe than that envisioned when formalist theories enjoyed higher regard. Nineteenth century commentary on legal ethics not only posited duties of law reform, but also expressly acknowledged that impartial application of civil law could occasionally result in "mistaken" or "perverted" judgments; for lawyers to lend assistance in these cases would be "revolting."

By contrast, the bar's current code envisions a more stoic stance. Reformist rhetoric is in decline. As long as attorneys continue representing a client, they are to "act with commitment and dedication to the interests of the client and with zeal in advocacy upon the client's behalf." Although lawyers retain "professional discretion in determining the means by which a matter should be pursued," they should defer to the client regarding "the purposes to be served by legal representation." If, during the course of representation, the client "insists upon pursuing an objective that the lawyer considers repugnant or imprudent," the lawyer has discretion but no duty to withdraw.

What is disquieting about this formalist approach is not simply its implicit hierarchy of values, but also the absence of any significant controversy over its terms. That of itself suggests the extent to which professional ideology has become detached from society's more general ethical norms. Relieved of any responsibility for substantive justice, lawyers can come to view it as peripheral to their own sense of achievement. Litigation becomes a game or ritual, and as William Simon notes, such perspectives relieve the process of any necessity to generate fair or rational results. Such a normative climate easily gives rise to the attitude expressed by one British barrister: "[I]t is sometimes more fun to have a bad case than a good one for it tests your powers of persuasion more severely. Certainly I have seldom felt better pleased than when I persuaded [the court] to come to a decision which I was convinced was wrong. ..."

This sporting theory of justice, however compatible with the profession's institutional incentives, fits poorly with its traditional ideals. Not only is such a perspective conducive to the procedural abuses described earlier, it seems fundamentally at odds with lawyers' aspirations to a public calling. To cope with that apparent contradiction, as well as with the vast range of representation in which adversarial safeguards are absent, bar ideology requires recourse to a second line of argument. This alternative approach legitimates partisanship norms not as instruments for achieving justice in particular cases, but as safeguards for values that are central to a just society.

B. Individualism: Private Ends as a Public Calling

The second premise of adversarial ideology is that lawyers' undivided client allegiance serves fundamental interests of individual dignity, privacy, and autonomy. From this essentially deontological perspective, justice depends not on the realization of substantively correct outcomes, but on the preservation of private rights. In Lord

Brougham's classic formulation, the advocate "knows in the discharge of that office but one person in the world—[the] client and no other." From this premise follow two corollaries. First, lawyers should remain neutral partisans who defend, not judge, their clients. In addition, norms that assist that partisanship function, such as those governing confidentiality, should assume precedence over other societal concerns.

The individualist premise, although frequently invoked, is almost never fully explicated in debates over professional responsibility. Most commentators on the *Model Rules* simply assume a societal preference for individual over collective interests. As in other rights-oriented discourse, the source of assertedly preeminent values remains unclear. Thus, the American Trial Lawyers Association reasons: "In a society such as ours, which places the highest value on the dignity and autonomy of the individual, lawyers serve the public interest by undivided fidelity to each client's interests as the client perceives them." This non sequitur presupposes a societal consensus that may not exist for civil matters comprising the bulk of legal practice.

The force of the bar's deontological claims derives in large measure from the criminal defense paradigm, where the case for undiluted partisanship is most compelling. When individuals' lives, liberties, or reputations are so immediately at risk, our constitutional tradition has sought to guarantee that they have advocates without competing loyalties to the state. The justifications for that guarantee have generated an extensive scholarly discourse that need not be rehearsed here. Given the small number of attorneys actively engaged in criminal defense work, the critical question is whether professional norms appropriate in that context should serve as the paradigm for all legal practice. Yet the bar's exaltation of individualism remains heavily parasitic on the criminal defense role. In commenting on the *Model Rules*, the ABA General Practice and Corporate Law Sections cast the lawyer as a "champion against a hostile world" and a "fearless advocate" protecting individuals in their struggles with the state.

Such rhetoric is not smoothly transposed to the social and economic landscape of most legal practice. To be sure, in some civil matters, the disparity of power between the parties, the potential for abusive state or private action, or the possible constraints on fundamental rights may raise concerns analogous to those at issue in criminal proceedings. While the bar's contribution in those circumstances has been of enormous societal importance, such cases do not constitute the mainstay of legal work. Only a few lawyers are actively engaged in poverty, civil rights, civil liberties, or analogous litigation; a high percentage focus on problems of corporations and wealthy individuals. In those more typical cases, even if the state is involved, the balance of power is often rather different than the ABA's self-portrait assumes. When a Wall Street firm representing a Fortune 500 corporation squares off against a woefully understaffed state regulatory agency, it strains credulity to paint the corporate defender as a champion against official tyranny.

Moreover, as an explanation of the lawyer's role in private ordering, the appeal to tyranny seems rather forced. According to many commentators, any effort to place the "interests of society over the interests of the individual ... [represents] a very significant move toward totalitariansim. It makes the lawyer an agent of the state." Not only does this logic confuse social responsibility with social control, it condemns one form of domination only to license another. The specter of the "collectivist" state serves to justify undivided partisanship in pursuit of private power, no matter how abusive. To assume that clients are entitled to assistance in any action not plainly prohibited collapses moral and legal rights. Only the most uninformed faith in legislative processes and unrefined concept of moral responsibility could sustain such a vision.

The individualist rationale retains force through a rarified conception of legal practice and a reified view of professional role. By assimilating all forms of legal assistance to a David and Goliath paradigm, the argument avoids testing its value assumptions against more realistic social and economic backdrops. From a rhetorical perspective, that assimilation makes eminent sense. It is far easier to defend a highly privatistic vision of the social good and the profession's responsibilities when the lawyer appears as protector of the persecuted rather than friend of the finance company. Yet highly abstracted encomiums to individualism fail to explain the wholesale appropriation of adversarial norms in the defense of organizational interests.

Among private practitioners, the traditional consensus has been that lawyers' societal responsibilities should be identical whether they represent institutions or individuals. Yet no serious efforts have been made to justify that position or to confront its discontinuity with values underpinning the partisanship role. In much contemporary legal practice, it is by no means clear who constitutes the corporate "client." Nor is it self-evident that concerns of human dignity and autonomy are best served by lawyers' undivided commitment to organizational objectives, whatever the consequences to individual third parties, such as consumers, employees, or victims of environmental violations. The less adequately those individual interests are represented, the less convincing becomes the defense of undiluted client allegiance.

In any event, however persuasive one finds the abstract appeal to dignitary values, its status as justification for particular professional standards is far more questionable. When rules governing access to the legal system and fidelity to client interests are examined in social context, it is difficult to defend their formulation by reference to individualist concerns.

An obvious threshold difficulty with that defense involves the financial underpinnings of advocacy, a point on which most proponents of the adversary ethos are diplomatically silent. Almost without exception, *Model Rules* commentators who invoked fundamental values simply ignored the vast array of civil matters in which the stakes do not justify or the claimant cannot secure a "champion against a hostile world."

Other professional standards affecting unrepresented parties reflect a comparable lapse in commitment to values of individual dignity and autonomy. For example, one regulation evoking almost no controversy among private practitioners prohibits the unauthorized practice of law. Yet considerable empirical evidence indicates that the bar's sweeping prohibitions have significantly, and unnecessarily, impeded access to the legal system. In this context, the profession's animating interest appears to be protecting its turf from lay encroachment, rather than maximizing opportunities for assertion of individual rights. Similarly, the interests of unrepresented litigants have little standing in official ideology. In response to vehement bar opposition, *Model Rules* draftsmen deleted provisions enjoining lawyers who appeared against pro se opponents from "unfairly exploiting ... ignorance of the law or the practices of the tribunal," and "procur[ing] an unconscionable result." Under the final draft, lawyers' sole responsibility when dealing with an unrepresented adversary is to avoid implying that they are disinterested and to make reasonable efforts to correct evident misunderstandings concerning their role.

Why attorneys, particularly those representing organizational clients, should be so unconstrained in exploiting the ignorance of undefended opponents is not readily explicable from an individualist perspective. Neither the *Model Rules* Commission nor its critics confronted the implications of such unqualified partisanship in a society marked by grossly unequal access to legal services. Rather, commentators' overriding concern seemed to be that opposing parties "too cheap to hire a lawyer" should not be "coddled" by special treatment. What these rules on unrepresented interests reflect is not simply an inconsistency in the bar's celebration of individualist values. Rather, such standards expose the fundamental inadequacy of any theory that defends partisanship on individualist grounds, where partisans are allocated by market methods.

That inadequacy is perhaps most apparent in the bar's recent debates on confidentiality, which remained at the forefront of controversy throughout the *Model Rules* ratification process. Bar opposition ultimately forced the deletion of almost all mandatory disclosure requirements from the proposed *Model Rules*, including those requirements designed to prevent a client from committing an act that would result in death or substantial bodily harm to a third party. In their final form, the *Rules* require disclosure by an attorney only where necessary to avoid assisting a client's criminal or fraudulent act in proceedings before a tribunal. Lawyers may, but need not, reveal confidences in only two other circumstances: to prevent crimes likely to result in imminent death or substantial bodily harm, or to assert their own claims in a controversy with the client. Thus official ideology not only permits but may require counsel to remain a silent witness to highly asocial conduct.

Absolving lawyers from disclosure obligations under such circumstances is not easily reconciled with individualist premises. Casting the lawyer's office as a secular "confessional for the troubled individual" scarcely justifies its status as a haven for corporate prerogative. Particularly where the tradeoff is between shareholder profit and human safety, it is by no means obvious why organizational interests should occupy such a preferred position in defining counsel's ethical responsibilities.

The profession's conventional defense of its limited disclosure obligations is too familiar to warrant extended exegis here. Nonetheless, the core arguments are readily summarized and reduce to two essential propositions: first, that any risk of disclosure would deter clients from freely confiding in counsel; and second, that the costs of such a chill on clients' access to legal assistance would outweigh any societal benefits. Such claims are not without some intuitive force. The public's distaste for tattling reflects deeply rooted convictions about the value of trust and candor in human relationships. The critical issue, however, is not whether those values are worth preserving, but to what extent they are reconcilable with fundamental interests in protecting innocent third parties. On this point, most professional discourse has been utterly unilluminating.

Defendants of broad confidentiality protections almost invariably assume what is to be proven, namely that *any* disclosure responsibilities would dismember lawyer–client relationships. Bar rejoinders to modest *Model Rules* proposals generally verged on the apocalyptic. The common assumption was that any qualification of confidentiality protections would "chill all client communications"; lawyers' access to "potentially sensitive information would be virtually eliminated," uprooting "a fundamental cornerstone of our legal system." Only where lawyers enjoyed a relationship of "total trust [and] candor" could they effectively assist clients in conforming their conduct to legal mandates.

Although rarely made explicit, the empirical basis for such assertions appears to be that attorneys' obligations are well known and that any qualification would induce clients to suppress critical facts that they now divulge. Neither supposition is self-evident. Prior disclosure standards have been riddled with exceptions and indeterminancies, with which few laymen are familiar. Moreover, many clients will withhold evidence of compromising conduct, regardless of the bar's formal rules or clients' perceptions of them. What knowledge their counsel acquires will often be the product of paper trails and external corroboration rather than voluntary revelations. In any event, concerns about personal as well as organizational liability frequently leave clients with no practical alternative but to consult attorneys, and it is unclear how often some risk of disclosure would materially alter the terms of counsel's involvement. From a historical and cross-cultural perspective, it appears that most professionals, including American lawyers, have managed to discharge confidential counseling functions without the absolute freedom from third-party obligations that the organized bar now claims.

Thus, claims predicated on the lawyer's role as an institutional superego by no means justify the breadth of modern confidentiality protections. Given the scope of the attorney–client privilege, little is known about the extent to which lawyers have managed to channel patrons along "proper paths." Yet certainly the current incidence of illegal or hazardous corporate conduct suggests room for improvement. It is at least conceivable that some qualified third-party responsibilities might incline attorneys toward greater activism in their prophylactic role.

Finally, it bears note that even the most fervent defenders of unqualified confidentiality have seldom pursued the logic of their position when attorneys' own interests are at issue. Few of the *Model Rules* evoked greater consensus than the provision allowing lawyers to reveal information necessary to collect fees or to establish their own position in a dispute with the client. Yet nothing in the Commission's text or commentary explains why disclosures to protect lay victims will erode client trust, while revelations to secure attorneys' financial interests will not. In effect the bar's selective endorsement of confidentiality exceptions concedes the empirical point at issue. Once one acknowledges that client's general expectation of confidentiality can be maintained despite some limited risk of betrayal, it is unclear why the pecuniary concerns of lawyers should assume priority over the potentially more significant claims of third-party victims.

NOTES AND QUESTIONS

1. While Rhode is writing in the US context, many of the rules of professional conduct to which she refers have counterparts in the proposed draft rules of professional conduct—for example, see rule 2.03 on confidential information and rule 6.07 on practice by unauthorized persons.

2. Does Rhode's critique of neutral partisanship also imply that, in fact, the traditional model fails in its claim to vindicate private interests?

CHAPTER FOUR

Challenges to the Traditional Model

I. INTRODUCTION

Critiques of the traditional model of adversarial adjudication have intensified, particularly over the past decade. These critiques have resulted in reforms to court-based litigation itself and in the spawning of "alternative" models of dispute resolution located entirely outside the courts. Many of these developments reflect, as Judith Resnick has argued, a "declining faith in adversarial exchanges as an adequate basis for adjudication, in adjudication as the essence of fair decision-making and in fair decision-making as essential for legitimate government action." (See Judith Resnick, "Failing Faith: Adjudicatory Procedure in Decline" (1986), 53 *University of Chicago Law Review* 494-560).

The critiques have been levied from a variety of perspectives, advocate multiple and often conflicting understandings of the appropriate or legitimate function of litigation, and both reflect and project different, and, again, frequently competing, values. The traditional model is variously critiqued as being too expensive; too slow; as engendering hostility; as alienating and destructive of relationships, be they personal or business; as failing to respect the central importance of participation in decision making; as obscuring rather than illuminating the truth; as derived from an outdated and inappropriate view of litigation as centrally engaged in the resolution of private disputes between individuals or corporate entities and thus unable to deal with complex, polycentric, "public" disputes; for failing to address the inequalities of resources between parties; as unable to address systemic issues, like discrimination; and for curbing the quest for creative solutions to problems.

These critiques have led to a variety of reforms, which, as noted above, include the creation of alternative models, as well as modifications to the traditional model of court-based litigation. In this chapter, we have grouped the critiques and the reforms that they have supported into four broad categories. It is important to emphasize that the categories that we have chosen serve only as devices to help conceptually organize the most significant recent developments. In reality, there are many significant overlaps between the categories and we have attempted in various parts of the text to draw attention to some of these overlaps.

We have called the first category "Adjudication Modified." While the modifications have occurred along a variety of dimensions and represent greater and lesser challenges to the core values and function of the traditional model, what unites this category is the continued presence of adjudication and the continued central, but not exclusive, role of the civil courts. Here, we first examine adjudication that is based on an inquisitorial method of fact finding, in which persons other than the "parties" (in some systems this is the judge or other court official) are charged with the responsibility for the factual and legal development of the case. This is a model that is prevalent in European countries using civil law. (The model was not adopted in Quebec despite its use of civil law.) The inquisitorial method obviously represents a fundamental departure from the principle of party prosecution underlying the adversarial system as discussed by Brooks in chapter 3, "The Core Features and Values of the Traditional Model." While it is no doubt fair to say that no civil justice system within Canada has moved to an inquisitorial method of presentation, evidence of shifts in this direction can be found in at least three areas: in the practices of many small claims courts (as described in chapter 1, "Introduction to Civil Actions and Courts"), in the practices of several administrative tribunals (discussed more fully under the heading "The Administrative State," below), and in the adoption of "case management."

The development of case management is our next point of inquiry. "Case management" is a device introduced into the traditional model that gives judges greater control over the conduct, particularly the timing, of litigation. As such, it reflects a shift away from a pure adversarial approach that is entirely dependent on the initiative of private parties. It is important to note that case management has come to be seen as a central pillar of modern day civil justice reform (a point that is developed more fully below in the article by Watson and Easthope). It largely concerns itself with efficiency—the costs and delays associated with the traditional model of litigation that have propelled the development and adoption of case management systems. Within both of these sub-categories (inquisitorially based adjudication and case management), adjudication is still understood to be primarily about the vindication of private rights, although case management has also been supported by some of its proponents as a device to better accommodate more diffuse, complex, and "public" litigation.

The third and final sub-category we consider under the broad heading of "Adjudication Modified" is that of "public law litigation." Unlike the previous sub-categories discussed, "public law litigation" does challenge the core of the traditional model. It is from this perspective that the traditional model is seen as inadequate to the resolution of many modern day "disputes," wherein large numbers of persons—the "public" or a significant portion thereof—seek redress for harm, or one or more persons seek an authoritative pronouncement of "public" values (such as those found in the Charter of Rights and Freedoms). The function of litigation is understood to be not only—perhaps not even primarily—about the vindication of private rights, but about the pronouncement of public values, and the shaping of public policy. This critique of the traditional model has led to the modification of several procedural rules governing litigation that we address more fully in subsequent chapters—joinder, standing, intervention, and class actions. This critique and the reforms that it has generated have also been understood as integrally tied to "access to justice." (See, for example, Mauro Cappelletti, "Alternative Dispute Resolution Processes Within the Framework of the World-Wide Access to Justice Movement" (1993), 56 *The Modern Law Review* 282-96.)

It is also significant to note the changing conceptualization of the role of judge, and the need to reconceptualize the role of lawyer, within this perspective. While the presentation of facts and arguments continues in an adversarial format, the judge has a more active role both in the conduct of the case and, occasionally, in overseeing remedial action. With respect to the role of the lawyer, the Canadian Bar Association's Model Code of Professional Conduct and the codes of each jurisdiction largely presuppose that lawyers act for individuals. Given the present day reality that lawyers frequently act for a wide variety of groups, the codes fail to provide much helpful guidance. The representation of groups gives rise to a series of ethical questions that are addressed, in part, in the article below by Ellman.

The second major category we explore in this chapter is that of "informalism." Unlike the first category, "Adjudication Modified," what unites the category of informalism is the rejection of adjudication. Much of what is discussed here is caught under the broad rubric of "alternative dispute resolution" (ADR); however, the descriptor "ADR" is frequently used to capture a much wider range of processes. Often ADR is used to refer to any method of dispute resolution that is not court-based adjudication and thus includes several processes in which adjudication—indeed adversarial adjudication—is preserved. At the outset of this section we have included some readings on ADR generally, and then turn to what has really caught the imagination of reformers in Canada—the informal, non-adjudicatory methods of dispute resolution, particularly mediation. Reforms have occurred and are occurring along a variety of fronts: the creation of private mediation; the creation of court-annexed mediation (sometimes "voluntary," sometimes not); and the modification to court-based litigation processes—for example, mandatory settlement conferences in which judges are expected to act qua mediators. As the materials discuss, a range of values, frequently competing ones at that—for example, efficiency and process values—are advanced in support of informal, non-adjudicatory methods of dispute resolution. So too, a range of "failings" of the traditional model are articulated.

In some jurisdictions, ADR is linked to case management (thus demonstrating the permeability of our categories) through particular forms of "case conferences" that are part of the case management design: a screening conference to determine which process is best suited to the particular dispute and a settlement conference, in which the judge is charged with the responsibility to attempt to bring about a settlement.

As with public interest adjudication, the shift toward informalism has been accompanied by a shift in the conceptualization of the function of litigation, and of the roles of judge and of lawyer. Moreover, like public interest litigation, ADR, especially informal processes, has been understood by many as integrally linked to "access to justice." (See Cappelletti, supra.)

In this section we have included many of the reform initiatives currently under consideration or recently introduced. Much of the material in support of these initiatives seems to rely on an idealized version of mediation or ADR and fails to attend not only to competing normative perspectives but also to the empirical literature. We have therefore included several excerpts that critique informalism, settlement, and ADR from a variety of perspectives and that challenge the claims linking ADR and access to justice.

The third major category we have called the "administrative state." Here we discuss the creation of a vast array of bodies within the administrative state for the resolution of particular kinds of disputes. These various bodies are frequently charged with an array of functions and responsibilities, with "adjudication" being only one. They also embrace a range of processes—for example, formal adversarial adjudication, mediation, and in-quisitorial adjudication. As described by Bogart later in the chapter, the impetus behind the administrative state lay in several observations about the limitations of court-based adjudication: lack of expertise to address certain issues; the volume of decisions to be made; and the need to locate adjudication within the broader goals and responsibilities of particular administrative bodies. Within this context we consider human rights com-missions, police complaints procedures, and public inquiries.

In this chapter's final category, we look at dispute resolution in the context of aboriginal communities. More so than with the other challenges reviewed, the critique of adversarial adjudication posited here is grounded in the embracement of a fundamentally different value system. The reforms posited include changes to the existing civil justice system and, more important and more radically, the creation of a parallel aboriginal civil and criminal justice system (an aspiration integrally linked to self-government).

Before embarking on an examination of the four categories of challenge to the traditional model, we turn first to an article by Watson and Easthope that describes current, major civil justice reforms in Canada, Great Britain, and the United States. As you will see, case management and ADR are central to each of the reform initiatives and the "failings" of the traditional model are understood to be primarily the delay and costs associated with the traditional model. Many of the reforms that they describe are exam-ined in greater detail later in the chapter.

Garry D. Watson and Dana Easthope, "The New Wave of Civil Justice Reform: Efficiency and Effectiveness"
(unpublished, 1997) (footnotes omitted)

Currently in many quarters it is felt that common law civil justice systems are in a state of crisis. Commentators point to numerous symptoms of civil justice malaise including the high cost of civil litigation, the lengthy period of time required to reach a disposition, significant case backlogs in some courts and general public apprehension about the entire process. Indeed, a common view is that our civil justice system is plagued by excessive cost and delay and has failed to provide a just, timely, and inexpensive resolution of disputes brought to the courthouse.

Given these circumstances, it is not surprising that demands for civil justice reform have increased in frequency and pitch. In response to these demands, governments and the profession in Canada, Great Britain, Australia and the United States have taken steps toward proposing fundamental changes in their systems of civil justice. This note reviews three recent reports, two from Canada and one from England. It then looks at an important evaluative study of reforms in the United States.

In November of 1996, the Ontario Civil Justice Review followed up its initial report with its *Supplemental and Final Report of the Civil Justice Review* (Toronto: Ontario Civil Justice Review, 1996) ("the OCJR"). Earlier that same year, the Canadian Bar Association released its *Report of the Systems of Civil Justice Task Force* (Ottawa: Canadian Bar Association, 1996) ("the CBA Report") which contained more generic proposals adaptable to all provinces. In Great Britain, Lord Woolf was given the task of recommending reforms of the civil justice system, and in his Interim and Final Reports entitled *Access to Justice* (London: HMSO 1995 and 1996), he set forth his ambitious recommendations for reform in England. ...

While obviously containing some variation, the OCJR, CBA Report, and *Access to Justice* all address similar themes and propose remarkably similar reforms: (1) judicial case management; (2) alternative dispute resolution (ADR); and (3) procedural and cultural reform to make the civil justice system more user friendly. (The first two reforms originated in the [United States].) However, the question remains whether the proposed reforms will increase the efficiency or effectiveness of the civil justice system and contribute to the reduction of costs and delay.

Judicial Case Management

All three reform packages conclude that many of the problems plaguing the civil justice system can be cured by wresting responsibility for the management of cases away from the parties and their lawyers and giving it to the courts.

Traditionally, under the adversary system the progress of a case through the various pre-trial stages of litigation is left up to the parties ("party initiative"). While the rules provide time frames for the completion of the various steps, the enforcement of these time frames is left up to the parties and most cases take a much longer time to reach trial (if they go to trial) than is anticipated by the time frame set out in the rules. Case flow management, or case management as it is now usually called, changes this by handing over the function of enforcement of time limits, the progress of cases generally, to the court. Case management has its origins in the United States, coming into common use there by the 1980s. During the 1990s numerous Canadian courts (but by no means all of them) started to experiment with or adopt case management regimes. (Interestingly, until the recommendations of Lord Woolf—see below—England had no experience with civil case management.)

The details of case management schemes differ from jurisdiction to jurisdiction and court to court. In some courts case management is reserved for complex litigation; in others it is applied to all cases within the system. Often "tracking" is employed, i.e. the regime provides for different tracks, e.g., fast track, standard track, complex track, and different time tables are provided for each track. Sometimes case management time tables are very detailed, e.g., 60 days for service, 20 days to serve and file a statement of defence, discovery to be completed within 120 or 240 days, pre-trial conference to be schedule 120 or 240 days after the close of the pleadings. Other case management systems involve less detailed regulation with many less time standards to be met. Under some systems judges (or masters) are given the power to mandate whatever timetable they feel is appropriate on a case-by-case basis. Whatever the system, the timetable is enforced by the court and the litigants require leave of court to proceed outside the time limits. Beginning in 1991 Ontario experimented with a variety of case management regimes in Toronto, Windsor and Sault Ste. Marie (largely employing detailed time-tables). These projects were monitored and evaluated and their evaluation formed the basis of the OCJR's recommendations on case management in Ontario.

The OCJR's *First Report* cited a number of evaluations of these pilot projects, each one concluding that case management was a success. Generally, the evaluations found that dispositions of case managed cases occurred at approximately twice the rate of cases which were not managed. Also, it was determined that case management reduced delay at most stages of proceedings and decreased overall costs. Finally, an independent study by the QUINDECA Corporation (*Justice in Ontario: A Change of Pace— Evaluation of the Case Management Pilot Projects*, October 1994) concluded that case management works, provided it is properly planned, supported and resourced.

Both of the Canadian reports recommend the introduction of judicial case management. The CBA Report implies that case management should only be used in complex cases where there is a need for ongoing judicial supervision or intervention. However, the OCJR recommends that case management be mandatory for all civil, non-family proceedings. The OCJR moves away from detailed case management by abandoning the idea of set time limits for each step of the process: instead there would be only two or three deadlines imposed on the parties. It also recommends the use of integrated case management techniques to be implemented by employing case management teams of judges and case management masters. (By contrast many US courts employ "individual calendar systems" by which cases are assigned at the outset to a particular judge. Where case management is being employed, that judge (together with his clerk) will individually supervise the management of each case.) Both of the Canadian reports recommend a "multi-track" system with the plaintiff being free to chose the track upon which he or she wishes to proceed.

In the area of case management Woolf's recommendations are clearly the most radical. His diagnosis is that civil justice is in crisis because it takes too long, it costs too much money and, even when people win, they are unhappy with the process. He concludes that the dual problems of cost and delay are largely caused by the excesses of the adversary system, with lawyers attempting to exploit every procedural and tactical advantage to benefit their client and impede the other side. For Woolf, the logical solution is to retreat from the adversary system and give judges the responsibility for managing every aspect of the case. For example, through case management conferences and pretrial reviews, managerial *judges* under Woolf's proposed system would assign the case to one of three "tracks" based on its monetary value, settle the pleadings, narrow the issues in dispute, set time lines for the progress of the case, approve the costs of the proceeding, and enforce managerial decisions through the use of sanctions. (As we will see below, the powers Woolf recommends being given to judges in controlling litigation go far beyond what is typically thought of as case management in North America.)

Alternative Dispute Resolution

Alternative Dispute Resolution is front and centre in the package of reforms proposed by the OCJR. That report recommends an early, three hour *mandatory* mediation session for all civil, non-family cases within a specified time after the statement of defence is delivered. Under its proposal, the mediation would be "court-connected" to lend the process legitimacy and to ensure accountability. The only way litigants could avoid mandatory ADR would be to obtain leave from a case management master, which presumably would be difficult to obtain.

The OCJR's recommendations were heavily influenced by an evaluation of the Toronto ADR Centre conducted by Dr. Julie Macfarlane (*Court-Based Mediation for Civil Cases: An Evaluation of the Ontario Court (General Division) ADR Centre*, November 1995). Two of the Macfarlane Evaluation's major findings were: first, there is strong support of ADR as part of the litigation process; and second, no significant opposition exists among lawyers or litigants to the program's mandatory nature.

The Macfarlane Evaluation also made several other notable findings. For instance, it reported that cases settled at the ADR Centre do so in approximately half the time of non-referred cases which settled before trial. Also, 15 percent of referred cases settled before the mediation session, suggesting that the fact of referral alone may promote earlier settlements. Finally, the majority of lawyers and clients reported that they were happy with the process and believed it saved them money. On the other hand, lawyers tended to be unhappy with the nature of the scheduling process and the mandatory selection of a mediator.

The CBA Report also recommends ADR, but with a slightly different emphasis. The most important difference is that under the CBA plan, ADR would not be mandatory. Rather, the *opportunity* to participate in ADR should be communicated to litigants and provided at the earliest possible stage in the process. In general terms, the CBA Report recommends increased reliance on mediation and other non-binding dispute resolution processes in lieu of litigation, or at the very least, that the parties avail themselves of the opportunity to use mediation as a precondition for the use of the civil justice system. This recommendation reflects the CBA's view that the civil justice system must be a "multi-option" system because the traditional adversarial approach to litigation often displaces "substantive communication, common sense, and a problem-solving orientation. ..."

Woolf does not emphasize ADR in his proposals and it remains almost peripheral to his major focus on case management. He discusses ADR at some length and makes various suggestions as to how it might be used, but stops short of mandating it as part of a multi-door court house. However, he does recommend that such developments in other common law countries should be monitored. (His only proposal in this area is that there be cost consequences if a party fails to attempt ADR after being directed to do so, or has been uncooperative during the ADR process.)

The OCJR recommendations led ultimately to the passage in Ontario of Rule 24.1 (in force January 1999) providing for early and mandatory mediation in case managed cases in Toronto and Ottawa. This is a pilot project and after detailed evaluation it will be extended province-wide if found to successful; the hope is that mandatory mediation will lead to earlier settlements at lower costs to litigants. Under the rule a mediation session has to take place within 90 days after the first defence is filed, unless the court orders otherwise. Mediations are to be conducted (a) by a person chosen by the agreement of the parties from an approved list of roster mediators, or (b) if the parties so agree, by a person who is not on the list; (c) and if the parties cannot agree to a mediator, or fail to proceed in a timely manner, the mediation coordinator will assign a person from the list of mediators to conduct the mediation session. The program is a *user-pay* program and if list mediators are used the charge for each party for a three-hour mediation session will be in the vicinity of $300. If a non-list mediator is used then such mediator is free to charge market rates for his or her services. The Ministry of the AG has established an "Access Plan" to ensure access for impecunious litigants. The plan requires mediators, as a condition precedent to placement on the roster under the program, to undertake to conduct up to twelve hours of pro bono mediations per year.

Procedural and Cultural Reform

In the area of procedural reform, Woolf is once again the most radical. He proposes a number of fundamental changes which empower the court rather than the parties to control the nature and presentation of the case. First, Woolf recommends that pleadings be replaced by "Statements of Case" whose content and form would be settled by the court. Second, Woolf would have procedural judges determine the amount and scope of document discovery. He would remove the present obligation on parties to search for relevant documents. Generally parties would only have to disclose relevant documents that are known to them at the time of discovery; full discovery of documents, with the requirement that parties search for such documents, would only be available in special cases by court order. Third, Woolf recommends the early exchange of witness statements *and* the use of such statements as evidence-in-chief at the trial. Moreover, he declares that it will be the judge who "will decide which witnesses he wishes to be called" and that "cross-examination on the contents of witness statements should only be allowed with a leave of the judge." Fourth, the use of expert witnesses would be totally within the court's discretion and the judge would have the authority, with or without the consent of the parties, to appoint a court expert to give evidence. Fifth, for cases between £3000 and 10,000 (cases under Woolf's "fast track procedure") there is a radical cost proposal. Providing a straight forward and limited procedure on the fast track is designed to make it possible to introduce standard *fixed* costs which would represent the extent of a party's liability to the opponent. Moreover, such fixed costs would also constitute an appropriate amount of solicitor and client costs payable to a party's own legal advisor, except in cases where there has been an explicit agreement to pay more which has been fully explained to the litigant.

> The results should be that not only would a party know what his maximum liability in relation to costs could be to the other side, he should be able to obtain legal representation for no greater sum than he would be liable to pay to the other side. I

envisage that the costs would normally represent a percentage of the claim and that there would be a basic fixed minimum of costs.

Woolf indicates that this recommendation is inspired by a similar regime that exists in Germany—an approach, he indicates, which does not appear to have had a deleterious effect on the income of German lawyers. (He noted that German fees are lower, although acceptable, and that there is still an acceptable level of access.) Other radical reforms proposed include allowing the judge to determine the length of the trial and giving the court the power to grant summary judgment on its own initiative if a case is viewed as having no realistic prospect of success. Clearly, Woolf's proposals in this area represent a significant step away from the traditional adversary system and party autonomy. At the centre of his report appears to be the profound wish to see the adversary system give way to one in which judges will become central and "run the show."

Woolf would also like to curb the adversary system by implementing a change in the litigation culture. He recommends legislating cooperative behaviour among parties and their lawyers, with their behaviour being a consideration in the determination of cost awards or in extending case management deadlines. Woolf also sees a need to change the mind set of judges whose role is usually characterized as that of a passive and neutral decision-maker. Also, with the rise of litigants acting in person (resulting from major cut backs in legal aid), Woolf recommends that the rules of civil procedure be rewritten in simple language understandable by lay persons.

The CBA Report is also strong on procedural reform. It recommends limiting the availability of oral discoveries. In their place, the parties would provide early written disclosure of anticipated evidence through "will-say" statements and early disclosure of expert reports. The CBA Report also recommends preventing abuses of interlocutory motions by restricting the right to appeal interlocutory orders and strengthening the cost sanctions against unsuccessful parties (as is already provided for in Ontario).

The CBA Report is also a strong advocate of cultural change, although not focused on the adversary conduct of lawyers which was Woolf's major concern. Many of its recommendations focus on making the civil justice system more user-friendly by changing the way lawyers conduct business. For example, the report identified one of the main weaknesses of the civil justice system as the lack of public understanding of the system's operation. To counteract this problem, the report proposes that lawyers be required by the Rules of Professional Conduct to fully explain and explore all prospects of settlement and available ADR alternatives (as is already required in Ontario). Also, a clearly-worded Statement of Client Rights should be made available. Finally, the report recommends that the legal profession move away from the billable hour and promote pre-paid legal services plans, contingency fees, and value-based or task-based billing.

The OCJR's only recommendation for procedural reform is a minor one: that venue provisions be reintroduced into Ontario law requiring many actions to be commenced in the county where the cause of action arose or where real estate involved in the litigation is located. In addition the Report would allow Senior Regional Justices to transfer cases to a different venue within the region for hearing or trial. Beyond this proposal, however, the OCJR is silent on other procedural issues. For example, the report concludes that further study is needed on the discovery process before recommendations for improvement can be made. Also, the OCJR concluded that additional research is needed on institutional and individual litigant costs. It did, however, echo the CBA Report by suggesting that alternatives to the billable hour be evaluated and that contingency fees be permitted for all matters except criminal and family proceedings. Regarding change in the legal culture, the OCJR seems to be of the view that culture cannot be legislated, but believes that lawyers will be "won over" once they gain experience with the new system. For judges to accept the new system, they must be convinced that it is not merely a new set of duties and responsibilities.

Effectiveness

The preceding material has briefly outlined the civil justice reforms proposed in Canada and Great Britain. In each instance their general mandate was to offer solutions to the problems of excessive cost and delay. But the question remains: will the recommended changes achieve their stated objective?

The United States: The Civil Justice Reform Act and the Rand Report

The 1990 federal *Civil Justice Reform Act* (CJRA) required each US federal district court to develop a plan to fight cost and delay in the civil justice system. The Act also mandated a pilot project whereby ten districts were directed to incorporate a number of different case management principles into their plans. To facilitate an evaluation of the case management techniques, ten comparison districts were chosen which were free to implement any plan they wished. The Rand Corporation's *Institute for Civil Justice* was selected to conduct an assessment of the CJRA's pilot programs. Its report, *An Evaluation of Judicial Case Management Under the Civil Justice Reform Act* (Santa Monica: Rand, 1996), by James Kakalik *et al.*, arrived at a variety of conclusions regarding several case management techniques and also provided some recommendations of its own.

The Rand Report concluded that although different types of cases require different types of case management, successfully assigning cases to "tracks" at an early stage is extremely difficult. The likely explanations for this problem are that judges do not have enough information when the track assignment must be made, or that judges prefer to use their own discretion rather than subjecting the case to the rigidity of a specified track. These findings suggest that judges will require more information at an earlier stage before assigning each case to a track.

Conversely, Rand found that early and ongoing judicial control of pretrial activities was an essential tool for reducing civil justice delay. The most important pretrial activity for reducing delay was setting a trial schedule at an early stage, but status conferences and other scheduling activities also produced beneficial effects. However, Rand found that while early judicial management decreases time to disposition, it also serves to increase lawyer work-hours as counsel respond to judicial management efforts. This in turn increases the dollar cost to litigants. This area of reform illustrates one of the essential conclusions of the Rand Report: different managerial and reform techniques often work at cross-purposes in the battle against cost and delay.

In terms of procedural reform, the Rand Report focused on the effects of discovery management. Rand concluded that the *Civil Justice Reform Act* produced substantial improvements in early disclosure and good-faith efforts to resolve discovery disputes. Furthermore, when judges set an early cut-off date for discovery, the time to disposition and cost to litigants are significantly reduced through reduced lawyer work-hours.

While Rand's Institute for Civil Justice also set out to study the effects of various ADR alternatives, its research was hampered by the small number of cases referred to ADR. Only mandatory arbitration had a sufficient number of cases referred to it to allow for evaluation, and Rand concluded that it had no major effects on time to disposition or costs. The Rand Report also noted that where ADR is voluntary, neither lawyers nor judges use it extensively.

In conclusion, while Rand concluded that a few case management techniques are effective at reducing delay, these techniques have offsetting or negative effects on lawyer work-hours and litigant costs. The stakes of the case and its complexity appear to be more important predictors of the amount of time a lawyer will spend on a case. Therefore, it appears from Rand's evaluation that civil justice reform will only have a minor role to play in reducing costs to litigants, although some progress can be made at controlling delay.

QUESTION

Note the extent to which lawyers—more specifically, adversarialism—are blamed for many of the pathologies of civil justice systems. What might Fried say about this? Rhode? (See chapter 3, "The Core Features and Values of the Traditional Model.")

II. ADJUDICATION MODIFIED

A. Inquisitorial Adjudication

This section examines those challenges to the traditional model of litigation that continue to embrace adjudication, but that see the traditional model as inadequate or inappropriate in several differing respects. We begin by examining inquisitorially based adjudication, particularly as practised in continental Europe. As the following article by Langbein emphasizes, continental procedure often reflects a mixed inquisitorial and adversarial model.

J.H. Langbein, "The German Advantage in Civil Procedure"
(1985), 52 *University of Chicago Law Review*, at 823-66 (footnotes omitted)

Our lawyer-dominated system of civil procedure has often been criticized both for its incentives to distort evidence and for the expense and complexity of its modes of discovery and trial. The shortcomings inhere in a system that leaves to partisans the work of gathering and producing the factual material upon which adjudication depends.

We have comforted ourselves with the thought that a lawyerless system would be worse. The excesses of American adversary justice would seem to pale by comparison with a literally nonadversarial system—one in which litigants would be remitted to faceless bureaucratic adjudicators and denied the safeguards that flow from lawyerly intermediation.

The German advantage. The main theme of this article is drawn from Continental civil procedure, exemplified for me by the system that I know reasonably well, the West German. My theme is that, by assigning judges rather than lawyers to investigate the facts, the Germans avoid the most troublesome aspects of our practice. But I shall emphasize that the familiar contrast between our adversarial procedure and the supposedly nonadversarial procedure of the Continental tradition has been grossly overdrawn.

To be sure, since the greater responsibility of the bench for fact-gathering is what distinguishes the Continental tradition, a necessary (and welcome) correlative is that counsel's role in eliciting evidence is greatly restricted. Apart from fact-gathering, however, the lawyers for the parties play major and broadly comparable roles in both the German and American systems. Both are adversary systems of civil procedure. There as here, the lawyers advance partisan positions from first pleadings to final arguments. German litigators suggest legal theories and lines of factual inquiry, they superintend and supplement judicial examination of witnesses, they urge inferences from fact, they discuss and distinguish precedent, they interpret statutes, and they formulate views of the law that further the interests of their clients. I shall urge that German experience shows that we would do better if we were greatly to restrict the adversaries' role in fact-gathering. ...

I. Overview of German Civil Procedure

There are two fundamental differences between German and Anglo-American civil procedure, and these differences lead in turn to many others. First, the court rather than the parties' lawyers takes the main responsibility for gathering and sifting evidence, although the lawyers exercise a watchful eye over the court's work. Second, there is no distinction between pretrial and trial, between discovering evidence and presenting it. Trial is not a single continuous event. Rather, the court gathers and evaluates evidence over a series of hearings, as many as the circumstances require.

Initiation. The plaintiff's lawyer commences a lawsuit in Germany with a complaint. Like its American counterpart, the German complaint narrates the key facts, sets forth a legal theory, and asks for a remedy in damages or specific relief. Unlike an American complaint, however, the German document proposes means of proof for its main factual contentions. The major documents in the plaintiff's possession that support his claim are scheduled and often appended; other documents (for example, hospital files or government records such as police accident reports or agency files) are indicated; witnesses who are thought to know something helpful to the plaintiff's position are identified. The defendant's answer follows the same pattern. It should be emphasized, however, that neither plaintiff's nor defendant's lawyer will have conducted any significant search for witnesses or for other evidence unknown to his client. Digging for facts is primarily the work of the judge.

Judicial preparation. The judge to whom the case is entrusted examines these pleadings and appended documents. He routinely sends for relevant public records. These materials form the beginnings of the official dossier, the court file. All subsequent submissions of counsel, and all subsequent evidence-gathering, will be entered in the dossier, which is open to counsel's inspection continuously.

When the judge develops a first sense of the dispute from these materials, he will schedule a hearing and notify the lawyers. He will often invite and sometimes summon the parties as well as their lawyers to this or subsequent hearings. If the pleadings have identified witnesses whose testimony seems central, the judge may summon them to the initial hearing as well.

Hearing. The circumstances of the case dictate the course of the hearing. Sometimes the court will be able to resolve the case by discussing it with the lawyers and parties and suggesting avenues of compromise. If the case remains contentious and witness testimony needs to be taken, the court will have learned enough about the case to determine a sequence for examining witnesses.

Examining and recording. The judge serves as the examiner-in-chief. At the conclusion of his interrogation of each witness, counsel for either party may pose additional questions, but counsel are not prominent as examiners. Witness testimony is seldom recorded verbatim; rather, the judge pauses from time to time to dictate a summary of the testimony into the dossier. The lawyers sometimes suggest improvements in the wording of these summaries, in order to preserve or to emphasize nuances important to one side or the other.

Since the proceedings in a difficult case may require several hearings extending across many months, these summaries of concluded testimony—by encapsulating succinctly the results of previous hearings—allow the court to refresh itself rapidly for subsequent hearings. The summaries also serve as building blocks from which the court will ultimately fashion the findings of fact for its written judgment. If the case is appealed, these concise summaries constitute the record for the reviewing court. ...

Expertise. If an issue of technical difficulty arises on which the court or counsel wishes to obtain the views of an expert, the court—in consultation with counsel—will select the expert and define his role. (This aspect of the procedure I shall discuss particularly in Part IV below.)

Further contributions of counsel. After the court takes witness testimony or receives some other infusion of evidence, counsel have the opportunity to comment orally or in writing. Counsel use these submissions in order to suggest further proofs or to advance legal theories. Thus, nonadversarial proof-taking alternates with adversarial dialogue across as many hearings as are necessary. The process merges the investigatory function of our pretrial discovery and the evidence-presenting function of our trial. Another manifestation of the comparative efficiency of German procedure is that a witness is ordinarily examined only once. Contrast the American practice of partisan interview and preparation, pretrial deposition, preparation for trial, and examination and cross-examination at trial. These many steps take their toll in expense and irritation.

Judgment. After developing the facts and hearing the adversaries' views, the court decides the case in a written judgment that must contain full findings of fact and make reasoned application of the law.

II. Judicial Control of Sequence

From the standpoint of comparative civil procedure, the most important consequence of having judges direct fact-gathering in this episodic fashion is that German procedure functions without the sequence rules to which we are accustomed in the Anglo-American procedural world. The implications for procedural economy are large. The very concepts of "plaintiff's case" and "defendant's case" are unknown. In our system those concepts function as traffic rules for the partisan presentation of evidence to a passive and ignorant trier. By contrast, in German procedure the court ranges over the entire case, constantly looking for the jugular—for the issue of law or fact that might dispose of the case. Free of constraints that arise from party presentation of evidence, the court investigates the dispute in the fashion most likely to narrow the inquiry. A major job of counsel is to guide the search by directing the court's attention to particularly cogent lines of inquiry.

Suppose that the court has before it a contract case that involves complicated factual or legal issues about whether the contract was formed, and if so, what its precise terms were. But suppose further that the court quickly recognizes (or is led by submission of counsel to recognize) that some factual investigation might establish an affirmative defense—illegality, let us say—that would vitiate the contract. Because the court functions without sequence rules, it can postpone any consideration of issues that we would think of as the plaintiff's case—here the questions concerning the formation and the terms of the contract. Instead, the court can concentrate the entire initial inquiry on what we would regard as a defense. If, in my example, the court were to unearth enough evidence to allow it to conclude that the contract was illegal, no investigation would ever be done on the issues of formation and terms. A defensive issue that could only surface in Anglo-American procedure following full pretrial and trial ventilation of the whole of the plaintiff's case can be brought to the fore in German procedure.

Part of what makes our discovery system so complex is that, on account of our division into pretrial and trial, we have to discover for the entire case. We investigate everything that could possibly come up at trial, because once we enter the trial phase we can seldom go back and search for further evidence. By contrast, the episodic character of German fact-gathering largely eliminates the danger of surprise; if the case takes an unexpected turn, the disadvantaged litigant can count on developing his response in another hearing at a later time. Because there is no pretrial discovery phase, fact-gathering occurs only once; and because the court establishes the sequence of fact-gathering according to criteria of relevance, unnecessary investigation is minimized. In the Anglo-American procedural world we value the early-disposition mechanism, especially summary judgment, for issues of law. But for fact-laden issues, our fixed-sequence rule (plaintif's case before defendant's case) and our single-continuous-trial rule largely foreclose it.

The episodic character of German civil procedure—Benjamin Kaplan called it the "conference method" of adjudication—has other virtues. It lessens tension and theatrics, and it encourages settlement. Countless novels, movies, plays, and broadcast serials attest to the dramatic potential of the Anglo-American trial. The contest between opposing counsel; the potential for surprise witnesses who cannot be rebutted in time; the tricks of adversary examination and cross-examination; the concentration of proof-taking and verdict into a single, continuous proceeding; the unpredictability of juries and the mysterious opacity of their conclusory verdicts—these attributes of the Anglo-American trial make for good theatre. German civil proceedings have the tone not of the theatre, but of a routine business meeting—serious rather than tense. When the court inquires and directs, it sets no stage for advocates to perform. The forensic skills of counsel can wrest no material advantage, and the appearance of a surprise witness would simply lead to the scheduling of a further hearing. In a system that cannot distinguish between dress rehearsal and opening night, there is scant occasion for stage fright.

In this business-like system of civil procedure the tradition is strong that the court promotes compromise. The judge who gathers the facts soon knows the case as well as the litigants do, and he concentrates each subsequent increment of fact-gathering on the most important issues still unresolved. As the case progresses the judge discusses it with the litigants, sometimes indicating provisional views of the likely outcome. He is, therefore, strongly positioned to encourage a litigant to abandon a case that is turning out to be weak or hopeless, or to recommend settlement. The loser-pays system of allocating the costs of litigation gives the parties further incentive to settle short of judgment.

III. Witnesses

Adversary control of fact-gathering in our procedure entails a high level of conflict between partisan advantage and orderly disclosure of the relevant information. Marvin Frankel put this point crisply when he said that "it is the rare case in which either side yearns to have the witnesses, or anyone, give *the whole truth*."

If we had deliberately set out to find a means of impairing the reliability of witness testimony, we could not have done much better than the existing system of having partisans prepare witnesses in advance of trial and examine and cross-examine them at trial. Jerome Frank described the problem a generation ago:

> [The witness] often detects what the lawyer hopes to prove at the trial. If the witness desires to have the lawyer's client win the case, he will often, unconsciously, mold his story accordingly. Telling and re-telling it to the lawyer, he will honestly believe that his story, as he narrates it in court, is true, although it importantly deviates from what he originally believed.

Thus, said Frank, "the partisan nature of trials tends to make partisans of the witnesses."

Cross-examination at trial—our only substantial safeguard against this systematic bias in the testimony that reaches our courts—is a frail and fitful palliative. Cross-examination is too often ineffective to undo the consequences of skillful coaching. Further, because cross-examination allows so much latitude for bullying and other truth-defeating stratagems, it is frequently the source of fresh distortion when brought to bear against truthful testimony. As a leading litigator boasted recently in an ABA publication: "By a carefully planned and executed cross-examination, I can raise at least a slight question about the accuracy of [an adverse] witness's story, or question his motives or impartiality."

When we cross the border into German civil procedure, we leave behind all traces of this system of partisan preparation, examination, and cross-examination of witnesses. German law distinguishes parties from witnesses. A German lawyer must necessarily discuss the facts with his client, and based on what his client tells him and on what the documentary record discloses, the lawyer will nominate witnesses whose testimony might turn out to be helpful to his client. As the proofs come in, they may reveal to the lawyer the need to nominate further witnesses for the court to examine. But the lawyer stops at nominating; virtually never will he have occasion for out-of-court contact with a witness. Not only would such contact be a serious ethical breach, it would be self-defeating. "German judges are given to marked and explicit doubts about the reliability of the testimony of witnesses who previously have discussed the case with counsel or who have consorted unduly with a party."

No less a critic than Jerome Frank was prepared to concede that in American procedure the adversaries "sometimes do bring into court evidence which, in a dispassionate inquiry, might be overlooked." That is a telling argument for including adversaries in the fact-gathering process, but not for letting them run it. German civil procedure preserves party interests in fact-gathering.

At trial, the battle of experts tends to baffle the trier, especially in jury courts. If the experts do not cancel each other out, the advantage is likely to be with the expert whose forensic skills are the more enticing. The system invites abusive cross-examination. Since each expert is party-selected and party-paid, he is vulnerable to attack on credibility regardless of the merits of his testimony. A defense lawyer recently bragged about his technique of cross-examining plaintiffs' experts in tort cases. Notice that nothing in his strategy varies with the truthfulness of the expert testimony he tries to discredit:

> A mode of attack ripe with potential is to pursue a line of questions which, by their form and the jury's studied observation of the witness in response, will tend to cast the expert as a "professional witness." By proceeding in this way, the cross-examiner will reap the benefit of a community attitude, certain to be present among several of the jurors, that bias can be purchased, almost like a commodity.

Thus, the systematic incentive in our procedure to distort expertise leads to a systematic distrust and devaluation of expertise. Short of forbidding the use of experts altogether, we probably could not have designed a procedure better suited to minimize the influence of expertise.

The Continental tradition. European legal systems are, by contrast, expert-prone. Expertise is frequently sought. The literature emphasizes the value attached to having expert assistance available to the courts in an age in which litigation involves facts of ever-greater technical difficulty. The essential insight of Continental civil procedure is that credible expertise must be neutral expertise. Thus, the responsibility for selecting and informing experts is placed upon the courts, although with important protections for party interests.

Selecting the expert. German courts obtain expert help in lawsuits the way Americans obtain expert help in business or personal affairs. If you need an architect, a dermatologist, or a plumber, you do not commission a pair of them to take pre-ordained and opposing positions on your problem, although you do sometimes take a second opinion. Rather, you take care to find an expert who is qualified to advise you in an objective manner; you probe his advice as best you can; and if you find his advice persuasive, you follow it.

When in the course of winnowing the issues in a lawsuit a German court determines that expertise might help resolve the case, the court selects and instructs the expert. The court may decide to seek expertise on its own motion, or at the request of one of the parties. The code of civil procedure allows the court to request nominations from the parties—indeed, the code requires the court to use any expert upon whom the parties agree—but neither practice is typical. In general, the court takes the initiative in nominating and selecting the expert. ...

Preparing the expert. The court that selects the expert instructs him, in the sense of propounding the facts that he is to assume or to investigate, and in framing the questions that the court wishes the expert to address. In formulating the expert's task, as in other important steps in the conduct of the case, the court welcomes adversary suggestions. If the expert should take a view of premises (for example, in an accident case or a building-construction dispute), counsel for both sides will accompany him.

Safeguards. The expert is ordinarily instructed to prepare a written opinion. When the court receives the report, it is circulated to the litigants. The litigants commonly file written comments, to which the expert is asked to reply. The court on its own motion may also request the expert to amplify his views. If the expert's report remains in contention, the court will schedule a hearing at which counsel for a dissatisfied litigant can confront and interrogate the expert.

The code of civil procedure reserves to the court the power to order a further report by another expert if the court should deem the first report unsatisfactory. A litigant dissatisfied with the expert may encourage the court to invoke its power to name a second expert. The code of criminal procedure has a more explicit standard for such cases, which is worth noticing because the literature suggests that courts have similar instincts in civil procedure. The court may refuse a litigant's motion to engage a further expert in a criminal case, the code says,

> if the contrary of the fact concerned has already been proved through the former expert opinion; this [authority to refuse to appoint a further expert] does not apply if the expertise of the former expert is doubted, if his report is based upon inaccurate factual presuppositions, if the report contains contradictions, or if the new expert has available means of research that appear superior to those of a former expert.

When, therefore, a litigant can persuade the court that an expert's report has been sloppy or partial, that it rests upon a view of the field that is not generally shared, or that the question referred to the expert is exceptionally difficult, the court will commission further expertise.

A litigant may also engage his own expert, much as is done in the Anglo-American procedural world, in order to rebut the court-appointed expert. The court will discount the views of a party-selected expert on account of his want of neutrality, but cases occur in which he nevertheless proves to be effective. Ordinarily, I am told, the court will not in such circumstances base its judgment directly upon the views of the party-selected expert; rather, the court will treat the rebuttal as ground for engaging a further court-appointed expert (called an *Oberexperte*, literally an "upper" or "superior" expert), whose opinion will take account of the rebuttal.

To conclude: In the use of expertise German civil procedure strikes an adroit balance between nonadversarial and adversarial values. Expertise is kept impartial, but litigants are protected against error or caprice through a variety of opportunities for consultation, confrontation, and rebuttal. ...

Outside the realm of fact-gathering, German civil procedure is about as adversarial as our own. Both systems welcome the lawyerly contribution to identifying legal issues and sharpening legal analysis. German civil procedure is materially less adversarial than our own only in the fact-gathering function, where partisanship has such potential to pollute the sources of truth.

Accordingly, the proper question is not whether to have lawyers, but how to use them; not whether to have an adversarial component to civil procedure, but how to prevent adversarial excesses. If we were to incorporate the essential lesson of the German system in our own procedure, we would still have a strongly adversarial civil procedure. We would not, however, have coached witnesses and litigation-biased experts. ...

Prejudgment. Perhaps the most influential justification for adversary domination of fact-gathering has been an agreement put forward by Lon Fuller: Nonadversarial procedure risks prejudgment—that is, prematurity in judgment. Fuller worried that the judge would make up his mind too soon.

> What generally occurs in practice is that at some early point a familiar pattern will seem to emerge from the evidence; an accustomed label is waiting for the case and, without awaiting further proofs, this label is promptly assigned to it. ...
>
> An adversary presentation seems the only effective means for combatting this natural human tendency to judge too swiftly in terms of the familiar that which is not yet fully known. The arguments of counsel hold the case, as it were, in suspension between two opposing interpretations of it. While the proper classification of the case is thus kept unresolved, there is time to explore all of its peculiarities and nuances.

This passage obtains much of its force from the all-or-nothing contrast that so misdescribes German civil procedure. In a system like the German, which combines judicial fact-gathering with vigorous and continuing adversarial efforts in nominating lines of factual inquiry and analyzing factual and legal issues, the adversaries perform just the role that Fuller lauds, helping hold the decision in suspension while issues are framed and facts explored.

In German procedure counsel oversees and has means to prompt a flagging judicial inquiry; but quite apart from that protection, is it really true that a "familiar pattern" would otherwise beguile the judge into investigating too sparingly? If so, it seems odd that this asserted "natural human tendency" towards premature judgment does not show up in ordinary business and personal decision-making, whose patterns of inquiry resemble the fact-gathering process in German civil procedure. Since the decision-maker does his own investigating in most of life's decisions, it seems odd to despair of prematurity only when that normal mode of decision-making is found to operate in a courtroom. Accordingly, I think that Fuller overstates the danger of prematurity that inheres in allowing the decision-maker to conduct the fact-gathering; but to the extent that the danger is real, German civil procedure applies just the adversarial remedy that Fuller recommends.

Depth. Fuller's concern about prematurity shades into a different issue: how to achieve appropriate levels of depth in fact-gathering. Extra investment in search can almost always turn up further proofs that would be at least tenuously related to the case. Adversary domination of fact-gathering privatizes the decision about what level of resources to invest in the case. The litigants who are directly interested in the outcome decide how much to spend on search. In German procedure, by contrast, these partisan calculations of self-interest are subordinated, for a variety of reasons. The initiative in fact-gathering is shared with the judge; and the German system of reckoning and allocating the costs of litigation is less sensitive to the cost of incremental investigative steps than in our system where each side pays for the proofs that it orders. On the other hand, the German judge cannot refuse to investigate party-nominated proofs without reason, and this measure of party control greatly narrows the difference between the two systems.

Writing in 1958, Kaplan and his co-authors recorded their "impression" that German civil "proceedings do not in practice serve as an engine of discovery comparable in strength to the modern American methods," in part because German courts are hostile to fishing. Further, the authors worried that the technique of recording witness testimony in succinct summaries could bleach out "[f]ine factual differentiations." They found German procedure to be "far less preoccupied than the American with minute investigation of factual detail of reliability of individual witnesses."

Defenders of the American status quo may take too much comfort from these observations. A main virtue of German civil procedure, we recall, is that the principle of judicial control of sequence works to confine the scope of fact-gathering to those avenues of inquiry deemed most likely to resolve the case. Fact-gathering occurs when the unfolding logic of the case dictates that investigation of particular issues is needed. That practice does indeed contrast markedly with the inclination of American litigators "to leave no stone unturned, provided, of course, they can charge by the stone." The primary reason that German courts do less fact-gathering than American lawyers is that the Germans eliminate the waste. Likewise, when American observers notice that there is less harrying of witnesses with "those elaborate testings of credibility familiar to American courtrooms," I incline to think that the balance of advantage rests with the Germans, since so much of what passes for cross-examination in our procedure is deliberately truth-defeating. ...

VI. Judicial Incentives

Viewed comparatively from the Anglo-American perspective, the greater authority of the German judge over fact-gathering comes at the expense of the lawyers for the parties. Adversary influence on fact-gathering is deliberately restrained. Furthermore, in routine civil procedure, German judges do not share power with jurors. There is no civil jury.

Because German procedure places upon the judge the responsibility for fact-gathering, the danger arises that the job will not be done well. The American system of partisan fact-gathering has the virtue of its vices: It aligns responsibility with incentive. Each side gathers and presents proofs according to its own calculation of self-interest. This privatization is an undoubted safeguard against official sloth. After all, who among us has not been treated shabbily by some lazy bureaucrat in a government department? And who would want to have that ugly character in charge of one's lawsuit?

The answer to that concern in the German tradition is straightforward: The judicial career must be designed in a fashion that creates incentives for diligence and excellence. The idea is to attract very able people to the bench, and to make their path of career advancement congruent with the legitimate interests of the litigants.

The career judiciary. The distinguishing attribute of the bench in Germany (and virtually everywhere else in Europe) is that the profession of judging is separate from the profession of lawyering. Save in exceptional circumstances, the judge is not an ex-lawyer like his Anglo-American counterpart. Rather, he begins his professional career as a judge.

In Germany judges and lawyers undergo a common preparatory schooling. After completing a prescribed course of university legal education that lasts several years, the young jurist sits a first state examination. After passing this examination satisfactorily, he enters upon an apprenticeship that now lasts two and one-half years. He clerks for judges in the civil and criminal courts, assists in the prosecutor's office, and works in a lawyer's office. At the conclusion of this tour of duty, the young jurist sits a second state examination, remotely akin to our bar examination, which concludes the certification process. Thereafter, the career lines of judge and lawyer diverge.

Recruitment. Although West Germany is a federal state, the state and federal courts comprise an integrated system. The courts of first instance and the first layer of appellate courts are state courts, while the second (and final) layer of appellate jurisdiction operates at the federal level. Thus, even though the basic codes of civil and criminal law and procedure are federal codes, the state courts have exclusive jurisdiction until the final appellate instance. It follows that most judges are state judges; and since appointment to the federal bench is by way of promotion from the state courts, all entry-level recruitment to the bench occurs at the state level.

In each of the eleven federal states, the ministry of justice is responsible for staffing the courts. Entry-level vacancies are advertised and applications entertained from young jurists. The judiciary is a prized career: influential, interesting, secure, and (by comparison with practice of the bar) prestigious and not badly compensated. "[O]nly the graduates with the best examination results have any chance of entering the judicial corps."

Advancement. A candidate who is accepted begins serving as a judge without any prior legal-professional experience, typically in his late twenties. At the outset his position is probationary, although he must be promoted to tenure or dismissed within five years. His first assignment may be to a court of petty jurisdiction (Amtsgericht), or else he will become the junior member of a collegial chamber of the main court of general jurisdiction (Landgericht, hereafter LG), where he can receive guidance from experienced judges.

The work of a German judge is overseen and evaluated by his peers throughout his career, initially in connection with his tenure review, and thereafter for promotion through the several levels of judicial office and salary grades. A judge knows that his every step will be grist for the regular periodic reviews that will fill his life-long personnel file. His "efficiency rating" is based in part upon objective factors, such as caseload discharge rates and reversal rates, and in part on subjective peer evaluation. The presiding judge of a chamber has special responsibility for evaluating the work of the younger judges who serve with him, but the young judges are rotated through various chambers in the course of their careers, and this reduces the influence of an aberrant rating from any one presiding judge. These evaluations by senior judges pay particular regard to (1) a judge's effectiveness in conducting legal proceeding, including fact-gathering, and his treatment of witnesses and litigants; and (2) the quality of his opinions—his success in mastering and applying the law to his cases.

This meritocratic system of review and promotion is meant to motivate the judge to perform at his best. In the main first-instance court (LG), which is sectioned into many three-judge panels called chambers, the judge aspires to advance to the position of presiding judge of a chamber, a job of greater importance and status with corresponding salary improvement. From there the main career path leads to the first appellate instance (Oberlandesgericht, hereafter OLG), which is also divided into many chambers, each led by a presiding judge who is promoted to that job after distinguishing himself as an ordinary judge of the court. And the final appellate instance, the federal supreme court for nonconstitutional law (Bundesgerichtshof, hereafter BGH), is staffed almost entirely with judges who have been promoted from the OLG.

Meritocratic review and promotion are meant to reward and thereby to inspire judges to be diligent on fact-gathering, to stay current in the law, and to be fair and accurate in the conduct of hearings and the rendering of judgments.

Specialization. I have been speaking throughout this article of the ordinary courts. Of the 17,000 judges who were sitting in Germany as of 1983, the most recent year for which the statistics are published, 13,000 sat in the ordinary courts. The others served in the specialized court systems for administrative law, tax and fiscal matters, labor and employment law, and social security. Furthermore, the Germans operate a separate supreme constitutional court (Bundesverfassungsgericht), to which the other courts refer some contentious constitutional business. Appointment to the constitutional court is by design highly political; members are seldom part of the career judiciary that I have been describing.

The specialized courts and the constitutional court siphon off business that Americans would expect to see in the ordinary courts. Within the German ordinary courts of first instance there are special divisions that have counterparts in our tradition—for crime, for what we would call probate, for domestic relations. In addition, commercial law matters are removed to specialized chambers. Thus, the German ordinary courts of first instance have a somewhat narrower diet than our own.

At the appellate level, including the first appellate instance (OLG) that proceeds by review de novo, there is extensive specialization. An OLG is quite large by our standards, sometimes staffed with more than a hundred judges, who sit in chambers containing four or five judges. Cases are allocated among these chambers on the basis of subject matter. All the medical malpractice cases go to one chamber, the maritime cases to another, and so forth. This system permits the judges to develop over the years just that sort of expertise in legal subspecialties that we expect of lawyers, particularly lawyers in large-firm practice, in the United States. The litigants get judges who know something about the field, in contra-distinction to the calculated amateurism of our appellate tradition.

Political influence. Judicial appointments and promotions issue in the name of the state or federal minister of justice, who is an important political official, usually a member of the state or federal parliament and of the cabinet. The minister acts in consultation with an advisory commission of senior judges; in some of the German states that commission has a formal veto power.

Directly political concerns appear to be very subordinated in the selection and advancement of judges. Because this subject is not much ventilated in the literature, I have inquired about it when talking with German judges and legal academics. The impression I have gained is that political considerations do not materially affect appointment or promotion until the level of the federal supreme court (BGH). Party balance is given weight in BGH appointments, but political connections do not substitute for merit. Positions on the BGH go to judges who have distinguished themselves on the OLG.

We must remember that the decision to isolate important components of constitutional and administrative-law jurisdiction outside the ordinary courts in Germany lowers the political stakes in judicial office, by comparison with our system, in which every federal district judge (and for that matter, every state judge) purports to brandish the Constitution and thus to be able to wreak major social and institutional change.

American contrasts. If I were put to the choice of civil litigation under the German procedure that I have been praising in this article or under the American procedure that I have been criticizing, I might have qualms about choosing the German. The likely venue of a lawsuit of mine would be the state court in Cook County, Illinois, and I must admit that I distrust the bench of that court. The judges are selected by a process in which the criterion of professional competence is at best an incidental value. Further, while decent people do reach the Cook County bench in surprising numbers, events have shown that some of their colleagues are crooks. If my lawsuit may fall into the hands of a dullard or a thug, I become queasy about increasing his authority over the proceedings.

German-style judicial responsibility for fact-gathering cannot be lodged with the Greylord judiciary. Remodeling of civil procedure is intimately connected to improvement in the selection of judges. I do not believe that we would have to institute a German-style career judiciary in order to reform American civil procedure along German lines, although I do think that Judge Frankel was right to "question whether we are wise" to disdain the Continental model, and to "wonder now whether we might benefit from some admixture of such [career judges] to leaven or test our trial benches of elderly lawyers." The difference in quality between the state and federal trial benches in places like Cook County is sufficient to remind us that measures far short of adopting the Continental career judiciary can bring about material improvement.

NOTES AND QUESTIONS

1. How are the two fundamental questions of procedural design posed by Brooks in chapter 3, "The Core Features and Values of the Traditional Model"—the allocation of function as between the judge and the parties for initiating and defining the dispute and for the development and presentation of proofs and arguments—resolved in the German procedural scheme? Later in the chapter we will examine instances in the administrative state where responsibility for the initiation, definition, and/or carriage of the case may be assigned neither to the decision maker nor to the parties but to an official attached to a statutory tribunal or agency.

2. Are you convinced of the German advantage in civil procedure? Is the procedural regime which Langbein describes likely to result in improved quality of testimony and greater efficiencies than a purely adversarial approach? Does it respond to some of the failings of the adversarial system identified by Rhode in chapter 3?

3. Recollect the recommendations of the Woolf report outlined in the article by Watson and Easthope, above. To what extent do they reflect an inquisitorially based system? Recollect the article by Zuker in chapter 1, "Introduction to Civil Actions and Courts," describing small claims court procedures. Do these procedures also reflect a mixed economy of adversarial and inquisitorial processes?

B. Case Management

As noted in the article by Watson and Easthope, case management has been at the centre of many recent civil justice reform efforts. As they observed, and as described in the readings that follow, case management reflects a significant departure in cultural mindset. There are arguably at least three ways in which case management reflects a departure from the mindset that created and sustained the traditional model. First there is the shift from party control to judicial control over the pace of the litigation—in other words, a shift away from strict reliance on the principle of party prosecution. As such, case management may be appropriately characterized as an incremental shift away from a purely adversarial model of adjudication completely dependent on party initiative. Second, and as discussed more fully below, case management also embraces ADR processes, particularly through the vehicles of the case conference (in which the judge plays a role in screening cases for alternative processes) and the settlement conference (in which the judge has a direct role in seeking to procure a settlement). Third, case management is regarded by some as representative of a fundamental shift in vision of the appropriate function of court-based litigation; a shift away from the vindication of private rights and toward simply getting cases settled in order to clear dockets.

Civil Justice Review, *First Report*
(Toronto: Ontario Civil Justice Review, March 1995) (footnotes omitted)

The notion of case management entails a significant shift in the cultural mind set that has characterized the processing of civil cases in our courts for generations.

In that tradition it has been the role of the lawyers, together with their clients, to decide if and when a lawsuit would proceed, and when various steps would be taken. They have done so within the framework of the Rules of Civil Procedure, and the time parameters laid out in those Rules. With few exceptions, however, the prevailing attitude in Ontario has always been that those time parameters are to be honoured more in the breach than in the observance.

There is a growing recognition that this mode of operation is no longer appropriate. It has ceased to work effectively in delivering civil justice to the public. Given the rising costs and unacceptable delays in litigation and the similarly escalating demands on the administration and the judiciary, it is apparent to us that we no longer have the resources as a society to permit this *laissez-faire* approach to the processing of cases to continue.

Caseflow management involves the transfer of principle responsibility for management of the pace of litigation to the judiciary. *It also involves the establishment of reasonable, but firm, time limits and the adherence to those parameters.* In short, caseflow management entails a more active form of management and intervention by the court in the various phases of litigation. It does so with a view to promoting the earlier resolution of cases, to eliminating unacceptable delays, and, ultimately, to reducing costs and enhancing the quality of justice.

Ideally, this intervention occurs early and also with some frequency during the life of the case. We have heard constantly from lawyers, administrators, judges and members of the public that *early intervention by the judiciary is of critical importance* in the disposition of cases. This is true in all cases, but is particularly true in family law cases. It is often, and in our view accurately, said that the more times one can build into the system an occasion when counsel has to pick up his or her file and think about it, the more likely it is that there will be an earlier resolution of the case.

We think this emphasis is important.

Studies show that approximately 55% of cases commenced never proceed to the point where a statement of defence is filed. They are either resolved by way of a default judgment, settled outside of the courts before reaching that stage, or any interest in pursuing them simply dissipates. The remaining 45% of the case load proceeds through various additional stages of litigation, with the vast majority settling at some point between the pleading stage and the eve or morning of trial.

The reality is that 95% to 97% of all civil cases are never tried. They are settled. This seems to be the experience in Anglo-Canadian-American court systems wherever located and regardless of the structure which is in place to process the flow of cases through the system.

If this is the reality, then, it makes sense that the overall mechanism for the disposition of disputes should focus on dealing with the vast majority of cases that settle, *as well as* focusing on those that have to be tried. Historically in Ontario, however, the primary focus has been on the processing of cases in preparation for trial.

Caseflow management permits the necessary broadening of perspective and emphasis from this primary focus to a duality of focus—disposition where possible, and trial where necessary. It does so by building in the potential for early—and if appropriate, repeated—judicial or quasi-judicial intervention. This is accomplished by means of case conferences which are either prescribed at fixed points in the process by the rules, or called at the instance of the case management judge or counsel. The case conference can take the form of an early evaluation or screening exercise; it can be used as an occasion to discuss the diversion of the dispute into one or another of the ADR channels; it can take the form of a settlement conference; or, if the case cannot be settled and is bound for trial, the case conference can take the form of a trial management conference. These events each provide occasions where the file must be dealt with by counsel. Moreover, they provide opportunities where the judge or the judicial support officer can work out with counsel how the case is to proceed.

Caseflow management is a concept which in our opinion offers great potential for combining and co-ordinating the various disparate elements of the civil justice system and integrating them into a more effective whole. It is able to do this by facilitating a combination of the following features:

  a) overall management of the case flow process by the judiciary;
  b) early intervention in a case either by a judge or by a quasi-judicial officer;
  c) the disposition of all interlocutory matters;
  d) the deployment of ADR mechanisms and techniques;
  e) the utilization of case conferences, settlement conferences and trial management conferences;
  f) the utilization of registrars, case management officers and judicial support officers to perform the administrative and quasi-judicial tasks which do not require a "section

96" judge to perform, thus freeing up judges to concentrate their efforts on the truly "judicial" activities of trying cases and assisting the parties in settling their disputes.

NOTES AND QUESTIONS

1. What operative vision of the function of the courts underpins case management?

2. What are the "public interests" articulated in favour of case management?

3. As noted in the introduction and in the above reading, while a central component of case management is active timetabling by the judiciary, case management systems often actively seek to promote settlement, particularly through the "conference." The Civil Justice Review in Ontario has led to the implementation of a new rule of practice before the Ontario Court (General Division), rule 77. The stated purposes of the rule are to reduce unnecessary cost and delay, to facilitate early and fair settlements, and to bring the proceedings expeditiously to a just determination (rule 77.02). The rule provides for three types of conferences: the case conference, the settlement conference, and the trial management conference. The purposes of the case management conference include the creation of a timetable, and the exploration of methods to resolve the contested issues (including a referral to ADR on consent). Settlement conferences are automatically scheduled at defined time intervals that vary depending on which of two tracks the case is proceeding on, the fast or standard track. As suggested in the introduction, case management, then, is potentially linked to our second broad conceptual category— informalism—through both the case conference and the settlement conference. Case management is to be gradually introduced throughout the province as various counties are added to the "schedule" to rule 77.

4. The implementation of case management is not without its critics. In an editorial in *The Advocates' Brief* (October 1998), Ronald G. Slaght, QC argues:

> As for me, I wish we had case management. Too bad we don't have case management. I doubt we'll get case management. We will probably get more of what we have now, which isn't case management.
>
> In Ontario, case management means team case management, with teams consisting of judges, a case management master and a case management bureaucracy, operating under a set of case management rules. Case management judges are not routinely appointed case by case, although this is contemplated by Rule 77.
>
> In that model, which I suggest is true case management, a judge is appointed to manage the litigation at some point early in the process, usually around the time a defence is filed. A variation on this theme is the combination of a case management judge and a fixed trial date, both in place early in the process. The latter is not achievable in Toronto for the foreseeable future. The ultimate in case management consists of the appointment of a case management judge, who will also try the case, and a fixed trial date, all early in the process.
>
> As we all now experience, much of case management in Toronto consists of managing the lawyers. Lawyers no longer have to work things out for themselves. Letters get fired around and positions are taken all with the secure knowledge that eventually someone calls up the judicial police, delays ensue, and matters get sorted out, at least for the time being. This, of course, does nothing for the time and costs of

litigation. Trial scheduling court for case managed actions takes longer, because the cases aren't ready when they get there.

The problem with our case management is that it is unfocused and defensive. The team approach is counter productive. No one is in charge. The case is dealt with piecemeal and mostly in reaction to procedural foul-ups for contentions, issue management is virtually impossible because there is no continuity. The office of the case management master is not a substitute for a well-informed judge who, with the credibility that knowledge and continuity bring, controls the lawyers, defines the issues and eliminates the chaff.

All of this is to say that, if we are to continue some form of case management, we should be sure that we are not just going through the motions but that the system we employ gets cases ready earlier with the hope that some costs are saved, and that issues are resolved or eliminated as part of the process so that trials are fewer or at least more reasonably managed.

Is this criticism justified?

5.   Lord Woolfe's reports (reviewed earlier) led to the introduction of entirely new rules in England, which came in to force in April 1999, embodying many of his recommendations. The very first rule sets out the overriding objective of the new rules and regime. To what extent do these objectives represent a modification of the adversary system model or radical change in how litigation is to be conducted?

The Overriding Objective

1.1(1) These Rules are a new procedural code with the overriding objective of enabling the court to deal with cases justly.

(2) Dealing with a case justly includes, so far as is practicable—

    (a) ensuring that the parties are on an equal footing;

    (b) saving expense;

    (c) dealing with the case in ways which are proportionate—

        (i) to the amount of money involved;

        (ii) to the importance of the case;

        (iii) to the complexity of the issues; and

        (iv) to the financial position of each party;

    (d) ensuring that it is dealt with expeditiously and fairly; and

    (e) allotting to it an appropriate share of the court's resources, while taking into account the need to allot resources to other cases.

Application by the Court of the Overriding Objective

1.2 The court must seek to give effect to the overriding objective when it—

    (a) exercises any power given to it by the Rules; or

    (b) interprets any rule.

Duty of the Parties

1.3 The parties are required to help the court to further the overriding objective.

Court's Duty To Manage Cases

1.4(1) The court must further the overriding objective by actively managing cases.

(2) Active case management includes—

(a) encouraging the parties to co-operate with each other in the conduct of the proceedings;

(b) identifying the issues at an early stage;

(c) deciding promptly which issues need full investigation and trial and accordingly disposing summarily of the others;

(d) deciding the order in which issues are to be resolved;

(e) encouraging the parties to use an alternative dispute resolution procedure if the court considers that appropriate and facilitating the use of such procedure;

(f) helping the parties to settle the whole or part of the case;

(g) fixing timetables or otherwise controlling the progress of the case;

(h) considering whether the likely benefits of taking a particular step justify the cost of taking it;

(i) dealing with as many aspects of the case as it can on the same occasion;

(j) dealing with the case without the parties needing to attend at court;

(k) making use of technology; and

(l) giving directions to ensure that the trial of a case proceeds quickly and efficiently.

6. For a review of the empirical data on the efficacy of various components of case management, see Kent Roach, "Fundamental Reforms to Civil Litigation," in Ontario Law Reform Commission, *Rethinking Civil Justice: Research Studies for the Civil Justice Review* (Toronto: Ontario Law Reform Commission, 1996), vol. 2, 381.

C. Public Law Litigation

The third and final sub-category under the broad category of "Adjudication Modified" is that of "public law litigation." Unlike the previous categories reviewed, it is neither the adversarial nature of adjudication nor the delay and costs associated with the traditional model that are understood to be the central failing of the traditional model. Rather, it is the preoccupation with the vindication of the rights of private individuals that is regarded as the central failing. As the following article by Chayes suggests, and about which there really is no debate, we are witnessing (both in Canada and the United States) the emergence of a new model of litigation, a model which some maintain is more "public law" oriented. The new model has emerged both through the introduction of specific procedural reforms and through the re-interpretation of existing common law doctrine and procedural rules (many of these specifics we examine in subsequent chapters). There has been, and continues to be, much debate about the desirability of these transformations to the traditional model.

Abram Chayes, "The Role of the Judge in Public Law Litigation"
(1976), 89 *Harvard Law Review* 1281 (footnotes omitted)

We are witnessing the emergence of a new model of civil litigation and, I believe, our traditional conception of adjudication and the assumptions upon which it is based provide an increasingly unhelpful, indeed misleading framework for assessing either the workability or the legitimacy of the roles of judge and court within this model.

In our received tradition, the lawsuit is a vehicle for settling disputes between private parties about private rights. The defining features of this conception of civil adjudication are:

(1) The lawsuit is *bipolar*. Litigation is organized as a contest between two individuals or at least two unitary interests, diametrically opposed, to be decided on a winner-takes-all basis.

(2) Litigation is *retrospective*. The controversy is about an identified set of completed events: whether they occurred, and if so with what consequences for the legal relations to the parties.

(3) *Right and remedy are interdependent.* The scope of the relief is derived more or less logically from the substantive violation under the general theory that the plaintiff will get compensation measured by the harm caused by the defendant's breach of duty—in contract by giving the plaintiff the money he would have had absent the breach; in tort by paying the value of the damage caused.

(4) The lawsuit is a *self-contained* episode. The impact of the judgment is confined to the parties. If plaintiff prevails there is a simple compensatory transfer, usually of money, but occasionally the return of a thing or the performance of a definite act. If defendant prevails, a loss lies where it has fallen. In either case, entry of judgment ends the court's involvement.

(5) The process is *party-initiated* and *party-controlled*. The case is organized and the issues defined by exchanges between the parties. Responsibility for fact development is theirs. The trial judge is a neutral arbiter of their interactions who decides questions of law only if they are put in issue by an appropriate move of a party. ...

Whatever its historical validity, the traditional model is clearly invalid as a description of much current civil litigation in the federal district courts. Perhaps the dominating characteristic of modern federal litigation is that lawsuits do not arise out of disputes between private parties about private rights. Instead, the object of litigation is the vindication of constitutional or statutory policies. The shift in the legal basis of the lawsuit explains many, but not all, facets of what is going on "in fact" in federal trial courts. For this reason, although the label is not wholly satisfactory, I shall call the emerging model "public law litigation."

The characteristic features of the public law model are very different from those of the traditional model. The party structure is sprawling and amorphous, subject to change over the course of the litigation. The traditional adversary relationship is suffused and intermixed with negotiating and mediating processes at every point. The judge is the dominant figure in organizing and guiding the case, and he draws for support not only on the parties and their counsel, but on a wide range of outsiders—masters, experts, and oversight personnel. Most important, the trial judge has increasingly become the creator and manager of complex forms of ongoing relief, which have widespread effects on persons not before the court and require the judge's continuing involvement in administration and implementation. School desegregation, employment discrimination, and prisoners' or inmates' rights cases come readily to mind as avatars of this new form of litigation. But it would be mistaken to suppose that it is confined to these areas. Antitrust, securities fraud and other aspects of the conduct of corporate business, bankruptcy and reorganizations, union governance, consumer fraud, housing discrimination, electoral reapportionment, environmental management—cases in all these fields display in varying degrees the features of public law litigation.

The object of this article is first to describe somewhat more fully the public law model and its departures from the traditional conception, and second, to suggest some of its consequences for the place of law and courts in the American political and legal system.

I. The Received Tradition

The traditional conception of adjudication reflected the late nineteenth century vision of society, which assumed that the major social and economic arrangements would result from the activities of autonomous individuals. In such a setting, the courts could be seen as an adjunct to private ordering, whose primary function was the resolution of disputes about the fair implications of individual interactions. The basic conceptions governing legal liability were "intention" and "fault." Intentional arrangements, not in conflict with more or less universal attitudes like opposition to force or fraud, were entitled to be respected, and other private activities to be protected unless culpable. Government regulatory action was presumptively suspect, and was tested by what was in form a common law action against the offending official in his private person. The predominating influence of the private law model can be seen even in constitutional litigation, which, from its first appearance in *Marbury v. Madison*, was understood as an outgrowth of the judicial duty to decide otherwise-existing private disputes.

Litigation also performed another important function—clarification of the law to guide future private actions. This understanding of the legal system, together with the common law doctrine of stare decisis, focussed professional and scholarly concern on adjudication at the appellate level, for only there did the process reach beyond the immediate parties to achieve a wider import through the elaboration of generally applicable legal rules. So, in the academic debate about the judicial function, the protagonist was the appellate judge (not, interestingly enough, the appellate *court*), and the spotlight of teaching, writing, and analysis was almost exclusively on appellate decisions. ...

In contrast to the appellate court, to which the motive power in the system was allocated, the functions of the trial judge were curiously neglected in the traditional model. Presumably, the trial judge, like the multitude of private persons who were supposed to order their affairs with reference to appellate pronouncements, would be governed by those decisions in disposing smoothly and expeditiously of the mine-run of cases. But if only by negative implication, the traditional conception of adjudication carried with it a set of strong notions about the role of the trial judge. In general he was passive. He was to decide only those issues identified by the parties, in accordance with the rules established by the appellate courts, or, infrequently, the legislature.

Passivity was not limited to the law aspects of the case. It was strikingly manifested in the limited involvement of the judge in factfinding. Indeed, the sharp distinction that Anglo-American law draws between factfinding and law declaration is itself remarkable. In the developed common law system, these were not only regarded as analytically distinct processes, but each was assigned to a different tribunal for performance. The jury found the facts. The judge was a neutral umpire, charged with little or no responsibility for the factual aspects of the case or for shaping and organizing the litigation for trial.

Because the immediate impact of the judgment was confined to the parties, the traditional model was relatively relaxed about the accuracy of its factfinding. If the facts were not assumed as stated in the pleadings or on the view most favorable to one of the parties or determined on the basis of burdens or presumptions, they were remitted to a kind of black box, the jury. True, some of the law of evidence reflects an active suspicion of the jury. And if the evidence adduced would not "rationally" support a finding for one party or the other, the case could be taken from the jury. But the limits of rationality are inevitably commodious. Even law application, unless there was a special verdict (never much favored in this country), was left to the jury's relatively untrammeled discretion. Indeed, one of the virtues of the jury was thought to be its exercise of a rough-hewn equity, deviating from the dictates of the law where justice or changing community mores required.

The emphasis on systematic statement of liability rules involved a corresponding disregard of the problems of relief. There was, to be sure, a good deal of discussion of measure of damages, as a corollary to the analysis of substantive rights and duties. Similarly, the question of the availability of specific performance and other equitable remedies came in for a share of attention. But the discussion was carried forward within the accepted framework that compensatory money damages was the usual form of relief. Prospective relief was highly exceptional in the traditional model and was largely remitted to the discretion of the trial judge. ...

Besides its inherent plausibility in the nineteenth century American setting, the traditional model of adjudication answered a number of important political and intellectual needs. The conception of litigation as a private contest between private parties with only minimal judicial intrusion confirmed the general view of government powers as stringently limited. The emphasis on the appellate function conceived as an exercise in deduction from a few embracing principles themselves induced from the data of the cases, supplied the demand of the new legal academics for an intellectual discipline comparable to that of their faculty colleagues in the sciences, and for a body of teachable materials. For practitioners and judges, the same conception provided a professional methodology that could be self-consciously employed. Most importantly, the formulation operated to legitimate the increasingly visible political consequences of the action of a judiciary that was not politically accountable in the usual sense.

II. The Public Law Litigation Model

Sometime after 1875, the private law theory of civil adjudication became increasingly precarious in the face of a growing body of legislation designed explicitly to modify and regulate basic social and economic arrangements. At the same time, the scientific and

deductive character of judicial lawmaking came under attack, as the political consequences of judicial review of that legislation became urgent.

These developments are well known and have become an accepted part of our
political and intellectual history. I want to address in somewhat greater detail the correlative changes that have occurred in the procedural structure of the lawsuit. Most
discussion of these procedural developments, while recognizing that change has been
far-reaching, proceeds on the assumption that the new devices are no more than piecemeal "reforms" aimed at improving the functional characteristics or the efficiency of
litigation conducted essentially in the traditional mode. I suggest, however, that these
developments are interrelated as members of a recognizable, if changing, system and
that taken together they display a new model of judicial action and the judicial role, both
of which depart sharply from received conceptions.

A. The Demise of the Bipolar Structure

Joinder of parties, which was strictly limited at common law, was verbally liberalized
under the codes to conform with the approach of equity calling for joinder of all parties
having an "interest" in the controversy. The codes, however, did not at first produce much
freedom of joinder. Instead, the courts defined the concept of "interest" narrowly to
exclude those without an independent legal right to the remedy to be given in the main
dispute. The definition itself illustrates the continuing power of the traditional model. The
limited interpretation of the joinder provisions ultimately fell before the banners of "rationality" and "efficiency." But the important point is that the narrow joinder rule could be
perceived as irrational or inefficient only because of a growing sense that the effects of the
litigation were not really confined to the persons at either end of the right-remedy axis.

The familiar story of the attempted liberalization of pleadings under the codes is not
dissimilar. Sweeping away the convolutions of the forms of action did not lead to the
hoped-for elimination of technicality and formality in pleading. The immediate response
was the construction of cause-of-action rules that turned out to be almost as intricate as
the forms themselves. The power of the right-remedy connection was at work here too,
but so also was the late nineteenth century impulse toward systemization, which tended
to focus attention on accurate statement of legal theory. The proponents of "efficiency"
argued for a more informal and flexible approach, to the end that the courts should not
have to rehear the same complex of events. This argument ultimately shifted the focus of
the lawsuit from legal theory to factual context—the "transaction or occurrence" from
which the action arose. This in turn made it easier to view the set of events in dispute as
giving rise to a range of legal consequences all of which ought to be considered together.

This more open-ended view of the subject matter of the litigation fed back upon
party questions and especially intervention. Here, too, the sharp constraints dictated by
the right-remedy nexus give way. And if the right to participate in litigation is no longer
determined by one's claim to relief at the hands of another party or one's potential
liability to satisfy the claim; it becomes hard to draw the line determining those who
may participate so as to eliminate anyone who is or might be significantly (a weasel
word) affected by the outcome—and the latest revision of the Federal Rules of Civil
Procedure has more or less abandoned the attempt.

The question of the right to intervene is inevitably linked to the question of standing to initiate litigation in the first place. The standing issue could hardly arise at common law or under early code pleading rules, that is, under the traditional model. There the question of plaintiff's standing merged with the legal merits: On the facts pleaded, does this particular plaintiff have a right to the particular relief sought from the particular defendant from whom he is seeking it? With the erosion of the tight structural integration of the lawsuit, the pressure to expand the circle of potential plaintiffs has been inexorable. Today, the Supreme Court is struggling manfully, but with questionable success, to establish a formula for delimiting who may sue that stops short of "anybody who might be significantly affected by the situation he seeks to litigate."

"Anybody"—even "almost anybody"—can be a lot of people, particularly where the matters in issue are not relatively individualized private transactions or encounters. Thus, the stage is set for the class action. ... Whatever the resolution of the current controversies surrounding class actions, I think it unlikely that the class action will ever be taught to behave in accordance with the precepts of the traditional model of adjudication. The class suit is a reflection of our growing awareness that a host of important public and private interactions—perhaps the most important in defining the conditions and opportunities of life for most people—are conducted on a routine or bureaucratized basis and can no longer be visualized as bilateral transactions between private individuals. From another angle, the class action responds to the proliferation of more or less well-organized groups in our society and the tendency to perceive interests as group interests, at least in very important aspects.

The emergence of the group as the real subject or object of the litigation not only transforms the party problem, but raises far-reaching new questions. How far can the group be extended and homogenized? To what extent and by what methods will we permit the presentation of views diverging from that of the group representative? When the judgment treads on numerous—perhaps innumerable—absentees, can the traditional doctrines of finality and preclusion hold? And in the absence of a particular client, capable of concretely defining his own interest, can we rely on the assumptions of the adversary system as a guide to the conduct and duty of the lawyer?

These questions are brought into sharp focus by the class action device. But it would be a mistake to think that they are confined to that procedural setting. The class action is only one mechanism for presenting group interests for adjudication, and the same basic questions will arise in a number of more familiar litigating contexts. Indeed, it may not be too much to say that they are pervasive in the new model.

B. *The Triumph of Equity*

One of the most striking procedural developments of this century is the increasing importance of equitable relief. It is perhaps too soon to reverse the traditional maxim to read that money damages will be awarded only when no suitable form of specific relief can be devised. But surely, the old sense of equitable remedies as "extraordinary" has faded.

I am not concerned here with specific performance—the compelled transfer of a piece of land or a unique thing. This remedy is structurally little different from traditional money-damages. It is a one-time, one-way transfer requiring for its enforcement no continuing involvement of the court. Injunctive relief, however, is different in kind, even when it takes the form of a simple negative order. Such an order is a presently operative prohibition, enforceable by contempt, and it is a much greater constraint on activity than the risk of future liability implicit in the damage remedy. Moreover, the injunction is continuing. Over time, the parties may resort to the court for enforcement or modification of the original order in light of changing circumstances. Finally, by issuing the injunction, the court takes public responsibility for any consequences of its decree that may adversely affect strangers to the action.

Beyond these differences, the prospective character of the relief introduces large elements of contingency and prediction into the proceedings. Instead of a dispute retrospectively oriented toward the consequences of a closed set of events, the court has a controversy about future probabilities. Equitable doctrine, naturally enough, given the intrusiveness of the injunction and the contingent nature of the harm, calls for a balancing of the interests of the parties. And if the immediate parties' interests were to be weighed and evaluated, it was not too difficult to proceed to a consideration of other interests that might be affected by the order. ...

C. The Changing Character of Factfinding

The traditional model of adjudication was primarily concerned with assessing the consequences for parties of specific past instances of conduct. This retrospective orientation is often inapposite in public law litigation, where the lawsuit generally seeks to enjoin future or threatened action, or to modify a course of conduct presently in train or a condition presently existing. In the former situation, the question whether threatened action will materialize, in what circumstances, and with what consequences can, in the nature of things, be answered only by an educated guess. In the latter case, the inquiry is only secondarily concerned with how the condition came about, and even less with the subjective attitudes of the actors, since positive regulatory goals are ordinarily defined without reference to such matters. Indeed, in dealing with the actions of large political or corporate aggregates, notions of will, intention, or fault increasingly become only metaphors.

In the remedial phases of public law litigation, factfinding is even more clearly prospective. ... [T]he contours of relief are not derived logically from the substantive wrong adjudged, as in the traditional model. The elaboration of a decree is largely a discretionary process within which the trial judge is called upon to assess and appraise the consequences of alternative programs that might correct the substantive fault. In both the liability and remedial phases, the relevant inquiry is largely the same: How can the policies of a public law best be served in a concrete case?

In public law litigation, then, factfinding is principally concerned with "legislative" rather than "adjudicative" fact. And "fact evaluation" is perhaps a more accurate term than "factfinding." The whole process begins to look like the traditional description of legislation: Attention is drawn to a "mischief," existing or threatened, and the activity of the parties and court is directed to the development of on-going measures designed to cure that mischief. Indeed, if, as is often the case, the decree sets up an affirmative regime governing the activities in controversy for the indefinite future and having binding force for persons within its ambit, then it is not very much of a stretch to see it as, pro tanto, a legislative act. ...

D. The Decree

The centerpiece of the emerging public law model is the decree. It differs in almost every relevant characteristic from relief in the traditional model of adjudication, not the least in that it *is* the centerpiece. The decree seeks to adjust future behavior, not to compensate for past wrong. It is deliberately fashioned rather than logically deduced from the nature of the legal harm suffered. It provides for a complex, on-going regime of performance rather than a simple, one-shot, one-way transfer. Finally, it prolongs and deepens, rather than terminates, the court's involvement with the dispute.

The decree is also an order of the court, signed by the judge and issued under his responsibility (itself a shift from the classical money judgment). But it cannot be supposed that the judge, at least in a case of any complexity, composes it out of his own head. How then is the relief formulated?

The reports provide little guidance on this question. Let me nonetheless suggest a prototype that I think finds some support in the available materials. The court will ask the parties to agree on an order or it will ask one party to prepare a draft. In the first case, a negotiation is stipulated. In the second, the dynamic leads almost inevitably in that direction. The draftsman understands that his proposed decree will be subject to comment and objection by the other side and that it must be approved by the court. He is therefore likely to submit it to his opponents in advance to see whether differences cannot be resolved. Even if the court itself should prepare the initial draft of the order, some form of negotiation will almost inevitably ensue upon submission of the draft to the parties for comment.

The negotiating process ought to minimize the need for judicial resolution of remedial issues. Each party recognizes that it must make some response to the demands of the other party, for issues left unresolved will be submitted to the court, a recourse that is always chancy and may result in a solution less acceptable than might be reached by horse-trading. Moreover, it will generally be advantageous to the demanding party to reach a solution through accommodation rather than through a judicial fiat that may be performed "in a literally compliant but substantively grudging and unsatisfactory way." Thus, the formulation of the decree in public law litigation introduces a good deal of party control over the practical outcome. Indeed, relief by way of order after a determination on the merits tends to converge with relief through a consent decree or voluntary settlement. And this in turn mitigates a major theoretical objection to affirmative relief— the danger of intruding on an elaborate and organic network of interparty relationships.

Nevertheless it cannot be supposed that this process will relieve the court entirely of responsibility for fashioning the remedy. The parties may fail to agree. Or the agreement reached may fail to comport with the requirements of substantive law as the judge sees them. Or the interests of absentees may be inadequately accommodated. In these situations, the judge will not, as in the traditional model, be able to derive his responses directly from the liability determination, since, as we have seen, the substantive law will point out only the general direction to be pursued and a few salient landmarks to be sought out or avoided. How then is the judge to prescribe an appropriate remedy?

If the parties are simply in disagreement, it seems plausible to suppose that the judge's choice among proposals advanced by the *quondam* negotiators will be governed by his appraisal of their good faith in seeking a way to implement the constitutional or statutory command as he has construed it. The interest in a decree that will be voluntarily obeyed can be promoted by enforcing a regime of good faith bargaining among the parties. Without detailed knowledge of the negotiations, however, any attempt to enforce such a regime can rest on little more than an uneasy base of intuition and impression. Where a proposed decree is agreed upon among the parties, but is inadequate because the interests shared by the litigants do not span the range that the court thinks must be taken into account, resubmission for further negotiation may not cure this fundamental defect. Here too, the judge will be unable to fill the gap without a detailed understanding of the issues at stake in the bargaining among the parties. ...

E. A Morphology of Public Law Litigation

The public law litigation model portrayed in this paper reverses many of the crucial characteristics and assumptions of the traditional concept of adjudication:

(1) The scope of the lawsuit is not exogenously given but is shaped primarily by the court and parties.

(2) The party structure is not rigidly bilateral but sprawling and amorphous.

(3) The fact inquiry is not historical and adjudicative but predictive and legislative.

(4) Relief is not conceived as compensation for past wrong in a form logically derived from the substantive liability and confined in its impact to the immediate parties; instead, it is forward looking, fashioned ad hoc on flexible and broadly remedial lines, often having important consequences for many persons including absentees.

(5) The remedy is not imposed but negotiated.

(6) The decree does not terminate judicial involvement in the affair: its administration requires the continuing participation of the court.

(7) The judge is not passive, his function limited to analysis and statement of governing legal rules; he is active, with responsibility not only for credible fact evaluation but for organizing and shaping the litigation to ensure a just and viable outcome.

(8) The subject matter of the lawsuit is not a dispute between private individuals about private rights, but a grievance about the operation of public policy.

In fact, one might say that, from the perspective of the traditional model, the proceeding is recognizable as a lawsuit only because it takes place in a courtroom before an official called a judge. But that is surely too sensational in tone. All of the procedural mechanisms outlined above were historically familiar in equity practice. It is not surprising that they should be adopted and strengthened as the importance of equity has grown in modern times. ...

III. A First Appraisal

• • •

In practice, all government officials, including judges, have exercised a large and messy admixture of powers, and that is as it must be. That is not to say that institutional

characteristics are irrelevant in assigning governmental tasks or that judges should unreservedly be thrust directly into political battles. But such considerations should be taken
as cautionary, not decisive; for despite its well rehearsed inadequacies, the judiciary may
have some important institutional advantages for the tasks it is assuming:

First, and perhaps most important, is that the process is presided over by a judge.
His professional tradition insulates him from narrow political pressures, but, given the
operation of the federal appointive power and the demands of contemporary law practice, he is likely to have some experience of the political process and acquaintance with
a fairly broad range of public policy problems. Moreover, he is governed by a professional
ideal of reflective and dispassionate analysis of the problem before him and is likely to
have had some experience in putting this ideal into practice.

Second, the public law model permits ad hoc applications of broad national policy
in situations of limited scope. The solution can be tailored to the needs of the particular
situation and flexibly administered or modified as experience develops with the regime
established in the particular case.

Third, the procedure permits a relatively high degree of participation by representatives of those who will be directly affected by the decision, without establishing a
liberum veto.

Fourth, the court, although traditionally thought less competent than legislatures or
administrative agencies in gathering and assessing information, may have unsuspected
advantages in this regard. Even the diffused adversarial structure of public law litigation
furnishes strong incentives for the parties to produce information. If the party structure
is sufficiently representative of the interests at stake, a considerable range of relevant
information will be forthcoming. And, because of the limited scope of the proceeding,
the information required can be effectively focused and specified. Information produced
will not only be subject to adversary review, but as we have seen, the judge can engage
his own experts to assist in evaluating the evidence. Moreover, the information that is
produced will not be filtered through the rigid structures and preconceptions of
bureaucracies.

Fifth, the judicial process is an effective mechanism for registering and responding to
grievances generated by the operation of public programs in a regulatory state. Unlike an
administrative bureaucracy or a legislature, the judiciary *must* respond to the complaints
of the aggrieved. It is also rather well situated to perform the task of balancing the
importance of competing policy interests in a specific situation. The legislature, perhaps,
could balance, but it cannot address specific situations. The bureaucracy deals with specific situations, but only from a position of commitment to particular policy interests.

Sixth, the judiciary has the advantage of being non-bureaucratic. It is effective in
tapping energies and resources outside itself and outside the government in the exploration of the situation and the assessment of remedies. It does not work through a rigid,
multilayered hierarchy of numerous officials, but through a smallish, representative task
force, assembled ad hoc, and easily dismantled when the problem is finally resolved. ...

There are also counter-instances and counter-arguments for each of the advantages of
the public law model suggested above. Can the disinterestedness of the judge be sustained, for example, when he is more visibly a part of the political process? Will the
consciously negotiated character of the relief ultimately erode the sense that what is being

applied is law? Can the relatively unspecialized trial judge, even with the aid of the new authority and techniques being developed in public law litigation, respond adequately to the demands for legislative and predictive factfinding in the new model? Against the asserted "responsiveness" of the courts, it may be argued that the insensitivity of other agencies represents a political judgment that should be left undisturbed. And although the courts may be well situated to balance competing policy interests in the particular case, if as is often true the decree calls for a substantial commitment of resources, the court has little basis for evaluating competing claims on the public purse. Each of these considerations needs exploration in much more detail—although I would hope that the discussion would proceed on the basis of what has been happening in the cases rather than a priori. ...

IV. Some Thoughts on Legitimacy

... As the traditional model has been displaced in recent years, ... questions of judicial legitimacy and accountability have reasserted themselves. ...

For it cannot be denied that public law litigation explicitly rejects many of the constraints of judicial method and procedure in which we have characteristically sought respite from the unease. Now, I do not deny that the law, like other creative and performing arts, encompasses a recognizable (and teachable) technique; and this technique plays an important part in the development of the medium and in the criticism and evaluation of its practitioners. But in the law, as elsewhere, technical virtuosity has never been a guarantee of acceptable performance.

Moreover, an amalgam of less tangible institutional factors will continue to operate to shape judicial performance in the public law system as in the past: general expectations as to the competence and conscientiousness of federal judges; professional traditions of conduct and performance; the accepted, often tacit, canons and leeways of office. These are amorphous. They mark no sharp boundaries. ...

More fundamentally, our transformed appreciation of the whole process of making, implementing, and modifying law in a public law system points to sources other than professional method and role for the legitimacy of the new model lawsuit. As we now begin to see it, that proces is plastic and fluid. Popular participation in it is not alone through the vote or by representation in the legislature. And judicial participation is not by way of sweeping and immutable statements of *the* law, but in the form of a continous and rather tentative dialogue with other political elements—Congress and the executive, administrative agencies, the profession and the academics, the press and wider publics. Bentham's "judge and company" has become a conglomerate. In such a setting, the ability of a judicial pronouncement to sustain itself in the dialogue and the power of judicial action to generate assent over the long haul become the ultimate touchstones of legitimacy.

In my view, judicial action only achieves such legitimacy by responding to, indeed by stirring, the deep and durable demand for justice in our society. I confess some difficulty in seeing how this is to be accomplished by erecting the barriers of the traditional conception to turn aside, for example, attacks on exclusionary zoning and police violence, two of the ugliest remaining manifestations of official racism in American life. In practice, if not in words, the American legal tradition has always acknowledged the importance of substantive results for the legitimacy and accountability of judicial action.

NOTES AND QUESTIONS

1. While Chayes is writing in the context of procedural developments in the United States, many of the same procedural developments have occurred in various Canadian jurisdictions. In later chapters we take up several of these specific changes—for example, those related to the scope of discovery, party structure, standing, intervention, and class actions. At the same time, not all of what Chayes describes accurately reflects the Canadian context. To date, the Canadian judiciary has been less involved in the sort of active judicial supervision that Chayes describes in relation to the decree, a point that is developed in the article by Roach, later in the chapter.

2. To what extent is the public law model favoured by Chayes premised on judges' receptivity to the substantive issues argued in such cases, including questions dealing with the environment, prisoners' rights, and civil rights. Given that the political complexion of the US judiciary, and in particular the Supreme Court, has recently been reshaped by conservative appointments by presidents Reagan and Bush, would Chayes be as optimistic concerning the public model today? What does Chayes mean, at the end of the excerpt, when he says, "In practice, if not in words, the American legal tradition has always acknowledged the importance of substantive results for the legitimacy and accountability of judicial action"?

3. The public model has many critics. One of the most articulate and thorough is D. Horowitz, *The Courts and Social Policy* (Washington, DC: Brookings Instituion, 1977).

4. Others have also written on models of civil procedure, contrasting a "behaviour modification" model (emphasizing prevention and deterrence) and a "conflict resolution" model (emphasizing retrospective compensation and dispute settlement): see, for example, Scott, "Two Models of the Civil Process" (1975), 27 *Stanford Law Review* 937; Garth, "Conflicts and Dissent in Class Actions: A Suggested Perspective" (1982), 77 *Northwestern University Law Review* 492; Wildsmith, "An American Model of Civil Process in a Canadian Landscape" (1980), 6 *Dalhousie Law Journal* 71; Lindblom, "Group Actions in Civil Procedure in Sweden" (published in the Swedish National Reports to the XIIIth International Congress of Comparative Law in Montreal 1990 (Uppsala, 1990)). Lindblom refers to the Swedish proceduralist Professor Ekelöf who, 50 years ago, conceived of civil procedure as having long-term effects on the morality and sense of duty of the citizens and thereby on their behaviour. By contrast, the US commentators (above) see behaviour modification as coming principally through deterrence resulting from "cost internalization"; the effects of the litigation on the defendant will or should lead others in the same position to find it economically rational to abstain from actions of a kind that might give rise to future legal actions. The goal of the competing model—the conflict resolution model—is different, and much more modest: "It is more important for society that the dispute be settled peacefully than it be settled in any particular way" (Scott, "Two Models of the Civil Process," above). It can be argued that the conflict resolution and behaviour modification models are not contradictory and competing (in the same way as the "crime control model" and the "due process model" are in criminal proceedings): effective conflict resolution at the individual level leads to behaviour modification at the general level, and vice versa. Consequently, it is argued, both models contribute to the overall function of civil procedure: the maximum realization of the values underlying the substantive law. But, in fact, the conflict resolution and behaviour modification models in civil procedure do not always walk hand in hand. For example,

various issues (such as standing, and the role of class actions in civil procedure) may be resolved in quite different ways according to which of the two models is emphasized.

Lindblom and Watson, "Courts and Lawyers Facing Complex Litigation Problems," in the *General Report to the Meeting of the International Association of Procedural Law* (Lisbon, August 1991), make the following observations:

> Conflict resolution resulting in retrospective compensation, with an emphasis on increased access to justice for the individual acting as plaintiff, is considered all over the world as a relevant (and by some the only relevant) function of civil procedure. Behaviour modification with its emphasis on deterrence is a more controversial perspective and model. Some proceduralists, such as Professor Ekelöf, define behaviour modification as the principal function and individual conflict resolution as a by-product. But some are unwilling to accept behaviour modification as a task for civil proceedings and private law at all. The development towards "public law litigation" in the [United States] during the 60s and 70s was well tuned to the efforts to use civil litigation as a tool for behaviour modification, but "the spirit of the 80s" gives expression to the opposite view. Discussions about the function of civil procedure in general, and group actions in particular, seem to have a parallel in the political arena.

The contrast that Chayes presents between the traditional dispute resolution model and the public law model has been brought to life by a debate between Owen Fiss and Ernest Weinrib. Owen Fiss is a US champion of the public law model that Chayes describes. He has argued that Weinrib's theory of corrective justice is deficient in modern contexts and that Canadian adjudication is not suited to the challenge of the Charter because it is based on Weinrib's theory of corrective justice. See Fiss, "Coda" (1988), 38 *University of Toronto Law Journal* 229.

In the following piece, Weinrib defends the traditional model as based on corrective justice, which for him provides the only coherent explanation of private law adjudication in courts as distinct from various distributive strategies, such as social security and "no fault" insurance schemes pursued by legislatures.

Ernest Weinrib, "Adjudication and Public Values: Fiss's Critique of Corrective Justice"
(1989), 39 *University of Toronto Law Journal* 1, at 3-17 (footnotes omitted)

Fiss's criticism of corrective justice is harsh. He concludes that

> [t]he corrective model might, as Weinrib hopes, achieve an elegance and neatness that will always be slightly beyond the reach of [the] structural model—whether it be in the field of torts or in constitutional litigation—but the fact remains that any court system held to it would become an empty and trivial institution. The "inner intelligibility" that Weinrib's model of corrective justice promises might be of great attraction to the scholastics and to others drawn to formal systems, but of no interest to anyone else, especially those seeking justice. ...

Corrective justice is part of a complex of ideas that goes to the significance of publicness for legal ordering. It underlies the intelligibility of *private* law in a way that brings to light the *public* character of such law. This is a paradox only to those who think words. Negatively, corrective justice involves the denial that publicness depends on collectively determined distributive considerations. Positively, the publicness of corrective justice arises out of the intelligible structure of doing and suffering. Thus, through corrective justice private law can be public in the truest and deepest sense: not merely the manifestation of a power to which all are subordinated, but an expression of the rationality common to all agents. ...

Before "Coda" the disfavoured position was what Fiss termed "dispute resolution." In Fiss's formulation, dispute resolution has no public dimension: the world that dispute resolution presupposes is exhaustively filled by the private desires of individuals. Disputes are purely private because "only the interests and behaviour of the immediate parties to the dispute are at issue." Clashes between individuals require some mechanism that restores the peace, because peace is itself a precondition of satisfying private ends. But the terms on which peace is restored are of concern only to the parties themselves. Just as only *their* interests are engaged in the dispute, so only *their* interests are engaged in its resolution. So indifferent is dispute resolution to public values that, from a public perspective, nothing would be lost if the dispute were to be settled by flipping a coin. ...

Corrective justice wreaks havoc on this too-easy contrast between the atomistic privacy of dispute resolution and the publicity that allows the structural model. Corrective justice is characterized by many of the features (individualized party structure, transactional causation, and so on) that Fiss had associated with dispute resolution. Under corrective justice, however, these features are not unadulteratedly private. By showing that the conception of litigation he disfavours has a public dimension, the theory of corrective justice engages Fiss on the very ground he sought to monopolize for his structural model. Corrective justice thus undermines the basis on which his advocacy of structural reform rests.

Corrective justice involves publicness in every way that dispute resolution does not. Consider, first, the connection between the parties. Under corrective justice, the parties are necessarily in a normative relationship to each other. Activity is not divorced from its potential effect on others, but is seen as inherently interactional. Far from being locked into the privacy of their own desires, actors are under the obligation always to execute their purposes subject to the constraints flowing from the presence of others. The world of corrective justice is social, not atomistic.

Moreover, corrective justice denies the disjunction between the existence and the resolution of controversy. Adjudication under corrective justice is not merely the production of a new effect that has no intelligible connection to the dispute that occasioned it. The point of litigation is to determine and undo the wrong. The correction is essentially connected to the contours of the dispute. The court's function in accomplishing this correction is to retrace the defendant's action and bring it into conformity with the norms inhering in interaction. The coin-flipping of Fiss's dispute resolution has no place here.

Nor does the dispute concern only the disputants. In corrective justice a specific episode of interaction is viewed from a general standpoint. The norms governing this episode of doing and suffering are applicable to all potential doers and sufferers. To be sure, each controversy is about a particular interaction. But because every adjudicated case requires an interpretation of the normativity latent in interaction generally, all interactors are implicated in the court's decision.

Because adjudication under corrective justice reflects the general nature of human interaction, the court's holdings are systematically related to one another. The presupposition of corrective justice is that the relationship of doer and sufferer is coherently normative. Therefore, the interpretations of this normativity in particular instances must themselves form a coherent whole. Under corrective justice, doing and suffering are explicated through a network of concepts that connect holdings to one another.

Thus, corrective justice matches the unremitting privacy of Fiss's "dispute resolution" with an equally extreme publicness. Where dispute resolution has an atomistic satisfaction of private desire, corrective justice has the social relationship of doer and sufferer. Where dispute resolution treats the disputants as irredeemably enclosed in private worlds, corrective justice makes them participants in a publicly intelligible interaction. Where dispute resolution posits no connection between dispute and resolution or among different resolutions, corrective justice requires that judgments systematically embody the norms implicit in doing and suffering. ...

Fiss comments on ... [the] universalism [of corrective justice] as follows:

> Corrective justice, as conceived by Weinrib, implies no particular conception of the good; the value it seeks to further is the presupposition of all human institutions. Corrective justice might thus be able to achieve an emphatic universalism of a transhistorical or transcultural character, while structural reform is limited by the constitutional or political or social context that shapes and informs the public values or social ideas that it seeks to further. But, of course, that is as it must be and should be. I believe with Weinrib that law cannot be the instrument of any partisan interest within a society, but I do not understand why it must be infused with the transhistorical or transcultural—the global—ambitions that Weinrib attributes to it. Law is the institution of a particular society, and must by necessity reflect the values and constitutional structure of that society. To aspire for a more universal scope is to confuse philosophy and law.

At the heart of this criticism lies a contrast between universalism and the "society-by-society, era-by-era relativism" that Fiss accepts. He sees relativism as a consequence of the tie between law and public values. Such values are geographically and temporally confined to the persons and communities who happen to be committed to them. Thus, "[T]oday, sexual equality is a public value of America and Canada, but not of Iran." What plays in New Haven does not play in Qum.

Now relativism is at least as ancient as the sophists, and this is not the place to rehearse its merits or demerits. What is notable here is Fiss's ringing assertion that his relativism "is not the kind of relativism that would undermine the inherent worth and dignity of the law." Fiss does not notice that this claim involves him in a contradiction. Consider societies such as Iran or Nazi Germany, where the public values are (let us suppose) moral abominations. Fiss's premise is that law takes its character from the particular public values that it reflects. Yet Fiss also believes that law has an inherent worth and dignity. Where does this inherent worth come from? It cannot derive from the public values of societies like Iran or Nazi Germany, because those particular values have, *ex hypothesi*, no worth or dignity. Neither can the law's inherent worth have some other source; if it did, the law's character would not be determined by the society's public values. ...

When the controversy over the structural model is put to one side, Fiss and I divide on two large issues. The first concerns the nature of adjudication. Fiss describes his own position in these terms: "My conception of adjudication starts from the top—the office of the judge—and works down ... I start with the conception of power embodied in the judge." For Fiss, the understanding of law begins with the recognition that the courts exercise power over those who are subordinate to them. This power is constrained by other manifestations of power: the professionally disciplining rules of interpretation and the public values, whether good or bad, that happen to obtain at a given time and place.

Corrective justice, in contrast, starts from the bottom and works up. The primary focus of understanding is on the inherently normative nature of action and interaction. The understanding of law begins with the structures of justification immanent in coherent juridical relationships. Law does not waft down from above; it percolates up from below, as courts shape legal reality to the contours of a rationality latent in interaction. The judge is not so much power embodied as (in Aristotle's immortal words) justice ensouled.

These two positions construe the relationship between power and reason in converse ways. Although Fiss sees adjudication as an opportunity "to use reason to confront state power," first and foremost he conceives of courts themselves as instrumentalities of state power. Reason is for him the reflex of official power as it interprets public values. Corrective justice, in contrast, begins with the possibility of coherent and intelligible juridical relationships. Power here is the reflex of reason as it elaborates the order of an inchoately ordered legal world.

The following article assesses the debate between Weinrib and Fiss in the context of law and politics in Canada and the United States.

Kent Roach, "Teaching Procedures: The Fiss/Weinrib Debate in Practice"
(1991), 41 *University of Toronto Law Journal* 247, at 247-86 (footnotes omitted)

[Professors Owen Fiss of Yale and Ernest Weinrib of Toronto have engaged in a provocative debate about adjudication. Fiss argues that adjudication must respond to the political and sociological realities of modern society and adjust its focus away from correcting discrete acts of wrongdoing between individuals and toward achieving greater compliance with public standards. The paradigmatic lawsuit for him is a case brought by a group, one that results in a judge's issuing a series of detailed "structural" injunctions designed to manage and eventually reform a public institution such as a school, hospital, or prison so that it comes closer to the standards set out in the constitution or other public laws. Weinrib argues that the very nature of private law is its ability to rectify identified acts of wrongdoing and correct the harms that one party causes to another. Thus, the paradigmatic lawsuit for him is the simplest of torts actions: one individual seeks correction for the damage that he or she received through the wrongful negligence of another. If courts abandon their task of correcting the wrongs that one party causes to another, they will pursue instrumental and distributive strategies that are best left, for reasons of institutional competence and democratic theory, to legislatures and agencies.]

In his 1987 Cecil Wright Memorial Lecture, Owen Fiss ventured beyond his critique of Ernest Weinrib's theory of corrective justice to make a broader point that Canadian legal culture is characterized by a traditional view of litigation as the settlement of disputes arising from discrete acts of wrongdoing. This view of law is consistent, and indeed, in Fiss's opinion, even influenced by Weinrib's theory. Fiss's characterization of Canadian legal culture is troubling at a time when courts and litigation are assuming important roles in Canada's political life. With the Charter, has not Canada's legal culture shifted away from Britain and towards the United States? Yet Fiss suggests that the Canadian understanding of adjudication is still well behind the times, "more English than American, more private than public, more oriented toward automobile accidents than the pursuit of equality."

No doubt Fiss underestimated some public law dimensions of Canadian litigation in the age of the Charter. However, those with a passing familiarity with American procedural innovations ... will find it difficult to dispute that he has a point about the present ability of litigation in Canada to achieve the type of structural reform he envisages American courts accomplishing. For example, stricter Anglo-Canadian pleading rules requiring specific factual allegations may inhibit novel legal claims that demand wide-ranging discovery to reveal complex patterns of causation. The procedural conservatism of the Canadian judiciary has prevented the judicial development of the class action as an effective means to stimulate reform litigation. Even if a judicial willingness to make procedural innovations in the absence of comprehensive legislation existed, formidable impediments produced by traditional Anglo-Canadian cost, fee, and financing structures would deter most plaintiffs from advancing innovative claims on behalf of diffuse groups. These procedural features, as well as the role played by workers' compensation and other legislative and administrative machinery that preclude civil actions, help explain why there has been little Canadian experience with public interest litigation.

On the constitutional side, litigation concerning conditions in custodial institutions in Canada has been successful in dealing with traditional problems of due process for the individual but not in achieving systemic reform. Although some Canadian courts have undertaken the difficult task of structural reform in order to implement language rights, they seem to be more comfortable with suggestions to legislatures that they, not the courts, implement the complex remedies required by new constitutional rights. This may be related to the retention of the traditional position that courts should not make coercive equitable orders against the Crown. Likewise, Canadian courts have not used masters or judicially enforced consent decrees to administer complex remedies. If Canadian proceduralists do not devote nearly as much attention to the public law model of courts engaging in structural reform, the reasons may be related to the relative absence of raw material as much as to any acceptance of Weinrib's understanding of adjudication over that of Fiss.

Fiss's attack on the Canadian legal system leaves him vulnerable to a counter-assault disputing the ability of the American political system to implement public values. Fiss fails to note that the shortcoming of Canadian litigation is at least partly compensated by the ability of Canadian political and social processes to implement reforms. Ian Scott, then Attorney General of Ontario, may, in Fiss's opinion, be a "Robert Kennedy of the North" tragically harnessed by a horse-and-buggy vision of adjudication, but that did not stop him from introducing legislative and administrative reforms whenever he could persuade his colleagues in Cabinet. Given Canadian traditions of parliamentary government, it is much easier for attorneys general to implement public values than their American counterparts. Likewise, the willingness of Canadian governments to refer structural reform matters to judges in reference cases or to commissions of inquiry should not be ignored, even if their findings sometimes are. The mandates and range of participants in both reference cases and commissions of inquiry would make the most activist of American judges blush. The viability of the Canadian political process is a matter of pride and opportunity for many Canadian commentators who reject Fiss's vision of adjudication, and even for those who believe that courts should play a greater role.

In turn the Canadian political process makes the limited role courts will play under corrective justice easier to tolerate. Ernest Weinrib as a Canadian citizen applauds the role of the Canadian state in providing social welfare, medical and insurance benefits for the injured, and criticizes the parsimony of the American social security system. He has argued that the policy-driven, distributive, and public law character of American tort law is related to: "the ineffectiveness of the legislative process, the consciousness of the revolutionary origins of legal order, the modeling of adjudication on the interpretation of a constitution continually beset by crisis"; while the preservation in Canada "of a more pristine conception of private law" is related to "the sustained liberal and even social democratic influence on the political process and by a conservative tradition that encouraged the realization of the public good through state action." The Canadian reluctance to rely on courts for social justice fits most comfortably within the broad structure of Weinrib's thought. Adjudication serves the corrective task of rectifying discrete wrongs between individuals by restoring the status quo ante of existing distributions. The prior distribution of resources between groups is left to the legislative process.

It is understandable why Fiss did not celebrate the Canadian attraction to legislative and administrative means to implement public values. Fiss's view of the judiciary as the body institutionally suited to give meaning to public values makes him suspicious of the use of negotiation designed to produce consent and accommodation in the political process. If pushed, Fiss might find support for his theory of adjudication in the practices of his homeland. "Adjudication American-style" for him is a source of pride and a tribute to a particular national commitment to justice exemplified in *Brown v. Board of Education*. Should Fiss's suspicions about the legislative process be checked at the border? If so, does this lead Canadians to accept Weinrib's view of adjudication? ...

The institutional preoccupations that Fiss and Weinrib share are in the end as important as their theoretical differences. They have judges speak in different but equally privileged tongues that diminish alternative forms of social ordering. Given the important role lawyers play in resolving not only legal but social, economic, and political conflicts and the need to recognize our individual, group, and communal identities in all these decisions, legal education should no longer be constrained by the individualistic vision of corrective justice or the collectivistic vision of public law litigation. Neither should it promote comfortable dichotomies between the work of courts and that of legislatures and agencies because of the dangers they present for those who cannot benefit within the individualistic structures of corrective justice or win reforms in the political arena. A society that cannot imagine its disadvantaged going to court to achieve reform will have an impoverished sense of justice; one that relies on such Herculean efforts will have an illusory one.

QUESTIONS

1. Is Roach arguing that we are not, in fact, so far behind the United States in terms of the sophistication of our legal procedures (in other words, that Fiss has the description wrong)? Or is his argument more along the lines that we are different (our legislatures are much more responsive and thus we need not resort to the courts in the ways that Americans have been obliged to) and we prefer it that way?

2. What does Roach mean when he states that "the Canadian political process makes the limited role courts will play under corrective justice easier to tolerate?" Would Weinrib agree? Does Roach take adequate account of the role that the Charter has played in many important issues such as abortion or gay rights?

Marchand v. The Simcoe County Board of Education
(1986), 55 OR (2d) 638 (HC)

SIROIS J: ... The plaintiff is a citizen of Canada, whose first language learned and still understood is that of the French linguistic minority population of the Province of Ontario. As such, he claims, pursuant to s. 23(1) of the *Canadian Charter of Rights and Freedoms*, to have with those he represents the right to have their children receive secondary school instruction in the French language, in French language educational facilities in or near the Town of Penetanguishene provided out of public funds. He claims that his minority language educational rights have been infringed or denied by the defendants.

He is seeking the following relief:

(1) As against both defendants:

(a) a declaration that the number of children whose parents have the right to have their children receive secondary school instruction in the French language in French language educational facilities in or near the Town of Penetanguishene is sufficient to warrant the provision of such instruction and facilities out of public funds;

(b) a declaration that the plaintiff and the members of the class of persons he represents have the right to have their children receive secondary school instruction in the French language in French language educational facilities which are equivalent to the instruction and facilities provided by the defendant Board in English language secondary school facilities in the County of Simcoe, and that such right has been denied or infringed;

(2) As against the defendant Her Majesty the Queen in right of Ontario, a declaration that Her Majesty is under a duty to ensure that the French language secondary school instruction and educational facilities provided to the children of the

plaintiff and of the members of the class of persons he represents, are equivalent to English language secondary school instruction and educational facilities provided within the County of Simcoe, and that such duty includes the provision of adequate funding for such purpose;

(3) As against the defendant Board:

(a) a mandatory order requiring the defendant Board to provide the facilities and funding necessary to achieve at L'école Secondaire Le Caron the provision of instruction and facilities equivalent to those provided to English language secondary schools by the defendant Board in the County of Simcoe;

(b) a mandatory order requiring the defendant Board to establish at the site of L'école Secondaire Le Caron facilities for industrial arts and shop programmes equivalent to those provided by the defendant Board in the English language secondary schools in the County of Simcoe.

The plaintiff, Jacques Marchand, is a business consultant, who resides in the Village of Lafontaine, a small town near Penetanguishene, in the County of Simcoe.

At the time the action was initiated, January 13, 1984, he had one child attending at L'école Secondaire Le Caron (Le Caron) in Penetanguishene and, at the time of trial, in May 1986, his other child was a student at Le Caron.

Le Caron is a secondary school established by the defendant the Simcoe County Board of Education (the Defendant Board) at which children of parents residing in or near the Town of Penetanguishene receive their secondary school education in the French language. It is the only secondary school in the County of Simcoe in which a secondary school education is provided to children in the French language.

Prior to 1966, there existed in the Penetanguishene area no authorized French language secondary school institution. In 1966, a school called Penetanguishene Secondary School (PSS) was opened in which a limited number of French language instruction courses gradually began to be offered. It was described as a mixed school and erroneously as a bilingual school. The language of instruction in that school is in English although there are certain classes in French.

There are four French language elementary feeder schools in the area in and around Penetanguishene attended by approximately 1,000 French-speaking students. According to the provincial average, 90% to 95% of such children would move to the French language homogeneous secondary school in Simcoe County. However, there were only 159 students registered at Le Caron in 1985-86. The other candidates have elected either to go to PSS or other English schools or simply have abandoned their studies.

In early 1980, the Minister of Education for the Province of Ontario, who supported the establishment of a French language secondary school in the Penetanguishene area, strongly urged the Defendant Board to establish such a facility. The ministry had earmarked the sum of $2,000,000 for the expected allocation of funds for the construction of a French language secondary school. As it turned out $1,200,000 roughly was spent. That is borne out by the evidence of Mr. John W. Storey, the then regional director of the ministry for the central region of the province.

Dr. Bette Stephenson, then Minister of Education, made a statement to the Defendant Board and FLAC [French Language Advisory Committee] dated March 6, 1980, filed as ex. 22, to provide accommodation for up to 240 francophone secondary students at the St. Joseph school site in Penetanguishene by September 1980. That was situated across the street from PSS. The statement described the intended facilities at a cost of $500,000 and the grants therefore as well as the programmes.

The ministry organized a working group chaired by the regional director Mr. John W. Storey, with three representatives from the Defendant Board, three from the ministry and three from FLAC to implement the plan of the Minister.

However, due to the refusal of the Corporation of the Town of Penetanguishene to amend the zoning by-law to permit the contemplated use by the Minister and all concerned, the school site had to be moved somewhere else.

Temporarily, Le Caron school was established in the Village of Lafontaine some five or six miles away from Penetanguishene in an abandoned school building, with the result that a fewer number of pupils registered, many preferring to remain in the Town of Penetanguishene. The principal had to proceed with alternate programmes which are illustrated in his letter of February 12, 1981 to his superintendent Mr. D.R. Beatty, filed as ex. 70.

When Le Caron was first established in its temporary location in Lafontaine, no facilities for industrial arts or shop instruction were provided. The parents of the students attending Le Caron at that time assisted the principal in setting up shop instruction programmes in the French language in facilities located in the community. The funds necessary to bring these facilities to acceptable standards were raised by the parents themselves. No funds from the province or from the board were provided for that purpose. During this period, students attending Le Caron were able to attend shop courses taught in the French language and the said courses were effective and well attended.

Finally, among several other sites, the present one on John St. was selected. In January of 1982, Le Caron high school was moved into the facility erected in the Town of Penetanguishene consisting of temporary structures of approximately 22,000 sq. ft. as described in the statement of claim, para. 15. The defendants refer to it as a demountable structure. It has no cafeteria nor any shops. In September of 1983, approximately 170 students were enrolled in Le Caron.

In or about March 1982, shortly after Le Caron was moved from its temporary location in Lafontaine to its existing facility in Penetanguishene, the Defendant Board announced that as of September 1982, it would no longer permit shop courses for Le Caron to be carried on as they had in the past.

The board required that the students wishing to take shop courses would have to attend at PSS. They would have to travel by bus for that purpose. Those courses would be in English unless a French-speaking teacher was available.

The students at Le Caron started attending their courses at PSS in March 1984. They were never allowed to *share* the facilities at PSS. They were permitted to use one room in which they could not touch anything, in which they had to bring their own defective equipment. This applies to both the technical shops and the home economics training.

For more than a year, the board has prohibited the teaching of the welding course and the small-motors shop because they could not safely be conducted in the same room as the wood work. During that time nothing was done to correct the safety aspects.

During his evidence, Mr. Boswell, Director of Education for the Defendant Board, indicated that the board had recently voted some moneys to improve the safety on the location of the technical shops and that they would be able then to do more than just wood work. He indicated that the home economics [classroom] would be supplied with sewing machines. He testified that the requirements of the shop training or the industrial arts training would have to be re-evaluated pursuant to the new general revision or reorganization throughout the Province of Ontario.

Mr. Boswell also confirmed that at present in Penetanguishene there are roughly 1,000 children in French language elementary schools, which is nearly twice as many children as in the English elementary schools, where the number is 516.

Comparisons were made during the trial with the facilities provided for English-speaking secondary school students at Elmvale High School, where presently there are roughly 310 students and where the impact report, filed as ex. 83, indicates a projected number for 1989 of 229 students.

The Defendant Board recommended an application for capital grants amounting to $1,500,000 to expand the facilities at Elmvale in order to construct a full-size gymnasium and add, amongst others, a second science room to the school.

Mr. Boswell confirmed, that with respect to Le Caron, there have been no requests by the board for capital funding for the school to the ministry, whereas several requests have been made in respect of Elmvale.

In re-examination, Mr. Boswell specifically stated on behalf of the board that Le Caron was built at the urging of the Minister and that the board felt that it was essentially a provincial enterprise: that FLAC had made the Minister aware of its requests to be provided for shops at Le Caron and that Dr. Stephenson had reviewed their requests and refused. Therefore, the board concluded that there would be no money for shops, that it was the Minister's position that there was no capital money for them.

There is no dispute as to the following facts:

(1) Le Caron is the only school operated by the Defendant Board without shop facilities on site.

(2) Le Caron has the least amount of laboratory and gymnasium equipment without regard to the relative enrollments.

(3) The ministry regulations as presently drafted will not allow the time spent in buses to be treated as teaching time unless an exception is applied for and granted by the Minister.

(4) It is also admitted that the ministry has maintained its mixed classes and its mixed school weighting factor for grants to benefit PSS after the establishment of Le Caron, contrary to its financial grant guidelines in an area served by a French language school.

The purpose of shop courses is to enable students to acquire basic skills in technical subjects such as drafting, wood working, mechanical repairs, home economics and other like subjects. Such courses are an extremely important part of the secondary school education of those children who will either terminate their formal education after graduation from high school and join the labour force or go on to a higher education in technical subjects.

The unsatisfactory arrangements respecting the teaching of industrial arts and conducting of shop courses, the continued uncertainty regarding the future provisions of such instruction, and the inadequacy of facilities and services, had a profoundly deleterious effect on the student body.

The evidence of the plaintiff's witnesses, and in particular Mrs. Claudette Paquin and Dr. Stacy Churchill, establishes that this has discouraged parents who, in the language of s. 23 of the *Charter*, possess the right to have their children receive French language instruction in a French language educational facility, from sending their children to Le Caron. ...

[Part II of the case, which deals with the rights of the plaintiffs under s. 23 of the Charter, is omitted; however, the text of s. 23, which is important for an understanding of the cases, follows:]

Minority Language Educational Rights

Language of instruction

> 23.(1) Citizens of Canada
>
> > (a) whose first language learned and still understood is that of the English or French linguistic minority population of the province in which they reside, or
> >
> > (b) who have received their primary school instruction in Canada in English or French and reside in a province where the language in which they received that instruction is the language of the English or French linguistic minority population of the province,
>
> have the right to have their children receive primary and secondary school instruction in that language in that province.

Continuity of language instruction

> (2) Citizens of Canada of whom any child has received or is receiving primary or secondary school instruction in English or French in Canada, have the right to have all their children receive primary and secondary school instruction in the same language.

Application where numbers warrant

> (3) The right of citizens of Canada under subsections (1) and (2) to have their children receive primary and secondary school instruction in the language of the English or French linguistic minority population of a province
>
> > (a) applies wherever in the province the number of children of citizens who have such a right is sufficient to warrant the provision to them out of public funds of minority language instruction; and
> >
> > (b) includes, where the number of those children so warrants, the right to have them receive that instruction in minority language educational facilities provided out of public funds.

Part III

Conclusion on the Claims

... [T]he plaintiff is entitled to be provided out of public funds for an *education* in French to his children. That means the *same education* as is given the majority but in the other official language. *This is to be a full and complete education not a limited, partial or truncated one, which necessarily would be an inferior education*, a second class one.

The costs of education to the majority is a relevant factor too, but not to a lesser extent nor a greater extent than for the minority. It is equally a limiting factor for both groups.

As long as the education provided to the minority is equivalent to that provided to the majority, then the constitutional rights of the minority can be said to have been respected.

There are no unequal rights under our *Charter*. The framers did not enshrine in the constitution a lesser right, an inferior right for the minority, in s. 23 (once the test has been met).

The s. 23 minority language educational rights of the plaintiff and those he represents to have their children receive their secondary school instruction in the French language in educational facilities, both provided by public funds, have been infringed and denied by the defendants.

Part IV

Remedies

The Legislature is under a duty to ensure that the French language secondary school instruction and educational facilities provided to the children of the plaintiff and the members of the class of persons he represents are equivalent to English language secondary school instruction and educational facilities provided within the County of Simcoe and such duty includes the provision of adequate funding for such purpose.

The plaintiff has had since April 17, 1982, the right to manage and control the minority French language classes of instruction and educational facilities. Since then, the Legislature has had the duty to enact legislation providing the plaintiff with the ways and means of exercising such right of exclusive management and control which the *Charter* has bestowed upon him as he has qualified under s. 23(1) and (2).

But the Legislature has not yet enacted a law to implement that right to manage and control. It is not just nor equitable in the meantime, to force the plaintiff and those he represents to have to depend upon the Defendant Board which continues to demonstrate the same negative attitude as already noted by the Court of Appeal.

In the words of the Court of Appeal in *Reference re Education Act of Ontario and Minority Language Education Rights*, supra, the minority language education rights of the plaintiff should not be left to the unfettered and undirected discretion of that local school board.

If the framers of the new Constitution had wanted it to be applied by steps they would have stated so. They suspended the application of the equality rights under s. 15 for three years. They did not for the rights under s. 23.

The framers must be taken to have intended the natural, normal and foreseeable financial consequence of their agreeing to the new Constitution in late 1981 and its proclamation in force on April 17, 1982.

Therefore, the plaintiff was entitled as of April 18, 1982, to claim the exercise and respect of such rights.

I find support for that conclusion in the decision of the Supreme Court of Canada, *A-G Que. v. Quebec Ass'n of Protestant School Boards*, supra, at p. 79 SCR, p. 331 DLR. The

Supreme Court of Canada concluded that the framers of the *Charter* knew and clearly had in mind at the time the following: the regimes governing the Anglophone and Francophone linguistic minorities in various provinces in Canada, and the history of these regimes; Regulation 17 limiting instruction in French in Ontario Separate Schools, Bill 101 in Quebec.

The framers regarded those regimes as inadequate and they intended to remedy the defects by uniform corrective measures, namely, s. 23.

The plaintiff, whose constitutional rights to minority language education have been denied, is entitled to such remedy "as this court considers appropriate and just in the circumstances," s. 24(1).

Counsel for Her Majesty the Queen in right of Ontario suggested to wait until the passing by the Legislature of the amendments to the *Education Act*, 1986 [Education Amendment Act, 1986 (Bill 75)] to provide for exclusive Governance of French Units. Bill 75 has received 2nd reading and was referred to committee.

Part XI-A would create a French language section of the board, which would govern for the board the French language instructional units operated by the board after January 1, 1989.

Part XI-B would create a French language education council which would have interim exclusive jurisdiction over the same matters as are specified for the above French language section of a board under Part XI-A from the date of the enactment of the law until January 1, 1989.

There is no assurance that it will be enacted at all, nor when it will be enacted. However, in the meantime, the plaintiff must no longer be denied his constitutional rights under s. 23.

In the present circumstances, it is just and appropriate that there be a declaration of the plaintiff's rights as requested in the statement of claim coupled with a mandatory injunction to implement his constitutional rights under s. 23 to prevent further infringement or denial.

Part V

Judgment

(1) As against both defendants:

(a) There shall be a declaration that the number of children whose parents have the right to have their children receive secondary school instruction in the French language in French language educational facilities in or near the Town of Penetanguishene is sufficient to warrant the provision of such instruction and facilities out of public funds;

(b) there shall be a declaration that the plaintiff and the members of the class of persons he represents have the right to have their children receive secondary school instruction in the French language in French language educational facilities which are equivalent to the instruction and facilities provided by the Defendant Board in English language secondary school facilities in the County of Simcoe, and that such right has been denied or infringed.

(2) As against the defendant Her Majesty the Queen in right of Ontario, there shall be a declaration that Her Majesty is under a duty to ensure that the French language secondary

school instruction and educational facilities provided to the children of the plaintiff and of the members of the class of persons he represents, are equivalent to English language secondary school instruction and educational facilities provided within the County of Simcoe, and that such duty includes the provision of adequate funding for such purpose.

(3) As against the Defendant Board there shall be:

(a) a mandatory order requiring the Defendant Board to provide the facilities and funding necessary to achieve at L'école Secondaire Le Caron the provision of instruction and facilities equivalent to those provided to English language secondary schools by the Defendant Board in the County of Simcoe;

(b) a mandatory order requiring the Defendant Board to establish at the site of L'école Secondaire Le Caron facilities for industrial arts and shop programmes equivalent to those provided by the Defendant Board in the English language secondary schools in the County of Simcoe.

(4) Counsel will have four weeks from this date to provide me with their written submissions concerning the costs of this action and each will have one week after receipt of the written submissions of the opposition to file their written reply.

Judgment for plaintiff.

Marchand v. The Simcoe County Board of Education (No. 2)
(1987), 61 OR (2d) 651 (HC)

SIROIS J (orally): This is a motion by the defendant, the Simcoe County Board of Education (the "Board"), to carry the judgment of July 22, 1986, into operation or to obtain other relief than that originally obtained pursuant to rule 59.06(2)(c) and (d)

Paragraph (a) of the notice of motion is for an order determining the nature and extent of the facilities that must be provided to carry into operation the judgment declaring the plaintiff's rights to equality and equivalence of education for his children under s. 23 of the *Canadian Charter of Rights and Freedoms*, in the *Constitution Act, 1982*.

Paragraph (b) is for an order determining the extent to which the province will participate to the cost of the construction pursuant to its duty to provide adequate funding to ensure equivalent facilities and education to the plaintiff's children and the children of those he represents.

On October 1, 1986, Bill 75 was enacted and became law [now Education Amendment Act (No. 2), 1986 (Ont.), c. 29]. The County of Simcoe, French-language Education Council (the "FLEC"), is now vested with exclusive authority to govern French units, including planning and the establishment and administration of French language schools and programmes. The said FLEC of the Board is represented also on this motion.

Because of the appeal, the parties agreed to an order dated October 29, 1986, by Mr. Justice Finlayson of the Court of Appeal to stay the judgment on the condition that: "the defendants (appellants) proceed forthwith with the planning, design and approval process for the educational facilities that appear to be required by the judgment." No definite plans have been accepted since and up to this time.

The appeals were abandoned in May 1987, by both the school board and the ministry.

As of today, though, the students still are deprived of their right, already recognized by the *Charter* in 1982, by the Court of Appeal's decision in *Reference re Education Act of Ontario and Minority Language Education Rights* (1984), 47 OR (2d) 1, 10 DLR (4th) 491, 11 CRR 17 (CA), and by the judgment of this court on July 22, 1986 [*Marchand v. Simcoe County Board of Education* (1986), 55 OR (2d) 638; 29 DLR (4th) 596; 25 CRR 139].

Conclusion

An immediate remedy is just and appropriate in the circumstances.

The Court of Appeal of this province in its decision on *Reference re Education Act of Ontario and Minority Language Education Rights*, supra, at p. 57 OR; p. 547 DLR stated: "The judiciary is not the sole guardian of the constitutional rights of Canadians ... Legislative action in the important and complex field of education is much to be preferred to judicial intervention."

But it went on to say that in cases of denial of constitutional rights this court had the power to act under s. 24 of the *Charter*.

However, as was already stated, Bill 75 was passed in October 1986, and by that act the province provided for the exclusive governance of French units until January 1, 1989, by the FLEC and thereafter by a French language section of the Board elected by the parents of the children who had the right to be educated in French. That council (FLEC) has on August 13, 1987 submitted a detailed proposal.

I need not intervene under s. 24(1) of the *Charter* as the province has legislated on the matter and its creature FLEC has accordingly determined the very issue I am asked to define.

The Ministry of Education filed the affidavit of Mr. Theo Grootenboer, the chief capital grants officer in the architectural services section, who swore in his affidavit of September 30, 1987 that the ministry considered as the best solution the transfer of the students of Le Caron to the building of the Penetang Secondary School, sending the actual or present students at PSS to the Midland Secondary School. As this proposal was not discussed in depth at the trial and has been raised only a few days ago, this tribunal does not consider it to be relevant to this motion under rule 59.06(2)(c) which deals with the execution of the judgment of July 22, 1986.

I propose to deal with the facts as of the date of the judgment and not to try and solve every possible change arising in the future.

My conclusion is that the proposal of August 13, 1987, by the FLEC, is within its exclusive powers. It meets the requirements of the judgment.

The duty of the province to provide adequate funding for the facilities required to carry the judgment into operation requires that it provide 94.4% of the capital cost of the proposition already mentioned, it being its ordinary share of funding for the construction of French-language secondary schools in the province. The share of the Board is the usual 5.6%.

I have endorsed the record as follows:

"The proposal of the French Language Education Council of the Board of Simcoe dated August 13, 1987 meets the requirement of this judgment and is to be funded according to the usual funding of French secondary schools, the province providing forthwith 94.4% and the Board of Simcoe 5.6%. Costs of the plaintiff to be paid by the defendant ministry on a solicitor-and-client basis."

Order accordingly.

NOTES AND QUESTIONS

1. While the action was brought by a single plaintiff, Marchand, at various points in his judgment Mr. Justice Sirois refers to "those he [Marchand] represents" and the "class of persons" he represents. What does he mean by these references? Is this an action for the vindication of private rights?

2. How, if at all, does the remedy granted in *Marchand* differ from that requested by the plaintiff? How does it differ from the damages remedy that might be sought in *Jane Doe* (see the introductory chapter)? Would the remedial issues have been more difficult in *Marchand* if the plaintiff had also asked for damages?

3. Does it make a difference that the right in *Marchand* is a positive right to certain governmental services? Might the same issues arise in cases dealing with unconstitutional conditions of confinement in custodial institutions?

4. Why did Sirois J not try a more deferential stance toward enforcing the government's obligation under s. 23 of the Charter? In *Dixon v. BC (AG)* (1989), 59 DLR (4th) 246 (BS SC), the court found that electoral boundaries were unconstitutional because their departure from constitutional standards of equal voting power were not justified. The court did not, however, either invalidate the existing boundaries or draw new ones that were closer to a one-person-one-vote standard. Instead, it declared the unconstitutional boundaries to be in force on a temporary basis to allow the government to enact new boundaries. McLachlin CJSC (as she was then) stated: "I need not enter into speculation of what might happen if remedial legislation were not passed within such time period as may be specified. I confine myself to the general enjoinder that just as the courts have a duty to measure the constitutionality of legislative acts against the Charter guarantees, so are they under an obligation to fashion effective remedies in order to give true substance to these rights."

Dixon is discussed in K. Roach, "Reapportionment in British Columbia" (1990), 24 *University of British Columbia Law Review* 79.

In "Coda" (1988), 38 *University of Toronto Law Journal* 229, referred to earlier in the chapter, Owen Fiss discussed a difficult remedial issue as follows (footnotes omitted):

> The example involved a statute requiring employers to provide maternity leave. I assumed that the statute, by its very terms, is applicable only to women and that it requires employers to provide up to four months' leave. Furthermore, I assumed that this leave can be used for child care, and is not restricted to the period of recovery from the birth itself. I also imagined a suit, perhaps brought by some women's organization, attacking this statute on the ground that it violates the constitutional guarantee of equality. The charge is that the statute tends to reinforce the social norm that links the child-bearing and child-rearing functions, or that, as Dorothy Dinnerstein put it, ties the

social divisions of labour to the biological one. The natural effect of the statute is to strengthen the assumption that a woman's place is in the home taking care of children, and it is this assumption, so it might be argued, that largely accounts for the exclusion of women from socially prestigious jobs, the creation of educational barriers, the values and forms of life prized in the public sphere, disparities in pay, and the kind of psychological oppression that Adrienne Rich described so movingly in the excerpt we read from her book.

Confronted with such a claim, the function of the judge is to ascertain whether the maternity leave statute does have this objectionable effect, and, if it does, to fashion an appropriate remedy. At first I had assumed that the remedy could only be a decree invalidating the statute in its entirety, allowing and encouraging (though obviously not requiring) the legislature to enact a more comprehensive statute, one that provided child-care leave for both men and women. But following the suggestion of a number of students in the class, it now seems to me that, as part of the remedy, the court could use a constitutional blue pencil—that is, eliminate the limitation in the statute that confines the duty to provide leave for child care to women. Such a remedy need not be based on the view that the constitution's equal protection clause itself directly commands the legislature to enact such a statute (though that would itself be sufficient ground for blue-pencilling), but rather that this statute might well be enacted by the legislature if it were given another opportunity to do so and if it fully appreciated the nature of the constitutional defect entailed in its previous effort at lawmaking. Of course, this prophecy might turn out to be mistaken, but given the disabilities women face in the political process, it appears fair and appropriate, for a change, to cast the burden of inertia in their favour. The legislature could always repeal the statute if the court was wrong in its assumption about what the legislature would do the second time around.

I called this form of adjudication—which defined the evil in group terms (the subordination of women) and then sought to reform the institution responsible for this hierarchial relationship—"structural reform." ... The end of a lawsuit is, of course, justice. This is true whether we speak in corrective or structural terms. There is, however, an important difference in how justice is achieved under each model. In the corrective one, the judge seeks through the award of damages or the infliction of punishment to restore the relationship of equality that existed between the parties before the unfortunate interaction. Sometimes the corrective judge might issue an injunction to prevent an anticipated wrong, but that is more exceptional, and in any event in such cases the anticipated wrong is defined in terms of the past. The defendant must not be allowed to act in a way that disturbs the relationship of equality that once existed between the plaintiff and defendant and that the plaintiff seeks to preserve. In the corrective context, justice is done when the relationship of equality—the status quo ante—is restored or preserved. In the structural context, however, justice is more forward-looking. The remedy that is exceptional in the corrective model—the injunction—here becomes favoured, and is used by the judiciary to bring social reality into conformity with a social ideal. In the feminist context, and in other forms of civil rights litigation, that particular ideal is "equality," but there is no necessary connection between justice and equality (and that is why I avoid the Aristotelian typology, which views "distributive justice" as the only alternative to "corrective justice"). Equality stands as but an example—an important but non-exhaustive example—of a larger category of social aspirations that are rendered authoritative by the law and against which social reality is to be measured. In feminist litigation, equality is the ideal that the judiciary seeks to actualize; in other cases it might be religious liberty, free speech, or personal safety. Moreover, even when equality is the ideal to be actualized, in the structural suit it refers not to a relationship between two individuals (the parties to the lawsuit), as it does in the corrective context, but rather to a state of affairs not yet in being—a projected or imagined view of the world, which the court embraces and seeks, through the use of its coercive power, to bring into being.

Canadian courts have recently used the "constitutional blue pencil" remedy that Fiss advocated. In *Schacter v. The Queen* (1990), 66 DLR (4th) 635 (FCA), the Federal Court determined that the extension of unemployment insurance benefits for parental leave to parents who adopted children but not those who give birth to their child violated the latter's s. 15 equality rights. Instead of nullifying the benefits of the former, the court extended the benefits so that in the case, the plaintiff, a biological father, could receive the parental leave benefit. The fiscal effects of the extension of such benefits were considerable (one estimate was over $500 million a year) and shortly afterwards the Unemployment Insurance Act was amended to lower from 15 to 10 the weeks of paren-tal leave benefits available. Nevertheless, the new provision provided parental leave benefits on a gender neutral basis to both adoptive and biological parents.

On appeal to the Supreme Court of Canada, the court held that the appropriate remedy would have been to declare the provision invalid and to have suspended the declaration to allow the legislative body in question to deal with all of the relevant factors in amending the legislation to meet constitutional requirements. In coming to this result the court held that reading in is permissible under s. 52 of the Charter in appropri-ate cases and provided several guidelines for a determination of the circumstances in which reading in (rather than severing, or striking down) would be an appropriate remedy. While setting down several steps in the analysis, the basic proposition advanced by the court is that reading in will be the appropriate remedy where to do so is more consistent with the legislative purpose of the impugned legislation than other remedial options and as such, would constitute the lessor intrusion into the legislative domain. In *Schacter*, considerations such as the nature of the benefit, the size of the excluded group to be read in, and the budgetary implications led to the conclusion that reading in was not an appropriate remedy.

Notwithstanding the guidelines set down in *Schacter*, no consistent approach to remedial questions has been taken by the courts. This is clearly evidenced by recent cases in which the exclusion of sexual orientation from prohibited grounds of discrimi-nation in various human rights statutes has been challenged. In the case of *Haig v. Canada* (1993), OR (3d) 495 (Ont. CA), Haig challenged the constitutionality of the Canadian Human Rights Act under s. 15 of the Charter because it did not include sexual orientation in its list of prohibited grounds of discrimination. The court concluded that sexual orientation was an analogous ground under s. 15, that s. 15 was violated by the exclusion of sexual orientation from the Canadian Human Rights Act because gay men and lesbians were deprived of a benefit available to other disadvantaged groups, and that the appropriate remedy would be to read in sexual orientation because this would be most consistent with the objective of the legislation in question. (Note also that the court relied on expressions of intention to amend the Code by various members of Parliament.) By contrast, in *Vriend v. Alberta* (1996), 37 Alta LR (3d) 364 (CA), the court, addressing the identical legal issue in the context of the Individual's Rights and Protection Act, dismissed Vriend's claim, admonishing "constitutionally-hyperactive judges" who thought it was their business to address such matters, and, at the same time, chastising members of the legislature for shipping "awkward political questions to the judiciary." The decision of the Court of Appeal was reversed by the Supreme Court of Canada (1998), 156 DLR (4th) 385.

On *Schacter*, see N. Duclos and K. Roach, "Constitutional Remedies as Constitutional Hints: A Comment on *The Queen v. Schacter*" (1991), 36 *McGill Law Journal* 1.

As suggested in the introduction, the public law model not only challenges our conceptualization of the purpose of litigation and the role of judge, but also the role of lawyer. As noted, codes of conduct largely presuppose that lawyers act for individuals and frequently fail to provide much meaningful guidance when lawyers represent entities of a variety of sorts. Of course, a great many lawyers represent corporate entities completely outside of a "public law" context. But like representation in a public law context, the representation of corporations gives rise to some of the same ethical issues, perhaps most important, to the centrally important question of precisely who is one's client. In the article that follows, Ellman illustrates effectively how our answer to the question who is our client substantially colours our thinking about issues such as conflict of interest and confidentiality. Unlike corporate representation, public law litigation gives rise to other important ethical questions, such as the selection of "test case" plaintiffs and worries about their potential exploitation, particularly if recruited on a conditional basis—for example, on the condition that they agree not to settle a claim or to do so only on particular terms.

S. Ellman, "Client-Centredness Multiplied"
(1992), 78 *Virginia Law Review* 1103, at 1104-70 (footnotes omitted)

This [a]rticle examines the conflicts between the themes of group participation and individual autonomy in the context of public interest lawyers' representation of groups. This is a critical area of legal practice, but one that neither current rules of legal ethics nor current models of lawyer–client interaction adequately illuminate. Indeed, the reader of the codes of legal ethics might be forgiven for assuming that most legal work is done on behalf of individuals. The Model Code of Professional Responsibility explains the fundamental duty of zealous representation as a consequence of the proposition that "[i]n our government of laws and not of men, each member of our society is entitled to have his conduct judged and regulated in accordance with the law. ..." The Model Rules of Professional Conduct, now a model for the ethical codes of most states, expressly regulate the conduct of lawyers who represent organizational clients—but only in a single rule.

In fact, however, a tremendous amount of what lawyers do they do for groups of people. The vast bulk of corporate representation is in a sense the representation of the many individual owners of the corporation's stock. Union representation is, probably a good deal more directly, representation of the union's members. Class action litigation expressly deals with the interests of groups of individuals who share common concerns but are too numerous to be individually represented, and the members of many smaller groups *are* individually named in the cases that concern them. There remain, to be sure, many cases or matters in which the only formal client is an individual, but few of these will implicate only that individual's interests. A single child may demand the desegration of a school system; one homeless family's vindication of a right to emergency housing may help others win the same benefit in the future; and the gains and losses from any transaction or litigation are likely to be reaped not only by the "client" but by the client's family.

For lawyers whose work is aimed at achieving social reform on behalf of people who would otherwise lack adequate representation—those lawyers whom I will call "public interest lawyers"—the role of groups is particularly significant. Faced with needs far greater than they can hope to meet, these lawyers must make decisions about what cases and causes to undertake. The problems their clients encounter are not the product of some series of unique individual accidents; rather, they result at least in part from social conditions that affect many people at once. Meaningful assistance to these clients depends, to some extent, on finding legal strategies that target broad situations rather than just individual circumstance, and public interest lawyers can properly make case selection decisions that take into account whether potential cases will have this broad impact. The success of these strategies, in turn, may depend on the extent to which they empower clients outside as well as inside the courts, and so may hinge on the degree to which they transform this multiplicity of people into a group.

The upshot is that a great deal of what public interest lawyers do will be done on behalf of groups, either explicitly or implicitly. But the various groups of disadvantaged or underrepresented people in our society are not monolithic. They consist of individuals, whose needs may in fact be unique and whose relations to the groups to which they may be said to belong may range from hostile to harmonious. Poor people, like rich people, are formed in and are part of communities. However, they equally may seek to change or even to shed some of the ties that bind them to these communities. Thus there is an inevitable danger that the lawyer who sets out to help disadvantaged people as members of groups may inadvertently succeed in oppressing them (or some of them) as individuals. So long as we acknowledge and value the capacity of individuals to make choices that are not entirely dictated by their preexisting group affiliations—in other words, so long as we value individual autonomy—we must be troubled by the danger to this autonomy inherent in a focus on group interests. My purpose in this [a]rticle is to examine the extent of this danger in certain forms of public interest lawyers' representation of client groups. I will argue that proper representation of groups demands radical alterations in our usual methods of protecting individual client autonomy in the lawyer–client relationship, but that it is possible for lawyers both to limit the intrusions on individual autonomy that group interactions generate and to protect a crucial element of individual autonomy—our choices to make connections—that would be jeopardized by a resistance to group representation. ...

That we are inescapably uncertain about the relative values of autonomy and community counsels against radically devaluing either one—a counsel this [a]rticle takes seriously. If lawyer–client relations can be shaped that provide effective representation of client groups and also secure real protection for the autonomy of those groups' members, these relationships are to be welcomed precisely because they do respect both sets of values. As I will argue, in some contexts such relationships are indeed within lawyers' reach. ...

I. The Definition of the Client

A. Four Frameworks for Representation

Defining the client is often difficult, even when only one person is being represented. In individual representation, the lawyer's task, and the client's, is to ensure that the lawyer comes to understand this particular client as he or she is, and not as the lawyer finds it natural, or convenient, or attractive to imagine the client to be. This is no easy matter, particularly for lawyers who are overburdened by caseload and look to routinized systems of legal triage for relief. Even lawyers who want to provide individualized service are in danger of misreading their clients, for the ways that clients describe themselves are inevitably influenced by the questions they are asked, and the desires clients articulate are affected by the sense of the possible that lawyers provide. These effects, moreover, are not merely a matter of self-presentation, because clients, like the rest of us, change in response to what they experience, so that what the lawyer says to the client may affect who a client *is*.

Whatever the intricacies of defining the individual client, matters are vastly more complex when the lawyer is dealing with more than one individual. Consider the following situation:

> Eight tenants from a particular apartment building meet with a lawyer at the local legal services office. The tenants explain that they, and the forty other families in the building, have struggled for years to make their landlord provide them with a minimally safe and habitable building. Many of them have, as individuals, protested to the landlord; some have temporarily withheld their rent; and some have moved out when they could. Now, however, these eight men and women have decided that conditions in their building are intolerable, and that they want to take action together to seek redress. In the course of the meeting, it becomes clear to the lawyer that although most of these eight people are quite determined to continue living in the building, two or three might be tempted to take a cash settlement that would enable them to find better housing elsewhere—even though their doing so might jeopardize the chance of the other tenants' obtaining needed repairs. The lawyer agrees to help them formulate and carry out a plan of attack that will put the maximum legal pressure on the landlord to accede to the tenants' demands.

This lawyer might characterize her relationship to the tenants in any of four quite different ways. These different characterizations, as we shall see, span a continuum from an insistence on the status of each individual as a client to a vision of these individuals, and their many other co-tenants, as a class. The consequences of these characterizations, not surprisingly, can powerfully affect the work the lawyer does for the tenants, and the relations the tenants will have with each other. Where individual representation is the model, the lawyer must assiduously work for each individual client, but may well have to withdraw altogether if the clients develop conflicts of interest. In group representation, on the other hand, the lawyer's fidelity to each individual is considerably curtailed, but her ability to help the individuals to achieve their collective ends is enhanced. These points will become more clear as we examine each of the four possible characterizations.

1. Individual Representation, Multiplied

First, a lawyer might see herself as representing eight separate individuals. This, of course, would be ethically unproblematic if the eight had identical interests, but they do not. Instead, after the first meeting it is already apparent that the tenants may eventually have quite different preferences as to the remedies they seek, and that these different preferences might result in sharp disagreements within the group. Under the Model Rules, however, "a possible conflict" does not necessarily bar the lawyer from representing all eight. If the lawyer reasonably believes, in light of her experience with such cases, that the tenants will ultimately agree on the issue of relief, or that each will be able to get his or her preferred relief without undercutting the others' positions vis-à-vis the landlord—and if the clients consent to her representing them all despite the possibility of future conflict—then she is free to do so. Each tenant will then be her client, and she will owe a duty of loyalty and confidentiality to each one as an individual. If a true conflict of interest does emerge, then she may well have to withdraw from the representation of all eight, whatever the difficulties they may face in finding alternative counsel.

2. Intermediation

Not every disagreement ripens into a conflict of interest, however, and if disagreement among the tenants on the issue of relief does develop, the lawyer can continue to represent all eight if she can characterize her relationship to the tenants in a second way—as a mediator or, in the language of the Model Rules, an "intermediary." Under this rubric, the lawyer is free to help the clients to reach a compromise that is in their collective best interest, rather than vigorously defending each individual's preexisting preferences. However, the lawyer can play the role of intermediary only in rather narrow circumstances. Each client must consent, after consultation, to the lawyer's playing of this part—and if any of the clients revoke their consent she must withdraw. In addition, she herself must

> reasonably believe that the matter can be resolved on terms compatible with the clients' best interests, that each client will be able to make adequately informed decisions in the matter and that there is little risk of material prejudice to the interests of any of the clients if the contemplated resolution is unsuccessful. ...

These conditions are not easily met. The lawyer is obliged to protect each client's confidentiality *and* to keep each client adequately informed, and these duties can be directly at odds: the more any client insists on confidentiality, the harder it will be for the lawyer to keep her other clients adequately informed. And because a failure of the mediation will likely preclude her from representing any of the clients and probably subject all of what any one of them has said to her to discovery by the others, she can hardly believe that there is little risk of material prejudice unless she can say that the matter not only *can* but *probably will* be resolved on terms compatible with the clients' best interests.

3. Organizational Representation

Given the vigilance on behalf of individual clients reflected in these first two formulations of the lawyer's role, it is startling—even stunning—to encounter the radically different regime envisaged by Model Rule 1.13. The first subsection of this rule declares that "[a] lawyer employed or retained by an organization represents the organization acting through its duly authorized constituents." This simple sentence adopts the "entity theory" of organizational representation, under which the lawyer for the organization does *not* represent its shareholders, or officers, or employees, but instead represents an artificial entity, the organization. No doubt the most frequent application of this proposition is in the field of corporate representation, but it may apply in a variety of other contexts, including our housing lawyer's relationship to this group of tenants.

Its bearing on this situation stems from the fact that Rule 1.13 applies to unincorporated associations as well as to organizations having corporate form. Neither the Rule itself nor the accompanying Comment defines "organization," but two influential commentators have urged a very expansive treatment of the term in this context. Geoffrey C. Hazard, Jr. and W. William Hodes suggest that the rule would also apply to seventeen homeowners who "form a group that hires lawyer L to prosecute a nuisance action" and agree that they will all abide by any settlement that twelve of their number approve. These facts, Hazard and Hodes indicate, give this set of people "an identity apart from the individuals who comprise it," and thus transform them into an organization.

On this logic, the eight tenants, too, can readily be seen as such an organization. It is true that these tenants have not, so far as the stated facts reveal, agreed among themselves on any such decisionmaking process. Perhaps they need not do so; perhaps they become an organization if they simply think of themselves as a group. But if they do need to adopt some structure, then their lawyer can help them do so. After all, lawyers help clients establish organizations all the time. The lawyer could suggest that the tenants agree on a procedure for resolving disagreements among themselves, and if, after proper counseling about the potential consequences, they did reach an appropriate agreement, the lawyer could represent them as an organization rather than as eight separate clients.

The consequences of this recharacterization are striking. Because the lawyer now represents the entity, she no longer owes unqualified loyalty or confidentiality to any of the eight tenants as individuals. Hence if one tenant provides her with information, she need not convey this information to each of the others unless doing so is required by her duty of loyalty to the organization. Conversely, if providing the information to the group is necessary in order to keep it adequately informed, the lawyer has no duty to protect the individual tenant's secrets. So, too, if the eight constituents of the organization develop disagreements, her obligation is *not* to remain neutral as between them. Rather, her obligation is to provide the best counsel she can to the organization (though adopting a neutral stance might still be appropriate, if neutrality best served the organization).

Even if the tenants' disagreements ripen into actual conflicts of interest, their lawyer will not automatically have to withdraw, for she does not represent the tenants as individuals. Her client is the group itself, and the fact that some constituents of the group now dissent from its collective decision does not automatically bar her from continuing to do the bidding of the group as an entity. So, for example, if the tenants have agreed to abide by any settlement that two-thirds of them approve, the lawyer can settle the case on behalf of the group despite the wishes of the minority. The shift from the norms of individual representation is particularly vivid here, for if the eight tenants constituted eight individual clients, each of them might have an *unwaivable* right to approve or reject any settlement. In short, the modest steps by which a set of people can transform themselves into a group sharply alter the role the lawyer can play, and in ways that facilitate group action at the expense of individual prerogatives.

4. Class Representation

The fourth characterization of the lawyer's relationship to this set of eight people is scarcely mentioned in either the Model Code or the Model Rules. This characterization treats the eight individuals as the named representatives of a class of all the tenants in the building (a group of perhaps 150 people or more). The lawyer cannot turn the tenants into class representatives without their consent, but once this consent has been granted the lawyer acquires a freedom from the wishes of the individual clients that in some ways exceeds even that conferred by Model Rule 1.13.

Indeed, whereas Rule 1.13 facilitates a group's collective *action*, the class action device is primarily concerned only with the group's collective *representation*. The result of class action status may well be to empower groups of people by facilitating their access to court, but the people so empowered are not empowered as against their lawyer. Certainly this is true as to the named class representatives, for according to the standard interpretation of Rule 23 of the Federal Rules of Civil Procedure, the lawyer owes her most fundamental duty of loyalty not to them but to the class itself. With judicial approval, she may settle the case despite the objections of a majority of the named representatives. Moreover, the existence of disagreements within the class by no means automatically precludes class certification, although if these disagreements are profound enough they may lead to the designation of subclasses with separate representation. Finally, even—or especially—the class as a whole lacks the power to direct the lawyer's actions, because the class typically has no decisionmaking structure through which it can act. As a result, the lawyer's responsibility for gauging what is in the class's best interests is profound, and a court may approve a settlement endorsed by the class lawyer even if most class members—and, it would seem, most named class representatives—object. ...

F. Advising the Group—and Allying with It

The guidelines offered in the preceding Sections have all been meant to assist the lawyer in eliciting the views of the group's members, and in dealing with the differences among the members that emerge in that process. Their focus has been primarily procedural, and certainly procedural issues are of great moment in group representation. But a client-centered lawyer must address the substantive choices before her client as well as the procedures to be used in making those choices. Most prosaically, she must provide the client with the information the client needs in order to make a decision based on an accurate understanding of the available options and their likely consequences. Somewhat more controversially, she may tell the client what she thinks the client ought to do. Binder, Bergman, and Price now accept—in my judgment, correctly—the propriety of the lawyer's giving advice, and indeed take the view that "reject[ing] requests for advice ... demeans clients' ability to make independent judgments." Though they suggest that normally the lawyer should give advice based on the client's values, discerned through the counseling process, they also affirm the propriety of the lawyer's expressing her own moral or political perspective when she disagrees with the client's intentions. So, too, a client-centered lawyer for a group can give advice based on the priorities the group has articulated during her work with it, and she can speak based on values she holds but that the group may not. But the implications of the advice-giving role change in certain respects when the client is a group rather than an individual.

First, the lawyer will often be unable to take a clearly defined set of client values and give advice that simply applies those values to the situation the client faces. To be sure, individual clients rarely present their lawyer with entirely clear sets of values either, and the lawyer who tries to give advice based on the client's values may not so much be telling the client what his values suggest he should do as helping him to reflect further on just what his values are. Nevertheless the lawyer's uncertainty about the client's values is often bound to be greater with a group client, for a straightforward reason: the group is unlikely to be unanimous about its values. In addition, because of the multiplicity of individual sentiments within the group and the impossibility of fully eliciting them, the lawyer often may not achieve as precise a feel for whatever values the group does share as she can attain when she deals with a single individual. As a result, the lawyer may be unable to give advice of the form, "Since you feel this is an important consideration, it makes sense to take this action." Instead, her advice may need to be, "*If* you decide that this is an important consideration, then this action makes sense." Sometimes she will need to add, "But if you decide that another consideration is also important, then a second course of action makes sense." Her advice, in short, may have to be even more tentative than when she speaks with an individual client, and the role of her advice frequently may be more to inform further debate than to bring the client to a quick resolution of uncertainty.

Second, if a lawyer contemplates giving advice based on her own values to a group, she must weigh against the benefit of her advice the risk of contributing to the disunity of the group. As we have seen, the lawyer for a group can have a special responsibility for promoting group harmony around decisions, a concern that disappears in individual representation. When the lawyer gives advice based on her own values, she inevitably runs the risk of being seen as a partisan, and very possibly also as an ally of one segment of the group against others. She may then be less able to win the conflicting members' trust in a process, whether of mediation or of structured discussion, that is meant to lead the members to see the logic of each others' positions and find common ground among them. If agreement is never achieved, moreover, the lawyer may have sacrificed some part of her credit with the dissenters, and thus be less able to assist them in their decision either to stay with the group or to abandon it.

Third, the lawyer who gives advice based on her own values when the group itself does not share those values is not likely to see her views prevail, at least unless she resorts to methods of persuasion that are emotive, and sometimes manipulative, rather than merely reasoned. It may never be easy for a lawyer to persuade a client to follow her values rather than his own. A group's values represent the confluence of many people's thinking, however, and may well be part of the very foundation of the group's existence. The chances of the lawyer's overcoming the group's contrary inclinations seem limited. It might seem, in sum, that there is little to be gained, and much to be lost, by lawyers who go beyond giving advice carefully keyed to the values of the group members.

When a lawyer gives only this modest advice and bends her efforts to promoting group harmony from a stance of neutrality, she *is* playing a valuable role, but there is another, much more assertive, possible part for the lawyer to take. If the lawyer who gives advice based on her own values risks alienating or dividing the group, perhaps she can partially overcome these dangers by showing the group members that she in fact shares their core convictions. Then her supporting one side rather than the other in an internal dispute might be couched in the context of her fellowship with all of the members, and even her arguing against a consensus of the group might be framed as an argument from a dependable ally rather than from a disengaged critic. To be sure, this visibly shared commitment will not always be a way to preserve credibility with the group's members. Some groups will be too divided for the lawyer to present herself as everyone's ally, and some issues will be too divisive for disagreement not to be seen as fundamental. In those cases, in fact, the lawyer's more active commitment might even make her a more divisive force than someone who, however irritating, was not seen as directly involved. But in some groups, the more engaged the lawyer is, the greater the impact she may make with her advice.

This full moral engagement between the lawyer and her client group, however, constitutes a relationship quite different from the characteristic client-centered interaction. In individual client-centered practice, perhaps the central emotional bond between lawyer and client is forged through the lawyer's empathy. Empathy, as Binder, Bergman, and Price characterize it, is the lawyer's nonjudgmental understanding and acceptance of the client. Empathy can be a powerful emotion, but it is a bounded one. In theory, at least, the lawyer who displays empathy does not offer actual approval of her client's feelings or beliefs, for such approval would be a form of judgment. Much as clients might respond to *positive* judgments from their lawyers, a focus on the centrality of empathy seems to weigh against the client-centered lawyer's expression of such approving evaluations. There is, indeed, good reason for lawyers to be wary of endorsing what their clients say, for the more a lawyer endorses any particular aspect of what the client tells her, the less the client will feel free to reveal other, inconsistent aspects of himself. If the client comes under such constraint, neither he nor his lawyer may be able to identify fully the real considerations facing the client, and so his decisions may be warped by the lawyer's approval. The lawyer who wants her clients to recognize that she shares their central values, however, must convey, explicitly or implicitly, just such endorsement or approval. Nothing less will express the sharing that she means to manifest.

In many situations, moreover, clients will insist on such commitment from the lawyer as a tacit condition of retaining her at all. It is inconceivable, for example, that a group of black parents pressing a school desegregation case would happily entrust their cause to a lawyer who did not consider segregation a profound injustice. A lawyer who expressed understanding of the parents' position, but never manifested her agreement with their fundamental grievance against the state, would also be more likely to receive the parents' suspicion and anger than their confidence. It seems plausible to generalize that the more a group understands itself as oppressed, and the more it sees its legal efforts as meant to challenge that oppression, the more it will seek such assurance of solidarity from its lawyer.

This moral or political alliance between lawyer and client is a potent force. It may well give the lawyer a credibility that melds together the expertise of the professional and the intimacy of the friend. The lawyer who acquires such credibility with her client group is in a position to influence her clients dramatically, a prospect fraught with potential and with danger. The potential is that the lawyer can inspire her clients to engage in a process of political mobilization. The danger is that the lawyer can mobilize demagogically or manipulatively. If lawyers could avoid forming such close alliances, they might be wise to do so in order to escape this risk of demagoguery, even at the cost of sacrificing the special potential for benign influence that this solidary relationship with client groups can give them. This would be a great sacrifice, for helping disadvantaged groups to find, and amplify, their political voice is a valuable step indeed. But in any event this choice is probably not open to lawyers, regardless of whether they wish it were, for, as I have already suggested, clients are often likely to insist on entering into such an alliance with their lawyers.

Such lawyers might still try to escape the danger of manipulating their clients by refraining from giving advice based on their own values. But this solution seems untenable as well. The lawyer who believes in school desegregation is unlikely to be neutral in a discussion of whether to settle a desegregation case by integrating the schools or by enhancing the funding to still segregated, black schools. For her to attempt to give neutral counsel would not be true to herself, and so would be a denial of her own autonomy. It might also be psychologically impossible for the lawyer, and even if she managed the feat, its falsity might be so palpable as to undercut her relationship with her clients. Indeed, clients who accept their lawyer as their ally in the perilous seas of politics may well invite the lawyer to push and challenge them, as we may invite our friends and family to pressure us without necessarily seeing our autonomy as diminished; but as with friends and family, so with lawyers, the line between invited suggestion and unsought interference may be easily crossed.

The lawyer-ally acquires as a result a particularly challenging obligation: an obligation of constant vigilance against her own overreaching. The lawyer's influence is too great for her to expect complete success in this self-scrutiny, but that does not mean the effort is to no avail. On the contrary, there are many manipulative steps that lawyers surely can refrain from taking. The lawyer who believed she had no obligation to respect her clients' autonomy, and sought only to press the political causes in which she believed, might advise her client groups in speeches using all the rhetorical maneuvers of a closing argument to a jury. She might incite her clients towards avoidable courtroom confrontations with the thought that provoking the judge into punitive behavior would reveal to the clients the true corruption of the legal system, or would reveal this reality to other members of the clients' community (at the clients' expense). No doubt the range of blatantly manipulative or coercive steps a Machiavellian lawyer-politician could take is vast. All of this a lawyer who seeks both to ally with her clients and to adhere to client-centered principles *can* avoid—and hopefully more.

NOTES AND QUESTIONS

1. The four models that Ellman proposes are not all mirrored in the proposed draft rules of professional conduct (see appendix II). See rules 2.04 and 2.05 and consider what models are available within the rules. Notwithstanding the differences in the codes of various jurisdictions, Ellman's broader point holds; how we conceptualize both who the client is and the nature of the relationship matters greatly with respect to the duties of loyalty, confidentiality, and the avoidance of conflicts.

2. What do you make of Ellman's balance between autonomy and community? Does Ellman's approach have wider implications for the general lawyer–client relationship?

III. BEYOND ADJUDICATION: "THE INFORMALISTS" AND THEIR CRITICS

As noted in the introduction to this chapter, what unites this category of processes is the rejection of adjudication, and the embrace of less formal, non-adjudicative forms of dispute resolution. Again, as noted, much of what we consider is caught under the broad rubric of alternative dispute resolution (ADR). While the term "ADR" has no fixed meaning (it is used by various commentators in differing ways), it is frequently employed to capture virtually every and any process other than institutionally based—that is, court-based or tribunal-based—adversarial adjudication. As such, the processes caught under the panoply of ADR are diverse. Indeed, some processes commonly captured by the term—for example, "arbitration" (essentially a form of privatized adversarial adjudication)—share more in common with court-based adversarial adjudication then they do with other ADR processes. While our attention in this section is focused primarily on those processes that reject adjudication and on mediation more specifically, we begin with some consideration of ADR more generally. As you will come to appreciate as you read through this section, proponents of ADR point to a variety of failings in the traditional model of adversarial adjudication, posit a variety of benefits of ADR (often as though it were a monolith), and frequently claim that some "alternatives," like mediation, are premised on and promote a differing set of values than does adversarial adjudication. It is also important to attend to the ways in which ADR rhetoric and practices are transforming court-based litigation itself, an issue that we take up in this section.

A. Alternative Dispute Resolution

D. Paul Emond, "Alternative Dispute Resolution: A Conceptual Overview"
in D. Paul Emond, ed., *Commercial Dispute Resolution: Alternatives to Litigation* (Aurora, ON: Canada Law Book, 1989) (footnotes omitted)

Alternative dispute resolution (ADR) describes the recent interest, perhaps even preoccupation, with finding an alternative to traditional litigation. The expression "ADR" tells the proponent of dispute resolution much about North American legal thinking about preferred dispute resolution processes. It asserts that adjudication in courts is the real thing and that other processes are peripheral and apart from the hard core of judicial dispute resolution. It tells the advocates of alternative processes that their disputes lie outside the mainstream and that their process is somehow atypical. And it makes these assertions even though the vast majority (95% to 98%) of disputes are resolved through negotiation and not adjudication. Furthermore, the expression assumes that the legal process is the baseline against which all other dispute resolution mechanisms are to be measured.

The expression does not, however, tell us very much about whether "alternative" refers to engrafting new dispute resolution mechanisms onto the existing process or whether it refers to creating completely different and separate processes for resolving disputes. One approach would merely lead to a modification of traditional litigation— perhaps rules to encourage and facilitate pretrial negotiation, mediation and ultimately settlement—the other would have society replace judicial litigation with, for example, private courts or mini-trials. It will not come as a surprise to learn that the judiciary tends to favour modification and streamlining of existing processes; critics of the judicial process tend to favour more dramatic change. The core of the movement is much closer to the modification school than to the radical change approach. It recognizes that judicial litigation has an important role to play in resolving private disputes, setting norms for acceptable conduct and resolving broader public/constitutional disputes.

The search for an "alternative" process, therefore, is the search for a more consensual approach to problem solving, more accessible and community-oriented forms of dispute resolution and less expensive, more efficient ways of resolving disputes, especially commercial disputes. In short, the search is for a more acceptable process(es) and more satisfying results. To use an expression that has gained in popularity, the search is for a process that generates "win/win" rather than "win/lose" or zero sum results. And generally, *all of this* is to take place within or as an adjunct to the existing litigation process. ...

The search for alternative dispute resolution processes stems from a number of perceived deficiencies with adjudication. These deficiencies may be lumped into three broad categories: cost (time and money spent to resolve the dispute); process (issues related to the participation of the parties in both the fact finding and decision-making process); and result (issues related to the imposition of a "remedy" by a "stranger" from a predetermined and limited range of options). ...

(1) Cost

Concern about the high cost of the adversarial process relates to transaction costs, that is, the cost to the parties (and society) of transacting with one another to reach a result. There are many reasons why the transaction costs associated with trial litigation are so high. First, as a highly competitive and adversarial process, the parties are encouraged to exaggerate their claims. Starting from such extravagant positions, the cost of finding the truth within such a highly structured setting will normally be higher than had the parties adopted more reasonable positions. Second, as a process that values individual rights and puts a very high premium on rigorously testing facts, witness credibility and propositions, it tends to be slow, cumbersome and riddled with opportunities for delay. Thoroughness, not efficiency, is the hallmark of judicial litigation. For many litigants, delay is just another word for expense. For others, delay may be fatal in the sense that "justice delayed is justice denied."

As an especially costly process, litigation impacts most harshly on certain segments of society. In the same way that sales taxes are regressive, so too are litigation costs. Start-up companies lack the resources to engage in costly litigation and thus may find the dispute resolution meted out by the courts is simply unavailable to them. It is no coincidence that much of the ADR movement is directed toward alternative forms of commercial dispute resolution, where the parties are especially sensitive to the costs of resolving disputes.

Furthermore, in those jurisdictions in which the losing party must pay the winner's costs as well as its own, there is a real financial disincentive to take on the highly speculative, but perhaps desirable "test case." Those who employ the judicial process to bring about broad social and economic change will inevitably pay a heavy price. This fact helps explain the growing popularity of the environmental mediation movement. Opponents of environmentally disruptive activities have sometimes had more success and with much less expense by participating at the negotiating table rather than in the courtroom. But it is the corporate sector, the group best *able* to afford costly litigation, that is so diligently seeking out alternatives. Again, perhaps it is no coincidence that the trend toward ADR has mirrored the rise of the multi-national firm and the growing recognition among those firms that corporations engaged in expensive, time-consuming and often unproductive litigation are simply not competitive in the world market. Even they cannot afford the high cost of *litigation*. ...

(2) Process

This section might be divided into a number of subparts, including: the process by which facts are determined; the process by which a decision is reached; and the extent and ways in which the process facilitates participation by the parties. I believe that many, if not all, of the process-related criticisms of judicial litigation can be explored by examining the participation issue. First, who qualifies as a participant or a party to a judicial or quasi-judicial proceeding is cause for concern. The right to participate, more often described as standing or *locus standi*, is limited to those with a relatively narrow and direct (usually proprietary or financial) interest. Others with an "interest" in the matter in dispute are often excluded. Thus, children and grandparents in a child-custody case, many members of the adversely affected public in an environmental case, and the injured party's relatives in a tort action may all be excluded from the process because they lack standing.

In fact many potential or would-be participants find themselves in a double bind. Their efforts to participate in their own right are usually frustrated by a successful standing challenge. Conversely, their efforts to participate as part of a class or group of affected persons are unsuccessful because they fail to comply with narrow class-action rules. Standing is denied to the individual because of a judicial fear that to open the gate to one participant may encourage a flood of similarly affected participants. Standing is

denied to the group because each member's interest in the dispute is sufficiently different and diverse that a single, collective action is, according to the court, inappropriate.
The result? Many persons who are affected by a dispute are denied access to the process
by which the dispute is to be resolved.

Second, the manner in which the parties participate is cause for criticism. Participation is indirect; not only do the parties not speak on their own behalf—that is done by
hired professionals—they do not speak to each other. Instead, they speak to a third party
decision-maker. The intimacy and conjoining effect of face-to-face contact is replaced
by the alienating and disjoining effect of a charade between strangers. Strategy is determined by professionals whose training and orientation emphasizes competition and
adversarialness. The parties participate, if at all, as well-rehearsed witnesses in a pre-set
drama. For many, the result is a sense of alienation and frustration. They are mere
observers, trying to comprehend the symbolism and the jargon of an incomprehensible,
highly formalistic charade.

The binary nature of the fact-finding and decision-making aspects of the process
shape participation in a number of potentially dysfunctional ways. First, because the
process demands a "yes/no," "right/wrong," "how much" answer from the decision-
maker, the parties are pushed out of the middle ground and forced to adopt extreme
positions. There is no room for the "maybe" or the "perhaps." Facts are "found" on a
balance of probabilities or beyond a reasonable doubt. While there will be occasions
where the parties require a clear cut answer (a precedent on an important and controversial issue), more often, the process will force the parties to pursue a "win/lose" strategy
that does not necessarily serve their long-term interests. The process discourages compromise by penalizing those who seek it; it offers few opportunities for the parties to
fashion a result that expands or enhances their relationship. Evidentiary rules, procedural safeguards and high standards of proof, all characteristic of a binary process,
combine to squeeze out the so-called "soft," fragile or unquantifiable values. Participation is channelled into a mode of discourse that effectively precludes a debate over
values or even an exploration of innovative solutions to the problem at hand.

In structure and in format the adjudicative process is essentially hierarchical. Peck-
ing orders are well determined, and the parties are well down on the scale. Once a
dispute goes to court, the parties have little control over the outcome. Swept up in a
process that is managed by a professional elite and played out before a detached "neutral," many participants feel disempowered.

(3) Results

By far the most serious criticism of the adjudicative process is that it often fails to
satisfy the needs of the parties, and thus of society. To use the economist's jargon, the
results are not Pareto optimal or efficient. Or, to use Fisher and Ury's expression, the
result is "inelegant." The process tends to "find" in favour of one party's interests, and
against another's. To repeat a point already made, the result will tend to have a
disjoining and alienating effect on the parties.

The judicial process limits remedies to two: damages and injunctive relief. With such
limited remedial options there is little opportunity for creative, innovative solutions. The

parties are forced to seek money damages as a proxy for the injury suffered. Any negotiation that does occur is conducted in "the shadow of the judicial process" and the parties seek to reproduce at the negotiating table what they hope to win in court.

The results of judicial dispute resolution are less certain and less predictable than theory would suggest. In theory, adjudicated decisions flow from the application of predetermined and widely accepted rules and principles to objectively determined facts. But there is much about the practice of adjudication that makes results highly problematic for the parties. First, there is seldom agreement over the specific content of a particular principle or over which of two or more competing principles apply to the case at hand. Decision-makers are urged by the parties to adopt one principle over another, to declare one applicable and the other not. Seldom are they invited or encouraged to accept the validity of each and seek a reconciliation of apparently competing principles. The "facts," as determined by the decision-maker, may bear little relationship to what actually happened or what is likely to happen. Finally, decision-makers are human. Personal or professional experience invariably impacts on the result.

None of these points necessarily means that some alternative decision-making or dispute resolution process is preferable to adjudication. Although adjudication has many dysfunctional characteristics, there is much about it that makes it very effective in resolving some types of disputes and for resolving disputes between some types of parties. Thus, our search for a preferable alternative must be tempered by a realization that no one process is necessarily best for all problems/disputes. Nor should our search for an alternative ignore the opportunities for reforming, improving and perhaps even expanding the present process. The search, therefore, must be both to locate adjudication on the dispute resolution process map and to do whatever is necessary to improve the process. The solution, it seems to me, is to fix what needs fixing, expand that which needs expanding and create new dispute resolution mechanisms for those disputes that do not fit within existing dispute resolution processes.

QUESTIONS

Emond suggests that we not abandon adversarial adjudication but, rather, "fix what needs fixing." What, according to Emond, needs to be fixed and how might he fix these failings? What would Fiss or Chayes argue needs to be fixed and what reforms would they advocate? And Weinrib?

The following excerpt is from a commentary prepared by Owen Fiss on a lengthy study paper by Roderick Macdonald for the Ontario Civil Justice Review, entitled "Prospects for Civil Justice" (in *Study Paper on Prospects for Civil Justice* (Toronto: Ontario Law Reform Commission, 1995)). In the excerpt, Fiss takes up the argument that it is possible to determine allocative criteria to ensure that the "forum fits the fuss"; in other words, that it is possible to discern which cases are best suited to particular dispute resolution processes. He offers several critiques of the various potential allocative criteria suggested by Macdonald. Notwithstanding Fiss' critique, you will see from the excerpt from the *First Report of the Civil Justice Review*, which follows the Fiss commentary, that its authors adopted a vision of the court as a multidoor dispute resolution centre, wherein particular "fusses" would be matched with the appropriate forum.

O. Fiss, "A Solution in Search of a Problem"
in Ontario Law Reform Commission, *Study Paper on Prospects for Civil Justice*
(Toronto: Ontario Law Reform Commission, 1995), 205, at 208-12 (footnotes omitted)

Professor Macdonald first considers the possibility of using justiciability as the allocative criterion. Disputes are to be allocated between courts and ADR mechanisms depending on whether the dispute is suitable for adjudication. He concludes, after a lengthy review of the American legal process literature, that this approach does not appear "encouraging." In this conclusion, Professor MacDonald is on firm ground; indeed, I would be a little harsher. The legal process school has never developed an adequate standard for deciding which cases are justiciable and which are not.

The most sustained effort in this regard has been Lon Fuller's notion of "polycentrism," but, as I have pointed out elsewhere, Fuller never satisfactorily explained why courts cannot handle polycentric disputes or why they can be handled better by arbitrators or mediators. Speaking more generally, I think it fair to say the experience of the 1960s in the United States—which involved the courts in school desegregation cases and all manner of structural reform litigation—suggests that no easy divide exists between disputes that are justiciable and those that are not. In fact, the experience of the Warren Court era suggests just the opposite. I read the history of that period to indicate that, in one way or another, all disputes could be formulated or reformulated in terms that make them amenable to adjudication.

At one point, Professor Macdonald mentions two types of disputes that he believes are not justiciable—custody hearings and commercial reorganizations. He writes, "Legal process analysis will permit the identification of various claims and entitlements currently allocated to the courts for decision that, as currently formulated, do not respond to the fundamental logic of adjudication (for example, custody hearings and commercial reorganizations)." I cannot speak to the Canadian experience, but in the United States both types of cases have been routinely handled by the courts; in fact, railroad reorganization was an important part of the civil docket of the federal courts in the late nineteenth century. In any event, note in the quoted sentence Macdonald's qualification "as currently formulated." A couple of lines later, he acknowledges that legal process cannot "guide the legislator in deciding whether ... certain disputes should still be allocated to any particular dispute resolution institution." Aside from the theoretical adequacy of the justiciability criterion, I wonder whether it is, as a purely pragmatic matter, responsive to the question put to Macdonald. Like most of those attracted to ADR, the Ontario Civil Justice Review starts with the existing civil docket now burdening the courts and asks whether some of these "cases" can be diverted to other dispute-resolving institutions (public or private). In framing the question this way, the Review presupposes that the disputes to be resolved are justiciable—after all they are already "cases"—and thus justiciability cannot possibly be used as the sorting criterion.

After he considers the justiciability criterion, Professor Macdonald addresses the possibility of implementing the two track strategy through a social ranking system—one that seeks to determine the relative importance of different kinds of disputes. Courts get the "important" cases, ADR institutions get the "trivial" ones.

In this context, Professor Macdonald makes two points with which I agree: first, that there can be no objection on principle to social rankings, and second, that such rankings are often implicitly made in the existing legal system (e.g., Small Claims Courts). A consensus seems to be emerging that "construction lien" cases should be taken out of the courts and put somewhere else. So be it. What troubles Professor Macdonald is the movement from implicit rankings, ones that have evolved over time, piecemeal, presumably in response to the development of a shared understanding, to a system of rankings that is explicit and fully comprehensive, imposed from the top down at a single moment in history. As Professor Macdonald, always the master of understatement, puts it, "Admittedly, the elaboration of a multi-dimensional civil disputes points system reflects the rationalistic spirit carried to the extreme."

I am probably more a believer in rationalism than Professor Macdonald, so I would not emphasize the intellectual difficulty of constructing the imagined comprehensive system of ranking, though it is obviously an enormously complex task. Rather, my concern is of another nature, arising from doubts as to whether such a comprehensive ranking scheme would be responsive to the social problem that presumably fuels this inquiry. Let us assume, as appears always to be the situation, that the caseload of the judiciary is "too great." Can the overload be due to the number of "trivial" cases before the courts? Of course, the number of filings of such "trivial" cases may be large, perhaps much larger than the "important" cases, but I suspect that the resources of the judiciary are primarily consumed by the "important" cases. "Trivial" cases can be and probably are handled by judges expeditiously, or settled.

I also fear that the social ranking criterion Macdonald envisions may prove to be counterproductive in practice. A comprehensive ranking system would require a screening mechanism that would require a judge or some court official to peek at the litigation that will eventually ensue. Such a peek will only compound delays and costs. Over the years we have become increasingly dissatisfied with ranking systems that look only to the status of the litigants (individual v. organization), the dollar amount of the claim, or the formal category of the law (e.g., family matters)—the easily administered criteria.

At one point in this report, Professor Macdonald makes use of a number of such easily administered criteria. In Appendix V, he lists 19 rules for determining which cases should be handled by the Ontario Court (General Division) and which should be handled by ADR mechanisms. Some of these rules, particularly those listed under the heading "Structure of the Dispute," are subject to the criticism just voiced—they will be counterproductive because they require an elaborate screening process. An example might be the proposed rule denying the Ontario Court (General Division) jurisdiction over any matter in which expert witnesses are required to prove either causation or economic damages. Others, like the rule saving the courts for cases involving "physical persons" or denying it jurisdiction over "commercial disputes," might be more easily administered. But, as pointed out by George Priest, the exclusions effectuated by this criteria could not possibly be justified on the ground that they are "trivial" or, for that matter, on the basis of the allocative criteria analyzed or discussed by Professor Macdonald. Indeed, such exclusions seem to express certain normative considerations, a kind of Canadian populism, that are never fully articulated, let alone defended, by Macdonald in his report. In the preface to the list of the 19 proposed rules, Professor Macdonald warns that the list is only "intended to stimulate discussions about values implicit in debates about alternative dispute resolution." He then adds, "This list itself has no intrinsic value."

After considering justiciability and social ranking, Professor Macdonald addresses the possibility of using consent or individual choice as an allocative criterion. Note that here, consent is not used to justify the preference for the solutions arrived at by certain ADR mechanisms (say, mediation or bilateral negotiation), but rather as sorting criterion, that is, as a basis for determining which cases should be handled by the courts and which ones by ADR. Under this theory, a dispute should be taken out of the courts and given to some other institution if all the parties genuinely agree to that placement (either at the time the disagreement arises or in a contract they enter beforehand).

I, for one, believe it more difficult to apply the consent criterion than Professor Macdonald allows. He acknowledges the risks of coercion and inequalities of bargaining power, but is not sufficiently attentive to the interests of third parties. That too would vitiate the normative force of the consent by litigants, and constitute a sufficient reason for not making the consent of the litigants dispositive. Many of the cases where the state mandates a judicial forum are precisely where third party interests may be in jeopardy, e.g., the dissolution of marriage. Moreover, even when the state allows choice, there may be good reason for second guessing the choice of forum or terms of settlement by the named parties. The litigants speak not just for themselves but may well be advancing the claims or defenses of social groups or organizations; their actions may compromise the rights of others. Almost obsessed by our individualistic ideology, we in the United States tend to slight the group dimensions of litigation. However, Canada has a much richer and more sophisticated understanding of group rights and thus should look more skeptically on the assumption usually made by ADR advocates that the conditions for true and genuine consent are present. This skepticism is particularly appropriate in the high profile cases that consume judicial resources and provoke political controversy.

But let us assume that the consent can be successfully obtained. Even then, I doubt whether treating individual choice as an allocative criterion will yield the results that the proponents of ADR promise. It is true, as Professor MacDonald points out, that there are a number of special situations where the state requires the parties to go to court even if both parties negotiate a settlement or agree to go through another kind of dispute resolution mechanism to resolve their disagreement. Mediators can work out a property settlement, but not dissolve a marriage even when it is childless. These situations are, however, relatively rare in number and cannot plausibly account for much of the judicial workload. Thus, even if we remove all bars to the choice of forum, it is hard to believe that we would have contributed much to alleviating what the Terms of Reference describes as "the pressures of modern litigation."

What the proponents of ADR want is not simply free choice among fora, which basically exists, but rather incentives, strong incentives, to guide that choice in favor of ADR, for only then would there be any meaningful diversion from the courts to alternative institutions. In that spirit, sometimes the search for strong incentives yields rules that are in fact coercive (e.g., in some jurisdictions in the United States a submission to arbitration is sometimes imposed as a condition of judicial access). In any event, whether we deal with incentives or coercion, we still need to identify the category of cases to which the incentives (or coercion) is to be applied—and consent or choice cannot be used for that purpose. Consent is the object acted upon and thus cannot be the sorting criterion.

At one point, Professor Macdonald appears to follow the lead of the proponents of ADR. In the conclusion of his consideration of the consent criterion, he states, "the legislature should not be reluctant ... to influence the streaming choices of individual litigants." But in failing to supply a criterion—choice can't be it—that would identify the cases where that influence should be applied, he leaves the Fundamental Issues Group pretty much as it started—searching for the allocative criteria needed to make ADR operational. Of course, Macdonald may believe that the incentives favoring ADR mechanisms should be created for *all* cases, and there is language on the page from which the last quotation is taken suggesting that is his view. But that is only to abandon the (pretense of the) two track strategy and return ADR to the form in which it was originally presented in the United States—as an expression of an unspecified unhappiness with the courts or government in general.

"The Multi-Door Concept and Alternative Dispute Resolution"
in Civil Justice Review, *First Report* (Toronto: Ontario Civil Justice Review, March 1995), 209-16 (footnotes omitted)

The "Multi-Door" Concept

Earlier in this Report we have alluded to the "multi-door" concept of civil justice.

By that we meant a system where the "Court," in a very broad sense, becomes a "dispute resolution centre"—a place where people go to have their differences resolved in a fashion which is most appropriate to their particular situation. That may—and often will—involve going through the traditional "courtroom door" for a court adjudicated resolution of their dispute. On the other hand, it may involve going through one or another of numerous "alternative dispute resolution" doors—the mediation door, the early neutral evaluation door, the mini-trial door, or the arbitration door, for example.

Central to the multi-door concept is the early evaluation and screening of cases with a view to directing them through the most appropriate "door." This is done through the application of various criteria designed to determine the dispute resolution mechanism most suited to the dispute. Such criteria include: the nature of the case; its complexity; the number of parties; the relationship of the parties; any disparity in bargaining power; the history of the negotiation between the disputants; the nature of the relief sought; and the size of the claim.

Members of the public should have the option to select the process which is most suitable to the resolution of their particular dispute, as well as the facilities to enable them to make that choice. Alternative dispute resolution—or "ADR" as it is commonly known—offers an important panoply of techniques for achieving this goal, particularly in conjunction with the rubric of caseflow management.

What Does It Offer?

ADR techniques are not a panacea for all that ails the civil justice system. They simply provide other methods of attacking the ever present need for human beings to settle their differences. They supplement the court system. They cannot—and should not be expected to—supplant it.

ADR offers a variety of techniques to assist disputants in arriving at resolutions which are more expeditious, less expensive, and, consequently, far less draining from an emotional and psychological point of view for the participants. The great advantage of these techniques is their flexibility—their "smorgasbord" nature. The disputants are free to pick and choose the technique which best suits their dispute, and to do so on their own schedule, in a more informal manner, and under the shield of confidentiality, if they so desire. In short, they can "fit the forum to the fuss," tailor-making their own procedure and, ultimately, their own solution.

The benefits provided by ADR processes have been summarized as follows:

(a) lower court caseloads and related public expense;

(b) more accessible forums to people with disputes;

(c) reduced expenditures of time and money for parties;

(d) speedy and informal settlement of disputes otherwise disruptive of the community or the lives of the parties and their families;

(e) enhanced public satisfaction with the justice system;

(f) tailored resolutions to the parties' needs;

(g) increased satisfaction and compliance with resolutions in which the parties have directly participated; and

(h) restoration of neighbourhood and community values and more cohesive communities.

The most commonly known forms of ADR include such techniques as mediation, arbitration, early neutral evaluation, neutral fact-finding, mini-trials and, of course, negotiation. Negotiation is the oldest form of dispute resolution, dating back as long as there have been two or more people on earth! It is also the best form of dispute resolution, because solutions are arrived at voluntarily rather than by imposition; because negotiation is empowering; because the parties control the process, and their own and everyone else's participation in it; and, finally, because the parties also create and control the final resolution of the issues. However, it does not always work, by itself. When it does not, the parties require the assistance of a third party, either as facilitator or adjudicator.

A great deal has been written on the subject of alternative dispute resolution, and it is not the purpose of the Civil Justice Review to repeat that wealth of information. A brief description of the basic forms of ADR might be useful, however.

Early Neutral Evaluation

Similar to the current process of pre-trials, early neutral evaluation requires the early assessment by an outside expert of the strengths of someone's case. This evaluation need not be by a judge but can be by a senior practitioner with particular expertise in the matter being litigated or by a trained ADR provider.

Pre-Trials

Pre-trials refer to meetings held between counsel and a judge (other than the one who will ultimately hear the case). Except in family law matters, it has not been common for parties to attend. Generally, counsel will file documentation outlining the facts of their case and the law and evidence that they will put forth at trial to support their position. The judge is asked to give an opinion as to how he or she would decide the case if they were the one making the decision. This allows the parties to reassess their positions before proceeding to trial. In a well-prepared for and well-run pre-trial, the judge and counsel will actively explore the possibilities of settlement.

Mini-Trials

A "mini-trial" is not a trial at all, but is a more structured presentation of the case than takes place at a pre-trial. It might be compared to a condensed version of the trial, with the presentation being made to a neutral person like a judge, or, preferably, to a neutral person plus a representative of each party. Evidence may be presented in the form of oral testimony and/or in affidavit form. The procedural details are usually determined by the parties in advance.

In the course of preparing for the mini-trial, the parties are required to give a thorough examination of the merits of their case. Once again, they have the benefit of an opinion from an outside evaluator.

Mediation

Mediation is a process in which a neutral person, agreeable to the disputing parties, acts as a facilitator to their negotiations and assists them in arriving at their own mutually acceptable solution. Mediation may occur before the litigation has commenced or at any time before trial. Generally, it is undertaken outside the court process, although judges will use mediating techniques in attempting to promote settlement discussions.

Settlement Conferences

In a case managed environment, there may be a number of meetings held in the course of the litigation between the parties and the assigned judge or team of judges. It is expected that at least once, before trial, there will be a meeting to actively explore the possibilities of settlement of all or part of the issues.

Arbitration (Binding and Non-Binding)

In this form of ADR, a neutral third party acts as an adjudicator. The parties can determine in advance if the decision of the arbitrator will be binding or non-binding. A non-binding decision will allow the party to proceed to the courts in the event that they are unhappy with the litigation and no reference will be made to the arbitrator's decision. In binding arbitration, the decision is enforceable. The parties will generally determine in advance what right and procedure of appeal will apply. If they do not, the provisions of *The Arbitrations Act* apply.

The Need for Standards for ADR Practitioners

Currently there exist few, if any, standards for qualification as an ADR practitioner. There are no accreditation facilities of a provincial or federal nature. There are individuals and organizations which provide training and courses in ADR. While much of this training is excellent, we believe it to be in the public interest that standards of accreditation be established, in order to ensure a high level of quality in the services provided to the public, both through the private sector and through any court-connected facilities that may be provided.

Should ADR Be Court-Connected?

There are two factors which, in our view, support the conclusion that ADR facilities should be available to the public as part of the "court" system (again using that concept in a broad sense).

The first, as we have already mentioned, is that the state has an obligation to make available to its members the means by which their disputes may be resolved through the medium of objective, independent and fair third party intervention, when they are unable to resolve those disputes themselves. ADR is an effective way of doing so for many civil disputes, albeit not for all. Parties should have the option of resorting to the private sector for ADR services—and, indeed, should be encouraged to exercise that option. There are many skilled ADR practitioners in the private sector. Civil justice ought not to be privatized, however, in the sense that the public is *required* to resort to private providers in order to enjoy the opportunities offered by ADR techniques. Such a circumstance could have the effect of limiting access to ADR options by those who are unable to resort to the private sector for one reason or another.

Secondly, ADR fits smoothly with the notion of caseflow management. Many of the techniques of ADR are already used by judges in settlement conferences. The use of these techniques can be expanded to other types of case conferences and, generally, to the process of managing the case throughout. Indeed, it could be argued that ADR itself *is* a multi-faceted form of case management. Since one of the important goals of case management is the early resolution of cases, the Court should have access to the range of ADR techniques which are available to effect that purpose, particularly the mechanism of early screening and evaluation of cases. If these procedures are to be effective in resolving some matters, it is critical that the Court have access to the tools.

Mr. Justice George Adams expressed the rationale for court-connected ADR in the following passage, in a paper on ADR, presented at Cornell University in July 1994:

> The inter-relationship between the courts, the rule of law and dispute resolution cannot be understated. Its importance to a viable democratic society has been underlined by the Supreme Court of Canada in the following passage from the decision of the Honourable Mr. Justice Cory in *Edmonton Journal v. Alta. (AG)*:
>
>> There can be no doubt that the courts play an important role in any democratic society. They are the forum not only for the resolution of disputes between citizens, but for the resolution of disputes between the citizens and the state in all its manifestations. The more complex society becomes, the more important becomes the function of the courts. ...

It is precisely this fundamental public function of the courts that makes court-annexed ADR so crucial. Our courts must reflect the growing complexity of Canadian society in the dispute resolution processes they offer to the public. We can no longer take efficient private self-ordering for granted. The law applying to efforts of the profession through settlement requires active support. It is not sufficient to provide only one specialized and formal dispute resolution procedure—the trial.

Whether one or another of the ADR options is an appropriate one for any case is a question that should be canvassed regularly during the course of the case's progress. Case management, with its more "hands on" judicial approach, and its more frequent resort to case conferences, is an ideal vehicle to permit the parties to do so, and to move their matter out of the litigation stream into ADR at any stage where it seems appropriate, either for the resolution of the dispute as a whole, or for the resolution of a particular issue or issues.

NOTES AND QUESTIONS

1. The authors of the *First Report* provide a list of the criteria to be used to determine the dispute resolution mechanism best suited to a particular dispute. These include "the nature of the case; its complexity; the number of parties; the relationship of the parties; any disparity in bargaining power; the history of the negotiations between the disputants; the nature of the relief sought; and the size of the claim." Does this list of criteria take at all seriously the critique offered by Fiss? To what type of dispute resolution process do these various criteria point?

2. Note the many benefits claimed for ADR (here, too, treated as a monolith) in the *First Report*. As you read the critiques of informalism later in the chapter, consider whether these claims can be sustained for any particular ADR process.

3. Recently, the benchers of the Law Society of Upper Canada unanimously endorsed the recommendations of the society's subcommittee on dispute resolution, designed to move ADR into the "mainstream of dispute resolution" and to provide lawyers with the necessary tools (see Law Society of Upper Canada Sub-Committee on Dispute Resolution, *Report Summary* (February 1993)). The benchers voted in May 1996 to add a new commentary to the Rules of Professional Conduct, which provides:

> The lawyer should consider the appropriateness of ADR to the resolution of issues in every case and if appropriate, the lawyer should inform the client of the ADR options and, if so instructed, take steps to pursue those options.

The benchers rejected a proposal for the creation of a new rule which would have imposed a positive duty to inform clients of ADR.

As the excerpt from Emond suggests, two approaches might be envisioned by the term "alternative." One approach would be the modification of traditional litigation, the other the replacement of judicial litigation with other mechanisms for dispute resolution. Of course, a third approach would be the creation of parallel structures—either court-annexed or entirely independent of the courts—that would expand the choice of at least some disputants. In chapter 6, "Pleadings and Disposition Without Trial," we consider some of the ways in which the rules governing traditional litigation have been modified to encourage negotiation or mediation. One of these modifications is the use of costs to penalize a party for the failure to accept a reasonable offer to settle (see rule 49.10 of the Ontario Rules of Practice). Another example is the "settlement conference," a mandatory procedure under rule 77 of the Ontario Rules of Practice, requiring the parties to attend before a judge to consider the settlement of any or all of the issues in the proceeding. Examples such as these are what Fiss arguably had in mind when he asserted that "what the proponents of ADR want is not simply free choice among fora, which basically exists, but rather incentives, strong incentives, to guide that choice in favor of ADR."

In the excerpt that follows, Menkel-Meadow discusses the mandatory settlement conference and, in particular, the different conceptions of role that judges bring to such conferences. These conceptions, Menkel-Meadow argues, are tied to some of the competing value claims made by proponents of ADR.

C. Menkel-Meadow, "For and Against Settlement: Uses and Abuses of the Mandatory Settlement Conference"
(1985), 33 *UCLA Law Review* 485, at 486-511 (footnotes omitted)

One of the most fundamental disputes about nonadjudicatory dispute resolution concerns the values it is intended to promote. Some commentators contrast the quantitative, efficiency, process axis to the qualitative, justice, substance axis. Some extol mandatory settlement conferences, arbitration, and mediation programs because they decrease delay of case processing time and promote judicial efficiency. This claim is not supported by the empirical research at this stage. Others assert (and I am affiliated with this school) that the *quality* of dispute resolution is improved when models other than the formal adjudication model are used. Solutions to disputes can be tailored to the parties' polycentric needs and can achieve greater party satisfaction and enforcement reliability because they are not binary, win/lose results. Still others assert that quality solutions are more likely to emerge when the dispute resolutions process is not privatized and individualized. This argument is characterized alternatively as the "cool efficiency/warm conciliation," "quanitative/qualitative," or "managerial/substantive" justifications for nonadjudicative dispute resolution.

A second dispute concerns the appropriate role of judges when they become involved in alternative dispute resolution or settlement conferences. The judges themselves characterize this issue as whether they should be "active" or "passive." Academics debate whether judges should be "managers" or "adjudicators."

A third dispute falls on the micro-macro axis of analysis. Is the appropriate unit of analysis the particular or individual disputes that are resolved and with which the parties and lawyers are satisfied or should the unit of analysis be the larger system as measured by judicial management statistics or by the quality of precedents produced? Owen Fiss has recently suggested that if too many cases are diverted from the courtroom into settlement, appellate judges will have an insufficient number and quality of cases from which to make the law. Fiss's prediction, if true, could have grave implications for the legitimacy of the entire legal system.

The three disputes outlined above raise issues that should affect significantly our assessment of the strengths and weaknesses of any dispute resolution device. In order to evaluate the arguments advanced in these disputes, we must explore the underlying values and the empirical claims made in support of these arguments.

There are, as I see it, three value claims. First, there is the efficient-justice claim: Full adjudicatory trials are too long, and there could be too many of them to permit expeditious justice. Ultimately, failure to provide "speedy and inexpensive justice" can become a substantive justice problem. Thus, proponents of mandatory settlement conferences, court-annexed arbitration, and mediation argue that more efficient justice is better justice.

Second, there is the substantive justice claim: The principal function of our legal system is to provide fair and just results to the individual disputants and to society. These results are dependent on rules, generated from other people's disputes, that help define appropriate behavior. Thus, in considering any dispute resolution device we should ask if this process is the most likely to produce a just result for the parties and/or the best result for the future guidance of society. (The answer to this compound question is sometimes different for each of its parts. This contributes to the difficulty of assessing whether settlement is appropriate.)

Third, there is a claim I will call a substantive process claim, made most recently by Judith Resnik. Proponents of substantive process argue that whether a process is public or private (subject to accountability), coercive or voluntary, reasoned or rationalized, matters a great deal, both for the substantive justice achieved and for the legitimacy of the entire process as viewed by those inside of the dispute and by those outside. A corollary substantive process claim, with a focus different from the locus of the claim asserted by Professor Resnik, is that the quality of the process (for example, the "warmer" modes of dispute processing such as conciliation and mediation which give greater involvement to the parties and permit greater flexibility in solution) serves important human values different from the value of a quality substantive outcome.

These three value claims are not as distinct as they may appear: All assume that the process chosen affects the outcome and the outcome desired affects the choice of process. To complicate matters further, as reviewed below, there are differences of opinion as to how effective particular dispute resolution forms are in advancing these values. ...

V. The Functions and Purposes of the Mandatory Settlement Conference: The How and Why of Settlement Practices

As greater numbers of judges and courts use settlement conferences, our information about particular practices increases. Our current sources of data include reports and articles written by judges and settlement officers, training materials written for new judges, some survey data collected by social scientists and court administrators, and descriptive and critical reports by academics. As we review this data, it is useful to think about how the manager of the settlement conference, whether judge or magistrate, views his or her role. What emerges from the data is a variety of role conceptions that parallel the various conceptions of the goals of settlement. For some, efficient case management is the primary role; for others, the primary role is the facilitation of substantive or procedural justice. For others still, the primary role is simple brokering of what would occur anyway in bilateral negotiations. Some judges avoid active settlement activity because they view adjudication as their primary role.

My concern with the settlement management role conception is twofold. First, role conception seems to have a direct effect on the choice of techniques used. In turn, the techniques may have a direct influence on the type of settlement reached. Second, without an open debate about the merits of particular technique choices, we may be unaware of both primary and secondary effects of making settlement conferences mandatory.

It is not surprising that the literature describing practices in settlement conferences reflects the full range of attitudes toward the appropriateness of judicial intervention. Those judges least comfortable with intervention in settlement describe the settlement process as a mere "by-product" of the mandatory pretrial conference. Such judges see themselves simply as facilitators of what the lawyers would do anyway, providing a meeting place for lawyers to get together and discuss their cases. In one well-documented case, the judge arranged several days of cocktail parties and country club dining to encourage a meeting of counsel in a complex case. Moving slightly closer to the activist line are those judges who maintain that the best intervention on behalf of settlement is the setting of a firm trial date, thereby expediting discovery, improving estimates of costs and predictions of trial outcomes, and setting firm deadlines for discovery and trial.

At the other extreme are the activist judges who see settlement of cases as one of their principal functions. In one of the more thoughtful judicial analyses of the advantages and disadvantages of judicial intervention, Judge Fox of the federal district court in western Michigan has analyzed both the quantitative efficiency, docket management arguments and the substantive values (results more closely related to the merits of the cases as the parties and their lawyers understand them) arguments in favor of intervention.

A. The Dangers of Efficiency-Seeking Settlement Techniques

For those who seek to use the settlement conference as a docket-clearing device, the conference becomes most problematic in terms of the substantive and process values (i.e., *quality* of solution) previously discussed. Judges see their role as simplifying the issues until the major issue separating the parties (usually described as money) is identified and the judge can attempt to "narrow the gap." In one study judges and lawyers were asked to report on judicial settlement activity. Seventy-two percent of the lawyers reported that they participated at least once in settlement conferences in which the judge requested the parties to "split the difference." The same study noted that when local rules require settlement conferences judges tend to be more assertive in their settlement techniques (using several techniques that some of the lawyers considered to be unethical). According to the study, jurisdictions with mandatory settlement conferences took more time in moving cases toward trial. This confirms the findings of earlier studies.

A much touted settlement technique is the use of the "Lloyds of London" formula: The settlement judge asks the parties to assess the probabilities of liability and damages and, if the figures are within reasonable range, to split the difference. The difficulty with such settlement techniques is that they tend to monetarize and compromise all the issues in the case. Although some cases are reducible to monetary issues, an approach to case evaluation on purely monetary grounds may decrease the likelihood of settlement by making fewer issues available for trade-offs. Furthermore, a wider definition of options may make compromise unnecessary. As the recent outpouring of popular and scholarly literature on negotiation illustrates, the greater the number of issues in controversy between the parties, the greater the likelihood of achieving a variety of solutions. Parties may place complementary values on different items. The irony is that settlement managers, who think they are making settlement easier by reducing the issues, may in fact be increasing the likelihood of deadlock by reducing the issues to one. Furthermore, as I have argued at length elsewhere, using money as a proxy for other interests the parties may have may thwart the possibilities for using party interests for mutual gain.

In addition to foreclosing a number of possible settlements, the efficiency-minded settlement officer seems prone to us[ing] coercive techniques such as suggesting a particular result, making threats about taking the case off the docket, directing meetings with clients or parties. Lawyers find these techniques problematic. Thus, the quest for efficiency may in fact be counterproductive.

B. The Search for Quality Solutions

Some recent data seem to indicate that greater satisfaction can be achieved with a different settlement management role—the facilitator of good settlements. Brazil's survey of lawyers practicing in four federal districts reveals that lawyers favored intervention techniques that sought to produce the "best result." Lawyers favored such techniques because judges who analyzed the particular facts of the case (as opposed to those who used formulas like "Lloyds of London"), offered explicit suggestions and assessments of the parties' positions, occasionally spoke directly to recalcitrant clients, and expressed views about the unfairness of particular results. Brazil's data are interesting in that they point to variations in the desirability of particular settlement techniques, depending on size of case, case type, defense or plaintiff practice, and other demographic factors.

What emerges from Brazil's data is that lawyers want different things in different cases. Thus, a routinized settlement agenda is not likely to be successful in satisfying their desires. More significantly, the data show that lawyers do not perceive judges' settlement role as significantly different from their adjudicative role when the judges employ the more favored settlement techniques. In alternative dispute resolution parlance, the lawyers of Brazil's study seek a hybrid of the adjudicator—the "med-arb" (mediator-arbitrator):

> They prefer that judges express opinions, offer suggestions, or analyze situations much more than they value judges asking the attorneys to make a presentation or conduct an analysis. Our respondents consistently give higher effective ratings to settlement conference procedures that revolve around inputs by judges than those that feature exposition by counsel. Thus, the lawyers' assessments of specific techniques reinforce the major theme that what litigators want most from judges in settlement conferences is *an expression of analytical opinion.*

The lawyers wanted help in achieving specific results through analysis and reasoned opinions, not formulaic compromises. Whether judges will deliver such help is another issue. If, as Resnik argues, there is a danger that judges will manipulate results to serve their own ends when the results do not have to be justified in print, we should view with distrust some of the techniques suggested here. But if judges (or magistrates) will serve as Howard Raiffa's "analytic mediators" (i.e., asking questions to explore the parties' interests and attempting to fashion tailor-made solutions from an "objective" outside-of-the-problem position, but with additional information), then judicial and magistrate settlement managers may be providing both better and more efficient (in the Pareto optimal sense) solutions to litigation problems.

Judges who perform these functions are not necessarily mediators, though they are frequently called that by themselves and others. Strictly speaking, a mediator facilitates communication between the parties and helps them to reach their own solution. As a mediator becomes more directly involved in suggesting the substantive solution, his or her role can change and he or she can become an arbitrator or adjudicator. It appears that the role judges and magistrates assume in many settlement conferences is this hybrid form of med-arb. Med-arb uses all the techniques associated with mediation and arbitration—caucusing (meeting with the parties separately), making suggestions to the parties, allowing closed or best-offer bidding, and meeting with principals (clients) who have authority to settle or to reconsider and reconceive the problem. As the med-arb process moves toward arbitration, "settlements" may closely resemble adjudication with rationalized, normative, or law-based solutions.

To the extent that settlement procedures are used to achieve substantive outcomes that are better than court-defined remedies, they have implications for how the settlement conference should be conducted and who should conduct it. First, those with knowledge about the larger implications of the litigation—the parties—should be present (this is the principle behind the mini-trial concept with business personnel in attendance) to offer or accept solutions that involve more than simple money settlements. Second, such conferences should be managed by someone other than the trial judge so that interests and considerations that might effect a settlement but would be inadmissible in court will not prejudice a later trial. Some argue for a separate "settlement officer" because the skills required for guiding negotiations are different from those required for trying cases. Third, some cases in which issues should not be traded off should not be subjected to the settlement process at all. For example, in employment discrimination cases, parties should not be asked to accept monetary settlements in lieu of a job for which they are qualified. Finally, a more traditional mediator's role may be more appropriate when the substantive process (i.e., direct communication between the parties) may be more important than the substantive outcome (i.e., employer–employee disputes, some civil rights cases).

QUESTION

Recall the excerpt from Tyler in chapter 2, "The Value of Procedure"; how, if at all, do these various approaches to the settlement conference mesh with people's expectations for procedural fairness?

B. The Case for Informalism: Mediation, in Particular

Mediation is a process located within the broad contours of the ADR movement. As suggested earlier, it is, perhaps, the process that has most captured the imagination and enthusiasm of civil justice reformers. Many of the arguments cast in favour of mediation are those arguments advanced by Emond with respect to ADR generally. Mediation is regarded by its proponents to be particularly relevant (and beneficial) in situations where conflict arises within the context of an ongoing relationship. An adversarial adjudicative process is seen to work a number of harms on long-term relationships. First, the adversary system often engenders hostility, it encourages each side to press its case to the fullest without regard to the consequences on one's opponent. Indeed, the very construction of "opponents" pits one party against the other. Second, as Emond notes, an adjudicative process produces a "winner" and a "loser." Not only does this render it difficult for the parties to continue their relationship into the future, but it also severely curtails the range of possible outcomes. Adjudication is also critiqued for its tendency to look back into the past in an attempt to reconstruct a completed life event and then to determine the appropriate remedy to correct this past state of affairs (assuming, that is, that the court in its reconstruction of the events actually determines that correction of some sort is required). Most adjudication fails to attend to the question of what is the most appropriate arrangement to guide the conduct and relationship of these parties into the future.

So, for example, in the context of an ongoing commercial relationship, where the parties would like the relationship to continue into the future, it will be important to them to try to resolve their existing disputes in a manner that will enhance, rather than impair, their future working relationship. An adversarial system of adjudication, it is argued, works harm upon the relationship. Mediation, by contrast, arguably enhances future outcomes.

In North America, mediation has had a strong presence within the context of industrial relations for years; terms of collective agreements (the contract between the employer and the union) are often settled through mediation, as are disputes that arise in the daily operation of the employer's business. But it has been only in the past decade or so, a period of time when mediation has been touted as the panacea for the resolution of disputes arising upon marital breakdown, that mediation has attracted much attention from legal academics, lawyers, and law-makers. The past few years have witnessed increasing numbers of mediation training courses, increasing momentum toward the requirement that parties to a family law proceeding participate in mediation, and increasing resort (volitional and compulsory) to mediation in the civil justice system more generally.

Jay Folberg and Alison Taylor, *Mediation*
(San Francisco: Jossey-Bass, 1984), 1-15 (footnotes omitted)

Mediation as an alternative to self-help or formal legal procedures is not entirely new. Forms of conflict resolution in which a third party helps disputants resolve their conflicts and come to their own decisions have probably been practiced since the existence of three or more people on earth. Mediation, like most concepts, is not a novel invention but an adaptation of that which has already existed in other cultures or in other times.

Historical and Cultural Roots

In ancient China, mediation was the principal means of resolving disputes. The Confucian view was that optimum resolution of a dispute was achieved by moral persuasion and agreement rather than sovereign coercion. Confucian beliefs proposed the existence of a natural harmony in human affairs that should not be disrupted. Unilateral self-help and adversary proceedings presume the end of a harmonious relationship and would thus be the antithesis of the peace and understanding central to Confucian thought. Mediation on a grand scale continues to be practiced today in the People's Republic of China through the institution of People's Conciliation Committees. Even in the formal Chinese legal system, considerable importance is placed on self-determination and mediation in the resolution of all types of disputes.

Conciliation and mediation have a rich history in Japanese law and customs. The leader of the village community was expected to help community members settle their disputes. Provision for conciliation of personal disputes in Japanese courts was enacted prior to World War II. Many writers, analyzing the litigious quality of American society, have noted the relative absence of lawyers in Japan. The tradition of conciliation and mediation is so imbued in Japan that there are rumored to be more flower arrangers in Japan than attorneys. However, this preference for mediation in Japan may reflect a system of procedural barriers to formal litigation as much as a popular preference for less formal dispute resolution.

In parts of Africa, the custom of assembling a *moot*, or neighborhood meeting, has long provided an informal mechanism for resolving a variety of interpersonal disputes. Any disputant or neighbor may call a moot where a respected notable or "big man" often serves as a mediator to help the involved parties resolve their conflict cooperatively. The role of the notable and the tradition of the moot vary from one community to another, but all appear to seek settlement without judge, arbitrator, or the use of sanctions. The success of the moot may be based, in part, on the extended kinship circles within many African communities.

The extended family and kinship circles have provided a mediation resource in many lands and cultures. Patriarchal as well as matriarchal family leaders have offered wisdom, precedents, and models to assist family members in resolving their disputes. As rural families gathered together in villages, as villages grew into cities, and as the nuclear family supplanted the extended family, the family structure began to provide less of a resource for conflict resolution. People turned increasingly to formal rather than informal mechanisms to resolve their disputes.

The church or temple has played an important part in resolving conflict among its members for centuries. The local parish priest, minister, or rabbi was frequently called upon to serve as a mediator, particularly in family disputes, to suggest ways that the disputants might learn to live with each other or reorganize their relationships. There is a rich New Testament tradition of mediation stemming from the recognition that Paul talked to the congregation at Corinth, suggesting that they should not take their disputes to the court but ought rather to appoint people of their own community to settle their disputes. Mediation is consistent with, if not central to, the biblical values of forgiveness, reconciliation, and community. There is both a biblical foundation and approval for mediators able to bring about peaceful coexistence: "Blessed be the peacemakers for they shall be called the sons of God."

Ethnic and religious groups, as well other subcultures, have historically established their own alternative systems for dispute resolution. They desired to avoid imposition of the majority government's values and sought to retain their own means of resolving conflicts. The Jewish Beth Din, a council of local rabbis, has existed for this purpose for many generations and in many different settings. Merchant groups, trade councils, gypsies, and even organized crime have all felt a common need to resolve disputes, one way or another, without the imposition of outside authority. Resolution of interpersonal and commercial conflicts between members of a subgroup with the assistance of respected third parties from the group was a way to retain a cherished independence and set of norms. Mediation, and to some extent arbitration, represented a form of personal, cultural, and religious empowerment without conceding the power to decide personal disputes to the king or other secular authority.

In the United States, Chinese immigrants set up the Chinese Benevolent Association to resolve by mediation disputes between members of the community and within the family. In 1920, the American Jewish community established its own mediation forum, the Jewish Conciliation Board, in New York City. The early Quakers in the United States practiced both mediation and arbitration to resolve their commercial disputes and marital disagreements without resorting to litigation. More recently, the Christian Conciliation Service has established several pilot projects to train and provide church mediators for the resolution of personal disputes.

The most familiar model for mediation in the United States comes from the dispute resolution procedures in labor/management relations. Labor disputes—like family disputes, neighborhood conflicts, environmental issues, and other relation-based tensions—represent a "polycentric," or many centered, situation. Labor relationships are long-term and depend on future cooperation of the parties, in contrast to isolated disputes dependent for resolution on findings of historical fact for the purpose of deciding upon a "winner" and "loser" who need have no further dealings with one another. Some of the early writing proposing the adaptation of alternative dispute settlement techniques for interpersonal conflict drew heavily from the background and experience of labor and industrial dispute resolution.

Definition

The history of mediation only begins to define what it is. Many questions about mediation are answered by understanding what mediation is and what it is not. The practice of mediation falls along a spectrum that defies a strict definition. The specifics of mediation depend on what is being mediated, the parties in dispute, who is doing the mediating, and the setting in which mediation is offered. Mediation is first and foremost a *process* that transcends the content of the conflict it is intended to resolve.

Mediation is an alternative to violence, self-help, or litigation that differs from the processes of counseling, negotiation, and arbitration. It can be defined as the process by which the participants, together with the assistance of a neutral person or persons, systematically isolate disputed issues in order to develop options, consider alternatives, and reach a consensual settlement that will accommodate their needs. Mediation is a process that emphasizes the participants' own responsibility for making decisions that affect their lives. It is therefore a self-empowering process.

Mediation has definite stages involving a series of techniques for accomplishing necessary tasks. It is a finite process that produces specific outcomes by utilizing the values, norms, and principles of the participants rather than those of mediators. The objectives of mediation are:

- Production of a plan (agreement) for the future that the participants can accept and comply [with]
    - Preparation of the participants to accept the consequences of their own decisions
    - Reduction of the anxiety and other negative effects of the conflict by helping the participants devise a consensual resolution

Mediation is usually a short-term process rather than a long-term intervention. It is interactive rather than interpersonal. The participants' personality structures and behavior (including manipulation, overt anger, withdrawal, power struggles) that may have created the interactional problems may be discussed, but personality is not the primary focus unless the behavior blocks the mediation process. Mediation is more concerned with how the parties will resolve the conflict and create a plan than with personal histories. In this respect, mediation is cognitive and behavioral in perspective rather than existential. It is more concerned with the present and the future than with the past. Mediation helps to:

- Reduce the obstacles to communication between participants
- Maximize the exploration of alternatives
- Address the needs of everyone involved
- Provide a model for future conflict resolution

Trust and confidence by the parties involved, as in any helping relationship, are necessary for an effective mediation process. The development of a therapeutic relationship between the parties and the mediator is not a goal, however. The relationship that is formed may be an important means, but it is subordinate to the orientation toward tasks and goals. Participation in mediation may or may not have a therapeutic effect on the parties. It is not intended to bring insight into past behavioral patterns or change personality. Mediation is task-directed and goal-oriented. It looks at results rather than the internal causes of conflict. It discourages dependence on the professional rather than promoting it.

Mediation is not primarily didactic. It is an experiential process requiring active participation. While there may be "take-home" knowledge that is derived from the experience of mediation, its primary focus is on the solution of the task and the development of a plan of action for the future. Mediation is not a new therapy method, nor is it a panacea for all psychological and interactive problems. It should be seen as a set of skills and a process that can be used selectively by professionals when the problems demand a coherent agreement between conflicting participants. Mediation will not replace present theories of behavior or therapy; it will not replace long-term therapy of behavioral, perceptual, or personality problems; nor will it replace the need for legal information and advice. It can, however, be a useful intervention technique when the situation calls for a structured agreement to a conflict.

Rationale

Both the rationale for mediation as an alternative to the adversary process and the effect of mediated agreements appear to make it a promising, if not compelling, process when compared to the adversarial model. Mediation can educate the participants about each other's needs and provide a personalized model for settling future disputes between them. It can thus help them learn to work together, isolate the issues to be decided, and see that through cooperation all can make positive gains.

Mediation offers this advantage because it is not bound by the rules of procedure and substantive law, as well as certain assumptions, that dominate the adversary process. The ultimate authority in mediation belongs to the participants themselves, and they may fashion a unique solution that will work for them without being strictly governed by precedent or being unduly concerned with the precedent they may set for others. They may, with the help of their mediator, consider a comprehensive mix of their needs, interests, and whatever else they deem relevant regardless of rules of evidence or strict adherence to substantive law. Unlike the adjudicatory process, the emphasis is not on who is right or wrong or who wins and who loses, but rather upon establishing a workable solution that meets the participant's unique needs. Mediation is a win/win process.

By definition, a consensual agreement, whether reached through mediation or direct negotiation, reflects the participants' own preferences and will be more acceptable in the long run than one imposed by a court. In the process of mediation, participants formulate their own agreement and make an emotional investment in its success. They are more likely to support its terms than those of an agreement negotiated or imposed by others. The lack of self-determination in adversary proceedings helps account for the never-ending litigation surrounding some conflicts.

The reduction of hostility—by encouraging direct communication between the participants through the process of mediation—facilitates the permanence of a settlement. It naturally reduces the likelihood that a legal battle will continue beyond the mediation process. Mediation tends to diffuse hostilities by promoting cooperation through a structured process. In contrast, litigation tends to focus hostilities and harden the disputants' anger into rigidly polarized positions. The adversarial process, with its dependence upon attorneys on behalf of the clients, tends to deny the parties the opportunity of taking control of their own situation and increases their dependence on outside authority. The self-esteem and sense of competence derived from the mediation process are important by-products that help to provide self-direction and lessen the need for participants to continue fighting.

Mediation works very well for many types of disputes. Groups and individuals who attempt to resolve their differences by using this process generally respond favorably to postmediation evaluations about its fairness and value.

Basic Propositions and Assumptions

Most mediators appear to share a set of principles, although these principles have rarely been systematically stated. ... The propositions listed below are intended to help form a framework of values and beliefs that will allow mediators to develop a shared theory of practice. Identifying, testing, and refining a set of principles upon which mediators can agree will allow mediation to grow into a separate and distinct profession. The "professionalization" of mediation will better serve the interests of the public as well as the needs of the mediator. These principles, which we shall call propositions, form the philosophy of mediation.

Propositions about mediation include beliefs about participants' abilities and motivation and beliefs about human processes in general. We propose the following eight propositions, further described in subsequent chapters, as the basis for a system of shared, unified beliefs for mediators:

- *Proposition 1.* People try to escape what they perceive as negative or destructive (pain) and go toward what they perceive as advantageous and positive (pleasure).
- *Proposition 2.* People make more complete, and therefore better, decisions when they are consciously aware of the feelings created by conflicts and deal effectively with those feelings. ("Dealing effectively" means integrating the feelings into decisions without allowing the emotions to overwhelm rational concerns.)
- *Proposition 3.* The participants in a personal dispute can generally make better decisions about their own lives than can an outside authority such as an arbitrator.
- *Proposition 4.* The participants to an agreement are more likely to abide by its terms if they feel some responsibility for the outcome and develop a commitment to the process used to reach agreement.
- *Proposition 5.* In mediation the past history of the participants is only important in relation to the present or as a basis for predicting future needs, intentions, abilities, and reactions to decisions.
- *Proposition 6.* The more accurately a mediated agreement reflects the needs, intentions, and abilities of the participants, the more likely it is to last.
- *Proposition 7.* Since the participants' needs, intentions, and abilities will probably change, the process should include a way of modifying the agreement in the future. Thus change is seen as a constructive and viable part of the agreement and must be considered in the mediation process.
- *Proposition 8.* The mediation process is substantially the same for all participants and all situations, but techniques, scheduling, and tasks to be accomplished must vary to match the circumstances, the participants, and the uniqueness of the mediator.

Acceptance of these propositions, or similar principles, is essential to the development of mediation as a process and a profession. While these propositions are quite basic, they are useful as a starting point for further development.

Although these eight propositions are thought to be universal, other basic assumptions need to be confirmed by the participants in each case. It is normally true, for example, that both participants in a mediation session wish for the conflicts between them to be resolved. This is particularly true when the mediation process is voluntary, but it may or may not be true in court-mandated mediation services. A further assumption that should be confirmed with the participants is that they must, to some degree, change their perceptions, feelings, beliefs, priorities, thoughts, or actions in order to bring about a resolution of the conflict.

Another assumption is that the participants are accepting the mediator as a guide to lead them through the mediation process. In private practice, this assumption should be double-checked and formalized into an employment agreement or agreement to mediate. Still another assumption is that the mediator's attitudes and conduct provide a model for the mediation process. The participants will expect the mediator to follow the same rules and offer structure and techniques they can use during the course of the mediation session. While this modeling may not be overtly discussed, the mediator must present a clear example of good communication skills and involvement in the process in order to elicit the same from the participants.

Most mediators who have gained expertise in the mediation process share one further assumption. Trained mediators can assist the process better than ad hoc mediators who have not had the benefit of specific education and experience, particularly when the issues have substantial impact. Thus disputes regarding use of natural resources, business mergers, or divorce and custody should be brought to trained mediators rather than well-intentioned but untrained friends or volunteers.

NOTES AND QUESTIONS

1. Currently the practice of mediation remains essentially unregulated. Anyone can hang out a mediator's shingle. As one can imagine, given the increasing resort to mediation as a process for the resolution of disputes, there is a growing concern that the practice be regulated in some fashion. In Ontario, the only restriction on the practice of mediation by lawyers is found in draft rule 4.08 of the Law Society of Upper Canada's Rules of Professional Conduct. (A similar provision has been proposed by the Canadian Bar Association for inclusion in the model code.)

> A lawyer who functions as a mediator shall at the outset ensure that the parties to the mediation process understand fully that: (a) the function being discharged is not part of the traditional practice of law; (b) the lawyer is not acting as a lawyer for either party, but as mediator acts to assist the parties to resolve the matters in issue; and (c) although communications pertaining to and arising out of the mediation process may be covered by some other common law privilege, they will not be covered by the solicitor–client privilege.

Commentary

1. The lawyer-mediator should suggest and encourage the parties to seek the advice of separate counsel before and during the mediation process if they have not already done so.

2. Where in the mediation process the lawyer-mediator prepares a draft contract for the consideration of the respective parties the lawyer-mediator should expressly advise and encourage them to seek separate independent legal advice concerning the draft contract.

3. The lawyer-mediator must at the outset inform the parties to the mediation that although communications pertaining to and arising out of the mediation process may be covered by some other common law privilege, they will not be covered by the solicitor-client privilege.

4. In acting in the capacity of a mediator the lawyer as a general rule should not give legal advice as opposed to legal information to the parties during the mediation process.

5. As a general rule, neither the lawyer-mediator nor a partner or associate of the lawyer-mediator should render legal representation or give legal advice to either party to the mediation bearing in mind the provisions of Rule 5 and its Commentaries and the common law authorities.

How, if at all, can one distinguish legal information from legal advice, as rule 25 purports to do? Could the failure to provide appropriate and adequate legal information constitute poor legal advice? Does this rule and commentary implicitly recognize that the norm in legal representation is adversarial and that mediation represents a marked departure from that norm?

2. As noted earlier, the Ontario Civil Justice Review's *Final Report* concluded that the Toronto ADR (mediation) project had been so successful that virtually all civil cases ought to be referred to mediation as a precondition to continuing in the litigation process. The Ministry of the Attorney General acted on this by proposing a new rule for consideration by the Rules Committee that ultimately led to the passage in Ontario of rule 24.1 (in force January 1999). The rule provides for early and mandatory mediation in case-managed cases in Toronto and Ottawa. This is a pilot project, which, if after detailed evaluation is found to be successful, will be extended province-wide; the hope is that mandatory mediation will lead to earlier settlements at lower costs to litigants.

Under the rule, a mediation session has to take place within 90 days after the first defence is filed, unless the court orders otherwise. Mediations are to be conducted by a person chosen by the agreement of the parties from an approved list of roster mediators; however, if the parties so agree, the mediation may be conducted by a person who is not on the list. If the parties cannot agree on a mediator or fail to proceed in a timely manner, the mediation coordinator will assign a person from the roster of mediators to conduct the mediation session. The program is a *user-pay* program and, if list mediators are used, the charge for each party for a three-hour mediation session will be in the vicinity of $300. If a non-list mediator is used then such mediator is free to charge market rates. The Ministry of the Attorney General has established an "access plan" to facilitate access for impecunious litigants. The plan requires mediators, as a condition precedent to placement on the roster, to undertake to conduct up to 12 hours of pro bono mediations per year.

Is this rule compatible with the "multi-door" approach to dispute resolution reviewed earlier? Does it undermine the purpose and efficacy of the case conference? Does the move to mandatory mediation reflect an abandonment of the notion of "fitting the fuss to the forum"?

Rule 25 of the Law Society of Upper Canada Rules of Professional Conduct (reviewed above) addresses the situation of a lawyer acting as mediator. In addition to this role in relation to mediation, a lawyer may play two further roles: that of an independent legal advisor to one of the parties to a mediation process, and that of a giver of advice and guidance to his or her client with respect to the appropriateness of mediation as a process. Many commentators have argued that as mediation moves into the "mainstream" of dispute resolution we will require a "new breed of lawyers," a breed less entrenched in adversarial norms. The article by Smiley that follows addresses these different roles for lawyers and critiques the adversarialism exhibited in the practices of many lawyers as undermining client dignity and autonomy, a claim that stands in stark contrast to the argument of Charles Fried (chapter 3, "The Core Features and Values of the Traditional Model"), for example, that zealous partisanship is morally defensible precisely because it respects and advances client autonomy.

A. Smiley, "Professional Codes and Neutral Lawyering"
(1993), 7 *Georgetown Journal of Legal Ethics* 213, at 214-42 (footnotes omitted)

Lawyers traditionally have thrived on the adversarial nature of the legal system. Their "standard philosophical map" has developed several assumptions which appear as lawyers serve as advocates for clients. Lawyers have come to focus on maximizing "victory" and the basic premise that disputes must be resolved through application of a rule of law by a third party. This "map" has become dominant, it is argued, because it comports with clients' expectations, helps achieve "winning results" within the adversary system, produces economic gains for both lawyers and clients, and makes the law appear clear and predictable.

The adversarial model is based upon a "stylized ritual of offer/response, counter-offer/counter-response" and reluctant concessions. However, adversarial rituals

> may not be of assistance when the issues are multi-dimensional and the parties seek to discuss a variety of solutions at the same time. Furthermore, these ... emphasize an argumentative, debate form of discussion that may force the parties into ... [aggressive] and defensive postures which then may inhibit creativity in finding solutions.

This adversarial debate tends to degenerate into competitive reactive dynamics, rather than a creative proactive dynamic, and the attorney's duty to represent this client zealously within the bounds of the law discourages concern for the opponents' welfare and the social effects of a dispute.

However, the process of dealing with events that produce conflicting interests need not be adversarial. Many attorneys instinctively address a dispute in terms of possession or benefit. Traditional and widely-held assumptions that the parties value a fixed resource equally or that there is only one issue at hand in a dispute cannot continue. Focusing on maximization of immediate individual gain causes an attorney to ignore the long-term and social consequences of a particular situation; indeed, the competitive strategies themselves may produce greater inefficiencies by taking more time and costing more money. Instead, lawyers should attempt to utilize a cooperative problem-solving model, which "substitutes a negotiation structure that does not require unnecessary compromise but permits the parties to come to agreement without having to give up their preferences." This cooperative model presents opportunities for discovering better, more diverse means of dispute resolution due to the underlying principle that "unearthing a greater number of the actual needs of the parties will create more possible solutions because not all needs will be mutually exclusive."

Many alternative dispute resolution mechanisms fit into the problem-solving model, but mediation is perhaps the best example of a process in which two parties can work together successfully to resolve a dispute without the complications and expenses attendant to adversarial advocacy and litigation. Efforts to fit mediation into the current adversarial structure, however, make the mediator's role difficult for attorneys. The emphasis on the adversarial model in current professional standards leaves lawyers ill-equipped to use cooperative dispute resolution techniques such as mediation effectively. ...

The strengths of mediation, however, have also discouraged lawyer participation. Mediation differs from the adversarial process in the conspicuous absence of formalistic procedural requirements, and this can present problems for an attorney because it is this system of checks and balances that fosters conceptions of fairness within the adversarial context. As one commentator notes:

> Adversarial traditions and litigations provide a structure for resolving disputes within an exacting set of procedures that have been tested and refined to achieve fairness.
> Mediation, as an alternative to the adversarial system, is less hemmed in by rules of procedure, substantive law, and precedent. It lacks the precise and perfected checks and balances that are the principal benefit of the adversary process.

These concerns about fairness, although serious, skirt the overriding feature and redeeming value of mediation—that it is a consensual process that seeks self-determined resolutions. In fact, the benefits of mediation can be enhanced by lawyer participation as neutral mediators.

B. The Neutral Lawyering Mediation Model

Placing one lawyer in a neutral position holds enormous potential for expanding mediation services while according adequate protection to the disputants' legal rights. Neutral lawyering can enhance the mediation process by giving people access to law in a way that diminishes the likelihood that law will dominate their decision-making. The neutral lawyer can reduce the societal dependency on lawyers and their resulting influence on the decision-making processes of individual parties. This may enable the parties to reach their own agreement and free them from the traditional, but not necessarily optimal, adversarial-materialistic perspective based on the "lawyers' standard philosophical map." The neutral attorney-mediator's expertise in law can free the parties from dependence on legal norms and allow them to find an independent solution that suits them, while still informing the parties of relevant legal information. Also, the neutral attorney-mediator may be better than the lay mediator at identifying issues, pressing parties for decisions, incorporating these decisions into a final settlement agreement, and drafting the final agreement.

Many lawyers currently see mediation as an economic threat which will inevitably drain lawyers' caseloads and change the parties' perceptions of the attorney-mediator such that clients will no longer seek his advocacy services in unrelated matters because they "no longer think of him as their valiant champion." These fears, while superficially forming a convincing rationale for avoiding involvement in mediation, fail to take into account two important counterarguments: first, the high settlement rate in mediation can provide the neutral attorney with two enthusiastic, satisfied parties who may refer others to them, as opposed to the adversarial system, which often creates one enemy and one client who may not be completely satisfied with the lawyer's courtroom performance. Second, with increased public understanding of mediation, there will be heightened demand and greater monetary rewards for those lawyers who effectively provide such services. ...

The concern with conflicts of interest traditionally arises in adversarial processes, where a lawyer must zealously advocate his client's interests. This concern may not be necessary in the mediation context, however. Without a representational relationship between any party and the neutral attorney, the mediator is not responsible for advocating the interests of one party which may be in conflict with the interests of the other party. Where legal information is given from a neutral perspective, client loyalty is absent and there is no adverse affect on the content or presentation of the legal information. Due to the mediation's emphasis on the parties' responsibility for resolving their dispute through mutual agreement on a fair settlement, the design of the mediation process eliminates the traditional legal concerns with conflicts of interest. Conflict of interest rules for the lawyer as mediator are "instinctive reactions of the legal profession's adversarial knee."

An attorney-mediator's dissemination of legal information (as opposed to legal advice) should not destroy the actual or perceived impartiality required of the mediator. ...

Ethics opinions, as well as most widely promulgated standards governing the conduct of attorney-mediators, recommend or require the mediating attorney to encourage the disputants to seek independent legal counsel. These opinions often convey, either implicitly or explicitly, the idea that parties cannot make wise decisions after education of their legal rights, without independent counsel. ...

Independent counsel can be helpful: "[a] prediction of the likely results of adversary processing is necessary for an informed, fully voluntary decision about a mediated solution." Lawyers may also aid in the process by encouraging their clients to accept a compromise that is reasonable. In addition, independent legal review may be considered a check on the fairness of a mediated agreement. As one commentator explains:

> The reviewing attorneys serve as a check to assure that all necessary items have been considered by the participants and that the proposed agreement accurately states their understanding. The reviewing attorneys might inform the individual participants of any other alternatives to the suggested terms and whether the points of agreement fall within acceptable legal norms. These norms are often raised in the context of the likely range of court decisions if agreement is not reached. ... The basic purpose of this independent legal review is to determine whether the agreement is "fair enough" not to take it back to the drawing board and if all necessary items have been covered.

Discussing the quality of alternative dispute resolution in general, another article questions whether results reached through ADR without lawyers' guidance are superior to those achieved through the trial process using adversarial counsel. The article suggests that "the presence of an advocate will guarantee that parties understand any relevant substantive law and the exact consequences of turning away from ADR to traditional court processes." The author further argues that mediation participants may not be equipped to notice that pertinent information has not been provided, while an attorney may better perceive the need for additional data. In addition, the author states that the presence of independent legal counsel can lend credibility to the mediation, enhancing the parties' perception that they have participated in an equitable and impartial process.

In the most commonly suggested format, both parties consult independent legal counsel before, during, and/or after the mediation process. When adversary lawyers do not participate in the mediation process, "the neutral lawyer must decide whether and how to accommodate interests normally protected by independent counsel." Proponents of independent legal counsel argue that when the mediator is obligated to focus on the legal merits of the litigation or to emphasize the importance of independent legal counsel during the mediation, "it is counterproductive because it tends to generate sterile discussion of how to win the case, rather than productive discussion of how to achieve settlement." Another commentator argues that if the mediator is allowed to give impartial legal advice after informing the parties of the risks to the mediation process in doing so, the mediator is presented with the problem of defining the level of risk to be disclosed to the parties, and neutrality may appear to be compromised if the law favors one disputant over the other. Given the strengths of these arguments, professional review can be beneficial in some cases.

However, "the infusion of professionalism and adversarial representation into the mediation process could subvert the individual autonomy, responsibility, and dignity" of the parties. Independent legal counsels' advice may undermine the mediation process itself; the advice may be delivered in a way that emphasizes the adversarial perspective and results in a party drawing away from the mediation. Although this corruption of the nonadversarial process would occur only if the party was not fully committed to the nonadversarial process, the risk is still posed, and its existence is problematic.

Further uneasiness about the effects of independent legal counsel on the mediation process is caused by the fact that such a rule implicitly sends a message "to the parties, and indeed even the mediator, that impartiality is impossible. As a result, trust in the mediator, essential to the mediation process, and developed in large part due to a perception of mediator neutrality, will be jeopardized." Additionally, an obligation to encourage independent legal advice at every step of the mediation process will increase the time and costs involved in resolving the dispute. This will dampen the demand for mediation, since saving time and money are important advantages of the process.

Finally, an independent legal advice recommendation sabotages the parties' self-determination of a fair settlement. Requiring independent legal counsel infuses the mediation process with an adversarial atmosphere, making the relationship between the parties and their attorneys paramount instead of the relationship between the parties. Through their involvement, the parties' lawyers will assume responsibility for decisions and agreements, creating "a process virtually analogous to the adversarial system," to the detriment of the parties' nonadversarial objectives.

It must be noted, however, that a significant risk may exist that agreements reached through mediation will be rejected by the courts without the "stamp of approval" of independent counsel. In this case, the rule obligating attorney-mediators to encourage parties to consult with independent counsel during mediation, or to have mediated agreements viewed, is necessary. If the courts come to accept mediated settlements without independent legal review, however, the attorney-mediator should determine whether information about the participants' legal positions should come from him or from independent legal counsel, considering the interests at stake, their complexity, the skill of the neutral lawyer, and the development of the participants' ideas of fairness. In this way, the neutral lawyer can and should be responsible for fostering the fairness interests in the cooperative process of mediation.

C. The Case Against Informalism

The enthusiasm for mediation and other informal methods of dispute resolution, while widely shared among civil justice reformers, has not been universal. Indeed, there is a well-developed theoretical critique, and, increasingly an empirically based critique, of many of the central claims advanced by mediation proponents.

Ian Morrison and Janet Mosher, "Barriers to Access to Civil Justice for Disadvantaged Groups"
in Ontario Law Reform Commission, *Rethinking Civil Justice: Research Studies for the Civil Justice Review* (Toronto: Ontario Law Reform Commission, 1996), 637, at 663-74 (footnotes omitted)

3. Models of Disputing and Their Relation to Disadvantage

... ADR is a catch-all phrase to refer to an enormous array of dispute resolution forums and processes; from privatized adversarial adjudication (rent-a-judge, arbitration), to settlement conferences, to mediation facilitated by social workers or "community" members. The claims made with respect to the strengths and benefits of ADR are equally expansive and frequently attributed to ADR in all of its manifestations as though it were a monolith. In what follows we focus on those processes and forums which are more likely to touch the lives of the "disadvantaged": few economically "disadvantaged persons" will be parties to rent-a-judge proceedings while many are likely to be affected by mediation and particularly by a move to mandatory mediation in the context of family law.

As described by many of its proponents, mediation, as a process, offers a range of benefits: win/win solutions; creative outcomes fashioned in the shadow of the law but not constricted by formal legal rationality; direct participation which makes good on the promise of dignity (unlike due process which fails to do so because participation is usually so attenuated); improved communication paving the way for a better future relationship; harmony; low cost (less cumbersome and costly formal procedures); speed; flexibility; greater participant satisfaction; and more lasting results. Beyond these process benefits it is claimed that mediation (and similar processes) will relieve court congestion, enhance community involvement, and facilitate access to justice. Challenges to each of these claims have been fully developed and many, we might add, are extremely persuasive. But, given time and space constraints, we propose to address specifically the potential of mediation (and other informal processes). In particular we want to consider whether mediation is capable of adequately taking account of the dependency, the on-going nature of the relationship, or the inequalities of resources in disputes between individuals and the state, or between private individuals.

The claim is frequently made that mediation is particularly well-suited to the resolution of disputes which arise in the context of an on-going relationship. Thus, disputes arising in families, in employment, in certain commercial contexts, and in housing (landlord and tenant) have often been identified as being well-suited for mediation. Other on-going relationships, such as those between welfare recipients and the state, have received relatively little attention in the ADR literature. With the exception of the commercial context, the relationships in each of these contexts are frequently marked by vast inequalities of resources and of power more generally. Coupled with these power imbalances are the ideologies of mediator "neutrality" and "harmony," both of which actively work in favour of the more powerful party. The ideology of mediator "neutrality" presupposes that the role of the mediator is simply to facilitate the communication necessary for the parties to come to their own agreement. For many, neutrality put into practice mandates non-intervention in aid of one of the parties to the mediation. As many authors have observed, the failure to intervene in circumstances where one party is taking advantage of the other can hardly be characterized as neutral. To the contrary, non-intervention works to actively promote the interests of the more powerful party.

The "harmony" ideology of mediation has a number of problematic ramifications. It signals that one ought to make concessions—it's a process of give and take to reach an amicable settlement. This can be problematic in a context where one is seeking to have a legal right acknowledged and enforced. Why should this party be expected to make any concessions? While we do not mean to suggest that one can never voluntarily agree to concede a legal right, nor that parties ought not to be permitted to resolve their disputes other than in accordance with the normative parameters recognized by law, we do think it critical to attend to the notion of voluntariness. Voluntariness requires more than the absence of explicit or indeed, subtle coercion. Explicit coercion in this context frequently comes in the form of mandatory mediation, or the "strong arm" of the mediator. Subtle coercion may be pervasive within the mediation process because of the expectation of settlement and compromise. Voluntariness requires a *real* choice of options, adequate information about one's legal rights and entitlements, and mechanisms that in some manner redress the inequalities of power. We emphasize *real* choice here to signal the importance of attending to the social and economic context in which choices are exercised. For those with few economic resources no meaningful choice exists if one option is enormously expensive, the other inexpensive. This observation has led many to express the concern that the creation of institutionalized ADR will result in its substitution for the right of "disadvantaged groups" to litigate and would create a two tier justice system, "that dispenses informal 'justice' to poor people with 'small claims' and 'minor' disputes, who cannot afford legal services, and who are denied access to courts."

This leads us to a second implication of the harmony ideology. It positions lawyers or other advocates as antithetical to "good" outcomes because their adversarial tactics are seen to undermine the process. While in the context of family law mediation, review of mediated agreements by lawyers is encouraged, all other forms of participation by advocates is usually discouraged. In the context where one party is much better resourced in terms of knowledge about the law, and experience in negotiating, this raises concerns that legal rights may be conceded through ignorance of them or an inability to successfully negotiate their respect.

The informality of mediation may also work in favour of more powerful parties. This claim has been particularly well developed in the context of disputes involving racial minority persons. Delgado et al. argue, based upon theories of prejudice which suggest that much prejudice is environmental (people express it because the setting encourages or tolerates it), that the rules and structures of formal justice tend to suppress bias, whereas informality tends to increase it. They argue that two features of formal settings decrease opportunities for the expression of racial bias; aspects of the role of judges (freedom from political pressure, commitment to apply rules, *stare decisis*, and codes of conduct); and several basic features of legal procedure (public trials, requirements of courts to give reasons, guaranteed opportunities to call and contest evidence, pre-trial discovery, and the rules of evidence). They conclude that formality and adversarial procedures counteract bias among legal decision-makers and disputants. They also maintain that minority group members are more apt to participate in processes which they believe will respond to reasonable efforts and thus, that "it is not surprising that a favoured forum for redress of race-based wrongs has been the traditional adjudicatory setting. Minorities recognize that public institutions, with their defined rules and formal structure, are more subject to rational control than private or informal structures."

While acknowledging that informal processes may less effectively curb racial and other biases than formal processes (this is not of course to suggest that formal processes are free of bias against "out groups"), other commentators have suggested that *if* the introduction of state-sponsored alternative disputes resolution processes and forums result in an over-all increase in the capacity of the system to deal with disputes, and in the availability of less costly alternatives (neither of which necessarily follows from the introduction of institutionalized ADR), access to justice for the poor may be enhanced in the sense that access may be had to at least some form of dispute resolution where none was available before. But if these alternatives fail to take seriously systemic inequalities of power and if "disadvantaged persons" are routinely encouraged (if not coerced) to concede legal rights, there is good reason to doubt that greater numbers will have access to a forum for dispute resolution—who would seek out such forums? There is equally good reason to doubt that justice in any substantive sense would be enhanced for "disadvantaged persons."

Many claim that mediation and other informal methods of dispute resolution are empowering, both for individuals and potentially for communities. At least for individuals, this is understood to be possible because disputants participate directly in the resolution of their own dispute. For many the experience may well be empowering. But it is unlikely to be for "disadvantaged persons" when pitted against powerful adversaries. The other piece of the empowerment claim is that because the disputants are not bound by the rational application of law, they are free to select the normative principles that will inform the resolution of the dispute. At the level of community, the claim has been made that community-based mediation (wherein the mediation is conducted by a panel of mediators from the community) offers the scope for the enunciation and development of community norms. This claim is one frequently made with respect to "neighbourhood justice centres." As Cohen notes, "in theory, neighbourhood programs allow prompt community resolution of disputes using community values instead of the rule of law ... . Applying shared values, [they] solve certain community problems more effectively than the court system. Nader appropriately questions this theory,

> ... Neighbourhood justice organizations, one outcropping of ADR reform, were set up on a Crown policy model: "Let's make believe that this is a self-contained community and let's make believe that within this community you can create your own organizations to increase access to justice." The community was a make-believe, the self-containment was a make-believe, and the idea that problems that they might take to justice were only between people who lived in the community was make-believe.

While we, like Nader, are wary about the claims regarding the application and evolution of community norms and values for the reasons she articulates, we do believe that there is at least one special case wherein community-based dispute resolution is genuinely *community*-based. Here we refer specifically to First Nations communities. While we discuss this in somewhat more detail *infra* we also want to emphasize that a mediation-style process, located within a culture respectful of the principle of harmony and based upon very different cultural traditions than those found in dominant Canadian society, is not subject to the whole of the critique of mediation which we have advanced above.

In sum, there seems to be no reason to believe that mediation, or other informal dispute resolution processes, hold out much promise for oppressed persons in terms of access to justice. The barriers to naming, blaming and claiming that impede access to a due process hearing also impede access to mediation. As a process of dispute resolution, mediation, while *potentially* less expensive, fares even less well than adversarial adjudication in addressing imbalances of power. It is hard to imagine that a person dependent upon the state (or abusive husband, or landlord) in an on-going way would be any more willing to take on conventional power through mediation, than through a due process hearing. It is not at all hard to imagine that such a person might fare less well if mediation is the process of dispute resolution.

Where does this leave us then in terms of dispute resolution processes? First, it is clear that simply creating opportunities for mediation will not improve access to justice for "disadvantaged groups"; nor indeed would simply creating additional opportunities for due process hearings. It seems to us that whatever the process, attention must be given to what would be the necessary pre-conditions for meaningful participation. As Tyler suggests in his research on small claims courts, "... disputants place great weight on having a dispute settled in a way which is perceived to be fair ... one important element in perceiving the procedure to be fair relates to the opportunity to participate in the process ... . Both mediation and adversarial adjudication claim to value party participation yet both have been criticized for failing to respect it in practice; the former largely because of inequalities of bargaining power and the latter because of the attenuated form that participation usually takes. What are the pre-conditions for meaningful participation? At a very general level these include an understanding of the process(es); real choice about entering the process, or as between processes; adequate information about legal rights, entitlements, obligations and remedies; advocacy supports; a conceptualization of advocacy which respects client narratives (see discussion *infra* of advocacy services); an opportunity to tell one's story; and a decision-maker or mediator who is able to hear and respect that story and its teller (see discussion *infra* on personnel of the justice system). While both mediation and adjudication could be dramatically improved should these pre-conditions be satisfied, it nevertheless is imperative that persons not be required to mediate disputes. As we stated at the outset, quoting from Walker and Fricker, "[w]e both begin [and end] our consideration of the issues from a belief in the validity and centrality of a formal process of litigation and the right of citizens to have access to justice in its most institutionalized form." For all of the reasons we have just canvassed then, any move to make mediation mandatory in the context of family law (as the new government has promised) or in the context of landlord–tenant law (as the *First Report* suggests) will further impede access to justice for disadvantaged groups.

Owen M. Fiss, "Against Settlement"
(1984), 93 *Yale Law Journal* 1073, at 1075-90 (footnotes omitted)

The advocates of ADR are led to support [measures to encourage settlement] and to exalt the idea of settlement more generally because they view adjudication as a process to resolve disputes. They act as though courts arose to resolve quarrels between neighbors who had reached an impasse and turned to a stranger for help. Courts are seen as an institutionalization of the stranger and adjudication is viewed as the process by which the stranger exercises power. The very fact that the neighbors have turned to someone else to resolve their dispute signifies a breakdown in their social relations; the advocates of ADR acknowledge this, but nonetheless hope that the neighbors will be able to reach agreement before the stranger renders judgment. Settlement is that agreement. It is a truce more than a true reconciliation, but it seems preferable to judgment because it rests on the consent of both parties and avoids the cost of a lengthy trial.

In my view, however, this account of adjudication and the case for settlement rests on questionable premises. I do not believe that settlement as a generic practice is preferable to judgment or should be institutionalized on a wholesale and indiscriminate basis. It should be treated instead as a highly problematic technique for streamlining dockets. Settlement is for me the civil analogue of plea bargaining: Consent is often coerced; the bargain may be struck by someone without authority; the absence of a trial and judgment renders subsequent judicial involvement troublesome; and although dockets are trimmed, justice may not be done. Like plea bargaining, settlement is a capitulation to the conditions of mass society and should be neither encouraged nor praised.

By viewing the lawsuit as a quarrel between two neighbors, the dispute-resolution story that underlies ADR implicitly asks us to assume a rough equality between the contending parties. It treats settlement as the anticipation of the outcome of trial and assumes that the terms of settlement are simply a product of the parties' predictions of that outcome. In truth, however, settlement is also a function of the resources available to each party to finance the litigation, and those resources are frequently distributed unequally. Many lawsuits do not involve a property dispute between two neighbors, or between AT&T and the government (to update the story), but rather concern a struggle between a member of a racial minority and a municipal police department over alleged brutality, or a claim by a worker against a large corporation over work-related injuries. In these cases, the distribution of financial resources, or the ability of one party to pass along its costs, will invariably infect the bargaining process, and the settlement will be at odds with a conception of justice that seeks to make the wealth of the parties irrelevant.

The disparities in resources between the parties can influence the settlement in three ways. First, the poorer party may be less able to amass and analyze the information needed to predict the outcome of the litigation, and thus be disadvantaged in the bargaining process. Second, he may need the damages he seeks immediately and thus be induced to settle as a way of accelerating payment, even though he realizes he would get less now than he might if he awaited judgment. All plaintiffs want their damages immediately, but an indigent plaintiff may be exploited by a rich defendant because his need is so great that the defendant can force him to accept a sum that is less than the ordinary present value of the judgment. Third, the poorer party might be forced to settle because he does not have the resources to finance the litigation, to cover either his own projected expenses, such as his lawyer's time, or the expenses his opponent can impose through the manipulation of procedural mechanisms such as discovery. It might seem that settlement benefits the plaintiff by allowing him to avoid the costs of litigation, but this is not so. The defendant can anticipate the plaintiff's costs if the case were to be tried fully and decrease his offer by that amount. The indigent plaintiff is a victim of the costs of litigation even if he settles.

There are exceptions. Seemingly rich defendants may sometimes be subject to financial pressures that make them as anxious to settle as indigent plaintiffs. But I doubt that these circumstances occur with any great frequency. I also doubt that institutional arrangements such as contingent fees or the provision of legal services to the poor will in fact equalize resources between contending parties: The contingent fee does not equalize resources; it only makes an indigent plaintiff vulnerable to the willingness of the private bar to invest in his case. In effect, the ability to exploit the plaintiff's lack of resources has been transferred from rich defendants to lawyers who insist upon a hefty slice of the plaintiff's recovery as their fee. These lawyers, moreover, will only work for contingent fees in certain kinds of cases, such as personal-injury suits. And the contingent fee is of no avail when the defendant is the disadvantaged party. Governmental subsidies for legal services have a broader potential, but in the civil domain the battle for these subsidies was hard-fought, and they are in fact extremely limited, especially when it comes to cases that seek systemic reform of government practices.

Of course, imbalances of power can distort judgment as well: Resources influence the quality of presentation, which in turn has an important bearing on who wins and the terms of victory. We count, however, on the guiding presence of the judge, who can employ a number of measures to lessen the impact of distributional inequalities. He can, for example, supplement the parties' presentations by asking questions, calling his own witnesses, and inviting other persons and institutions to participate as amici. These measures are likely to make only a small contribution toward moderating the influence of distributional inequalities, but should not be ignored for that reason. Not even these small steps are possible with settlement. There is, moreover, a critical difference between a process like settlement, which is based on bargaining and accepts inequalities of wealth as an integral and legitimate component of the process, and a process like judgment, which knowingly struggles against those inequalities. Judgment aspires to an autonomy from distributional inequalities, and it gathers much of its appeal from this aspiration. ...

Justice Rather Than Peace

The dispute-resolution story makes settlement appear as a perfect substitute for judgment, as we just saw, by trivializing the remedial dimensions of a lawsuit, and also by reducing the social function of the lawsuit to one of resolving private disputes: In that story, settlement appears to achieve exactly the same purpose as judgment—peace between the parties—but at considerably less expense to society. The two quarreling neighbors turn to a court in order to resolve their dispute, and society makes courts available because it wants to aid in the achievement of their private ends or to secure the peace.

In my view, however, the purpose of adjudication should be understood in broader terms. Adjudication uses public resources, and employs not strangers chosen by the parties but public officials chosen by a process in which the public participates. These officials, like members of the legislative and executive branches, possess a power that has been defined and conferred by public law, not by private agreement. Their job is not to maximize the ends of private parties, nor simply to secure the peace, but to explicate and give force to the values embodied in authoritative texts such as the Constitution and statutes: to interpret those values and to bring reality into accord with them. This duty is not discharged when the parties settle.

In our political system, courts are reactive institutions. They do not search out interpretive occasions, but instead wait for others to bring matters to their attention. They also rely for the most part on others to investigate and present the law and facts. A settlement will thereby deprive a court of the occasion, and perhaps even the ability, to render an interpretation. A court cannot proceed (or not proceed very far) in the face of a settlement. To be against settlement is not to urge that parties be "forced" to litigate, since that would interfere with their autonomy and distort the adjudicative process; the parties will be inclined to make the court believe that their bargain is justice. To be against settlement is only to suggest that when the parties settle, society gets less than what appears, and for a price it does not know it is paying. Parties might settle while leaving justice undone. The settlement of a school suit might secure the peace, but not racial equality. Although the parties are prepared to live under the terms they bargained for, and although such peaceful coexistence may be a necessary precondition of justice, and itself a state of affairs to be valued, it is not justice itself. To settle for something means to accept less than some ideal.

I recognize that judges often announce settlements not with a sense of frustration or disappointment, as my account of adjudication might suggest, but with a sigh of relief. But this sigh should be seen for precisely what it is: It is not a recognition that a job is done, nor an acknowledgment that a job need not be done because justice has been secured. It is instead based on another sentiment altogether, namely, that another case has been "moved along," which is true whether or not justice has been done or even needs to be done. Or the sigh might be based on the fact that the agency of judgment has been avoided. ...

Someone like Bok sees adjudication in essentially private terms: The purpose of lawsuits and the civil courts is to resolve disputes, and the amount of litigation we encounter is evidence of the needlessly combative and quarrelsome character of Americans. Or as Bok put it, using a more diplomatic idiom: "At bottom, ours is a society built on individualism, competition, and success." I, on the other hand, see adjudication in more public terms: Civil litigation is an institutional arrangement for using state power to bring a recalcitrant reality closer to our chosen ideals. We turn to the courts because we need to, not because of some quirk in our personalities. We train our students in the tougher arts so that they may help secure all that the law promises, not because we want them to become gladiators or because we take a special pleasure in combat.

NOTES AND QUESTIONS

1. The author of the preceding excerpt is the same Fiss whose ideas were analyzed earlier in the chapter in the context of a debate with Weinrib regarding the function of litigation. Are the ideas here compatible with those reviewed earlier? Do the critiques of Fiss considered earlier apply to "Against Settlement"? Specifically, what would Roach say about this Fiss article? One of Fiss' arguments against settlement is that the opportunity is lost for the judiciary "to bring a recalcitrant reality closer to our chosen ideals." What is the vision of adjudication that underlies this claim? How is it that judges are able to see beyond the recalcitrant reality and identify societal values that transcend this reality?

2. While Fiss may be correct in highlighting the pitfalls of too great reliance on settlement, is it reasonable to think that the solution is to force most cases to proceed to trial? If you do not share Fiss' enthusiasm for courts as the forum of choice for the development of public values, how would you respond to the difficulties with settlement that Fiss criticizes?

3. Are you as confident as Fiss that inequalities of bargaining power are less worrisome in the context of adjudication (where Fiss claims that the judge can intervene to redress the inequalities) than in the context of negotiation? Recall the cases that you read in chapter 3, "The Core Features and Values of the Traditional Model," on the role of the judge in the adversary system. What scope does a judge have to enter the fray to redress the inequalities?

Robert F. Reid and Richard E. Holland wrote in 1984, at a time when both were judges of the then Supreme Court of Ontario: "Judges are not investigators; they are watchers and listeners. Counsel have the active role; they 'present' the case. If the presentation is deficient it is not the judge's fault. If a witness is not called or an argument not made the error is not for the judge to rectify, however hard the self-restraint might be. ... In essence, the judge's task is to sit patiently, watch closely, listen carefully and decide justly." (*Views from the Bench* (Aurora, ON: Canada Law Book, 1984), at 23.)

4. Even if one accepts all of Fiss's arguments against settlement does he not fail to address two crucial issues? First, if he is saying that parties who *agree* to settle should be forced on to trial, who is going to pay for the legal costs involved? Second, if parties

are to be forced on to trial, what has happened to the concept of "party autonomy?" If the parties *choose* to settle, by what principle can they be forced to continue litigating?

5. Note that the centre piece of Fiss's defence of adjudication is the US desegregation case of *Brown v. Board of Education* and the role of the courts in implementing its mandate. Derrick Bell, a professor at Harvard Law School, has criticized the implementation of that case as being insensitive to the concerns of African-American communities that their children's education be improved and not disrupted by judicial remedies. He also raises the question of who is the lawyer's client in politicized class action litigation. See D. Bell, "Serving Two Masters: Integration Ideals and Client Interests in Desegregation Litigation" (1975), 85 *Yale Law Journal* 470. Would settlements between boards of education and minority communities better reflect the priorities and aspirations of the communities to be reformed? Or are Fiss' concerns about inequality of bargaining power still relevant? Even if a "fair" settlement could be reached, perhaps by increasing funds available for education in minority communities, would Fiss still not have problems with settlements that did not reflect integration values he sees in the constitution?

Notwithstanding these various critiques and, in particular, the concerns that they raise in relation to the potential harms of informalism for members of various disadvantaged groups, one can certainly find instances where "alternative," and less formal, processes arguably have contributed significantly to "just" outcomes for members of disadvantaged groups. One example is the "Grandview Agreement," an agreement reached between the Grandview Survivors Support Group (survivors of institutional abuses in a custodial facility for girls operated by the Ontario government) and the Government of Ontario. The excerpt from the agreement that follows describes the process used to come to the agreement. The process led to important substantive outcomes, most of which could not have been achieved through the civil courts: groups benefits, such as the creation of a helpline for any former ward of Grandview; and individual benefits, including direct financial support (determined in accordance with a grid), access to counselling and therapy, and access to vocational or educational training or upgrading. Individual benefits were determined through a non-adversarial process in which a woman claiming benefits told her story to an adjudicator. Importantly, the government agreed to amend social assistance legislation so that payments received pursuant to the agreement would not be deducted dollar for dollar from family benefits or welfare benefits that a woman was receiving.

Agreement Between: The Grandview Survivors Support Group and the Government of Ontario

Overview

This Agreement is based on a recognition that abuse or mistreatment as defined in this Agreement cannot be tolerated nor condoned. It is further based on a recognition that society has a direct responsibility to provide the support necessary to facilitate the healing process of survivors of sexual and institutionalized abuse, particularly when such abuse arises in the context of an institution housing children. It also recognizes [that] the current individual-based solutions offered by the civil justice system are inadequate responses to institutionalized and sexual abuse. These problems are prevalent enough in our society so as to warrant a social based response which seeks, ultimately, to facilitate the healing of survivors of such abuse and mistreatment.

In an effort to empower the voices of those who are to be the beneficiaries of this Agreement, it was agreed that the negotiating representatives would embark on an alternative dispute resolution process. This process was carefully designed to give real voice to those who would be directly affected by the results sought to be achieved, in a process that was not overburdened with legalistic tactics. Accordingly, four former residents at Grandview who were executive members of the Grandview Survivors Support Group representing in this endeavour more than 130 members participated with their counsel in the various negotiation sessions.

The initial agenda was, indeed, formulated by the needs identified by the executive of the group in consultation with the membership of the Grandview Survivors Support Group so that as broad a base for discussion as possible could be developed. The Government was represented by experienced legal counsel and by a civil servant who had much experience in dealing with the issues of violence against women as a community advocate. The Grandview Survivors Group was also represented by the legal counsel of their choice. Finally, a facilitator was present at these sessions. Her commitment to these issues and her equality driven process was critical to ensuring that all voices were heard at the table, with dignity.

These sessions were typically full day sessions and occurred once and then twice monthly over a period of six months. A process of mutual education was engaged upon and was a critical feature of the negotiations. In between meetings, each party assumed the obligation to keep their respective membership or client groups fully informed and to prepare for addressing specific matters at subsequent sessions.

The purpose of this Agreement is to engage in a process to afford to any eligible person real opportunities to heal and to introduce real hope for a better future.

The Agreement does not seek to single out any particular individual for blame. It, in fact, recognizes that there were within the administration of the training school system many persons who sincerely believed in the remedial philosophy of the institutions and who were personally committed to the creation of a just and protective environment for those in their care.

How any particular person or why such person was committed to the training school system and why Grandview was determined to be an appropriate placement for any individual are not in issue here. In each case, a judicial determination was made based on criteria considered appropriate.

It is acknowledged that, in individual cases, allegations have been made that officials employed by the Government and placed in positions of trust and authority over their wards abused that trust in ways that if proven would constitute serious criminal misconduct. There are criminal charges pending in a number of cases and further charges against other persons are expected.

It is recognized that every effort should be made to ensure that nothing contemplated to be done under the terms of this Agreement affects the integrity of the criminal justice process. However, if there are needs that are identified which must be addressed now, every effort will be made to meet those needs but without jeopardizing any prosecution.

The Grandview Training School for Girls ("Grandview") opened in 1932, and was formally known as the Ontario Training School for Girls—Galt. It was located at what is now known as Cambridge, Ontario.

Grandview was an institution housing, at any one time, approximately 120 girls with 30-35 girls housed in Churchill House, a secure facility. It appears that these girls were wards of the Ontario Government or of Grandview at the time of their committal to Grandview. By the terms of the governing legislation in place from time to time (repealed in 1982), the girls' parents lost their parental rights through the wardship process.

This Agreement is designed to address the consequences of "abuse" and "mistreatment" as those terms are defined, of those who were actually resident at Grandview.

It is understood that the beneficiaries of these arrangements were children at the time of admittance to Grandview.

Actions that are gender based and result in physical, sexual or psychological harm or suffering to women including threats of same, coercion or arbitrary deprivation of liberty are abusive and this Agreement reflects the abhorrence of such conduct. This Agareement will support efforts both of a policy and of a legislative nature to prevent and remedy the consequences of the kind of conduct described here, in recognition that these issues require a society based response to supplement the case by case dispute resolution system which informs our civil justice process.

Early detection of the circumstances and instances of abuse, intervention in effective ways and support for the healing of the consequences of this conduct are recognized as essential. The loss of trust in the institutions responsible for the care of young people and the personnel running them represents a legitimate social concern. The loss of self confidence and self esteem and ability to freely enter relationships of intimacy requiring trust and the corresponding distrust of authority exact lifelong penalties for the individual survivor of abuse. As well, unacceptable financial burdens are imposed on the social services, health and court systems in what are often disjointed responses to complaints of abuse.

It is an objective of the various components of this Agreement to facilitate a path of healing and recognition of self fulfilment for its beneficiaries. It is hoped that the coordination of the various components, will, as an integrated whole, produce a more accountable and effective response for survivors of institutionalized and sexual abuse.

It is recognized that greater success may be achieved by early attention to the needs of the beneficiaries and that the failure to carry through with the promise of this Agreement will carry with it the risk of further harm.

It is the hope of the parties to this Agreement and each individual who seeks to access the benefits of these arrangements that the provisions of this Agreement provide the best alternative of all likely to permit healing and reintegration of the beneficiaries into full partnership with society.

It is also recognized that barriers based on gender, race and class considerations exist, that these "biases" exist in any system [currently] in place to address the needs of women and this Agreement seeks to identify and eliminate these systemic issues that would otherwise prevent the promise of this Agreement being realized. There is an interrelationship between sexism, racial and class distinctions which together foster violent actions.

It is the intention here to develop a non court based process to address the needs of those affected by certain conduct, to suggest a model adaptable to other circumstances. For it to work, various Government ministries, private and public advocates and the survivors have all committed their cooperation to craft a unique response to sexual and institutional abuse.

It is a key feature of these arrangements that the encounter of a survivor of abuse with the community be supportive and that the response by the community be collective and coordinated.

A commitment to help eradicate abuse and its underlying causes is shared by all who participated in the development of the approach disclosed in the text of this Agreement.

It is hoped that this text and its underlying process will be a new starting point in ultimately achieving this commitment.

QUESTIONS

In what respects do the process and agreement concluded respond to the deficiencies of the civil justice system? Would a different approach be preferable? What terms would you seek in the agreement and how, if at all, might these substantive terms be linked to the process adopted?

IV. THE ADMINISTRATIVE STATE

In this section we explore the third major challenge to the traditional model of litigation; a challenge connected to the evolution of the "administrative state." As discussed in the excerpt from W. Bogart's *Courts and Country*, the rise of the administrative state has been accompanied by the development of a vast array of decision-making bodies. The nature of the decision-making responsibility assigned by statute to these bodies varies, but frequently includes responsibility for the resolution of particular types of disputes. In resolving disputes within their assigned jurisdiction, these bodies embrace a range of processes—for example, formal adversarial adjudication, mediation, and inquisitorial adjudication. As Bogart discusses, the impetus for the assignment by statute of jurisdiction over particular kinds of disputes to administrative agencies and tribunals lay in several observations about the limitations of court-based adjudication: lack of expertise to address certain issues; the volume of decisions to be made; and the need to locate adjudication within the broader goals and responsibilities of particular administrative bodies.

Administrative agencies and tribunals and their activities in quantitative terms dwarf both the number and activity of courts. For example, Evans et al. report that a 1977 survey of agencies, boards, commissions, and advisory bodies conducted by the Ontario Economic Council identified 36 regulatory bodies (not including 22 specific marketing boards), 44 licensing appeal bodies, 8 compensation bodies, 19 arbitral bodies, and 95 advisory bodies (Evans et al., *Administrative Law*, 3d ed. (Toronto: Emond Montgomery, 1995)).

Agencies and tribunals are key instruments in the activity of the modern regulatory state. Agencies are used to regulate most areas of the economy and society, including communications, financial markets, transportation, the environment, income support, labour relations, pay equity, professional discipline, immigration, and human rights.

The functions of agencies and tribunals obviously differ depending on the particular context and, as such, it is not surprising that their procedures and composition also differ greatly. Although we will focus on the adjudicative activities of agencies and tribunals, it is important to remember that they also may make rules and policies, educate, prosecute, or engage in administrative and political decision making.

The procedures of agencies and tribunals may be very similar to a court when they focus on a dispute between a particular individual and the state. On the other hand, other agencies have relatively informal procedures and deal with multi-faceted problems with the input of a wide variety of interested parties. Examples would include a hearing to determine the licensing of a radio station or a nuclear energy plant or the allowable rate increase of a public utility.

Some tribunals, such as a human rights tribunal, are generally composed of legally trained persons who are aware of the relevant law and the procedures used in court. Other agencies are composed of those who are expert in a particular subject matter. Labour relations boards are deliberately composed of representatives of labour and management as well as experts appointed by the government.

W. Bogart, *Courts and Country*
(Toronto: Oxford, 1994), 107-24 (footnotes omitted)

This chapter deals with the relationship between courts and the huge administrative state that has developed in Canada and may be summarized as follows. First, courts over the last century blocked many progressive attempts to deal with widely applicable issues such as compensation for injury in the workplace, unionization, and human rights, with the result that the administrative state frequently displaced courts in dealing with such issues. Competition law provides a more complex example where the courts' failure to enforce laws regarding economic competition echoed vacillation in the political process that continues today. Second, courts continue to exert at least ideological influence through a review process (that is mostly constructed by themselves) of administrative actors' decisions. Such a process has the capacity to prune administrative programs in the name of the highly contentious concept of "jurisdiction." Finally, the foregoing suggests little basis for concluding that courts are capable of or willing to intervene systematically and to devise effective solutions to social problems in the face of powerful economic forces. ...

In administrative issues our judges have mostly been the keepers of pure liberal ideology: the state assigned minimalist policing functions, and the market was the best distributor of goods and services. Whether it was in such matters as occupational health and safety, the development of human rights, or the advent of unions and collective bargaining, the courts' activities wove a pattern of indifference, even hostility towards state activities. With a few notable exceptions, judges have raised the sanctity of the common law, which brought market principles to bear on the resolution of such issues: that everyone should be free to contract and negotiate the terms on an individual basis, and that only establishing fault should determine the basis for compensation of injury. Yet, under the guise of principles that seemed to treat everyone equally, the health and safety of workers were ignored with abandon, poisons were dumped into the environment, and the most insidious acts of prejudice were taken as a hallmark of self-regarding behaviour.

Change to curb the most dire consequences of such rules came from the legislatures, but was resisted by the courts. This opposition had two clear consequences. First, it led to the removal of several important areas of law from the courts. Second, when the areas were taken from the courts and a new regime was established and carried out by an administrative board, the courts insisted on overseeing their activities through a process of judicial review, which provoked much controversy among legal commentators.

The Establishment of Tribunals as Alternatives to Courts

While many instances exist (for example, regarding the environment or in terms of public interest groups participating in the process itself) three prominent illustrations spanning the better part of the twentieth century will be discussed regarding the courts' resistance to change aimed at altering the minimalist state. As a result of such resistance, the legislatures not only had to alter judge-made law but also took the task of implementing the new regime away from the courts. We will look at a fourth example—competition policy and law—which illustrates a more complex set of attitudes on the part of the courts and legislatures and a more ambiguous solution.

Workers' Compensation, Labour Relations, and Human Rights

The first illustration of resistance by courts and intervention by the administrative state concerns compensation of workers who were injured as a result of industrial accident. By the mid-nineteenth century, it was clear that only the most hardened could be indifferent to the toll industrialization had taken on human lives. Mishaps in the workplace injured and killed workers with alarming frequency, but the courts' response to this demonstrated a distressing rigidity. They insisted that fault must be established as a basis for recovery. In such a regime, individual workers fighting over a specific claim were almost always no match for employers, who were better organized and more financially able to resist. Courts placed workers at an even greater disadvantage with such holdings as that negligence of fellow workers would bar injured ones from recovering on the theory that they must have agreed to the joint enterprise that resulted in the damage. This "fellow servant" rule and other doctrines propounded by the courts were compatible with broader ideas about the role of the common law. Its purpose was to augment autonomy by creating spheres where individuals were free from state or any other interference. Accompanying such independence was a person's responsibility for his own fate. Such responsibility depended upon free will, with fault both a moral failing and a condition of liability.

Studies done of court cases just before substantial change was effected by legislation suggest that despite impediments, those workers who turned to litigation may have been successful more often than the rules would suggest, but these few cases may illustrate how pathetic some work conditions actually were. These results conveyed a possibility for compensation while leaving untampered a severe regime weighted against the injured labourer:

> Recovery by a few workers could satisfy the impulse of sympathy without challenging the settled doctrine and without making a shift in the balance of power between employers and labour or a threat to the established economic order. It may also be seen as giving the subtle control that can come from being merciful.

After much debate, the legislatures in many industrialized countries, including Canada, established a regime to compensate workers injured on the job. The details varied markedly, but the schemes had two characteristics. First, recovery was to be based on "no fault"; that is, the injured worker had to prove that she was injured as a result of an accident in the workplace, regardless of whose responsibility it was. Second, the regime of compensation was taken from the courts and handed to an administrative agency. Injuries were compensated by a system that provided for filing and adjudication of claims (where necessary) and for a system of appeals, all housed within an administrative structure established by the statutory regime.

A similar pattern developed with workers' rights to organize and bargain collectively, providing the second example of resistance by courts and intervention by the administrative state. During the nineteenth century, employees began to consolidate to demand some minimum benefits that came with the Industrial Revolution. Concerns for safety, exploitation of women and children, limits to hours worked, and the desire for increased wages all drove the union movement on. When it was not attacked by brute force, it was assaulted in the courts, where judges were mostly the allies of management. The cudgel was the concept of restraint of trade. Liberal values, at least in this context, espoused free markets where goods and services could flow unimpeded. Any clog was to be removed, hence any agreements or activities that restrained trade were to be suppressed. Courts used this concept to pummel any formal organizing by workers and attempts to bargain collectively.

Again, it was for the legislatures to reformulate the structure between employees and management by recognizing the workers' rights to form unions and requiring employers to bargain with them collectively and, of course, freeing them from the threat of criminal conspiracy for asserting their own interests: "the statutory freeing of unions from criminal responsibility for conspiracy or combination in restraint of trade is the cornerstone on which the trade movement rests. From it flows also collective bargaining and the later legislation dealing with labour relations."

Further, the implementation of such a regime was ultimately handed to administrative tribunals. A number of attempts to leave the issues with the courts foundered. Their focus on one-time disposition based on winners and losers, their adherence to a passive model where all aspects of an issue were to be brought and shaped by the parties, and their abiding hostility to the notion that workers should be able to bind together to improve their lot doomed the courts' role to failure. Ultimately, all legislatures in Canada ousted them from a direct role in collective bargaining issues. Yet the courts did not ease silently away but reasserted themselves in another role, a matter discussed below.

The last example of resistance by courts and intervention by the administrative state comes from the law's treatment of discrimination. One of the most cherished ideals of justice is the law's equal treatment of everyone. But like so many ideals, it is utterly compelling as an abstraction and extraordinarily difficult as a reality. Does everyone have at least a basic claim to society's economic resources for minimum food, shelter, medical care, education, and access to the justice system? Does equality always mean equal treatment or is it sometimes necessary to treat individuals differently so as to achieve equal results?

Whatever equality should convey, it has come to mean at least a claim to treatment freed from discrimination based on religion, race, and sex. A man's chances for being hired for a job should be based on his competence as compared with that of other applicants. His ethnic background should be irrelevant. A black woman's desire to rent an apartment should depend on her ability to pay and her willingness to use the premises reasonably. The fact that she is a woman and black should be beside the point. Even this negative sense of equality can be problematic. Should it allow for affirmative action programs to rectify past injustices? Should a criminal record be taken into account when hiring or should it be regarded as irrelevant like religion, at least for some positions? Is it appropriate to allow certain institutions that overtly espouse a particular religion or set of beliefs to hire only those who adhere to those beliefs in order to foster the institution itself?

These issues illustrate the complexity of the concepts of equality and discrimination regardless of which government agency grapples with them. What is clear from the historical record is the courts' antagonism to even minimum notions of equality of freedom from discrimination. For decades the courts were given a number of opportunities to nurture or at least tolerate the concepts, but, with few exceptions, they were hostile and unyielding.

The market was once again the frequent watchword. The free and uninterrupted flow of goods and services needed to be enhanced, while individual proprietors of those goods and services decided to contract with whomever they wished. If an owner refused to serve blacks, that was his right, subject to discipline by the market, because he would be deprived of that group's commerce. That a group as weak and diffuse as blacks in this country at that time could actually discipline bigotry through market forces was a fantasy that escaped the courts' notice.

This fidelity to freedom of contract was not subtle in any way. In one of the most notorious cases in Quebec before the Second World War, a black was refused service by a tavern owner. In upholding his right to do so, the Supreme Court of Canada made these comments:

[T]he general principle of the law of Quebec was that of complete freedom of commerce. ... Any merchant is free to deal as he may choose with any individual member of the public. It is not a question of motives or reasons for deciding to deal or not to deal; he is free to do either. The only restriction to this general principle would be the existence of a specific law, or, in the carrying out of the principle, the adoption of a rule contrary to good morals or public order ... [and it cannot] be argued that the rule adopted by the respondent in the conduct of its establishment was contrary to good morals or public order.

Over time, there were a number of cases dealing with similar issues that venerated contract and dishonoured human dignity.

A similar atmosphere surrounded the "Persons" case, which raised the question of whether women could be appointed to the Senate as "qualified persons," a case we will return to in the next chapter. In denying the entitlement to women, the Supreme Court of Canada engaged in tortuous reasoning based on the historical intent when the provision was created in 1876. That is how things would have stood had an English appellate court, the Judicial Committee of the Privy Council (at that time Canada's highest court of appeal), not disagreed, ruling that women were qualified. This case is but one example of how the courts treated women … .

To be sure, the legislatures perpetuated their own discriminatory horrors. But again, challenges to these wrongs, particularly against the Chinese, were continually rebuffed by the courts. Often the legislation restricted the rights of the Chinese to gain a livelihood or employ certain people, particularly "white women." On these occasions freedom of contract was subordinated to the higher cause of "morals" and "bodily health." This is typical judicial reaction:

> It would require some evidence of it to convince me that the right and opportunity to employ white women is, in any business sense, a necessary condition for the effective carrying on by Orientals of restaurants and laundries and like establishments. … Neither is there any ground for supposing that this legislation is designed to deprive Orientals of the opportunity to gain a livelihood.

Hesitantly and piece by piece, the legislatures eradicated discrimination after the Second World War. Though fragmentary and incomplete, the idea behind the statutes was basic: equal treatment for all individuals without regard to particular characteristics that are irrelevant to the decision being made. It is well to remember that the process is still unfolding and is almost always controversial. In Ontario, it has only been a few years since gay men and women have received at least some of the law's protection, and in a few jurisdictions in Canada, it is still denied to them altogether.

Yet the process continues and these issues have been removed from the courts' jurisdiction. Human rights commissions have been established to implement the legislation, fight discrimination with education, conciliation and, if necessary, through adjudication that brands particular actions as wrong and awards compensation to victims when the allegations are proven. Reviewing the courts' performance and legislative reaction, a leading text on discrimination concludes, "[I]t is no wonder, then, that the legislatures, with no aid from the judiciary, had to move into the field and start to enact anti-discrimination legislation, the administration and application of which have largely been taken out of the courts."

The examples drawn from these three areas are merely illustrative of a pattern: initially, the courts' propounding of rules that mostly honoured strict liberal notions of individual responsibility, autonomy, and freedom centred on economic entitlement; then a reaction by legislatures that adopted a more communitarian perspective, inquired into the actual results, and recognized other values (such as need for compensation, legitimacy of collective action, and claims to equal treatment), frequently combined with the creation of an administrative body. Finally, the removal of these issues, in large part, from the courts, at least in terms of initial decision-making and the creation of some administrative agency to decide such questions. Other contemporary examples include pay equity, redress for environmental harm, and compensation for injuries from motor vehicle accidents. Issues concerning the last example will be taken up in Chapter Six regarding tort litigation.

This is not to say that the legislative response has been flawless. Workers' compensation boards, grappling with rising costs, have come to be seen as unresponsive to very serious issues that affect health in the workplace, such as occupational disease, though most standard claims are handled promptly and to the satisfaction of the injured. Human rights tribunals are criticized for being slow and backlogged. Indeed, such problems have grown to crisis proportions in Ontario and have been the subject of a very critical report. There are many examples of discrepancy between the high ideals espoused by these tribunals and related initiatives and the underlying reality. For example, despite strict laws prohibiting discrimination against the disabled, Canada's record for employing people with disabilities appears to be among the worst.

Yet in terms of responding with solutions other than those centred on economic individualism when it comes to issues that affect ordinary men and women, there has been a consistent division in this century between the courts and the legislatures and their agencies. Reviewing the historical record on this question, Arthurs has flatly asserted, "the courts utterly failed to deal with the most significant legal repercussions of the Industrial Revolution in the nineteenth century and with the revolution of rising expectations in the twentieth." In suggesting that judges by and large should not deal with human rights cases, a former justice of the Ontario courts has observed recently that:

> Judges as a group have been traditionally drawn from social classes unsympathetic to social change. This has been perceived as clouding their judgment by inclining them to decide against the change the legislation seeks to achieve. Judges have been perceived as unsympathetic to the problems of the "common-man."

• • •

Judicial Review of Administrative Action

The clash between the judiciary and the administrative state—illustrated by our discussion of workers' compensation, labour relations, and human rights—developed on another front. Even before the advent of industrialization and capitalism, the courts had claimed the right to review the workings of government, though actual review was unsystematic. The growth of government was accompanied by the courts' increasing propensity to intervene and set aside orders made illegally.

But how was illegality to be determined? The courts vowed that this review was focused not on the correctness of the ultimate decision but on whether the decision-maker was empowered by the authorizing legislation to make the decision and the procedures the decision-maker was required to use. But even if this was the ambit of review, deciding what legislation empowered and what procedures could be used left plenty of scope for review. It was easy to see how a view that suggested the courts should not have such power of scrutiny would arise. Such an opinion was grounded in the belief that each administrative actor was as well situated or even better situated because of expertise to determine how his decisions ought to be made. Any review or appeal should come from that structure. The courts should keep out, as history indicates this was not a task for them, either as initial decision-makers or as reviewers of administrative actors' decisions, unless there was some appeal made to them that was authorized by statute.

Those who subscribed to this view were outraged that legislatures often inserted in relevant statutes sections declaring that the tribunal's decision was final and not to be reviewed in any way, specifically by a court. Yet these admonitions—known as "privative clauses"—were frequently defied by courts. To do this, they declared that all administrative tribunals had limited jurisdiction assigned to them by the legislatures. Therefore, whenever the tribunal made decisions that exceeded the limits of the jurisdiction assigned to them, they stepped outside the ambit of protection afforded by these clauses and the courts as protectors of the rule of law could—and indeed were obliged to—step in and corral them.

As logic, this manoeuvre was fine; as policy, it was highly dubious. It was true that administrative tribunals were assigned limited functions. Labour relation boards were to deal with issues arising between properly certified unions and management but were not to set milk production quotas. But the flaw was that issues submitted to the court as jurisdictional ones were far less clear than that. They almost always dealt with questions critical to the task the administrative actor was performing. The courts were frequently ignorant and even hostile to the thrust of the underlying legislative policy. When they brought to the interpretive exercise notions about the rule of law that idealized courts and the common law as its embodiment, there were bound to be clashes.

Perhaps at this point an example would be helpful. Any number could be provided, but let us take a classic one from the wranglings between courts and human rights tribunals, since we have already looked at the courts' response to issues of discrimination in the previous section. In 1968 McKay, a black, phoned about renting an apartment in the home of Bell. When he arrived to look at it, Bell informed him that the flat was rented. McKay, who was suspicious of the circumstances, had an acquaintance of his phone Bell soon after and she was told it was still available. Faced with this revelation, McKay went to the Ontario Human Rights Commission and filed a complaint. Bell explained that he lied because he did not rent to young men who could be students, and lying was a means to avoid argument and confrontation. However, at the board of inquiry—the hearing to adjudicate whether a discriminatory act had taken place—Bell raised a more formidable point that, if accepted, would prevent the board from proceeding at all.

Preventing discrimination has been given a high value in our society through the statutory prohibitions against it, but compromises have been made. Rightly or wrongly—at the time of this case—the legislation only prohibited discrimination in rental accommodation for "self-contained dwelling units." The idea behind the qualification was that the physical setup is likely to engender even more hostility between bigot and victim if the bigot is forced to accept the victim into what is basically her own home.

However, the matter for debate was what qualified as a "self-contained dwelling unit" since this term was not defined in the code. Bell went to court to have the judges stop the board of inquiry on the grounds that the flat was not a self-contained dwelling unit and, therefore, the board had no "jurisdiction" to decide whether acts of discrimination had occurred. Despite dissents, Bell won in the Supreme Court of Canada, the majority characterizing the issue as a "perfectly simple, short and neat question of law."

What irks defendants of administrative tribunals is the attitude typified by this quote. In fact the issue is complex and heavily dependent on a sense of the entire antidiscrimination structure and where and how to draw boundary lines in terms of, on the one hand, resisting discrimination and, on the other, realizing that insistence on enforcing the Human Rights Code will result in even more rancour. Such a decision should not be reached in the abstract, but only after carefully examining the facts in the particular case and relating them to appropriate circumstances where boundary lines have had to be drawn to enforce human rights legislation and mindful of the fact that premises such as the one in the *Bell* case are likely to be rented by individuals most in need of protection from discrimination.

Instead the Court based the meaning it attributed to "self-contained dwelling unit" on a mechanical and selective application of the previous formulation of the legislation. Initially the code forbade discrimination in "any apartment in any building that contains more than six self-contained dwelling units." An amendment in 1965 included buildings with more than three such units. Finally, in 1967 the legislation was altered again to prevent discrimination because of race to "any self-contained dwelling unit." Responding to these evolving formulations, the Court asserted that: "[T]he premises leased by the appellant, located in his upstairs floors, may well be 'dwelling units' but they were not 'self-contained' dwelling units."

It is small wonder then, with the *Bell* case as an example, that courts' review of administrative action has been characterized as subjective, inconsistent, hostile to the purpose of the agency and the legislation being scrutinized, and just plain muddled. Adams, a leading author in labour law (and himself now a judge) explains that since substantive rules of law applicable to judicial control of administrative action are so general in nature, they may actually invite intervention based on "subjective judicial opinion." Statutes like those dealing with labour relations issues were enacted to reflect particular economic and social policy, but any number of judges' personal views may be quite contradictory and lead to any number of conflicting decisions. ...

The landscape is even more complex. In addition, whatever should be the appropriate point for courts overturning administrative actors' decisions about the proper scope of their statutory regime, courts have also sought to fulfil a second function with their review. In this second role, they recognize the importance of reviewing an administrative decision to ensure that one who has been affected by a decision has been accorded minimal procedural decencies. At first glance, this too may seem intrusive since the courts' power to intervene is so embracing. Still, most of the criticism of courts' interference with tribunals, much of it justified, has been directed towards their mangling of the agencies' substantive programs by second-guessing how their legislative mandate is to be carried out. Critics have been much less bothered by the courts' role in assuring that decisions accord with appropriate procedural safeguards—free of bad faith and bias, and giving those who are affected adequate opportunities to participate in the process. That these two processes—supervising the scope of administrative agencies' power and scrutinizing the procedures used to arrive at their decisions—can be very different is obvious if one realizes that former Chief Justice Dickson, the primary architect of deference to boards working out their regulatory scheme, was also one of the judges who favoured the most intervention to ensure that individuals affected by administrative actors' decisions have an adequate opportunity to present their arguments and evidence.

Deference to an agency's decisions in determining its mandate will alleviate problems of courts crippling tribunals' substantive programs. On the other hand, respect for persons—not just in terms of economic rights but in all aspects of individual integrity—should inform any kind of decision made by anyone empowered to decide. Even the staunchest defenders of administrative law are willing to admit that agencies' records at times have not been good in this regard. While indicating their willingness to intervene on this basis, the courts have simultaneously indicated that they will not use a fixed and immutable standard for evaluating the decencies of the procedures used unless required to do so by some statutory directive. The person affected must be given an adequate opportunity to participate and be treated fairly, but what is adequate and fair will vary from the most perfunctory right of oral reply to written submissions to a more formal hearing.

V. DISPUTE RESOLUTION IN ABORIGINAL SOCIETIES

The methods traditionally used to resolve disputes in various aboriginal societies differ fundamentally from those examined in this chapter. Also, different aboriginal societies have their own distinctive methods of resolving disputes.

The following excerpt is taken from Manitoba's report on aboriginal justice. The commissioners were A.C. Hamilton and C.M. Sinclair JJ. Among their recommendations was that aboriginal justice systems be established in aboriginal communities as part of the inherent right of self-government. A tribal court system would include youth, family, criminal, civil, and appellate court systems and a mediation/counselling system based in part on the role played by the Peacemaker Court in the Navajo tribal justice system. All of these institutions would "look toward the development of culturally appropriate rules and processes which have as their aim the establishment of a less formalistic approach to courtroom procedures."

The inquiry also recommended that aboriginal communities be entitled to enact their own criminal, civil, and family laws based on their traditions and customs and that they should not be bound by the Canadian Charter of Rights and Freedoms, but rather by a First Nations charter reflecting aboriginal customs and values.

Public Inquiry into the Administration of Justice and Aboriginal People
in *The Justice System and Aboriginal People*, vol. 1, c. 3
(Winnipeg: Queen's Printer, 1991) (footnotes omitted)

The differences between Aboriginal processes and the processes of the Canadian justice system are profound. The Canadian justice system, like other justice systems in the

European tradition, is adversarial. When an accusation has been made against an individual, legal advisers representing plaintiff and defendant confront one another before an impartial judge or jury. Witnesses are called to testify for or against the accused; that is, to criticize or explain the actions of another. Guilt or innocence was decided on the basis of the argument that takes place between legal representatives. Retribution is demanded if the person accused is considered guilty.

The concepts of adversarialism, accusation, confrontation, guilt, argument, criticism and retribution are alien to the Aboriginal value system, although perhaps not totally unknown to Aboriginal peoples. In the context of Aboriginal value systems, adversarialism and confrontation are antagonistic to the high value placed on harmony and the peaceful coexistence of all living beings, both human and non-human, with one another and with nature. Criticism of others is at odds with the principles of non-interference and individual autonomy and freedom. The idea that guilt and innocence can be decided on the basis of argument is incompatible with a firmly rooted belief in honesty and integrity that does not permit lying. Retribution as an end in itself, and as an aim of society, becomes a meaningless notion in a value system which requires the reconciliation of an offender with the community and restitution for victims. ...

The same contradictions between Aboriginal values and the dominant justice system result in a heavy burden being placed on Aboriginal accused, plaintiffs and witnesses who enter into the "white" justice system. Accusation and criticism (giving adverse testimony), while required in the Canadian justice system, are precluded in an Aboriginal value system which makes every effort to avoid criticism and confrontation. "Refusal or reluctance to testify, or when testifying, to give anything but the barest and most emotionless recital of events" appears to be the result of deeply rooted cultural behaviour in which "giving testimony face to face with the accused is simply wrong ... [and] where in fact every effort seems to have been made to avoid such direct confrontation. In Aboriginal societies, it may be ethically wrong to say hostile, critical, implicitly angry things about someone in his or her presence, precisely what our adversarial trial rules require.

Methods and processes for solving disputes in Aboriginal societies have developed, of course, out of the basic value systems of the people. Belief in the inherent decency and wisdom of each individual person implies that any person will have useful opinions in any given situation, and should be listened to respectfully. Aboriginal methods of dispute resolution, therefore, allow for any interested party to volunteer an opinion or make a comment. The "truth" of an incident is arrived at through hearing many descriptions of the event and of related, perhaps extenuating, circumstances.

Impossible though it is to arrive at "the whole truth" in any circumstance, as Aboriginal people are aware, they believe that more of the truth can be determined when everyone is free to contribute information, as opposed to a system where only a chosen number are called to testify on subjects carefully chosen by adversarial counsel, where certain topics or information are inadmissible, and where questions can be asked in ways that dictate the answers. ...

At the most basic level of understanding, justice is understood differently by Aboriginal people. The dominant society tries to control actions it considers potentially or actually harmful to society as a whole, to individuals or to the wrongdoers themselves by interdiction, enforcement or apprehension, in order to prevent or punish harmful or deviant behaviour. The emphasis is on the punishment of the deviants as a means of making that person conform, or as a means of protecting other members of society.

The purpose of a justice system in an Aboriginal society is to restore the peace and equilibrium within the community, and to reconcile the accused with his or her own conscience and with the individual or family who has been wronged. This is a primary difference. It is a difference that significantly challenges the appropriateness of the present legal and justice system for Aboriginal people in the resolution of conflict, the reconciliation and the maintenance of community harmony and good order.

NOTES AND QUESTIONS

1. The aboriginal justice inquiry reported that about 145 US Indian tribes have some form of their own court systems. A further 14 tribes function in full or in part under a traditional or customary law system. Most tribal courts are limited to matters that arise within the boundaries of their reservations. In *Williams v. Lee*, 358 US 217 (1959), the court upheld the exclusive jurisdiction of the Navajo tribal court to decide an action brought by a non-Indian to enforce a debt under a contract entered into with the Indian defendant on the reservation.

2. The Navajo Peacemaker Court is examined in James Zion, "The Navajo Peacemaker Court: Deference to the Old and Accommodation to the New" (1985), 11 *American Indian Law Review* 89. See also Michael Coyle, "Traditional Indian Justice in Ontario: A Role for the Present" (1986), 24 *Osgoode Hall Law Journal* 605.

3. While there is much that could be done to improve access to existing legal structures and to change our delivery models to ensure that they are more culturally responsive, conceptualizing the problems in this manner obscures what is a deeper challenge. The challenge, advanced by aboriginal communities in particular, is that the existing order cannot, by its very nature, take seriously the cultures of First Nations peoples. For many, tinkering at the edges of what is, at its core, a white man's justice system will never lead to justice for aboriginal communities.

Sam Stevens, in "Access to Civil Justice for Aboriginal Peoples," in A. Hutchinson, ed., *Access to Civil Justice* (Toronto: Carswell, 1990) 203, at 212-13 discussed these issues and presented a structure for solutions:

> [I]t may be useful to summarize the reasons for why aboriginal people do not feel they can gain access to the civil justice system.
>
> 1. Aboriginal people have been conditioned to distrust the Canadian judicial system, part of which includes the civil court process. They will therefore not usually use the civil justice system.
>
> 2. The Canadian justice system does not recognize aboriginal customary laws, laws that have been used by aboriginal peoples, in some cases, for thousands of years. As a result, aboriginal people feel their disputes cannot be resolved by the present justice system in a meaningful way.
>
> 3. The adversarial system used by the Canadian judicial system is antithetical to the traditional aboriginal dispute resolution system.

4. The aboriginal people in Canada are unfamiliar with the courts and their rights as Canadians; they therefore do not generally assert their rights as recognized under federal or provincial laws.

5. Until recently, there has been an obvious lack of representation in the Canadian judicial system by aboriginal lawyers and judges.

6. A majority of aboriginal people have incomes substantially less than those of average Canadians, and, as a result, many of the problems that aboriginal people experience are "poor people problems." Lawyers generally do not want to deal with these "poor people problems."

7. The time it takes to solve their legal problem is something that aboriginal people cannot accept.

8. The cost of having a civil suit adjudicated by the court is prohibitive.

9. The socio-economic position of aboriginal peoples makes the courts more inaccessible for aboriginal peoples than for non-aboriginal peoples.

10. The civil court system is an inappropriate forum for the resolution of issues dealing with claims and aboriginal rights.

To begin to solve these problems, I have proposed solutions based on three broad approaches. First, there are disputes of a private, individual nature, involving an aboriginal person and a non-aboriginal person or one of the governments. These disputes should continue to be settled by the present civil courts. So, what can be done to ensure that the civil courts are more accessible to aboriginal people or other people in circumstances similar to those of aboriginal peoples? Second, there are disputes that are of a civil, private law nature but that are between two aboriginal people from the same community or from another aboriginal community. Aboriginal people have proposed, and it seems reasonable and indeed feasible, to have these disputes resolved by the aboriginal community and according to their laws and standards. Third, there are disputes that are of a public law nature and that involve aboriginal community rights on the one hand, and either the Canadian or provincial community or private law rights on the other hand. The civil courts are being asked to resolve increasingly more disputes of this nature. It is questionable whether the present civil courts are necessarily the best forums to settle these kinds of dispute. If we continue to use the present civil court system to resolve some of these disputes, what can we do to ensure aboriginal people get a just resolution of their disputes, and are there other alternative dispute resolution forums that can be implemented to resolve these types of dispute?

What criteria should be employed in evaluating these proposals? Who should decide?

The following excerpt from the Royal Commission on Aboriginal Peoples, while not specifically addressed to procedures for resolving civil disputes, provides important insights into the nature of "traditional" or "customary" law, governance, decision making, and value systems, all of which are relevant to conceptualizing civil processes within separate justice systems.

Canada, Report of the Royal Commission on Aboriginal Peoples, "Governance"
in *Restructuring the Relationship*, vol. 2, chapter 3,
(Ottawa: Queen's Printer, 1996), 115-39

1.2 Traditions of Governance

In most Aboriginal nations, political life has always been closely connected with the family, the land and a strong sense of spirituality. In speaking to the Commission of their governance traditions, many Aboriginal people emphasized the integrated nature of the spiritual, familial, economic and political spheres. While some Canadians tend to see government as remote, divorced from the people and everyday life, Aboriginal people generally view government in a more holistic way, as inseparable from the totality of communal practices that make up a way of life.

This outlook is reflected in Aboriginal languages that express the concept of government in words meaning "our way of life" or "our life":

> If you take the word *bemodezewan*, you will find that it is a way of life ... That is why it is difficult when you ask an Indian person to describe self-government. How do you describe a way of life and its total inclusion of religious rights, social rights, government rights, justice rights and the use of the family as a system by which we live? ... We are not prepared at this time to separate those things. They are a way of life for our people.

> Leonard Nelson
> Roseau River, Manitoba
> 8 December 1992

Most Aboriginal people continue to be guided, to some degree, by traditional outlooks in their approach to matters of governance. In some instances, Aboriginal communities have made traditional laws, practices and modes of leadership the basis of their contemporary governmental institutions. In other cases, however, traditional systems of governance have fallen into disuse or been replaced by new systems, such as those imposed by the *Indian Act*.

Faced with these changes, many Aboriginal people have called for a revitalization of traditional values and practices and their reintegration into institutions of government. Aboriginal people see this process occurring in a variety of ways. A number of representations made to the Commission emphasized the need to root contemporary governmental initiatives in traditional attitudes and institutions:

> If self-government is to become the vehicle by which Native people resume their rightful place in North American society, it must grow, unaffected, out of a strong knowledge of the past. Only in this way, is it assured that the Anishinabek, and other traditional governing structures, will be resuscitated for future growth and development. ... Knowledge of pre-contact Native societies will serve as the proper base upon which we can carefully and slowly construct models of governance. These models will be founded in the past and developed to consider environmental changes and the realities of today.

Nevertheless, in calling for governmental structures that are grounded in Aboriginal peoples' cultures and values, some interveners also spoke of the need to adopt certain features of mainstream Canadian governments.

> The Lheit-Lit'en solution was to recognize what had been lost, which is a traditional form of government. What had been lost was culture. What had been lost was any relationship between the community, the children, the adults and the elders as well as language. And that needed to be regained, the community decided.
>
> But at the same time, the community also felt that since we live in a contemporary non-Aboriginal world that it would be impossible to regain that out of context. ... As a consequence, the Lheit-Lit'en decided to combine traditional and contemporary methods of governments, contemporary as well as traditional methods of justice.

> Erling Christensen
> Prince George, British Columbia
> 1 June 1993

In what follows, we consider some important aspects of Aboriginal traditions of governance, drawing on testimony in the Commission's hearings, briefs and studies. These aspects are

- the centrality of the land
- individual autonomy and responsibility
- the rule of law
- the role of women
- the role of elders
- the role of the family and clan
- leadership
- consensus in decision making
- the restoration of traditional institutions.

There is no uniform Aboriginal outlook on these topics, many of which are the focus of lively discussion and exchange among Aboriginal people. Nevertheless, the very fact that they are the object of such interest shows their continuing importance in the panoply of indigenous approaches to governance.

One point needs to be emphasized. For most Aboriginal people, "tradition" does not consist of static practices and institutions that existed in the distant past. It is an evolving body of ways of life that adapts to changing situations and readily integrates new attitudes and practices. As a study of traditional Inuit governance explains:

> This ... Inuit approach to "traditions" and the "traditional culture" moves "traditional culture" away from its exoticized state depicted in books and displayed in museums and presents it instead in the everyday actions of northern individuals. This insider view grounds "traditional culture" not in a time frame (the pre-contact period) but instead in a set of practices engaged in by Inuit of both the recent or distant past.

Here, Aboriginal people are no more prisoners of the past than other Canadians are. They do not need to replicate the customs of bygone ages to stay in touch with their traditions, just as Parliament does not need to observe all the practices of eighteenth-century Westminster in order to honour the parliamentary tradition. Aboriginal people, like other contemporary people, are constantly reworking their institutions to cope with new circumstances and demands. In doing so, they freely borrow and adapt cultural traits that they find useful and appealing. It is not the heedless reproduction of outmoded practices that makes a vigorous tradition, but a strong connection with the living past. ...

Individual Autonomy and Responsibility

In most Aboriginal societies, an individual is imbued with a strong sense of personal autonomy and an equally strong sense of responsibility to the community. Since the welfare of the community depends on the ingenuity, initiative and self-reliance of its individual members, individual rights and responsibilities are viewed as serving rather than opposing collective interests.

> One of the most important and respected attributes of a person in Inuit society is their degree of independence and ability to meet life challenges with innovation, resourcefulness and perserverance. Traditionally, these were traits that would greatly increase the chance of survival for the individual and group. ... In addition to a strong value being place on individual independence, the practice of sharing was held to be of the utmost importance.
>
> In general, the Dene governed themselves with recognition and acceptance of the individual's right and responsibility to live according to the demands and needs of the gifts which the individual carried. ... It is in the context of mutual benefit to all individuals concerned that collective rights and responsibilities are exercised.

Understanding the individual's status and role has important implications for governance. In a number of Aboriginal societies, this understanding has fostered a strong spirit of egalitarianism in communal life. As the Deh Cho Tribal Council affirms, "No one can decide for another person. Everyone is involved in the discussion and ... the decision [is] made by everyone."

From this perspective, interfering with the fulfilment of an individual's responsibilities can be seen as interfering with natural law. It is only when the actions of individuals threaten the balance of society and the fulfilment of collective responsibilities that justice, as a mechanism of government, is brought to bear:

> Justice was prescribed as a code of individual duties and responsibilities first; then when the correction of a wrong was ignored, the community could and would institute sanctions—ranging from restitution by apology, retribution, to outright ostracism. But always the rehabilitation and healing of the individual was central to the wellness and normal functioning of the community within the nation.

The Rule of Law

In Aboriginal societies, as in mainstream Canadian society, the rule of law is accepted as a fundamental guiding principle. However, the law is not understood in an exclusively secular sense. For many Aboriginal people, the law is grounded in instructions from the Creator or, alternatively, a body of basic principles embedded in the natural order. Thus basic law is viewed as the "law of God" or "natural law." This basic law gives direction to individuals in fulfilling their responsibilities as stewards of the earth and, by extension, other human beings. The law tells people how to conduct themselves in their relations with one another and with the rest of creation.

> The Creator gave us our instructions in which are ordained our duties and freedoms; our roles and responsibilities; our customs and traditions; our languages; our place on Mother Earth within which we are to enjoy peace, security, and prosperity. These are the spiritual ways by which we live.
> Included in the spiritual laws were the laws of the land. These were developed through the sacred traditions of each tribe of red nations by the guidance of the spirit world. We each had our sacred traditions of how to look after and use medicines from the plant, winged and animal kingdoms. The law of use is sacred to traditional people today.

Dennis Thorne
Edmonton, Alberta
11 June 1992

Since the law ultimately stems from God, any failure to live by the law is to turn one's back on the Creator's gifts, to abdicate responsibility and to deny a way of life. The law helps people fulfil their responsibilities as individuals and members of the community.

The traditional laws of most Aboriginal peoples are customary and usually unwritten. They are embodied in maxims, oral traditions and daily observances and are transmitted from generation to generation through precept and example. This practice is often misunderstood. Some outside observers, accustomed to thinking of the law as rules laid down by legislatures and embodied in written statutes, have denied that custom truly can constitute law. They forget that, even in mainstream society, few individuals are familiar with more than a small portion of the written law; in practice, ordinary people conduct their lives in accordance with what amounts to a living customary system. Moreover, English common law, which is the basis of the legal system in Canada outside Quebec, originated as a body of customary law under the supervision of the courts. To this day, it is largely uncodified. ...

Some Aboriginal people, with the help of their elders, have remained in close touch with their traditional legal systems. These systems are not static but continue to evolve and provide a strong basis for contemporary communal life. Other communities have not been as fortunate and are only just beginning to rediscover and revitalize their traditional laws. They recognize that the process may not be easy and will require time, sustained effort and the commitment of scarce resources. Nevertheless, they are hopeful they will succeed.

> Our traditional laws are not dead. They are bruised and battered but alive within the hearts and minds of the indigenous peoples across our lands. Our elders hold these laws within their hearts for us. We have only to reach out and live the laws. We do not need the sanction of the non-indigenous world to implement our laws. These laws are given

to us by the Creator to use. We are going to begin by using them as they were intended. It is our obligation to the children yet unborn.

Sharon Venne
Saulteau First Nation
Fort St. John, British Columbia
20 November 1992

• • •

The Role of the Family and Clan

Traditionally, the family or clan constituted the basic unit of governance for many Aboriginal peoples. For more detailed discussion, see Volume 3, Chapter 2.

Before the white nations had any dealings with the Indian people of this nation, the whole realm of Indian being Indian meant that we had a clan system. It's a system of relationships that are defined by our birth right.

The clan system is a social order. The clan system is a justice system. The clan system is a government. The clan system is an extended family unit.

Leonard Nelson
Roseau River, Manitoba
8 December 1992

It is my personal view that the culture of any people is centred and perpetuated through the family unit. It is for this reason that I do not believe one can legislate the perpetuation of cultural values. I believe that if you destroy the family unit you will also lose the culture of a people. In this regard, I cannot overstate the importance of recognizing the integrity of the family unit as an integral part of any initiative leading toward Aboriginal self-government.

Dennis Surrendi
Elizabeth, Alberta
16 June 1993

Families and clans fulfilled a number of essential governmental functions. They determined who belonged to the group, provided for the needs of members, regulated internal relations, dealt with offenders and regulated use of lands and resources. They also imbued individuals with a sense of basic identity and guided them in cultivating their special gifts and fulfilling their responsibilities.

The clan system gives each member of the community clear knowledge of his or her place, in a number of ways. In a community with a functioning clan system, it tells individuals who their spiritual and political leaders are. It tells the person where to sit in the ceremonies. It often tells people about the others to whom they bear a special set of obligations—to help and guide them, but also that they are responsible and accountable to a particular individual as well as to all members of the clan.

• • •

Consensus in Decision Making

> The art of consensus decision making is dying. We are greatly concerned that Aboriginal people are increasingly equating "democracy" with the act of voting. ... [W]e are convinced that the practice of consensus decision making is essential to the culture of our peoples, as well as being the only tested and effective means of Aboriginal community self-government.

Decision making took a variety of forms in traditional Aboriginal societies. For example, decentralized systems of government often relied on the family and its internal structures to make decisions. In such societies, the autonomy of family groups was a fundamental principle. Societies with a more complex political organization made decisions not only at the level of the family but also through broader communal institutions. The potlatch, as practised among the peoples of the northwest coast, is an example of a communal institution serving multiple functions.

> The potlatch was a gathering of people, often including people from surrounding nations. According to the Lheit-Lit'en Nation, the potlatch was usually a culmination of smaller earlier meetings where individual issues were dealt with. At this final gathering, all people were included so that everyone could participate in final discussions and be aware of the decisions and agreement reached. The gathering dealt with territorial and justice issues and was generally the main instrument of community control, community watch, defence of territory and any issues relating to the community.

Whatever their system of government, many Aboriginal people have spoken of the principle of consensus as a fundamental part of their traditions. Under this principle, all community members should be involved in the process of reaching agreement on matters of common interest. Among some peoples, discussions generally begin at the level of the family. In this way, the views of women, children and all who are not spokespersons may help shape the view expressed by the family or clan. Discussions may then proceed at a broader level and involve all family spokespersons, clan leaders or chiefs. In certain cases, all members of the community meet in assembly. Through a prolonged process of formulation and reformulation, consensus gradually emerges, representing a blend of individual perspectives.

In describing how an Anishnabe nation with seven clans came to decisions through a consensus-seeking process, an intervener made these observations:

> Peter Ochise ... said seven twice is eight. ... It's taken me some time to grasp what he meant. Seven perspectives blended, seven perspectives working in harmony together to truly define the problem, truly define the action that is needed makes for an eighth understanding. It's a tough lesson that we don't know all the answers, we don't know all the problems. We really own only one-seventh of the understanding of it and we only know one-seventh of what to do about it. We need each other in harmony to know how to do things. ... This process that we had was 100 per cent ownership of the problem.

Mark Douglas
Orillia, Ontario
14 May 1993

In consensus-based political systems, the concept of "the loyal opposition," as in parliamentary systems, does not exist. As Williams and Nelson point out, decision making by consensus, often referred to as coming to one mind, is gradual, and the resolution of issues is built piece by piece, without confrontation.

A study of Dene governance traditions notes that "consensus among the Dene is more a quality of life than a distinct process, structure or outcome." It permeates all levels of decision making, from the extended family to local and regional communities and the nation as a whole. Nevertheless, the same study observes that certain conditions are necessary for consensus systems to operate properly. These include face-to-face contact among members and the opportunity for those affected by decisions to take part in them. Consensus systems also require a broad pool of shared knowledge, including recognition of the leadership qualities of particular individuals, their family, history, spiritual training and so on. These conditions presuppose a basic political unit having strong continuing ties, such as those found in the extended family. ...

The Restoration of Traditional Institutions

Many Aboriginal people see revitalization of their traditions of governance as playing an important role in reform of current governmental systems. The Assembly of First Nations states:

> The move to re-establish and strengthen First Nation governments must be encouraged by all levels of government. The establishment of First Nation governments based on First Nation traditions, including hereditary systems, clan systems and other governing structures, should be encouraged and innovative institutions developed to reflect both these traditions and contemporary governing needs.

For some groups, a return to traditional systems of government would mean the restoration of the primary role played by extended families and clans. For example, the extended family might be given initial responsibility for matters affecting the welfare of individuals and the family, such as domestic conflict, child welfare and some aspects of the administration of justice, such as the healing of offenders. Representatives of families or clans might come together as a community council, which would exercise a range of governmental functions and responsibilities. Chiefs or chief spokespersons would then be selected in a traditional manner, which in some cases might involve mutual agreement among families. Such arrangements would be designed to avoid the situation that sometimes results under conventional electoral arrangements, whereby one or two families in a community are able to dominate the entire apparatus of government.

In some approaches, special roles and responsibilities should be assigned to women and elders in a revival of traditional institutions. Such approaches would place women and elders at the centre of government and decision making and give them particular responsibilities for the selection and removal of leaders. Other approaches would assign women and elders mainly advisory and supportive roles. Approaches of the latter kind are cause for scepticism and concern for many Aboriginal women, who express the fear that such arrangements may disenfranchise them or muffle their voices under a blanket of tradition.

Such concerns are not confined to women. Several men have expressed the view that any revival of traditional institutions and laws need not (and should not) involve reinstating practices that discriminate against certain individuals and groups.

> I think a lot of the traditional laws and traditional concepts make a lot of sense and that is how our society functioned in the past and it can function again very well, but in doing so we have to be careful that we do not take away rights from people and that individual rights and collective rights are properly addressed and that traditional laws are clearly defined and apply to everybody, not only to certain groups and not to other groups.

Chief Jean-Guy Whiteduck
Maniwaki, Quebec
2 December 1992

The Teslin Tlingit Nation in the Yukon is an example of a group that has taken significant steps toward restoring its traditional system of government, particularly in the areas of leadership and decision making. It has done so as part of a self-government initiative that is parallel to its negotiation of a comprehensive land claims settlement. The new arrangements are embodied in a written constitution developed pursuant to the self-government agreement. The constitution represents an adapted version of traditions that have been observed from time immemorial. It envisages a multi-level governmental structure, with institutions both at the clan level and at the level of the nation as a whole.

The five clans of the nation play an important role in the new arrangements. They determine who is a member, select leaders and assume certain governmental responsibilities for the internal affairs of the clan. For example, each clan has its own court structure called a peacemaker court. At the level of the nation, there are several distinct branches of government, including an executive council, an elders council, a justice council and a general council, which acts as the main legislative body. While these councils are not exact duplicates of traditional Tlingit institutions, they reflect the nation's clan-based structure and strike a balance among the various sectors of the community. Thus, each clan is awarded five representatives on the general council. Council decisions are taken by consensus and require the presence of at least three members from each clan as a quorum. Moreover, the leader of each clan has a seat on both the executive council and the justice council.

L. Chartrand, "The Appropriateness of Lawyer as Advocate in Contemporary Aboriginal Justice Initiatives"
(1995), XXXIII *Alberta Law Review* 874-81 (footnotes omitted)

There is an increasing number of alternative responses to the existing criminal justice system. These responses are motivated by a number of different factors. Aboriginal communities and non-aboriginal communities see these initiatives as a means to address or minimize the over-representation of aboriginal offenders in the prison system. However, aboriginal communities also see these initiatives as a means of acquiring greater control of or input into the decision-making processes of the justice system.

This article will focus on "circle sentencing," which is one particular response that is growing in usage. However, the discussion that follows also has implications for other aboriginal justice initiatives. Circle sentencing is increasingly being relied upon by the system as an alternative to the regular sentencing approach. This unique sentencing approach, however, raises serious questions about the role of the lawyer as an advocate for her client. There is arguably an irreconcilable inconsistency between the circle sentencing process as a means of community decision-making and the role of the lawyer as advocate.

II. The Lawyer as Advocate

One of the most fundamental professional rules of conduct for lawyers is their duty to act as advocates for their clients. The Alberta Law Society states the rule as follows:

> When acting as an advocate the lawyer must, while treating the tribunal with courtesy and respect, represent his client resolutely, honourably and within the limits of the law.

This duty applies throughout the criminal process, including the sentencing stage. For example, a defence lawyer is arguably responsible to a client for ensuring that he or she has obtained the best plea bargain if the client intends to plead guilty. The lawyer must ensure that the facts to be "read in" are appropriate and do not unduly prejudice the client. The lawyer must protect the client's rights while ensuring that the client gets the best possible outcome. The prosecutor is not under any different duty as advocate except that the client he or she represents is the "interests of the state."

In an adversarial system, such duties of advocacy by counsel are necessary to ensure the fair representation of each party. However, do these same concerns apply in a circle sentencing proceeding? Do lawyers have a continuing duty to be advocates for their clients in circle sentencing? If so, is not the integrity and purpose of the circle sentencing thereby compromised?

III. Circle Sentencing

Circle sentencing is an alternative to regular sentencing. The client or community will ask the judge to consider establishing a circle court for determining a sentence. The aboriginal community is usually enthusiastic about participating in circle sentencing because such a process is more conducive to traditional aboriginal concepts of justice.

Circle sentencing is used regularly in the Yukon, Northwest Territories and in the northern reaches of many provinces. Its use as an alternative to the adversarial sentencing approach is gaining prominence in southern parts of the provinces, as well as in urban centres. For example, the Stoney Indian band of the Alexis reserve, west of Edmonton, is in the process of establishing circle sentencing as a "regular" part of the criminal justice system for their community.

The circle process begins by having the usual participants of the justice system sit in a circle with members of the community who have expressed an interest in participating. As Judge Barry Stuart stated in *R v. Moses*:

By arranging the court in a circle without desks or tables, with all participants facing each other, with equal access and equal exposure to each other, the dynamics of the decision-making process were profoundly changed. ... The circle setting dramatically changed the roles of all participants, as well as the focus, tone, content and scope of discussions.

Stuart J specifically identified a number of "benefits" that the circle process is said to provide the court. They are:

(1) It challenges the monopoly of professionals.
(2) It encourages lay participation.
(3) It enhances the transfer of information.
(4) It facilitates a creative search for new options.
(5) It promotes a sharing of responsibility.
(6) It encourages the offender's participation.
(7) It involves victims in sentencing.
(8) It creates a constructive environment.
(9) It generates a greater understanding of justice system limitations.
(10) It extends the focus of the criminal justice system.
(11) It mobilizes community resources.
(12) It merges values of First Nation and western governments.

The non-adversarial, consensus-based nature of the circle sentencing process is seen as more conducive to aboriginal values of dispute resolution. In the circle sentencing process, the values of aboriginal society gain prominence. Thus, emphasis is placed on rehabilitation rather than punishment, with a view to resolving disputes that will promote the achievement of harmony within the community. As a result, the circle sentence is seen as an alternative that respects aboriginal values and processes of dispute resolution. ...

At first appearance, it might seem that by accepting the circle sentence approach, the lawyer is compromising his or her duty to the client as advocate. Since the purpose of the circle sentence is to achieve a consensus as to the appropriate sentence for the accused, is the lawyer not relinquishing his or her responsibility to represent the client resolutely? In particular, is the lawyer in breach of the rules of professional misconduct? On the duty as advocate, Commentary 1(d) of the Law Society of Alberta's *Handbook*, states that the lawyer must not

endeavour or allow anyone else to endeavour, directly or indirectly, to influence the decision or action of a tribunal or any of its officials in any case or matter, whether by bribery, personal approach or any means other than open persuasion as an advocate.

In other words, a lawyer is allowing members of the community to influence the judge in circle sentencing, and it is possible that such influence may not be in the best interests of the client. Unlike a pre-sentence report, for example, individuals give more than just information about the client for the judge's benefit. Members of the community often give their opinions on what the sentence should be, opinions that may be adverse to what the client thinks he or she should reasonably receive.

However, certain members of the bar and judiciary would argue that it is possible to maintain one's duty as an advocate to the client and still allow the client to participate in the circle sentence process. Stuart J in *Moses* stated that the "traditional and essential functions of Crown and defence counsel are not excluded by the circle." Both defence and Crown are given the usual opportunities to speak to sentence. The only difference is that the community is then allowed to provide its input. Stuart J argues that the role of the Crown is actually facilitated because he or she can use the comments and views of the members of the community in the circle to determine what sentence would be best to protect that community. After all, it is that very community which Crown submissions are designed to protect. Defence counsel, too, can constructively use the circle to develop a sentencing option to advance both the immediate and long-term interests of the client in a process in which community support can create alternatives to jail.

Certain members of the bar who have been involved in circle sentencing maintain that it is the lawyer's responsibility to the client to continue being an advocate to ensure that the client's interests are protected. Allowing the community to participate in the sentencing process is a decision that rests with the accused. The accused has the ultimate decision as to whether he will participate in a circle sentencing process or not. As long as the lawyer informs her client of the options and risks involved, she is not in breach of her duty to her client. Furthermore, if the client elects to participate in the circle sentencing process, the lawyer can still maintain the role of an advocate. If a member of the community begins to make statements against the client's best interests, the lawyer can take on a more active role as advocate within the circle. For example, the lawyer could protect the client by challenging a speaker's credibility.

There comes a point, however, where the lawyer's protection of the client's interests threatens the very purpose of having the circle sentencing process in the first place. The more the lawyer acts as an advocate in directing his remarks to the judge, knowing that the decision of sentencing remains within the judge's discretion, the more the process is transformed. Essentially, the role of the community becomes depreciated and weakened, to the point where its members become mere observers, in a traditional adversarial setting.

In other words, the role of the lawyer as advocate diminishes the role of the community as a participant in the process. From an aboriginal community healing perspective, this outcome is contrary to the very purpose of the circle sentencing process, which is to have the aboriginal community regain a measure of control over the justice system in a manner more conducive to its traditional methods of dispute resolution.

Can a lawyer be respectful of the community and maintain her role as advocate? In the United States, aboriginal tribes have jurisdiction over criminal law. The Navajo Nation, for example, has established a dispute resolution process called the Peacemaker Court. The purpose of this court is to provide the Navajo community with an inexpensive and simple system based on standards of Navajo tradition and custom. Under the system, the "Peacemaker" acts very much like a mediator, helping the parties to come to a consensus on what is the most harmonious solution to the dispute. One of the most important rules of this court is that no lawyers are allowed to participate. The adversarial process is avoided and the role of the lawyer as advocate is no longer appropriate. Indeed, it is felt to be counter-productive.

In other words, for the circle sentencing process to function as intended (i.e. as a process for the community to actively participate in reaching an appropriate sentence based on community consensus), and not as a more elaborate version of a pre-sentence report, the lawyer must relinquish the role of advocate. This is a case where the best of both worlds is simply not possible.

A client must either fully accept or fully reject the circle sentencing process. If the client accepts it, the client must understand that his lawyer is no longer an advocate. The lawyer can still participate, but as a resource person and not as an advocate. If this role change is made clear to the client, and the client accepts this non-adversarial role, then the lawyer should remain within the boundaries of ethical propriety while according full respect to the aboriginal community. ...

If the judge is to give full respect to the aboriginal community, then his or her role must also change from being the focus of attention and authority to one where he or she largely concedes the decision-making authority to the community. The role of the judge has traditionally been one where the judge is intended to be passive and neutral. The proper role of the judge is one where he or she sits back and listens to counsel for each side, intervening as little as possible. Of fundamental importance is the requirement that the judge be completely impartial to the parties involved. Such is the hallmark of ensuring that the rule of law is maintained and the system is truly just.

The judge's role in circle sentencing, if he or she is to even have a role, would be that of a mediator. In such a role, the judge would assist the community in arriving at a consensus of the best disposition for the accused. In undertaking such a role, judicial responsibility for ensuring impartiality and neutrality is not jeopardized. As a mediator, the judge can still maintain his or her neutrality in guiding the community to a consensus. As a mediator, however, the judge's role would change from one of passivity to one of active intervention as a facilitator in the process. Although such a role is not normal judicial behaviour, it does not necessarily threaten the rule of law or the ultimate fairness of the hearing.

Until the procedural laws change, the judge still holds the ultimate discretion over sentencing under the *Criminal Code*. Nonetheless, it is possible to give the aboriginal community the respect it deserves by according it full decision-making authority, assuming, of course, that the judge would uphold every decision made by the community. Furthermore, the judge can be instrumental in encouraging counsel to acknowledge the incompatibility of the role as advocate in the circle sentencing process.

NOTES AND QUESTIONS

1. Can a non-aboriginal lawyer give sound advice to an aboriginal accused with respect to his or her participation in a sentencing circle? If so, what might be the necessary preconditions? What must a lawyer know and understand?

2. Contrary to what Chartrand suggests, the Rules of Professional Conduct do envision different roles for defence counsel and prosecutors; see proposed draft rules of professional conduct, rule 4.01 (see appendix II).

The Litigation Process

CHAPTER FIVE

Commencement of Proceedings

I. THE RULES OF CIVIL PROCEDURE

A. The Codification of Rules

Much of this casebook deals with the interpretation and application of the rules of civil procedure. It is helpful at this early stage to get a sense of the nature and function of such rules. As we have seen, each civil jurisdiction in Canada (provincial, territorial, and federal) has legislation that established the court system, defines its substantive jurisdiction, provides for certain basic procedural and substantive rules respecting civil actions, and, perhaps most important, provides for a procedure by which rules of civil procedure may be enacted from time to time by regulation. In Ontario, these tasks are accomplished in the Courts of Justice Act. For example and contrast, the same topics are dealt with in British Columbia in the Supreme Court Act, RSBC 1996, c. 443, the Court of Appeal Act, RSBC 1996 c. 77, the Court Order Enforcement Act, RSBC 1996, c. 78, and the Law and Equity Act, RSBC 1996, c. 253.

Read ss. 65 and 66 of the Ontario Courts of Justice Act, which are typical of the statutory provisions that authorize the making of rules of civil procedure and consider the following:

1. Why should the rules of civil procedure be enacted as regulations rather than statutes? Is it merely administrative convenience due to the fact that they are amended with great frequency?

2. In the overall legislative process, the rules of civil procedure are relatively invisible, and changes to the rules rarely attract public notice or debate. Is this an appropriate result of nature and composition of the Civil Rules Committee? Are all potentially relevant interests represented on the committee?

The rules of civil procedure are intended to be a complete code of procedure for civil proceedings. They provide a general framework for the litigation of disputes. Justice John Morden of the Ontario Court of Appeal has commented as follows about the rules in "An Overview of the Rules of Civil Procedure in Ontario" (1984), 5 *Advocates Quarterly* 257:

> If I may indulge in a generality, it seems to me that there is a fairly widespread attitude among those involved in the legal process that relegates procedure to a position vastly inferior to that of substantive law and regards procedural rules somewhat as a nuisance. This is unfortunate for two reasons.
>
> First, without fair and effective procedural law there cannot be substantive justice. Professor Harold Potter did not put the matter too highly when he said: "The fight for human justice must be on a procedural plane, since procedure may determine how far the truth can come out." (*The Quest of Justice* (1951), p. 28).
>
> Secondly, in the field of civil litigation there is no other law which will receive as much daily interpretation and application as the rules. The facts in any dispute in the litigation process are bound to differ from those in all other cases. The applicable substantive law from case to case will vary accordingly. However, there can be no variation in the basic procedural law which is applicable to every civil case. All civil cases must pass through the same procedural mould, after giving effect, of course, to the kind of proceeding in question and to the differences between cases which will make certain parts of the rules relevant to some cases and not to others. Generally, all actions are treated the same and all applications are treated the same. Accordingly, it makes sense for those regularly involved in litigation to recognize the importance of procedural law and to achieve a practical mastery of it. The nuisance is caused when we fail to do this.

B. Rules: Substance or Mere Procedure

An issue that will be confronted throughout this casebook is the substantive vision that may or may not exist behind procedural rules. The traditional view has been that procedural rules should and do provide a neutral framework for the resolution of disputes. Matters of value are left to the substantive law. This vision of the neutrality of procedure has come increasingly under attack.

If rules are neutral then it may make sense that they be formulated by a body of experts who need not be elected or representative. If, however, rules embody substantive values, the case for greater involvement by the elected legislature is probably greater.

Section 66(2) of the Courts of Justice Act specifically empowers the Civil Rules Committee to make rules, "even thought they alter ... the substantive law." What is the purpose of this provision? When is it possible or appropriate for the Rules Committee, in the course of making rules, to alter substantive law?

Example. Under rule 49, one party may make a written offer to settle a case, which, if not accepted, may have cost consequences in certain circumstances. Rule 49.07(2) expressly provides that a rejection of an offer to settle or the making of a counteroffer does not put an end to an offer to settle; unless withdrawn, the offer to settle remains open for acceptance until the court has disposed of the claim in respect of which it was made. This is a substantial change to the common law of contract, which holds that a rejection of the offer or making a counteroffer precludes subsequent acceptance of the original offer. See *Re Desanto et al. and Cretzman et al.* (1986), 53 OR (2d) 732 (DC). Is this an appropriate use of the power to alter substantive law?

When is it more appropriate for procedural change to proceed by way of statute rather than rule? When Ontario and British Columbia took steps to provide for a modern form of class actions, they each decided to pass a separate act, rather than proceed by making new rules or, in the alternative, amending an existing act. In the *Report of the Attorney General's Advisory Committee on Class Action Reform* (Ontario, 1990), that committee recommended that any provision for class action be made in an act, rather than through rules changes. In doing so, the committee referred to the following factors:

> The procedure represents a significant development in the administration of justice in Ontario. It has been the subject of controversy and debate. The recommended reforms call for the removal of substantive obstacles to class proceedings. ...
>
> The new procedure requires a specificity and, in some cases, a priority over other litigation which the Rules of Civil Procedure are unaccustomed and inappropriate in providing.

Which, if any, of these factors justify the choice made?

C. Procedural Pathways

Modern rules of civil procedure can be distinguished from the common law writs and forms of action that they sought to displace by the fact that they are intended for application to adjudication arising out of all forms of disputes between private parties. In contrast, common law writs were fashioned for particular kinds of disputes such as, for example, the recent eviction of a tenant or the tort of deceit.

Does the fact that "all civil cases must pass through the same procedural mould" have an effect on substantive law? Is it correct to assume that all litigation must be treated the same? Although the rules of civil procedure apply generally to all civil disputes, there has been an increasing tendency for procedures to be moulded to fit particular types of action. They may have their source in specific provisions of the rules or more informal practices of the court.

The rules of civil proceedings contain a significant number of supplements to or variations to the generally applicable rules for use in specific types of litigation. In the Ontario rules, these are found in rules 64-71 and 73-75, and relate to such matters as mortgage actions, proceedings for judicial review of administrative action, divorce actions, family law proceedings, and estate matters.

Procedural approaches can also be varied on the basis of the perceived complexity of litigation, which is usually roughly measured by the value of the matters in dispute. Mention has already been made of the Small Claims Court. An effort to provide a procedural pathway that is intermediate between the very simple procedures of that court and the full-fledged procedure of the General Division may be seen in rule 76, which provides for a simplified procedure for actions where the matters in dispute are below a certain value.

In addition, the courts have used practice directions and other administrative means to create procedures for special categories of litigation. The most far-reaching example of this is the creation of the Commercial List in the Ontario Court of Justice. The *Commercial List Practice Direction* (1995), 24 OR (3d) 455 not only creates a distinct administrative structure for the handling of specified categories of commercial disputes, but provides a number of specific procedural innovations in the handling of those disputes.

More specialized pathways for litigation raise a number of specific issues. What is the rationale for the establishment of such alternative pathways? Some are the result of historical accident, whereas others reflect a more recent decision to allocate additional resources to specific disputes (that is, the Commercial List). Some of these pathways are discussed in the next section, which deals with choices in the commencement of proceedings.

II. CONSIDERATIONS IN THE COMMENCEMENT OF PROCEEDINGS

There are various factors which are relevant to the decision to sue in a particular court at a particular time. These factors include:

1. Does the court have jurisdiction to hear the case?
2. Is it too late to sue?

In addition, assuming that these questions can be answered yes and no, respectively, there are a number of preliminary procedural decisions that must be made in the course of carrying out that decision to sue. These include:

1. Who will be named as parties in the lawsuit?
2. What claim or claim will be asserted?
3. What general procedural choices as available with respect to the kind of proceeding to be commenced?

4. What specialized procedures may be used to supplement or replace the general rules of civil procedure?

The choices in (1) and (2), which deal with the joinder of claims and parties, are the subject matter of chapter 7, "The Size and Scope of Litigation." The remaining questions are considered in this section.

A. Jurisdiction

In the context of a civil dispute, "jurisdiction" simply refers to the power or authority of the court to hear and decide the dispute. With respect to the Ontario Court (General Division), the Courts of Justice Act simply states in s. 11(2) that "[t]he General Division has all the jurisdiction, power and authority historically exercised by courts of common law and equity in England and Ontario." How broad is that power?

80 Wellesley St. East Ltd. v. Fundy Bay Builders Ltd. et al.
[1972] 2 OR 280 (CA)

[In this case, the plaintiff agreed to sell a piece of property to one of the defendants. Before the date for closing, that defendant assigned the agreement to another defendant, who registered the assignment of the agreement against the title to the property. The transaction did not close and a dispute arose whether the deposit should be refunded and whether the registration of the assignment on title should be discharged. The plaintiff took the position that the deal was at an end, that the registration of the assignment (which blocked any further sale) should be discharged, and that the plaintiff should be able to keep the deposit. The defendants argued that the deposit should not be forfeited. A lawsuit ensued.

In the course of the litigation, the plaintiff wished to sell the property to another person and brought an application to discharge the assignment to allow the new sale to proceed. The plaintiff offered to post security in respect of the defendant's claim to a refund of the deposit. The application was dismissed by Wright J. The plaintiff appealed.]

BROOKE JA:—

[The judge set out the factual history summarized above and continued:]

It appears Wright J believed that the security which was proposed was adequate but found that he had no jurisdiction to require the defendants to look to such security for satisfaction of their claim in lieu of the assignment. His brief reasons for judgment are as follows:

> Although I agree with Mr. Teplitsky that what he offers is reasonably better than what the defendants now have, I consider that I have no power to force it on an unwilling defendant as trustee.

In our view, Wright J was in error. As a superior Court of general jurisdiction, the Supreme Court of Ontario has all of the powers that are necessary to do justice between the parties. Except where provided specifically to the contrary, the Court's jurisdiction is unlimited and unrestricted in substantive law in civil matters. In *Re Michie Estate and City of Toronto et al.*, [1968] 1 OR 266 at pp. 268-9, 66 DLR (2d) 213 at pp. 215-6, Stark J, after considering the relevant provisions of the *Judicature Act* and the authorities, said:

> It appears clear that the Supreme Court of Ontario has broad universal jurisdiction over all matters of substantive law unless the Legislature divests from this universal jurisdiction by legislation in unequivocal terms. The rule of law relating to the jurisdiction of superior Courts was laid down at least as early as 1667 in the case of *Peacock v. Bell and Kendall* (1667), 1 Wms. Saund. 73 at p. 74, 85 ER 84:
>
>> ... And the rule for jurisdiction is, that nothing shall be intended to be out of the jurisdiction of a Superior Court, but that which specifically appears to be so; and, on the contrary, nothing shall be intended to be within the jurisdiction of an Inferior Court but that which is so expressly alleged.

In *Board v. Board* (1919), 48 DLR 13 at pp. 17-8, [1919] AC 956, [1919] 2 WWR 940, Viscount Haldane for the Privy Council in dealing with the question of the nature of jurisdiction of a superior Court said: If the right exists, the presumption is that there is a Court which can enforce it, for if no other mode of enforcing is prescribed, that alone is sufficient to give jurisdiction to the King's Courts of Justice. In order to oust jurisdiction, it is necessary, in the absence of a special law excluding it altogether, to plead that jurisdiction exists in some other Court. This is the effect of authorities, such as the well-known judgment of Lord Mansfield in *Mostyn v. Fabrigas* (1774), 1 Cowp. 161, 98 ER 1021, and the judgment of Lord Hardwicke in *Earl of Derby v. Duke of Athol* (1749), 1 Ves. Sen. 201, 27 ER 982. They are collected in the admirable opinion of Stuart J, in the Supreme Court in the present case, from whose reasoning, as well as from the arguments employed by the other learned Judges there, their Lordships have derived much assistance. They only desire to add that independently of the rule just referred to, there is another principle of construction which would in their opinion have been by itself sufficient to dispose of the question whether the words of the Act of 1907 excluded matrimonial jurisdiction. That Act set up a superior Court, and it is the rule as regards presumption of jurisdiction in such a Court that, as stated by Willes J in *Mayor of London v. Cox* (1867), 1 E & I App. 239, at p. 259, nothing shall be intended to be out of the jurisdiction of a superior Court, but that which specially appears to be so.

In addition, and of importance, is that the justice of the situation requires a cause such as this will not fail for want of a remedy. In *Williams and Rees v. Local Union No. 1562 of United Mine Workers of America* (1919), 45 DLR 150 at p. 178, [1919] 1 WWR 217, 14 Alta. LR 251 [reversed on other grounds 59 SCR 240, 49 DLR 578, [1919] 3 WWR 828], Beck J said, and I agree with his view:

> I believe my brother judges accept the opinion I expressed some time ago as follows:—
>
>> That every superior court is the master of its own practice is a proposition laid down by Tindal CJ in *Scales v. Cheese* (1844), 12 M & W 685, 152 ER 1374, and

adopting this, I think that, without any statutory rules of practice, the court can, should a case arise, even though the law be fixed as to the substantial rights of the parties, award such remedies, though they be new, as may appear to be necessary to work out justice between the parties.

Where the plaintiff is desirous of selling its land and provides adequate security to meet its possible obligations to the defendants, surely it has a right to have its title cleared and proceed, and this Court has the power to make any order necessary in the circumstances. In my opinion, then, the Court had jurisdiction at law to deal with this matter in addition to its powers by reason of its equitable jurisdiction. ...

In all of the circumstances, then, we think that Mr. Justice Wright was in error—that he had jurisdiction to make the order sought before him and an order should go that upon the providing of the security proposes, which is a second mortgage on the property which matures June 30, 1975, in the sum of $130,000 bearing interest at the rate of 8½% payable to the defendants and assigned to a trustee, to be agreed upon, to abide the outcome of this action, the defendants should remove from the title to the lands the assignment of the agreement of purchase and sale here in question.

Appeal allowed.

NOTES AND QUESTIONS

1. The Court of Appeal in *Wellesley* discusses the jurisdiction of the Supreme Court, the predecessor to the Superior Court of Ontario, from two points of view:

   a. the power of the court to grant an appropriate remedy; and
   b. the power of the court to control its own process.

How true is it to say, as Brooke JA states, that "the Court's jurisdiction is unlimited and unrestricted in substantive law in civil matters"? His reasons envisage cases where the legislature explicitly excludes the jurisdiction of the court. What other limits to jurisdiction may exist?

2. A court's power and authority can ultimately be traced to and is limited by the constitutional and legislative power of the government that creates it. The Constitution Act, 1867, s. 92 includes the following in a list of matters over which the provinces have exclusive legislative power:

   13. Property and Civil Rights in the Province.
   14. The Administration of Justice in the Province, including the Constitution, Maintenance, and Organization of Provincial Courts, both of Civil and of Criminal Jurisdiction, and including Procedure in Civil Matters in those Courts.

In this context, what is meant by "Civil Rights"?

3. The same Act, s. 91 includes the following in a list of federal government powers:

   2. The Regulation of Trade and Commerce,
   18. Bills of Exchange and Promissory Notes,
   21. Bankruptcy and Insolvency,

22. Patents of Invention and Discovery, and

23. Copyrights.

To the extent that federal legislation respecting these matters creates civil causes of action, it is for the federal legislation to determine where and how those causes of action are to be dealt with.

For example, s. 34 of the Copyright Act provides:

> 34.(1) Where copyright in any work has been infringed, the owner of the copyright is, subject to this Act, entitled to all remedies by way of injunction, damages, accounts and otherwise that are or may be conferred by law for the infringement of a right.

This section of a piece of federal legislation creates a civil cause of action, and another section of the same act specifies where those causes of action are to be heard:

> 37. The Federal Court shall have concurrent jurisdiction with provincial courts to hear and determine all civil actions, suits or proceedings that may be instituted for contravention of any of the provisions of this Act or to enforce the civil remedies provided by this Act.

In the absence of such a provision, would a provincial superior court have the jurisdiction to hear a copyright infringement case?

4. The question of who has civil jurisdiction in areas of federal legislative power is addressed either, as in the case of the Copyright Act, in the relevant federal legislation or, if the federal legislation is silent, in the Federal Court Act, or through the interaction of the relevant substantive legislation and the Federal Court Act. Notwithstanding legislative attempts to simplify, jurisdiction in civil causes of action arising out of federal legislation and the role of the Federal Court remains complex and difficult. See generally, Sgiayas et al., *Federal Court Practice* (annual), part 1.

5. Apart from the potential limits on the power of the Superior Court flowing from the constitutional division of powers, and areas where the provincial legislature has specifically excluded the jurisdiction of the court, what other limits are there on the jurisdiction of the Superior Court? Does the Superior Court have jurisdiction to deal with cases dealing with persons resident outside Ontario? With respect to property situate outside Ontario? The general common law principle is that the jurisdiction of a court is limited to the territory of that court's state or province. Why is that? If that is the case, how does the court determine whether it has jurisdiction over a person who may have several different residences or places of work in a number of jurisdictions? When should this determination take place? These matters are discussed later in this chapter in the context of service out of the jurisdiction.

B. Limitation Periods

1. General

Each province has enacted legislation that specifies time periods within which court proceedings must be commenced. This legislation is generally called the Limitations Act, or some other similar name. There is no single limitation period applicable generally to all proceedings. There are different limitation periods and their length varies with the nature of the claim.

There are two major policies underlying statutory limitation periods. The first is a concern for fairness for the defendant. It is felt that a defendant ought not to be forever under the threat of an ancient claim and the economic and psychological disruptions associated with it. There has to come a time when defendants can order their affairs secure in the knowledge that the past is beyond inquiry. If a person has to defend an action, he or she should be assured of a reasonably timely notice so that there is an opportunity to preserve and marshal the evidence needed at the hearing. The second policy is the general concern of the legal system that its processes of disputed fact resolution be efficient, and that they be so regarded by litigants and the community generally. This policy is closely related to the first and recognizes that a court cannot effectively resolve factual disputes if it has to decide what happened in the remote past after memories have faded, witnesses are dead or have disappeared, and documents are lost or have been destroyed. Surmise and speculation should not be allowed to substitute for findings enlightened by positive information. See James, *Civil Procedure* (1965), at 174 *et seq.*; "Developments in the Law-Statutes of Limitations" (1950), 63 *Harvard Law Review* 1177, 1185 *et seq.*

Consider the following extracts from the Ontario Limitations Act, RSO 1990, c. L.15.

Part III
Personal Actions

Limitation of time for commencing particular actions

35. The following actions shall be commenced within and not after the times respectively hereinafter mentioned,

    (a) an action for rent, upon an indenture of demise;

    (b) an action upon a bond, or other specialty, except upon a covenant contained in an indenture of mortgage made on or after the 1st day of July, 1894;

    (c) an action upon a judgment or recognizance,

within twenty years after the cause of action arose,

    (d) an action upon an award where the submission is not by specialty;

    (e) an action for an escape;

    (f) an action for money levied on execution; or

    (g) upon any lending or contract without specialty, debt for arrears of rent, detinue, replevin or upon the case other than for slander,

within six years after the cause of action arose,

    (h) an action for a penalty, damages, or a sum of money given by any statute to the Crown or the party aggrieved, within two years after the cause of action arose;

    (i) an action upon the case for words, within two years after the words spoken;

    (j) an action for assault, battery, wounding or imprisonment, within four years after the cause of action arose;

    (k) an action upon a covenant contained in an indenture of mortgage or any other instrument made on or after the 1st day of July, 1894, to repay the whole or part of any money secured by a mortgage, within ten years after the cause of action arose or within ten years after the date upon which the person liable on the covenant conveyed or transferred the person's interest in the mortgaged lands, whichever is later in point of time;

(l) an action by a mortgagee against a grantee of the equity of redemption under section 20 of the *Mortgages Act*, within ten years after the cause of action arose;

(m) an action for a penalty imposed by any statute brought by any informer suing for the informer alone, or for the Crown as well, or by any person authorized to sue for the same, not being the person aggrieved,

within one year after the cause of action arose.

NOTES AND QUESTIONS

1. Can you easily tell from the above what the limitation period is for a negligence action? A contract action? The wording of the Ontario Act dates back, in part, to the original English limitations legislation in the 17th century. Accordingly, in using the Ontario Act, it is necessary to know that a negligence action is historically considered to be an "action ... upon the case."

2. Most provinces other than Ontario have limitations legislation that is more modern in scope and approach. This situation in Ontario is widely considered to be absurd and was condemned as long ago as 1969 by the Ontario Law Reform Commission, which proposed a new limitations act. Although draft legislation of one sort or another has been under consideration by the Ontario Ministry of the Attorney General for many years, none has been enacted. As you read the material following, consider the possible reasons why? The latest version of the draft Ontario legislation is reproduced later in this topic.

3. The existence of a limitation period does not mean that the action must be tried or completed within the period. The statute is satisfied if the action is *commenced* within the limitation period and, as we have already seen, it is the issue of the originating process that marks the commencement of the proceeding. A claim becomes statute-barred once the applicable period has expired and no originating process has been issued. Technically, however, the commencement of an action outside the limitation period does not lead to automatic dismissal. Non-compliance with a limitation period is a defence that must be pleaded specifically by the defendant, and if he or she does not raise the plea in the statement of defence, he or she will not be able to rely on the statute. See 1 Williston and Rolls, *The Law of Civil Procedure*, at 692; *Pollakis v. Corner* (1975), 9 OR (2d) 691. But, as might be expected, defendants rarely fail to plead a limitation period in cases where the defence will defeat the plaintiff's claim.

4. Although the Limitations Act contains many limitation periods (there are other parts of the act dealing with actions involving property and trusts), it does not purport to be exhaustive. Many limitation periods will be found in other statutes. Consider the following examples. What impact do each of them have on the application of s. 35 of the Limitations Act with respect to contract and tort actions?

Public Authorities Protection Act, RSO 1990, c. P.38:

7(1) No action, prosecution or other proceeding lies or shall be instituted against any person for an act done in pursuance or execution or intended execution of any statutory or other public duty or authority, or in respect of any alleged neglect or default in the execution of any such duty or authority, unless it is commenced within six months next after the cause of action arose, or, in case of continuance of injury or damage, within six months after the ceasing thereof.

Public Hospitals Act, RSO 1990, c. P.40:

31. Any action against a hospital or any nurse or person employed therein for damages for injury caused by negligence in the admission, care, treatment or discharge of a patient shall be brought within two years after the patient is discharged from or ceases to receive treatment at the hospital and not afterwards.

Regulated Health Professions Act, SO 1991, c. 18, Sched. 2:

89.(1) No person who is or was a member [of a College of any regulated health profession] is liable to any action arising out of negligence or malpractice in respect of professional services requested of or rendered by the person unless the action is commenced within one year after the date when the person commencing the action knew or ought to have known the fact or facts upon which the negligence or malpractice is alleged.

Do these short limitation periods reflect the particular need of such defendants to receive early notice of litigation, or are they, in fact, "special interest" legislation?

5. The existence of a large number of special limitation periods outside of the Limitations Act raises serious questions of professional competence and liability, especially considering that there is no officially sanctioned comprehensive index of limitation periods that can be consulted. For commercial attempts (including appropriate liability disclaimers see, *Ontario Limitation Periods* (Butterworths, 1978, updated), and *The Ontario Legal Desk Book* (Carswell, annual). The Lawyers Professional Indemnity Company (LPIC), a company that insures lawyers in Ontario and Newfoundland for professional liability, in recognition of the fact that a significant percentage of claims reported against lawyers relate to missed limitation periods, has placed a list of key limitation periods online: see <http://practicepro.lpic.ca/practice/limitation.asp>. How can a lawyer ensure that all reasonable steps have been taken to identify the applicable limitation period? Should the lawyer be the guarantor of complying with limitation periods?

6. If a lawyer fails to recognize the applicability of a special (read shorter) limitation period to a certain kind of defendant, and the action is not commenced before the expiration of that period, the client will lose the ability to sue to on the cause of action. The lawyer will then be exposed to a lawsuit by the client for professional negligence. In such circumstances, how will the court determine whether the lawyer has been negligent? Do you agree with the following comments of Scrutton LJ in *Fletcher & Son v. Jubb, Booth & Helliwell*, [1920] 1 KB 275, at 281-82:

Now it is not the duty of a solicitor to know the contents of every statute of the realm. But there are some statutes which it is his duty to know; and in these days when the defendants in so many actions are public authorities the *Public Authorities Protection Act*, 1893, is one of those statutes … . What is the duty of a solicitor who is retained to institute an action which will be barred by statute if not commenced in six months? His first duty is to be aware of the statute. His next is to inform his client of the position … .

The period of limitation was one of those matters which the respondents as the appellants' legal advisers ought to have borne in mind. It was negligence not to bear it in mind.

2. When Does Time Run?

As already noted, limitation periods are satisfied and time ceases to run once the originating process is issued. But what is the starting point of the limitation period? Typically, the statutory provisions require that an action be brought within a certain time of "the accrual of the cause of action." But when does a cause of action accrue? In many instances the answer will be quite clear—for example, in an automobile accident where the negligent act and the injuries of the plaintiff are virtually contemporaneous. But in some cases the problem is much more difficult. For example, from what event is the running of the limitation period to be measured in the following cases?

1. The walls of a building are negligently constructed and 10 years later the building collapses; an action is brought by the owner of the building (who contracted for its construction) and by an injured passer-by.

2. A lawyer is negligent in closing a real estate transaction. As a result the client obtains a defective title; however, this only becomes apparent when the client attempts to sell the house 12 years later.

3. A doctor negligently performs an operation, but the patient's injuries only manifest themselves three years later, and it is a further five years before the cause of the injury is identified as a negligently performed operation?

Until recently, the accepted rule was that in contract the cause of action accrues, and the limitation period starts to run, when the breach of contract takes place—for example, when the building is constructed or the conveyancing services are rendered by the lawyer—not when damage results; still less when the damage comes to light. In a *negligence action in tort*, however, the cause of action is not complete (and hence the limitation period does not start to run) until the plaintiff suffers damage from the defendant's breach of duty. As the following case indicates, the courts have found the results produced by mechanical application of these rules to be unacceptable.

Consumers Glass Co. Ltd. v. Foundation Co. of Canada Ltd.
(1985), 51 OR (2d) 385 (Ont. CA)

DUBIN JA: … The appellant, The Foundation Company of Canada Limited/La Compagnie Foundation du Canada Limitee (hereinafter referred to as Foundation), is a builder and general contractor in the construction industry. The appellant, Foundation of Canada Engineering Corporation Limited/La Compagnie de Genie Foundation Limitee (hereinafter referred to as Foundation Engineering), is a corporation carrying on the business of design and structural engineers.

The respondent entered into a contract with Foundation for the construction of a wareshed on the respondent's premises in Toronto. Foundation engaged Foundation Engineering to design or to assist in the design and to supervise or to assist in the supervision of the wareshed. Foundation Engineering also entered into a contract with the respondent for that purpose.

The wareshed was designed and erected by the appellants and was completed in 1963. It is alleged that on August 4, 1981, a section of the roof collapsed.

The action against both appellants was framed in tort and in contract.

In the statement of claim the respondent alleged that the appellants negligently designed the wareshed and were negligent in carrying out the work.

It was further alleged that the negligent acts of the appellants did not become known to the respondent until after August 4, 1981, the date of the collapse. The writ was issued on November 19, 1982.

The appellants moved before J. Holland J to dismiss the action on the ground that it was statute-barred by reason of the *Limitations Act*, which motion was dismissed. Subsequently, Trainor J ordered the issues to be referred to the Court of Appeal pursuant to s. 34 of the *Judicature Act*.

Concurrent Actions in Tort and in Contract

Notwithstanding the submissions by counsel for the appellants to the contrary, it is now firmly established in this province, as well as in other jurisdictions, that there can be concurrent actions in tort and in contract, and such remedies are available both with respect to Foundation and Foundation Engineering.

[There follows a discussion of *Dominion Chain Co. Ltd. v. Eastern Construction Co. Ltd.* (1976), 12 OR (2d) 201 (CA) and *John Maryon Int'l. Ltd. et al. v. New Brunswick Telephone Co. Ltd.* (1982), 141 DLR (3d) 193 (NB CA).]

Since an action in negligence has not been precluded by the contract between the parties, the respondent's claim can be equally asserted both in contract and in tort.

Statute of Limitations

The relevant provisions of the *Limitations Act*, s. 45, are as follows:

> 45(1) The following actions shall be commenced within and not after the times respectively hereinafter mentioned, ...
>> (g) an action ... upon the case other than for slander,
> *within six years after the cause of action arose* ...

(Emphasis added.)

The classic definition of a cause of action as stated by Diplock LJ in *Letang v. Cooper*, [1964] 2 All ER 929 at p. 934, is as follows:

> A cause of action is simply a factual situation the existence of which entitles one person
> to obtain from the court a remedy against another person.

I would have thought that it would follow that a cause of action does not arise until a plaintiff has knowledge or means of acquiring knowledge of the existence of the facts which entitles him to seek a remedy by the institution of an action. However, the question of when a cause of action arises for the purposes of determining when the statute of limitations begins to run has been the subject of a plethora of judicial decisions both in Canada and in the United Kingdom.

With respect to an action in tort, that issue has been finally resolved by the Supreme Court of Canada in *City of Kamloops v. Nielson et al.*, [1984] 2 SCR 2, 10 DLR (4th) 641, [1984] 5 WWR 1. In that case the Supreme Court of Canada preferred the judgment of the Court of Appeal in *Sparham-Souter et al. v. Town & Country Developments (Essex) Ltd. et al.*, [1976] 2 All ER 65, and rejected the decision of the House of Lords in *Pirelli General Cable Works Ltd. v. Oscar Faber & Partners (a firm)*, [1983] 1 All ER 65, which subsequently held to the contrary.

In *Sparham-Souter* the Court of Appeal held that time does not begin to run for the purposes of the limitations statute until the acquisition of knowledge or the means of acquiring knowledge of the facts giving rise to the cause of action.

In so holding, Lord Denning noted at p. 68:

> A statute of limitations cannot begin to run unless there are two things present: "A party capable of suing and a party liable to be sued." It was so stated by Vaughan Williams LJ in *Thompson v. Lord Clanmorris*, [1900] 1 Ch. 718, at 729, [1900-03] All ER Rep. 804, at 809, and there is good sense in it. *It would be unjust that time should run against a plaintiff when there is no possibility of bringing an action to enforce it.*

(Emphasis added.) He continued at p. 70:

> It may seem hard on the builder or the council surveyor that he may find himself sued many years after he left the work; but it would be harder on the householder that he should be without remedy, seeing that the surveyor passed the bad work and the builder covered it up, and thus prevented it being discovered earlier. And, when one finds such cases as *Dutton v. Dognor Regis United Building Co Ltd.*, [1972] 1 All ER 462, [1972] 1 QB 3731, (where the house was built on a rubbish tip), or *Higgins v. Arfon Borough Council*, [1975] 2 All ER 589, [1975] 1 WLR 5241, (where it was built on bare earth), or *Anns v. Walcraft Property Co Ltd.*, [1976] 2 WLR 5121, (where the foundations were too thin)—and the inspector negligently or conveniently overlooked it—it is only fair that the plaintiff should have a remedy.

And Lord Justice Geoffrey Lane stated at p. 80:

> ... the period of limitation may be postponed indefinitely as already pointed out. This I regard as less obnoxious than the alternative, which is that a house owner may be deprived of his remedy against a negligent defendant by the arbitrary imposition of a

limitation period which started to run before the damage caused by the defendant could even be detected.

In rejecting the House of Lords decision in *Pirelli*, which held that a cause of action in negligence is completed as soon as the damage comes into existence, Madam Justice Wilson, delivering the judgment of the court in *Kamloops*, commented as follows at p. 40 SCR, pp. 684-5 DLR:

> There are obvious problems in applying *Pirelli*. To what extent does physical damage have to have manifested itself? Is a hair-line crack enough or does there have to be a more substantial manifestation? And what of an owner who discovers that his building is constructed of materials which will cause it to collapse in five years time? According to *Pirelli* he has no cause of action until it starts to crumble. *But perhaps the most serious concern is the injustice of a law which statute-bars a claim before the plaintiff is even aware of its existence.* Lord Fraser and Lord Scarman were clearly concerned over this but considered themselves bound by *Cartledge* [*Cartledge v. E. Jopling & Sons Ltd.*, [1963] AC 758]. The only solution in their eyes was the intervention of the legislature.

(Emphasis added.)

Thus, if there was no contractual relationship between the respondent and the appellants, this action would have to proceed to trial to determine when the damage occurred, or when it could reasonably have been discovered.

However, it is submitted, that even assuming that there can be concurrent actions in tort and in contract, where what is alleged is a breach of duty by persons undertaking to render special skills or personal services, the action must be brought within six years from the breach, which in this case at the latest would have been at the time that the work was completed.

In support of this proposition, counsel for the appellants principally relied on the judgment of this Court in *Schwebel v. Telekes*, [1967] 1 OR 541, 61 DLR (2d) 470. In that case, the defendant, a notary public, represented the plaintiff in a matrimonial dispute in the course of which he was engaged in the purchase of a home to which, the plaintiff alleged, she was to have sole title. Her husband later successfully asserted an interest in the land. The plaintiff subsequently sued the defendant for negligence for his failure to have provided her with sole title to the land. This action was brought more than six years after the transaction, and her action was dismissed on the ground that the writ was issued beyond the applicable limitation period ...

The authority of *Schwebel* has been very much undermined by the subsequent judgment of this Court in *Dominion Chain Co. Ltd. v. Eastern Construction Co. Ltd.* (1976), 12 OR (2d) 201, 68 DLR (3d) 385, 1 CPC 13. ...

As has been observed in both *Dominion Chain and John Maryon Int'l. Ltd.*, the modern trend in Canada is to hold that a person who is negligent in the performance of a contract may be liable concurrently both for the tort of negligence and for breach of contract even in the case where the alleged breach relates to professional services. This modern trend was also recognized in *A-G NS v. Aza Avramovitch Associates Ltd.* (1984), 11 DLR (4th) 588, 63 NSR (2d) 181, where Chief Justice Mackeigan, delivering the judgment of the Nova Scotia Court of Appeal, stated at p. 595:

I reject the ground of appeal which relies upon the contrary view that a person who negligently breaches a contract, especially one for professional services, can be sued only for breach of contract and not for negligence and cannot be a tortfeasor.

Given the right to sue concurrently in tort and in contract, it must follow, in my respectful opinion, that the respondent cannot be deprived of such a right by holding its action in negligence to be statute-barred before damage occurred and therefore before the respondent had a right to sue in negligence.

If *Schwebel* were to be followed in this case, the action against Foundation Engineering would have to be dismissed on the pleadings as having been statute-barred before the plaintiff could possibly have been aware of any of the facts upon which the action could have been instituted. In so far as Foundation is concerned, not being one who professes skills in a calling within the principle set forth in *Schwebel*, the action, it would appear, could proceed to trial to determine when damage occurred or when it could first have been reasonably discovered.

Such a result, in my opinion, would not only be grossly unjust, but it would be illogical. It would result in professionals like engineers, architects and solicitors being protected from actions when the less skilled would not be. It would expose professionals who serve gratuitously to suit when professionals who are paid would be immune. It would also follow that Foundation Engineering would be liable to suit by a subsequent purchaser of the premises but not by the contracting party. It is also to be noted that a contracting party could be protected from subsequent liability by the terms of the contract, and yet, in the absence of such a provision, would nevertheless be immune by statute.

Conclusion

For the above reasons, I am respectfully of the opinion that the case of *Schwebel v. Telekes, supra*, is no longer authoritative in this province. In my opinion, in cases which are based on a breach of duty to take care, a cause of action does not arise, and time does not begin to run for the purposes of the *Limitations Act*, until such time as the plaintiff discovers or ought reasonably to have discovered the facts with respect to which the remedy is being sought, whether the issue arises in contract or in tort.

As I read the judgment of the Supreme Court of Canada in *Kamloops, supra*, the underlying policy consideration was "the injustice of a law which statute-bars a claim before the plaintiff is even aware of its existence." That principle, in my opinion, is equally applicable where the issue arises in cases sounding in contract or in tort. That is not to say that the plaintiff would have to know the extent of the damage complained of before the time begins to run, but the cause of action does not arise, in my opinion, until the plaintiff could first have brought an action and proved sufficient facts to sustain it, or ought reasonably to have discovered the facts upon which the cause of action is premised. ...

I am not unmindful that the conclusion that I have arrived at may cause wider exposure to some potential defendants than is now current, but it would be a greater injustice to deprive a plaintiff, through no fault of its own, of a cause of action premised upon a breach of duty by the person seeking immunity. This exposure, of course, is tempered by the fact that in many cases the plaintiff by the very lapse of time will be hard pressed to prove a causal connection between the alleged breach and the damage. ...

I would therefore dismiss this appeal and permit the action to proceed to trial. Since this appeal comes to us by way of a reference because of the uncertainty of the law, I do not think that this is a proper case for costs.

NOTES AND QUESTIONS

1. The discoverability principle was reaffirmed by the Supreme Court of Canada in *Central Trust Co. v. Rafuse* (1986), 31 DLR (4th) 481. The case was one of professional negligence against a solicitor, once again arising from a situation where the plaintiff was not aware of a claim until six years after the negligent act occurred. Writing for the court, LeDain J set out the following principle (at 535-36):

> I am thus of the view that the judgment of the majority in *Kamloops* laid down a general rule that a cause of action arises for purposes of a limitation period when the material facts on which it is based have been discovered or ought to have been discovered by the plaintiff by the exercise of reasonable diligence, and that that rule should be followed and applied to the appellant's cause of action in tort against the respondents under the Nova Scotia Statutes of Limitations. There is no principled reason, in my opinion, for distinguishing in this regard between an action for injury to property and an action for the recovery of purely financial loss caused by professional negligence ... Since the respondents gave the Nova Scotia Trust Company a certificate on January 17, 1969 that the mortgage was a first charge on the Stonehouse property, thereby implying that it was a valid mortgage, the earliest that it can be said that the appellant discovered or should have discovered the respondents' negligence by the exercise of reasonable diligence was in April or May, 1977, when the validity of the mortgage was challenged in the action for foreclosure. Accordingly the appellant's cause of action in tort did not arise before that date and its action for negligence against the respondents is not statute-barred.

2. Consider whether the Jane Doe case described in the narrative is timely. Jane Doe was assaulted on August 24, 1986. Her assailant was arrested and charged on October 3, 1986. The preliminary hearing (described in the narrative) commenced on February 2, 1987 and on February 20, 1987, Callow, the assailant, entered a plea of guilty to all charges. Jane's action was commenced on August 10, 1987. Assume that the relevant statute of limitations is the Public Authorities Protection Act, RSO 1980, c. 406, which provides that an action must be brought within six months "after the cause of action arose." When, according to the discoverability principle discussed in the above cases, did the cause of action arise?

3. Does the application of the discoverability rule depend on the choice of words in the limitations provision? The Ontario Highway Traffic Act, s. 206 stipulates that actions for "damages occasioned by a motor vehicle" must be commenced within two years of the time when the "damages were sustained." Does discoverability apply? In *Peixeiro v. Haberman*, [1997] 3 SCR 549, the Supreme Court held it did, per Major J:

> The appellant submitted here that the general rule of discoverability was ousted because the legislature used the words "damages were sustained," rather than the date "when the cause of action arose." It is unlikely that by using the words "damages were sustained," the legislature intended that the determination of the starting point of the limitation

period should take place without regard to the injured party's knowledge. It would require clearer language to displace the general rule of discoverability. The use of the phrase "damages were sustained" rather than "cause of action arose," in the context of the HTA, is a distinction without a difference. The discoverability rule has been applied by this Court even to statutes of limitation in which plain construction of the language used would appear to exclude the operation of the rule.

Are there limits to this approach?

4. All limitations legislation contains provisions that postpone or suspend the operation of limitation periods in certain exceptional circumstances. For example, s. 47 of the Limitations Act provides that a limitation period in respect of minors'—that is, children's—claims does not commence to run until the age of majority is reached. The same section also prevents the running of limitation periods against persons who are under a mental or other disability.

M.(K.) v. M.(H.)
[1992] 3 SCR 6

[Appellant was the victim of incest. It began with fondling by her father and, after the age of 10 or 11, involved regular sexual intercourse with him. Her cooperation and silence were elicited by various threats that appellant had good reason to take seriously. She was also rewarded with pop, potato chips, and money. In time, respondent gave her the responsibility for initiating sexual contact. Appellant tried several times to disclose this abuse to no avail. At the age of 10 or 11 appellant tried to tell her mother and at age 16 she told a high school guidance counsellor, who referred her to a school psychologist. Her father had her recant both to the psychologist and to a lawyer for the local school board. Other disclosures made after leaving home came to nothing until she finally attended meetings of a self-help group for incest victims and realized that her psychological problems as an adult were caused by the incest. With therapy, appellant also came to realize that it was her father rather than herself who was at fault. Professional opinion was that appellant was unable to assess her situation rationally until she entered this therapy.

In 1985, at the age of 28, appellant sued her father for damages arising from the incest and for breach of a parent's fiduciary duty. A jury found that the respondent had sexually assaulted his daughter, and assessed tort damages of $50,000. The trial judge ruled, however, that the action was barred by s. 45 of the Limitations Act. The Ontario Court of Appeal dismissed an appeal from the trial judge's ruling.]

LA FOREST J: This case concerns the procedural obstacles facing victims of childhood incestuous abuse who attempt to vindicate their rights in a civil action for damages against the perpetrator of the incest. While the problem of incest is not new, it has only recently gained recognition as one of the more serious depredations plaguing Canadian families. Its incidence is alarming and profoundly disturbing. The damages wrought by incest are peculiarly complex and devastating, often manifesting themselves slowly and imperceptibly, so that the victim may only come to realize the harms she (and at times he) has suffered, and their cause, long after the statute of limitations has ostensibly proscribed a civil remedy. It has been said that the statute of limitations remains the primary stumbling block for adult survivors of incest, and this has proved to be the case thus far for the appellant in the present action. The appellant commenced this action for damages occasioned as a result of recurrent sexual assaults between the ages of eight and sixteen when she was twenty-eight. A jury found that the respondent committed sexual assault upon the appellant and assessed damages at $50,000, but her action was dismissed on the basis of a statute of limitations. ...

In 1985 the appellant sued her father for damages arising from the incest, or in the alternative for the infliction of mental distress. Further damages were claimed for breach of a parent's fiduciary duty to care for and minister to his child. The claims of mental distress and breach of fiduciary duty were also made against the appellant's mother. Before the trial began, counsel for the respondent moved for dismissal of the action on the ground that it was barred by the passage of time pursuant to s. 45 of the *Limitations Act*, RSO 1980, c. 240. ...

Issues

Several issues were argued by the appellant, and for the sake of completeness, I will enumerate them all here: (1) incest is a separate and distinct tort which is not subject to any limitation period; (2) incest constitutes a breach of fiduciary duty by a parent and is not subject to any limitation period; (3) if a limitation period applies, the cause of action does not accrue until it is reasonably discoverable; (4) the appellant was of unsound mind pursuant to s. 47 of the *Limitations Act*; (5) the tort is continuous in nature and the limitation period does not begin to run until the plaintiff is no longer subjected to parental authority and conditioning; and (6) the equitable doctrine of fraudulent conceal-ment operates to postpone the limitation period.

For the reasons that follow, I am of the view that this appeal should be allowed. Incest is both a tortious assault and a breach of fiduciary duty. The tort claim, although subject to limitations legislation, does not accrue until the plaintiff is reasonably capable of discovering the wrongful nature of the defendant's acts and the nexus between those acts and her injuries. In this case, that discovery took place only when the appellant entered therapy, and the lawsuit was commenced promptly thereafter. The time for bringing a claim for breach of a fiduciary duty is not limited by statute in Ontario, and therefore stands along with the tort claim as a basis for recovery by the appellant. ...

The Limitations Act and Reasonable Discoverability

The appellant argues that her cause of action did not accrue until she went through a form of therapy, because her psychological injuries were largely imperceptible until later in her adult life and thus not reasonably discoverable until she was able to confront her past with the assistance of therapy. During the hearing, counsel for the respondent conceded that the doctrine of reasonable discoverability had application to an action grounded in assault and battery for incest. He submitted, however, that the appellant was aware of her cause of action no later than when she reached the age of majority. In order to determine the time of accrual of the cause of action in a manner consistent with the purposes of the *Limitations Act*, I believe it is helpful to first examine its underlying rationales. There are three, and they may be described as the certainty, evidentiary, and diligence rationales; see Rosenfeld, "The Statute of Limitations Barrier in Childhood Sexual Abuse Cases: The Equitable Estoppel Remedy" (1989), 12 *Harv. Women's LJ* 206, at p. 211.

Statutes of limitation have long been said to be statutes of repose; see *Doe on the demise of Count Duroure v. Jones* (1791), 4 TR 301, 100 ER 1031, and *A'Court v. Cross* (1825), 3 Bing. 329, 130 ER 540. The reasoning is straightforward enough. There comes a time, it is said, when a potential defendant should be secure in his reasonable expectation that he will not be held to account for ancient obligations. In my view this is a singularly unpersuasive ground for a strict application of the statute of limitations in this context. While there are instances where the public interest is served by granting repose to certain classes of defendants, for example the cost of professional services if practitioners are exposed to unlimited liability, there is absolutely no corresponding public benefit in protecting individuals who perpetrate incest from the consequences of their wrongful actions. The patent inequity of allowing these individuals to go on with their life without liability, while the victim continues to suffer the consequences, clearly militates against any guarantee of repose.

The second rationale is evidentiary and concerns the desire to foreclose claims based on stale evidence. Once the limitation period has lapsed, the potential defendant should no longer be concerned about the preservation of evidence relevant to the claim; see *Dundee Harbour Trustees v. Dougall* (1852), 1 Macq. 317 (HL), and *Deaville v. Boegeman* (1984), 48 OR (2d) 725 (CA). However, it should be borne in mind that in childhood incest cases the relevant evidence will often be "stale" under the most expedient trial process. It may be ten or more years before the plaintiff is no longer under a legal disability by virtue of age, and is thus entitled to sue in her own name; see *Tyson v. Tyson*, 727 P2d 226 (Wash. 1986), at p. 232, *per* Pearson J (dissenting). In any event, I am not convinced that in this type of case evidence is automatically made stale merely by the passage of time. Moreover, the loss of corroborative evidence over time will not normally be a concern in incest cases, since the typical case will involve direct evidence solely from the parties themselves.

Finally, plaintiffs are expected to act diligently and not "sleep on their rights"; statutes of limitation are an incentive for plaintiffs to bring suit in a timely fashion. This rationale again finds expression in several cases of some antiquity. For example in *Cholmondeley v. Clinton* (1820), 2 Jac. & W 1, 37 ER 527, the Master of the Rolls had this to say in connection with limitation periods for real property actions, at p. 140 and p. 577, respectively:

> The statute is founded upon the wisest policy and is consonant to the municipal law of every country. It stands upon the general principle of public utility. *Interest rei publicae ut sit finis litium*, is a favorite and universal maxim. The public have a great interest, in having a known limit fixed by law to litigation, for the quiet of the community, and that there may be a certain fixed period, after which the possessor may know that his title and right cannot be called in question. It is better that the negligent owner, who has

omitted to assert his right within the prescribed period, should lose his right, than that an opening should be given to interminable litigation, exposing parties to be harassed by stale demands, after the witnesses of the facts are dead, and the evidence of the title lost. *The individual hardship will, upon the whole, be less, by withholding from one who has slept upon his right.* ... [Emphasis added.]

There are, however, several reasons why this rationale for a rigorous application of the statute of limitations is particularly inapposite for incest actions.

As I mentioned earlier, many, if not most, of the damages flowing from incestuous abuse remain latent until the victim is well into adulthood. Secondly, and I shall elaborate on this further, when the damages begin to become apparent, the causal connection between the incestuous activity and present psychological injuries is often unknown to the victim; see DeRose, "Adult Incest Survivors and the Statute of Limitations: The Delayed Discovery Rule and Long-Term Damages" (1985), 25 *Santa Clara L Rev.* 191, at p. 196. This Court has already taken cognizance of the role that the perpetrator plays in delaying the reporting of incest; see *R v. L. (W.K.)*, [1991] 1 SCR 1091. That case concerned a stay of criminal proceedings, arising out of alleged childhood sexual abuse, commenced after a lengthy delay. Stevenson J, speaking for the Court, observed, at p. 1101:

> For victims of sexual abuse to complain would take courage and emotional strength in revealing those personal secrets, in opening old wounds. If proceedings were to be stayed based solely on the passage of time between the abuse and the charge, victims would be required to report incidents before they were psychologically prepared for the consequences of that reporting.
>
> That delay in reporting sexual abuse is a common and expected consequence of that abuse has been recognized in other contexts. In the United States, many states have enacted legislation modifying or extending the limitation period for the prosecution of sexual abuse cases, in recognition of the fact that *sexual abuse often goes unreported, and even undiscovered by the complainant, for years* ... . Establishing a judicial statute of limitations would mean that *sexual abusers would be able to take advantage of the failure to report which they themselves, in many cases, caused.* This is not a result which we should encourage. There is no place for an arbitrary rule. [Emphasis added.]

Needless to say, a statute of limitations provides little incentive for victims of incest to prosecute their actions in a timely fashion if they have been rendered psychologically incapable of recognizing that a cause of action exists.

Further, one cannot ignore the larger social context that has prevented the problem of incest from coming to the fore. Until recently, powerful taboos surrounding sexual abuse have conspired with the perpetrators of incest to silence victims and maintain a veil of secrecy around the activity. The cogency of these social forces would inevitably discourage victims from coming forward and seeking compensation from their abusers. The English Court of Appeal in *Stubbings v. Webb*, [1991] 3 All ER 949 (CA), recently acknowledged that the social climate during the mid-1970s was not at all conducive to bringing an action of this nature. That case involved a remarkably similar fact situation to that in the present case. Although the relevant statute of limitations is quite different from the Ontario Act, the following remarks made by Sir Nicolas Browne-Wilkinson V-C, at p. 960, are nevertheless telling:

> The question is whether, in 1975, the plaintiff acted reasonably in not then suing Mr. Webb and Stephen Webb for the serious wrongs alleged to have been done to her. In my judgment it is important not to consider the question by reference to the social habits and conventions of 1991. Over recent years, for the first time civil actions have been brought by victims of adult rape against their assailants. As to actions against child abusers, this is apparently the first case in which the alleged victim has sought to sue her abusers. In the present climate and state of knowledge it would in my judgment be very difficult, if not impossible, for a plaintiff coming of age in the late 1980s to establish that she acted "reasonably" in not starting proceedings alleging child abuse within three years of attaining her majority. But we are concerned with the reasonableness of the plaintiff's behaviour in the period 1975-78. At that time civil actions based on sexual assaults were unknown in this country. In my judgment, it was accordingly reasonable for the plaintiff not to have considered the injuries done to her sufficiently serious to justify starting proceedings against her adoptive father and brother. In 1975 such proceedings were unthought of and it was therefore reasonable for her not to have started such proceedings.

I would adopt these comments as a reasonable description of the situation in this country at that same time.

The foregoing discussion has examined the policy reasons for limitations from the perspective of fairness to the potential defendant. However this Court has also said that fairness to the plaintiff must also animate a principled approach to determining the accrual of a cause of action. In *Kamloops (City of) v. Nielsen*, [1984] 2 SCR 2, one of the issues that arose was whether the plaintiff's action was statute-barred by the British Columbia *Municipal Act*, RSBC 1960, c. 255, where the plaintiff first became aware of the damage after the one year prescription. Wilson J, writing for the majority, observed that the injustice which statute-bars a claim before the plaintiff is aware of its existence takes precedence over any difficulty encountered in the investigation of facts many years after the occurrence of the allegedly tortious conduct.

This principle was later adopted in *Central Trust Co. v. Rafuse*, [1986] 2 SCR 147, where the Court held that the reasonable discoverability rule was as applicable to cases involving professional negligence as it was to actions involving injury to property. Le Dain J thus articulated the general rule, at p. 224:

> ... a cause of action arises for purposes of a limitation period when the material facts on which it is based have been discovered or ought to have been discovered by the plaintiff by the exercise of reasonable diligence. ...

Application of the Discoverability Rule to Incest

In my view the only sensible application of the discoverability rule in a case such as this is one that establishes a prerequisite that the plaintiff have a substantial awareness of the harm and its likely cause before the limitations period begins to toll. It is at the moment when the incest victim discovers the connection between the harm she has suffered and her childhood history that her cause of action crystallizes. I am in complete agreement with Professor Des Rosiers that the causal link between fault and damage is an important fact, essential to the formulation of the right of action, that is so often missing in cases of incest; see "Les recours des victimes d'inceste et d'agression sexuelle" to be published in Legrand, ed., *Common law d'un siècle à l'autre* (1992). What is more, I am satisfied that the weight of scientific evidence establishes that in most cases the victim of incest only comes to an awareness of the connection between fault and damage when she realizes who is truly responsible for her childhood abuse. Presumptively, that awareness will materialize when she receives some form of therapeutic assistance, either professionally or in the general community. I have come to this conclusion after studying the expert evidence in this case and the American jurisprudence which has wrestled with this problem over the past decade. The presumption will, of course, be displaced when the evidence establishes that the victim discovered the harm and its likely cause at some other time. ...

In *Gray v. Reeves* (1992), 64 BCLR (2d) 275 (SC), Hall J concluded that the victim's recognition of the nexus between her injuries and the earlier incest is the point when time should begin to run against the victim. In that case the plaintiff was sexually assaulted by her uncle on approximately fifteen occasions between the ages of four and twelve. She commenced action at the age of thirty, after receiving therapy which identified the true cause of certain psychological problems suffered by the plaintiff during her adult life. This is clearly a "Type 1" case, as the plaintiff always remembered the assaults, had revealed the incestuous abuse to her family, and indeed had fought continuously to have her uncle excluded from family gatherings during her adult life. Nevertheless, the trial judge found as follows, at p. 306:

> Here, the plaintiff Ms. Gray knew from a very early age that the assaultive behaviour of her uncle, the defendant, was disgusting to her. She knew at least from the time when she was a teenager that these acts were wrong and she sought to protect younger children from any assaults by the defendant. I am of the view that the evidence in the case discloses that, although the plaintiff was repelled by the assaults, she had no reason to believe and did not believe that she had suffered any material harm, mental or physical, from the assaults. While she had these feelings of revulsion or repugnance to the activities of the defendant concerning herself or others, I am quite unable to find that she was able, until a point in time after the commencement of her therapy with Dr. Way in 1988, to perceive any link between the earlier wrongful conduct of the plaintiff and her depression and inability to establish a satisfactory relationship with a member of the opposite sex.

British Columbia's limitations legislation (*Limitation Act*, RSBC 1979, c. 236) is very different from the statute before us in the instant case. It creates a form of statutory reasonable discoverability test, and I note with interest that this legislation emphasizes the importance of professional treatment and advice by stating the test (s. 6(3)) as the knowledge of a reasonable person "having taken the appropriate advice." (The meaning of this provision has most recently been considered by British Columbia's Court of Appeal in *Levitt v. Carr* (1992), 66 BCLR (2d) 58.) Despite the differences in legislation, the conclusions of Hall J in *Gray v. Reeves*, at p. 309, are worthy of note:

... it seems to me that the hypothetical reasonable person in the shoes of the plaintiff here would not have been acting sensibly in commencing an action until such a person came to appreciate that a wrong or wrongs that had occasioned significant harm to her wellbeing could be established.

This is essentially the test I propose in the instant case.

It is clear from the evidence and the scientific literature that a misapplied sense of responsibility is instrumental in conditioning the child victim to submit silently to the abuse, while at the same time serving as the catalyst for much of the consequential psychological and emotional damages that emerge over time. More importantly, though, it is the redirection of responsibility for the abuse to whom it properly belongs that initiates the therapeutic process, such that the victim becomes aware of the causal connection between her childhood history and resulting injuries. Summit, *supra*, put it succinctly in his article, at p. 183:

> Without a consistent therapeutic affirmation of innocence, the victim tends to become filled with self-condemnation and self-hate for somehow inviting and allowing the sexual assaults.

In short, the issue of responsibility plays a pivotal role in both the genesis and the cessation of the harms caused by incestuous abuse.

The close connection between therapy and the shifting of responsibility is typical in incest cases. In my view, this observed phenomenon is sufficient to create a presumption that certain incest victims only discover the necessary connection between their injuries and the wrong done to them (thus discovering their cause of action) during some form of psychotherapy. I base this proposition on the scientific evidence presented at trial and to this Court which confirms a post-incest syndrome amongst incest survivors. If the evidence in a particular case is consistent with the typical features of this syndrome, then the presumption will arise. Of course, it will be open to the defendant to refute the presumption by leading evidence showing that the plaintiff appreciated the causal link between the harm and its origin without the benefit of therapy.

Application to the Present Case

After hearing the evidence, the trial judge concluded that from the age of sixteen the appellant was aware that she had been wronged and had suffered adverse effects. I will not expound on the role of an appellate court when reviewing findings of fact. Here, in my view, the trial judge did not address himself to the critical issue—i.e., when did the appellant discover her cause of action in the sense of having a substantial awareness of the harm and its likely cause? With respect, the trial judge made no finding that the appellant had made the necessary connection at any time before entering therapy.

In my view, this is a case in which it can be presumed that the nexus between the appellant's injuries and incest was discovered only when the appellant received therapy. The evidence presented at trial shows the appellant to be a typical incest survivor. Her experiences as a child and later in life correspond closely to the symptoms of post-incest syndrome. As a child, she was subjected to the threats and bribes that enforce secrecy on the assaults. Her mental defence mechanism was dissociation, typical in incest cases. Later in life, her attempts at disclosure were met with scepticism, denial and evasion, again a typical feature of post-incest syndrome. As an adult she suffers from depression and difficulty with intimate relationships, which are classic symptoms of the syndrome.

Aside from the presumption available to the appellant, the evidence overwhelmingly indicates that she did not make the causative link between her injuries and childhood history until she received therapeutic assistance, and the evidence proffered to the contrary was entirely speculative. In any event there was no direct evidence to overcome the presumption that the appellant's therapy was the triggering event for discovering her cause of action. As such, the statute of limitations did not begin to run against her until that time, and this action was commenced within all relevant statutory limitation periods. On this basis, together with the reasons which follow, I would allow the appeal and restore the jury's verdict both as to liability and damages.

I cannot leave this topic without adding my voice to the chorus calling for reform in this area of limitations law. I note that a recent consultation draft prepared by the Attorney General of Ontario has proposed the abolition of limitation periods in cases of incestuous sexual assault: A Consultation Draft of the General Limitations Act, s. 18(h), in "Recommendations for a New Limitations Act," report of the Limitations Act Consultation Group. As well, British Columbia has recently amended its *Limitation Act* to permit survivors of childhood sexual abuse to pursue legal action at any time; see *Limitation Amendment Act*, 1992, SBC 1992, c. 44. In light of the existing evidence on the nature and extent of the problems faced by incest survivors, these are welcome developments. ...

Recovery for Breach of Fiduciary Obligation

The appellant argues that incest constitutes not only the tort of assault and battery, but is also a breach of the fiduciary relationship between parent and child. The appellant submits that Ontario's *Limitations Act* does not apply to fiduciary duties, and as such the plaintiff's delay is no defence to the fiduciary action. I agree. Incest is a breach of both common law and equitable duties, and the latter claim is not foreclosed by the Act. Certain equitable defences may, however, be available to the respondent. ...

By way of summary, fiduciary obligation has apparently not been raised in previous incest cases as an independent head of liability. However, it is clear that such an option is available subject to statutory and other limitation defences specific to equitable claims. It is to these defences that I now turn.

Defences

As with the appellant's claim in tort, her delay in bringing the claim for breach of fiduciary duty raises several possible defences. The first is limitations legislation; the second is the application of that legislation by analogy, and finally there is the equitable doctrine of laches. In my view, none of these defences is made out in this case, and the appellant's claim should stand. As will become apparent, many of the factors activating the reasonable discoverability principle in tort are also applicable in assessing these equitable defences. While there is some overlap, there are also different considerations that arise solely in the realm of equity.

Limitations Legislation

Ontario's *Limitations Act* is one of the few remaining limitations statutes in Canada that is not made applicable to civil actions in general. Such provisions capture any common law or equitable claim, and reference can be made to six provincial statutes in this regard: *Limitation Act*, RSBC 1979, c. 236, s. 3(4); *Limitation of Actions Act*, RSA 1980, c. L-15, s. 4(1)(g); *The Limitation of Actions Act*, RSS 1978, c. L-15, s. 3(1)(j); *Statute of Limitations*, RSPEI 1988, c. S-7, s. 2(1)(g); *The Limitation of Actions Act*, RSM 1987, c. L150, s. 2(1)(n); *Limitation of Actions Act*, RSNB 1973, c. L-8, s. 6. In Ontario, by contrast, the Act applies only to a closed list of enumerated causes of action. Counsel for both parties have apparently conceded that this list does not include fiduciary obligations, and it is therefore unnecessary to consider this question in great depth. However, some comment on the issue may be helpful in understanding the next defence under consideration, namely, limitation by analogy to the statute.

Section 2 of the Ontario *Limitations Act* reads as follows:

> 2. Nothing in this Act interferes with any rule of equity in refusing relief on the ground of acquiescence, or otherwise, to any person whose right to bring an action is not barred by virtue of this Act.

This section makes clear that the Act does not exhaust the defences available to a defendant because of the passage of time. Thus, certain actions expressly made subject to the *Limitations Act* may not yet be out of time under the terms of that statute, but may be precluded by equitable defences that apply notwithstanding the terms of the Act. The section also gives rise to the inference that there is a category of equitable claims not subject to the Act at all, and that the equitable defences survive in those cases. Such is the case here. The Act does not apply to fiduciary obligations, but the respondent may nonetheless argue that the equitable defence of laches is available to the respondent. ...

Statutory Limitation by Analogy

While a breach of fiduciary duty is not expressly limited by Ontario's *Limitations Act*, can it be said that equity should apply the Act by analogy to bar the appellant's claim? That is, should the limitation period applicable to tortious assault be applied on the fiduciary side because both claims arise out of the same facts? There is a short answer to this question. Having already found that the limitation period was tolled by the reasonable discoverability principle, analogous application of the statute is, of course, not fatal to the appellant's claim in equity. But even apart from this, I think the same result would follow. While there is no doubt that in some cases equity will operate by analogy and adopt a statutory limitation period that does not otherwise expressly apply, in my view this is *not* such a case. And this for several reasons. First, equity has rarely limited a claim by analogy when a case falls within its exclusive jurisdiction, as in this claim for breach of fiduciary duty. Moreover, even if it is appropriate to analogize from the common law, the analogy will be governed by the parameters of the equitable doctrine of laches. More will be said about laches later when it will become evident that it is of no assistance to the respondent. Finally, any analogy drawn in this case would be nullified by the doctrine of fraudulent concealment. ...

Laches

Historically, statutes of limitation did not apply to equitable claims, and as such courts of equity developed their own limitation defences. Limitation by analogy was one of these, but the more important development was the defence of laches. While laches must be considered here as in any delayed equitable claim, in my view it does not afford the respondent redress. ...

A good discussion of the rule and of laches in general is found in Meagher, Gummow and Lehane ... [R.P. Meagher, W.M.C. Gummow, and J.R.F. Lehane, *Equity Doctrines and Remedies* (Sydney: Butterworths, 1984)], at pp. 755-65, where the authors distill the doctrine in this manner, at p. 755:

> It is a defence which requires that a defendant can successfully resist an equitable (although not a legal) claim made against him if he can demonstrate that the plaintiff, by delaying the institution or prosecution of his case, has either (a) acquiesced in the defendant's conduct or (b) caused the defendant to alter his position in reasonable reliance on the plaintiff's acceptance of the status quo, or otherwise permitted a situation to arise which it would be unjust to disturb. ...

Thus there are two distinct branches to the laches doctrine, and either will suffice as a defence to a claim in equity. What is immediately obvious from all of the authorities is that mere delay is insufficient to trigger laches under either of its two branches. Rather, the doctrine considers whether the delay of the plaintiff constitutes acquiescence or results in circumstances that make the prosecution of the action unreasonable. Ultimately, laches must be resolved as a matter of justice as between the parties, as is the case with any equitable doctrine. ...

In the present case, was it reasonable for the appellant to know the facts of her abuse and yet be unable to determine that her father was in the wrong and that a suit in equity could be launched? I believe that in the circumstances of the typical incest survivor the failure to know that one has been wronged is entirely reasonable. I have already discussed the medical evidence which indicates a post-incest syndrome of denial, memory repression, and self-guilt. The very existence of this syndrome is evidence that the reasonable incest survivor is incapable of appreciating her rights in equity or in law, and as such is incapable of acquiescing in the conduct that has breached those rights.

As is now apparent, the considerations outlined in detail under the common law discoverability doctrine must also be considered under the rubric of acquiesence. However, I would not wish to be taken as suggesting that an inquiry under the common law will reach the same result as in equity in every case. Rather, there is an important distinction between the two that has not yet been considered. As I have stated, both doctrines share the common requirement of knowledge on the part of the plaintiff. However, a consequence of that knowledge is that the reasonable discoverability inquiry is at an end, and the statutory limitations period begins to run. In equity, however, there is a residual inquiry: in light of the plaintiff's knowledge, can it reasonably be inferred that the plaintiff has acquiesced in the defendant's conduct? That question depends on the circumstances of each case, but in my view it would require particularly compelling evidence to demonstrate that an incest victim had "acquiesced" in the sexual assaults made against her. In this case I need not consider this second inquiry, as the appellant did not have real knowledge of the wrongfulness of the respondent's conduct until shortly before commencing this action. However, I see nothing in the facts of this case to suggest that the appellant truly acquiesced in her father's abuse.

NOTES AND QUESTIONS

1. One of the intervenors in the case, LEAF, argued that the Limitations Act, in so far as its provisions bar incest claims, violates s. 15 of the Canadian Charter of Rights and Freedoms. It submitted that the provisions bar claims of women in a disproportionate fashion and so constitutes discrimination on the basis of sex. The Supreme Court held that in view of its disposition of the case on other grounds, it was not necessary to decide that issue. Is the Charter argument a valid argument?

2. *Constitutionality of Limitations.* The previous note raises the question of constitutional validity of limitations provisions and the extent to which they may be subject to attack under the Canadian Charter of Rights and Freedoms, and specifically s. 15. A number of cases have unsuccessfully attempted to argue that a special limitation period in favour of a profession or organization contravenes the equality rights under s. 15. Before 1989, cases were generally decided on the basis of the "similarly situated" test for discrimination which looked to define a class of persons similarly situated, and then see whether members of that class were subject to unlawful discrimination. Most cases held that all plainitffs suing subject to a special limitation period who were similarly situated should be considered the class of persons within which one tested for unlawful discrimination. Since members of such a class were all treated the same under the legislation, there was no discrimination among them and no basis for a s. 15 claim. See, for example, *Colangelo v. City of Mississauga* (1988) 66 OR (2d) 29 (CA); *Brochner v. MacDonald* (1989), 34 CPC (2d) 314 (Alta. CA).

In 1989, the Supreme Court of Canada decided *Andrews v. Law Society (BC)*, [1989] 1 SCR 143. In that case, the court rejected the "similarly situated" approach to defining discrimination under s. 15 in favour of a test that limited its protection to the groups listed in the section or those analogous to them. This had the effect of narrowing the scope of s. 15 and further limiting or eliminating its potential application to limitation periods. See, for example, *Mirhadizadeh v. Ontario* (1989), 69 OR (2d) 422 (CA).

A separate theme sounded in many of the decisions dealing with the Ontario limitations legislation is the need for reform of the existing Limitations Act, and the rationalization of the multitude of individual limitation periods. What are the most obvious areas for revision?

In 1992, the Ontario government introduced Bill 99, An Act To Revise the Limitations Act. Consider the provisions of the Bill reproduced below. What are the nature of the reforms proposed? Are they appropriate? Are they effective to implement the 1969 recommendation of the Ontario Law Reform Commission that a single limitation period be enacted?

3. Limitation Reform

Bill 99, An Act To Revise the Limitations Act
2d Sess., 35th Leg. Ont., 1992 (1st Reading on November 25, 1992)

Basic Limitation Period

4. Unless this Act provides otherwise, a proceeding shall not be commenced in respect of a claim after the second anniversary of the day on which the claim was discovered.

Discovery

5.(1) A claim is discovered on the earlier of,
    (a) the day on which the person with the claim first knew,
        (i) that the injury, loss or damage had occurred,
        (ii) that the injury, loss or damage was caused by or contributed to by an act or omission,
        (iii) that the act or omission was that of the person against whom the claim is made, and
        (iv) that, having regard to the nature of the injury, loss or damage, a proceeding would be an appropriate means to seek to remedy it; and
    (b) the day on which a reasonable person with the abilities and in the circumstances of the person with the claim first ought to have known of the matters referred to in clause (a).

Presumption

(2) A person with a claim shall be presumed to have known of the matters referred to in clause (1)(a) on the day the act or omission on which the claim is based took place, unless the contrary is proved.

Minors

6. The limitation period established by section 4 does not run during any time in which the person with the claim is a minor and is not represented by a court-appointed litigation guardian.

Incapable Persons

7.(1) The limitation period established by section 4 does not run during any time in which the person with the claim,
    (a) is incapable of commencing a proceeding in respect of the claim because of his or her physical, mental or psychological condition or because of physical restraint, war or war-like conditions; and
    (b) is not represented by a court appointed litigation guardian.

Presumption

(2) A person shall be presumed to have been capable of commencing a proceeding in respect of a claim at all times unless the contrary is proved.

Extension

(3) If the running of a limitation period is postponed or suspended under this section and the period has less than six months to run when the postponement or suspension ends, the period is extended to include the day that is six months after the day on which the postponement or suspension ends.

Exception

(4) This section does not apply in respect of a claim referred to in section 9. ...

Assaults and Sexual Assaults

9.(1) The limitation period established by section 4 does not run in respect of a claim based on assault or sexual assault during any time in which the person with the claim is incapable of commencing the proceeding because of his or her physical, mental or psychological condition.

Presumption

(2) Unless the contrary is proved, a person with a claim based on an assault shall be presumed to have been incapable of commencing the proceeding earlier than it was commenced if at the time of the assault one of the parties to the assault had an intimate relationship with the person or was someone on whom the person was dependent, whether or not financially.

Same

(3) Unless the contrary is proved, a person with a claim based on a sexual assault shall be presumed to have been incapable of commencing the proceeding earlier than it was commenced. ...

Ultimate Limitation Periods

15.(1) Even if the limitation period established by any other section of this Act in respect of a claim has not expired, no proceeding shall be commenced in respect of the claim after the expiry of a limitation period established by this section.

(2) No proceeding shall be commenced in respect of any claim after the thirtieth anniversary of the day on which the act or omission on which the claim is based took place.

Health Facilities

(3) No proceeding shall be commenced in respect of a claim based on the negligent act or omission of a health facility or a health facility employee after the tenth anniversary of the day on which the act or omission took place.

Health Practitioners

(4) No proceeding shall be commenced in respect of a claim based on the malpractice or negligent act or omission of a health practitioner after the tenth anniversary of the day on which the malpractice or negligent. act or omission took place.

Exception

(5) Subsections (3) and (4) do not apply if the claim is based on the leaving of a foreign object having no therapeutic or diagnostic purpose in the body of the person with the claim.

Improvements

(6) In the case of an improvement to real property carried out under a contract, no proceeding shall be commenced in respect of a claim based on a deficiency in the design, construction or general review of the improvement after the tenth anniversary of the first day on which the contract was substantially performed within the meaning of the *Construction Lien Act.*

Periods Not To Run

(7) The limitation periods established by subsections (2), (3), (4) and (6) do not run in respect of a claim during any time in which,
> (a) the person with the claim,
>> (i) is incapable of commencing a proceeding in respect of the claim because of his or her physical, mental or psychological condition or because of physical restraint, war or war-like conditions, and
>> (ii) is not represented by a court appointed litigation guardian; or
> (b) the person against whom the claim is made,
>> (i) wilfully conceals from the person with the claim the fact that injury, loss or damage has occurred, that it was caused by or contributed to by an act or omission or that the act or omission was that of the person against whom the claim is made, or
>> (ii) wilfully misleads the person with the claim as to the appropriateness of a proceeding as a mean of remedying the injury, loss or damage.

(8) The limitation periods established by subsections (3), (4) and (6) do not run in respect of a claim during any time in which the person with the claim is a minor and is not represented by a court-appointed litigation guardian.

(9) Subject to section 9, the burden of proving that subsection (7) or (8) applies is on the person with the claim. ...

No Limitation Period

16. There is no limitation period in respect of, ...

(h) a proceeding arising from a sexual assault if at the time of the assault one of the parties to it had charge of the person assaulted, was in a position of trust or authority in relation to the person or was someone on whom he or she was dependent, whether or not financially. ...

18.(1) A limitation period set out in another Act that applies to a claim as defined in this Act is of no effect unless,

(a) the provision establishing it is listed in the Schedule to this Act; or

(b) the provision establishing it incorporates by reference a provision listed in the Schedule to this Act.

(2) If there is a conflict between a limitation period established by a provision referred to in subsection (1) and one established by any other provision of this Act, the limitation period established by the provision referred to in subsection (1) prevails.

Adding Party

19.(1) If a limitation period in respect of a claim against a person has expired, the claim shall not be pursued by adding the person as a party to any existing proceeding.

Misdescription

(2) Subsection (1) does not prevent the correction of a misnaming or misdescription of a party.

C. Choice of Proceeding and Originating Process

1. Actions and Applications

In courts with a very simplified procedure—for example, Small Claims Courts—there is only one form or type of proceeding. In higher courts, however, two different forms of proceedings typically are available. It is relevant to discuss these at this point because, not only do the general procedures applicable to the two forms of proceedings differ, the two forms involve different originating processes.

The first of the two types of proceedings is commonly referred to in Canada as an "action." With regard to the other type of proceeding, however, the terminology is not uniform. A common term is "originating notice"—for example, Alberta, Saskatchewan, and the former Ontario rules—but "originating application" is also used in British Columbia and New Brunswick. The Ontario, Nova Scotia, Newfoundland, and Prince

Edward Island rules use the term "application." (In this book, "originating notice" or "application" will be used interchangeably to refer to the second type of proceeding.)

There is a basic functional distinction between the two types of proceedings: each is designed to deal with different types of cases. An *action* is appropriate in cases where there are likely to be seriously contested issues of fact (for example, tort claims). Such cases require a more elaborate procedure—that is, pleadings, discovery, and the opportunity to adduce oral evidence at a trial. An application, on the other hand, is appropriate for cases where issues of fact are unlikely to be seriously disputed—for example, where what is primarily at issue is the interpretation of a legal document, such as a will, trust, contract, statute, or regulations.

The development of the two types of proceedings must be seen in historical context. The traditional position of the common law was—and largely continues to be—that issues of fact should be resolved at an oral trial, by witnesses testifying in open court where they are subject to cross-examination before the trier of fact.

The difference between the two proceedings lies in the procedure taken before the ultimate hearing and the nature of that hearing. In an action, pleadings are exchanged and the parties usually employ the various discovery devices that the rules provide to learn as much as possible about their opponent's case before the hearing. These steps are time-consuming and sometimes two or three years may elapse before an action reaches a trial in which oral testimony is given in open court. In most cases, the parties dispute the facts and, at the hearing, the court resolves the contest on the basis of oral testimony and any documentary evidence given by the parties and their witnesses.

By comparison, proceedings brought by an application are summary in nature: no pleadings are required and discovery is not available. It is possible, though not usual, for an application to be heard within one or two weeks after the proceedings commenced. An application is far less costly because many of the pre-trial procedures attached to an action are dispensed with. The relevant facts and supporting evidence are set out in affidavits and the party seeking relief may be required to file and give to the other party a concise statement of the facts of law on which he or she relies. Cross-examination may take place on the affidavits before the hearing. The cross-examination is not held before the judge who is to hear the application, but before a court reporter who prepares a transcript of the cross-examination. When the application comes on for hearing the judge will resolve any disputed matters of fact by reference to the affidavits and to any cross-examination on them. However, the court has power on the hearing to *direct the trial of an issue* on oral evidence if a major factual dispute develops. Typically, this will involve pleadings and discovery, and more or less converts the proceedings into an action.

The typical pattern across Canada is that a party may always commence a proceeding by means of an action, but he or she may only proceed by way of an originating motion or application when the rules or statutes so provide (see, for example, Alberta rule 6(1), British Columbia rule 8(1), Ontario rule 14.02, Nova Scotia rule 9.04, Saskatchewan rule 13(1), and Manitoba rule 14.02). For the most part, this book concentrates on the procedure applicable to and the dynamics of actions rather than the less widely available application. However, proceedings by way of application are extremely important in certain areas of litigation—for example, trusts and estates and judicial review administrative boards and tribunals.

Proceedings by way of application have been less useful when courts are concerned that there will be important disputes about facts. In *Re Seaway Trust and the Queen* (1983), 41 OR (2d) 501 the applicants sought to challenge legislation and orders in council allowing the government to take over trust companies with an apparent deficiency of assets under the Charter and by way of an application. Cory JA held that an application was not appropriate and stated:

> The nature of the legislation attacked and the Charter infringements alleged make it clear that the interests of justice would best be served if all issues were determined on the trial of an action commenced by writ.
>
> The interests of the parties appearing on this application as well as those of others concerned with the eventual outcome of the issues raised (for example, the intervenants) will best be served by the trial process.
>
> The trial procedure offers a number of safeguards and protections which are essential to the proper and just resolution of this matter. It will permit all interested parties to be joined and, if they wish, to assert claims against others. The issues can be clearly defined by the pleadings. The parties will have the benefit of production and discovery. Most importantly it will permit the essential assessments of credibility and finding of facts to be made based upon the hearing of *viva voce* evidence tested by cross-examination.

However, the courts have not been oblivious to the fact that parties who wish to mount a constitutional challenge may wish to resort to the speedier and less expensive procedures by way of an application. The reason why an applicant may wish to so proceed, and why he or she may have a just claim to do so, was succinctly stated in *Canadian Newspapers Co. v. AG Canada* (1985), 49 OR (2d) 557, at 572 (CA): "It is important that persons who allege that their rights under the Charter have been infringed should have an opportunity of having their legal position determined expeditiously." Frequently the courts will permit Charter issues today to be resolved on an application, but this approach is not universal, particularly where the court is of the view that there are complex or disputed issues of fact that render proceedings by way of an application inappropriate. In Ontario, rule 14.05 specifically authorizes the commencement of Charter challenges by way of application.

In *Re Maltby et al. and Attorney General of Saskatchewan* (1984), 10 DLR (4th) 745, the Saskatchewan Court of Appeal held that a constitutional challenge to the conditions of confinement at a provincial detention centre could not proceed by way of application for a declaration: per Bayda CJS, at 750:

> The material comprises affidavit evidence only, containing but minimum information untested by cross-examination and unelucidated by further inquiry and probing. There is not sufficient evidence to enable an adjudicator to test and adjudge objectively the reasonableness or otherwise of the impugned practices, or to compare the practices with those of similar institutions in Canada and other parts of the democratized world. The material leaves unanswered a myriad of questions. What is the *rationale* for the practices? What statistical studies have been made and what are the empirical data showing the need for these practices in a democracy? What are the alternatives for security? What are the detrimental effects upon the individual who is subjected to these practices? Are the effects temporary? Permanent? What are the views of psychiatrists,

psychologists, penologists, reformed inmates and other knowledgeable persons in this respect? For example, is it the *fact* of the "strip search" that is objectionable or the *manner* in which it is carried out? Is it possible to conduct a "strip search" in a way that does not offend? And the list goes on. I can only reiterate that while the issues may be valid ones to raise for the type of adjudication the applicants seek, for this court to rule on those issues and in effect condemn or approve a huge part of the custodial aspect of the remand system would be an injudicious use of this court's power, given the sparse circumstances disclosed here.

The documents by which the proceedings are commenced are generically referred to as the *originating process*. Different originating processes are used for actions and applications. Where the proceeding is an application or originating motion, the document is an "originating notice of motion" or "notice of application." But whatever the name, it is a notice setting forth succinctly the relief sought by the applicant (the facts on which the claim is based will be set forth in an accompanying affidavit or affidavits).

The originating process for an action varies not only in name, but in substance, according to the jurisdiction. Basically, Canadian jurisdictions fall into one of two categories. Some use the traditional method of commencing an action by a *writ of summons* (for example, British Columbia). This is a command in the name of the sovereign, endorsed with a very brief statement of the plaintiff's claim, and warning the defendant to respond to the writ or suffer judgment by default. Since this document gives no details as to the plaintiff's claim it must be subsequently followed by the service of the plaintiff's pleading—that is, the statement of claim. To avoid this two step procedure many Canadian jurisdictions (for example, Alberta, Manitoba, New Brunswick, Newfoundland, Ontario, Saskatchewan, and the Federal Court of Canada) now provide that actions are commenced by the plaintiff's statement of claim accompanied by standardized warnings to the defendant that if he or she does not respond he or she may suffer judgment by default.

Actions for divorce differ slightly from other types of actions in that they are commenced not by a writ or statement of claim but by a *petition*. Apart from its name this is really indistinguishable from a statement of claim. A petition is used because the Divorce Act (Canada) requires a proceeding for divorce to be commenced by a document called a "petition."

The contents of the originating process can be divided into three elements. The first is the *title of the proceeding* or the "style of cause," as it is sometimes called, in which the parties are named. (In an action they are usually called the "plaintiff" and "defendant"; in an application they are referred to as the "applicant" and the "respondent.") Who should be made parties to a proceeding is governed by both substantive and procedural considerations that will be discussed subsequently. When a party sues or is sued in a capacity other than a personal capacity, the title or the body of the proceeding must indicate the capacity in which the party sues or is sued. This refers to situations where a person sues or is sued not personally but as a representative of another person. The representative is in a sense a nominal party; the real party in interest is the person on whose behalf the action is brought or defended. The representative will have to pay costs if he or she loses, though he or she generally will be entitled to recover them from the person represented. The distinction between a nominal party and represented persons is illustrated by the case of an action involving the estate of a deceased person. If a person dies with money due to him or her, an action can be brought to recover the debt for the benefit of those entitled to the estate of the deceased. The plaintiff in the action will be the person who has the responsibility of administering the deceased's estate, called the personal representative (either an executor or an administrator depending on whether the creditor died leaving a will). In the case of an action on behalf of the estate of a deceased person, the plaintiff must state in the title of the proceeding whether he or she sues as "executor of the will of XY deceased" or as "administrator of the estate of AB deceased," as the case may be. It must be emphasized that a plaintiff who sues as executor or administrator is not seeking to recover the debt for his or her own benefit, but for the benefit of those entitled to the deceased's estate (which might include the plaintiff). Similarly, an action to recover a debt due by a person at his or her death will be brought against the executor or administrator representing the estate, and the capacity in which the defendant is sued will have to be specified in the title of the proceeding.

The second element of the content of the originating process is a statement about the nature of the claim made and the relief sought. Where the proceeding is commenced by a writ of summons or a notice of application these statements will be brief and not very informative about the details underlying the claim. However, when the originating process is the plaintiff's statement of claim, much more detail will be revealed. The contents of pleadings, including statements of claim, is dealt with in chapter 6, "Pleadings and Disposition Without Trial."

The third element of the originating process informs the defendant of what steps must be taken in response to the service of the originating process—that is, signify an intention to defend the proceeding, for example, by delivering an appearance or a statement of defence—and warns the defendant of the consequences of not responding (for example, judgment may be given by default).

A proceeding is commenced when the originating process is *issued*. To accomplish this, the lawyer for the plaintiff or, more rarely, the plaintiff prepares the originating process and takes the original and a copy to the court office. On payment of the prescribed fee, a court officer will issue the process by stamping the original with the seal of the court and by signing, dating, and numbering it. After inserting these details on the copy of the originating process, the court officer will return the original to the lawyer and retain the copy for the court's file.

The issuing of the originating process is an administrative act and is ordinarily a matter of right and the plaintiff does not require leave of the court before commencing the proceeding.

When is an application more or less appropriate than an action? What, if any, guidance is afforded by the following decision?

E.J. Hannafin Enterprises Ltd. v. Esso Petroleum Canada
(1994), 17 OR (3d) 258 (Gen. Div.)

BLAIR J (orally): This is a motion by the respondents to convert the within application to an action.

Background and Overview

The applicant E.J. Hannafin Enterprises Ltd. ("Hannafin") operates a passenger car and truck stop retail enterprise near Belleville in the province of Ontario. It carries on such operation in conjunction, now, with Esso Petroleum Canada ("Esso") pursuant to three agreements earlier entered into between Hannafin and Esso's predecessor Texaco Canada Inc. By a head lease dated June 12, 1989, Hannafin leased the lands and premises in question to Texaco and pursuant to a sublease Texaco leased the premises back to Hannafin. The third agreement between the parties consists of an agreement called the Dealer Sales and Equipment Loan Agreement (which I will refer to as "the supply agreement"). ...

A dispute has arisen between Hannafin and Esso as to whether or not Hannafin is in default in the making of payments due under the supply agreement. Esso takes the position that Hannafin is in default and has served notice accordingly to terminate the supply agreement pursuant to subs. 5(b) thereof. ...

Hannafin disputes that it is in default under the supply agreement and disputes the right of Esso to terminate that agreement. In order to protect its position, however, and without prejudice to its rights, it served notice electing to continue the supply agreement in effect for a further six-month period, which expires on March 22, 1994. In addition, by notice dated December 17, 1993, Hannafin served notice, pursuant to para. 20 of the head lease, that it was exercising its option to purchase the option facilities. ...

Paragraph 20 of the head lease, as I have indicated, provides for the installation and financing of the option facilities, and concludes with the following provision:

> Upon the termination or expiration of this lease for any reason whether by effluxion of time or otherwise, but save and except for termination by reason of the Lessor's default, the Lessor shall have the option to purchase the Option Facilities at a price equal to the unamortized balance (if any) of the Installation Cost determined and certified by a Lessee as of the date of completion of such purchase, such option to purchase to be exercised by delivery of written notice to the Lessee not less than forty-five (45) days prior to the date of termination or expiration of this lease.

Hannafin has brought the within application seeking "a declaration that the Head Lease, and in particular, the option to purchase referred to in Clause 20, is in full force and effect."

The respondents take the position that this relief cannot be granted without a determination and a finding, first, that Hannafin is in default of its obligations under the supply agreement. The parties agree that there is a triable issue with respect to this question and, accordingly, Mr. Ledger argues on behalf of Esso that the entire application should be converted into an action so that that question may be determined upon *viva voce* evidence at a trial.

In response, Mr. Solmon submits on behalf of the applicant that there is a separate and discreet question which can be determined in isolation on the basis of non-disputed facts and which, if decided in favour of Hannafin, will be determinative of the issues between the parties. That question, he submits, is whether Hannafin is entitled to exercise its option under Clause 20 of the head lease *whether or not it is in default under the supply agreement.* He argues that the words "lessor's default" in the passage quoted above from Clause 20 refers only to lessor's default under the head lease and not to a default by the lessor, Hannafin, in its capacity as purchaser under the supply agreement. Mr. Ledger on behalf of Esso, of course, takes the opposite position and argues that the words "lessor's default" in the head lease must be taken to encompass a default by Hannafin under the supply agreement.

Law and Analysis

It is clear that if the parties must litigate the question of Hannafin's default under the supply agreement there is a triable issue in that respect and that a trial must be heard to determine that question. It is less clear to me, but not pressed by Mr. Ledger, whether a trial may be necessary to enable the court either to make the link or to reject the making of the link between the head lease, the sublease and the supply agreement. As Mr. Ledger did not press this point, however, I take it to be some indication that that issue may well be determinable by a court on the basis of the agreements themselves and the non-contested evidence before the court.

I would have thought that it made considerable sense in the proper case, from a commercial point of view, and also, in these days of protracted and expensive litigation, for a court to determine in a summary proceeding, if possible, an issue which might well be determinative of the overall dispute, thus saving the parties the time, effort and significant expense of what could be a lengthy trial. Accordingly, I would have had little hesitation in determining that the matter could be dealt with by way of application were it not for a line of authorities put before the court by Mr. Ledger which stand, essentially, for the proposition that the court should not act in half measures on applications and that it should not deal with issues in a bifurcated fashion if, on one outcome of the argument, the matter should be required to proceed to trial in any event. ...

In my view these authorities ... , most of which pre-date the extensive revisions to the Rules of Practice in 1985, must be read with caution and in light of those changes to the Rules of Practice and in light of the exigencies of modern day litigation. ...

In my view, fragmentation of the trial and lack of finality are not evils in themselves, in the context of an application, if the end result is to enable the parties to process their dispute more expeditiously and efficiently, and provided there are no material facts which require a trial for their disposition *in relation to the fragmented issue,* and provided there is some reasonable prospect that the resolution of that issue may resolve the *lis* between the parties.

Rule 14 [of] the Rules of Civil Procedure is the rule which provides for the making of an application by way of originating process. In many ways that process is comparable to the earlier proceedings by way of originating motion. Rule 38.10 of the Rules of Civil Procedure, however, gives the presiding judge upon an application the discretion [to],

> (a) *grant the relief sought* or dismiss or adjourn the application, in whole or *in part* and with or without terms; or,
>
> (b) *order* that the whole application or *any issue* proceed to trial and give such directions as are just. (Emphasis added.)

That provision did not exist in the previous rules.

As I interpret r. 38.10(1), the court is empowered to sever an issue from the whole of the application and to deal with that issue as part of the application, while directing that the remaining issues in the application, if necessary, proceed to trial. Generally speaking, of course, a court will only do so if the separate discrete issue can be determined on the basis of non-contested facts, that is to say, that there are no material facts in dispute in relation to that issue.

In this matter there does seem to me to be a separate and distinct issue which, depending upon how it is decided, could be determinative of the *lis* between the parties. That is the question of whether or not, even if it is in default under the supply agreement, Hannafin has the right to exercise its option under the head lease. If the answer to that question is "yes," then the issue of Hannafin's default need not [be] litigated, at least in the context of the right to exercise the option to purchase the option facilities. If the answer is "no," of course, then the question of Hannafin's default under the supply agreement will have to be litigated and a trial of that issue will be necessary.

I am satisfied that r. 38.10(1) authorizes such a procedure, and I intend to follow that route. The court must be cautious, I think, in embarking upon a procedure which may result in the litigation, and a litigant's right to a trial, being broken up into too many chunks. As long as the court exercises its discretion in a judicial fashion, however, that danger can be controlled, in my view.

I take comfort from the fact that Mr. Justice Steele appears to have followed a similarly broader approach to the resort to the application procedure under r. 14 in *McKay Estate v. Love* (1991), 6 OR (3d) 511 (Gen. Div.) where, in an estate administration case, he allowed an application regarding the approval of the sale of a piece of property by an executor to proceed, notwithstanding that there were facts in dispute. The issue is not whether there are material facts in dispute, necessarily, but whether there are material facts in relation to the question to be dealt with that are in dispute. Steele J said, at p. 514:

> On the jurisdictional issue, counsel for Kenneth McKay argued that the power given under all of the paragraphs in rule 14.05(3) should not be exercised where there were material facts in dispute. In my opinion, that would impose para. (h) as a condition to hear any matter under the preceding paragraphs. This would be clearly contrary to the disjunctive wording of subs. (3). I believe that the court has power to hear an application under paras. (a) to (g) inclusive, even if there are material facts in dispute. *This does not mean that in an appropriate case the court may decide to direct the trial of an issue or otherwise deal with the application.* [Emphasis added.]

Accordingly, the motion is dismissed and the application will proceed.

Motion dismissed.

---

2. Simplifying Procedure

A. Zuckerman, "A Reform of Civil Procedure—Rationing Procedure Rather Than Access to Justice"
(1995), 22 *Journal of Law and Society* 157

It would be absurd to say that we are entitled to the best possible legal procedure, however expensive, when we cannot lay a credible claim to the best possible health service or to the best possible transport system.

There is little doubt that the structure of our legal procedure, in both the lower and the upper judicial tiers, facilitates a good deal of avoidable procedural waste. As a result, critics and reformers have tended to devote most of their attention to improving court and case management and to simplifying the processes involved. Most significantly, Lord Woolf, who is chairing a committee appointed by the Lord Chancellor to consider reform of the administration of justice, seems to think that the solution lies in more extensive court supervision of the litigation process and in the enforcement of adherence to tight timetables. It is, however, insufficiently appreciated that the capacity of our procedure to absorb ever increasing amounts of funds is not due just to poor management of case flows or to the complex and cumbersome nature of the civil process. It is also promoted by certain underlying factors. The method of paying lawyers on hourly basis ensures that they have no incentive to economize in the provision of legal services. Publicly funded legal aid provision was, at least until recently, determined by reference to the standard of legal services commonly employed by the affluent, rather than by what the taxpayer could reasonably afford to pay. These and other factors have reacted upon each other to produce conditions that favour rising costs and mounting delays.

A lack of attention to the interaction of different elements of the legal process has undermined at times the object of reform. For instance, when the legal aid system was introduced, hardly any consideration was given to the possibility that the injection of a massive subsidy into the purchase of legal services will combine with existing inflationary factors to produce a tremendous upward pressure on costs. Similarly, a failure to have regard to the possibility that while a new measure could achieve savings in certain respects, it might produce an equal or greater expense in another respect has led to waste. Thus, one of the purposes of exchange of witness statements on the eve of the trial was to obtain savings by obviating examination in chief. But the indications are that the resources invested in preparing witness statements may at times exceed the cost involved in oral testimony.

Future reform must avoid these pitfalls and ensure that it does not merely result in localized savings but does succeed in securing a reduction in overall cost and delays. To this end we need to fashion an overall strategy which takes account of the potential interaction between different aspects of the system. There would be little point, for instance, in simplifying procedure unless we also remove the incentives for increasing the complexity and duration of litigation. Similarly, it would be self-defeating to speed up the rate of case disposal, if this were going to produce an exponential increase in the volume of litigation that could overwhelm the courts.

The purpose of this paper is to highlight the main factors that contribute to cost and delay and to outline a strategy for reversing existing trends. Reform, it will be argued, should be guided by the idea that, when procedural resources are finite, we should ration their employment and not, as is the case at present, restrict access to court by means of prohibitive costs. To implement this idea, we need to fashion a comprehensive and integrated approach consisting of three major limbs. First, we must render procedure simpler and cheaper in the majority of cases so as to make access to justice affordable by those who need it, even if this means some reduction in the quality of judgments. Second, we must ensure that litigation remains affordable in the long run by providing effective incentives to both lawyers and their clients to keep down costs. Third, we would need to counteract the likelihood that greater accessibility to justice will stimulate litigation by erecting powerful disincentives to litigation which, unlike the present ones, are fair and non-discriminatory.

Before outlining these proposals, however, two preliminary matters need to be addressed: the connection between the adversarial character of our procedure and its complexity, and the relationship between cost and justice.

Adversarial Freedom and Proportionality in Procedure

There seems to be a perception that, in an adversarial system, latitude in the conduct of one's case is a requirement of justice. The reasoning runs as follows. Since the courts do not take it upon themselves to investigate the issues but confine themselves to the role of impartial umpires, litigants must be afforded the means with which to prepare their case and present it at the trial. Thus they need facilities for eliciting information about the opponent's case and the evidence he or she holds, for compelling witnesses to testify, for examining witnesses at the trial, and the like. The processes of pleadings, interrogatories, discovery, exchange of witness statements, and the rules of evidence are designed to meet these needs.

Given that these facilities have been placed at the parties' disposal, so the thinking proceeds, the law cannot then restrict the parties' freedom to use them. For example, if litigants have the right to obtain discovery of documents necessary for disposing of the matter or saving costs, the court can hardly turn round and say that this or that request for disclosure is not really necessary or that the parties should content themselves with a more limited and cheaper form of discovery. Nor can a court tell the parties that the importance of the case or the nature of the issues involved do not justify the extensive and expensive procedural steps they propose to take. In an adversaries' system, litigants are free within the contours of the permissible, the argument concludes, to exploit to their own advantage the procedural devices that the law provides.

Even if the usefulness of the procedural devices provided by the law can be accepted, it does not follow that they are equally important or necessary in all cases, regardless of complexity of issues and of the gravity of subject matter. Just as not all medical conditions require the employment of all the available diagnostic methods, so not all disputes in the courts justify the use of all available pre-trial tactics regardless of cost. It might be objected that merely because we might think that a case does not justify the deployment of all available procedural devices, it does not mean that such deployment should be restricted or forbidden. For just as citizens cannot be forbidden to have recourse to excessive medical services, if they choose to pay for them, litigants should be free to invest as much as they wish in legal services, including litigation. But this analogy is clearly flawed, because disproportionate legal measures affect not only the resources of those litigants who employ them but also increase the burden on their opponents and consume the resources of the court.

The idea of complete adversarial freedom is in any event at odds with the present state of the law, because some limitations are already placed on the use of procedure. Litigants who have only a flimsy defence may not insist on having recourse to the normal pre-trial and trial procedures. All they can expect is a summary adjudication. Thus, plaintiffs who believe that their defendant has no reasonable or credible defence, may apply for summary judgment under RSC, Ord. 14. Similarly, upon an application by one party, whether plaintiff or defendant, a court may strike out any pleading that "discloses no reasonable cause of action or defence in accordance with RSC, Ord. 18, r. 19(1)(a). The object of these provisions is to block access to full pre-trial and trial procedures and enable litigants to obtain a quick judgment where the opponent's case is so weak as not to justify recourse to the normal process."

The point to be noticed about these summary methods of adjudication is that they are concerned with proportionality. The full procedure is not waived because it is incapable of making a difference to the eventual out-come. A summary dismissal of a claim or of a defence may not be as reliable as a dismissal after trial. An argument which appears flimsy when tested by a summary process might turn out to be well-founded, once the full pre-trial processes of pleadings, interrogatories, and discovery have been employed and once the parties' respective cases have been exposed to close scrutiny at the trial. Discovery, for instance, may turn up something that sheds a different light on a defence which appears insubstantial at first glance, or cross-examination may show an otherwise unanswerable claim to be ill-founded. Rather, the standard procedure is waived because, as the case stands at the time, it is unlikely to make a difference and it is therefore wasteful to employ it. These summary processes are accordingly illustrative of the notion of procedural proportionality, which holds that a dispute has to be sufficiently substantial to justify the use of the normal process.

Not only is the system prepared to shed some procedural provision where the issues are abundantly clear, it is also prepared to do so in situations of urgency. When a party is concerned that his or her rights would be harmed during the pendency of litigation, he or she may apply for an interlocutory injunction. Applications for interlocutory injunctions are determined without recourse to pleadings, interrogatories, discovery, exchange of witness statements, and oral testimony. They are decided instead on the basis of affidavit evidence. It is important to appreciate that it is not the consideration that an interlocutory injunction does not finally dispose of the case which provides the justification for doing away with the pre-trial processes. For this consideration does not always apply. Indeed, interlocutory injunctions may be obtained, provided that the criteria of urgency have been met, notwithstanding that they may permanently dispose of the case to all intents and purposes. Further, even where the interlocutory decision does not finally and conclusively dispose of the whole suit, it may still leave one party facing an irreparable loss, and thus permanently compromise his or her rights. As a result, the idea that at the interlocutory stage the court need not concern itself with the merits of the parties' respective claims has been much criticized and effectively abandoned. The processes that are otherwise regarded as important for obtaining accurate decisions are shed in the interlocutory procedure not because of provisionality but due to the necessity of reaching a decision within a short time.

It would therefore appear that, even as things stand, the system does not allow an unqualified access to the full procedural menu. The notion of proportionality, that not every dispute deserves equal procedural investment, is already ingrained in our procedural arrangements. There is therefore nothing in principle to prevent us from considering whether access to the full process of the law is too widely defined at present, and whether the balance between summary adjudication and standard adjudication should not be tilted further towards the former.

Accuracy and Economy in Procedure—A Matter of Compromise

The realization that procedural provision may be relative leads to a more general discussion about the extent to which a system of procedure has to strive to ascertain the truth. It is axiomatic that the object of procedure is to render litigants their due; namely, to return judgments which correctly apply the law to the true facts. But this does not mean that the state has an obligation to provide the most accurate civil procedure regardless of cost. It would be absurd to say that we are entitled to the best possible legal procedure, however expensive, when we cannot lay a credible claim to the best possible health service or to the best possible transport system. Yet it would be equally absurd to suggest that procedure need not strive to achieve any level of accuracy to satisfy the demands of justice. We are therefore entitled to expect procedures which strive to provide a reasonable measure of protection of rights, commensurable with the resources that we can afford to spend on the administration of justice.

Once we have accepted that the commitment to accuracy is not absolute and boundless, we must also accept that the choice of procedure must involve compromises. First and foremost, a compromise has to be struck between accuracy and cost. A highly accurate system of adjudication would require intensive preparation and extensive judicial personnel and would therefore be very expensive. By contrast, a very cheap system may produce a very low level of accuracy. A legislature who cannot afford a limitless investment in the administration of justice must achieve compromise whereby the level of accuracy that the administration of justice could produce will reflect the level of support that the state can reasonably be expected to give to legal services. It follows that, in devising a system of procedure, the legislature has considerable scope for choice between different ways of balancing accuracy against cost.

Our existing system of civil justice represents, therefore, no more than one possible way of balancing cost and accuracy. Of course, it is not suggested that this system is the outcome of a deliberate and conscious cost benefit exercise carried out at a certain point in the past. Civil procedure has evolved into its present shape through a succession of choices, made by the law maker over many decades, which were necessitated by diverse legal, economic and other social factors. The important point to realize is that the present procedural arrangements are not sacrosanct. On the contrary, it is desirable that we should ask periodically whether the administration of justice reflects an optimal compromise between accuracy and cost and whether it fulfills the needs of the community at the time.

This way of looking at procedure should help us deal with the kind of objection that is usually raised against suggestions for introducing measures of economies in the administration of justice: namely, that economies that compromise accuracy also compromise justice. Quality, it might be said, must not be sacrificed for the sake of economy. We do not live in the days of Solomon but in a far more complex society which demands intricate legal arrangements. Under such conditions, correct judgments may be obtained only through the investment of a good deal of time and resources. Justice bought cheaply and in haste, it could be suggested, may be so inferior as not to be worth having. The response to this type of objection has already been hinted at. There is simply no way of avoiding compromises. It is therefore inevitable that quality should, to some degree, be sacrificed for the sake of economy. The real question is whether any given procedural arrangements produce a satisfactory compromise.

In today's conditions, civil procedure may be criticized for striking a compromise which tilts too far towards accuracy at the expense of economy. Our procedural arrangements demonstrate a willingness to tolerate high costs for the sake of high standards of accuracy in judgments. As a result, it is becoming uncomfortably clear that access to the courts is being placed beyond the means of the vast majority of the population and that the exchequer is finding it increasingly hard to shoulder the support of poor litigants. It is therefore legitimate to ask whether it is really better to offer high quality justice to a few, rather than dispense justice, albeit of lesser quality, to a wider segment of society. Further, we may well wonder whether it is justified to ask the taxpayer to pour vast sums of money into the administration of civil justice, when justice may be bought more cheaply, if a little less accurately.

There is a further dimension to the tension between cost and accuracy in procedure, for a compromise must also be struck between accuracy and speed. We tend to think that the only requirement of justice is that a judgment should give the parties what is theirs by right. But time is also a dimension of justice, for, as we like to remind ourselves, justice delayed is justice denied. Delay may undermine the practical utility of judgments for the purpose of redressing rights and a judgment may come too late to be capable of putting things right. Clearly, a system of procedure which systematically allows delays to rob judgments of their practical usefulness, cannot be said to be a just procedure. It follows that while a just procedure cannot be wholly indifferent to the need to establish the truth, it also cannot be altogether indifferent to delay, because a just procedure must aim to deliver judgments when they can still do some good. Yet, no system can be expected to invest limitless resources in achieving speedy justice. Accordingly, where resources are limited, accuracy in judgments may have to be sacrificed to some extent not only for the sake of economy but also for the sake of obtaining timely judgments.

When we consider the reform of civil procedure, we must therefore not be deterred by arguments that the introduction of savings may lead to a deterioration in the accuracy of judgments. What matters is not any particular level of accuracy but the correct balance between accuracy of justice and timeliness of justice, and between accuracy and affordability.

A Ratcheting Up Mechanism—The Clogs on Access to Justice

A most cursory examination of statistical data is enough to make the grim picture of rising costs abundantly clear. During 1987-88, legal aid payments amounted to £426m., but by 1993-94 they rose to £1,020m., of which £350m. was spent on civil proceedings. These figures are expected to rise to £1,633m. and £685m. by 1996-97. The cost of litigation, whether funded publicly or privately, has been on an inexorable rising curve. In 1974 hourly rates charged by solicitors were in the region of £25, but by 1994 they rose to an average of £185, with a high of £310; the price retail index for the same period rose only six times. Legal aid statistics suggest that in 1974-75 the average cost of a non-matrimonial case in the High Court was £338, but by 1993-94 this figure rose to £4,462.37. Over the last twenty years the income of solicitors and barristers has risen much faster than the retail price index or the average income in the country. Several factors may have contributed to this upward movement, but there can be little doubt about the contributory effect of two features of our procedural arrangements: the method of remunerating lawyers on an hourly basis and the legal aid system. A discussion of reform must therefore start by looking at these factors.

In England, solicitors are paid for their services on an hourly basis. While barristers traditionally charged according to the complexity of the case, there is now an increasing trend for them too to charge on an hourly basis. Whether charging is by the hour or in proportion to complexity, it seems obvious that lawyers have no direct incentive to economize in the provision of services. On the contrary, the more complex and pro-tracted litigation becomes, the more they earn. It is not suggested that lawyers deliber-ately inflate their services for gain. But it is in the nature of things that economic activity should, probably without any self-conscious decision on the part of the actors, follow the most rewarding path.

Normally, resistance to price comes from the consumers of services. In the present context, however, this moderating mechanism is blunted by several factors. Lay persons have to rely on lawyers to judge how necessary costs are in order to defend their rights and, further, it is largely in the hands of lawyers to render costs necessary. As a result, clients are poorly placed to bring down the cost of litigation. The indemnity rule, whereby the loser in litigation has to pay the winner's costs, also makes a contribution here. As we shall shortly see, the main effect of this rule is to discourage litigation, but once it is clear that litigation is destined to go all the way to trial and beyond, it tends to erode resistance to cost. Given that success brings with it not only the sum claimed but also the expenses laid out in securing judgment, a litigant who believes that an increase in the amount spent on litigation will increase his or her chances of success has a very good reason for progressively raising the stakes. Once one party has increased the stakes, opponents would feel compelled to follow suit for fear that by using inferior procedural devices, be it a less celebrated lawyer or a less qualified expert, they would compromise their chances of success and run a greater risk of having to pay the other party's costs as well on losing the subject matter in dispute. Indeed, a point may come where the parties would have reason to persist with investment in litigation not so much for the sake of a favourable judgment on the merits, as for the purpose of recovering the money already expended in the dispute, which may well outstrip the value of the subject matter in issue.

NOTES AND QUESTIONS

1. Under the usual rules of civil procedure, the procedures relating to an action or an application apply equally to all proceedings, regardless of complexity or amount at stake. The much simpler procedures of the Small Claims Courts are available only where the amount at stake is small (in Ontario $6,000 or less).

2. Since 1996, the Ontario Rules of Civil Procedure have made provision in rule 76 for a simplified procedure where the amount at stake is less than $25,000. These rules were made to address the perception that the cost of litigating claims that were "modest" under the rules (that is, more than the limit of the Small Claims Court and less than $25,000) was greatly out of proportion to the amount recovered. Studies of litigation in Ontario had disclosed that while the median judgment amount was $15,000, the costs to the client of successfully litigating the claim (even after recovering costs from the other side) was as high as $10,000—two-thirds of the amount recovered. The subcommittee studying the question discussed the problem in the following terms:

> In considering the causes of the problem of unaffordable litigation, we saw high lawyer fees as more a product of the problem than the cause of it. In General Division litigation involving small amounts, lawyers face a seemingly insoluble dilemma. If the lawyer does not invoke all of the procedures available, even if the cost effectiveness of those procedures is out of proportion to the amount involved, the lawyer may be accused of indifference to the client's interests or be exposed to an allegation of negligence. Alternatively, a lawyer simply may be unable to steer an inexpensive course because the opponent invokes all of the procedures available. We felt that, although the current Rules are admirably suited to litigation involving large sums of money, those same Rules, when applied to disputes over lesser sums of money, generate prohibitive costs.
>
> To find a way to make litigation more affordable, we were guided by two principles. The first was that it is the procedure and not the lawyers that should be regulated. Thus, we rejected imposing fixed limits on party-and-party costs or on solicitor-and-client costs. The second was a proportionality principle that there should be a relationship between the procedures available to pursue or defend a claim and the magnitude of that claim. We tried to reduce the costs by striking a balance between the expense of procedures before trial and the value of the potential outcome. We concluded that there should be a simplified procedure, perhaps more accurately, a truncated procedure, for the lower range of monetary and property claims.

3. Overall, the aim of rule 76 is to curtail the costs of litigation by truncating or eliminating procedural steps that normally apply to actions commenced under the rules. Significant areas affected are discovery, cross-examination on affidavits, and summary judgment. As each of these topics are dealt with later in this book, consider the limitations imposed by the simplified procedure provisions, and whether their impact is justified by the likely cost savings. Having regard to the arguments of Zuckerman, are these shortcuts justified?

4. Under the Ontario simplified procedure rule, the procedure is, in effect, mandatory for cases involving up to $25,000 but optional for cases involving larger amounts. Given the problems of the costs of litigation, is $25,000 a meaningful figure? Should the procedure be mandatory for much larger lawsuits—say, up to $100,000?

III. SERVICE OF ORIGINATING PROCESS

A. Personal Service and Alternatives

Consider the rules respecting service of the originating process—that is, Ontario rule 16 and the following case.

Rupertsland Mtge. Inv. Ltd. v. Winnipeg
(1981), 23 CPC 208 (Man. Co. Ct.)

JEWERS CO. CT. J: This case raises the question of whether documents have been personally served when the process server has not himself delivered them to, but they have nevertheless reached, the intended recipient.

Rupertsland Mortgage Investment is appealing against four orders issued by the City of Winnipeg Health Department pursuant to The Public Health Act of Manitoba, CCSM 1970, c. P210 requiring Rupertsland to effect certain repairs and do certain things at 530 Corydon Avenue in the City, being residential premises owned by Rupertsland.

One of the grounds of appeal is that the orders were not properly served upon Rupertsland. If that is a valid ground of appeal, consideration of other grounds of appeal raised by Rupertsland would not be necessary.

A sheriff's officer delivered two copies of the orders to Esther Matz at 187 Montrose Street in the City of Winnipeg on December 30, 1980. That address is the head office and business address of Rupertsland. Mrs. Matz is neither a director nor officer, nor employee, of Rupertsland, but she is the company's solicitor. As well, she is the wife of the sole director of Rupertsland, Mr. Waldemar H. Matz. Mrs. Matz is not authorized to accept service of process on Rupertsland. Nevertheless, she accepted delivery of the orders and, in turn, delivered them to her husband who received them not later than December 31, 1980. The question is whether, in these circumstances, the documents can be said to have been personally served upon Rupertsland.

The City of Winnipeg was proceeding pursuant to revised regulation P210-R3, being a regulation respecting sanitation under The Public Health Act. Section 6(1) of that regulation provides that, where the medical officer of health or an inspector becomes aware of the existence of any insanitary condition, he shall serve on the person responsible, a written order to abate the condition. The Act does not expressly authorize substituted service and, unless authorized by statute, there is no substitute for personal service. See *Smith v. Smith* (1952), 7 WWR (NS) 163, affirmed 9 WWR (NS) 144, 61 Man. R 105, [1953] 3 DLR 682 (CA). There is no doubt that Rupertsland is the person responsible for any alleged insanitary condition, and so the service of the orders must be effected personally on Rupertsland.

There is no definition in the Act or the Regulations of "personal service." A good discussion of what is meant by the term "personal service" may be found in the case of *Orazio v. Ciulla* (1966), 57 WWR 641, 59 DLR (2d) 208 (BC SC) a decision of Kirke Smith LJSC. That learned Judge adopted, as I do, the following statement of Lord Cransworth LC in *Hope v. Hope* (1854), 4 De GM & G 328, 43 ER 534 [at 664 WWR]:

The object of all service is of course only to give notice to the party on whom it is made, so that he may be made aware of and may be able to resist that which is sought against him; and when that has been substantially done, so that the Court may feel perfectly confident that service has reached him, everything has been done that is required.

In the instant case, the object referred to by Lord Cranworth has been attained. Mr. Matz, a responsible officer of Rupertsland, actually received the orders not later than December 31st, 1980, and was fully apprised of their contents. The material makes it clear that he read the orders and knew precisely what was required of Rupertsland. Does it legally make any difference that the orders were not given to him directly by the process server but rather through the intermediary, Mrs. Matz?

The case of *Re Consiglio*, [1971] 3 OR 798 (MC), a decision of Senior Master Rodger, is instructive. In the headnote of that case, which dealt with an application to set aside a writ on the ground that it had not been personally served, it is stated that, "If the writ comes to the knowledge, or into the possession, of the person to be served, either directly or indirectly from a third party, then it may be found that there has been personal service."

In that case, the process server attempted to serve the writ upon the defendant's brother-in-law, outside of certain residential premises, in the mistaken belief that the brother-in-law was the proper party to be served. The brother-in-law refused to accept the document and went into the premises, whereupon the process server followed, and, as the brother-in-law closed the door of the premises, the server threw the papers between the screen and the door. The Senior Master held that, if it could be established that the papers had actually come into the possession of the defendant, it could be considered that there has been personal service upon him. He therefore ordered the brother-in-law to attend and be cross-examined on an affidavit which he had filed in the proceedings, so that he could answer questions bearing upon that point.

In the course of his reasons, the Senior Master referred to the following cases:

(a) *O'Neil v. O'Neil* (1913), 4 WWR 478, 11 DLR 440, a Saskatchewan decision in which there was obiter to the effect that, if the plaintiff could show that a copy of the writ ultimately came to the knowledge or possession of the defendant, the Court would have been disposed to allow the service of the writ to stand;

(b) *Rhodes v. Innes* (1831), 7 Bing. 329, 131 ER 127, where a copy of the writ enclosed in a letter was left with the defendant's son at the defendant's residence; the son was asked to give the letter to his father, which he promised to do, and such service was held to be equivalent to personal service;

(c) *Vidito v. Veinot* (1912), 3 DLR 179, 10 ELR 292, where the writ of summons was given to the defendant's wife and there was evidence that she had given it to her husband on the same day when he returned from his work (that, of course, is essentially the case at Bar);

(d) *Phillips v. Ensell* (1834), 1 CM & R 374, 149 ER 1124, where the writ was given to the defendant's brother living in the same house and where, because it was not sworn that the writ did not come to the knowledge or possession of the defendant, the application to set aside the writ was refused.

It is clear, then, that there is precedent for the proposition that, for "personal service" to be effected, the process need not be delivered directly by the process server to the intended recipient, just as long as the party to be served actually does receive the process into his possession. I am content to adopt and follow these precedents, which recognize, and apply, the essential principle: that the whole purpose of service is to apprise, and give a party notice of, proceedings intended to be taken against him, and if that object has been satisfied, and the process has actually reached the party, the precise manner in which that has occurred should not be of concern.

I hold, therefore, that, in this case, the orders were personally served upon the appellant, Rupertsland, on December 31st, 1980.

NOTES AND QUESTIONS

1. Consider Ontario rule 16. What would constitute valid service of an originating process on Rupertsland if it were in Ontario? Would the facts in that case constitute valid or potentially valid service in Ontario? What specific rules would you rely on?

2. The general rule in the various rules of civil procedure is that the originating process must be served on the defendant personally. See Alta. rules 14-15, BC rule 11, Man. rule 16.01(1), NB rule 18.01, Nfld. rule 6, NS rule 10, Ont. rule 16.01, PEI rule 10, and Sask. rule 18. Personal service of an individual generally requires leaving a copy with the individual.

3. The rules make specific provision for what constitutes personal service on various types of defendants. Consider, for example, the provisions relating to service on a corporation. In the case of a large corporation with many places of business, their effect is to provide the plaintiff with many options with respect to service. What are the potential risks to a corporation in terms of ensuring a timely response to any lawsuits against it?

4. In *Bhatnager v. Canada (Minister of Employment and Secretary of State for External Affairs)* (1990), 71 DLR (4th) 84, the issue before the Supreme Court of Canada was whether two ministers could be held in contempt for disobeying a court order to produce immigration files when the order was served on government lawyers but not the ministers personally. The Supreme Court held unanimously that personal service was necessary, overturning a decision of the Federal Court of Appeal that the federal rules authorized service on the solicitor. Sopinka J stated:

> With respect to Urie J, I cannot interpret the *Federal Court Rules* as having the effect he
> ascribed to them, apart altogether from any *Charter* considerations that might have
> come into play if I had held otherwise. While it is true that there are provisions in the
> Rules for personal service (e.g. r. 355(4)), it does not follow that the permission in Rule
> 308 to effect service other than personally is determinative of the issue of knowledge in
> a contempt of court proceeding. The relevant Rules define what is effective service for
> the purposes of the expeditious conduct of litigation in the Federal Court, but they do
> not purport to detract from the elements necessary to establish contempt. It seems to me
> that a crucial requirement for the proof of a serious offence such as contempt of court
> could not be implicitly abrogated by a provision in subordinate legislation; such an
> alteration of the general law would require explicit language. As Hogg JA stated in *Re
> Gordon MacKay & Co. and Dominion Rubber Co.*, [1946] 3 DLR 422 (Ont. CA), at p. 425:
>
> > The common law rights of the subject are not to be taken away or affected except
> > only to such extent as may be necessary to give effect to the intention of Parliament

when clearly expressed or when such result must follow by necessary implication, and if the rights of persons are encroached upon, this intention must be made manifest by the language of the statute, if not by express words then by clear implication and beyond reasonable doubt.

Note that under the Ontario Rules of Civil Procedure, personal service of an originating process on the government and the attorney general is defined broadly so that, for example, personal service of the attorney general can be achieved by leaving a copy of the document with a solicitor in the Crown Law Office (Civil Law) of the Ministry of Attorney General (rule 16.02(h)). What, if anything, justifies the "more personal" personal service of the order in *Bhatnager*?

The Supreme Court saw personal service of the order as an important element of due process before the two ministers were exposed to possible incarceration as a result of a finding of contempt for disobeying the order. Do the same type of considerations apply in the civil context?

5. Why the insistence that the originating process must be served on the defendant personally? Can we design more convenient and less expensive methods of service that will ensure that the defendant receives actual notice of the proceeding?

6. One alternative to personal service has long been recognized. Personal service of the originating process is not necessary where the solicitor for the defendant accepts service on behalf of the defendant. (See, for example, Ontario and New Brunswick rules 18.03(2), BC rule 11(8), and NS rule 10.03(2)). This is a useful procedure for a plaintiff because it avoids the necessity of finding and serving the defendant. Obviously, though, it can only be used if the plaintiff knows the defendant is represented in the matter and the solicitor is prepared to accept service. It may only occur, however, where the solicitor is authorized by the client to accept services

7. Some jurisdictions have gone much further in relaxing the requirement of personal service. For example, New Brunswick (rule 18.03) and Ontario (rule 16.03) permit, subject to certain safeguards (see rules 18.08 and 16.08), service by mail or by leaving a copy of the document at the residence of the person to be served with a person who appears to be an adult member of the household. Saskatchewan rule 19 also permits service by mail in certain types of cases. Are such relaxations of the requirements of personal service appropriate?

8. After the service of the originating process, subsequent documents are then usually served on each party's solicitor of record, and there is usually considerable flexibility in terms of service by mail, facsimile, and courier delivery. In Ontario, for example, see rules 16.01(4)(a) and 16.05. Typically, the rules provide that if a party has a solicitor on the record, the solicitor, and not the party, must be served.

B. Substituted Service

Gallacher v. Hashim
[1989] OJ no. 1642 (HC)

DANDIE LJSC:—The petitioner wife asks for an order dispensing with the service of the petition of divorce on the grounds that the petitioner has no knowledge of the whereabouts of the respondent and on the further ground that the respondent suffers from schizophrenia and has threatened the petitioner's life in the past and that the petitioner is fearful that the respondent may become violent and attack her upon receipt of the petition. Rule 16.04(1) reads as follows:

> 16.04(1) Where it appears to the court that it is impractical for any reason to effect prompt service of an originating process or any other document required to be served personally or by an alternative to personal service under these rules, the court may make an order for substituted service or, where necessary in the interest of justice, may dispense with service.

Service of a process is so fundamental to our system of justice that it would appear, at first blush, that the present application should be denied. It is clear to me that there are two branches to Rule 16.04(1), namely where it appears to the Court that it is impractical to serve the document and where it is necessary in the interests of justice, the Court may dispense with service. It may be that when a petitioner has reasonable cause to fear for his or her life in the event a petition is served on the respondent, that service of the petition may be dispensed with. Although such relief may be available, the issue must be established by more than an affidavit of the petitioner. The least degree of proof required is an opinion by the attending psychiatrist, Dr. Ahmed, that service needs to be dispensed with. It is apparent from the material that such a letter will not be forthcoming and I am not prepared to dispense with service in these circumstances on the untested affidavit of the petitioner. As the relief asked is for an order dispensing with service, the motion is denied. I would think that if the petitioner were to make an application asking for substitutional service upon Dr. Ahmed and provided there are sufficient facts to determine that the petition will come to the respondent's attention then I might be persuaded to order substitutional service upon Dr. Ahmed.

NOTES AND QUESTIONS

1. Do you agree with this decision? Why would it matter in this case whether the respondent husband was served or not? Would it be wise to order substitutional service on Dr. Ahmed? What will he do with the originating process?

2. As we have seen, typically the plaintiff is required to serve the originating process on the defendant personally. However, in some cases this may be impossible—for example, where the defendant cannot be found or is avoiding service. To overcome this problem, and to prevent the plaintiff from being stopped in his tracks by the inability to serve the defendant personally, throughout Canada courts are given power to order substituted service—that is, service by some other means. See Alta. rule 23, BC rule 12, Man. rule 16.04, NB rule 18.04, Nfld. rule 6.10, NS rule 10.10, Ont. rule 16.04, PEI rule 10.10, and Sask. rule 23.

An order for substituted service is obtained by applying to the court "*ex parte*" (that is, without notice). What facts do you think the plaintiff will have to set forth in his supporting affidavit?

3. Common modes of substituted service include by mail addressed to the defendant at his or her last known address; by leaving the writ with a person who is shown to

be in communication with the defendant or likely to be in communication—for example, the spouse or other relative of the defendant or a solicitor known to have represented the defendant in other matters; by leaving the writ at the defendant's last known address; or by advertisement in a newspaper circulating in the area where the defendant is believed to be living.

4. In motor vehicle litigation, because of insurance, the named defendant is not often the "real" defendant. The defendant's insurer will be entitled and required by the policy to take charge of defending the action and to pay any judgment. In cases where the named defendant cannot be found, and an application for substituted service is made, the court must, in effect, decide whether the injured plaintiff or the insurer should bear the risk of the defendant's disappearance. If the insurer has notice of the claim, why should the court require that the named defendant be served? Is it fair to force the insurer to defend without the assistance of the defendant? Would the defendant be prejudiced in any way? Consider the solution adopted by Cory J in *Meius v. Pippy* (1980), 20 CPC 215 (Ont. HC), a decision followed and approved in *Kalser et al. v. Brine* (1981), 126 DLR (3d) 190, aff'd. 133 DLR (3d) 512 (Ont. Div. Ct.):

> In this case the plaintiff has taken every reasonable step to locate the defendant, Pippy. When the sheriff was unable to effect service at the last noted addresses of Patricia Pippy, a special investigator was retained. The special investigator, by his report, indicated that Patricia Pippy was no longer within the jurisdiction and could not be located. An application was then made for the substitutional service upon the insurer.
>
> On behalf of the insurer it has been argued firstly, that there is no indication that the insurer was able to conduct its investigation at least to the extent of conferring with its insured, the defendant Pippy. Secondly, it was pointed out that in light of the difficulty the insurer would have in producing Pippy for discovery that substitutional service ought not to be permitted.
>
> The material indicates that the insurer was sufficiently satisfied with its investigations to confirm in writing on two occasions that its "investigations" had reached such a stage that it was able to deny liability on behalf of its insured Pippy.
>
> In light of the correspondence from the insurer, there is no prejudice at least at this stage in permitting the substitutional service. Further, I am satisfied that the plaintiff has taken all requisite steps and proceeded with all due diligence both with regard to the action itself and with regard to the attempts to locate the defendant Pippy. Substitutional service therefore should be permitted upon the defendant. I would ordinarily have been more concerned with the problems that would arise and beset the insurer in attempting to produce the missing Patricia Pippy for discovery. However, that problem has been resolved by the undertaking of counsel which is confirmed by this order that the plaintiff will not move to strike out the defence of the defendant Pippy if the insurer is unable to produce Patricia Pippy for discovery.
>
> The application will therefore be granted. Costs in the cause.

C. Time for Service and Extensions

Once the originating process is issued, the rules of civil procedure provide a fixed period of time within which it must be served on the defendant. You will recall that limitation periods are satisfied by the act of issuing the originating process—an act that is not designed to come to the attention of the defendant. However, the ultimate purpose of limitation periods is timely notice to the defendant that he is being sued; this is not met by the mere issuing of the originating process, but by service on the defendant. Hence, in a very real sense, the time limit for service by the rules forms part and parcel of the overall scheme of the limitation periods. Note that the court has no general power to relieve against limitation periods—that is, if the plaintiff fails to commence the action within the limitation period by issuing the originating process, the court is generally powerless to protect the plaintiff from the bar of the limitation period. But what if the plaintiff fails to *serve* the originating process within the time limit set by the rules and the relevant limitation period expires during that period of time?

The court has the power to extend the time for service, either through and application of the general power in the court to extend time limits under the rules (for example, Ontario rule 3.02), or pursuant to a specific power to "renew" the originating process (for example, BC rule 9). How should that power be exercised where the expiry of a limitation period has intervened? Consider the approach in the following case.

Buleychuk v. Danson
(1992), 8 OR (3d) 762 (Ont. Gen. Div.)

O'LEARY J:—The issue on this appeal is the test to be applied where a solicitor asks the court to extend time for service of a statement of claim that he has failed to serve within the six-month period provided for in rule 14.08(1) of the *Rules of Civil Procedure*, O. Reg. 560/84.

The master, who refused to extend the time for service and from whose decision this appeal is taken, seems to have reasoned as follows.

(1) Not only had the six-month period for service of the statement of claim expired, but the statutory two-year limitation period for commencing an action under the *Highway Traffic Act*, RSO 1990, c. H.8, had also long expired by the time the solicitor asked the court to extend time for service.

(2) The statutory limitation period having expired, the principles laid down by the Court of Appeal in *Deaville v. Boegeman* (1984), 48 OR (2d) 725, 14 DLR (4th) 81, and *Aliferis v. Parfenuik* (1985), 1 CPC (2d) 41, 9 OAC 215, come into play, those principles being:

(a) The expiry of a limitation period created by statute for the commencement of an action creates a presumption the defendant has been prejudiced through not having been served with the document that commenced the action.

(b) The plaintiff must rebut (and here he has failed to rebut) this presumption of prejudice to the defendant before the court will extend time for service of the statement of claim and, presumably but not so expressed by the master, "special circumstances" or "exceptional circumstances" must exist before it can be said such prejudice has been rebutted.

(3) In any event, an order extending time for service of the statement of claim should be refused because to adopt the words of Lacourcière JA in *Laurin v. Foldesi*

(1979), 23 OR (2d) 321, 96 DLR (3d) 503 (CA), this was "an unpardonable and inexcusable laxity" on the part of the plaintiffs' solicitor.

I agree with the learned master that *Deaville* and *Aliferis* appear to enunciate the principles he has outlined. I suggest, however, that based on their facts those two cases have little in common. In *Deaville* the Court of Appeal was dealing with the question as to when, following the expiry of a statutory limitation period, it is permissible to add a new plaintiff to an action that was commenced within the statutory limitation period. In *Aliferis* the Court of Appeal was dealing with the question as to when it is proper to renew a writ of summons issued within the statutory limitation period but not served within one year from the date it was issued as was required by the former Rules of Practice, RRO 1980, Reg. 540.

The court has no power (except to correct administrative error or avoid a fraud or like impropriety) to permit the commencement of an action that is barred by statute. It is not surprising then that the court allows a new plaintiff to be added beyond the statutory limitation period in only "special circumstances." That is the basis for the reasoning behind *Deaville*.

But once an action has been commenced within the period allowed by statute, as was the case in *Aliferis*, it is only a rule that requires service on the defendant within a specified period. As was stated by MacKay JA in *Brown v. Humble*, [1959] OR 586, 21 DLR (2d) 38 (CA), at p. 594 OR, p. 55 DLR:

> I am in agreement with the statement of McRuer CJHC in the *Robinson* case [*Robinson v. Cornwall*, [1951] OR 587, [1951] 4 DLR 161] … . At p. 597 he said
>
>> With the greatest respect, I do not think there is a strict analogy between a case where a writ has been issued within the time allowed by a statute of limitations but not served until after the time has expired and one where no action is brought against a party until after the period has run.

The words of Laskin JA in *Clairmonte v. Canadian Imperial Bank of Commerce*, [1970] 3 OR 97, 12 DLR (3d) 425 (CA), at p. 113 OR, p. 441 DLR, are to the like effect but more enlightening:

> I say, with respect, that where an action has been commenced within the proper limitation period, there can be no pretence that any right of a defendant to rely on a limitation period is prejudiced, because the course of the action is protracted … .
> Indeed, to speak of prejudice to the defendant on the basis of the expiry of a limitation period which would protect him only if the application to dismiss the action for want of prosecution succeeded, is to beg the very question that has to be decided; it is to use the results of success on the application as a ground for granting it.

It is evident then that the question before the court in *Aliferis* was quite different from that facing the court in *Deaville*. While Cory JA, speaking for the court in *Aliferis*, did say, "The disposition of this appeal is in accord with the most recent decision of this Court pertaining to extension of limitation periods: see *Deaville v. Boegeman* (1984), 48 OR (2d) 725," I suggest it is obvious that the ratio of the decision in *Aliferis* is that it is proper to renew a writ that has not been served when such renewal will not prejudice the defendant. Indeed Cory JA said as much at p. 43 CPC, pp. 216-17 OAC:

With all due respect to the Judge hearing the motion, we are of the opinion that he erred in concluding that the plaintiff had failed to satisfy the onus resting upon him to demonstrate that the defendant would not be prejudiced by an order renewing the writ. Here the facts are quite exceptional and make it clear that the defendant will not, in fact, be prejudiced by an extension of time.

So even if this application had been dealt with under the former Rules of Practice, time for service should have been extended, for counsel for the defendant admitted before me that, save for the loss of the six-month time limit for service fixed by rule 14.08(1), the defendant will not be prejudiced by late service of the statement of claim.

I respectfully disagree with the learned master that Lacourcière JA in *Laurin v. Foldesi*, supra, purported to enunciate an inflexible rule that a plaintiff will be denied an extension of time for service where his solicitor has been guilty of unpardonable and inexcusable laxity. Rather, Lacourcière JA said in *Laurin*, at p. 323 OR, p. 505 DLR:

> The basic consideration in these matters is whether the renewal *post diem* will advance the just resolution of the dispute, without prejudice or unfairness to the parties.

That then was the test for renewal or extension of time for service under the former *Rules of Practice* and, in my view, remains the test under the *Rules of Civil Procedure*, which came into force in 1985. That such is the test can be established by the mere recitation of rules 1.04(1), 2.01(1) and 3.02(1) and (2):

> 1.04(1) These rules shall be liberally construed to secure the just, most expeditious and least expensive determination of every civil proceeding on its merits.
>
> 2.01(1) A failure to comply with these rules is an irregularity and does not render a proceeding or a step, document or order in a proceeding a nullity, and the court,
>
>   (a) may grant all necessary amendments or other relief, on such terms as are just, to secure the just determination of the real matters in dispute; or ...
>
> 3.02(1) Subject to subrule (3), the court may by order extend or abridge any time prescribed by these rules or an order, on such terms as are just.
>
> (2) A motion for an order extending time may be made before or after the expiration of the time prescribed.

The court must then examine the facts in each case to determine whether time for service of the statement of claim can be extended and the terms on which such time can be extended in an effort to secure a just determination of the real matters in dispute.

The task of the court is easy and time for service should be extended where the defendant frankly admits, or it is in any event obvious, that extending time for service will cause the defendant no prejudice. Such is the case here.

This action arises out of a motor vehicle accident that occurred on January 30, 1987. The police accident report indicates that the defendant, who had been travelling westbound on Highway 26, lost control of his vehicle, crossed the centre line and came into collision with the plaintiffs' motor vehicle which had been travelling eastbound. It appears the defendant was completely responsible for the accident.

The plaintiffs retained a solicitor on February 6, 1987. On February 9, 1987 that solicitor sent a letter to the defendant, which reads as follows:

RE: *BULEYCHUK & DANSON*—AUTO ACCIDENT

We have been retained on behalf of Mr. & Mrs. Walter Buleychuk in connection with injuries and damages sustained by them in a motor vehicle accident which occurred on or about the 30th day of January, 1987.

Please accept this correspondence as notice of an intention on the part of Mr. & Mrs. Buleychuk to claim prejudgment interest in connection with damages arising out of this accident.

We understand that the adjuster will be in touch with us in due course.

The solicitor sent a copy of this letter to the Advocate Insurance Company, the defendant's insurer. On February 2, 1987, Advocate Insurance appointed A.W. Masterton to be its adjuster in the matter and he became aware on that date of the particulars surrounding the accident. Mr. Masterton had a telephone conversation with the plaintiff, Walter Buleychuk, on February 17, 1987. In October 1987 Masterton had a further telephone conversation with Walter Buleychuk at which time he obtained from Walter Buleychuk the name of his solicitor. Masterton could also have obtained that information from Advocate Insurance.

On January 29, 1988 Masterton telephoned the office of the plaintiffs' solicitor and left a message for him to contact Masterton with respect to the plaintiffs' claims. On February 11, 1988 the plaintiffs' solicitor's secretary telephoned Masterton's secretary and advised that medical reports on the plaintiffs' injuries would be forthcoming.

On April 12, 1988 Masterton wrote to the plaintiffs' solicitor as follows:

> Re: Your Client: Buleychuk
> Our Insureds: Isobel & Barnett Danson
> Date of Loss: January 30, 1987

In February 1988 we contacted your office in an effort to learn the status of your client's claim. We were told you were awaiting medical reports.

Have you now received any medical reports on Mr. Buleychuk's condition? If so, we would be pleased to pay for the acquisition costs of those reports. If none have been obtained then perhaps now would be the appropriate time to have examinations done. Again, our principals would be willing to reimburse those costs.

It is my understanding that Mr. Buleychuk is back at work but we have no idea at this time as to the extent of the special damage claim and I would be grateful for an opportunity to discuss that portion of his claim so our principals can have an opportunity to reserve their funds accordingly.

In spite of further letters and telephone calls made during the following months to the office of the plaintiffs' solicitor, Masterton received no information about the plaintiffs' injuries. Finally, in January 1989, Masterton spoke to the plaintiffs' solicitor who advised him that he would send him medical reports with respect to the claims of both plaintiffs. The solicitor advised Masterton at that time that a statement of claim had been issued. On April 17, 1989 Masterton wrote to the solicitor again asking for medicals, details of the special damages and a copy of the statement of claim. Those were not sent to him. Not having heard from the solicitor, Masterton closed his file on this claim on December 11, 1989.

As indicated, the accident occurred January 30, 1987. If the plaintiffs had waited two years before issuing their statement of claim and then had waited a further six months before serving it, the defendant and his insurer might not have learned until approximately the end of July 1989 that he was being sued as a result of the accident. In fact the defendant, and perhaps more importantly his insurer, knew within a few days of the accident that the plaintiffs were claiming damages for their injuries.

The neglect and incompetence of the solicitor for the plaintiff is obvious and little is to be gained by dwelling on it. The fact is, however, it did not prejudice the defendant, that is to say, the evidence does not suggest that the defendant is less able because of it to defend in regard to liability or damages.

The statement of claim was issued December 20, 1988 and so should have been served by June 20, 1989. The solicitor's affidavit in support of his motion to extend the time for service of the statement of claim was sworn on May 10, 1990, although the evidence before me does not disclose just when the notice of motion was served. The fact that Advocate General Insurance Company, the defendant's insurer, went into receivership at some point has tended to delay this matter and the parties are in agreement that any delay since June 15, 1990, when the motion was first returnable, is not to be held against the plaintiffs.

Since the solicitor for the defendant admits that in fact the defendant has suffered no prejudice by the delay in serving the statement of claim and since the evidence in any event makes that obvious, the defendant should not have resisted the motion to extend time for service, unless he wanted some conditions attached to any order extending time for service. No such conditions have been asked for.

I, therefore, allow the appeal and extend time for service of the statement of claim for one month from this date. Costs both before me and before the master to the plaintiff in any event of the cause.

Appeal allowed.

NOTES AND QUESTIONS

1. Would the result have been different if the lawyer in *Danson* had failed to issue a statement of claim at all? Why?

2. What would have happened if the time for service had not been extended? Would the client have a good cause of action in negligence against the lawyer? To what extent do you think that factor played a role in the decision of the judge to extend service?

3. Was the cost order here appropriate? See Ontario rule 57.07.

IV. TERRITORIAL LIMITS AND SERVICE OUT OF THE JURISDICTION

The traditional common law rule: service in the jurisdiction or consent. The traditional common law rule was that the jurisdiction of the courts was territorially limited and they could take jurisdiction over a civil case only where the defendant had been served with the originating process within the jurisdiction of the court—that is, an Ontario court would have jurisdiction only where the defendant had been served in

Ontario, or an Alberta court would have jurisdiction only where the defendant was served in Alberta. This was sometimes called jurisdiction "as of right."

In addition, the courts would have authority over the matter if the defendant consented. If the defendant had agreed by contract to litigate in the courts in which the plaintiff commenced the claim, or if the defendant appeared and defended the claim on its merits, the court would generally be regarded as having authority to decide the matter.

Under this traditional common law rule, if the defendant could not be served in the jurisdiction, had not agreed to suit in that forum, and would not submit to the court's authority, the plaintiff had no alternative but to go to a jurisdiction in which one of these requirements could be met (for example, where the defendant resided) and institute proceedings there.

Expanded rules for service outside the jurisdiction. The inconvenient common law rules based on service and consent have long been modified by rules that authorize service "*ex juris*"—that is, the service of process on a defendant outside the territory of the issuing court. This makes sense because in some situations the old requirements cannot be met but the forum is still the most suitable for the resolution of the dispute by reason of substantial connections to the matter. For example, if the events giving rise to the matter occurred there, access to evidence and witnesses might be facilitated by trial there. Moreover, in situations involving consumers, workers, and other plaintiffs who are unlikely to be able to travel to sue defendants in distant fora, it can seem unfair to require them to do so.

For example, in *Moran v. Pyle National (Canada) Ltd.*, [1975] 1 SCR 393, the Supreme Court of Canada considered a situation in which the widow of a man, who had been electrocuted in Saskatchewan when removing a spent light bulb that had been manufactured in Ontario by the defendant, commenced an action in Saskatchewan. The Supreme Court was asked to consider where the tort occurred and, consequently, whether the Saskatchewan court had jurisdiction to hear the matter. Mr. Justice Dickson held that, in determining where a tort has occurred for the purposes of establishing jurisdiction, "it is unnecessary, and unwise, to have resort to any arbitrary set of rules." Further, following the US tradition of emphasis on fairness to the defendant, he reasoned that "where a foreign defendant carelessly manufactures a product in a foreign jurisdiction which enters into the normal channels of trade and he knows or ought to know both that as a result of his carelessness a consumer may well be injured and it is reasonably foreseeable that the product would be used or consumed where the plaintiff used or consumed it, then the forum in which the plaintiff suffered damage is entitled to exercise judicial jurisdiction over that foreign defendant."

The "service out" (or "long arm" as they are called in the United States) rules, which permit defendants to be served outside the jurisdiction in which the proceeding has been commenced, vary from province to province. Initially the rules were relatively narrow but in Canada in the 1970s and 1980s, they were gradually extended to become more "pro-plaintiff." Today, in some provinces, the rules permit service *ex juris* in cases that have very little connection to the forum province. For example, under Ontario rules 17.02(h) and (o), defendants can be served without leave in cases in which the damage was suffered in Ontario regardless where the wrong was committed, or in which the defendant is simply a necessary party to a proceeding against another defendant served in Ontario; and under NS rule 10.07, a defendant can be served without leave anywhere in Canada or the United States, apparently in any type of case. Further, in regimes like that established by the Ontario rule, there is generally provision for plaintiffs to seek the leave of the court to serve out if their case does not fit into one of the categories of cases for service out without leave. See Ontario rule 17.03.

Despite its increasing prevalence, jurisdiction based on service out traditionally has been exercised with some degree of caution and the courts in some Canadian provinces still require plaintiffs to obtain leave to serve out on persuading the court that it is an appropriate forum for the resolution of the dispute. Even in places such as Ontario where the rules have been amended to permit service out without leave in certain established categories of cases, it has been held that this does not signal a change in the reservations courts have about assuming jurisdiction over cases against foreigners. (See *Frymer v. Brettschneider* (1994), 19 OR (3d) 60 (CA).)

One important practical problem in using service out rules to sue a foreign party is how to effect service in a foreign country. Rules about service differ substantially from country to country. For example, while anyone can serve an originating process under the Ontario rules, in some jurisdictions service must be effected by a state official. Whose rules as to the form of service apply? For many countries, this is answered by The Hague Convention on the Service Abroad of Judicial and Extrajudicial Documents in Civil or Commercial Matters, which establishes the regime for how service abroad is to be effected. In Ontario, rule 17.05 provides for the application of the convention, and sets out how service is to be effected in countries who have not acceded to the convention.

Service out and the enforcement of judgments. Even if jurisdiction is assumed over a foreign defendant the resulting judgment might not be enforceable in the places where the foreign defendant's assets are located. A judgment granted by a court, say, in Ontario is, of course, enforceable in Ontario, but if the defendant has no assets in Ontario, the plaintiff (now a judgment creditor) must take the Ontario judgment to a jurisdiction where the defendant's assets are located and bring an action on the judgment there.

Until very recently the rules about when a court would recognize and enforce the judgments of other courts were narrower than the jurisdiction asserted by the recognizing court itself under its own service out rules—that is, courts would generally recognize and enforce the judgments of courts only in cases in which the defendant had been served in the territory of the court or had submitted to the court's jurisdiction. There was no obligation, or requirement of "comity," to respect the jurisdiction of a court when it had been assumed over a defendant outside the court's territory (by service out) without the defendants' consent. These narrow enforcement rules helped to make the expanded service *ex juris* rules tolerable because defendants who were served out under the expanded rules and who had no assets in the jurisdiction could ignore the proceeding and the default judgment would not be enforceable in the place where their assets were located. Effectively, this gave plaintiffs the opportunity to choose a forum for the proceeding other than the defendants' home forum or one which the defendants had previously approved, and it gave defendants a veto over the plaintiffs' choice.

The Morguard revolution. This asymmetry in the rules for jurisdiction and for judgments continues to prevail between the majority of *independent sovereign states*. Courts will assume jurisdiction over foreigners in certain situations in which there are connections between the forum and the action but they are not prepared to recognize the jurisdiction of other courts that do so when asked to enforce the other courts' judgments. But is this an appropriate model for jurisdictional relations or comity between the courts of the provinces *within the Canadian federation*? The founders of the American, Australian and European unions thought not. Instead, they created special rules for the assumption of jurisdiction and the enforcement of judgments by the courts of the constituent parts of their unions. Article IV of the US constitution requires the courts of the states to give "full faith and credit" to the judgments of the courts of other states, as does the Australian constitution. Article 220 of the Rome Treaty, which was the basis for the Brussels Convention, provides for similarly generous rules for the recognition of judgments.

It was not, however, until 1990 that the Canadian courts addressed this question. Until this time it had been said that, for the purposes of jurisdictional relations, the superior courts of the Canadian provinces had treated one another as if they were the courts of different countries. The decision that hailed the advent of this new approach to jurisdiction and the recognition and enforcement of judgments was that of the Supreme Court of Canada in *Morguard Investments Ltd. v. De Savoye*, [1990] 3 SCR 1077. In that case, the court unanimously upheld the enforceability of an Alberta judgment for the shortfall from a mortgage of Alberta land on which a BC resident had defaulted despite the fact that the BC defendant had not been served in Alberta (the judgment was based on service out, in British Columbia) nor had he consented to adjudication of the matter there. Speaking for the court, La Forest J acknowledged that the facts of *Morguard* would not satisfy the common law rule of recognition because the defendant was outside the jurisdiction of the Alberta court at the time of the action and had never submitted to the jurisdiction. But La Forest J said that Canadian courts had in the past "made a serious error in transposing the rules developed for the enforcement of foreign judgments to the enforcement of judgments from sister-provinces" and he noted that the old rules for jurisdiction and judgments "seem ... to fly in the face of the obvious intention of the Constitution to create a single country." For the purpose of recognizing each other's judgments, the provinces should not be regarded as "foreign" jurisdictions—they were part of one nation; and that "various constitutional and sub-constitutional arrangements and practices make unnecessary a 'full faith and credit' clause. ... [T]he application of the underlying principles of comity and private international law must be adapted to the situations where they are applied, and that in a federation this implies a fuller and more generous acceptance of the judgments of the courts of other constituent units of the federation."

Despite the emphasis on the constitutional basis for expanding the bases for enforcing judgments from other provinces, Canadian courts were quick to extend this generous approach to the enforcement of truly foreign judgments. In doing so, they relied on the extensive discussion in *Morguard* of the importance to international trade of liberal rules for the recognition and enforcement of judgments. Observations of La Forest J like "modern states ... cannot live in splendid isolation" and "accommodating the flow of wealth, skills and people across state lines has now become imperative" supported the view that this new approach should be applied to all judgments, whether issued in other provinces or other countries.

The implications of the Morguard principles for jurisdiction. This expansive approach to the recognition of judgments is fair to defendants only if the courts exercise restraint in the assumption of jurisdiction over persons in other provinces and confine themselves to cases in which there was a "real and substantial connection" between the matter and the province in which the action was to be tried. In *Morguard*, La Forest J limited the obligation to enforce to such cases. Accordingly, our courts still retain the power to refuse to deny enforcement of a judgment where there was no real and substantial connection between the matter and the forum in which the judgment was issued.

Although the *Morguard* case was neither argued nor decided in constitutional terms, the subsequent decision of the Supreme Court of Canada in *Hunt v. T & N plc*, [1993] 4 SCR 289 held that the jurisdictional principles it enunciated were constitutional principles. Accordingly, the "real and substantial connection" test for the jurisdiction of the superior provincial courts supersedes the rules for judicial jurisdiction. This, however, has not had a significant impact on the approach courts have taken to jurisdictional challenges. When we take a closer look at the "real and substantial connection test" we find that possible examples of such connections are those contained in the categories of cases set out in the rules for service *ex juris*. Indeed, the Uniform Jurisdiction and Proceedings Transfer Act proposed by the Uniform Law Commissioners treats such categories as presumptively "real and substantial connections" for establishing jurisdiction.

Thus the question arises: if a court takes jurisdiction over a case that meets the requirements of the rules for service out but, on closer inspection, has no real and substantial connection to the forum, could the assumption of jurisdiction be challenged on constitutional grounds? It would seem that this is the clear implication of *Morguard* combined with *Hunt*—that is, if service out under the rules would lead to an assertion of jurisdiction where there is no "real and substantial connection" then it is unconstitutional for the court to proceed to assert jurisdiction over the defendant. However, with few exceptions, Canadian courts have been reluctant to find themselves constitutionally incapable of deciding a case. Instead they have preferred to exercise their broad discretion to stay proceedings pursuant to the doctrine of *forum non conveniens*. This is illustrated in the decision excerpted below from *SDI Simulation Group Inc. v. Chameleon Technologies Inc.*

Forum non conveniens—stays and injunctions. The broad authority to assume jurisdiction described above would give rise to overreaching if it were not for the fact that Canadian courts (including Quebec courts), like other common law courts, may exercise discretion to decline to hear a matter where there is a clearly more appropriate forum elsewhere. The law governing discretionary relief from jurisdiction is derived from the Scottish doctrine of *forum non conveniens* and it forms a potent remedy for defendants who wish to resist trial in the forum chosen by the plaintiff where that forum is unsuitable. In fact, the doctrine of *forum non conveniens* fulfils such a fundamental role in discouraging plaintiffs from commencing proceedings in inappropriate fora that it is an integral feature of the law of jurisdiction in common law countries. As Lord Goff explained in *Airbus Industrie GIE v. Patel*, [1998] 2 All ER 257:

> In the common law world ... (t)here is, so to speak, a jungle of separate, broadly based, jurisdictions all over the world ... . But the potential excesses of common law jurisdictions are generally curtailed by the adoption of the principle of forum non conveniens—a self-denying ordinance under which the court will stay (or dismiss)

proceedings in favour of another clearly more appropriate forum ... . The principle is directed against cases being brought in inappropriate jurisdictions and so tends to ensure that, as between common law jurisdictions, cases will only be brought in a jurisdiction which is appropriate for their resolution ... . It is however dependent on the voluntary adoption of the principle by the state in question; and ... if one state does not adopt the principle, the delicate balance which the universal adoption of the principle could achieve will to that extent break down.

Relying on this doctrine, defendants have two remedies. They may bring a motion in the proceeding commenced by the plaintiff to ask that court to *stay* its proceedings; or, they may apply to another court (one that has jurisdiction over the plaintiff and that is an appropriate forum for the action) for an order injoining the plaintiff from continuing the proceeding. Although an "anti-suit injunction" is binding only on the plaintiff in the foreign action, it has the potential to pre-empt the decision of a foreign court regarding its own jurisdiction. This raises sensitive issues of comity and so injunctions are treated with considerable caution. To maintain the "delicate balance" described by Lord Goff, the leading common law courts, including the Supreme Court of Canada in its judgment in *Amchem v. British Columbia Worker's Compensation Board*, [1993] 1 SCR 897, have demonstrated an interest in aligning their principles with those guiding judicial discretion in other countries.

The following excerpt from the decision in *SDI Simulation Group Inc. v. Chameleon Technologies Inc.* provides a good illustration of the approach Canadian courts take to the properly restrained exercise of jurisdiction and the discretion to grant a stay in cases in which there is a clearly more appropriate forum elsewhere. This judgment is particularly instructive because it shows that in cases involving connections to other jurisdictions, even where the plaintiff has been able to serve the defendant in Ontario, the court will not hesitate to stay the matter if there is a clearly more appropriate forum elsewhere. Notice how the court chastises the plaintiff by awarding solicitor-and-client costs against it in part for "the opportunistic selection of an entirely inappropriate forum in which to litigate this dispute." Notice also that by readily invoking its discretion to stay the proceeding the court has no need to address the constitutionality of the assumption of jurisdiction over the matter.

SDI Simulation Group Inc. v. Chameleon Technologies Inc.
(1994), 34 CPC (3d) 346 (Ont. Gen. Div.)

[This action was to collect a debt that had arisen in the United States. The debt, related to repairs performed on image generators for virtual reality amusement rides, was originally owed by the defendant Chameleon to Ball, but had been assigned by Ball to the plaintiff.]

BORINS J:—This is a motion by the plaintiff to continue until trial a *Mareva* injunction granted without notice to the defendant by Wein J on September 1, 1994, which, with the consent of the parties, on September 2, 1994 I extended to September 14, 1994. The plaintiff also seeks leave to add Simulation Devices Inc. as a plaintiff. By way of cross-motion the defendant seeks an order to stay the action on the basis that Ontario is not a convenient forum, it being the defendant's position that either the state of Virginia or the state of California is clearly a more appropriate forum.

I heard argument on the defendant's cross-motion only. Of necessity, the submissions of counsel included the history of the relationship between the parties, which is relevant to both the forum non-conveniens issue and the *Mareva* injunction issue. When I heard the plaintiff's motion on September 2, 1994 to continue the order of Wein J the defendant had not had an opportunity to provide responding evidence. It has now had this opportunity. As well, the plaintiff has provided further evidence. As a result, I have a far different picture of the relationship between the parties now than I had on September 2, 1994. At the conclusion of the argument I granted an order staying the action and vacating the interim injunctive relief granted by Wein J and myself and advised counsel that I would provide reasons for my decision at a later date.

This is an action to collect a debt which arose in the United States of America ... . The debt has its origin in a contract entered into on May 26, 1992 between Chameleon and Ball Systems Engineering ("Ball") which provided for the supply by Ball to Chameleon of image generators and technical support for a period of five years. Chameleon manufactures "virtual reality" amusement park rides and purchased from Ball, as well as other manufacturers, image generators which constitute a vital component of the ride. In 1993 Chameleon purchased a 944 image generator from Ball which it incorporated into one of its rides which, from January to May, 1994, was located in Daytona Beach, Florida. Because Chameleon was experiencing problems with the 944 image generator, Ball sent a number of technicians to Daytona Beach between February 1, 1994 and April 1, 1994 to deal with the problems. The cost of these services was allegedly $615,319 US. ...

It is unnecessary to describe in detail the disputes which exist between the parties. However, in resolving these disputes it will be necessary for the court to interpret the agreement of May 26, 1992 which Chameleon entered into in Virginia and which Ball entered into in California and which contains the provision that it is to be interpreted pursuant to the law of Virginia. As well, it will be necessary to interpret the May 1, 1994 contract between SDI and Ball which was entered into in the United States. The disputed debt and disputed invoice relate to factual circumstances which occurred in Daytona Beach, Florida and San Diego, California where work was performed on the 944 image generator. SDI is a Delaware company. Its operational facilities and all of its employees are in San Diego. It has an executive office but no paid employees in Toronto. Chameleon is also a Delaware company with its head office in Alexandria, Virginia and an engineering and manufacturing facility in Ivyland, Pennsylvania. Chameleon brings its "virtual reality" rides to fairs and exhibitions in the United States, and occasionally, in Canada. Communications between the parties with respect to their disputes flowed exclusively between the plaintiff's employees in San Diego and the defendant's employees in Alexandria, until the intervention of the plaintiff's Toronto solicitors on or about August 24, 1994. None of the witnesses essential to the resolution of the issues raised by this case are in Ontario. They are all in the United States in Virginia, California and Florida and possibly elsewhere.

How did it come about that the plaintiff commenced this action in Ontario? It somehow came to the plaintiff's attention that the defendant was operating two "virtual reality" rides at the Canadian National Exhibition ("CNE") which was to close on September 5, 1994. It was believed that one of the rides contained a Ball 944 image generator. Whether or not it was the one which had been repaired in Daytona Beach is not clear. The plaintiff's Toronto solicitors wrote to Chameleon threatening to obtain a court order to seize the rides on the basis of an alleged security interest in any Ball components contained in the rides if the amount of $353,785 US was not paid. The plaintiff's alleged security interest—and hence its alleged possessory interest in the rides—emanates, it is submitted, from the May 1, 1994 contract between it and Ball which was terminated on September 7, 1994 as well as the contract between Ball and Chameleon. When it came to the plaintiff's attention that Chameleon had removed one of its rides from the CNE and was transporting it to the United States and that it appeared to be about to remove the second ride the plaintiff appeared without notice to the defendant before Wein J in the late afternoon of September 1, 1994. I am satisfied on the evidence that the defendant had removed the first ride, which contained the Ball image generator, to fulfill a contract signed several weeks ago which required the defendant to have it in Charlotte, North Carolina by September 9, 1994. I am also satisfied that it had no intention of removing the second ride on September 1. In fact, it moved this ride to a fair in London, Ontario when the CNE closed. This ride was to remain there until September 18, 1994 when the fair closed. During the evening of September 1, 1994 representatives of the defendant were served at the CNE with the plaintiff's notice of action, notice of motion and the order of Wein J. Thus, the defendant was served in Ontario.

The law with respect to forum non-conveniens has been the subject of a number of recent cases ... . In my view, on the basis of these authorities the test is not one of convenience, but one of "a more appropriate jurisdiction based on the relevant factors in which to litigate the plaintiff's claim." In the *Gordon Capital* case Ground J identified the following as the factors to be considered in determining the appropriate forum and, in the case of two appropriate forums, which is the more appropriate:

(a) the location where the contract in dispute was signed;
(b) the applicable law of the contract;
(c) the location in which the majority of witnesses reside;
(d) the location of key witnesses;
(e) the location where the bulk of the evidence will come from;
(f) the jurisdiction in which the factual matters arose; and
(g) the residence or place of business of the parties.

Applying these factors, and on the basis of the facts which I have reviewed, this case has absolutely no connection with Ontario. In my view, the only reason that it was brought in Ontario was the fact that the defendant happened to have two of its rides at the CNE. It does not otherwise do business in Ontario and has no permanent assets there. I will say more about this subsequently. Clearly there is a more appropriate jurisdiction in which to litigate this dispute. The relevant factors point overwhelmingly to at least two more appropriate jurisdictions in the United States and, possibly, a third—Virginia, California and Florida. In my view, it is unnecessary for the court to identify the most appropriate foreign jurisdiction in order to grant a stay of an Ontario action. The court need only determine that clearly a more appropriate forum exists in order to reach the conclusion that Ontario should decline jurisdiction. In summary, it is my view that this is a case which contains very complex issues which will require the application of United States law to resolve and which have no factual connection to this jurisdiction. The essence of this case is a dispute between two American companies in regard to products manufactured in the United States and repairs made to them in the United States pursuant to contracts entered into in the United States and involving negotiations between representatives of the companies in the United States. The only possible connection with Ontario is that the alleged assignee of the debt, Simulation Devices Inc., is an Ontario company.

I appreciate that SDI takes the position that it has a security and possessory interest in the property of Chameleon under s. 62 of the *Personal Property Security Act*, RSO 1990, c. P.10 and s. 14 of the *Repair and Storage Liens Act*, RSO 1990, c. R.25. I also appreciate that I did not call on the parties to argue the *Mareva* injunction issue although, as I have said, many of the points relative to this issue were argued in the context of the forum non-conveniens issue. However, it is my opinion that the evidence and the law in respect to the plaintiff's alleged security and possessory interests in the defendant's property is so vague and speculative that had I been required to consider the *Mareva* injunction issue it would have been my view that the plaintiff had failed to establish a prima facie case in respect to these interests. As well, I have serious doubt that the plaintiff made full and fair disclosure to Wein J and to me. Indeed, it is my view that this case raises the concern expressed by Estey J in *Aetna Financial Services v. Feigelman*, [1985] 1 SCR 2, at 37 where he said that a plaintiff cannot use a *Mareva* injunction to "tie up the assets of the defendant, nor for the purpose of their preservation until judgment, but to force, by litigious blackmail, a settlement on a defendant who, for any one of many reasons, cannot afford to await the ultimate vindication after trial."

The remaining issue to be resolved is the costs of this motion, including the costs of the appearance before me on September 2, 1994. There is no dispute that the defendant is entitled to its costs. However, counsel for the plaintiff disputes the submission of the defendant's counsel that this is an appropriate motion in which to order that costs be awarded on a solicitor-and-client scale. In *Mortimer v. Cameron* (1994), 17 OR (3d) 1, at 23, the Court of Appeal recently confirmed the principle that "it is only in the rare and exceptional case that costs are awarded on a solicitor-and-client scale rather than on a party-and-party scale." Robins JA on behalf of the Court of Appeal quoted with approval the following passage from Orkin, *The Law of Costs*, 2d ed. (1993), at pages 2-91 to 2-92:

> Costs on the solicitor-and-client scale should not be awarded unless special grounds exist to justify a departure from the usual scale.
>
> Such orders are not to be made by way of damages, or on the view that the award of damages should reach the plaintiff intact, and are inappropriate where there has been no wrongdoing.
>
> An award of costs on the solicitor-and-client scale, it has been said, is ordered only in rare and exceptional cases to mark the court's disapproval of the conduct of a party in the litigation. The principle guiding the decision to award solicitor-and-client costs has been enunciated thus:

> [S]olicitor-and-client costs should not be awarded unless there is some
> form of reprehensible conduct, either in the circumstances giving rise to
> the cause of action, or in the proceedings, which makes such costs
> desirable as a form of chastisement.

On the basis of the principles contained in the *Mortimer* case I am satisfied that this is an appropriate motion in which to award costs on a solicitor-and-client scale. In my view, what has occurred in this case deserves the chastisement of the court. There are three factors which lead me to this conclusion. First, there is the opportunistic selection of an entirely inappropriate forum in which to litigate this dispute. Second, there is the attempt to use the *Mareva* injunction for the inappropriate purposes which received the disapproval of Estey J in the *Fiegelman* case. Third, there is the plaintiff's failure to make full and fair disclosure before Wein J and me. As a result, the defendant was put to considerable expense in responding to the plaintiff's motion.

In the result, there will be an order staying the plaintiff's action and vacating the interim injunctive relief granted by Wein J and myself. The plaintiff's motion to add Simulation Devices Inc. is allowed but its action, of course, is also stayed. The defendant will have its costs fixed at $6,000 plus GST payable forthwith.

NOTES AND QUESTIONS

1. The court referred to "the opportunistic selection of an entirely inappropriate forum in which to litigate this dispute." In *SDI*, the plaintiff's tactics seem, in part, to have been motivated by a desire to tie up the defendant's assets locally through the Mareva injunction, but the case raises more general questions and practices. When a plaintiff retains a lawyer in jurisdiction X to advise on litigating a claim, often the lawyer will have to advise on (or should be thinking about) *where* the action should be brought. If there are interprovincial or international aspects to the case a lawyer should not assume that jurisdiction X is where the action should be brought. Generally speaking, unless the action is commenced in jurisdiction X, the lawyer will have to refer the matter and the client to a law firm in another jurisdiction where the action is to be commenced, and the fees generated by the litigation will go to the new law firm, not to the lawyer in jurisdiction X. In this sense the lawyer in jurisdiction X has a conflict of interest with the client. Much of the case law suggests that this conflict is not well handled or that, when retained, local lawyers do not think carefully enough about whether some other jurisdiction is really the more appropriate forum for the litigation.

2. As we will see in chapter 7, "The Size and Scope of Litigation, in order to avoid a multiplicity of litigation and *the risk of inconsistent determinations*, there are broad rules permitting the joinder of multiple defendants in one lawsuit. Also, there are further broad rules permitting a defendant to bring into the plaintiff's action other persons as "third parties" in order to have them bound by the decision in the main action or obtain recovery over against the third party in respect of claims being made against the defendant by the plaintiff. Typically, there are also extremely broad service-out-of-the-jurisdiction rules with regard to such added defendants or third parties: see, for example, Ontario rule 17.02(o) (necessary and proper parties) and (q) (third parties).

Consider the case of *Jannock Corp. Limited v. R.T. Tamblyn and Partners Limited* (1975), 8 OR (2d) 622 (CA). The plaintiff brought an action for damages in Ontario against the defendant Tamblyn, an Ontario company, alleging defects in a system for storing and refrigerating fish that Tamblyn had designed for the plaintiff. The system, after it was designed by Tamblyn, was manufactured by Vickers, a Quebec company, and then installed in a ship that was built for the plaintiff in British Columbia by Yarrows, a company incorporated in that province. The ship-building agreement between the plaintiff and Yarrows provided that the laws of British Columbia should govern and that the courts of the province should have jurisdiction. In its defence, Tamblyn alleged that the plaintiff's loss was caused by the fault or negligence of the manufacturer Vickers and the ship-builder Yarrows. The plaintiff then amended its statement of claim to name Vickers and Yarrows as defendants and made comparable allegations (to those which Tamblyn made) against Vickers and Yarrows. The plaintiff then served Yarrows out of the jurisdiction. Yarrows unsuccessfully moved to set aside service out of the jurisdiction. The court concluded that the clause in the contract did not confer exclusive jurisdiction on the BC court. Moreover, the court was concerned about the possibility of a multiplicity of actions with inconsistent determinations and concluded that Yarrows was a necessary and proper party and on that ground could be served outside of the jurisdiction:

> Tamblyn, of course, had the right to defend by asserting that Yarrows had caused plaintiff's loss and to prove it at the trial of the action in Ontario. If Tamblyn succeeds in its defence that Yarrows was at fault and Yarrows is not a party, while the finding is binding [as between] the appellant [Jannock] and Tamblyn, it is of no moment for the appellant must sue Yarrows in British Columbia where Yarrows may well successfully defend by heaping the blame on Tamblyn.
>
> The result is the possibility of two trials with different results, both finding that the plaintiff suffered loss by reason of the faulty brine tanks but without final judgment against the wrongdoer. To me this is an important reason why the defendants would be joined if all were in Ontario and it is an important consideration as to whether one can conclude that the defendant Yarrows is a necessary and proper party in an action against Tamblyn under [rule 17.02(o)]. In cases such as this where persons, whose work and skill are combined to fashion a unit for a purchaser, defend its suit by seeking to blame each other when the plaintiff seeks to allege fault on the part of each or all of them, each and all of them are necessary and proper parties.

How would *Jannock* be decided subsequent to *Morguard*?

3. *A new approach to choice of law.* Given that a plaintiff may resort to the rules for service out of the jurisdiction, or may go and sue in a jurisdiction where the defendant can be served locally, the plaintiff is often presented with a choice of fora in which to sue. This may give rise to what is often referred to as "forum shopping"—that is, in deciding where to sue, the plaintiff may seek out a forum that is not only convenient for the plaintiff, but one that will apply substantive law favourable to the plaintiff.

Although courts assume jurisdiction over matters involving foreign defendants and claims arising in foreign countries, this does not necessarily mean that they will apply their own law to resolve the dispute. For example, a BC court might hear an action for breach of contract that occurred in Saskatchewan but apply Saskatchewan law to decide the case. If one of the parties argues that the connections between the case and a foreign country (or another province) warrant the application of the law of that country to the dispute, the court will engage in what is known in the conflict of laws as "choice of law" analysis to decide which law will govern the dispute.

The *Morguard* decision marked the beginning of a revolution, not only in the approach taken in Canadian law to the relations between the courts of different provinces in the rules for assuming jurisdiction and enforcing judgments, but also in the rules for choice of law. In *Tolofson v. Jensen*, [1994] 3 SCR 1022, the Supreme Court held that the territoriality principle should be respected through the application of the law of the place where the wrong occurred and that exceptions to this rule should be carefully defined.

In *Tolofson*, the plaintiff in an automobile accident case sued in British Columbia, the province in which he resided, rather than in Saskatchewan, the province in which he was injured, because he hoped to avoid the application of the shorter limitation period in Saskatchewan. Even if the court decided to apply the law of Saskatchewan, he hoped that the court would apply the BC limitation period. This litigation strategy relied both on the well-established rule that courts always apply their own rules on procedural issues, even where a foreign law governs the substance of the rights and obligations of the parties, and on an old common law rule that statutes of limitation were classified as procedural and not substantive in nature. Accordingly, even if a BC court determined that it should apply the law of Saskatchewan, it was likely to apply the BC limitation period. The routine application of local limitation periods, coupled with choice of law rules that could lead courts to apply their own tort law rather than the law of the place where the accident occurred, led to a great deal of "forum shopping" in personal injury cases in Canada.

When *Tolofson* reached the Supreme Court of Canada, La Forest J held that these rules were out of place in the modern context and that courts had to apply the law of the place where the tort occurred, including its limitation period—that is, limitation periods were no longer to be characterized as procedural for choice of law purposes, but as substantive law. He reasoned that "to permit the court of the forum to impose its views over those of the legislature endowed with power to determine the consequences of wrongs that take place within its jurisdiction would invite the forum shopping that is to be avoided if we are to attain the consistency of result an effective system of conflict of laws should seek to foster." Accordingly, our courts will continue to apply the local rules of procedure that are essential to the efficient adjudication of the matter but limitation periods will no longer be regarded as fitting in that category.

V. RESPONDING TO ORIGINATING PROCESS

A. Delivery of Pleadings

The rules of civil procedure for each province set out not only the time within which the originating process must be served, subject to the power to renew or extend (as the case may be), but also the time periods for the delivery of the required response to the originating process.

The nature of the required response will depend on the rules of the particular jurisdiction. If the originating process is a statement of claim, then the defendant will be required to "deliver"—that is, serve on the plaintiff and file with the court—a statement of defence within the specified time. Where the originating process is a writ of summons, the defendant is required to file an "appearance"—a document signifying an intention to defend and indicating which law firm, if any, is representing him or her. Where a writ of summons is in use, the defendant's obligation to deliver a statement of defence does not arise until he or she is served with the plaintiff's statement of claim.

The time for response following service of the originating process varies considerably. In Ontario, the time for delivery of the statement of defence under rule 18 varies from 20 to 60 days, depending on where the defendant is served, and the defendant may gain a further 10 days to respond by filing a 1-page notice of intention to defend. In British Columbia, where a writ is the originating process, the time for appearance is only 7 days, and the defence must be delivered within 14 days after the delivery of the statement of claim, regardless of where the defendant is served. What is a reasonable amount of time for the rules to allow for a defendant served to review and understand what is required by the originating process, retain a lawyer, brief the lawyer adequately, and allow the lawyer sufficient time to advise and draft the appropriate response? The answer is probably that there is no single standard, as the time reasonably required will depend on such factors as the sophistication of the client, where the client is served, the complexity of the action, and the extent to which the client is aware of the claim and already prepared to meet it. Do the rules really matter, having regard to the power of the court to extend time limit, and the general professional practice between lawyers (supported by the rules of professional conduct) of granting reasonable extensions of time? This question should be borne in mind when considering the potential consequences of failing to respond in a timely manner, considered below.

B. Alternative Responses and Raising Defects

Although the procedural model assumes that the defendant will respond substantively to the claim via the filing of a statement of defence, that is not the only possibility. First, the defendant may decide not to respond to the lawsuit. In what circumstances might this be the best course of action for the defendant?

Second, the defendant may wish to raise a substantive or procedural defect in the originating process, or its service, at an early stage. If the defendant wishes to raise some form of non-compliance with the rules, there may be a specific provision in the applicable rule as to how the non-compliance is to be raised, or the defendant may have recourse to the general provisions in the rules relating to raising matters that are not in compliance with the rules. For examples of the former, see Ontario rule 17.06 and BC rule 13(10) (application to set aside service out of the jurisdiction). For the general power to deal with non-compliance, see rule 2 in both Ontario and BC.

Consider Ontario rule 2.02 or BC rule 2(4), which requires that any attack on a step for failure to comply with the rules must be made within a reasonable time and before "any further step" is taken by the party in the proceeding. Failure to do so will be considered a waiver of the procedural defect.

With respect to service out of the jurisdiction, not only does Ontario rule 17.06 require that any motion to challenge service under the rules be brought before the delivery of the statement of defence, it has been held that delivering a defence waives any ability of the foreign defendant to raise an objection to the territorial jurisdiction of the court: *Gourmet Resources International Inc. v. Paramount Capital Corporation* (1991), 5 CPC (3d) 140.

Ordinarily, substantive matters that the defendant may wish to use to defeat the lawsuit are pleaded in the statement of defence and adjudicated at the trial of the proceeding; however, the rules enable some of them to be raised before the filing of a statement of defence. In Ontario, rule 21 enables a court, at any time, to determine a question of law raised by the pleadings whether the court has subject matter jurisdiction over the action; whether the plaintiff has the capacity to sue; whether the action should be stayed because there is another proceeding pending; and whether the action is frivolous, vexatious, or an abuse of process. While this rule, unlike rule 17.06, does not require that the objection be raised before the filing of the statement of defence, the grounds set out in the rule are those that are typically raised at the earliest possible moment, and are often raised by a defendant before delivering a statement of defence. Note the requirement in rule 21 that any such objections are to be raised promptly. Is there any reason why the defendant would not want to raise such a defect at the earliest possible moment? Rule 21 in relation to pleadings will be considered in more detail in chapter 6, "Pleadings and Disposition Without Trial."

C. Failure To Respond: Default Proceedings

If the defendant fails to respond to the originating process within the time required, the plaintiff may use provisions in the rules—default proceedings—that allow the plaintiff to proceed to judgment. Note that in most jurisidctions, the defendant has the right to respond notwithstanding the expiry of the time for response, unless the plaintiff has taken steps toward default judgment that have the effect, under the rules, of preventing the defendant from filing a response.

Recall the warning to the defendant on the form of the originating process, which states in emphatic terms that if the defendant fails to respond in the time limited, judgment may be given without further notice to the defendant. While notice of proceedings to the defendant is a fundamental aspect of the procedural system and the basis of the requirement of personal service, once that notice is given and the defendant does not respond, there is no requirement that further notice be given to the defendant. Accordingly, the rules make specific provision that if a defendant properly served does not respond to the originating process as required, the defendant is generally not entitled to further notice of steps in the proceedings.

The precise path available to a plaintiff where the defendant does not respond is defined in the specific rules dealing with default proceedings (that is, Ontario rule 19 or BC rules 17 and 25). While the precise terminology may vary from province to province, the essential elements follow:

1. The time for response has expired.

2. The plaintiff files proof of service with the court, with a request that causes the court to cut off the ability of the defendant to file response. (In Ontario, this is known as requisitioning the Registrar to note the defendant in default.)

3. Where the default is in delivering a statement of defence, the rules deem the defendant to have admitted all allegations in the statement of claim.

4. The defendant is not entitled to notice of further steps in the action except in specified situations.

Following that, the manner in which the plaintiff proceeds to judgment following the defendant's default depends on the type of claim advanced. Consider the distinctions in the rules between, on the one hand, debts or liquidated claims and, on the other hand, other types of claims. There is a long judicial history considering when a claim is either a "debt or liquidated demand" or not, because this distinction was important for other reasons that predate the present rules. The definition generally accepted is as quoted by the Master in *J. Cooke (Concrete Blocks) Ltd. v. Campbell*, [1947] OWN 713:

> A claim is liquidated "whenever the amount to which the plaintiff is entitled (if he is entitled to anything) can be ascertained by calculation or fixed by any scale of charges or other positive data."

What is the difference in procedure between the granting of default judgment in the case of debts or liquidated demands and other situations? What is the justification for the difference in treatment?

The first notice that a defendant will have that a default judgment has been granted will ordinarily be when the plaintiff takes steps to have the judgment enforced against the defendant. The rules give the court the power to set aside a default judgment (and, in jurisdictions that treat the noting in default as a separate step, a noting in default). When should the court exercise its power to set aside a default judgment and allow a defendant who has not responded to the originating process the opportunity to defend the lawsuit? Do you agree with the judge's exercise of discretion in the following decision?

Lenskis v. Roncaioli
(1992), 11 CPC (3d) 99 (Ont. Gen. Div.)

MACDONALD J (orally): ... This motion was brought by the defendants, Ibi Roncaioli and Joseph Roncaioli for an order setting aside the noting of pleadings closed, and the default judgment signed against the defendants on Monday, February 10, 1992, pursuant to r. 19.09(1) of the *Rules of Civil Procedure*.

The motion record discloses that default judgment was signed by the Honourable Mr. Justice Webb. The judgment ordered the defendants, the moving party in this motion, to pay to the plaintiff Raisa Lenskis ("Lenskis"), the responding party in this motion, the sum of $44,399.48. The judgment further ordered that the defendants would pay to the plaintiff Sonia Grimman ("Grimman") the sum of $13,513.36, and costs as assessed by the court.

The essential grounds for the motion brought by the defendants is that they now allege that they have a good defence to the plaintiffs' claim. In support of their position, the defendant Mrs. Roncaioli has sworn an affidavit dated March 11, 1992 deposing to a number of facts and circumstances. She was cross-examined on this affidavit and I was referred on several occasions during argument to the transcript of her cross-examination.

Without going into the background in detail, the statement of claim as initially issued, seeks repayment of moneys alleged to be owed by the defendants to the plaintiffs. It is alleged that during the course of the relationship between the parties, substantial amounts of money were lent by the plaintiffs to the defendants. There are allegations of illicit activities made by the defendant Ibi Roncaioli in her affidavit wherein she states that prior to the issuing of the statement of claim, the plaintiff Lenskis owned a variety store and sold illegal contraband cigarettes through her business. She states that at no time did she borrow money from Lenskis, but that Lenskis gave her money to buy cigarettes for Lenskis, and that she did so without making a profit.

The defendant Ibi Roncaioli was charged in Provincial Court for defrauding the plaintiffs of moneys exceeding $1,000. At the preliminary hearing before the Honourable Mr. Justice Crossland, the defendant Ibi Roncaioli was discharged. In her affidavit, the defendant Ibi Roncaioli relies on this discharge in support of her position that in these civil proceedings she now has a defence to the plaintiffs' action. The defendant Ibi Roncaioli acknowledges that she executed documents purporting to settle her claims with the plaintiffs in the office of Mr. David Sloan, the solicitor of record for the plaintiffs.

In her affidavit filed in support of this motion, the defendant Mrs. Roncaioli attempts to put a different interpretation on the settlement documents and suggests that they were merely documents that she described as "settlement agenda containing figures in a format for payment." She also argues that she was under extreme duress by reason of the following circumstances:

1. She was unrepresented by counsel.

2. She did not want her husband to find out what was going on, as the plaintiffs were actively pressuring her and threatening to expose their illegal enterprises to him.

3. She was under heavy medication at the time, including morphine, as a result of pain and discomfort associated with a serious complication that developed from a broken ankle that had left her partially disabled.

4. She thought if she repaid the plaintiffs' losses she would be able to prevent further trouble.

After having made two settlement agreements, both of which she defaulted on, the plaintiffs appeared to have decided not to pursue the matter, but the defendant, Ibi Roncaioli, did not take any steps to dismiss the plaintiffs' claim.

Things changed significantly when the defendant, Ibi Roncaioli, won $5 million dollars in the Lotto 649. She now states that she is a very wealthy woman and alleges that the plaintiffs who took no steps in the interim to pursue the matter are now attempting "a fast grab." The plaintiffs' motion record is comprised of two affidavits. One is sworn May 5, 1992 by Suzie Larado, who alleges that she is a former friend of the defendants and that she was involved with the defendants on a direct basis in her dealings with the plaintiffs in late 1985 and 1986. She states that the moving party told her that she owed the money to Ms. Lenskis and that she was agreeable to paying the money back.

As a result of her feeling that she owed the money and agreeing to paying it back, the defendant, Ibi Roncaioli, attended at the offices of J. David Sloan, the plaintiffs' solicitor, in January 1986, and in the presence of the deponent of the affidavit that I have just identified, the negotiations were carried out directly between Mr. Sloan and Mrs. Roncaioli.

These negotiations resulted in a settlement. I find that there was a settlement, although this settlement was referred to in argument before me as a purported settlement, I see nothing on the face of the documents before me that would suggest that it was not in fact a settlement. The word "purported" was used only to indicate that while a settlement had been reached it was purported in that Mrs. Roncaioli did not meet the obligations for repayment which [was] contemplated in the settlement.

In *Dealers Supply (Agriculture) Ltd. v. Tweed Farm & Garden Supplies Ltd.* (1987), 22 CPC (2d) 257 (Ont. Dist. Ct.), the Honourable Mr. Justice Miesener sets out three requirements that a moving party must meet in order to have judgment against him or her set aside. The requirements are as follows [at 262–63]:

1. The motion to set aside a default judgment should be made as soon as possible after the applicant becomes aware of the judgment.

2. More importantly, the moving party's affidavit must set out circumstances under which the default arose that give a plausible explanation for the default.

3. The moving party must set forth facts to support the conclusion that there is at least an arguable case to present on its merits.

In addition, Miesener DCJ commented that there is still a broad obligation to look at all the circumstances and to be satisfied that no injustice is done to the innocent party, the respondent to the motion, in any order that is finally made. Miesener DCJ cited with approval the decision of Urquhart J in *Nelligan v. Lindsay*, [1945] OWN 295 (HC), and while it is an older case, it is still good authority for the principles that are to be followed in a motion of this sort.

In *Nelligan v. Lindsay*, supra, the delay was short, and it occurred by reason of a misunderstanding between the solicitors for the parties, with the result that the pleadings were noted closed. The delay was negligible and the court found that there could be no prejudice caused to the plaintiff who was capable of being compensated for in costs. In addition, and most importantly, the defendant set out in his motion material circumstances which could afford a defence. Urquhart J quoted from *Klein v. Schile*, [1921] 2 WWR 78, 14 Sask. LR 220, 59 DLR 102 (CA), at p. 221 [Sask. LR] as follows:

> It is not sufficient to merely state that the defendant has a good defence upon the merits. The affidavits must show the nature of the defence and set forth facts which will enable the Court or Judge to decide whether or not there was a matter which would afford a defence to the action.

Counsel for the moving party has drawn to my attention a recent decision of the Ontario Court of Appeal; *Earl v. Koloszar*, [1991] OJ 45, oral reasons released January 17, 1991 [(Doc. CA 506/89), Tarnopolsky, Finlayson and Galligan JJA]. Counsel on behalf of the moving party today, strenuously argued that the decision of the Court of Appeal in *Earl v. Koloszar* relaxes the tests and considerations which were set forth in

Nelligan v. Lindsay, supra. The Court of Appeal made the following comments with respect to the setting aside a default judgment [at 1-2, unreported]:

> While the decision whether or not to set aside a default judgment is a matter of discretion, the exercise of that discretion is reviewable by an appellant court. The principles to be applied in such cases have been set out in numerous decisions. It is not necessary to make any review of authority because the factors and principles can vary depending on the circumstances. However, among the factors which always have to be considered and which apply in this case are the following:
>
> 1. the delay between the default and the noting pleadings closed;
> 2. the delay on the part of the defendant between learning of the default judgment and moving to set it aside;
> 3. the reasons for the delay;
> 4. the prejudice, if any, which either or both of those delays caused the plaintiff;
> 5. whether or not there was a matter disclosed which could afford a defence to the motion.

I do not agree with counsel that the Court of Appeal decision relaxes the tests or in any way departs from the principles which emerge from *Dealers Supply v. Tweed Farm*, ... [(1987), 22 CPC (2d) 257 (Ont. Dist. Ct.)], and *Nelligan v. Lindsay*, supra.

In this case, I find Mrs. Roncaioli did move with relative speed and accordingly I do not find anything under this heading of the test which deprives her of her right to bring the motion. I do not find however that Mrs. Roncaioli has set out in her affidavit material, circumstances which are acceptable to this court that explain the reasons why the default arose. In addition, she has not set forth in the material filed, facts which support the conclusion that she would have an arguable case to present on the merits. In addition, I do not find anything that suggests to me that the moving party when she reached her settlement, was incapacitated and I am cognizant of the extensive medical material that was provided to me which suggests that this moving party had a history of medical problems. There is nothing in the material that convinces me that when she attended at Mr. Sloan's office, she was suffering in any way from any disability which made her unable to understand what she was attempting to do in achieving settlement.

On the material in this motion before me, I do not find facts that afford a valid defence. As I have indicated, I do not accept what appears to be some defence related to duress in respect of the settlement negotiations, nor do I find the fact that there was a discharge in the criminal proceedings ... one which I should take as being compelling or conclusive in my considerations with respect to this civil matter. ...

In view of the absence of a defence, or if the defendant has a valid defence, it is not adequately set out in the pleadings as mandated by the authorities. The motion to set aside the default judgment is dismissed accordingly.

Motion dismissed.

VI. COSTS IN A PROCEEDING

With this section we begin to talk specifically about how litigation is financed. There are two basic sets of costs that need to be addressed. The first is the costs to the client of paying his or her own lawyer. These costs are often referred to as "solicitor-and-client" costs and are briefly discussed in the first section. The second set of costs are those that may be payable by one party to another party in the litigation. These costs are often referred to as "party-and-party" costs and they are dealt with in detail in this section. For further details concerning the law of costs, see M. Orkin, *The Law of Costs*, 2d ed. (Aurora, ON: Canada Law Book, 1987).

A. The Private Funding of Litigation

1. Lawyer–Client Relationship

Subject to a number of broad limitations, the financial relationship between lawyer and client is a matter of agreement between them. However, for much civil litigation, no specific agreement is made as to what clients will pay their lawyer for acting for them. In such situations, an agreement that the legal services are to be paid for is simply implied from the fact that the client has requested these services to be performed and the lawyer has provided them. As to the amount of the lawyer's remuneration, the term implied is that it is to be the reasonable value of the services. Many jurisdictions' rules of professional conduct address the relationship; see, for example, Ontario *Rules of Professional Conduct*, rules 9 and 12.

In the following discussion of the financial relationship between lawyer and client, we will look first at the situation where there is no specific agreement as to the amount the lawyer will be paid and consider how disputes about what is a reasonable sum are resolved when the parties cannot agree. Next, we will examine the situation where the lawyer and the client agree to the lawyer's fee in advance and the permissible limits of such agreements. We will also look generally at the question of the contractual arrangement or "retainer" between lawyer and client. It should be noted that, while the following analysis relates specifically to the financial relationship between lawyer and client where the lawyer is acting for the client in litigation, much of what is said applies equally to all types of legal services that a lawyer may perform, such as representing a client on the purchase of a house, in drafting a will, or in seeking a licence to carry on a business.

2. The Retainer

When a solicitor is retained in a litigious matter, it is the normal practice for a lawyer to take written instructions; see Frederic T. Home, *Cordery's Law Relating to Solicitors*, 8th ed., 76 et seq. In essence, a retainer is a contract whereby in return for the client's offer to employ the solicitor, the solicitor expressly or by implication undertakes to fulfill certain obligations. The retainer will describe the ambit of the legal services that are to be provided by the lawyer and, for contentious business, it should be given with respect to specific proceedings. It is for the lawyer to prove the existence or terms of the retainer: see *Roberts v. Kroll*, [1971] 5 WWR 133 (BC Co. Ct.). Though directed to specific proceedings, most retainers in litigation are broadly drafted. For example, a retainer might provide as follows:

> I, John Smith, of the City of Toronto, hereby retain and employ Harry Johns, Esq., of the City of Hamilton as my solicitor and hereby authorize him to commence and prosecute an action in the Supreme Court of Ontario against XYZ Ltd. of the City of Windsor for damages occasioned to me as a result of injuries sustained by the consumption of certain goods manufactured and sold by the said XYZ Ltd. and to take such actions and conduct such proceedings as he may consider necessary or proper for the conduct of such action on my behalf.

A lawyer is merely the client's agent. Since the client is the principal, the lawyer is obliged to take instructions from the client. Thus, a lawyer who acts outside of the authority granted by the client may end up in serious difficulties. For example, if a lawyer commences an action on behalf of the plaintiff without the authority of the plaintiff, the proceedings are subject to being stayed and the lawyer may be ordered to pay the costs of the client, any costs which the client might have been ordered to pay the defendant and the additional costs of the defendant; see *Dumart Packing Co. v. Dumart* (1927), 61 OLR 478. For a discussion of other consequences resulting from a lawyer acting outside of his authority, see 1 Williston and Rolls, 61 et seq.; Frederic T. Home, *Cordery's Law Relating to Solicitors*, 8th ed., 76 et seq.

3. The Solicitor's Account

When retained, the solicitor may request some payment from the client to cover disbursements and, perhaps, partial payment of the ultimate fee. Also, the solicitor may deliver an interim bill to the client in the course of the litigation. In any event, when the services are completed, the solicitor will normally render a final account to the client. Frequently, this final account will contain merely a description of the services rendered with a lump sum charge. However, the usual form of a bill rendered in respect of civil litigation will be less succinct and will list in detail the various actions taken by the lawyer on the client's behalf.

4. Assessment of the Solicitor's Account

What if the client fails or refuses to pay the lawyer's bill? As in any similar situation of an unpaid creditor, the lawyer may bring an action for the debt. However, most provinces have introduced a much more expeditious method of recovering legal fees: see, for example, the Solicitors Act, RSO 1990, c. S.15.

Provided that the retainer is not disputed, either the solicitor or the client may apply to have the bill assessed. (In some provinces, the term used is "taxation.") These provisions work in two ways. They permit a lawyer who has not been paid to have the bill assessed (and to enforce the resulting order as a judgment of the court). They also provide a client who is dissatisfied with the amount of the fees charged by a lawyer to have the bill assessed. It would appear that the right of a client to have the amount of a bill assessed is not something that is widely publicized. Do you think that it should be made a requirement for every lawyer to set forth a notice on a bill advising the client of the right to assessment?

In Ontario, the right to proceed to assessment is limited to situations where the retainer of the solicitor is not disputed. Where it is disputed—that is, where the client denies having engaged the lawyer at all or disputes some part of the services billed—an order for assessment should not be made. Instead, the solicitor should bring an action: see *Re Solicitor*, [1940] OWN 438, aff'd. [1940] 4 DLR 821 (CA). If on the assessment the client disputes the retainer, the assessment should be stayed leaving the solicitor to proceed by way of action. The issue of the retainer and the liability of the client will then be determined in the action: see *Re A Solicitor*, [1945] OWN 494; *Re Solicitor*, [1965] 1 OR 189.

On assessment, the assessment officer will determine the appropriate fee on the basis of established principles (see below). The assessment officer will advise the solicitor and the client of his determination by way of a report. Unless set aside or varied on appeal, such a report is final, and has the effect of a judgment. Consequently, if the report holds that a client is indebted to his solicitor (or vice versa, as where it is determined that the client has overpaid the solicitor) recourse may be had to the procedures available for the enforcement of a judgment for an amount found due and owing. For example, the solicitor may obtain a writ of execution for the seizure and sale of the client's personal and real property.

However, the solicitor has a further and very effective remedy to enforce the payment of the fees due. This is the device of the "solicitor's lien": see, for example, Alberta rule 625. This entitles the solicitor, even without assessment, to retain possession of the client's property, whether it be books, papers, etc. or money, including the proceeds of a judgment, until the outstanding fees have been paid. The solicitor's lien can have a very serious effect on the rights of the client where, for example, the solicitor and client terminate their relationship midway through litigation. Since the property of the client in the hands of the solicitor includes the file pertaining to the case, the client can be seriously prejudiced if the solicitor refuses to release the file until his fees have been paid. In one case the Ontario Court of Appeal provided some relief against the hardship created by this doctrine. In *Re Gladstone*, [1972] 2 OR 127, the court interfered with the solicitor's lien for his unpaid costs because the assertion of the lien affected other parties interested in the procedures, in this case the children of a marriage and their maintenance. However, the court did not suggest that had the interests of third parties not been affected, they would have deprived the solicitor of his lien. Although the Ontario Law Reform Commission recommended the abolition of the solicitors' lien (see *Report on the Solicitors Act* (1973), 36-38; *Report on the Administration of Ontario Courts Part III* (1973), 206-07), it still remains: see the Solicitors Act, s. 34.

5. Agreements as to a Solicitor's Remuneration

Before considering the principles applied by the assessment officer on an assessment between lawyers and their clients, it is best to examine the scope for specific agreements between lawyers and clients, in advance of litigation, as to the remuneration a lawyer will receive. A lawyer may enter into an agreement with a client with regard to the amount of fees that the client will be charged for the services that the lawyer is contracting to perform. Such agreements must be in writing. Also, there are provisions to ensure that such agreements can or must be validated by the courts. For instance, Ontario and British Columbia insist that the agreement must be "fair and reasonable"; see the Solicitors Act, s. 18 and the Legal Profession Act, RSBC 1996, c. 255, s. 87(15). As regards the enforcement of such agreements, some provinces allow actions but restrict costs and default judgments; see Nova Scotia rule 63.27 and Alberta rule 626. However, Ontario prohibits actions to enforce such agreements but allows recovery through an application to the courts; see the Solicitors Act, s. 23.

Even where an agreement in writing exists, the assessment provisions are available for the lawyer or client to fix the total amount actually payable, because most fee agreements refer to hourly rates or a formula for charging and do not set a fixed amount in advance.

6. Criteria Applied on Solicitor-and-Client Assessment

A major problem confronting the assessment officer is the criteria to be used in determining whether the fee a solicitor has charged the client is appropriate. In some jurisdictions legislation spells out the criteria. For instance, in Nova Scotia, rule 63.16 lays down the criteria to be used in assessing the reasonableness of the costs claimed:

(a) the nature, importance and urgency of the matters involved,

(b) the circumstances and interest of the person by whom the costs are payable,

(c) the fund out of which they are payable,

(d) the general conduct and costs of the proceeding,

(e) the skill, labour and responsibility involved, and

(f) all other circumstances, including, to the extent hereinafter authorized, the contingencies involved.

However, in Ontario, the assessment officer is given a general power with no specific instructions for its exercise. Nonetheless, rules have developed over the years as to the criteria to be used; see, for example, in *Re Solicitor*, [1972] 3 OR 433 (SC), at 436-37, where the officer explained that the following factors are usually examined:

1. The time expended by the solicitor.
2. The legal complexity of the matters dealt with.
3. The degree of responsibility assumed by the solicitor.
4. The monetary value of the matters in issue.
5. The importance of the matters to the client.
6. The degree of skill and competence demonstrated by the solicitor.
7. The results achieved.
8. The ability of the client to pay.

The cases abound with statements about the principles and criteria that should govern the assessment of a fair and reasonable bill between a solicitor and client. For example, in *Re Solicitors* (1911), 2 OWN 596, at 597, Middleton J stated:

The amount of fee charged can only be based upon the nature of the case and the skill and ability brought to bear upon it. When a solicitor is employed to adjust a matter of difficulty, nothing more injurious to the client could be suggested than that the solicitor's remuneration must depend upon the length of time taken and the number of interviews had. One may grasp a situation with great rapidity and his skill and experience may lead to its satisfactory solution in a way that after the event appears easy. Another, lacking the necessary skill and experience, may plod away at great length and in the end fail to reach as satisfactory a result.

One important criterion is the effect of any fee quotation or fee estimate. The cases make it quite clear that if the lawyer is not to be bound by a fee estimate, the fact that the estimate does not commit the lawyer should be made very clear to the client when it is made, and the lawyer must advise the client promptly if the circumstance change such that it is likely the quote will be exceeded. Otherwise, the lawyer may be bound by the estimate. See *Cohen v. Kealey* (1985), 26 CPC (2d) 211 (Ont. CA); *Thomson, Rogers v. Croydon Furniture Systems Inc.* (1982), 30 CPC 298 (Ont. SC, Taxing Office).

Most members of the public are unaware of the powers of the assessment officer. What devices could be adopted to advise the public of its ability to have a lawyer's bill assessed. Would it be sufficient for the law society to post an advertisement in the *Yellow Pages* as, for example, the Law Society of Upper Canada does now?

B. "Fee Shifting": The General Rule and Its Effect

1. The General Rule

The power to order one party to a lawsuit to pay the costs of another is statutory. Each jurisdiction empowers the courts to award costs in language similar to s. 131(1) of the Ontario Courts of Justice Act:

> Subject to the provisions of an Act or rules of court, the costs of and incidental to a proceeding or a step in a proceeding are in the discretion of the court, and the court may determine by whom and to what extent the costs shall be paid.

The rules of court in some jurisdictions provide some structure to this discretion by establishing a list of factors that the court may take into account in exercising its discretion to award costs. See, for example, Ontario rule 57.01. Most of these factors have also been historically recognized by the courts as factors in the exercise of the discretion as to costs even in the absence of such a rule. Note the wide range of factors in rule 57.01 that the court may take into consideration. How is a court to balance such disparate factors as, for example, degree of success, amount in issue, public interest aspects, or party misconduct and arrive at an appropriate costs order?

The answer is that while the written laws and rules respecting costs seem to establish a broad discretion as to costs, the practice that has developed in Canada and the Commonwealth focuses primarily on *success in the litigation* as the factor governing most costs orders. As the English Court of Appeal described it in *Campbell (Donald) & Co. v. Pollak*, [1927] AC 32:

A successful Defendant ... has no doubt, in the absence of special circumstances, a reasonable expectation of obtaining an order for the payment of costs by the Plaintiffs; but he has no right to costs unless and until the court awards them to him, and the court has an absolute and unfettered discretion to award or not to award them. This discretion, like any other discretion, must of course be exercised judicially and the Judge ought not to exercise it against the successful party except for some reason connected with the case.

The principle that, absent other circumstances, the victorious party should get an award of costs, applies equally to a successful plaintiff.

In the light of this general practice, consider the exercise of discretion in the following decision.

Pittman Estate v. Bain
(1994), 35 CPC (3d) 55 (Ont. Gen. Div.)

LANG J: ... These reasons address the issue of what costs, if any, should be awarded to the plaintiffs.

This action included claims by the plaintiffs that, in November 1984, the Canadian Red Cross Society (Red Cross) was negligent in screening blood donations and, further, that the Canadian Red Cross and the Toronto Hospital were negligent in the implementation of their respective lookback programs. Those programs were intended to trace potentially tainted donations to the recipients of the blood products.

In addition to the tort action, the plaintiffs argued that the Toronto Hospital was liable in contract for breach of warranty as to the quality of the blood. Finally, the plaintiffs claimed against Dr. Bain, the family doctor, because, once he learned of the potentially tainted transfusion, he failed to warn the plaintiffs of the risks of HIV. The plaintiffs, while they achieved a substantial damages award, were not successful on all issues.

The proceedings were lengthy. The trial, originally estimated at 20 days, lasted 91, including 13 days of argument. During the course of the evidence, the plaintiffs called 20 witnesses, and the three defendants, between them, called 30 witnesses. While the trial was much longer than expected, it would have been still longer had all counsel not agreed, with the assistance of the pre-trial judge, to delineate the issues outstanding between them. As a result of the length of the trial, the costs will be significant, including more than $147,000 of disbursements, mostly for expert witnesses. The purpose of these reasons, however, is simply to award costs. A later appointment has been arranged to decide whether I will fix those costs, or refer them to a master for assessment, with certain directions.

In awarding costs, I will consider the relevant enumerated factors of r. 57.01(1) of the Rules of Practice. In particular, I will consider the amount claimed and recovered, the apportionment of liability, the complexity of the proceeding, the importance of the issues, and the conduct of the parties. I will also consider that r. 57.01(4) authorizes a court to award, or refuse, costs in respect of a particular issue, and permits a court to award a percentage of costs.

Amount Claimed

In their statement of claim, the plaintiffs sought damages of more than $2,000,000. During final argument, the amount requested was $1,400,000, exclusive of prejudgment interest. The amount awarded was about $630,000, inclusive of prejudgment interest. The plaintiffs clearly received a significantly lower award than they had sought. This factor will bear on the costs award. No r. 49 offers to settle were made by any party.

Apportionment of Liability

In deciding costs, I must also consider the apportionment of liability among the three defendants. The judgment divided that liability among the defendants as 30 per cent against each of the hospital and the Red Cross, with the balance of 40 per cent attributed to Dr. Bain. By itself, apportionment of liability in a particular case may not be a significant consideration. That is so because the apportionment may not reflect the trial time spent on the issues, or the complexity of the matter or the importance of the issues. In *Pittman* the cases against the different defendants occupied significantly different amounts of trial time.

It may be unfair to apportion costs on the basis of the apportionment of liability between the parties if the cases against them did not occupy an amount of trial time commensurate with that apportionment. However, on the successful issues in *Pittman*, as will be discussed, the case took, very roughly, equal amounts of time against each of the three defendants. Accordingly, the costs awarded will be shared among the three defendants in a manner reflecting the various considerations set out in these reasons, of which apportionment of liability is one.

Complexity of the Proceeding

The proceeding was complex, both from a factual and from a legal perspective, but it was more complex with respect to some defendants than with respect to others. The case against the Red Cross and the hospital with respect to donor screening and lookback was scientifically complex. The court had to be educated on HIV and AIDS from the time the disease was first identified. To understand HIV and AIDS, it was necessary to educate the court on the epidemiology and etiology of AIDS. Experts were called in, amongst other disciplines, infectious diseases, virology, transfusion medicine, and public health. It was necessary to present a chronology of information over time to establish what steps, if any, should have been taken by the Red Cross, by the hospital, and by Dr. Bain at the relevant times. In addition, the case against the Red Cross was complicated by the legal argument about the applicable standard of care and causation. This included a review of the American authorities on blood transfusion cases. In addition, the case against the hospital, while not factually difficult, was complicated by the legal argument of implied warranty in contract. The case against Dr. Bain was more straightforward, resting as it did on the allegation of failure to warn. All these matters were difficult because the evidence had to be presented to establish standards of care some ten years ago so that the court did not render a decision based on the benefit of hindsight. In determining the appropriate disposition of costs, I bear in mind that the matter was complicated.

That complexity was more apparent in the case against the Red Cross, and to a lesser extent against the hospital. The case against Dr. Bain was not unusually complicated.

Importance of the Issues

There can be no doubt that the trial was conducted in a manner that reflected the importance of its result to each party. It was followed by many not involved in the litigation, as it was the first civil AIDS transfusion case to reach trial in Canada. While, in the end, the decision was fact specific on the issue of donor screening, it was viewed by many as an important factor in settlement negotiations in similar cases. As a result, it was necessary for all counsel to ensure that all relevant evidence was before the court. Further, given the nature of AIDS, and its inevitably fatal results, it was important that the evidence presented be complete. A new trial after appeal would not only be lengthy, but would be difficult if many witnesses had died meanwhile. For example, in this case, the evidence of Mr. L was taken long before trial, and indeed Mr. L died before the trial began. The importance of the proceeding and the pressure on counsel to ensure that their case presentation was thorough are factors that affected the duration of the trial, and accordingly its costs.

Conduct of the Parties

I turn now to consider the issue of the conduct of the parties, or their counsel. Mr. Armstrong, supported by the other defendants, said that Mr. Arenson, counsel for the plaintiffs, unduly prolonged the trial of this action.

It is my view that the trial took significantly longer than it might otherwise have taken for several reasons. While I will comment specifically about the allegation against Mr. Arenson later, I also recognize that the length of the trial was affected by certain of my evidentiary rulings. One of those was my decision to admit certain evidence, rather than ruling it irrelevant. An example of this was my decision to allow the plaintiffs to lead evidence about the knowledge of and steps taken by US blood banks. While in the end this evidence did not achieve a successful result for the plaintiffs on the donor screening issue, I could not reach that conclusion without first hearing the evidence. Certainly, plaintiffs' counsel should not be held financially responsible for my decision to admit such evidence.

As well, as counsel for the Red Cross argued throughout the trial, the issue before the court on donor screening was a narrow one, restricted to the procedures in place when and where Mr. L donated blood. While the Red Cross did so persuade me, the matter was initially difficult because Red Cross practices differed significantly between clinics and between personnel. It was not until after the summer recess that the Red Cross located the documents to show which personnel were at the particular clinic on the day of Mr. L's donation. Indeed, the Red Cross was slow in producing many relevant documents, and production was ongoing late into the trial. As a result, further discoveries were necessary mid-trial. This delay in production was attributed to the voluminous documents available to the Red Cross, and to the difficulty it had in locating documents because its head office had been moved to Ottawa. Nonetheless, it is a circumstance that must also be taken into account in apportioning responsibility for costs.

On the other hand, counsel for the plaintiffs did, in my view, cause a certain amount of delay that, while perhaps understandable, was a delay the costs of which should not be borne by the defendants. For example, rather than concentrating on the issues particular to the Pittman case, Mr. Arenson examined and cross-examined very broadly. I have no doubt that he did so with a clear view to obtaining information for the numerous other plaintiffs whom he represents in other tainted blood cases. While he may well have obtained useful information in that regard, responsibility for the costs of obtaining that information should not rest with the defendants in this case. Accordingly, I have notionally reduced the time spent on the evidence of Dr. Francis and Dr. Lange, which was either days, as, in my view, their evidence in this trial went further than was necessary for the issues in this action.

I turn now to the defendants' allegations that plaintiffs' counsel prolonged the trial by his failure to appreciate the rules of evidence, and his failure to prepare adequately. Indeed, some time was taken when counsel for the plaintiffs encountered difficulty in phrasing his questions in a manner that complied with the usual requirements for examination-in-chief. It was striking too that when the defendants began their case, counsel for the plaintiffs developed a marked ability that had not been exhibited during his case, to distinguish between a question that was leading and one that was not.

In addition, there was a certain amount of delay near the beginning of trial, when, in order to follow the evidence, counsel and the court had to number individually pages of voluminous exhibits that had not been numbered by counsel for the plaintiffs. In addition, it would have been helpful had the plaintiffs consistently, and in a timely manner, provided adequate copies of the material that was being presented by witnesses. As well, while it is difficult to criticize counsel for underestimating the time needed for a particular witness, counsel that did so most frequently in this case was the plaintiffs'. As a result, the evidence of witnesses, including experts from the US, was interrupted, sometimes for weeks. Such interruptions complicated the scheduling of the trial and impeded the flow of the evidence, causing both delays and additional work for all.

Counsel for the plaintiffs attributed much of his difficulty in these matters to the fact that he came from a small firm and was therefore operating without the benefit of the significant resources available to counsel for the defendants, who, besides having the resources of large firms, acted as a team on many issues. Certainly it would be wrong to criticize a counsel for the occasional inability, because of limited resources, to produce a perfectly polished product. On the other hand, a case of the complexity of this one warranted particular attention to detail. In such circumstances, counsel who does not have the resources to conduct such a trial appropriately cannot expect opposing counsel to pay the costs of the resulting delays.

As well, apart from procedural difficulties, there were instances when the plaintiffs displayed more tenacity on a losing issue than was appropriate. One such issue was that of the weight to be given to the test kit of 3,000 randomly selected Red Cross donors. Even though the plaintiffs' own expert was concerned about the reliability of the test kit results, counsel pursued the issue with vigour at every opportunity.

In addition, there was one incident that caused further concern when, in the midst of cross-examination, counsel for the plaintiffs, during lunch with their witness during her testimony, told her that she had erred about a certain piece of factual information.

All these matters of conduct must be considered in deciding an appropriate award of costs. The court must be careful not to penalize the individual litigant with limited resources who is up against large institutions that possess the resources to frustrate the trial process. However, this case was not one, in my view, where the defendants' counsel took advantage of the plaintiffs' limited resources. Instead, this was a case where the plaintiffs' counsel could have exercised more care in his conduct of the litigation.

Distributive Costs

I turn now to consider whether a distributive costs award is appropriate in this case. A distributive costs award gives costs on a successful issue to the successful party.

In the *Pittman* case, success can be divided by issue. The plaintiffs were successful on the issues of the defendants' lookback programs and of Dr. Bain's failure to warn. They were unsuccessful in establishing negligence against the Red Cross for its donor screening program that was in place on November 24, 1984, at the Ajax mobile clinic. They were unsuccessful in their claim of contractual warranty against the hospital. They were successful in achieving a substantial damages award, but that award did not meet that requested in the pleadings or in argument.

Using a distributive costs order, the court could award costs to the Red Cross on the donor screening issue, costs to the hospital on the contractual warranty issue, and costs to the plaintiffs on the lookback and the failure to warn issues.

In order to assist the calculations necessary for such an order, counsel for the Red Cross, with the help of the registrar's detailed court log, provided a breakdown of the time spent on each issue. The necessary background evidence, applicable to all issues included evidence from family members and included expert evidence on AIDS. It occupied ten days of trial time. The lookback evidence against the Red Cross occupied about five days, and the lookback evidence against the hospital occupied about seven days. The case against Dr. Bain took about 13 days of evidence. In addition, the damages evidence consumed 10.5 days of court time.

According to the Red Cross calculations, the single biggest issue in terms of time devoted to it was that of Red Cross donor screening, with over 23 days of evidence, and an additional number of days of motions and other matters.

In theory, an assessment officer could separate the costs for each issue and assess them to the successful party. This approach presents a number of problems, not the least of which is the judicial concern expressed about it. The Court of Appeal discouraged distributive orders of costs in *Oakville Storage & Forwarders Ltd. v. Canadian National Railway* (1991), 5 OR (3d) 1 (indexed as *Armak Chemicals Ltd. v. Canadian National Railway Co.*).

In that decision Carthy JA discussed a distributive costs order made by the trial judge after a lengthy trial involving several parties and multiple issues in one of 19 actions being tried together. The trial judge had made awards giving the plaintiff costs on its successful issues and had made other awards giving the defendant costs on its successful issues. In discussing the proper disposition of costs, Carthy JA pointed out that litigation is result-oriented and asked [at 8]:

> Why make an offer of settlement equivalent to a gross judgment if the trial judge is going to allocate costs by success on issues?

He went on to say that success, or want of it, on individual issues can be addressed by the application of the factors set out in r. 57.01(1). The decision shows a concern that a division of costs by success on particular issues ignores a litigant's interest in the overall result and concentrates it artificially on the success of specific issues. Offers to settle are based on the result without particularizing success by issue; accordingly, a distributive costs approach is not in keeping with the structure of offers to settle. The court expressed concern about such orders even in cases such as the one before me where there are no offers to settle.

In *Laven Associates Ltd. v. Price* (1993), 20 CPC (3d) 86 (Ont. Gen. Div.), Sheard J considered the Court of Appeal's comments in determining appropriate costs in a situation where a plaintiff claimed $73,785.22. The plaintiff was awarded that amount less $7,605 allowed to the defendants for one item on their counterclaim. After noting the *Armak Chemicals* negative comments on distributive orders, Sheard J stated that it would not be just to allow a plaintiff to assess costs for time spent upon issues decided against it. However, given his ruling on the claim and counterclaim, he could make a cost award that satisfied the concern for justice without making a distributive award. In the result, relying upon r. 57.01(4), Sheard J reduced the plaintiff's costs by 10 per cent to reflect the result that the plaintiff had achieved 90 per cent of the amount it sought, after subtracting from that sum the amount allowed to the defendants on their counterclaim.

In my view, a distributive costs order in this case would not be the appropriate disposition of costs. The great expense of an already lengthy trial would be exacerbated by the need for an assessment officer to examine individually every piece of evidence to determine its appropriate attribution to a specific issue. Such a process would be unnecessarily time-consuming when, in my view, in this case, the same result could be achieved by a r. 57.01(4) award of a percentage of costs, though one determined by somewhat different criteria than those employed by Sheard J in *Laven Associates*.

Percentage Award

I turn, then, to consider the appropriate percentage award that should be made under the authority of r. 57.01(4), bearing in mind all of the factors referred to in these reasons.

In doing so, I will consider, amongst other things, the amounts of time devoted to issues where the plaintiffs did or did not achieve success.

On the donor screening issue, the Red Cross argued that, including related motions, a total of about 30 days, or one third of trial time, was devoted to the unsuccessful donor screening issue. With this, I cannot agree. While certainly a substantial amount of time was spent on donor screening, a certain amount of that time was necessary to give the court the required perspective for evaluating the design and implementation of the lookback programs.

Without that evidence concerning the chronology of HIV/AIDS, the state of knowledge of the Red Cross policies, the court would have been unable to determine what lookback programs should have been implemented in the period from 1986 until 1989. The lookback programs could not be judged in isolation. Accordingly, in my view, roughly one quarter of the time spent on donor screening was necessary background to the Red Cross and hospital lookback programs. I estimate that by combining this portion of the donor screening evidence with the almost five days spent on Red Cross lookback, and by attributing an appropriate proportion of the background and damages evidence to the case against the Red Cross, as well as some time for motions and argument, about 25 per cent of trial time was spent on the matters about which the plaintiffs were successful.

With respect to the case against the hospital, while the hospital was successful in defending the contractual warranty issue, the evidence for that issue occupied very little trial time in evidence as the question rested primarily on legal argument. By far the bulk of the case against the hospital, in terms of court time expended, related to the hospital's administrative implementation of its lookback program. If a proportionate share of the background, damages evidence, motions, and argument is added to the approximately seven days spent on the hospital lookback program, about 20 per cent of trial time was spent on issues that were resolved in favour of the plaintiffs.

With respect to the case against Dr. Bain, the plaintiffs were successful. That portion of the trial occupied about 13 days of evidence. Again, adding to that time spent on background, damages, motions, and argument, about 27 per cent, of trial time was spent on issues that were resolved in favour of the plaintiffs.

Dispositions of Costs

Accordingly, if one used an arithmetical calculation of the time spent on the plaintiffs' successful issues, it would be on the basis that a total of about 72 per cent of trial time was spent on those issues. In this case, this is not a satisfactory basis to make the type of distributive order by giving the plaintiffs 72 per cent of their costs. Such a result would fail to reflect the fact that the defendants were successful on certain significant issues, that many issues were in fact overlapping, and that, in all the circumstances, arithmetical precision is not possible.

Further, the costs award should reflect the necessity for the plaintiffs to bring the action and proceed to trial in order to obtain compensation. As well, as mentioned earlier, the case was complex, and the issues, important. On the other hand, the award should be reduced to some extent to reflect the conduct of the plaintiffs' case. In all the circumstances, a fair result is achieved by awarding the plaintiffs 60 per cent of their party-and-party costs.

The plaintiffs are entitled to costs that are reflective of each of those considerations. This cannot be done with mathematical precision. After considering all the factors mentioned in these reasons, it is my view that a fair result is achieved by awarding the plaintiffs 60 per cent of their party-and-party costs.

Allocation of Costs

Given that disposition, I must now determine the allocation of the responsibility for those costs among the three defendants.

In so doing, some of the comments made above are applicable. For example, the case against Dr. Bain was not complex. It involved a rather straightforward issue about a doctor's obligation to warn. On the other hand, it occupied the most trial time and raised interesting ethical issues.

The case against the Red Cross was more complex in considering the background, design, and implementation of its lookback program from 1986 onwards. The case against the hospital was not as complex as that against the Red Cross, at least with respect to the lookback issue. There were not the same issues as to the knowledge of the hospital and the appropriate response given that knowledge. Rather, the case against the hospital concentrated on the propriety of its administrative response to a hazard that, by 1987, it knew existed.

The success of the Red Cross and hospital was reflected in the costs percentage award of 60 per cent. In those circumstances, and considering the slightly greater amount of time spent on the case against Dr. Bain, it is appropriate that the costs are borne in the same proportion as liability. Costs will be paid 30 per cent by the Red Cross, 30 per cent by the hospital, and 40 per cent by Dr. Bain.

Disbursements

While I will apply the principles set out in these reasons to the issue of disbursements, I prefer to consider disbursements on an individual basis, particularly when it comes to the expense incurred for expert witnesses called to give evidence on specific issues. Clearly, the plaintiffs should not recover any disbursements incurred on unsuccessful issues. Counsel have agreed to argue the next step of the costs issue on June 28, and we will address that and other issues relevant to the assessment of costs at that time.

Summary

In summary, the plaintiffs are entitled to 60 per cent of their party-and-party costs, payable 30 per cent by each of the Red Cross and the hospital, and 40 per cent by Dr. Bain. Other costs issues will be addressed on June 28 [reproduced below].

Plaintiffs awarded 60 per cent of their party-and-party costs.

NOTES AND QUESTIONS

1. Having regard to the relative positions of the plaintiff and defendants, is this a fair outcome for costs? Is it appropriate to discount the costs award to the plaintiff by the lack of success on certain issues? What effect may this have on the way similar cases might be litigated in the future?

2. When it comes to determining the fee that the plaintiff's counsel will charge the client (the solicitor-and-client fees), is the counsel entitled to his or her full fee for all work actually done, or is the counsel obliged to reduce his or her fees in the light of the court's reduction of the party-and-party costs?

3. In *Bain*, the judge awarded costs on an overall percentage basis, but refused to consider a distributive order—that is, one where the judge separates the issues and makes an order for costs on the basis of the success on each issue. What are the pros and cons of a distributive order, as opposed to a percentage order, where there is mixed success?

4. Why should success be the dominant factor in an award of costs? Whether they win or lose, all parties to the litigation will have incurred considerable expense in conducting the proceedings. When the litigation is over, how should responsibility for these expenses be allocated? Should each party bear its own expenses? Should the loser pay the expenses or the winner? If so, should the loser pay all of the winner's costs or only part of them?

5. The genesis of the cost-shifting rule seems to be that a successful plaintiff could, under the name of "damages," obtain compensation that would cover the costs of litigation as well as all other harm sustained. In other words, the costs of the litigation—the expense of having to go to court to vindicate one's rights—was seen as a compensable head of damage suffered by the plaintiff that could be recovered from the defendant. The rationale, then, of this principle seems historically to be that of compensation based on *fault*—that is, by defending or instituting an action the loser wrongly caused the victor to incur legal expenses, for which the loser must pay. Success in the lawsuit has, in general, been seen as a sufficient reason for shifting the costs of litigation from the victor to the loser. A consequence of the rule that, in general, costs follow the event is the discouragement of marginal litigation. Before deciding to commence an action, the plaintiff must take into account the fact that should the case be lost, liability for his or her own expenses as well as those of the defendant will follow. Similarly, in deciding whether to defend an action, a defendant must weigh the possibility of losing and having two sets of costs—his or her own plus the plaintiff's costs. On the other hand, the victorious party can expect to have his or her costs paid by the loser.

6. There has been a wealth of literature on the advantages and disadvantages of each approach to costs. The general conclusion is that neither of the solutions is without its drawbacks and each can produce hardship. The Anglo-Canadian rule, based on the notion of fault, exacerbates the already harsh consequences of the all-or-nothing character of litigation. Also, while it may serve to discourage frivolous litigation, it may result in meritorious and novel claims, which might be in the public interest to have litigated. On the other hand, the US rule, it is argued, increases the volume of litigation and, therefore, contributes to court congestion. Further, it fails to justly compensate the winner whose claim has been vindicated, and it discourages the litigation of small claims.

7. In view of the general principle that, in litigation, costs follow the event, a lawyer has an important obligation to explain carefully to a client the nature of the costs system and how it operates in the civil litigation process. When a client enters a lawyer's office and seeks advice about whether to bring a civil action, the lawyer has the obligation to explain the financial consequences of losing the action and, indeed, the financial consequences of winning. Similarly, when a defendant seeks the advice of a lawyer, the lawyer has the obligation of explaining the financial consequences of defending the action, not only in relation to a successful defence but also in relation to an unsuccessful one. In other words, whether a lawyer is advising a plaintiff or a defendant, it is imperative for the lawyer to carefully explain to the client the financial ramifications of winning or losing an action.

8. In the United States, the general rule with regard to the recovery of costs is different from that which exists in Anglo-Canadian jurisdictions: see *Alyeska Pipeline Service Co. v. Wilderness Society*, 421 US 240 (1975). There is no general power in US courts to order that a losing party pay the lawyer's fees and general disbursements of the

successful litigant. US courts do have a limited general power with regard to costs—that is, to order that the losing party pay the successful litigant's court filing fees. But these represent a very small portion of the total costs incurred by either side. However, within the last decade or so, and particularly with regard to litigation in the federal courts, there have been numerous specific statutory authorizations to permit the courts to award costs (referred to as attorneys' fees). A 1981 survey reported that there were approximately 125 fee-shifting statutory provisions: see Cohen, *Awards of Attorneys' Fees by Federal Courts and Federal Agencies*, Report no. 81-30A, Congressional Research Service, 11-17 (1981). Basically, these provisions allow for awards of costs only in favour of successful plaintiffs and are based on a view that in some areas costs rules should be used to encourage the vindication of specific rights; see, for example, the Fair Labor Standards Act, 29 USC §21 6(b). Are such "one way" provisions slanted in a plaintiff's favour? The use of costs as a means of encouraging (or discouraging) particular kinds of proceedings (and litigants) is addressed in several places in this chapter, including the Prichard paper, reproduced below. For further discussion of the relative merits of different systems, see Leubsdorf, "Toward a History of the American Rule on Attorney Fee Recovery," [1984] 47 L & CP 9; and Rowe, "The Legal Theory of Attorney Fee Shifting," [1982] *Duke Law Journal* 651.

The following excerpt shows how expensive litigation can be, particularly in the context of assessment of costs. Are the proposals adequate to deal with the issues raised?

The Report of the Ontario Courts Inquiry (The Zuber Inquiry)
(Toronto: Attorney General of Ontario), 1987, at 51-52

The most common complaint about the justice system is that the cost of litigation is prohibitive.

It is generally conceded that only the very wealthy, or the poor on legal aid, can afford to go to court. With the exception of matters within the jurisdiction of the Provincial Court (Civil Division), civil cases of less than $5,000 may not be worth taking to court because the costs will equal or exceed the amount in issue. Even minor criminal matters can be expensive to defend, making it more attractive to plead guilty, since the fine will cost substantially less than any legal fees. The cost of litigating property division disputes in matrimonial cases has been known to exceed the value of all the assets accumulated by the divorcing couple.

Compounding the expense picture is a system of awarding costs at the end of a case which rewards inefficiency and prolixity by basing the assessment of costs on the number of motions, days at trial, and hours spent on preparation. Legal aid fees are calculated in much the same manner.

Assessment officers have noted that costs have risen dramatically over the last two to three years. Once upon a time, a bill of costs assessed on a party-and-party scale represented about two-thirds of the costs the client would actually have to pay. Currently, that proportion has shrunk to less than one-half of the bill of costs.

This fact directly affects the amount which the winning litigant can actually expect to receive after he or she has paid the solicitor, and the losing litigant has paid the judgment, interest and assessed costs. From a cursory examination of typical bills of costs in the District Court and the High Court of Justice it was apparent that, after a winning litigation has paid his or her lawyer, only 20 to 30 percent of a District Court judgment (including interest and costs) will remain. This proportion rises to 40 to 60 percent of a judgment in the High Court.

The Inquiry conducted a survey of the average cost of certain types of civil cases in the District Court. ... The survey showed that an average bill of costs, assessed on a party-and-party basis, was nearly $4,000. Preparation for trial and the counsel fee were the most expensive items on the bill, representing slightly more than one-half of the total bill.

When it is remembered that an assessed bill of costs represents less than one-half of the actual bill a solicitor would present to his or her client, it is not difficult to understand how even a winning litigant can end up with little more than a paper victory. One assessment officer told the Inquiry that he had assessed costs in the District Court which exceeded the monetary jurisdiction of the District Court (i.e. $25,000).

[Later in formulating its recommendations the Report states (at 217-218):]

In some systems of justice, there are no awards of costs as we know them in Ontario. Costs in some jurisdictions involve only the actual expenses of litigation such as the filing fees and cost of the service of process.

In Ontario, costs include large amounts, which at least partially cover lawyers fees. The award of costs fulfills two general purposes: compensation to the party aggrieved and a sanction against the party who is in the wrong.

There are improvements that can be made in the award of costs. Firstly, the award should be more discriminate. Currently, awards of costs are simply made to the winner almost as a matter of course. There is very little "fine tuning" of the award of costs. A successful party who has been guilty of unduly prolonging the proceeding should not be rewarded for it. Even a successful party should be awarded only costs calculated on the basis of the amount of time that the matter ought to have taken. Judges and judicial officers should be encouraged in their award of costs to specify the basis of calculation. There is no necessity to amend statutes or rules to award this kind of power since it already exists. The assessment officer, who of course is not present at the trial or other proceeding, would find it impossible to assess how long a proceeding ought to have taken when he or she was not present.

In extreme cases, the order awarding costs on the basis of how long the proceedings ought to have taken might oblige the successful party to compensate the unsuccessful party for the time wasted.

Entirely apart from such qualifications in the order awarding costs, the paramount principle in the assessment of costs should be the value of the work done and not the amount of time spent or the number of steps taken.

It is recommended that for the assistance of assessment officers, the rules of the various courts be amended to spell out the principle that the paramount consideration in the assessment of costs is the value of the work done.

---

2. The Amount Recoverable

If at the conclusion of an action, one litigant is ordered to pay the costs of another, what is the amount of costs that must be paid? Looked at from the point of view of the successful party, must the loser pay all of the successful party's legal bill or only part? The general rule is that recoverable costs (those ordered on a "party-and-party" scale) should only provide a partial indemnity for the costs actually incurred by a litigant. This represents a compromise on the part of our legal system. While it is felt that as a rule the loser should be ordered to pay the winner's costs, it is realized that in most cases to require payment of all of an opponent's costs will normally be too severe a sanction. Consequently, in general, the loser will be required to pay only what amounts to a reasonable proportion of the winner's expenses.

However, in many jurisdictions, the court can vary the degree to which the recoverable costs provide the successful party with an indemnity for the legal costs by the specific type of order it makes. The court does this by specifying the "scale of costs" on which the quantum of recoverable costs is to be assessed. There are two such scales, referred to as (1) party-and-party and (2) solicitor-and-client. In British Columbia, the latter are now called "special costs." Generally, it can be said that costs on a party-and-party scale give the party in whose favour the order is made partial compensation for the expenses incurred; costs on a solicitor-and-client scale will usually provide a complete indemnity for the costs of the litigation.

Unless the court orders otherwise, an award of costs is on the party-and-party scale. For example, a judgment concluding with the words "judgment for the plaintiff with costs" or "judgment for the defendant with costs" will mean costs to be assessed on the party-and-party scale. Costs on this scale will be ordered by the court in the vast majority of cases. Costs on the higher scale, solicitor-and-client costs, are only occasionally awarded. Such an award would usually be made in two types of situations. The first is where there is a punitive element in the costs award—that is, where the court wishes to punish a party for the way in which it has conducted the litigation. The second type of situation is quite different. Where the litigation concerns a fund of money, those parties who have an interest in the fund, or who are responsible for its maintenance, will usually be awarded costs to be paid out of the fund. Litigation involving the construction of a will or the administration of a trust are common examples. If the executor, trustee, or beneficiaries are awarded costs, as is usually the case, such costs will as a rule be awarded on a solicitor-and-client scale out of the fund.

Costs awarded on a solicitor-and-client scale are intended to provide close to a full indemnity to the recipient for legal costs—that is, fees and disbursements—excluding only the costs incurred for services not reasonably necessary to permit the full and fair prosecution or defence of the action. Hence, in the vast majority of cases where costs on a solicitor-and-client scale are awarded, they will represent the complete account that the client will have to pay the lawyer. However, in rare cases there may remain extra costs which a successful party will not be able to recover from the opponent. This will occur, for example, when a client instructs a lawyer to do something that is held to be unreasonable or unnecessary in the circumstances—for example, retaining an excessive number of counsel or expert witnesses at trial.

Apart from power of the court to determine the scale of costs, the court has the power to affect the amount of costs in a number of different ways. While, normally, the amount of costs payable are determined following the trial in a process called assessment (or "taxation" in some provinces and previously in Ontario), the court itself can fix the amount of costs payable. The court may also disallow the costs of a portion of the proceedings.

In the following case, the trial judge in the *Pittman* case, above, exercises her power (see Ontario rule 57.01(3)) to fix the costs of the trial, following her initial costs order.

Pittman Estate v. Bain
(1994), 35 CPC (3d) 67 (Ont. Gen. Div.)

LANG J (supplementary reasons): ... For reasons released on June 10, 1994 [reproduced above], I awarded the plaintiffs 60 per cent of their party-and-party costs, apportioned 30 per cent to the Red Cross, 30 per cent to the Hospital, and 40 per cent to Dr. Bain. Counsel have asked me to fix those costs and I do so pursuant to r. 57.01(3). The plaintiffs' bill of costs requests $602,587, comprising $455,901.50 in fees and $146,685.66 in disbursements.

General Principles

In fixing costs, I am mindful of the comments in *Apotex Inc. v. Egis Pharmaceuticals* (1991), 4 OR (3d) 321 (Gen. Div.), at p. 326: a judge fixing costs does so as a "determination of what the services ... are worth," using the tariff as a reference point. The judge is not assessing costs on an item-by-item tariff basis, as would be done by an assessment officer. Indeed, r. 57.01(3) provides that "[i]n awarding costs, the court may fix all or part of the costs with or without reference to the Tariffs, instead of referring them for assessment."

Before looking at the hours attributed by counsel to the various stages of the litigation, I first consider the appropriate hourly rates. Those rates will apply to the work done by senior counsel, Mr. Arenson, by junior counsel, Mr. Harvey, and by the law clerk, Judy Hercbergs.

In that regard, I agree with O'Brien J's holding in *Minuteman Press of Canada Co. v. Touche Ross & Co.*, a judgment of the Ontario Court of Justice released February 28, 1994 [reported at 27 CPC (3d) 70 (Ont. Gen. Div.)]. In that case he said that the "going rates" of $110 to $120 hourly on a party-and-party basis, approved in *Canadian Express Ltd. v. Blair* (1992), 10 CPC (3d) 141 (Ont. Gen. Div.), are insufficient in many cases to reflect the current cost of litigation of this nature. O'Brien J considered an hourly rate of $175 appropriate for senior counsel in party-and-party assessments and he applied that hourly rate to a counsel who had been called to the bar for about 25 years.

Mr. Arenson advised that he was called to the bar of Manitoba in 1973, and to the Ontario bar in 1983. With that seniority and experience, and in the circumstances of this case, his work merits an hourly rate of $175 as set out in his bill of costs. Defendants' counsel have agreed that the hourly rate of $85 is an appropriate one for the work done by Mr. Harvey as junior counsel. Similarly, the $40 attributed to Ms Hercbergs's work as a law clerk was accepted as appropriate.

I turn now to consider the work done by the plaintiffs' team to bring these proceedings from their inception to final disposition. It is helpful to consider that work using the stages of litigation contemplated by the tariff, although in the final analysis I will fix costs on a general view of the work encompassed by the tariff item.

With respect to the early stages of the case, Mr. Arenson said that he spent 33 hours on pleadings, 30 hours on motions exclusive of motions in which costs were otherwise fixed, 111 hours on discovery, and 30 hours on judicial pre-trials.

I will consider those preparatory stages of the litigation first. In doing so I note that the time spent by plaintiffs' counsel was relatively little when compared with the cost of the actual trial and its preparation. Indeed, counsel asks for only about $50,000 for the stages from inception to final preparation for trial, while he asks for $407,000 for trial preparation and counsel fees at trial.

Pleadings

While the claimed amount of 33 hours spent on pleadings might be considered unusual in the ordinary party-and-party assessment, it is not in the circumstances of this case. Here, Mr. Arenson was required to plead against three defendants on many issues that were both factually and legally novel in Canada. Accordingly, he is entitled to compensation for a reasonable amount of time spent on the preparation of and response to pleadings. In total, Mr. Arenson's dockets show time spent purely on pleadings of approximately 26 hours, rather than 33 hours. That is not unreasonable in the circumstances of this case, and I would allow it in its entirety in the amount of $4,550.

Motions

Despite the complexity of the issues and the absence of timely production by the Red Cross, the plaintiffs engaged in very little by way of interlocutory motions. In fixing a reasonable amount for motions, I will include the motions where costs were fixed, those where costs were awarded but not fixed, and those where no costs were awarded to any of the parties.

On two motions, the plaintiffs were awarded fixed costs totalling $650. On two other motions, costs were refused.

In a motion about the examination of the blood donor, the plaintiffs were awarded costs in the cause payable by the Red Cross. For that important motion, Mr. Arenson docketed 14.2 hours. When I consider that significant investment of time, the time actually spent before Master Sandler, and the result, it is my view that costs of $1,500 are appropriate. From that amount should be deducted a $300 costs award given to the Red Cross on another related appearance. Accordingly, the net award of costs to the plaintiffs payable by the Red Cross for those motions is $1,200.

In addition, the Red Cross brought a motion about refusals on discovery, and no order was made as to costs. That motion appears to have been a standard one, and not unduly complex. In those circumstances, its costs would not reflect the same degree of complexity or preparation. An amount of $750 should be paid to the plaintiffs by the Red Cross for that motion.

Finally, on a motion against the Red Cross for a better affidavit of documents, the plaintiffs were awarded costs in the cause. This was apparently a half-day motion, and I fix its costs at $750, also payable by the Red Cross.

In summary with respect to motions, the plaintiffs are entitled from all defendants to the $650 costs already fixed by masters hearing some motions. The plaintiffs are also entitled to a further $2,700 against the Red Cross for other motions, as discussed above.

Discovery

In total, there were 10 days of examinations for discovery, representing 111 hours of work by both senior and junior counsel. At first glance, it is a commendably brief time given the allegations in this proceeding. However, one reason for the brevity of formal discovery was the lack of early production of documents by the Red Cross. Indeed, even well into the trial of these proceedings, production and discovery continued.

Mr. Arenson argued that he obtained more productive discovery in this case by questioning witnesses in similar parallel litigation. Further, he, or others from his office, attended a significant amount of the disciplinary proceeding against Dr. Bain before the College of Physicians and Surgeons. In that manner, he says that they obtained information helpful to this proceeding. While I do not allow compensation for all the time spent at the disciplinary proceeding, or for the time spent in examining witnesses in other cases, these are factors that I can, and do, consider in fixing a reasonable amount for discovery in these proceedings.

In all those circumstances, I fix costs for discovery at $28,000.

Pre-trials

Counsel attended two pre-trials, which, according to Mr. Arenson, took about 30 hours of his time and that of junior counsel. One pre-trial was held prior to the trial, while the other was held in the midst of the trial, at my request, in the vain hope that counsel could resolve some damages issues. Given the need to prepare and attend upon two separate occasions on fairly substantial pre-trials, I fix costs to the plaintiffs at $4,500 inclusive of fees for both senior and junior counsel.

Pre-trial Preparation Totals

In summary, and subject to the comments below, the plaintiffs would be entitled from all defendants to their party-and-party work exclusive of trial preparation and counsel fee as follows:

Pleadings	$ 4,550.00
Motions	650.00
Discovery	28,000.00
Pre-trials	4,500.00
	$37,700.00

The plaintiffs are entitled to a further $2,700 from the Red Cross alone.

However, there is another factor which must be considered. In my supplementary reasons awarding costs, I reduced the plaintiffs costs to only 60 per cent of their party-and-party costs. I did so for two reasons. First, I found that only 72 per cent of the 50-day trial time could be attributed to issues where the plaintiffs succeeded. Second, I reduced the award for reasons relating to the conduct of the trial. It is clear from a reading of those reasons that in so reducing costs, my attention was directed at the trial of the matter and conduct during that trial.

I see no evidence that the preliminary pre-trial matters were in any way prolonged by the conduct of the process. On the contrary, I consider that the actual time spent on pleadings, discovery, motions, and pre-trials was modest given the issues to be addressed in the proceedings. In those circumstances, the costs for pleadings, discovery, motions, and pre-trial matters should not be subject to the 40 per cent reduction suggested in my earlier reasons. In all the circumstances, they should be fixed at $37,700.

Accordingly, the plaintiffs are entitled to costs for this portion of their bill fixed at $37,700, and a further $2,700 against the Red Cross alone.

Trial Preparation

Trial preparation and counsel fee at trial are by far the most significant part of the bill of costs, totalling some $409,000. Following my earlier supplementary reasons, the costs for this portion of the bill will be 60 per cent of what would have otherwise been fixed.

In total, the plaintiffs' bill of costs for trial preparation shows 1,048.6 hours spent by senior counsel and 477.5 hours spent by junior counsel.

Normally, when assessing such bills, trial preparation done during the trial outside court hours is incorporated into the counsel fee daily rate. In that way the counsel fee reflects both the actual time at trial and the amount of time necessary to prepare witnesses and argument for the next day's attendance. For reasons that I will address under counsel fee, it is appropriate in this case to approach the costs differently. Here, I will allow an hourly rate for all trial preparation regardless of whether it was done before trial, during trial while the court was in session, or during the weeks when the court was not in session on this case. In doing so I recognize that time spent in trial preparation should not be out of proportion to the time spent in court.

After reviewing the docket summaries provided by Mr. Arenson, I am satisfied that senior counsel spent additional time during the trial of an average of 2.5 hours daily for trial preparation. As there were 81 full days and 12 half days of trial time, I will consider that there was significant additional trial preparation during the time that the trial was in session.

In addition, there was trial preparation done before the trial began and preparation on the many days after the trial began that the court was not sitting on this case. As well, after the conclusion of evidence, senior counsel spent considerable time in preparation for written and oral argument.

In estimating a reasonable quantum for all trial preparation done at any time, I note that Mr. Arenson's bill of costs reflects total time in excess of 1,000 hours. I have reviewed his time summary and cannot attribute that much time to pure trial preparation.

I have, for example, not included time spent by Mr. Arenson with his client preparing for the discipline proceeding, or for preparing for press conferences. As far as the discipline hearing is concerned, I have allowed some of that time under the heading of discoveries, and so will not allow it again under trial preparation. I have also excluded many meetings Mr. Arenson had with his client that did not involve trial preparation.

After taking into consideration the above factors, a reasonable time for all trial preparation for Mr. Arenson is a total of 850 hours, yielding a cost for his time of $148,750 based on an hourly rate of $175.

In looking at Mr. Harvey's time summaries and deducting time spent for some overlap of his work with that of Mr. Arenson, I fix his trial preparation time at $38,000 and allow $740 for that of the law clerk.

Accordingly, the total costs for all trial preparation are $187,490. Allowing the plaintiffs 60 per cent of that amount, they are entitled to net costs under this item of $112,494.

Counsel Fee

In my view, it is reasonable for the plaintiffs' counsel to calculate trial time on an hourly basis, rather than on the more traditional approach of a daily rate. This is so because this case did not proceed in the usual fashion. Usually, the most significant amount of trial preparation is completed before the case opens. It is then only for counsel to prepare witnesses and argument on a daily basis. Here, however, trial preparation continued and was extensive throughout the trial.

In part, this was necessary because the case was complex and centred on different issues at different times. In part, it was because the direction of the trial changed from time to time with the disclosure of new information, or with changes in the understanding of the progression of HIV/AIDS. At times, the trial adjourned to accommodate witnesses or other commitments. During those breaks, counsel did extensive preparation for the next segment of the trial. Accordingly, I cannot quantify costs based on a daily counsel fee. Rather, it is more equitable to apply an hourly rate to the counsel fee as well as to trial preparation.

In making the calculation, though, I have difficulty with Mr. Arenson's estimate of eight hours a day of actual in-court time. More commonly, the court schedule was from 10 a.m. until 4:45 p.m. with recesses and lunch. Accordingly, even considering those occasions when the court sat late or started early to accommodate witnesses, court time, on the average, would not exceed six hours daily.

In those circumstances, I fix costs for actual trial time at $137,475. That sum is calculated by multiplying Mr. Arenson's hourly rate of $175 by 6 hours a day for 81 full trial days, 12 half days, and 1 additional day for the r. 36 examination of the donor. Similarly, it includes Mr. Harvey's hourly rate of $85 times 6 hours a day for 86.5 trial days. As well, I have included the law clerk's trial time of 24 hours at her hourly rate of $40.

In summary, for trial time the plaintiffs will be allowed 60 per cent of $137,475, or $82,485.

Post-trial Matters

After the conclusion of the trial, counsel reattended before me to assist with matters concerning damages. It was also necessary for them to review lengthy reasons for judgment, and attend once to argue the award of costs and a second time to argue the amount at which costs should be fixed.

In total, Mr. Arenson shows that he spent about 57 hours on these items, that Mr. Harvey spent 31 hours, and that the law clerk, Ms Hercbergs, spent 12.5 hours. In the result, the bill of costs asks $13,092.50 for post-trial matters that included seven attendances before me, either in court, in chambers, or by telephone conference.

While I would reduce the amount of time spent on these matters somewhat, the attendances and preparation for them were necessary. As they occurred after the trial and as, in my view, there was no waste of court time, I would allow party-and-party costs for post-trial matters at $10,000, without further reduction.

Summary of Fees Allowed

In summary, I fix the plaintiffs' fees at $242,679 plus GST, for a total of $259,667, calculated as follows:

Pleadings	$ 4,550.00
Motions	650.00
Discoveries	28,000.00
Pre-trials	4,500.00
Trial Preparation	112,494.00
Counsel Fee	82,485.00
Post-trial Matters	10,000.00
GST	16,987.00
Total	$259,667.00

As well, the plaintiffs are entitled to a further $2,700 plus GST from the Red Cross for the motions costs discussed above.

Disbursements

I turn now to consider the requested disbursements of $146,685.66, comprised mainly of experts' fees. In doing so, I bear in mind that the onus is on the plaintiffs to establish that, at the time, the disbursement was a reasonable one, necessary for the trial of the matters. If the plaintiffs submit an account that satisfies those requirements, I will allow it unless there is some reason to persuade me to the contrary conclusion.

The defendants have agreed to various disbursements totalling $1,287.60 for Doctors Vellend, Shumak, Braude, Walmsley, Rowe, James, Barrettara, and McLaughlin. They have also agreed to the expenses for Mount Sinai and North York General records of $952.25. As well, they acknowledged as appropriate the costs for the donor's transcript of $6,434.62, as well as the net cost for discovery transcripts of $3,396.46. In total, counsel have agreed to $12,070.93 of the disbursements claimed.

The defendants took significant issue with the costs for the main medical witnesses and for the damages experts.

Medical Experts

There can be no issue that the nature of the negligence claim required extensive expert evidence. That evidence concentrated on the development of knowledge about AIDS from its first appearance through the period at issue. It was necessary to have that evidence not only for the donor screening issue on which the plaintiffs were unsuccessful, but also as background for the issue of the obligation of the defendants to trace blood donated by persons possibly infected with HIV and to warn recipients of the ramifications of receiving tainted blood.

I begin with the experts from the United States, as their accounts represent by far the largest portion of the disputed disbursements. Dr. Lange's bill for court appearances and expenses totals $26,085.60, while that of Dr. Francis totals $28,797.41.

In my view, the testimony was essential to give the state of knowledge about HIV and AIDS in the United States and the reaction in that country to the identification of AIDS in the early 1980s. In considering the accounts of Dr. Francis and Dr. Lange, I realize that they claim a higher hourly rate than is usual for experts in our courts. However, they were essential witnesses whose charges are apparently commensurate with those of other experts from their jurisdiction. The plaintiffs had no choice but to retain such experts, as none [was] available to them in Canada. They should be compensated for the accounts rendered, if those accounts are reasonable in all the circumstances.

Dr. Lange testified on March 22, 23, 25, 26, and 31, for a total of 3.5 days of evidence. In addition, he spent 25 hours from January to the beginning of his evidence in reviewing Mrs. Pittman's files, preparing a written report, preparing slides to assist the court, and meeting with counsel in preparation for his testimony.

While Mr. Arenson suggested to Dr. Lange that an appropriate rate would be $3,000 US daily, or $300 hourly, Dr. Lange felt that $2,500 daily or $250 hourly was more appropriate. These fees are apparently in line with those of US experts in this area. As Dr. Lange was, in my view, a necessary witness, I would allow those rates. However, his evidence was broken up over three separate appearances. I am of the view that his evidence was thereby unnecessarily fragmented over several days and was, as a result, longer than necessary to canvass the issues. An experienced counsel should have realized that this witness should set aside some significant time in which to give his evidence and be cross-examined. Accordingly, in fixing the costs for this item I consider that Dr. Lange's evidence was spread over five days when it could have been heard in less. As well, his travel expenses reflected three round trip flights from New York, rather than the one trip which would have been necessary had his trial time been adequately gauged. I fix this disbursement in total at $20,000.

Where Dr. Lange charged his time at $250 hourly, or $2,500 daily, Dr. Francis, another US expert, billed his time at $300 US hourly, or $3,000 daily. He billed 19.25 hours of preparation time, including the preparation of his report, and a further $15,000 for the five days when he gave his evidence. Like Dr. Lange, Dr. Francis could not complete his evidence in the time allotted by counsel for the plaintiffs. As a result, he first gave evidence at the end of March for two days, and then again in mid-May for a further three days. Examination-in-chief took 3.5 days, while cross-examination by all defendants was finished in one day. In my view, the evidence elicited from Dr. Francis was broader than was necessary to address the issues in this proceeding. While it may have been helpful to other clients of Mr. Arenson, it was not all necessary for the presentation of Mrs. Pittman's case and, accordingly, cannot be fully compensated even on a party-and-party basis.

A fair remuneration on a party-and-party basis for Dr. Francis's evidence should not exceed the amount allowed for Dr. Lange. I fix this disbursement at $20,000.

I now turn to consider the disbursements for the Canadian experts, and, in particular, those for Dr. Hébert and Dr. Rock. ...

[The judge then proceeded to deal with the disbursements for various other experts.]

Office Costs

I turn, finally, to the costs for miscellaneous expenses. I have no difficulty in accepting the fax and photocopy charges at 25 cents per page, nor the off-premises printing expense. As well, the amounts are reasonable for filing and witness fees. I would allow courier fees at a reduced amount. As counsel could not explain the miscellaneous expenses in certain respects, and in other respects these reflect normal overhead costs for paper and supplies, I do not allow that claim. I allow expenses in the total amount of $12,000 inclusive of GST where applicable.

Conclusion

In summary of the costs fixed, the plaintiffs are entitled to $259,667 for fees and $110,381.70 for disbursements, for a rounded total of $370,000. That amount is attributed 30 per cent to the Red Cross and the hospital, or $111,000 each. The balance of $148,000 is fixed against Dr. Bain. Those amounts are subject to adjustment for other matters.

With regard to the Red Cross, the amount is increased by the $2,889 inclusive of GST for the additional motions, and by another $755 paid by the plaintiffs' counsel to the Red Cross for photocopies. From that total, the Red Cross is entitled to a deduction for $282.27 it has already paid counsel for the plaintiffs. In total, the plaintiffs are entitled to $114,381.73 from the Red Cross.

The amount fixed against the hospital must be adjusted by $235.64 paid by the hospital to counsel for the plaintiffs. Accordingly, the amount due the plaintiffs from the hospital is $110,764.36. Similarly, the sum of $195.32 must be deducted from the amount due from Dr. Bain, leaving a net costs award of $147,804.68.

An order will go, then, fixing the plaintiffs' costs at $114,381.73 payable by the Red Cross, $110,764.36 payable by the hospital, and $147,804.68 payable by Dr. Bain.

Order accordingly.

NOTES AND QUESTIONS

1. It was open for the trial judge in *Pittman*, after making the initial award of costs, to order that costs be assessed pursuant to rule 58, which establishes a mechanism for determination of the amount of costs pursuant to the court's order. In such circumstances, in Ontario, the assessment is carried out by a court officer who is neither a judge nor master, and is generally not legally trained. What are the pros and cons of having the trial judge fix costs, as opposed to being determined during the separate assessment procedure? The two procedures may lead to very different results as to the amount actually recovered: see Robert D. Malen, "To Assess or To Fix Costs: That Is the Question?" (1998), 20 *Advocates' Quarterly* 85. The Court of Appeal has cautioned Ontario judges against fixing costs on an inadequate evidentiary basis: *Polish National Union of Canada Inc. v. Palais Royale Ltd.* (1998), 111 OAC 165 (CA).

2. The method by which the amount to be paid by the losing party to the winning party is arrived at varies. In some jurisdictions, such as Alberta rule 605, the party-and-party tariff provides fixed amounts in respect of each major step in an action. However, the amount fixed varies with the amount in dispute in the action. This is achieved by providing for a number of columns of costs, each column dealing with a different "amount in dispute" range. Other jurisdictions, such as Ontario, allow more flexibility and tend to award a greater level of indemnification. Ontario's practice is described here. On being awarded the costs of an action, a successful party will prepare a "bill of costs" and submit it to the unsuccessful party. If the latter party agrees on the amount of the bill, the costs will usually be paid and that ends the matter. However, if the loser disagrees with the amount of the bill, or refuses to pay, the party who is awarded costs can have the bill of costs assessed by a court officer called an assessment or taxing officer.

3. The Rules of Civil Procedure contain numerous principles that an assessment officer must apply on a party-and-party assessment: see rule 58 and, in particular, rule 58.07. The assessment officer may disallow the costs of proceedings unnecessarily taken, incurred through overcaution, negligence, or mistake (rule 58.07(1)(f)(ii)). If a party at trial should have admitted certain matters but did not do so, thereby requiring the other party to prove the facts in question, the assessment officer may order that party to pay the costs occasioned by this refusal or neglect (rule 58.07(1), (9)).

4. In the assessment of party-and-party costs the assessment officer must be guided by rule 58.06 and the tariff of fees and disbursements that are annexed to the rules: costs can only be allowed according to the tariffs. The assessment officer concludes the assessment by issuing a certificate specifying the amount at which costs have been assessed. If either of the parties request him to do so, the officer must withhold the certificate in order to allow a party who is dissatisfied to deliver to the other parties interested in the assessment, and to the officer, objections in writing to the manner in which the assessment officer has assessed the costs (rule 58.11). The assessment officer is then bound to reconsider and review the assessment in the light of such objections, after which the certificate will be issued. Any party dissatisfied with the decision of the assessment officer on any question of principle or on any item respecting which objections have been filed may appeal from the certificate of the assessment officer to a judge (rule 58.12). A party who has been awarded costs at a trial is in the position of a judgment creditor. Therefore, once it has been issued, the certificate of the assessment

officer, unless set aside or varied, is final and conclusive as to the amount thereof and payment of that amount may be enforced forthwith against the judgment debtor: *Gostick v. CBC*, [1966] 1 OR 583, aff'd. [1966] 1 OR 789.

5. *The differential impact of litigation costs.* Costs will affect different types of parties differently. Corporations and individuals involved in business-related litigation will be entitled to deduct legal fees as a business expense for the purpose of taxation, and if the applicable tax rate is high the after tax cost is substantially reduced. Also, for individuals who are successful in litigation and recover substantial damages, having to pay their own lawyer will at least be manageable since they can "dip into" the damages to pay the lawyer (although the risk of having to pay the other side's party-and-party costs may be a deterrent to suing). Family law litigation creates serious cost problems: the litigants are individuals, the legal expenses are not business expenses and they are not tax deductible, and there is no "pot of gold" at the end of the litigation for anybody since the dispute is typically about assets that the parties already owned or shared.

3. Impact of the Indemnity Rule

We have already observed that while cost indemnity is the general rule in Canada (and in all Commonwealth and most civil law jurisdictions), in the United States the rule is to the contrary—the "American rule" is that there is no general regime of two-way cost indemnity or "attorney fee shifting." This gives rise to the question of what is the impact of having (or not having) a cost indemnity system? In general terms this can be explored by examining the cost consequences of winning and losing litigation that goes to trial under either system.

Consider the following hypothetical, premised on an actual incident. At the time of closing a residential real estate deal (in a falling market), the purchaser refused to close unless the vendor reduced the purchase price by $35,000. In order to close the deal (and to avoid owning two houses in a falling market) the vendor agreed. The vendor was understandably upset by this turn of events and considered suing to recover $35,000 damages (the difference between the original contract price and the price at which the deal closed) on a theory of economic duress. On the existing case law it was not clear that the plaintiff would succeed. (For the purpose of the hypothetical the underlying facts are not of particular importance, except the fact that it is unclear if the plaintiff will win.) The table on the next page presents an analysis of the impact of cost rules on a plaintiff bringing such litigation under an indemnity and a no-indemnity system under win–lose scenarios. Note that under the *indemnity system* the plaintiff risks losing $15,000 to get $30,000, while under the *no-indemnity system* the plaintiff risks losing $10,000 to get $25,000.

Several observations can be made with regard to this example.

1. From the plaintiff's perspective, under either system litigating is a risky business.

2. However, litigating under the indemnity system is riskier because litigants face the "downside risk" of having to pay (part of) the other side's costs if they lose.

3. Note that if the level of cost indemnity is increased from 50 percent to 100 percent, under the indemnity system the deterrent effect becomes even greater. (Using the figures given in the table, the plaintiff would be risking $20,000 to get $35,000.)

	Indemnity	*No indemnity*
1. Plaintiff wins		
Damages	35,000	35,000
Party-and-party		
costs	5,000	n/a
Recovery	40,000	35,000
Less fees to own		
lawyer	10,000	10,000
Net recovery	30,000	25,000
2. Plaintiff loses		
Damages	0	0
Party-and-party		
costs payable . . .	5,000	n/a
Fees payable to		
own lawyer	10,000	10,000
Net loss	15,000	10,000

4. If the plaintiff can retain his or her lawyer's services on a *contingent fee basis* (no-win, no-pay) the situation changes, but more dramatically under the no-indemnity system than under the indemnity system. Under the indemnity system (using the figures in the table) the plaintiff would risk losing $5,000 to obtain $30,000 (or something less if a premium is charged by the lawyer for bearing the risk), while under the US no-indemnity system, the plaintiff would risk *nothing* in order to obtain $25,000 (or something less if a premium is charged by the lawyer for bearing the risk).

5. Under the indemnity system a *successful plaintiff* will always do better (because there will be at least a partial indemnity for costs), but because the plaintiff also runs the risk of having to pay costs if unsuccessful the deterrent effect will always be greater.

An enormous literature in the United States has developed on whether the legal rules governing the assignment of trial costs will affect the likelihood of settlement—that is, will the parties be more likely to settle the case if their action is pending in a jurisdiction operating under the US rule rather than one operating under an indemnity rule—see for example, R. Posner, *Economic Analysis of Law*, 3d ed. (1986), 537-42; Shavell, "Suit, Settlement and Trial: A Theoretical Analysis Under Alternative Models for Allocation of Legal Costs" (1982), 11 *Journal of Legal Studies* 55; Donohue, "Commentary" (1991), 104 *Harvard Law Review* 1093 (listing much of the literature). For a pioneering analysis of this issue, see Mause, "Winner Takes All: A Re-examination of the Indemnity System" (1969), 55 *Iowa Law Review* 26. Initially, Judge Richard Posner concluded that the greater risk associated with the indemnity rule—parties can win more or lose more under this rule than under the US rule—would lead risk-adverse litigants to settle more cases. Subsequently, Judge Posner and Professor Steven Shavell developed a model of the litigation decision to settle or try a case that produced the opposite result:

the British rule would reduce the likelihood of settlement. It seems fair to say that intuitively most Canadian lawyers disagree and feel that a cost-indemnity system increases the rate of settlement because of the "downside risk" of proceeding to trial and losing. This risk is daunting for the many "risk-averse" parties, particularly individuals of limited means. Although precise figures are not readily available, it would seem that settlement rates are, in fact, higher in Canada and England than in the United States.

J. Robert and S. Prichard, "A Systemic Approach to Comparative Law: The Effect of Cost, Fee, and Financing Rules on the Development of the Substantive Law"
(1988), 17 *Journal of Legal Studies* 451, at 460-75 (footnotes omitted)

It is possible to summarize five differential incentives between the American and English costs rules:

First, in England [and Canada], relative to the United States, plaintiffs are encouraged to litigate relatively strong or safe cases, that is, those cases with a relatively high probability of success. The intuitive explanation for this effect is that the English rule, by shifting costs, increases the stakes of the litigation and increases the expected value of the litigation to the plaintiff for cases that are likely to succeed.

Second, in England, relative to the United States, plaintiffs are discouraged from initiating relatively novel or risky cases, that is, those cases with a relatively low probability of success. Again, to clarify, the English rule increases the downside risks associated with the litigation and reduces the expected value to the plaintiff, thus making relatively low probability cases less attractive in England than in the United States.

Third, this relative support for novel cases in the United States, as opposed to England, is reinforced by contingent fee arrangements, which allow the risk of the litigation to be shifted from the client to the lawyer whenever the lawyer is best placed to evaluate the value of the action or bear its risk.

Fourth, class, derivative, and other forms of group litigation are virtually prohibited in Britain by the cost rules associated with class actions, the unavailability of legal aid, the prohibition on contingency fees, and the absence of public interest firms. By contrast, group litigation in the United States is actively encouraged.

Fifth, the second, third, and fourth effects are all magnified by the increasing frequency of proplaintiff fee awards in the United States under various federal and state statutes and various judicially created incentives in the state courts. ...

III

The effects of procedures on the development of the substantive law may usefully be divided into two categories: litigation effects and substitution effects. By *litigation effects* I mean developments in the substantive law that arise through the elaboration of legal doctrine by courts in response to litigation. By *substitution effects* I mean legal changes initiated by nonjudicial lawmaking bodies (for example, the legislature) with knowledge of the incentive effects governing litigation activity. In what follows, I first address litigation effects and then, in much briefer form, some possible substitution effects.

The influence of cost and fee rules on substantive doctrine can be either explicit or implicit. Explicit recognition arises whenever the court expressly makes reference to the applicable procedural rules in reasoning its way to a proposition of substantive law. For example, many American courts refer to cost and fee rules to justify expansive recovery of punitive damages. ...

Implicit recognition arises in the same way, but it does not depend on actual judicial articulation of the relationship between the cost and fee rules and the substantive doctrine. For example, a second striking difference between American and British tort law relates to the substantially greater pain and suffering damages that are recoverable in America. What causes this point to stand out is that most other heads of damage in personal injury litigation are very similar within the common-law world. But this more generous attitude toward pain and suffering can readily be traced to the widespread understanding that a major purpose of pain and suffering damages in America is to leave the plaintiff fully compensated with respect to special or pecuniary damages, while providing an additional form of damages sufficient to meet the lawyer's contingent fee. In England no such expansive measure is required since the lawyer's claim on his own client's recovery is limited to that portion of his fees which is not indemnified by the losing party. Thus, in England pain and suffering awards are far more modest, and an inflation-adjusted numerical maximum has been placed on them elsewhere in the Commonwealth. ...

The second set of hypotheses concerning the development of substantive law relates to the virtual absence of class and other forms of group litigation in Britain and their frequency and importance in the United States. I will illustrate these effects by reference to nuisance law and derivative actions in corporate law.

At one level, the absence of group litigation makes English law seem less rich, diverse, and complex in any area that relies primarily on group-based litigation. Thus, for example, in corporate law, while the statutory regimes enabling the creation of corporations are very similar in England and America, the judicial interpretation of those statutes appears quite different, particularly with respect to those portions of the statute that rely on group litigation for their enforcement. For this reason, in discussing the relative development of English and American corporate law, Gower stated, "American corporate law is now incomparably richer and more highly developed than its English parent."

Given, however, that the law will appear to be different, more complex, and more diverse, it is not necessarily also true that the law is in any fundamental sense very different. It simply means that the law, say, of shareholder and derivative actions will have been applied to a greater number of fact situations than its English counterpart. In America, the complexity and subtlety of the doctrines will have been played out in decided cases, while in England it is left as a matter for abstract speculation. That suggests, however, that the relative richness of American law may diminish in importance over time, so long as the incentive to litigate does not absolutely prohibit the bringing of cases in Britain. Thus, one would expect that so long as even a small number of cases is brought each year, eventually the British law would begin to appear more and more similar to its American counterpart. Yet the long run may be a long time away, and in the meantime the pace of legal evolution may have appeared to be quite different. In newer developing areas of law the differences should be particularly stark.

These differences in the appearance of the law and the relative rate of maturity are in some ways less important than what I will call the "cross-fertilization" effect that group litigation may have on doctrinal development. My suggestion is that group-based litigation does more than just put different types of cases before the court. In addition, the judicial resolution of these cases is likely to influence the substantive law that applies to *both* group and nongroup cases.

For example, within nuisance law, group litigation asserting environmental claims raises types of issues in America that British nuisance law virtually never needs to address. My hypothesis is that addressing these issues forces American courts to confront complex problems that call for the delicate balancing of competing interests. ...

To generalize the point, I hypothesize that doctrinal developments that arise first with respect to group litigation will, in time, influence the development of doctrine applicable to individual litigation. Thus, I predict that there will be greater differences in the substantive law between England and America in those areas of law with differentially greater group litigation in the United States than those areas in which most litigation in both jurisdictions is limited to individual suits. The point is, in a sense, quite simple. Courts are both limited to and driven by the cases that litigants put before them. Their understanding of legal problems is limited to the cases before them. At the same time, however, courts are driven to develop substantive doctrines to respond satisfactorily to the full array of cases they are called upon to decide. In elaborating substantive doctrines, courts are unlikely to separate entirely the individual and group claims. Rather, their understanding of the one type will likely influence, and sometimes profoundly influence, their resolution of the other and vice versa. The net effect will be an interdependence and a cross-fertilization of ideas that will, over time, lead to doctrinal divergences between America and Britain. ...

My third hypothesis is that the incentives for lawyers under the American system provide a spur for bringing provocative and novel claims. If one were to ask English or Commonwealth lawyers to describe what they find most remarkable about American litigation, a common response would identify the startling or provocative or novel extension of existing principle: "Can you imagine arguing that?" captures the type of reaction. My argument is that the origin of these novel developments lies in the incentive structure.

Novel claims are low-probability claims and are favored in American law by the cost rule, by the availability of contingent fees, and by the existence of public interest firms. They are further accentuated by the proplaintiff fee statutes in substantive areas. Low-probability cases, if brought often enough, succeed sometimes. Having succeeded once, they are brought repeatedly. Furthermore, once a number of cases have succeeded at trial, the supporting legal principle is then tested at the appellate level. Often the novel claim loses at the appellate level and little more is heard of the development apart from the memory of the headlines. On the other hand, sometimes these novel cases are affirmed on appeal: through a number of these decisions new legal principles are articulated and elaborated. It is these new principles and new theories that lead to a pace of legal change that is greater in America than in the United Kingdom, as cases at the frontier of the law tend to be brought in American courts. ...

My fourth hypothesis is really the converse of the second and third. Where the incentives to litigate are relatively similar in the two jurisdictions, I would anticipate that the evolution of the substantive law will also be relatively similar. Thus, in those areas of law that are relatively certain, where litigation costs are relatively small as a proportion of the amount in dispute, where contingent fees are not a significant factor, where there is unlikely to be differential risk adversity between the parties, where most litigation is done in individual form, where litigation is not influenced by proplaintiff fee statutes, and where differences in the rate of litigation are relatively unimportant (for example, in relatively more mature areas of the law), differences in substantive law are less likely. Furthermore, to the extent they do exist, they are in some sense more significant. Since these differences in the law cannot be causally related to differential incentives to litigate, the differences must necessarily reflect some broader difference between jurisdictions, traceable to cultural, social, or economic values, for example.

The fifth hypothesis is perhaps the most speculative of all. It builds upon the second, third, and fourth hypotheses stated above. I believe that the relatively more rapid decline of judicial formalism and the far more significant emergence of public law litigation (to use Chayes's phrase) in America as opposed to Britain both owe their origins, in part, to the differential incentives to litigate. On both of these questions it is possible to note the coalescence of the factors previously identified, that is, the greater American propensity to novel legal theories, the permissibility of group litigation, and the existence of public interest law firms and financing and proplaintiff fee statutes.

Turning first to formalism, it seems likely that the inadequacies of a formalist approach to legal decision making will be made more apparent in novel or group claims where the limits of precedent and the conflict of underlying principles are necessarily more intense and apparent. Thus, if American law is characterized by a greater frequency of such cases, then one would anticipate that the limits of legal formalism would be thrust upon courts with greater frequency and greater force in America. This, in turn, will cause American judges and legal commentators to have greater difficulty retaining a belief that law is best understood as a system of rules as opposed to a system of underlying principles, policies, and value judgments that are only converted into rules as required by the circumstances. For this reason, one might anticipate a greater number of occasions calling for a rather more open-textured, policy-oriented, less formal, more functionalist style of judicial reasoning in America than in England.

The differential incentives to litigate may also influence the style of judicial craftsmanship. It is arguable that in the British system, judges, when faced with cases that are in any sense novel or speculative, should try to give relatively more guidance through their decisions since they know that the frequency of such cases is much lower and the risk and cost to the plaintiffs of bringing them is greater. Thus, one might anticipate a more legislative style of judicial decision making (for example, *Rookes v. Barnard*) and a style of writing involving large numbers of hypothetical fact situations that serve as alternatives to actual cases for indicating the court's appreciation of the contours of the law once applied to a variety of such situations. Furthermore, this consideration may contribute to the infrequency of dissents and concurring judgments that might reduce the predictive value of judgments.

The emergence in America of public law litigation, the consequent modification of the bipolar paradigm of individual litigation, the development of structural remedies (to use Fiss's phrase), and the relative absence of these phenomena outside America can also be understood, in part, in the terms I have suggested. The origins of these phenomena lie primarily in the assertion of group-oriented claims through litigation: civil rights, school desegregation, prisoners' rights, reapportionment, environmental protection, and so on. These are, however, the very kind of claims that are so actively discouraged by the British incentives to litigate. ...

IV

These differential incentives to litigate are not the whole story. Let me now turn briefly to some substitution effect, by which I mean the decisions taken by nonjudicial lawmaking bodies to shape the law in light of the cost, fee, and financing rules in their respective jurisdictions.

The first tendency one would anticipate outside America is toward alternative forums for dispute resolution. These forums are characterized by different incentive rules for bringing cases wherever the disincentives to relying on civil litigation are greatest in the British system. Thus, my analysis predicts heavier British reliance on administrative agencies that typically, at a minimum, use the American cost rules and frequently supplement, if not virtually replace, the plaintiff's legal expenditures. With situations involving civil rights or corporate law, one would anticipate greater reliance on administrative agencies such as civil rights commissions and securities commissions as the primary, and often exclusive, forums for adjudication. Similarly, in new areas of law, my analysis suggests a tendency to rely initially on nonjudicial forums.

Second, British-style systems do not permit effective reliance on private enforcement through litigation except in high-probability and non-group-oriented cases. Articulating the jurisprudence of human and civil rights cases is apt to prove especially troublesome given the broad-textured language that characterizes these statutes. The high level of uncertainty posed for litigation in this area means that private litigation could not thrive in the absence of significant modification of the cost rules, a point that has been recognized implicitly by proposals to modify the fee and cost rules for certain classes of favored cases.

Third, assuming the need for legal change is relatively equal among jurisdictions, the relative dearth of litigation activity in these areas should lead to more frequent legislative intervention, updating, and reform in Britain as opposed to the United States, particularly in those areas characterized by very low absolute levels of litigation. This effect will, of course, be particularly prominent in areas that rely primarily on group cases, such as corporations statutes.

V

... [M]y emphasis on a systemic approach should be a productive source of prediction even if it falls short of an ultimate explanation of differences among legal systems. That is, even if the force of my argument is limited to establishing systematic causal relationships between the incentives to litigate and the underlying substantive law, it should support predictions concerning the likely direction of doctrinal changes if and when the underlying incentives are altered. This power of prediction is of particular importance at a time when there is an active debate whether to retain or modify the major litigation rules, which has resulted in some changes in both the Commonwealth and America.

In Canada, for example, in the past decade the cost rules for corporate derivative actions have been overhauled; the Province of Quebec has adopted a class action statute with public funding in response to the prior disincentives; Ontario is actively studying new class action rules that would substantially mimic American federal procedure, including a contingency-based fee arrangement; community-based legal centers receiving public funds have been established in a number of provinces; public interest law firms enjoying both public and private support are emerging; the new Charter of Rights and Freedoms includes a broad remedial provision that has already attracted special judicial treatment of costs in cases raising novel constitutional claims, and the application of the traditional two-way cost rule to environmental litigation has become a source of controversy and criticism. Similarly, England and Australia have made or are contemplating procedural reforms that lessen the financial disincentives to group litigation. In the United States, the past decade has seen significant extensions of proplaintiff fee statutes, although at the same time the period has also witnessed some moderation of fee awards in group litigation and severe restrictions on the public funding of legal services.

Understood systemically, these changes in the incentives to litigate are important not only in their own terms but also in terms of the effects they are likely to have on those areas of substantive law that fall within their reach. If incentives to litigate play the casual role that I have attributed to them, we should anticipate, for example, a narrowing of the differences of law with respect to group-based litigation as a result of the developments just listed. Furthermore, these substantive changes and the newly viable litigation from which they arise may cause a change in the judicial perception of its role. While that may not ease the task of explanation, it surely would focus the comparativist's search on the right place: on the procedural innovations, not on the substantive developments.

Fifth, and finally, by way of response to the hypothetical critic, I want to argue that a systemic emphasis in understanding differences in substantive law may contribute to an enhanced understanding of "the migration of legal ideas." To illustrate the point, I will refer again to my arguments concerning the acceptance of novel claims and their subsequent transnational portability. My argument suggests that the lag in adoption reflects not a cultural or social lag but rather the rational and predictable response of litigants to the differential incentives to litigate. In this sense, the analysis allows one to discriminate among examples of the transnational flow of ideas, distinguishing those that can be explained in the terms I suggest from those for which alternative explanations need to be found. ...

In conclusion, I want to refer briefly to the implications of my analysis for the general fee-shifting debate that has achieved such prominence recently in America and has been as least a source of some agitation within the Commonwealth. If I am right—if differential incentives to litigate under different systems of cost, fee, and financing rules do systematically affect the substantive law, the process and pace of legal change, the nature of legal reasoning, and the role of judges and their relationship to other lawmaking institutions—then the debate on fee shifting and related issues takes on a new significance. Now the debate cannot be confined to issues of increasing access to justice, increasing or decreasing the rate of litigation, discouraging less meritorious suits, and similar concerns. Rather, at the analytical level, the debate must be broadened to include the full range of consequences of the type that I have identified. And at the normative level, that recognition further complicates an already complicated problem, because it forces us to ask not just what sort of procedures we want, but also what kind of law we want—a subject that is the paradigmatic example of a matter on which reasonable people may disagree. ...

C. Disciplinary Use of Costs

1. Parties

The normal practice of ordering costs to follow the event is itself a rule for regulating the conduct of litigation because it is designed to discourage unmeritorious litigation. The instances that follow, however, are all exceptions to the normal rule that costs on a party-and-party basis follow the event. They should be taken as illustrations of how the court can use the device of costs to discourage abuse of the procedural system; to regulate the conduct of parties and their lawyers; and, in some small way, to deal more equitably with distributing the cost of litigation.

The court's use of costs as a disciplinary tool has as its starting point the generally expected outcome that the successful party will receive an award of costs on a party-and-party scale. If the court wants to discipline a successful party, all or part of that expected award of costs may be disallowed. If the court wanted to discipline an unsuccessful party, the court may increase the ordinary award of costs on a party-and-party scale to an award of costs on a solicitor-and-client scale. The latter scale is intended to be a more complete indemnity for the actual costs and fees incurred in the litigation.

There is considerable confusion in the case law as to when a court will intervene to award solicitor-and-client costs for disciplinary reasons. The criteria expressed in the rules are not intended to be exhaustive; there are a multitude of judicial decisions considering the factual circumstances for an award of costs on a solicitor-and-client scale and the results often seem to be contradictory.

The basic principles are clear. While the award of costs is within the discretionary power of a court, the court's discretion must be exercised in accordance with accepted principles and with regard to relevant considerations. It has been held that the award of costs on a solicitor-and-client basis "should only be made in very exceptional circumstances." See *Procor Ltd. v. USWA* (1990), 71 OR (2d) 410, at 434 (HC). The policy underlying this approach was articulated by Dubin JA (as he then was) in *Foulis v. Robinson* (1978), 21 OR (2d) 769, at 776 (CA):

> The expense of litigation is a matter of concern for all those interested in the administration of justice, but one must have regard for the burden which such costs place on all parties. Generally speaking, an award of costs on a party-and-party scale to the successful party strikes a proper balance as to the burden of costs which should be borne by the winner without putting litigation beyond the reach of the loser. There are, of course, cases in which justice can only be done by a complete indemnification for costs, but, in my respectful opinion, this is not such a case.

These principles leave open the question of what circumstances qualify as "exceptional." Generally, the court will order solicitior–client costs against a party who has made unfounded or unproven allegations of fraud or dishonesty. See, for example, *Murano v. Bank of Montreal* (1995), 41 CPC (3d) 143, additional reasons (July 3, 1996), doc. B314/93 (Ont. Gen. Div., Com. List). Certainly, where are party is shown to have engaged in dishonest or misleading conduct in relation to the pre-trial or trial process (for example, committed perjury), solicitor-and-client costs are justified. See *539618 Ontario Inc. v. Olympic Foods (Thunder Bay) Ltd.* (1987), 22 CPC (2d) 195 (Ont. SC), aff'd. 65 CBR (NS) 285 (Ont. SC).

Apart from proven or unproven allegations of fraud or dishonest conduct, the assessment of the basis for solicitor-and-client costs is fact-specific and guided by prior examples and the court's own assessment of what is "exceptional."

One of the issues raised by disciplinary costs orders is whether they are the most effective means of disciplining a party's conduct in litigation. Disciplinary costs orders also raise the question of the allocation or responsibility for wrongful acts in litigation between a party and his or her lawyer or in relation to non-parties. This question is considered in the following section.

2. Lawyers and Non-Parties

Young v. Young
[1993] 4 SCR 3

[Appellant's and respondent's separation was marked by a protracted series of court battles. Appellant was awarded custody of the couple's three daughters and respondent was granted access subject to court-imposed restrictions arising from appellant's objection to respondent's religious activity with the children. Respondent was ordered not to discuss the Jehovah's Witness religion with the children; not to take them to any religious services, canvassing, or meetings; or expose them to religious discussions with third parties without appellant's prior consent. Organized religion was not important to appellant although she wanted the children to be raised within the United Church.

The two older daughters liked their father but came to dislike his religious instruction to the extent that it was damaging his relationship with them and was contributing to the stress the children were experiencing in adjusting to their parents' separation.

The trial judge also made orders for the distribution of property and for costs. The respondent's interest in the matrimonial home was ordered transferred to the appellant because any remaining interest in the house, after respondent paid what was already owing to appellant, was to be transferred in the form of lump sum maintenance. Respondent was found responsible for debts incurred by the appellant for the support of herself and the children pending maintenance and for a debt made to a family corporation. Costs were awarded on a solicitor-client basis against respondent, his lawyer, and a religious society not a party to the proceedings.

Respondent appealed. The Court of Appeal set aside the limitations on religious discussion and attendance, on the ground that it was in the best interests of the children that they come to know their non-custodial parent fully, including his religious beliefs, unless the evidence established the existence of or the potential for real harm or the child did not consent to being subject to the access parent's views or practices. The Court of Appeal also altered the division of property and the awards of costs made by the trial judge.]

McLACHLIN J:

[On the substantive issues in the lawsuit, McLachlin J upheld the findings of the Court of Appeal, except with respect to certain property issues, and then considered the question of costs.]

1. *Costs Against the Respondent*

The trial judge ordered solicitor–client costs against the respondent. This award was made on the basis that the custody claim had "little merit," that the respondent attempted to mislead the court, that the respondent was recalcitrant on matters of custody and maintenance and, finally, on the basis that unnecessary proceedings had resulted. The trial judge also referred to the fact that someone else was promoting and paying for the legal action and that repetitive and irrelevant evidence was tendered.

The Court of Appeal, *per* Cumming JA, upheld the imposition of solicitor–client costs for four days of the trial and for four days of the interlocutory proceedings concerned with financial issues, on the basis of the husband's non-disclosure of financial information. Otherwise, costs against the respondent were reduced to party-and-party costs.

The Court of Appeal's order was based on the following principles, with which I agree. Solicitor–client costs are generally awarded only where there has been reprehensible, scandalous or outrageous conduct on the part of one of the parties. Accordingly, the fact that an application has little merit is no basis for awarding solicitor–client costs; nor is the fact that part of the cost of the litigation may have been paid for by others. The Court of Appeal meticulously considered all the proceedings in the light of these principles to arrive at its conclusion that only partial solicitor–client costs were justified.

Finding no error in the reasoning or conclusion of the Court of Appeal on this question, I conclude that its order for costs should remain, save to the extent different conclusions on the merits in this Court require that an adjustment be made. As I have made clear, the only respect in which I would vary the order of the Court of Appeal is that instead of ordering lump sum maintenance and a moratorium on the sale of the matrimonial home, I would restore the trial judge's order that the entire interest in the home be conferred on the wife. In my view, this difference does not warrant altering the award of costs against the respondent made below.

2. *Costs Against the Respondent's Counsel*

The trial judge ordered solicitor–client costs against counsel for the husband, Mr. How. For the reasons recited above in connection with costs against the respondent, she concluded that the proceedings had been unnecessarily lengthened. She also referred, at

p. 216, to the fact that "[c]ounsel for the respondent had a forum and a cause to pursue. Unfortunately, what was in the best interests of the children, their welfare, was totally lost by the respondent and his counsel in these protracted proceedings .... The court was subjected to unwarranted abuse, criticism and insult." She made no finding, however, that Mr. How had been in contempt of court.

The Court of Appeal held that no order for costs should have been made against Mr. How. There is no need to repeat that entirely satisfactory analysis. The basic principle on which costs are awarded is as *compensation* for the successful party, not in order to punish a barrister. Any member of the legal profession might be subject to a compensatory order for costs if it is shown that repetitive and irrelevant material, and excessive motions and applications, characterized the proceedings in which they were involved, and that the lawyer acted in bad faith in encouraging this abuse and delay. It is clear that the courts possess jurisdiction to make such an award, often under statute and, in any event, as part of their inherent jurisdiction to control abuse of process and contempt of court. But the fault that might give rise to a costs award against Mr. How does not characterize these proceedings, despite their great length and acrimonious progress. Moreover, courts must be extremely cautious in awarding costs personally against a lawyer, given the duties upon a lawyer to guard confidentiality of instructions and to bring forward with courage even unpopular causes. A lawyer should not be placed in a situation where his or her fear of an adverse order of costs may conflict with these fundamental duties of his or her calling.

The Court of Appeal found that the trial judge's criticism of Mr. How related to his conduct in bringing the action. Assuming that costs might, in certain circumstances, be imposed for contempt of court, none was found. Accordingly, no order for costs should have been made against Mr. How. I see no error in the conclusion of the Court of Appeal in this regard.

3. *Costs Against Burnaby Unit (Watch Tower Bible and Tract Society)*

Since the Watch Tower Bible and Tract Society (the Society) did not appear as a party, the costs awarded against it must be taken to have been premised on the fact that it supported the litigation financially. In effect, this was equivalent to an award for the tort of maintenance: see *Re Sturmer and Town of Beaverton* (1912), 25 OLR 566 (Div. Ct.), at pp. 568-69. To be liable for maintenance, a person must intervene "officiously or improperly": *Goodman v. The King*, [1939] SCR 446. Provision of financial assistance to a litigant by a non-party will not always constitute maintenance. Funding by a relative or out of charity must be distinguished from cases where a person wilfully and improperly stirs up litigation and strife: *Newswander v. Giegerich* (1907), 39 SCR 354.

In this case there was no evidence that the respondent had been induced to allow the Society to use his name in order that it might avoid liability for costs while advancing its own interests, that he would not have advanced his own interests in the absence of its help, that the Society's funding was for other than charitable motives, or that it controlled or directed the proceedings. Its support was "out of charity and religious sympathy" and did not constitute maintenance. The fact that the Society had a common interest with the respondent (as followers of the same religion) did not affect this.

Cumming JA so found, and then qualified his position at p. 85 by stating:

I hasten to add that it does not follow that the resources of the Watch Tower Bible & Tract Society can be brought to bear in every dispute between a Jehovah's Witness parent and a non-Jehovah's Witness parent. Once an issue of constitutional law of the kind raised here is settled then, if further litigation of the point between other litigants is supported, another question might arise. It may be that the right to assist without facing an award of costs cannot itself be used by the rich and powerful, no matter how great their interest in the issue, as an instrument of the oppression of those who must fight their battles alone.

I find again that no error has been made in the Court of Appeal's reasoning or conclusion. The evidence established that the respondent paid for a considerable portion of the cost of the proceedings personally, that the dispute was instigated at least in part by the appellant, and that the Society could not be considered to have stirred up the litigation, much less to have done so wilfully or improperly.

One argument, however, was not touched on by the Court of Appeal. This is the argument that the Society was an unnamed party to the litigation and, as such, should properly bear its portion of the costs. I would not discount the possibility that a court might properly hold an unnamed party liable for costs. The rule is that a non-party who has put forward another person in whose name the proceedings are taken cannot escape liability for costs in putting forward another: *R v. Sturmer and Town of Beaverton, supra*. However, it seems to me that the evidence here falls short of establishing that the society was a party in this sense. Even on the constitutional issue, it cannot be said that the Society put Mr. Young forward, in effect bringing its own action in his name. The constitutional issue was first raised by Mrs. Young's objection to Mr. Young's communicating his religious beliefs to the children and was validly pursued by Mr. Young in his own interest. The Society's interest in the constitutional issue is insufficient, as I see it, to distinguish it from intervenors who appear on constitutional cases and who have never been liable for costs.

NOTES AND QUESTIONS

1. Compare with *Young* how the courts dealt with costs in two other Jehovah's Witnesses cases.

In *Lawson v. British Columbia (Solicitor-General)* (1992), 88 DLR (4th) 533 (BC CA), a woman who was a Jehovah's Witness died as a result of a refusal to have a blood transfusion after having had a caesarean section. As a result of concerns by the woman's family that her refusal was made under pressure from other Jehovah's Witnesses who attended at the hospital, an inquest was ordered. A petition was brought by the deceased's husband to quash the decision of the respondent ordering the inquest. At first instance, the petition was dismissed and an award of costs on a solicitor-and-client basis was awarded against the Community of Jehovah's Witnesses in favour of the deceased woman's mother, the respondent solicitor general, and the coroner. On appeal, held, the appeal should be dismissed; the award of costs to be varied.

When the respondent solicitor general made the decision that the original inquiry did not fulfill the purpose of a coroner's inquest and ordered an inquest, he made an administrative decision. No *lis inter partes* was created. No person's rights were decided although some persons' interests might be affected during and by the inquest. There were adequate reasons why the respondent could conclude an inquest ought to be held, therefore the order was validly made.

Solicitor-and-client costs should be awarded only in exceptional cases where there has been reprehensible, scandalous or outrageous conduct deserving of chastisement. The evidence indicated that the real litigant in the launching of the petition was not the deceased's husband but rather the Jehovah's Witnesses community. Where the interest of the supporters becomes the motivating force then the proper course for those supporters is to seek intervener status. If accorded that status, they become liable for costs to the extent determined by the courts to be just in the circumstances. In the circumstances, costs should properly be awarded against the community; however, a case had not been made out for solicitor-and-client costs as no reasons indicated that the community's conduct deserved chastisement. Thus, the award of costs ought to be on a party-and-party basis.

Kennett Estate v. Health Sciences Centre, [1992] 1 WWR 60 (Man. CA) was another case involving Jehovah's Witnesses.

> HUBAND JA: ... The plaintiffs Steven and Velina Kennett husband and wife and are the natural parents of Daniel Kennett who died at the Health Sciences Centre on January 25, 1986 at age 15. Daniel Kennett had been admitted to that facility on January 14, 1986 suffering from an infection with an enlarged spleen. ...
>
> The Health Sciences Centre in Winnipeg is sued along with a number of employees. The employees are nurses and hospital administrators. A large number of doctors are also made party to the action on the basis of what they either did or failed to do in terms of the treatment of Daniel Kennett. Finally, the Attorney General of Manitoba is made a party to the action because at the heart of the case is a constitutional issue. The pleadings assert that Daniel Kennett's Charter rights were violated, and that certain portions of child welfare legislation in Manitoba and of the Criminal Code of Canada, RSC 1985, c. C-46, violate the constitutional protections guaranteed under the Charter.
>
> Daniel Kennett and his family were Jehovah's Witnesses and objected to the use of blood products in medical care. On the day prior to his death, Daniel Kennett was apprehended pursuant to the Child Welfare Act, SM 1974, c. 30 (also CCSM, c. C80), as his spleen had ruptured, and he required surgery which the attending physician felt could only be performed with the use of blood products. Late on January 24th, however, the attending physician decided that Daniel Kennett's condition was medically irreversible, and consequently no surgery was performed. He died in the early hours of January 25th.
>
> One aspect of the claim is based on allegations of negligence and breach of contract by those involved in the care of Daniel Kennett. The statement of claim seeks special and general damages as one might normally expect in a case of a fatality allegedly caused by negligence or a negligent breach of contract.
>
> However, the claim for damages based on negligence or breach of contract is secondary to the main purpose of the litigation, which is to have the court rule on the constitutional issues which have been raised in the pleadings. ...

The individual defendants sought an order for security of costs on the ground that the plaintiffs are resident in Ontario and on the ground that it would be just to make such an order in the circumstances of this case. In denying the defendants' motion seeking security for costs, Schwartz J took into account a number of factors. It was not the choice of the Kennett family that Daniel Kennett be moved from Ontario health care facilities to Manitoba ...

In my opinion, however, there are other factors which were not sufficiently considered, and which lead to the conclusion that security for costs should be ordered.

The affidavit material demonstrates that the Kennett family does not have the resources to post security. Indeed, they lack the resources to pay their own counsel the legal fees involved in litigating the action which has been commenced on their behalf. They look for support to co-religionists. The action in question provides the mechanism to raise constitutional issues of particular importance to Jehovah's Witnesses. The Kennett family has been well represented from the outset. Three lawyers attended on their behalf throughout a lengthy inquest hearing. A complex statement of claim, twice revised, has been filed. On examination upon his affidavit concerning the issue of security for costs, Steven Kennett was again represented by three lawyers. At that time he acknowledged that he had not been billed for legal services and did not expect to be.

Counsel for the plaintiffs proposes to examine each of the defendant doctors and nurses, and the various hospital administrators, in order to lay a factual foundation upon which constitutional issues will be argued. It will be an expensive process and an inconvenience to the individual defendants. The constitutional case for damages against the defendants other than the Attorney General of Manitoba is a tenuous one. The defendants are being drawn into a complex action, not because of a negligence claim, but in order to facilitate the plaintiffs and their co-religionists in attacking laws passed by the legislature. The right to involve the individual defendants in this constitutional challenge must be counter-balanced with the responsibility of securing their costs. This is particularly important where persons not directly responsible for costs are financing the litigation. ...

As to amount, the learned motions judge indicated [at 302 Man. R] that had he awarded security for costs he would have ordered $2,500 with respect to the Ontario hospitals, $3,500 for the Health Sciences Centre group, and $5,000 for the defendant doctors. These amounts are significantly less than the anticipated taxable costs on a party/party basis to which the defendants would be entitled through the examination for discovery stage if costs were awarded in their favour. In a case where these defendants are implicated because of the plaintiffs' expectation that their evidence will assist in establishing a constitutional case, the amounts should be set at a sum that more closely approximates the anticipated costs. I would order security of $10,000 with respect to the Ontario hospitals, $14,000 for the Health Sciences Centre group of defendants, and $22,000 for the defendant doctors.

2. The power to award costs against lawyers and non-parties flows in part from the wording of the basic power of the court to award costs, which speaks of the power to determine "by whom" costs are to be paid. Courts have historically treated this power as enabling the court to reach beyond the parties to the litigation to award costs against

non-parties and lawyers in appropriate cases. See *Rockwell Developments Ltd. v. Newtonbrook Plaza Ltd.*, [1972] 3 OR 199 (CA).

3. Some jurisdictions, such as Ontario (rule 57.07), Nova Scotia (rule 63.15(2)), and British Columbia (rule 57(30)), now deal specifically with the subject of costs orders against a solicitor. The NS rule 63.15(2) provides as follows:

Where in a proceeding, costs are incurred improperly, or without reasonable cause, or arise because of undue delay, neglect or other default, the court may, when the solicitor whom it considers to be responsible, whether personally or through a servant or agent, is before the court or has notice, make an order,

(a) disallowing the costs as between the solicitor and his client;

(b) directing the solicitor to repay to his client costs which the client has been ordered to pay to any other party;

(c) directing the solicitor personally to indemnify any other party against costs payable by the party;

(d) directing a taxing officer to inquire into the act or omission, with power to order or disallow costs as provided in clauses (a) to (c).

4. A typical example of a case under such rules is *Aliferis v. Parfeniuk* (1985), 1 CPC (2d) 41 (Ont. CA). There the court awarded costs against the solicitor for the plaintiff in respect of interlocutory proceedings to extend the time for service of an originating process where the extension of time was required as a result of the solicitor's negligence. Refer to the decision above in *Buleychuk v. Danson*, in section III.C. "Time for Service and Extensions." Should costs in that case have been awarded against the plaintiff's lawyer, instead of against the defendant?

5. Another example is the decision to award solicitor-and-client costs of an unsuccessful class proceeding against the non-party promoters of the action who had had purported to sell rights in the proceeds of the action to the public: see *Smith v. Canadian Tire Acceptance Ltd.* (1995), 36 CPC (3d) 175 (Ont. Gen. Div.), aff'd. (November 8, 1995), doc. CA C21786, C21811 (Ont. CA).

6. Could the threat of costs being awarded against a lawyer inhibit the lawyer's pursuit of a client's claims or interfere with the solicitor–client relationship? Consider *Naeyaert v. Elias* (1985), 4 CPC (2d) 298 (Ont. HC). The plaintiff's action was dismissed at trial and the judge gave notice that he might award costs against the solicitor. However, the material on the motion to determine the question demonstrated that the decision to proceed with the trial was made by the plaintiff, contrary to the advice of her lawyer, who had substantial reservations about liability and who had obtained an offer of settlement from the defendant, and thus no order was made against the lawyer. The material on the motion was available only because the client waived the solicitor-and-client privilege. How could the lawyer have established his position if the privilege had not been waived? How can lawyers protect themselves in the future in these kinds of circumstances?

7. For articles on the use of costs as a regulatory device, see Neil Gold, "The Court's Authority To Award Costs Against Lawyers," in E. Gertner, ed., *Studies in Civil Procedure* (1979), chapter 4, and P. Lantz, "Costs as a Regulatory Device" (1981), 2 *Advocates' Quarterly* 396.

D. Settlement and Formal Offers To Settle

Only a very small percentage of actions that are commenced are resolved through a trial. In Canada, this figure is about 5 percent or less. While the rate of cases ending in a default judgment (typically debt-collection cases) is high (estimated to be 40 percent or greater in Ontario), a substantial number of cases commenced are resolved through a settlement negotiated by the parties. Settlement, therefore, is an essential component of the system because it helps maintain at an acceptable level the number of actions that require a trial (or other adjudication—that is, a motion for summary judgment) for resolution. However, settlement also mirrors essential characteristics of the adversarial system that have been already discussed. If the adversarial system is founded on ideals of autonomy of the individual as reflected in party initiation and control of litigation, settlement is an apt element because it permits each side to the litigation to negotiate and bargain for resolution of the dispute through a process driven by self-interest and evaluation of the comparative strengths and weaknesses of the respective parties. Recall the discussion of the arguments for and against settlement in chapter 4, "Challenges to the Traditional Model," in this context.

As we have seen already in this chapter, costs can be used as a regulatory device to encourage or discourage particular kinds of litigation or specific claims. With the process of settlement, costs can be used to encourage acceptance of reasonable offers and, conversely, to punish recalcitrant litigants who refuse to consider appropriate offers and thus increase the volume of disputes resolved through negotiation. Indeed, most jurisdictions have such a device to do just that: see, for example, Ont. rule 49, BC Rules of the Supreme Court, rule 57(18), NB rule 49, and Sask. rule 184C. Moreover, many jurisdictions have rules of professional conduct designed to encourage settlement (for example, Ontario rule 3, commentary 5: "The lawyer should advise and encourage the client to compromise or settle a dispute whenever it is possible to do so on a reasonable basis"; see also Ontario rule 10, commentary 6).

Although the details of the "offer to settle" rules in the different jurisdictions vary, these particular costs rules share essential elements. Parties are, of course, free at any time to negotiate their way to resolution of a claim. However, if one party is willing to compromise but the other steadfastly clings to a position, the party willing to terminate the proceeding on particular terms (usually the payment of a sum of money) makes a formal written offer of settlement. If the opposite party accepts it, then the proceeding is ended. However, if the opposite party refuses to settle on those terms and if, at the end of the proceedings (usually the trial), the opposite party is awarded less than what was offered, particular costs sanctions are applicable unless the court makes a specific ruling to the contrary. Thus, through this device, parties can be exposed to increased liability for costs if they refuse to engage in the settlement process and to seriously consider an offer of settlement.

Many of the same issues that arise in respect of access to justice re-emerge in the context of settlement. The same barriers that prevent access to the litigation process may render a party incapable of pursuing the legal process through to its conclusion. An imbalance of factors such as economic wealth, expertise, and bargaining power may cause a party to accept a poor settlement rather than proceed with the litigation. Often, the practical choice is to accept a poor settlement or to abandon the litigation process entirely. Given this, to what extent to should settlement incentives focus on the early stages of litigation rather than on costs awards at the end of the process? Recall that the new Ontario mandatory mediation rule, rule 24.1, has as its goal the achievement of settlements in the early stages.

Niagara Structural Steel (St. Catharines) Ltd. v. W.D. LaFlamme Ltd.
(1987), 58 OR (2d) 773 (CA)

The judgment of the Court was delivered by MORDEN JA (orally):

The defendant appeals from a judgment in the amount of $48,942.53 ($35,531.91 and $13,410.62 for prejudgment interest) on the plaintiff's claim against it for the balance owing on a construction contract between these parties. The plaintiff, having obtained leave, cross-appeals against the trial Judge's disposition of costs.

The issue in the appeal is whether the trial Judge was right in concluding that the defendant agreed to extend the time for completion by the plaintiff of its subcontract with the defendant to perform the structural steel work on a bridge-widening project for the Ministry of Transportation and Communications. The defendant was the general contractor on the project.

Having arrived at the conclusion that the subcontract was extended, the trial Judge held that the plaintiff was entitled to recover from the defendant the balance owing to it under the subcontract (which was agreed at trial to be $35,531.91) and that the defendant was not entitled to recover any damages on its counter-claim flowing from the alleged delay of the plaintiff in completing the subcontract. The trial Judge assessed these damages at $23,636.37. The defendant had claimed $44,700.92. On the appeal the defendant has submitted that the assessment should be increased to $27,116.37.

[The court considered and dismissed the appeal from the judgment.]

With respect to the cross-appeal the facts are as follows. The plaintiff served an offer to settle on the defendant on April 26, 1985, some two months before the trial. It read:

> The Plaintiff offers to settle the claim and counterclaim including all claims for prejudgment interest in these proceedings on the following terms:
>   1. The Defendant shall pay to the Plaintiff the sum of $35,600.00.
>   2. The disposition of costs shall be reserved to the Trial Judge.

We note that the amount of the claim in the statement of claim was $36,040.13 together with prejudgment interest. As indicated earlier, the total amount of the plaintiff's recovery in the judgment was $48,942.53.

The applicable provision in the Rules of Civil Procedure is contained in r. 49.01(1) which reads:

> 49.10(1) Where an offer to settle,
>   (a) is made by a plaintiff at least seven days before the commencement of the hearing;

> (b) is not withdrawn and does not expire before the commencement of the hearing; and
>
> (c) is not accepted by the defendant,

and the plaintiff obtains a judgement as favourable as or more favourable than the terms of the offer to settle, the plaintiff is entitled to party-and-party costs to the date the offer to settle was served and solicitor-and-client costs from that date, unless the court orders otherwise.

The plaintiff asked for costs on a party-and-party basis to April 26, 1985 and on a solicitor-and-client basis from that date forward, on the basis of this provision. The trial Judge "ordered otherwise" under the exception to the rule. Her reasons, in full, are as follows:

> It is clear that the plaintiff's judgment is more favourable than the offer and that ordinarily the plaintiff would be entitled to solicitor-and-client costs from the date the offer was served. Rule 49.10(1)(c) states this to be the case "unless the court orders otherwise." I have decided this is a proper case in which the court should rule otherwise.
>
> The case involved the construction of a rather complex contract into which were incorporated terms from another complex contract. The prospective result for either party was either complete success or complete defeat, subject to the actual ascertainment of the items constituting the claim and the counterclaim. It was not a situation of negotiating damages as in motor vehicle or wrongful dismissal cases. The offer of the plaintiff maintained the plaintiff's entitlement to the whole of its claim and the denial of the defendant's counterclaim. The inducement to settle was the waiver of any prejudgment interest. It was a reasonable offer to settle from the plaintiff's viewpoint.
>
> The parties were entitled to an adjudication of the issue between them by having the court construe the contract. I do not think that rule 49.10, though designed to encourage settlement, should be invoked to force a defendant to abandon a position put forward in good faith because of the risk of the added burden of solicitor-and-client costs. I am of the opinion that the defendant did advance its position in good faith throughout.

With respect, we think that the learned trial Judge erred in principle in resorting to the exception in r. 49.10(1) on the facts of this case.

While the most general provision respecting costs, which is set forth in s. 141(1) of the *Courts of Justice Act*, SO 1984, c. 11, is that costs are in the discretion of the Court, it may be noted that in this provision itself there is the qualification "[s]ubject to the provisions of ... rules of court." The relevant rule in the case where there has been an offer of settlement by a plaintiff is r. 49.10(1). The importance of written offers to settle is emphasized by the reference to them in the opening part of r. 57.01, which is concerned with the awarding of costs. The general, or basic, rule contained in r. 49.10(1) is intended to be an incentive to the settlement of litigation. While r. 49.10(1) does not set forth the basis for resorting to the exception to it, it is reasonable to assume that the occasions for the application of the exception should not be so widespread or common that the result would be that the general rule is no longer, in fact, the general rule. If this were to happen, the presumption in favour of the general rule and the resulting reasonable degree of predictability respecting the incidence of costs would disappear and the incentive policy of the rule would be substantially frustrated. Another consequence would be a more uneven application of the rule in litigation generally.

As far as the occasions for resort to the exception are concerned, if the framers of the rules could have expressed the relevant bases or factors with any degree of comprehensive detail it may be assumed that this would have been done. Accordingly, it would be wrong, for several reasons, to attempt to do so by judicial declaration. Keeping the matter on a general plane, it can be said that resort should only be had to the exception where, after giving proper weight to the policy of the general rule and the importance of reasonable predictability and the even application of the rule, the interests of justice require a departure.

In the present case, as we have indicated, we do not think that the circumstances justified a departure. First, the rule is not confined to non-complex cases or cases of claims for damages of the "negotiable" type referred to in the reasons. (In any event, the defendant's counterclaim, which was asserted as a defence to the plaintiff's claim, was for damages of the "negotiable" kind.) These considerations clearly were not the most important basis of the trial Judge's decision but they apparently carried some weight in her reasoning. Secondly, we think that the offer to forgo prejudgment interest on the facts of this case resulted in a genuine offer of compromise of the plaintiff's claim. Thirdly, we do not think that in the circumstances of this case, and indeed of most cases, the good faith of a party should be given significant weight. Until there is some evidence or indication to the contrary, the good faith of parties is to be generally assumed.

We note that the decisions which have come to our attention are generally in accord with our approach to the proper application of r. 49.10(1). In the following decisions the Court applied the basic provision in subr. 49.10(1) and (2), and not the exception: ... [many cases cited omitted]. In the following cases, in which the Court considered that there was insufficient or no compromise element in the offer, resort was had to the exception: ... [cases cited omitted].

In the result, the appeal is dismissed with costs and the cross-appeal is allowed with costs, including those of the motion for leave to appeal, and the costs order in the judgment below is varied to provide that the plaintiff be awarded its costs of the action on a solicitor-and-client basis from and after April 26, 1985.

Appeal dismissed. Cross-appeal allowed.

NOTE AND QUESTION

Subsequently, in *Data General (Canada) Ltd. v. Molnar Systems Group Inc.* (1991), 6 OR (3d) 409 (CA), the court held that an offer to settle need not contain an element of compromise and a plaintiff's offer to settle for 100 percent of a liquidated claim may result in an award of solicitor-and-client costs (however, the absence of an element of compromise is a fact that the court may consider in exercising its discretion to "order otherwise"). In short, the court sanctioned the use of rule 49 by plaintiffs in debt-collection cases to obtain solicitor-and-client costs (rather than party-and-party costs) throughout, by the simple device of serving an offer to settle for 100 percent of the debt owed at the outset of the litigation. Is this a fair and reasonable application of the rule?

E. Security for Costs

Most jurisdictions have rules that attempt to ensure that a defendant falling within certain categories and who is successful at trial will receive at least partial payment of costs. A typical illustration is afforded by rule 56 of the Ontario Rules:

WHERE AVAILABLE
 56.01(1) In a proceeding where it appears that,
   (a) the plaintiff or applicant is ordinarily resident outside Ontario;
   (b) the plaintiff or applicant has another proceeding for the same relief pending in Ontario or elsewhere;
   (c) the defendant or respondent has an order against the plaintiff or applicant for costs in the same or another proceeding that remain unpaid in whole or in part;
   (d) the plaintiff or applicant is a corporation or a nominal plaintiff or applicant, and there is good reason to believe that the plaintiff or applicant has insufficient assets in Ontario to pay the costs of the defendant or respondent;
   (e) there is good reason to believe that the action or application is frivolous and vexatious and that the plaintiff or applicant has insufficient assets in Ontario to pay the costs of the defendant or respondent; or
   (f) a statute entitles the defendant or respondent to security for costs, the court, on motion by the defendant or respondent, may make such order for security for costs as is just. [am. O. Reg. 221/86, s. 161]
 (2) Subrule (1) applies with necessary modifications to a party to a garnishment, interpleader or other issue who is an active claimant and would, if a plaintiff, be liable to give security for costs. [am. O. Reg. 364/89, s. 6]

(See also Alta. rules 593-599, NB rule 58, NS rule 42, PEI rule 42, Sask. rule 547, and fzederal rule 446.)

To what classes of persons or organizations does this rule apply and not apply? What is the rationale for the inclusion or exclusion of each class? Can a defendant in an action be required to give security?

A similar power to order security exists with respect to appeals. See rule 61.06. If a defendant seeks to appeal a trial judgment, can the court order security for costs against the defendant-appellant?

CHAPTER SIX

Pleadings and Disposition
Without Trial

I. INTRODUCTION

In this chapter and in chapter 9, "Discovery," we address the issue of the pre-trial exchange of information between the parties to an action. There are two major aspects to this issue: how much information exchange should be required and how should it be achieved?

Of course a threshold question is why have information exchange at all, and, if so, for what purpose? (To what extent does the adoption of the adversary system necessitate information exchange?) It is generally accepted that, in advance of trial, it is necessary to define what are the issues in the case—to identify what it is the plaintiff says the defendant did and how the defendant responds. This aids efficiency, since the parties and the court then need not worry about matters that are agreed. More important, it is essential to procedural fairness. Recall from chapter 1, "Introduction to Civil Actions and Courts," that "fair process," in the trial context, entails the right to participate in the proceedings by calling evidence and challenging the evidence put forward by one's opponent. The right to participate in the proceedings is not of much use unless you know the case against you so that you can marshal relevant evidence and argument.

The major mechanism for defining the issues and giving notice has traditionally been pleadings: responsive written statements setting out the position of the parties. However, as we will see, today discovery has come to play an increasingly important role in issue definition and notice giving.

There are two main forms of discovery—oral and documentary. Oral examination for discovery refers to the process whereby a party is entitled to put questions to his or her opponent before the trial to obtain a fuller and more complete account of the basis of the claim or defence. Documentary discovery refers to the pre-trial exchange between the parties of relevant documents. Given that the discovery process provides an opportunity to define the issues and to put the parties on notice of the nature of the claims and defences to be advanced at trial, the question arises how best to allocate the function of issue definition and notice giving between pleadings and the discovery process. How much weight should pleadings be expected to bear? How much information should the parties be required to include in their pleadings, given that much additional information will come to light during the discovery process? In turn, this raises questions about the relative effectiveness, efficiency, and cost of information exchange through pleadings and the discovery process.

Pleadings and the discovery process largely reflect the traditional, adversarial, and bipolar model of disputing. For instance, the pleading rules presuppose that the dispute will be defined and shaped by the parties, without the intervention of a judge. Moreover, the rules largely contemplate an all-or-nothing approach to participation in the pre-trial process; either one is a named party and entitled to participate fully or is a non-party with no rights to participate at all. While modern discovery rules permit the examination for discovery of a non-party with the leave of the court, such examinations remain exceptional in the litigation process.

This chapter begins with an overview of pleadings and the mechanics of their exchange between the parties. We then consider in detail the content requirements of pleadings. The principal requirement is that pleadings contain a statement of "all material facts." What are material facts? How can one know all of the material facts at the time of pleading? What are the consequences of the failure to set forth all material facts? If material facts come to light after the exchange of pleadings, can the pleadings be amended? These are some of the questions to be considered in section II, Nature and Function of Pleadings, below.

In sections III, Substantive Adequacy, and IV, Summary Judgment: Piercing the Pleadings, below, a variety of avenues available to a litigant to attack the pleadings of his or her opponent are explored. Using these various devices, one may challenge the pleadings and, if successful, prevent the litigation from proceeding beyond the pleading stage. For example, if a party's pleading does not allege facts that, if proven at trial, would constitute a legally valid cause of action or defence, they can be struck out (and the litigation stopped) for lack of substantive adequacy. Even if the pleadings do allege facts that, if proven at trial, would constitute a valid legal cause of action, a party may try to end the litigation at the pleading stage by moving for "summary judgment." This process is often described as "piercing the pleadings." It is discussed below in section IV. The court may look behind the pleadings in order to consider whether, for instance, evidence is available to establish the facts alleged in the pleading. If the court is satisfied that no evidence is available to establish the facts as alleged—that there is no genuine issue for trial—the court will grant summary judgment. The court will also grant summary judgment in the event that, assuming all the facts could be established, there really is no genuine issue to be tried in that on the basis of the facts alleged, it is clear which of the parties is entitled to judgment as a matter of law.

II. NATURE AND FUNCTION OF PLEADINGS

A. An Overview of the Pleading Process

Trial is the culmination of the litigation process. It is then that the court resolves the conflicting assertions of law and fact of the parties and finds for one against the other. For the trial to be fair, it is essential that each party know in advance what the assertions of the opponent will be. A court hearing is not spasmodic but a single episode, and adjournment is an indulgence not a right. Each party must therefore be ready with evidence to prove whatever parts of his or her case the opponent has put in issue and to repel those assertions of the opponent which are disputed.

Surprise can never be entirely eliminated from any process of fact determination that depends on the oral presentation of witnesses in the dramatic setting of a courtroom. But surprise is objectionable if there is evidence to meet the unexpected thrust and the affected party is not able to find and present it in time. All of the common law systems have endeavoured to minimize the risk of surprise by the pre-trial procedures of pleadings and discovery. Together, these procedures require the parties to give notice to each other of their respective claims and defences and to afford each party the means of obtaining a further elaboration of the case that has to be met. The method of administering the two devices, the extent to which they are relied on, and the relationship between them vary considerably from jurisdiction to jurisdiction. They remain, however, the basic notice-serving tools of the procedural system of all the common law jurisdictions.

Pleadings are statements in writing of the claim and defence of the plaintiff and defendant respectively that are exchanged between them before trial. The pleading of the plaintiff is called the statement of claim. In this document, the plaintiff has to set out the remedy claimed from the defendant—for example, damages or specific performance—and describe the events that took place that would justify the court awarding this remedy—for example, the defendant assaulted the plaintiff or the defendant refuses to perform a contract to sell land to the plaintiff. Under the pleading rules this description in the statement of claim of the relevant events is called a "statement of the material facts on which the party pleading relies."

If the defendant wishes to defend the action—that is, to avoid suffering judgment by default—a response to the statement of claim is required. Unless the defendant wishes to make a preliminary attack on the adequacy of the plaintiff's pleading (we will discuss this possibility later in section III, Substantive Adequacy) the defendant must respond by delivering a pleading: the statement of defence. In the statement of defence, the defendant must respond to each of the plaintiff's allegations. Logic dictates that there are three types of responses a defendant can make to the plaintiff's allegation.

1. *Admissions.* If an allegation made by the plaintiff is true, the defendant can and should respond by admitting the allegation. Indeed, the rules so require. However, if a defendant admits allegations made by the plaintiff and, taken together, these allegations entitle the plaintiff to relief as a matter of law, the defendant will have admitted the plaintiff's claim and the plaintiff will be entitled to judgment based on the admissions. Given this consequence, one can well understand that defendants are slow to deliver a statement of defence admitting all of the plaintiff's allegations. (Indeed, a defendant who is prepared to admit all of the plaintiff's allegations is not likely to deliver a statement of defence at all, thus permitting the plaintiff to take default proceedings.) Typically, the defendant will admit allegations that are obviously true—for example, that the parties are accurately identified or that in fact an accident occurred on the stated date—but beyond this defendants are often slow to make admissions. Facts once admitted in the pleadings are no longer in controversy and do not have to be proven at trial.

2. *Denials.* If the defendant denies that an allegation made by the plaintiff is true, or if the defendant is not prepared to admit the allegation because of uncertainty about its truth or falsity, the defendant will deny the allegation. For instance, in a contract action, the defendant might admit that the contract was entered into, but deny any failure to perform it. Or in a product liability case a soft drink manufacturer, because of a lack of knowledge at the pleading stage about whether these facts are true, may deny that the plaintiff purchased the product and that it subsequently exploded. A denial (sometimes called a "traverse") puts the facts denied in issue, and the plaintiff then has the burden of proving those facts to the satisfaction of the court at trial.

3. *Lack of knowledge.* It is not always possible for a defendant to know whether or not a given factual allegation is true or not. It is therefore open to the defendant to plead lack of knowledge about the truth or falsity of the allegation. This does not constitute an admission, and the plaintiff is required to be able to prove this fact at trial.

Affirmative defences—confession and avoidance. "Confession and avoidance" is legal terminology used to describe another logical alternative that is open to the defendant—that is, admit the relevant allegation made by the plaintiff but set forth further facts that, if true, avoid the legal consequences argued for by the plaintiff. A simple example would be for the defendant in an assault action to admit striking the plaintiff but to plead that it was done in self-defence. Similarly, in our contract example, the defendant might admit the contract and non-performance but plead that a subsequent agreement with the plaintiff dissolved any obligation of performance. This form of defence, an admission ("confession") coupled with the pleading of further facts that, if true, destroy the legal effect of the admission ("avoidance"), amount to the pleading of an affirmative defence—that is, something beyond a mere denial—and places on the defendant the burden of proving at trial the new facts pleaded by way of defence—that is, avoidance. In practice, a plea of confession and avoidance is often combined with a denial: the defendant will first deny the plaintiff's allegations and then, usually in a separate paragraph, in the alternative, admit those allegations and allege further facts by way of avoidance. Such pleading in the alternative is permitted by the rules. Take the contract example again. A defendant may first deny that a contract was made and then go on to plead, in the alternative, that, if there was a contract, it was subsequently terminated by further agreement. The defendant is in effect saying, "I deny there was a contract, but if there was one it is now at an end."

In this way the defendant is setting up two lines of defence. If the first fails, there is always the second to fall back on. At trial, the plaintiff will have to prove the contract. If necessary, the defendant will have to prove the subsequent agreement.

In any case a defendant may in the statement of defence employ each of the responses discussed above: admit certain allegations, deny others, plead lack of knowledge to others, assert one or more alternative defences, or plead in the alternative.

Reply. The pleadings will "close"—that is, the process ends—after delivery of the statement of defence if the defendant's defence rests on a mere denial of the plaintiff's allegations. However, if the defendant has raised an affirmative defence—that is, pleaded in confession and avoidance—a further pleading from the plaintiff may be called for. This pleading of the plaintiff is called a *reply*. A reply is not strictly necessary and, in some jurisdictions, is not permitted, if the plaintiff simply denies the facts pleaded affirmatively by the defendant—for example, that by a subsequent agreement the plaintiff discharged the defendant from performance of the original agreement. In the absence of a reply, the plaintiff is deemed to have denied the defendant's allegations and to have put them in issue. If the plaintiff elects to deliver a reply, the express denial of the defendant's allegations is called a joinder of issue. However, if the plaintiff wishes not merely to deny the defendant's defence but to assert an affirmative defence, a reply must be delivered. For example, a reply will be necessary if the plaintiff in a contract action admits the defendant's allegation that a subsequent agreement ostensibly discharged the defendant from any obligations under the original contract, but pleads that this later agreement was obtained by the fraud of the defendant. The plaintiff thus has raised a plea in confession and avoidance and will have the burden at trial of proving the facts asserted. This is but one example of circumstances where a reply will be necessary. It illustrates, however, the more general principle that a reply will be required whenever the plaintiff intends, in response to the defence, to rely on issues or a version of the facts that have not been raised by the earlier pleadings. The requirement of a reply in these circumstances serves the function of notice giving and issue defining. Further pleadings beyond reply are possible, but leave is required before they can be delivered. They are encountered rarely and it is not necessary to describe them.

One variant of the above pattern needs to be mentioned. As discussed, the defendant may assert a claim against the plaintiff through a counterclaim or may bring in new parties through a third-party claim. Additionally, in cases where there are two or more defendants, one or more of them may make a cross-claim against the other(s). Each of these types of proceedings will entail specific pleading documents. While we will not take up the rules governing each, the mechanics of these pleadings can be understood by analogy to those of the statement of claim and the statement of defence.

So far we have looked at the advantages of pleadings to the parties in preparing for trial by giving them notice and by defining the issues. Another advantage usually attributed to pleadings concerns the result of the trial. Since the pleadings are filed in court, the precise questions raised and determined in the action will be placed on record. In a proceeding where a party seeks to prevent relitigation of a cause of action or an issue by relying on the doctrine of *res judicata* (discussed in chapter 7, "The Size and Scope of Litigation"). The court will be able to consult the pleadings and the judgment in the original action to determine what issues were raised and decided.

Pleadings are the first step in the translation and filtering process, wherein the story or narrative that your client recounts is cast into legal form. This is significant in that aspects of your client's story are divided into those that are legally relevant (in your view) and those that are not. As we will discuss in the following section, the requirement to plead "all material facts" presupposes that the facts pleaded will be relevant to a legally recognized cause of action, and that no facts will be included that are not material to that cause of action. Thus, the rules require that you engage in this filtering process. As the dispute winds its way through the various legal processes, the problem often becomes less and less recognizable to the client as his or her problem. Many commentators have been critical of this aspect of the legal process, arguing that it results in the decontextualization of the problem. This is considered problematic for at least two reasons. First, by stripping away context, the "moral crux" of the matter may never be addressed; what is really at the nub of the dispute may go unresolved. Second, by stripping away context, we may lose sight of other interests and persons who may be affected by the litigation and whose perspective may be vital to a just resolution of the dispute. As you read this chapter, think about the ways in which the rules of procedure result in the stripping away of context. What types of rules would be appropriate if we desired a more contextualized approach?

B. The Mechanics of Pleading

The rules of each jurisdiction set time limits for the exchange of pleadings. If the action is commenced by a statement of claim, time for service is measured from the issuance of the claim. For example, in Ontario, the time permitted for service of the statement of claim is six months from the date of issuance (see rule 14.08). In jurisdictions where the action is commenced by a writ, time for the delivery of the statement of claim will be measured from the date of the defendant's appearance (a document the defendant is obliged to file in response to receipt of the writ of summons if he or she intends to defend the action). Similarly, the statement of defence is required to be "delivered" within a specified time frame. "Delivery" is a technical term used in most jurisdictions to refer to the dual requirement of "serving and filing." Thus, the defendant must both serve the plaintiff and file the statement of defence with the court within the allotted time. In Ontario, the statement of defence must be delivered within 20 days after service of the statement of claim where the defendant is served in Ontario (see rule 18.01(a)).

As previously discussed, the court has a discretion to extend the time for service prescribed by the rules. Additionally, it is common practice for the parties to extend the time requirements by agreement, with the result that the pleading stage is often more drawn out than the timetable prescribed by the rules would suggest. Where a party fails to meet the time requirements prescribed by the rules or agreed on by the parties, the opposing party may take action to note his or her opponent in default.

C. The Form and Contents of the Pleadings

The rules of pleading in Canada are uniform and represent a particular form or system of pleading. The central requirement, as alluded to earlier, is that the pleadings contain a "precise statement of the material facts on which the party relies for his or her claim or defence." But such a system of pleading is not universal. It was not followed at common law; at that stage of our history, "issue pleading" was in vogue. Nor is it in use in the United States, where "notice pleading" is the order of the day.

As already noted, in Canada, the exchange of pleadings is not the only mechanism we have for formulating the issues before trial. Once the pleading process is complete, discovery is available to further narrow and define more sharply the matters in dispute. The question then presents itself of how the issue defining function is to be allocated between pleadings and discovery. Given the broad range of pre-trial discovery, what should be the function of pleadings? In particular, how much detail should we require the pleadings to give? When broad pre-trial discovery was introduced in the United States, it was accompanied by a shift from detailed "fact pleading"' to more general "notice pleading." Not so in Canada. Although we have adopted broad discovery devices, we have retained detailed fact-pleading rules, inherited from England where, because of the lack even today of broad pre-trial discovery, pleadings must alone bear the function of issue definition. In England, discovery of documents is available, but examination for discovery is unknown. Fact discovery is theoretically possible through the less effective device of written interrogatories, but these may only be administered with the leave of court and in practice are not greatly used. Recently, the English rules were radically changed to permit a judge to require the pre-trial exchange of witness statements. A major issue in Canada is how much detail must be contained in the pleadings.

In the materials below, we first consider the meaning of "material facts," and the extent of detail required to be contained in the pleadings. While at first blush this may appear to entail no more than an examination of the procedural requirements of the pleading process, it is important to bear in mind that the procedural requirements are directly linked to the substantive issues underlying the case. For instance, the requirement to plead all material facts seeks to ensure that the party pleading has set forth a sufficient factual foundation for the claim in law that he or she seeks to advance. In the event that the pleading fails to set forth all facts necessary to establish a substantive cause of action, the action will be vulnerable to attack and possible dismissal. The links between the procedural requirements and the substantive issues raised by the case will become increasingly clear as we explore challenges to pleadings below, in sections III and IV. After considering in detail the "material fact" requirement, we will return to the discussion of the comparison of the pre-trial procedures in Canada and the United States in order to consider the appropriate allocation of issue defining and notice giving between pleadings and discovery.

The following two cases discuss the concept of "material facts." Both cases are the result of decisions rendered in motions brought by defendants for "particulars." In order to fully appreciate these cases, a few words about "particulars" are necessary. After the receipt of the pleading of an opposing party, the rules permit a party to seek "particulars" of any allegation contained in the pleading—for example, see Ontario rule 25.10. A court entertaining a request for particulars will order that they be provided if this information is required by the moving party in order to prepare its response, and such information is not within the knowledge of that party. Often, "particulars" are described in relation to "material facts" as providing further details of the material facts alleged in the pleadings. In the cases below, the moving parties seek particulars of allegations contained in the pleadings. In each case, the respective courts conclude that the pleadings are defective in that they have failed to set out the material facts and the pleadings have failed to meet the more general requirement of pre-trial disclosure.

Copland v. Commodore Business Machines Ltd.
(1985), 3 CPC (2d) 77 (Ont. Sup. Ct.)

MASTER SANDLER: This motion raises the question of how much information must be set forth in a statement of defence, in a wrongful dismissal action, when the defendant employer seeks to plead dismissal for cause. This issue has practical significance because of the frequency with which this type of action and this type of defence comes before this Court.

The statement of claim reveals that the plaintiff started his employment in May of 1982 as a national sales manager. This employment was terminated on July 5, 1984, without any prior warning. There follows the usual claims for relief.

The key paragraph in the statement of defence is para. 9, containing the pleas of "cause," and I now set out each of the subparagraphs of para. 9, together with the relief that the moving party-plaintiff seeks in relation to each subparagraph.

> 9(a) The plaintiff attempted to mislead representatives of the defendant as to the amount of his salary and as to his obligation to repay advances provided to him by the defendant;

The plaintiff seeks "particulars" of the "times" at which and the "nature of the attempts" which the plaintiff is alleged to have made, to "mislead" the defendant as alleged; and also particulars of the "circumstances in which such attempts are alleged to have been made."

> 9(b) The plaintiff knowingly or incompetently permitted excessive costs of sales;

The plaintiff seeks particulars of the "instances of and the manner in which the plaintiff permitted excessive costs of sales."

> 9(c) The plaintiff entered into imprudent personal transactions which brought his personal interests into conflict with his duties to the defendant;

The plaintiff seeks particulars of the "imprudent personal transactions ... as pleaded in para. 9(c)."

> 9(e) The plaintiff abused limousine and entertainment privileges provided to him at the defendant's expense;

The plaintiff seeks "particulars of the instances and circumstances" in which he is alleged to have abused these privileges.

> 9(f) The plaintiff was insubordinate at and systematically attempted to undermine the position and authority of the defendant's president by mispresentations [sic] made with respect to the latter's conduct and abilities;

The plaintiff seeks "particulars of the occasions and circumstances in which the plaintiff is alleged to have been insubordinate" and how he attempted to "undermine the position and authority of the defendant's president," and particulars of the "misrepresentation" referred to in para. 9(f).

9(g) On the final day of his employment the plaintiff openly confronted the defendant's president in the presence of another employee, in a manner which was abusive, improper, and incompatible with the continuance of the plaintiff's employment relationship with the defendant.

The plaintiff seeks particulars of this "confrontation" which would include a general description of exactly what the defendant did on this particular occasion.

The plaintiff's counsel argued that these particulars are not within the plaintiff's knowledge and that they are necessary in order to enable the plaintiff to plead to the statement of defence. There is no affidavit filed by the plaintiff (or by anyone else) to this effect.

Under r. 25.06(1), "Every pleading shall contain a concise statement of the material facts on which the party relies ... , but not the evidence by which those facts are to be proved." This rule is almost identical to former R. 143. Material facts must be pleaded; evidence must not be pleaded. In between the concept of "material facts" and the concept of "evidence" is the concept of "particulars." These are additional bits of information, or data, or detail, that flush out the "material facts," but they are not so detailed as to amount to "evidence." These additional bits of information, known as "particulars," can be obtained by a party under new r. 25.10, if the party swears an affidavit showing that the particulars are necessary to enable him *to plead* to the attacked pleading, and that the "particulars" are not within the knowledge of the party asking for them. An affidavit is not necessary only where the pleading is so bald that the need for particulars is patently obvious from the pleading itself. New r. 25.10 is substantially the same as former R. 140, and in my view, the law on this subject has not changed by reason of the change from the Rules of Practice to the Rules of Civil Procedure. ...

Rule 25.06(1) mandates a minimum level of material fact disclosure and if this level is not reached, the remedy is not a motion for "particulars," but, rather, a motion to strike out the pleading as irregular. It is only where the minimum level of material fact disclosure has been reached that the pleading becomes regular. Thereafter, the discretionary remedy of "particulars" under r. 25.10 becomes available, if the party seeking particulars can qualify for the relief under the provisions of that rule.

Thus it becomes necessary, in any specific type of action, to determine the minimum level of material fact disclosure required for any particular pleading, in order to determine if the pleading is or is not regular. This is not an easy task by any means, and much common sense must be brought to bear in this endeavour. As well, the purpose and function of pleadings in modern litigation must be kept constantly in mind. It is often difficult to differentiate between, and articulate the difference between material facts, particulars, and evidence.

Some assistance is obtained, as to statements of defence, from new r. 25.07(4) which seems to be the successor to parts of former Rr. 144 and 145. Under this new rule, a party must plead "... any matter on which the party intends to rely to defeat the claim of the opposite party ... ," and the "material facts" in relation to such matters must be set forth as required by r. 25.06(1).

Further assistance is obtained from Bullen and Leake and Jacob's Precedents of Pleadings (12th ed., 1975) at pp. 1207 to 1208, where the precedent sets forth a plea of misconduct of an employee, in wilfully disobeying the reasonable orders of his employer, or by habitually neglecting his duties, or by dishonestly converting to his own use money which he had received to the use of the employer. The precedent then indicates that the pleading is to "state the particulars of the misconduct which justified the dismissal according to the fact." Further on, the notes say "The ground of dismissal must be specifically pleaded (*Tomlinson v. London Midland & Scottish Ry.*, [1944] 1 All ER 537 at 541 (CA))." And further, "The defendant must in his defence give particulars of the misconduct to show clearly in what it consisted, so as to enable the plaintiff to meet the charge, and if this is not done, further particulars will be ordered: see *Saunders v. Jones* (1877), 7 Ch. D 435 (CA)." ...

In my view, the minimum level of material fact disclosure for a statement of defence in a wrongful dismissal action, where the defendant employer relies on cause for the dismissal, is very high, and the pleading must contain sufficient detail so that the employee and the Court can ascertain the exact nature of the questions to be tried, and so that the employee can meet the charge and respond in his reply accordingly.

As one studies the allegations in paras. 9(a) through 9(g) of this statement of defence, it becomes apparent that material facts relating to each of these allegations are missing and have not been pleaded. For example, the material facts of the "imprudent personal transactions" referred in 9(c) are missing. The material facts concerning which employees were abusively and improperly treated and of what the plaintiff's conduct consisted are missing from 9(d). The material facts concerning how the plaintiff abused his limousine and entertainment privileges, as pleaded in para. 9(e), are missing.

I am satisfied that each of paras. 9(a) through 9(g) fails to meet the minimum level of material fact disclosure required by rule 25.06(1) in the particular context of this particular action, and I thus strike out para. 9 in its entirety, with leave to the defendant to amend as it may be advised. (I suggest that the amended para. 9 be divided into additional paras. 9A, 9B, etc. containing all the necessary material facts, so that the numbering of the remaining paras. 10-18 of the statement of defence is not changed, which will make any subsequent review of the amended pleading much easier.)

Costs of this motion to the plaintiff in the cause.

Order striking out paragraphs of statement of defence granted.

NOTES AND QUESTIONS

1. Note that in the *Copland* decision, Master Sandler refers to Ontario rule 25.06(1), which states that "every pleading shall contain a statement of the material facts upon which the party relies ... but not the evidence by which those facts are to be proved." It is generally accepted that the "no evidence" rule flows from the requirement to plead material facts—that is, the requirement to plead material facts is interpreted to mean "plead material facts only, not evidence." As Master Sandler points out, the dis-

tinction between material facts and evidence is sometimes tenuous. At the core of the distinction is the notion that it is not necessary to plead circumstances that merely tend to prove the facts already alleged. For example, the *material fact* might be whether a traffic signal was red or green at a particular moment in time. The evidence that will prove that material fact might consist of the eyewitness testimony of pedestrians who recall seeing that the light was green at that particular moment.

2. Master Sandler notes that the precise content of material facts must be determined by reference to the function and purpose of modern-day pleadings. How ought we to assess the purpose of modern-day pleadings in the light of the fact that the rules now permit wide-ranging discovery? Given the availability of discovery, how much detail should we require in the pleadings? In coming to his decision, Master Sandler relies on Bullen and Leake and Jacob's *Precedents of Pleadings*. Observe that these authors were writing in a jurisdiction where examination for discovery is unknown. In the light of this, is his reliance on this authority appropriate?

3. What was achieved by requiring the defendant to provide this information at the pleading stage, rather than permitting the plaintiff to seek this information during discovery?

4. Master Sandler concludes that when an employer relies on "cause" in a wrongful dismissal suit by a fired employee "the minimum level of material fact disclosure ... is very high." Should greater specificity be required in the defendant's as opposed to the plaintiff's pleading?

5. *Material facts and improper pleading.* The flip side of the requirement that all material facts be contained in the pleading is the requirement that only material facts be asserted. We noted earlier that one aspect of the requirement of "material facts only," is that the allegations be facts and not evidence. Another component of this is that the facts that are included be material. Thus, facts that are immaterial or irrelevant are not to be included. While this prohibition is at least implicit in the material facts rule, the rules go further and specifically provide that such material may be struck out. They do so by using archaic and confusing language, to the effect that the court may strike out "scandalous" or "embarrassing" material. See Alta. rule 129, BC rule 19(24), Nfld. rule 14.24, NS rule 14.25, Ont. rule 25.11, NB rule 27.09, PEI rule 14.25, and Sask. rule 173. The case law indicates that, despite the pretension of the language, these rules amount to a prohibition against pleading irrelevant facts.

A pleading is *scandalous* if it contains indecent or offensive matter or allegations made for the purpose of abusing or prejudicing the opposite party. But nothing that is relevant can be scandalous. The test is whether the matter alleged to be scandalous would be admissible to establish the case of the pleading party. For instance, it would not be scandalous for the defendant to plead that the plaintiff had committed an infamous crime to support a defence of justification in a defamation action in which the plaintiff complained that the defendant had published a statement that the plaintiff was a criminal.

As far as *embarrassing* material is concerned, "to warrant striking out on the ground of embarrassment, a pleading must be embarrassing in the legal sense of the word." (*Le Merchant v. Irish & Maulson Ltd.*, [1940] OWN 506, at 507).

> No pleading can be said to be embarrassing if it alleged only facts which may be
> proved—the opposite party may be perplexed, astonished, startled, confused, troubled,

annoyed, taken aback, and worried by such a pleading—but in the legal sense he cannot be "embarrassed." But no pleading should set out a fact which would not be allowed to be proved—that is embarrassing. ... Even if a pleading set out a fact that is not necessary to be proved. Still, if it can be proved, the pleading will not be embarrassing. Anything which can have any effect at all in determining the rights of the parties can be proved, and consequently can be pleaded—but the Court will not allow any fact to be alleged which is wholly immaterial and can have no effect upon the result.

(Riddell J in *Duryea v. Kauffman* (1910), 21 OLR 161, at 168.)

This statement about what constitutes embarrassing material is, on first reading, confusing if one takes too literally the notion that the pleadings determine what can be proven at trial. Not everything and anything pleaded can be proven at trial. It can only be proven at trial if it is properly pleaded, and it is only properly pleaded if it is relevant (legally) to the claims or defences made out by the pleadings. An illustration will help.

If D sues K for the payment of royalties due under a patent licensing agreement and K admits using the patent under the agreement, K cannot plead that D is not the owner of the patent without also alleging an express warranty of the validity of the patent or fraud. The reason is that, absent these further allegations—the invalidity of the patent—D's non-ownership of it, is wholly immaterial—K has promised to pay and D's action is on that promise.

A mundane analogy may drive the point home. In a typical left-hand-turn automobile collision case, the defendant may not plead or prove at trial that the plaintiff is purveyor of child pornography or a member of Heritage Front. Such an allegation would be simply legally irrelevant to the issues raised by the pleadings.

Famous Players Canadian Corporation Limited v. J.J. Turner and Sons Ltd.
[1948] OWN 221 (HC)

GALE J: In this action the plaintiff, as owner of certain lands in Peterborough, asks for a declaration that the defendant, the owner of the adjoining property, has encroached on those lands, for an injunction restraining the maintenance of such encroachment and for its removal, or, in the alternative, for damages. The statement of defence raises many issues which will be discussed separately at a later stage. It is enough to say now that upon application made to him, the learned Senior Master struck out paras. 3, 4, 5 and 10 and portions of paras. 6 and 11 of the defence, with leave to amend. This is an appeal from that order. The several paragraphs to which objection is taken will be dealt with in the order in which they appear in the statement of defence.

The first paragraph attacked is para. 3. In it the defendant pleads that if any encroachment exists it was not caused by the negligence of the defendant or of any person for whom the defendant is legally responsible. A denial of negligence is clearly irrelevant to the claim set up by the plaintiff and accordingly the paragraph was quite properly struck out as embarrassing.

In para. 4 the defendant alleges that if the footings of its building encroach, "the defendant's predecessors in title by a Conveyance to them dated October 25th, 1911, and

registered on the 27th day of October, 1911, as Number M-7146 became lawfully entitled to such lands." The learned Senior Master held that the closing phrase was a plea of
a legal conclusion and he struck out the whole paragraph with leave to amend. May I say
at once that I do not understand that a conclusion of law, as such, may never be pleaded.
It is quite proper and necessary to set forth the legal conclusion which the party will ask
the Court to adopt, provided that conclusion is adequately supported by a statement of
facts which are material to that result. I concede, of course, that the plea of a legal
proposition cannot be allowed to stand alone; the facts upon which it is based must be
given. On the other hand, it is equally objectionable simply to plead facts without
mentioning the legal consequences which the party will contend flow from the existence
of those facts, for otherwise the opposite party and the Court may be left under a
complete misapprehension as to the outcome which the party pleading will seek to
secure at the trial. Pleadings are meant to disclose fairly the proposition being presented
by the party pleading, and many examples come to mind where to limit the document to
a recital of facts would be to defeat that fundamental purpose. Moreover, Rule 141
requires pleadings to contain a statement of material facts; how can it be ascertained
whether the facts chosen are material if the document is silent as to the legal conclusions
upon which the party relies? Rule 143 would also seem to sanction the view just expressed, and accordingly I say with confidence that it is wrong to suggest that under our
Rules a conclusion of law as such may not be included in a pleading.

Applying those principles to this statement of defence, it is obvious that para. 4
should be restored, for although a legal consequence is set out, it is sustained by a
statement of facts which are material to it. Admittedly, the paragraph could have been
drafted so as to give greater clarity, but it does not otherwise offend the ordinary
conventions of pleading.

Order accordingly.

NOTES AND QUESTIONS

1. Consider the present wording of the rule respecting the pleading of material facts
and conclusions of law; see, for example, Ontario rule 25.06(2). On what basis should
the court go beyond that and require a party to plead a legal conclusion to or characterization of the material facts? How important is that requirement to the notice-giving or
issue-defining function of pleadings? Should this be a general rule?

2. In *Allen v. Mt. Sinai Hospital* (1980), 28 OR (2d) 356, the trial court held that the
failure to specifically plead battery in the statement of claim did not preclude the plaintiff
from advancing this theory at trial. In this case, the plaintiff had pleaded all facts
material to a claim in battery or in negligence but had stated in the claim that the facts as
alleged constituted negligence. On appeal, the Ontario Court of Appeal reversed, holding
that the plaintiff was precluded from advancing the case in battery, but granted the
plaintiff leave to amend the statement of claim. Is there something special about a cause
of action founded on battery that requires that a defendant receive specific notice of the
plaintiff's intention to advance his or her case on this basis?

3. Often, the party pleading will simply not be in a position to know the facts supporting his or her claim. In simply pleading a conclusion of law, a party runs a substantial risk that his or her pleading will be struck out. Is there an alternative? Consider a situation where the plaintiff sues for damages arising out of a slip and fall on an icy sidewalk. One of the causes of action that might be alleged is negligence. The authorities are clear that simply alleging that the defendant was negligent is not proper pleading: *Thompson v. TTC*, [1947] OWN 920 (Master). While the plaintiff may be convinced that the owner of the property was negligent, the plaintiff may not know the precise negligent act of the plaintiff. In the case of the icy sidewalk, the negligent act(s) might be one or more of, for example, failing to check the sidewalk to see if it were icy, knowing that it was icy but failing to apply ice melter, or applying insufficient ice melter. In practice, it means that in order to comply with the pleading rules, a plaintiff in this situation must speculate about what might have been the negligent act and set out several alternative factual scenarios that it will then test in the course of the discovery process. Is this appropriate?

4. *The nature of statements in pleadings.* The nature of the statements made in the pleadings is to be noted. They are statements of the parties' contentions. Although they often take the form of statements of fact, they are nothing more than allegations. They are not evidence, like statements in an affidavit, evidence—that is, sworn statements of fact that are admissible in court. Rather, they are statements about what the party believes occurred and hopes to prove at trial. Using various discovery devices, the lawyer will hope to elicit the necessary information before trial. Where the pleader does not know or is uncertain of the material facts, he or she must rely on knowledge of the substantive law and of the rules of evidence and also exercise a considerable degree of imagination and creativity in anticipating what information will emerge as the action develops. For assistance and perhaps inspiration, the lawyer may consult the pleadings in similar cases in the past.

5. *Truth in pleadings.* Before leaving this topic, it is important to note that "truth in a pleading" has been and continues to be a problem. In most lawsuits that go to trial, the result turns on the inability of one of the parties to prove the facts necessary to support the positions taken in his or her pleading—that is, most lawsuits are decided on the facts. Given this state of affairs, would the whole process be improved, simplified, and shortened by requiring the parties to verify their pleadings, to swear that the allegations made are true? The answer, based on US experience, would seem to be "no." Often in that country the parties are or were at one time required to verify their pleadings. Despite this requirement, the pleadings remained a statement of the parties' contentions, positions or allegations. All that the requirement of verification did, as one learned law professor pointed out, was to lead US attorneys "to lie every day" (if the appropriate test was whether they were possessed of the information necessary to establish the contentions set forth in their pleadings). See, generally, J.J. Cound, J.H. Friedenthal, A.R. Miller, and J.E. Sexton, *Civil Procedure, Cases and Materials*, 4th ed. (1985), 508-16; and D.W. Louisell and G.C. Hazard, *Cases and Materials on Pleading and Procedure*, 4th ed. (1979), 754, 779. Verification of pleadings fails to achieve its aim because it misconceives the purpose of pleading, which is merely to record the parties' contentions and allegations. Since these are not present statements of fact, they are not an appropriate subject for verification.

However, situations arise where positions taken in allegations made in pleadings are demonstrably untrue—that is, they are either unprovable or evidence exists to disprove them. Is there a mechanism for disposing of such cases, short of lengthy pre-trial procedures and a trial? The answer is to be found in the device of a motion for summary judgment, discussed in section IV, below.

6. *US pleadings.* The system of pleading employed in Canada and elsewhere in the Commonwealth is sometimes referred to as "fact pleading," because of the obligation on the pleader to plead the material facts relied on. In the United States, a different system prevails (at least in theory) and the pleader is not required to plead material facts but to identify in more general terms the transactions in issue and the claims arising therefrom. This is referred to as "notice pleading." So, for example, it is sufficient in the United States in a motor vehicle accident case to allege the place and date of the accident and that the plaintiff's injuries were caused by the defendant's negligence (without particularizing the negligence). The idea is that the issues will become further defined through employment of a broad range of discovery devices and will ultimately be defined through pretrial conference orders specifying the issues to be tried. Do you see advantages or disadvantages in this different system?

Rule 11 of the US Rules of Civil Procedure, applicable to matters litigated in the federal courts, while not requiring that the pleader swear to the truth of the allegations contained in the pleading, does go some way to ensure that only claims that are grounded in both fact and law proceed through the litigation process. The rule requires lawyers (and parties, if not represented) to sign pleadings in order to indicate that the pleading,

> to the best of the signer's knowledge, information and belief formed after reasonable inquiry ... is well grounded in fact and is warranted by existing law or a good faith argument for the extension, modification, or reversal of existing law, and that it is not interposed for an improper purpose, such as to harass or to cause unnecessary delay or needless increase in the cost of litigation.

If a pleading is signed in violation of the above, a court may, on its own motion or a motion brought by a party, impose appropriate sanctions, including an order to pay reasonable expenses that the opposing parties incurred because of the pleading.

What are some of the factors that have led to this requirement? In the United States there is increasing concern about excessive and meritless litigation. Recall that Ontario has devised rules that are also aimed at lawyers who cause "costs to be incurred without reasonable cause or to be wasted by undue delay, negligence or other default." Under Ontario rule 57.07, the court may disallow costs between a lawyer and his or her client and order the lawyer to repay or reimburse the client money paid on account of costs. When this rule is applied to pleadings, how does it resemble and differ from rule 11? Are both rules justified? Why or why not?

D. The Relationship of Pleading to Proof: Variance

Pleadings, and the material facts contained therein, are vital because they determine the outer parameters of the case. While other pre-trial processes, such as particulars and discovery, may shrink the dimensions of the dispute, pleadings set its outer limits. Generally speaking, these outer limits cannot be expanded without the consent of all parties or the leave of the court. Recall that a party is required to state all material facts on which he or she relies in support of his or her claim or defence at the pleading stage.

Pleadings are not an end in themselves. They have a function—to define the issues that have to be determined and to give each party notice of the case he or she has to meet. As a corollary, a party will not normally be permitted to advance a claim or defence at trial that was not raised in the pleadings. The purpose of pleading would be frustrated, and due process denied, if the parties were not bound by the positions taken in their pleadings.

The following case illustrates in part what, ultimately, pleading is all about. It demonstrates the problem that will be encountered at trial by a party who has not fully pleaded the case he or she seeks to rely on—the divergence between pleading and proof or, as it is often called, the problem of variance.

MacDonald Construction Company v. Ross
(1980), 17 CPC 142 (PEI SC)

McQUAID J: This is an action for damages which the plaintiff is alleged to have suffered by reason of the negligence of the defendant.

Briefly, the plaintiff is a building contractor and the defendant was, at all material times, solicitor to the plaintiff. One of the plaintiff's properties was destroyed by fire, and the plaintiff instructed the defendant, as its solicitor, to take the necessary steps to realize upon a fire insurance policy earlier placed on the property. The main action arises out of the defendant's alleged negligence in not so doing until after the limitation period of one year had expired, thus rendering any such claim barred by statute.

Upon the completion of the taking of evidence, counsel for the defendant proceeded to make his argument. During the course of his presentation he advanced the proposition that even if the defendant were negligent, which he did not admit, and even if he had pursued the claim for insurance with due diligence, he would not have been successful in any event, since the property in question was vacant on the date of the loss, contrary to the terms of the policy. Since the plaintiff's claim against the defendant was for loss allegedly incurred in the defendant's failure to pursue the insurance claim to recovery, his alleged loss being the amount which he claims he should have recovered, the defendant's argument was that no loss would have been recovered in any event, the policy being voided by vacancy, and hence the plaintiff had no recoverable claim against the defendant.

Counsel for the plaintiff objected to the defendant being permitted to advance this line of argument, since it had never been pleaded, that had such been pleaded as a defence, his examination of witnesses would have taken a different course, and that he was taken by surprise and therefore prejudiced. Counsel for the defendant argued that this defence was implicit in his pleadings, or in the alternative, that he be permitted to amend his pleadings, and moved accordingly.

The issues presently before the Court are twofold, first whether he is to be permitted to pursue this argument without amendment, or is he precluded from so doing by his pleadings; second, whether he be permitted to amend, and, if so, the implications of any such amendment.

In his defence, the defendant pleaded:

> 2. The Defendant denies that the Plaintiff retained the defendant as its solicitor as alleged or at all.
>
> 3. If the Plaintiff retained the Defendant as its solicitor (which is denied) the Defendant denies that he was instructed to take any action against The Casualty Company of Canada within the limitation period, or at all.
>
> 4. The Defendant does not admit that the Plaintiff suffered the damages alleged or at all.

The proposed amendment would be in the following words:

> 5. In the alternative, the Defendant denies liability to the Plaintiff for his failure to take action against The Casualty Company of Canada as alleged in paragraph 6 of the Plaintiff's Statement of Claim, because such an action, had it been taken within the limitation period, would have been unsuccessful by reason that the Plaintiff's building referred to in the Statement of Claim at the time of the fire had been vacant for more than thirty (30) consecutive days and, therefore, was a loss excluded under the Plaintiff's fire insurance policy with The Casualty Company of Canada.

Paragraphs 2 and 3 of the defence are, I think, immaterial to the issue at hand. The first question to be determined here is whether para. 4 is sufficiently broad to encompass the particular line of argument on defence.

The purpose of pleadings is to enunciate to the opposing party, and to the Court, precisely and with some degree of definition the issues in dispute as between the parties, to enable each to know, in advance of trial the issues to be met, the evidence which will be required, and the shape which the trial is likely to take.

Rule 14.04 provides:

> Every pleading shall contain a statement in summary form of the material facts on which the party pleaded relies on for his claim or defence. ... and the statement shall be as brief as the nature of the case admits.

And Rule 14.14:

> Subject to Rules 14.15 to 14.18 [not relevant here], a party in his defence or in any subsequent pleading shall,
>
> (c) specifically plead any matter, for example, performance, release, payment, or any relevant statute of limitation, statute of frauds, fraud, or any fact showing illegality that,
>
> > (i) might make any claim or defence of the opposing party not maintainable;
> > (ii) if not specifically pleaded, might take the opposing party by surprise;
> > (iii) raises issues of fact not arising out of the preceding pleadings.

The requirement is, therefore, that pleadings are required to be so framed that they contain all material facts and matters in a manner sufficiently clear and concise to present the nature of the claim, or defence, so that the opposing party will not reasonably be taken by surprise, or which, in themselves will not raise collateral or subsidiary issues not otherwise pleaded. (*Cherry v. Petch*, [1946] OWN 383; *Saliarius v. Saunders; Saunders v. Saliarius*, [1948] 2 WWR 706). The commentary on the corresponding English Rule, 18/8, as it appears at p. 271 of the 1976 Annual Practice indicates that the defendant must make it quite clear what line of defence he is adopting.

Referring back to the defence as filed, "The Defendant does not admit that the Plaintiff suffered the damages alleged or at all," this does not, in my opinion, meet the requirements of the Rule. It is a simple traverse which, in effect, does little other than to put the plaintiff to the proof of his allegations. It does not, as I suggest it should, alert the plaintiff to the line of defence which the defendant intends to advance, that is to say, that the plaintiff was in breach of his insurance contract, and by reason of such breach could not have recovered in any event.

I would therefore be of the opinion, and so hold, that, on the basis of the pleadings as they stood at the time of trial, the defendant is precluded from pursuing this line of argument.

Rule 15 provides that a party may amend his pleadings at any time with leave of the Court. The granting or withholding of such leave is discretionary in the Court, and although the evidence, but not the argument, had been completed, the application for amendment was made "at trial," and hence not out of time. The wording of the proposed amendment is appropriate in that it clearly defines the issue and line of argument on which the defendant presumably will rest his defence.

The first question is: should I exercise that discretion, and permit such an amendment? I am grateful to counsel for providing me with their many authorities, all of which I have reviewed, but out of which I will refer only to those which appear to me to be the most applicable.

In *Re Robinson's Settlement; Gant v. Hobbs*, [1912] 1 Ch. 717 (CA) Fletcher Moulton LJ states at p. 726,

> With regard to the other question, I would point out that these rules are meant to assist the administration of the judicial functions of the Court, and they are not meant to introduce rigid technicalities which would militate against full justice being done by the Court. They are there to protect litigants, and in cases where there is no wrong done, and nobody is taken by surprise or put at a disadvantage thereby, it is perfectly open to the Court either to grant an amendment or to decline to enforce strict obedience to these rules, more especially in the case of rules to the breach of which no penalty is affixed.

In the same case at p. 728, Buckley LJ said:

> The effect of the rule is, I think, for reasons of practice and justice and convenience to require the party to tell his opponent what he is coming to the Court to prove. If he does not do that the Court will deal with him in one of two ways. It may say that it is not open to him, that he has not raised it and will not be allowed to rely on it; or it may give him leave to amend by raising it, and protect the other party if necessary by letting the case stand over. The rule is not one that excludes from the consideration of the Court the relevant subject-matter for decision simply on the ground that it is not pleaded. It leaves the party in mercy and the Court will deal with him as is just.

This case was cited as an authoritative statement of the law in *Pirie v. Richardson*, [1927] 1 KB 448, Lord Hanworth MR at p. 453. Two Canadian cases on point are *Toronto v. Hutton*, [1951] OWN 639, and *Simrod v. Cooper*, [1952] OWN 720.

Thus, the principle is established that the Rules of Court, at least insofar as they apply to pleadings, are intended to constitute the criteria required to be met in case disclosure, for the information of the litigants, and, insofar as the Court is concerned, to enable it to adjudicate with equal fairness to those litigants on all matters in issue as between them. Where, however, either party may not have complied with those criteria, the Rules should not be strictly and rigidly construed to preclude amendment, and thus defeat justice being done. This is not to say that in all cases will such amendment be allowed, or if allowed, without terms and conditions. ...

Having reviewed these authorities, it now becomes necessary to attempt to relate them to the present matter. Reference has already been made to the defendant's pleadings with respect to which I have held that they are, in themselves, insufficient to permit the defendant to develop the line of defence upon which he launched in his argument.

Next, I think the evidence must be looked at to determine whether the question of vacancy was raised. I have examined the evidence of Earl Beaton, the representative of the insuring company and can find no reference therein to the possibility that the property was vacant, or even that he was aware or suspected it might have been. The matter was not in any way broached.

The cross-examination of Dewar MacDonald, president of the plaintiff company contains the following exchange beginning at the foot of p. 34 of the transcript:

Q. Did anybody live in it after the first week of September?
A. No.
Q. So, the property was vacant until September 1 until the fire, is that correct?
A. Oh, six weeks, a month, somewheres around there.
Q. I see. When you obtained your insurance, did you advise Mr. Beaton that the property was vacant?
A. It wasn't vacant at the time I put insurance on it.
Q. I see, but it was vacant from somewhere around September the 1st, on?
A. Approximately there.
Q. And this fire occurred when?
A. October the 31st, '75.
Q. That's normally Hallowe'en night?
A. That's right.
Q. And you knew on Hallowe'en night that this property was vacant?
A. That's right.
Q. And this property was not a summer or seasonal dwelling, this was a property you had for purposes of rental the full year around, is that correct?
A. That's right.

Apart from a casual reference to vacancy on Halloween night on p. 78(a), there appears to be no other mention of the fact of vacancy.

It is on the basis of this brief passage of evidence that the defendant would introduce his proposed line of argument. It could be said, that, in a subtle way, a groundwork had been laid. However, there was nothing in the defendant's pleadings which would alert the plaintiff, which, of course, is the purpose of pleadings. The evidence of MacDonald, above quoted, was subsequent to that of the insurer, Beaton. I am quite sure, knowing the examining capabilities of both counsel, had there been any prior intimation that the vacancy element would be a factor, the examination of Beaton might well have taken a different course. Indeed one can speculate that the entire thrust of the plaintiff's case, pleadings, discovery and evidence, might well have been different. I think it would be extremely difficult for any counsel, upon reading para. 4 of the defence, to anticipate this line of defence.

I do not believe that, as the pleadings now stand, the defendant should be permitted to pursue it.

However, as Fletcher Moulton LJ pointed out in *Re Robinson's Settlement*, supra, the function of rules is to present the respective position of the litigants in such a manner as will enable the Court to administer justice between them, and where they appear to militate against this end, they should either be interpreted flexibly, or where this is not possible, amendment on terms should be permitted in the discretion of the Court.

It is possible that had the defendant's suggested defence been properly pleaded, rather than approached obliquely, it might conceivably constitute a good defence to the action, and he should not be denied his defence by a rigid application of the rule. On the other hand, had the defendant so pleaded, it is equally conceivable that the plaintiff might well have countered it either by way of a pleading in reply, or by evidence led.

I would be of the opinion that the proposed amendment should be allowed in order to bring all proper issues before the Court, for that is the purpose of the trial process. To allow the amendment may change substantially the entire thrust of the proceeding, and this should not be done to the prejudice of the plaintiff.

The amendment will be allowed on the following terms. The pleadings will be deemed to be re-opened with the plaintiff being allowed to reply, if he considers it appropriate to do so; the plaintiff may discover, or rediscover any witness; when trial resumes either party should have the right to recall and re-examine any witness on matters touching or arising out of the substance of the amendment.

In addition the plaintiff shall have its costs as taxed in any event from the time of the close of the initial pleadings to the date of resumption of trial. In addition, if it should be that the end result of the trial shall be in favor of the plaintiff, the plaintiff will be entitled to interest, at present bank rates, from the date on which the application to amend was made to the date on which the taking of any further evidence which either counsel may elect to adduce, as a result of such amendment, shall be concluded.

Application allowed.

NOTES AND QUESTIONS

1. Precisely which aspect of the rules of pleading did the defendant in *MacDonald* breach? Why was it important for the facts alleged at trial to have been disclosed in the statement of defence? What would the defendant have been required to plead in order to avoid the objection made by the plaintiff?

2. Consider the terms imposed in *MacDonald*. What impact would those terms
have on the parties in terms of the future course of the litigation or the likelihood of a
settlement?

3. *Defences.* Pleading in the statement of defence is subject to the general requirement that the defendant set forth all material facts on which he or she relies in support of
the defence advanced. In the past, it was not uncommon for defendants to simply plead a
general denial. While the requirement to plead all material facts makes clear that a mere
denial is inadequate, the rules go even further. In Ontario, for instance, rule 25.07 provides:

Admissions

25.07(1) In a defence, a party shall admit every allegation of fact in the opposite
party's pleading that the party does not dispute.

Denials

(2) Subject to subrule (6), all allegations of fact that are not denied in a party's
defence shall be deemed to be admitted unless the party pleads that he or she has no
knowledge in respect of the fact.

Different Version of Facts

(3) Where a party intends to prove a version of the facts different from that pleaded
by the opposite party, a denial of the version so pleaded is not sufficient, but the party
shall plead his or her own version of the facts in the defence.

Affirmative Defences

(4) In a defence, a party shall plead any matter on which the party intends to rely to
defeat the claim of the opposite party and which, if not specifically pleaded, might take
the opposite party by surprise or raise an issue that has not been raised in the opposite
party's pleading.

4. *Power to amend.* As we can see from *MacDonald*, a variance between pleading
and proof may not be fatal, because of the court's power to grant an amendment to the
pleadings, even at trial. All modern procedural codes give the court broad amendment
powers over the proceedings, including the amendment of pleadings. The following
Ontario amendment rule is representative; note the sweeping language of the rule.

26.01 On motion at any stage of an action the court shall grant leave to amend a
pleading on such terms as are just, unless prejudice would result that could not be
compensated for by costs or an adjournment.

While the courts grant amendments liberally during the pre-trial stages of the litigation, once the matter reaches trial, the courts are more reluctant to grant an amendment.
In the *MacDonald* case, the defendant was given the opportunity to rely on a defence
that it had not raised by its pleading. It was given leave to amend the pleading to allege
the facts supporting the new defence. The price for this indulgence was the payment of
the plaintiff's costs of an adjournment. The adjournment was necessary to enable the

defence to be amended and to give the plaintiff time to meet the new plea. As we saw, the price was small in view of the final outcome. But as the next two cases show, a party may not always be as successful as the defendant was in the *MacDonald* case in his attempt to rely on a new ground of claim or defence at trial.

In *Severin v. Vroom* (1977), 3 CPC 183 (Ont. CA), the plaintiff sued to enforce an agreement to lease land for 21 years. The plaintiff's evidence indicated that the agreement was an oral one. At the close of the plaintiff's case, the defendant successfully moved to have the action dismissed on the ground that the agreement was unenforceable by reason of the Statute of Frauds, which requires such a contract to be enforceable, to be "in writing and signed by the party to be charged therewith." The plaintiff appealed and was successful. The Court of Appeal held that the defence of the Statute was an affirmative defence that must be pleaded before it can be relied on and the defendant had not pleaded the Statute in the statement of defence. The defendant did not request leave to amend at the trial. The Court of Appeal held that this failure to so request an amendment was a waiver of the right to an amendment and an admission that the Statute was not applicable. (In addition, the court found evidence of past performance that was sufficient to make the agreement enforceable, notwithstanding the Statute of Frauds.)

In *Assie v. Sask. Telecommunications* (1978), 7 CPC 299 (Sask. CA), the plaintiff's cultivator was damaged when it became entangled in sagging wires belonging to the defendant telephone company. The plaintiff sued in negligence, alleging that the wires had sagged six feet below their proper height. The defendants' employees had been working on the wires two days before, and they testified that they had left the wires intact at the proper height. The trial judge found no negligence on the part of the defendant, but instead of dismissing the action found the defendant liable in nuisance and awarded damages on the basis of strict liability. The defendant appealed and in its reasons the Court of Appeal rejected the possibility of an amendment:

> The second issue in this appeal is whether the learned trial Judge was right in considering the plaintiff's claim on the basis of nuisance when such a claim had been neither pleaded nor argued before him.
>
> Courts in Saskatchewan are given a wide discretion by Rule 210 of the Queen's Bench Rules to make all necessary amendments for the purpose of determining the real question or issue raised or depending on the proceedings. It is well established, however, that an amendment to the pleadings setting up an alternative cause of action should not be allowed after all the evidence has been heard, unless the Court is satisfied that all the evidence possible on the new issue has been submitted ... and there is no prejudice to the other side ...
>
> Hughes J said he could not see any prejudice to the defendant either as to the manner in which it would have put its own case or in which the cross-examination of the plaintiff's witnesses would have been conducted. However, with deference, I do not see how it is possible to arrive at that conclusion without consulting counsel for the defendant to ascertain whether there is any further evidence which he might wish to call and to hear argument as to whether the proposed amendment will prejudice his position. In my respectful opinion, it would have been preferable in this case for the learned trial Judge to have called in counsel for both parties to inform them of what he was

contemplating doing and giving them an opportunity to make submissions. On the facts of this case, it is difficult to escape the feeling that the defendant suffered some prejudice when judgment was founded upon a basis which was not pleaded, on which no opportunity to adduce evidence was afforded, and on which no argument of counsel was heard, and, had the defendant so pleaded, it is equally conceivable that the plaintiff might well have countered it either by way of a pleading in reply, or by evidence led.

(The court then proceeded to hold that, in any event, there was no evidence to support the conclusion that the defendant allowed the wires to fall into disrepair and, hence, no nuisance.)

The amendment rules typically require a court to grant amendments at any stage of the proceedings, unless there is prejudice that cannot be compensated for. Practically, this means that while an amendment will be entertain and may be granted at any stage of the process, a party is under some responsibility to move for amendments at a reasonable time after the need for an amendment is realized. The later the party moves for an amendment, the more likely the allegation of prejudice from the other side, and the more likely the court will impose costly terms on the amendment to compensate the other party for the inconvenience involved.

5. *The relevance of discovery to the variance problem.* We have already noted that pleadings are not the only mechanisms for parties to inform each other about their contentions and the facts they rely on—discovery may do this, and often with greater detail than pleadings. When a question of variance arises at trial, of what relevance is what took place at the discovery? In *Sullivan v. Hoffman Bros. Ltd.*, [1968] 2 OR 201 (HC), the jury found the defendant Cullen to have been negligent in failing to sound his horn. Cullen sought to have the jury's verdict set aside on the ground that the finding of negligence against him was not open to them, because neither the plaintiff nor the co-defendant had pleaded that Cullen had failed to sound his horn. The plaintiff and co-defendant sought leave to amend if necessary. The trial judge agreed that there was no specific pleading of Cullen's failure to sound his horn, although it was alleged that "even after the collision arose he could by the exercise of reasonable care have avoided the same." He refused to set aside the verdict and allowed the requested amendment, noting that the matter had been covered on Cullen's examination for discovery.

The foregoing cases demonstrate the problem that will be encountered at trial by a party who has not fully pleaded the case he or she seeks to rely on—the divergence between pleading and proof or, as it is often called, the problem of variance. The basic principle is that at trial each party is bound by his pleadings and may only rely on claims or defences that are pleaded, unless the court grants leave to amend the pleadings. As the foregoing cases indicate, a party will be ill advised to rely on obtaining leave to amend at trial, because the court may refuse leave or, if it is granted, the trial may be adjourned with the costs of the adjournment to be paid by the party seeking the amendment.

However, as we have noted, a party seeking to have unpleaded matters excluded at trial may fail in the objection if it appears that, through pre-trial discovery, he or she had notice that his or her opponent intended to rely on the new ground. This reflects the fact that the courts have come to recognize that not only pleading, but also discovery, serve an important notice-giving function.

6. *The scope of pleadings.* Given that pleadings define the outer parameters of the dispute, one can appreciate that the pleading party will seek both to define his or her claim or defence as widely as possible and to narrow the claim or defence of his or her opponent. But how is one to do this, particularly given that, at the time of pleading, so much of the information relevant to the case has yet to come to light? Interestingly, particularization of a pleading is a strategy often employed to do both. First, let us consider how particularization may be used to limit the scope of the inquiry.

Consider the consequences of the plaintiff simply pleading that the defendant was negligent, without providing any material facts of the negligence. If the defendant did not move to strike out the pleading for the failure to plead all material facts, or if the defendant did not move for particulars of the negligence but allowed the case to proceed to discovery, the plaintiff at discovery would be entitled to ask any questions relevant to the negligence of the defendant, and at trial would be free to prove any act or omission whatsoever on the part of the defendant showing negligence. The reason is that the pleading of the plaintiff has defined the outer parameters of the suit broadly—a general allegation of negligence that has not been limited to specific acts or omissions. From the defendant's viewpoint, this will be an undesirable state of affairs. The defendant will not wish to give the plaintiff such scope on discovery or at trial and will almost invariably seek to narrow the scope of the inquiry. He or she may accomplish this either by seeking to strike the claim for the failure to disclose material facts or by seeking particulars. If particulars or further material facts are provided, the result is to limit the generality of the initial claim. Thereafter, the inquiry will be limited to the acts or omissions particularized. Similarly, at trial the plaintiff may only prove negligence of the kind specified by the particulars. Evidence of other conduct would amount to a variance and the defendant could properly object to the plaintiff adducing it. Thus, a motion for particulars is often not used to obtain further information but, rather, in an attempt to limit the scope of the inquiry by committing one's opponent to a specific account of the events.

As noted, a detailed pleading may also be used to expand the scope of the dispute in issue. The experienced pleader (whether in the initial pleading or in response to a request for particulars) will usually give extensive particulars, striving to make the particulars as comprehensive as possible since they will control the later conduct of the action. Recall that a pleader may often set forth details of matters in respect of which there at present no supporting evidence. Thus, the pleader may set out numerous bases for the foundation of liability and a host of different factual contentions. For example, in a motor vehicle injury case, it is not uncommon to find a rather "standardized" list of plausible foundations for liability—failure to keep a proper look-out, driving while intoxicated, and failure to maintain the car in proper working order. It is not uncommon (and in order) for a party to abandon, either before or at trial itself, various grounds of liability alleged in the pleading or certain particulars for which the party has not been able to muster the supporting evidence. Is this a satisfactory state of affairs? Does it suggest that whatever the rules, the adversarial energies of the parties will find ways to accomplish their desired ends?

7. *Amending after the expiry of the limitation period.* As we have seen the court has a very broad power to grant amendments. However, problems arise for plaintiffs if at the time an amendment is requested a relevant limitation period has expired. In this

situation, the defendant will invariably argue that the amendment should not be allowed on the ground that to do so will deprive her of a defence that has accrued under the relevant limitation statute. How powerful is this argument? When, if ever, should it prevail? Consider the following case and comments.

Basarsky v. Quinlan
(1971), 24 DLR (3d) 720 (SCC)

HALL J: This is an appeal from the Appellate Division of the Supreme Court of Alberta in which an application by the appellant to amend the statement of claim in the action was dismissed.

Gordon Stewart Onishenko was killed in an automobile accident on September 9, 1967, near Lacombe in the Province of Alberta. The appellant Basarsky was appointed administrator of the estate of the deceased Onishenko under letters of administration granted to him on January 17, 1968. On October 18, 1968, the appellant commenced an action against the respondents.

The defendants entered a statement of defence in the action and para. I of that defence reads:

> THAT the Defendants admit the accident referred to in the Statement of Claim and further admit that the said accident occurred as a result of the negligence of the Defendant, JOE QUINLAN.

The action proceeded limited to the quantum of damages recoverable as liability had been admitted.

On August 26, 1970, the appellant applied to the presiding Judge in Chambers at Edmonton for leave to amend the statement of claim in certain particulars which were not objected to by the respondents and for which leave was given, and in the same application the appellant asked leave to amend the statement of claim by adding two new paragraphs, 7(a) and (b), as follows:

> 7(a) The said Gordon Stewart Onishenko before the time of his death was 43 years of age, employed as a sheet metal shop foreman and his wife and children aforesaid were entirely dependent upon his earnings as such, for their support and education, and in consequence of the death of the said Gordon Stewart Onishenko they have been deprived of that means of support and education.
>
> 7(b) The plaintiff, as Administrator aforesaid, incurred expense for the burial of the said Gordon Stewart Onishenko and therefore claims the sum of $500.00.

and by changing the prayer for relief to read:

> (c) Under the provisions of the Fatal Accidents Act and on behalf of the widow and children of Gordon Stewart Onishenko, deceased, damages in the sum of $150,000.00.

The application was dismissed without written reasons by Primrose J and on an appeal to the Appellate Division the appeal from Primrose J was dismissed, again with no written reasons.

The issue here is as to whether the proposed amendments could be made, having regard to the fact that the two-year period under which an action could be brought under the *Fatal Accidents Act*, RSA 1955, c. 111 [now RSA 1970, c. 138] had expired before the application to amend was made.

The respondents in their factum rely principally on what is known as the rule in *Weldon v. Neal* (1887), 56 LJQB 621, and the jurisprudence emanating therefrom and quote from Lord Esher MR in that case as follows:

> It has been urged that if the Court were to allow an amendment by adding a cause of action which, if the writ were issued at the time when such amendment is allowed, would be barred, this would be giving the plaintiff an advantage and taking away from the defendant a right which he would have had—the effect of such an amendment being to allow the plaintiff to take advantage of the original writ of summons for the purpose of defeating the Statute of Limitations.

and:

> The effect of allowing these amendments would be to deprive the defendant of his right to plead the Statute of Limitations ...

It must be pointed out that there was omitted from the remarks attributed to Lord Esher MR in the Law Journal Queen's Bench Report between the two quotations as given above the following:

> *The Court, inasmuch as they have power to allow amendment, would, under very peculiar circumstances, allow it to be made;* but, as a general rule, such an amendment will not be allowed. There are no peculiar circumstances here. The plaintiff originally brought an action for slander alone; and if the matters now sought to be put into the statement of claim had been included in the writ of summons, they would not have been barred; whereas if a new writ were to be issued in respect of these matters they would be barred. (Emphasis added.)

It is of some significance to point out that Lord Esher MR's judgment in *Weldon v. Neal* is also reported in the Law Reports, 19 QBD 394, and the complete text of his judgment in the latter report of the case is as follows:

> We must act on the settled rule of practice, which is that amendments are not admissible when they prejudice the rights of the opposite party as existing at the date of such amendments. If an amendment were allowed setting up a cause of action, which, if the writ were issued in respect thereof at the date of the amendment, would be barred by the Statute of Limitations, it would be allowing the plaintiff to take advantage of her former writ to defeat the statute and taking away an existing right from the defendant, a proceeding which, as a general rule, would be, in my opinion, improper and unjust. Under very peculiar circumstances the Court might perhaps have power to allow such an amendment, but certainly as a general rule it will not do so.
>
> This case comes within that rule of practice, and there are no peculiar circumstances of any sort to constitute it an exception to such rule. For these reasons I think the order of the Divisional Court was right and should be affirmed. (Emphasis added.)

In the light of the special circumstances existing in this case, I would allow the appeal and order that the statement of claim be amended as asked for. The appellant will have his costs in this Court and in the Appellate Division. The respondents are entitled to their costs of the application before Primrose J.

NOTES AND QUESTIONS

The problem discussed in *Basarsky*—that is, adding parties or claims after the expiry of the limitation period—arises with great frequency. Which of the following two approaches do you prefer?

1. *Deaville v. Boegeman* (1984), 48 OR (2d) 725, at 729-30, *per* Mackinnon ACJO:

A number of courts have made rather heavy weather out of the meaning of "special circumstances" and have sought to establish conditions or detailed guide-lines for the granting of relief after the expiry of the limitation period. This is a discretionary matter where the facts of the individual case are the most important consideration in the exercise of that discretion. While it is true that the discretion is not one that is to be exercised at the will or caprice of the court, it is possible to outline only general guidelines to cover the myriad of factual situations that may arise.

When limitation periods were under consideration by the common law courts in the 18th and the 19th centuries, the judges described these limitation statutes as "statutes of repose" or "statutes of peace": *Tolson v. Kaye* (1822), 3 Brod. & B 217, 129 ER 1267; *A'Court v. Cross* (1825), 3 Bing. 329 at p. 332, 130 ER 540; *Hunter v. Gibbons* (1856), 26 LJ Ex. 1 at p. 5; *Scales v. Jacob* (1826), 3 Bing. 638 at p. 645, 130 ER 660. The emphasis then was as it is today, on the necessity of giving security to members of society. Citizens would not expect to be disturbed once the limitation period had expired. Today when a limitation period has expired it is considered that, generally speaking, a defendant need no longer be concerned about the location or preservation of evidence relevant to the particular claim or relevant to a claim which has not been made. Further, the defendant is, presumably, at the stage free to act and plan his life without concern for stale claims or claims of which he has no knowledge which have arisen out of the original incident. When considering the purpose of limitation periods, the maxim, although used frequently in other connections, *expedit reipublicae ut sit finis litium* is appropriate; it is indeed in the public interest that there should be an end to litigation: *Smith v. Clay* (1767), 3 Bro. CC 646, 29 ER 743.

Some courts have suggested that in applications of the nature of the one in the instant case, limitation periods can be ignored. Limitation periods, however, were not enacted to be ignored. It has also been suggested that the mere bringing of such an application as in the instant case immediately shifts the burden of establishing prejudice to the defendant. I do not agree. In my view, the expiry of the limitation period creates a presumption, however slight in some cases, of prejudice to the defendant. It may be that the mere recitation of the facts and history of the case makes it clear there is no prejudice to the defendant and it can be inferred that he knew, within the limitation period, of the case and the nature of the claims now being made against him. Alternatively the defendant may file material which establishes prejudice. If matters are

left in balance, the usual rules apply and the applicant upon whom the burden lies has
not discharged that burden. The facts of the case and the claims and the history of the
dealings with the defendant are within the knowledge of the plaintiff and there is no
unfairness in placing upon the plaintiff the burden of establishing those facts.

2. Watson, "Amendment of Proceedings After Limitation Periods" (1975), 53
Canadian Bar Review 237, at 276-78:

In exercising the amendment power the goal must be to strike a balance between the
plaintiff's interest in fully developing the action he has diligently commenced and the
interests of the defendant which the limitation period seeks to protect. As we have
already seen, the policies underlying statutes of limitations seek to protect two interests
of the defendant through the device of timely notice of the plaintiff's claim. The first is
that the defendant need no longer preserve or seek out evidence to use in defence of the
claim. The second is that he need no longer fear the insecurity that his business and
social activities will be disrupted by the reactivation of claims which he reasonably
believes are dead. To the extent consistent with the protection of these interests the
plaintiff should be entitled to freely amend his action.

Hence, where a plaintiff seeks leave to amend after the expiration of the limitation
period, then (irrespective of whether analytically it may involve the addition of a new
cause of action, a change of parties or the curing of a nullity) the amendment should be
allowed whenever the defendant has received such timely notice that he will not be
prejudiced by an actual infringement of either of the interests sought to be protected by
the limitations statute. As to the "evidentiary interest" the amendment should only be
refused when the defendant can show that through lack of notice the change sought will
require the use of evidence now unavailable to him but which would have been
available had the action been constituted in this manner at the outset. With regard to his
"interest in security" the amendment should be permitted unless the defendant can show
that through lack of notice of the claim now sought to be asserted he actually changed
his position, to his detriment, in reasonable reliance on the fact that the claim now
sought to be asserted was dead.

It will be observed that, while giving a plaintiff broad scope for amendment, two
requirements are contained in this suggested approach. The first is timely notice to the
defendant. Notice is the device by which the interests sought to be protected by the
statute of limitations are protected in the ordinary course and this is retained. But here
the concept of notice should not be restricted merely to formal notice of the kind given
by the writ or the statement of claim. As many courts have already done in the context
of amendments after the limitation period, and analogous situations, all sources of
notice formal and informal (for instance, correspondence or discovery) should be taken
into account.

The second requirement is that an amendment will not be permitted if it can be
shown that actual prejudice to the defendant will result from his lack of timely notice.
This requirement assures that the legitimate interests of the defendant sought to be
protected by the statute of limitations remain inviolate but beyond this, amendments
should be freely allowed. It is also explicit in the above formulation that the burden of
proving the existence of actual prejudice should be placed on the defendant. This seems

reasonable and is in accord with the general principle that where the facts necessary to establish a proposition are peculiarly within the knowledge of one of the parties, that party should bear the burden of proof. If the amendment will cause actual prejudice to the defendant, he is in the better position to prove it. Generally, the plaintiff will not know whether the defendant is prejudiced or not, and if the burden were placed on him he will be faced with the difficulty of establishing a negative proposition.

III. SUBSTANTIVE ADEQUACY

A first requirement of a pleading is that it disclose a legally valid cause of action or defence. This means that the plaintiff must make allegations that, if true, will amount to a valid legal claim. Similarly, a defendant must plead matters by way of defence that, if true, will as a matter of law amount to a defence to the plaintiff's claim.

The reason for the basic requirement that pleadings be substantively adequate and why this issue can be raised and determined at the outset of the litigation is an obvious one—protracted pre-trial proceedings and the trial itself are unnecessary if the plaintiff's pleading does not set out a claim that is legally recognized or if the defendant's statement of defence is, in law, no valid answer to the plaintiff's claim.

In this context, it is important to recall that pleadings are not expressed in terms of direct statements of law. Pleadings are required to contain a "concise statement of material facts upon which the party pleading relies." Such statements of fact, however, must invoke a valid legal theory of claim or defence. We have seen that various jurisdictions may take different approaches to the question what form must pleadings take; contrast the situation in Canada and the United States. However, the requirement that pleadings be substantively adequate is a basic requirement of every common law procedure system. All provide machinery by which the substantive adequacy of a plaintiff's statement of claim or of the defendant's statement of defence may be challenged and the question determined at the outset. The following provision (Ontario rule 21.01) is typical. (See also Alta. rules 129 and 220, BC rules 19(24) and 34, NB rule 23, NS rules 14.25 and 25.01, PEI rules 14.25 and 25.01, and Sask. rules 173 and 188-89.)

> 21.01(1) A party may move before a judge,
>
> (a) for the determination, before trial, of a question of law raised by a pleading in an action where the determination of the question may dispose of all or part of the action [and] substantially shorten the trial or result in a substantial saving of costs; or
>
> (b) to strike out a pleading on the ground that it discloses no reasonable cause of action or defence, and the judge may make an order or grant judgment accordingly.
>
> (2) No evidence is admissible on a motion,
>
> (a) under clause (1)(a), except with leave of a judge or on consent of the parties;
>
> (b) under clause (1)(b).

The provision is typical in providing for two methods of raising the question of substantive adequacy. How do clauses 21.01(1)(a) and (b) differ?

It is important to understand that, as a consequence of these devices for testing the substantive adequacy of a pleading, substantive and procedural law meet at the commencement of the action. Unless the pleader is able to allege facts that in law invoke a valid theory of recovery or defence, there is a strong possibility that the opposite party will move to have the offending pleading struck out. It is not surprising that there should be this intersection of substantive and procedural law at the pleading stage, for it is something that the lawyer must assess when his or her client asks, "Do I have a good case?"

The rules governing the form of the pleadings, in particular the requirement to plead all material facts, are obviously linked to the requirement of substantive adequacy. Unless you have set out in your pleading all facts material to the establishment of a legally recognizable cause of action or defence, your pleading is subject to attack by your opponent. For instance, in the *Jane Doe* litigation, assume that Jane Doe advances her claim in negligence. A possible line of attack on the plaintiff's pleading might be that the statement of claim fails to allege facts that, if true, would establish that the police owed a duty of care to Jane. In other words, the pleading fails to allege all facts material to the cause of action and is thus defective. Here one might argue either that the pleadings fail to disclose a reasonable cause of action or that the pleadings fail to comply with the requirement to plead all material facts. In essence, these are two ways of raising the same complaint. Here, in all likelihood, the plaintiff will be able to amend her claim to set out the necessary facts.

In the following decision, the Court of Appeal for Ontario, on an appeal from a decision on a motion granting summary judgment under rule 20, had occasion to consider the scope of rule 21 as it applies to attacks on pleadings and compare it to the next rule to be considered in this chapter, rule 20 dealing with summary judgment.

Dawson v. Rexcraft Storage and Warehouse Inc.
[1998] OJ no. 3240 (CA)

BORINS JA: ... In my view, a helpful way to discuss these issues [relating to summary judgment] is to compare the principal devices provided by the Rules of Civil Procedure for the pre-trial resolution of a claim or a defence. The first is a motion under rule 21.01(1)(b) to strike out a pleading on the ground that it discloses no reasonable cause of action or defence. The second is a motion for summary judgment under rule 20.01(1) or (3) on the ground, provided by rule 20.04(2), that there is no genuine issue for trial with respect to a claim or defence. Generically, each may be characterized as a device to challenge the merits of the plaintiff's claim, or the defendant's defence, before trial, with the goal of foreclosing the need for a trial to resolve all, or part, of the lawsuit. As background to this discussion, it is necessary to recognize the paramountcy of the due process requirements which apply to the resolution of disputes which have been incorporated in the Rules of Civil Procedure, notably pre-trial discovery and a plenary trial on the merits before a trial judge presiding alone, or with a jury. ...

Under rule 21.01(1)(b), a defendant may move to strike out a plaintiff's statement of claim on the ground that it does not disclose a reasonable cause of action. The essence of the defendant's motion is that the "wrong," described in the statement of claim, is not recognized as a violation of the plaintiff's legal rights, with the result that the court would be unable to grant a remedy, even if the plaintiff proved all the facts alleged. Thus, to permit the plaintiff to litigate the claim through discovery and trial would be a waste of both the parties' and the court's time.

Because the purpose of a rule 21.01(1)(b) motion is to test whether the plaintiff's allegations (assuming they can be proved) state a claim for which a court may grant relief, the only question posed by the motion is whether the statement of claim states a legally sufficient claim, i.e., whether it is substantively adequate. Consequently, the motions judge, as mandated by rule 21.01(2)(b), does not consider any evidence in deciding the motion. The motions judge addresses a purely legal question: whether, assuming the plaintiff can prove the allegations pleaded in the statement of claim, he or she will have established a cause of action entitling him or her to some form of relief from the defendant. Because dismissal of an action for failure to state a reasonable cause of action is a drastic measure, the court is required to give a generous reading to the statement of claim, construe it in the light most favourable to the plaintiff, and be satisfied that it is plain and obvious that the plaintiff cannot succeed. See *Hunt v. Carey Canada Inc.*, [1990] 2 SCR 959.

In some cases, a statement of claim will be vulnerable to dismissal under rule 21.01(1)(b) because the plaintiff has sought relief for acts that are not proscribed under the law. The typical textbook example is a statement of claim that alleges that the defendant made a face at the plaintiff, or that the defendant drove a car of an offensive colour. In other cases, however, the statement of claim may be defective because it has failed to allege the necessary elements of a claim that, if properly pleaded, would constitute a reasonable cause of action.

To illustrate the second situation, suppose, for example, that P sues D for damages for malicious prosecution. To recover for malicious prosecution, a plaintiff must establish these elements: institution of criminal proceedings by the defendant without reasonable and probable cause; an improper purpose in instituting the proceedings such as malice, or a primary purpose other than that of carrying the law into effect; termination of the criminal proceedings in favour of the plaintiff; and damages: J. Fleming, *The Law of Torts* (8th ed., 1992, The Law Book Co. Ltd.) at 610. If P fails to plead favourable termination of the criminal proceedings, D may move to strike out the statement of claim on the ground that P failed to allege a necessary element of the tort. P's failure to plead favourable termination may simply be an oversight. If so, the court should allow P to amend the statement of claim to add this allegation, and the lawsuit will proceed. See *AGF Canadian Equity Fund v. Transamerica Commercial Finance Corp. Canada* (1993), 14 OR (3d) 161 at 172-74 (Gen. Div.).

Although I have analyzed rule 21.01(1)(b) from the perspective of a defendant's motion to strike out a statement of claim on the ground that it is substantively inadequate, a similar analysis applies to a plaintiff's motion to strike out a statement of defence on the ground that it does not state a reasonable defence.

In contrast, a motion for summary judgment under Rule 20 permits the motions judge to consult not only the pleadings, but affidavits, cross-examination of the deponents, examinations for discovery, admissions and other evidence to determine whether there is a genuine factual dispute between the parties. No witnesses testify (unless, in exceptional circumstances, leave is granted under rule 39.03(4)). The essential

purpose of summary judgment is to isolate, and then terminate, claims and defences that
are factually unsupported. Because a motion for summary judgment is decided on the basis
of documentary evidence, American commentators have described summary judgment as
"a form of quick 'paper trial.'" See S.C. Yeazell, J.M. Landers and J.A. Martin, Civil
Procedure, (3rd ed., 1992, Little, Brown & Co.) at 653. Rule 24.04(2), which is mandatory, provides that a motion for summary judgment is to be granted where the record
shows "[t]here is no genuine issue for trial with respect to a claim or a defence," and the
moving party is entitled to judgment as a matter of law. See *T1T2 Ltd. Partnership v.
Canada* (1995), 23 OR (3d) 81 (Gen. Div.), aff'd. (1995), 24 OR (3d) 546 (CA). The
second part of this requirement is essentially a replay of a rule 21.01(1)(b) motion.
However, as most motions for summary judgment focus on the factual foundation of the
claim, or defence, their legal sufficiency does not arise frequently on a motion for summary
judgment. Even though there is no genuine issue for trial with respect to the facts, a plaintiff
is not entitled to summary judgment if the facts do not establish a cause of action which
entitles the plaintiff to some remedy from the defendant. However, as I will discuss, where
the court determines that the material facts are not in dispute, and the only genuine issue
is a question of law, the motions judge has the discretion under rule 24.04(4) to either
determine the question and grant judgment accordingly, or to send the action on to trial.

Thus, while a rule 21.01(1)(b) motion focuses on the substantive adequacy of a
claim, or a defence, it offers no assistance in weeding out cases where a substantively
adequate claim, or defence, has been pleaded, but cannot be proved. This is the function
of a motion for summary judgment. This can be illustrated by reference to the hypothetical action for malicious prosecution. Suppose that P has pleaded the essential elements
of the tort, and D knows that the case was stayed by the court, rather than dismissed. If
this disposition does not constitute "favourable termination," P cannot win his malicious
prosecution action. Under Rule 20, D may challenge P's ability to prove favourable
termination by moving for summary judgment, supported by evidence that provides proof
that the case was stayed without a finding, and legal argument that a stay is insufficient
to meet the "favourable termination" element of a malicious prosecution action.

NOTES AND QUESTIONS

1. Where a motion is brought to strike for no reasonable cause of action, should the
court hearing the motion decide the underlying question of law? Here the courts seem to
be divided. This division is clearly demonstrated in *Nelles v. The Queen in Right of
Ontario* (1989), 60 DLR (4th) 609 (SCC). The plaintiff, Susan Nelles, brought an action
against the attorney general of Ontario and others in which she alleged that the defendants had maliciously prosecuted her. She had been charged with the death of four infant
patients at the Hospital for Sick Children but was discharged after a preliminary hearing.
The defendants challenged the pleading, alleging that the claim disclosed no reasonable
cause of action and, in the alternative, asking for the determination of a question of law
as to whether the attorney general enjoyed immunity from prosecution for malicious
prosecution. Justice MacIntyre held that "before laying down any proposition to the
effect that the Attorney General and his agents enjoy absolute immunity from civil suit,
there must be a trial to permit a conclusion of the question of prosecutorial immunity

and to furnish—in the event that it is decided that the immunity is not absolute—a factual basis for a determination of whether or not in this case the conduct of the prosecution was such that the appellant is entitled to a remedy."

Justice Lamer (Dickson, Wilson, and La Forest JJ concurring), while agreeing that the case ought not to be struck for the failure to disclose no reasonable cause of action, took a different view about the determination of the question of law raised by the pleading:

> I am of the opinion that the question of immunity should be addressed by this court in this case, and that nothing prevents the court from so doing. I set out the relevant rules of the Ontario Rules of Practice, RRO 1980, Reg. 540, as they were at the time of the case for ease of reference:
>
> 124. Either party is entitled to raise by his pleadings any point of law, and by consent of the parties or by leave of a judge, the point of law may be set down for hearing at any time before the trial, otherwise it shall be disposed of at the trial. ...
>
> 126. A judge may order any pleading to be struck out on the ground that it discloses no reasonable cause of action or answer, and in any such case, or in the case of the action or defence being shown to be frivolous or vexatious, may order the action to be stayed or dismissed, or judgment to be entered accordingly.
>
> A review of the cases dealing with the application of Rule 124 [rule 21.01(1)(a)] and Rule 126 [rule 21.01(1)(b)] reveals the following. The difference between the two rules lies in the summary nature of Rule 126 as opposed to the more detailed consideration of issues under Rule 124. A court should strike a pleading under Rule 126 only in plain and obvious cases where the pleading is bad beyond argument. Rule 124 is designed to provide a means of determining, without deciding the issues of fact raised by the pleadings, a question of law that goes to the root of the action. I would like to point out that what is at issue here is not whether malicious prosecution is a reasonable cause of action. A suit for malicious prosecution has been recognized at common law for centuries dating back to the reign of Edward I. What is at issue is whether the Crown, Attorney General and Crown Attorneys are absolutely immune from suit for the well-established tort of malicious prosecution. This particular issue has been given careful consideration both by the Court of Appeal and in argument before this court. The Court of Appeal for Ontario undertook a thorough review of authorities in the course of a lengthy discussion of arguments on both sides of the issue. As such it matters not in my view whether the matter was disposed of under Rule 124 or 126. To send this matter back for trial without resolving the issue of prosecutorial immunity would not be expeditious and would add both time and cost to an already lengthy case.
>
> Furthermore, I am of the view that the rules of civil procedure should not act as obstacles to a just and expeditious resolution of a case. Rule 1.04(1) of the Rules of Civil Procedure in Ontario, OReg. 560/84, confirms this principle in stating that "[T]hese rules shall be liberally construed to secure the just, most expeditious and least expensive determination of every civil proceeding on its merits."

Lamer J then proceeded to conclude that the attorney general did not enjoy immunity from civil suit founded upon a claim of malicious prosecution. L'Heureux-Dubé J, in dissent, agreed with Lamer J that the court ought to determine the legal issue, but decided the issue in favour of the attorney general.

Which of these approaches do you prefer and why? While the rules clearly contemplate that a question of law can be determined at the outset, what do you think might underlie the reluctance of the court to do so?

The *Nelles* case also raises the issue of the effect of preliminary challenges on the litigation of novel claims. What impact is the unsuccessful challenge by the defendants to strike out the claim and the ruling of Lamer J likely to have on future settlement negotiations between the parties, on the financial and emotional resources of the plaintiff? What is the possible impact of the delay of seven years from the commencement of the action to the decision of the Supreme Court of Canada? The *Nelles* case was ultimately settled. What, if anything, is lost when a case such as *Nelles* is not litigated to a final conclusion on the merits?

2. In *D.H.L. v. G.A.F.* (1987), 28 CPC 78 (Ont. HC), a case similar on its facts to *M. v. M.* (see the materials on limitation periods in chapter 5, "Commencement of Proceedings"), the plaintiff alleged that her mother, one of the defendants, was negligent in failing to protect her from the abuse of the plaintiff's father. The mother moved to strike out the action against her as disclosing no reasonable cause of action. The court dismissed the motion, noting that while the claim might have been novel, it was not a clear case where the plaintiff could not succeed at trial. This case and *M. v. M.* demonstrate the difficulties encountered in attempting to expand the boundaries of causes of action. Until recently, claims for damages arising out of an incestuous relationship have been unknown to the courts. Many societal factors continue to discourage naming, blaming, and claiming in these situations. Obviously, one of the impediments is the conduct of litigation itself—limitation periods drafted without this in mind, the very public nature of trials, and the delay and expense that can be incurred in litigation, especially when it is challenged at the preliminary proceeding stage.

Jane Doe v. Board of Commissioners of Police for the Municipality of Metropolitan Toronto
(1990), 74 OR (2d) 225 (Div. Ct.)

[A motion to strike the claim as disclosing no reasonable cause of action was first heard by a master, who granted leave to the plaintiff to amend her statement of claim. Another motion was then brought before Henry J to strike the amended statement of claim at (1989), 58 DLR (4th) 396 (Ont. HC). Henry J dismissed the motion, again granting leave to the plaintiff to amend her pleading. The decision was appealed to the Ontario Divisional Court. The reasons of the court appear below. Again, the motion was dismissed. The defendants were denied leave to appeal to the Ontario Court of Appeal. Jane Doe was ultimately successful at trial: [1998] OJ no. 2861.

The defendants in *Jane Doe* pursued two lines of attack under the "no reasonable cause of action" rubric. One line of attack was to claim that the law did not recognize such a claim and, thus the pleadings disclosed no reasonable cause of action. The second line of attack was to claim that even if the law recognized such a cause of action, the pleading failed to disclose the facts necessary to make out such a claim. In other words, the pleading failed to disclose all material facts.]

MOLDAVER J:

Brief Summary of Case

On August 24, 1986 Jane Doe was confronted by an intruder. He had gained access to her second floor apartment by forcible entry through a locked balcony door. Ms. Doe was raped. The attacker fled. The police were called immediately.

Several months later, the attacker was captured. He ultimately pleaded guilty to a number of sexual assaults. These included the attack upon Ms. Doe and assaults upon several other women who had been previously violated in a manner similar to Ms. Doe. The accused was sentenced to 20 years' imprisonment.

All of the prior attacks had occurred within a one-year period in the vicinity of Church and Wellesley Streets, Toronto. They involved white, single women, living in second or third floor apartments. In each case, the attacker had gained entry through a balcony door.

Ms. Doe has now started a civil action against:

(1) Kim Derry and William Cameron, the investigating officers in charge of the case;

(2) Jack Marks, Chief of the Metropolitan Toronto Police Force at that time; and

(3) the Board of Commissioners of Police for the Municipality of Metropolitan Toronto.

She seeks damages for pain and suffering, inconvenience and loss of enjoyment of life. In addition, she has incurred expenses and lost income. She suffers from serious and prolonged bouts of depression and anxiety. This has led to psychiatric counselling and therapy.

Ms. Doe has raised two causes of action against each of the defendants. The first of these is framed in tort. The second seeks a declaration that her right to security of the person and her right to equal protection of the law under ss. 7 and 15(1) of the Canadian Charter of Rights and Freedoms respectively, have been violated. …

Issues

There are three main issues to be determined by this court. They are:

(1) Do the pleadings support a cause of action against the defendants, or any of them, in tort?

(2) Do the pleadings support a cause of action against the defendants, or any of them, for violating the plaintiff's Charter rights?

(3) Have these causes of action been properly pleaded?

The History of the Action

The matter came to this court by way of appeal from the decision of Mr. Justice Henry, released March 31, 1989 [reported 58 DLR (4th) 396 (HC)]. Leave to appeal was granted by Madam Justice MacFarland on July 17, 1989.

All of the submissions presented to this court were thoroughly canvassed before Henry J in a hearing which lasted some five days. Henry J reserved judgment and later delivered thorough and extensive reasons. He concluded that the causes of action advanced by Ms. Doe were both legally founded and properly pleaded. However, he granted Ms. Doe leave to amend the pleadings, if counsel so advised, as follows:

(1) to specifically allege the necessary proximity of relationship between herself and the defendants; and

(2) to specifically allege that the defendants irresponsibly failed to exercise or improperly exercised their power to make policy decisions.

In his judgment, Mr. Justice Henry reviewed each and every argument advanced by the defendants. As well, he carefully and thoroughly considered the case law.

I do not intend to embark upon such a detailed analysis. For the reasons which follow, I am satisfied that Ms. Doe is entitled to proceed with her action against each of the defendants by way of tort. She is also entitled to continue her action against each of the defendants for a declaration that her s. 7 and s. 15(1) Charter rights have been violated. As well, I find that both causes of action have been properly pleaded.

General Principles Applicable to All Pleadings

Before considering the several causes of actions pleaded, it may be helpful to review some of the principles relating to statements of claim generally. The following factors are significant:

(1) The pleadings must disclose a cause of action founded in law. So long as this criterion is met, the novelty of the cause is of no concern. See *Johnson v. Adamson* (1981), 34 OR (2d) 236, 128 DLR (3d) 470, 18 CCLT 282 (CA) [leave to appeal to SCC refused (1982), 35 OR (2d) 64n; 41 NR 447n].

(2) In determining whether a cause of action exists, the material facts pleaded are to be taken as proved. However, this principle does not apply where the alleged facts are based on assumptive or speculative conclusions which are incapable of proof. See *Operation Dismantle Inc. v. R*, [1985] 1 SCR 441, 13 CRR 287, 12 Admin. LR 16, 18 DLR (4th) 481, 59 NR 1.

(3) If the facts, taken as proved, disclose a reasonable cause of action, that is, one with some chance of success, then the action may proceed. See *Operation Dismantle Inc., supra.*

(4) The statement of claim must be read as generously as possible, with a view to accommodating any inadequacies in the form of the allegations due to drafting deficiencies. See *Operation Dismantle Inc., supra.*

With these principles in mind, I now turn to a consideration of issue one.

Issue One

Do the Pleadings Support a Legal Cause of Action Against the Defendants, or Any of Them, in Tort?

Under what circumstances will the police owe a private law duty of care to a member of the public?

Section 57 of the Police Act, RSO 1980, c. 381, reads as follows:

> 57. The members of police forces appointed under Part II except assistants and
> civilian employees, are charged with the duty of preserving the peace, preventing
> robberies and other crimes and offences, including offences against the by-laws of the
> municipality and apprehending offenders, and commencing proceedings before the
> proper tribunal, and prosecuting and aiding in the prosecuting of offenders, and have
> generally all of the powers and privileges and are liable to all the duties and
> responsibilities that belong to constables.

This section imposes certain duties upon the police. They include (1) preserving the
peace; (2) preventing crimes; and (3) apprehending offenders. The police are charged
with the duty of preserving law and order within our society, including the protection of
the public from those who would commit or have committed crimes.

When a crime has been committed, society is best protected by the ultimate detection and apprehension of the offender. This holds especially true when the criminal is at
large and likely to commit further offences.

For the most part, the police are free to go about their task of detecting and apprehending criminals without fear of being sued by individual members of society who
have been victimized. The reason for this is simple. While the police owe certain duties
to the public at large, they cannot be expected to owe a private law duty of care to every
member of society who might be at risk.

Foreseeability of risk alone is not sufficient to impose a private law duty of care. See
Hill v. Chief Constable of West Yorkshire, [1989] 1 AC 53, 11988] 2 All ER 238 (HL).

To establish a private law duty of care, foreseeability of risk must coexist with a
special relationship of proximity. In the leading case of *Anns v. Merton (London Bor-
ough)*, [1978] AC 728, [1977] 2 All ER 492, 121 Sol. Jo. 377 (HL), Lord Wilberforce
defined the requirements of this special relationship as follows at pp. 751-52 AC:

> First one has to ask whether, as between the alleged wrongdoer and the person who has
> suffered damage there is a sufficient relationship of proximity or neighbourhood such
> that, in the reasonable contemplation of the former, carelessness on his part may be
> likely to cause damage to the latter—in which case a prima facie duty of care arises.

This principle has been approved by the Supreme Court of Canada in *Kamloops
(City) v. Nielsen*, [1984] 2 SCR 2, 66 BCLR 273, 29 CCLT 97, 8 CLR 1, 10 DLR (4th)
641, 26 MPLR 81, 54 NR 1, [1984] 5 WWR 1.

Do the Pleadings Support a Private Law Duty of Care by the Defendants in This Case?

The plaintiff alleges that the defendants knew of the existence of a serial rapist. It was
eminently foreseeable that he would strike again and cause harm to yet another victim.
The allegations therefore support foreseeability of risk.

The plaintiff further alleges that by the time she was raped, the defendants knew or
ought to have known that she had become part of a narrow and distinct group of
potential victims, sufficient to support a special relationship of proximity. According to
the allegations, the defendants knew:

(1) that the rapist confined his attacks to the Church-Wellesley area of Toronto;
(2) that the victims all resided in second or third floor apartments;
(3) that entry in each case was gained through a balcony door; and
(4) that the victims were all white, single and female.

Accepting as I must the facts as pleaded, I agree with Henry J that they do support the requisite knowledge on the part of the police sufficient to establish a private law duty of care. The harm was foreseeable and a special relationship of proximity existed.

Do the Pleadings Support a Breach of the Private Law Duty of Care?

The law is clear that in certain circumstances, the police have a duty to warn citizens of foreseeable harm. See *Schact v. R*, [1973] 1 OR 221, 30 DLR (3d) 641 (CA), aff'd. *sub nom. O'Rourke v. Schact*, [1976] 1 SCR 53, 55 DLR (3d) 96, 3 NR 453, and *Beutler v. Beutler; Adams v. Beutler* (1983), 26 CCLT 229 (Ont. HCJ). The obvious purpose of the warning is to protect the citizens.

I would add to this by saying that in some circumstances where foreseeable harm and a special relationship of proximity exist, the police might reasonably conclude that a warning ought not to be given. For example, it might be decided that a warning would cause general and unnecessary panic on the part of the public which could lead to greater harm.

It would, however, be improper to suggest that a legitimate decision not to warn would excuse a failure to protect. The duty to protect would still remain. It would simply have to be accomplished by other means.

In this case the plaintiff claims, *inter alia*, that the duty owed to her by the defendants required (1) that she be warned of the impending danger; or (2) in the absence of such a warning, that she be adequately protected. It is alleged that the police did neither.

Instead, she claims they made a conscious decision to sacrifice her in order to apprehend the suspect. They decided to use her as "bait." They chose not to warn her due to a stereotypical belief that because she was a woman, she and others like her would become hysterical. This would have "scared off" the attacker, making his capture more difficult.

It should here be noted that the plaintiff cannot say which of the defendants made the decisions not to warn or adequately protect her. It is alleged that the investigating officers and the Chief of Police took part in this.

However, the pleadings also allege that both the Chief of Police and the Board of Commissioners were negligent in allowing or authorizing a decision which favoured apprehension of the suspect over the protection of his likely victims. Further, it is alleged that both the Chief of Police and the Board of Commissioners failed to provide adequate resources to investigate and apprehend the rapist, even though they knew or ought to have known that he would strike again against Ms. Doe or others like her. The failure to properly protect the plaintiff is implicit in this latter allegation.

Pleadings of this nature have been upheld by the Ontario Court of Appeal in the case of *Johnson v. Adamson, supra.*

Basis Upon Which the Police Chose Not To Warn

The defendants submitted that the decision not to warn was obviously one of policy. As such, it could not form the basis of a cause of action in tort so long as it was reasonably and responsibly made. Mere error in judgment, if such was the case here, would not support the claim.

This principle is well established. It has been recognized and approved by the Supreme Court of Canada. See *Kamloops (City) v. Nielsen, supra*. In that case, Madam Justice Wilson, speaking for the majority of the court, stated that even if a private law duty of care exists, policy decisions made by public officials will not attract liability in tort so long as they are reasonably and responsibly made. On the other hand, when it comes to the implementation of policy decisions, *i.e.*, the operational area, public officials who owe a private law duty of care will be exposed to the same liability as others if they fail to take reasonable care in discharging their duties.

While this distinction will undoubtedly be important at trial, in my opinion it does not affect the validity of these pleadings. Whether the decision not to warn was one of policy made in the operational context or an operational decision made in the context of some broader policy, the facts pleaded support a claim in either case.

If the decision not to warn was based on policy, the plaintiff implicitly alleges that it was made arbitrarily, unreasonably and irresponsibly. It stemmed from a conscious decision to use the plaintiff as "bait," combined with an unwarranted stereotypical belief that such warning would cause hysteria.

I would go further and suggest that even if the decision not to warn was one of policy and was responsibly made, it may have carried with it an enhanced duty to provide the necessary resources and personnel to protect the plaintiff and others like her. As already indicated, the plaintiff has alleged that the defendants failed to do this.

Causation

This leaves the question of causation. How can it be proved that if the police had discharged their private law duty of care to the plaintiff, she would not have been assaulted?

In my opinion, it is open to the plaintiff to show that had she been warned, she could have taken steps to prevent the attacker from entering her apartment. Alternatively, she could have moved, stayed with a friend or had someone stay with her. Many options would have been available to her, all of which she was denied as a result of the failure to warn.

Furthermore, the plaintiff pleads that in the absence of warning, if the police had properly protected her, she would not have been assaulted.

Where the negligent conduct alleged is the failure to take reasonable care to guard against the very happening which was foreseeable, the claim should not be dismissed for want of causal connection. See *Funk v. Clapp* (1986), 35 BCLR (2d) 222, 68 DLR (4th) 229 (CA).

For all of these reasons, the claim in tort against all defendants must be allowed to proceed.

Issue Two

Do the pleadings support a cause of action against the defendants, or any of them, for violating the plaintiff's Charter rights?

Do the pleadings support a violation of the plaintiff's rights under s. 15(1) of the Charter?
    Section 15(1) reads as follows:

> 15.(1) Every individual is equal before and under the law and has the right to equal protection and equal benefit of the law, without discrimination and, in particular, without discrimination based on race, national or ethnic origin, colour, religion, sex, age or mental or physical disability.

The plaintiff alleges that her s. 15(1) right to equal protection and benefit of the law, without discrimination, was violated. She states that the defendants had a legal duty to warn her of impending danger. They chose, or at least adopted a policy not to warn her because of a stereotypical and therefore discriminatory belief that as a woman, she and others like her would become hysterical and "scare off" the attacker. As a result, she was turned into "bait," without her knowledge or consent. A man would have been warned and perhaps given the choice of exposing himself to danger to help capture the criminal. She was denied this choice because she was a woman.

It is immediately apparent that the alleged violation of s. 15(1) does not relate to discriminatory legislation. Instead, it points to discriminatory conduct by state officials in the carrying out and enforcing of the law.

In my opinion, these pleadings do support a violation of the plaintiff's rights under s. 15(1) of the Charter.

Do the pleadings support a violation of the plaintiff's rights under s. 7 of the Charter?
    Section 7 reads as follows:

> 7. Everyone has the right to life, liberty and security of the person and the right not to be deprived thereof except in accordance with the principles of fundamental justice.

The plaintiff claims that she was deprived of her right to security of the person. The defendants chose, or at least adopted a policy which favoured the apprehension of the criminal over her protection as a targeted rape victim. By using Ms. Doe as "bait," without her knowledge or consent, the police knowingly placed her security interest at risk. This stemmed from the same stereotypical and therefore discriminatory belief already referred to.

According to the plaintiff, she was deprived of her right to security of the person in a manner which did not accord with the principles of fundamental justice. These principles, while entitled to broad and generous interpretation, especially in the area of law enforcement, could not be said to embrace a discretion exercised arbitrarily or for improper motives. See *R v. Bearer; R v. Higgins*, [1988] 2 SCR 387, 36 CRR 90, 45 CCC (3d) 57, 66 CR (3d) 97, 55 DLR (4th) 481, 88 NR 205, 71 Sask. R 1, [1989] 1 WWR 97.

As a result, the plaintiff claims that her rights under s. 7 of the Charter were violated. Again, in my opinion, these pleadings do support such a violation.

The Position of the Defendants

The defendants submit that the Charter has no application in this case for the following reasons:

(1) The purpose of the Charter is to limit state action. It does not guarantee certain minimal levels of government services. Here, there was no state action that caused injury to the plaintiff. The harm she suffered was caused by her attacker.

(2) Even if the failure to act on the part of the state could give rise to a Charter violation, such a claim should be narrowly limited to cases involving a special relationship between the state and the victim. This relationship can only exist when the victim is in the custody or control of the state.

(3) Mere negligence on the part of the state cannot support such a claim.

(4) The allegations of the plaintiff are conclusory. They fail to set out facts demonstrating a particularized pattern or series of constitutionally invalid acts.

(5) Even assuming that the plaintiff's Charter rights were violated, such violations were reasonably and demonstrably justified in a free and democratic society in accordance with s. 1 of the Charter.

(6) Section 15(1) of the Charter has no application here. The plaintiff asserts that the classes to be compared are men and women. Women are discriminated against because they are not afforded the equal protection of the law provided to men. But, since men are not subject to the material risk of sexual assault, no amount of police protection could achieve "equality" in these circumstances.

I will now deal with each of these arguments separately.

Argument 1

The proposition advanced is essentially derived from the thoughts expressed by Mr. Justice Dickson (as he then was) in the case of *Hunter v. Southam Inc.*, [1984] 2 SCR 145, 9 CRR 355, 33 Alta. LR (2d) 193, 55 AR 291, 27 BLR 297, 14 CCC (3d) 97, 2 CPR (3d) 1, 41 CR (3d) 97 *sub nom. Director of Investigation and Research, Combines Investigation Branch v. Southam Inc.*, 11 DLR (4th) 641, 84 DTC 6467, 55 NR 241, [1984] 6 WWR 577. At pp. 156-57 SCR, p. 365 CRR, p. 650 DLR, Dickson J stated:

> I begin with the obvious. The Canadian Charter of Rights and Freedoms is a purposive document. Its purpose is to guarantee and to protect, within the limits of reason, the enjoyment of the rights and freedoms it enshrines. It is intended to constrain governmental action inconsistent with those rights and freedoms; it is not in itself an authorization for governmental action.

The defendants further rely on the decision of the United States Supreme Court in *DeShaney v. Winnebago County Department of Social Services*, 109 SCt. 998 (1989). There, Chief Justice Rehnquist, speaking for the majority of the court, held that the due process clause of the Fourteenth Amendment to the Constitution imposed no duty on the state to provide members of the public with adequate protective services. The relevant portion of the Fourteenth Amendment reads as follows:

... nor shall any State deprive any person of life, liberty or property, without due process of law; nor deny to any person within its jurisdiction the equal protection of the laws.

This clause was phrased as a limitation on the state's power to act, not a guarantee of certain minimal levels of safety and security. While it forbade the state itself from depriving individuals of life, liberty and property without due process of law, it did not impose an affirmative obligation on the state to ensure that those interests did not come to harm through other means.

I agree with these propositions. However, they have no bearing on this case.

This case involves the imposition by law of a positive duty upon the police to act. They are required by the Police Act to preserve the peace, prevent crimes and apprehend offenders. Their failure to perform a duty mandated by law for improper reasons may well amount to an infringement of the rights guaranteed by ss. 7 and 15(1) of the Charter. This was clearly recognized by Chief Justice Rehnquist in *DeShaney*, *supra*, where he said:

> If the due process clause does not require the state to provide its citizens with particular protective services, it follows that the state cannot be held liable under the clause for injuries that could have been averted had it chosen to provide them.

Having said this, Chief Justice Rehnquist immediately pointed out, by way of footnote, the following:

> The state may not, of course, selectively deny its protective services to certain disfavoured minorities without violating this equal protection clause. But no such argument has been made here. See *Yick Wo v. Hopkins*, 118 US 356, 6 SCt. 1064, 30 LEd. 220 (1886).

Surely, that is exactly the situation alleged here.

Argument 2

The defendants rely again on *DeShaney*, *supra*, for the proposition that a special relationship can only exist when the state takes a person into custody and holds that person against his or her will. Only then does the Constitution impose a corresponding duty to assume some responsibility for the safety and general well-being of that individual. The affirmative duty to protect arises not from the state's knowledge of the individual's predicament or from its expression of intent to help, but from the limitation which is imposed on the individual's freedom to act.

Again, with respect, this has nothing to do with this case. The positive duty here which requires government officials to act arises under s. 57 of the Police Act. Whether a special relationship exists or not will depend on the circumstances of each case. I have already found that the allegations here support such a finding.

In any event, there is no suggestion on the part of Chief Justice Rehnquist that state denial of protective services *mandated by law* will only arise if persons entitled to protection are in the custody of the state against their will. Such a proposition would make no sense.

It would be absurd to suggest that a police officer who observed a citizen under attack could simply walk away because the citizen was not involuntarily in the custody of the state. In my view, the police officer would have a duty to intervene in accordance with s. 57 of the Police Act. Furthermore, a special relationship of proximity would clearly exist. Finally, if the police officer chose not to intervene because of bias or prejudice against the victim, this would amount to a violation of the victim's s. 7 and s. 15(1) Charter rights.

Argument 3

It is not necessary to decide whether mere negligence on the part of the state is sufficient to support a violation of an individual's Charter rights.

The plaintiff here does not allege that her rights under s. 15(1) and s. 7 of the Charter were violated as a result of mere negligence. Instead, she alleges that the police chose, or at least adopted a policy not to warn her because of a stereotypical and therefore discriminatory belief that a warning to women would lead to hysteria.

Argument 4

This argument must fail for the reasons stated by Henry J at pp. 95-97 of his decision. In particular, I adopt the following passage at pp. 96-97 [at 445 DLR]:

> In the case at bar, however, the plaintiff has asserted the nature of the alleged violations and has particularized to the extent known to the plaintiff the manner in which the defendants have done so. In the case of the Board and to some extent in the case of the chief, the allegation of default will concern functions in the policy field which because of their supervisory powers and duties, are of a different character from the powers and duties of the constables. In the case of all the defendants, however, the allegations even if conclusory may be made, as the Court of Appeal found in *Johnson v. Adamson*, and in my opinion are not incapable of proof, both as to the allegations of failure to adopt adequate policies, regulations and procedures to protect the plaintiff's Charter rights and to the causal connection.

Argument 5

In my opinion, s. 1 of the Charter can play no part in this application. This section may afford a defence at trial, if the trial judge finds that the plaintiff's Charter rights under either s. 7 or s. 15(1) have been violated.

Argument 6

As I perceive it, the defendants submit that it is impossible to find discrimination against women because men are not generally subject to this type of offence. Indeed, the plaintiff has so pleaded.

How then can the treatment of women be compared to the treatment of men in order to decide whether or not such treatment is discriminatory?

While superficially attractive, in my opinion this argument must fail.

The fact that men are generally not subject to this type of crime cannot be determinative. The discriminatory treatment alleged here stems not from the nature of the crime but from a stereotypical view of women held or adopted by the defendants.

The issue may be more clearly defined by altering the facts somewhat. Suppose instead of a serial rapist, a serial murderer who preyed upon men was at large. Assuming that a special relationship of proximity existed between the police and a certain definable group of men, would the police have warned the men? According to the plaintiff, the answer would be "*yes*" since the decision to warn would not have been clouded by the stereotypical presumption that men are prone to hysteria.

When considered this way, it is apparent that the position of the defendants cannot be sustained.

For all of these reasons, the plaintiff is entitled to pursue her action against all of the defendants on the basis that her s. 7 and s. 15(1) Charter rights have been violated.

Issue Three

Have the causes of action been properly pleaded?

In my opinion, having regard to the general principles that apply to all statements of claim, these pleadings are sufficient.

So far as the alleged failure on the part of the plaintiff to specifically plead a special proximate relationship between her and the police, I am satisfied that the facts alleged implicitly support this.

As regards the submission that in the area of policy, the plaintiff has failed to specifically plead that the discretion of the defendants or any of them was irresponsibly made, this too is implicit in the facts alleged.

In my view, these arguments go to form as opposed to substance. In accordance with the guidelines set out by Dickson J (as he then was) in *Operation Dismantle, supra*, the claim must be read as generously as possible, with a view to accommodating any inadequacies in the form of the allegations due to drafting deficiencies. With this principle in mind, I am satisfied that these pleadings may stand.

Conclusion

The plaintiff is entitled to proceed with both causes of action against each of the defendants. Furthermore, the pleadings need not be amended.

I wish to make it perfectly clear that this decision merely entitles the plaintiff to continue her action. It should not be taken as an indication that the allegations or any of them against the defendants are true or that the defendants are liable to the plaintiff. These are matters for trial.

Costs of this appeal to the plaintiff (respondent).

Appeal dismissed.

IV. SUMMARY JUDGMENT: "PIERCING THE PLEADINGS"

A motion to dismiss for failure to state a cause of action involves an attack on the substantive adequacy of the opponent's pleading. The moving party contends that, even if what has been alleged can be proven, as a matter of law no relief is available. On such a motion only the substantive validity of the claim or defence is in issue; the facts alleged are assumed to be true and capable of proof. Consequently, on such a motion affidavit, evidence is generally not receivable.

But what if a party wishes to attack the opponent's pleading, not on the ground that it lacks substantive validity but on the ground that the facts pleaded in the claim fail to disclose a genuine claim or defence, because, for instance, evidence necessary to establish a material fact cannot be proven or a material fact alleged is untrue. Historically, the answer was that such an objection could not be raised at the pleading stage; under the procedural system in common law jurisdictions, factual inquiries about the merits of claims and defences were a matter to be determined after the taking of oral evidence at trial. A party would not be permitted to precipitate a "trial by affidavit" by bringing a motion, supported by affidavit evidence, attacking the factual allegations of the opponent. While this approach is, *prima facie*, reasonable, it is not without its difficulties, for it is easy for an unscrupulous party to make it appear that there are genuine controverted issues of fact by making false allegations and denials in the pleadings. Since pleadings are statements, allegations, or contentions that are not sworn, an unscrupulous party may be tempted to make assertions known to be untrue. Given this state of affairs, civil procedure can become a device for harassment if the system clings steadfastly to the concept that controverted issues of fact can only be resolved at trial after lengthy and expensive pre-trial procedures.

A. The Initial Approach

Dissatisfaction with the motion to dismiss for failure to state a cause of action (or "demurrer" as it was then called) as the only way of avoiding a plenary trial emerged in the 19th century. One cause of this was the practice of people who were liable on bills of exchange of asserting spurious defences to delay collection of their debts. "In 1855 the [English] Parliament enacted legislation to enable the courts to 'pierce the pleadings' in such cases, in order to render prompt decisions without trial against deadbeats taking advantage of the law's delay to the injury of their honest creditors": Carrington and Babcock, *Civil Procedure* 744.

Since 1855, procedures for obtaining summary judgment have broadened gradually, though summary judgment varies from jurisdiction to jurisdiction. In some provinces it is available only to a plaintiff, but in others such as British Columbia, New Brunswick, and Ontario, it is also available to a defendant. In many provinces, it is now available in any type of case. The details of the procedure vary, but the essential element is the same in all jurisdictions—a motion for a final judgment in which the parties put forward affidavit evidence (with or without cross-examination thereon) with the moving party attempting to establish that there is no "triable issue" or no "genuine issue of fact requiring a trial" and that he or she is entitled to judgment as a matter of law. For the rules governing summary judgment in the various provinces see Alta. rules 159-64, BC rule 18, Man. rule 20, NB rule 22, NS and PEI rule 13, Nfld. rule 17, Ont. rule 20, and Sask. rules 129-137. Before considering the following cases read carefully the summary judgment rule in the jurisdiction you are studying. Consider how these cases would have been handled both by the lawyers and the court under those rules.

The summary judgment rule in Ontario in its current form was enacted with the intent of broadening the scope of the summary judgment procedure, and was considered a major change from the earlier procedure. Initially the courts struggled with the powers under the rule and, in particular, with the scope of what constituted a "genuine issue for trial," in the absence of which the court could grant summary judgment.

Early cases that considered "the no genuine issue for trial test" evidenced a continuing debate between judges about the extent to which the evidence and ultimate merits of each party's case raised a genuine issue for trial. The majority of cases appeared to conclude that a "hard look" at the merits of the action was required. This approach was best captured in the frequently quoted reasons of Boland J in *Vaughan v. Warner Communications Inc.* (1986), 56 OR (2d) 242 (HC):

> The specific changes to the summary judgment rules and the spirit in which other rules are changed indicates in my respectful view that Rule 20 should not be eviscerated by the practice of deferring actions for trial at the mere suggestion that further evidence may be made available or that the law is in a state of confusion. The responding party has a positive responsibility to go beyond mere supposition and the court now has the duty to take a hard look at the merits of an action at this preliminary stage.

A more constrained approach to the "hard look" test was provided by Watt J in *Menash v. Robinson* (unreported, February 22, 1989) (Ont. HC), who, borrowing from the approach taken in the area of a defendant discharging an evidential burden in the criminal trial context, opted for a test calling for the court to determine whether "the claim in respect of which summary judgment is sought has an air of reality in light of the evidence upon which reliance is placed on the motion." Watt J went on to state his suggested approach as follows:

> The critical issue, however, is whether, assuming the evidence in support of the claim to be true, it is sufficient to justify the consideration of the claim by the trier of fact. The evidence will be sufficient for such purpose where there is at least some evidence upon the basis of which a reasonable trier of fact, properly instructed, could find in favour of the responding party upon the issue at trial.
>
> In practical terms, the sufficiency of proof upon a particular issue by a party bearing the onus in respect of that issue can be but rarely adjudged on the basis of controverted affidavit material even with cross-examination. Indeed, it has been elsewhere said that when there are controverted facts relating to matters essential to a decision, such facts cannot be found by an assessment of the credibility of deponents who have been neither seen nor heard by the trier of fact. See *R v. Jetco Manufacturing Ltd. and Alexander* (1987), 31 CCC (3d) 171 (Ont. CA), at p. 176. It is nonetheless so where what is being determined is whether summary judgment should issue where the facts which underlie the claim or defence are controverted. As it would appear to me, it will be a comparatively rare case where controverted factual issues may be resolved

upon a motion for summary judgment. If indeed they could be so as a matter of routine, one might be forgiven for wondering as to the purpose of a trial.

The constrained approach as exemplified in *Menash* and other similar decisions was expressly criticized by Henry J in *Pizza Pizza Ltd. v. Gillespie* (1990), 75 OR (2d) 225 (Gen. Div.) as an approach that "emasculates the developing concept of the new Rule 20." After a detailed review of the various approaches taken by Ontario courts in interpreting and applying the summary judgment rules to date, Henry J summarized the general approach as follows:

- Rule 20 contemplates a radically new attitude to motions for judgment; the objective is to screen out claims that in the opinion of the court, based on evidence furnished as directed by the rule, ought not to proceed to trial because they cannot survive the "good hard look."
- There is no arbitrary or fixed criterion that the motions judge must apply. It is a case by case decision to be made on the law and on the facts that he is able to find on the evidence submitted to him in support of the claim or defence, whether the plaintiff has laid a proper foundation in its affidavit and other evidence to sustain the claims made.
- It is not sufficient for the responding party to say that more and better evidence will (or may) be available at trial. The occasion is now. The respondent must set out specific facts and coherent evidence organized to show that there is a genuine issue for trial.
- Apparent factual conflict in evidence does not end the inquiry.
- The court may, on a common sense basis, draw interferences from the evidence.
- The court may look at the overall credibility of the plaintiff's action, i.e. does the plaintiff's case have the ring of truth about it such that it would justify consideration by the trier of fact?
- Matters of credibility requiring resolution in a case of conflicting evidence ought to go to trial; however, that depends upon the circumstances of the case; the court in taking the "hard look" at the merits must decide if any conflict is more apparent than real, i.e. whether there is really an issue of credibility that must be resolved in order to adjudicate on the merits.
- Motions under Rule 20 must be made sparingly and judiciously; the court will control abuse of this process if necessary by its order for costs.

The approach adopted by Henry J in *Pizza Pizza*, which requires the court to take a critical and close look at the merits of each party's case on a motion for summary judgment, quickly became the dominant approach to the hearing of summary judgment motions.

B. The Developing Approach

Irving Ungerman Ltd. v. Galanis
(1991), 4 OR (3d) 545 (CA)

MORDEN ACJO: The appellants, Irving Ungerman Limited and Karl Ungerman Limited, appeal from a summary judgment against them granted by Sutherland J under R. 20 of the Rules of Civil Procedure. His reasons are reported at (1990), 13 RPR (2d) 102 (Ont. HC).

The only issue raised is whether the learned motions court judge erred in concluding that there was no "genuine issue for trial" (r. 20.04(2)). ...

Mr. Galanis, who is a defendant and plaintiff-by-counterclaim in this proceeding, brought his motion for summary judgment on the counterclaim following the exchange of pleadings. The appellants brought a countermotion for summary judgment on their claim in the action. The parties placed extensive evidence before the court on these motions, including affidavits of the parties or their representatives, affidavits of witnesses, transcripts of cross-examinations on these affidavits and of the examination for discovery of Mr. Galanis which was combined with his cross-examination. (I might mention that the appellants' countermotion was dismissed in light of the judge's conclusion on Mr. Galanis's motion. There is no appeal from this particular decision.)

Sutherland J reviewed the evidence in considerable detail and I shall not repeat what he has done. The appellants' contention was that Mr. Galanis had not validly exercised his option to buy the property because he had not presented to Mrs. Haut, within the requisite time (before midnight on October 21, 1988), an offer matching the appellants' offer accompanied by a deposit cheque for $10,000 payable to "Howard Ungerman in Trust." Howard Ungerman was Mrs. Haut's lawyer in the transaction with the appellants.

The appellants submitted to Sutherland J that there were several genuine issues of fact which required a trial. He ruled against each submission. In the argument before us, the appellants confined their submissions to two issues: (1) that Mr. Galanis had not presented Mrs. Haut with an offer matching that of the appellants; and (2) that he did not present her with the requisite deposit cheque for $10,000. Clearly, on the evidence, the second submission raises more difficulties than the first as far as Mr. Galanis is concerned.

Before considering the relevant law relating to the granting of summary judgment and its application to the evidence in this case, I shall refer to those passages in Sutherland J's reasons which indicate how he approached the issues before him.

He quoted the following passage from the judgment of Anderson J in *209991 Ontario Ltd. v. Canadian Imperial Bank of Commerce* (1988), 24 CPC (2d) 248, 8 PPSAC 135, 39 BLR 44 (Ont. HC) at 261 [CPC]:

> No doubt the extent to which it is appropriate for the Court on a motion such as this to investigate questions of fact, and the nature of the issues of fact which will comprise a "genuine issue for trial," will vary from case to case. ...

Sutherland J then said at pp. 134-135 [RPR]:

> I am respectfully and wholly in agreement with that statement. Anderson J continues, at p. 261, as follows:
>
> > As a matter of present impression, I see nothing in the language of the rule, or in the review of the law contained in Vaughan [*Vaughan v. Warner Communications Inc.* (1986), 56 OR (2d) 242 (H Ct.)], to suggest any clear or arbitrary limit, although it seems safe to say that, where there are contested issues of fact involving the credibility of witnesses, the only

appropriate forum remains a trial Court. A lawyer … schooled in the
tradition that almost any substantial issue was to be determined at trial
requires a material change in attitude to give appropriate effect to the rule.

I am more comfortable with the last quoted sentence than with the sentence that
precedes it. I note that the second last sentence is obiter for the reason that Anderson J
as he stated, did not on the facts before him have to choose between contradictory
factual allegations. My reservation about the penultimate quoted sentence is that it tends
to give too much effect to what may be mere vehement and self-serving assertion. In my
view the question of a genuine issue for trial means that, admittedly within narrow
limits not often attainable, the Court can look at the whole of the evidence and consider
the inherent probability or improbability of an assertion of fact, having regard to the
number of other assertions by the same witness or witnesses that have subsequently
been admitted to be or clearly shown to be incorrect. Regard should also be had to how
self-serving or conclusory the factual assertion may be. The rule does not, in my opinion
require an admission that a previously asserted fact is not or may not be the truth. In the
absence of admission, the Court will properly proceed with great caution, requiring a
very high level of probability, but in my view the Court must not be stopped in its tracks
by a vehement and dogged assertion where the person's other evidence has been
repeatedly, and often admittedly, shown to be incorrect and where the doggedly asserted
fact is both inherently improbable and contrary to the evidence of witnesses, the body of
whose evidence has not been shown to be significantly or inherently improbable. …

   In this case I have reviewed the evidence with care—and at what I am confident
many will agree to be tedious length—in order to satisfy myself that, and to demonstrate
the reasons why, this is one of the rare and exceptional cases where in the face of
controverted evidence as to a material matter there is no genuine issue for trial and the
defendant Galanis is entitled to the order for specific performance that he seeks and to
related declarations and relief to be referred to below.

Specifically, with respect to the issue of whether or not Mr. Galanis delivered a
deposit cheque of $10,000 to Mrs. Haut on October 21, 1988, he concluded at p. 139
[RPR]:

   On all the evidence and despite Haut's persistent denials, I am satisfied that there is no
   genuine issue for trial on the question of whether on Friday, October 21 Galanis left
   with Haut along with the second Galanis offer an uncertified deposit cheque dated
   October 21, 1988, and payable to Howard Ungerman in trust in the amount of $10,000.
   That means that Galanis properly exercised his option on October 21, 1988 and I so
   find.

Rule 20, which came into force on January 1, 1985 as part of the *Rules of Civil
Procedure*, O Reg. 560/84, substantially expanded the potential scope of a litigant's right
to move for summary judgment beyond that provided for in the former Rules of Practice, RRO 1980, Reg. 540, as amended. Under the former rules, only a plaintiff could
move for summary judgment and only in actions where the writ of summons was
specially endorsed (see former R. 33 and 58). Now, either party may so move
(r. 20.01(1) and 20.01(3)).

Under the former rules, only the defendant had to support his or her position by affidavit (see former R. 42 and 58). The new rule contemplates both parties "delivering affidavit material or other evidence" (r. 20.01(1) and 20.01(3)). There are other distinctions between the former and the new rules which need not be mentioned.

The key provision in the new practice, as far as the present appeal is concerned, is r. 20.04(2), which reads:

> Where the court is satisfied that there is no genuine issue for trial with respect to a claim or defence, the court shall grant summary judgment accordingly.

The expression "genuine issue" was borrowed from the third sentence in R. 56(c) in the Federal Rules of Civil Procedure in the United States which were adopted in 1938. It reads:

> The judgment sought shall be rendered forthwith if the pleadings, depositions, answers to interrogatories, and admissions on file, together with the affidavits, if any, show that there is no genuine issue as to any material fact and that the moving party is entitled to a judgment as a matter of law.

Our rule does not contain, after "genuine issue," the additional words "as to any material fact." Such a requirement is implicit. If a fact is not material to an action, in the sense that the result of the proceeding does not turn on its existence or non-existence, then it cannot relate to a "genuine issue for trial." (See 10A Wright, Miller and Kane, *Federal Practice and Procedure*, 2d ed. (Saint Paul, Mn.: West Publishing Co., 1983) at 93-95.) Similar reasoning applies to the absence from our rule of the words "and the moving party is entitled to a judgment as a matter of law." This is implicit.

Because the term "genuine issue" is taken from R. 56(c), it is reasonable to think that some of the judicial experience with that provision would be of assistance in applying the term. In a relatively early United States decision concerned with R. 56(c), *Engl v. Aetna Life Insurance Co.*, 139 F2d 469 (1943), Judge Charles E. Clark, one of the drafters of the Federal Rules of Civil Procedure, said at p. 472:

> But the matter is sufficiently important so that we should go beyond the bare words of the summary-judgment rule to the reasons behind it. The federal summary judgment proceeding is the most extensive of any jurisdiction in that it is equally available to plaintiffs and defendants and in all forms and kinds of civil actions. But the history of the development of this procedure shows that it is intended to permit "a party to pierce the allegations of fact in the pleadings and to obtain relief by summary judgment where facts set forth in detail in affidavits, depositions, and admissions on file show that there are no genuine issues of fact to be tried." 3 Moore's Federal Practice 3175.

I refer, in particular, to the intention of enabling "a party to pierce the allegations of fact in the [other party's] pleadings." This means that, in addition to having a right to move for early resolution of a question of law, as a means of avoiding a trial or shortening a proceeding as provided for in R. 21 and 22, it is now possible to avoid a trial or shorten the proceeding on satisfying a court that there is no need for a trial because there is no genuine issue of fact requiring one.

The summary judgment rule, properly applied, is one of several rules which enables the policy expressed in r. 1.04(1) to be given effect. It reads:

These rules shall be liberally construed to secure the just, most expeditious and least expensive determination of every civil proceeding on its merits.

A litigant's "day in court," in the sense of a trial, may have traditionally been regarded as the essence of procedural justice and its deprivation the mark of procedural injustice. There can, however, be proceedings in which, because they do not involve any genuine issue which requires a trial, the holding of a trial is unnecessary and, accordingly, represents a failure of procedural justice. In such proceedings, the successful party has been both unnecessarily delayed in the obtaining of substantive justice and been obliged to incur added expense. Rule 20 exists as a mechanism for avoiding these failures of procedural justice.

It would be convenient if the term "genuine issue" could be expressed in a precise formula for the ease of its application. Having regard, however, to the varied and unpredictable ways in which issues under R. 20 may arise, it cannot—and the experience with R. 56(c) in the United States has shown that it can be harmful to gloss the wording of the rule with expressions that fail to capture its meaning. (See 10A Wright, Miller and Kane, op. cit. at pp. 97-107 and 176-177.)

It is safe to say that "genuine" means "not spurious" and, more specifically, that the words "for trial" assist in showing meaning of the term. If the evidence on a motion for summary judgment satisfies the court that there is no issue of fact which requires a trial for its resolution, the requirements of the rule have been met. It must be clear that a trial is unnecessary. The burden is on the moving party to *satisfy* the court that the requirements of the rule have been met. Further, it is important to keep in mind that the court's function is not to resolve an issue of fact but to determine whether a genuine issue of fact exists. (See 6 James W. Moore, *Moore's Federal Practice*, 2d ed. (New York: Bender, Matthew & Co. Inc., 1989), p. 56-391; 10A Wright, Miller and Kane, op. cit., at pp. 574-575.)

At the heart of the proceeding before us is the issue of credibility. Mrs. Haut has steadfastly maintained in her evidence that she did not receive a deposit cheque for $10,000 on October 21, 1988. The evidence on behalf of the respondent is that a cheque for $10,000 was delivered to her in the evening of October 21, 1988.

It is a sensible general proposition that, if there is an issue of credibility, a trial is required and summary judgment should not be granted. This is reflected in the settled practice under R. 56(c) in the United States. In 6 *Moore's Federal Practice*, 2d ed. (1989) [supra], at p. 56-519 the following appears:

> The general and well settled rule is that the court should not resolve a genuine issue of credibility at the hearing on the motion for summary judgment, whether the case be a jury or court case; and if such an issue is present the motion should be denied and the issue resolved at trial by the appropriate trier of the facts, where, to the extent that witnesses are available, he will have the opportunity to observe their demeanor.

At pp. 56-521 to 56-522 the following appears in Moore with respect to whether an issue of credibility exists:

> Judge Hutcheson's statement as to the test to be applied in determining whether the materials favorable to the opposing party present an issue of credibility will bear repetition:

> To proceed to summary judgment it is not sufficient then that the judge may not credit testimony proffered on a tendered issue. It must appear that there is no substantial evidence on it, that is, either that the tendered evidence is in its nature too incredible to be accepted by reasonable minds, or that conceding its truth, it is without legal probative force. [*Whitaker v. Coleman* (1940), 115 F2d 305, 306]
>
> The test has been applied and often quoted. Evidence, then, that is too incredible to be accepted by reasonable minds does not raise an issue of credibility. Conversely, if the evidence is such that a jury would not be at liberty to disbelieve it no issue of credibility is present. Or, stated differently, a summary judgment may be granted on evidence that would compel the direction of a verdict; and should be denied when a directed verdict would be improper.

As the first passage indicates, the proposition that an issue of credibility precludes the granting of summary judgment applies only when what is said to be an issue of credibility is a genuine issue of credibility. In the present case, Sutherland J was satisfied that "this is one of the rare and exceptional cases where in the face of controverted evidence as to a material matter there is no genuine issue for trial ..." (p. 135 [RPR])

With respect, I do not think that the evidence before the court reasonably justifies this conclusion.

Sutherland J formed the view, and it was open to him to do so on the evidence, that Mrs. Haut was an unsatisfactory witness. He also was impressed by the evidence of the witnesses who testified that the cheque had been presented to Mrs. Haut on October 21. This evidence was referred to by the respondent before us as undisputed objective evidence. With respect, I think that this puts the matter too highly. It would be open to a trier of fact to reject the evidence of Mr. Galanis and his son with respect to presenting the cheque. The acceptance of this evidence, ultimately, turns on the credibility of these witnesses and that of Mrs. Haut. ...

I shall refer to one further matter covered in the evidence. Both Mrs. Haut and Irving Ungerman gave evidence that on the evening of October 21, 1988, around 10:00 to 10:30 p.m., Mrs. Haut telephoned Mr. Ungerman and told him that no deal had been made with Mr. Galanis. No matching offer had been presented and Mr. Galanis had not brought a cheque. Mr. Ungerman was not clear on whether Mrs. Haut said "certified cheque" or simply "cheque." To match the terms of the Ungerman offer the cheque did not have to be certified. In any event, although this evidence might not ultimately prove anything in favour of the appellants it is evidence that tends to support them in that it reflects Mrs. Haut's position, on the very evening in question, that she had no agreement with Mr. Galanis. She would not appear to have had any reason to mislead Mr. Ungerman at that time.

As indicated, I think Sutherland J erred in concluding that there was no genuine issue for trial. No doubt there are contradictions in Mrs. Haut's evidence. There are also circumstantial features which support, perhaps strongly so, the probability that the $10,000 deposit cheque was presented to Mrs. Haut on October 21, 1988. The motions court judge obviously thought that the level of probability was such that Mrs. Haut's evidence could be rejected as incredible. With respect, on the basis of the evidence to which I have referred, including that of Mrs. Haut, I do not think that the materials before the court were such that the court could properly be "satisfied" that there was no genuine issue requiring a trial.

Appeal allowed.

NOTES AND QUESTIONS

1. *Genuine issue for trial.* The genuine issue for trial in *Ungerman*, according to the Court of Appeal, was whether the evidence of Mr. Galanis and his son should be preferred to the evidence of Mrs. Haut. Why is a trial a more appropriate place for such a determination to be made? Does this mean that any conflict in evidence on an essential point requires a trial, no matter how strange or implausible the story of one of the parties? Consider this situation. Someone yells, "Fire!" in a crowded theatre, provoking a stampede in which a number of people are injured. One person in the crowd is accused of negligently or deliberately making the statement and is sued as a result. Five people swear in affidavits on a motion for summary judgment that the defendant is the person who caused the stampede. The defendant files an affidavit in which he denies the allegation. Should a motion for summary judgment succeed? Would it matter if 50 people so identify the defendant?

2. *Onus on the responding party.* What approach should a respondent take to a summary judgment motion? It is clear that the onus lies on the moving party to show that there is no genuine issue for trial. However, many summary judgment rules specifically require that, in response to a summary judgment motion, "a party may not rely on the mere allegations or denials of the party's pleading, but must set out, in affidavit material or other evidence, specific facts showing that there is a genuine issue for trial." See Ont. rule 20.04(1), Man. rule 20.02(1), NWT rule 176(1), PEI rule 20.04(1), Sask. rule 131(1), and federal rule 432.2(1). Why have this requirement? What is the practical impact of this on a respondent?

3. *The need for discovery to contest a motion for summary judgment.* How does summary judgment relate to discovery? In most provinces, a motion may be brought any time after the delivery of the statement of defence and before discovery has taken place. Does this mean that a party has to be prepared to prove his or her case in possible response to a motion for summary judgment at the time pleadings are delivered? What of the case where the plaintiff alleges negligence but does not know the precise act of the defendant that constitutes negligence? Authority in Ontario has held that a party may not respond to a motion for summary judgment by stating that it requires discovery first or that more evidence may be available at trial: *645952 Ontario Inc. v. Guardian Insurance Co. of Canada* (1989), 69 OR (2d) 341 (HC) (the US federal rules specifically permit such a response). Does this raise the risk that an early motion for summary judgment may unfairly eliminate valid claims or defences? Consider this in the light of the provisions of the rules relating to evidence on motions and the options available to a party to a summary judgment motion in obtaining evidence for the motion. Contrast the rule relating to evidence on motions and applications (rule 39) and the general ability to examine non-party witnesses out of court under that rule (rules 39.02 and 39.03) with the scope of oral examination for discovery (rule 31) and the limitations on the discov-

ery of non-parties (rule 39.10). In short, does the summary judgment process itself offer the parties the equivalent of discovery; procedures that are broader than examination for discovery? Compare rules 39.03 and 31.10; which of these two rules is broader?

4. *Comparing applications and motions for summary judgment.* Compare the procedure used on a motion for summary judgment and the test for summary judgment to those where the application procedure is used. Is a motion for summary judgment a mechanism that enables a defendant to convert an action to a *de facto* application? To what extent are the procedures similar or different?

Rogers Cable TV Ltd. v. 373041 Ontario Ltd.
(1994), 22 OR (3d) 25 (Gen. Div.)

BORINS J: This is a motion by the plaintiff pursuant to rule 20.01(1) of the Rules of Civil Procedure for summary judgment for $40,582.72 together with pre-judgment interest. The issue raised by this motion is whether the plaintiff has established that there is no genuine issue for trial. The issue arises in the context of an admission by the defendant that although at one time it owed this amount to the plaintiff, the plaintiff subsequently agreed to forgive payment of the debt by the defendant. The position of the defendant is that the evidence it has presented raises a credibility issue which, on the authority of *Irving Ungerman Ltd. v. Galanis* (1991), 4 OR (3d) 545, cannot be resolved by a motions court judge and, therefore, constitutes a genuine issue for trial.

The debt of $40,582.72 is the balance owing by the defendant to the plaintiff pursuant to a Bulk Cable Agreement into which they entered in January, 1988, and which the defendant, under the terms of the agreement, terminated as of November 30, 1992. The agreement in fact continued until December 31, 1992 at which time the defendant owed the plaintiff $54,376.97. On March 18, 1993, Bernice Stitt, the plaintiff's area sales supervisor, met with Kurt Pieckenhagen, president of the defendant, who gave her four post-dated cheques from the defendant in full satisfaction of the debt. The first cheque was negotiated but the other three cheques were returned by the bank marked NSF. The plaintiff, despite attempts to do so, has been unable to recover the balance of $40,582.72. When cross-examined in respect to a separate action between the parties Mr. Pieckenhagen admitted that the defendant owed the plaintiff in excess of $45,000 and that the defendant had provided the plaintiff with four post-dated cheques in satisfaction of the debt, which is the subject of this action.

In an affidavit delivered on behalf of the defendant Mr. Pieckenhagen states that at the termination of the Bulk Cable Agreement the defendant gave permission to the plaintiff to enter into individual contracts with its tenants for the provision of cable television services as consideration for the plaintiff agreeing to forgive payment of the arrears. He also stated that another reason why the plaintiff forgave payment of the arrears was "as a reflection of the poor quality cable service which had been provided." He points to a letter written to the defendant by Ms. Stitt on September 28, 1992 as confirmation by the plaintiff that it has forgiven payment of the debt. Ms. Stitt has denied forgiveness of the debt. Mr. Pieckenhagen's affidavit is silent in respect to the plaintiff's evidence of the defendant's admission of the debt and its provision of four post-dated cheques in full satisfaction of the debt in March, 1993. He was not cross-examined. In my view, there is not one word in Ms. Stitt's letter of September 28, 1992 which supports Mr. Pieckenhagen's contention that the plaintiff forgave payment of the debt. Therefore, what the defence amounts to is Mr. Pieckenhagen's uncorroborated evidence that the plaintiff forgave payment of the debt. It is this evidence which the defendant's counsel submits raises a "credibility issue" which constitutes a genuine issue for trial.

Rule 20 contemplates that a complete evidentiary record will be before the motions court judge. The parties must put their "best foot forward" at that time: *Pollon v. American Home Assurance Co.* (1991), 3 OR (3d) 59 at 61 (CA), citing with approval *Pizza Pizza Ltd. v. Gillespie* (1990), 75 OR (2d) 225. This requirement was again emphasized by the Court of Appeal in *Bluestone v. Enroute Restaurants Inc.* (1994), 18 OR (3d) 481 at 492. I am entitled to assume, therefore, that the defendant has done so and that if this case were to go to trial it would present no additional evidence. I am, thus, entitled to assume that the defendant will be unable to provide any explanation for its admission of the debt and the four post-dated cheques it gave the plaintiff to pay the debt. The requirement that the parties put their "best foot forward" goes together with the requirement that the motions court judge "take a hard look at the merits of the action at this preliminary stage" to determine whether the moving party has succeeded in establishing that there is no genuine issue for trial: *National Trust Co. v. Maxwell* (1989), 34 CPC (2d) 211 at 217 (High Ct.). This is because, in determining whether or not there is a genuine issue for trial, it must be clear that a trial is unnecessary: *Ungerman*, supra, at 551; *Farm Credit Corp. v. Pipe* (1993), 16 OR (3d) 49 at 61 (CA).

What other evidence is contained in the record, in addition to Mr. Pieckenhagen's evidence, that the plaintiff forgave payment of the debt? The answer is none. All of the other evidence points to the conclusion that Rogers did not forgive the debt. There is the provision by the defendant in March, 1993—six months after Mr. Pieckenhagen claims Ms. Stitt wrote to him forgiving the debt—of four post-dated cheques in full satisfaction of the debt. There is Mr. Pieckenhagen's admission when cross-examined in other proceedings between the parties that the debt existed and that the defendant had provided the four post-dated cheques in payment of it. Mr. Pieckenhagen made no reference to the cheques or his admissions in his affidavit. He did not produce any document emanating from the defendant, or the plaintiff, expressly acknowledging that payment of the debt had been forgiven. Finally, there is Ms. Stitt's evidence that payment of the debt was never forgiven by the plaintiff. It would make no sense for the plaintiff to pursue the defendant for payment of the debt if its payment had been forgiven. It would make less sense for the defendant to provide cheques for its payment in March, 1993, if it had been forgiven its obligation to do so in September, 1992—or, indeed, at any other time.

I am completely satisfied that the plaintiff has established that there is no genuine issue for trial. What the defendant's position amounts to is this—a genuine issue for trial is raised in every case in which a defendant swears that it does not owe a debt, notwithstanding overwhelming evidence to the contrary presented by the plaintiff, and in the absence of any additional evidence by the defendant to support its denial. Although in one sense an issue of credibility is raised on the assumption that a trial judge may believe the defendant, in my view in the context of the record in this case this does not constitute a genuine issue for trial with respect to the defence put forward within the meaning of rule 20.04(2). In my opinion, no *genuine* issue of fact exists which requires a trial.

In my respectful view, this conclusion is in conformity with the principles discussed by Morden ACJO on behalf of the Court of Appeal in the *Ungerman* case, supra, at 549-552. At best, the issue raised by the defendant is spurious. The following passage from the reasons for judgment of Morden ACJO at 552 has direct application to the facts of this motion: "As the first passage indicates, the proposition that an issue of credibility precludes the granting of summary judgment applies *only when what is said to be an issue of credibility is a genuine issue of credibility*." (Emphasis added). Although the defendant may have raised an issue of credibility, it is far removed from constituting a genuine issue of credibility. Therefore, the plaintiff has established that there is no genuine issue for trial in this case.

In the result, the plaintiff will have judgment for $40,582.72 together with pre-judgment interest at the statutory rate from January 1, 1993 to the date of judgment. As well, the plaintiff will have its costs of the motion fixed at $1,500 and its costs of the action fixed at $850, each inclusive of disbursements, for a total of $2,350 plus GST.

Judgment for plaintiff.

NOTES AND QUESTIONS

1. What if the facts in *Rogers* had been slightly different? What if the defendant had not tendered cheques in purported payment of the debt after the date it was supposedly forgiven? What if, in the responding affidavit, the defendant described in detail a meeting at which the plaintiff stated that it was waiving the debt? Would either of these have been sufficient to demonstrate a genuine issue for trial? How can you reconcile the approach of the judge in *Rogers* in reviewing the evidence of the defendant with the approach of the court in *Ungerman*?

2. If the court concludes that there is a "triable issue" but it suspects that the defence is likely to fail, there are other alternatives to simply allowing the defendant to defend in the normal course. The court may impose terms—for example, that the defendant pay the amount into court as a condition of being permitted to defend. Another alternative is for the court to order a speedy trial—that is, within a few weeks; see, for example, Ont. rule 20.05(1)(a). What objectives do such terms seek to achieve? These rules are, however, rarely invoked. Why is this so?

3. *Costs of and on a motion for summary judgment.* How expensive is it to bring or defend a motion for summary judgment? A simple motion (as in *Rogers*) might cost each side about $6,000. However, a motion of any complexity can cost the parties $30,000 or more.

While summary judgment rules seek to address the concern that matters that need not go to trial be determined at a preliminary stage in the litigation process, the rules also attempt to address the situation where resort to summary judgment is used inappropriately. Note, for example, that Ontario rule 20.06(1) provides that where the moving party obtains no relief, "the court shall fix the opposite party's costs of the motion on a solicitor and client basis ... unless the court is satisfied that the making of the motion, although unsuccessful, was nevertheless reasonable." When can it be considered that a motion for summary judgment, though unsuccessful, was reasonably brought? What is the likely impact of this provision on the bringing of such motions?

4. It can be said that while the decision in *Ungerman* sounded a note of caution in the aggressive use of the summary judgment procedure, the decision in *Rogers*, and similar cases that preceded and followed it, seemed to encourage a more active use of the procedure by allowing the court to focus on and make judgments about the *genuineness* of the issue for trial. This resulted in a number of cases where the court found that an apparent conflict or testimony on a material issue did not preclude a court from taking a "hard look" at the evidence and the basis for the conflict to determine whether, in fact, there was a *genuine* issue for trial.

5. Most recently, the Ontario Court of Appeal has sounded a further cautionary note in two decisions released in 1998 that have further clarified the role of the motions judge on a rule 20 motion. In *Aguonie v. Galion Solid Waste Material Inc.*, [1998] OJ no. 459 (CA) Borins JA (the same judge who decided the *Rogers* case as a trial judge) expounded further on the meaning of "genuine issue for trial," where he explained at para. 32:

> An issue of fact must relate to a material fact. As Morden ACJO pointed out in *Ungerman*, *supra*, at p. 550: "[I]f a fact is not material to an action, in the sense that the result of the proceeding does not turn on its existence or non-existence, then it cannot relate to a 'genuine issue for trial.' " In ruling on a motion for summary judgment, the court will never assess credibility, weigh the evidence, or find the facts. Instead, the court's role is narrowly limited to assessing the threshold issue of whether a genuine issue exists as to material facts requiring a trial. Evaluating credibility, weighing evidence, and drawing factual inferences are all functions reserved for the trier of fact ...
>
> Summary judgment, valuable as it is for striking through sham claims and defences which stand in the way to a direct approach to the truth of a case, was not intended to, nor can it, deprive a litigant of his or her right to a trial unless there is a clear demonstration that no genuine issue exists, material to the claim or defence, which is within the traditional province of a trial judge to resolve.

Subsequently, in *Dawson v. Rexcraft Storage and Warehouse Inc.*, [1998] OJ no. 3240 (CA), Borins JA recommended to Ontario judges the approach that their US counterparts adopt in adjudicating motions for summary judgment (referring favourably to the analysis of summary judgment by Wright J in *(Paula) Jones v. (William) Clinton*, 990 F Supp. 657 (1998) (US Dist. Ct., E Dist. Ark.)):

> In applying a test which focuses on whether the entire record could lead a rational trier of fact to find for the non-moving party, what the court is saying is that there is no evidence on which the plaintiff's claim, or the defendant's defence, can succeed. In a sense, the courts have come to equate "genuine issue for trial" with "genuine need for trial." However, at the end of the day, it is clear that the courts accord significant deference to the trial process as the final arbiter of the dispute which has brought the parties to litigation. If there is a genuine issue with respect to material facts then, no matter how weak, or how strong, may appear the claim, or the defence, which has been

attacked by the moving party, the case must be sent to trial. It is not for the motions judge to resolve the issue.

Borins JA recommended the following analytical approach in deciding a motion for summary judgment. The elements of the plaintiff's claim need to be identified. The case law relating to the claim should be reviewed to determine the range of facts that courts have accepted as establishing the claim. Finally, the entire evidentiary record should be examined with a view to determining whether it discloses a genuine issue for trial with respect to a fact material to the proof of the claim.

Would this change the result in *Rogers*?

6. See, generally, K. Kelertas, "The Evolution of Summary Judgment in Ontario" (1999), 21 *Advocates' Quarterly* 265.

C. The Wave of the Future?

Two complaints are perennially levelled at the litigation process—it takes too long and it costs too much. These two complaints are generally seen to be interrelated—that is, one of the reasons that litigation costs too much is that too much time is spent preparing the case for the ultimate trial. The current jurisprudence on summary judgment, as reflected in *Agounie*, *Dawson*, and *Ungerman*, above, clings to the traditional notion that due process in a civil context requires a trial wherever there are issues that require the assessment of credibility or the weighing of evidence.

Is this principle inviolate? Manitoba and British Columbia have attempted to come to grips with this problem with a different procedure. In British Columbia, in addition to a summary judgment procedure under rule 18, the Supreme Court rules make separate provision for an application for judgment under rule 18A. Under this procedure, which has come to be called the summary trial procedure, the court has an additional ability to grant judgment on the merits without a trial. In Manitoba, a BC-style summary trial provision is blended with an Ontario summary judgment provision, as follows:

Disposition of Motion

Where no genuine issue

20.03(1) Where the court is satisfied that there is no genuine issue for trial with respect to a claim or defence, the court shall grant summary judgment accordingly.

Only genuine issue is amount

20.03(2) Where the court is satisfied that the only genuine issue is the amount to which the moving party is entitled, the court may order a trial of that issue or grant judgment with a reference to determine the amount.

Only genuine issue is question of law

20.03(3) Where the court is satisfied that the only genuine issue is a question of law, the court may determine the question and grant judgment accordingly.

Trial on affidavit evidence

20.03(4) Where the court decides there is a genuine issue with respect to a claim or defence, a judge may nevertheless grant judgment in favour of any party, either upon an issue or generally, unless
>(a) the judge is unable on the whole of the evidence before the court on the motion to find the facts necessary to decide the questions of fact or law; or
>(b) it would be unjust to decide the issues on the motion.

Trial and expedited trial

20.03(5) Where a motion for summary judgment is dismissed, either in whole or in part, a judge may order the action, or the issues in the action not disposed of by summary judgment, to proceed to trial in the ordinary way, but upon the request of any party, the judge may order an expedited trial under rule 20.06.

No further motion without leave

20.03(6) Where a motion for summary judgment is dismissed, the moving party may not make a further motion under rule 20.01 without leave of the court.

Effect of Summary Judgment

20.04 A plaintiff who obtains judgment under rule 20.03 may proceed against the same defendant for any other relief and against any other defendant for the same or any other relief.

The following case, decided under the BC summary trial rule, illustrates the operation of these rules.

Inspiration Management Ltd. v. McDermid St. Lawrence Limited
(1989), 36 BCLR (2d) 202 (CA)

McEACHERN CJBC (Seaton, Esson and Wallace JJA concurring):—

I. The Nature of the Appeal

This appeal is against an order made in chambers dismissing the plaintiffs' (appellants') application for judgment under R. 18A in an action for restitution or damages for shares of the plaintiffs sold by the defendant broker.

The plaintiff Robert J. McGowan ("McGowan") is the principal and sole shareholder of both of the other plaintiffs, Inspiration Management Ltd. ("Inspiration") and Wabenung Resources Ltd. ("Wabenung"). McGowan is also the owner of a "control" block of shares in Dragoon Resources Ltd. ("Dragoon").

The defendant McDermid St. Lawrence Limited ("MSL") is a licensed security brokerage house and the defendant, John Wheeler ("Wheeler") is a registered representative in the employment of MSL.

Prior to the events in question in this action, the plaintiffs Inspiration and Wabenung had accounts with MSL. In Inspiration's account were a number of shares in Dragoon which were endorsed for transfer. It is the defendants' sale of Dragoon shares out of the accounts of Inspiration and Wabenung about which the plaintiffs complain in this action.

The chambers judge dismissed the plaintiff's motion for judgment under R. 18A because she considered the test for disposition of such an application was such that judgment should not be given "unless it is clear that a trial in the usual way could not possibly make any difference in the outcome."

We have convened this five-judge court for the purpose of pronouncing upon the proper application of R. 18A. In addition, of course, it is necessary properly to dispose of the plaintiff's appeal. These issues require an examination of the facts.

I propose first to state in an overview what I am able to discern from the material which was before the chambers judge, and secondly to examined the pleadings and affidavits.

II. Overview

Each of Inspiration and Wabenung opened an account with MSL pursuant to client account agreements which, amongst other things, permitted the broker to sell shares in any account which was in a debit position, but neither McGowan personally nor either of the companies guaranteed the debts of the others.

As of 1st October 1987 and at all material times Inspiration's account was long 197,580 shares in Dragoon and there was a small cash credit balance.

The account of Wabenung on the other hand was in a debit position but there were some securities in the account including 10,000 shares in Dragoon.

Early in October 1987 McGowan, who was desperate for money, arranged a one-week loan of $77,000 from the defendants or one of them (it does not matter which) for which he agreed to pay a fee of $3,000. These funds were paid by MSL or Wheeler into the account of Wabenung on 6th October 1987 on which date McGowan signed a letter addressed to Wheeler in the following terms:

October 6, 1987

John Wheeler,
McDermid St. Lawrence Limited,
601 West Hastings Street
Vancouver, BC

Dear John,

On October 14, 1987, I promise to repay $80,000.00 in return against the $77,000.00 loan of October 6, 1987.

Yours truly,

Robert J. McGowan,

Wabenung Resources Ltd.

McGowan says this letter was prepared by Wheeler's assistant. Wheeler says its terms were dictated by McGowan to his assistant at the time McGowan picked up the proceeds of the loan at the defendant's office. The loan proceeds were first paid into and then out of the account of Wabenung which thereby fell into a debit position.

There is a serious conflict of evidence about the collateral for this loan which became important when the market crashed during the one-week period of the loan and McGowan was unable to repay as promised.

McGowan says a "liquidation agreement" was reached after default in which he agreed to furnish a quantity of shares of Geostar Resources Ltd. ("Geostar") to Wabenung sufficient to significantly reduce its debt; that MSL would sell all Wabenung's securities except the Dragoon shares first; and that MSL would not sell any Dragoon shares without consultation.

Wabenung's ledger card shows the sale previously by McGowan of 21,000 shares of Geostar between 6th and 14th October at prices of between 61 and 65; the deposit of 150,000 Geostar shares into that account on 21st October 1987; and the sale of 169,000 Geostar shares between 23rd and 27th October at prices from 38 to 44 .

Wheeler, on the other hand, starts the collateral narrative earlier. He says the loan of $77,000 was a personal loan to McGowan; that McGowan agreed that all the securities in all companies accounts were to be available as collateral for the loan; and that when McGowan failed to repay the loan more security was demanded which led McGowan to deposit 150,000 shares of Geostar; that he told McGowan that all the accounts had to be out of a debit position by the end of the month; that he never agreed not to sell Dragoon shares; that McGowan later promised further Geostar shares but he failed to deliver them, so at the month end Wheeler sold 10,000 shares of Dragoon out of the Wabenung account at 30 to 31 and 55,000 shares in Dragoon out of the Inspiration account at prices of 21 to 40.

McGowan did deposit an additional 19,000 shares in Geostar into Wabenung's account around the end of October. McGowan says the shares were deposited at 11:00 a.m. on 30th October but Wheeler says they did not arrive until 2nd November after the Dragoon shares had already been sold. Wabenung's ledger card records the deposit on 30th October 1987 but it is not clear whether this was an accounting date or a transaction date.

McGowan says that at a later conversation Wheeler admitted he caused these sales to be made and that "he had made a mistake." Counsel for the plaintiffs point to this as an admission by Wheeler of absence of authority to sell shares from the Inspiration account. However, the defendants say that it can be understood merely as a statement by Wheeler that he did not know that the additional Geostar shares had been deposited.

There is a letter dated 29th October 1987 from Inspiration, signed by McGowan, to MSL authorizing payment of the $3,000 loan fee out of Inspiration's account. McGowan says he signed this in early November before he knew of the sale of any Dragoon shares and that he did this in appreciation for the cooperation he thought he was receiving from MSL. The plaintiffs say that this letter helps prove their case because, had Inspiration been liable on the $77,000 loan, the letter would have been unnecessary. The defendants say that the letter is entirely equivocal on that question.

There is also some correspondence between solicitors which I do not think is relevant to any issue of fact or law.

It is obvious that the terms of the loan agreement are crucial to the outcome of this case and that the defendants' authority for MSL or Wheeler to sell shares out of the Inspiration account, if any, could only arise by the agreement of McGowan as Inspiration's account was always in a credit position. This is the crucial issue in the case.

There is, however, a subsidiary issue and that is whether Wheeler sold more Dragoon shares than was necessary to liquidate the loan. In addition to other securities, Wheeler sold 10,000 shares in Dragoon out of the Wabenung account and 55,000 shares in Dragoon out of the Inspiration account, all at post-crash prices.

With the foregoing overview I shall now review the material which was before the chambers judge.

III. Pleadings and Affidavits

The chambers judge had to wrestle with the following disjointed volume of information.

There is no mention of the $77,000 loan in the statement of claim. It alleges that the Wabenung account was in a debit position in October 1987; that there was a debit repayment arrangement, one of the terms of which was that MSL would not unilaterally exercise any of its contractual rights to sell Dragoon shares; that McGowan would provide shares in Geostar Resources Ltd. as security; and that in no event would MSL sell any shares of Dragoon without first consulting with McGowan. This was alleged to be a "liquidation agreement." The statement of claim then goes on to allege that at all material times the Inspiration account remained in a credit position, and relief is claimed both for the unauthorized sale of Dragoon shares out of the Wabenung account and for the sale of any shares out of the Inspiration account.

The defence, filed 28th January 1988, is a pro forma, four line denial of all the allegations in the statement of claim. Pleading this way, which furnishes no answer to the statement of claim, is to be deplored. It was not filed by counsel appearing for the defendants on this appeal.

It is not therefore surprising that the plaintiffs on 23rd February brought a motion for summary judgment under R. 18A.

In his first affidavit sworn 23rd February 1988 McGowan does not mention the $77,000 loan or the words which passed between himself and Mr. Wheeler regarding security for or repayment of such loan. He merely verifies the allegations contained in the statement of claim (which did not mention the $77,000 loan), and he describes the state of the trading accounts of the two companies and verifies the separate existence of Inspiration, and the "unauthorized" sale of its shares in Dragoon.

In para. 30 of this affidavit McGowan says that between 19th December 1987 and 5th January 1988, in discussions with Wheeler about the sales of Dragoon shares from the Inspiration account, "Mr. Wheeler admitted to me that he had caused the said sales to be made, explaining that he had made 'a mistake.' "

On 23rd March McKenzie J made an order in chambers acceding to an application to adjourn the R. 18A motion and he ordered the defendants to provide to the solicitor for the plaintiffs draft copies of an amended statement of defence and the defendants' material to be filed in opposition to the R. 18A application, unexecuted, by 30th March 1988. This amended defence, although not filed until 28th April, recites the $77,000 loan and alleges in para. 2(c):

(c) As security for the loan, Mr. McGowen [sic] was required to provide collateral of 150,000 shares in Geostar Mining Corp. and in addition, all of the shares in the accounts of Inspiration and Wabenung were to stand as security for the debt.

Mr. Wheeler's first affidavit sworn 7th April 1988 describes the $77,000 loan in the following terms:

4. THAT on or about October 5, 1987, Mr. McGowen [sic] approached me for a loan in the amount of $77,000.00 which he said he required within 24 hours in order to prevent the forfeiture of certain assets that he owned in respect of a mining company that he was involved with.

5. THAT Mr. McGowen advised me that a private placement for Dragoon had been completed and that he had money in an account in a London brokerage house or Bank but that he needed the loan as he was unable to get these monies transferred quickly enough.

6. THAT Mr. McGowen suggested and it was agreed that he would pay the funds within 7 days and would pay a fee of $3,000.00 in respect of the loan. Mr. McGowen further agreed that in order to collateralize the loan, he would deposit a further 150,000 shares of Geostar Mining Corp. *in addition to all shares on deposit at McDermid St. Lawrence in all of the Plaintiff's accounts* [my emphasis]. ...

10. THAT I started to commence selling the shares of Geostar Mining Corp. in order to realize upon the loan security. At this time, Mr. McGowen requested that I not sell his Dragoon shares. However, I did not at any time specifically agree that the Dragoon shares would not be sold. I told Mr. McGowen that the Plaintiff's accounts would be liquidated at month end.

Mr. McGowan swore his second affidavit on 5th April (filed 8th April 1988) but he had obviously seen the amended defence and Mr. Wheeler's first affidavit, in draft, because he purports to respond to them in this second affidavit. He describes the loan agreement as follows:

(b) The description of the said loan agreement referred to in the Amended Statement of Defence and the Wheeler Affidavit is not true in any event. The said agreement actually transpired as set out herein below;

(c) On or about October 6, 1987 I, for and on behalf of the Plaintiff Wabenung Resources Ltd. (hereinafter called "Wabenung"), arranged with Wheeler to borrow $77,000.00 from the Defendant McDermid St. Lawrence Limited (hereinafter called "MSL"). The said amount was to be repaid on October 14, 1987, together with interest in the amount of $3,000.00;

(d) My said agreement with MSL was documented in a letter dated October 6, 1987 and signed by me for and on behalf of Wabenung. The said letter was prepared by Ms. Bernice Kosiur of MSL on Wheeler's instructions. At no time was Inspiration or any securities, or other property held by it, made a part of the said loan agreement.

Mr. Wheeler swore his second affidavit on 14th April 1988 which was filed the same day. He says:

(a) the loan was made to Mr. McGowan personally by me personally and the agreement that I made with McGowan and the Plaintiffs was that the shares in the accounts of all of the Plaintiffs would stand as security for the loan made to McGowan. More specifically Mr. McGowan pleaded that I lend him money and that I should do so as I had all of the securities in the Plaintiffs [sic] accounts as collateral. He told me that I was the only person in Vancouver that he could turn to.

(b) the monies were advanced to Mr. McGowan personally through the Wabenung Resources Ltd. account and the indebtedness was registered as a debit in the Wabenung Resources Ltd. account.

(c) the letter of October 6, 1987 attached as Exhibit "C" to Mr. McGowan's affidavit recorded only the promise of Mr. McGowan to repay $80,000 on October 14, 1987. The purpose of this letter was to record only the promise to pay made by McGowan and did not refer to any of the security provisions granted by McGowan, Wabenung Resources Ltd., or Inspiration Management Ltd. The letter was dictated by Mr. McGowan to Bernice Kosiur in my absence as Mr. McGowan required the money immediately on that day and I was not in my office at that time.

Mr. McGowan's third affidavit was sworn 22nd April 1988 (filed 25th April 1988). It does not purport to answer Wheeler's allegations about the terms of the loan agreement. Presumably McGowan thought this had been done sufficiently in his second affidavit.

IV. Rule 18A

As I have said, the learned chambers judge dismissed the McGowan application for judgment under R. 18A because she considered the test to be applied under this rule precluded her from giving judgment unless it was "clear that a trial in the usual way could not possibly make any difference to the outcome."

Before us Mr. Campbell argued that the test described by the chambers judge was not the correct one. It is accordingly necessary as a first step in the determination of this appeal to settle this and other important questions concerning the operation of R. 18A.

The Rules of Court have prescribed a summary judgment procedure for many years. Until our present rules were adopted, this procedure was found in O. 14, R. 1 (MR 115) of the old rules which was limited to liquidated demands and a number of other special kinds of cases. This summary judgment procedure was carried forward into the present rules in 1976, particularly R. 18 which permits judgment to be given in any action on the ground that there is no defence to the whole or any part of the claim or any defence except as to amount (R. 18(1)). This rule understandably received a restricted construction having regard to its provisions. In *Golden Gate Seafood (Vancouver) Co. v. Osborn & Lange Inc.* (1986), 1 BCLR (2d) 145, 13 CPC (2d) 227, Lambert JA at p. 171 said:

> Rule 18 is entitled "Summary Judgment in Action." The ground of the application must be that there is no defence to the whole or a part of the claim or, if the application is made by the defendant, no merit in the whole or a part of the claim. The judge before whom the application is brought is not to decide questions of fact or law as on a trial; his function is restricted to determining whether there is a bona fide triable issue. If there is, he must dismiss the application. See *Hughes v. Sharp* (1969), 68 WWR 706, 5 DLR (3d) 760 (BC CA), and *Memphis Rogues Ltd. v. Skalbania* (1982), 38 BCLR 193, 29 CPC 105 (CA). If there is not, he may give judgment.

The problem with R. 18 of course is that artful pleaders are usually able to set up an arguable claim or defence and any affidavit that raises any contested question of fact or law is enough to defeat a motion for judgment. Rule 18 was often ineffective in avoiding unjust delay or in avoiding unnecessary expense in the determination of many cases.

As a consequence, R. 18A was added to the Rules of Court in 1983 in an attempt to expedite the early resolution of many cases by authorizing a judge in chambers to give judgment in any case where he can decide disputed questions of fact on affidavits or by any of the other proceedings authorized by R. 18A(5) unless it would be unjust to decide the issues in such a way.

I endeavoured to state the differences between applications under RR. 18 and 18A in *Soni v. Malik* (1985), 61 BCLR 36, 1 CPC (2d) 53 (SC), which was quoted with apparent approval by Taggart JA, speaking for this court in *Placer Dev. Ltd. v. Skyline Explor. Ltd.* (1985), 67 BCLR 366 at 377. At pp. 40-41 of *Soni* I said:

> There are substantial differences between an application under RR. 18 and 18A. Under the former, summary judgment should not be given if "there is a bona fide triable issue": *Memphis Rogues Ltd. v. Skalbania* (1982), 38 BCLR 193 at 202, 29 CPC 105 (CA).
>
> Under R. 18A, on the other hand, the court actually tries the issues raised by the pleadings on affidavits. The hearing of a R. 18A application has been called a summary trial: *Imbrook Properties Ltd. v. Bordignon Const. Ltd.* (1984), 51 BCLR 66 at 73, 7 DLR (4th) 602, 4 CLR 223 (CA).
>
> This is a useful way to illustrate the distinction between the two rules although I would have preferred to reserve the term summary trial for expedited proceedings under R. 18A(5). For convenience I am content to describe the various proceedings under RR. 18, 18A and 18A(5) as summary judgment, summary trial and expedited trial respectively.
>
> The important point, however, is that the raising of a triable issue or arguable defence will not always defeat an application under R. 18A, for the court is authorized under that rule to conduct a summary trial of that issue or defence. The court's function is described in R. 18A(3), which provides that on such an application the court "... may grant judgment ... unless (a) the court is unable on the whole of the evidence [that is, affidavits] ... to find the facts necessary to decide the issues of fact or law ..." or unless it is unjust to do so: *Royal Bank v. Vista Homes Ltd.* (1984), 54 BCLR 252 (SC).
>
> While the court must always be careful in exercising this new jurisdiction, it is clearly the intention and expectation of the rule that cases will be decided summarily if the court is able to find the facts necessary for that purpose, even though there may be disputed issues of fact and law.

In *Placer Dev. Ltd. v. Skyline Explor. Ltd.* Taggart JA also referred to R. 1(5) which provides:

> (5) The object of these rules is to secure the just, speedy and inexpensive determination of every proceeding on its merits.

Taggart JA then reviewed a number of authorities and said at pp. 385-86:

> Clearly the opening language of subr. (3) of R. 18A contemplates the possibility of judgment being entered on one or more or all issues raised by the pleadings. But that

contemplation is, for the judge hearing the application, tempered by the language of paras. (a) and (b) of subr. (3). They clothe the judge with a broad discretion to refuse to proceed with the application where he decides he cannot find the facts necessary to decide the issues of fact or law or if it would be unjust to decide the issues raised on the application. Although those two matters are stated in separate clauses of subr. (3), they will often have to be considered together. I can envisage circumstances where the judge will decide on the whole of the evidence that while it is possible to find the facts necessary to decide the issues of fact or law it would be unjust to decide those issues. On the other hand, I cannot think of a case where, notwithstanding his inability to find the necessary facts, the judge would be justified in proceeding with the application.

Having said that, however, I am far from saying that the judge is precluded from finding facts where he has before him affidavits which conflict. The ability of the judge to find the necessary facts and to decide if it is just to resolve the issues before him will to a large extent depend on the nature and quality of the material before him. I think the rule contemplates that the judge may make the necessary findings of fact on conflicting evidence. Here I think the judgment of the Chief Justice of the Supreme Court in the *Soni* case, the statement of Macdonald J in the *Anglo-Amer. Cedar Prod.* case, including his quotation from the judgment of the Privy Counsel in *Eng Mee Yong v. Letchumanan*, and the statements of principle by Leggatt Co. Ct. J in the *J.M. Stafford & Assoc.* case, may all have application.

In summary, the rule is a means whereby the general principles stated by R. 1(5) may be attained. The rule must, however, be applied only where it is possible to do justice between the parties in accordance with the requirements of the rule itself and in accordance with the general principles which govern judges in their daily task of ensuring that justice is done.

With respect, I think the foregoing accurately describes the proper practice to be followed by a judge hearing an application under R. 18A.

Notwithstanding this, R. 18A has not received a consistent application. In some cases judgment has been given in fairly complicated cases such as *Bank of BC v. Anglo-Amer. Cedar Prod. Ltd.* (1984), 57 BCLR 350, 47 CPC 89 (SC), and in *Soni Placer* and *Golden Gate*. Other decisions point out the usefulness of R. 18A such as *United Services Fund v. Ward* (1986), 1 BCLR (2d) 396 (CA); and *Wolf Mountain Coal Ltd. Partnership v. Netherlands Pac. Mining Co.* (1988), 31 BCLR (2d) 16 (SC). But other decisions have adopted an extremely cautious approach resulting in the development of the test adopted by the chambers judge in this case. Such cases include *Stuart v. Russell*, [1988] BCWLD 1649, CA, Vancouver No. CA006892, 2nd March 1988 (not yet reported), and *Lafleur v. Maryniuk* (1988), 23 BCLR (2d) 131, 28 CPC (2d) 67 (CA). In *Royal Bank v. Stonehocker* (1985), 61 BCLR 265 (CA), it was held that where there are conflicting affidavits it is not open to a judge hearing an application for judgment under R. 18A to prefer the affidavit of one party over that of the other and in such cases the proper course is to dismiss the motion for judgment and remit the matter to the trial list.

It is timely, in my view, for this court to settle the practice to be followed on applications brought under R. 18A keeping always in mind that the variable circumstances under which such applications may be made are unlimited and it may not be possible to foresee every eventuality which may arise.

In my judgment, it must be accepted that while every effort must be made to ensure a just result, the volumes of litigation presently before our courts, the urgency of some cases, and the cost of litigation do not always permit the luxury of a full trial with all traditional safeguards in every case, particularly if a just result can be achieved by a less expensive and more expeditious procedure. I agree with Hinkson JA when he said in *United Services Fund v. Ward* at p. 399:

> My concern is with respect to the intention of promulgating R. 18A. McEachern CJSC has referred to it as a summary trial proceeding, adopting a decision of this court in that respect. It seems to me that that was the intention in R. 18A, that it not be a full-blown trial with all the rights and safeguards that accompany such a trial, but indeed it involved shortcutting some of the normal processes that are involved in a trial and expedited the administration of justice.

In fact R. 18A substitutes other safeguards which are sufficient to ensure the proper attainment of justice. First, 14 days' notice of the application must be given (R. 18A(1.1)); secondly, the chambers judge cannot give judgment unless he can find the facts necessary to decide issues of fact or law (R. 18A(3)(a)); and thirdly, the chambers judge, even if he can decide the necessary factual and legal issues, may nevertheless decline to give judgment if he thinks it would be unjust to do so. The procedure prescribed by R. 18A may not furnish perfect justice in every case, but that elusive and unattainable goal cannot always be assured even after a conventional trial and I believe the safeguards furnished by the rule and the common sense of the chambers judge are sufficient for the attainment of justice in any case likely to be found suitable for this procedure. Chambers judges should be careful but not timid in using R. 18A for the purpose for which it was intended.

In deciding whether it will be unjust to give judgment the chambers judge is entitled to consider, *inter alia*, the amount involved, the complexity of the matter, its urgency, any prejudice likely to arise by reason of delay, the cost of taking the case forward to a conventional trial in relation to the amount involved, the course of the proceedings and any other matters which arise for consideration on this important question. ...

The test for R. 18A, in my view, is the same as on a trial. Upon the facts being found the chambers judge must apply the law and all appropriate legal principles. If then satisfied that the claim or defence has been established according to the appropriate onus of proof he must give judgment according to law unless he has the opinion that it will be unjust to give such judgment.

In deciding whether the case is an appropriate one for judgment under R. 18A, the chambers judge will always give full consideration to all of the evidence which counsel place before him but he will also consider whether the evidence is sufficient for adjudication. For example, the absence of an affidavit from a principal player in the piece, unless its absence is adequately explained, may cause the judge to conclude either that he cannot find the facts necessary to decide the issues, or that it would be unjust to do so. But even then, as the process is adversarial, the judge may be able fairly and justly to find the facts necessary to decide the issue.

Lastly, I do not agree, as suggested in *Royal Bank v. Stonehocker* that a chambers judge is obliged to remit a case to the trial list just because there are conflicting affidavits. In this connection I prefer the view expressed by Taggart JA in *Placer*, ... [at 212-13] of these reasons. Subject to what I am about to say, a judge should not decide an issue of fact or law solely on the basis of conflicting affidavits even if he prefers one version to the other. It may be, however, notwithstanding sworn affidavit evidence to the contrary, that other admissible evidence will make it possible to find the facts necessary for judgment to be given. For example, in an action on a cheque, the alleged maker might by affidavit deny his signature while other believable evidence may satisfy the court that he did indeed sign it. Again, the variety of different kinds of cases which will arise is unlimited. In such cases, absent other circumstances or defences, judgment should be given.

But even if there is a conflict of evidence which cannot easily be resolved on affidavits, as is often the case, the chambers judge is still not required to remit the case to the trial list. He could, for example, adjourn the application and order cross-examination on one or more affidavits, or he could order the deponents to appear to be cross-examined before him or another judge after which time it may be possible to find the facts necessary to give judgment. The chambers judge also has the option of employing any of the other procedures included in R. 18A(5) instead of remitting the case to the trial list.

I have no doubt that R. 18A is destined to play an increasingly important role in the efficient disposition of litigation, and experience has already shown that its use is not limited to simple or straightforward cases. Many complex cases properly prepared and argued can be resolved summarily without compromising justice in any way.

But it is necessary to recognize that it is essential on all applications under R. 18A for counsel to bring an appropriate measure of professional skill to the preparation of both the substance and the form of their material. It is unfair to scoop-shovel volumes of disjointed affidavits and exhibits upon the chambers judge and expect him or her to make an informed judgment. While I also have the view that many of these applications will in future be heard [i]n Chambers Division III which will inevitably be expanded, many of these applications will continue to be heard on a chambers list or by a referral judge where there is little or no opportunity for judicial preparation. Thus it is incumbent upon counsel to ensure, as the old pleaders used to say, that there is a proper joinder of issues on all questions on fact and law, and the practice of serial affidavits as in this case should be avoided.

It should not be good enough in such serious matters for counsel to throw up volumes of ill-considered affidavits and exhibits which do not squarely raise or answer the real issues in the case. The preparation of affidavits for an application or defence under R. 18A is a serious matter which requires the careful professional attention of counsel.

Fortunately, most counsel take great care in the preparation of their material. If they do not do this the chambers judge is entitled to send them away to put their material in proper order. Serial affidavits, as in this case, should be avoided if possible. One of counsel's objectives is to persuade, and they cannot expect to succeed in this endeavour if they permit confusion in the form of masses of disorganized fact and paper to intrude into the decisional process.

V. Judgment on This Appeal

In my view, the learned chambers judge applied the wrong test in this case. Instead of the test she applied (that a conventional trial could not possibly make any difference), she should have followed the process I have just discussed.

But even if the chambers judge had applied the proper test it is my view that she could not have found the facts with sufficient certainty to give judgment because the real question was whether McGowan agreed, as Wheeler alleges, that all of the shares in the accounts of all of the plaintiffs would stand as security for the loan made by the defendants. McGowan in his second affidavit denies this and says that the loan agreement is described in the brief letter of 6th October 1987 and he adds: "At no time was Inspiration or any securities or other property held by it made a part of the said loan agreement." His position is that the only security he gave for this loan was his personal covenant, the securities in the Wabenung account and of course, the debt owed by the company.

Notwithstanding the fact that the conflict between these two deponents could not be resolved on affidavits, the chambers judge was not required to dismiss the application and leave the action to be tried in the usual way. She could have required McGowan and Wheeler to be cross-examined on their affidavits because such cross-examination would put her in a position to decide this crucial question and all other questions which would dispose of the action, or she could have exercised any one or more of the other jurisdictions conferred by R. 18A(5) in an endeavour to bring this relatively straightforward litigation to an early and inexpensive disposition. The learned chambers judge did give leave to the plaintiff to bring a fresh application under R. 18A after examination for discovery. That was an option that was also open to her but it seems to me, with respect, that cross-examination before a judge would have been the preferable course to follow.

At the end of the day I am left with the view that the use of an improper test by the chambers judge may have led her to conclude that she had no choice but to dismiss the application.

Because of the urgency of this matter to the parties (a trial date was pending) the court, on 21st April 1989, allowed this appeal and authorized the plaintiffs, if they wished, to renew their application for judgment under R. 18A on the ground that, if Mr. McGowan and Mr. Wheeler were cross-examined on their affidavits before the judgment, either on an issue or generally, under R. 18A(3). These are my reasons for allowing this appeal to the extent just mentioned.

Appeal allowed.

NOTES AND QUESTIONS

1. This case was decided under the BC summary trial rule. Compare the application of that rule with the approach of the Ontario courts in the summary judgment decisions already considered. Is the BC approach fair? Is it justified as a form of "rough and ready" justice that is cheaper and faster? Should other provinces adopt a similar provision?

2. It should be noted that in British Columbia, there is no right to cross-examine on affidavits filed with the court. Compare Ontario rule 39.02. How would the difference affect the hearing and disposition of a motion for summary judgment?

3. Review the Ontario simplified procedure rule (rule 76) and the provision in that rule providing for the hearing of summary judgment motions on affidavit evidence without cross-examination. Is summary judgment more likely or less likely to be granted on such motions?

CHAPTER SEVEN

The Size and Scope of Litigation

I. INTRODUCTION

A feature of modern litigation and adjudication is that litigation must deal with problems that are much more diffuse and public in nature than traditional thinking or practice anticipated. As chapter 4, "Challenges to the Traditional Model," suggested, this has required judges and courts to reappraise their approach to the demanding task of decision making and its institutional character. The pressures for such a change have obviously exerted themselves at many different stages of the litigation process and on many different concepts of traditional procedure. A particular and pressing challenge has been the need to reformulate the rules and principles that determine the appropriate parties and interests that can and should be heard and considered by a court before it reaches its final decision. The result has been the development of new procedural vehicles and the revision of old doctrines to ensure adequate opportunities for broader and more effective participation in lawsuits.

This move away from more restrictive traditional rules to more expansive modern principles has not been uncontroversial or uncontested. The fear is that we might have jumped out of the formalist fire of procedural technicalities only to leap into the realist frying pan of open-ended discretion. Whereas old claims ran the risk of being defeated by the rigid application of limiting rules, modern actions will be stifled by an overabundance of parties and issues. Throughout this chapter, this tension between limiting and enlarging the number and identity of interests that are permitted to be brought and appear before the court informs the historical development and contemporary interpretation of the relevant rules and common law principles.

This chapter examines five areas of procedure that touch on these questions about the interests that may be furthered in litigation. As with the balance of this book, the areas are organized chronologically, much as they would arise in the course of pursuing litigation. However, as will be seen, each area provides an occasion to consider the ongoing tension between "private" and "public" models of litigation.

We first examine the rules that govern who can become a party to any lawsuit through a review of the doctrine of *standing*. The key question in this section is "Who can sue?." Still, as the cases and commentary will show, standing is as much a matter of the nature of the rights capable of vindication in litigation as it is a matter of the persons permitted to sue.

It would seem logical to move from the question "Who can sue?" to the questions "Who can they sue?" and "What claims should be asserted?" but we suspend that question for a time to consider the basis for deciding those issues. The doctrine of *res judicata* is designed to prevent duplicative litigation. While it generally becomes an issue only in subsequent litigation, it operates as a key consideration in framing the initial litigation from the outset.

Having considered "Who and what should be included?" in the litigation, we then turn to the rules governing the ways in which claims and parties may be included in a proceeding: "Who may sue and be sued?." This subject is know as "*joinder*." As we will see, the desire to prevent duplicative litigation, which has given rise to liberal joinder rules, is balanced by the countervailing concern that the litigation will become unduly complex and burdensome.

If the first half of this chapter is, broadly speaking, about framing the litigation, then the second half is about expanding the litigation once it has been commenced. Joinder bridges the divide. Thus, the second half of this section considers joinder from the defendants' perspective: "Who may defendants join in litigation to ensure that all interests affected are party to the proceeding?"

The fourth section looks at the relatively new rules developed to allow others— those who have not been joined by the plaintiff or defendant—to be involved in litigation. This is known as "*intervention*."

Finally, the fifth section considers the contemporary efforts to broaden the circumstances in which one person can bring an action on behalf of a large number of others. This is known as a "*class proceeding*."

II. STANDING

What interest does a person seeking to litigate have to demonstrate in order to be permitted to sue and how does he or she demonstrate such an interest? With the advent of the Canadian Charter of Rights and Freedoms, the question of standing has arisen in the context of public interest litigation when the plaintiff is trying to vindicate rights not possessed by him or her personally, but rather by the public. But the question of which claims ought to be recognized and allowed to be litigated can be viewed more fundamentally. Take an obvious case: Why do we let someone who has been run down by a car and has had an arm broken sue? The answer, of course, is because he or she has suffered physical damages for which he or she seeks compensation based on harm done by the negligence of the driver. However, we do not permit someone who has observed the incident and is horrified by the mayhem caused by negligent driving to sue. Why not? Is it because such an individual has no interest in what has transpired or is it because the interest is one that the law is not, in any event as yet, willing to protect? Is the difference that, in the former case, the plaintiff can show harm that can be compensated in damage or some other form of relief and that will benefit that person directly, or is it something more fundamental? We do not, after all, protect all claims for relief that allege injury even if the injury is a traditional one. In the classic case of *Donoghue v. Stevenson*, the plaintiff had to go to the House of Lords and even there only a majority of that court decided that the interest she was asserting ought to be protected. If the decision to recognize a claim does depend on something more fundamental, what is it?

Lets return to the question of standing when someone wishes to litigate and cannot claim an invasion of any interest to himself or herself directly, at least as traditionally conceived, and, therefore, seeks to litigate in the "public interest" or to vindicate "public rights." What does "public interest" or "public rights" mean? Does it mean only that if a court decides to allow the litigation for other reasons it is in the "public interest" but, if the plaintiff is refused standing, the litigation is not in the "public interest"?

The following is a description of how courts have traditionally treated standing to litigate "public rights." Why do you think the attorney general was accorded such deference? How did the attorney general know where the public interest lay in any question?

W.A. Bogart, "Developments in the Canadian Law of Standing"
(1984), *Civil Justice Quarterly* 340-42 (footnotes omitted)

The traditional common law position in Canada is based on standing rules formulated by the English courts, which in turn, had their origins in the law of public nuisance. Gradually, the rules formulated in that context spread to other areas, namely "public rights," where individuals were attempting to seek redress for wrongs which affected many people but no one of them in particular.

The basic rule which developed is that suits to redress infringement of public rights are a matter for the Attorney-General to enforce. The Attorney-General may enforce the rights in two ways: either he initiates and prosecutes the action himself or he permits some private individual or public authority to bring a relator action which is an action in the name of the Attorney-General "on the relation of" that private individual or public authority. The Attorney-General is exclusively empowered to refuse or permit an individual to commence a relator action and his decision is not reviewable by a court.

However, the need to vindicate public rights through the Attorney-General by having him initiate the litigation himself or through a relator action can be circumvented if the individual can demonstrate that either his private right will be infringed or that he will suffer "special damages." What constitutes "special damages" has spawned all sorts of litigation. A favourite question is whether the damage to the individual seeking to litigate has to be of a different kind and not just different in degree from that suffered by the rest of the public.

Canadian courts have recognised some exceptions to the "special damages" rule. The first allowed municipal ratepayers standing where a municipality made an expenditure alleged to be *ultra vires*, that is, outside the scope of its authority. Even in these cases some deference was paid to the notion of special damages, for the courts said that they presumed that the ratepayer suffered special damages in the form of increased taxes over and above other residents in the municipality and the public in general. Moreover, the municipal ratepayers exception has been, at least by some courts, only tolerated and has often been interpreted narrowly.

The second kind of exception to the "special damages" rule was that found in statutes which widened standing in order to permit a body, a class, or specific individuals to maintain suits, without the need to demonstrate special damages arising out of the subject of the litigation, or without the need to obtain the Attorney-General's consent. These statutory standing provisions break down into three categories. In the first category are statutes which allow the governing body of a profession to seek court orders when the governing statute is being infringed. Canadian courts have held that in the absence of such statutory provisions, a professional body cannot seek an injunction to restrain persons from acting in breach of the statute unless the Attorney-General is joined as a plaintiff. Secondly, under certain provincial acts, municipalities are given the right to obtain an injunction to restrain a breach of the municipality's by-laws. In addition, sometimes an elector or "person interested in a by-law" is granted standing to apply to have a by-law quashed. Thirdly, certain acts, particularly those designed to protect consumers' interests, grant broad standing to individuals to apply to court when the act in question is being contravened.

The third type of exception focusses on the remedies sought. While it is not entirely clear, it seems that the courts are more disposed to give an individual standing when review by the court of administrative action is sought. The reasons for the courts' more liberal view have never been fully articulated though the courts' general desire to check administrative action may be significant. There is evidence that courts treat the question of standing as a matter of discretion when review of administrative action is in issue though, again, it is uncertain how this discretion is to be exercised.

NOTES AND QUESTIONS

1. *The expansion of standing in public interest litigation.* In the last two decades the Supreme Court of Canada has decided a number of cases dealing with challenges to

the plaintiff's standing to raise constitutional and other issues and each time has confirmed the plaintiff's entitlement to sue. The first three of these, *Thorson v. Attorney General of Canada*, [1975] 1 SCR 138, *Nova Scotia Board of Censors v. McNeil*, [1976] 2 SCR 265, and *Minister of Justice of Canada v. Borowski*, [1981] 2 SCR 575 greatly liberalized the test for granting standing in public interest litigation.

Thorson, a constitutional challenge to the Official Languages Act, was framed as being brought by a taxpayer on behalf of all taxpayers. This basis for standing was rejected because "the claim to legal standing could not be founded solely on the damage resulting from an illegal expenditure of public funds." However, it was recognized that "the Act was not a regulatory type of statute, but was declaratory and directory in respect of the use of English and French by and in federal authorities and agencies and did not, itself, create offences or impose penalties. There was thus no person or class of persons particularly aggrieved who might raise the issue of its constitutional validity." Accordingly, standing was granted to prevent such legislation from being immune from judicial review.

Thorson was soon followed by a challenge to the constitutional validity of censorship provisions of the Nova Scotia Theatres and Amusements Act in *McNeil*. Standing was granted by the court in a decision by Laskin J who said,

> [M]embers of the Nova Scotia public are directly affected in what they may view in a Nova Scotia theatre, albeit there is a more direct effect on the business enterprises which are regulated by the legislation. The challenged legislation does not appear to me to be legislation directed only to the regulation of operators and film distributors. It strikes at the members of the public in one of its central aspects.
>
> In my view, this is enough, in the light of the fact that there appears to be no other way, practically speaking, to subject the challenged Act to judicial review to support the claim of the respondent to have the discretion of the Court exercised in his favour to give him standing.

In the third decision of the trilogy, *Borowski*, the issue of standing arose in a challenge pursuant to the Canadian Bill of Rights by an anti-abortionist to certain exclupatory provisions to the Criminal Code that permitted doctors to perform abortions when authorized to do so by a hospital committee. The court granted standing (Laskin J dissenting) based on the following reasoning:

> The legislation under attack here is not declaratory or directory as in the case of *the Official Languages Act* nor is it regulatory as in the case of the *Theatres and Amusements Act*. It is exculpatory in nature. It provides that in certain specified circumstances conduct which otherwise would be criminal is permissible. It does not impose duties, but instead provides exemption from criminal liability. That being so, it is difficult to find any class of person directly affected or exceptionally prejudiced by it who have cause to attack the legislation.
>
> Doctors who perform therapeutic abortions are protected by the legislation and would have no reason to attack it. Doctors who do not perform therapeutic abortions have no direct interest to protect by attacking it, and, consequently, an attack by a doctor in that category would be no different from that made by any other concerned citizen. The same thing applies to hospitals. A hospital which appoints a therapeutic abortion

committee has no reason to attack the legislation. A hospital which does not appoint such a committee has no direct reason to attack the legislation.

There is no reason why a pregnant woman desirous of obtaining an abortion should challenge the legislation which is for her benefit. The husband of a pregnant wife who desires to prevent an abortion which she desires may be said to be directly affected by the legislation in issue in the sense that by reason of that legislation she might obtain a certificate permitting the abortion if her continued pregnancy would be likely to endanger her life or health and thus prevent the abortion from constituting a crime. However, the possibility of the husband bringing proceedings to attack the legislation is illusory. The progress of the pregnancy would not await the inevitable lengthy lapse of time involved in court proceedings leading to a final judgment. The abortion would have occurred, or a child would have been born long before the case had been finally terminated, perhaps in this Court.

The legislation proposed to be attacked has a direct impact upon the unborn human foetuses whose existence may be terminated by legalized abortions. They obviously cannot be parties to proceedings in court and yet the issue as to the scope of the *Canadian Bill of Rights* in the protection of the human right to life is a matter of considerable importance. There is no reasonable way in which that issue can be brought into court unless proceedings are launched by some interested citizen.

In the light of the *Thorson* and *McNeil* cases, it is my opinion that the respondent should be recognized as having legal standing to continue with his action. In the *Thorson* case, the plaintiff, as an interested citizen, challenged the constitutional validity of the *Official Languages Act*. The legislation did not directly affect him, save in his position as a taxpayer. He had sought, without avail, to have the constitutional issue raised by other means. He was recognized to have status. The position is the same in the present case. The respondent is a concerned citizen and a taxpayer. He has sought unsuccessfully to have the issue determined by other means.

In the *McNeil* case, the plaintiff was concerned about censorship of films in Nova Scotia. He had sought by other means to have the validity of the *Theatres and Amusements Act* tested, but without success. In that case there were other classes of persons directly affected by the legislation who might have challenged it. Nonetheless, he was recognized as having legal standing because it also affected the rights of the public. The position of the respondent in this case is at least as strong. There are in this case no persons directly affected who could effectively challenge the legislation.

I interpret these cases as deciding that to establish status as a plaintiff in a suit seeking a declaration that legislation is invalid, if there is a serious issue as to its invalidity, a person need only to show that he is affected by it directly or that he has a genuine interest as a citizen in the validity of the legislation and that there is no other reasonable and effective manner in which the issue may be brought before the Court. In my opinion, the respondent has met this test and should be permitted to proceed with his action.

2. *Extension of public interest standing to challenges to administrative action.* In 1986, Finlay, a Manitoba resident who relied upon social assistance, sought declaratory and injunctive relief from the Federal Court to the effect that the transfer payments made

by the federal government to Manitoba under the Canada Assistance Plan, RSC 1970, c. C-1 were illegal in *Finlay v. Canada (Minister of Finance)*, [1986] 2 SCR 608. The basis for this claim was that the relevant Manitoba social welfare legislation did not comply with the Plan's requirements for transfer payments to the provinces. Compliance allegedly would have produced a higher level of assistance for Finlay whose assistance payments were clawed back when a previous overpayment was discovered. His claim was struck out at the trial level but restored on appeal. On appeal by the Crown to the Supreme Court of Canada, standing was upheld. The court found that although Finlay had a direct, personal interest in provincial non-compliance with the Plan, the relationship between the prejudice suffered and the illegality of the transfer payments was too remote for standing under traditional rules. However, the court reviewed the *Thorson*, *McNeil*, *Borowski* trilogy and held that public interest standing could be applied as a matter of judicial discretion to cases such as *Finlay* in which the challenge was not made to the constitutionality of legislation but to administrative action.

3. *The tide turns: the limits of public interest standing.* It appears that the trend to more liberal rules for standing in public interest litigation has run its course. The effects of such rules on the allocation of scarce judicial resources and on the need to have actions prosecuted by those most affected began to be considered by the courts as was predicted in a provocative piece by David Mullan and Andrew Roman, *"Minister of Justice v. Borowski*: The Extent of the Citizens' Right To Litigate the Lawfulness of Government Action" (1984), 4 *Windsor Yearbook of Access to Justice* 303. Mullan and Roman caution against the wholesale application of constitutional rules to administrative settings:

> Useful focus can be given to this discussion by reference to the case of *Re Ratepayers of the School District of the New Ross Consolidated School*. There, Glube J (as she then was) of the Nova Scotia Supreme Court, Trial Division granted a group of ratepayers in a particular school district standing to challenge the dismissal of a school principal. Like *Borowski*, this decision raises the issue of whether there are certain types of wrong which should give rise to relief only at the suit of persons directly affected. After all, in the private law sphere, no matter how great a value some courts place on adherence to contractual promises as a matter of public policy, they would assuredly not recognize the status of the "Canadians for Contract Society" to seek a declaration that there had been a breach of contract as between Smith and Jones, albeit that neither Jones nor Smith had chosen to sue. The principle of private autonomy rejects *jus tertii* claims; only those wronged have control over whether there should be a suit. To us, that also provides a reason why the "Canadians for Procedural Fairness Society" should not *automatically* be able to sue to vindicate the rights of the teacher dismissed under a statute but contrary to the rules of natural justice. First, dismissal of a teacher, albeit under a statutory scheme, comes very close to the area where public and private law intersect and, secondly, and perhaps stemming from the first, the claim to *procedural* fairness in a particular case is much more of an individual, private claim than it is a public claim.
>
> This, therefore, suggests that the courts should exercise caution in the automatic application of *Thorson*, *McNeil* and *Borowski* in the administrative law arena. Not all administrative law cases raise the same public issues as is generally the case with

challenges to the constitutionality of legislation or the legality of other kinds of government action. Indeed, it is also clear that application of the *Canadian Bill of Rights* and *Charter of Rights* to individuals may raise the same considerations as the procedural fairness example just discussed. In the situation of particular, executive applications of statutes to individual citizens allegedly contrary to the *Bill* or *Charter*, as opposed to challenges to legislation or executive rule-making implementing legislation, the courts may very well hesitate to allow X to vindicate Y's claim, *Borowski* notwithstanding. Seen in this light, the proper solution to the administrative law dilemma may well be to acknowledge the relevance of the *Thorson*, *McNeil* and *Borowski* factors to many administrative law situations but also, to recognize that sometimes, indeed frequently, administrative law claims are very close to being purely private claims and that this deserves weight as a countervailing factor.

Viewed from this perspective the *New Ross* case was not necessarily wrongly decided. The ratepayers are affected, as parents of pupils, when the principal is dismissed; not as directly, of course, as the principal, but he may have no objection to their trying to vindicate his rights as well. Moreover, should the pattern continue and school principals be dismissed constantly without fair procedures, the situation achieves a far more dramatic public aspect and the private rights argument becomes submerged, at least to the extent of allowing the parents to seek declaratory relief as to the illegality of the pattern of conduct.

Ultimately, what this discussion is meant to demonstrate is that the principles of *Borowski* and the rights of citizens to constitutional behaviour should not extend to the totality of action by governments and public authorities. Challenges to legislation and programmes and rules allegedly justified by legislation may well be a different matter than individualized decisions for which legislative authority is claimed. Even where the challenge to such individualized action is *Charter* or *Bill of Rights* based and because of that generally regarded as "constitutional" in basis, the nature of the decision may be such as to open it to challenge only at the suit of the person directly affected. Putting it another way, *Borowski* should not be seen as approving public interest challenges whenever a question of legality is raised in relation to public authority activity.

Indeed, as far as the *Charter* is concerned, there is a potential roadblock in section 24, the remedies provisions. This gives the Courts extensive remedial powers to rectify breaches of the *Charter* but only at the suit of persons "whose rights or freedoms … have been infringed or denied." Up to this point, commentators have argued against this being interpreted as imposing a restrictive standing requirement in *Charter* cases. One point of view is that section 24 is not intended to be a codification of the remedial possibilities for breaches of the *Charter*. Such rights to seek declaratory relief as general public law allows are said to continue to exist outside of the *Charter*. Another contention is that section 24 covers a situation such as *Borowski* anyway; if the abortion provisions violate the *Charter*, they infringe the rights of all citizens including Borowski. Nevertheless, converting the *New Ross Consolidated School* decision into a *Charter* case, it is easy to see a court using section 24 to deny the ratepayers a remedy on the basis that the denial of natural justice to the principal did not infringe or deny the ratepayers' rights or freedoms in any way and at the same time seeing section 24 as establishing a criterion by which access to the courts in such cases must be judged.

Canadian Council of Churches v. The Queen
[1992] 1 SCR 236

CORY J: … At issue on this appeal is whether the Canadian Council of Churches should be granted status to proceed with an action challenging, almost in its entirety, the validity of the amended *Immigration Act, 1976*, which came into effect January 1, 1989.

Factual Background

The Canadian Council of Churches ("the council"), a federal corporation, represents the interests of a broad group of member churches. Through an inter-church committee for refugees it coordinates the work of the churches aimed at the protection and resettlement of refugees. The council, together with other interested organizations, has created an organization known as the Concerned Delegation of Church, Legal, Medical and Humanitarian Organizations. Through this body the council has commented on the development of refugee policy and procedures both in this country and in others.

In 1988 the Parliament of Canada passed amendments to the *Immigration Act, 1976*, SC 1976-77, c. 52, by SC 1988, c. 35 and c. 36. The amended Act came into force on January 1, 1989. It completely changed the procedures for determining whether applicants come within the definition of a Convention refugee. While the amendments were still under consideration the council expressed its concerns about the proposed new refugee determination process to members of the government and to the parliamentary committees which considered the legislation. On the first business day after the amended Act came into force, the council commenced this action, seeking a declaration that many if not most of the amended provisions violated the *Canadian Charter of Rights and Freedoms* and the *Canadian Bill of Rights*, RSC 1985, App. III. The Attorney General of Canada brought a motion to strike out the claim on the basis that the council did not have standing to bring the action and had not demonstrated a cause of action.

The Question of Standing in Canada

Courts in Canada, like those in other common law jurisdictions, traditionally dealt with individuals. For example, courts determine whether an individual is guilty of a crime; they determine rights as between individuals; they determine the rights of individuals in their relationships with the state in all its various manifestations. One great advantage of operating in the traditional mode is that the courts can reach their decisions based on facts that have been clearly established. It was by acting in this manner that the courts established the rule of law and provided a peaceful means of resolving disputes. Operating primarily, if not almost exclusively, in the traditional manner, courts in most regions operate to capacity. Courts play an important role in our society. If they are to continue to do so care must be taken to ensure that judicial resources are not overextended. This is a factor that will always have to be placed in the balance when consideration is given to extending standing.

On the other hand there can be no doubt that the complexity of society has spawned ever more complex issues for resolution by the courts. Modern society requires regulation to survive. Transportation by motor vehicle and aircraft requires greater regulation for public safety than did travel by covered wagon. Light and power provided by nuclear energy require greater control than did the kerosene lamp.

The State has been required to intervene in an ever more extensive manner in the affairs of its citizens. The increase of State activism has led to the growth of the concept of public rights. The validity of government intervention must be reviewed by courts. Even before the passage of the Charter this court had considered and weighed the merits of broadening access to the courts against the need to conserve scarce judicial resources. It expanded the rules of standing in a trilogy of cases; *Thorson v. Canada (Attorney General)*, supra, *McNeil v. Nova Scotia (Board of Censors)* (1975), [1976] 2 SCR 265, 12 NSR (2d) 85, 32 CRNS 376, 5 NR 43, 55 DLR (3d) 632, and *Borowski v. Canada (Minister of Justice)*, [1981] 2 SCR 575, [1982] 1 WWR 97, 24 CPC 62, 24 CR (3d) 352, 12 Sask. R 420, 64 CCC (2d) 97, 130 DLR (3d) 588, 39 NR 331. Writing for the majority in *Borowski*, Martland J set forth the conditions which a plaintiff must satisfy in order to be granted standing, at p. 598 [SCR]:

> [T]o establish status as a plaintiff in a suit seeking a declaration that legislation is invalid, if there is a serious issue as to its invalidity, a person need only to show that he is affected by it directly or that he has a genuine interest as a citizen in the validity of the legislation and that there is no other reasonable and effective manner in which the issue may be brought before the Court.

Those then were the conditions which had to be met in 1981.

In 1982, with the passage of the Charter, there was for the first time a restraint placed on the sovereignty of Parliament to pass legislation that fell within its jurisdiction. The Charter enshrines the rights and freedoms of Canadians. It is the courts which have the jurisdiction to preserve and to enforce those Charter rights. This is achieved, in part, by ensuring that legislation does not infringe the provisions of the Charter. By its terms the Charter indicates that a generous and liberal approach should be taken to the issue of standing. If that were not done, Charter rights might be unenforced and Charter freedoms shackled. The *Constitution Act, 1982* does not of course affect the discretion courts possess to grant standing to public litigants. What it does is entrench the fundamental right of the public to government in accordance with the law.

The rule of law is recognized in the preamble of the Charter, which reads:

> Whereas Canada is founded upon principles that recognize the supremacy of God and the rule of law:

The rule of law is thus recognized as a cornerstone of our democratic form of government. It is the rule of law which guarantees the rights of citizens to protection against arbitrary and unconstitutional government action. The same right is affirmed in s. 52(1), which states:

> 52.(1) The Constitution of Canada is the supreme law of Canada, and any law that is inconsistent with the provisions of the Constitution is, to the extent of the inconsistency, of no force or effect.

Parliament and the legislatures are thus required to act within the bounds of the Constitution and in accordance with the *Canadian Charter of Rights and Freedoms*. Courts are the final arbiters as to when that duty has been breached. As a result, courts will undoubtedly seek to ensure that their discretion is exercised so that standing is granted in those situations where it is necessary to ensure that legislation conforms to the Constitution and *Canadian Charter of Rights and Freedoms.*

The question of standing was first reviewed in the post-Charter era in *Finlay v. Canada (Minister of Finance)*, [1986] 2 SCR 607, 23 Admin. LR 197, [1987] 1 WWR 603, 17 CPC (2d) 289, 71 NR 338, 33 DLR (4th) 321, 8 CHRR D/3789. In that case Le Dain J, speaking for the court, extended the scope of the trilogy and held that courts have a discretion to award public interest standing to challenge an exercise of administrative authority as well as legislation. He based this conclusion on the underlying principle of discretionary standing which he defined as a recognition of the public interest in maintaining respect for "the limits of statutory authority."

The standard set by this court for public interest plaintiffs to receive standing also addresses the concern for the proper allocation of judicial resources. This is achieved by limiting the granting of status to situations in which no directly affected individual might be expected to initiate litigation. In Finlay, it was specifically recognized that the traditional concerns about widening access to the courts are addressed by the conditions imposed for the exercise of judicial discretion to grant public interest standing set out in the trilogy. Le Dain J put it in this way, at p. 631 [SCR]:

> [T]he concern about the allocation of scarce judicial resources and the need to screen out the mere busybody; the concern that in the determination of issues the courts should have the benefit of the contending points of view of those most directly affected by them; and the concern about the proper role of the courts and their constitutional relationship to the other branches of government. These concerns are addressed by the criteria for the exercise of the judicial discretion to recognize public interest standing to bring an action for a declaration that were laid down in *Thorson*, *McNeil* and *Borowski*.

Should the Current Test for Public Interest Standing Be Extended?

The increasing recognition of the importance of public rights in our society confirms the need to extend the right to standing from the private law tradition which limited party status to those who possessed a private interest. In addition, some extension of standing beyond the traditional parties accords with the provisions of the *Constitution Act, 1982.* However, I would stress that the recognition of the need to grant public interest standing in some circumstances does not amount to a blanket approval to grant standing to all who wish to litigate an issue. It is essential that a balance be struck between ensuring access to the courts and preserving judicial resources. It would be disastrous if the courts were allowed to become hopelessly overburdened as a result of the unnecessary proliferation of marginal or redundant suits brought by well-meaning organizations pursuing their own particular cases certain in the knowledge that their cause is all-important. It would be detrimental, if not devastating, to our system of justice and unfair to private litigants.

The whole purpose of granting status is to prevent the immunization of legislation or public acts from any challenge. The granting of public interest standing is not required when, on a balance of probabilities, it can be shown that the measure will be subject to attack by a private litigant. The principles for granting public standing set forth by this court need not and should not be expanded. The decision whether to grant status is a discretionary one with all which that designation implies. Thus, undeserving applications may be refused. Nonetheless, when exercising the discretion the applicable principles should be interpreted in a liberal and generous manner.

The Application of the Principles for Public Interest Standing to This Case

It has been seen that when public interest standing is sought, consideration must be given to three aspects. First, is there a serious issue raised as to the invalidity of legislation in question? Second, has it been established that the plaintiff is directly affected by the legislation or if not does the plaintiff have a genuine interest in its validity? Third, is there another reasonable and effective way to bring the issue before the court?

(1) Serious Issue of Invalidity

It was noted in *Finlay, supra,* that the issues of standing and of whether there is a reasonable cause of action are closely related and indeed tend to merge. In the case at bar the Federal Court of Appeal in its careful reasons turned its attention to the question of whether the amended statement of claim raised a reasonable cause of action. The claim makes a wide-sweeping and somewhat disjointed attack upon most of the multitudinous amendments to the *Immigration Act, 1976.* Some of the allegations are so hypothetical in nature that it would be impossible for any court to make a determination with regard to them. In many ways the statement of claim more closely resembles submissions that might be made to a parliamentary committee considering the legislation than it does an attack on the validity of the provisions of the legislation. No doubt the similarity can be explained by the fact that the action was brought on the first working day following the passage of the legislation. It is perhaps unfortunate that this court is asked to fulfil the function of a motions court judge reviewing the provisions of a statement of claim. However, I am prepared to accept that some aspects of the statement of claim could be said to raise a serious issue as to the validity of the legislation.

(2) Has the Plaintiff Demonstrated a Genuine Interest?

There can be no doubt that the applicant has satisfied this part of the test. The council enjoys the highest possible reputation and has demonstrated a real and continuing interest in the problems of the refugees and immigrants.

(3) Whether There Is Another Reasonable and Effective Way To Bring the Issue Before the Court

It is this third issue that gives rise to the real difficulty in this case. The challenged legislation is regulatory in nature and directly affects all refugee claimants in this country. Each one of them has standing to initiate a constitutional challenge to secure his or her own rights under the Charter. The applicant council recognizes the possibility that such actions could be brought but argues that the disadvantages which refugees face as a group preclude their effective use of access to the court. I cannot accept that submission. Since the institution of this action by the council, a great many refugee claimants have, pursuant to the provisions of the statute, appealed administrative decisions which affected them. The respondents have advised that nearly 33,000 claims for refugee status were submitted in the first 15 months following the enactment of the legislation. In 1990, some 3,000 individuals initiated claims every month. The Federal Court of Appeal has a wide experience in this field. MacGuigan JA, writing for the court, took judicial notice of the fact that refugee claimants were bringing forward claims akin to those brought by the council on a daily basis. I accept without hesitation this observation. It is clear therefore that many refugee claimants can and have appealed administrative decisions under the statute. These actions have frequently been before the courts. Each case presented a clear, concrete factual background upon which the decision of the court could be based.

The appellant also argued that the possibility of the imposition of a 72-hour removal order against refugee claimants undermines their ability to challenge the legislative scheme. I cannot accept that contention. It is clear that the Federal Court has jurisdiction to grant injunctive relief against a removal order: see *Toth v. Canada (Minister of Employment & Immigration)* (1988), 6 Imm. LR (2d) 123, (sub nom. *Toth v. Minister of Employment & Immigration*) 86 NR 302 (Fed. CA). Further, from the information sub-mitted by the respondents it is evident that persons submitting claims to refugee status in Canada are in no danger of early or speedy removal. As of March 31, 1990, it required an average of five months for a claim to be considered at the initial "credible basis" hearing. It is therefore clear that in the ordinary case there is more than adequate time for a claimant to prepare to litigate the possible rejection of the claim. However, even where the claims have not been accepted "the majority of removal orders affecting refugee claimants have not been carried out." (See *Report of the Auditor General of Canada to the House of Commons, Fiscal Year Ended 31 March 1990*, at pp. 352-353, para. 14.43.) Even though the Federal Court has been prepared in appropriate cases to exercise its jurisdiction to prevent removal of refugee claimants there is apparently very little need for it to do so. The means exist to ensure that the issues which are sought to be litigated on behalf of individual applicants may readily be brought before the court without any fear that a 72-hour removal order will deprive them of their rights.

From the material presented, it is clear that individual claimants for refugee status, who have every right to challenge the legislation, have in fact done so. There are, therefore, other reasonable methods of bringing the matter before the court. On this ground the applicant council must fail. I would hasten to add that this should not be interpreted as a mechanistic application of a technical requirement. Rather it must be remembered that the basic purpose for allowing public interest standing is to ensure that legislation is not immunized from challenge. Here there is no such immunization as plaintiff refugee claimants are challenging the legislation. Thus the very rationale for the public interest litigation party disappears. The council must, therefore, be denied stand-ing on each of the counts of the statement of claims. This is sufficient to dispose of the appeal. The respondents must also succeed on their cross-appeal to strike out what remained of the claim as the plaintiff council does not satisfy the test for standing on any part of the statement of claim. I would simply mention two other matters.

Intervenor Status

It has been seen that a public interest litigant is more likely to be granted standing in Canada than in other common law jurisdictions. Indeed, if the basis for granting status were significantly broadened, these public interest litigants would displace the private litigant. Yet the views of the public litigant who cannot obtain standing need not be lost. Public interest organizations are, as they should be, frequently granted intervenor status. The views and submissions of intervenors on issues of public importance frequently provide great assistance to the courts. Yet that assistance is given against a background of established facts and in a time-frame and context that is controlled by the courts. A proper balance between providing for the submissions of public interest groups and preserving judicial resources is maintained.

Disposition of the Result.

In the result I would dismiss the appeal and allow the cross-appeal on the basis that the plaintiff does not satisfy the test for public interest standing. Both the dismissal of the appeal and the allowance of the cross-appeal are to be without costs.

Appeal dismissed; cross-appeal allowed.

NOTES AND QUESTIONS

1. What is the relationship between "cause of action" and "standing"? Is "standing" simply about the ability to be heard or is it the "public" part to the "private" "cause of action"—that is, a recognition of entitlement so long as the underlying factual basis is established? In his book *Locus Standi* (Toronto: Carswell, 1986), at 208, T.A. Cromwell suggests that standing should essentially be confined to the ability to be heard: "[I]f the definition of standing includes such issues [relating to cause of action], it fails to isolate a set of legal issues concerned solely with access to adjudication that may be usefully analysed as a unit."

2. In contrast, consider the position of the Ontario Law Reform Commission in its *Report on the Law of Standing* (1989), at 87-91:

> Any new test to be proposed by the Commission must guide courts to make decisions that are consistent with the legitimate rationalia of standing rules. Moreover, the test must be animated by a recognition of what courts really do when they make standing decisions. The Commission believes that, in deciding questions of standing in any type of civil proceeding, courts essentially determine whether a particular claim or interest, advocated by a particular plaintiff, should be recognized as worthy of protection by, and therefore deserving of advancement in, the courts.
>
> In our view, it is critical for the law of standing to recognize a broadened array of interests. In order to do so, courts must necessarily become sensitive to the existence and implications of various values in our society—values that have dramatically altered from the time when the public nuisance rule first developed. Focusing on normative values will permit courts to utilize decision-making tools that further a serious

consideration of potentially novel kinds of interest and a sensitivity to the place of such interests in various contexts. Courts need to abandon tools to the extent that they promote the notion that standing decisions are made according to rigid rules, and in a sort of normative vacuum.

Reflecting on the circumstances and situations where standing issues have arisen or will likely arise suggests that there is no single factor, no one element, that should invariably lead to the grant or denial of standing in any particular case. Instead, as we shall see below, it is sensitivity to the existence of a variety of factors, and a sophisticated evaluation and balancing of them, that we believe should lie at the heart of the court's decision-making process.

This is not easy or uncontroversial. Deciding which interests to recognize and for what purposes is a complex and sensitive task, one in which courts are always actively engaged, whether explicitly recognized or not. By granting standing, a court indicates that it is prepared to place a certain value on an interest and to protect it by allowing it to be the subject of litigation, and that the individual or group seeking to litigate is not disputing something of, for example, merely idiosyncratic interest. One commentator has described the process in this way: "What we need to attend to is separating out interests sincerely held, but which nevertheless are too embryonic or too idiosyncratic, from those which represent a common interest of sufficient importance to merit the law's protection."

This process, in our view, links the notion of standing and the notion of cause of action at the theoretical, and certainly at the practical, level. Both concepts essentially involve asking the same questions. Accordingly, whether or not courts explicitly acknowledge the link—and whether they use the term "standing" or "cause of action"— the process of decision-making in respect of both "private" and "public" litigation does not, in fact, "keep the recognition of rights and standing as separate exercises." Courts do focus, in effect, on the normative values underlying any determination of standing (and therefore, cause of action) and do not in practice make decisions that reflect a rigid dichotomy between who should be permitted to proceed and what claims, whether traditional or otherwise, should be recognized. We believe this is the correct approach for all types of civil litigation—a rational and principled approach to the issue of entitlement to seek relief in the courts under the rubric of standing or cause of action. One commentator has put the matter in this way:

> Toward the end of his judgment in *Finlay* Le Dain J, in responding to an argument of the defendant that even if Finlay had standing the proceedings should nonetheless be struck out because the plaintiff still had no cause of action, made a brief but critical observation:
>
>> I question whether there is a true issue of reasonable cause of action distinguishable, as an alternative issue from that of standing. ... Clearly, if a plaintiff has the requisite standing an action will lie for a declaration that an administrative authority has acted without statutory authority.

This is important because it indicates that recognizing someone's standing and founding a cause of action are closely related processes, that there is no clear line of division between different kinds of interest and that the recognition of any interest is grounded in a common process—the law's pronouncement about which values it will enhance and protect.

The regime that we propose in this report is intended to, and will, deal fully and adequately with what courts and commentators have hitherto called either "cause of action" or "standing" (although, as indicated in the General Introduction, for convenience we use only the latter term throughout this report). In the end then, we believe that cause of action and standing are sufficiently intertwined and co-extensive, if not identical, to warrant their continued assimilation in practice by the courts.

The assimilation of these two concepts—which, as we have said, is a feature of existing practice in all civil proceedings—is reflected in the manner in which a plaintiff's entitlement to commence and maintain a proceeding is challenged. In Ontario, there is no discrete rule permitting a challenge on the basis of "standing." However, rule 21.01(1)(b) of the Rules of Civil Procedure provides for motions "to strike out a pleading on the ground that it discloses no reasonable cause of action. ... Notwithstanding this terminology, it is clear that where a defendant wishes to challenge the plaintiff's standing," he may wish to proceed under this rule.

It is, we believe, critically important to understand the essential nature of the defendant's attack on the plaintiff's right to commence and maintain an action, and to emphasize that no change in principle or practice is intended to be made by the proposals set forth in this report. Whether this view of the practical effect of our recommendations requires the amendment of any rule, or of any other provision, is a matter we leave to the appropriate authority.

Which view do you prefer? Why? In answering, is there a particular model of litigation you are drawing upon?

III. RES JUDICATA

A. Introduction

In general terms, the doctrine of *res judicata* prevents the relitigation of matters already decided. So, for example, it will prevent a losing plaintiff from suing the defendant again on the same cause of action. The operation of the doctrine is summarized in G. Spencer Bower and A.K. Turner, *The Doctrine of Res Judicata*, 2d ed. (London: Butterworths, 1969), at 9:

> The rule of estoppel by *res judicata* ... is a rule of evidence [and] may thus be stated:
>
> > [W]here a final judicial decision has been pronounced by ... [a] judicial tribunal of competent jurisdiction over the parties to, and the subject of, the litigation, any party or privy to such litigation, as against any other party or privy thereto ... is estopped in any subsequent litigation from disputing or questioning such decision on the merits, whether it be used as the foundation of an action, or relied upon as a bar to any claim, indictment or complaint, or to any affirmative defence, case or allegation.

Although united in the same doctrine, there are two quite distinct limbs to the general principle of *res judicata*.

1. Claim Preclusion or Cause of Action Estoppel

The first limb arises when a court has adjudicated a claim between two or more parties and a second action is brought between the same parties that is in some way related to the first. The decision in the first action may bind the parties. If the same cause of action is involved in both actions, the second action is precluded and must fail. (If the plaintiff wins the first action, his or her cause of action is said to *merge* in the judgment and it cannot be reasserted.) If the plaintiff was unsuccessful in the first action, the cause of action is said to be *barred* by the judgment for the defendant.) This is called merger and bar or, more commonly, "cause of action estoppel." The term used in the United States—"claim preclusion"—is the most descriptive: what the rule does is preclude a party from relitigating a claim.

2. Issue Preclusion or Issue Estoppel

The second limb of the doctrine arises when the second action does not involve the same cause of action or claim. In certain circumstances, the courts are prepared to treat any issues decided in the first case that also arise in the second case as settled and, therefore, not open to relitigation. This is known as issue estoppel or issue preclusion: the rule estops or precludes a party from relitigating an issue.

It is important to distinguish the operation of *res judicata* from the doctrine of *stare decisis*. A rule of law decided in an earlier case can determine or control the result in a later case but, under *stare decisis*, the parties to the second case are free to argue that the principle does not apply to their particular set of facts. Nonetheless, the courts give considerable weight to earlier precedents and past decisions therefore exert a gravitational pull on later decisions.

The difference between *stare decisis* and *res judicata*, and how the latter binds more strictly than the former, is dramatically illustrated by the *Re Waring* decisions. In *Re Waring (No. 1)*, [1942] Ch. 426, trustees under a will applied to the court for the determination of the question whether two annuities granted under the will were subject to taxation. The Court of Appeal interpreted the relevant statute as making the annuities taxable. Subsequently, in *Berkeley v. Berkeley*, [1946] AC 555, the House of Lords overruled the Court of Appeal's decision in *Re Waring (No. 1)* and its interpretation of the taxing statute. The trustees of the Waring estate then made another application, *Re Waring (No. 2)*, [1948] 1 Ch. 221, to determine the liability of the annuities to taxation. There were two annuities payable under the will; one of the annuitants was a party in *Re Waring (No. 1)*, and one was not. Surprisingly, it was held that the action by the annuitant who was a party to the first action was *res judicata*, but the action by the annuitant who was not a party to the original proceeding could take advantage of the *Berkeley* decision and take the annuity tax-free. The English courts have since granted relief against such a rigorous application of issue estoppel in "special circumstances." In *Arnold v. Westminster Bank plc*, [1991] 3 All ER 41 (HL), a continuing contractual obligation by way of long lease was held to be sufficient to permit the courts to reopen the issue already decided between the same parties where, since the original decision, the law had been judicially changed.

3. Hypothetical

In reading the following materials, consider this situation. An accident occurs between two cars at an intersection. The driver of one car, Allan, is charged with proceeding from a stop sign before it was safe to do so. He was acquitted. He then brought an action against the other driver, Nancy, in the Small Claims Court to recover $1,000 for damage to his car. What should be the effect, if any, of his earlier acquittal on the outcome of this action? Would it make any difference if he had been convicted? Assume that Allan succeeds in his action against Nancy. He now brings an action against Nancy to recover $50,000 in damages for personal injuries. Allan's daughter, Sarah, was also injured in the action and she joins her father's action as another plaintiff; her claim is also for $50,000. Also, Nancy counterclaims for $1,000 for property damage and $50,000 for personal injuries. Can Allan claim that Nancy is estopped from defending his action? And that she is estopped from proceeding with her counterclaim? Or can Nancy claim that Allan is estopped from proceeding with his claim? And can she claim a similar estoppel against Sarah's action? Or can Sarah plead that Nancy is estopped from defending Sarah's action?

B. Claim Preclusion/Cause of Action Estoppel

Las Vegas Strip Ltd. v. Toronto (City)
(1996) 30 OR (3d) 286 (Gen. Div.)

SHARPE J: ... Since December 1993, Las Vegas Strip Ltd. has operated a strip bar featuring live nude dancing at 361 Yonge Street, Toronto. Abdul Hilmy and Mohammad Zak Khan are principals of Las Vegas. The City of Toronto and Zanzibar Tavern Inc. (which operates a similar establishment next door) take the position that the Las Vegas operation is contrary to the City's Zoning By-law 438-86 which prohibits "adult entertainment parlours" in the downtown core. Initially, Las Vegas took the position that its operation constituted a legal non-conforming use. That claim was dismissed by a judgment of this court in June 1995 following the trial together of an action by Zanzibar against Las Vegas for an injunction and an action by Las Vegas against the City for a declaration.

Las Vegas now seeks to challenge the adult entertainment by-law on the grounds that it is vague or uncertain according to the principles of municipal law and that it violates s. 7 of the Canadian Charter of Rights and Freedoms on grounds of vagueness or overbreadth.

There are before me three related matters. First is an application by Las Vegas seeking a declaration against the City to the effect that the by-law is invalid. Zanzibar has been granted intervenor status in that application. Second, Annina Sohmer, an individual with certain associations with Mohammad Zak Khan, applies for identical declaratory relief with respect to the validity of the same by-law, asserting that she wishes to establish an adult entertainment operation at 645 Yonge Street, Toronto. Third, Las Vegas moves in the earlier Zanzibar action for an order setting aside the judgment and injunction in the event the by-law is found to be invalid. ...

In October 1993 Las Vegas sought permission from the appropriate municipal licensing authorities to commence operations as a live nude strip bar. It took the position that this use was a legal non-conforming use and filed certain affidavits regarding the prior use of the premises. In December 1993, the City granted zoning clearance on the basis of this material but that permission was withdrawn by the City in March 1994 at the insistence of Zanzibar which alleged that the premises had not previously been used as an adult entertainment parlour.

Two actions were then commenced. On April 15, 1994 Las Vegas commenced an action against the City claiming a declaration that the business constituted a legal non-conforming use. On July 12, 1994, Zanzibar commenced an action claiming a declaration that the Las Vegas operation did not constitute a legal non-conforming use and seeking injunctive relief. In its statement of defence to the Zanzibar action Las Vegas admitted that its adult entertainment parlour business was "not a permitted use of the subject premises" under the by-law but went on to assert "that the subject premises has been used continuously since 1979 as an adult entertainment parlour within the meaning of the City of Toronto by-law number 438-86 and as such, enjoys a legal non-conforming use status as an adult entertainment parlour." In its action against the City, Las Vegas took a similar position in its pleadings, admitting that it did operate an adult entertainment parlour, that such use was not currently permitted under the zoning by-law, but asserting that use enjoyed protection as a legal non-conforming use. I should perhaps note here that at the time, Las Vegas was represented by different counsel than appeared in the present proceedings.

These actions were tried together before Dennis Lane J who heard evidence over the course of several days. Dennis Lane J rendered judgment on June 1, 1995 rejecting the claim of Las Vegas that its use enjoyed protection as a legal non-conforming use and granting Zanzibar a permanent injunction prohibiting Las Vegas from operating an adult entertainment parlour at the location in question. In the course of his detailed reasons for judgment, Dennis Lane J found the evidence submitted by Khan on behalf of Las Vegas to be entirely unreliable:

> In my view this evidence shows that Mr. Khan set out upon a deliberate campaign of deception with the second batch of affidavits. The evidence of Ross [a solicitor for Las Vegas Strip] makes clear the central role of Mr. Khan in the preparation of these affidavits and Mr. Khan's explanations of their falsity are simply incredible. It is an irresistible inference that Mr. Khan knew what evidence would satisfy the City's Building Department and provided false affidavits that said what was necessary. The affiants who referred to such services either did not testify or confirmed that these services were not provided continuously. I am not prepared to accept any evidence of Mr. Khan as reliable.

Las Vegas's appeal to the Court of Appeal for Ontario was dismissed on April 23, 1996. On the appeal, Las Vegas attempted to raise the argument that the by-law was void for uncertainty.

The Court of Appeal refused to entertain this argument:

> At the commencement of these proceedings we directed the appellants that they were
> not permitted to argue that the definition of "adult entertainment parlour" in the zoning
> by-law is void for uncertainty. This argument was not raised in the pleadings, not raised
> at trial and not raised in the notice of appeal. *It is totally inconsistent with the*
> *appellants' position, set out in the pleadings and at trial, that the current operation*
> *contravenes the by-law but is a protected activity because it is a legal non-conforming*
> *use.* (Emphasis added.)

Las Vegas has filed an application for leave to appeal to the Supreme Court of
Canada which is still pending. It has continued its operations to the present time by
virtue of various orders staying the injunction pending final determination of the
appeals. ...

Are the Applicants Barred from Claiming Relief by the Doctrines of Res Judicata or Abuse of Process?

The City and Zanzibar submit that these applications are barred by the principles of res
judicata or abuse of process. They rely upon the general principle that a judgment between parties to litigation is conclusive upon issues actually brought before the court and
upon any issues which the parties, exercising reasonable diligence, should have brought
forward on that occasion. Reliance is placed on the often quoted passage from *Henderson
v. Henderson* (1843), 3 Hare 100 at p. 115, 67 ER 313 at p. 319, per Wigram VC:

> ... where a given matter becomes the subject of litigation in, and of adjudication by, a
> Court of competent jurisdiction the Court requires the parties to the litigation to bring
> forward their whole case, and will not (except under special circumstances) permit the
> same parties to open the same subject of litigation in respect of matter which might have
> been brought forward as part of the subject in contest, but which was not brought
> forward, only because they have, from negligence, inadvertence, or even accident,
> omitted part of their case. *The plea of res judicata applies, except in special cases, not*
> *only to points upon which the Court was actually required by the parties to form an*
> *opinion and pronounce a judgment, but to every point which properly belonged to the*
> *subject of litigation, and which the parties, exercising reasonable diligence, might have*
> *brought forward at the time.* (Emphasis added.)

As has been frequently mentioned in the cases, there is a dual purpose behind the res
judicata principle. First, it is in the public interest that there should be an end to litigation. Second, no individual should be subjected to proceedings more than once for the
same cause: see Spencer, Bower and Turner, *The Doctrine of Res Judicata*, 2d ed.
(1969), at p. 10.

It is clear that the related doctrine of issue estoppel has no bearing upon the case at
bar. The issue of whether the by-law is invalid was not put to Dennis Lane J and the
Court of Appeal refused to deal with that issue. The respondents submit, however, that
the broader principle of res judicata, as enunciated in the Henderson case, does apply.
They say that the points now raised by Las Vegas properly belonged to the subject of the

earlier litigation and that having failed to advance those points then, Las Vegas has lost the right to do so now. It is their position that the question of the entitlement of Las Vegas to operate a strip bar with reference to City of Toronto zoning was squarely before the court, both by virtue of the claim of Zanzibar and by virtue of Las Vegas's claim against the City.

Counsel for Las Vegas, on the other hand, takes the position that the present claim of Las Vegas is not barred as it constitutes a separate and distinct "cause of action." In his submission, the earlier proceedings dealt with the cause of action asserted by Las Vegas that its operation constituted a legal non-conforming use while the present application concerns the cause of action that the by-law itself is invalid. Having attempted to raise that issue before the Court of Appeal and having been refused, Las Vegas says it should be permitted to proceed now to have those questions determined.

It is apparent that analysis of the question must focus on the causes of action that were asserted in the prior proceedings. "Cause of action" does not appear to have been precisely defined in the authorities cited by the parties. Standard dictionary definitions, however, suggest that it refers to a set of facts giving rise to a legal claim or entitlement: see Yogis, *Canadian Law Dictionary*, 2d ed. (1990): "cause of action. A claim in law sufficient to demand judicial attention; the composite of facts necessary to give rise to the enforcement of a right"; Dukelow and Nuse, *The Dictionary of Canadian Law* (1990), "cause of action. 1. The factual circumstances which give rise to a right to sue"; Walker, *The Oxford Companion to Law* (1980), "cause of action. The fact or set of facts which gives a person a right of action"; *Black's Law Dictionary*, 6th ed. (1990), "cause of action. The fact or facts which give a person a right to judicial redress or relief against another."

In the prior proceedings tried by Dennis Lane J, there were two separate actions tried together and two causes of action asserted. In the Zanzibar action, Las Vegas was the defendant. To identify what was decided and what issues that judgment now precludes, it is necessary to have reference to the claim Zanzibar asserted and the defences Las Vegas did or could have advanced to that claim. The cause of action asserted was that of Zanzibar claiming that Las Vegas was not entitled to operate a strip bar on account of the City's adult entertainment by-law. Zanzibar's action for a declaration and an injunction put directly in issue the right of Las Vegas to carry on its operation in the face of By-law 438-86. In the statement of claim, Zanzibar specifically alleged that "Las Vegas is an illegal business operation which contravenes the provisions of the City of Toronto's By-Law No. 438-86 as amended" and claimed declaratory as well as injunctive relief restraining the defendants "from using or causing to be used the premises municipally known as 361 Yonge Street, in the City of Toronto, for purposes of an adult entertainment parlour as defined in the City of Toronto's Zoning By-Law No. 438-86, as amended." While the focus of the detailed facts pleaded in the statement of claim concerned the prior use of the premises, Zanzibar put squarely in issue the legal right of Las Vegas to carry on its operation. There can be no doubt but that Las Vegas could have raised as a defence to the Zanzibar action the argument it now seeks to assert, that the By-law is invalid, had it chosen to do so. A defence based on the invalidity of the By-Law would have been inconsistent with the defence of legal non-conforming use that Las Vegas did assert. It is clear, however, that the invalidity defence could have been pleaded in the alternative.

In my view, the failure of Las Vegas to come forward in the prior action with the invalidity defence is fatal to its attempt now to advance that claim with a view to reversing the result in the Zanzibar action. In *Glatt v. Glatt*, [1937] SCR 347 at p. 350, [1937] 1 DLR 794, the Supreme Court of Canada affirmed a judgment of the Ontario Court of Appeal in which Middleton JA had stated as follows:

> It is I think clear beyond possibility of a doubt that a defendant who is sued must in the action in which he is sued put forward all defences which he has to the plaintiff's claim. He cannot allow the action to go to trial upon a certain defence which he sets up and when that defence fails set up another and inconsistent defence by bringing an action to set aside the judgment. If in the original action he applies for some relief, his application will be scrutinized with the greatest of care, but there would be no end to litigation if proceedings such as these received the sanction of the court.

Las Vegas had the opportunity to present its case in the earlier action and chose to do so on a certain footing. For whatever reason, it chose not to advance the invalidity defence. To permit the present application by Las Vegas would run directly counter to the principle enunciated by Middleton JA. It would also run counter to the underlying policy that it is in the public interest that there be finality to litigation and that individual parties such as Zanzibar be protected against the burden of repeat litigation. The situation is plainly distinguishable from a case relied on by Las Vegas, *Greymac Properties Inc. v. Feldman* (1990), 1 OR (3d) 686, 46 CPC (2d) 125 (Gen. Div.), where it was held that the plaintiff was not barred from proceeding with a claim that might have been advanced as a set-off in an earlier action. As Dennis Lane J explained in that case (at p. 692):

> There is a large and important difference between, on the one hand, a defence which is intimately related to the issues in the earlier litigation and, on the other hand, a separate litigation against a party to the earlier litigation, a claim which stands on its own separate set of facts and could have been brought at any time without reference to the issues in the earlier action.

While this is sufficient to dispose of the matter as both Las Vegas and the City were parties to the Zanzibar action, I will also consider the impact of the Las Vegas action upon the present proceedings. In the action brought by Las Vegas against the City, the cause of action asserted was that Las Vegas was entitled to operate a strip bar despite the City's adult entertainment by-law on account of the prior use of the premises. Does the failure of Las Vegas to advance the invalidity defence in that action bar it from doing so now? Can Las Vegas escape the earlier finding by asserting a different legal argument which does not depend upon the same factual elements as the non-conforming use position taken in the earlier action?

In my view, the present application cannot be said to be based upon a different set of facts for the purposes of res judicata. Las Vegas has, in effect, subtracted certain facts from the earlier claim, those concerning the prior use of the premises, but the issue remains whether its operation is illegal under the by-law. In *Grandview (Town) v. Doering*, [1976] 2 SCR 621, 61 DLR (3d) 455, the Supreme Court of Canada held that a party cannot claim to assert a new and distinct cause of action by manipulation of the factual elements if what remains is essentially the same claim. In that case, the plaintiff sought to add certain facts giving rise to a new basis for its contention that acts of the defendant had caused flooding of his lands. In the earlier action, brought with respect to an earlier period of time, the plaintiff asserted that a dam erected by the defendant caused water to overflow the banks of a river and flood the plaintiff's land. In the subsequent action, with reference to a different time period, the plaintiff alleged that the impounding of the water caused flooding by an aquifer, a factual theory of causation not previously advanced. The Supreme Court of Canada held the subsequent claim to be barred. Speaking for the majority, Ritchie J stated (at p. 635 SCR, p. 459 DLR):

> Nothing had changed between the bringing of the first action and the second one except that the respondent had received advice from a soil expert who expounded the aquifer theory. Such an expert could probably have been consulted before the first action, and if he had been then the matter would no doubt have been put in issue at that time.

The situation can surely not be improved from the plaintiffs' perspective where it is sought to subtract rather than add facts. All of the facts upon which Las Vegas's present contention rests were available in its earlier action and precisely the same relief is sought, namely, a declaration that the by-law does not in law prevent Las Vegas from carrying on its operation. In my view, this means that for the purposes of the doctrine of res judicata, as defined by the dictum of Wigram VC in Henderson, supra, Las Vegas cannot claim to be advancing a separate and distinct cause of action.

Does the fact that Las Vegas now relies upon a different legal theory remove the present claim from the reach of the old? In my view it does not. The authorities establish that a litigant cannot establish a new and fresh cause of action by advancing a new legal theory in support of a claim based upon essentially the same facts. As was stated by the Privy Council in *Hoystead v. Taxation Commissioner*, [1926] AC 155 at pp. 165-66, [1925] All ER Rep. 56 (a passage quoted with approval by the Supreme Court of Canada in *Maynard v. Maynard*, [1951] SCR 346 at p. 354, [1951] 1 DLR 241 at p. 254, per Cartwright J):

> Parties are not permitted to begin fresh litigations because of new views they may entertain of the law of the case, or new versions which they present as to what should be proper apprehension by the Court of the legal result either of the construction of the documents or the weight of certain circumstances.
>
> If this were permitted, litigation would have no end, except when legal ingenuity is exhausted. It is a principle of law that this cannot be permitted, and there is abundant authority reiterating that principle.

I conclude, therefore, that the contentions now advanced by Las Vegas do not constitute a separate and distinct cause of action. There are no new facts, merely new legal arguments, and these could readily have been advanced in the earlier proceeding. To permit Las Vegas to advance them now would run directly counter to the legal rules enunciated in the *Henderson, Grandview (Town)* and *Hoystead* cases. It would also, in my view, violate the policies previously mentioned as underlying those rules, namely, the public interest in finality to litigation and the private interest in being protected from repeat litigation.

Moreover, I see no unfairness to Las Vegas in the circumstances. It has been well represented by experienced counsel throughout, and it made certain decisions about how best to present its case. The many cases cited by Las Vegas on the vagueness argument demonstrate that the contention that this very by-law suffers that infirmity is anything but novel. Having had the full opportunity of presenting every available argument in the earlier proceeding, Las Vegas must, in my view, live with its decision to restrict itself to the non-conforming use claim.

Accordingly, whether one views the matter from the perspective of the defences Las Vegas could have asserted to the Zanzibar claim or from the perspective of the arguments it could have advanced in its action against the City, the Las Vegas application is barred by res judicata.

Abdul Hilmy and Mohammad Zak Khan are applicants in this proceeding but were not named in the prior proceedings. It is clear, however, that their claims are also barred as they are in privity of interest with Las Vegas. In a leading text on the subject, Spencer, Bower and Turner, *The Doctrine of Res Judicata*, *supra*, the authors state (at p. 210):

> And it has been suggested that the doctrine may be extended so as to include the case where a party against whom a previous decision has been pronounced may employ a servant or agent or engage third party to do something which infringes the right established in the earlier litigation, thus raising the whole matter again in his interest; it would be unjust to allow the successful party to be so vexed by relitigating the original question by means of the device of putting forward a third party.

… It is apparent from the material presented that Messrs. Hilmy and Khan are principals behind Las Vegas. Indeed, they are themselves bound by the terms of the injunction granted by Dennis Lane J which applied to Las Vegas's "officers, directors, servants, employees, agents, contractors, shareholders and assigns." With respect to the claims at issue here, they are in privity with Las Vegas for the purposes of the doctrine of res judicata.

Is the claim of Annina Sohmer to declaratory relief also barred by the doctrine of res judicata? In my view the evidence before me indicates beyond any serious question that Mohammad Zak Khan is in fact the moving force behind the Sohmer application and that it has been brought with a view to avoid the effect of res judicata on the Las Vegas application.

The following facts, established from the affidavit and cross-examination of Annina Sohmer, have led me to this conclusion. Ms Sohmer has been an acquaintance or friend of Mr. Khan for seven years. Sohmer resides in Lindsay with her husband and stated that she does not like Toronto. She has no prior involvement with or experience in the Adult Entertainment Parlour business and appears to have little if any connection with Toronto. On the application for an adult entertainment parlour licence, she gave an address on Gerrard Street as her place of residence. This is an apartment rented by Khan. At first Sohmer said she subleased the apartment but then she stated "I don't sublease it. I stay there when I am in the city" which, she admitted, was not often. The premises at 645 Yonge Street where she alleges she wishes to establish an adult entertainment parlour are owned by Mr. Khan. Sohmer has never occupied or carried on any business at this location. In support of her application she produced a lease which she signed on April 16, 1996 listing her and "Erotica Entertainments" as the lessee. Sohmer states that very shortly after signing the lease, she sublet these premises to Hade Hamade who was introduced to her by Mr. Khan. The business carried on by Hamade is not that of "Restaurant and/or Tavern, including reasonably associated activities (such as Adult Entertainment, Catering etc.)" as Sohmer's lease with Khan purports to require. Sohmer was able to produce no records or receipts for any of the transactions concerning the premises at 645 Yonge Street other than receipts from Khan. She stated that all payments had been made in cash and that when Hamade pays her, she hands the money over to Khan. Most of the transactions she says took place in her car. She was unable to identify the architect she claims to have retained and instructed to develop plans for the adult entertainment parlour attached to the application to the City Building and Inspections Department, nor could she remember the precise amount she had paid for those services. She is represented by the same solicitors and her application simply adopts the arguments advanced in the Las Vegas application.

In my view, these facts lead to the inevitable conclusion that the application of Annina Sohmer is a claim advanced by or on behalf of Mohammad Zak Khan. In *Gleeson v. J. Wippell & Co.*, [1977] 3 All ER 54 at p. 60, [1977] 1 WLR 510, Megarry VC defined privity as "a sufficient degree of identification between the two to make it just to hold that the decision to which one was a party should be binding in proceedings to which the other is party." In my view, on the facts before me there is a sufficient degree of identification to hold that Annina Sohmer is in privity of interest with Khan and Las Vegas.

If I am wrong with respect to the privity point, it is my view that the Sohmer application may also be dismissed as an abuse of process. This doctrine has been applied to respond to certain technical limitations of res judicata: see *Nigro v. Agnew-Surpass Shoe Stores Ltd.* (1977), 18 OR (2d) 215 at p. 218, 82 DLR (3d) 302 at p. 305 (HCJ), affirmed (1977), 18 OR (2d) 714n, 84 DLR (3d) 256n (CA); *Hunter v. Chief Constable of West Midlands*, [1981] 3 All ER 727 at p. 729 (HL); see also *Solomon v. Smith* (1987), 45 DLR (4th) 266 (Man. CA) at p. 275, per Lyon JA:

> By encouraging the determination of each case on its own facts against the general principle of the plea of abuse, serious prejudice to either party as well as to the proper administration of justice can best be avoided. Maintaining open and ready access to the courts by all legitimate suitors is fundamental to our system of justice. However, to achieve this worthy purpose, we must be vigilant to ensure that the system does not become unnecessarily clogged with repetitious litigation of the kind here attempted.

... For the foregoing reasons, the applications are dismissed.

NOTES AND QUESTIONS

1. How does the court in *Las Vegas* define "cause of action"? Why must it include issues that were never raised? Is the decision in *Las Vegas* a fair one? If so, in what sense is it fair? What policies justify the decision?

Las Vegas is fairly representative of the modern day approach of courts to attempts to relitigate matters that could have been, but were not, raised in earlier proceedings— that is, typically, the second action will be held to be barred. But the outcome of such cases is not always predictable as the following (quite rare) examples illustrate: *Gallant v. Bembridge* (1993), 140 NBR (2d) 119 (QB) (where a plaintiff's first action for defamation had been dismissed for failure to comply with notice provisions, the court refused to dismiss a second action against the same defendants for tortious conspiracy for conspiring to injure him by disseminating certain information; the second action was not grounded on defamation nor on conspiracy to commit libel and, therefore, a *res judicata* argument was without merit); *Batchelor v. Morden* (1985), 50 CPC 39 (Ont. Dist. Ct.) (the court refused to dismiss an action by a tenant against a landlord claiming a rent rebate and damages for invasion of privacy where the tenant had brought an earlier action for breach of a covenant of quiet enjoyment in which the claims might have been included; although the claims could have been set up in the first action, they had no relevancy to the first action and the tenant was not precluded from now advancing them); and *Decorby v. Decorby* (1985), 34 Man. R (2d) 124 (QB), affirmed 37 Man. R (2d) 271 (CA) (a son who had previously unsuccessfully challenged the interpretation of his father's will was not barred from bringing a subsequent action claiming entitlement to all his father's land pursuant to an agreement, or alternatively claiming unjust enrichment or quantum meruit).

2. *Defining "cause of action" or "claim."* The different approaches to defining "cause of action" or "claim" are canvassed in American Law Institute, *Restatement of the Law (Second), Judgments* (1982), 196-97:

"Claim" in the context of res judicata, has never been broader than the transaction to which it related. But in the days when civil procedure still bore the imprint of the forms of action and the division between law and equity, the courts were prone to associate claim with a single theory of recovery, so that, with respect to one transaction, a plaintiff might have as many claims as there were theories of the substantive law upon which he could seek relief against the defendant. Thus, defeated in an action based on one theory, the plaintiff might be able to maintain another action based on a different theory, even though both actions were grounded upon the defendant's identical act or connected acts forming a single life-situation. In those earlier days there was also some adherence to a view that associated claim with the assertion of a single primary right as accorded by the substantive law, so that, if it appeared that the defendant had invaded a number of primary rights conceived to be held by the plaintiff, the plaintiff had the same number of claims, even though they all sprang from a unitary occurrence. There was difficulty in knowing which rights were primary and what was their extent, but a primary right and the corresponding claim might turn out to be narrow. Thus it was held by some courts that a judgment for or against the plaintiff in an action for personal injuries did not preclude an action by him for property damage occasioned by the same negligent conduct on the part of the defendant—this deriving from the idea that the right to be free of bodily injury was distinct from the property right. Still another view of [cause of action] looked to sameness of evidence; a second action was precluded where the evidence to support it was the same as that needed to support the first. Sometimes this was made the sole test of identity of claim; sometimes it figured as a second action might be precluded although the evidence material to it varied from that in the first action. Even so, claim was not coterminous with the transaction itself.

The present trend is to see claim in factual terms and to make it coterminous with the transaction regardless of the number of substantive theories, or variant forms of relief flowing from those theories, that may be available to the plaintiff; regardless of the number of primary rights that may have been invaded; and regardless of the variations in the evidence needed to support the theories or rights. The transaction is the basis of the litigative unit or entity which may not be split.

In Canadian law, this trend is illustrated by contrasting *Brunsden v. Humphrey* (1884), 14 QBD 141 and *Cahoon v. Franks*, [1967] SCR 455. In *Brunsden v. Humphrey*, on facts similar to those referred to above, the Court of Appeal concluded that the second action was not barred by the first, holding that different rights were infringed in the two actions: that a tort causing both injury to the person and injury to the property gave rise to two distinct causes of action. In *Cahoon v. Franks*, the plaintiff commenced an action for property damage suffered in an automobile accident. After the expiry of the relevant limitation period, the plaintiff sought leave to amend to add a claim for $150,000 for personal injuries. The defendant opposed leave on the ground that the plaintiff was attempting to add a new cause of action (citing *Brunsden*) after the expiry of the limitation period (discussed in chapter 6, "Pleadings and Disposition Without Trial"). The Supreme Court of Canada held that the tort of negligence involves a breach by the defendant of the duty owed to the plaintiff resulting in damage to the plaintiff, and that there is only one cause of action notwithstanding that plaintiff suffers both personal injury and property damage. In so holding the court concluded that *Brunsden* is not good law in Canada and ought not to be followed. (Since on this reasoning the amendment did not set up a new cause of action, the court held *Weldon v. Neal* to be irrelevant and granted leave to amend.)

3. *Splitting the cause of action in negligence.* In *Cox v. Robert Simpson Co. Ltd.* (1973), 1 OR (2d) 333, plaintiff sued in Small Claims Court for damage to his automobile. The defendant paid the amount claimed into court and the plaintiff took the money out in satisfaction of his claim. Subsequently, the plaintiff commenced a County Court action in respect of the same accident claiming damages for personal injury. The defendant moved for an order dismissing the action by reason of what had occurred in the Small Claims Court proceedings. Section 84 of the Small Claims Court Act, RSO 1980, c. 476 provided that "the sum so paid shall be paid to the plaintiff, and he shall be deemed to have accepted it in full satisfaction of his claim, and all proceedings in the action shall be stayed." The Ontario Court of Appeal, following *Cahoon*, held that the negligence of the defendant gave the plaintiff but one cause of action, which could not be split, and the plaintiff's second action was barred. (The court indicated that this may be a harsh result as far as the plaintiff is concerned, particularly having regard to the fact that he conducted the first action himself.)

Should it make any difference if A had collision insurance on his automobile and the insurance company had paid A the amount of the damages to the vehicle, whereupon, in accordance with a provision in his insurance policy, A assigned to the insurer his claim for such damage, and subsequently the insurer instituted the first action in A's name and A subsequently institutes his own action for his personal injuries? Some courts in the United States have created an exception to the rule against splitting a cause of action that permits a separate suit for property damage to be brought by the insurer without jeopardizing the insured's own claim for personal injuries. See the cases referred to in *Weekes v. Atlantic National Insurance Company*, 370 F2d 264 (9th Cir. 1966).

In *Vaughan v. Scott* (1980), 15 CPC 219 (Ont. CC) in June 1976, the plaintiff suffered both property damage and personal injuries in a motor vehicle accident with the defendant. The plaintiff's insurer paid the property damage claim and, in November 1976, commenced an action in the plaintiff's name pursuant to its subrogation rights. Default judgment was obtained against the defendant and damages were assessed in June 1977. In May 1978, the plaintiff personally commenced an action for personal injuries and the defendant applied to dismiss the action as being an abuse of process— that is, *res judicata*—and the application was dismissed. *Cox v. Robert Simpson* was distinguished as a case turning on the interpretation of s. 8 of the Small Claims Court Act. While plaintiffs may not split their cause of action, the reality here was that it was the insurance contract and the Insurance Act (not the plaintiff) that split the cause of action. The insurer is given the subrogation right when it has paid the property claim, whereas the plaintiff personally retains the right to sue for personal injuries. For a similar result see *Malcolm v. Carr* (1996), 40 Alta LR (3d) 29 (QB).

4. *What are the policy goals of res judicata?* How important is ending disputes to the traditional model of adjudication and corrective justice discussed by Chayes and Weinrib in chapter 4, "Challenges to the Traditional Model"? Whatever the policy goals of *res judicata*, can they be reconciled with the policy of deciding cases on the merits?

5. *How should the question of attempts to relitigate claims be approached?* It will be clear that it is often not easy to determine what is a cause of action. Louisell and Hazard have suggested that it would facilitate "analysis of the problem of bar and merger to eliminate 'cause of action' as an intermediate terminological repository and to put the [real issue] directly: Is there any satisfactory explanation why this claim was not presented in the prior action?" Their basic position is that "a plaintiff should be com-pelled to join all those claims arising from the same out-of-court transaction that he could have joined" on penalty of being barred from bringing any subsequent action for such claims: Louisell and Hazard, *Cases and Material on Pleading and Procedure*, 2d ed. (Mineola, NY: Foundation Press, 1968), at 590. Do you agree with them? Are their views consistent with the decision in *Las Vegas*?

Edward Cleary, in "*Res Judicata* Re-examined" (1948), 57 *Yale Law Journal* 339, takes a very different view. First, he would like to see the bar and merger doctrine given a quite narrow scope. He argues that broad tests, like that proposed by Louisell and Hazard, requiring extensive joinder of claims "usually effect no saving except paper and filing fees and [result] as a practical matter in breaking the case back down into some sort of units for the purposes of trial." Second, he believes that the present penalty for "splitting" a cause of action—dismissal of the latter action—is too severe. Instead, he would impose, in the US context, the sanction of requiring the plaintiff to pay the defendant's costs, including attorney's fees, of litigating the second action. Do you agree? Adapting his suggestions to the Canadian context, would a preferable solution in *Las Vegas* have been to allow the plaintiff to proceed but on condition that it pay the defendant's costs, on a solicitor-and-his-client scale, in any event? (It should be noted that Cleary would retain the present rules relating to issue estoppel to prevent relitigation of matters actually decided in the first action.)

In respect of Cleary's second proposal, Louisell and Hazard, above, at 591 ask, Does the proposed sanction "take adequate account of the human and social costs of litigation?

What about compensation for defendant's mental anguish? Doesn't final disposition of the controversy, even on terms less than fully just have a value in and of itself?"

In *"Res Judicata* Redux" (1986), 24 *Osgoode Hall Law Journal* 713, at 735, Tim Pinos suggests a similar policy-based solution:

> The first temptation is to try to supplant the concept of a *cause of action* with another concept that directs the court's attention more broadly. In other contexts, and other jurisdictions, the concepts *matter*, or *transaction* have been construed fairly broadly, and may provide possible candidates for a *test*. An alternate approach would be to say that when litigation arises between two parties, both are under an obligation to raise all claims, counterclaims, and defences arising out of or connected to the original subject-matter of the lawsuit, and whether raised or not, they may not be raised in a subsequent proceeding.
>
> Regardless of the choice, it is suggested that the following criteria are relevant to the scope of the judge's power under either formulation of the rule:
>
> 1. Would a reasonably diligent party, acting with reasonably diligent legal advice, have been aware of the opportunity to advance the claim or defence?
> 2. Was the claim or defence connected in any way with the subject-matter of the earlier litigation?
> 3. Was the claim or defence available at the time of the earlier proceeding, in the sense of having accrued?
> 4. Did the court in the prior proceeding have jurisdiction over the claim or defence asserted in the subsequent proceeding?
>
> If the answer to these questions is yes, then *prima facie*, the attempt to litigate the claim or defence in a subsequent proceeding should fail.

6. *What types of former adjudications attract claim preclusion?* The application of claim preclusion is pervasive and it applies not only to judgments rendered by domestic courts after a contested hearing, but extends also to *default judgments* (see, for example, *Miscouche Sales & Service Ltd. v. Massey Ferguson Industries Ltd.* (1992), 12 CPC (3d) 63 (PEI TD) (where a first action resulted in a default judgment, a subsequent action relating to the same transaction was dismissed on the grounds of *res judicata*; the claim now sought to be asserted by the plaintiff should have been raised in the earlier action instead of permitting default judgment to be taken)); to *consent judgments* (see, for example, *Patterson v. Antonucci*, [1988] WDFL 1744 (Ont. CA) (in a family law case a woman was not permitted to claim damages for assault when she could have made such a claim in earlier proceedings between the parties that had been settled)); to *decisions rendered by an administrative or arbitration tribunal* of competent jurisdiction (see, for example, *Balanyk v. Greater Niagara General Hospital* (April 3, 1996) (Ont. Gen. Div.) (where the majority of claims in an action arose out of issues previously determined by the Labour Relations Board, and the court held the action was barred by the principle of res judicata) and *Venneri v. Bascom* (1996), 28 OR (3d) 281 (Gen. Div.) (the court held that an attempt by the plaintiff to relitigate an issue that had already been conclusively decided by a board of arbitration was an abuse of process)); and to *foreign judgments* entitled to recognition under conflicts of laws principles (see, for example, *Pervez*

(Litigation Guardian of) v. Carpenter Technology (Canada) Ltd. (February 10, 1992), (Ont. Gen. Div.), affirmed (December 15, 1995) (Ont. CA) (where, in an Ontario action that was virtually identical to one in the United States that had been dismissed, the court held that the matter was *res judicata* and to allow it to continue against the defendants would be an abuse of process).

7. *Application of claim preclusion to counterclaims.* Claim preclusion clearly applies to a defendant in requring him or her to put forward any and all defences to the plaintiffs claim in the first action (see, for example, *Four Embarcadero Centre Venture v. Kalen* (1988), 65 OR (2d) 551 (HC) (a default judgment results in the merits becoming *res judicata*; a foreign money judgment which is final and enforceable settles the issues between the parties just as an Ontario judgment would do; when sued on the foreign judgment the defendant may not attack it on the ground that the foreign court never considered the merits of the claim). But what if the claim the defendant now seeks to assert could have been asserted by the defendant as a counterclaim in an earlier action by the plaintiff? In the United States, the Federal Rules of Civil Procedure, rule 13(a) specifically makes "compulsory" any counterclaim that the defendant may have *that arises out of the same transaction or occurrence* on which the plaintiff sues. Canadian authority on the issue is sparse, but compare *Ranch des Prairies Ltée (Prairie Ranch Ltd.) v. Bank of Montreal* (1988), 69 CBR (NS) 180 (Man. CA) (shareholders of a bankrupt company were precluded from suing a bank, the company's receiver/manager, and their solicitors for damages because the shareholder's claims should have been raised in earlier proceedings—that is, when the receiver was appointed by the court, when the sale of the company's assets was approved by the court, or when default judgment was signed against the shareholders) with *Roque v. Brown* (1977), 2 CPC 243 (Ont. HC) (the present plaintiff, P, had been unsuccessfully sued by the defendant, D, in earlier proceedings for malicious prosecution where there was a finding that D had assaulted P, who then commenced this action; commencement of action that might have been raised as a counterclaim in prior proceedings between the same parties may amount in certain circumstances to an abuse of process, but in normal circumstances (as here) there is a right to wait and bring a separate and subsequent action, although the plaintiff may in consequence be deprived of costs in the second action).

8. *Requirements for the application of res judicata (both claim and issue preclusion).* There are several requirements for the application of both limbs of *res judicata.*

(a) *Generally, the two actions must involve the same parties or their privies*
As a matter of due process or fundamental justice a person's legal rights should not be determined without an opportunity to litigate them. This principle is so important that any exceptions to it are carefully and narrowly defined in the law of *res judicata*. There are only two exceptions to the general rule in which a judgment may have preclusive effects with respect to a nonparty. One exception is that for privies—a person may be bound by the decision in former litigation to which he or she was not a party because he or she was "in privity" with a person who was a party to the earlier litigation. We saw this illustrated in *Las Vegas* re the claims of the owners of the company and the claim made by Annina Sohmer, and Sharpe J gave a (very broad) defintion of privity. The other is non-mutual issue estoppel, discussed below under the heading, "Issue Estoppel."

(The debate concerning the abandonment of the requirement of "same parties" (mutuality) in the context of issue estoppel has no application to claim preclusion; the only exception to the "same parties" requirement re claim preclusion is privity.)

(b) *Claim now sought to be asserted must have been within the prior court's jurisdiction*
The reason for this requirement is straightforward and obvious; for the defence of *res judicata* to succeed, a plaintiff must have had the opportunity to recover in the first action and but for his own fault might have recovered then what he seeks to recover in the second: *Horsman Bros. Holdings Ltd. v. Dolphin Electrical Contractors Ltd.* (1987), 10 BCLR (2d) 213 (CA).

(c) *Prior adjudication must have been on the merits*
What this requirement does is to deny preclusive effect to adjudications that result in the first action being dismissed for procedural reasons not going to the merits of the claim asserted—for example, dismissal for want of prosecution or for lack of jurisdiction: Ontario rule 24.05; *Sharma v. Ouellette* (1991), 2 CPC (3d) 289 (Ont. Gen. Div.) (for *res judicata* to apply, the judgment in the first action must have been on its merits and where the previous action against an insurer was dismissed solely on the basis of a finding that the plaintiff did not commence the action within the limitation period that action was therefore not determined on its merits; the limitation period did not apply to the claim made in the second action for declaratory relief). The rationale is that if the prior court did not get to the merits of the plaintiff's claim, but dismissed the proceeding on some preliminary or procedural point, it would be too harsh to foreclose the plaintiff; an adjudication on the merits of the plaintiff's claim is a prerequisite to this. However, note that there are limits to this reasoning and to the principle. Where it is held that the claim now sought to be asserted is barred because, though it was not asserted in the prior proceeding it should have been (as in *Las Vegas*), the claim will be barred even though there was no adjudication on the merits of that claim. Also for the purposes of this principle a default judgment is an adjudication of the merits; in rendering a default judgment a court intends to finally adjudicate on the merits of the plaintiff's claim, albeit without considering the merits.

(d) *The prior decision must have been a final judgment*
As to this requirement—that of finality of the prior decision—F. James and G.C. Hazard, *Civil Procedure*, 3d ed. (Boston: Little, Brown, 1985), 591 state:

> Both branches of the rules of res judicata, that is claim preclusion and issue preclusion, depend on there having been a final determination of the claim or issue with respect to which rules are applied. The reason is virtually definitional: The rules preclude relitigation of a matter previously determined, and a matter has not been "determined" until a judgment has been rendered concerning it. It follows that the rules of res judicata do not come into operation before a final judgment.

For examples of the principle that the prior decision must have been a final judgment, see *Westcoast Energy Inc. v. Husky Oil Operations Ltd.* (March 13, 1995), Doc. Calgary Appeal 13415 (Alta. CA) (the court held that because of the broad powers granted to the provincial Public Utilities Board by its enabling legislation, there was no finality to its earlier decision refusing to make an award of interest that would invoke the doctrine of *res judicata*); and *Barwell Food Sales Inc. v. Snyder & Fils Inc.* (1988), 38 CPC (2d) 192 (Ont. HC) (where the plaintiff commenced separate actions in Quebec and Ontario for the same relief, the failure to obtain an interlocutory injunction in Quebec did not render the interlocutory injunction motion in Ontario *res judicata*; the refusal to grant injunctive relief did not constitute a final order and hence *res judicata* was not applicable).

James and Hazard point out that a troubling point is whether preclusive effect should be given to a judgment that is under appeal and that the US decisions are divided on the issue, reflecting the dilemma posed. On the one hand, it makes little sense to give preclusive effect to a determination that may be reversed on appeal; on the other hand, it may be a waste of effort to retry an issue just because an appeal is pending in the earlier case (and hence there is no "final judgment"). Note that in *Las Vegas* in the earlier litigation an application for leave to appeal to the Supreme Court of Canada was still pending.

9. *Exceptions to the application of res judicata (both claim and issue preclusion).* The law recognizes certain exceptional circumstances where some overriding question of fairness requires a re-hearing of a matter which is otherwise *res judicata*. The two most important exceptions are (1) fraud or other misconduct in the earlier proceedings, or (2) the discovery of fresh evidence that "entirely changes the aspect of the case," that could not, by the exercise of reasonable diligence, have been adduced in the earlier proceeding. Both exceptions are discussed by Lord Denning in *McIlkenney*, below; both are narrowly construed and rarely (if ever) applied.

10. *Review exercise.* Consider the hypothetical case, above, that precedes the *Las Vegas* case. How many of the questions posed can you now answer? What are the answers?

C. Issue Preclusion/Issue Estoppel

The legal doctrine of issue estoppel is in a state of considerable flux in Canadian law. Pulled between the traditional rigidity of English law and the modern flexibility of US law, Canadian courts are cautiously addressing the topic and seeking to fashion an appropriate solution. After an introduction to the area by Garry Watson of Osgoode Hall Law School, we rely on three cases to capture the direction and tension of the law in English, US, and Canadian jurisdictions.

1. The Basic Requirements of Issue Estoppel and an Introduction to Non-Mutuality

Garry D. Watson, "Duplicative Litigation: Issue Estoppel, Abuse of Process, and the Death of Mutuality"
(1990), 69 *Canadian Bar Review* 623 (footnotes omitted)

1. *Issue Estopel Defined*

Res Judicata is a form of estoppel and operates through the application of two doctrines or species: cause of action estoppel (called by the Americans "claim preclusion") and issue estoppel (called by the Americans "collateral estoppel" or "issue preclusion"). Cause of action estoppel simply means that where the legal claims and liabilities of two parties have been determined in a prior action, the *claims* may not be relitigated. If the cause of action was determined to exist, it is said to be *merged* in the judgment. If it was determined not to exist any subsequent action is *barred*.

Issue estoppel is an extension of the same rule of public policy, but it focuses not on claims or causes of actions, but on *issues*. It precludes relitigation of issues that a court has decided in a prior suit. If the cause of action involved in a subsequent proceeding is a separate and distinct one, cause of action estoppel will not apply. However, within a given cause of action there may be several issues that have to be adjudicated. If an issue has been determined in prior litigation, issue estoppel—even if the new litigation involves a different cause of action—will prevent relitigation of the issue already decided.

For issue estoppel to apply, certain requirements must be met. Three of the four requirements for the application of issue estoppel are uncontroversial and generally accepted in all jurisdictions: (1) the same issue must be involved in the initial and subsequent litigation; (2) the issue must have been actually litigated and determined in the first suit and its determination must have been necessary to the result in the litigation; and (3) the decision on the issue in question must have been final.

In the classic statements of issue estoppel in Anglo-Canadian law (see *Carl Reiss Stifting v. Rayner & Keeler Ltd. (No. 2)*, [1967] AC 853 and *Angle v. Minister of National Revenue*, [1975] 2 SCR 248) there is a fourth requirement—the only persons who can take advantage of the estoppel, or be bound by it, are the parties to the previous proceedings or their privies; no other person can take advantage of it or be bound by it because they were not a party to the previous proceeding. This privity requirement is also expressed in terms of *mutuality*: in order for there to be an estoppel the party must be bound by the estoppel, whichever way it goes. If, for example, A and B had been parties to litigation that established the authenticity of a signature, neither can relitigate the authenticity question in a subsequent suit between them, even in one involving a different claim or defence. But either can litigate the question in a suit with X, who was not a party to the first suit. Since X was not a party to the first suit, he is not bound by the decision therein (that is, he can disavow it if it is unfavourable to him) and consequently he cannot rely on it if it is favourable to him. Mutuality requires that he be bound whichever way the first case was decided. Since mutuality is lacking, X cannot bind either A or B to the earlier judgment. While there is a general agreement as to the appropriateness of the first three requirements, the final requirement—mutuality—has been subject to considerable criticism which has led to its abandonment in most United States jurisdictions.

The mutuality (or "same parties") requirement—that favourable preclusion from a former judgment is only available to persons who would have been bound by any unfavourable preclusion—has always been recognized as being subject to the exception for "privies." Over the years, and even today, courts have often manipulated the notion of privity to permit non-parties to preclude the relitigation of issues that earlier law suits have determined. At times the privity concept has assumed wondrous attributes of flexibility as courts attempt to apply their subjective sense of fairness to situations that do not fit neatly within the traditional requirements for preclusion.

2. The Abandonment of Mutuality in the United States

To set the scene for a discussion of the English and Canadian case law and an analysis of the benefits and problems associated with the abandonment of mutuality, it is necessary to tell the story of the history of the abandonment of this requirement in the United States. So long as issue estoppel is confined by the mutuality/privity requirement its impact is quite limited. However, abrogating mutuality makes it possible for a single case's fact-finding to have a wide ranging impact by effectively determining issues in later cases involving only one of the original parties.

A. History of Abandonment

The abandonment of mutuality in the United States involved many court decisions and the contribution of numerous commentators, but the story can be reduced ultimately to the contribution of two people—Jeremy Bentham and Mr. Justice Roger Traynor—and three landmark cases.

In the nineteenth century Jeremy Bentham had called the mutuality requirement illogical and ill-founded:

> There is no reason for saying that a man shall not lose his cause in consequence of the verdict given in a former proceeding to which he was not a party; but there is no reason whatever for saying that he shall not lose his cause in consequence of the verdict in a proceeding to which he *was* a party, merely because his adversary was not. It is right enough that the verdict obtained by A against B should not bar the claim of a third party, C; but that it should not be evidence in favour of C against B, seems the very height of absurdity.

Bentham referred to the rule as "a curious one, the reason given for it still more so" and characterized it as "destitute of ... [a] semblance of reason" and that it was a "maxim which one would suppose to have found its way from the gambling-table to the bench." It is to be noted that Bentham was concerned less with judicial efficiency than with what he saw as a superfluous and illogical prerequisite to collateral estoppel. He believed that the law entitled the litigant to only one day in court on a given issue and that thereafter the findings should bind him and prevent him from relitigating the same question.

The first landmark case on the abandonment of mutuality in the United States was the 1942 decision by Traynor J in *Bernhard v. Bank of America Nat. Trust & Savings Assn.*, 122 P2d 892, 19 Cal. 2d 807 (SC Cal., 1942). In action #1, P (a beneficiary) had sued D1 (the executor) with respect to an estate and it was held that the deceased had made a gift during her lifetime to the executor of her bank account. Subsequently, in action #2, P (the beneficiary) sued D2 (the bank) to recover the amount in the bank account on the ground that the deceased had never authorized the executor to withdraw it. The court allowed the bank to invoke the first judgment as a collateral estoppel on the issue as to the ownership of the money, even though the bank would not have been bound had the earlier court determined that the deceased had never given the money to her executor. In so holding, Traynor J explicitly rejected the requirement of mutuality, concluding that no satisfactory rationalization had been advanced for it. The benefits of *res judicata* found in "the sound policy of limiting litigation by preventing a party who has had one fair trial on an issue from again drawing it into controversy" make it "unjust to permit one who has had his day in court to reopen identical issues by merely switching adversaries." He applied a three-part test for determining when preclusion is appropriated:

> Was the issue decided in the prior adjudication identical with the one presented in the action in question? Was there a final judgment on the merits? Was the party against whom the plea is asserted a party or in privity with the party to the prior adjudication?

Two points are to be noted about the *Bernhard* decision. First, on its facts it sanctioned only the *defensive* use of non-mutual issue estoppel, and as we will see, it is the subsequent approval of *offensive* non-mutual issue estoppel which is the more powerful, and problematic, development. Second, the abandonment of mutuality only permits the use of the estoppel against a person *who was a party to the original litigation.* While it was no longer necessary that there be the same parties to both the former and the present action, it *is* essential that the person against whom the estoppel is to be pleaded was a party to the earlier proceeding. To hold otherwise would simply be to deny subsequent plaintiffs their day in court and to deprive them of due process by binding them to a decision in which they never had an opportunity to participate.

In 1971 in *Blonder-Tongue Laboratories Inc. v. University of Illinois Foundation*, 402 US 313 (1971) the United States Supreme Court joined the growing number of state jurisdictions that had abandoned the mutuality requirement where issue estoppel was sought to be used defensively, that is, in situations in which a (new) defendant sought to preclude an issue that the plaintiff had already litigated and lost against another party. The case concerned a patent infringement action in respect of a patent that had already been declared invalid in an earlier action brought by the plaintiff against another party. Citing the burden on judicial administration and the misallocation of resources resulting from relitigation of decided issues, the court followed *Bernhard* and rejected the mutuality requirement. But the court imposed the *caveat* that an earlier judgment could not preclude a losing party from relitigating an issue if he could demonstrate that the first action failed to allow him a "fair opportunity procedurally, substantively, and evidentially to pursue his claim."

The defensive use of non-mutual issue estoppel is straight forward. If P, having litigated an issue with D1 and lost, subsequently sues D2 raising the same issue, D2 can rely defensively on the issue estoppel arising from the former action, unless the first action did not provide a full and fair opportunity to litigate or other factors make it unfair or unwise to permit preclusion. The rationale is that P should not be allowed to relitigate an issue already lost by simply changing defendants, as was the case in *Blonder* itself.

Like *Bernhard*, *Blonder-Tongue* approved only this *defensive* use of non-mutual issue estoppel, and the court expressly refused to rule on its offensive application. However, eight years later, the Supreme Court took the remaining step and, in *Parklane Hosiery Co. v. Shore*, 439 US 322 (1979) it approved *the offensive* application of non-mutual issue estoppel, subject to certain conditions. Its affirmation of this final step in the abandonment of mutuality has been largely followed by state courts. In *Parklane*, the Securities and Exchange Commission had obtained injunctive relief against the defendants in prior litigation on the ground that they had violated the securities law by false and misleading proxy statements in connection with a merger. In a subsequent private shareholders class action to recover damages arising from the false and misleading proxy statements, the court held that the plaintiffs could use the earlier determination to preclude the defendants from relitigating any of the issues decided against them.

The power of this offensive non-mutual issue estoppel doctrine is illustrated by single event disaster cases, such as an airline crash. Assume P1 sues Airline for negligence in the operation of the aircraft and in that action Airline is found to have been negligent. Offensive non-mutual issue estoppel permits P2 through P20, *etc.*, now to sue Airline and successfully plead issue estoppel on the question of the airline's negligence. The rationale is that if Airline fully and fairly litigated the issue of its negligence in action #1 it has had its day in court; it has had due process and it should not be permitted to re-litigate the negligence issue. However, the court in *Parklane* realized that in order to ensure fairness in the operation of offensive non-mutual issue estoppel the doctrine has to be subject to qualifications. ...

3. Rationale for Non-Mutuality

The purpose of issue estoppel is to "relieve parties of the cost and vexation of multiple lawsuits, conserve judicial resources, and, by preventing inconsistent decisions, encourage reliance on adjudication." The basic arguments in favour of nonmutual preclusion are that it reduces the risk of inconsistent adjudication, spares one party the cost of ever litigating the issue, and protects the court system and other litigants against the delay and burdens entailed by relitigation. These are substantial values, which go far to support the argument that one full and fair opportunity to litigate an issue is enough.

But the abandonment of mutuality, and the use of offensive non-mutual collateral estoppel in particular, has its opponents and there are policy arguments to the contrary. The first is that the case for non-mutual preclusion is weaker than that which supports preclusion between the same parties. The need to foster repose and reliance on judgments that support the general doctrine of preclusion is greatly diluted in the context of non-mutual issue preclusion. Moreover, the argument that a party should not be "twice-vexed"—burdened with relitigating the same issues—is inapplicable to offensive non-mutual preclusion. The defendant in the second action usually resists the application of issue estoppel and is quite happy to be "twice-vexed," if this means that he or she will have a second chance at a better result. In the final analysis it is the justice system, and other litigants within the system with unrelated disputes, that benefit from non-mutual preclusion's avoidance of duplicative litigation.

A second argument against non-mutual preclusion points to the fact that the first determination of an issue is not always correct, and refers to special dangers peculiar to non-mutual preclusion. Experienced litigators know that any decision may be strongly affected by the identity of the parties. For example, a badly disfigured survivor of an accident may have a much better chance of recovery than the estate of someone killed in the accident. Moreover, chance may not determine the identity of the plaintiff in the first action, since plaintiffs' lawyers may see to it that the most sympathetic claim is tried first. This argument rejects the notion that "fact finders compartmentalize their decision making and ignore 'irrelevant' information that one case is as good as another for establishing the liability facts for future cases. ... The damages proof often spills over into liability issues so that a case weak on liability is saved if the damages are strong and vice-versa." That the first court may be ignorant of the potential impact of its findings is seen as aggravating these difficulties. "No one involved in the first case can be sure whether its outcome will have collateral estoppel effects." The court "may yield to the temptation to make a sympathetic award, even if the liability proof does not quite justify it, if it appears that the defendant can easily afford to pay."

A third argument questions the contribution of non-mutual preclusion in preventing the legal system from embarrassing itself through inconsistent determinations. Although it "somewhat reduces the potential for inconsistent decisions," it in no way ensures this because (a) it is unavailable where its application would be unfair to the defendant, and (b) it does nothing to prevent relitigation of the same question if the plaintiff loses the first case.

Even accepting the merit of these arguments, offensive non-mutual preclusion remains justified because of (a) "its contribution to judicial efficiency" (sparing one party the cost of ever litigating the issue and protecting the court system and other litigants against the delay and burdens entailed by relitigation) and (b) its ability to bring about at least a partial reduction of inconsistent decisions. And surely these are sufficient justifications. To be acceptable, however, the doctrine must ensure fairness to the defendant by a careful determination that, in the first action, the defendant had a full and fair opportunity to litigate and that, therefore, to apply preclusion would be fair. Moreover, the doctrine must be administered in such a way as to disarm the "option effect" (the "free-riderism") that it offers to "wait and see" plaintiffs.

NOTES AND QUESTIONS

1. To what extent does Watson allow considerations of efficiency to outweigh notions of substantive fairness in favouring non-mutual preclusion? Does the kind of defendant involved matter—that is, large or small resources? Why is the prospect of inconsistent decisions so daunting?

2. At the beginning of the piece, Watson notes the clear leaning that a move to non-mutuality has toward a more publicly based conception of litigation (at 626):

> The resolution of doctrinal difficulties, of course, takes place in the context of broader
> normative concerns that infuse and inform legal rules and policy. Although I will not
> explore the implications of this important understanding, it is essential to acknowledge
> the play and pull of competing visions of procedural justice. In short, this article aligns
> itself with the more expansive "public" view of litigation rather than the more
> traditional "private" conception. The conventional principle of non-mutuality draws its
> normative justification from a theory of corrective justice whose primary focus is the
> processing of individualized disputes in line with a restricted, individual and rights-
> centred ideology. On the other hand, the broader approach advocated in this article
> situates itself within a vision of law that is more sensitive to the need to ensure a more
> effective use of social resources and that recognizes the public consequences of any
> procedural regime. As such, this article is part of the growing trend within legal

scholarship that favours broader rules of standing, intervention, class actions and the increased aggregation of litigation.

2. The Emergence of Non-Mutual Issue Estoppel (or Abuse of Process)

McIlkenny v. Chief Constable of the West Midlands
[1980] QB 283 (English Court of Appeal)

[The plaintiffs, who were alleged to be members of the IRA, had been previously convicted of the horrible bombing of a hotel which caused the death of numerous people. Subsequently they brought a damage action against the police for allegedly beating them during their interrogation. During the course of the earlier criminal trial the accused had specifically raised this issue by alleging that their confessions had been beaten out of them, and both the judge (on the *voir dire*) and the jury had rejected this contention and held the confessions to be voluntary. In the subsequent civil action the police argued that there was an issue estoppel arising from earlier criminal proceedings. In the Court of Appeal, Lord Denning based the dismissal of the action on the ground of non-mutual issue estoppel, holding that, for issue estoppel to apply, it should no longer be necessary, as required by traditional doctrine, that there be the same parties in both the former and the present action. What was essential, he held, is that the person against whom the estoppel was now sought to be pleaded (that is, the present plaintiff) have been a party to the earlier proceeding. In so doing Lord Denning referred to, and specifically embraced, the doctrine of non-mutual issue estoppel as developed in the United States. On the question of abandoning mutuality, Goff LJ dissented, insisting that mutuality and privity must remain, but holding that the action should be dismissed on the grounds of "abuse of process" arising from the fact that the very issue that the plaintiffs sought to raise had already been decided against them in the prior proceeding on the criminal standard of proof beyond a reasonable doubt. In his reasons Lord Denning anticipated Goff LJ's invocation of abuse of process, and stated that "the real reason why the claim was struck out was because the self same issue had previously been determined *against* the party by a court of competent jurisdiction. What is that but issue estoppel?"]

DENNING MR: In seeking to strike out these actions, the police rely first on the law as to issue estoppel. They say that the six men are estopped from raising again an issue which was decided by Bridge J. Secondly, if that be wrong, the police say that these actions are an abuse of the process of the court. Now of these two propositions, I feel that priority should be given to issue estoppel. For this reason: It is admitted that the six men, if they are to be believed, have a reasonable cause of action for damages against the police officers: just as they have against the prison officers. On the ground that they, the six men, say that they were subjected to serious assaults—violence and threats—whilst in custody. The action itself is not therefore an abuse of the process. If it is to be called an abuse, it is because of the previous decision against them in the "trial within a trial." If they are to be stopped, it must be by way of an estoppel of some kind or other.

For the word "estoppel" only means stopped. You will find it explained by Coke in his *Commentaries on Littleton* (19th ed., 1832), vol. II, s. 667, 352a. It was brought over by the Normans. They used the old French "estoupail." That meant a bung or cork by which you stopped something from coming out. It was in common use in our courts when they carried on all their proceedings in Norman-French. Littleton writes in the law-French of his day (15th century) using the words "pur ceo que le baron est estoppe a dire," meaning simply that the husband is *stopped from* saying something.

From that simple origin there has been built up over the centuries in our law a big house with many rooms. It is the house called Estoppel. In Coke's time it was a small house with only three rooms, namely, estoppel by matter of record, by matter in writing, and by matter in pais. But by our time we have so many rooms that we are apt to get confused between them. Estoppel per rem judicatam, issue estoppel, estoppel by deed, estoppel by representation, estoppel by conduct, estoppel by acquiescence, estoppel by election or waiver, estoppel by negligence, promissory estoppel, proprietary estoppel, and goodness knows what else. These several rooms have this much in common: They are all under one roof. Someone is stopped from saying something or other, or doing something or other, or contesting something or other. But each room is used differently from the others. If you go into one room, you will find a notice saying, "Estoppel is only a rule of evidence." If you go into another room you will find a different notice, "Estoppel can give rise to a cause of action." Each room has its own separate notices. It is a mistake to suppose that what you find in one room, you will also find in the others.

Privity and Mutuality

Today we go into a room described as estoppel per rem judicatam: in which there is an alcove which has sometimes passed unnoticed. It is called issue estoppel. In this room there are several chairs to sit on. One is called the doctrine of privity. The other is the doctrine of mutuality. The two look all right but they are both a bit rickety.

The doctrine of *privity* says that the only persons who can take advantage of the estoppel or be bound by it are the two parties to the previous proceedings themselves or their privies. No third person can take advantage of it or be bound by it; because he was no party to the previous proceedings. Those proceedings, so far as the third person is concerned, were res inter alios acta.

The doctrine of *mutuality* says that, in order that there should be an estoppel, it must be such that both of the two parties and their privies must be bound by the estoppel, whichever way it goes. Win or lose, each party must be bound. It is said that, in any contest, that is the only fair thing.

Now although those two chairs look all right to start with, you will soon find that they are quite unsafe. Jeremy Bentham as long ago as 1827 told people not to rely on them. In his "Rationale of Judicial Evidence," *Jeremy Bentham's Works* (Bowring ed., 1843), vol. VII, Book VI, p. 171, he said that: "This rule of *mutuality* is destitute of even that semblance of reason, which there is for the rule concerning *res inter alios acta*." And 10 years later in 1837 John William Smith in the 1st edition of his *Smith's Leading Cases* gave a warning more politely: "Yet this rule that an *estoppel must be mutual, otherwise neither party is bound*, must be taken with some limitation." Then in 1856

Martin B. in *Petrie v. Nuttall (1856)*, 11 Exch. 569, 576-577, castigated the consequences of it as "absurd" and said it should be reconsidered by the court of error.

Our friends in the United States have been just as scathing as Jeremy Bentham.
They have rejected the doctrine of mutuality altogether: and they have limited the
doctrine of privity. They take a distinction between a decision *in favour* of man and a
decision *against* him. If a decision has been given *against* a man on the identical issue
arising in previous proceedings—and he had full and fair opportunity of defending
himself in it—then he is estopped from contesting it again in subsequent proceedings.
Not only is he estopped but so are those in privity with him. But there is no corresponding estoppel on the person in whose favour it operates.

This is no new departure. It was foreseen as long ago as 1776 when the judges of
England advised the House of Lords in the *Duchess of Kingston's Case* (1776), 2 Smith
LC (13th ed., 1929), pp. 644, 647-648:

> But in all these cases, the parties to the suits, or at least the parties against whom the
> evidence was received, were parties to the sentence, or had acquiesced under it; or
> claimed under those who were parties and had acquiesced. ...

Exceptions

It has long been recognised that estoppel per rem judicatam or issue estoppel is not an
absolute bar to the matter in dispute being tried again. The party concerned can avoid the
effect of the previous decision if he can prove the same to have been obtained by fraud or
collusion. That was the unanimous opinion of the judges in the *Duchess of Kingston's
Case*, 2 Smith LC (13th ed.), pp. 644, 652. To which we can add now that the party
concerned can avoid the effect of the previous decision if he can show that a new fact has
come to light (which he could not have ascertained before by reasonable diligence) which
entirely changes the aspect of the case: see *Phosphate Sewage Co. Ltd. v. Molleson*
(1879), 4 App. Cas. 801, 814, *per* Earl Cairns LC This is a much stricter test than we
require when we admit fresh evidence on an appeal. On an appeal (which is a re-hearing)
we have said that the fresh evidence must be such that, if given, it would probably have
an important influence on the result of the case, though it need not be decisive: see *Ladd v.
Marshall*, [1954] 1 WLR 1489, 1491, and *Skone v. Skone*, [1971] 1 WLR 812, 815. But in
order to avoid the effect of an estoppel (when there is no re-hearing) the fresh evidence
must, I think, be decisive. It must be such as to show that the previous decision was wrong.
Oath against oath will not do. An "important influence on the result" will not do. ...

[I]it seems to me that a previous decision in a civil case against a man operates as
an estoppel preventing him from challenging it in subsequent proceedings unless he can
show that it was obtained by fraud or collusion: or he can adduce fresh evidence (which
he could not have obtained by reasonable diligence before) to show conclusively that the
previous decision was wrong. ...

To illustrate my view of the present law, I would take this example. Suppose there is
a road accident in which a lorry driver runs down a group of people on the pavement
waiting for a bus. One of the injured persons sues the lorry driver for negligence and
succeeds. Suppose now that another of the injured persons sues the lorry driver for

damages also. Has he to prove the negligence all over again? Can the lorry driver (*against* whom the previous decision went) dispute his liability to the other injured person? It seems to me that if the lorry driver (with the backing of his employer) has had a full and fair opportunity of contesting the issue of negligence in the first action, he should be estopped from disputing it in the second action. He was a party to the first action and should be bound by the result of it. Not only the lorry driver, but also his employer should be estopped from disputing the issue of negligence in a second action: on the ground that the employer was in privity with the lorry driver.

Thus in all cases, both criminal and civil, our law is now brought into line with that of the United States. This should give an English lawyer satisfaction just as it did Lord Atkin in *Donoghue v. Stevenson*, [1932] AC 562, 598. As he paid tribute to the judgment of Cardozo J so I would pay tribute to the illuminating judgment of my friend Traynor J in *Bernhard v. Bank of America* (1942), 122 P2d 892 and equally of my friend White J in the Supreme Court in *Blonder-Tongue Laboratories v. University of Illinois* (1971), 402 US 313. ...

Abuse of the Process of the Court

In some cases in the past when the self-same issue has been decided *against* a party in previous proceedings, the courts have said that they will not allow him to raise it again in a subsequent proceeding. These decisions have been put on the ground that it is an abuse of the process of the court. ...

The truth is that at the date of those cases the doctrine of issue estoppel had not emerged as a separate doctrine. So the courts found it necessary to put it on "abuse of the process of the court." Now that issue estoppel is fully recognised, it is better to reach the decision on that ground: rather than on the vague phrase "abuse of the process of the court." Each doctrine is based on the same considerations and produces the same result.

Conclusion

This case shows what a civilised country we are. Here are six men who have been proved guilty of the most wicked murder of 21 innocent people. They have no money. Yet the state lavished large sums on their defence. They were convicted of murder and sentenced to imprisonment for life. In their evidence they were guilty of gross perjury. Yet the state continued to lavish large sums on them—in their actions against the police. It is high time that it stopped. It is really an attempt to set aside the convictions by a sidewind. It is a scandal that it should be allowed to continue. The issue was fully tried out and decided by Bridge J at the "trial within a trial." His finding on that issue is decisive unless there are circumstances which make it fair or just to reopen it. I see no such circumstances. I would allow the appeal and strike out these actions on the ground of issue estoppel.

NOTES AND QUESTIONS

1. On appeal to the House of Lords, in *McIlkenny* (*sub nom. Hunter v. Chief Constable of the West Midlands*, [1982] AC 529 (HL)) the court rejected Denning MR's

attempt to reform the mutuality requirement of issue estoppel stating that it preferred the reasoning of Goff LJ. The following is an excerpt from the speech of Lord Diplock:

My Lords, this is a case about abuse of the process of the High Court. It concerns the inherent power which any court of justice must possess to prevent misuse of its procedure in a way which, although not inconsistent with the literal application of its procedural rules, would nevertheless be manifestly unfair to a party to litigation before it, or would otherwise bring the administration of justice into disrepute among right-thinking people. The circumstances in which abuse of process can arise are very varied; those which give rise to the instant appeal must surely be unique. It would, in my view, be most unwise if this House were to use this occasion to say anything that might be taken as limiting to fixed categories the kinds of circumstances in which the court has a duty (I disavow the word discretion) to exercise this salutary power. ...

Lord Denning MR and Sir George Baker were also in favour of extending the description "issue estoppel" to cover the particular example of abuse of process of the court presented by the instant case—a question to which much of the judgment of Lord Denning is addressed. Goff LJ, on the other hand, expressed his own view, which had been shared by Cantley J, that such extension would involve a misuse of that expression. But if what Hunter is seeking to do in initiating this civil action is an abuse of the process of the court, as I understand all your Lordships are satisfied that it is, the question whether it also qualifies to bear the label "issue estoppel" is a matter not of substance but of semantics. Counsel for the appellant was therefore invited to address this House first upon the broader question of abuse of process and to deal in particular with the reasoning contained in the judgment of Goff LJ who dealt with the matter more closely than the other members of the court and bases his decision solely on that ground. In the result, counsel for the appellant, Hunter, who argued the case with their accustomed ability and diligence, were quite unable to persuade any of us that there was any error in the reasoning of Goff LJ in what proved to be the last judgment that he prepared before his much lamented and untimely death. In the result it became unnecessary to call on counsel for the police. So the debate upon semantics did not take place. It could not possibly affect the outcome of the appeal or justify the public expense that would have been involved in prolonging the hearing any further.

Nevertheless it is my own view, which I understand is shared by all your Lordships, that it would be best, in order to avoid confusion, if the use of the description "issue estoppel" *in English law, at any rate* (it does not appear to have been adopted in the United States), were restricted to that species of estoppel per rem judicatam that may arise in civil actions between the same parties or their privies, of which the characteristics are stated in a judgment of my own in *Mills v. Cooper*, [1967] 2 QB 459, 468-469 that was adopted and approved by this House in *Reg. v. Humphrys*, [1977] AC 1, the case in which it was also held that "issue estoppel" had no place in English criminal law.

The abuse of process which the instant case exemplifies is the initiation of proceedings in a court of justice for the purpose of mounting a collateral attack upon a final decision against the intending plaintiff which has been made by another court of competent jurisdiction in previous proceedings in which the intending plaintiff had a full opportunity of contesting the decision in the court by which it was made.

The proper method of attacking the decision by Bridge J in the murder trial that Hunter was not assaulted by the police before his oral confession was obtained would have been to make the contention that the judge's ruling that the confession was admissible had been erroneous a ground of his appeal against his conviction to the Criminal Division of the Court of Appeal. This Hunter did not do. Had he or any of his fellow murderers done so, application could have been made on that appeal to tender to the court as "fresh evidence" all material upon which Hunter would now seek to rely in his civil action against the police for damages for assault, if it were allowed to continue.

2. *Does it matter whether we eliminate the mutuality requirement for issue estoppel or rely on abuse of process?* What is at stake in this distinction between issue estoppel and abuse of process? Is it important that one is a rule and the other a discretion? Is it a debate of technical significance or does it have practical significance?

Whether or not the distinction affects the outcome in any particular case, the rejection of Denning's position by the House of Lords in *Hunter* (coupled with the adoption of the reasoning of *Hunter* by the Ontario Court of Appeal in *Demeter*, see below) has introduced considerable confusion into Anglo-Canadian law on the continuing requirement of mutuality. Current case law suggests that English and Canadian judges no longer "buy" mutuality as a requirement of issue estoppel—that is, they agree with Denning and the US authorities—but they feel they must resort to abuse of process when faced with a case in which this requirement is not met. (Could it be that they do this just to confuse law students?)

In an article in (1986), 64 *Canadian Bar Review* 437, at 453, Michael Herman and Gerald Hayden argue that *McIlkenny* collapsed the two questions into one:

> It does seem that this attempt to collaterally attack the finding of the trial judge in the criminal proceedings is an abuse of process, and it may well be that this is another, independent ground on which the civil action for assault could have been dismissed or stayed. However, to preserve clear thinking, it is important to realize that the application of the doctrine of abuse of process for their purpose is quite different and distinct from the narrower and more specific doctrine of issue estoppel, which seems to deal with the more salient complaint in the case; namely that the defendants ought not to be able to relitigate a matter which has already been found against them in the prior criminal adjudication. In the instant case, the application of the doctrine of issue estoppel was sufficient to dispose of the case, whether or not the plaintiffs' conduct in the subsequent civil proceeding was abusive as an improper collateral attack on the criminal trial judge's findings. By simply relying on the generalized and multi-purpose principle of abuse of process, the House of Lords has muddied the waters, and has failed to distinguish between two distinct, albeit complementary, bases on which the civil cause of action was properly dismissed.

Do you agree?

3. *How should the legal system deal with wrongful convictions?* Subsequent to their civil action, the case was investigated by a different police force whose findings were considered by the Court of Appeal in January 1987, at which time the court upheld the convictions. In March 1990, the Home Secretary ordered that the police inquiry into the case be reopened to examine new evidence that might provide grounds

for further reference to the Court of Appeal. The new evidence included revelations that several members of the now disbanded West Midlands Serious Crime Squad (which had investigated the Bombers) extracted confessions from men, allegedly by brutality. Subsequently, the Home Secretary again referred the case to the Court of Appeal on the ground that new evidence "might be thought to cast doubt on the safety of the convictions," notwithstanding that the pending police inquiry was not expected to be completed for several months. In March 1991, the six were acquitted and released.

It eventually came to light that the police had withheld exculpatory evidence, had fabricated inculpatory evidence, and had indeed extracted confessions through the use of force and intimidation. As Gerry Hunter, one of the six men, stated, the only thing he was guilty of was being Irish and leaving on a train from Birmingham to Belfast to attend an IRA funeral.

These events may seem to make it ironic to use their civil case as a major basis for an argument for issue preclusion, particularly in the light of the ultimate acquittal of the "Guildford Four" (whose bombing convictions were referred to and quashed by the Court of Appeal after they had spent fifteen years in prison) and the release of the "Maguire Seven" (whose convictions for operating a bomb factory were declared by the Director of Public Prosecutions to be unsafe after the accused had spent ten years in jail). In cases like these, to avoid the chaos of relitigation of all criminal convictions, should we leave reconsideration of unsound verdicts to the type of rehearings used in those cases (satisfactory or unsatisfactory as they may be), rather than to private attempts at collateral attack?

In Canada, the wrongful convictions of Donald Marshall, David Milgaard, and Guy Paul Morin have heightened public concern about wrongful convictions generally. The Royal Commission on the Donald Marshall Jr. Prosecution recommended the establishment of an independent review body to investigate cases of alleged wrongful conviction. As a public inquiry, this body would have coercive powers to compel witnesses to testify and provide evidence.

Some still contend that to blame the application of a *res judicata* principle for wrongful convictions is to miss the point and purpose of the principle. Those who blame a rigorous use of estoppel argue that it is important that every opportunity must be given to ensure that truth is arrived at in the judicial process: systemic efficiency ought not to trump substantive justice. Others disagree. While the appeal process is primarily directed to ensuring adequate safeguards against erroneous decisions, the doctrine of *res judicata* is more concerned with matters of judicial efficiency and procedural fairness— it wishes to allocate scarce institutional resources sensibly and to ensure that everyone has a full and fair opportunity to present their case, but only once. Does the ultimate outcome affect your confidence in a rigorous application of estoppel? Could there have been a more appropriate result?

4. In the opposite vein, many were puzzled that the families of Nicole Brown and Ronald Goldman were able to obtain determinations of liability against O.J. Simpson in civil actions for wrongful death after Simpson had been acquitted of criminal charges based on the same events. Why was the civil action not a collateral attack upon the result of the criminal trial?

Parklane Hosiery Co. v. Shore
439 US 322 (1979)

MR. JUSTICE STEWART: This case presents the question whether a party who has had issues of fact adjudicated adversely to it in an equitable action may be collaterally estopped from relitigating the same issues before a jury in a subsequent legal action brought against it by a new party.

The respondent brought this stockholder's class action against the petitioners in a Federal District Court. The complaint alleged that the petitioners, Parklane Hosiery Co., Inc. (Parklane), and 13 of its officers, directors, and stockholders, had issued a materially false and misleading proxy statement in connection with a merger. The proxy statement, according to the complaint, had violated §§ 14(a), 10(b), and 20(a) of the Securities Exchange Act of 1934, 48 Stat. 895, 891, 899, as amended, 15 USC §§ 78n(a), 78j(b), and 78t(a), as well as various rules and regulations promulgated by the Securities and Exchange Commission (SEC). The complaint sought damages, rescission of the merger, and recovery of costs.

Before this action came to trial, the SEC filed suit against the same defendants in the Federal District Court, alleging that the proxy statement that had been issued by Parklane was materially false and misleading in essentially the same respects as those that had been alleged in the respondent's complaint. Injunctive relief was requested. After a 4-day trial, the District Court found that the proxy statement was materially false and misleading in the respects alleged, and entered a declaratory judgment to that effect. *SEC v. Parklane Hosiery Co.*, 422 F Supp. 477. The Court of Appeals for the Second Circuit affirmed this judgment. 558 F2d 1083.

The respondent in the present case then moved for partial summary judgment against the petitioners, asserting that the petitioners were collaterally estopped from relitigating the issues that had been resolved against them in the action brought by the SEC. The District Court denied the motion on the ground that such an application of collateral estoppel would deny the petitioners their Seventh Amendment right to a jury trial. The Court of Appeals for the Second Circuit reversed, holding that a party who has had issues of fact determined against him after a full and fair opportunity to litigate in a nonjury trial is collaterally estopped from obtaining a subsequent jury trial of these same issues of fact. 565 F2d 815. The appellate court concluded that "the Seventh Amendment preserves the right to jury trial only with respect to issues of fact, [and] once those issues have been fully and fairly adjudicated in a prior proceeding, nothing remains for trial, either with or without a jury." *Id.*, at 819. Because of an intercircuit conflict, we granted certiorari. 435 US 1006.

I

The threshold question to be considered is whether, quite apart from the right to a jury trial under the Seventh Amendment, the petitioners can be precluded from relitigating facts resolved adversely to them in a prior equitable proceeding with another party under the general law of collateral estoppel. Specifically, we must determine whether a litigant who was not a party to a prior judgment may nevertheless use that judgment "offensively" to prevent a defendant from relitigating issues resolved in the earlier proceeding.

[In a footnote, Stewart J observed: "In this context, offensive use of collateral estoppel occurs when the plaintiff seeks to foreclose the defendant from litigating an issue the defendant has previously litigated unsuccessfully in an action with another party. Defensive use occurs when a defendant seeks to prevent a plaintiff from asserting a claim the plaintiff has previously litigated and lost against another defendant."]

A

Collateral estoppel, like the related doctrine of res judicata, has the dual purpose of protecting litigants from the burden of relitigating an identical issue with the same party or his privy and of promoting judicial economy by preventing needless litigation. *Blonder-Tongue Laboratories, Inc. v. University of Illinois Foundation*, 402 US 313, 328-329. Until relatively recently, however, the scope of collateral estoppel was limited by the doctrine of mutuality of parties. Under this mutuality doctrine, neither party could use a prior judgment as an estoppel against the other unless both parties were bound by the judgment. Based on the premise that it is somehow unfair to allow a party to use a prior judgment when he himself would not be so bound, the mutuality requirement provided a party who had litigated and lost in a previous action an opportunity to relitigate identical issues with new parties.

By failing to recognize the obvious difference in position between a party who has never litigated an issue and one who has fully litigated and lost, the mutuality requirement was criticized almost from its inception. Recognizing the validity of this criticism, the Court in *Blonder-Tongue Laboratories, Inc. v. University of Illinois Foundation, supra*, abandoned the mutuality requirement, at least in cases where a patentee seeks to relitigate the validity of a patent after a federal court in a previous lawsuit has already declared it invalid. The "broader question" before the Court, however, was "whether it is any longer tenable to afford a litigant more than one full and fair opportunity for judicial resolution of the same issue." 402 US, at 328. The Court strongly suggested a negative answer to that question:

> In any lawsuit where a defendant, because of the mutuality principle, is forced to present a complete defense on the merits to a claim which the plaintiff has fully litigated and lost in a prior action, there is an arguable misallocation of resources. To the extent the defendant in the second suit may not win by asserting, without contradiction, that the plaintiff had fully and fairly, but unsuccessfully, litigated the same claim in the prior suit, the defendant's time and money are diverted from alternative uses—productive or otherwise—to relitigation of a decided issue. And, still assuming that the issue was resolved correctly in the first suit, there is reason to be concerned about the plaintiff's allocation of resources. Permitting repeated litigation of the same issue as long as the supply of unrelated defendants holds out reflects either the aura of the gaming table or "a lack of discipline and of disinterestedness on the part of the lower courts, hardly a worthy or wise basis for fashioning rules of procedure." *Kerotest Mfg. Co. v. C-O-Two*

Co., 342 US 180, 185 (1952). Although neither judges, the parties, nor the adversary system performs perfectly in all cases, the requirement of determining whether the party against whom an estoppel is asserted had a full and fair opportunity to litigate is a most significant safeguard. Id., at 329.

B

The *Blonder-Tongue* case involved defensive use of collateral estoppel—a plaintiff was estopped from asserting a claim that the plaintiff had previously litigated and lost against another defendant. The present case, by contrast, involves offensive use of collateral estoppel—a plaintiff is seeking to estop a defendant from relitigating the issues which the defendant previously litigated and lost against another plaintiff. In both the offensive and defensive use situations, the party against whom estoppel is asserted has litigated and lost in an earlier action. Nevertheless, several reasons have been advanced why the two situations should be treated differently.

First, offensive use of collateral estoppel does not promote judicial economy in the same manner as defensive use does. Defensive use of collateral estoppel precludes a plaintiff from relitigating identical issues by merely "switching adversaries." *Bernhard v. Bank of America Nat. Trust & Savings Assn.*, 19 Cal. 2d, at 813, 122 P2d, at 895. Thus defensive collateral estoppel gives a plaintiff a strong incentive to join all potential defendants in the first action if possible. Offensive use of collateral estoppel, on the other hand, creates precisely the opposite incentive. Since a plaintiff will be able to rely on a previous judgment against a defendant but will not be bound by that judgment if the defendant wins, the plaintiff has every incentive to adopt a "wait and see" attitude, in the hope that the first action by another plaintiff will result in a favorable judgment. *E.g., Nevarov v. Caldwell*, 161 Cal. App. 2d 762, 767-768, 327 P2d 111, 115; *Reardon v. Allen*, 88 NJ Super. 560 571-572, 213 A2d 26, 32. Thus offensive use of collateral estoppel will likely increase rather than decrease the total amount of litigation, since potential plaintiffs will have everything to gain and nothing to lose by not intervening in the first action.

A second argument against offensive use of collateral estoppel is that it may be unfair to a defendant. If a defendant in the first action is sued for small or nominal damages, he may have little incentive to defend vigorously, particularly if future suits are not foreseeable. *The Evergreens v. Nunan*, 141 F2d 927, 929 (CA2); cf. *Berner v. British Commonwealth Pac. Airlines*, 346 F2d 532 (CA2) (application of offensive collateral estoppel denied where defendant did not appeal an adverse judgment awarding damages of $35,000 and defendant was later sued for over $7 million). Allowing offensive collateral estoppel may also be unfair to a defendant if the judgment relied upon as a basis for the estoppel is itself inconsistent with one or more previous judgments in favor of the defendant. [Footnote: In Professor Currie's familiar example, a railroad collision injures 50 passengers all of whom bring separate actions against the railroad. After the railroad wins the first 25 suits, a plaintiff wins suit 26. Professor Currie argues that offensive use of collateral estoppel should not be applied so as to allow plaintiffs 27 through 50 automatically to recover. Currie, "Mutality of Estoppel: Limits of the *Bernhard* Doctrine" (1957), 9 *Stan. L Rev.*, at 304. See Restatement (Second) of Judgments

§ 88(4).] Still another situation where it might be unfair to apply offensive estoppel is where the second action affords the defendant procedural opportunities unavailable in the first action that could readily cause a diferent result. [Footnote: If, for example, the defendant in the first action was forced to defend in an inconvenient forum and therefore was unable to engage in full scale discovery or call witnesses, application of offensive collateral estoppel may be unwarranted. Indeed, differences in available procedures may sometimes justify not allowing a prior judgment to have estoppel effect in a subsequent action even between the same parties, or where defensive estoppel is asserted against a plaintiff who has litigated and lost. The problem of unfairness is particularly acute in cases of offensive estoppel, however, because the defendant against whom estoppel is asserted typically will not have chosen the forum in the first action.]

C

We have concluded that the preferable approach for dealing with these problems in the federal courts is not to preclude the use of offensive collateral estoppel, but to grant trial courts broad discretion to determine when it should be applied. The general rule should be that in cases where a plaintiff could easily have joined in the earlier action or where, either for the reasons discussed above or for other reasons, the application of offensive estoppel would be unfair to a defendant, a trial judge should not allow the use of offensive collateral estoppel.

In the present case, however, none of the circumstances that might justify reluctance to allow the offensive use of collateral estoppel is present. The application of offensive collateral estoppel will not here reward a private plaintiff who could have joined in the previous action, since the respondent probably could not have joined in the injunction action brought by the SEC even had he so desired. Similarly, there is no unfairness to the petitioners in applying offensive collateral estoppel in this case. First, in light of the serious allegations made in the SEC's complaint against the petitioners, as well as the foreseeability of subsequent private suits that typically follow a successful Government judgment, the petitioners had every incentive to litigate the SEC lawsuit fully and vigorously. Second, the judgment in the SEC action was not inconsistent with any previous decision. Finally, there will in the respondent's action be no procedural opportunities available to the petitioners that were unavailable in the first action of a kind that might be likely to cause a different result.

We conclude, therefore, that none of the considerations that would justify a refusal to allow the use of offensive collateral estoppel is present in this case. Since the petitioners received a "full and fair" opportunity to litigate their claims in the SEC action, the contemporary law of collateral estoppel leads inescapably to the conclusion that the petitioners are collaterally estopped from relitigating the question of whether the proxy statement was materially false and misleading. …

[The balance of the judgment and the dissenting opinion of Rehnquist J, dealing with the question whether offensive collateral estoppel violates the Seventh Amendment right to jury trial, are omitted.]

NOTES AND QUESTIONS

1. *The power of offensive non-mutual estoppel and its problems.* A plane crashes killing all 250 passengers and wrongful death actions are commenced by the next of kin of the deceased against the airline. Of these actions, 24 are consolidated for trial and result in a verdict for the plaintiffs based on a finding of negligence on the part of the airline. Subsequently in 10 further actions the plaintiffs move for summary judgment on the issue of liability on the ground that in view of the earlier decision the issue is *res judicata*. What will the decision be? Compare *United States v. United Airlines, Inc.*, 216 F Supp. 701, aff'd. *sub nom. United Airlines v. Wiener*, 335 F2d 379 (9th Cir. 1964) and *Zdanok v. Glidden Co.*, 327 F2d 944 (2d Cir. 1964) with *Berner v. British Common-wealth Pacific Airlines, Ltd.*, 346 F2d 532 (2d Cir. 1965).

What if instead the 24 plaintiffs had sued the airline in successive actions and lost and a 25th plaintiff sues and wins. May the 26th plaintiff (and all other persons suing in respect of the death of the passengers) rely on the judgment in the 25th case?

P1 sues D for demolishing his new car in an auto accident; D is found negligent and ordered to pay $20,000. D is then sued by P1's passenger, P2, for $500,000 for personal injuries. May P2 rely on issue estoppel? What if D had won the first action on a finding that he had not been negligent. Can D rely on this finding as issue estoppel in P2's action?

2. In *Bomac Construction Ltd. v. Stevenson* (1986), 48 Sask. R 62, two people were injured in a plane accident. The first plaintiff succeeded in a negligence action and damages against the plane owners and the pilot. A second plaintiff brought a similar action. The plaintiff moved to have the defendants' defence struck out. In allowing the application, the Saskatchewan Court of Appeal stated that:

> It is usual to consider that the concept of abuse of process is applicable only to a plaintiff's claim to prevent the commencement of certain types of actions, but there is no apparent reason for its restriction to such circumstances when it is considered that the purpose is to prevent the raising of an issue which has already been squarely before the courts once before and decision rendered. There seems little justification for concluding that such an issue cannot be raised by a plaintiff but may be raised in defence by a defendant. If the concern is a valid one, it should not matter by what process the concern is raised.
>
> In any event, there would be great difficulty in thinking that courts would permit a rule to evolve which in negligence cases involving a claim and counterclaim the defendant could be permitted to challenge the previous trial finding out of the same occurrence but as plaintiff by counterclaim he would be precluded from doing so on the basis of abuse of process.
>
> What is involved here is that the plaintiff wishes to deny the defence the opportunity to have a second chance to avoid liability, whereas the defence contend that by not joining in the first action the plaintiff has sought to assure its opportunity for two chances to succeed. If the first action was successful she would seek to rely on it, whereas if the first action was not successful she would have a second chance to succeed by proceeding with this case. One cannot conclude that the ends of justice are best served by permitting such a situation to prevail. If the plaintiffs in separate actions

wish to stand on their right to a separate trial where the facts and issues and defendants are identical with another claim, they must take the chance of having their claim follow the result of the first action. Similarly, the defendant liability must be taken as having been established in the first action. To rule otherwise would be to permit an abuse of process through the prospect of a multiplicity of actions, inconsistent results and no fitting end to the litigation process.

Courts are always reluctant to prevent an issue from proceeding to trial. This reluctance has been expressed time and time again, particularly in relation to applications to set aside statements of claim as disclosing no cause of action. The same reluctance arises here but it is tempered somewhat by the knowledge that the basic issues raised by the plaintiff and the third party claim have been fully canvassed, and if any injustice arises from an inability to litigate the said issues again it is less than the potential injustice perpetuated both on the parties and the judicial system by having the same basic issues dealt with in two or perhaps three separate trials.

3. *Offensive non-mutual estoppel in Canadian courts.* In his survey of Anglo-Canadian doctrine, "Duplicative Litigation": Issue Estoppel, Abuse of Process, and the Death of Mutuality" (1990), 69 *Canadian Bar Review* 623, Garry Watson argues that while Canada lacks a landmark decision of an appellate court clearly abandoning the mutuality requirement in favour of non-mutual issue estoppel, the *Bomac* decision (above), and the following cases (among others) spell the death of mutuality in Canada, albeit by resorting to the application of the doctrine of "abuse of process."

In *Bjarnarsen v. Manitoba* (1987), 22 CPC (2d) 302, an attempt was made to invoke offensive non-mutual estoppel. There the trial court held that a defendant, who had been found liable in a previous action on the same facts brought by a different plaintiff, should not be allowed to relitigate the issue where it had had a full opportunity to deal with the issue, and the defendant was held to be bound by issue estoppel as to liability. The court held that, although the Canadian doctrine of issue estoppel did not apply (because they were not the same parties), this was a special case, and the court followed the position, advocated by Lord Denning in England, and adopted by the United States Supreme Court in *Parklane*, and relaxed the requirement that they be the same parties. On appeal, the Manitoba Court of Appeal held that the "same parties" is still a requirement for the application of issue estoppel. However, the court affirmed the trial judgment on the ground that "it would be an abuse of process to permit the defendant to dispute its negligence again in this action."

Similarly, in *Germscheid v. Valois* (1989), 68 OR (2d) 670 (HC), Judge Kurisko confronted the problem that unfairness may result if estoppel is applied without qualification in favour of a "wait and see" plaintiff—that is, a plaintiff who deliberately stays out of the first proceeding and then subsequently attempts to rely upon a favourable decision arrived at in that proceeding. The case involved a fire in a bunk house complex on a construction site. In an earlier action one of the injured workmen, Pl, sued six defendants and, at a jury trial, four of the defendants were found to be liable. This decision was affirmed on appeal. Subsequently, another injured workman, P2, commenced a similar action against the defendants in the first action plus a new defendant, and brought a motion for summary judgment against those who were losing defendants in the first action on the issue of liability (and for an order directing a trial respecting contributory negligence and damages). Two of the defendants who had been found (minimally) liable in the first action, together with the new defendant, supported the plaintiff's motion. The motion was opposed by four defendants (two of whom had been found liable in the first action and two of whom had not been found liable). In holding that the losing defendants who were common to both actions were to be precluded on the liability issue, Judge Kurisko observed that Canadian courts have declined to abandon the requirement of mutuality (because of the Supreme Court of Canada's decision in *Angle v. Minister of National Revenue* (1974), 47 DLR (3d) 544), but that they have arrived at the same conclusion by invoking abuse of process. He decided that on this ground the defendants were precluded from relitigating the issue of negligence.

However, he confronted the fact that the plaintiff clearly had played "wait and see." He rejected the US solution (which is to refuse to allow non-mutual issue estoppel in such circumstances), because to do so would open the risk of inconsistent decisions, involve the squandering of judicial time and do injustice to the defendants who now supported the present plaintiff and had nothing to do with that plaintiff's conduct. Instead, Judge Kurisko addressed the "wait and see" problem by imposing costs sanctions with a two-fold purpose: to deter other litigants from adopting unjustified or unexplained "wait and see" tactics, and to indemnify the present defendants for the expenses that they were now incurring because the plaintiff had failed to participate during the first trial. The court ordered the plaintiff to pay the costs of all of the defendants on the motion on a solicitor-and-client basis and, to carry through the deterrent principle, it recommended that the trial judge should consider a similar order at trial in relation to any matters that were duplicated by reason of the failure of a plaintiff to have been involved in the first trial.

In *Hamelin v. Davis* (1996), 18 BCLR (3d) 85 (CA), Newbury J stated:

> There is by now considerable Canadian and other authority for the proposition that even in the absence of mutuality, a person who has had had a "full and fair" opportunity (per Denning MR in *McIlkenny*) to meet the case against him should not generally be permitted to relitigate an adverse finding made as an essential part of the ruling of another court. Where the first adjudicating body is not a court of law but a regulatory tribunal such as the Commission, with a recognized mandate and expertise, the same rule should generally apply, again subject to any particular prejudice being shown.

In *Vos v. Canadian Red Cross Society*, [1998] OJ no. 4369 (Gen. Div.), a motion was brought on the basis of issue estoppel and abuse of process for an order that the Red Cross ("CRCS") was bound by the finding of Borins J in *Walker Estate v. York Finch General Hospital* (1997), 39 CCLT (2d) 1 (Ont. Gen. Div.) that the screening methods used by the Red Cross in 1984 to deter HIV carriers among blood donors fell below acceptable standards. Benotto J granted the order and held that:

> It is only issues which deal with the standard of care of the CRCS and which I have referred to as the first step in the [*Walker Estate*] negligence inquiry which the CRCS is estopped from challenging. This order will not affect issues specific to the donor GR or the plaintiffs.

Benotto J held that the plaintiffs in *Vos* still had to fulfil what she referred to as the second step of the *Walker Estate* approach—namely, to establish the causal link between the negligence of the Red Cross and the HIV infections of the plaintiffs.

In arriving at her decision, Benotto J had to deal with numerous objections to the applicability of issue estoppel. The first was the fact that the "same-parties" requirement for issue estoppel was not met in *Vos*, because Vos was not a party to the *Walker Estate* litigation. She held that this was no longer a requirement.

> Clearly, the parties Vos are not the same as in [*Walker Estate*] because the plaintiffs are different. This precludes the operation of issue estoppel as defined in *Angle*. However, courts in the United States and Canada have achieved a similar result through a different process. Courts have considered that, even when parties are not the same, there is a duty to maintain the integrity of the major policy consideration underlying issue estoppel: that litigants be protected from the burden of relitigating an issue with the party who has previously had a full and fair judicial hearing on the issue. American courts have abandoned the requirement of mutuality and developed "offensive non-mutual estoppel" to estop a defendant from relitigating issues which it lost against another plaintiff. ....
> There, the court has discretion to dispense with the mutuality requirement where the party against whom the estoppel is directed has had a full and fair opportunity to litigate that same position in an earlier proceeding.
>
> In Canada, the courts have not embraced the notion of offensive non-mutual estoppel. They have, however, used their inherent power to prevent an abuse of process. (Citing *Bjarnson v. Government of Manitoba* (1987), 21 CPC (2d) 302 (Man. QB), affirmed on appeal 21 CPC (2d) 312 (Man. CA) and *Germscheid v. Valois* (1989), 34 CPC (2d) 268.)

The Red Cross also argued that the two restrictions on the use of non-mutual offensive estoppel developed in the United States should apply to the application of abuse of process—that is, that a plaintiff cannot rely on estoppel if he or she could easily have joined in the earlier action (as a "wait-and-see" plaintiff) and that an estoppel will not be used where it would be "unfair to the defendant" because of conflicting decisions on the issue. Benotto J rejected both contentions.

> It is suggested by the CRCS that the plaintiffs in *Vos* were wait and see plaintiffs. I do not agree. There are multiple actions involving the CRCS. The court has been actively involved in the management of these cases through the case management process. Throughout the process, an attempt has been made to "have as many relevant issues decided in the most economical way with the view to establishing the basis for possible settlement of the cases yet to be scheduled." ... This has involved an enormous number of case conferences and planning meetings with all parties. Moreover, even if the plaintiffs were wait and see plaintiffs, the sanction, in Canada, has been not to deny relief, but to consider the issue in costs. [See *Germscheid v. Valois* (1989), 34 CPC (2d) 267, at 291.]

Benotto J also rejected the argument that it would be unfair to prevent the Red Cross from contesting the standard-of-care issues because the decision in *Walker Estate* was inconsistent with the previous decision of the court in *Pittman Estate v. Bain* (1994), 19 CCLT (2d) 1.

> [B]etween the trials of *Pittman* and [*Walker Estate*], information became available as a result of the Krever Inquiry ... which did not start until the evidence in *Pittman* was complete. This was information not available to the Pittmans. It was available to the [*Walker Estate*]. Most notably, a series of memos were available in [*Walker Estate*], which were not before Lang J and which cast doubt on some of her findings favourable to the CRCS. One of the memos, written by Ms Janet Wells, the acting Toronto area manager for the CRCS, indicated that "quite often" the blood clinics would run out of pamphlets. She was called as a witness in [*Walker Estate*] and confirmed that there were not enough pamphlets to give one to everybody. This evidence was not available in *Pittman* and was contrary to the CRCS evidence in *Pittman*.

What is to be made of the following statement from the judgment of Laskin JA in *Minott v. O'Shanter Development Co.* (1999), 42 OR (3d) 321 (CA) (reproduced, in part, below under III.C.4, "The Impact of the Decisions of Administrative Tribunals on Civil Proceedings"), where he was discussing the "same-parties" requirement of issue estoppel and his finding that the employer in *Minott* was not a party to the administrative proceeding?

> Implicit in this discussion is my rejection of any notion of non-mutual issue estoppel. The doctrine of non-mutual issue estoppel, which was not argued before us, has roots in American jurisprudence. [See Holmested and Watson, *Ontario Civil Procedure*, vol. II (looseleaf), at s. 21, subs. 24.] It permits a judgment to operate in favour of a non-party. Applied here, it might permit an employer to refrain from participating in a hearing before a Board of Referees yet rely on a favourable Board decision in a subsequent wrongful dismissal action. By adopting a "wait and see" approach to the Board's decision, an employer could rely on issue estoppel if the employee lost, but be no worse off if the employee won, because issue estoppel could not be applied against an employer who had not had its day in court. Applying non-mutual issue estoppel would allow the employer to "have it both ways". In my view, in these cases issue estoppel should be mutual. [See, generally, Spencer, Bower, Turner, and Handley, *The Doctrine of Res Judicata*, 3d ed. (1996), at 110-11.] An employer should only be able to invoke issue estoppel for a favourable decision if issue estoppel could also be invoked against it for an unfavourable decision. I do not consider O'Shanter bound by the Board's decision any more than I consider it would have been bound in the wrongful dismissal action had Minott succeeded in his appeal before the Board of Referees. O'Shanter was not a party for the purpose of issue estoppel and the third requirement is therefore not satisfied.

Is Laskin JA's initial, sweeping statement—"Implicit in this discussion is my rejection of any notion of non-mutual issue estoppel"—to be taken literally, or is it to be qualified and narrowed to the context in which he was speaking—"In my view, *in these cases* issue estoppel should be mutual" (emphasis added)? Do you agree that the latter reading seems the preferable one? Surely Laskin JA would have given a more carefully reasoned opinion (and the judiciary and the public are certainly entitled to one) on this important issue in the light of the number of Canadian decisions embracing some form of non-mutual issue estoppel.

4. *Discouraging "wait and see" plaintiffs in a non-mutual estoppel regime.* In "Duplicative Litigation," above, Garry Watson recommends that the courts should openly adopt non-mutual issue estoppel. However, he recognizes potential drawbacks and inequities that need to be addressed if the handling of duplicative litigation is to be more efficient. In particular, regarding the need to discourage "wait and see" plaintiffs in a regime of offensive non-mutual issue estoppel, he recommends the following:

> As the United States Supreme Court in *Parklane* recognized, the offensive use of nonmutual issue estoppel carries with it the problem that potential plaintiffs may play "wait and see." Unless the rules as to the applicability of the doctrine take this into account, the unmodified use of the doctrine *encourages* "wait and see" and hence duplicative litigation. By staying out of action #1, P2 escapes being bound by a decision adverse to the plaintiff in action #1, but if P1 is successful in that action in establishing the defendant's liability, the subsequent plaintiff can use issue estoppel against the common defendant in action #2. Professor Ratliff has observed that this "option effect" is part and parcel of the doctrine. In *Parklane* the court acknowledged what Professor Currie had earlier identified as this "multiple claimant anomaly," and proposed as part of the doctrine that preclusion should be denied "in cases where a plaintiff could easily have joined in the earlier action." Experience has indicated that for two reasons the Supreme Court's qualification of the doctrine is ineffective. First, the sanction that follows (the plaintiff in action #2 may not rely on issue estoppel and hence must reprove the claim) is an insufficient deterrent, since it puts the plaintiff in no worse a position than he would have been in action #1 (of having to prove his claim), but he is still ahead because he escapes the risk of an adverse decision in action #1 and he may have learned a great deal—in terms of proving his claim—from "observing" the earlier litigation. (Moreover, where P2 is permitted to obtain preclusive effect from the decision in action #1, he or she escapes the cost of establishing liability). Second, the United States caselaw indicates that, in any event, the courts have been extremely slow to impose even the suggested sanction and have generally declined to do so.

Where does this leave us? Does offensive non-mutual issue estoppel ultimately have to be rejected because of an "incurable" option effect? I suggest not. Instead, what is necessary are strategies to avoid the problem. These fall into two categories—"second case strategies" to discourage litigants from holding back, and "first case strategies" designed to marshall together in the first action all related claims against a common defendant to bring about one common determination. Both approaches involve adopting a policy perspective that to maximize judicial efficiency and to remove the unfairness of the option effect, the legal system should generally require that like and related claims should be subject to only one adjudication.

"Second case strategies" are rules to be imposed in case #2 to discourage P2 from holding back from participating in case #1. There is a range of them which can be used individually or collectively. The first is a strengthening of the *Parklane* qualification: P2 must satisfy the court in the second action that he or she has a "cast iron" reason for not having joined in action #1. Desire to sue alone, rather than with others, should be an insufficient excuse. The test should be: if P2 was aware of action #1 and joinder or consolidation would have been permitted had P2 sued at the time of action #1, then he or she should be treated as a wait and see plaintiff. Second, the defendant's conduct should be taken into account. If at the time of action #1 action #2 was pending and the defendant did not request consolidation (where it would have been granted), then P2 should be entitled to rely on issue estoppel. In such circumstances the "option effect" is not unfair, it is of the defendant's own making.

The next issue is what consequences should follow from P2 being declared to be an improper wait and see plaintiff. The *Parklane* sanction (the plaintiff cannot rely on issue estoppel and must prove his case) is obviously inadequate. Two possibilities present themselves and both have been suggested in Canadian cases. The first, and less draconian, is to use the Anglo-Canadian device of general cost indemnity (fee shifting) to punish and discourage the wait and see plaintiff, that is, by ordering the plaintiff to pay the defendant's costs in action #2 on a solicitor and client basis, or, requiring the plaintiff to bear part of the costs incurred in the first action—an action the plaintiff should have joined in and the benefit of which the plaintiff now seeks to reap. A second, draconian sanction is that proposed in *Bomac Construction Limited v. Stevenson*—that a true "wait and see" plaintiff should be held to be bound by any *adverse* decision in the first action. (While this is certainly an extreme position it is not to be mistaken as simply unthinking, non-party issue estoppel. Rather, it is based upon P2's own "abuse of process": under the policy perspective adopted here, there is an obligation on P2 to join in the earlier litigation and the sanction for not so doing is that P2 is bound by any adverse decision in that action, that is, P2 is bound by the earlier adverse decision not simply because it was made, but because P2 was under a duty to have participated in the first action and did not).

An alternative approach is to call in aid the device of using the former judgment as "*prima facie* evidence subject to rebuttal." Not only is this strategy less draconian than the *Bomac* solution, it is potentially more powerful. A drawback to the "should have joined or consolidated" rule is that it is ineffective as against plaintiffs who cannot be shown to be improper "wait and see" plaintiffs, because they did not have knowledge of the earlier proceeding. Obviously, in such circumstances, the argument for doing anything is much weaker since such plaintiffs are not, by definition, exercising any "option effect." However, even with respect to such plaintiffs there is respectable precedent for making some fair usage of the prior adjudication, thus maximizing judicial efficiency. Where such usage is made of the prior determination as against an improper "wait and see" plaintiff, it should be effective in discouraging wait and see tactics. If a plaintiff realizes that an adverse decision in action #1 will become *prima facie* evidence subject to rebuttal in action #2, the plaintiff will presumably think very carefully before abstaining from participation in the first action where the *prima facie* adjudication will be made.

5. *Has the use of "abuse of process" as a surrogate for non-mutual issue estoppel lost its way in England?* In the decision of the English Court of Appeal in *Ashmore v. British Coal Corp.*, [1990] 2 All ER 981, the applicability of *Hunter* to civil cases arose. In 1982, about 1,500 applications for equal pay were made by women canteen workers, including the appellant, employed by the respondent employer, claiming that they were

doing like work with male comparators on less favourable terms. On the direction of the industrial tribunal, 14 cases were selected as sample cases and the proceedings in the other applications, including the appellant's, were stayed. On the hearing of the sample cases, the applications were dismissed on the grounds that none of the claimants were employed on like work with the selected male comparator and the variation in pay between him and the claimants was genuinely due to a material factor other than the difference in sex. The appellant then applied to have the stay on her application removed and the case listed for hearing, on the ground that in her case she was employed on like work with the selected male comparator. The employers applied to have the appellant's claim struck out on the grounds that it was frivolous and vexatious. The industrial tribunal struck out the claim on the grounds that although the decision in the sample cases was not technically binding on the appellant, it would be an abuse of process to relitigate the same factual issue that had been decided in those cases and the appellant's claim was bound to fail. The appellant appealed to the Employment Appeal Tribunal, which dismissed her appeal. The appellant appealed to the Court of Appeal, contending that in the absence of *res judicata*, issue estoppel or an agreement to be bound by the findings in the sample cases, the appellant had an absolute right to have her claim litigated.

The Court of Appeal held that no absolute right existed. Abuse of process was not limited to sham claims by way of collateral attacks on earlier decisions. In giving judgment, Stuart-Smith LJ said (at p. 985):

> Counsel for the board accepted that the appellant's claim is not a collateral attack on the decision of the tribunal in the *Thomas* case; but he submits that it is analogous to it. He submits that where sample cases have been chosen so that the tribunal can investigate all the relevant evidence as fully as possible, and findings have been made on that evidence, it is contrary to the interests of justice and public policy to allow those same issues to be litigated again, unless there is fresh evidence which justifies re-opening the issue. I agree; it is no answer to say that if the appellant's claim fails, the board can be compensated in costs. Even if an award of costs is made, and it is not necessarily so in the industrial tribunal (see rule 11 of the 1985 rules of procedure), it does not always amount to an indemnity, and is seldom compensation for inconvenience and disruption caused by litigation. Moreover, it is not in the interests of justice that the time of the courts or tribunals is taken litigating claims that have effectively been already decided. Furthermore, if the appellant is to be at liberty to pursue her claim, I can see no reason in principle why the 1486 other applicants, who were not among the sample claimants, should not also have a similar right. It is true that in their cases they have two hurdles to surmount, namely both grounds on which the tribunal found in favour of the board, while the appellant has only one; but, if the appellant is to be permitted to re-open one issue, I cannot see why the others cannot re-open two. This would plainly defeat the whole object of having the 14 sample cases.

Was Ms Ashmore treated fairly? How would a US court, applying non-mutual issue estoppel, have decided her case?

Is the decision in *Whiteoak Lincoln Mercury Sales Ltd. v. Canadian Pacific Ltd.* (1982), 30 CPC 136 (Ont. HC) distinguishable from *Ashmore*? In *Whiteoak*, as a result of a major train derailment that occurred at Mississauga, Ontario in November 1979, some 389 actions were commenced against Canadian Pacific Limited. In order to streamline the litigation, an application was brought to have all of the actions joined to be tried together. Montgomery J stated as follows:

> Since counsel attended before me on January 28, 1982, many leading counsel for plaintiffs and defence have met with a view to streamlining the Mississauga litigation.
>
> A form of draft order was circulated with the notice of motion and comment was invited from all interested parties.
>
> The order which follows is largely the product of counsel involved. It may not satisfy all parties but it does, in my view, represent the desire of all counsel to create a workable system out of chaos.
>
> No plaintiff's rights are taken away. By electing to become a "Scheduled Plaintiff," rather than assuming conduct of a lead case, plaintiff's rights are secured without the onerous burden of conducting a protracted lawsuit. ...
>
> I am strongly of the view that all actions must be tried together with the option of plaintiffs not to appear at trial, in the confidence that all issues of liability will be disposed of in the test cases that emerge. Clients electing to await the outcome of liability should not enjoy a free ride. Some modest contribution to the costs of lead counsel may be provided in the discretion of the trial Judge.
>
> If counsel having primary carriage of a category settles prior to trial, another case in that category will be entitled to apply before me for carriage. If settlement occurs during trial, it will be a matter for the determination of the trial Judge.
>
> For these reasons, the following order shall issue:
>
> > IT IS ORDERED that this action and all other actions set out in Schedule A hereto, being actions in this Court arising out of the Mississauga derailment and evacuation (hereinafter referred to as "Mississauga Actions") shall, subject to the interlocutory directions hereinafter, be set out and, subject to the direction of the trial Judge, shall be tried together *so that the findings of the trial Judge with respect to liability and recoverable categories of damages in the scheduled actions shall be binding upon all plaintiffs and all defendants in the Mississauga actions.* [Emphasis added.]

In class proceedings a decision on the common issues binds every class member who has not opted out of the class proceeding: Ontario Class Proceedings Act, s. 27(3). Given this, is there anything wrong with the *Ashmore* decision? Or are there aspects of a class proceeding that make it quite different to the proceeding in *Ashmore*?

Incidentally, the Ontario Class Proceedings Act, s. 27(2) further provides that where a person opts out of a class proceeding that person is not bound by a judgment on the common issues and, moreover, the judgment is not binding on any party to the class proceeding—for example, a defendant found liable—in any subsequent proceeding brought by a person who opts out of the class. This later provision appears to be a clear recognition of non-mutual issue estoppel that the section makes inoperative re persons opting out of the class proceeding.

6. *A restatement of the issue estoppel rule and an explanation of certain of its requirements.* For issue estoppel to apply, certain requirements must be met. Leaving aside the issues discussed above (mutuality/same parties and the common requirements that apply to both claim and issue preclusion), there are additional requirements for the application of issue estoppel that we have not yet discussed. These are uncontroversial and generally accepted in all jurisdictions: (1) the same issue must be involved in the initial and subsequent litigation; (2) the issue must have been actually litigated and determined in the first suit; and (3) its determination must have been necessary to the result in the litigation. Hence, assuming the acceptance of non-mutual issue estoppel, the basic elements of the issue estoppel rule can be restated as follows:

> Issue estoppel applies in respect of an issue in present litigation, against a party who was a party (or a privy) to a former adjudication, where the same issue (a) was actually decided, (b) after a full and fair opportunity to litigate, and (c) was necessary to the decision in the former litigation: compare the *Restatement (Second) of Judgments* s. 27 (1980).

Because of the requirement "that the issue must have been actually litigated and determined in the first suit," we can see immediately that issue estoppel is much narrower and of more limited effect than claim preclusion. The reason is that the two rules have somewhat different objectives. Claim preclusion is concerned with preventing relitigation of claims and defences arising out of a transaction or occurrence. To achieve this objective, that rule requires the parties in the first action to put forward all their claims and defences arising out of the transaction or occurrence and may lead to there never being a consideration on the merits of a particular claim in either the first or the second action. (This is what we saw happen in *Las Vegas.*) By contrast, issue estoppel only comes in to play when, for some reason, claim preclusion is inapplicable—for example, the second action involves a different cause of action or claim, the second claim was beyond the jurisdiction of the first court, or, as in the case of non-mutual estoppel, the parties are not the same—but action #2 involves an issue that arose and was decided in action#1. What issue estoppel seeks to do is to prevent relitigation of the decided issue—for example, for reasons of efficiency, or to avoid inconsistent determinations; *ex hypothesi*, for issue estoppel to come into play, action #2 must involve an issue that was litigated and decided in action #1. "Not only must the matter or point have been put in issue by the parties, but it must also have been determined by the tribunal in the first action": James and Hazard, *Civil Procedure*, 3d ed. (Boston: Little, Brown, 1985), § 11.18, citing *Restatement of the Law (Second) Judgments*, § 27. Although we will not go into the issue or look at the case law, it is not always easy to ascertain that a particular issue was actually determined in action #1; for example, if action #1 resulted in a default judgment, what issues did the court determine?

As to the requirement that "the determination of the issues must have been necessary to the result in the litigation," James and Hazard, *Civil Procedure*, above, § 11.19 explain the rationale for this requirement as follows:

> Three considerations tend to support this rule. (1) The parties' attention and efforts are likely to be focused on points and matters that are necessary to the result. (2) The tribunal's attention is likely to be focused on the grounds necessary for its decision.

Findings that are not necessary partake of the nature of obiter dicta and the reasons for the distinction between dictum and holding in applying the rule of stare decisis also favor denying collateral estoppel effect to unnecessary findings. Both are unlikely to receive the full judicial consideration with respect either to premises or consequences that is given to the very grounds of decision. (3) Unnecessary findings are usually not subject to appellate review. While the availability of such review ... is probably not an essential predicate of res judicata, yet its absence here does seem to furnish an additional valid reason for the rule under discussion.

7. *Application of issue estoppel to interlocutory orders and to decisions made within one proceeding.* Here there are two distinct situations and questions. The first is what preclusive effect will be given in action #2 to a decision made in action #1 where the decision is one that did not dispose of action #1—that is, it was not embodied in the final judgment but was merely embodied in an order giving some form of interim relief or deciding some interlocutory procedural point—for example, whether a claim for privilege was valid? Generally, the answer in this situation is that since the decision was not a final one (said to be a prerequisite to the application of any form of *res judicata*), issue estoppel is inapplicable and there is no preclusion: see, for example, *Barwell Food Sales Inc. v. Snyder & Fils Inc.* (1988), 38 CPC (2d) 192 (Ont. HC) (where the plaintiff commenced separate actions in Quebec and Ontario for the same relief the failure to obtain an interlocutory injunction in Quebec did not render the interlocutory injunction application in Ontario *res judicata*; the refusal to grant injunctive relief did not constitute a final order and hence *res judicata* was not applicable).

The second situation is what preclusive effect will be given to issues decided within a given proceeding—that is, if an issue is raised and decided at one stage in the proceeding, may the parties relitigate it at a later stage—for example, on a subsequent interlocutory motion or at trial? The answer is that, in terms of statements of general principle, the case law is in hopeless confusion. Compare the following rulings. *Res judicata* applies to interlocutory orders in the abscence of an appeal, a material change in circumstances, or new evidence that had been previously suppressed or unavailable: *Newmarch Mechanical Constructors Ltd. v. Hyundai Auto Canada Inc.* (1994), 26 CPC (3d) 289 (Ont. Gen. Div.). For issue estoppel to apply, the subject order must finally determine an issue; since the interlocutory injunction in question was not final but interlocutory in nature, the court was prepared to review the issue afresh: *Trilea Centres Inc. v. Cumming Cockburn Ltd.* (1991), 5 OR (3d) 598 (Gen. Div.). Where an issue is raised and determined in the context of an interlocutory motion, as a general rule issue estoppel applies and neither party will be permitted to relitigate the issue in the same or a subsequent proceeding: *Ward v. Dana D. Colson Management Ltd.* (1994), 24 CPC (3d) 211 (Ont. Gen. Div.). Where the plaintiff had been refused an order for disclosure of documents in the defendant's possession on the ground that they were protected by public interest immunity, the court held that a further application by the plaintiff would be considered; a ruling on an interlocutory application that does not adjudicate on issues of fact or law raised by the pleadings is not *res judicata* if the same interlocutory issue is raised again: *Pocklington Foods Inc. v. Alberta (Provincial Treasurer)* (1993), 25 CPC (3d) 292 (Alta. QB), varied (1995), 28 Alta. LR (3d) 96 (CA).

In part, these conflicting statements reflect uncertainty about the role and application of the "final order" requirement to issues decided within a given proceeding. In the United States, much of the confusion found in the Canadian case law in our attempts to apply the *res judicata* principles to issues decided within a given proceeding, has been avoided by removing such cases from the operation of *res judicata* and subjecting them to a separate (but clearly related) doctrine called "the law of the case." James and Hazard, *Civil Procedure*, 593 explain this doctrine as follows:

> The rules of *res judicata* are to be distinguished from a related but distinct rule, that of the "law of the case." The law-of-the-case rule has application to a determination of a question of law at an earlier stage of a proceeding. The rule is that a determination once made will be treated as correct through all subsequent stages of the proceeding except when the question comes before a higher court. Thus, a trial court will treat its own earlier rulings as conclusive in subsequent trial proceedings. Similarly, when there has been an interlocutory appeal in which a legal question was decided, that decision will be treated as conclusive by the same appellate court if the case later comes before it on an appeal from the final judgment. The law of the case rule thus applies within one action regarding issues of law previously determined that action, while the rules of *res judicata* apply between successive actions.

3. The Impact of Criminal Convictions on Civil Proceedings

Demeter v. British Pacific Life Insurance Co.
(1983), 150 DLR (3d) 249 (Ont. SC)

OSLER J: These three actions, which are, with the exception of minor details, identical, are brought by the plaintiff against the three defendant insurance companies upon policies of insurance whereby the defendants, respectively, agreed to pay to the survivor of the plaintiff and Christine Demeter, his wife, specific sums of money upon the death of the other. The statements of claim allege that on July 18, 1973, the plaintiff's wife, Christine Demeter, died; that proof of her death was duly filed; that each of the policies was in full force and effect at the material time; and that payment has been refused by each of the defendants. In their amended statements of defence each of the defendants plead that Christine Demeter came to her death by reason of the criminal conduct of the plaintiff and that the purported policy was thereby rendered void and unenforceable, that public policy precludes any person benefiting from his own criminal act, and the death of the life insured resulted from a criminal act of the plaintiff. They add certain technical defences.

[The defendants moved for an order to determine as a question of law the effect of the criminal conviction on the civil claims and for an order dismissing the claims as an abuse of process. Counsel for the plaintiff relied heavily on the decision of the English Court of Appeal in *Hollington v. F. Hewthorn & Co. Ltd.*, [1943] 1 KB 587, holding that in a motor vehicle action, evidence of the defendant's conviction for driving without due care and attention was inadmissible. Osler J reviewed the authorities dealing with *Hollington* and concluded that it had not been followed in Canada, had been overruled by the House of Lords in *McIlkenny*, *supra*, and that proof of the conviction of the plaintiff for the murder of his wife may be adduced in evidence and, if this is done, should be regarded as *prima facie* proof of that issue, subject to rebuttal by the plaintiff on the merits.]

That, however, does not end the matter. [The defendants contend that] the claim of the plaintiff in the statements of claim constitutes an abuse of the process of the court in light of the conviction of the plaintiff for the murder of his wife.

In *McIlkenny*, Lord Diplock was careful to emphasize that the inherent jurisdiction of the court to dismiss or stay an action as an abuse of its own process was one to be sparingly exercised but one that undoubtedly existed and should be exercised if the circumstances should warrant. In *McIlkenney's* case, what was said to be an abuse of the process of the court was the collateral attack inherent in the civil action upon not simply and plainly the prior criminal conviction but really upon a subordinate finding that it must have been assumed the jury made, as well as the trial judge, in the light of the verdict it reached. ...

The gravamen of the abuse is the attempt to relitigate an issue already tried. True, Lord Diplock did refer to what he concluded was an improper motive for proceeding with the action, namely, the desire to influence the Home Secretary to pardon the offenders rather than the purported aim of the action to secure damages. He reached this conclusion because one of the defendants, the Home Secretary on behalf of prison guards, had caused a payment to be made into court or an offer to be tendered which the plaintiffs disregarded. It is, therefore, perhaps not entirely out of place to refer to what was placed before me as an excerpt from the *de bene esse* examination of Csaba Szilagyi on April 17, 1978, when the plaintiff, conducting the examination on his own behalf, stated in part:

> ... I am not here for the money, I am here to reopen my case. The only reason I decided to—planning this on the record—the reason I am going to publish in the first volume only until the night of my wife's death, July 18th, '73, which is mostly about us, mostly about Mr. Szilagyi and my wife. To put him into the position to have to go to court and refute it, because only through these reactions and an action he has to start, can I reopen my case, can I bring my new witnesses and prove my total innocence and vindicate myself.

Those words do not suggest a man who is single-mindedly pursuing a series of actions for purely financial reasons.

In fairness, however, it must be said that Ms Belman put it forcefully that such an interpretation does not accord with reason and common sense. The plaintiff Demeter has now served almost ten years of a life sentence for non-capital murder. He is now on day parole and stands an excellent chance of being placed on full parole in the very near future. An attempt to prove his innocence, Ms Belman says, might well result in a new trial being ordered, a trial which would of necessity be for first degree murder and which would carry with it the risk of conviction and a sentence of not less than 25 years, with no credit for the time already served.

The motive of the plaintiff, then, may be dubious. Nevertheless, the circumstances of this case, the fact of conviction for the non-capital murder of his wife, the dismissal of his appeals up to and including the Supreme Court of Canada, and the refusal of the

Minister of Justice to reopen the case, persuade me beyond peradventure that to permit these actions to go forward would result in a travesty of justice and would bring the administration of justice into disrepute. It would be, in the most fitting phrase of Schroeder JA, in *Kennedy v. Tomlinson et al.* (1959), 20 DLR (2d) 273, 126 CCC 175, "an unedifying spectacle." ...

Nothing is put forward, therefore, by the plaintiff to justify me in concluding that, if the prior conviction were admitted in the present actions as *prima facie* evidence of the fact that the plaintiff killed his wife, any evidence is available to the plaintiff that would cast doubt upon that proposition. In view of the solemn verdict of the jury, properly charged with respect to the burden of proof, the fact that proof must be beyond a reasonable doubt, and the identity of the issue before the jury with the issue in the present actions, it would be an affront to one's sense of justice and would be regarded as an outrage by the reasonable layman to let these actions go forward. In the exercise of the court's inherent jurisdiction they will each be dismissed with costs.

Actions dismissed.

[Demeter's appeal to the Ontario Court of Appeal was dismissed: (1984), 13 DLR (4th) 318, per MacKinnon ACJO]:

We agree with Mr. Justice Osler's careful and thoughtful analysis of the authorities and his conclusions that *Hollington v. F. Hewthorn & Co., Ltd. et al.*, [1943] 1 KB 587, which held that the fact that the defendant driver in that case had been convicted of careless driving at the time and place of the accident did not amount to even *prima facie* evidence of his negligent driving at the time and place, is not the law in Ontario. We are equally of the view that the use of a civil action to initiate a collateral attack on a final decision of a criminal court of competent jurisdiction in an attempt to relitigate an issue already tried is an abuse of the process of the court. The alleged fresh evidence or evidence of fraud or collusion falls far short of supporting an argument that an exception should be made to the general rule of public policy.

On the facts of this case it would be, as the learned motions court judge pointed out, an affront to one's sense of justice to let these actions go forward and, for the reasons given by him, the appeals are dismissed with costs as of one appeal.

Appeal dismissed.

NOTES AND QUESTIONS

1. The British Columbia Evidence Act, RSBC 1979, c. 116, ss. 80 and 81, provides that evidence of a prior conviction may be admitted in a subsequent civil action, and that the weight to be given to the conviction is a matter for the trier of fact. In other provinces, the matter is governed by the common law. For instance, in Ontario, there is authority that a criminal conviction is admissible as *prima facie* evidence only and the reasons for conviction or findings of fact in support of the conviction are not admissible in evidence in civil proceedings; see *Re Del Core and Ontario College of Pharmacists*

(1985), 51 OR (2d) 1 (CA) (discipline hearing following a criminal conviction) and *Taylor v. Baribeau* (1985), 51 OR (2d) 541 (Div. Ct.) (personal injury action following a conviction for dangerous driving).

2. Was *Q. v. Minto Management Ltd. and Halliday* (1984), 15 DLR (4th) 581 (Ont. HC) correctly decided? The plaintiff sued for damages resulting from an assault committed by the defendant Halliday, an employee of the corporate defendant, Minto. The plaintiff resided in a building owned by Minto, and alleged that Minto was negligent in permitting Halliday to have access to her apartment. Prior to the civil action, Halliday had been convicted of sexual assault and sentenced to seven years' imprisonment. Steele J held that proof of the conviction was admissible against *both* defendants, but that *both* should be permitted to challenge the correctness of the conviction on the ground that it could not be said they were guilty of abuse of process, since they had not initiated the proceedings but were merely defending themselves.

3. *How should criminal convictions be used in subsequent civil actions?* Should a distinction be drawn between criminal convictions for serious criminal offences, and convictions for less serious matters, such as careless driving and other traffic offences? In the United States, many jurisdictions prevent a party from relitigating issues determined by conviction where the offence was a serious one (such as in *Demeter* or *Q. v. Minto Management Ltd. et al.*) but provide that in less serious matters (such as traffic offences) the conviction should be evidence only. The distinction is explained in H. Karlson, "Criminal Judgments as Proof of Civil Liability" (1982), 31 *Defense Law Journal* 173:

> In order for a criminal conviction to preclude a party from relitigating issues determined in the criminal proceeding, the defendant must have had an adequate opportunity and incentive to obtain a full and fair adjudication in the criminal action. When a criminal trial concerns a serious offense, the accused clearly has motivation to defend himself fully, and the procedural requirements of our criminal justice system ensure a fair day in court. These characteristics, however, are not always present in proceedings arising out of minor traffic offenses. Unless a defendant is aware that the outcome of the traffic court proceeding will create a substantial risk of civil liability, he usually has little incentive to contest the issue of guilt. Minor fines imposed by traffic courts create no desire on the part of a defendant to expend the funds necessary to obtain an attorney and litigate the issues. A driver may plead guilty to a minor traffic offense because the cost of defending outweighs the burden of having such a conviction on his record.
>
> Even where a driver has the incentive to contest his guilt, traffic courts are neither designed nor equipped to become the crucial forums in deciding issues for civil actions. The incredible volume of convictions generated by traffic courts must be routinely handled in as expeditious a manner as possible. If the effect of a minor traffic conviction is to preclude relitigation of important issues in a civil action, drivers involved in traffic accidents will have a strong incentive to contest traffic citations. This would increase, not decrease, litigation. Therefore, one of the main justifications for the doctrine of collateral estoppel, the reduction of litigation, will not result from permitting traffic convictions to be used in subsequent civil actions. The overwhelming majority of jurisdictions that have considered the questions have, by either statute or court decision, refused to permit a minor traffic conviction to preclude relitigation of issues in a civil action.

In his "Duplicative Litigation" article, above, Garry Watson notes that generally the Canadian case law envisages prior judgments being used in subsequent proceedings in two different ways: as truly preclusive issue estoppel (which prevents re-litigation), and as *prima facie* evidence subject to rebuttal (which permits re-litigation, but with the prior judgment being admitted in evidence in the second litigation). The first approach has been taken with regard to the use of prior civil determinations, while the second approach has been taken with the use of prior criminal convictions.

He then poses some questions. If mutuality is openly abandoned, and nonmutual preclusion is adopted subject to appropriate qualifications, why should criminal convictions be treated any differently from civil determinations? He also raises the question whether there is any role at all for prior determinations as merely "*prima facie*" evidence subject to rebuttal?

He argues that reason dictates that where the conditions for non-mutual preclusion are met, this "stronger" doctrine should apply, leaving no room for the *prima facie* evidence approach. If the dual components of the doctrine, fairness and efficiency, are met, then issue estoppel should apply and the former judgment should preclude re-litigation: preclusive effect should be given to the prior judgment, rather than merely making it a matter of evidence.

> But accepting this general proposition still leaves circumstances where it will be appropriate to use the evidentiary approach. This can be seen by examining the *Hollington v. Hewthorn* type of scenario, that is, a prior traffic conviction followed by a subsequent civil motor vehicle action. Here, if we apply the tests necessary to determine whether nonmutual preclusion should be available it will often lead to the conclusion that it is inapplicable. First, frequently in such cases the "full and fair opportunity to defend" test will not be met because given the nature of most traffic court proceedings the now convicted person will often have lacked the incentive to litigate fully the issue in the traffic court. Second, if we accept the notion that the driving force behind non-mutual preclusion is judicial efficiency and that it should not apply where efficiencies are minimal or non-existent, then there may be a further reason for not applying preclusion in the subsequent civil negligence action. Often in such cases, issues other than the liability of the convicted person are present (for example, the plaintiff's contributory negligence and the comparative negligence of other defendants) so that all the evidence relating to the accident has to be adduced (including the evidence relating to the convicted person's negligence). The end result is that there may be no efficiency gains and, moreover, giving preclusive effect to the conviction may actually complicate the second adjudication. (A further argument for not giving preclusive effect to traffic convictions, involving both fairness and efficiency, is that often the real party in interest in the subsequent civil action will be an insurance company, which will not have participated in the criminal defence of the insured. From an efficiency point of view, the last thing we want to do is to have insurance companies defending every traffic prosecution against their insured on the off chance that there may subsequently be a civil negligence claim.
>
> If, however, in any given circumstances it is inappropriate to give preclusive effect to a prior judgment, resort may still be had to admitting the prior judgment as *prima facie* evidence subject to rebuttal, since the fairness rights of all persons affected are

protected by their ability to call evidence to rebut the *prima facie* evidence arising from the earlier judgment. But in some cases involving the use of prior criminal convictions in subsequent civil actions, non-mutual preclusion will be quite appropriate, for example, after a fully contested rape trial where the accused was vigorously represented and faced a substantial period of imprisonment, and was convicted. If the convicted person is subsequently sued for damages for assault, a court should normally conclude that such an accused had a full and fair opportunity to defend. [Footnote: This will also be true of some traffic convictions, for example, for impaired driving, where there was a vigorous defence. I am not suggesting a separate rule for traffic convictions and other convictions (but see, *supra*, as to the role of insurance). In all cases a functional analysis is required.] The conditions for non-mutual preclusion will have been met and issue estoppel should apply to the exclusion of giving the previous conviction effect as *prima facie* evidence subject to rebuttal.

4. *Review exercise.* Reconsider the hypothetical case, above, preceding the *Las Vegas* case. How many more of the questions posed can you now answer? What are the answers?

4. The Impact of the Decisions of Administrative Tribunals on Civil Proceedings

We have already noted earlier in this section that preclusion may arise from decisions rendered by administrative tribunals of competent jurisdiction. In an earlier chapter we observed that the procedures followed by some administrative tribunals may be very simple—summary and quite uncourt-like. The combination of these two factors produces its own problems as the following case and notes demonstrate.

Rasanen v. Rosemount Instruments Ltd.

(1994), 17 OR (3d) 267 (CA)

[The plaintiff was employed by the defendant as Manager of Nuclear/Aerospace, Marketing and Sales, based in Toronto, and reported directly to the defendant's Canadian president. In 1984, as a result of a corporate restructuring, the plaintiff's position became redundant. He was offered two alternative positions, both at the same salary level as his old position, one in Calgary, reporting to the president, and one in Toronto, reporting to the president through the sales manager. The plaintiff, through his lawyer, stated that he viewed both alternatives as representing a unilateral and fundamental change in his employment position amounting to a constructive dismissal. The defendant's response was to terminate the plaintiff's employment because of his refusal to accept either offer. The plaintiff made a claim under s. 40 of the Employment Standards Act ("the ESA") for eight weeks' termination pay and commenced an action for damages for wrongful dismissal.]

ABELLA JA:—This is an appeal from a judgment dismissing Henry Rasanen's action for wrongful dismissal. Prior to instituting his wrongful dismissal action, Rasanen had made a claim for termination pay, pursuant to s. 40 (now s. 57) of the Employment Standards

Act, RSO 1980, c. 137 (now RSO 1990, c. E.14). After a hearing during which Rasanen and his employer gave evidence, the referee, appointed pursuant to s. 50(1) (now s. 68(1)) of the Employment Standards Act, concluded that no money for termination pay was owing to Rasanen. Because the trial judge was of the view that the issues before him and the referee were the same, he dismissed Rasanen's claim on the basis of issue estoppel. This application of the doctrine of issue estoppel forms the basis for this appeal. ...

Rasanen left Rosemount on September 30th and instituted two legal proceedings. His Employment Standards Act claim and his wrongful dismissal action were started almost contemporaneously at the end of 1984. The hearing before the referee took place on January 14, 1986. The trial, on the other hand, did not take place until June 21, 1989. ...

[Abella JA then reviewed the process under the Employment Standards Act by which it was determined that Rasanen was not entitled to termination pay.]

At the trial over three years later, both Rasanen and Rosemount were represented by counsel. As in the hearing before the referee, the only witness called on behalf of Rasanen was Rasanen himself. No one testified on behalf of Rosemount. The evidence was completed on the first day.

The trial judge reviewed both the facts of the case and the reasons of the referee before concluding that the doctrine of issue estoppel applied. In the alternative, it was his view that if the doctrine was inapplicable, there was, in any event, no fundamental breach of the employment contract given what he considered to be equally advantageous status, pay and benefits in the Calgary position. While he disagreed with the referee as to which of the Toronto or Calgary jobs Rasanen ought to have accepted, the trial judge agreed that because a sufficiently reasonable job alternative was made available by Rosemount, no liability attached. He rejected Rasanen's submission that the reassignment constituted constructive dismissal by quoting extensively from the reasons of Finlayson JA in *Smith v. Viking Helicopter Ltd.* (1989), 68 OR (2d) 228, 31 OAC 368, who in turn reiterated the "good faith" test in *Canadian Bechtel*, supra, relied upon by the referee.

In other words, an analysis under either the Employment Standards scheme or the "wrongful dismissal" jurisprudence would, according to the trial judge, yield no remedy for Rasanen.

Analysis

The appellant argued that none of the conditions precedent to the application of issue estoppel existed in this case; the matters to be decided in the wrongful dismissal action and the Employment Standards Act claim were not the same; the issue determined by the referee was not necessary to the result; the hearing before the referee was neither judicial nor final, and the parties were not the same in both proceedings. Additionally, the appellant maintained that the Employment Standards Act itself, by stating in s. 6 that no civil remedy is affected by the Act, mandates the parallel pursuit of remedies in the courts. ...

In my view, the question to be decided in these proceedings is the same question that was, and was necessarily, decided in the earlier Employment Standards Act proceedings:

was there any entitlement by the employee to compensation from the employer arising from the termination of his employment? There is no doubt that under the Employment Standards Act this question has a different linguistic and quantitative formulation than at common law. But a different characterization and process does not, in this case, mean a different question. ...

The second requirement is that there be a prior, final, judicial decision. The appellant argued that the procedure before the referee was not sufficiently "judicial," and that the absence of discovery, costs, production of documents and a judge rendered it so dissimilar a process to that of the courts that no decision resulting from it should be binding.

This is an argument, in my opinion, which seriously misperceives the role and function of administrative tribunals. They were expressly created as independent bodies for the purpose of being an alternative to the judicial process, including its procedural panoplies. Designed to be less cumbersome, less expensive, less formal and less delayed, these impartial decision-making bodies were to resolve disputes in their area of specialization more expeditiously and more accessibly, but no less effectively or credibly. ...

As long as the hearing process in the tribunal provides parties with an opportunity to know and meet the case against them, and so long as the decision is within the tribunal's jurisdiction, then regardless of how closely the process mirrors a trial or its procedural antecedents, I can see no principled basis for exempting issues adjudicated by tribunals from the operation of issue estoppel in a subsequent action. If the purpose of issue estoppel is to prevent the retrial of "[a]ny right, question, or fact distinctly put in issue and directly determined by a court of competent jurisdiction" (*McIntosh v. Parent*, supra), then it is difficult to see why the decisions of an administrative tribunal having jurisdiction to decide the issue, would not qualify as decisions of a court of competent jurisdiction so as to preclude the redetermination of the same issues. ... On the contrary, the policy objectives underlying issue estoppel, such as avoiding duplicative litigation, inconsistent results, undue costs, and inconclusive proceedings, are enhanced in appropriate circumstances by acknowledging as binding the integrity of tribunal decisions. ...

There is no basis for restricting the application of issue estoppel to decisions made by judges in the ordinary course of litigation. By analogy, the hearing by the referee, if not technically "judicial," is designed to be an independent, fair, impartial and binding adjudicative process, and therefore satisfies the spirit of the requirement. It was a decision made in a hearing in which the appellant knew the case he had to meet, had a chance to meet it, and lost. Had he won, the decision would have been no less binding.

The remaining aspect of this second requirement is that the decision be final and conclusive of the relevant issues. Of this there can be no doubt. Section 50(7) (now s. 68(7)) of the Employment Standards Act states:

> 50(7) A decision of the referee under this section is final and binding upon the parties ...

The referee's decision is subject only to judicial review. No judicial review was sought. The decision is therefore final.

No one disputes that the referee had the jurisdiction to decide the questions he decided, and I have earlier expressed my view that the questions he decided were conclusive of the issues in the wrongful dismissal action. What remains is the appellant's contention that the referee's decision was not final and binding as against him because he was not a party to the hearing held pursuant to s. 50 of the Act. This leads to an examination of whether the third requirement of issue estoppel was met in this case, namely, whether the same parties or their privies are common to both proceedings.

The respondent argued that even if there was no privity or mutuality because the parties were not the same, this court should none the less follow leading American decisions and several Canadian judgments by embracing non-mutual issue estoppel. (An excellent review of the jurisprudence and analysis of this development can be found in Garry D. Watson, "Duplicative Litigation: Issue Estoppel, Abuse of Process and the Death of Mutuality" (1990), 69 Can. Bar Rev. 623.)

In my view, it is not necessary to apply the non-mutual preclusion because the appellant was, if not a party to the earlier proceeding, certainly a privy. It was a hearing resulting from a claim he initiated. He participated in the two stages which preceded a referee hearing under the Employment Standards Act—the initial investigation and the officer's review of the investigation. The Ministry of Labour, through counsel, appeared on the appellant's behalf for the purpose of promoting his claim and defending the officer's decision in his favour. He not only had notice of every step of the process and hearing, he was present at the hearing, gave evidence, heard the evidence and argument of all parties, and submitted or reviewed the relevant documentation filed. ...

The referee hearing is the final stage in the process the appellant initiated. ... [T]he process is a dispute between an employer and an employee. The appellant Rasanen was the "Employee." The employer Rosemount was the "Applicant" who applied for the hearing in appeal from the officer's decision. The "Appearances" refer to two sets of personnel: those appearing for the Applicant employer and those appearing for the ministry. Since the two disputants are designated as being the "Applicant" and the "Employee," and since the Applicant employer is represented by counsel and Rosemount's president, the remaining appearances must of necessity be on behalf of the Employee Rasanen. The ministry appears, therefore, on behalf of the Employee Rasanen and in support of his favourable order. There was a clear community of interest between Rasanen, the employee whose claim was the subject of the proceedings culminating in the referee hearing, and the Ministry of Labour: both were seeking to uphold the prior determination made by an employment standards officer in those proceedings.

The appellant clearly called the witnesses he wanted, introduced the relevant evidence he needed, and had the chance to respond to the evidence and arguments against him. He had the assistance of counsel provided by the Ministry of Labour and there was no evidence that he sought his own counsel or that his choice would have been denied if sought. He enjoyed, in short, the full benefits that an official "party" designation would have provided, regardless of whether he was referred to specifically as a party in s. 50(4) (now s. 68(4)) of the Employment Standards Act [ESA]. He had a meaningful voice, through his own evidence and through the assistance of the ministry, in a proceeding which decided the very issue he sought to raise in his subsequent action. The third requirement that he be a party or privy to the prior proceeding has therefore been satisfied. ...

The trial judge was correct in applying issue estoppel in the circumstances of this case. ...

CARTHY JA (concurring in the result):—I have read the reasons of Abella JA and respectfully disagree with her view as to the application of issue estoppel, although I agree as to the ultimate disposition of this appeal. ...

[O]ne of the features of issue estoppel is that the parties or their privies are the same in the present and earlier dispute. In the present case, the trial judge concluded that the appellant and respondent were parties to the proceedings under the ESA. This does not appear to be so.

As noted above, the parties to the earlier hearing were the employer, represented by his counsel, and the employment standards officer, represented by counsel from the ministry. The employee was in attendance and gave evidence but was not represented by counsel, except to the extent that the ministry was defending the earlier order. ...

The issue before this court is whether, on a policy basis, issue estoppel should apply against the appellant, notwithstanding that he was not a party to the earlier proceedings.

The ESA provisions assure employees that a wide variety of minimum standards of employment are maintained. The Act also provides for quick and efficient administrative procedures to enforce those standards. The Act does not contemplate a wide-open and time-consuming confrontation between the contestants. At the hearing stage in the present proceedings, the employment standards officer took control on behalf of the employee, presumably for the sake of efficiency and to save the employee the expense of retaining a lawyer. There is no suggestion in the prescribed procedure that the ESA purports to usurp the normal function of the courts in applying the common law, which includes full discovery and trial, and representation throughout. Section 6 is a positive statement to the contrary.

The right of discovery is not a nominal factor. In wrongful dismissal cases oral and documentary discovery can potentially change the entire texture of the factual basis for the claim or defence from what can be identified on a peremptory procedure directed at quick justice. Further, the right of personal representation is fundamental to the assertion of common law rights, and its denial, except by discretionary leave, is an indicator that common law rights are not being affected. In my view it is not a case of conflict between the function of a tribunal and the courts, or a lack of respect of one for the decision of the other. It is rather that a tribunal has been assigned its function of providing expeditious, but limited, relief and the court is left to provide the more thorough and time-consuming common law relief.

The evidence of the appellant as to the steps he took fits with my view of the intended operation of the Act. He says that he applied for unemployment insurance but found there would be an extensive waiting period because his employer indicated that he had quit his employment. He therefore applied for the limited benefits under the ESA in order to tide him over. That is what the Act appears to invite.

It would be unfair to an employee who sought out immediate and limited relief of $4,000, forsaking discovery and representation in doing so, to then say that he is bound to the result as it affects a claim for ten times that amount. Neither representation nor discovery is affordable for a $4,000 claim and that is undoubtedly why the Act provides for representation on behalf of the employee by a representative of the ministry. I would adopt the language of Lord Upjohn in *Carl-Zeiss-Stiftung*, supra, at p. 947:

> All estoppels are not odious but must be applied so as to work justice and not injustice, and I think that the principle of issue estoppel must be applied to the circumstances of the subsequent case with this overriding consideration in mind.

It is my conclusion that, in this case, it would be unfair to the appellant to consider him as so closely associated with the proceeding under the ESA as to invoke issue estoppel against his common law claim for wrongful dismissal damages. ...

Turning then to the merits of the appellant's wrongful dismissal claim, ... this employer was entitled to restructure its operations as it did, and was being perfectly fair in offering the appellant a comparable position located in Calgary with a back-up alternative of a lesser position in Toronto. The appellant's reasons for rejecting a move to Calgary may have been perfectly valid from a personal viewpoint, but they cannot be imposed upon an employer who is operating reasonably in the conduct of its business. Further, the appellant acknowledged in his evidence that the job market was very tight at the time and, having made his decision to stay in Toronto, he should have taken the alternative position to mitigate his potential loss and to provide him with an employed base from which to seek out a new position.

For these reasons I would dismiss the appeal with costs.

[The concurring judgment of Morden ACJO is omitted.]

NOTES AND QUESTIONS

1. *What degree of procedural fairness in the tribunal hearing should be required before persons who go before them are held to be estopped in litigating their claim in court?* Recall that in *Parklane Hosiery* the court said that it might be unfair to apply issue estoppel where the second action affords the party against whom the estoppel is sought procedural advantages that were unavailable in the first proceeding. The American Law Institute, *Restatement of the Law (Second), Judgments* (1982) provides as one of the exceptions to the general rule of issue preclusion in § 28(3), "A new determination of the issue is warranted by differences in the quality or extensiveness of the procedures followed in the two courts." Although not referring to these authorities, was Carthy JA in *Rasanen* essentially saying the same thing? On the issue estoppel point whose decision is preferable, that of Abella JA or that of Carthy JA?

Rasanen has spawned a body of case law applying determinations in administrative proceedings to court proceedings. Many of the cases, like *Rasanen* itself, have concerned employment-standards tribunals in Ontario and elsewhere. Several of the cases have applied *Rasanen* in the context of a finding of "misconduct" on the part of a dismissed employee by a board under the Unemployment Insurance Act (where the employee had applied for UIC and also brought an action for wrongful dismissal). In some of these decisions the judges found that the board under the Act was required to answer the same question that was raised in the wrongful dismissal action—see, for example, *Schweneke v. Ontario* (1996), 1 CPC (4th) 35 (Ont. Gen. Div.) (employee bound by unfavourable finding by Board); *Randhawa v. Everest & Jennings Canadian Ltd.* (1996), 22 CCEL (2d) 19 (Ont. Gen. Div.) (employer bound by finding, favourable to employee, that he did not quit his job and was not dismissed for cause); and *Bowen v. Ritchie Brothers Auctioneers Ltd.*, Court File no. C13081/93, December 20, 1996. Generally, these case have not seriously questioned the reasoning of the majority in *Rasanen*, but there have been exceptions.

Morden ACJO in his concurring judgment in *Rasanen* left open the possibility that deficiencies in the procedure relating to the first decision could be taken into account in determining whether to apply issue estoppel. He stated:

> I do not exclude the possibility that deficiencies in the procedure relating to the first decision could properly be a factor in deciding whether or not to apply issue estoppel. However, in this case, whatever the procedure was that governed the statutory proceeding, the appellant frankly admitted that it placed him at no disadvantage in the presentation of his case and so I do not think that the procedural aspect is relevant in this case.

In *British Columbia (Minister of Forests) v. Bugbusters Pest Mgt. Inc.* (1998), 19 CPC 1 (BC CA), the court referred to *Rasanen* but refused to apply issue estoppel to the finding of an administrative tribunal (the deputy chief forester) on the ground that (1) the parties could not reasonably expect the deputy's decision to be final, and (2) that even where the requirements of issue estoppel are satisfied, there is no automatic application; the rule is to be applied at the discretion of the court to achieve fairness and here it would be unfair to hold the Crown bound by the earlier decision.

2. *Privity, and in its absence, the question of applying non-mutual issue estoppel.* In *Rasanen* was the plaintiff a privy to the officials conducting the hearing under the Employment Standards Act? If so, why? Note that Abella JA specifically stated that because of the finding of privity it was unnecessary to consider non-mutuality, which had been argued. In his reasons in *Minott* (see the next note), Laskin JA discusses non-mutuality. What do you make of his discussion?

3. *The Ontario Court of Appeal's post-Rasanen decisions.* The law with regard to the issue estoppel effect of the decisions of administrative tribunals on court proceedings is in somewhat of a state of disarray as a result of two Ontario Court of Appeal decisions subsequent to *Rasanen*. As we have seen, in *Rasanen*, the court held that issue estoppel applied to decisions of administrative tribunals even where the procedural context of the decision making (and the procedure available to the parties) was very different from that of a court. In *Danyluk v. Ainsworth Technologies Inc.*, [1998] OJ no. 5047 (December 2, 1998), the Court of Appeal held that issue estoppel applied to a decision of an administrative tribunal, even where the procedure employed by the tribunal violated natural justice, if the litigant before the tribunal had an internal administrative right of appeal and did not exercise it. In *Minott v. O'Shanter Development Co.*, [1999] OJ no. 5 (January 7, 1999), the court held (without reference to *Danyluk*) that courts should be slow and wary to give issue estoppel effect to decisions of administrative tribunals (notwithstanding that there the unsuccessful administrative law litigant in the case before it had an internal right of appeal and did not exercise it).

Danyluk case. The facts here were similar to the facts in *Rasanen* with two differences. First, while in *Rasanen* there was no complaint of unfairness in the process before the referee, the employments standards officer, who heard Danyluk's complaints and decided against her in a material aspect of the case, acted unfairly and failed to act "judicially." Second, whereas Rasanen had exercised his internal right of review under the Employment Standards Act, Danyluk did not avail herself of the internal right of review.

The officer in *Danyluk* did not hold a conventional hearing and she did not receive oral evidence from the parties. She proceeded by speaking to Danyluk by telephone and meeting with her for an hour. Subsequently, the solicitors for the employer wrote to the officer responding to Danyluk's claim. The employer's letter included a number of documents to substantiate its position. The officer did not provide this material to Danyluk, nor did she ask Danyluk to respond to it. This, the court concluded, was a breach of the officer's administrative law obligations to act fairly and judicially.

Notwithstanding that finding, the court concluded that Danyluk faced issue estoppel with respect to the employment standard officer's decision by invoking (and extending) an administrative law doctrine that holds that the discretionary remedies of judicial review will be refused when an adequate alternative remedy exists—that is, a party may not seek judicial review of an administrative decision where the party has failed to avail itself of an internal administrative tribunal right of appeal. The court did not extensively examine whether this administrative law doctrine, developed in the context of judicial review, should be extended to the different context of giving issue estoppel effect to administrative decisions in a court action. The court simply stated that "the courts should not use their discretion to promote delay and expenditure unless there is no other way to protect a right. These policy considerations are also applicable to the present appeal."

Minott case. This involved an appeal by the defendant employer from the trial judge's decision to award the plaintiff employee, Minott, a wrongful dismissal award of $40,537.47. Minott worked in O'Shanter's maintenance department for 11 years. He was a loyal worker with a good work record. However, after a dispute with a supervisor, he took two days off without permission and received a two-day suspension. He was then fired when he did not come to work on the day after his suspension. He was 43 years old and had little formal education or skills. There was a job slump in construction. He applied for unemployment insurance (UI) benefits. The UI Board of Referees found that Minott was disqualified from receiving benefits for three weeks because he had lost his job by reason of his own conduct. Minott then sued O'Shanter for damages for wrongful dismissal. At trial, O'Shanter moved to dismiss the action on the ground of issue estoppel based on the board's finding that Minott was fired for cause. The trial judge dismissed the motion, allowed the action, and awarded damages. O'Shanter's appeal was dismissed by the Court of Appeal.

Following is part of the court's judgment written by Laskin JA (with numerous footnotes omitted). Earlier in the judgment, Laskin JA held that the board's finding did not give rise to issue estoppel because the issues were not the same in the two proceedings. The board's finding did not answer the same question that had to be answered in the wrongful dismissal action. Misconduct under the Unemployment Insurance Act and just cause for dismissal at common law did not necessarily raise the same question.

Minott v. O'Shanter Development Co.
[1999] OJ no. 5 (CA)

(iii) Were the Parties the Same?

To apply issue estoppel, the parties to the first proceeding must be the same as the parties to the second proceeding. Deciding whether this requirement has been met

causes difficulty when one of the parties to the second proceeding is entitled to participate actively in the first proceeding and to exercise fully the rights of a party in that
proceeding, but chooses not to do so. That is the case here. Although O'Shanter could
have taken part in the oral hearing before the Board of Referees, it declined to do so. In
such cases, whether a person is a party for the purpose of issue estoppel depends on its
degree of participation. Because O'Shanter did not actively participate in the hearing
before the Board of Referees, I conclude that it was not a party for the purpose of issue
estoppel.

The provisions of the *Employment Insurance Act* and the regulations passed under
it, the *Employment Insurance Regulations* ... give the employer the right to participate
at the various stages of the proceedings before the Commission, the Board of Referees
and the Umpire. The employer is entitled to notice, has the right to make representations
at the hearings, is notified of the outcome and has a right to appeal a decision of the
Commission or of the Board of Referees. ... For example, s. 83(1) of the Regulations,
which contemplates that an employer is a party, states: "A board of referees shall give
each of the parties interested in an appeal a reasonable opportunity to make representations concerning any matter before the board."

O'Shanter took no part in the proceedings before the Board of Referees, although it
received notice of Minott's appeal. O'Shanter did not appear before the Board; it did not
seek to introduce any evidence; and it made no written representations. It did, however,
file with a Commission a written statement in response to Minott's application for
benefits. This statement, to which I referred earlier, was given at the invitation of the
Commission under s. 42 of the Unemployment Insurance Act, which provided:

> 42. Where, in considering a claim for benefit, the Commission finds an indication
> from the documents relating to the claim that the loss of employment resulted from the
> claimant's own misconduct or that the claimant voluntarily left employment, the
> Commission shall
> (a) provide an opportunity to the claimant and the employer to provide
> information as to the reasons for the loss of employment; and
> (b) where any such information is provided, take it into account in
> determining the claim. ...

This statement, which said that Minott had received written warnings and had been
offered a job he could reach by public transportation, was in the Board's file on appeal
and was apparently relied on by the Board in reaching its decision. The giving of this
statement, however, was the only way that O'Shanter participated in the proceedings
before the Commission and the Board. In my view, that limited participation was not
sufficient to make O'Shanter a party for the purpose of issue estoppel.

Recent caselaw in this province suggests that a person must actively participate in
administrative proceedings to meet the "same parties" requirement of issue estoppel. In
both *Schweneke v. Ontario* (1996), 1 CPC (4th) 35 (Ont. Gen. Div.) and *Randhawa v.
Everest & Jennings Canadian Ltd.* (1996), 22 CCEL (2d) 19 (Ont. Gen. Div.), also cases
concerning proceedings under the *Unemployment Insurance Act*, the employer actively
participated in the hearing before the Umpire or the Board of Referees and was therefore
held to be a party. Similarly, in *Rasanen*, Abella JA held that the appellant, the employee,

if not a party to the proceedings under the *Employment Standards Act*, was at least a privy. She wrote:

> The appellant clearly called the witnesses he wanted, introduced the relevant evidence he needed, and had the chance to respond to the evidence and arguments against him. ... He had a meaningful voice, through his own evidence and through the assistance of the ministry, in a proceeding which decided the very issue he sought to raise in his subsequent action. ...

In contrast, in the recent case of *Wood v. Nor-Sham (Markham) Hotels Inc.* (1998), 35 CCEL (2d) 206 (Ont. Gen. Div.) Sharpe J held that an employer who chose not to contest an employee's appeal before a Board of Referees under the Act was not bound by the Board's decision in the subsequent wrongful dismissal action. As in the case before us, in *Wood* the employer had provided information about the employee's dismissal to the unemployment insurance officer adjudicating the claim for benefits. The employer, however, did not attend the hearing before the Board of Referees and instead wrote the Chairman of the Board saying it would not attend. Sharpe J held that "the letter, together with the other conduct of the employer taken as a whole, do not constitute participation in the process sufficient to render the employer bound by the Board of Referees' decision."

In their article, "Ties that Bind at Common Law: Issue Estoppel, Employment Standards and Unemployment Insurance Adjudication" (1997), 24 CCEL (2d) 291, at 310, Jeffrey Goodman and Jeff Murray accurately summarize the caselaw:

> The caselaw to date suggests that employers can avoid creating an estoppel either by not appealing a decision favourable to an employee or not attending an employee's appeal. The cases have held that by appealing or attending at an employee's appeal, the employer becomes a party to that appeal.

The recent Australian High Court case, *Australian Securities Commission v. Marlborough Gold Mines Limited* (1993), 177 CLR 485 (Aust. HC), also lends support to the need for active participation to become a party for the purpose of issue estoppel. A company had applied to the trial court for an order to summons a meeting of its members to consider a scheme to convert the company from one of limited liability to one of no liability. The Australian Securities Commission appeared and told the court that it neither consented to nor opposed the application. The order was made and a meeting was held to approve the scheme. The Commission then learned of a recent judgment suggesting that the scheme was illegal. The trial court approved the scheme and the Commission filed a notice to intervene, opposing the approval and then appealing against the approval. The Australian High Court had to consider whether issue estoppel arose in this context, estopping the Commission from its opposition. The High Court held that the Commission's appearance before the court on the application for leave to summons a meeting was not sufficient to make it a party for the purpose of issue estoppel. The High Court wrote: ...

> The fact that the Law requires that notice be given to the Commission does not make the Commission a party. Nor, in our view, does the fact that the Commission appeared to announce its attitude make it a party. That, if anything, was something done by way of making information available to the Court.

A person can be a party for one purpose and not for another. In the present case, O'Shanter provided information to the Commission. By doing so it did not become a party for the purpose of issue estoppel. In addition to the caselaw, I think that policy considerations justify focussing on the degree of participation to determine whether an employer in O'Shanter's position is a party for the purpose of issue estoppel. Holding that an employer who merely provides information to an insurance officer becomes a party and thus bound by the Commission's or the Board's findings could turn a right to participate into a practical obligation to do so. Ordinarily, employers do not appear on applications for unemployment insurance benefits or even on appeals because the stakes are small and they do not have a direct financial interest in the outcome, although they may be liable under s. 46(1) of the Act to repay any benefits received by an employee who subsequently succeeds in a wrongful dismissal action. Thus, to give employers in O'Shanter's position party status for the purpose of issue estoppel would provide a perverse incentive for employers to participate actively in hearings before the Board of Referees or before an Umpire.

Implicit in this discussion is my rejection of any notion of non-mutual issue estoppel. The doctrine of non-mutual issue estoppel, which was not argued before us, has roots in American jurisprudence. ... It permits a judgment to operate in favour of a non-party. Applied here, it might permit an employer to refrain from participating in a hearing before a Board of Referees yet rely on a favourable Board decision in a subsequent wrongful dismissal action. By adopting a "wait and see" approach to the Board's decision, an employer could rely on issue estoppel if the employee lost, but be no worse off if the employee won, because issue estoppel could not be applied against an employer who had not had its day in court. Applying non-mutual issue estoppel would allow the employer to "have it both ways." In my view, in these cases issue estoppel should be mutual ... . An employer should only be able to invoke issue estoppel for a favourable decision if issue estoppel could also be invoked against it for an unfavourable decision. I do not consider O'Shanter bound by the Board's decision any more than I consider it would have been bound in the wrongful dismissal action had Minott succeeded in his appeal before the Board of Referees. O'Shanter was not a party for the purpose of issue estoppel and the third requirement is therefore not satisfied.

I have concluded that the Board's finding of misconduct under the Act does not satisfy the first and third requirements of issue estoppel. Therefore the Board's finding did not prevent Minott from maintaining his action for wrongful dismissal. Even had the three requirements been met, however, in my view the court has always retained discretion to refuse to apply issue estoppel when to do so would cause unfairness or work an injustice. As Lord Upjohn observed in *Carl Zeiss Stiftung v. Rayner Keeler Ltd.*, [1967] 1 AC 853, at 947, "[a]ll estoppels are not odious but must be applied so as to work justice and not injustice, and I think the principle of issue estoppel must be applied to the circumstances of the subsequent case with this overriding consideration in mind."

Issue estoppel is a rule of public policy and, as a rule of public policy, it seeks to balance the public interest in the finality of litigation with the private interest in achieving justice between litigants. Sometimes these two interests will be in conflict, or at least there will be tension between them. Judicial discretion is required to achieve practical justice without undermining the principles on which issue estoppel is founded. Issue estoppel should be applied flexibly where an unyielding application of it would be unfair to a party who is precluded from relitigating an issue.

That the courts have always exercised this discretion is apparent from the authorities. For example, courts have refused to apply issue estoppel in "special circumstances," which include a change in the law or the availability of further relevant material. If the decision of a court on a point of law in an earlier proceeding is shown to be wrong by a later judicial decision, issue estoppel will not prevent relitigating that issue in subsequent proceedings. It would be unfair to do otherwise. In *Arnold v. National Westminster Bank plc*, [1991] 3 All ER 41, at 50 (HL), Lord Keith wrote:

> ... there may be an exception to issue estoppel in the special circumstance that there has become available to a party further material relevant to the correct determination of a point involved in the earlier proceedings, whether or not that point was specifically raised and decided, being material which could not by reasonable diligence have been adduced in those proceedings. One of the purposes of estoppel being to work justice between the parties, it is open to courts to recognize that in special circumstances inflexible application of it may have the opposite result. ...

Applying issue estoppel to the findings of an administrative tribunal to foreclose a subsequent civil proceeding may also be unfair or work an injustice. Its application to findings made in proceedings under the Employment Insurance Act is a good example. Looking at legislative intent, nothing either in the scheme of the Act or in its individual provisions suggests, for example, that the finding of misconduct by a Board of Referees or by an Umpire is binding in a civil action for wrongful dismissal. Issue estoppel is a common law rule and therefore the courts must consider the appropriateness of applying it to the findings of a tribunal under the Act to prevent those finding from being relitigated in a subsequent action for wrongful dismissal.

In my opinion, invoking issue estoppel for the findings of a Board of Referees or of an Umpire raises several concerns. Some of these concerns are alleviated by holding that the "same parties" requirement turns on the employer's degree of participation. But issue estoppel affects employees as well as employers and thus other concerns remain, which I will discuss briefly.

First, the scheme of the Act contemplates that claims for unemployment insurance benefits be adjudicated quickly, inexpensively and summarily. To inject issue estoppel into these claims adjudications would undermine the aim of the legislative scheme. [See also N. Grosman, "No Estoppel" (April 1997), 7 EMP Bul. 2.] Employers and employees may overlitigate these adjudications, hire lawyers unnecessarily or pursue appeals they might not otherwise take out of fear of the consequences in later civil litigation. As Molloy J [the trial judge in *Minott*] sensibly observed:

> If the decisions of Boards of Referees as to misconduct are held to always be determinative of whether there has been cause for dismissal at common law, it will be necessary for employees to retain counsel and litigate before the Board in the same manner as before a court ina wrongful dismissal action. This would not be a desirable result for any of the parties involved, including the administrative board itself which would soon find its expeditious summary process clogged with parties litigating their civil causes of action.

Second, employees apply for benefits when they are most vulnerable, immediately after losing their job. The urgency with which they must invariably seek relief compromises their ability to adequately put forward their case for benefits or to respond to the case against them. [See *Restatement of the Law (Second), Judgments*, 2d (1982), s. 83(2)(e).] Applying issue estoppel may therefore cause real injustice to an aggrieved employee. As Langdon J noted in *Hough v. Brunswick Centres*, "[t]o become unemployed is a fairly universal experience in modern days. It is an almost automatic reaction for anyone who is terminated or laid off to file for benefits. One does not do so with the thought in mind that if one loses one's claim, one is at risk of having all legal remedies foreclosed."...

Third, the financial stakes in an application for unemployment insurance benefits are typically insignificant compared to the financial stakes in an action for wrongful dismissal. [*Restatement*, at 279.] Here, before the Board of Referees, only a few weeks of benefits were at stake, but in the wrongful dismissal action $40,000 was at stake. As Sharpe J observed in *Randhawa* [above], "there may well be situations where one would hesitate to apply the doctrine of issue estoppel where a party participated in an administrative hearing having insignificant consequences and the result of that hearing was then raised later in a suit which had enormous consequences." To apply issue estoppel in such a case may be as unfair to the employer as to the employee.

Fourth, the procedural differences between a hearing under the Act and a civil action for wrongful dismissal may cause a court to exercise its discretion against applying issue estoppel. The Restatement (Second) of Judgments sets out several exceptions to the application of issue estoppel. [See *Restatement*, para. 28, "Exceptions to the General Rule of Issue Preclusion."] One exception recognizes that procedural differences in the two proceedings may be a sufficient reason not to apply issue estoppel. Section 28(3) of the Restatement states that "a new determination of the issue is warranted by differences in the quality or extensiveness of the procedures followed in the two courts ... ." Morden ACJO expressed a similar view in his concurring judgment in *Rasanen* when he said "I do not exclude the possibility that deficiencies in the procedure relating to the first decision could properly be a factor in deciding whether or not to apply issue estoppel." In *Rasanen* itself, Morden ACJO held that the tribunal procedures were sufficient to apply issue estoppel. Carthy JA, dissenting on this point, held that they were insufficient.

Procedural differences should be looked at in practical terms. In the present case, Minott did not have a prehearing discovery. Although he had limited formal education, he appeared before the Board of Referees unrepresented, led no evidence, called no witnesses and had no opportunity to build his case through cross-examination. His claim failed because the Board had in its file, and apparently acted on, information from O'Shanter later proved incorrect in the wrongful dismissal action. I do not say that the procedures before the Board of Referees were deficient. They may have been appropriate for the purpose of the Act and for the summary determination of the disqualification period to be made by the Board, but entirely inappropriate for the determination in the wrongful dismissal action of Minott's claim for damages and of O'Shanter's defence of just cause.

Finally, the expertise of the Board of Referees is quite different from the expertise needed to decide a wrongful dismissal action. The Board of Referees must consider misconduct in the context of a claim for unemployment insurance not in the context of a dispute between an employer and an employee over just cause. [See *Re Toronto Police Services Board and Toronto Police Association* (1998), 71 LAC (4th) 289, at 306-7.]

Because I take the view that O'Shanter has not met all of the three basic require-ments of issue estoppel, I need not invoke discretion to hold that the Board's finding of misconduct does not prevent Minott from maintaining his action for wrongful dismissal. Had I concluded otherwise, however, I would have been prompted by the concerns that I have listed to exercise my discretion to refuse to apply issue estoppel to the finding of misconduct made by the Board of Referees. I do not intend by anything I have said to undermine the role of the tribunals under the Employment Insurance Act. They play a vital role because they decide entitlement to benefits that are of great importance to many workers. But because of the very different characteristics of decision making under the Act, the findings of these tribunals should not automatically be imported into a subsequent civil action. I would not give effect to this ground of appeal.

QUESTION

Was the court in *Minott* effectively overruling *Rasanen*?

IV. JOINDER OF CLAIMS AND PARTIES

A lawsuit in its simplest form involves a single plaintiff asserting a single claim against a single defendant. However, few cases assume that simple form. Most situations are more complex. In this part, the rules governing the extent to which a lawsuit can be expanded or confined within particular limits are examined. The first section looks to the ways in which a plaintiff can (or must) add multiple claims and parties. The second section explores the ways in which a defendant can expand the size of the litigation by claiming relief against the plaintiff (counterclaims), against other defendants (cross-claims) or against an entirely new party (third-party claims). The last section considers the circum-stances in which separate actions can be united in the proceeding (consolidation).

The essential starting point in any discussion of joinder is the proposition that, in general, the interests of society and of the litigants are better served by one lawsuit than by several. It is usually more economical—for the litigants and for the court system—to litigate matters in one action than in numerous separate actions. For example, in most cases the trial in a single action of all the matters in dispute between the parties will take less time, trouble, and money than several actions. Thus, the gain to be derived from broad joinder is the convenience and utility of settling all differences between parties at the one time. There is a further factor that will often favour a single action rather than a multiplicity of actions. It is that frequently there will arise situations in which, if the plaintiff is required to bring separate actions, there will be the risk of inconsistent verdicts in the different actions, both adverse to the plaintiff, and finish with no recovery at all, whereas had the plaintiff brought one action asserting all of the claims he or she would have succeeded against someone. The possibility of inconsistent verdicts is viewed by the law as something to be avoided.

This general policy in favour of a single action rather than a multiplicity of actions is implemented, *inter alia*, by (1) rules making generous provision for the joinder of multiple claims and parties, (2) a rule that prohibits the splitting of a cause of action (the principle of *res judicata*), and (3) the practice of allowing either party to obtain consolidation or the trial of actions together. However, the policy in favour of joinder of claims and parties is not an absolute one. An unlimited right of joinder could lead to confusion and complexity, a situation that would result if too many and possibly diverse issues were attempted to be litigated in one action. Consequently, the court has a broad discretion to refuse to permit claims or parties to be joined in the same action. This is a discretion that will be exercised when it is demonstrated that fairness and trial convenience favour separate actions rather than a single action.

Though not always the case, progressive amendment and continuing reformulation of the modern joinder rules allow parties and actions to be joined in almost any circumstances, leaving the court with a residual discretion to forbid joinder if it would lead to inconvenience or injustice. In the following sections, the emphasis is upon explaining the situations in which the different mechanisms for joinder might be utilized and locating the limits that ought to be respected if the litigation is not to become so unwieldy and complex as to defeat the general objectives (efficiency and justice) that led to expansive joinder rules in the first place.

A. Addition of Claims and Parties by the Plaintiff

1. Introduction

In this subsection, we look specifically at the scope of the plaintiff's option to increase the size of litigation beyond the simple situation of one plaintiff asserting one claim against one defendant. The plaintiff may do this (1) by uniting multiple claims against one defendant in one action (joinder of claims); (2) by uniting multiple plaintiffs or multiple defendants or *both* in an action (joinder of parties); or (3) by uniting both multiple claims and multiple parties. Thus, in its most elaborate form, joinder may result in multiple plaintiffs suing multiple defendants concerning multiple claims.

The major issue is how far plaintiffs may go in joining multiple claims and parties in one action when they believe such joinder, referred to as permissive joinder, is desirable. In other words, what limits are there on the maximum size of the litigation expanded by the plaintiffs using permissive joinder? We will see that the rules of procedure and the courts tend to be very liberal in allowing permissive joinder. Why is this? When courts do confine joinder, is a consistent guideline applied?

There is also a less obvious issue concerning not the maximum but rather the minimum size of the litigation. As we will see, rules exist that may compel a plaintiff in a narrow range of circumstances to join multiple parties and to assert multiple claims. When a plaintiff is required to join either parties or claims or both, this is referred to as compulsory joinder. How can requiring a plaintiff to add certain parties or claims be reconciled with party control of litigation, one of the hallmarks of the adversary system?

At common law, quite restrictive rules prevailed regarding the joinder of multiple claims and multiple parties. For an account of these rules see James and Hazard, *Civil*

Procedure, 3d ed. (1985), at 462-65 and 469-70 and Louisell and Hazard, *Cases and Materials on Pleading and Procedure*, 4th ed. (Mineola, NY: Foundation Press, 1979), at 540-42. In the following pages, we will concern ourselves only with the modern rules on the subject.

2. Joinder of Multiple Claims

a. *Permissive Joinder*

See Ontario rules 5.01 and 5.05. Other examples are BC rule 5(1), Man. rule 5.01, NB rule 5.01, NS rule 5.01, and Sask. rule 35.

Foley v. Signtech Inc.
(1989), 66 OR (2d) 729 (Ont. HC)

GRANGER J: The defendants appeal from Master Garfield's order dated July 7, 1988, dismissing their motion to strike out paras. 1(b), 17 and 18 of the plaintiffs' statement of claim on the ground that such paragraphs are a claim for damages for defamation or loss of reputation which should not be joined with a claim for wrongful dismissal. The plaintiffs appeal those parts of the order which require particulars of the claim in para. 17 and strike either of subparas. 1(d) and (e) as being redundant.

The plaintiffs had been employed by Signtech Inc. for periods ranging from 8 to 21 months before their termination without notice during December, 1987. The plaintiffs allege that as a result of their termination without notice or cause they have suffered loss of remuneration and have been denied the right to enhance their reputation in their field of endeavour. The plaintiffs also allege in para. 17 that the defendants made false and malicious allegations against the plaintiffs:

> 17. The defendant Candy and other representatives and agents of the defendant Signtech Inc., in dismissing the plaintiffs, falsely and maliciously accused them of being involved in the alleged disappearances of a large quantity of inventory.
>
> 18. In making this allegation, the defendants have irreparably damaged the reputations of the plaintiffs and have effectively precluded them from finding other equivalent employment.

Master Garfield held that para. 17 was "not a combination of a claim for wrongful dismissal and one for defamation," but rather a claim for loss of reputation, and following *Makkar v. City of Scarborough* (1985), 48 CPC 141 (Ont. HCJ), was properly joined with a claim for wrongful dismissal.

The defendants in their appeal raise three issues for determination:

1. Can damages for loss of reputation resulting from the termination itself be claimed in an action for wrongful dismissal?

2. Are the plaintiffs asserting a claim for defamation resulting from statements made by the defendants to third parties, in the guise of a claim for loss of reputation?

3. Can a claim for defamation be joined with a claim for wrongful dismissal?

Issue 1

. . .

[Grainger J referred to older cases, from the House of Lords and the Supreme Court of Canada, holding (the defendants argued) that claims for loss of reputation and wrongful dismissal cannot be joined. In fact, as later cases have pointed out, those cases were not really concerned with joinder at all, but with the different question of whether damages for loss of reputation *were recoverable as a head of damages* in a claim for wrongful dismissal. The older cases held that they were not but the case law now permits such recovery in appropriate circumstances. Grainger J concluded.]

[P]leadings should only be struck in the clearest of cases. If the master was correct in his understanding that the claim was a claim for loss of reputation as opposed to a claim for defamation, then in view of the conflicting case-law in this area, he was correct in allowing the claim to stand.

Issue 2

... Quite clearly, the plaintiffs' allegation that the defendants' conduct in discussing the circumstances of the plaintiffs' dismissal falls outside the ambit of a claim for loss of reputation that may ordinarily flow from a dismissal. It is squarely within the definition of defamation.

Issue 3

... The defendants rely on a number of cases in support of their proposition that a claim for wrongful dismissal cannot be joined with one for defamation: *Baker v. Weller* (1981), 10 ACWS (2d) 278 (Ont. Master's Ch.); *Braun v. Fleisher* (1983), 2 CCEL 305 (Ont. Div. Ct.); *Kelly v. American Airlines Inc.* (1981), 32 OR (2d) 626 (HCJ), and *Rotenberg v. Rosenberg*, [1964] 1 OR 160 (Masters' Ch.).

The bases for these decisions appear to be that because loss of reputation claims cannot be tried with wrongful dismissal then defamation, which is closely related to loss of reputation, cannot survive either; and the now eroded principle, that wrongful dismissal cases cannot be tried by a jury. ...

In my view, it is obvious that the principles of *Addis, supra*, have been eroded to a significant extent. Properly instructed, juries are fully capable of considering and dealing with several issues. Given the tremendous expense and protracted nature of litigation today it appears to me to be nonsensical to sever these two claims.

If the defendants' position is upheld there will be two separate trials arising from the same facts. I am convinced that a trier of fact whether it be a judge or jury is capable of dealing with this action as framed.

The prohibition against joining a claim for defamation and wrongful dismissal is no longer valid and should be disregarded, as was the prohibition against joining a claim for loss of reputation and wrongful dismissal, in order to minimize the costs of the litigation.

In most cases employers are better able financially to withstand the financial strain of litigation and to require an employee to finance two separate trials would be unfair, and in many cases preclude the employee making a legitimate claim.

Accordingly, the defendants' appeal is dismissed. The defendants are entitled to particulars of the plaintiffs' claim as set out in para. 17 in order to properly prepare for discovery and trial. The plaintiffs' cross-appeal is dismissed. Costs of both appeals reserved to the trial judge.

NOTES AND QUESTIONS

1. What procedural objectives were served by permitting Foley to join the claims relating to his dismissal and the defamation claim? Are there any disadvantages? How can the disadvantages be overcome? Consider Ontario rule 5.05.

2. *Joining claims that may cause prejudice.* In some relatively rare circumstances a defendant can make a credible argument that joining claim B with claim A will prejudice the defendant in his defence of claim B—see, for example, *Heider v. Levine*, [1955] OWN 936 (the court held improper the joinder of a claim for indecent assault with one for breach of contract, although a causal connection between the two was alleged); *Sporn v. Hudson Transit Lines*, 265 App. Div. 360, 38 NYS 2d 512 (NY 1942) (the plaintiffs, the driver of a car and his passengers, joined claims that each of them had against the defendant bus company for personal injuries sustained in a collision between the car and the bus allegedly due to the negligent operation of the bus, with a claim by one of them, the driver, for malicious prosecution; the basis of the second claim was that following the accident the defendant had maliciously caused the arrest of the driver for reckless driving; joinder was held to be improper). Are the decisions in *Sporn* and *Heider* justifiable? Contrast the following statement by Friedenthal, "Joinder of Claims, Counterclaims and Cross-Complaints: Suggested Revision of the California Provisions," 23 *Stanford Law Review* 1, at 5-6.:

> Any undesirable effects resulting from unlimited joinder of causes can be remedied by a severance of causes for trial. Joinder of causes, in and of itself, is never harmful. A joint trial of causes may be unjustified, however, either because the trial may become too complex for rational decision, or because evidence introduced on one cause may so tend to prejudice the trier of fact that it will be unlikely to render a fair decision on another cause.

3. *Joinder and relief against joinder.* As the *Foley* case illustrates, the rules regarding the joinder of multiple claims by a plaintiff are extremely broad. Under the rules the plaintiff may join any number of claims against the same defendant, subject to the power of the court to exclude or to direct separate trials in respect of any causes of action that cannot be conveniently disposed of together. Essentially, the question is determined on the basis of fairness and convenience and it involves a balancing of interests. On the one hand, the court seeks to avoid prejudice to the defendant by joinder of multiple causes of action. On the other hand, it seeks to avoid putting the plaintiff to unwarranted expense by forcing separate proceedings where the claims could more conveniently and less expensively be tried together.

When the court exercises its power it will usually simply order separate trials of the plaintiff's claim rather than total exclusion of some of the claims from the plaintiff's action. (But note the decisions in *Sporn* and *Heider*.) If the court orders claims initially joined to be excluded, then the plaintiff is forced to abandon these claims altogether or to assert them in a separate action. However, where separate trials are ordered, all the claims remain in the action and the separation takes place only at the trial stage. That is, instead of there being one trial at which all the claims will be tried and determined, separate trials on the different claims will take place. Usually the issue of whether or not there should be separate trials is left to the trial judge to decide.

b. *Compulsory Joinder*

Usually it is said that the plaintiff is free to assert any or all claims against a defendant but there is no obligation to do so. This is true in the sense that a court will not, in a particular action, force a plaintiff to assert any particular claim. But recall the treatment of *res judicata*. Is it not in policy and consequence designed to require joinder of claims?

It is in the sense illustrated by the *Las Vegas* case that *res judicata* can operate as compulsory joinder of claims. Failure to join a claim in an action does not prevent the plaintiff from proceeding with the action. However, *res judicata* may operate to bar any other related claims from ever being asserted in any other proceedings and it, therefore, places the onus on the plaintiff to ensure that all relevant issues and aspects of a claim or claims are argued in the one proceeding or to suffer the consequences.

3. Joinder of Multiple Parties

a. *Permissive Joinder*

Here our concern is with the maximum size of the litigation. In terms of parties, how large may the plaintiff make the litigation through joinder of multiple plaintiffs or defendants? This issue arises regularly since it is a common occurrence for a number of plaintiffs to wish to join together in bringing an action, or for one or more plaintiffs to seek to sue multiple defendants.

The rules relating to the joinder of multiple plaintiffs and defendants in one action are very broad and permissive. But such joinder is not unlimited. Multiple joinder of either plaintiffs or defendants is only proper if the conditions set out in the applicable rules of practice, as interpreted by the courts, are met. Even if the joinder attempted in a particular case satisfies the requirements of the appropriate rule, the court has a broad discretion to order separate trials where fairness and convenience so require.

Multiple plaintiffs. See Ontario rules 5.02(1) and 5.05. Other examples are Alta. rule 36, BC rule 5.02, Man. rule 5.02, NB rule 5.03(1), NS rule 5.02, and PEI rule 5.02(1).

Typical cases in which joinder of multiple plaintiffs would be proper occur where the defendant owes an obligation jointly to numerous plaintiffs—for example, where the plaintiffs are partners who have entered into a contract with the defendant that they allege has been broken—and cases in which a number of persons are injured as a result of an automobile accident—for example, where three persons travelling in a car are all injured in a collision. In what way does the automobile accident case just described satisfy the conditions of the rules concerning joinder? What policy objectives justify joinder of the claims of several plaintiffs injured in an automobile accident in one action? Consider the following statement of the policy relating to joinder (*per* Fletcher Moulton LJ, in *Markt & Co. Ltd. v. Knight Steamship Co. Ltd.*, [1910] 2 KB 1021, at 1037):

> Judgment may be given for such of the plaintiffs as succeed, and the defendant is protected with regard to the costs which relate to the plaintiffs who are unsuccessful. This makes it clear that (subject to the control of the Court) persons can unite as plaintiffs, though seeking individual relief, in cases where the investigation would to a great extent be identical in each individual case.
>
> The policy of the rule is to avoid needless expense where it can be done without doing injustice to any one. And it carries out its object. No plaintiff can complain, for he cannot be made a plaintiff without his consent, so that if he avails himself of the rule it is because he desires to do so. The defendant has no cause to complain, because the plaintiffs are liable for his costs if he succeeds, and he has just the same rights in the action against each plaintiff as if a separate action had been brought against him by that plaintiff.

NOTES AND QUESTIONS

1. *Tactical consequences.* There are some tactical considerations to be borne in mind by a plaintiff contemplating bringing suit with other co-plaintiffs including liability for costs, possible conflict of interest or division of opinion, the possible delay and expense that might result from the defendant's counterclaiming against a co-plaintiff or bringing in a third party with reference to the co-plaintiff's claim, and the possible prejudice resulting from discovery of a co-plaintiff. To these may be added the consideration that all the plaintiffs have to be represented by the same counsel (see Ontario rule 5.02(1)).

2. In *Bath v. Birnstihl* (1975), 11 OR (2d) 770 (HC), more than 100 plaintiffs joined in one action claiming return of the moneys paid by each of them, together with general damages for breach of contract, for a package tour holiday to Acapulco that they alleged went badly wrong—for example, inferior, as opposed to the promised first-class hotels and sewage in the swimming pool. In situations like the *Bath* case, where a large number of plaintiffs wish to sue, an alternative to joinder of plaintiffs may now be a class action in which one or a few persons sue on behalf of themselves and all others similarly affected by the defendant's conduct. Such a procedure can be particularly useful where the persons affected by the conduct are so numerous as to defy ascertainment—for example, where an industrial plant has been illegally discharging pollutants over a wide metropolitan area or where a publicly regulated telephone company or bus company has been overcharging users of its services. The subject of class actions is taken up in a subsequent part of this chapter.

3. *Multiple defendants.* See Ontario rules 5.02(2) and 5.05. Other examples are Alta. rule 36, 39, Man. rule 50.2(2), NB rule 5.03(2), NS rule 5.02, PEI rule 5.02, and Sask. rule 37(2).

Garry D. Watson, "Joinder of Defendants Sued in the Alternative: Solicitors as Co-Defendants"
(1981), 2 *Advocates' Quarterly* 365

Joinder of multiple defendants is permitted for two basic policy reasons; reasons which underlie many civil procedural rules: economy and justice. Typically, in most cases where joinder is sought both policies will be operative. However, as we will see, this will not always be so.

Economy. A plaintiff is permitted to join multiple defendants to achieve a saving of time and costs, both to himself and to the court, through the avoidance of a multiplicity of actions where there are questions of law or fact common to the claims asserted. This is *one* of the policies which justifies, for example, the most common instance of multiple joinder of defendants—that of several defendants sued in respect of the plaintiff's injuries incurred in an automobile accident. To require the plaintiff to sue each defendant separately would involve the plaintiff in additional costs and would require the court to go over much of the same area twice.

Justice and the risk of inconsistent determination. Economy (or convenience) is not the only policy underlying multiple joinder. There is a second and, it is submitted, a more important one: to assure that justice is done by avoiding the risk of inconsistent determinations. This risk arises because, under the traditional rules of *res judicata*, only the parties to the litigation (and privies) are bound thereby. Hence, if P sues D1 and is unsuccessful because the court concludes that the injuries were a result not of the negligence of D, but rather of the negligence of D2 (who is not a party), and P then turns around and sues D2, D2 is in no way bound by the "decision" in the first action that his negligence caused the plaintiff's injuries. He is completely free to relitigate the question and, moreover, to blame the accident on D1's negligence. A major reason for allowing the joinder of multiple defendants is to spare the plaintiff this risk of inconsistent determinations: to force both defendants where the plaintiff is in doubt as to the persons from whom he is entitled to relief to defend in one action. A primary purpose of multiple joinder of defendants is to get D2 bound by the decision as against D1, and *vice-versa*. It stops D1 from blaming D2 in D2's absence, and then D2 blaming D1 in Dl's absence (or, put more generally, it stops the second defendant from questioning the underlying basis of the decision in favour of the first defendant) which may leave the plaintiff unjustly uncompensated.

The second policy is arguably the more important of the two because it involves a more significant value. It is concerned not merely with convenience and economy, but with justice in terms of the ultimate outcome. It assures that a fair and proper result is achieved and that if the plaintiff is to lose he does so on the merits, rather than as a result of procedural manoeuvering. However, the existence and importance of the second policy is often overlooked, for several reasons. In most cases the two policies favouring joinder will be operative where multiple joinder is sought. This is because the existence of a common question of law or fact normally invokes both policies: it will usually make it convenient to try the claims together and it will present the plaintiff with the risk of inconsistent determinations if joinder is disallowed. Moreover, the economy-convenience policy is the more obvious of the two and the one most often referred to. Recognition of the second policy has been somewhat obscured by the judge-made rule which has emerged in Ontario as the test for the propriety of multiple joinder of defendants: "it depends upon convenience and the existence of a common question of law or fact." This formulation, while it makes overt reference to convenience (economy), makes no explicit reference to the second policy.

The following cases were decided under the earlier Ontario rules. What rules would now apply? Would joinder be easier to justify under the present rules?

Thomas W. Sayle Transport Ltd. v. Rivers
[1955] OWN 321 (SC)

An application by the defendant Prentice for an order compelling the plaintiff to elect.

MARRIOTT, SENIOR MASTER: It is alleged by the plaintiff company in its statement of claim that its tractor-trailor was forced off the highway and into the ditch by the negligent act of the defendant Allair, driving a car owned by the defendant Rivers, with consequent damage to the plaintiff's vehicle. It is further claimed by the plaintiff that the defendant Prentice, who operates a garage near the scene of the accident, orally contracted with the plaintiff to pull its vehicle back onto the highway, and that while he was in the process of doing so the tractor-trailor rolled back into the ditch and sustained further damage. The plaintiff claims damages of $2,000 to the vehicle against all the defendants and states that it is unable to distinguish how much damage was sustained by reason of each event.

This application is by the defendant Prentice for an order requiring the plaintiff to elect against whom it will proceed, on the ground that it has no right to join these two causes of action, against different defendants, in one action. Counsel relies on [former] Rules 67, 68, 69 and 73 and numerous decisions thereunder. In support of the application an affidavit is filed by the applicant wherein he says that in his opinion the damage caused by his negligence did not exceed $200. This is denied by counsel for the plaintiff and I think it is clear that it is a matter of controversy.

First, there is no doubt that if there were no issue as to the respective responsibility of each defendant (treating Rivers and Allair as one defendant) for the damage suffered by the plaintiff, there would be no justification for the joinder of these two distinct and separate causes of action. However, that issue is raised and I do not see how it can be fairly adjudicated upon in the absence of either defendant. If the action proceeds as constituted the Court can first determine the amount of the total damage suffered by the plaintiff and by weighing the evidence respecting the damage caused by each event, proceed to apportion the responsibility against the respective defendants. In this way the plaintiff will be fully compensated. If separate actions are brought there is no assurance that this will be the result. There might be a tendency for the defendant in each action to blame the absent defendant, and it might be difficult for the Court to determine the true extent of the liability of each defendant, resulting possibly in inconsistent verdicts:

Rodway v. Williams (1929), 37 OWN 116. One cannot say that in proceeding in this fashion there may not be some inconvenience and extra expense caused to the applicant and perhaps to the other defendants, but I am of the view that this is outweighed by the primary consideration of getting at the truth of the matter and thereby doing justice to the parties. If it appears at the trial that the plaintiff had no substantial reason for proceeding as it has done the trial judge can compensate the defendants by an adjustment of the costs: see *Canadian Steel Corporation Ltd. v. Standard Lithographic Co. Ltd. et al.*, [1933] OR 624. This being my conclusion on the merits, is there anything in the Rules or authorities to preclude the Court from allowing the plaintiff to proceed in this manner? I do not think so. The plaintiff "is in doubt as to the person from whom [it] is entitled to redress," in the sense that it does not know the extent of the liability of each of the defendants, and therefore comes within Rule 67. As to the authorities, the precise point in question does not appear to have been dealt with in any reported decision. However, Scrutton LJ said in *Payne v. British Time Recorder Company, Limited et al.*, [1921] 2 KB 1, at p. 16, that where there are common questions of law or fact involved in different causes of action the Court has a discretion to allow the joinder. Here it is to be noted that there is a common question of fact which, it appears, cannot be properly adjudicated upon in the absence of any of the defendants. This circumstance distinguishes this case from those relied upon by counsel and warrants the Court in exercising its discretion and allowing the joinder, bearing in mind the fact that the plaintiff has brought itself within Rule 67, as already mentioned.

For these reasons the plaintiff should be allowed to proceed with its action as constituted. It may be feasible, following the provisions of Rule 73, to direct that the issues between the plaintiff and each defendant as to negligence and contractual liability respectively be tried separately and that the issue as to damages be tried jointly, subject, of course, to the discretion of the trial judge, and that this separation of issues be followed on the examinations for discovery, in order to minimize embarrassment, expense and inconvenience to the parties.

For the above reasons the application will be dismissed. Costs will be reserved to be dealt with by the trial judge.

Application dismissed.

Pryshlack v. Urbancic
(1975), 10 OR (2d) 263 (HC)

LERNER J: This is an application by the defendant Roy M. Kostuk, a solicitor, for an order striking out the statement of claim and dismissing the action as against him or, in the alternative, perpetually staying the action on the grounds that the statement of claim discloses no cause of action and that the action is frivolous and vexatious as it relates to him.

The plaintiff, as the vendor of his residential home, sued the defendant Urbancic, as the purchaser for damages for failing to complete the transaction. He also sued Kostuk, his own solicitor in the aborted transaction, for damages for (a) acting outside his authority,

(b) without the plaintiff's instructions, and (c) for negligence in failing to protect the plaintiff's rights of action against Urbancic. The plaintiff did not claim in the alternative for specific performance against the defendant Urbancic.

The decision herein is, of necessity, based solely on allegations of fact found in the statement of claim, the statement of defence of Urbancic and the particulars provided through the demand of the defendant Kostuk who has, as yet, not filed and served a statement of defence.

The pleadings and particulars are, *ad idem*, that Urbancic, as purchaser, refused or was unable to complete the purchase because of lack of funds. The statement of claim could hardly be classed as an example of good pleading.

[The plaintiff's allegations against his solicitor included that the solicitor had failed to make proper tender at the closing and failed to make a proper election on behalf of the plaintiff to preserve his right of action for damages against the purchaser Urbancic. The defendant Urbancic filed a statement of defence putting the plaintiff's claim "seriously in issue" alleging, among other things that the "plaintiff failed to make tender and was not ready willing and able to close" and "chose to treat the agreement at an end and attempted to resell the property at his own risk."]

Before the plaintiff can maintain any action against the defendant solicitor, he must establish that he suffered damages as the result of the defendant's failure as purchaser to complete the sale. As stated earlier, the defendant purchaser raised what I consider to be real issues going directly to the plaintiff's right to recover quite apart from any alleged loss to the plaintiff on the basis of the allegations made against his solicitor as a defendant in the statement of claim or any other ground.

I refrain from being too specific because I would not want to prejudice the position of any of the parties if the action proceeds further. Those issues are of such a nature they might very well not involve the solicitor. It may be that the plaintiff could have made out a case for specific performance and by his election chose to claim damages. Furthermore, was the plaintiff ready, willing and able to close the transaction? If the defendant purchaser clearly indicated that he would not complete the transaction, the formal tender by the plaintiff might not be necessary, depending on the circumstances.

I am not unmindful that multiplicity of proceedings is to be discouraged. The allegations raised by the plaintiff in his statement of claim do not make that proposition a matter to be considered in this action. The priority with respect to these allegations is whether the trial should be confused by premature issues between the plaintiff and the defendant solicitor. It is a consideration whether a litigant should be put to his defence for an anticipated claim. …

There is another basis for my conclusion. The claims against the solicitor and the proposed purchaser are not based on the same allegations of fact (*e.g.*, as in a damage action arising out of a motor vehicle collision involving several defendants). Nor are the claims on the same legal premise. It is trite to say that different causes of action against different parties cannot be joined in the same proceedings. The plaintiff's claims against the defendant solicitor are founded in negligence in carrying out duties of his retainer and secondly, that he acted outside his authority as the plaintiff's agent. Negligence and failure to carry out his duties as a solicitor, in a sense, are a breach of contract but not that kind of breach alleged against the defendant purchaser, which are for breach of contract to complete a purchaser of land. ...

[A discussion of authorities is omitted.]

[It may be that] the plaintiff as vendor may have a cause of action against his own solicitor. If the solicitor Kostuk, as a defendant, negotiated a settlement for $1,000 without his client's authority but the third party (the purchaser) was not aware of the lack of authority, the result of the negotiations between the solicitor and third party might be binding upon the plaintiff but he could still have recourse against his solicitor.

Were it not for the fact that I have found that there are distinct and separate causes of action against both defendants, the proper disposition of this case may have been to stay the action against the defendant solicitor until the action against his co-defendant had been concluded. But since I have concluded that there are two separate causes of action against different parties, it would be incongruous to stay the action against the solicitor. Therefore, to be consistent, an order will go dismissing the action as against the defendant solicitor Kostuk, without prejudice to the plaintiff's right to bring such further or other proceedings as he may be advised against this defendant. The defendant Kostuk will therefore have his costs of the action and of his motion forthwith after taxation.

NOTES AND QUESTIONS

1. Was *Pryshlack* correctly decided? What distinguishes *Pryshlack* from *Sayle*? What do you think motivated the plaintiffs to join both defendants in one action? Is it "trite to say that different causes of action against different parties cannot be joined in the same proceedings"? What provisions in the applicable rules would you rely on if representing a plaintiff who sought joinder in a case like *Pryshlack*?

2. *A different solution to the Pryshlack problem.* In his article above, Garry Watson offers a different solution to the problem presented by the "solicitor" cases:

> The solution to these cases of alternate joinder of multiple defendants, where there are common questions but also significant non-common questions, is *not* to deny joinder and thus expose the plaintiff to the risk of inconsistent determinations. Rather, the solution is ... to permit the joinder and to deal with the problem of the presence of significant non-common issues by the creative exercise of the court discretion as to how the actions should be tried. In this context it is worth recalling that both the joinder rule and the *Payne* test refer to the orderings of separate trials as a major device or relieving against difficulties caused by multiple joinder. ...
>
> [T]his approach gives D2 [an option]: he can defend or not defend on the common questions, but in any event he is to be bound by the determination thereof. There may be situations where D2 is prepared to abide by the court's determination on the common questions without his participation. Where he is not prepared to do this, and wishes to defend on the common issues, so be it (thus proving that he was not so unconcerned with the issues as between the plaintiff and D1 as many solicitors have argued, to date).

A further step, already specifically provided for in some jurisdictions, is desirable in rounding out this approach. The courts should strive to orchestrate the trial in such a way as to isolate, as far as possible, the common issues so that D2's involvement in the trial of the claim between the plaintiff and D1 can be minimized.

A further refinement of the approach suggested here was put forward in the Victorian case of *Birtles v. Commonwealth of Australia*, [1960] VR 247, an excellent, carefully reasoned decision providing a strong functional analysis of the alternate joinder problem. The facts in *Birtles*, somewhat simplified, were that the plaintiff, who had suffered personal injuries, sued several "public authority" defendants who raised, *inter alia*, the defence that the plaintiff had failed to give timely notice of the action as required by statute. The plaintiff responded by denying the need for, and the lack of, notice and by applying to join his former solicitor, in the alternative, alleging that if the defence of the original defendants were successful he was entitled to recovery against the solicitor in negligence. The solicitors opposed joinder, arguing that joinder would involve them in the trial of issues with which they were not concerned. The judge, Adam J, accepted the defendants' contention, but prescribed a different solution, for he viewed saving the plaintiff from the risk of "falling between two stools" as the paramount concern. First, he directed that the trial (if any) of the claim against the solicitors should be separate from, and subsequent to, the trial of the claims against the other defendants. Second, he granted to the solicitors a stay of action as against them until the conclusion of the trial against the original defendants, *but only on condition* that at the trial (if any) against them they agreed not to dispute the findings made as against the original defendants on the common issues. if the solicitors refused to accept this condition, then he ordered that the joinder would stand and no stay would be effective. As Adam J concluded:

> By this order the principal object of the plaintiff in seeking to have the [solicitors] joined in the one action with the original defendants will be achieved, and the inconvenience and embarrassment of trying all causes of action together will be avoided.

The Birtles conditional stay approach focuses directly on the "common questions-risk of inconsistent determination" problem, and explicitly gives the alternate defendant a choice. If he is prepared to abide the outcome of the court's determination of the common questions in the action between the plaintiff and D1, then he may accept the condition and obtain a stay of the proceedings against him. However, if he does not wish to accept the court's determination of these issues in his absence and would seek to relitigate them in the plaintiff's action against him (with a risk to the plaintiff of inconsistent determination) then, quite properly, a stay should be refused and joinder permitted. The *Birtles* approach also satisfies both of the policies underlying joinder. It avoids the inconvenience associated with a multiplicity of actions and also the risk of inconsistent determinations. If D2 wishes to participate in the resolution of the plaintiff's claim against D1, *i.e.*, he desires to contest the determination as between the plaintiff and D1, then it is not unreasonable that he should be subjected to the inconvenience of being involved in that action. The new proposed Ontario Rules specifically provide that the court may make a *Birtles* type order as a response to a challenge to the joinder of multiple defendants (see R. 5.05(d)).

Where a defendant is offered a conditional stay and refuses, or where a joinder is simply permitted without a conditional stay, the court should (as already indicated) use its discretion as to the manner of trial to protect D2 from excessive involvement in the trial of the claim against D1. Similarly, the court should be prepared to tailor discovery to protect D2. Typically, the claim against D, will be ordered to be tried first. D2's involvement in this trial will usually be limited to the common issues, so discovery by and against him should initially be limited to those issues. After all, if the plaintiff succeeds against D, the action against D, will be at an end, and so wider discovery is premature.

3. *"Beautiful Losers": Persons injured in successive accidents.* Is joinder of multiple defendants permissible in what might be termed the case of the "beautiful loser" plaintiff—the plaintiff who is allegedly injured by two different defendants acting independently and at different times. For example, (1) plaintiff's injuries were purportedly sustained by the negligence of A and were aggravated by the subsequent negligence of B, an ambulance driver, while taking the plaintiff to the hospital; (2) plaintiff was a passenger in a car that was struck from the rear twice in one day—once when en route to work in the morning, and again when returning home in the afternoon; or (3) in an accident caused by the first defendant the plaintiff loses a leg and suffers a whiplash, while in the accident caused one year later by the second defendant the plaintiff suffers brain damage and a further whiplash. Is joinder of both defendants proper? See Ontario rule 5.02(2)(d).

[A] practice has been established which may be summarized in this way. If a plaintiff has had his injuries aggravated by involvement in a second vehicle accident following the first such accident, the proper method of computing the damage is as follows:

(1) assess the amount the plaintiff would have recovered against the first tortfeasor on the day before the second occurrence;
(2) assess the total damages for both accidents at the date of the trial; and
(3) subtract the first amount from the second, awarding the remainder as the amount of the damages against the second tortfeasor. *Bain v. Schudel* (1988), 67 OR (2d) 221 (HC).

The importance, if not the necessity, of one tribunal trying the two actions is, in my view, obvious. To allow the two actions to be tried by separate tribunals, even if possible, having regard to the principles applicable respecting the determination of such damages, involves a substantial and unnecessary risk of injustice to at least one of the parties. *Rita v. Perrotta* (1974), 4 OR (2d) 175, 177 (HC) [*per*] Morden J (as he then was).

4. *Costs in actions against two or more defendants.* While it may seem a good idea on the part of plaintiffs to sue "everyone in sight," this may prove to be an imprudent tactic. It must be remembered that the general rule with regard to costs is that a winning party is usually entitled to costs against the loser. Consequently, a plaintiff who sues two defendants and recovers against only one of them faces the prospect of being ordered to pay costs to the successful defendant.

A special rule has been developed to deal with costs in this type of situation if, and only if, it was reasonable for the plaintiff to join multiple defendants. Let us take the situation of a plaintiff in a personal injury action who was involved as a passenger in a two-car collision, and joins as defendants the drivers of both cars. At trial the driver of the car in which the plaintiff was a passenger is successful but the plaintiff succeeds against the driver of the other vehicle. Applying general costs principles the successful defendant will be entitled to an order for costs against the plaintiff. But here—if it were reasonable for the plaintiff to have joined the successful defendant—the plaintiff will receive an order permitting any costs due to the successful defendant to be added to the costs that the unsuccessful defendant is ordered to pay the plaintiff. This form of order is known as a "Bullock order" after the case of *Bullock v. London General Omnibus Co.*, [1907] 1 KB 264 (CA). If the plaintiff is unable to recover the necessary moneys from the unsuccessful defendant, the plaintiff still remains primarily liable to pay the costs of the successful defendant. For another example, see *Badger v. Surkan* (1973), 32 DLR (3d) 216 (Sask. CA).

The consequences of a Bullock order may be disastrous for one of several defendants who alone is ultimately held liable to the plaintiff. Thus, where a number of defendants are sued by a plaintiff who appears to have a good cause of action against one of them (though against which one it is not clear), the defendants may be well advised to pool their resources and make a settlement with the plaintiff. See Ontario rule 49.11.

5. *Joinder and examination for discovery.* Generally, in Canada, only parties may be orally examined for discovery, although there are exceptions as we shall see in the chapter on discovery. This general limitation on who may be examined for discovery may lead a plaintiff to name a person as a defendant partly to ensure the right to examine that person for discovery. A typical example is where a plaintiff sues an employer alleging that the employer is vicariously liable for a tort committed by an employee against the plaintiff. In such a case the plaintiff would normally join the employee as a co-defendant. One reason for so doing would be to ensure that right to examine the employee for discovery.

This tactic of joining a party "for the purposes of discovery" is subject to one obvious limitation: a plaintiff may not simply name a person as a defendant for the purpose of obtaining discovery. The plaintiff may join a person as a defendant only if there is a claim for relief against that person in the action: *Langleys Ltd. v. Martin* (1924), 25 OWN 596.

b. *Compulsory Joinder*

The concern here is with the minimum size of the litigation—how few parties may a plaintiff join in the litigation and still have the court adjudicate a claim? Whereas issues of the permissive joinder of parties—that is, how large may the action become through joinder of parties?—arise quite frequently, problems of compulsory joinder are a relatively rare occurrence.

Ordinarily it is up to the plaintiff to decide which persons will be involved in the litigation. Should the plaintiff choose to sue B alone and not B and A, that is ordinarily of no concern to B or to A or to the court. So also where the plaintiff, without A as co-plaintiff, sues B. But, while this is the general rule, the plaintiff's choice as to the minimum number of parties to the lawsuit will not always be conclusive. Occasionally, there are persons whose presence before the court is "necessary" in the sense that on the application of the defendant the court will order them to be joined as a precondition to the court deciding the case. To this extent the question of who are to be the parties to the litigation is not always in the sole discretion of the original plaintiff. See Reed, "Compulsory Joinder of Parties in Court Actions" (1957), 55 *Michigan Law Review* 327.

James and Hazard, *Civil Procedure*, 3d ed. (1985), at 534-38, explain the rationale for the necessary parties/compulsory joinder rule, and the narrow range of its operation, as follows:

> The absence of C as a party to an action may work prejudice to D, who is a party, in at least two ways. In the first place it may expose D to multiplicity of suits, which is itself something of an evil. But beyond that is the exposure to possible injustice, particularly double liability, if inconsistent results are reached in two or more lawsuits where the nonparty is not bound by the first judgment.
>
> An example of simple multiplicity is found in the case of partial assignment or subrogation: when debtors have incurred a single obligation they ought not to be subjected to multiple suits for its breach. Partial assignees are therefore regarded as necessary parties.
>
> Multiplicity of suits is a burden not only on [the] defendant, but also on society because of the expense to the taxpayers and the burden of crowded dockets on the administration of justice. Curiously, this interest has been given little recognition when it comes to joinder of plaintiffs. As expressed in Federal Rule 20 [see Ont. rule 5.02(1)], plaintiffs who have claims arising out of the same transaction may join in one action but are not obliged to do so. This reflects the old common law's preference for simple lawsuits, but it does not make sense in [the] modern context, especially in two frequently recurring situations. One is where several members of a family are hurt in the same accident, for example in an automobile accident. Since their interests are compatible, and often overlap so far as damages are concerned, and since they are usually represented by the same counsel, it would seem that they should be compelled to sue in one action. But the rules do not so require, except that in a few jurisdictions a spouse's claim for loss of consortium by reason of injury to the other spouse can be asserted only if joined in the latter's own action for his or her injury. The reason why plaintiffs bring separate actions in such situations sometimes is to avoid the possibility that the jury may be inclined to put a "cap" on defendant's total liability, or to get "two bites" at the issue of defendant's liability—since one family member is not bound by a judgment against another family member.
>
> The other situation is where a large number of persons are injured in one transaction—for example, a plane crash. As we shall see, defendants in such situations are usually bound in subsequent litigation if they lose, but unjoined plaintiffs are free to sue even if some of their number have lost. Yet the rules do not require joinder, with [the] result that the same issue of liability can be thoroughly litigated more than once, at resultant public expense.

In insisting upon compulsory joinder, the court is usually pursuing one or both of the policies offered by James and Hazard. Consider the applicable rules regarding compulsory joinder of parties—for example, Ont. rule 5.03(1), NB rule 5.02(2), Man. rule 5.03(1), and the following (earlier) cases decided under substantially similar rules. Can you deduce when a party will be considered a "necessary" party? Does it depend on the party to be joined being "jointly entitled"? If so, how do courts conceive of joint entitlement?

Dix v. Great Western Railway Co.
(1886), 34 WR 712 (Ch. D, England)

Summons by the defendants, asking for the joinder of certain persons as parties to the above action.

By an indenture of the 30th of May, 1884, certain pieces of land belonging to the plaintiff, to Owen, and to Jallion respectively were conveyed to the defendant company, and the company covenanted with each of the vendors, his heirs and assigns, separately, that the defendant company would make a road between certain points on the land bought, and would allow the plaintiff, Owen, and Jallion, and their respective heirs, tenants, and assigns, to use the road for all purposes.

The action was for specific performance of the covenant, and damages.

Neither Owen nor Jallion had been made parties to the action; the summons sought their joinder.

KAY J: The court, under Ord. 16 r. 11, has a wide discretion in cases like the present, and I have to consider here whether I should use that discretion in the sense of ordering these two covenantees to be added as parties to this action. They might entertain different views from the plaintiff as to the line of road. Again, part of the covenant is that the company will allow all the covenantees, their heirs, tenants, and assigns, to use the road. Consequently, it becomes impossible for the court "effectually and completely to adjudicate upon and settle all the questions involved in the cause or matter without the presence of" all the covenantees. They will be necessary parties in fact if it becomes necessary to specify in the order how and where the road is to be made, which will have to be done if this action is successful which I must assume to be possible.

I accede to the present application, but I shall reserve the costs of it. The order should be prefaced with the statement that it was made on the application of the defendant company.

NOTES AND QUESTIONS

1. In *Looker v. Imperial Oil Limited*, [1944] OWN 167 (SC), the court faced a similar problem. Looker sought a declaration that she was the owner of certain share warrants issued by Imperial Oil that had been destroyed and an order requiring Imperial Oil to issue her new share warrants on the basis that the shares had been left to her in her brother's will. Imperial Oil had refused to do so because a Mr. Shutes had informed Imperial Oil that the shares had been left with Shutes by the plaintiff's brother to be given to one Barbara Hollinger in the event of his death and that Shutes had accidentally destroyed them. Although the plaintiff argued that she should not be compelled to join Shutes and Hollinger in her claim, the court required her to do so "to enable the Court

effectually and completely to adjudicate upon the questions involved in the action." On appeal Rose CJHC agreed, observing that the Imperial Oil "would be in a very awkward position if, complying with the plaintiff's demand, they issued new share warrants to the plaintiff, and if afterwards Barbara Hollinger claimed the warrant and succeeded in establishing her title. That being so, it is eminently right that before any judgment is pronounced against the defendants in this action, the real ownership of the warrant shall be determined."

2. Professors Louisell and Hazard, *Cases and Materials on Pleading and Procedure*, 4th ed. (Mineola, NY: Foundation Press, 1979), at 571 summarize the reasons for the compulsory joinder of necessary parties very succinctly as follows:

> [T]he objectives of the rule were, and still are, simple enough: from the Viewpoint of the court, to do a complete job on the controversy in one sitting; from the view-point of those already parties, to protect them against the consequences of subsequent litigation reaching inconsistent results; from the viewpoint of those not made parties but by the rule required to be brought in, to assure that their practical out-of-court situation would not be adversely affected by changes in the *status quo* wrought in consequence of the judgment.

3. *Today, should the absence of a "necessary party" be the plaintiff's or the defendant's problem?* Modern third-party rules like Ontario rule 29.01 now specifically provide a means by which a defendant can solve the absent party problem himself or herself:

> A defendant may commence a third party claim against any person who is not a party to the action and who, ...
>
> (c) should be bound by the determination of an issue arising between the plaintiff and the defendant.

Instead of bringing a motion to force the plaintiff to join a necessary party, clearly the defendant could simply join the party as a third party under the above provision. But can the plaintiff argue that, in the light of this relatively new provision, that is the proper approach and he is now relieved of the obligation to join a necessary party? Probably not, if only because (1) the necessary parties law is old and well established, and (2) the question of who may become liable to pay the necessary party's costs is possibly different depending upon who joins that party. Compare *Hannah v. Canadian General Insurance Co.*, later in this section under heading B.4., "Third-Party Claims."

4. As already indicated, the compulsory joinder principle is a narrow exception to the general rule that a plaintiff is free (within the limits of the permissive joinder rules) to decide who to sue. This is well illustrated by the attitude of the courts to joinder in most tort cases. If injured in a multiple-car collision, the plaintiff is free to select one of several tortfeasors as a sole defendant. As we will see in the next section, the plaintiff will usually be most unwise to take this approach, but the court will not order that the other possible tortfeasors be joined as defendants as a precondition to hearing the case.

In view of the law's strong policy against a multiplicity of actions this attitude, perhaps, seems somewhat odd since there is nothing (except limitation periods and rules forbidding double recovery) to stop the plaintiff subsequently suing the other tortfeasors. The explanation is to be found, it would seem, in several factors.

First is the basic commitment of our law to the adversary system with its principle of party presentation and formulation of the case as opposed to presentation and formulation by the court. The court will force a party on the plaintiff only where the absent party or the defendant will be prejudiced by the absence, even though by so doing the court may also avoid a multiplicity of actions. The principle of party formulation of the case, coupled with the risks involved in non-joinder, will usually result in the plaintiff suing all persons reasonably thought to be liable. Thus, defining the minimum size of the litigation can generally be safely left to the plaintiff and this relieves the court of having to concern itself with the problem. On balance the legal system is probably better served by leaving the choice of parties to the plaintiff, since enforced joinder will lead to a larger present lawsuit to avoid a subsequent lawsuit that may never eventuate anyway. Second, rules of compulsory joinder may cause expense for and even produce injustice to the plaintiff, since an additional party must then be found, served and fought in the litigation. Finally, the problem of a multiplicity of proceedings of a kind that compulsory joinder might avoid are perhaps more theoretical than real. The subsequent litigation usually does not materialize, either because the plaintiff chooses not to sue or because the running of limitation periods prevents it.

B. Addition of Claims and Parties by the Defendant

1. Introduction

We now turn to a discussion of how the litigation may be expanded by the defendant. We will see that expansion can occur in three ways. First, defendants can assert claims against the plaintiff through *counterclaims*. Second, they can assert claims against each other by means of *cross-claims*. Third, they can assert claims against persons, not yet formal parties to the litigation, by initiating *third-party proceedings*. Are there common concerns regarding these three devices in terms of their capacity for expanding a lawsuit and proper limits on them?

2. Counterclaims

See Ontario rule 27. If the defendant has a claim against the plaintiff, is it necessary for a separate action to be instigated, or can the claim be asserted and relief recovered from the plaintiff in the original action? Considerations of economy and convenience favour a determination of the claims of each party against the other by the same tribunal at the same time in a single action. In other cases, to require the defendant to bring a separate action against the plaintiff might cause financial hardship. If the plaintiff is successful on the initial claim the defendant will become immediately liable to satisfy such a judgment, notwithstanding that the defendant may have a claim against the plaintiff, possibly for an amount equal to or greater than the judgment debt.

At one time, a defendant could assert a claim in the plaintiff's action in only a restricted number of situations. Today a defendant can assert any claim against the plaintiff by counterclaim, subject only to the power of the court to exclude the defendant's claim where it cannot be conveniently dealt with in the plaintiff's action.

Rotenberg v. Rosenberg
[1964] 1 OR 160 (SC)

Application by the plaintiff for an order striking out the counterclaim and for other relief with respect to the statement of defence.

SENIOR MASTER (MARRIOTT): This is an application by the plaintiff for an order striking out the counterclaim.

I disposed of the application to strike out parts of the statement of defence except para. 14. The allegations in that paragraph are inconsistent with those contained in para. 6 of the statement of defence. If the defendants wish to maintain it, it should be couched in different language—perhaps in the alternative. Therefore, while it is struck out, leave should be given to amend.

Dealing then with the counterclaim, the main action is for rescission of a contract, for an accounting of secret profits and commissions received by the defendants Rosenberg and the defendant firm for breach of fiduciary duty and breach of duty as the plaintiff's solicitors. The counterclaim is by the defendants for $2,000 for damages for slander against the plaintiff and her husband.

It is almost a rule of thumb that the Court will not permit actions for defamation to be tried with other actions. In support of this I refer to *Holmested & Langton's Judicature Act* (5th ed.), at pp. 586-588, where in examples of counterclaims not excluded I see not one where the action of counterclaim was for damages for libel or slander. On the other hand in the examples of counterclaims excluded on pp. 588-590 there are several in that category: See also *Williams Tool Corp. of Canada Ltd. v. Merrickville Engineering Co.*, [1944] OWN 384. Counsel for the defendants, however, strongly urges that the circumstances of this case warranted the Court in permitting the counterclaim to stand, his chief reason being that the circumstances surrounding the plaintiff's claim and the counterclaim are so interwoven to require them to be tried together and therefore form an exception to the general rule. Upon reading the pleadings I think it is true that part of the evidence relevant to the plaintiff's claim may be relevant to the counterclaim. However, that in itself is not sufficient to warrant the Court in allowing the action and counterclaim to proceed together. In *Edward v. Ing*, [1938] OWN 330, that argument was rejected by the Master in a case where the plaintiff's action was for malicious prosecution and the counterclaim was for damages for conversion of mining shares.

The reason which prompts the Court to separate claims for damages for defamation from others, which overrides almost all other considerations, is the one that appears in all of the authorities, and that is that such a claim being of a very technical nature, it is extremely inconvenient and inexpedient to try those causes of action with others. Furthermore, the counterclaim in this case, of course, must be tried by a jury, whereas it is unlikely that a jury notice will be served in the main action. So that one action is one in which the judge controls the law and the jury the facts and the other in which the judge will decide both law and facts. This is a complication which should not be allowed to arise. See the remarks of O'Connor J, in *McLean v. Hamilton Street Ry. Co.* (1885), 11 PR 193 approved by the Court in *Odell v. Bennett* (1889), 13 PR 10.

In the result an order will go striking out the words objected to in paras. 5 and 10, all of para. 14 and the second sentence of para. 15 of the statement of defence with leave to amend paras. 14 and 15. The application for an order striking out the counterclaim will also be granted. Costs to the plaintiff in the cause.

[An appeal from this order was dismissed by Fraser J, without written or recorded reasons, on December 17, 1963.]

NOTES AND QUESTIONS

1. What are the policy reasons for allowing a defendant to counterclaim at all? What interests is the court attempting to balance in deciding whether or not to allow a counterclaim?

Why was the defendant in *Rotenberg* not permitted to use the device? Can the decision in *Rotenberg* be reconciled with *Foley*, above? Notwithstanding *Foley*, there is still likely vitality in the *Rotenberg* decision. Would it not be too easy for defendants to try and deter all plaintiffs by the simple device of responding with a defamation action asserted as a counterclaim?

2. *Counterclaims for the tort of abuse of process.* A recent phenomonen is for some defendants to assert, by way of counterclaim, that the very bringing of the main action by the plaintiff constitutes the tort of abuse of process. The following case illustrates "the problem" and how the courts are handling it.

Teledata Communications Inc. v. Westburne Industrial Enterprises Ltd.
(1990), 71 OR (2d) 466 (HC)

EBERLE J:—This is an application by the defendants by counterclaim to strike out the counterclaim. For brevity I will refer to the opposing sides on this motion as the plaintiffs and the defendants, the former being the applicants and the latter the respondents. The circumstances are as follows. The plaintiffs sue for breaches of contract, breaches of fiduciary duty and for conspiracy. The plaintiffs, sellers and installers of communications equipment, allege a contract with the defendant Westburne, a supplier of such equipment, to become a dealer for the latter. The plaintiffs say that the defendant breached the contract by refusing to supply the equipment. Subsequently, some employees of the plaintiff left it and joined the defendant, and assisted the latter in obtaining the benefit of certain contracts with customers for the supply and installation of communications equipment, which contracts it is alleged, should have gone to the plaintiffs. A conspiracy to put the plaintiff out of business is alleged and there are other related allegations and claims.

The defendants deny all those allegations and claims and have launched the counterclaim, which is now under attack, for damages and for punitive damages. The defendants say that the plaintiffs know that their claims have no factual foundations and further say that the action was begun to (1) create an illusion that the plaintiff is financially viable, and (2) inflict vengeance and cause personal embarrassment to one of the individual defendants, who it is alleged, rebuffed efforts of the principal officer of the plaintiffs to establish a personal relationship with her. In short, it is alleged that the plaintiffs' motivation in bringing the action is simply malicious, and the defendants counterclaim for punitive damages in the sum of $25,000.

Further, the defendants allege that the plaintiffs' abusive use of the court process to harass the defendants has and will cause commercial embarrassment and commercial damage to the defendants, by creating an illusion of conspiratorial conduct on the part of the defendants. For the commercial and economic harm, the defendants counterclaim for damages of $100,000.

To some extent the counterclaim has aspects of a defamation action. However the law is clear that no action will lie for defamatory statements contained in a document properly used in the course of any proceedings before a court of justice. ...

Rather the defendants' submissions focused on the tort of abuse of process, the necessary elements for which are now well established and confine its ambit very narrowly. In *Atland Containers v. Macs Corp. Ltd.* (1974), 7 OR (2d) 107 at pp. 109-10, 54 DLR (3d) 363 at p. 365-6, 17 CPR (2d) 16 (HCJ), Parker J (as he then was) said:

> By way of counterclaim the defendant corporation repeats the allegations contained in its statement of defence and alleges that the institution and prosecution of this action has already caused and will continue to cause serious financial loss to the defendants in their business undertakings. The defendant then pleads that the plaintiff has instituted and prosecuted this action for an improper purpose, namely, to limit lawful competition within the corrugated box industry.
>
> The corporate defendant is in fact pleading for damages for the tort of abuse of process although the words are not used in the pleading and counsel for the defendant agreed that this was so.

So far the content of the counterclaim in that case resembles closely the counterclaim in the present one. At p. 111 OR, p. 367 DLR, Parker J continued as follows:

> In the case at bar the defendant claims for damages because the institution and prosecution of the plaintiff's action has caused and will continue to cause serious financial loss to the defendant. If followed to its logical conclusion every plaintiff would be open to such a claim. However, the law re the abuse of process is very narrow in scope. It is only where the process of the Court is used for an improper purpose and where there is a definite act or threat in furtherance of such a purpose. No such act or threat is pleaded in this case.

Nor is any such act or threat pleaded in the case at bar.

The defendants relied on *Tsiopoulos v. Commercial Union Assurance Co.* (1986), 57 OR (2d) 117, 32 DLR (4th) 614, 21 CCLI 212 (HCJ), in support of their position. In that case at pp. 119-20 OR, p. 616 DLR, Henry J wrote as follows:

> It is well settled that there is at law a tort known as abuse of process. This cause of action arises when the processes of law are used for an ulterior or collateral purpose. It is defined as the misusing of the process of the courts to coerce someone in some way entirely outside the ambit of the legal claim upon which the court is asked to adjudicate. It occurs when the process of the court is used for an improper purpose and where there is a definite act or threat in furtherance of such purpose.

Finally, in *Beckingham v. Sparrow* (1977), 2 CCLT 214 (Ont. HCJ), Grange J (as he then was) struck out a counterclaim in somewhat similar circumstances, relying upon the decision of Parker J in *Atland Containers Ltd. v. Macs, supra*. He said at p. 217:

> The cause of action in abuse of process cannot be extended to embrace a counterclaim arising out of the action itself. ...
>
> As is apparent from the judgment of all the judges in *Grainger v. Hill* the root of the action is the attempt by the defendant to gain something to which he has no colour of right.

On the following page, he said:

> Certainly the action brought by the plaintiffs, with or without the assistance of their co-defendants by counterclaim, may have a chastening or inhibiting effect upon the defendant's future statements, but that is not outside the scope of the process. The most that can be said of it is that it is a potential collateral benefit.

He struck out the counterclaim which was based upon an alleged abuse of process.

I conclude therefore that the bringing of an action, even if factually groundless, together with wrongful motives for bringing the action, are not sufficient to constitute the tort of abuse of process. What lies at the heart of the cause of action is an act, or threat of an act, outside the ambit of the action. The essence of the action therefore is the use of legal process to gain an end which the legal process does not entitle the plaintiff to obtain.

This essential ingredient in the cause of action relied upon is entirely missing from the counterclaim in this case. The focus is clearly on the action brought by the plaintiff together with the allegations in the statement of claim as the basis for the counterclaim.

On this point the case may be usefully compared with *Grainger v. Hill* (1838), 4 Bing. (NC) 212, 132 ER 769, a case which is generally viewed as the foundation for the tort of abuse of process. There the defendant Hill had earlier sued the plaintiff for a debt, in connection with which action he also issued a writ by which the plaintiff could be arrested unless he could pay the debt at once. The defendant's real object was to obtain possession of the register of the plaintiff's ship, to which the lawsuit did not and could not entitle the defendant. When the defendant's agents demanded the register, the plaintiff, in order to escape arrest, handed it over. Subsequently, the plaintiff sued the defendant for having abused the process of the court. He succeeded, it being held that the defendant had abused the legal process by employing it to extort property from the plaintiff to which property the defendant had no right. The difference between *Grainger* and the present case is clear.

Here, there is no allegation of any act which the plaintiffs were enabled to commit, or threatened to commit, because of the existence of the lawsuit but lying outside its scope. It is solely the bringing of the lawsuit, together with the allegations in the statement of claim, upon which the defendants rely to found the counterclaim. Paragraph 26 of that pleading may be referred to as an example. This, even assuming the truth of the improper motives alleged for the bringing of the action, is not enough.

The defendants argued that an award of costs will not be a sufficient deterrent to the plaintiffs nor remedy for the defendants, who as they say, find themselves faced with an action which has no factual foundation. Counsel argued that in the communication industries, a company has a peculiar vulnerability to any hint of weakness. This point, however, is not pleaded. Even if it were, effect could not be given to it for I agree with the authors of 25 Hals., 3d ed., p. 367, under the heading of "Malicious Abuse of Civil Proceedings" where they write as follows:

> The law allows every person to employ its process for the purpose of asserting his rights without subjecting him to any liability other than the liability to pay the costs of the proceedings if unsuccessful.

This is the basis on which our system of litigation operates and has long operated. It is a principle which marches hand in hand with the one quoted from the Sussman case earlier, that defamatory statements contained in a document properly used in the course of any proceedings before a court cannot give rise to an action. These two principles are important cornerstones of the right of full and free access to the courts for all persons who feel, even wrongly, that they have a ground of complaint against another.

For the above reasons the counterclaim will be struck out. The costs of this motion will be to the defendants by counterclaim forthwith after taxation.

NOTES AND QUESTIONS

1. What do you think of the decision in *Teledata*? What if the defendant's allegations were solidly grounded—that is, they represented the truth? Does the problem lie in the law as quoted from *Halsbury's* (near the end of the judgment)? Should that law be changed and should we recognize a tort of "malicious abuse of civil proceedings" without a requirement of "an act, or threat of an act, outside the ambit of the action"? Or is this requirement a wise one? Would the dynamics of litigation change if we made such a change to the law? If the law were changed, would it be wise to hold that such a claim could not, however, be asserted by counterclaim in the plaintiff's action that the defendant contends is the abuse of process? Why?

2. *Joining other persons as defendants to the counterclaim.* The rules permit a defendant asserting a counterclaim to further expand the size of the litigation by joining other persons as defendants to the counterclaim. Until recently, the defendant's right to add additional parties as defendants to a counterclaim was limited—that is, the defendant could bring in new parties by counterclaim only where the relief claimed related to or was connected with the original subject of the plaintiff's claim. Modern rules (for example, Ontario rule 27.01(2)) typically impose no such limitation; the only requirement now is that the person to be added as a defendant to the counterclaim "is a necessary or proper party to the counterclaim." Hence, the counterclaim may be unrelated to the plaintiff's claim and may involve bringing in a new party as defendant to the counterclaim. Of course, the court has power "where it appears that a counterclaim may unduly complicate or delay the trial of the main action, or cause undue prejudice to a party," to order separate trials or order that the counterclaim proceed as a separate action: Ontario rule 27.08(2).

3. *Ordering a separate trial or severance (separate actions).* The wording of rules such as Ontario rule 27.01(1) seems to indicate that the defendant has an unlimited right to set up "any ... claim by way of counterclaim against the original plaintiff." But, as

was illustrated by *Rotenberg*, the rule has to be read with rule 27.08(2) giving the court a residual power to order that a counterclaim be tried separately or that it be servered and proceed as a spearage action.

4. *Granting leave to a defendant to counterclaim after delivering the defence.* In *Lid Brokerage & Realty Co. (1977) Ltd. v. Budd*, [1992] 2 WWR 45, a produce broker- age firm claimed against former employees and others for conspiring to use information gained during their employment to compete against the brokerage firm. In discoveries, the defendants learned of activities by the former employer and others that formed the basis for a claim against the brokerage firm for conspiring to injure their business. The court permitted the defendants to counterclaim, even though the limitation period had passed and it would involve the addition of new parties, because this would enable the real issues in the case to be determined. Further, although the counterclaim would undoubtedly delay and complicate the main action, there would be little overall net benefit to any of the parties in requiring the defendants to commence a separate action. That action might, in any event, be consolidated at a later stage with the current action, producing a similar result. The court summarized the principles governing the exercise of discretion to grant leave to amend pleadings to permit a counterclaim as follows:

> 1. Leave should be granted to the applicant (the paramount consideration being convenience and the avoidance of multiple proceedings) unless the party opposing the proposed counterclaim establishes that:
>
> a. the counterclaim, even if delivered on time, could have been struck … on the basis it discloses no cause of action; or
>
> b. there are extenuating circumstances which would render it inequitable to grant leave (such as an intervening limitation period barring the defendant from bringing a separate action); or
>
> c. the proposed counterclaim will so unduly complicate or delay the trial of the main action that the benefits of avoiding multiple legal actions are outweighed by prejudice to the plaintiff that cannot reasonably or adequately be compensated by conditions attached to such leave.
>
> 2. Leave should be granted on conditions where the plaintiff will otherwise suffer prejudice due to the delay on the part of the defendant in bringing the counterclaim in time. Such conditions should, as far as reasonably possible, adequately compensate the plaintiff for such unnecessary prejudice. …

5. *History of counterclaims and set-off.* Originally at common law, with one very minor exception, the defendant could not assert in the same action a claim against the plaintiff. (The exception was that a defendant could defeat or reduce the plaintiff's recovery on a claim for the price of goods sold and delivered or of work and labour done by pleading, as a defence, the plaintiff's breach of warranty.) A complaint about a different transaction necessitated a separate action. The inconvenience caused by these restrictions produced some legislative reform in England early in the 18th century. The legislation consisted of two enactments, known as the statutes of set-off. (For example, in Ontario, see now s. 111 of the Courts of Justice Act and in Manitoba, see Queen's Bench Act, ss. 78-79).

The statutes of set-off allowed *mutual debts* to be set off. The right of the defendant to plead damages for breach of warranty in diminution of the price was preserved, and the right to assert in, extinction or diminution, a debt arising out of another transaction was created. However, the defendant could not set off a debt that was incurred by the plaintiff after the issue of the writ in the action, and if the amount of the defendant's debt was less than that due by the plaintiff the excess was not recoverable. Moreover, since the statutes allowed only *mutual debts* to be set off, the defendant could not set off *a claim that sounded in damages* nor could a debt be set off in answer to a claim by the plaintiff for damages. It is important to note that both set-off and a plea of breach of warranty in diminution of the price were considered to be *defences*, rather than cross-actions by the defendant. This was so because the common law would not accept the notion of the defendant pursuing a claim in the plaintiff's action. The major consequence of this view was that the excess of the defendant's claim over that of the plaintiff was never recoverable. A separate action would have to be commenced to recover this excess.

The counterclaim is a creature of the late 19th century Judicature Act reforms. It was devised in order to overcome the restrictions that applied to set-off. A defendant may now assert any counterclaim against a plaintiff, whatever the nature of the claim and the date of its accrual, and whether it arises out of the same transaction as that relied on by the plaintiff or not. In short, provided that it is substantively adequate, the defendant may assert any claim against the plaintiff as a counterclaim. This right is subject only to the discretionary power in the court to sever the claims where the trial of claim and counterclaim together might be inconvenient or cause unfairness.

It might have been expected that the statutory provisions relating to set-off would be repealed with the creation of the more liberal device of the counterclaim. However, this did not occur and set-off continues to exist with the counterclaim. Set-off is still largely subject to the same restrictions that applied before the counterclaim was devised (see—for example, Ontario Courts of Justice Act, s. 111), although the subject has been further complicated, even recently, by the expansion of what is known as equitable set-off: *Ferrum Inc. v. Three Dees Management Ltd.* (1992), 7 OR (3d) 660 (Gen. Div.) (equitable set-off is available whether or not the cross-obligations are mutual debts, or even debts at all, provided there is a relationship between the cross-obligations such that it would be inequitable to permit one to proceed without taking the other into account; it is enough that the opposing claims flow from the same transaction or relationship between the parties). See, generally, Holmested and Watson, *Ontario Civil Procedure*, CJA s. 111, and K. Palmer, *The Law of Set-Off in Canada* (Canada Law Book, 1993).

Today a defendant can counterclaim against the plaintiff for any relief that could be claimed against the plaintiff in an independent action, subject to the power of the court to direct a separate trial of the counterclaim, or to exclude the counterclaim altogether and so require the defendant to commence a fresh action, where the claim and counterclaim cannot be conveniently dealt with together. Moreover, the defendant is also permitted to counterclaim against both the plaintiff and a person who is not already a party to the action, but who is a proper party defendant to the counterclaim.

6. *Modern consequences of the distinction between set-off and counterclaim.* As already indicated, since set-off has survived the creation of the counterclaim, in certain situations the defendant can plead a claim against the plaintiff either as a counterclaim or by way of *set-off*. Today there are still some significant procedural differences between counterclaim and set-off.

Suppose that A claims $1,000 from B for the price of goods sold and delivered and, at the date of commencement of A's action, A owes a sum to B for money lent. B's liability for the price of the goods can be set off against the unpaid loan. Since set-off is a defence proper to the plaintiff's claim, where it is pleaded there will be but a single judgment in the action. If the amount of the set-off equals or exceeds the amount of the plaintiff's claim, there will be judgment for the defendant. If it is for less, the plaintiff will be given judgment for the balance. Since the set-off is a defence, a shield for the defendant, the defendant originally could not recover any excess from the plaintiff. This is now altered by statute. See Courts of Justice Act, s. 111(3). Where a counterclaim is asserted, it is for the purposes of judgment treated as a separate action and there will be not one judgment but two—one on the plaintiff's claim and the other on the defendant's. This means that if the defendant counterclaims and both parties are successful, there will be judgment for the plaintiff against the defendant with costs on the claim, and judgment for the defendant against the plaintiff with costs on the counterclaim. For the purposes of execution, however, one judgment will usually be set off against the other.

As already noted, set-off is much narrower in scope than the counterclaim. In almost every case where a defendant has a claim against the plaintiff, the claim can be asserted by way of counterclaim. However, the defendant can plead by way of set-off only in situations of mutual debts. But apart from the different forms of judgment that are pronounced according to whether the defendant has pleaded a set-off or delivered a counterclaim, does the distinction today produce any important practical consequences?

The continued distinction between set-off and counterclaim has two important practical consequences—the awarding of costs and the operation of limitation periods.

Costs. Since set-off is a defence, if it is successful for the full amount of the plaintiff's claim, the action will be dismissed and the defendant will therefore be entitled to the costs of the action. By contrast, in the case of a counterclaim, when a plaintiff succeeds on a claim and the defendant on a counterclaim, each party, subject to judicial discretion, is entitled to the costs incurred to recover the claim and counterclaim respectively. For the purposes of costs a claim that could be pleaded by way of set-off does not lose its real character by being asserted as a counterclaim. Of course, it should be noted that a set-off, since it is a defence (see the Courts of Justice Act, s. 111), can simply be pleaded in the defendant's statement of defence or can be asserted as a counterclaim. However, claims that can only be the subject of a counterclaim cannot be asserted in the statement of defence, but must be asserted in a separate defendant's pleading entitled a "counterclaim" (see rule 27.02).

Is any useful purpose served by retaining the dichotomy between set-off and counterclaim? Does it make any sense to have the issue of costs depend on whether the defendant's claim is a set-off or a counterclaim? If so, why?

The decision in *Reid (E.D.) Produce Ltd. v. Bayside Transport Ltd.* (1986), 64 Nfld. & PEI R 55 (PEI TD) illustrates the costs consequences of proceeding by counterclaim rather than set-off. The plaintiff was a buyer of empty beer bottles and whenever it had assembled enough to make up a trailer load, it would contact the defendant, a licensed carrier, which had an arrangement with a Saint John brewery for delivery. The defendant would purchase the load of bottles from the plaintiff, for which it would either pay cash immediately upon loading, or, as sometimes happened, the first business day following, if the pick-up was made on a weekend. The loading of the trailer would normally be at the cost of the plaintiff. The plaintiff obtained judgment against the defendant for $3,500.50 for a dishonoured cheque and other shortages in payment. Of the defendant's counterclaim of $8,840 made up of six different and distinct accounts, two items were allowed in part for a total amount of $2,800. Since the defendant was successful, at least in part, on two of six counts, but unsuccessful on the remaining four, it was entitled to recover one-third of its taxed costs against the plaintiff.

Limitation periods. With regard to set-off the rule is that a defendant may assert the claim provided that it was not statute-barred at the time the plaintiff commenced the action. Consequently, though the limitation period has expired by the time the defendant delivers a statement of defence, the set-off may be pleaded provided that the limitation period had not run on this claim at the date of the writ. The general rule regarding counterclaims and limitation periods is narrower. The limitation period continues to run against a claim asserted by counterclaim until the counterclaim is actually delivered. Consequently, if the limitation period expires between the plaintiff commencing the action and the defendant delivering the counterclaim, the counterclaim will be statute-barred. The different rule in respect of set-off is said to be a consequence of the character of a set-off as a defence.

7. *Compulsory counterclaims.* Consider the following problem. Ross claims he was assaulted by Brown as he attempted to drive his new car away from Brown's car lot. Ross lays criminal charges against Brown, which are dismissed. Brown then sues Ross for malicious prosecution. At the trial Ross succeeds, the trial judge holding that Ross's conduct in bringing the criminal prosecution was justified by reason of the fact that he had been assaulted by Brown. Subsequently Ross sues Brown for damages for assault. Brown seeks to have the action dismissed as an abuse of the process of the court on the ground that Ross's present claim should have been asserted as a counterclaim in Brown's malicious prosecution action. What decision and why? As we noted earlier (in note 7, following the *Las Vegas* case in the *res judicata* section) the Canadian authorities appear to be in conflict on this issue, but there is authority that the later action is not barred: see *Roque v. Brown* (1977), 2 CPC 239 and 243 (Ont. HC) (the fact that a prior defendant—now plaintiff—could have, but did not, counterclaim in the prior action does not prevent that party from bringing a subsequent action.)

Court rules in the United States now usually provide that the defendant *must* assert as a counterclaim in the plaintiff's action any claim that arises out of *the transaction or occurrence that is the subject of the plaintiffs claim*—see, for example, FRCP rule 13(a). If the defendant fails to make such a counterclaim the matter may not be subsequently asserted in a separate action. What is the policy behind this type of provision? Does it have any drawbacks? Should such a provision be incorporated into the rules of Canadian courts?

8. *Setting off judgments on the claim and counterclaim.* Suppose the plaintiff succeeds on a claim and is awarded $25,000 and the defendant is successful on a counterclaim and is awarded $19,000. In most such situations it will be convenient and just to order that, for the purposes of execution, the two judgments be set off and that the defendant pay the plaintiff the balance of $6,000. And this is indeed the general practice followed by the court. But what if the action and counterclaim are for personal injuries arising out of an automobile accident involving two fully insured parties? Since both

have succeeded on their respective claims, each must have contributed to the accident by their own negligence. Is it just in such a situation to order a set-off of the judgments for the purposes of execution? Ontario courts have generally held it is not: see *Wells v. Russell*, [1952] OWN 521 (CA) and *Lewenza v. Ruszczak*, [1960] OWN 40 (CA). But other courts have permitted the judgments to be set off: see *Schellenberg v. Cook* (1960), 25 DLR (2d) 607 (Sask. CA); *Johnny's Taxi v. Ostoforoff* (1962), 33 DLR (2d) 85 (Sask. CA), at 89; and *McConnell v. Alexander*, [1954] OWN 266. Do decisions ordering set-off of the judgments in these circumstances defeat the very underlying social purpose of requiring mandatory auto insurance and simply lead to injured persons going uncompensated, and insurance companies avoiding the responsibility of paying legitimate claims?

3. Cross-Claims

See Ontario rule 28. Other examples are NB rule 29 and Sask. rule 106. Cross-claims permit claims between co-defendants and are provided for in some jurisdictions. We have already seen that a defendant can claim against a plaintiff by use of a counterclaim, but what if a defendant wishes to claim against a co-defendant? Such a situation can easily arise. Take for example the situation where P, a passenger in a car, suffers injuries in a collision and sues D1 (the owner-driver of the vehicle in which P was a passenger) and D2 (the driver of the other vehicle). Assume that after the action is commenced D1 wishes to claim against D2 for personal injuries and property damage. Note that D1 cannot simply assert this claim by serving a counterclaim on D2 because the rules clearly assume that a counterclaim is only available for use by a defendant against a plaintiff either alone or with another person. In what other situations might resort be had to cross-claims?

Cross-claims were introduced in Ontario in 1985. They were adopted from the United States and make good sense. Before their introduction, in the situation above, D1 could not cross-claim against D2. Instead, he or she would have to bring a separate action against D2 and then either D1 or D2 would have to move for an order to have the two actions tried together (see Ontario rule 6). While cross-claims are closely related to counterclaims, the model for the cross-claim rule is the third-party rule (Ontario rule 29, discussed below) rather than the counterclaim rule (Ontario rule 27).

In *Jordan v. Guardian Insurance Co.* (1985), 50 OR (2d) 673 (HC), negotiations between the plaintiff's solicitor and the plaintiff's insurer failed to produce a settlement within the limitation period so the plaintiff commenced a claim against the insurer and, in the alternative, her solicitor. The solicitor, a US resident, did not defend and was noted in default but he moved to deliver a cross-claim against the other defendants. Although this was not specifically contemplated by the rules, Master Peppiatt reasoned that this claim operated like a third-party claim, albeit by one who was already a party to the action, and the solicitor should, therefore, be permitted to claim over without defending as he would if he were a third party. Requiring him to deliver a defence in which he had no real faith, or that merely admitted the allegations against him, would not contribute to "the just, most expeditious and least expensive determination of every civil proceeding on its merits."

4. Third-Party Claims

a. *Nature and Purpose*

Suppose a defendant in an action believes that he or she has a claim against someone who is not a party and that claim is related to the issues that have arisen or could arise between the plaintiff and the defendant. As we have seen, if such a claim is against the plaintiff, that defendant may assert it by counterclaim, or, if it is against another defendant, it may be asserted by cross-claim. However, if the claim is against someone else, the defendant will have to bring that person into the action by way of third-party proceedings. The defendant may assert such a claim because he or she believes that there is a right of contribution or indemnity against the third party—that is, if the defendant is liable to the plaintiff, he or she has a right to demand compensation from the third party, in whole or in part, for the relief the defendant will be ordered to pay the plaintiff. Historically, third-party procedures were limited to this situation, which still arises frequently. However, under many modern rules, a defendant may also initiate a third-party proceeding for a claim against the third party regardless of whether the plaintiff prevails against the defendant.

An example will illustrate how a defendant might have a claim over against a person not a party to the action in respect of the relief claimed against him by the plaintiff. Suppose that X has entered into a contract with Air Canada to have a quantity of goods shipped from Toronto to Vancouver. Air Canada, in turn, enters into a contract with Y to have the goods picked up and taken to the Toronto airport. On the way to the airport the goods, while in the custody of Y, disappear. X now sues Air Canada claiming damages for breach of the contract to deliver the goods from Toronto to Vancouver. Air Canada is likely to be primarily liable to X, but since the goods were lost while in the possession of Y, Air Canada feels that Y should have to pay Air Canada the amount that it must pay X. Air Canada could wait until X has obtained judgment against it and then bring a separate action against Y claiming the amount of damages that it had to pay to X. However, to have to bring a second action in such a situation is not only cumbersome and expensive and violates the principle that a multiplicity of proceedings should be avoided, but it also exposes Air Canada to the risk of inconsistent decisions in the two actions—that is, it might lose to X and then lose against Y. It was for this reason that the third-party procedure was developed. Thus, Air Canada, rather than bringing a separate action against Y, in which it would have to prove the matters already determined in the action brought by X, may join Y as a third party in that action. What results is really two actions under the umbrella of a single action in which the title of proceedings would read:

Between:
X   Plaintiff
            and
Air Canada   Defendant
            and
Y   Third Party

If, in addition, Air Canada wished to assert a claim against Y for return of money paid under the contract because of non-performance by Y, such an assertion would illustrate the use of third-party procedures to assert a claim by the defendant regardless of the plaintiff's claim. Should Air Canada be able to assert an unrelated claim by means of third-party proceedings?

Although the special words "contribution or indemnity" may no longer be in many rules (although they are clearly encompassed by such language as appears in Ontario rule 27.01(a)), they represent situations in which third-party proceedings will be frequently employed. The term *indemnity* applies to the situation where the defendant claims as against the third party that in the event of the defendant being found liable to the plaintiff, the third party must provide full compensation to the defendant including any costs awarded the plaintiff and the defendant's personal costs. When *contribution* is sought the defendant claims that the third party is liable to pay *part* of any amount for which the defendant is adjudged liable to the plaintiff. The extent of the contribution and the way it is determined will depend on the nature of the relationship between the defendant and the third party out of which the liability to contribute arises.

The following are examples of relationships between two persons that give one the right to be indemnified by the other: an agent by a principal for liabilities incurred in the course of the agency; a guarantor by the principal debtor in respect of liability to the creditor under the guarantee to satisfy the debt; and any contract by which one party agrees to indemnify the other—for example, an insurance contract. There are two other relationships in which there is a right of indemnity that are especially significant in automobile accident litigation. In each case the right is implied by law. A servant is liable to indemnify a master for a tort committed in the course of employment for which the master is vicariously responsible (*Lister v. Romford Ice and Cold Storage Co. Ltd.*, [1957] AC 555), and, where an automobile owned by one person is driven by another with the consent of the owner, the driver is liable to indemnify the owner for any loss or damage caused by negligent driving for which, by virtue of legislation like s. 166(1) of the Highway Traffic Act, RSO 1990, c. H.8, the owner is responsible (*McFee v. Joss* (1924), 56 OLR 578 (App. Div.)).

As regards contribution, this right is implied by law in relationships such as that existing between partners, trustees, guarantors, and joint debtors. Further, there is a statutory right of contribution between concurrent tortfeasors.

The character of third-party procedure where contribution or indemnity is claimed was noted by Cassels J in *Horden-Richmond Ltd. v. Duncan*, [1947] KB 545 at 551-52, in these words:

> One has to bear in mind that third-party proceedings are proceedings in the nature of a separate action brought by a defendant against a third party, in which the cause of action is by no means necessarily the same as the cause of action which brings the plaintiff and the defendant before the court. The cause of action which brings a plaintiff and a defendant before the court in such a case as may arise out of this accident is negligence. The cause of action which entitles a defendant to bring a third party before the court is the liability of the third party to make contribution or to pay an indemnity. That cause of action has not arisen until the liability of the defendant has been ascertained. Under [the provisions] governing third-party proceedings, notice of them is given to a third party before liability is established. It is one of the peculiarities of that procedure which enables this to take place before there is any liability. But the plaintiff can never get a

judgment against the third party, it is only the defendant who gets a judgment against the third party. Neither, in such proceedings, could the defendant succeed and yet leave the plaintiff with judgment against the third party. It is only on the defendant being made liabile that the defendant has any cause of action against the third party. Whatever for convenience of procedure may be the order for directions for the trial, however the witnesses may be called and heard, or whether the proceedings by the plaintiff against the defendant are tried at the same time as the proceedings by the defendant against the third party matters not. The position is quite clear. The proceedings by the defendant against the third party are independent of and separate from the proceedings by the plaintiff against the defendant, except that, when the defendant is made liable to the plaintiff, he then has his right open against the third party to establish, if he can, that he possesses a right to indemnity and contribution from that third party.

However, as observed initially, third-party procedings in many jurisdictions are not limited to situations involving claims for contribution or indemnity. For example, Ontario rule 29 clearly contemplates assertion of claims by the defendant independent of the claims of the plaintiff (Watson and McGowan, *Ontario Supreme and District Court Procedure* (1987), at 349:

> Rule 29.01(b) expressly authorizes the assertion by a third party claim of an "independent claim" the defendant may have against the third party, provided it arises out of the transactions or occurrences involved in the main action or a related series of transactions or occurrences. So, for example, if P (a passenger) sues D (the driver) for damage arising out of an automobile accident, D may, by a third party claim, seek to recover from X (the driver of another car) the damages that D suffered in the same accident.
>
> The significance of this change should not be underestimated. It changes the very nature of a third party claim. No longer is it limited to situations designed to obtain "a flow through of recovery" to D from the third party because of the judgment that the plaintiff may obtain against the defendant. Instead, it is now a general joinder device by which a defendant may engraft on to the main action any "related claim" he or she may have against non-parties, subject to the power given to the court by rule 29.09. (Compare the analogous "same transaction or occurrence" language used in the various general joinder rules; see rule 5.02(1)(a) and (2)(a) (joinder of multiple plaintiffs and defendants), and rule 6.01(1)(b) (consolidation)). Since the availability of third party claims against non-parties and crossclaims against co-defendants are designed to be parallel, rule 28.01(1) and rule 29.01 use virtually identical language.

One of the most significant features of third-party procedure is that the decision reached by the court on the issues between the plaintiff and the defendant binds the third party. This follows because the rules permit the third party not only to defend against the defendant's claim, but also to participate in the main action and defend the claim of the plaintiff against the defendant. Of course, it is very much in the interest of the third party to defend the plaintiff's claim against the defendant, if the situation is one in which should that claim fail, the third-party claim will also fail. The third party has substantial leeway in defending the main action and can raise not only any defence open to the defendant, but also defences not raised by the defendant or defences that contradict those presented by the defendant: *Smith v. Brown*, [1955] OWN 201; *Hi-Grade Welding Co. Ltd. v. Lytle Engineering Specialities Ltd.*, [l965] 1 OR 697 (action for damages against seller of goods for breach of warranty as to quality, with claim by seller against supplier for indemnity. Third party allowed to deny contract between plaintiff and defendant although defendant had admitted contract and merely denied a breach.)

Negligence Act. Since it has a major impact on joinder generally, and on third-party claims in particular, this is a convenient place to say something about the Negligence Act, RSO 1990. This legislation, and similar legislation in most Commonwealth jurisdictions, does two things. First, it does away with contributory negligence as a complete defence, which was the situation at common law—that is, if the plaintiff caused or contributed to her own injuries through her own negligence—to any degree—that was a complete defence to any claim by the plaintiff. Instead, under the legislation, the absolute defence is abolished in favour of a regime in which the plaintiff's contributory negligence merely goes to reduce *pro rata* the plaintiff's recovery, according to the relative degrees of negligence. So even a plaintiff whose own negligence is 90 percent the cause of his injuries can still recover 10 percent of his assessed damages. However, it is the second aspect of the legislation that is most important regarding joinder. The legislation makes all concurrent tortfeasors jointly and severally liable for the plaintiffs injuries—that is, if D1 and D2 equally contribute to the plaintiff's injuries through their negligence, the plaintiff is entitled to (and will normally be given) a judgment against both of them for the full amount of the damages. While the plaintiff is only entitled to satisfaction of the amount of the judgment once, the plaintiff can (if need be—for example, if one defendant is insolvent) execute for the whole of the amount of the judgment against any one of the defendants. The legislation further provides a right of contribution between tortfeasors who are held jointly and severally liable—that is, if one of them is called to pay the plaintiff more than her *pro rata* share of the damages then she can recover that amount from the other (a right that will be worth nothing if the other is insolvent). The overall effect of this regime is to place on the defendants, rather than the plaintiff, the risk of insolvency of one of the defendants. This contributory negligence regime is in contrast to the "comparative negligence" regime in place in many US states under which a defendant is only ever liable for his *pro rata* share. The contributory negligence regime can be characterized as an "in for a penny, in for a pound" regime because it can lead to a defendant who is only slightly to blame for the plaintiff's injuries—for example, 1 percent) being held liable for, and having to satisfy, 100 percent of the plaintiff's damages. It will often lead injured plaintiffs to search out and sue "deep pocket" defendants who merely made a small contribution to the plaintiff's injuries.

The contributory negligence regime of the Negligence Act impacts on joinder decisions in various other ways. A plaintiff may join both D1 and D2 as defendants, not merely because she is in doubt about from whom she is entitled to relief, but to guard against the risk that one of them will not be able to satisfy the whole judgment. While the legislation gives joint tortfeasors a right of contribution, this right (like any right) is one for which a claim has to be asserted and a judgment obtained. Consequently, in an action where contributory negligence is alleged against multiple defendants, those defendants should, and normally will, "claim over" against each other for contribution by means of a cross-claim. What if the plaintiff sues D1 alone and D1 believes that D2 contributed to the plaintiff's injuries? Here D1 can join D2 as a third party, asserting the latter's negligence and claiming contribution. (This, in turn, will likely lead the plaintiff to amend to add D2 as a defendant because if D2 is merely a third party and is found to be 100 percent the cause of the injuries, the plaintiff will fail in the action because in order to recover he or she must establish that *a defendant* caused his or her injuries; the plaintiff can never obtain a judgment against a third party.) We have already discussed compulsory counterclaims and have seen that there is conflicting Canadian authority on the issue.

The following cases are intended primarily to illustrate the use of third-party claims, and to give you a feel for third-party proceedings.

Daniel Industries Inc. v. Alberta Energy Co.
(1989), 37 CPC (2d) 118 (Alta. CA)

Appeal from order staying third party notice pending trial of main action.

PER CURIAM (Memorandum of judgment): ... At issue here is a stay of a third party proceeding.

The plaintiff contracted with the defendant (or its distributor) to supply 16 valves manufactured by the defendant for an oil pipeline. The plaintiff also contracted with the third party to design how to install them, and to supervise installation. After operation for some time, one of the valves blew up. Another valve was removed for inspection. On advice of the third party, all the valves from the defendant were removed and replaced by valves from another manufacturer.

The plaintiff sued only the defendant manufacturer (and its distributor). It did not sue the third party. The defendant issued a third party notice against the third party. The plaintiff moved to strike out the third party notice, or in the alternative to stay it until after trial. The chambers judge stayed it, and the defendant appeals.

The learned judge's reasons are not recorded. The plaintiff first argues that the third party notice contravenes a rule of law. The appellant agrees that the rule of law exists, so the question is its application. The rule forbids a third party notice which is based solely on facts which, if proved, would give a complete defence to the main action. In such a case the very facts which would make the third party liable to the defendant would make the defendant not liable to the plaintiff. So the main action would be dismissed, and there would be no need for contribution or indemnity.

Some cases have applied that rule in situations where the plaintiff and the third party are identified with and responsible for each other's fault, by statute, for example, a passenger and his driver; or the government guaranteeing a student loan, and the lending bank. The defendant here offered to abandon its appeal and its third party notice if the plaintiff would agree to be identified with any fault or liability of the third party. But the plaintiff did not volunteer such liability. No one argued that the plaintiff and the third party are in law identified or vicariously liable for each other here, so the identification doctrine does not apply.

Here the third party notice denies liability to the plaintiff. But should there be such liability, it claims indemnity "in whole or in part." It alleges that the third party (a) inspected and approved the valves, (b) had fabrications built incorporating those valves, (c) undertook to inspect and ensure proper construction, (d) did all those things "negligently" and failed to do them properly (with extensive particulars), (e) caused the one explosion by those defaults, and (f) improperly advised the plaintiff after one valve exploded that all the rest should be replaced, and did not tell the plaintiff that the cause was its own previous defaults.

The plaintiff suggests that the facts alleged in the third party notice will either be found or not be found at trial. It says if they are found, they will give a complete defence to the action, and so render the third party notice unnecessary. That may be so at common law, but the defendant points out that s. 3 of Alberta's Tort-Feasors Act and s. 2 of its Contributory Negligence Act change that. They allow for partial defences and percentages of liability. If the defendant is partly to blame, the plaintiff will recover a judgment for all its loss against the defendant. The defendant may then claim contribution against the other tortfeasor for the portion which was the latter's fault. The courts have often held that such a claim over for contribution may be made by third party notice.

Therefore, the trial or the third party notice need not produce an all-or-nothing situation. The trial judge might find that the first valve exploded because of the combined effects of the defendant's poor design or manufacture, and of the third party's poor inspection or installation method or supervision. He might also find that the other valves were removed and replaced because of the combined effects of some of those things plus poor advice by the third party. In any such event, the third party claim would be well-founded. The third party claim is necessary, since the plaintiff chose not to sue one of the alleged original tortfeasors.

Counsel for the plaintiff admitted in argument that such trial results were possible, but contended that they were very unlikely, especially respecting the one valve which exploded. Counsel for the defendant contended that such results were not improbable. There have been fairly extensive examinations for discovery to date, which are detailed by an affidavit of the plaintiff's officer for discovery. That affidavit is the only evidence. It says nothing about the merits of the main lawsuit, or the merits of the third party claim. We are unwilling to assume that it is very unlikely that there could be a mixed result in this three-cornered suit. Such mixed results are not uncommon in construction litigation. We cannot see that finding bad manufacture of the valves would render bad installation improbable. Negligence by the manufacturer and the installer could co-exist and compound each other.

Therefore, in our view, the third party notice cannot be struck out, and must be taken to be a proper third party notice.

The chambers judge granted the alternative relief of a stay, and counsel gave us brief argument on that topic. A few days have been reserved for further examination for discovery by both parties. The plaintiff's counsel believes that the main action will then be ready to set down for trial, but the defendant's counsel believes that it will not. How long the third party proceedings would delay trial (if not stayed) is not clear. But the evidence before us is that a great deal of the third party's information and documents have already been produced to the defendant in the main action. In argument, the plaintiff suggests that little, if any, has not. Therefore, the only evidence suggests that additional discovery from the third party would not take long, and so would not long postpone trial. The benefits of having the identical fact issue tried once by one judge and not twice by two judges are always great, and must be doubled in such a technical suit. Inconsistent findings by the two judges would be a disaster, and the cost of trying the same issues twice would be no kindness to anyone.

The plaintiff suggests that the third party notice may have been issued only to get discovery and not in good faith because the third party is out of business. The defendant's counsel assures us that is not so, and there is no evidence that the third party lacks assets or lacks insurance. We would not find bad faith or oblique motives without evidence.

The plaintiff briefly suggested delay by the defendant, but the only affidavit does not address that point. The motion to strike out the third party notice was filed over two years after the third party notice was issued. It is alleged that the defendant had issued formal notices against the third party for discovery of documents and examination for discovery many months before the notice of motion. There is no basis in evidence for finding delay, let alone undue delay.

That covers all the grounds argued to support the order for a stay. We allow the appeal, discharge the order of the learned chambers judge, and dismiss the motion to strike out or stay the third party proceedings. As each party sought costs of the appeal, the defendant will have costs of the appeal. As the reasons of the chambers judge and the arguments before him are not known, costs of the Queen's Bench motion to strike out or stay the third party notice will be awarded by the trial judge.

Appeal allowed.

Carswell v. Traders General Insurance Co.
(1987), 19 CPC (2d) 126 (Ont. Dist. Ct.)

Motion by third party pursuant to r. 21.01(1)(b) to strike out third party claim.

TROTTER DCJ: This is a motion by the Corporation of the Town of Bracebridge to strike out the third party claim on the ground that it discloses no cause of action. The plaintiffs, Gordon and Hazel Carswell commenced an action against the defendant, Traders General Insurance Company, for compensation under an insurance policy issued by the defendant to the plaintiffs. Damage had resulted to the plaintiffs' property as a result of flooding which was caused by blasting operations conducted adjacent to the plaintiffs' property. The defendant denied liability under the insurance policy. The defendant issued a third party claim against the Corporation of the Town of Bracebridge.

The grounds for the third party's motion was that pursuant to s. 242 of the Insurance Act, RSO 1980, c. 218:

> Only an insurer who makes payment pursuant to an insurance contract is subrogated to the insurance right of action and can bring an action in the name of the insured.

In its factum, the third party stated that:

The right of subrogation does not arise unless and until the insurer has admitted the insured's claim and paid the sum payable pursuant to the policy;

and:

Insurance companies have no independent right to maintain in their own names, and without reference to the person insured, an action for damage to the thing insured.

Counsel for the defendant argued that r. 29.01 of the Ontario Rules of Civil Procedure aborted its claim. Rule 29.01 reads as follows:

29.01 A defendant may commence a third party claim against any person who is not a party to the action and, who,

(a) is or may be liable to the defendant for all or part of the plaintiff's claim;

(b) is or may be liable to the defendant for an independent claim for damages or other relief arising out of,

(i) a transaction or occurrence or series of transactions or occurrences involved in the main action, or

(ii) a related transaction or occurrence or series of transactions or occurrences; or

(c) should be bound by the determination of an issue arising between the plaintiff and the defendant.

Counsel for the defendant particularly relied on r. 29.01(c) arguing that:

A defendant is entitled to commence a third party claim against any person who should be bound by the determination of an issue arising between the plaintiff and the defendant.

The defendant also relied on r. 29.01(a) in stating that:

A defendant may commence a third party claim against any person who is or may be liable to the defendant for all or part of the plaintiff's claim.

The defendant further relied on s. 148 of the Courts of Justice Act, SO 1984, c. 11, which reads as follows:

148. As far as possible, multiplicity of legal proceedings shall be avoided.

The issue is whether r. 29.01 effects a substantial change in the law permitting the issuance of a third party claim against the Corporation of the Town of Bracebridge. Any resolution of this matter entails an examination of the competing issues of subrogation under insurance law, versus the desire under the new Rules to simplify third party procedure, and to avoid multiplicity of proceedings.

Under the new R. 29, there are significant changes in the availability of third party proceedings. Under the former Rules, a third party claim was available only in respect of claims for contribution or indemnity "or other relief over." This latter phrase was restrictive and did not permit the assertion by the defendant against a third party of a claim that was independent of the outcome of the main action. However, the new R. 29 does not use the phrase "other relief over." Rule 29.01(b) expressly authorizes the assertion by a third party claim of an "independent claim" the defendant may have against the third party, provided it arises out of the transactions or occurrences involved in the main action or a related series of transactions or occurrences. As stated in Holmested and Watson's Ontario Civil Procedure (loose leaf), p. 29-6 [rule 29, s. 3[2]]:

> The significance of this change should not be under-estimated. It changes the very nature of a third party claim. No longer is it limited to situations designed to obtain "a flow through of recovery" to [the defendant] from the third party because of the judgment that the plaintiff may obtain against the defendant. Instead, it is now a general joinder device by which a defendant may engraft on to the main action any "related claim" he or she may have against nonparties, subject to the power given to the court by rule 29.09.

Several cases have arisen on this subject pursuant to the enactment of the new Rules of Civil Procedure. In *Rupolo v. Tulshi* (1985), 51 OR (2d) 288 at 289 (Ont. Master), affirmed (1985), 51 OR (2d) 288 (Ont. HC), it was held that in a motor vehicle action against the tortfeasor and the plaintiff's own insurer under the uninsured motorist coverage, that it was permissible for the defendant insurer to assert a third party claim against the putative insurer of the tortfeasors to determine whether it was liable to the tortfeasor. It was held that the Rule clearly permitted a defendant to commence a third party claim against the person who should be bound by the determination of an issue arising between the plaintiffs and the defendant and in so doing effected a substantial change in the law. It must be noted that in this case, the plaintiffs' own insurer was entitled to issue third party proceedings before the plaintiffs had obtained judgment against the defendants.

Master Sandler stated [49 CPC, at 19-20]:

> Further, from the plaintiffs' point of view, if this action went to trial with only the plaintiffs, the alleged wrongdoers Tulshi and Hardeo, and the defendant Wawanesa, as parties, and if the plaintiffs were unsuccessful against the defendant Wawanesa, because of a finding that the Tulshi-Hardeo vehicle was insured by Royal/Skutnik, Royal/Skutnik would not be bound by such finding, and in any subsequent action against them under s. 226(1) of the Insurance Act, ... Royal/Skutnik could again raise the issue that they did not issue a policy of insurance, and the plaintiffs might also fail against Royal/Skutnik on the basis that they were not the insurer of the Tulshi-Hardeo vehicle, an inconsistency of result that would lead to a serious injustice.

On appeal, Smith J stated [1 CPC (2d), at 13; OR, at 297-98]:

> The scope of the Rule having now been considerably broadened to include cases in which indemnity and contribution may have no part, it seems to me that the dilemma facing and plaguing the Courts in cases involving the issue as to whether the defendant was insured or not can be resolved by the very simple expedient of the addition of the alleged insurer of the defendant as a third party. No claim can be asserted against that insurer in the action since liability under the Insurance Act, RSO 1980, c. 218, only arises upon a judgment being recovered. However, once having been given an opportunity to participate in the trial and being bound by the findings made, it is difficult to accept that in a case in which the defendant was held to be insured by the third party, the plaintiff would still be put to the expense of the separation action under s. 226 of the Insurance Act. There would be no conceivable defence to such a claim advanced by the victim against the defendant's insurer.

... It has been argued before me that the right of subrogation does not arise unless and until the insurers have admitted the assured's claim, and have paid the sum payable under the policy. However, as held in the Rupolo case [49 CPC, headnote]:

> It was in the legitimate interest of W Co. [the insurer] and the plaintiffs that W Co. obtain production and discovery from R Co. and S and that R Co. and S be bound by the findings in the plaintiffs' action. Although R Co. and S could not have been added as third parties under former Ontario R. 167, r. 29.01 of Ontario's new Rules of Civil Procedure had effected a substantial change in the law, and permitted a defendant to commence a third party claim against a person who should be bound by the determination of an issue arising between the plaintiffs and the defendants.

Therefore, if the Corporation of the Town of Bracebridge were added as third party, the expense of a separate later action against it might be avoided. Subrogation would still apply, in that the defendant could only obtain judgment from the third party after the defendant had been found to be liable to the plaintiff.

In my view, the primary consideration is to see to it that all parties involved in the same factual situation have their rights determined without a multiplicity of proceedings. Therefore, with this in mind, and for the reasons set forth above, this motion is dismissed. Costs in the cause.

Motion dismissed.

Hannah v. Canadian General Insurance Co.
(1989) 90 NSR (2d) 83 (SC)

HALLETT J: This is a motion made by the defendant at the pretrial conference that the action be adjourned and an order made requiring the plaintiff to add a blasting contractor as a defendant. The plaintiff's action is against the insurer of his home for damages caused to his home from blasting carried out on an adjacent lot. The insurance contract provides for coverage caused by "explosion."

Civil Procedure Rule 5.04(2)(b) provides:

> 5.04(2) At any stage of a proceeding the court may, on such terms as it thinks just and either of its own motion or on application, ...
>
> (b) order any person, who ought to have been joined as a party or whose participation in the proceeding is necessary to ensure that all matters in the proceeding may be effectually adjudicated upon, be added as a party.

This motion comes very late in the proceedings, just four days prior to trial, the action having been commenced in November of 1987, and the trial dates set many months ago. The defendant raises the point that if the trial goes ahead and the plaintiff succeeds and the defendant then exercises his right of subrogation and sues the blasting contractor, there is a danger of inconsistent findings as to what damage was caused by the blasting as a result of two proceedings dealing with this issue and, secondly, by not joining the blasting contractor as a defendant, there will be a duplicity of proceedings and the attendant increased costs; he suggests this is not in the interest of justice. ...

In *Canada Permanent Trust Co. v. Rao et al.* (1981), 46 NSR (2d) 336; 89 APR 236, at p. 343, Cowan CJTD, quoted from *The Law of Civil Procedure*, Williston and Rolls, vol. 1, p. 426, that the objects of third party proceedings are:

> (1) to avoid a multiplicity of actions. The procedure provides a substitute for another action, and disposes of all issues arising out of a transaction as between the plaintiff and the defendant, and between the defendant and a third party;
>
> (2) to avoid the possibility that there might otherwise be contradictory or inconsistent findings in two different actions on the same facts;
>
> (3) to allow the third party to defend the plaintiff's claim against the defendant;
>
> (4) to save costs; and
>
> (5) to enable the defendant to have the issue against the third party decided as soon as possible, in order that the plaintiff can not enforce a judgment against him before the third party issue is determined.

In *Burry v. Centennial Properties Ltd.* (1979), 38 NSR (2d) 450; 69 APR 450, the court, in considering the scope of rule 17.02, stated at paragraph 32:

> The only real limitation on the use of third party proceedings is contained in the *Judicature Act* where the second cause of action must be "relating to or connected with the original subject of the proceeding," but once that connection is established then procedurally all common issues should be tried and disposed of at the one time.

In my view, the defendant's counsel puts too narrow an interpretation on rule 17.02 as the blasting contractor should, in the interest of the efficient administration of justice, be bound by a determination of the issue of causation and damages that arises between the plaintiff and the defendant in these proceedings. The defendant could have applied to join the blasting contractor as a third party as provided for by rule 17.02(1)(c); it chose not to do so. The plaintiff is entitled to choose his remedy and has chosen to sue his insurer under the insurance contract which provides for extended coverage, including damage from explosion. The plaintiff opposes the granting of the order. This motion, on the eve of the trial, comes too late. While it would be desirable to have the blasting contractor before the court, it would be unfair and not in the best interests of the administration of justice to adjourn this case four days before trial when trial dates were set so many months ago and the defendant could have applied months ago to join the blasting contractor. I am dismissing the motion.

NOTES AND QUESTIONS

1. Under the former Ontario practice, the availability of third-party claims was extremely limited and was restricted to claims for contribution or indemnity "or other relief over." This latter phrase did not permit a defendant to assert against a third party a claim that was *independent* of the outcome of the main action. The new rule does not use the phrase "other relief over." Moreover, rule 29.01(b) *expressly* authorizes the assertion by a third-party claim of an "independent claim" the defendant may have

against a third party, provided that it arises out of the transaction or occurrence involved in the main action or a related series of transactions or occurences. Under the former practice, in *Allen v. Bushnell TV Co.*, [1968] 1 OR 720 (CA), Laskin JA attempted to give meaning and definition to the words "other relief over" and held that in order to resort to third-party proceedings "there must be a connection of fact or subject matter between the cause of action upon which the plaintiff sued and the claim of the defendant for redress against the third party; and, such claim would ordinarily arise out of relations between the defendant and the third party anterior to those between the plaintiff and the defendant which precipitated the main action."

The purpose of the rule makers in drafting rule 29 was to (1) expand greatly the availability of third-party claims, and (2) get rid of the vague phrase "other relief over" (the definition of which was the subject of Laskin JA's judgment in *Allen*). Should rule 29 be interpreted by reference to its language and to the overall purposes of the new third-party proceedings and not by reference to prior court decisions which it was the purpose of the rule to overcome?

2. Matters do not necessarily stop with third parties. The rules provide that a third party may in turn make, for example, a fourth party claim: see Ontario rule 29.11.

3. *The mechanics of third-party proceedings.* See Ontario rule 29. For other examples see Alta. rules 66-79, BC rule 22, NB rule 30, NS rule 17, and Sask. rules 1070-1071.

The defendant is required to serve the third-party notice within a stipulated time after delivering the statement of defence or the time limited for its delivery has expired. The defendant must also serve the third party with a copy of the pleadings previously delivered. (Where a defendant counterclaims, any defendant to the counterclaim may take third-party proceedings—for example, see, Ont. rule 29.13.)

Under the former practice, challenges to the availability of third-party proceedings were almost always raised by the third party, rather than by the plaintiff in the main action. This practice is difficult to support because it amounts to the third party's questioning at the outset the defendant's procedural right to sue him or her, a right the third party would not enjoy if he or she were simply made a defendant to an action in which the (now defendant) were plaintiff. In reality all that third-party proceedings are is another action (defendant v. third party) engrafted on to the main action.

On the other hand, the *plaintiff* is the party whose procedural rights may be adversely affected by the addition of third-party claims. For this reason, under Ontario rule 29 only the plaintiff in the main action, and not the third party, is given the express right to challenge the propriety of a third-party claim: rule 29.09. It is, however, open to the third party to move under the general relief against joinder provision (rule 5.05) in an appropriate case.

If the motion is unsuccessful, or if no motion is brought, the third party is required to file a statement of defence and the defendant may then deliver a reply. As previously indicated, the third party may also deliver a statement of defence to the plaintiff's statement of claim. The third party and the defendant (and the third party and the plaintiff where the main action is being defended by the third party) may have production and discovery from each other in the same manner as between a plaintiff and a defendant. The third-party issue is to be set down for trial at the same sitting of the court for which the action between the plaintiff and defendant was set down. However, it should be observed that rule 29.09 provides that "a plaintiff is not to be prejudiced or unnecessarily delayed by reason of a third-party claim."

Where a third party in turn has a claim to assert, fourth-party proceedings are available, and claims by fourth and subsequent parties may also be asserted: see—for example, Ont. rule 29.11.

4. *Conduct of the trial where third-party proceedings are taken.* The third-party action is placed on the list for trial next following the main action: see, for example, Ont. rule 29.08(1). The rule also provides that the third-party action shall be tried at or after the trial of the main action as the trial judge may direct; that the third party shall be at liberty to appear at the trial of the action and to take part therein in such manner and to such extent as the trial judge may direct; and that the third party shall be bound by any judgment or decision in the action. The extent to which there will be a separate trial in the third-party action depends on the nature of the main action and the claims asserted in the third-party proceeding.

In the typical automobile case where the defendant joins a third party alleging that the third party caused or contributed to the accident, and is thus liable to contribute under the Negligence Act, all of the issues between the defendant and the third party will, typically, simply be litigated in the trial of the main action and there will be no separate trial in the third-party proceeding. The reason for this is that usually in such a case the only issue between the defendant and the third party is who caused the plaintiff's injuries and, if both defendant and third party are found at fault, their respective degrees of responsibility. In this kind of action it is clearly convenient for the court and the parties, when considering the issues between the plaintiff and the defendant, to consider also those between the defendant and the third party. However, in other types of actions there may be issues between the defendant and third party—for example, where the defendant is asserting an independent claim—that are unrelated to any issues between the plaintiff and the defendant. In such a case, the main action will be disposed of and then the third-party proceedings will be heard.

C. Relief from Joinder: Consolidation and Orders for the Trial of Actions Together

As we have seen, the rules give the court power to relieve against the consequences of joinder when the court sees them as being serious. See Ontario rule 5.05 and the specific provisions under the rules relating to counterclaims (rule 27.08(2)), cross-claims (rule 28.10), and third-party claims (rule 28.09).

What can a party do if, though joinder, cross-claims, counterclaims, or third-party procedures are possible, the party capable of using such procedures does not do so but, instead, commences a separate action? For example, take the following situation: a car driven by A and in which B is a passenger is involved in a collision with a car owned and operated by C. A institutes an action for personal injuries against C claiming that the latter's negligence caused the injuries. B institutes a separate action against C making similar allegations. Can C force A and B to join their claims together or must C face the prospect of two trials?

The answer is to be found in provisions, such as Ontario rule 6, giving the court power to order *consolidation* of actions or the trial of actions together. Generally speaking the court will order consolidation of actions whenever joinder would have been proper. There are, however, certain exceptions—for example, the court will not order the plaintiffs to consolidate their actions if they are represented by different solicitors. Also, as a general rule, an order for consolidation will be refused if a trial of the claims together would not be convenient.

However, in those situations in which the court will refuse to consolidate actions, it nevertheless has a broad discretion to invoke a closely analogous device—to direct that the actions be tried together. The difference between consolidation and an order that the actions be tried together is as follows: if actions are consolidated, the two actions are completely melded into one and proceed in all respects as if there had been initial joinder of the claims. There is but one set of pleadings, one set of discoveries, one judgment, and one bill of costs. If an order is made that actions be tried together, the actions maintain their separate identity and there are separate pleadings, discoveries, judgments, and bills of costs. But the actions are set down on the list one after the other to be "tried in such manner as the court directs." Usually, the trial judge will order that the evidence in one action is to be taken as evidence in the other action or actions. In this way both or all of the actions are tried together by the same judge or jury. The purpose of directing the trial of actions together is the same as consolidation—to save time and to avoid inconsistent determinations. The difference between consolidation and an order directing the trial of actions together is more technical than real.

It is important to note that to apply for an order for trial of actions together may be an appropriate step for a plaintiff to take when an initial joinder of claims and parties has been successfully challenged by the defendant. In other words, denial of the plaintiffs' right to join multiple claims and parties may not be all that significant, for in many such cases the plaintiff may be able to obtain an order for trial of the actions together.

Bain v. Schudel
(1988) 67 OR (2d) 221 (HC)

CRAIG J (orally): This is an appeal by the plaintiff John Bain from the order of Master Sandler dated November 14th last, wherein the master ordered that the plaintiff's motion for the trial of this action, together with three other actions, be dismissed.

The within action arises as a result of a motor vehicle collision which occurred on May 19, 1988. In that action it is alleged that the plaintiff John Bain sustained serious injury to his neck, shoulders and back, including headaches and nervousness, emotional and physical upset, together with a general tearing and straining of the muscles and ligaments throughout his body.

The three other actions referred to above are, first, an action by John Bain against the Toronto Transit Commission and James Wright in action No. 12986/82 arising out of a motor vehicle collision which occurred on November 20, 1981, in which Bain alleges he sustained serious injuries of the same kind that he sustained in the accident of May 19, 1988.

The plaintiff also brought an action against London Life Insurance Company on July 25, 1984 (now action No. 25666/88), arising out of an allegation that London Life failed to pay disability benefits to the plaintiff due to the disability he suffered as a result of the 1981 motor vehicle collision.

On November 27, 1987, McRae J ordered that the London Life action be transferred to the Supreme Court to be tried together with the action by Bain against the Toronto Transit Commission No. 12986/82. The third action was brought by the plaintiff against Commercial Union Assurance Company in February 1984. That action has now been settled. It was settled subsequent to the order made by Master Sandler.

There is some uncontradicted evidence that the injuries sustained by the plaintiff in the two motor vehicle collisions are similar and overlapping, although no medical reports were produced on the hearing before Master Sandler. Also it is alleged that the plaintiff has remained unable to perform the duties of his employment since the first motor vehicle accident, with the exception of unsuccessful attempts at rehabilitation. He takes the position that both accidents have lessened his ability to earn a livelihood. ...

Certain cases discussed on this appeal were not brought to the attention of Master Sandler. ... As a result of those and other similar cases, a practice has been established which may be summarized in this way. If a plaintiff has had his injuries aggravated by involvement in a second vehicle accident following the first such accident, the proper method of computing the damage is as follows:

(1) assess the amount the plaintiff would have recovered against the first tortfeasor on the day before the second occurrence;

(2) assess the total damages for both accidents at the date of the trial, and

(3) subtract the first amount from the second, awarding the remainder as the amount of the damages against the second tortfeasor.

Even where a substantial period of time intervenes between the first and second accident, but because the injuries in the second are superimposed on those suffered in the first, the award of damages for each injury will be a matter of great difficulty and both cases should be tried together before a judge without a jury.

As I indicated a moment ago, there is some uncontradicted evidence before me that there is overlapping of injuries. Counsel sought to introduce medical evidence before me that was not before Master Sandler. I declined to admit this evidence.

The defendant Schudel herein is not represented on this appeal but counsel for the appellant informs me that counsel for Schudel consents to the order sought on this appeal. Also an examination for discovery in this action has been arranged for January 27th next. Counsel for the defendant in the first motor vehicle accident (of 1981) does not seriously oppose the appeal so long as there will not be any lengthy delays before trial.

The cases to which I have made reference do not create any rule of law but the practice is well established. For example, in *Rita v. Perrotta*, supra, Morden J (as he then was), stated at p. 177:

The importance, if not the necessity, of one tribunal trying the two actions is, in my view, obvious. To allow the two actions to be tried by separate tribunals, even if possible, having regard to the principles applicable respecting the determination of such damages, involves a substantial and unnecessary risk of injustice to at least one of the parties.

For the above reasons it is my opinion that these cases should be tried together.

In allowing this appeal I am not suggesting that the other two cases be struck from the trial list. I should have said earlier that those cases are now on the ready list for trial. In fact in the instant case I order that notice of listing for trial be dispensed with, that the time for placing this case on the trial list be abridged and that this action be placed on the ready list, Toronto non-jury, to be tried together with the other two actions mentioned on or before January 10, 1989.

Rae-Dawn Construction Ltd. v. Edmonton (City)
(1992) 10 CPC (3d) 356 (Alta. CA)

COTÉ JA (for the court): In 1986 and 1987, a number of construction suits were begun, two of them being builders' lien suits. They all involve the same construction failure, and unpaid construction bills. In 1987, by agreement those parties all sued the common construction insurers. In 1987, there was a motion to have all the suits tried together, but after discussion that was dropped. Instead, a master was simply asked to order that the construction suits be tried together, and he so ordered.

Since then, a large number of discoveries have been held in the construction suits, and they are close to being ready for trial, and have been so ready for about a year. Counsel for the insurers has taken no part in them. Much less has been done about discoveries in the insurance suit. If its discoveries are to plow any of the same ground, they will take a long time to complete. But little has been done with the insurers' counsel to discuss or agree on whether the construction suit discoveries can be used in the insurance suit. One of the parties to one construction suit accepted the money paid into court respecting his part of the insurance suit, and so he and his claim are now gone from the insurance suit. The insurers never were parties to any construction suit.

After those things occurred, one party common to both suits secured an order from a justice in chambers. The order directs that the construction suits cannot be tried until after judgment is given in the insurance suit. It also directs that the same trial judge is to try all the suits, and that the evidence from the insurance suit is to apply in the construction suits. Many of the other parties opposed that order, and now appeal.

It is desirable to try to do something to avoid duplication of proceedings or inconsistent verdicts. But in our view that cannot always be done, and should not be done where it unfairly retards litigation.

The construction suits are as much as six years old. It is entirely possible that at least one of the plaintiffs is free of blame for the construction failure. Many seem to have large prima facie debts owing to them, and the defence is essentially a set-off for the loss from the construction failure. Two of the suits are builders' lien actions, and the *Builders' Lien Act*, RSA 1980, c. B-12, contains a number of provisions suggesting that such suits should move speedily. One such plaintiff is no longer a party to the insurance suit, and so has no responsibility to keep it moving, and no interest whatever in it. While some issues overlap between the construction suits and the insurance suit, not all do. Even the issue of responsibility for the construction failure may not be legally identical in the two suits.

What is more, all parties agree that even under the order appealed some evidence would be led in the construction trial which would not be led in the earlier insurance trial. And as counsel differ somewhat, different arguments might well be heard at the two trials, even on supposedly identical issues. Therefore, even if the same trial judge heard both, inconsistent verdicts in the two trials would be possible.

The order appealed directs that the construction trial not start until after judgment has been rendered in the insurance suit. As there must be some waiting time between setting down and trial, and as one cannot tell how long judgment would be reserved in the insurance suit, that could easily add another year or two of delay. What is more, if the trial judgment in the insurance suit were appealed by any party (as seems fairly likely), that could add yet another two years' delay. Therefore, it might be years before the trial of the construction suits could begin.

Therefore, it seems to us that far too high a price has been paid in an uncertain attempt to achieve consistency and economy.

The construction suits should not have to wait for the insurance suit. The construction suits should be set down for trial as soon as they are ready, even though the insurance suit may well not be ready then. If they are tried before the insurance suit, or even by different judge, so be it.

Of course we do not forbid trial of the construction suits and the insurance suits at different times, but before the same judge. When the suit which is ready for trial later comes to be set down, if the judge who heard the other suits happens to be available, or can be made available, doubtless all concerned would prefer that she or he hear the later trial.

The respondents argued that the insurance suit can be got ready for trial as quickly as can the construction suits. As noted, we doubt that that is possible, and will not hold up the construction suits to see if that is so. But if it should happen that in fact the insurance suit is made ready as quickly, our decision does not preclude an application putting down both trials consecutively on the same trial list before the same trial judge.

However, it seems to us that trial together is not now possible. The parties differ in the construction and insurance suits, and many issues and pleadings are radically different. For example, in the insurance suit only the insurers are defendants. All the other players (except the one who has settled) are co-plaintiffs with no issues framed between them. When parties and issues differ significantly and there is no consent, we cannot imagine how simultaneous trials could be made to work. Nor is trial together what was directed by the order now appealed, nor is it the real thrust of any party's factum.

A large feature of trial together would presumably [be] the use of common evidence, rather than its segregation. In any event, that was ordered here. The evidence in the insurance suit is automatically to apply in the construction suits. How that would work is not entirely clear.

And we see some grave objections to that. First, the subcontractor who settled with the insurer (long before the motions in question were launched) would not take any part in the insurance suit. It could not object to the admissibility of evidence, nor cross-examine. That violates natural justice. Nor would it make sense to make that subcontractor again a party for that purpose, for its quarrel is with its former co-plaintiffs, not with the insurers who are the only defendants. Those insurers strenuously and correctly object to having to fight afresh in any respect with someone whom they have paid to go away and drop his claim.

Second, it is most unusual to tell a trial judge in advance what evidence he can and cannot admit. What evidence is proper often depends on the course of trial, and what evidence has preceded. No one can foresee all the twists and turns of a long trial. Ever since the Judicature Acts, civil trials have been before one trial judge who decides all the issues, factual, procedural and legal, and decides those issues in whatever order to him seems most fit.

Therefore, the order that the evidence in one trial apply maybe years later in a different trial with somewhat different players, appears to us to be unjust and unworkable.

The appeal is allowed and the order appealed is set aside.

V. INTERVENTION

Intervention deals with the circumstances under which courts will permit persons who are not parties to participate in the litigation and the roles they will play in the litigation. Not all jurisdictions have rules that deal with this issue and those that do vary in the manner in which they address it. Ontario rule 13 provides both for intervention as an added party and for intervention as a friend of the court.

The extract by Jillian Welch summarizes judicial attitudes to intervention and the reasons why intervention is controversial. Which traditional values of the adversarial system does intervention challenge and which ones does it foster? Should the courts' attitude be different for intervention in "public" as opposed to "private" litigation? What do these terms mean in this context?

**J. Welch, "No Room at the Top: Interest Group Intervenors and
Charter Litigation in the Supreme Court of Canada"**
(1985), 43 *University of Toronto Faculty of Law Review* 204, at 205

It is clear that the Supreme Court is not alone in struggling to deal with the role that interest group intervenors can and should play. Generally there is no right to intervene, and leave is discretionary in the court, so that courts have been largely left on their own to evolve criteria for granting and denying leave. An examination of the written decisions offered by lower courts in response to leave applications reveals a lack of consensus about who should be allowed to inject themselves into litigation which is not their "own."

Intervention is based upon a recognition that a lawsuit or criminal trial may involve the interests of a wider group than simply those of the two parties to the dispute. Thus, those who will be affected by the outcome in some way are given a chance to participate in the argument of the issues. As one commentator has noted, such a recognition runs counter to the traditional Anglo-American view of private law litigation, which assumes that litigation is a "closed" dispute between two individuals asserting directly opposite interests. As a result, intervention has been only rarely allowed. The courts have structured their discretion in a restrictive manner, potential intervenors having to prove not only that they had a direct interest in the outcome of the specific dispute and that their interests would not be adequately represented by the original parties, but that these factors outweighed considerations of prejudice to the original parties and the orderly and efficient handling of cases by the court.

However, where private litigation raises issues which are clearly "multi-polar" or even public in scope and potential intervenors are interest groups who have no direct interest in the specific dispute but rather in the development of legal doctrine over many cases, the traditional private law model of litigation is strained to a breaking point. Yet, as can be seen from the caselaw, courts are still using the traditional criteria of sufficient interest in the dispute and adequate representation of viewpoint to deal with intervention applications, and often the effect is to bar interest groups from involvement in private litigation, regardless of the social, economic, or political impact the decision might have.

In the following decision in *Schofield*, the court demonstrates the traditional view of litigation as a means of determining the law *only* for the parties. Note the care with which the court defines the interests of parties through reference to the operation of *stare decisis*.

Re Schofield and Minister of Consumer and Commercial Relations
(1980), 112 DLR (3d) 132 (Ont. CA)

[The applicant, a solicitor, sought an order permitting him to intervene on behalf of two clients in an appeal in which neither the solicitor nor the clients were directly involved. The appeal raised the issue whether no-fault benefits paid by the minister of consumer and commercial relations to a plaintiff injured in an accident involving an uninsured motor vehicle are to be deducted from the amount of the plaintiff's judgment or are to be deducted from the maximum amount payable by the minister out of the Motor Vehicle Accident Claims Fund in respect of the claim. The applicant solicitor represented a client ("Client A") who was involved in a pending case in which the same issue had been raised, and also represented a client ("Client B") who had settled her action on the basis that the amount of her recovery would be calculated with reference to the outcome of the present appeal.]

WILSON JA: Mr. Cherniak's application raises two questions, namely:

(1) Are Mr. Cherniak's clients persons "interested" in the *Schofield* appeal within the meaning of [former] Rule 504a?

(2) If they are, is this an appropriate case for the exercise of the Court's discretion to grant leave under the Rule?

With respect to Client A, there can be little doubt that he is "interested" in the *Schofield* appeal in the widest sense of that term. He is concerned with the outcome of it because he may be affected by the outcome of it. Indeed, he may be affected by the outcome of it more intimately and more immediately than members of the public generally who have no litigation currently outstanding involving the issue under review. Is he not then a person "interested" in the *Schofield* appeal within the meaning of the Rule?

In order to answer this question, it is necessary to analyze the nature of Client A's "interest" in the *Schofield* appeal. It is said by Mr. Cherniak that his interest is that he will be bound by the Court's order in *Schofield*. It will constitute a precedent governing the facts of his case because his case raises the same issue as is raised in *Schofield*. "How could one have a greater interest?" Mr. Cherniak asks. His client's rights will be determined on this appeal.

Is this correct? Is it appropriate for this Court to determine whether or not the decision in *Schofield* will govern Client A's case and then, on the basis of an affirmative answer to that question, find that Client A is a person "interested" in this appeal? I do not think so. I think this is "putting the cart before the horse." It is surely for the Court hearing Client A's case to decide whether or not *Schofield* is applicable to the facts of that case. This is fundamental, I believe, to the operation of the doctrine of precedent.

Assuming, however, that we accept Mr. Cherniak's approach to precedent, is this the type of "interest" contemplated by Rule 504a? ...

[Having reviewed cases decided under a similar federal rule, Wilson JA continued:]

It seems to me that [other cases] stand for the proposition that, in order to obtain standing as a person "interested" in litigation between other parties, the applicant must have an interest in the actual *lis* between those parties. While I would not be prepared to construe rule 504a so narrowly, it seems to me that the fact that the decision of that *lis* may be applied subsequently by another Court as a precedent in resolving a *lis* between other parties is not a sufficient interest to justify a grant of standing to one of those other parties. ...

Mr. Cherniak acknowledges that Client B's case will not proceed to trial having regard to the settlement and that therefore an interest based on precedent cannot be put forward on behalf of Client B, but he submits that the above clause gives Client B a "direct" interest in the *Schofield* appeal. Client B, he points out, will get more or less money under the terms of the settlement depending on the disposition of the appeal in *Schofield*.

With respect, I do not think this gives Client B any more "direct" an interest in the *Schofield* appeal than Client A has. It certainly makes Client B's contractual rights under the settlement hinge on the outcome of *Schofield* but this is surely a different thing from giving his client an interest in the *Schofield* appeal. Commercial agreements are drafted every day by solicitors with an eye to tax jurisprudence but I do not think it has ever been suggested that such agreements provide their clients with a basis for *locus standi* in someone else's tax appeal.

I appreciate that the Supreme Court of Canada granted *locus standi* recently under its comparable Rule ... . I believe, however, that in both cases the interveners were confined to public law issues such as legislative authority and the effect of the *Canadian Bill of Rights*, RSC 1970 (App. 111), and were not permitted to get into the merits of the *lis inter partes*.

We also have in Canada a lengthy tradition inherited from England of appointing persons to act as *amici curiae* but it seems clear that Mr. Cherniak's obligations to his two clients disqualifies him for that role. ...

There have, however, been a number of cases in the Supreme Court of Ontario, particularly in application for judicial review before the Divisional Court, in which non-parties have sought to be added as parties under Rule 136 of the Rules of Practice on the ground that they were in some manner interested in the issue under review. ...

In my opinion, no principle emerges from these authorities as to the nature of the interest an applicant must have in order to obtain joinder under that Rule. The one thing that does seem to emerge from them is that a person should not be added as a party if his interest is already adequately represented.

I believe that the same principle should be applied under Rule 504a and that, even if Mr. Cherniak's clients or either of them are persons "interested" in the *Schofield* appeal within the meaning of the Rule, the interest which he seeks to represent is already very capably represented by Mr. Wigie. This is not an application on behalf of a private or public interest group which might bring a different perspective to the issue before the Court. It is an application on behalf of an individual private litigant said to be identical in interest to the appellant.

I would therefore dismiss the application but, in the circumstances, without costs.

THORSON JA: I agree with the conclusion reached by my colleague Wilson that on the facts present before us on this application, this is not an appropriate case in which to grant leave to intervene in the within appeal. Having had the benefit of reading my colleagues reasons, I should like to add certain comments of my own, and to record my disagreement with one aspect of her reasons. ...

However the Court's discretion in this case ought to be exercised, and whatever decisions ought to guide the exercise of its discretion, it is obvious that the discretion must be exercised in such a way that appeals which are now pending or are brought before the Court in the future can continue to be dealt with and disposed of in an orderly way, fairly and impartially as between the parties, and without unnecessary costs or delays being imposed upon the parties. It must also be exercised in such a way as to preserve for the Court its ability to ensure that the orderly and efficient processing and handling of the cases before it can be maintained.

In my view, the accomplishment of both of these objectives could be jeopardized if a person were to be permitted to intervene in an appeal between other parties solely because, in the words of Jackett CJ, in the passage in *R v. Bolton*, [1976] 1 FC 252 at p. 253, quoted by my colleague, "he has an interest in another controversy where the same question of law will or may arise as that which will arise in the controversy that is before the Court." As my colleague Wilson has observed in her comments on the doctrine of precedent and how it is applied by our Courts, "It is surely for the Court hearing Client A's case to decide whether or not [the decision in this appeal] is applicable to the facts of that case."

Were it not so, the class of persons who might be argued to be "interested" in an appeal involving a particular question of law would be potentially unlimited, since virtually everyone can be said to have an interest in how the laws of general application are interpreted and given meaning and effect by the Courts. This is particularly the case with new laws which give rise to litigation before the Courts the outcome of which predictably will affect many persons beyond those immediately involved as parties to the litigation.

On the other hand, few if any of these persons have an "interest" in the outcome of the litigation in the sense of having any direct interest in the *lis inter partes*.

It seems to me that there are circumstances in which an applicant can properly be granted leave to intervene in an appeal between other parties, without his necessarily having any interest in that appeal which may be prejudicially affected in any "direct sense," within the meaning of that expression as used by Le Dain J, in *Rothmans of Pall Mall et al. v. Minister of National Revenue et al.* (1976), 67 DLR (3d) 505, [1976] 2 FC 500, [1976] CTC 339.

As an example of one such situation, one can envisage an applicant with no interest in the outcome of an appeal in any such direct sense but with an interest, because of the particular concerns which the applicant has or represents, such that the applicant is in an especially advantageous and perhaps even unique position to illuminate some aspect or facet of the appeal which ought to be considered by the Court in reaching its decision but which, but for the applicant's intervention, might not receive any attention or prominence, given the quite different interests of the immediate parties to the appeal.

The fact that such situations may not arise with any great frequency or that, when they do, the Court's discretion may have to be exercised on terms and conditions such as to confine the intervener to certain defined issues so as to avoid getting into the merits of the *lis interpartes*, does not persuade me that the door should be closed on them by a test which insists on the demonstration of an interest which is affected in the "direct sense" earlier discussed, to the exclusion of any interest which is not affected in that sense.

In my view it would be unwise, and would do a disservice to the jurisprudence which must be allowed to develop in the ordinary way around Rule 504a, based on a case-by-case approach to its application, to attempt to forecast, on the occasion of this application, the circumstances in which applications brought under the Rule at some future time might be granted in other classes of cases. The example given above is no more than a single illustration of one situation in which, as I see it, the door ought not to be closed by the application of one particular test of interest. This said, however, it seems evident to me that the kind of interest that the applicant in this case has been able to demonstrate in the outcome of this appeal cannot form a basis for the exercise of the Court's discretion to grant leave to the applicant to intervene in this appeal, given the need to draw a line which will avoid the very real practical difficulties already mentioned.

My colleague Wilson has alluded to the subject of tax litigation. This class of litigation affords a particularly dramatic illustration of the practical difficulties that could be encountered, both by litigants and by the Court concerned, if every taxpayer who might be prejudicially affected by the outcome of an appeal brought by one taxpayer on a particular question involving the interpretation of the law were free to seek and be granted standing to intervene in that appeal.

Because of the practical difficulties, the fact that the appellant's counsel in this case has consented to this application cannot, in my view, be a governing factor in this

Court's decision. Nor does the fact that there is a common respondent involved in this case make a difference which ought to be reflected in the disposition of the application.

By the same token, I am also unconvinced by the argument that the Court can afford to adopt a somewhat "relaxed" approach to the granting of leave under Rule 504a on the reasoning that, although the immediate result of granting any such leave may be to leave unanswered some of the practical problems here touched upon, it remains open to the Court under the Rule to impose upon an intervener such terms and conditions as the Court sees fit. This argument assumes that the unanswered problems can be met on a case-by-case basis by whatever terms and conditions are in fact then imposed. In my view, to adopt this approach is simply to transfer the problems to a second or later stage or level in the appeal process.

In the concluding portion of her reasons my colleague Wilson introduces a consideration with which I must, with deference, express my disagreement. After referring to a number of cases in the Supreme Court of Ontario in which non-parties to an action have sought to be added as parties under Rule 136 on the basis of their having an interest in the action such that they ought to be joined, or such that their presence is necessary to a complete adjudication of the issues, she comments that the one point that seems to emerge from these cases is that "a person should not be added as a party if his interest is adequately represented." She then adds that the same principle ought to be applied under Rule 504a, and that even if, in this case, the applicant's clients or either of them are persons "interested" in the appeal, "the interest which he seeks to represent is already very capably represented" by counsel for the appellant.

In my view this is not a consideration which this Court should take into account in an application under Rule 504a. To apply the Rule in such a way that the Court is in effect invited to assess, or feels it necessary to assess, whether a particular appellant is or is not capably or even adequately represented by counsel would be to put the Court in a most difficult position. However cautiously an invitation to embark upon such an assessment might be advanced by counsel for an applicant, it would still amount to an invitation to the Court to reach a conclusion as to the competence of another counsel, and to attach consequences to its conclusion in terms of how the application is disposed of by it. The acceptance of such an invitation would, in my opinion, place a severe strain on the ability of both Bench and Bar to maintain that proper balance between them which is so essential to the functioning of our Court system. I therefore reject this approach as a consideration to be taken into account in any application under Rule 504a.

In the result, however, I agree with my colleague Wilson that the application should be dismissed, and in the circumstances without costs.

ZUBER JA (dissenting): I have had the benefit of reading the reasons of my colleague Madam Justice Wilson but find that I am unable to subscribe to the result.

[I]t is to be observed that both Client A and Client B, like Edith Schofield, had claims against the Minister of Consumer and Commercial Relations. I agree with Madam Justice Wilson that the case of Client A falls short of providing a sufficient basis for this application. The case of Client A whose case against the Minister of Consumer and Commercial Relations is pending in the High Court will be affected by the result in this appeal by virtue of the operation of the doctrine of *stare decisis* and this alone in cases which do not affect the public interest is not sufficient. The case of Client B, however, is different. Client B has settled his case with the Minister of Consumer and Commercial Relations but the minutes of settlement make the quantum of the settlement dependent upon the outcome of this appeal. The respondent, by using this mechanism to settle the claim of Client B, has given him a significant contractual interest in the outcome of this appeal. I should add that the Minister does not object to the participation of Mr. Cherniak in this appeal, nor does Mr. Wigie, counsel for Edith Schofield. In my view, the position of Client B provides Mr. Cherniak with a sufficient interest in this appeal to warrant a Court exercising its authority under Rule 504a to grant him leave to intervene. I would, however, impose the condition that the intervenant shall not seek costs in this appeal but may be subject to them, depending on the result.

NOTES AND QUESTIONS

1. Consider how in Zuber J's dissent in *Schofield*, and in the following case, rulings regarding costs were made, in part, to control the participation of the intervenor. What are the strengths and weaknesses of such an approach?

2. The following decision is another in the case that earlier gave rise to the question of public interest standing. On reading it, try to articulate the distinctions between the initial concern to have the matter prosecuted (or defended) by the appropriate persons and the subsequent interest in ensuring that the court has the benefit of the participation of those who will best assist it in the appropriate resolution of the controversy.

Borowski v. Minister of Justice of Canada; Canadian Civil Liberties Association
(1983), 144 DLR (3d) 657 (Sask. QB)

NATHESON J: In separate applications the proposed intervenants applied for leave to intervene in this action. The plaintiff opposed all of the applications, whereas the defendants neither opposed nor supported the applications.

All of the applications were heard at the same time, and following the hearing thereof all of the applications were dismissed, with written reasons to follow.

I

The Canadian Civil Liberties Association ("CCLA") and Campaign Life Canada ("CLC") each applied to intervene as *amicus curiae* for the purpose of participating at the trial solely to the extent of presenting written arguments with respect to the question of the constitutionality of s. 251 of the *Criminal Code*.

The Canadian Abortion Rights Action League ("CARAL") applied for leave to intervene, but not as *amicus curiae*. The object of CARAL is to decriminalize abortion by removing it from the *Criminal Code*, and it was proposed that CARAL be permitted to intervene to enable it to fully participate in the trial to the extent of adducing evidence, cross-examining witnesses, adducing rebuttal evidence and submitting argument.

II

The plaintiff has alleged, generally speaking, that an individual, from the moment of his conception, is a living human being and an "individual" within the meaning of the *Canadian Bill of Rights*. Consequently, it has been alleged that the constitution, operation and conduct of "therapeutic abortion committees," and the acts of medical practitioners in effecting abortions, permitted pursuant to the provisions of s-ss. (4), (5) and (6) of s. 251 of the *Criminal Code*, are illegal and constitute a trespass to, and a violation of the fundamental rights of, an individual to his right to life. Presumably it will also be alleged that these subsections violate the legal rights of "everyone" embodied in s. 7 of the *Canadian Charter of Rights and Freedoms*.

The Minister of Finance has been named as a defendant by virtue of the allegation that he, his servants and agents, allocate money from the Consolidated Revenue Fund, comprised of taxes levied upon and collected from the plaintiff and all other taxpayers of Canada, for various purposes, including the provision of health care and treatment services throughout Canada, and that a portion of the money so allocated is designated for, and expended in, the establishment and maintenance of therapeutic abortion committees. Because, it is alleged, the objects and conduct of therapeutic abortion committees are illegal, it has therefore been alleged that the distribution of money by the Minister of Finance for these specific programs is illegal. ...

VII

Without attempting to even outline the developments in the United States whereby intervention in cases viewed as "causes celebre" is now apparently broadly permitted, it does appear that most interventions have been permitted, under the guise of designating the intervenor as *amicus curiae*, to permit submissions on behalf of a group of citizens who desire that the legal question before the court be resolved in a particular manner—a result is desired which will be consonant with the views advocated by that group. One may very well accept the proposition that publicly organized bodies may be more concerned than specific litigants with the development of laws related to general social interests, particularly when moral questions are interwoven with a challenge to existing laws, but it is still necessary to question whether a trial in a properly constituted court is the proper forum to permit such concerns to be expressed, particularly when expressed by counsel in the guise of *amicus curiae*.

Counsel for CARAL did not suggest that he, on behalf of his client, should be permitted to intervene as *amicus curiae*. CARAL was unquestionably desirous of advocating a position in opposition to that of the plaintiff. Although there is quite likely a moral issue interwoven in the plaintiff's challenge to the validity of the specific subsections of s. 251 of the *Criminal Code*, it would indeed be presumptuous of me to inferentially conclude that the Minister of Justice, through his agents, is perhaps incapable of effactually facing this challenge. It would be even more presumptuous at this stage to permit one or more parties to intervene for the purpose of fully participating in the trial, including the adducing of evidence. It is the trial judge's prerogative to decide whether any evidence preferred is relevant and therefore admissible. This prerogative would be substantially eroded if an organization such as CARAL should be granted leave, prior to the trial, to participate fully in the trial, because the granting of such leave would necessarily entail permission to adduce evidence which would presumably be adduced to advance the interests of CARAL, which may not necessarily be relevant to the issues which the trial judge perceives he must resolve.

CLC requested permission to intervene as *amicus curiae*, suggesting that its written submissions would supplement the arguments of the plaintiff and defendants. Nevertheless, it was quite apparent that CLC intended, if granted permission to intervene, to substantially support the position advocated by the plaintiff. ...

Intervention should not be permitted, prior to trial, to groups advocating a partisan position under the guise of *amicus curiae*. In any event, if the court requires a "friend" to assist it in the resolution of the issues raised by the parties to the action, the trial judge, after hearing the evidence adduced and arguments presented as a result thereof, is the only person who can make the appropriate assessment in this respect.

The material filed by the CCLA did not clearly reveal that this organization would, if permitted to intervene, adopt a partisan position. The CCLA desired only to be permitted to make written submissions to supplement the submissions of the plaintiff and the defendants. If permission had been granted to intervene for this restricted purpose, the CCLA would be required to make its submissions on the basis of evidence which it could not in any way influence. Its submissions would necessarily have to be based on the record of evidence, which is exactly the position with which it would be faced if it should attempt to intervene at an appellate level, such as in the Supreme Court of Canada pursuant to a rule promulgated for this very purpose.

It was for these reasons that all of the applications to intervene were dismissed.

Re Association of Parents for Fairness in Education
(1984), 8 DLR (4th) 238 (NB CA)

[An action was brought by the Société and Conseillers to obtain a declaration that the teaching of French to French-speaking students in the board's English schools was contrary to a number of provincial statutes. The court found, *inter alia*, that there was no parental right to enroll a student who is able to function in a language into an immersion program or that language. The rulings in the case had the effect of barring some 86 students from continuing in the extended core French program. The parents of at least 57 of the students formed an association to respond to the ruling. They were unsuccessful in persuading the school board to appeal the ruling and so they brought a motions for leave to appeal and to be granted intervenor status. The court found that it had inherent jurisdiction to grant leave to appeal to persons, though not party to an action, who alleged that they had been aggrieved or prejudiced by a decision in the action. The court went on to consider the intervention as follows:]

There can, however, be little doubt that the parents concerned in this case would feel aggrieved or prejudicially affected by the decision sought to be appealed against. Such a parent can hardly be described, in Lord Denning's expression, as "a mere busybody who is interfering in things which do not concern him"; rather he is "a person who has a genuine grievance because [a decision] has been made which prejudicially affects his interests": ... The children of a substantial number of these parents, according to the affidavit of the president of the Association, have been forced out of an educational programme in which they wished to participate, and the children of the other parents will be unable to avail themselves of this programme. They clearly have a ... personal stake in the outcome of the controversy" to use the words of Justice Brennan in *Baker v. Carr* (1962), 369 US 186 at p. 204. ...

The interest of the Board was obviously to ensure that its actions complied with the law; it does not seek to appeal the decision. The individuals really affected by the decision are the children and their parents in what they conceive to be their rights to educate their children under the programmes whose validity was contested in the action. It seems right and proper, in a case like this, that a person whose interests are seriously affected by a judicial decision be accorded the opportunity to be heard so that he can himself raise the issues he considers important in his own way.

It is not as if the parents had been neglectful of their interests. Some of them took steps to initiate a motion to intervene at trial but this was refused. As well, the assertion in the affidavit of the president of the Association that the parents, or at least many of them, did not fully appreciate the implications of the action until the judgment and the clarifications to it were issued cannot fairly be ignored. It was only when the clarification was issued in October that these implications were fully brought home to them.

The Société and Conseillers also claim they would suffer inconvenience if leave were granted. But apart from the inconvenience of responding to the appeal, a risk a person undertakes when he initiates an action, there does not appear to be any particular inconvenience. The Association has agreed to be bound by the record and to be joined as a defendant. The issues proposed to be raised on appeal are of a legal nature and, counsel for the Société and Conseillers conceded, fairly arise out of the judgment of Chief Justice Richard. Under the circumstances, the situation does not appear to be substantially different from other appeals.

NOTES AND QUESTIONS

1. What is the relevance of the diligence of the intervenors in seeking standing to participate in the litigation? What is the relevance of the potential inconvenience to the existing parties to the litigation? Does the relevance of these questions depend on whether a proposed intervenor seeks standing to intervene as a party or as a friend of the court?

2. The public funding and administration of education raises issues that frequently have significant effects on several different groups of interested parties: schoolchildren, their parents, taxpayers, educators, school officials, and the government. Accordingly, it is not surprising that when disputes arise and come to be litigated, they raise questions of standing and intervention. (Recall the concern canvassed by Mullan and Roman regarding the *New Ross Consolidated School* case and whether the parents of the children attending the school should have standing to challenge the dismissal of a teacher.) In the following decision, the court considers six applications for leave to intervene in a

constitutional challenge to the failure to fund Jewish day school education in Ontario. Note the way in which the court considers each of the applications on its own particular merits and, where it grants the application, tailors the terms of the intervention to maximize the usefulness of the intervention.

Re Adler
(1992) 9 OR (3d) 676 (Gen. Div.)

ANDERSON J: The six moving parties listed above seek to intervene in the above application (the Application) brought by Adler et al. The motions were heard in succession in the order set out above. Although all present varying questions for consideration and decision, there are principles of a general nature which will be applicable to each. These relate in large measure to the manner in which the discretion of the court should be exercised in dealing with a motion to intervene. Because of these common considerations, I have deemed it advisable to combine the reasons for judgment as they relate to each motion in one document so that portions which are applicable to all will not have to be repeated. ...

The applicants, Adler et al., are parents of children in Jewish day schools. ...

In conventional litigation between subject and subject, this rule has, for the most part, been narrowly construed. That is probably because the interests considered in such cases are usually financial, and considerations of stare decisis and issue estoppel are of concern. Constitutional litigation presents a range of considerations which is much broader and much more difficult to define. Interests of various kinds may be affected by the decision in a constitutional case, which are almost impossible either to number or identify.

Orders made on motions under Rule 13 are discretionary. In exercising the discretion, a court is faced by twin hazards. On the one hand, the rule should not be so narrowly construed as to exclude persons who may have a real, substantial and identifiable interest in the outcome of the proceedings. On the other hand, the proceedings ought not to be rendered unduly ponderous, onerous and unwieldy by the admission of parties whose interests are illusory, insubstantial, or excessively difficult to identify.

The original parties ought not to be unduly prejudiced or delayed by the intervention. The issues ought not to be so treated as to inhibit or fetter the judge before whom the substantive proceeding comes for disposition. Yet they must be sufficiently explored to deal intelligently with the motion to intervene.

Rule 13.01 deals with intervention as an added party. An order granting such status usually carries with it a right to adduce evidence and to participate generally in the proceeding. Intervention of a somewhat different kind is contemplated by rule 13.02. Somewhat similar considerations apply to both types of intervention. However, there is a significant distinction in that a party intervening as a friend of the court cannot adduce evidence, but is confined to making argument on the record as produced by the parties. ...

Motion by the Metropolitan Toronto School Board (MTSB) and Ontario Public School Boards Association (OPSBA)

... On the primary constitutional issue, I am not persuaded that MTSB has any special contribution to make. It seems to me that the constitutional interest of MTSB and its constituent elements will be fully and adequately represented by counsel for the respondents.

Should a prima facie case be made out by the applicants that their constitutional rights have been infringed, then the application will require consideration of s. 1 of the *Canadian Charter of Rights and Freedoms*, and whether such infringement is justified. A cursory review of the background material filed by MTSB on this motion, reinforced by the tenor of the factum and oral argument of its counsel, indicates that it is in this area that MTSB has the greatest interest and the greatest knowledge and expertise. Its interest and concern is with the maintenance of the public school system in its traditional form, and with the potential threat to that system which might result from success in the Application. The applicants do not resist intervention by MTSB as a friend of the court, but submit that its intervention should be so limited and that it should take the record as it is assembled by the parties. While I feel that the constitutional issue will be quite adequately dealt with by counsel for the respondents, and on the material which they will bring forward, it must be remembered that constitutional validity is their primary concern. I think it quite possible that in a detailed consideration of the potential effects of the application on the public school system, MTSB may not only contribute usefully to the argument, but may have useful evidence to advance. It must be left to the discretion and good judgment of counsel not to unduly encumber the record or to advance evidence that is simply duplication or corroboration.

I have concluded that MTSB has made out a satisfactory foundation for its motion to intervene as a party. However, its intervention should be limited to supplementing the record in areas which are of particular concern to it, and related to the application of s. 1 of the Charter, to filing a factum, and to participating in the oral argument to the extent deemed appropriate by the judge hearing the Application. ...

Canadian Civil Liberties Association

Canadian Civil Liberties Association (CCLA) ... supports non-denominational public schools and entertains the view that such schools provide an opportunity for various religious groups to develop appreciation and respect for each other, and that such tolerance will, in turn, foster religious freedom. It has a substantial record of involvement as intervener in various public interest causes. It seeks intervention for the purpose of opposing the Application. ...

It is interesting to an impartial observer to note that both the applicants and CCLA see in the application an issue of religious freedom and both, no doubt, are in favour of it. Given that common approach, it is interesting to see that they are potential adversaries on the Application.

Given this apparent anomaly, and given the objective consistently commended in the cases, of having the court assisted by information from different points of view, it seems to me appropriate that CCLA should be heard as a friend of the court. It shall be permitted to file a factum and participate in the oral argument, once again, to the extent permitted by the judge hearing the application.

The Multi-Faith Coalition for Equity in Education

... I would have grave reservations about admitting the coalition as an intervener because of its acknowledged wish to expand the issues to be dealt with upon the application. It seems to me that the issues which arise on the application, as constituted, are sufficiently complicated. I would be concerned that such enlargement of the issues would make the proceedings unduly ponderous and unwieldy and would result in prejudice to the applicants in the pursuit of the application.

The motion of the coalition for intervention shall be dismissed.

The Ontario Federation of Independent Schools

... In my view, the motion on behalf of the federation does not have appropriate bases for the granting of an order under Rule 13 as a party to the application. It seeks other relief and on quite different grounds.

Viewing its potential intervention, not as a party but as a friend of the court, it may well be that in the infinitely complex world of constitutional litigation, its ends may be not unrelated to those which are sought by the applicants, and it may well have a useful contribution to make.

Neither the applicants nor the respondents raise any objection to the intervention of the federation as a friend of the court, and an order permitting them to intervene in that character shall issue. They shall be entitled to file a factum and to participate in the argument to the extent permitted by the judge hearing the application.

Reverend William D.F. Morris

Mr. Morris is an ordained clergyman of the United Church of Canada who is now retired from the active ministry. Mr. Morris seeks to intervene as a knowledgeable and concerned citizen who wishes to oppose the application. I hope I do it no injustice when I express his concern as being chiefly related to the desirability and health of the public school system and the detrimental consequences for that system which might ensue if the application were granted. He has been an intervener in various proceedings of a public nature.

I am much in sympathy with Mr. Morris, and I think it admirable and desirable that concerned citizens should devote time and energy and substance to the advancing of causes in which they believe. However, I am not persuaded that his motion can be properly brought within the ambit of Rule 13 without giving to that rule an interpretation much broader than it has heretofore received. Mr. Morris has not demonstrated either an interest in the subject-matter of the proceeding, or that he may be adversely affected by the judgment, save as any individual Canadian might be affected. However desirable it might be that every citizen should be heard from, it is obviously impractical to give that effect to the rule. The motion by Mr. Morris shall be dismissed.

Conditions of Intervention

All of the orders permitting intervention shall be on the following terms and conditions:

(1) That the parties shall exercise their best efforts to adhere to the timetable for the proceedings set out above.

(2) That no intervening party shall seek or be made subject to any order as to costs.

The hearing and disposition of these motions has not been a simple matter, and it is entirely possible that I have overlooked some detail. In that case I may be spoken to. I can also envisage the possibility that there may be problems related to scheduling which will require further consideration and adjustment, and on those topics also I may be spoken to.

Judgment accordingly.

NOTES AND QUESTIONS

1. There has been debate on the move to liberalize intervention. The debate touches on many of the larger questions raised earlier in this casebook about the nature and scope of litigation and the courts' suitability as a forum for effecting social change. Jillian Welch, above, summarizes the main advantages of liberal intervention and emphasizes the connection between responsible decision making and broad participation:

> First, if interest groups are allowed to participate in cases of broad social import, become involved in delineating group rights, or effect the redistribution of benefits in society, then the courts will reach better, in the sense of more informed, decisions. Certainly they will be better than if there had been no participation at all. ... This clearly raises the serious problem of the sort of material these groups might put before the court and how its truth might be tested. Nevertheless, the involvement of non-parties will necessarily ensure that a more comprehensive range of issues and remediable possibilities will be put before the court than might be chosen by the contesting parties themselves.
>
> The second argument is one which rests upon the notion of "strategic litigation"—a long-term program of litigation in selected cases in order to influence the development of jurisprudence favourable to one's interests. The essence of the argument ... is that the beneficial characteristic of intervention is the protection it offers non-parties. Strategic litigation by interest groups is impossible unless they can inject themselves into cases, brought by their interest "opposites," which would potentially cut down or alter, through precedent, their jurisprudential gains.
>
> Third, if interest groups are included, courts will reach more acceptable decisions than those achieved from a narrow range of viewpoints. This will increase, not decrease as courts seem to fear, the legitimacy of their decisions. In short, one can argue that the reasons for allowing increased participation by non-parties in civil rights litigation go beyond the "self-interested" goal of protecting the interests of non-participants. Professor Chayes argues that, where courts must engage in social orderings affecting many interests, what he calls "public law litigation," securing the participation by representatives from a broad range of interests, helps assure the court that "it will not only properly shape relief but will increase the legitimacy of the final relief."

A stronger form of the argument would be that excluding interest groups from the litigation of "public" issues will inevitably result in excluding the voices of minorities. Yet to make a decision on "the fate of minority aspirations," as much *Charter* litigation will ask the courts to do, without minority participation, is to leave these groups largely at the mercy of the majority and to discount their rights. Further, it undermines the very claim to impartiality and apoliticism which might prompt the courts to deny any participation at all. "The legitimacy of judicial authority and leadership in resolving fundamental social conflicts is eroded where minorities are excluded."

2. To what degree is Welch's reasoning persuasive? Would the reasons she advances apply to all cases in the Supreme Court of Canada whether raising Charter or other issues? Would the reasons apply to all levels of courts? Is the case for restricting intervention stronger in lower courts, particularly at the trial level? Might the answer depend on the purposes for which intervention is sought?

3. In a comprehensive survey, "Public Interest Intervention in the Courts" (1987), 66 *Canadian Bar Review* 490, at 513, Philip Bryden of UBC Law School advances three arguments against a broad approach:

> The first are what might be described as arguments of principle. What is considered objectionable about public interest intervention is that it is believed to be incompatible with the proper functioning of the judicial system, or that it is unfair to the parties, who may be deprived of control over the litigation. The second type of objection can be termed arguments of practicality. Public interest intervention is not considered undesirable in and of itself, but only to the extent that it represents an unproductive use of the court's time and energy. The third type of argument is one of balance. The concern here is not that intervention is wrong or impractical but that it will not work well enough, so that the courts will be presented with an unequal or unrepresentative sample of the views of members of the public. I do not think that these objections can be dismissed out of hand, but I do believe that they must be weighed carefully in light of the positive contribution that public interest intervention can make to the process of judicial law-making.

Are you persuaded by these arguments? Do the judges in *Schofield et al.* appreciate or consider the arguments?

4. Do you think that persons or groups other than the parties to the *Jane Doe* litigation may wish to be involved? Could you identify an interest that is not represented by the current constellation of parties and that ought to be included?

VI. CLASS PROCEEDINGS

A class action is a device that allows a named plaintiff to assert a claim on behalf of a large number of others who have similar claims. In some aspects, a class action can be viewed as a massive joinder, allowing one action to resolve all relevant issues instead of a number of individual actions. But, perhaps more important, a class action also allows claims to be aggregated that would not otherwise be asserted because of the costs involved in doing so on an individual basis: each individual claim may be for a relatively small amount compared with the economics of litigation, but, if asserted, in total all the claims involve a substantial sum, or would involve a significant and broad-based relief if the remedy were non-monetary in nature—for example, an injunction.

Class actions are relatively new in common law Canada, though they have existed in the United States for some 30 years. The Ontario Class Proceedings Act, 1992 was proclaimed in force January 1, 1993. Ontario was the second Canadian jurisdiction to pass legislation in this area. Quebec has had such a procedure since 1978 under the Act respecting the Class Action, RSQ 1977, c. R-2.1. The British Columbia Class Proceedings Act, RSBC 1996, c. 50 came into force in 1995.

A. An Overview of Class Proceedings Legislation

Garry D. Watson, "Ontario's New Class Proceedings Legislation—An Analysis"
in Watson and McGowan, *Ontario Civil Practice 1999*
(Toronto: Carswell, 1999)

Introduction

Ontario's class proceedings legislation consists of two Acts—the Class Proceedings Act, 1992, SO 1992, c. 6, which establishes the procedure for class actions, and the Law Society Amendment Act (Class Proceedings Funding), 1992, SO 1992, c. 7, which provides a funding mechanism for class actions. In addition, a regulation has been made under the latter Act (O Reg. 771/92) and the former Rule 12 (Representative Proceedings) has been revoked and replaced with a new Rule 12 (Class Proceedings) (O Reg. 770/92).

The legislation uses the term "class proceedings" rather than the more familiar term "class actions," simply because the legislation contemplates that the proceedings may be either by way of action or application. However, since most such proceedings are more likely to be brought by an action, rather than an application, the terms "class action" and "class proceeding" are here used interchangeably.

Ontario's is not the first Canadian legislation specifically providing for class actions— Quebec passed such legislation in 1978. In broad outline the Ontario legislation is comparable to that of Quebec. Moreover, the legislation in both provinces is, in general terms, structurally similar to the well known American class action procedure provided in the US Federal Rules of Civil Procedure, Rule 23—but in many respects the Ontario procedure is more liberal in terms of facilitating class actions than the American or Quebec counterpart.

In attempting to predict the likely impact of the Ontario legislation, it is interesting to examine the Quebec experience. (See S. Potter and J.-C. René, "Class Actions— Quebec's Experience," in *Insight, New Class Proceedings Legislation*, April 11, 1991.) Initially, the Quebec courts took a restrictive approach to the interpretation and application of the class action legislation. Over time this attitude has changed and the class action is no longer perceived to be an exceptional judicial measure and is readily authorized when the basic certification requirements are met. But overall, in the 12 years immediately following the enactment of the Quebec class action legislation, the number of class actions generated was by no means massive or unmanageable. There were a total of 244 applications to certify class actions, resulting in 62 actions being certified and 71 denied certification (with 75 applications being settled or abandoned before any determination on the certification issue and 36 pending). While these statistics indicate that in Quebec certification is (slightly) more likely to be refused than granted, in those cases in which certification is granted the plaintiff's chances of success are greatly enhanced. Of the 62 class actions certified, 55 evolved into fully fledged actions; 12 of these actions were successful and only 4 were dismissed. (As of April 1991, 37 of these cases were still pending, with the 2 remaining cases either settled or abandoned.)

The Ontario legislation is clearly pro-class actions and removes most procedural barriers to the bringing of class actions. Whether it will lead to a significant volume of litigation will depend upon whether there exist groups of injured persons (and potential representative plaintiffs) who will now make use of the new procedure or, perhaps more realistically, whether the Ontario legal profession will spawn "legal entrepreneurs" who will assemble class actions and assume the attendant financial risks (and rewards) of conducting such litigation. This in turn will depend largely upon whether the costs regime established by the legislation will be sufficiently attractive to both potential representative plaintiffs and their lawyers.

1. Class Proceedings Procedure

(a) General

In general the conduct of class proceedings is governed by the Rules of Civil Procedure and such proceedings are commenced in the ordinary way. However, the Class Proceedings Act, 1992 contains a variety of special procedures for class proceedings. The key elements of the Act include the provisions for a certification procedure, the giving of notice to class members, the ability of class members to opt out, the regulation of discovery rights, the ability to make global or aggregate awards and discretionary judgment distribution, court approval of settlements and court-controlled contingency fees. (The legislation provides not only for plaintiff's class actions but also for actions against defendant classes. Since actions against defendant classes are likely to be relatively rare, to simplify the analysis presented here the focus is on plaintiffs' class actions. All section citations that follow are to the Class Proceedings Act, 1992 unless otherwise indicated.)

(b) Certification

At the outset of class litigation, the person commencing the action is required to seek an order certifying the proceeding as a class proceeding and appointing the person as the representative plaintiff: s. 2(2). (It is also open to a defendant to two or more proceedings to move to certify the proceedings and have a representative plaintiff appointed: s. 3). Although an order certifying a class proceeding is in no sense a ruling on its merits (s. 5(5)) (other than a determination that the pleadings disclose a cause of action), the motion for certification is a significant event in any proceeding because, unless certified, it may not proceed as a class action. Certification requires that the court screen potential class actions and the applicant must satisfy five criteria. As long as these criteria are met the judge has no discretion to deny certification: s. 5(1). The criteria are as follows:

1. the pleadings disclose a cause of action: s. 5(1)(a);

2. there is an identifiable class of two or more persons who are to be represented in the proceedings: s. 5(1)(b);

3. the claims of the class members raise common (but not necessarily identical) issues: ss. 1 and 5(1)(c);

4. a class proceeding will be the preferable procedure for the resolution of the common issues: s. 5(1)(d); and

5. the proposed class representative will fairly and adequately represent the interests of the class, has a plan for advancing the proceeding and does not have a conflict of interest with other class members: s. 5(1)(e).

Under the former procedure there were a number of factors, which if present precluded class proceedings. These have now been removed by the new Act. It is specifically provided in s. 6 that certification is not to be refused solely because the relief claimed involves (1) separate contracts, (2) different remedies for different class members, or (3) individual damage assessments: s. 6. Nor will certification be precluded solely because the number of class members is unknown or because the class includes a subclass whose members have claims or defences that raise common issues not shared by all class members.

If, following certification, the certification criteria are no longer met, the court is given power to decertify the proceeding: s. 10.

(c) Notice

Once a class action is certified, notice of the action is to be given by the representative party to the class members: s. 17(1). However, in this matter the court is given a very broad discretion—as to the manner in which notice is to be given (e.g. it can be by posting, advertising, publishing or leafleting, s. 17(4)(b)) and as to the contents of the notice: s. 17(6). Indeed, the court is given power to dispense with notice to the class members where it seems appropriate to do so (s. 17(2)) and the court may even require the defendant, rather than the representative party, to deliver the notice where this is more practical: s. 21. Moreover, the court may order that the costs of notification be paid by either party or apportioned between the parties: s. 22(1). In addition, a representative plaintiff may apply to have such notification costs funded by the "Class Proceedings Fund" (discussed below).

Where class members are required to participate in the determination of individual issues (e.g., the assessment of damages), however, notice is mandatory: s. 18(1).

(d) Opting Out

Once the proceeding is certified, members of the class are presumed to be in the proceeding and bound by the court's determination, unless they take active steps to "opt out" within a time set by the court: s. 9. Those who opt out will not share in any judgment or settlement obtained in the class action, but they are free to commence separate proceedings and any applicable limitation period is suspended during the time they were members of the class: s. 28(1)(a). However, parties who opt out of the class proceeding are denied both the benefit and burden of res judicata, i.e. they are not bound by any judgment on the common issues in the class action nor may they rely in any subsequent proceeding on any determination made in the class action against any party to the class action: s. 27(2).

(e) Discovery

Discovery (e.g. the production of documents and examination for discovery) is prima facie limited to the named parties to the proceeding, i.e. the defendant is given only the right to discovery of the class representative and not of other individual class members: s. 15(1). However, after discovering the class representative, the defendant may request leave for discovery against other individual class members: s. 15(2). The court may grant such leave, taking into account such factors as the defences raised by the defendant, the monetary value of individual claims and whether discovery will result in oppression or an undue annoyance, burden or expense of the class member sought to be discovered: s. 15(3).

    Similarly, unless leave is obtained, only the representative party and not other class members may be examined as a witness under rule 39.03 to obtain evidence for the hearing of a motion or application: s. 16.

(f) Conduct of Class Proceedings

The legislation envisages that the issues common to the class (e.g, the defendant's liability) will be determined first and the individual issues, requiring the participation of individual class members (e.g., some types of damage assessments), will be resolved subsequently and individually: s. 11. Generally the court is given great flexibility and may make "any order it considers appropriate respecting the conduct of a class proceeding to ensure its fair and expeditious determination": s. 12. As a case management measure it is provided that the same judge will hear all motions before the trial of the common issues, but unless the parties agree otherwise that judge shall not preside at the trial of the common issues: s. 34.

(g) Assessment of Damages

Where liability has been determined in favour of a plaintiff class the court is given a discretion as to how damages are to be assessed. Obviously, provision is made for individual proof and assessment of the damages suffered by individual class members, on a case-by-case basis, where that is appropriate: s. 25. However, the court is also given the power to direct an "aggregate assessment of damages" (i.e. to make a determination, as a common issue, of the total liability of the defendant to the class members without resort to individual trial proceedings), where the underlying facts permit this to be done with an acceptable degree of accuracy: s. 24(1). The court may calculate monetary relief on an aggregate basis if the defendant's total liability can be reasonably determined without proof by individual class members: s. 24(1)(c).

By way of illustration, this would permit a court to make the type of aggregate assessment made in two US cases. (Both cases are discussed in the Ontario Law Reform Commission's Report on Class Actions (1982), 541-542.) In the first, a class action by credit card holders against a bank on the ground that charges made against their accounts were usurious, the defendant kept computerized records. Consequently, the identity of the 90,000 class members and the amount of any overcharge could be determined by reference to these records, without individualized proof. The second action was one by non-converting debenture holders claiming that the company had given insufficient notice of its intention to call the debentures and as a result the class members were unable to exercise their conversion rights in time. Evidence adduced during the liability phase indicated the principal amount of unregistered debentures that had not been converted and, hence, the court could calculate in aggregate the amount of damages suffered by the class.

Aggregate assessment provides a particularly effective way of assessing damages where individual claims are small or where there is no economical way of determining each member's individual loss. For this purpose the court is specifically given power to admit statistical evidence, including sampling, on the issues of quantum and the distribution of monetary awards: s. 23(1).

(h) Distribution of Monetary Awards

Where it would be impractical to ascertain the identity of each member or the exact amount of their claims, an aggregate award may be distributed among class members on an average or proportional basis: s. 24(2) and (3). As further alternatives to distribution based on proof of individual entitlement, the court may order direct distribution by the defendant, abatement, credits, payment into court or other methods deemed appropriate: s. 26(2).

A provision for "cy-près" distribution empowers the court to order a defendant to apply all or part of an aggregate award to a purpose which generally benefits class members even though non-class members might benefit as well: s. 26(4) and (6). For example, in cases of overcharging by a regulated cable television company the defendant could be ordered to credit each current subscriber's next bill, or in cases of price fixing the defendant might be ordered to reduce its prices for a given period until the amount of an aggregate assessment has been disgorged to consumers generally.

However, where damages remain undistributed after a time set by the court, they are to be returned to the defendant: s. 26(10).

(i) Settlement

To ensure the protection of absent class members, all settlements of class proceedings must be approved by the court: s. 29(2). This requirement is essential since the settlement will be binding on every class member other than those who have chosen to opt out: s. 29(3).

(j) Interrelationship of the Act and the Rules of Civil Procedure

Since it is specifically provided (s. 35) that the "rules of court apply to class proceedings," the general procedure to be followed in class proceedings is that provided in the

Rules of Civil Procedure, supplemented by the additional procedures provided for in the the Class Proceedings Act, 1992. However, there are a few areas in which it has been felt necessary to rationalize the operation of the Act and the Rules, or to specifically supplement the provisions of the Act and these provisions are contained in the new Rule 12 (Class Proceedings).

2. Costs and Funding

In the final analysis the economics of class action litigation will likely determine the volume of such proceedings. The crucial determinants are (a) the mechanisms for funding the legal fees and disbursements of the plaintiff class and (b) the liability of the represenative plaintiff for the costs of the defendant in the event that the class proceeding is unsuccessful (i.e. the "down-side risk").

Under the Quebec legislation, the funding of the legal expenses of the plaintiff class is facilitated by the establishment of a government agency (the "Fonds") which provides financial assistance to plaintiff class representatives to defray the costs of paying both lawyer's fees and disbursements incurred in the class action. In Ontario a different approach has been taken. While the Law Society Amendment Act (Class Proceedings Funding), 1992 establishes a "Class Proceedings Fund," to provide financial support for plaintiffs in respect of disbursements in appropriate cases, it is not available for the payment of plaintiffs' lawyer's fees: Law Society Act, s. 59.1(1) and (2). Instead, this latter aspect is dealt with by provisions in the Class Proceedings Act authorizing non-percentage contingent fees for successful plaintiffs' lawyers in class actions, fees which must be approved by the court. Adopting criteria developed by US courts in fixing lawyers' fees recoverable in class actions, the legislation specifies that the calculation of this fee be tied to three factors: the hourly rate of the lawyer, the number of hours worked and the discretionary application of a "multiplier" that can be used to compensate the lawyer for the risk of engaging in litigation which might have been unsuccessful: ss. 32 and 33.

In terms of the "down-side risk" of litigation, the prima facie rule is that an unsuccessful representative plaintiff (but not the class members) is personally liable for the defendant's party and party costs: s. 31(2). However, the impact of this deterrent to litigation is mitigated by a unique provision in the legislation making the Fund, where a plaintiff has received assistance from the Fund, liable to pay the defendant's costs and, in such circumstances, relieving the plaintiff from any liability for the defendant's costs: Law Society Act, s. 59.4.

Absent disbursement funding from the Fund, the representative plaintiff remains personally exposed to the risk of having to pay the defendant's costs if the class action is unsuccessful and a costs order is made in favour of the defendant (as to which see s. 31). For many plaintiffs (who, after all, are suing primarily on behalf of others) this risk will likely be daunting and unacceptable. Consequently it may be anticipated that many representative plaintiffs, if refused disbursement funding from the Fund, will not proceed with the class action. This could lead to the curious situation that the most important and significant step in class proceedings may not be in court, but will be the class representative's application to the Class Proceedings Committee for what will be (in form) a request for disbursement funding, but is in reality a desire to obtain an immunity from the "down-side risk" of liability for the defendant's costs. (The legislation provides for plaintiffs' funding applications to be heard by the Class Proceedings Committee: Law Society Act, ss. 59.2 and 59.3.)

It is worth noting that initially in Quebec the full rigour of the "loser pays" rule was applicable to class actions, but in 1982 (after a case in which Canadian Honda Motors Limited claimed $675,650 in costs) the Code of Civil Procedure was amended to provide that where costs are ordered in class actions they are to be computed as if the action was one for $1,000-$3,000—classes of actions for which recoverable costs are modest. See L. Fox, "Liability for costs: A Comparison of Bill 28 and Bill 29 and the Quebec Legislation," in *Proceedings of the First Yves Pratte Conference* (Wilson & Lafleur, 1992) at 123 et seq. The Ontario legislation in fact authorizes the making of regulations "establishing limits and tariffs" for costs awards recoverable by defendants against the fund (Law Society Act, s. 59.5(d)), but the government has not seen fit to exercise this power, at least at present.

In retaining the normal Anglo-Canadian cost shifting principle in class proceedings, the legislation rejected a key recomendation of the Ontario Law Reform Commission ("OLRC") in its Report on Class Actions (1982) at p. 704:

> We believe that, irrespective of the amount of his potential personal recovery, an individual will be deterred from initiating a class action by the risk that party and party costs will be awarded against him in an unsuccessful action. Accordingly, we recommend that the ordinary party and party costs rule should be abrogated and replaced by a general rule that, at the certification hearing and the common question stage of a class action, no party and party costs may be awarded to either party.

However, despite this rejection there is in one sense a surprising similarity between the overall scheme proposed by the OLRC and that which emerges from the legislation. In recommending the abrogation of cost shifting in class actions, the OLRC pointed out that the policy objective of deterring specious actions, performed by cost shifting, would be achieved under its proposals by a stringent certification procedure requiring the plaintiff to satisfy the court of the merits of the action (Report, p. 706). However, these requirements did not find their way into the certification procedure of the Class Proceedings Act and consequently a class action plaintiff does not have to satisfy the court of the merits of the class action in order for it to be certified. But the Fund, if it is to maintain its solvency, will need to be very careful in funding class actions which will be unsuccessful. Indeed, it may be expected that funding will be given only to cases which the Class Proceedings Committee sees as being "winners." If this occurs a preliminary merits test will in fact apply, but it will be applied by the Class Proceedings Committee rather than by the court.

A significant aspect of this unusual Ontario scheme is how the Fund receives its funding. In Quebec the "Fonds" is regularly "topped up" as a result of legislative provisions that require a percentage of class action awards to be paid into the fund. The Ontario approach is similar. The legislation provides that the Fund is to be initially financed to the extent of $500,000 by funds to be provided by the Law Foundation (Law Society Act, s. 59.1) although it is silent as to whether the provincial government is also to contribute directly to the Fund. The Law Society Act (s. 59.5(g)) confers power to make regulations "providing for levies in favour of the Class Proceedings Fund against awards and settlement funds in proceedings in respect of which a party receives financial support from the Class Proceedings Fund." This power has been exercised in O Reg. 771/92, s. 10, which provides that the amount of the levy is to be the amount of any financial support paid by the Fund to the plaintiff plus 10 per cent of the amount of any award or settlement funds.

NOTES

1. *The British Columbia legislation.* The British Columbia class proceedings legislation differs in several important ways from the Ontario legislation. These differences relate to the test for cerification; the provision made for persons from outside the province who wish to participate in the proceeding as members of the class; and the approach taken to costs, fees, and funding.

The test for certification. The focus of the analysis of many certification decisions in Ontario class proceedings has been on the s. 5 requirement that a class proceeding be the preferable procedure for the resolution of the common issues. In drafting the BC Act, legislators provided the following guidance for making this determination:

> 4(2) In determining whether a class proceeding would be the preferable procedure for the fair and efficient resolution of the common issues, the court must consider all relevant matters including
> (a) whether questions of fact or law common to the members of the class predominate over any questions affecting only individual members;
> (b) whether a significant number of the members of the class have a valid interest in individually controlling the prosecution of separate actions;
> (c) whether the class proceeding would involve claims that are or have been the subject of any other proceedings;
> (d) whether other means of resolving the claims are less practical or less efficient; and
> (e) whether the administration of the class proceeding would create greater difficulties than those likely to be experienced if relief were sought by other means.

Non-resident class members. The legislation in Quebec and Ontario is silent on the question of the participation of non-residents in class proceedings as members of a plaintiff class. However, the BC Act specifically provides for non-resident class members by requiring non-residents who wish to participate to take steps to opt into the class.

Costs, fees, and funding. While the basic cost-shifting rule is retained with some modification in the Ontario legislation, the BC legislation takes a quite different approach. In BC class proceedings, no costs awards are made except when the court considers there has been vexatious, frivolous, or abusive conduct; or an improper or unnecessary step has been taken for the purpose of delay or increasing costs or other improper purpose; or when exceptional circumstances make it unjust to deprive the successful party of costs. Since contingent fees are permitted in British Columbia, the legislation is silent on this issue. Moreover, the legislation makes no provision for a funding vehicle like the Ontario Class Proceedings Fund or the Quebec "Fonds."

2. *Class action activity to date.* Class proceedings in Ontario have indeed spawned "legal entrepreneurs" (including three specialist law firms) who have brought a remarkable number and range of class actions in a relatively short time span. In doing so they have achieved a major goal of the legislation—seeking to hold accountable wrongdoers who in the absence of class actions may well have escaped accountability.

What types of cases have been commenced under the Act and how many? As of mid-1999 more than 120 proceedings have been commenced under the legislation. They represent a broad range of types of cases but can be broken down into the following sample listing of categories.

Tort cases include products liability relating to breast implants, pacemakers, HIV-contaminated blood, medical negligence causing Hepatitis B, the manufacture and sale of tobacco products, the release of toxic gases from an industrial plant, defamation, a subway accident, and nuisance.

Contract cases include a range of consumer class actions, involving defective products such as vinyl siding, household dryers, plastic blinds, furnace venting systems, misrepresentation in the provision of services (for example, fast food), allegations of improper calculation of interest rates on credit card and utility bills, and claims arising out of "vanishing premium" life insurance policies, actions by employees against employers for wages and wrongful dismissal, and real estate and commercial transactions.

Other cases. Class actions have also been employed in corporate disputes, pension cases and a variety of miscellaneous cases ranging all the way from native land claims to actions for breach of copyright and an internal union dispute.

The vast majority of the actions remain presently unresolved. However it is worth noting that several cases have been disposed of on interlocutory motions—for example, striking for failure to state a cause of action or motions for summary judgment—brought prior to any application for certification. It appears that only two cases have resulted in a trial on the merits—a successful claim by owners of condominiums against the developer for interest on monies paid as deposits, and an unsuccessful claim that the government was not entitled to refuse salary increases to senior level employees. There have also been numerous settlements, some well publicized.

Class actions also appear to be developing (though less rapidly) in British Columbia. Among the reported certifications are claims relating to overheating radiant ceiling panels, cracking toilet tanks, blood products contaminated with Hepatitis C and silicon gel breast implants.

B. Certification

1. The Court's Evolving Approach to Certification

Numerous cases in Ontario have reached the stage of a motion for certification. Given the liberal and minimal requirements for certification under the Ontario Act, it is not surprising that the majority of certification applications have been successful. After all, reading only the words of the statute, the plaintiff merely has to show that the pleadings disclose a cause of action, that the claims of the class members raise common (though not necessarily identical issues) and that a class proceeding will be the preferable procedure for the resolution of the *common issues*. At the certification stage there is no enquiry into the (factual) merits of the action. However, in some cases, courts have imposed other evidentiary requirements: see *Hollick v. City of Toronto* (1998), 168 DLR (4th) 760 (Ont. Div. Ct.) (leave to appeal to the Court of Appeal granted) (the court refused to certify a class action for nuisance on behalf of persons residing near a landfill site because there was no evidence each of proposed class members likely had a cause of action against the defendant); *Taub v. Manufacturers Life Insurance Co.* (1998), 40 OR (3d) 379 (Gen. Div.) (if widespread harm is not inherent in a class action claim, such as in air crash or pollution cases, the plaintiff must provide evidence that more than one person was affected; in this toxic mould class action, the court required evidence that at least one person other than the plaintiff had a similar claim). Are these decisions sound?

Of the Ontario cases refusing certification to date, two raise concerns about the interpretation being given to the criteria for certification.

In *Abdool v. Anaheim Management Ltd.* (1995), 21 OR (3d) 453 (Div. Ct.), the court refused to certify a class action by condominium investors where there were numerous individual issues, individual discovery of class members was likely, and the class members' claims were individually viable. *Abdool* involved an action by the purchasers of condominiums in a tax driven real estate development scheme. When the real estate market took a downturn, the financiers called the promissory notes signed by the purchasers as part of the transaction (and sued them) and the purchasers then instituted this class action against those involved in the development—the developer, the real estate agents, the financing institutions, the lawyers who acted for the developer, and the accountants who had provided a letter setting out the financial projections for the scheme. The allegations consisted of breach of warranty, breach of fiduciary duty, negligence, and misrepresentation.

While the court cleared up some errors made at first instance, it demonstrated apparent hostility to the breadth of language of the legislation and made statements that could seriously limit the scope of class proceedings in the future. In particular, in analyzing the goal of "judicial economy," Moldaver J interpreted s. 6 in such a way as to reintroduce the existence of individual issues into the formula for determining certification criteria. Section 6 states that a court is not to refuse certification *solely* if any one of the five delineated grounds is found to exist. He found this to imply that a court is entitled to consider whether the cumulative effect of two or more of these grounds legitimately precluded certification. On the facts of *Abdool* he found four of the five grounds enumerated in s. 6 to be present—damages requiring individual assessment, the relief claimed related to separate contracts, different remedies were sought for different class members, and the class included a sub-class whose members have claims of defence that raised issues not shared by all class members. He stated that while not necessarily fatal to certification, the presence of four of the five grounds referred to in the section weighs in the balance against certification. Courts have since declined to follow this reasoning.

Does the statutory language provide an adequate framework for resolving a certification motion in a case like *Abdool*? Arguably it was a weak case on the merits, especially as regards certain of the defendants less closely involved in the transaction, and there was a real likelihood that it was commenced as a means of forestalling the claims that were pending against the plaintiffs on their promissory notes. Should the court have granted certification as against the promoters of the project (who were by that time no longer capable of satisfying a judgment) but denied certification as against the financial institutions, accountants, and solicitors who provided services to the project? It would seem unfortunate for an apparently aberrant case to skew the approach taken to the certification of more straightforward cases. Nevertheless, bearing in mind the concerns that have arisen in the United States regarding abusive securities fraud class action litigation, it seems the underlying issues raised in this case will be likely to resurface in other certification decisions.

The other questionable decision was that in which certification was refused in *Sutherland v. Canadian Red Cross Society* (1994), 17 OR (3d) 645 (Gen. Div.) in a proposed class action to recover damages for people who had contracted HIV as a result of receiving contaminated blood and blood products. Although the Ontario Law Reform Commission's 1982 draft Act had included a requirement that a class action be "superior to other available methods for the fair and efficient resolution of the *controversy*" and a consideration of whether the common issues predominate over the individual issues, this language did not find its way into the legislation. Still, certification was refused, *inter alia*, on the ground that a class action was not the preferable procedure to resolve *the controversy*. Moreover, the determination that certification should be refused on the ground that the claims asserted by class members did not raise common issues seemed at odds with the findings emanating from the Krever blood inquiry (which was under way at the time of the decision). Among possible common issues were whether the Red Cross waited too long in warning donors that homosexual sex between males or intravenous drug use increased the risks to recipients of transmitting HIV and so should preclude them from donating, and whether the authorities waited too long before introducing heat treatment of blood products for hemophiliacs. As a result of this, Ontario decision cases have since been pursued individually and not as a class action. This led to the back-to-back trials of two HIV cases in Toronto—each taking more than 100 days at trial. Whether such claims were certifiable was revisited in *Anderson v. Wilson* (1998), 37 OR (3d) 235 (Div. Ct.). The further appeal in *Anderson* is the only decision to date by the Ontario Court of Appeal dealing with certification.

Anderson v. Wilson
[1999] OJ no. 2494 (CA)

CARTHY JA:—This appeal, by leave from the Divisional Court, concerns the certification of a class action in a medical negligence proceeding under the Class Proceedings Act, 1992, SO 1992, c. 6.

Facts

The respondent, Dr. Wilson, operated five clinics that provided electroencephalogram tests (EEGs) between 1989 and 1996 in the Durham Region and in the eastern part of Metropolitan Toronto. The respondent, Kyprianou, was a technician who administered

EEG tests. The defendants, John Doe and Jane Doe, represent the other, presently uni-identified, workers in Dr. Wilson's clinics who also administered EEG tests.

In 1996, a public health inspector identified a possible link between the defendant's clinics and an outbreak of hepatitis B. Public Health Authorities notified over 18,000 patients, by letter, that they may have been infected and that they should be tested. At least seventy-five of the patients are known to have contracted the disease and three became violently ill and were hospitalized.

Of those who responded, 75 persons showed symptoms of recent infection, and approximately 1100 were termed "suspect cases" because there was evidence of earlier infection with hepatitis B. Because there are no symptoms in a substantial percentage of infected persons, these numbers are expected to increase. These two groups, plus some carriers of hepatitis B, comprise the class of "infected" patients identified by both Jenkins J on the motion for certification and the Divisional Court on appeal. The patients who received the notification letter and showed no symptoms after testing comprise the "uninfected" portion of the class.

The representative plaintiffs claim in negligence and breach of contract alleging that they contracted hepatitis B during performance of EEGs at the clinics operated by Dr. Wilson.

Robert Anderson, one of the proposed representative plaintiffs, is 57 years old. He is married with three children and is not presently employed. Mr. Anderson attended Dr. Wilson's Ajax clinic for an EEG on June 29, 1993. Mr. Anderson now carries the hepatitis B virus. He is expected to remain an infection carrier for the rest of his life. The other proposed representative plaintiff, Deborah Fischer, is a 45-year-old bank manager. She is married with two children. She attended Dr. Wilson's North York clinic for an EEG on March 23, 1995. She contracted hepatitis B. Ms. Fischer became severely ill and twice neared death. She was hospitalized for about ten days and was off work for approximately ten weeks.

Procedural History

The initial certification motion proceeded before Jenkins J on January 13, 1997. In reasons reported at (1996), 7 CPC (4th) 244 (Ont. Gen. Div.), Jenkins J certified the plaintiffs' action as a class proceeding and defined the class to include:

    1. All patients of Dr. Wilson any time after January 1, 1990 who contracted hepatitis B after being given an EEG at one of the clinics, or the estate of those now deceased;
    2. All persons who contracted the disease from an infected patient (or their estates); [herein called "derivative claimants"]
    3. All patients any time after January 1, 1990 who did not contract the disease from the test but who nonetheless were sent a notice by public health officials to be tested and were tested (or their estates);
    4. All living parents, grandparents, children, grandchildren, siblings and spouses of infected patients, cross-infected persons and uninfected patients (family law claimants).

Jenkins J defined the common issue as "liability and punitive and exemplary damages."

On appeal to the Divisional Court, Campbell J, in reasons reported at (1998), 37 OR (3d) 235 (Div. Ct.), upheld certification of the class but removed from it the group of plaintiffs who did not contract hepatitis B but had been informed of the possibility and were tested. The basis for their claim was in nervous shock, i.e., the psychological trauma of being told of the possibility of infection and the resultant uncertainty as to their condition until they received negative test results. Campbell J stated that the weight of Ontario law does not recognize claims for fear and nervous shock in the absence of a diagnosed psychological or psychiatric illness.

Further, Campbell J amended the description of the common issues in the certification order. Campbell J redefined the common issues as follows:

1. Did the defendants breach the standard of care for infection control procedures?
2. Did the clinics provide a common source of infection for those patients who contracted hepatitis B?
3. Does the evidence of causation, in the absence of evidence to the contrary, amount to proof of causation on a balance of probabilities?
4. Is this a case for punitive and exemplary damages?

Thus, both courts concluded that a class should be certified, the Divisional Court confining the class to infected persons, and the Divisional Court selecting a more particularized statement of the common issues.

The plaintiffs sought, and were granted, leave to appeal the decision of the Divisional Court. They seek to restore the order of Jenkins J. The defendants were granted leave to cross-appeal and seek to have the certification application dismissed in its entirety.

Analysis

This is the first time this court has considered the certification of a class action and I am mindful of the deference which is due to the Superior Court judges who have developed expertise in this very sophisticated area of practice. The Act provides for flexibility and adjustment at all stages of the proceeding and any intervention by this court at the certification level should be restricted to matters of general principle.

1. Does the statement of claim disclose a cause of action for uninfected patients?

In my view the Divisional Court was wrong to put aside the class of persons who received notice from the Public Health Authorities of the possibility of infection, were tested and are unaffected. The basis for their claim is in nervous shock. Although the House of Lords [Note 1: *White and Others v. Chief Constable of South Yorkshire and Others*, unreported decision of the House of Lords released December 3, 1998.] has decided that emotional suffering without psychiatric symptoms does not qualify for tort relief, two recent Ontario Superior Court judges have held to the contrary. In *Mason v. Westside Cemeteries Ltd.* (1996), 135 DLR (4th) 361 (Ont. Gen. Div.), Madam Justice Molloy awarded damages for nervous shock to a son when a funeral home lost the cremated remains of his parents' bodies. Similarly, in *Vanek v. Great Atlantic & Pacific*

Co. of Canada, [1997] OJ No. 3304 (Gen. Div.), Cosgrove J adopted Molloy J's reasoning in *Mason* and awarded damages for mental distress to a father who suffered chronic anxiety after his daughter swallowed some contaminated juice.

In *Nespolon v. Alford et al.* (1998), 161 DLR (4th) 646 (Ont. CA) at 660-61 [Note 2: Court of Appeal decision released before *White and Others*, but thereafter application for leave to the Supreme Court of Canada dismissed, January 21, 1999.] this court, in a majority decision, denied damages for nervous shock arising out of a motor vehicle accident, but in doing so Abella JA commented as follows:

> A number of circumstances have been held by the courts to fall within the ambit of risk leading to liability for nervous shock. These include whether there was a relationship between the tortfeasor and the injured person, whether the injured person was acting as a rescuer, and whether the injured person anticipated or saw the accident. None of these circumstances are present here. The issue then becomes whether there are any policy reasons to add someone in Nespolon's circumstances to this class of persons entitled to recover damages for nervous shock. In *Hall v. Herbert*, [1993] 2 SCR 159 at p. 203, 101 DLR (4th) 129, Cory J said:
>
> > ... even if a duty of care is found to exist, the court will have to determine whether, for public policy reasons, that duty should be limited in part or in whole.
>
> The cautionary words of Griffiths JA [in *Bechard v. Haliburton Estate* (1991), 5 OR (3d) 512 (CA) at p. 520], are particularly apposite in deciding whether policy grounds justify Nespolon recovering damages from the three boys:
>
> > The "policy grounds" that have concerned the courts in these cases is that there should not be unlimited liability to persons who suffer nervous shock. The perceived danger is that every accident may generate an ever-widening circle of plaintiffs including, possibly, the casual passerby who witnesses the accident and those who come to gaze at the scene later, as well as the relatives of all of those to whom the details will be recounted.
> >
> > In my view, there are no policy reasons to justify expanding the category of those whose nervous shock is compensable, to include a stranger in Nespolon's circumstances.

Section 5(1)(a) of the *Class Proceedings Act* states:

The court *shall certify* a class proceeding on a motion under section 2, 3 or 4 if,
    (a) *the pleadings or the notice of application discloses a cause of action;*
[Emphasis added.]

Wilson J articulated the general test for whether a pleading discloses a cause of action in *Hunt v. T & N plc* (1990), 43 CPC (2d) 105 (SCC), at 123:

> Thus, the Ontario Court of Appeal has firmly embraced the "plain and obvious" test, and has made clear that it too is of the view that the test is rooted in the need for courts to ensure that their process is not abused. The fact that the case the plaintiff wishes to present may involve complex issues of fact and law or may raise a novel legal proposition should not prevent a plaintiff from proceedings with his action.

Superior Court judges have applied this "plain and obvious" test in the context of class actions: see, for example, *Chippewas of Sarnia Band v. Canada (AG)* (1996), 29 OR (3d) 549 (Gen. Div.) at 564.

In the present case it is at least arguable that the defendant's alleged negligence had the foreseeable consequence of a general notice to patients that a test was required to determine if they were infected. It was also arguably foreseeable that some suffering from shock would be occasioned by the notice. When the claimants are limited to those who received the notice and family law claimants it can further be argued that there is no ever widening circle of potential liability created in these circumstances and that there is no policy concern to justify excluding recovery.

Given the uncertain state of the law on tort relief for nervous shock, it is not appropriate that the court should reach a conclusion at this early stage and without a complete factual foundation. It cannot be said, in this case, that it is plain and obvious that the claim for the tort of mental distress standing alone will fail. On the assumption that a legal obligation may exist, this segment of the class proceeding is ideally suited for certification. There are many persons with the same complaint, each of which would typically represent a modest claim that would not itself justify an independent action. In addition, the nature of the overall claim lends itself to aggregate treatment because individual reactions to the notices would likely be similar in each case—fear of a serious infection and anxiety during the waiting period for a test result. If evidence from patients to support such reactions to the notices is necessary, it would probably suffice to hear from a few typical claimants. The balance of the evidence as to liability would relate to the conduct of the clinics, the reaction of the Public Health Authorities and foreseeability issues.

Thus, in my view, the claim in tort for mental distress for this group of persons should proceed as the preferable mode of bringing these claims forward.

2. What is the appropriate definition of the common issues for uninfected persons who received the notice?

Section 8(1)(e) of the *Class Proceedings Act* provides:

8.(1) An order certifying a proceeding as a class proceeding shall, ...
      (e) set out the common issues for the class;

Section 1 of the CPA defines "common issues" as

(a) common but not necessarily identical issues of fact, or (b) common but not necessarily identical issues of law that arise from common but not necessarily identical facts.

Section 8(2) of the Act contemplates a subclass and the order of Jenkins J includes both infected and uninfected patients in separate paragraphs describing a single class. I consider the uninfected a subclass of the whole. The infected patients must establish that the clinics failed to meet an appropriate standard of care for infection control and that they were infected as a result. The factual basis for the uninfected patients will obviously not include the same causation factor. Their claim is based on an allegation that the conduct of the defendants occasioned the notices which, in turn, foreseeably caused them nervous shock. The difference in what each group must prove affects the definition of the common issues for each group.

I would define the common issue for the uninfected patients, and their derivative claimants, in the broadest terms, as did Jenkins J. The common issues for trial should be "liability and punitive and exemplary damages."

This is in contemplation that the evidence as to the alleged negligence and reaction of the authorities can be conveniently tried without a significant involvement of the uninfected members of this subclass and, if appropriate, the use of s. 24 of the Act to assess aggregate relief and proportional or average application of that relief.

The Infected Patients

I have no difficulty agreeing with both Jenkins J and the Divisional Court and their reasons for finding that these patients comprise a class, that the pleadings disclose a cause of action, and that there is a commonality which suggests resolution in the context of a class action. My concern is with the definition of the common issues and whether it can encompass liability and damages. In particular, I am concerned about causation, and its necessary link to each individual claimant.

The defendants put their position as follows in the factum of the respondent Wilson, referring to affidavit evidence of Dr. Loutman:

> 16. In order to determine if there is a causal relationship between a patient receiving an EEG at one of the clinics and their hepatitis B status, serologic data on each patient is necessary. While not being conclusive proof of causation, the serologic data is a critical factor in assessing whether there is a temporal and therefore, causal relationship between the EEG and infection.
>
> 17. In addition to obtaining and analysing this serologic data, each plaintiff must be assessed for other risk factors for hepatitis B such as lifestyle, age, blood transfusions, recent travel to high risk areas, sexual partners and IV drug use. This examination is required to determine whether a particular event, namely an EEG, was the source of infection. The mere fact that an individual underwent an EEG at one of the clinics and presently shows a positive test for hepatitis B is insufficient to establish a causal relationship between the two events.

The reasons of Campbell J deal with the issue of causation at p. 243:

> But if the plaintiffs can establish a common breach of the standard of care for infection control practices, a common highly infectious EEG technician, with a particular strain of the Hepatitis B virus and a common body of epidemiological evidence that patients treated at these clinics by that infected technician are over 500 times more likely than the general population to come down with Hepatitis B, then they have gone a long way towards discharging the onus of proof. A trial judge might easily conclude that proof of those facts, *in the absence of evidence to the contrary*, amounts to proof of causation on a balance of probabilities.
>
>   The certification of the class action in respect of the infected patients would not reverse the onus of proof. Relatively simple elements can be added to the litigation plan

to ensure, if the plaintiffs prove what they say they can prove, that the defendants have a fair opportunity to test the possibility that any one or more of the infected clinic patients contracted their hepatitis B elsewhere. [Emphasis added.]

My concern is that Campbell J has been too expansive in his approach to defining the common issues and has imposed a consequent unfairness upon the defendants; in particular by his inclusion of the issue: "Does the evidence of causation, in the absence of evidence to the contrary, amount to proof of causation on a balance of probabilities?"

Causation is an individual issue with respect to every infected member of the class. Some of the patients who answered the questionnaire were carriers and probably contracted the virus prior to attending the clinic. The evidence of causation as to some individuals may be equivocal in the sense that there may be other competent sources. In such cases the only approach is for one judge to assess the evidence concerning all competent sources and make a finding of liability on the basis of probability on all the evidence. If there were only one plaintiff, the trial would deal with the appropriate standard of care, the actual standard of care, the plaintiff's evidence as to treatment, and the plaintiff's medical and lifestyle history. Evidence on all of these issues would be necessary to arrive at a balanced conclusion as to whether there was negligent conduct and whether this was the probable cause of the plaintiff's complaint.

The order under appeal contemplates a hearing as to causation without the involvement of the class members. It invites a judgment on only a portion of the issue of causation, which under the Act, is a *res judicata* against the parties, and not only stands in the way of a balancing of all evidence by one judge at one hearing, but also will appear as a reversal of the onus of proof. Assuming an initial finding against Dr. Wilson and Mr. Kyprianou, it will be left to them to produce evidence and satisfy a court that actual causation is elsewhere.

I think that what Campbell J had in mind was the reasoning in *Farrell v. Snell* (1990), 72 DLR (4th) 289 (SCC), to the effect that it is not essential to have a positive medical opinion to determine causation. The trial judge may apply common sense to the evidence and thus draw an inference that the failure to meet the required standard of competence was the cause of the injury. That may be the ultimate test, but it is too soon to anticipate it, and it should only follow discoveries and a trial involving each claimant.

No case has been produced either here or in the United States where the class members and their evidence and medical records were essential to a finding of liability. Implants [Note 3: See, for example, *Bendall v. McGhan Medical Corp.* (1993), 14 OR (3d) 734 (Gen. Div.); *Harrington v. Dow Corning Corp.* (1996), 48 CPC (3d) 28 (BCSC).], motor vehicle malfunctions [Note 4: See, for example, *GM (Canada) v. Naken*, [1983] 1 SCR 72.], improper interest charges [Note 5: *Abdool et al. v. Anaheim Management Ltd. et al.* (1995), 21 OR (3d) 453 (Div. Ct.).], and such, all lend themselves to resolution as to liability without involvement of the injured parties. That is not the situation here, where an injured person may or may not be able to relate the infection to the defendants and their clinics.

If causation cannot be handled as a common issue, then liability and damages must also fall. The question then becomes whether there are sufficient common issues left to justify certification. In my view, it seems sensible with this number of potential plaintiffs and the similarities that are evident in their claims, that any potential efficiency in advancement of their claims through the flexibility provided by the CPA should, where reasonable, be utilized.

Counsel for Dr. Wilson argued that the representative plaintiffs have failed to identify common issues and in fact, are unable to do so because this is a medical negligence action. They submit that in medical negligence actions liability turns on the medical presentation of each patient. Mr. Kyprianou adopted this position.

In my view, this argument is far too broad. Unlike typical medical negligence cases this action concerns allegations of a general practice over a number of years falling below acceptable standards. Those general allegations can be pulled out and tried separately, to the benefit of all parties.

I agree with the British Columbia Court of Appeal's observation, as did Campbell J, that the common issues need only involve a matter, that if determined, would move the litigation forward. In *Campbell v. Flexwatt Corp.* (1998), 15 CPC (4th) 1 (BCCA), leave to appeal to the Supreme Court of Canada denied, Cumming JA, speaking for the court, at pp. 17-18 reasoned:

> The *Class Proceedings Act* requires that the claims of the class members raise common issues which, for reasons of fairness and efficiency, ought to be determined within one proceeding. Common issues can be issues of fact or law and do not have to be identical for every member of the class. ...
>
> *When examining the existence of common issues it is important to understand that the common issues do not have to be issues which are determinative of liability; they need only be issues of fact or law that move the litigation forward.* The resolution of a common issue does not have to be, in and of itself, sufficient to support relief. To require every common issue to be determinative of liability for every plaintiff and every defendant would make class proceedings with more than one defendant virtually impossible. (Emphasis added.)

In this case, the common issue as to the standard of conduct expected from the clinics from time to time, and whether they fell below the standard, can fairly be tried as a common issue. Resolving this issue would move the litigation forward. The participation of the class members is not needed for that inquiry, although their later evidence may bear upon whether standards, such as the use of gloves, were actually met in individual cases. Isolating this one major issue, the class action proceeding clearly appears to be the preferable method of resolution to the benefit of all parties.

Thus, it is my view that the common issues for the uninfected patients and their family law claimants should extend from liability through damages but that the common issue for the infected patients and their derivative claimants should be restricted to whether the defendants breached the standard of care for infection control practices.

These reasons should not be read as saying that there cannot be a certification or a common issue if the claimants' evidence is individually necessary. Sub-classes and sub-issues are recognized by the Act. I have noted above that in this case claimants may have to give evidence as to whether protective gloves were used when they were treated, as one example of what could develop from a finding on the common issue. The use of gloves is something that can be dealt with on discovery and in a mini-trial without prejudice to the defendant. It would be quite otherwise if a general finding was made of prima facie causation and the defendant then had to overcome that by establishing another cause.

In the result, I have, in effect, identified a subclass of uninfected patients and family law claimants and should consider whether separate representation is required as provided in s. 5(2) of the Act. Although the representative plaintiffs are infected patients, and the Act contemplates representatives that have the same complaints as the class, I cannot see any reality at this stage to the argument that they would not fairly and adequately represent the interest of all patients or that there is presently any conflict of interest. Most of the facts pertaining to the issues to be tried are common to all. If and when real problems arise it will not be difficult to create separate representation. In the meantime, economy favours single representation.

There were other arguments concerning family claimants and cross-infected claimants and the creation of sub-classes for each. I agree with the disposition of these issues by the Divisional Court and Jenkins J. There will be later opportunities to make adjustments as may be justified by events, and, with the more restricted common issue, there is little likelihood that this will be necessary before the trial of the issue.

I would, therefore, set aside the order of the Divisional Court and vary the order of Jenkins J in accordance with these reasons.

As in the Divisional Court, success has been divided and I would order no costs of the appeal or motion for leave to appeal.

McMURTRY CJO:—I agree. WEILER JA:—I agree.

NOTES AND QUESTIONS

1. *The "it will advance the claims to an appreciable extent" approach.* This standard based on the presence of issues the resolution of which "will advance the claims to an appreciable extent" developed in the BC cases, and adopted by the Court of Appeal in *Anderson* is having a liberalizing effect on certification. The principle is that with regard to common issues the question to be asked is not whether the resolution of common issues will be dispositive of liability, but whether the resolution of the common issues will "advance the litigation." But see *Carom v. Bre-X Minerals Ltd.*, below, note 3.

2. *Common versus individual issues.* Keep in mind that the presence of individual issues does not automatically defeat certification. In fact, Ontario legislators took a more liberal approach than was taken in the United States regime on which they modelled the Ontario Act. The requirement that common issues predominate over individual issues and that a class action be superior to other methods for the fair and efficient adjudication of the controversy was replaced by the more discretionary "preferable procedure" requirement in the Ontario legislation. The Ontario legislation envisages a bifurcated proceeding: a common issues hearing at which issues common to the class—for example, was the defendant's product defective?—will generally be determined first and the individual issues, requiring the participation of individual class members—for example, did the individual rely on the defendant's representation; was the individual contributorily negligent; and what damages did the individual suffer?—will be resolved subsequently and individually: s. 11. Generally, the court is given great flexibility and may make "any order it

considers appropriate respecting the conduct of a class proceeding to ensure its fair and expeditious determination": s. 12. Such an order was given in *Maxwell v. MLG Ventures Ltd.* (1995), 40 CPC (3d) 304, a claim for misrepresentation in an offering circular where there was a potentially dispositive individual issue regarding whether a plaintiff's knowledge was not based only on the offering circular. The court on the motion for certification held that the difficulty could be overcome by requiring those joining the class to file an affidavit concerning the state of their knowledge at the relevant time.

3. *Certification where the plaintiffs' claim is based on misrepresentation.* A significant recent development is the refusal to grant certification in class actions based on misrepresentation on two separate grounds.

Lack of a common issue. In a number of cases certification has been refused on the ground of the lack of a common issue. In *Rosedale Motors Inc. v. Petro-Canada Inc.* (1998), 42 OR (3d) 776 (Gen. Div.), the court refused to certify an action by a class of franchisees based on various misrepresentations made largely in separate meetings with each franchisee. The court stated that while, in principle, misrepresentation class actions may be certified, in this case there were no common issues the adjudication of which would move the litigation forward in a meaningful way. Similarly, in *Controltech Engineering Inc. v. Ontario Hydro*, [1998] OJ no. 5350 (Gen. Div.), the court refused to certify a claim for misrepresentation on behalf of a class of participants in a contract-bidding process. The court held that where the defendant allegedly made various misrepresentations to various class members, there was no common issue for certification purposes. However, the court stated that misrepresentation claims may raise common issues where a single misrepresentation is made to all class members or where the defendant uses a standard deceptive sales pitch. Again, in *Mouhteros v. DeVry Canada Inc.* (1998), 41 OR (3d) 63 (Gen. Div.), certification of misrepresentation claims against an educational institution was refused: whereas in some cases misrepresentation claims might raise a common issue (as in *Abdool v. Anaheim Management Ltd.* (1995), 21 OR (3d) 453 (Div. Ct.), where the representation was contained in a single letter), in the present case there were no common misrepresentation issues because the various representations were published by the defendant in 67 different television commercials and 30 different newspaper advertisements or were made verbally by some 122 admissions officers over a 6-year period.

Class proceeding was not the preferable procedure. In the certification decision in the seven Bre-X class actions, *Carom v. Bre-X Minerals Ltd.*, [1999] OJ no. 1662, Winkler J held that the claims made against the brokerage firms who were alleged to have promoted Bre-X stock based on negligent and fraudulent misrepresentation raised common issues, but that certification should be refused on the ground that a class proceeding was not the preferable procedure for their resolution.

In sharp contrast to the "lack-of-a-common-issue" cases, discussed above, is *Dabbs v. Sun Life Assurance Co. of Canada* (1998), 40 OR (3d) 429 (Gen. Div.), where the court certified for the purpose of settlement a "vanishing-premium" class action against a life insurer based on alleged misrepresentations by its individual agents as to future investment performance. (See also *McKrow v. Manufacturers Life Insurance Co.*, [1998] OJ no. 4692 (Gen. Div.) (approval of the settlement of another "vanishing-premium" life-insurance-policy case)). In *Dabbs*, the plaintiff alleged that in marketing these

so-called "vanishing-premium" life-insurance policies, Sun Life and its agents represented to purchasers that dividends to policy holders would pay the required premiums
within a specified number of years. Sales illustrations projected a "premium-offset date"
after which no further premiums would be required. In fact, dividends were lower than
projected and policy holders had to pay premiums for a longer period than the projected
premium offset date. The defendant Sun Life had made it clear that it denied the allegations of misrepresentation. The motion before the court in *Dabbs* was to certify the
action as a class action following a settlement entered into between the parties (the
approval of the settlement itself was dealt with on a subsequent motion). Hence, both
parties supported certification, although there were objectors opposing the motion. What
is interesting about *Dabbs* is that the case was based on misrepresentations made by the
defendant's 100s of agents to 400,000 individual policy purchasers and hence potentially
or actually raised all the objections to certification raised in the misrepresentation cases
referred to above. Sharpe J held that the statement of claim did raise a common issue—
namely, the following:

> Did the use of illustrations and/or any representations, in writing or verbal, create an
> obligation on the part of Sun Life with respect to a specified offset date despite the
> terms of the policy itself and the terms of any illustration?

Given the number of policy holders and agents involved, the lack-of-a-common-issue
cases, discussed above, would suggest that what Sharpe J called a common issue was a
mass of individual issues. Perhaps the key to the common-issue finding is to be found in
the terms of the Settlement Agreement, which gave "global benefits"—that is, "no-
proof" benefits—without inquiry as to the nature of the representations that were made
to the class member at the time he or she purchased the policy. There are also elaborate
ADR arrangements for claimants to prove individual misrepresentations and obtain
more generous benefits (which, however, underlines the individual nature of the misrepresentations).

What *Dabbs* would appear to stand for, however, is that the courts are prepared to
apply different standards where certification is sought for the purposes of settlement
rather than for the purposes of a contested adjudication. In the United States, these are
described as "settlement-only class certifications" and have become the subject of widespread criticism: see John Coffee, "Class Wars: The Dilemma of the Mass Tort Class
Action" (1995), 95 *Columbia Law Review* 1343 and "Symposium: Mass Tortes: Serving
Up Just Desserts" (1995), 80 *Cornell Law Review* 811-1235. Ultimately these criticisms
led the US Supreme Court largely to outlaw separate standards for settlement-only class
certifications: *Amchem Products Inc. v. Windsor*, 117 S Ct. 2231 (1997) (a district court
faced with a request for settlement-only class certification need not inquire whether the
case would present intractable problems of trial management, but other requirements for
certification must still be satisfied, and here the requirements for class certification of
commonality of issues of fact and law and adequacy of representation were not met).
See also *Ortiz v. Fibreboard Corporation*, 1999 WL 412604 (US Sup. Ct.). It is not
suggested that the excesses present in *Amchem* were present in *Dabbs*, but that the US
experience indicates that the establishment of different certification standards for settlement-only cases can be a slippery slope.

4. *Policy goals of the class proceedings legislation.* In its report, the OLRC identified three main objects of the class proceeding legislation that were described in *Abdool* as "(i) *judicial economy*, or the efficient handling of potentially complex cases of mass wrongs; (ii) *improved access to the courts* for those whose actions might not otherwise be asserted; this involves claims which might have merit but legal costs of proceeding are disproportionate to the amount of each claim and hence many plaintiffs would be unable to pursue their legal remedies; and (iii) *modification of behaviour* of actual or potential wrongdoers who might otherwise be tempted to ignore public obligations." The courts have regularly cited these objectives in determining whether to certify a claim, usually on the issue of "preferable procedure." Is this appropriate for them to do in the light of the legislative endorsement of a detailed analytical framework that does not include reference to such objectives?

5. *Use of a class action by the defendant as a way to deal with the "wait-and-see" plaintiff.* When sued by a class, defendants will typically oppose certification of the action as a class proceeding. It is most unusual for defendants to seek to have a non-class proceeding converted into a class proceeding, although s. 4 of the Ontario Class Proceedings Act makes specific provision for doing so. This is exactly what happened in *Anderson Exploration Limited v. Pan-Alberta Gas Limited* (1997), 12 CPC (4th) 59 (Alta. QB). In that action the plaintiffs were 9 of 425 natural gas producers who had contracted with the defendant to provide natural gas for a specific pool, relying on the defendant to market the gas in accordance with contractual and statutory guidelines and to distribute to each plaintiff its proportionate share of the profits. When the plaintiff sued for breach of fiduciary duty, the defendant proposed that the action be converted into a representative action on behalf of all producers so that the result of the action would be binding on the remaining 416 producers. The court concluded that it was a proper case for a class proceeding: the class was clearly capable of definition, the significant issues of fact and law were the same for all producers, and the parties were subject to the same legislative regime and similar fundamental contractual terms. Since the defendant conceded that if a fiduciary duty was owed to these plaintiffs all producers were owed the same fiduciary duty, there needed to be no individual assessment of damages as the price difference and the volume of gas that the defendants allegedly sold in breach of its duty resulted in an ascertainable amount from which a common fund could be established. The case provides an interesting example of how, at least in these circumstances, the defendant can protect itself from "wait-and-see" plaintiffs—that is, plaintiffs who stay out of an action with a view to later bringing their own subsequent action in which they will rely on the decision in the first action if it is adverse to the defendant (invoking non-mutual issue estoppel or abuse of process), but avoiding any issue estoppel effect from the decision in the first action that is favourable to the defendant.

2. Certification of "National" Classes and Their Constitutionality

Can a Canada-wide plaintiff class be certified under the provincial legislation governing class proceedings or must the class be restricted to residents of the province in which the action is commenced? The legislation in Quebec and Ontario is silent on this question. The BC legislation specifically provides that persons from other provinces (and countries) may participate in a class proceeding commenced by a BC resident provided that they opt in.

Permitting a national class action has two consequences. First, it can provide something that we presently lack in Canada—that is, a national forum for the litigation of nation-wide mass tort cases—for example, breast implants. (The lack of a national forum results from the decisions of the Supreme Court holding that the Federal Court may not, constitutionally, be given jurisdiction generally as between subject and subject: see, for example, *R v. Thomas Fuller Const. Co. (1958) Ltd.*, [1980] 1 SCR 695.) The importance of this becomes clear when we consider that many of the class proceedings certified to date have involved consumer products or services and that the consumer market in Canada is frequently a multi-province or nationwide one. Second, the existence of a national class can have a very substantial impact on the total amount of the claim of the plaintiff class and hence the potential liability of the defendant. Defendants are likely to be conflicted over their support for national class actions. They may wish at the certification stage to oppose certification of a national class to reduce its total damage exposure in the litigation. However, when it comes to settlement, and court approval of the settlement, defendants may well wish to buy "national peace" and bring closure to the matter through an approval that binds a national class rather than leaving it open to subsequent similar suits in the other provinces.

But there are arguably potential constitutional difficulties associated with certifying a national class action in the Canadian context under the provincial class proceedings legislation. The defendant may argue on certification that the provincial superior court lacks jurisdiction, as a matter of constitutional law, to adjudicate the claims of non-residents. Also where a national class has been certified, and the action has been dismissed, residents of other provinces may in subsequent proceedings argue that the Ontario court was constitutionally incapable of binding them even though they fell within the description of the class. This can be illustrated with the following hypothetical. Assume that in a products liability case in Ontario a national class is certified but the class proceeding is unsuccessful on the liability issue and the action is dismissed against the defendant. Subsequently, persons in Winnipeg (who were notified of the Ontario class proceedings but who took no steps to "opt out") commence an action in Manitoba against the party who was the successful defendant in the Ontario class proceeding, asserting the same claim as that litigated in the Ontario proceeding. The defendant then pleads in the Manitoba proceeding that the plaintiffs' claims are barred by s. 27(2) of the Class Proceedings Act (a judgment on common issues binds every class member who has not opted out of the class proceeding). An obvious response of the Manitoba plaintiffs would be to argue that the Ontario legislation does not extend to them—constitutionally Ontario has no authority to pass extra-territorial legislation binding on them where they had no contact with Ontario.

In the following excerpt from *Nantais v. Telectronics Proprietary (Canada) Ltd.*, an action relating to the functioning of pacemaker leads, the court considers its capacity to certify a national class and the underlying reasons for doing so. Do you agree with Zuber J's observation that "it seems eminently sensible, for all the reasons given by La Forest J in *Morguard*, and the policy reasons given for passage of the Act, to have the questions of liability of these defendants determined as far as possible once and for all, for all Canadians"?

Nantais v. Telectronics Proprietary (Canada) Ltd.
(1995), 25 OR (3d) 331 (Gen. Div.), aff'd. (Div. Ct.), at 347

BROCKENSHIRE J: The defendants are all members of an international family of associated and/or related corporations, with an Australian parent, which manufactures and markets medical devices including Telectronics Accufix Atrial "J" Leads 329-701 and 330-801 ("the leads") complained of. The leads implanted in Canada were made in the USA and France, and marketed in Canada through Ontario, by members of the corporate family of defendants. The defendants that did not appear to argue on this motion are appealing an earlier ruling of mine on the jurisdiction of this court to authorize service upon them.

A pacemaker controls the beating of a malfunctioning heart by transmitting electrical impulses to the heart through a lead—an insulated wire or wires inserted through an artery into the heart and affixed to the heart muscle. The heart beats around 100,000 times each day. The leads complained of have a short "J" shaped flattened retention wire under the lead insulation at the end attached in the heart, that can fracture. On fracturing, the jagged end can cut through the lead insulation, and then through the heart, with disastrous results. Despite this risk, the current defence medical opinion is that there is a greater medical risk in undertaking the removal of a lead whose retention wire has not yet broken. Various studies now show breaks in 16 per cent to 25 per cent of the retention wires in these leads.

The health authorities in Canada and the USA have issued recall orders, and they and the defendant corporations are working on trying to find out what has caused the problem, and how best medically to deal with the implanted persons. They do not yet have clear answers, but have recommended continuing monitoring, by fluoroscopy and otherwise, of all implanted persons. Some 1,125 Canadians have been implanted with these leads, some 700 of whom reside in Ontario. The leads were sold to hospitals, which provided them for implantation by doctors of their patients. There was no contractual relationship between the patients and these defendants.

The proposed representative plaintiffs, Patricia S. Nantais and Mary Margaret Gavel, both were implanted with these leads. Mrs. Gavel's lead was explanted. Mrs. Nantais' was not. Neither lead failed. The remaining plaintiffs are the spouses and family members of Mrs. Nantais and Mrs. Gavel. Plaintiffs' counsel proposes a class composed of the persons implanted with these leads in Canada and a secondary class composed of the spouses and close family members of the implanted persons. ...

Analysis—Extra-Provincial Plaintiffs

Argument here centred around an article by Garry D. Watson, QC, published in 18 CPC (3d) 344 on initial interpretation of the Act, and particularly his question of whether there can be a national class, and the cases of *Morguard Investments Ltd. v. De Savoye*, [1990] 3 SCR 1077, 76 DLR (4th) 256, *Hunt v. T & N plc*, [1993] 4 SCR 289, 109 DLR (4th) 16, and *Phillips Petroleum Coal v. Shutes*, 105 S Ct. 2965 (1985).

In *Phillips Petroleum*, Justice Rehnquist of the US Supreme Court held that in a class action proceeding, reasonable notice plus an opportunity to opt out provides "at a minimum" sufficient due process for the judgment of one state to be given full faith and credit by the courts of other states so that class members in the first state would be prevented from taking action in other states.

In *Morguard*, La Forest J speaking for the entire court spoke of the modern need to deal nationally with problems, and at p. 1079 [the head note] said that:

> The courts in one province should give "full faith and credit" to the judgments given by a court in another province or territory, so long as that court has properly, or appropriately, exercised jurisdiction in the action.

In *Hunt*, La Forest J, again for the entire court, revisited *Morguard* and at p. 325 said:

> The basic thrust of *Morguard* was that in our federation a greater degree of recognition and enforcement of judgments given in other provinces was called for. *Morguard* was careful to indicate, however, that a court must have reasonable grounds for assuming jurisdiction. One must emphasize that the ideas of "comity" are not an end in themselves, but are grounded in notions of order and fairness to participants in litigation with connections to the multiple jurisdictions.

Further, at pp. 326-27, he suggested that the federal government had power and authority to pass legislation to solve any problems, and continued:

> But subject to these overriding powers, I see no reason why the provinces should not be able to legislate in the area, subject however, to the principles in *Morguard* and to the demands of territoriality as expounded in the cases. ...

Morguard was a case involving enforcement in BC of a foreclosure action in Alberta against a BC resident, served in BC per Alberta rules. *Hunt* involved interpretation by the BC court of the constitutionality of Quebec statute. Our Supreme Court has not dealt directly with the issue addressed in *Phillips Petroleum*.

I find the reasoning in *Phillips Petroleum* to be most persuasive. The reference by La Forest J to provincial authority may be helpful. So also may the certification by Montgomery J of a national class in *Bendall v. McGhan*, supra. The different procedure adopted by the BC statute for non-residents certainly provides grounds for an argument, but it is not "plain and obvious" that such an argument would succeed.

However, I do not see how this potential problem can prejudice the defendants. If, indeed, class members outside of Ontario are free to sue despite a class judgment here, how are the defendants any worse off than if the class was limited to residents of Ontario? Would the defendants, being aware of the potential possible problem, be any worse off if non-resident class members should later argue they were not bound by a decision, than if those persons simply opted out now?

Further, is this potentially possible problem really relevant to this action? It seems to me to be something to be resolved in another action (by a non-resident class member) before another court in another jurisdiction.

Part of the proposed plan of the plaintiffs is the sending of questionnaires to each class member. Perhaps prudence would dictate that such questionnaires include an opting in provision for non-residents, to avoid any doubt as to jurisdiction.

It seems eminently sensible, for all the reasons given by La Forest J in *Morguard*, and the policy reasons given for passage of the Act, to have the questions of liability of these defendants determined as far as possible once and for all, for all Canadians. There is nothing in the Act to prevent it. Any questions of the treatment of non-members of the class either through opting out or through some future successful jurisdictional argument, would be dealt with separately. I do not see the possibility of a future adverse finding on jurisdiction as a present bar to certification of all affected Canadian residents.

Certification

For these reasons, I grant certification as asked.

APPLICATION FOR LEAVE TO APPEAL—October 4, 1995

ZUBER J: This is an application for leave to appeal to the Divisional Court from an order of Mr. Justice Brockenshire dated August 29, 1995 [above, at 331], which certified this proceeding as a class proceeding. ...

National Class

Mr. Nordheimer has pointed out that the order in question is the only one made under the Class Proceedings Act, 1992 that has set up a national class. The 1,100 members of the class are spread out across the country although most, approximately 700, reside in Ontario.

The Class Proceedings Act, 1992 is a relatively new statute and the mere fact of novelty does not suggest error. There are two aspects to the concern respecting a national class, one legal and one practical.

At the legal level it may be asked what is the reach of the Ontario legislature and the Ontario courts acting under it, and how does this process involve those who do not reside in Ontario.

It is clear that the Ontario legislature and the Ontario courts are not simply imposing jurisdiction on non-residents. Those outside the jurisdiction who are included in the class are free to opt out in the same manner as those inside Ontario may do.

Whether the result reached in [an] Ontario court in a class proceeding will bind members of the class in other provinces who remained passive and simply did not opt out, remains to be seen. The law of res judicata may have to adapt itself to the class proceeding concept. In my respectful view the order of Brockenshire J setting out a national class, finds powerful support in the judgment of La Forest J in *Morguard Investments Ltd. v. De Savoye*, [1990] 3 SCR 1077, 76 DLR (4th) 256.

On a more practical level it is argued that a court attempting to try this class proceeding will face a multiplicity of laws from all of the provinces which may confuse the matter. This argument in my view is largely speculative. I am not aware of any difference in the law respecting product liability or negligence in the common law provinces and I have not been shown that there is any real difference between the common law on this matter and the law in the Province of Quebec.

It is also argued that other class proceedings may be certified in other provinces relating to the matter which is the subject of this class proceeding. In my respectful view any of these practical difficulties which may develop as the matter proceeds can be met by amending the order in question to adjust the size of the class. If it is shown that the law of another province is so substantially different as to make the trial with respect to class members from that province very difficult, the class can be redefined. Additionally, if a class is certified in another province that group can be deleted from the Ontario class.

In the result I am not persuaded that there is good reason to doubt the correctness of the order in question.

NOTES AND QUESTIONS

1. *Constitutionality of National Cases.* Recall the discussion of *Morguard* in chapter 5, "Commencement of Proceedings"—that is, the constitutional requirement that Canadian courts take jurisdiction over cases only where there is a real and substantial connection to the province. How might the courts describe such a connection where the plaintiff class involves non-residents whose claims have arisen in other provinces? Much could depend on whether the court determines that the real and substantial connection must be between the *individual* and the forum province or whether the requisite connection is merely one between the forum province and the *subject matter* of the litigation. The court in *Harrington v. Dow Corning Corp.* (1997), 29 BCLR (3d) 88 (SC) seems to have made a quantum shift in the analysis of connections to the forum province by identifying the existence of common issues as itself a basis for assuming jurisdiction. The court in *Harrington* observed:

> MACKENZIE J: This is an action for damages against manufacturers and distributors of breast implants. It was certified as a class proceeding under the Class Proceedings Act, SBC 1995, c. 21, on April 11, 1996.
>
> Certain issues relating to the certification order, including the extent of a non-resident sub-class, were deferred for further argument. The plaintiff, by this application, seeks to include "all women who have been implanted with one or more breast implant mammary prosthetic devices and are resident in Canada, anywhere other than Ontario and Quebec, or were implanted in Canada, anywhere other than Ontario and Quebec."
>
> The defendants do not contest the recognition of a non-resident class per se but they contend it should be limited to women, now non-resident, who were implanted in BC. They argue further that the BC resident sub-class must also exclude women who were implanted outside the province because this court does not have jurisdiction over those claims. ...
>
> The issues on this application are whether this court can assume jurisdiction over claims subject to the substantive law of other Canadian jurisdictions ... .
>
> I am satisfied that the legislation is sufficiently open-ended that it can be read as confined by necessary implication to the limits of provincial jurisdiction, whatever those limits are, and no question of the constitutionality of the statute therefore arises. In practical terms, however, the BC legislature has enacted a procedure not available in other provinces and territories, Ontario and Quebec excepted, which facilitates the litigation of multiple claims on a class basis. Should residents of other jurisdictions in Canada, having no individual connection to BC jurisdiction, be permitted to avail

themselves of the BC procedure essentially because a similar procedure is unavailable at home? British Columbia is not the jurisdiction of manufacture of breast implants and the availability of class proceedings here is the main reason why non-residents seek to participate.

The defendants contend that recognition of a broad non-resident sub-class is an unwarranted intrusion into other jurisdictions and interferes with the evident choice of those jurisdictions not to allow class proceedings. They contend that order and fairness require that the choices of the other jurisdictions be respected. They raise the spectre of British Columbia as "Texas north," and class proceedings as an undesirable growth industry taking scarce resources of the courts at the expense of domestic litigation with greater merit. Counsel for the plaintiff respond that the extension of BC class proceedings to non-residents was a conscious policy decision of the BC legislature and that it is not for the courts to second-guess the legislature's decision, providing constitutional limits of jurisdiction are respected. I have already stated above that I am satisfied the legislation does not attempt to exceed constitutional limits, but neither does it attempt to define those limits. ...

In *Amchem Products Inc. v. British Columbia (Workers' Compensation Board)*, [1993] 1 SCR 897, Sopinka J commented (at p. 911-2):

> With the increase of free trade and the rapid growth of multi-national corporations it has become more difficult to identify one clearly appropriate forum for this type of litigation. The defendant may not be identified with only one jurisdiction. Moreover, there are frequently multiple defendants carrying on business in a number of jurisdictions and distributing their products or services world wide. As well, the plaintiffs may be a large class residing in different jurisdictions. It is often difficult to pinpoint the place where the transaction giving rise to the action took place. Frequently, there is no single forum that is clearly the most convenient or appropriate for the trial of the action but rather several which are equally suitable alternatives.

I think those comments are pertinent here, and they go to the jurisdictional issue and not just to forum conveniens. The demands of multi-claimant manufacturers' liability litigation require recognition of concurrent jurisdiction of courts within Canada. In such cases there is no utility in having the same factual issues litigated in several jurisdictions if the claims can be consolidated. I do not think that *Nitsuko* and *Con Pro* stand in the way of concurrent jurisdiction as they do not deal with claims inside and outside the province which raise the same common issue. It is that common issue which establishes the real and substantial connection necessary for jurisdiction. *Nantais* is a considered decision on the question which is otherwise largely a matter of first impression. I am not persuaded that *Nantais* is clearly wrong or inapplicable and accordingly I intend to follow it.

2. In *Carom v. Bre-X Minerals Ltd.*, [1999] OJ no. 281 (Gen. Div.), a class action arising out of the Bre-X mining share scandal, Winkler J upheld the use of a national class, stating as follows:

Morguard and *Hunt* permit the extra-territorial application of legislation where the enacting province has a real and substantial connection with the subject matter of the action and it accords with order and fairness to assume jurisdiction.

As for the first consideration, there is no rigid test which a court can apply when determining whether there is a real and substantial connection between the action and the jurisdiction. As La Forest J stated in *Hunt* at 326:

> Whatever approach is used, the assumption of and the discretion not to exercise jurisdiction must ultimately be guided by the requirements of order and fairness, not a mechanical counting of contacts or connections.

However, as stated in *Morguard* at 1103:

> ... it hardly accords with principles of order and fairness to permit a person to sue another in any jurisdiction, without regard to the contacts that jurisdiction may have to the defendant or the subject-matter of the suit. ...

The plaintiffs assert that there are a multiplicity of contacts between these actions and this jurisdiction. The corporate defendants in these actions are either Ontario corporations, have subsidiary operations in Ontario or engage in business activities within the province. The shares of Bre-X traded through the Toronto Stock Exchange. The causes of action framed in the statements of claim, at their essence, relate to the negligent, intentional or reckless public dissemination of inaccurate or misleading information concerning Bre-X. The brokerage firm research departments disseminating the information regarding Bre-X were headquartered in Toronto. The information emanated from research analysts, who are also named defendants, located in Ontario. The information was supplied by Bre-X to the brokerages and to the media in Ontario. The Bre-X insider defendants were involved with preparing this information for release in Ontario. The information was supported by the allegedly negligent verification of the Bre-X drill core results by the SNC group of companies, one of which is located in Ontario.

I am therefore satisfied that there is a "real and substantial connection" between the defendants and the subject matter of the actions to Ontario, thus meeting that requirement in *Morguard* and *Hunt* for the assumption of jurisdiction.

This leads to the second consideration of "order and fairness."

It is not in dispute that Ontario is the appropriate jurisdiction for these proceedings as they relate to Ontario resident plaintiffs. However, the defendants argue that the inclusion of non-resident plaintiffs as members of the class offends the principle of "order and fairness." They contend that they, and these plaintiffs, will be prejudiced by such a class.

These arguments do not withstand scrutiny. The CPA is a procedural statute replete with provisions guaranteeing order and fairness. Section 9 permits any member to opt out of the class proceeding within the time provided. Section 10 provides for monitoring of the proceeding and empowers the court to amend or terminate the certification order where the s. 5(1) or (2) requirements are no longer met. Section 12 allows any party or class member to bring a motion for an order regarding the fair conduct of the proceeding. Section 13 permits the court to stay a proceeding, on its own motion if necessary. Under s. 14, individual class members may be permitted to take part in the proceedings "to ensure fair and adequate representation of the interests of the class or any subclass or for any other appropriate reason." A class member may be ordered to attend discovery if necessary under s. 15.

In addition s. 17 requires that proper notice of the certification, in a court approved form, must be provided to all class members. The notice must include the "manner by which and time within which class members may opt out of the proceeding." Additional notices to ensure that the interests of the class members are protected may be ordered by the court under s. 19.

The defendants maintain that the requirement of s. 27(3), that any judgment on the common issues is to be binding on all class members, cannot be met if the class includes non-resident plaintiffs. The essence of the argument is that these non-resident "opt out" plaintiffs can take a "wait and see" approach to the Ontario litigation and if dissatisfied with the result, commence an action in another jurisdiction.

This argument overlooks the fact that Ontario has a "real and substantial connection" to the actions. Thus, any final disposition will be binding and will foreclose any further litigation on the same facts in Ontario by operation of the statute. Furthermore, without presuming a determination elsewhere, an attempted exercise of concurrent jurisdiction by a court in another province will undoubtedly be met with an argument based on the principles in *Morguard* and *Hunt*. As stated by La Forest J in *Morguard* at 1103:

> ... the taking of jurisdiction by a court in one province and its recognition in another must be viewed as correlatives and ... recognition in other provinces should be dependent on the fact that the court giving judgment "properly" or "appropriately" exercised jurisdiction.

3. If national classes are permissible, why not worldwide classes?

4. *Certifying mass tort cases as class actions.* How do the class proceeding policy objectives of judicial economy and access to justice relate to one another?

> [A] central question of modern class action theory [is] whether the function of the class action is to consolidate suits that would otherwise be brought (and thus to reduce the caseload of the judiciary) or to facilitate the bringing of suits that would otherwise not be brought because the individual stakes are too small (and thus increase the accessibility of adjudication). The first alternative aims at reducing existing litigation, the second at enabling potential litigation to occur; at some level the two stand at tension.

(S.C. Yeazell, *From Medieval Group Litigation to the Modern Class Action* (New Haven, CT: Yale University Press, 1987), at 25.)

Is judicial economy independently sufficient to warrant certification—that is, should a court certify class actions for mass torts (for example, breast implants, HIV contaminated blood, asbestos cases, and subway disasters) *where the plaintiffs' claims are individually recoverable*? Or should the fact that claims are individually recoverable foreclose class actions for mass torts?

This issue was addressed in *Sutherland* where certification was refused, in part, because the claims were individually recoverable, the court pointing they were already pending in Ontario more than 80 individual lawsuits arising from HIV infection. The individual viability of claims also played a part in the decision not to certify a class in *Abdool*. However, the substantial damages claimed by individual plaintiffs did not prevent certification in the breast implant cases or in *Nantais* although in these cases it was asserted that the claims were not individually viable or recoverable.

In 1982, the Ontario Law Reform Commission criticized the resistance in the US courts to the certification of mass tort claims. Since then, the tide turned (temporarily) in favour of mass tort claims in the United States and several class actions were certified in situations of mass tort, such as in the Agent Orange case, the Dalkon Shield case (*Re: A.H. Robbins Co. Inc.*, 880 F2d 709 (4th Cir., 1989)) and the breast implant cases. It seemed that the courts were reacting to the "horror show" produced by asbestos litigation and other mass torts litigated repetitively as individual claims. But the tide has turned again in the United States against the certification of mass torts as a result of a rising concern about the handling of "immature torts," which has led to cases being decertified. Notable actions to be decertified include those brought with respect to the use of tobacco, penile implants, and contaminated blood. In decertifying these mass tort class actions, courts have been concerned that certification of a class action involving a new and emerging tort or legal theory should be forestalled to permit them and counsel time to acquire the necessary experience through individual actions to do justice to the claim. As Judge Smith, speaking for the 5th Circuit Court of Appeals in *Castano v. American Tobacco Co.*, 84 F3d (5th Cir., 1996), "[t]he collective wisdom of individual juries is necessary before this court commits the fate of an entire industry or, indeed, the fate of a class of millions, to a single jury."

While it is unlikely that class actions in this country will be tried by a jury, in the Canadian context arguments in support of such an approach would include the fact that breast implant litigation has a different aspect and is more informed after the Supreme Court's decision in *Hollis v. Dow Corning Corporation*, [1995] 4 SCR 635 and that tainted blood litigation is much better informed after the disclosure and findings of the Krever commission than it was before that inquiry.

5. Some commentators have argued that a need for judicial economy should outweigh the notion of the right of individual litigants to individually and repeatedly litigate the same issue time and time again. As David Rosenberg of the Harvard Law School has put it (in "Class Actions for Mass Torts: Doing Individual Justice by Collective Means" (1987), 62 *Indiana Law Journal* 561, at 563-64):

> The case-by-case mode of adjudication magnifies [the burden on the judicial system] by requiring the parties in the courts to reinvent the wheel for each claim. The merits of each claim are determined *de novo* even though the major liability issues are common to every claim arising from the mass tort accident, and even then they may have been previously determined several times by full and fair trials.

Is it better in cases based on emerging torts such as those related to HIV infected blood to opt for multiple separate actions—with the potential for numerous separate trials on the common issues—when the legislature has provided that in such cases a class action may be certified to provide judicial economy and to avoid a multiplicity of proceedings? Is the concern about "immature torts" well founded? Where there are plaintiffs who have individually recoverable claims and wish to sue individually, is the simple answer that they can "opt out" of the class action if they wish? Is it fair to the defendant to have to face both a class action and individual actions arising from the same mass tort? (Note that under the legislation the right of a plaintif to opt out appears to be absolute.) If plaintiffs do opt out is it likely that they will have personally made that decision or is it likely that their lawyer will have made the decision, possibly influenced by the fact that he or she will get a much larger fee through an individual action than a class action? If so, should the legal system concern itself with this?

C. Fees: Remunerating the Class Lawyer

As we have seen, the legislation has led to considerable class action activity in Ontario and legal entreprenuers have indeed emerged. Whether this has occurred within the fee framework actually provided for in the statute, or contemplated by the legislators, is another question.

Sections 32 and 33 of the Ontario Act deal with lawyers fees in class proceedings and provide, for the first time ever in Ontario, legalized contingency fees. However, the initial consensus was that the (far from perfectly drafted) provisions authorized only one particular type of contingent fee—a non-percentage, "multiplier" fee which must be approved by the court. Adopting criteria developed by US courts in fixing lawyers' fees recoverable in class actions, the legislation specifies that the calculation of this fee be tied to three factors: the hourly rate of the lawyer, the number of hours worked, and the discretionary application of a "multiplier" that can be used to compensate the lawyer for the risk of engaging in litigation that might have been unsuccessful. This formula has been applied in several cases, two of which resulted in substantial and generous multiplier fees. Fees of $750,000 for a $2.6 million award, and $2 milion for a settlement of some $29 million have been approved, but in other cases substantial or incresed fees were refused where the court concluded, in effect, that hourly rates were too high, too many hours were spent, and there was little risk involved or where the multiplier was inappropriate because the solicitors had no material risk in accepting the retainer and the base fee provided fair compensation. Most recently, in *Gagne v. Silcorp Limited* (1998), 41 OR (3d) 417 (CA), the court held that the legislative objective of enhanced access to justice requires that solicitors conducting class proceedings have a real opportunity to obtain a multiple of the base fee and that the multiplier should generally be in the range of one to four.

However, plaintiffs' counsel have argued, successfully, that the types of contingency fees authorized by the Act are not limited to a "multiplier fee." In the pacemaker case, *Nantais v. Telectronics Proprietary (Can.) Ltd.* (1996), 134 DLR (4th) 47 (Ont. Gen. Div.), the court so held and approved, early in the litigation, a "*lump-sum*" contingent counsel fee of $5,000 per class member (plus party-and-party costs, together with any disbursements not recovered as party-and-party costs), which ultimately yielded some $6 million in counsel fees. In *Crown Bay Hotel Ltd. Partnership v. Zurich Indemnity Company of Canada* (1998), 40 OR (3d) 83 (Gen. Div.), Winkler J held that percentage fee agreements are permissible (and he approved a 20 percent fee), but that ordinarily the fee arrangement ought not to be approved by the court in advance—that is, before the judgment is rendered on the common issues or a settlement is concluded.

> At issue on this motion is the question of whether a contingency fee based on a percentage of the settlement is within the contemplation of the Act. In my view it falls within the ambit of section 32 of the Act, subject to approval by the court. The use of the term "otherwise" in clause (c) of subsection (1) in reference to the method of payment, when considered in the context of the terms "lump sum" and "salary," support this view. Clause (b) makes reference to the estimated fee, " ...whether contingent on success ... or not." It is within the discretion of the judge, in the exercise of his or her discretion as set out in section 32 of the legislation, to approve such a fee arrangement in the appropriate circumstances. ...

> The scheme of the CPA seems to envisage that sections 32 and 33 operate independently of one another. Hence the duplicate provisions for court approval. Moreover, a restrictive construction of the Act is contrary to the policy of the statute, one of the purposes of which is to promote judicial economy. A contingency fee arrangement limited to the notion of a multiple of the time spent may, depending upon the circumstances, have the effect of encouraging counsel to prolong the proceeding unnecessarily and of hindering settlement, especially in those cases where the chance of some recovery at trial seems fairly certain. On the other hand, where a percentage fee, or some other arrangement such as that in *Nantais*, is in place, such a fee arrangement encourages rather than discourages settlement. In the case before this court the settlement averted a seven to ten day trial. Fee arrangements which reward efficiency and results should not be discouraged.

> However, it seems to me to be equally clear that ordinarily the fee arrangement ought not to be approved by the court until after the judgment is rendered on the common issues or the settlement concluded. It is only then that a court can be satisfied that it has all of the relevant facts before it necessary for approval of the fee arrangement. Given that a percentage arrangement represents a melding of a base fee and multiplier, the court will determine a reasonable percentage having regard to the degree of risk undertaken by counsel, the degree of success in the proceeding, and the other criteria enunciated in *Serwaczek v. Medical Engineering Corp.* (1996), 3 CPC (4th) 386 (Ont. Gen. Div.).

Notwithstanding Winkler J's last statement, there are unreported cases approving percentage contingent fees at the outset of the litigation, but with an express reservation of power in the court to review the fee at the end of the litigation.

It is unclear whether the approval in advance of percentage contingent fees are consistent with the legislators' intent to have the multiplier fee provisions specifically provide that in determining the base fee "the court shall allow only a *reasonable fee*" (s. 33(8)) and that the multiplier is to be one that results in "fair and *reasonable compensation* to the solicitor." If, for example, the litigation settles shortly after the fee is approved the class counsel could receive an unduly large fee. On the other hand, a percentage fee fixed in advance may be attractive to class members who may find the multiplier fee incomprehensible and too uncertain; at least with a percentage fee they have some ground to decide whether to opt out because the lawyers' fees are "too rich."

This is an important subject, not simply because it determines what will go into class counsel's pocket, but because it will determine whether or not the legislation is successful. In the final analysis, whether or not the class proceedings legislation achieves its objectives largely depends on whether there are plaintiff class lawyers who are prepared to act for the class and bring the actions. This in turn depends both on whether class counsel are *adequately remunerated* for the time, effort, and skill put into the litigation *and* for the risk they assume (under contingency fee arrangements) of receiving nothing and on whether such remuneration is *reasonably predictable*—that is, that class counsel can take on class actions with a reasonable expectation that in the event of success they will receive reasonable remuneration.

A further issue raised by the fee-fixing process is the potential conflict of interest between class counsel and the class members in the amount to be set aside for counsel fees from the judgment or settlement offer. When a motion is made for approval of counsel fees, whether in advance or on disposition of the matter, should the interests of class members be represented by somebody other than class counsel? Is it proper in these circumstances to proceed in a non-adversarial context? Are judges able to make the decision to approve counsel fees appropriately and to arrive at reasonable results, without the benefit of hearing any opposing argument? Is it wise for court in a common law system (steeped in the adversarial tradition and inexperienced in inquisitorial decision making) to proceed to make decisions in the absence of an adversarial presentation?

If it would be a wise policy to have the class represented by somebody other than class counsel on these fee hearings, who should play that role? Would this be an appropriate role to be assigned to the public guardian and trustee, or for counsel appointed *ad hoc* by the judge? If so, do we need to take added steps to ensure or encourage whoever is given this task to perform it diligently?

D. Costs: The "Downside" Risk and Class Action Litigation

The exposure of the representative plaintiff to liability for costs is a crucial aspect of class proceedings. As the Ontario Law Reform Commission observed in its 1982 *Report on Class Actions* (at 647), "In our view, the question of costs is the single most important issue this Commission has considered in designing an expanded class action procedure for Ontario. ... The matter of costs will not merely affect the efficacy of class actions, but in fact will determine whether this procedure will be utilized at all." The OLRC was well aware that if the representative plaintiff remained exposed to the risk of having to personally pay the defendant's costs if the action was unsuccessful, there was a very real likelihood that people would not come forward to act as representative plaintiffs. (Why take on the risk of the very substantial costs of a class action when the representative plaintiff will only ever recover his or her own individual damages?) To this end the OLRC proposed a regime in which class proceedings satisfying rigorous certification criteria would not be subject to adverse costs awards. Instead, the Ontario Class Proceedings Act retains cost shifting and provides that the court in exercising its discretion with respect to costs may consider whether the class proceeding "was a test case, raised a novel point of law or involved a matter of public interest": s. 31(1).

The BC legislation takes the opposite approach to costs by prohibiting costs awards in s. 37 except when the court considers there has been vexatious, frivolous, or abusive conduct; or an improper or unnecessary step has been taken for the purpose of delay or increasing costs or other improper purpose; or when exceptional circumstances make it unjust to deprive the successful party of costs. However, given the room for discretion in making and declining to make costs awards contained in both the Ontario and the BC legislation, it remains to be seen whether there will be a substantial difference in the operation of these provisions. Nevertheless, the question remains for Ontario counsel as to how they must responsibly advise representative plaintiffs regarding the potential for adverse costs awards in the absence of funding by the Class Proceedings Fund.

Despite the retention of traditional cost shifting, the courts have shown their sensitivity to the threat that the "downside risk" of costs presents to class actions. For example, in *Garland v. Consumers Gas Co. Ltd.* (1995), 22 OR (3d) 451 (Gen. Div.) the plaintiff unsuccessfully argued that the utility's late payment penalty policy offended the Criminal Code (now reversed on this issue by the Supreme Court of Canada, [1998] 3 SCR 112). On dismissing the claim at first instance on a summary judgment motion, Winkler J was unmoved by submissions on behalf of the Law Foundation of Ontario that an adverse costs award "could seriously deplete the resources of the Class Proceedings Fund and thereby impair the ability of the Fund to provide full financial assistance in the future." He held that "the impact of a costs award on the Class Proceedings Fund is not an appropriate consideration for the court in determining whether to award costs to a worthy party in an appropriate case. Rather, the impact of such an award should be taken into consideration by the Class Proceedings Committee in deciding whether to grant funding to a particular plaintiff." Nevertheless, he denied costs to the successful defendant where the case met the legislative criteria because it was a test case, raised a novel point of law, and involved a matter of public interest.

While Ontario courts have shown some sympathy to unsuccessful representative plaintiffs in awarding costs, they have also shown resistance to efforts by plaintiff classes to shield themselves from the potential for adverse costs awards. This resistance turned to open hostility in the following case when a judgment-proof representative plaintiff was put forward to shield the "real" plaintiffs from adverse costs awards in a case that was simply too "entrepreneurial" for the court's liking. Read the following excerpt from *Smith v. Canadian Tire Acceptance Ltd.*, and consider whether the court has struck the right balance between the traditional approach to litigation as a means of righting wrongs and the more "entrepreneurial" quality of class proceedings.

Smith v. Canadian Tire Acceptance Ltd.
(1995) 22 OR (3d) 433 (Gen. Div.)

WINKLER J: This is a motion brought by the Defendant, Canadian Tire Acceptance Limited ("CTAL") for an order that the costs of this action be paid by the Borrowers' Action Society (Society) and Larry Whaley, as non-parties to these proceedings. ...

For the reasons which follow, costs shall be awarded jointly and severally against the Society and Mr. Whaley on a solicitor and client scale. ...

The facts of this matter are essentially not in dispute.

Mr. Whaley was, at all times material to this proceedings, the president of and spokesperson for the Society. The Society represents itself to be a non-profit organisation, the objectives of which are to organize, coordinate and promote class action lawsuits on behalf of credit customers against Canadian corporations.

Prior to the commencement of this action and throughout the conduct of the lawsuit, the Society and Mr. Whaley have represented to the public, in their solicitations, communications and media statements, that they were the instigators and controllers of the proceedings. In short, they held out the lawsuit to be that of the Society. The Society retained counsel to act for the named Plaintiffs in this action, and paid the costs of commencing the action.

Neither the Society, nor Mr. Whaley are named plaintiffs in the action. The reason advanced for the Society not being a named plaintiff was that it was understood to lack standing to sue in this province. No explanation was proffered as to why Mr. Whaley was not a named plaintiff.

The Society and Mr. Whaley began soliciting funds from CTAL Cardholders and other credit card holders prior to the enactment of the *Class Proceedings Act*, to pay for this and other proposed class proceedings. This promotion, which also continued after passage of the Act, was conducted through advertisements which were broadcast on radio and television, placed in newspapers and transmitted through other media. Through these solicitations, it was represented to the public that, for a fee, potential plaintiffs in class action lawsuits, who participated by registering with the Society, would have the opportunity to obtain substantial monetary returns, over and above any damages to which they would be entitled, if the class action lawsuit were successful.

This action involved the allegation that CTAL had been exacting rates of interest on credit cards issued to its customers which contravened the *Interest Act*, RSC 1985, c. I-15. The relief sought was the restitution of interest collected from Cardholders by CTAL, which exceeded that permitted by the *Interest Act*.

The scheme devised by the Society went beyond the mere funding of the action by the Cardholders. Pursuant to the scheme, Cardholders could register with the Society for an initial fee of $100. Additional shares could be purchased for $50 per share. These funds were purported to be used in funding the action. If the lawsuit were successful, Cardholders who had registered with the Society would be entitled to a proportionate share of a contingent fee which, the Society asserted, would be available for distribution, subject to the approval of the Court. Cardholders who had not registered with the Society, but who were members of the class, would only be entitled to the amount by which their interest payments had exceeded those permitted by the *Interest Act*.

Mr. Whaley has acknowledged that this fund-raising arrangement involved the sale of shares in a lawsuit.

In promoting this scheme, the Society and Mr. Whaley made the following representations, which are set out at para. 9 of the Defendant's factum:

(a) The law provides a way in which the Society could obtain a share of the damages award in the event that the class action were successful.

(b) The Society's share or contingency is subject to court approval, but could be between 10% and 30% of the award in the lawsuit.

(c) If 500 Canadian Tire cards are registered with the Society, each registered cardholder will receive $129,000. If 5,000 are registered, the share will be $12,900.

(d) The cost of registration is $100 plus GST.

(e) Cardholders qualify to register and share in the contingency even if they pay no interest and even if their card is cancelled.

(f) The Society will retain 10% of any share before dividing the contingency among the registered cardholders.

(g) Cardholders are able to purchase an additional share of the award for an additional $50 contribution.

These representations were made across Canada in newspapers and letter solicitations of the Society, interviews broadcast on radio, television and reported in newspaper. There were also advertisements placed in daily newspapers in British Columbia, Manitoba and Ontario, and a video "infomercial" which was broadcast in Edmonton and which was viewed by this Court. 1,750 person are registered with the Society.

In a news release, dated June 15, 1992, which was sent to Dean Groussman, the president of Canadian Tire Corporation, it was stated:

Canadian Tire has been selected as the first Credit Card Company to be sued in the Borrowers' Action Society's Billion Dollar Class Action.

Our calculations indicate that this company has pocketed over 400 million dollars in interest overcharges since 1981," says borrowers' advocate Larry Whaley. "Canadian Tire Customers are entitled to this money back. And if the Canada Interest Act is applied they will also be entitled to the difference between the amount they agreed to pay and the 5% limit the law imposes on lenders who do not disclose properly.

In an interview broadcast on CFRB-1010 AM Radio, on March 16, 1993, when asked what Cardholders would receive in return for their $100 contribution, as re-stated in the Defendant's factum, Mr. Whaley stated:

Well, they become a supporter of the action that this Borrowers' Action Society is taking. And, in exchange for that, if we are successful, they will receive an (sic) share of the contingency that we will be seeking from the court, and the legislation provides for this. So, we'll be seeking a contingency. If we get our $720-million award and 10% of that comes to us, if there are 500 card holders registered with us, those 500 will share that 10 per cent equally, which would mean $129,600 each. If there are 5,000 registered with us, that will be $12,960 each.

Although Mr. Whaley's evidence was vague and evasive on this point, I find that neither the Society nor Mr. Whaley obtained legal advice as to whether a court in Ontario would have jurisdiction to award the Society a contingency if the action were successful. This was so both before and after the decision on the motion for summary judgment was released, as well as after notice was given by the Defendant that it was seeking costs against the Society and Mr. Whaley, personally.

The Society has not ceased campaigning for funds. In a Society newsletter dated September 15, 1994, the Society stated that it would proceed to the Court of Appeal and that Cardholders currently registered with the Society could "buy an additional share of each action" in which they were registered for an additional $50. In the *BA Update*, a newsletter published by the Society, vol. 4, no. 5, August 1994, the Society stated that despite the decision on the summary judgment motion, it was still of the view that the Plaintiffs' position was legally correct and that it required further funds for the appeal of the action.

In an earlier *BA Update*, released prior to May 30, 1993, entitled: Collect your share of a Billion Dollar Award, it was stated:

> If you have ever had a credit card you can join a Borrowers' Action Society Class Action and share in what could amount to several billion dollars while helping to bring justice to all Canadian borrowers. You can participate at no risk.
>
> Actions are being filed in Ontario, where law that was proclaimed on January 1, 1993 makes the procedure clear. The law provides a way for the Borrowers' Action Society to obtain a share of the award and divide it with card holders who support the action. The Society's share is subject to court approval but could be between 10% and 30% of each award. In the Canadian Tire case the award could be as much as $720 million. If the Society share is 10% and the award is $720 million we will have $72 million to divide.

An advertisement placed by the Society in the Edmonton Journal, dated April 7, 1994, read in part:

> Would you risk $100 on the chance you will get back up to $64,500? $150 for a chance at double that? Sounds like a get-rich quick scam? It's not, it's a class action. And it looks like it has a very good chance at success. The first of 35 planned actions was launched against Canadian Tire Acceptance Corporation in an Ontario court by the Edmonton-Based Borrowers' Action Society in 1993. Society president, Larry Whaley is inviting people from right across the country to join and share in the awards.

Mr. Whaley's name and persona can be seen to figure prominently in advancing the goals of the Society.

The scheme masterminded by the Society and Mr. Whaley involves the taking of 10 per cent of the interest refund which would otherwise be payable to members of the class if the action were successful and diverting that 10 per cent to the Society and those having purchased shares in the lawsuit. It would appear, from the evidence and statements of Mr. Whaley, that he receives a salary for work done for the Society and that he is hopeful he will gain financially if the action is successful.

As Mr. Whaley stated in an interview on Canada AM, in respect of successful class actions generally, as re-stated in the Defendant's factum:

> **Mr. Whaley**: We're doing a lot of work, and we've been in this business looking at this for a long period of time, and we think that we're entitled to a share.
>
> **Interviewer**: Mind you, a share of a billion dollars from each of however many credit card issuers you're going to go after ... sounds like you may become Canada's next billionaire.
>
> **Mr. Whaley**: Well, we certainly hope so. We'll have to see how that goes ...

The video "infomercial" reveals three aspects of the promotion which are noteworthy in this proceeding. First, pursuant to the scheme advanced by the Society, there were to be two types of Cardholders; those who did not register with the Society, who would realize small damages awards; and those who registered who, in a successful proceeding, would realize larger amounts than the unregistered cardholders, based on a share of the contingency. Second, concerning the matter of costs sanctions in the event of an unsuccessful proceeding. In response to being questioned on this subject, Mr. Whaley stated that costs, if awarded, would be insignificant, as little as 25 cents against any individual member of the class. Third, Mr. Whaley indicated that the Society would be pursuing class proceedings against 35 Canadian corporations. This action was, therefore, part of a broader plan to promote, organize and control class actions of this nature across the country. ...

By virtue of s. 131(1) of the *Courts of Justice Act*, RSO 1990, c. C.43, this Court has the discretion to award "the costs of and incidental to a proceeding or a step in a proceeding" and to "determine by whom and to what extent the costs shall be paid." Costs will be awarded against non-parties to proceedings only in exceptional circumstances. Such an award may be made, however, where the non-party is the real plaintiff, although not a de facto plaintiff, in the proceedings, and where the non-party has engaged in improper conduct in respect of the litigation. Courts have held that structuring a lawsuit to avoid liability for costs or engaging in maintenance or champerty or similar conduct constitute improper conduct for the purposes of non-party costs awards. ...

Having reviewed all of the evidence of the campaign mounted by the Society and Mr. Whaley, to provide a foundation for this action, including interviews, press releases and other promotional materials, I am satisfied that the Society and Mr. Whaley are the real Plaintiffs in this action. They instigated, promoted and financed the litigation throughout. Although they were not the *de facto* Plaintiffs in the action, they each had a financial stake in its outcome. They actively solicited funds from Cardholders to commence the action; they retained and instructed counsel to act on behalf of the named Plaintiffs, and they controlled the conduct of the litigation from its inception. They conceptualized the scheme underlying this action and targeted the Defendant as the corporation against which they wished to proceed first. They held out to the public that this was the Society's case.

As stated, neither the Society, nor Mr. Whaley are *de facto* parties to these proceedings. It was stated by the Society that it did not believe that it had standing to sue in an Ontario court. This supports the conclusion that, except for this, the Society would have been named as a plaintiff. No explanation was advanced as to why Mr. Whaley is not a party to the proceedings. It is clear from the infomercial that the potential costs consequences of litigation was a forefront issue. From all of the facts, I draw the inference that the reason the real Plaintiffs, the Society and Mr. Whaley, were not named as plaintiffs in this proceeding, was to avoid possible costs consequences.

However, in addition to the attempt to avoid costs sanctions, other aspects of the scheme upon which this lawsuit was advanced, are more disturbing. The Society and Mr. Whaley, have made and continue to make, promises that, if the action is successful, registrants will obtain sums of money far in excess of that to which they might have been entitled as damages. As stated, all this was done without having obtained a legal opinion concerning the propriety of the scheme, which would have appeared problematic to any observer, or the likelihood of being able to deliver on these promises, which was even more problematic. By Mr. Whaley's own admission, the solicitation of funds from class members and potential class members was tantamount to the marketing and selling of shares in this lawsuit. 1,750 persons registered with the Society, based on these representations.

The Society and Mr. Whaley were cautious to state that registrants could lose their registration fee if the action were unsuccessful. This much is correct. They stated further, that the ultimate reward to registrants was dependent upon the Court's approval. Although, on its face innocuous, it is implicit in this statement that the Court's approval will be forthcoming. No issue was raised concerning the inevitability of the Court's approval if this action were successful. On the contrary, this statement adds a degree of legitimacy to this scheme. In the absence of a legal opinion, and given the nature of the scheme, this representation was irresponsible.

The promises made by the Society and Mr. Whaley could not have been realized. A windfall, of the sort envisaged here, could not occur under the *Class Proceedings Act*. The approval of the Court would not have been granted.

This scheme was ill-founded and flawed both conceptually and in law. The promises of financial gain for registrants were irresponsible, and the conduct of the Society and Mr. Whaley in attempting to gain financially from the action was akin to maintenance and champerty.

Maintenance and champerty are defined in the *Canadian Encyclopedic Digest* (Ont. 3d), Title 139, at p. 100, as follows:

> The tort of maintenance arises when an individual intermeddles in a lawsuit in which he or she does not have a genuine interest. Champerty arises when the intermeddling occurs by virtue of an agreement. Maintenance involves providing financial support for another to bring or defend an action, champerty involves not only the provision of such support, but an agreement to share the profits of the action. Historically, both champerty and maintenance were also common law criminal offences but with the abolition of non-statutory criminal offences there is now only a civil law action. [Footnotes omitted.]

At p. 101, it is further stated:

> There must also be an improper motive present to found the action. A person who, without malice or any desire to stir up strife or litigation or to officiously interfere with the business of others, assists another to recover his or her legal rights has not committed maintenance. The person providing the assistance is not required to ascertain whether or not there is reasonable ground for the litigation. It is sufficient to possess a bona fide belief in the litigant's inability to sustain the costs. A common interest, either direct or indirect, in the litigation will constitute a proper motive. [Footnotes omitted.]

The words of the Supreme Court of Canada in *Goodman v. The Queen*, [1939] SCR 446, provide wise counsel, to the effect that to allow a person who had no interest whatever in a lawsuit, to intermeddle, purely with the object of personal gain, might lead to a grave abuse.

Counsel for the society argued, citing *S. (J.E.) v. K. (P.)* (1986), 55 OR (2d) 111 (Dist. Ct.) as authority, that in order for champerty or maintenance to have occurred, there must have been an improper motive on the part of the party providing support to the litigation. I agree. The objective of the Society and Mr. Whaley to personally gain from the litigation, taken together with the hollowness of the representations made to solicit registrations with the Society, constitute ample evidence of this.

Mr. Whaley submitted that, throughout this litigation, he had acted only in his capacity as the president of the Society. He argued, therefore, that if costs were awarded on this motion, they should be awarded against the Society only, and not against him. In my opinion, the Society and Mr. Whaley are alter egos of one another, both in promoting their scheme and for all other purposes of this litigation.

The *Class Proceedings Act* was never intended to insulate representative plaintiffs, or class members, from the possible costs consequences of unsuccessful litigation. The goal of the Act is not to encourage the promotion of litigation. Rather, it is designed to provide a procedure whereby the courts will be more readily accessible to groups of plaintiffs. It is the intention of the legislation that representative plaintiffs initiate, organize and manage these actions. The legislative purpose was succinctly summarized by Mr. Justice O'Brien, writing for the Divisional Court, in *Abdool*, at para. 60 [31 CPC (3d), at 210]:

> The goal is to permit advancement of small claims where legal costs make it uneconomic to advance them.

At para. 44, he addressed the issue of costs as follows:

> Under the Act, once certification is granted, class plaintiffs face little, if any, exposure to legal costs. Contingency fees are permitted for plaintiffs' counsel and s. 31 of the Act provides for the court to exercise its discretion regarding costs, and indicates class members are not liable for those costs except with respect to the determination of their own individual interests.

Pursuant to s. 131(1) of the *Courts of Justice Act*, the discretion of the Court to award costs and the custom that the unsuccessful party will pay the successful party's costs also applies in class proceedings. There is provision, however, for the amelioration of an adverse costs award. First, a successful defendant may seek costs from the Class Proceedings Fund where the representative plaintiff has obtained assistance. Second, s. 31(1) of the *Class Proceedings Act* states:

> In exercising its discretion with respect to costs under subsection 131(1) of the Courts of Justice Act, the court may consider whether the class proceeding was a test case, raised a novel point of law or involved a matter of public interest.

Hence, in a case of a novel nature, and absent any circumstances which militate to the contrary, the Court may exercise its discretion and decline to award costs to the successful party. This was done in the instant case on the motion for summary judgment in respect of the named Plaintiffs.

This section was never intended, however, to permit a representative plaintiff, as distinct from a real plaintiff, to invoke the courts' discretion so as to avoid an adverse costs award. This is especially so where the real plaintiff would not have had a valid stance upon which to do so. In general, see *Lavigne v. OPSEU* (1989), 67 OR (2d) 536 (CA).

It must be recognized that, in a class proceeding, there is a real vulnerability that an impecunious representative plaintiff will be put forward with this purpose in mind. Such a plaintiff is, strictly speaking, a real plaintiff in the sense of having an interest the same as others in the class, while at the same time being immune from costs sanctions. In such circumstances, the Court must exercise its supervisory jurisdiction with vigilance and, where circumstances dictate, apply the appropriate principles of law. In a proper case, a court may examine the role of counsel. ...

The scheme which was advanced by the Society and Mr. Whaley, for the funding of this and other class proceedings, is beyond the contemplation of the *Class Proceedings Act*. This legislation does not envisage that causes of action, legitimate though they may be, will be identified and class members recruited, for the ultimate financial gain of the organizers. Instead, the legislation anticipates a genuine representative plaintiff. The purpose of the legislation is to facilitate the litigation of causes of action and not to generate them for financial gain.

The Society and Mr. Whaley are the real Plaintiffs in this proceeding. The representative plaintiffs, while interested in the outcome of the litigation, were not the real Plaintiffs for the purposes of the *Class Proceedings Act*. The objective in not naming the real Plaintiffs was to avoid an adverse costs award. The scheme conceived of by the Society and Mr. Whaley to fund the litigation was akin to maintenance and champerty. The holding out of a Court approval of this scheme and the projected rewards flowing therefrom was presumptuous; to some, it may appear contumacious.

For all of these reasons, in the exercise of my discretion, costs shall be awarded as follows:

> The Borrowers' Action Society and Mr. Whaley, personally, shall pay to the Defendant, Canadian Tire Acceptance Ltd., the costs of this action, including costs incurred on the motion for summary judgment, Mr. Whaley's motion to re-open the matter and this motion, on a solicitor and client scale, for which the Society and Mr. Whaley shall be jointly and severally liable.

The costs of these proceedings shall be assessed.

NOTES AND QUESTIONS

1. *Financing class actions.* This will always be an issue for plaintiffs' class counsel who act on a "no win–no pay" contingency basis. As they work on the case, unbilled lawyer time builds up (some of it for associates whose salaries need to be paid) and disbursements are incurred that may have to be paid long before the litigation ends. This raises the question of how the litigation is to be financed. In the fee determination decision in the breast implant litigation, *Serwaczek v. Medical Engineering Corp.* (1996), 3 CPC (4th) 386 (Ont. Gen. Div.), it was stated that the disbursements were financed by a bank loan on which the class counsel paid interest at the prime rate. As reported in the *The Toronto Star*, February 22, 1998, in the heart pacemaker litigation, *Nantais v. Telectronics Proprietary (Can.) Ltd.* (in which the ultimate disbursements allowed were $800,000), a less conventional financing method was used. Class counsel Harvey Strosberg "convinced a handful of wealthy investors to ... [invest] a total of $350,000 to help finance [the] class action." "If the heart patients won, the investors would be first in line to get their money back, plus 20 per cent annual interest. If not, they'd lose the entire amount." It is reported that Mr. Strosberg stated that this financing method "had the okay of the judge hearing the case." Had the *Nantais* action failed, could the defendants have argued, on the authority of *Smith*, that they were entitled to

their costs against either Mr. Strosberg or his investors as persons who had promoted the action through champerty and maintenance? Or should it be accepted that, in order for the legislatively created class action regime to work (one which unabashedly relies on lawyer entrepreneurs for its operation), lawyers must be permitted to make such financing arrangements even if they appear to offend traditional notions of champerty and maintenance? What are the acceptable methods of financing? Should class actions be permitted to become investment vehicles and "maintenance" abolished? See Poonam Puri, "Financing of Lawsuits by Third Party Investors: A Share of Justice?" (1998), 36 *Osgoode Hall Law Journal* 515, proposing that class actions be permitted to become investment vehicles.

2. *Seeking funding from the Class Proceedings Committee.* Questions remain as to how plaintiffs' counsel should advise representatives about the "downside cost risk." By no means all representative plaintiffs are applying to the Class Proceedings Committee for funding which, if granted, immunizes the representative plaintiffs from the risk of having to pay an adverse cost award. Indeed, as of mid-1999, there had been less than 30 applications. But routinely advising representative plaintiffs to apply to the Class Proceedings Committee does not itself resolve the issue when the claim is a novel one. In *Edwards v. Law Society of Upper Canada* (1994), 36 CPC (3d) 116 (Ont. Class Proc. Cmte.), the committee discussed its criteria for funding of class actions and made it clear that the merits of the case is the most important consideration. The committee's current view is that applicants must convince it that the committee should become a partner with the applicant. As of mid-1999 the committee had only funded five class actions, but was already concerned about the fund's potential solvency.

Given that well in excess of 100 class actions have been commenced to date in Ontario, why have there been so few applications to the Class Proceedings Committee? Are lawyers acting prudently in not advising their clients to apply?

E. Settlement of Class Actions

Like most litigation, many class actions tend to end in settlement. But unlike most other litigation, the settlement of class actions requires court approval (Class Proceedings Act s. 29(2)) to ensure the protection of absent class members. This requirement is essential since the settlement will be binding on every class member other than those who have chosen to opt out: s. 29(3).

Reports of numerous class action settlements have come from the courts and the media. For example, the court approved settlements in *Godi v. TTC* (unreported, court file 95-CU-89529—a personal injury case arising out of the August 1995 collision of two subway trains operated by the Toronto Transit Commission) and *Gagne v. Silcorp Ltd.* (unreported, court file 97-CU-120941—a wrongful dismissal case arising out of the merger of the Mac's and Beckers convenience store chains and the ensuing dismissal of about 120 employees). Both settlements provided for mini-hearings to assess individual damages, preserved the defendants right to raise individual defences in the mini-hearing process, and made extensive and creative use of ADR.

The court also approved a settlement in the pacemaker case, *Nantais*. The following details are taken from an account in *The Globe and Mail*, Monday, October 6, 1997. The total amount of the settlement is reported to be $23.1 million with the 1,005 class members sharing approximately $15 million. One point eight million dollars is to be paid to provincial health plans. Under the terms of the settlement, the defendant will pay the plaintiffs' solicitors $6 million in fees including $800,000 in disbursements. The estates of class members who have died will receive either $1,500 or $3,000; claimants who are still alive stand to receive at least $10,000 each and those who had their pacemakers replaced will get at least $15,000. A further $5 million fund has been set aside for those who feel they deserve more and who have suffered very serious injuries. These claims for additional compensation had to be dealt with by special referees from the ADR Chambers. The newspaper report states that the settlement figure represents the full amount of the defendants' North American insurance coverage and by reason of the settlement Canadian plaintiffs will access these funds to the exclusion of 40,000 class action claimants in the United States. In a letter to the class members, class counsel Harvey Strosberg stated that there was a risk of losing at trial and that not to settle would likely have resulted in a delay of at least five years because of appeals, damage assessments, and the time required to collect.

In a settlement in the breast implant cases reported in *The Globe and Mail*, Friday April 3, 1998, Dow Corning has agreed to pay $35 million to plaintiffs in the class action against it. As many as 10,000 women would be eligible for compensation under the agreement, which still requires the approval of the US Bankruptcy Court as well as courts in Ontario and Quebec. Dow is the third major maker of silicone breast implants to settle class action law suits with Canadian women. In 1995 a $20.5 million settlement was negotiated against Bristol-Myers Squibb, and in March 1998 a $15.3 million settlement with Baxter Health Care Corp. was approved by the courts. Mr. Eizenga, one of the plaintiff's lawyers, was quoted as saying that the recent settlements justify the decision to reject the possibility of sharing in the $64 million global compensation fund offered in a US settlement by the breast implant manufacturers. He noted that the three settlements on behalf of Quebec and Ontario alone would amount to $75 million when the implant removal program is included. A breast implant class action against all the major manufacturers of implants is still pending in British Columbia.

In June 1998, a motion was brought to approve a settlement arrived at in *Dabbs v. Sun Life Assurance Co.* (1997), 35 OR (3d) 708 (Gen. Div.) (leave to appeal refused January 22, 1998), a "vanishing premiums" insurance policy case brought on behalf of policy holders. The settlement was estimated to be worth a total of $65 million. Although this seems a sizable amount, if shared equally among some 400,000 class member policy holders (should all of them claim a share), it would yield only about $162.50 per claimant. In *Dabbs* a number of policy holders were granted standing to participate in the motion to approve the settlement or to oppose the terms of the settlement. The approval motion was complicated by the fact that the settlement agreement contained an arbitration agreement with a mechanism for determining class counsel's fee (which was to be decided by arbitration before a neutral third party) and was required to fall within the range of $1.4 million and $6.5 million. The figure of $1.4 million was the minimum figure to be awarded, and was based on estimates of the actual time spent by counsel. According to the agreement, the arbitrated fee was to be paid by the defendant directly, from monies separate from the settlement funds, and to be divided among class counsel from three provinces. Although class counsel had previously executed a separate fee agreement with the representative plaintiff, they did not move for approval of that agreement. Instead they advised the court that they did not intend to seek payment from the class members over and above that provided for in the settlement. The objecting class members brought a motion to have class counsel disqualified on the basis of a conflict of interest alleged to have arisen from the simultaneous negotiation of the agreement respecting counsel's fees and the settlement of the action. This motion was unsuccessful. In *Dabbs v. Sun Life Assurance Co.* (1997), 35 OR (3d) 708 (Gen. Div.), O'Driscoll J refused the objectors leave to appeal this decision and awarded solicitor-and-client costs against them on the ground that they had unnecessarily sought to remove class counsel and cast unfounded aspersions on the integrity of class counsel. Was this costs order wise, fair, or deserved?

NOTES AND QUESTIONS

1. *How should the court approach its role as settlement approver?* A variety of issues and challenges are posed by class action settlements and the court's obligation under the Act is to scrutinize the settlements and to refuse to approve them if they are not fair and reasonable. Should the court itself take steps to precipitate an adversarial hearing with regard to the adequacy of the settlement? What should be the standard of scrutiny to be applied by the court in approving the settlement? Should the court be concerned if plaintiff's and defendant's counsel have simultaneously negotiated both a settlement for the class and class counsel's fees?

In this context, it helps to keep in mind the two sources of the legitimacy of decisions resolving litigation. The legitimacy for court decisions resolving litigation—adjudication—comes from the reasoned decisions given by an independant judiciary. By contrast, the legitimacy for the resolution of cases through settlement comes from the consent of those who are to be bound—that is, the named parties whether or not the settlements might be regarded as fair by others. As Judith Resnik has pointed out (in "Aggregation, Settlement, and Dismay" (1995), 80 *Cornell Law Review* 918 and "Litigating and Settling Class Actions: The Prerequisites of Entry and Exit" (1997), 30 *University of California at Davis Law Review* 835), for various reasons (one being judicial self-interest), we have elevated settlements to being the best form of resolution, preferable to adjudication, and the current judicial regime often pushes for them. This is summed up in the statement, attributed to some judges, "a bad settlement is better than a good trial." Does this reasoning apply to class actions? Consider the following arguments put forward by Resnick:

> With class actions the situation is quite different. Because the settlement will finally determine the rights of absent parties and consent of all class members is not possible, nor required, *courts* are charged with the responsibility of passing on the adequacy and fairness of class action settlements. This function must be taken seriously and class action settlements must be carefully scrutinized by judges—difficult as this task may be. This is a situation where the courts are dealing with "other people's money"—the rights of people who are not before the court. The settlement of a class action is not the same

as the settlement of an individual action. Not only is it impossible to establish the consent of all the parties, but also there is a potential conflict of interest for those who negotiate the settlement, i.e., the plaintiff's lawyer and the defendant, who might [have] a personal interest in settlement (rendering a fee certain on the one hand and capping liability on the other) which may not be congruent with the interest of class members. As Professor John Coffee has observed, *Class Wars: The Dilemma of the Mass Tort Class Action* (1995) 95 Colum. L. Rev. 1343, the risk with the settlement of class actions is that the defendant will seek to achieve a lower than market price settlement by taking steps to see that the plaintiff's lawyer receives some form of above-market lawyer's fee.

Moreover, the court has to keep in mind that when class counsel is acting on a contingency fee basis, he or she might be under pressure from partners to settle the case. The risks and expense of taking complex class actions to trial are undoubtedly formidable. If the case is one of any complexity and length, class counsel will steadily build up unbilled fees and sizeable (or even huge) disbursements (e.g. these were $800,000 in *Nantais*). This may mean that for many class actions the prospect of the plaintiff taking the case to trial is remote. Class counsel will likely settle the case. The court's role is to assure that that settlement is adequate, fair and reasonable. As Resnik and others have pointed out evaluating the adequacy of settlements will always be difficult. However, this does not justify abandoning the enterprise which is a statutorily imposed duty and one that is crucial to the fairness of class actions and their credibility in the public eye. Judges need to handle this task in such a way that the public does not develop the jaundiced view recently expressed by a US defence lawyer: "a class action is where the class members each get a new toaster (or something like that) and the class lawyers get $1 or $2 million." This is not a task which should be characterized by "umpirial judging" (with its approach of "hands off" and impartiality); rather it is a task which calls for the assertivness of "managerial judging" and a serious enquiry into the substantive merit of the proposed settlement.

Do you agree or disagree with this analysis?

2. Prior to the actual hearing to consider approval of the *Dabbs* settlement, Sharpe J held a hearing to determine the appropriate procedure. In the course of the resulting reasons, *Dabbs v. Sun Life Assurance Co. of Canada*, [1998] OJ no. 1598 (Gen. Div.), he made the following observations:

> With respect to specific objections raised by the objectors, there is an additional factor to be kept in mind. The role of the court is to determine whether the settlement is fair, reasonable and in the best interests of the class as a whole, not whether it meets the demands of a particular class member. As approval is sought at the same time as certification, even if the settlement is approved, class members will be afforded the right to opt out. There is, accordingly an element of control that may be exercised to alleviate matters of particular concern to individual class members.
>
> Various definitions of "reasonableness" were offered in argument. The word suggests that there is a range within which the settlement must fall that makes some allowance for differences of view, as an American court put it, "a range which recognizes the uncertainties of law and fact in any particular case and the concomitant risks and costs necessarily inherent in taking any litigation to completion." (*Newman v. Stein*, 464 F (2d) 689 (1972) at 693).

(c) Factors to be considered by the court for approval of the agreement

A leading American text, *Newberg on Class Actions* (3rd ed.), para. 11.43 offers the following useful list of criteria:

1. Likelihood of recovery, or likelihood of success
2. Amount and nature of discovery evidence
3. Settlement terms and conditions
4. Recommendation and experience of counsel
5. Future expense and likely duration of litigation
6. Recommendation of neutral parties if any
7. Number of objectors and nature of objections
8. The presence of good faith and the absence of collusion

I also find the following passage from the judgment of Callaghan ACJHC in *Sparling v. Southam Inc.* (1988), 66 OR (2d) 225 at 230-1 to be most helpful. Callaghan ACJHC was considering approval of a settlement in a derivative action, but his comments are equally applicable to the approval of settlements of class action:

> In approaching this matter, I believe it should be observed at the outset that the courts consistently favour the settlement of lawsuits in general. To put it another way, there is an overriding public interest in favour of settlement. This policy promotes the interests of litigants generally by saving them the expense of trial of disputed issues, and it reduces the strain upon an already overburdened provincial court system.
>
> In deciding whether or not to approve a proposed settlement under s. 235(2) of the Act, the court must be satisfied that the proposal is fair and reasonable to all shareholders. In considering these matters, the court must recognize that settlements are by their very nature compromises, which need not and usually do not satisfy every single concern of all parties affected. Acceptable settlements may fall within a broad range of upper and lower limits.
>
> In cases such as this, it is not the court's function to substitute its judgment for that of the parties who negotiate the settlement. Nor is it the court's function to litigate the merits of the action. I would also state that it is not the function of the court to simply rubber-stamp the proposal.
>
> The court must consider the nature of the claims that were advanced in the action, the nature of the defences to those claims that were advanced in the pleadings, and the benefits accruing and lost to the parties as a result of the settlement. ...
>
> The matter was aptly put in two American cases that were cited to me in the course of argument. In a decision of the Federal Third Circuit Court in *Yonge v. Katz*, 447 F (2d) 431 (1971), it is stated:
>
> > It is not necessary in order to determine whether an agreement of settlement and compromise shall be approved that the court try the case which is before it for settlement. Such procedures would emasculate the very purpose for which settlements are made. The court is only called upon to consider and weigh the nature of the claim, the possible defences, the situation of the parties, and the

exercise of business judgment in determining whether the proposed settlement is reasonable.

In another case cited by all parties in these proceedings, *Greenspun v. Bogan*, 492 F (2d) 375 at p. 381 (1974), it is stated:

> … any settlement is the result of a compromise—each party surrendering something in order to prevent unprofitable litigation, and the risks and costs inherent in taking litigation to completion. A district court, in reviewing a settlement proposal, need not engage in a trial of the merits, for the purpose of settlement is precisely to avoid such a trial. See *United Founders Life Ins. Co. v. Consumer's National Life Inc. Co.*, 447 F (2d) 647 (7th Cir. 1971); *Florida Trailer & Equipment Co. v. Deal*, 284 F (2d) 567, 571 (5th Cir. 1960). It is only when one side is so obviously correct in its assertions of law and fact that it would be clearly unreasonable to require it to compromise in the extent of the settlement, that to approve the settlement would be an abuse of discretion. …

It is apparent that the court cannot exercise its function without evidence. The court is entitled to insist on sufficient evidence to permit the judge to exercise an objective, impartial and independent assessment of the fairness of the settlement in all the circumstances.

Subsequently, after a hearing at which certain class members opposed the settlement, Sharpe J approved the settlement of the class action against the life insurer: *Dabbs v. Sun Life Assurance Co. of Canada* (1998), 40 OR (3d) 429 (Gen. Div.).

Access to Justice

I. INTRODUCTION

No matter how well-organized or progressive, societies cannot avoid generating a large number of disputes. While efforts must be made to ensure that the extent and character of such disputes are kept within reasonable limits, every society must ensure that there are readily available forums and devices through which disputes can be effectively and fairly resolved. Traditionally, the legal system has been at the heart of this dispute resolution process. In societies devoted to the virtues of the rule of law, judges and lawyers have been entrusted with the task of fulfilling this responsibility in a manner that works for the general benefit at large. However, in recent years, widespread dissatisfaction with the performance of the legal process has developed. In blunt terms, it is contended that existing arrangements are too expensive (the costs of obtaining justice too often outweigh the benefits of the justice obtained), too delayed (the inordinate time it takes to obtain justice amounts to a denial of any justice), too distant (people are not actively involved in the pursuit of justice, but function only as the statistical objects of a bureaucratic processing), and too individualistic (the legal system is oriented around the resolution of individual disputes and is unable to deal with or comprehend disputes of a more collective or structural nature).

In addition to these concerns, we need to consider whether access to the legal system necessarily means access to *justice*—that is, the existence of barriers that impede access to the legal system may constitute an injustice, but it does not necessarily follow that the removal of these barriers will result in access to justice. While this chapter focuses largely on the economic barriers to access to the legal system, we begin by sketching the broader issues of access to justice and then locate economic and other non-economic barriers within that context. After that, we examine the different mechanisms—contingency fees, private insurance, paralegals, and public funds—that are or might be used to facilitate better access to the justice system. The next section looks at legal aid, the major device used to compensate for people's economic inability to access legals services—an area of intense political pressure and debate. The last section initiates a short inquiry into the responsibility that the legal profession might have to provide broader access to its services for those who cannot afford them.

As you read the following extract ask yourself whether the existence of barriers that impede access to the legal system is unjust. Should access be available on an equal basis? After all, there are many goods and services that are not equally available in our society and we tolerate (perhaps even approve of) such disparities. What exactly is wrong with allowing people to have as much as or as little law as they are willing to pay for and can afford? If access to the legal system is not synonymous with access to justice then should it be a matter of concern that access to legal services is not equally available to all?

Rod MacDonald, "Access to Justice and Law Reform"
(1990), 10 *Windsor Yearbook of Access to Justice* 287 (footnotes omitted)

In order to work oneself back to an integrated, social construction of complex justice which is both more encompassing than, and prior to, our current conception of justice according to law, it is helpful to examine the premises of the access debate, at least as it now stands. As I read it, mainstream access to justice literature is largely instrumental; it is a literature about access to law, rather than access to justice. In this perspective, whatever else justice might be for philosophers, it is, for access to justice proselytizers, fundamentally a product marketed by the state through its dispute processing agencies to which all citizens should have access. Justice is neither an aspiration, nor an ideal which demands engagement by those who pursue it. Rather, like data-banks stored by computer systems, justice is a commodity which can be made more accessable by removing interface obstacles. Access to justice is, therefore, really about access to the systemic equivalent of hardware—to the processes and institutions of formalized law.

Given this model of justice and its accessibility, it is hardly surprising that the law reform agenda consists of a series of issues relating to operation of various state agencies. The *problematique* is simply: "What measures can be implemented in order to facilitate the recognition and exercise by citizens of those rights and entitlements which existing law puts at their disposal?" It is on this ground, and not on the ground of re-examining the existing distribution of rights and entitlements, or of questioning the centrality of the concept of rights to the achievement of justice that most lawyers and politicans who are interested in "access to justice" take their stand. The identification and removal of obstacles to the deployment of the legal instruments with which they are familiar and over which they exercise some control exhausts the law reform agenda.

Yet it is not evident that the lay population of the country has willingly accepted its preordained non-role in the officially-organized justice system. For example, many citizens reject the idea that the definition of those procedures and institutions to which access must be enhanced should be entirely captured by groups who have a personal interest in maintaining a monopoly over a limited set of such dispute-processing institutions. Non-state agencies of affect and dis-affect, and especially those from which lawyers are routinely excluded, still play important roles in assisting people to discern the entailments of justice. The scepticism of ordinary citizens goes even much deeper: for they under-stand that it is the acquisition of *knowledge* and not just the availability of "expertise" which is a precondition to achieving justice. Thus, most citizens can still draw a distinction between access to legal services (and to official institutions such as courts) and access to legal knowledge. As in health care, the maxim "an ounce of prevention" applies; and knowledge is believed to be a prerequisite to prevention. Nevertheless, as in health care, instrumental maxims about the virtue of prevention present only a small part of the picture of legal knowledge. If the object of knowledge is seen only in these instrumental terms, it can easily be captured by special interests. That is, if the concept of legal information is restricted to data about rights or about the powers of the police, or more generally to data about those claims arguable in official institutions, capture is complete.

I would claim that enhancing access to legal knowledge is a valuable goal not just because it can serve to further the agenda of preventive law. Law is powerfully symbolic. Legal knowledge is about control over law's symbolism as well as over its instruments. Unfortunately, even as uninstitutional a theme as access to legal knowledge typically has been co-opted into a reinforcing mechanism of the existing legal order. Rather than knowledge about law being used to situate formal legal institutions and processes in a wider, more democratic and less professional normative context, the dissemination of legal information is often consciously advanced in professional circles as a means to expand the reach of law.

The same is true of attempts to make legal jargon more conprehensible—in legisla-tion, contracts, court documents, and so on. To the extent that the arcane vocabulary of official law remains largely inaccessible and incomprehensible, subtle legal ordering outside the domain of this official law retains a healthy presence in people's lives. Legal text, like scripture or religious canon, is the preserve of the priesthood. And fortunately, just as not all spiritual needs require the ministry of clergy, neither do all social needs require the attornment of lawyers. Once the processes of formal law are democratized, however, and especially once its texts are rendered "vulgar," the penetration of formal law into everyday life is enhanced. In the present state of Canadian political life, dejargonizing the law does not empower the citizen by disseminating broadly the previ-ously private knowledge of legal professionals; quite the contrary, by legalizing the vocabulary of routine human interaction it makes the services of professional advisers and decoders even more indispensible to everyday life. And so, even though access to justice could mean access to legal knowledge for the symbolic reasons suggested, to all intents and purposes it means access to legal information for the instrumental purpose of reinforcing the centrality of those formal institutions and procedures which comprise the real field on which the contemporary access to justice agenda is played out.

Not surprisingly, therefore, in both the public and professional sectors access to justice is strongly focussed on the delivery of traditional legal services. Access to information is only a beginning. For true believers, the principle of equality before the law (now conveniently entered in the most hallowed ground—section 15 of the *Charter of Rights and Freedoms*) can only be made operational if all citizens have equal access, as a very first step, to those state institutions charged with applying the law and allocating its sanctions. Hence, the conditions for ensuring equal access to courts and administrative tribunals assume a primary place in policy recommendations. The lawyer's trite saying that "a right which one cannot vindicate in court is no right at all" is the touchstone of this conception of access.

But little attention is devoted by those who are concerned with access to justice to ensuring access to other state institutions for the production of law which are closely associated with these adjudicative and quasi-adjudicative bodies. I have in mind here the executive, and to a lesser extent the legislature. Among executive agencies one could identify the police, licensing bodies, inspectorates, and various officials in the public service. It is at this level of administration of the law that the principle of equal access (even in the limited sense here used) is most often put to its severest test. For it is often at the level of street contact with the police that the various injustices of law are most manifest to ordinary citizens.

In an even larger perspective of formal law one must also consider access to legislative institutions. Should not the notion of equal access also comprise equal access to the legislative body which most often announces the state normative order defining the rights and entitlements thought to ensure justice? Conceived in this fashion, equal access would demand the allocation of equal resources to all citizens in order to influence policy by way of lobbying, pressure groups or the submission of briefs to working groups, consultative committees and legislative hearings. Those who dismiss these concerns as hyperbolic by pointing to the equality of access which is reflected in the exercise of the electoral franchise make two mistakes. First, they conflate politics with law, and second they conflate the state in its various managerial roles with the state as legislator.

These last forms of equal access lead to a conception of access to justice which is congruent with the major concern of most commissioned studies of the phenomenon—equal access to legal services, whether provided by lawyers or licensed para-legals. The recognition that access to institutions in a purely formal sense is an inadequate conceptualization (after all, every criminal accused has equal formal access to the criminal courts) leads to concern for equal access to the means to make use of that institution. Nevertheless, given the professionalization of modern social reflexes, just as equal access to health is immediately translated into medicare—equal access to doctors—so too the primary thrust of the movement to equal access to justice is translated into some variant of judicare—equal access to lawyers. Only on the margins of the system, and only under strict control of the primary profession, does this notion of judicare suggest the need for equal access to para-legals, legal technicians and so on.

This preoccupation with the delivery of legal services is a reflection of a conception of justice which discounts true preventive law as an object of concern. The curative focus of investigations into access to justice not only makes a mockery of the idea that equal access to law-making and law administering institutions is important, but also minimizes the idea of equal access to public legal education. Hence, in addition to a neglect of para-legals or their telescoping into the professional hierarchy, one finds that access to formal legal education, community clinics, information provided via the mass media, and even indirect behaviour modifying inducements designed to forestall legal difficulty are not privileged as access to justice themes.

As a final observation about the professional model of access to justice, it is worth noting that, consistent with its etymology, access is conceived largely in individualized and instrumental terms. The notion of access is individualized because late-20th century notions of rights are localized in individuals, and justice is seen almost exclusively in Aristotelian "commutative justice" terms. Social justice, or the idea of just distributions even in existing legal arrangements is discounted because of its aggregative orientation. Thus, concepts such as class actions, broadened standing for non-hohfeldian plaintiffs, and the possibility of impleading unspecified "industry defendants" get marginalized as policy initiatives. Moreover, institutional considerations like the representativity of the police, the bar, the judiciary, faculties of law, are not viewed as important aspects of the access agenda. Here the individual orientation merges with [the] instrumental. Law, being neutral, is not in need of aggregated representativity in order to maintain its symbolic efficacy. Put bluntly, access to justice is the access of a disembodied individual to the institutions of formal law, when the latter are seen only as instruments for enforcing pre-established "just" rights and claims.

C. Of Metaphors and Barriers

Having sketched this preliminary landscape of what the concepts access and justice might comprise, and how their current composition in the access to justice debate is so limited, let me now reflect briefly upon the rhetoric by which we have come to understand the current policy agenda. To me it is highly significant that the logic of access leads to the metaphor of barrier—as if justice comprised simply a consumer product there to be delivered to all were only some obstacle external to it to be removed. Necessarily, talk of barriers evokes preliminary and collateral (or ancillary) concerns. And this preoccupation with the ancillary, of course, is perfectly captured by the distinction now being drawn between availability and accessibility. The argument typically runs as follows: justice is available—lawyers and courts actually exist—but that barriers to availability mean that access is denied. While I reject the metaphor of barrier as an approach to solving problems of access to justice, it can serve a useful purpose in illustrating its own inadequacy; I shall, consequently, explore how it features in current discussions of law reform.

Analytically, the barriers to equal access to justice can be distinguished as being either subjective or objective. The former, it is said, depend on the knowledge or lack of knowledge and perceptions (as well as capacities) of individual citizens; the latter reflect the constraints which limit the ability of citizens to call in aid the formal institutions of legal justice. It is hardly surprising that legal commentators focus almost exclusively on objective barriers, for it is objective barriers which are most closely connected to instrumental understandings of the legal enterprise. Furthermore, even to characterize subjective barriers as barriers seems to denature the metaphor. That is, to qualify the rejection by ordinary citizens of legal recourses as a barrier to access, is to miss the obvious point that the reason for the rejection is the perception that there is no justice in the scheme or institution to which objective access is sought to be guaranteed.

For this reason, what have been called subjective barriers are the most difficult to assess. They touch issues relating both to psychological attitudes and to knowledge: they touch, that is to say, the law primarily in its symbolic aspect. Age, physical or intellectual deficiency, ethnic and socio-cultural background and internalized class perceptions about the attitude of state functionaries such as the police, lawyers and judges constitute major impediments to the achievement of equal access to the instruments of legal justice. As is the case with so many of our cultural artifacts, the state legal system is designed with the average, middle-class, middle-aged, white male primarily in view. The young, the old, the poor, the immigrant, visible minorities, aboriginal peoples, and the intellectually or (in certain cases) the physically disabled are each seen as deviations from the norm rather than as constituting aspects of normality. Hence, the psychological barriers attaching to such status are typically screened out of assessments of how equal access to justice really is. That is, because psychological and intellectual barriers go to the very substance of what we mean by justice, the metaphor of barriers is inapt to describe them. Together these subjective failings of the system have been recast by law-and-economics scholars as reflecting informational shortfalls. For such commentators, there is a market for justice, to which, *ceteris paribus*, all would adhere voluntarily if only they had complete information about how it worked. The optimal solution to inaccessibility caused by psychological barriers, therefore, is simply more information—to the young, the old, immigrants, the poor, aboriginal peoples, women.

This second type of subjective barrier—lack of knowledge—affects not only the abnormal, but is at the root of most denials of justice to all citizens. Its real nature has already been alluded to: lack of information is not just an instrumental defect; it is a symbolic defect. Instrumentally, one can concede that the world's best legal aid system, or most flexible small claims court structure, or broadly drawn class-action procedure, or expeditious workers' compensation scheme means nothing if a large percentage of those whom it was designed to service do not either know of its existence, or know how to invoke its competence. So too, with ordinary rules and regulatory norms: unknown labour standards norms may just as well be unenacted. So finally with contractual language printed in small type and in incomprehensible jargon: indecipherable commitments hardly speak to informed private law-making. In other words, if knowledge is power, then the ability to recognize the formal legal dimension of any problem which arises is, from an instrumental perspective, a key component of access. But information is also powerfully symbolic. Empowerment comes from knowing that no one else has private information or knowledge which you lack. And since the informational stakes are so high, the best way of achieving informational equality is to make someone else's informational advantage irrelevant.

In standard access to justice studies it is claimed that just as important as (if not more important than) these subjective barriers to access are objective barriers. This category comprises an odd collection of defects with the current legal system. Objective barriers may relate to physical access to legal services (be these, for example, opening hours, distances to travel, lack of wheelchair access, or of facilities for overcoming audio and visual deficit, etc.), to economic considerations (such as the cost of obtaining legal redress), to delay in legal proceedings, or to the structural complexity of the legal system. For obvious reasons it is these objective barriers which most conveniently fit the instrumental metaphor of barrier, and hence are highest on the agenda of reformers. They are statistically measurable, can be accounted for on a balance sheet, and lend themselves to follow-up studies which generate self-congratulation.

Among those barriers which can be characterized as purely physical could be included: the availability of courts, tribunals, registries, inspectorates, claims officers, and especially lawyers and paralegals within a reasonable distance of all citizens; the availability of services at convenient hours; the provision of front-line legal information by telephone (reverse charge calls, taped messages, *etc.*) and wheelchair access and analogous services for persons having a physical deficiency. It is to be observed that all these physical barriers do not speak to the content of justice, or even to its direct achievement, but rather to the structural management of the institutions by which the state legal system purveys its version of justice. Indeed, none of the identified physical barriers speaks to the substantive or procedural operation of the formal adjudicative, facilities that have been developed to manage disputing. But it is precisely these latter types of barrier that most implicate the quality of justice rendered.

Probably because North American social policy tends today to be driven by economic considerations, financial barriers are those which attract the most attention in access to justice studies. These include, of course, institutional costs: filing fees, court costs, the cost of expert witnesses and other judicial disbursements. But they also comprise lawyer's fees—the single greatest economic barrier—and indirect costs such as lost wages, opportunity costs, and for those in outlying areas, transportation and subsistence costs. It is often not an exaggeration when people parrot Voltaire's quip: "I've been ruined financially twice in my life: once when I lost a lawsuit and once when I won one." The irony of cost (understood as a barrier) is that the principal feature of the cost barrier to access to justice is the sole cost which is fundamentally market-driven: the cost of privately provided legal services.

Delay is yet another barrier to access which is often decried. This is not to claim that all delay is inappropriate, but in many cases it can be. The inability to reconstruct evidence after a long period; the diminished value of compensation resulting from inflation; the uncertainty or opprobrium attaching to pending criminal charges; the pressure on economically less resilient parties to settle; the additional opportunity costs occasioned to the parties, and the disruption of family life. Once the delay which is necessary in order to permit the parties to gain some distance on their dispute and to develop a degree of dispassion is passed, any further delay can be understood as a barrier.

A final barrier which is typically characterized in studies as objective can be traced to the complexity of the law, its institutions, its vocabulary and its procedures. It is, of course, interesting that recharacterizing law's complexity as a barrier to access is yet another tactic to instrumentalize the psychological impediments to achieving justice. It is not the notion of state law itself, or of formal rationality as a conception of interpersonal relations, or of a universal abstract justice which requires removal; rather energy should be directed to removing the barrier caused by excessive complexity in the system. So, the argument goes, one need think only of the diversity of courts and tribunals, the multiplicity of procedural regimes, including varying limitation periods or filing delays, and the arcane vocabulary of judicial proceedings—including that which is common on writs, summonses and other court documents—to realize that the information costs to obtaining justice are overwhelming. Additional complexities flow from the language of the law itself, both in statutes and in ordinary legal correspondence and contracts, as well as in judicial decisions. In each case, the law reveals a labyrinthian complexity hardly guaranteed to make the justice which it proffers more accessible. Finally, it is often argued that the poor drafting of legislation and the desire to obtain "perfect individual justice" produce a desire for institutional recourses even in cases where private dispute resolution would be preferable. Not only is law complex, but its very structure demands lawyers and courts to unravel personal problems. Here one sees writ large how justice, in its transformation into justice according to law operates to generate an unnecessary complexity.

These then are the principal injustices and non-justices in the system of formal law which have been recharacterized as barriers to access to justice in mainstream access to justice literature. Yet, even despite this recharacterization, they retain enough distinctiveness to show that access to justice is not simply a matter of cost or of financing. Most often problems of access to justice are problems of perception and formulation. Issues of no access which can be framed in terms of barriers only arise once a "legal problem" has been perceived, and once a commitment to solving the problem through the formal legal system has been generated.

II. Access to Justice and Legal Theory

It is hardly a startling proposition that the standard approaches to most problems thought to have a legal component will implicitly confirm dominant tendencies in legal theory. The essence of the metaphenomenon is to conceive solutions only within the intellectual framework which has generated the problem. At the risk of using a hackneyed example, let me suggest that much access to justice thinking is of the same type as the placement of yet another epicycle on the Ptolomeic model of planetary motion. The system's two fundamental postulates, that the earth must be in the centre of the planetary system, and that planetary motion may only be described by reference to the perfect geometric form—the circle—, are not open for challenge or revision. As I attempted to illustrate in the previous section, such confirmation of basic postulates can be found in the very definition of the topic "access to justice," and in the logic which sustains its conception of the problems to be overcome—the elimination of barriers. The logic of access to justice is, therefore, a classic illustration of the old adage: "if all you have is a hammer, every problem looks like a nail."

What is, of course, surprising is that even though the logic of the system controls the conception of the problem and its solutions, this logic rarely is made explicit. When lawyers get together to talk about "access to justice" they have very clear notions of what the issues are. And, of course, they also have very clear ideas about the solutions: not necessarily about specific palliatives (of which there are many divergent and conflicting opinions), but more importantly, about the need for "Law Reform" to accomplish the task, and the particular kind of law reform which is required. For this reason, I should now like to examine some of the theoretical assumptions and understandings of law and legal ordering which underlie the logic of access to justice which is currently in vogue, and to suggest (if only tentatively) alternative theoretical frameworks.

I believe that there are five interrelated theoretical beliefs, each of which is at least tacitly accepted by most professional participants in the debate, which drive the agenda of access to justice law reform. First, and most importantly since this is the ground on which we as lawyers and law professors claim authority to lead the debate on the question, is the belief that justice is a concept inseparable from that of law; not only do we set our goal as seeking "justice according to law," we hold that in the absence of law there can be no justice. Second, and almost as importantly since this justifies the formal and institutional approach at which we claim particular (if not exclusive) expertise, we believe that the law is a concept inseparable from that of the state; the legal order which alone can ensure the attainment of social justice is the state legal order. Third, as a confirmation of our special expertise in deciphering the formal product of state institutions, we believe that fidelity to the rules authoritatively laid down by formal institutions is the highest legal virtue—that rule-following and role-fetishism are the best guarantees of justice; the only legal rules which enter the temple of law are those which are consciously and formally elaborated by legitimated institutions for a particular purpose. Fourth, given our reluctance to conceive that political judgments about distributive justice may have their own compelling rationality, and given our inability to perceive both the politics and the distributive consequences of the special rationality called legalism, we believe that rigorous adjudicative due process as a procedural theme is the optimal means for ensuring objective, substantive justice; equality of access to the legal institutions and procedures of commutative justice induces the achievement of, and even stands surrogate for, substantive justice. Finally, because the rules, institutions and procedures of formal, state law are so numerous and complex, we believe that ensuring access to the services of legal professionals is necessary to ensure access to justice and, by ricochet to ensure the achievement of justice itself; lawyers and notaries are the instruments of a legal instrumentalism which is designed exclusively to resolve the very disputes which it shapes.

It is obvious from the way I have peresented these beliefs that I reject them as necessarily reflecting how the problem of access to justice must be conceived in theoretical terms. But, as long as our basic professional concept of justice is rendered by such notions, and is only presented or made accessible to citizens on such terms—that is, as long as access to justice is viewed as the marketing of a commodity (or series of commodities) rather than as an exercise of education about, and reconstruction of, an ideal— law reform in this field will retain its current "barrier elimination" orientations. As long as our theoretical frame conceives justice as (i) exclusively the product of formally rational law, (ii) emerging only from a state legal order, (iii) explicitly made for the purpose of institutional disputing, (iv) to be set in motion through adjudicative processes, [and] (v) as a purely instrumental project, we will fall victim to the successive displacement of the primary by the secondary in our attempts to structure our law reform project.

NOTES AND QUESTIONS

1. Even if we accept that access to legal services may not be synonymous with access to justice, might we nonetheless want to take the position that access to the legal system should be equally available to all? Although we have taken some public goods out of the market—such as education and health—we still feel that it is appropriate to distribute legal services largely on the basis of people's ability to pay. What does this say about our conception of justice? Is there a realistic alternative?

2. In his essay, does MacDonald engage in an analysis that is theoretically illuminating, but practically of little use? In a society that is increasing its attachment to "commodification," not lessening it, what suggestions might MacDonald make about how to reverse this trend in the field of legal services? What can individual lawyers do to respond to this situation?

3. In a study of civil disputes in Ontario, it was found that a tendency to complain about a perceived problem (even without necessarily initiating formal legal process) was heavily dependent on the type of problem. See Bogart and Vidmar, "Personal Experience with the Ontario Civil Justice System: An Empirical Assessment," in A. Hutchinson, ed., *Access to Justice* (Toronto: Carswell, 1990). For example, people with perceived problems arising out of auto accidents were much more likely to complain than those with problems concerning discrimination. What does this tell us? Do people complain about auto accidents because they see them as a legal problem, as opposed to discrimination? Or do they perceive that an automobile accident is worth complaining about but that discrimination is not?

II. ECONOMIC BARRIERS TO ACCESS

The following excerpt illustrates how expensive litigation can be. Reread the extract from *The Report of the Ontario Courts Inquiry*, reproduced in chapter 5, "Commencement of Proceedings," under heading VI. "Costs in a Proceeding."

Ontario Civil Justice Review, *First Report*
(Toronto: Queen's Printer, March 1995)

Table 3: Cost of the Typical Civil Case to Litigant
(assuming the plaintiff's side through a three day General Division Trial and a solicitor's time at $200 per hour)

Steps:

Initial interview, information gathering and research:	10 hours
Draft Statement of Claim:	5 hours
Prepare and Finalize Affidavit of Documents:	10 hours
Assume two motions (including prep):	15 hours
One cross-examination on Affidavits (one day plus prep):	15 hours
Discovery (two days plus prep):	25 hours
Pre-Trial:	10 hours

Notices including Request to Admit: ....   5 hours
Trial Preparation: ....   30 hours
Trial Time: ....   30 hours
Miscellaneous letters, telephone calls, reports (assume one hour
   per month over 3 years from start to finish): ....   36 hours

Total ....   191 hours

191 Hours at $200 .... $38,200.00
   Plus Disbursements
   Plus GST

"Plus disbursements" may appear to be an innocuous addition to this list. It is not. Disbursements can be very substantial. We have been advised, for instance, that the disbursements in a simple uncontested divorce proceeding usually exceed the amount of the legal fees. In other instances, the cost of retaining experts or preparing drawings or surveys—to name but a few examples—can run into the many thousands of dollars. In addition, the litigant must pay 7% GST on fees and disbursements.

A Survey of Lawyers' Fees

The Civil Justice Review commissioned a survey of the private Bar in an effort to gather more substantive information about costs to litigants. 8,300 surveys were sent to civil litigation practitioners around the Province. A response of 521 completed surveys (6.3%)—a statistically valid average—was received.

The demographics of the respondents were as follows:

- average year of call was 1981/82;
- 38% practised in Toronto;
- 16% (mostly Toronto) practised in firms of 51 lawyers or more; and
- 79.5% devoted at least half of their practice to civil litigation.

These demographics appear to be representative of the civil bar in Ontario.

The average hourly rate was $195.

The responses indicated that the median of the largest bill for judge and jury trials in the last two years (only 16% responding) was $38,500.00. This compares almost exactly to the estimate set out in the Table above, which was prepared quite independently of the survey. 85% of respondents said that less than 1/4 of their bill was due to systemic delay.

Another interesting survey relating, at least indirectly, to lawyers' fees was conducted for the Simplified Rules Sub-Committee. It examined party and party costs in a random sampling of 98 court files from six different court centres in the Province. This survey reveals that the average claim in the General Division is approximately $197,000; the average judgment is approximately $58,000; the average allowance of party and party costs, approximately $8,500. In terms of "medians," as opposed to "averages," the median claim is approximately $32,000; the median judgment is approximately $15,000; the median award of party and party costs is approximately $4,300.

Keeping in mind that the foregoing figures represent only the costs awarded to one of the litigants, and that those costs are only a portion of what that litigant pays to counsel, the inference is strong that the combined legal costs of the parties to a lawsuit are, on average, about ¾ of the judgment obtained; and on a median basis, are perhaps more than the judgment obtained.

NOTES AND QUESTIONS

1. How troubling is the fact that, in median terms, the party-and-party costs account for about 30% of the judgment recovered? Mindful that party-and-party costs account for only part of one party's reimbursement, how can a system claim to be operating with any degree of efficiency or fairness if the total costs in the case amount to over 60% of the judgment ultimately recovered?

2. Although traditional billing practices are being revised in non-litigious areas of work, they still remain a common feature of most litigation work. The following extract by K. Pratt, "Airlines Going to Billable Hours?" (1995), 42 *Law Practice Management* 25-28, places lawyers' billing practices in a revealing and unflattering light. Why do clients put up with such archaic and unfair practices?

The Denver lawyer stepped up to the airline ticket counter and asked to buy a ticket for a flight to Chicago.

"No problem," said the clerk, "but before I issue the ticket, I should remind you of the new way we charge for tickets. This year we have adopted a 'basic rate' of three dollars a minute for our flights. The clock starts when you check in at the gate and stops when you pick up your luggage. We mail you a bill about two months after the flight."

"Well, I guess that's okay," commented the lawyer.

The clerk continued, "Remember, we call it a 'basic rate' because we sometimes adjust that rate up or down if the flight is very empty or very full. Too, we may multiply that rate if the flight is very empty or very full. Too, we may multiply that rate if our expert pilot finds a tail wind. We also adjust the rate according to what you will be doing in Chicago. You look like a lawyer, so I'll assume it's very important that you get there by plane, so we quadruple our basic rate. Another thing, how much is your annual income? You see, if you earn a great deal and it turns out the plane crashes, we will have to pay more on your spouse's damage claim; and we have, of course, to consider that increased risk to the airline."

The astounded lawyer choked, "But how much will this trip cost me? How do I know you don't slow down on purpose? How do I know your bill will be correct?"

The clerk stared down over the end of his nose, "I can see you're not familiar with the complexities of airline work. There are so many things we just can't know in advance—the winds, the traffic delays, the weather, the routing. Airlines are a business and we have to make a profit to stay in business. Now don't worry, we're very honest and sensitive about all this billing business and I'm sure you'll be pleased with the fully itemized bill when you get it. If so, we understand each other. If you don't pay the bill in full and promptly, you'll never fly on this airline again."

"Oh," grunted the Denver lawyer. "Is there anything else I should know?"

The clerk smiled thoughtfully and murmured, "On your flight there is a new copilot in training and so we charge an additional 50 cents a mile. Copilots are really very important, you know, to carry the pilot's charts, to fly on clear, calm days, even to land the plane if the pilot is busy with other matters. Too, if you fly with us again your copilot may have become your pilot. Wouldn't that be great? One other thing, if the copilot uses computerized flight routing there will be an additional $75 charge. But of course, computerized flight routing is almost standard charge with technologically advanced airlines."

"But I just wanted to get to my meeting in Chicago and come home. Now, I don't even know if I should fly at all," groaned the lawyer.

The clerk smiled again, "Mature passengers come to understand that flying is just a cost of doing business. They never know how much it costs 'til we bill them. But then, there's really no choice, is there?"

"No," conceded the lawyer, "I guess not."

And then the lawyer tried again, "[C]an't you just give me a fixed price and I'll decide if I'll go or not?"

The clerk frowned, "But we can't do that. That wouldn't be fair to you. We might overcharge you and then you'd be unhappy; or we might underestimate and then the airlines would lose money and couldn't maintain their planes, and we certainly don't want that.

And so the Denver lawyer came to hate airlines and took his revenge by regaling acquaintances at cocktail parties about the new pitfalls of airline travel.

III. NON-ECONOMIC BARRIERS TO ACCESS

There is considerable literature that emphasises that how and why disputes come to be recognised and identified is of great significance; it is not the simple or value-free process that many assume. The following extract explores this neglected issue in civil litigation and general discussions about access to justice.

William L.F. Felstiner et al., "The Emergence and Transformation of Disputes: Naming, Blaming, Claiming ..."
(1980-81), 15 *Law and Society Review* 631 (footnotes omitted)

The sociology of law has been dominated by studies of officials and formal institutions and their work products. This agenda has shaped the way disputes are understood and portrayed. Institutions reify cases by reducing them to records; they embody disputes in a concrete form that can be studied retrospectively by attending to the words used by lay persons and officials and by examining the economic and legal context in which cases occur. But disputes are not things: they are social constructs. Their shapes reflect whatever definition the observer gives to the concept. Moreover, a significant portion of any dispute exists only in the minds of the disputants.

These ideas, though certainly not novel, are important because they draw attention to a neglected topic in the sociology of law—the emergence and transformation of disputes—the way in which experiences become grievances, grievances become disputes, and disputes take various shapes, follow particular dispute processing paths, and lead to new forms of understanding. Studying the emergence and transformation of disputes means studying a social process as it occurs. It means studying the conditions under which injuries are perceived or go unnoticed and how people respond to the experience of injustice and conflict. ...

Assume a population living downwind from a nuclear test site. Some portion of that population has developed cancer as a result of the exposure and some has not. Some of those stricken know that they are sick and some do not. In order for disputes to emerge and remedial action to be taken, an unperceived injurious experience (unPIE, for short) must be transformed into a perceived injurious experience (PIE). The uninformed cancer victims must learn that they are sick. The transformation perspective directs our attention to the differential transformation of unPIEs into PIEs. It urges us to examine, in this case, differences in class, education, work situation, social networks, etc. between those who become aware of their cancer and those who do not, as well as attend to the possible manipulation of information by those responsible for the radiation. ...

The next step is the transformation of a perceived injurious experience into a grievance. This occurs when a person attributes an injury to the fault of another individual or social entity. By including fault within the definition of grievance, we limit the concept to injuries viewed both as violations of norms and as remediable. The definition takes the grievant's perspective: the injured person must feel wronged and believe that something might be done in response to the injury, however politically or sociologically improbable such a response might be. A grievance must be distinguished from a complaint against no one in particular (about the weather, or perhaps inflation) and from a mere wish unaccompanied by a sense of injury for which another is held responsible (I might like to be more attractive). We call the transformation from perceived injurious experience to grievance *blaming*. ...

The third transformation occurs when someone with a grievance voices it to the person or entity believed to be responsible and asks for some remedy. We call this communication *claiming*. A claim is transformed into a dispute when it is rejected in whole or in part. Rejection need not be expressed by words. Delay that the claimant construes as resistance is just as much a rejection as is a compromise offer (partial rejection) or an outright refusal.

The sociology of law should pay more attention to the early stages of disputes and to the factors that determine whether naming, blaming, and claiming will occur. Learning more about the existence, absence, or reversal of these basic transformations will increase our understanding of the disputing process and our ability to evaluate dispute processing institutions. We know that only a small fraction of injurious experiences ever mature into disputes. Furthermore, we know that most of the attrition occurs at the early stages: experiences are not perceived as injurious; perceptions do not ripen into grievances; grievances are voiced to intimates but not to the person deemed responsible. A theory of disputing that looked only at institutions mobilized by disputants and the strategies pursued within them would be seriously deficient. It would be like constructing a theory of politics entirely on the basis of voting patterns when we know that most people do not vote in most elections.

NOTES AND QUESTIONS

1. As highlighted in the extract from Felstiner et al., disputes are social constructs, their boundaries flexible, changing over time in response to the social context in which the conduct is situated. Marc Galanter, in an article entitled, "Reading the Landscape of Disputes: What We Know and Don't Know (And Think We Know) About Our Allegedly Contentious Society" (1983), 31 *UCLA Law Review* 4, describes the process of dispute formation as follows:

> Disputes are drawn from a vast sea of events, encounters, collisions, rivalries, disappointments, discomforts and injuries. The span and composition of that sea depend on the broad contours of social life. For example, the introduction of machinery brings increases in non-intentional injuries; higher population densities and cash crops bring raised expectations and rivalry for scarce land; advances in knowledge enlarge possibilities of control and expectations of care.

2. What are the factors which will influence whether one names, blames, and/or claims? In what ways might the organization and distribution of legal services play a role? Consider, for example, that most legal services are provided on a fee-for-service basis, such that, by and large, only persons with considerable economic resources can access legal information and advice.

Reread the Jane Doe narrative and consider what factors would bear on whether Jane names, blames, and/or claims. Whom would she blame and what would she claim? The narrative involves an obvious criminal violation, but it may also be possible to pursue a civil remedy. Indeed, in the actual case on which the narrative is based, not only was Jane Doe's assailant convicted and imprisoned, but Jane Doe began a civil action against the police. The *Jane Doe* litigation, currently before the Ontario Court (General Division), is significant in that it represents an attempt to shift the sea of disputes. To appreciate the significance of the case a brief historical note is necessary.

The earliest rape laws in England were designed to ensure the protection of a woman as the property of her father or husband, so, for instance, punishment often included pecuniary compensation to the family of the woman. The violation was seen not as one committed on the person of a woman, but on the property of a man. Over time, the crime has evolved slowly from one of interference with the line of descent to one of a violation of women. (See Marilyn Stanley, *The Experience of the Rape Victim With the Criminal Justice System Prior to Bill C-127* (Ottawa: Communications and Public Affairs, 1987) for a more detailed historical account.) In the criminal law context we can thus trace an evolution in the way in which the dispute was characterized. Another significant development can be seen in the law's response to allegations of rape in the context of marriage. Until 1983, Canadian law did not recognize a crime of rape within marriage.

In the past decade or so there have been a great many amendments to the Criminal Code in an attempt to address some of the concerns relating to prosecution of rape cases. Also, recently, women have brought civil actions for assault in response to being raped. However, the *Jane Doe* case is the first attempt to seek civil redress from the police for the manner in which they handled a sexual assault case. *Jane Doe* puts directly in issue the question of the responsibility of the police to ensure that women are adequately protected against sexual assault. In other words, *Jane Doe* further challenges the existing sea of disputes by claiming a civil cause of action in circumstances where none to date has been recognized.

The reasons that might help us to understand the evolution of "disputing" in the area of sexual assault (and where we are at present) are of course very complex. While it is not our intention to canvass this fully, one aspect of the explanation is particularly relevant in the context of *Jane Doe*. This explanation posits that the law is premised on a complex stereotype of both women and men. In the context of sexual assault, the stereotyping has constructed women who can and cannot be raped. The extract by Lorenne Clark and Debra Lewis that follows describes this stereotype and, in particular, how that stereotype has come to shape police responses to the complaints of women. Although the article was written in 1977, the findings continue to be relevant—for example, see Susan Estrich's recent book *Real Rape* (Cambridge, MA: Harvard University Press, 1987)).

While reading the extract, think about how the stereotype that Clark and Lewis describe might help explain the police conduct in the *Jane Doe* case. Do you think it would have occurred to the police not to warn potential victims if the crime and victims had been different—for example, robbers holding up store owners or burglars robbing and assaulting elderly persons?

In contemplating the questions raised at the outset—that is, which factors will bear on whether Jane Doe names or blames—it is important to consider the events in their social context. Recall that whether an event is ultimately cast as a dispute will turn to a great extent on the current social context in which it is situated. Can you identify factors in our current social context which might bear on whether Jane Doe names or blames?

Lorenne Clark and Debra Lewis, *Rape: The Price of Coercive Sexuality*
(Toronto: The Women's Press, 1977) (footnotes omitted)

The progress of a rape case through the criminal justice system reflects a highly selective process of elimination. Only a fraction of all rapes are reported; only a fraction of reported rapes are classified as founded; only a fraction of founded cases lead to an arrest; and only a fraction of suspects arrested are convicted. Our own study provided us with a vivid illustration of how few rapes ever lead to trial and conviction. We believed that a rape had most likely occurred in 104 of the 116 cases we studied. If only 40% of all rapes are reported (the highest of all estimated reporting rates), then these 104 reported rapes represented the approximately 260 rapes which actually occurred. The police classified only 42 of the 116 reported rapes as founded, and arrested 32 suspects. Given an average conviction rate of 51.2%, approximately 17 suspects were probably convicted. Thus only 17 out of approximately 260 rapists are likely to be convicted in Metropolitan Toronto—only 7%. That is the highest estimate that any of the figures, at any stage of the process, would justify. As such, it stands as something of a monument to injustice, and a serious indictment of our criminal justice system. ...

Women Who "Can't Be Raped"

We have now examined in detail the victim-related variables determining police classification of rape reports. The police process of classification is intended to filter out all cases in which an offence did not occur, and all cases which look particularly difficult to prosecute. But as we remarked at the beginning of this chapter, all of the major factors which make a case a "bad" one, are directly linked to the victim. To a very large extent, it is the character of the reporting rape victim which determines whether or not a reported offence will be classified as founded, and passed on in the judicial system. This process of selection may have nothing to do with whether or not the complainant was actually raped. In effect, the law is saying that some women can be raped and some women can't, and it is instructive to summarize the features of those women whose cases are by and large classified as unfounded.

The rape victim whose case does not make it past the first stage of the criminal justice system may be perceived as "drunk" when she is first interviewed by the police. She may be a teenager, who does not live at home, has a record of "unmanageable" behaviour, or has already come to the attention of school authorities, the Children's Aid Society, or the Juvenile Court. She may be between thirty and forty years of age, and either separated, divorced, or living in a common-law relationship. Regardless of her age, she may be "idle," unemployed, or on welfare. She may also have been under previous psychiatric care; she probably wasn't hysterical when she reported the crime; she may not have reported the offence to the first possible person following its commission. And, as we have discussed in the chapter on "The Crime," she may have "known" the offender, she may have voluntarily accompanied her assailant to his residence and been raped there, or she may have voluntarily accepted a ride in his car.

Women who display a number of these features will not have their sexual assault defined as rape. They quite literally cannot be raped, because "rape" is a social and legal definition, and these are not the sort of women that society believes *can* be raped. It is virtually impossible for these women to complain of rape and have their complaint taken seriously. Their vulnerable position in society—itself a function of age, lack of occupational skills, and, in general, low socio-economic status—leaves them open to rape with very little hope of redress.

A number of women in our study whose cases were classified as unfounded were notified that they could, if they wished, swear out a warrant with a Justice of the Peace and proceed on their own. Understandably, no women were willing to take this course of action. These women must not only endure social and economic oppression; they must also sustain physical and sexual abuse without either legal redress or emotional support. As the following examples show, these women are easily victimized.

One case involved a woman whom the police described as being on welfare, and having a history of mental illness. She had been separated from her husband for seven years, and had borne an "illegitimate" child since that time. Despite strong medical and material evidence that she had been raped, her report was later classified as unfounded, largely because she had a history of drinking, and because she was unwilling to co-operate further in the investigation. Her unwillingness to co-operate was hardly surprising in the light of her past; people who have had previous dealings with public institutions are often justifiably reluctant to have any more contact with "professionals" than is absolutely necessary. Moreover, it is likely that this victim knew how little chance her case had of reaching successful prosecution. It was also clear, through interviews which the police conducted with her landlord and with the godfather of her child, that at least some of her associates did not believe her story. They described her as a habitual drunk, given to "shacking up with coloureds."

This woman displayed many of the characteristics which appear to lead to an "unfounded" classification. She was a single parent, on welfare, and had undergone psychiatric care, albeit for a short period of time. She had a reputation (whether founded or not) for "excessive" drinking and for unacceptable sexual behaviour. The facts of her case strongly support her contention that she was raped; nevertheless, she was not believed. It is not difficult to imagine a different response had she been a middle-class married woman with a "good" reputation in the community; she would certainly have received (at least overtly) a more sympathetic response from friends, relatives, and public institutions.

NOTES AND QUESTIONS

1. Is the goal of the *Jane Doe* litigation individual redress, or is it not, at least as much, about altering patterns and practices of police departments regarding women and sexual assault? Should Jane Doe have to initiate and maintain this litigation herself? If not, what means are available to support Jane Doe with respect to this lawsuit? What means should be available? See below, as well as chapter 4, "Challenges to the Traditional Model," regarding the costs of litigation and chapter 7, "The Size and Scope of Litigation," regarding group litigation.

2. In the situation where one seeks, through litigation, to advance a novel claim—that is, a claim that to date has not been specifically recognized by the law—one's opponent will often try to pre-empt the litigation. The party who seeks to pre-empt the litigation will ask the court to dismiss the action before trial on the ground that the claim advanced is not one which the law recognizes. If successful, the claim will be dismissed after a summary hearing and without a complete examination of the facts. Thus, attempts to reconstruct the sea of "legal disputes" can be met with considerable resistance. However, courts are increasingly reluctant to pre-empt novel litigation in this summary manner. In *Jane Doe*, the court rejected attempts by the defendant to pre-empt the litigation.

In attempting to define the phrase "access to justice," various commentators have identified two discreet, yet related, issues—equal access to the system and access to a system that generates results that are individually and socially just. In other words, as MacDonald insisted, one cannot simply equate, without inquiry, access to the legal system with access to justice. Indeed, many individuals and groups lack confidence that access to the legal system will ensure access to justice and for this reason choose not to enter the legal arena. How might the question of who the judge is make a difference about whether a particular litigant's claim is, and is perceived to be, treated fairly or justly? Consider these questions as you read the following excerpts.

N. Duclos, "Passion for Justice in a Multicultural Canada"
(1990, unpublished)

Being aware of one's own cultural history in relation to the cultural backgrounds of others is an important beginning in bridging the gaps across differences in the courtroom. It lets the judge begin to understand how he or she perceives a particular person or group and why that perception is what it is.

The ability to recognize difference is learned. People from non-English linguistic backgrounds frequently cannot recognize the difference between British and American English. Some Caucasians say that all Blacks or all Orientals "look the same." Such comments may reflect racist attitudes, but they also reflect a failure of perception. If your eyes or ears are not sensitive, you cannot perceive the world that is apparent to others. Sensitivity to these kinds of difference is obviously important for judges who adjudicate controversies involving people from different cultures. Judicial impressions as to the trustworthiness and reliability of a witness, a litigant and even counsel influence outcomes. From the litigants' perspective, their impressions about the perceptions of the judge influence their views about the fairness of the judicial process. The cultural affiliation and consequent ethnocentrism of those involved in a particular legal proceeding attunes each individual to certain differences or characteristics but obscures others. This is not a very new idea. One of the original rationales for the jury system was a recognition that one's peers—members of one's community—would be most closely attuned to and thus the best judges of a party's conduct. In Canada today, where it is increasingly likely that a judge will not share the culture of those who appear before him or her, learning sensitivity to other cultures is vital to the fairness of the adjudicative process.

To illustrate the claim that sensitivity to cultural difference, that is, awareness of the particular tilt of one's own ethnocentrism and the acquisition of knowledge about different cultures to compensate for one's ethnocentrism, makes a difference, consider the likely impact of lack of cultural awareness on the part of a decision-maker in the following scenarios:

1. A key witness comes from a culture in which nodding one's head up and down means "no" and not "yes." Thus, as this witness is cross-examined, s/he nods as s/he verbally disagrees with counsel.

2. In a complicated litigation, many of the witnesses have names which are unfamiliar to the judge—they sound very similar and it is hard to remember which name goes with which face.

3. A key female witness comes from a culture in which it is inappropriate for women to make eye contact with men. As a result, this woman constantly avoids the gaze of counsel and the judge. Her testimony is also given in an almost inaudible voice.

4. An expert witness testifies in a heavily accented voice. In cross-examination, he often hesitates and appears to contradict what he has said earlier which gives an impression that he does not really know what he is talking about although in fact due to difficulty in translating concepts which he knows in his native tongue which have no ready English equivalent.

Consider how you would feel about the judicial process if you were a party [in a] civil or criminal action involving a police officer (or a plumber or a woman Muslim or a Black or a Francophone) and everyone in the room except you [were a] police officer (or a plumber etc.). Your impressions of the fairness of the process might be significantly affected by your assessment of how sensitive the judge, or other participants, was to your difference. Subtle signals that your difference was understood and acknowledged together with overt gestures to accommodate difference, where appropriate, by both lawyers and judges would mitigate considerably your unease at being the odd one out in a situation where the stakes are high.

NOTE

The Duclos article is suggestive of one strategy to try to bridge the gulf of difference that often exists between a judge and a litigant—a bridge that is essential to a just resolution. An alternative, and arguably complementary strategy, was put forward earlier in the materials: see chapter 4, "Challenges to the Traditional Model." That strategy is to increase the diversity of the judiciary as a mechanism to ensure "impartiality." A report entitled "Access to Legal Education in Canada, Datebook 1990," prepared by Brian M. Mazer and M. Samantha G. Peeris, gives us some indication of the lack of diversity in the Canadian bar, from whom judges are ultimately chosen:

> In 1986, according to the census, there were 41,330 lawyers across Canada, 0.8% and 2.8% of which were aboriginal and visible minorities, respectively. Aboriginal people represent 2.3% of the Canadian population aged 15 and over, while visible minorities account for 5.9%. Aboriginal women represented 1.2% of the total population, age 15 and over, and 0.3% of the legal profession and 0.3% of the university professorate. Visible minority women accounted for 0.3% of the total population aged 15 and over, and 0.8% of the legal profession and 1.6% of the University professorate.

The two extracts that follow take a slightly different tack. The first describes access to "social services" in Metropolitan Toronto. While the investigators were not examining legal services as such, consider what relevance the findings may have for the provision of legal services. What role might legal services themselves play in addressing the inequities in the provision of other social services?

The second extract looks at the challenge to disabled persons in gaining access to the courts and, therefore, justice.

**Robert Doyle and Livy Wisano, "Equality and Multiculturalism:
Access to Community Services"**
(1988), 3 *Journal of Law and Social Policy* 21-35

An Unequal Society

Canadians have recently witnessed a proliferation of public inquiries, media accounts and research attention on equality. The long awaited equality provisions of the *Charter of Rights and Freedoms* as well as the much celebrated policies on multiculturalism continue to evoke a degree of unreasonable optimism. Legal protections and multicultural initiatives are of dubious value when unaccompanied by meaningful programs which embrace universal entitlements.

Historically, equality in Canada has been characterized by attractive legal palliatives replete with convenient mythologies. For example, long before the equality sections of the Charter came into effect in 1985, Canada was a signatory of the Universal Declaration of Human Rights in 1948. Accordingly, Article 25 affirmed a number of moral principles which included provisions for a standard of living adequate for the health and wellbeing of the individual and his/her family, such as food, clothing, housing, medical care and social services, as well as the right to security in the event of disability and/or unemployment. Likewise, in 1982 the Charter clearly indicated that within the operation of law, every individual was to be treated without discrimination. Section 15(1) states:

> 15.(1) Every individual is equal before and under the law and has the right to the equal protection and equal benefit of the law without discrimination and, in particular, without discrimination based on race, national or ethnic origin, colour, religion, sex, age or mental or physical disability.

But this provision alone does not ensure equality. ...

Despite the "spirit of equality" enshrined in the Charter, studies have documented ways in which visible minorities are denied access to employment, personnel procedures discriminate in recruitment practices and little effort exists to eliminate discrimination. The lingering "spirit" of the Charter to which many politicians and bureaucrats allude warrants careful scrutiny.

Persistent inequality is the most basic source of tension in our society. The admonitions of Miller and Roby regarding the dangers of inequality to social stability are applicable to Canada in the 1980s. Moreover, they argue that:

> A minimum approach by government in any society with significant inequalities must provide for using minimum levels, not only of (1) incomes, (2) assets, and (3) basic services, but also of (4) self-respect and (5) opportunities for education and social mobility and (6) participation in many forms of decision-making.

In other words, a commitment to equality can only be measured by its contribution to social reform. Exaggerated claims of equality juxtaposed against actual provisions of fundamental services will serve to unravel and challenge prevailing myths about multiculturalism and the renewed spirit of the Charter. There is, for example, little evidence of organizational changes designed to remove direct obstacles to equality. Nowhere is this more apparent than in the most fundamental features of subsistence and basic entitlements of citizenry as in the health and social services. Equality requires equitable access to these resources.

Access to Services as an Equality Issue

People who need and who are entitled to human services do not generally receive assistance in an equitable manner. Rahn notes a number of reasons for this: the complexity and bureaucratic nature of the service system; discrimination; variations among citizens in knowledge and understanding of rights or in appreciation of the values of certain resources, benefits and entitlements, and; geographic distance between people and services. ...

[I]nterviews with "multicultural" consumers indicated that an overwhelmingly large number of clients experience difficulties in securing access. They attribute obstacles to factors such as their lack of information, the styles and techniques of agency interaction, and the poor level of understanding of cultural and linguistic factors which complicate delivery patterns. Consumers, in general, expressed feelings of uncertainty, powerlessness and distance from agencies designed to serve them. For example, a middle aged woman who arrived from Poland in 1957 described: "No one ever tried to understand my accent."

Moreover, it was found that prevailing cultural factors either inhibit consumers from approaching agencies or effectively negate the value of assistance by failing to recognize the respective values of consumers. A young man who arrived from El Salvador in 1981 notes: "I didn't feel good when I was there. I was afraid, so I did what they wanted."

There is widespread discontent among consumers about the staff and the services obtained at agencies. The most frequent criticism directed at service providers concerned their ignorance—their failure to appreciate the predicament experienced by newcomers from different cultures. Admittedly, consumers from racial and cultural groups encounter problems which are common to other consumers but their difficulties are more intensified because of their limited knowledge of rights and entitlements; their limited language ability; and their cultural differences which make them more susceptible to misconceptions and negative judgements. They risk double exclusion, making it difficult for them to be considered as full and equal members of the society.

In general, minorities are not participating fully in programs ostensibly designed for them. Current practices succeed, however, only in fostering further discrimination and alienation. Just as consumers are ill-informed about services to which they are entitled, providers are extremely insensitive and ignorant of cultural diversity. Despite the rhetoric of multiculturalism and the benevolence of social assistance, providers willingly admit that the services they offer are inappropriate. Surprisingly, providers candidly acknowledge the debilitating effects of a number of impediments and yet they fail not only to proffer suggestions in improving their immediate organizational responses but miserably refuse to even hypothetically consider changes at the systemic level.

D. Lepofsky, "Equal Access to Canada's Judicial System for Persons with Disabilities: A Time for Reform"
(1995, unpublished) (footnotes omitted)

The Status of Persons with Disabilities in Canada

It is now accepted as virtually axiomatic that persons with disabilities in Canada constitute a substantial and a substantially disadvantaged minority in our society. They now number as high as 15 to 17% of the Canadian population. Since advancing age is the most common direct cause of disability, the proportion of Canada's population which has physical or mental disabilities will increase in the immediate future. This is because the proportion of elderly persons in our society is increasing.

Numbering in excess of four million, persons with disabilities in Canada as a group often experience conditions of serious socio-economic disadvantage. For most people in Canada, national unemployment rates are considered to be entirely unacceptable when they climb as high as 10 or 11%. This common perception becomes striking if it is grafted on the experience of persons with disabilities in Canada. According to 1991 federal data, employable age persons with disabilities faced unemployment rates of 52%. For them, an average unemployment rate of 11% would seem a massive improvement.

People with disabilities are over represented among the poor in this country. They are underrepresented among those persons who have graduated from post-secondary educational institutions. Generally, they tend to be underrepresented in the mainstream of Canadian society where upward mobility is most likely to be possible.

Barriers Impeding Persons with Disabilities in Canada's Courts

There are a number of serious barriers which impede the full and equal participation of persons with disabilities in the Canadian judicial process. This is particularly troubling since the courts are supposed to be the place where persons with disabilities can go to have their equality rights vindicated when they are infringed by government or private parties. If our courts themselves have significant barriers, persons with disabilities cannot expect that the judicial process will be able to effectively enforce their equality rights and human rights.

The first and perhaps the most immediate barrier confronting persons with disabilities in the justice system is architectural. Many Canadian courtrooms and courthouses have not been designed or retro-fitted to enable persons with disabilities to have full physical access to them. The most obvious barrier can be stairs in front of a courthouse. Many structural barriers can be found inside a courthouse as well, such as steps within the hallways, steps up to the Judges bench, to the witness stand or to the jury box. Counsel tables may be too low to enable a lawyer in a wheelchair to sit right up at the desk, and make use of the desktop to spread out materials needed for the proceeding. Courthouses are not necessarily equipped with conveniently-located bathrooms which can accommodate persons in wheelchairs, or with doorways that are wide enough for a person in a wheelchair to pass through. In addition to these barriers to the mobility impaired, courthouses and courtrooms may not be designed to accommodate the mobility needs of persons with visual handicaps, including persons with low vision, as well as those with no vision. For example, signs may be positioned in the middle of a floor, or sticking out from a wall, so as not to be easily detectable by a white cane.

It is commonly believed that all buildings, or at least all new public buildings, must be accessible to persons with disabilities and that the legislated accessibility standards are rigorous and effective. Unfortunately, this is a myth. Legislated physical access requirements often tend to be inadequate. They also tend to apply to new structures, rather than pre-existing buildings. Most courthouses in Canada are undoubtedly older structures which did not even have to conform to insufficient building codes when they were constructed.

Who are the victims of these architectural barriers? They include persons with disabilities who come to court as parties to civil proceedings seeking vindication of their legal rights, as criminally accused persons whom the state seeks to convict and incarcerate, as witnesses who appear either voluntarily or under court order to perform the civil duty of testifying, and as prospective jurors who seek to fulfil the democratic duty of jury service. They also include those persons with disabilities who wish to pursue a career in the administration of justice, such as judges, court staff or lawyers with mobility impairments. If a litigation lawyer in a wheelchair lives in a community whose courthouse is physically inaccessible, they can be rendered unable to practice in their chosen field of law for reasons that have no relation to their professional competence.

These structural barriers can also impede members of the public who have mobility disabilities from exercising their fundamental common law, statutory and constitutional right to attend and observe court proceedings. Canadian courts have held that Charter s. 2(b)'s guarantee of freedom of expression includes a constitutional right of members of the public to attend and observe court proceedings. This right is meaningless to persons with mobility disabilities, where courthouses are physically inaccessible. Thus, physical barriers to their access to the courthouse violate not only their rights under Charter s. 15, but under s. 2(b) as well.

To some, it might first seem sufficient to simply provide some physical assistance to persons with disabilities who cannot gain access to a courthouse or courtroom. Why not simply carry a person with a mobility disability up a flight of stairs, and then place them back in their wheelchair? To a person with a disability, this is not meaningful access. Rather, it is an affront to their independence, dignity and autonomy. Equality of access includes a right to enter premises with dignity on one's own power. Able-bodied persons would not tolerate it if they had to undergo the demanding spectacle of being carried into and out of a courtroom or courthouse as a precondition to securing admission. Persons with disabilities have no greater desire to suffer such treatment.

A second barrier in the justice system confronts persons with hearing disabilities. Our courts do not have readily available sign language interpretation or real-time transcription of court proceedings where a deaf person is a party, witness, juror, lawyer, or public spectator. Charter section 14 covers part of the terrain, in so far as hearing-impaired persons who are parties to or witnesses in a proceeding are concerned. It provides: ... ["]A party or witness in any proceedings who does not understand or speak the language in which the proceedings are conducted or who is deaf has the right to the assistance of an interpreter.["] However, Charter s. 14 does not address the needs of hearing-impaired jurors, lawyers, judges or public spectators who are present during a court proceeding. Even though s. 14 speaks to the right to interpretation for parties or witnesses to a proceeding, the simple fact that the Charter articulates this right does not mean that court staff actually comply with it in a timely fashion across Canada whenever needed.

Third, much of the information which is placed before a court, during a proceeding may be in printed form e.g. documentary exhibits. For a person with a visual handicap, or a person with a learning disability such as dyslexia, this can impede full participation in the court process as juror, litigant, counsel, witness, judge or public spectator. There are a number of alternative formats, such as Braille, large type, computer speech synthesizers, and the like, which can make printed materials available to a print-handicapped individual in a useable form. Courts are now generally not equipped to make printed information available in any of these alternative formats. This is part of a larger problem with government generally. While freedom of information laws have extended to the public a right of access to public information in government hands, governments have generally not set up comprehensive systems for ensuring timely access to information for visually handicapped and otherwise print-handicapped persons in alternative formats, even though the cost and time needed to produce such alternative formats has [been] dramatically reduced in recent years.

Fourth, a number of persons who come before the courts as witnesses or parties may have developmental disabilities. For them, a significant barrier to full participation in the justice system is the complex and abstruse language which judges and lawyers often use in court. Plain language in court can be as important for persons with developmental disabilities to be able to follow the case and to participate in them to the extent of their abilities, as is Braille for a visually impaired person, or sign language interpretation for a hearing-impaired person.

A fifth barrier in the judicial process concerns impediments to persons with disabilities serving as jurors. Jury service is a fundamental aspect of the rights and duties of a citizen in a democratic society. It is only through jury service that most members of the public can play a decision-making role in the administration of justice. In fact, apart from the exercise of the vote during an election, jury service is probably the only way that most people can participate in the democratic process of self-government.

The Supreme Court of Canada has emphasized that it is fundamentally important that juries be representative of the greater community. Jury representativeness helps ensure public confidence in the fair administration of justice. As well, the jury has an intersticial law-making role which requires that it be able to draw upon the broad experiences of all facets of the community. Since people with disabilities are a substantial group in Canadian society, it is important that there be an opportunity for their experiences to be reflected in the jury room.

Historically there have been a number of barriers impeding persons with disabilities from serving as jurors. As discussed above, court facilities, including jury boxes, have often not been designed to be accessible to persons using wheelchairs. Exacerbating these physical impediments have been legislative barriers. Juries legislation often excluded many persons with disabilities from jury service whether or not they were incapable of effectively discharging the duties of a juror, with or without reasonable accommodation.

For example, Ontario's previous version of its Juries Act provided in s. 4(a) and (b) that a person is ineligible to serve as a juror who "is infirm, decrepit or afflicted with blindness, deafness or other physical infirmity incompatible with the discharge of the duties of a juror" or "not in the possession of his natural faculties." This reflected a stereotype-driven categorical legislative judgement that none of these individuals would ever be able to serve as jurors, whether or not their disability did in fact impede their capacity to perform the functions of a juror, and whether or not that disability could be accommodated without undue hardship, so they could fulfil a juror's essential functions.

Ontario amended this provision in an effort to modernize it. It now provides in material part as follows:

Jurors Act, section 4: A person is ineligible to serve as a juror who:

    a) has a physical or mental disability that would seriously impair his or her ability to discharge duties of a juror.

This provision's "seriously impaired" standard properly construed, should only preclude a person with a disability from serving as a juror if he or she could not perform a juror's essential duties due to a disability even after his or her disability-related needs are accommodated to the point of undue hardship. This is because the jurors legislation must be construed in a manner consistent with the strictures of the Charter and human rights legislation, including the requirement to meet the constitutional and statutory human rights duty to accommodate. While it would be preferable for this duty to be explicitly incorporated into the jury legislation, its absence there does not take away the obligation of the courts and courts administration officials to comply with the duty to accommodate arising under the Charter and human rights codes.

NOTES AND QUESTIONS

1. While there is much that could be done to improve access to existing legal structures and to change our delivery models to ensure that they are more culturally responsive, conceptualizing the problems in this manner obscures what is a deeper challenge. The challenge, advanced by aboriginal communities in particular, is that the existing order cannot, by its very nature, take seriously the culture of the First Nations peoples. For many, tinkering at the edges of what is, at its core, a white man's justice system, will never lead to justice for aboriginal communities. See the Royal Commission on Aboriginal Peoples (Ottawa: Supply and Services, 1996).

2. Sam Stevens, "Access to Civil Justice for Aboriginal Peoples," in A. Hutchinson, ed., *Access to Civil Justice* (Toronto: Carswell, 1990), 203, at 212-13, discussed these issues and presented a structure for solutions:

> It may be useful to summarize the reasons why aboriginal people do not feel they can gain access to the civil justice system.
>
>   1. Aboriginal people have been conditioned to distrust the Canadian judicial system, part of which includes the civil court process. They will therefore not usefully use the civil justice system.
>
>   2. The Canadian justice system does not recognize aboriginal customary laws, laws that have been used by aboriginal peoples, in some cases, for thousands of years. As a result, aboriginal people feel their disputes cannot be resolved by the present justice system in a meaningful way.
>
>   3. The adversarial system used by the Canadian judicial system is antithetical to the traditional aboriginal dispute resolution system.
>
>   4. The aboriginal people in Canada are unfamiliar with the courts and their right as Canadians; they therefore do not generally assert their rights as recognized under federal or provincial laws.
>
>   5. Until recently, there has been an obvious lack of representation in the Canadian judicial system by aboriginal lawyers and judges.

6. A majority of aboriginal people have incomes substantially less than those of average Canadians, and, as a result, many of the problems that aboriginal people experience are "poor people problems." Lawyers generally do not want to deal with these "poor people problems."

7. The time it takes to solve their legal problem is something that aboriginal people cannot accept.

8. The cost of having a civil suit adjudicated by the court is prohibitive.

9. The socio-economic position of aboriginal peoples makes the court more inaccessible for aboriginal peoples than for non-aboriginal peoples.

10. The civil court system is an inappropriate forum for the resolution of issues dealing with claims and aboriginal rights.

To begin to solve these problems, I have proposed solutions based on three broad approaches. First, there are disputes of a private, individual nature, involving an aboriginal person and a non-aboriginal person or one of the governments. These disputes should continue to be settled by the present civil courts. So, what can be done to ensure that the civil courts are more accessible to aboriginal people or other people in circumstances similar to those of aboriginal peoples? Second, there are disputes that are of a civil, private law nature but that are between two aboriginal people from the same community or from another aboriginal community. Aboriginal people have proposed, and it seems reasonable and indeed feasible, to have these disputes resolved by the aboriginal community and according to their laws and standards. Third, there are disputes that are of a public law nature and that involve aboriginal community rights on the one hand, and either the Canadian or provincial community or private law rights on the other hand. The civil courts are being asked to resolve increasingly more disputes of this nature. It is questionable whether the present civil courts are necessarily the best forums to settle these kinds of disputes. If we continue to use the present civil court system to resolve some of these disputes, what can we do to ensure aboriginal people get a just resolution of their disputes, and are there other alternative dispute resolution forums that can be implemented to resolve these types of dispute?

What criteria should be employed in evaluating these proposals? Who should decide?

IV. MECHANISMS TO FACILITATE ACCESS

A. Contingency Fees

In the United States, it has long been common practice for lawyers to enter into contingent fee agreements with their clients (at least with plaintiff clients) (see *Wylie v. Coxe*, 56 US 415 (1853). In a contingent fee agreement, usually, if the client is successful, the lawyer takes a certain percentage of the proceeds of the litigation as a fee; in the event that the client is unsuccessful, the lawyer will make no charge for the services rendered. In Canada, the acceptance of such arrangements is recent. In all Canadian jurisdictions except Ontario, some types of contingency arrangements are now permitted by statute, rule, case law, or as a matter of practice. A typical set of limiting provisions are those of Nova Scotia—see rules 63.16 to 63.31. Even in Ontario, a limited form of contingency arrangement is possible in class actions.

These rules permit a solicitor to enter into a contingency fee arrangement with a client; the fee may be an amount that is the same, greater, or less than that which the solicitor normally receives as remuneration. However, such an arrangement is still subject to a solicitor-and-client taxation in the normal way. A contingent fee arrangement must be entered in writing, signed by the client, and contain, *inter alia*, a statement of the contingency on which the compensation is to be paid and whether and to what extent the client will be liable to pay compensation other than from amounts collected by the solicitor. It must also contain a statement that reasonable contingent compensation is to be paid for the services; the maximum amount or rate which the compensation is not to exceed, after deduction of all reasonable and proper disbursements; and a statement to the following effect (see NSR 63, 18(2)(f).):

> This agreement may be reviewed by a taxing officer at the client's request, and may either at the instance of the taxing officer or the client be further reviewed by the court, and either the taxing officer or the court may vary, modify or disallow the agreement.

Within ten days after it is signed, a copy of the agreement must be filed with the court. The agreement is not available for inspection by any person other than the client, the solicitor, or a taxing officer engaged in its taxation. If the agreement is not in proper form nor properly filed, the solicitor's compensation is limited to that normally expected in the absence of a contingency arrangement. At any time until six months after the date on which a solicitor received any part of the fee, the agreement may be reviewed by the taxing officer at the instance of the client. On review, the taxing officer may approve the agreement, vary, modify or disallow any of its provisions and if the agreement is disallowed determine the solicitor's fee as on a normal solicitor and client taxation. The rules also make void any provision in an agreement purporting to provide that a proceeding cannot be abandoned, discontinued, or settled without the consent of the solicitor. It is also provided that, notwithstanding anything to the contrary in an agreement, a client may change solicitors before the conclusion of the retainer.

At a purely abstract level are there not many arguments to be made against payment-in-any-event provisions as well? Is not a lawyer who will be paid in any event tempted to take any case regardless of its merits and to encourage its continuation even in the face of a reasonable offer? Furthermore, can it not be argued that for many individuals of limited means the choice is between legal services with a contingency fee arrangement or no legal services at all. Should the focus not be on controlling the potential abuse of contingency fees rather than on prohibiting contingency fees altogether? Of what relevance is the public's view? The next article explores these issues.

M. Trebilcock, "The Case for Contingent Fees: The Ontario Legal Profession Rethinks Its Position"
(1989), 15 *Canadian Business Law Journal* 360-68 (footnotes omitted)

1. Introduction

The virtues and vices of contingent fee arrangements for the remuneration of claimants' lawyers in civil litigation have been a matter of long-standing debate in the legal profession.

They are liberally permitted in the United States, but have been accorded much more qualified acceptance in most Commonwealth legal systems. In Canada, all provinces now permit some form of contingent fee arrangement except Ontario where they are prohibited by provincial statute. However, even in Ontario, much civil litigation is *de facto* conducted on a contingent fee basis, *i.e.*, a substantial fee in the event of success, only disbursements in the event of failure. Moreover, the Taxing Master explicitly recognizes that the results obtained in litigation are a factor to be weighed in taxing a lawyer's bill of costs.

Many provinces in Canada have only moved in the last two decades to authorize contingent fees, and it was inevitable that the Ontario legal profession would sooner or later feel compelled by these developments to re-evaluate its own long-standing hostility to such arrangements. ...

In a report of May 27, 1988, of a Special Committee of the Law Society of Upper Canada, subsequently adopted with minor amendments by Convocation, the committee recommended that contingent fees be permitted in most classes of litigation (other than criminal and most family law matters). A committee of the Canadian Bar Association (Ontario) in a submission to the Attorney-General of Ontario of June 10, 1988, has adopted a similar view. Both reports contain detailed comparative accounts of the historical evolution of the law relating to contingent fees and provide balanced, careful and thoughtful evaluations of the arguments for and against such arrangements. Both reports acknowledge that, if permitted, there will be a need to formulate some regulatory parameters to govern these arrangements, and canvass at some length the regulatory alternatives, leaving open for further discussion within the profession and with the government detailed choices amongst these alternatives.

2. The Basic Arguments for and Against Contingent Fees

Let me briefly review the major arguments conventionally made for and against contingent fees.

For:

1. If there is disparity in the legal knowledge between the client and the lawyer, so that the client is unable to evaluate correctly the merits of the case, then a contingent fee contract gives the client a contract which provides an incentive for the lawyer to act in the client's best interests. Under an hourly fee contract, the lawyer may not have any direct economic incentive to work for the client's victory or to discourage the bringing of unmeritorious suits, because the lawyer's returns (at least in theory, except for reputation effects) are unrelated to the outcome of the case.

2. Contingent fee contracts may provide access to the courts for certain groups, especially the poor and those not eligible for legal aid, who under a certain hourly fee contract may not be able to initiate litigation. A similar argument is presented for risk averse individuals who are unwilling to initiate legal proceedings under a certain hourly fee basis because of the risk of having to pay a substantial lawyer's bill if the case is not successful. Essentially, a contingent fee contract allows a client to "borrow" from the lawyer and provides a shifting of risk from the client to the lawyer. It is assumed that the

lawyer is more able to diversify this risk than the client by taking on a "portfolio" of cases.

3. Under a certain hourly fee contract, even if the client can evaluate the merits of the case, the client either cannot monitor the actual time a lawyer works on a case or can monitor but at a cost. A contingent fee contract minimizes this type of moral hazard problem.

Against:

1. Because a lawyer's remuneration is contingent on the success of an action, his objectivity in advising his client will be compromised, and indeed he may have heightened incentives to engage in unethical practices, *e.g.*, suppressing evidence, suborning witnesses.

2. In meritorious cases, plaintiffs will receive lower net recoveries (after payment of contingent fees) than they would under a standard hourly fee contract, thus in affect being required to cross-subsidize claimants in unsuccessful suits.

3. Damages awarded in successful suits may be inflated by the courts over time in order to ensure adequate net recoveries by meritorious claimants, thus unfairly penalizing defendants and increasing insurance costs.

4. Contingent fees will encourage the bringing of nuisance or harassing claims with a low probability of success, with a view to coercing settlements from defendants or landing the occasional jackpot, but further congesting the courts with low-quality claims.

5. Contingent fees, like certain hourly fee contracts, also present their own form of moral hazard problem. If lawyers possess better information than clients on the likely success of an action and the likely scale of recovery if the action is successful, there is the potential for lawyers to charge their clients a percentage of the recovery that is excessive relative to the amount of lawyer's time required on the case and the amount of risk entailed. That is, a lawyer may correctly assess a case as a "sure thing" but induce his client to believe that the odds are less favourable, in order to justify a higher fee.

My assessment of these arguments for and against contingent fees is that their advantages are substantial in terms of risk shifting, which facilitates some meritorious litigation that would otherwise be discouraged, and in terms of aligning plaintiffs' and lawyers' incentives and interests in achieving the best possible outcome at the lowest cost. Some of the arguments against contingent fees can be better met by more finely targeted responses than complete prohibition, *e.g.*, rules on particular forms of unethical behaviour. The nuisance or harassing claim argument seems of little substance—the lawyer only gets paid if he wins a case, so there is even less incentive than under certain hourly fee contracts to bring claims that are unlikely to succeed. Moreover, under the Anglo-Canadian two-way cost rule, in contrast to the standard US no-way cost rule, the losing plaintiff even under a contingent fee arrangement will still be liable for a substantial portion of the other side's costs, again discouraging frivolous or nuisance suits.

However, I question the wisdom of retaining this latter rule in its present form in a contingent fee context. This rule still leaves substantial risk on plaintiffs even in non-frivolous suits and may discourage meritorious litigation. In a class action context, I, Dewees and Prichard have shown that such a rule, which places the brunt of party-and-party costs on the class representative in a losing case, will discourage most class actions. Consideration should be given to permitting the plaintiff in individual actions, or the class representative in class actions, and his or her lawyer, to negotiate a fee arrangement that shifts party-and-party costs to the lawyer personally, thus removing all risk from the plaintiff or class representative while increasing risk for the plaintiff's lawyer, for which increased compensation will appropriately be demanded. There seems to me to be no reason why the plaintiff's disbursements should not also be amenable to this kind of arrangement. Frivolous or nuisance suits will still be discouraged, because the lawyer for the plaintiff will not find it rational to bear the risk of loss of the value of his time, disbursements, and personal liability for party-and-party costs, but meritorious suits will be encouraged that would otherwise be discouraged by the plaintiff's or class representative's aversion to the downside risk of liability to the defendant for his costs. In this respect, I believe the committees' proposals do not go far enough.

One difficulty that my proposal would need to confront relates to incentives to settle. If all risks to the plaintiff of bearing legal costs in the event of a losing suit are shifted to the plaintiff's lawyer, there is no incentive for the plaintiff to agree to a settlement as long as the private expected additional returns from pressing forward with the suit are positive, abstracting from legal costs. But if legal costs on both sides are accounted for, the expected additional returns from pressing forward may be socially negative (as well as unprofitable for the plaintiff's lawyer).

One response to this problem is that full cost indemnification is only proposed as an option for lawyer and client and may be rejected if the lawyer is concerned that the client will be obdurate in agreeing to reasonable settlement proposals. Another response is that the lawyer can simply factor this additional risk into the percentage fee he negotiates with the client, although this in itself may not discourage socially wasteful litigation. Yet a further response might be to allow a provision in a full-cost indemnification contingent fee contract that permits the lawyer to terminate his involvement in the case on the rejection by his client of what the lawyer considers a reasonable settlement offer, with the client then being liable to compensate his lawyer for services performed to that point on a normal hourly fee basis.

However, it may be necessary to subject such termination decisions to approval by a judge in chambers or Master in order to discourage lawyers from attempting to turn contingent fee contracts into certain hourly fee contracts when the prospects of substantial success in a suit begin to appear dim during the litigation process, thus improperly reallocating the risk of a negative outcome to the client. A variant on this proposal, suggested in the Canadian Bar Association's report, is to allow the lawyer to terminate the contingency fee arrangement where he considers that his client is acting unreasonably, but with no right to any fees, other than disbursements. This again reflects a risk that a lawyer would wish to factor into the initial contingency arrangement.

I now turn to the need to impose some regulatory constraints on contingent fees in order to respond in particular to the legitimate concerns reflected in (5) above (over-charging).

3. Regulatory Constraints on Excessive Fees

The committees sensibly propose a prescribed written form of contingent fee agreement, signed by both lawyer and client, that sets out in clear language the rights and obligations of parties. It is important that this agreement clearly indicate to the client the process by which the fee arrangement may subsequently be reviewed (by whatever third party review agency—court or taxing officer—is appointed under the regulations). I believe that the committees also rightly reject as too cumbersome and as entailing needless expense prior judicial or administrative approval of each contingent fee arrangement. While both committees contemplate some form of *ex post* review mechanism (judge in chambers or assessment officer or some combination of the two) which the client can invoke if he or she wishes, both committees take seriously the possible need to superimpose on the process detailed fee caps or sliding scales. I am sceptical of the wisdom or feasibility of this. ...

Because of the complexities raised by prescribed fee caps, I advocate much greater flexibility (including individualized upward and downward sloping scales) in the fee arrangements that lawyers and clients are permitted to negotiate with each other.

Consistently with this suggestion, I propose the following possibility for consideration. After a lawyer and client have signed a contingent fee arrangement, the lawyer should be required to mail to an officer of the Law society a standardized computer coded card indicating the type of litigation involved, the damages sought, and the fee band or bands into which the negotiated fees fall, along with the lawyer's name. The Law Society could then very easily compile and disseminate (without lawyers' names) to the public periodically general distributions of contingent fees commonly charged for standard classes of litigation thus (a) helping clients *ex ante* to negotiate in a more informed way with their lawyers (indeed lawyers could be required to furnish clients with this information before concluding an agreement), (b) alerting clients *ex post* to possible causes of complaint warranting review, (c) providing the *ex post* review agency with some meaningful benchmarks, and (d) in extreme cases alerting the Law Society to possible patterns of egregious individual over-charging warranting investigation and possible disciplinary action.

In this way, maximum flexibility is maintained in permissible fee arrangements, reflecting the myriad of individual circumstances that have to be accommodated, while providing a meaningful set of checks on over-charging. It is crucially important that the Law Society not fall into the trap (as I believe it has in its rules on lawyers' advertising) of approaching the innovation of contingent fees with such deep apprehension of possible evils that it regulates them to death before they have been given a chance to breathe.

4. The Lawyer as Entrepreneur

The contingent fee debate should be seen as part of a broader emerging debate about the entrepreneurial role of lawyers. In this broader setting, rules on advertising, solicitation, class actions, maintenance, champerty, pre-paid legal service plans, expanded roles for para-professionals, incorporation, multi-disciplinary, province-wide, national and international law firms exploiting brand-names, all require re-evaluation along with rules relating to permissible fee arrangements.

If one believes that at present our problem is not a litigation "explosion," with an avalanche of insubstantial claims inundating the court system, but rather the opposite problem—a significant number of meritorious claims that are going unrecognized and unredressed—then a liberalization of various rules that constrain the entrepreneurial role of lawyers may be needed to stimulate heightened claim recognition and enhance capacity to redress a claim once recognized. By encouraging lawyers to communicate more freely with members of the public about their rights and the price and availability of legal services, and to assume risks of litigation (at a price) that would otherwise deter meritorious claims, access to justice may well be significantly enhanced. But removing the remaining vestiges of a guild mentality in the legal profession is a precursor to this more enterprising, catalytic role.

We cannot go on assuming that the only way of improving access to the legal system is to have governments throw ever larger amounts of public moneys at the system. Beyond providing an adequately staffed and efficiently operated legal infrastructure (*e.g.*, courts, tribunals, alternative dispute resolution mechanisms, land title and other registration systems for facilitating transactions), and providing adequate legal aid for the indigent, many other improvements in access may entail more efficient and enterprising deployment of private legal resources.

NOTES AND QUESTIONS

1. How adequately does Trebilcock address the problem of settlement offers refused by the plaintiff? Can a similar set of problems arise, in a different aspect, when plaintiffs—for example, corporations with a continuing relationship with the law firm—have a fee for service—that is, hourly rate—arrangement with their lawyers? In these circumstances do lawyers have an incentive to keep the litigation going and put more work into a file than is required? Does the system adequately guard against this problem?

2. In Ontario, contingency arrangements are not permitted in litigious matters, except in class actions. They are allowed in non-contentious business and conveyancing (see Solicitors Act, RSO 1980, ss. 18 and 30). The prohibition stems from Ontario's continued retention of the old common law position. At common law, there existed the crimes and torts of champerty and maintenance (see P.H. Winfield (1919), 35 *Law Quarterly Review* 50).

"Maintenance" is giving of assistance or encouragement to one of the parties to an action by a person who has neither an interest in the action nor any other motive recognized by the law as justifying this interference. "Champerty" is a particular kind of maintenance—namely, maintenance of an action in consideration of a promise to give to the maintainer a share in the subject matter or proceeds thereof. At common law, these two doctrines clearly forbid an agreement to remunerate a solicitor by a share of, percentage of, or sum proportioned to the amount of property to be recovered in an action.

These anachronistic vestiges of the common law still form part of the law of Ontario. The Champerty Act, RSO 1897, c. 327, now reprinted in RSO 1980, appendix A, which declares champertous agreements to be illegal, has never been repealed. Moreover, s. 30 of the Solicitors Act sets forth a sweeping prohibition on fee arrangements involving champerty and maintenance or (so it would appear) involving any contingent element. It provides that nothing in s. 18 of the Act (which permits solicitor and client agreements as to compensation)

> gives validity to a purchase by a solicitor of the interest or any part of the interest of his client in any action or other contentious proceeding to be brought or maintained, *or gives validity to an agreement by which a solicitor retained or employed to prosecute an*

action or proceeding stipulates for payment only in the event of success in the action or proceeding, or where the amount to be paid to him is a percentage of the amount or value of the property recovered or preserved or otherwise determinable by such amount or value or dependent upon the result of the action or proceeding. [Emphasis added.]

As a consequence of this provision, percentage contingent fee arrangements are not used in Ontario, and any lawyer entering into such an arrangement will be subject to disciplinary proceedings by the Law Society although the rules are under review by that Law Society. Notwithstanding the Solicitors Act, it is now unknown in Ontario in personal injury litigation for a solicitor to undertake an action on behalf of a plaintiff on the understanding that the solicitor will ask for a minimal fee or no fee at all if the action should fail: see H. Kritzer, "Fee Arrangements and Fee Shifting: Lessons from the Experience in Ontario" (1983), 47 *Law and Contemporary Problems* 125.

3. What are the reasons for the traditional prohibitions against champerty and maintenance? Do they have anything to do with the traditional or corrective model of adjudication, discussed in chapter 4, "Challenges to the Traditional Model," which imputes sole ownership of a dispute to the parties affected by it?

4. Although contingency fees remain prohibited in Ontario, except in class actions, most lawyers know that if they undertake certain cases they will only be paid if they succeed and that their costs will come out of the settlement or judgment funds. It is estimated that between 60 and 70 percent of personal injury cases use this type of arrangement.

B. Private Insurance

In recent years, considerable interest has developed in the use of insurance as a means to overcome the prohibitive costs of legal services. These are schemes under which the costs of possible future legal services are paid in advance by or on behalf of the clients who will receive the services. The scheme is generally offered on a group basis—for example, to members of trade unions. Underlying the schemes is the basic insurance principle—contributions to the scheme are pooled and the risk is spread out between users and non-users, thereby decreasing the cost of legal services to individuals who require legal advice and assistance.

The plan can take various forms. Essentially, individuals contribute (or contributions are made by employers) to an insurance plan of sorts. In return, they receive a predetermined set of legal services, generally defined in terms of types of services, with maximum ceilings stated in dollar amounts. The range of plans varies greatly. Some offer only consultation; others are practically unlimited in services. Specifically, some cover the costs of litigation, others only a portion, and others exclude litigious matters. Perhaps the most contentious issue is how the participant chooses a lawyer. In "fully open plans," the individual can choose any lawyer for services that the plan covers. A "partly open plan" restricts choice to lawyers within a small geographical area or lawyers who are members of the plan. "Fully closed plans" refer to plans in which all claims are handled by a full-time staff lawyer.

In Western Europe, legal-cost insurance dates from the first quarter of the 20th century and is now widespread and highly developed. For example, in West Germany there are some 5,000,000 insurance contracts in force covering approximately 25 percent of the population. In Europe it appears that this type of insurance is primarily concerned with covering the expenses of litigation, including not only the legal fees of the insured but also any costs that might be awarded to the opponent. For an examination of why schemes that have succeeded in Europe have failed to take hold in North America, see W. Pfenningstorf, *Legal Expense Insurance: The European Experience in Financing Legal Services* (Chicago: American Bar Foundation, 1975). Interest in legal-cost insurance has increased rapidly in North America in the last few years, although various limited forms of group legal services—for example, automobile clubs and trade associations—have existed in the United States for some time.

The Canadian experience has been limited and halting. The following extract offers a glimpse at the development of these schemes in Canada. It is taken from a study of the prepaid legal services plan implemented by the Canadian Auto Workers. Originally, the Law Society of Upper Canada opposed the plan and sued to prevent it from operating. Litigation focused on how "open" or "closed" the plan would be. Litigation was settled and this study investigated the operation of that plan.

Wydrzynski, Hildebrandt, and Blonde, "The CAW Prepaid Legal Services Plan: A Case Study of an Alternative Funding and Delivery Method for Legal Services" (1991), 10 *Windsor Yearbook of Access to Justice* 22-78 (footnotes omitted)

The Idea of Prepaid Legal Services

The modern concept of prepaid legal services plans was largely developed in the United States in the late sixties and early seventies, although its origins go back much further. Canadian developments have not kept pace with those in the United States for a variety of reasons; in general, the concept was not as readily accepted by Canadian lawyers, consumers and regulators as appropriate or desirable for our jurisdictions. It was assumed that the historical *"fee-for-service"* model, combined with provision for legal aid for those unable to afford legal service, was sufficient to meet the legal needs of the public. This attitude has been changing. Canadian consumers, lawyers and regulators look much more favourably on the prepaid or group method of delivering legal services than they have in the recent past. The overall results of this study demonstrate this positive perspective.

The basic prepaid model for legal services plans is a means for individuals or groups of consumers (usually middle-income) to finance the cost of specific legal services for individual members of the group by pooling their economic resources to enhance their economic bargaining power. The pool of financial resources can then be used by the group to bargain with the providers for the delivery of legal services to the individual members. Thus, the mechanism is self-induced and self-funded. Annual individual contributions to the plan will be less than the value of legal services to which the individual is entitled, assuming a utilization rate of less than 100%. Therefore the nature of prepaid legal services is only innovative because it applies the idea of cost-sharing to the market for legal services. The recognition that collective activity to solve individual problems is a standard mode of social organization rather than a radical deviation from the norm allowed for the growth of such plans in the United States. Even in Canada the introduction of similar plans should be viewed as an evolution rather than a revolution in legal services delivery.

Legal services plans seek to solve the dilemma of cost for the middle-income consumer of legal services, and to assist in providing greater access to legal providers. Although the problem of access can be viewed primarily as one of cost, it also has other dimensions. Persons may not know how to find a lawyer suitable for their problems; they may not even conceive of their problem as "legal" in nature; they may only utilize legal services when a crisis situation occurs, rather than for advice, planning and prevention. This is in contrast to the wealthy who are able to more readily afford legal services, and even the poor who at least have access to government funded legal aid programs. Middle-income earners are thus viewed as having unmet legal needs which can be rectified through the use of legal services plans. These legal needs are "unmet" in the sense that there are not adequate delivery systems to bring lawyers and clients together, or that such needs are "unperceived" by the consumer and therefore go unserviced.

There is no generic model for legal services plans, they are dependent on the groups' resources and the groups' needs. Typically, employers fund legal services plans as a fringe benefit for their employees. These plans have been partly encouraged in the belief that assistance for employees' personal legal problems would lead to greater job productivity. This was the basic model which spawned rapid growth of plans in the United States in the 1970s. More recently, profit-driven institutions such as insurance companies, similar benefit organizations, and even credit card companies have established plans in which individuals voluntarily subscribe through payment of a premium. In the United States, "telephone access plans," in which a member may phone an attorney for advice at any time, and "referral/discount plans," which provide a member with lower hourly rates for services provided, have also become popular. Flexible tailoring of a plan to serve the needs and desires of the plan users is one of the most attractive features of legal services plans. The advantage of all such plans is that the client has immediate access to legal information and legal advice. This allows for prevention and avoidance of legal entanglements, something not generally available to middle-income consumers in the fee-for-service market.

The significant social benefit to be derived from legal services plans is the advancement of access to justice fostered through a movement toward the equalization of the availability of professional services for all members of the community. Exercise of legal rights is often dependent on access to legal service providers. Groups and individuals can use collective risk-sharing, cost-sharing and budgeting as the methods to help ensure access to the means whereby their rights may be exercised in the most effective manner. ...

General Conclusions and Recommendations

When we began the study we were greatly concerned about the unsettled atmosphere in which legal services plans had to operate within Canada. Lawyers were concerned about the economic impact of such plans on private practices. Law societies were unsure of the proper regulation of such plans. Potential clients were unaware and unsure of the potential benefits of legal services plans. While this study does not suggest legal services plans as a miracle cure for the issues of access to justice for middle income consumers, it argues that such plans are an efficient and effective method to deliver some legal services to the community. The initial fears of the practising bar have not been supported by this research. Instead, the positive features recommended prepaid plans as legitimate, alternative methods of legal service delivery that do not compromise professional values. We recommend that governments, lawyers' groups, plan sponsors and consumers work together for the growth and development of legal services plans.

The CAW Legal Services Plan has been shown to deliver legal services to its clients in an efficient and professional manner. Staff lawyers appear to be well-satisfied with their employment context. They have developed a very satisfactory method of dealing with their union clients and have demonstrated a positive and confident attitude. Not surprisingly, staff lawyers rated their service as superior to that of co-operating and non-co-operating lawyers (8.3 on a 10 point scale, as opposed to 6). Our survey and the Plan's CSQs [client satisfaction questionnaires] suggest that clients agree with this assessment. Staff lawyers have learned to provide quality service in a responsive manner to their middle-income union clients.

The value of the Plan to the members can be assessed in monetary and non-monetary terms. As members contribute approximately $120.00 per year, a single legal service use per year would give members good value for their contribution. Not surprisingly, therefore, Plan users are overwhelmingly satisfied with the plan and wish to retain it. At the same time, a large majority of non-users also wishes to keep the benefit. The value to the non-users (if they are thought to be rational) must therefore be a non-monetary one, similar to participating in an insurance scheme. Obviously, users obtain this non-monetary benefit as well, and both reasons lead non-eligible members to desire participation in this benefit. This strong endorsement of the Plan must be viewed as a significant finding of this study.

One question which was not (and could not be) addressed in this research is whether the CAW Prepaid Plan provides a less expensive legal service delivery method, compared to private practice. The CAW Plan was no more willing (and perhaps no more able) than private practitioners would have been to give us as researchers actual per case costs for different types of cases, or the raw numbers to allow us to make such calculations ourselves. However, there are two pieces of circumstantial evidence which suggest that the effect of the Plan may be to reduce legal costs overall. First, we suspect that any obvious higher per-case costs under the CAW Plan would have been pointed out by the private bar; since no such argument has been attempted, the Plan's cost are probably no higher than the Bar's. Second, as we noted above, the 1988 per-hour fee of $70 under the Plan was below the Windsor averages of both co-operating and non-co-operating lawyers. In fact, many non-co-operating lawyers admitted that, at least sometimes, they charged Plan members less than their customary fees, thus reducing legal costs. Hence, while careful cost-accounting could not be part of this research, we are convinced that legal services are delivered cost-effectively by the CAW Plan.

One of the goals of this study was to determine whether legal services plans increase access to justice and access to law for middle income consumers. It is not possible to draw a definitive conclusion on this essential issue, but we can state that Plan users think it increases their access to law and justice. Perhaps this is a no less important test. On the other hand, there probably has been no significant additional usage of the legal system because of the existence of the Plan. Use of the Plan has not been as high as might have been expected, and Plan members continue to use lawyers outside the Plan, including those who have chosen to continue established relationships with their own lawyers. In addition, some matters (e.g. business law, criminal matters, etc.) are not presently covered by the Plan. For this reason, legal services plans should periodically re-examine the extension of coverage based on clients' needs and demands, in order to provide access to needed services.

There is little doubt that legal services plans provide improved access to lawyers; improved access to legal services and peace of mind for the consumer. Knowing that legal advice and information is freely and conveniently available, often over the phone, provides the consumer with a degree of comfort not available in other legal service settings. This aspect of the benefit should not be overlooked; it allows the consumer to engage in prevention before serious legal problems even arise. ...

Legal services plans can also be seen as one method to help improve the public image of lawyers as a group. Throughout this research we have seen that the more contact legal consumers have with lawyers, the better their impression of the legal profession. ...

The issue of legal information appears at many levels, but the root of the problem appears to be that the community needs to be better educated about when a lawyer is needed and the benefit of using lawyers. This is apparent among the members of the CAW Plan itself; they desire more knowledge about the services of the Plan and education about legal problems. This function of the Plan should be enhanced: legal services plans should include legal education programs for their members. Increased information will help clients better understand their needs, so that they can utilize a plan most effectively. But the problem of public legal education has a much broader perspective as well. If legal services plans in general should be encouraged as a matter of public policy as alternatives for the delivery of legal services to the community, community education must be improved by groups other than the plans themselves. Indeed, in some types of privately offered plans, plan organizers could think it contrary to their own economic interests to encourage greater use of lawyers. Therefore, other groups like governmental agencies, educational institutions, consumer groups, law societies and other lawyer groups should provide education. The public in general needs to be informed about the benefits of legal services plans as an alternative mechanism to fulfill their legal needs, but they also need education to better perceive those needs in the first place. ...

Given our positive evaluation of the CAW Legal Services Plan, similar plans should receive promotion throughout Canada. Regulatory measures could assist this development further, such as changing the taxation status of legal services plans to make contributions tax exempt, as they have been in the United States for many years. We see no reason medical benefits receive a favourable taxation status, but legal plans do not. Legal services plans provide for essential needs, and ultimately aid in the resolution of society's problems. In addition to government, the agencies which govern the conduct of lawyers, the law societies, should play a positive role. The CAW Legal Services Plan was able to operate by reaching an agreement with the Law Society of Upper Canada which mandated that members should have the freedom to obtain covered legal services from any lawyer in the community. In the interest of also preserving the consumer's freedom to obtain different forms of legal services plans, including plans with a closed panel model, such restrictions on lawyer use as imposed by the Law Society of Upper Canada should not be made mandatory. Such plans have proven to be effective and compatible with professionalism in the United States, and we see no reason why they would not be so in this country.

C. Paralegals

For at least the last two decades in Canada, particularly in Ontario, an interesting phenomenon has been growing. Individuals, not legally trained, have been assisting others with legal problems. This assistance is done for compensation and without supervision of lawyers. Such problems include defences to minor criminal matters, small claim court actions, drafting of wills, immigration matters, and real estate transactions. These individuals are known as paralegals and should not be confused with law clerks who perform some of the same services under the supervision of lawyers. The following material explores some of the issues raised by the activities of paralegals.

Regina v. Lawrie and Points Ltd.
(1987), 59 OR (2d) 161

BLAIR JA: The question in this case is whether a paid agent acting for persons charged with traffic offences under the *Highway Traffic Act*, RSO 1980, c. 198, pursuant to s. 51(1) of the *Provincial Offences Act*, RSO 1980, c. 400, can be prosecuted for acting as a barrister or solicitor under s. 50(2) of the *Law Society Act*, RSO 1980, c. 233. ...

Lawrie is not a barrister or solicitor. He is a retired policeman with considerable experience in the conduct of traffic cases under the *Provincial Offences Act*. He incorporated the company for the purpose of representing persons charged with traffic offences under the *Highway Traffic Act*. Each customer or client is required to sign a form appointing the company as agent to act on his or her behalf "within the meaning of the *Provincial Offences Act*." Lawrie controls the company. At the time of trial, two former police officers were also employed by the company and represented its clients in proceedings under the *Provincial Offences Act*.

The relevant provisions in the *Law Society Act* are:

> 50(1) *Except where otherwise provided by law*, no person, other than a member whose rights and privileges are not suspended, shall act as a barrister or solicitor or hold himself out as or represent himself to be a barrister or solicitor or practise as a barrister or solicitor.
>
> (2) Every person who contravenes any provision of subsection (1) is guilty of an offence and on conviction is liable to a fine of not more than $1,000.

(Emphasis added.)

The prosecution was conducted under the *Provincial Offences Act*, which provides:

> 51(1) A defendant may appear and act personally or by counsel or *agent*. ...
>
> (3) The court may bar any person from appearing as an agent who is not a barrister and solicitor entitled to practise in Ontario if the court finds that the person is not competent properly to represent or advise the person for whom he appears as agent or does not understand and comply with the duties and responsibilities of an agent.

(Emphasis added.)

The learned trial judge found that both respondents had acted as barristers or solicitors within the meaning of s. 50(1) of the *Law Society Act*. This finding was challenged by the respondents in this appeal but, since it is amply supported by the evidence, it should not be disturbed. The respondents were charged only with acting as barristers or solicitors and not with holding themselves out or practising as barristers or solicitors which are the other activities prohibited by s. 50(1). ...

[A review of the judgments below is omitted.]

Mr. Kellock, in his able argument, contended that the *Provincial Offences Act*, by permitting accused persons to be represented by agents, did not thereby confer upon agents, who were not qualified as barristers or solicitors, the authority to carry on the business of advising and defending accused persons and to charge them for so acting. He, therefore, argued that s. 51 of the *Provincial Offences Act* did not constitute an exception to s. 50(1) of the *Law Society Act* and, additionally, did not constitute an implied amendment to s. 1 of the *Solicitors Act*, RSO 1980, c. 478, to which I will refer later. In his submissions, the hallmark of the profession of barristers and solicitors is the provision of legal advice and representation on a repetitive basis and the charging of fees for such services. He maintained that the agent whose appearance was authorized by the *Provincial Offences Act* was not intended to be a person engaged in the business of representation for a fee. Rather, the agent was intended by the legislation to be a relative or friend who spoke for a party without remuneration.

The *Provincial Offences Act*, which governs the prosecution of provincial offences created by the Legislature, was enacted in 1979 by 1979 (Ont.), c. 4. It replaced the *Summary Convictions Act*, RSO 1970, c. 450, which, in large part, incorporated the provisions of Part XXIV of the *Criminal Code*, RSC 1970, c. C-34 , dealing with summary convictions. The *Criminal Code* since 1906 (RSC 1906, c. 146, s. 720) has permitted defendants to appear through agents in summary conviction proceedings as is now provided in s. 735(2) of the *Code*.

Appearances through agents, who are not barristers or solicitors, are permitted by other statutes. ...

[A discussion of these statutes is omitted.]

Rule 20 of the Law Society's Rules of Professional Conduct permits delegation of many tasks by lawyers to employees who are not lawyers or articled students. The delegable tasks include conveyancing, drafting corporate and commercial documents,

administration of estates and trusts, and research and preparation of documents in litigation. The rule states that "[g]enerally speaking a non-lawyer shall not attend on examinations or in court except in support of a lawyer also in attendance." The rule makes an
exception for appearances by law clerks employed by only one lawyer or law firm in a
variety of cases. These include appearances as agents where statutes or regulations
permit non-lawyers to appear and on routine adjournments in Provincial Court. Law
clerks may also attend on routine examinations in uncontested matters, *ex parte* or
consent orders before a master and the taxation of costs.

The common thread that runs through these examples of employment of law students and non-lawyers is that their work is done under the direction and supervision of
lawyers who are responsible to clients and the public for the work's proper performance.
Moreover, the work is done by salaried employees whose remuneration, unlike that of
lawyers, is fixed and not related to fees charged for specific services.

The position of the respondents in this case is different. They operate their own
business independent of any direction or supervision by qualified lawyers. The respondents, when acting as agents under the *Provincial Offences Act*, perform the same services as lawyers and, like them, are paid on a fee-for-service basis. They are not barred,
as the legal profession is, from carrying on their business through corporations. As
recently as 1980 "The Report of the Professional Organizations Committee," April,
1980, at p. 69, reported that law clerks appearing before the committee did not seek
independent status: see also "The Market for Legal Services: Paraprofessionals and
Specialists," Working Paper No. 10 of the Professional Organizations Committee. It is
the growth since that report of independent paralegal businesses carrying on lawyer-like
activities free from the direction and supervision of the legal profession that elevates the
public importance of this case.

Agents have been authorized to act in some proceedings for more than a century.
They were first permitted in small claims matters before Division Courts in 1872: "An
Act to empower all persons to appear on behalf of others in the Divisional Courts in the
Province of Ontario," 1872 (Ont.), c. 8, s. 1, and in mechanics' lien proceedings in 1910:
Mechanics and Wage-Earners Lien Act 1910 (Ont.), c. 69, s. 37(7). As previously men-
tioned they have acted in summary conviction proceedings under the *Criminal Code*
since 1906. Their appearance before coroners' inquests was authorized by the *Coroners
Act*, 1972 (Ont.), c. 98, s. 33, and their limited participation in proceedings under the
Landlord and Tenant Act dates from 1975: *Landlord and Tenant Amendment Act*, 1975
(Ont.) (2nd Sess.), c. 13, s. 6. The first statutory reference to their appearance before
administrative tribunals was in the *Statutory Powers Procedure Act*, 1971 (Ont.), c. 47,
s. 23(3), but it is known that laymen appeared as advocates before such tribunals prior to
that date.

Despite the long participation of agents in judicial proceedings, they have been the
subject of only one reported decision and little has been written about them. In *R v.
Duggan* (1976), 31 CCC (2d) 167, this court held that right of audience of an agent was
confined to the court which was specifically authorized by statute. ...

One is entitled, in my opinion, to take judicial notice of the extent of the business
carried on in this province by persons acting as agents under the *Province Offences Act*
quite apart from those performing other paralegal services. While it is the view of the

law society that agents are not entitled to operate a business for reward, the obvious fact is that they do and have done so for many years. Writing in 1971 about encroachments on the legal profession, Mark M. Orkin observed: "[T]he 'small claims' field of practice is no longer financially attractive to most lawyers, hence the emergence of division court 'agents,' non-lawyers who openly carry on this type of business." (Orkin, Mark M. "Professional Autonomy and the Public Interest: A Study of the Law Society of Upper Canada," D Jur. dissertation, York University, 1971 at p. 182.)

The hiring of agents as a common practice in provincial offence proceedings is acknowledged in the leading textbook on the *Provincial Offences Act*: see Drinkwalter and Ewart, *Ontario Provincial Offences Procedure* (1980), note 46 at p. 57. It is beyond dispute that paid agents are employed in proceedings before administrative tribunals or under the *Construction Lien Act*. The fact that agents do carry on business for reward does not, of course, determine the legal question whether they are authorized to do so under the *Law Society Act*. It does, however, place this case in its proper context. It is not an isolated occurrence but appears rather to be an example of a reasonably common practice.

It is not the role of this court to determine whether, as a matter of policy, the operations of the respondents serve the public interest. It is obvious from the business they have attracted that they are providing an unmet need for service to the public. While no reflection of any kind was made in this case on the respondents, there must be concern about the absence of any control over the education, qualification, competence and probity of all agents. They deal with serious matters because penalties of up to six months imprisonment apply to some offences under the *Highway Traffic Act*. No provision exists for disciplining or supervising agents and protecting the public from financial loss arising from the improper performance of their responsibilities by way of an insurance scheme like that of the law society.

It has been observed many times that the prohibition against the unauthorized practice of law is not merely to protect qualified lawyers from infringement of their right to practise their profession. ...

It is the responsibility of the Legislature to resolve these issues of policy. The task of this court is to determine whether, on a proper construction of the relevant statutes, they prohibit what the respondents were doing.

If only s. 50 of the *Law Society Act* had to be considered, there would be little difficulty in deciding that the respondents are not prohibited from carrying on the business of acting as agents for a fee under the *Provincial Offences Act*, I can find nothing in the Act that limits the exception in s. 50 of the *Law Society Act* of persons "otherwise authorized" to friends and relatives acting as agents without remuneration. Absent a specific limitation to this effect in the *Law Society Act*, the court could not read such a restriction into the statute.

The *Law Society Act*, however, is not the only statute to be considered. Under the heading of "Unauthorized Practice," s. 1 of the *Solicitors Act* provides:

> 1. If a person, unless himself a party to the proceeding, commences, prosecutes or defends in his own name, or that of any other person, any action or proceeding without having been admitted and enrolled as a solicitor, he is *incapable of recovering any fee,*

reward or disbursements on account thereof, and is guilty of a contempt of the court in which such proceeding was commenced, carried on or defended, and is punishable accordingly.

(Emphasis added.) I accept Mr. Kellock's argument that the *Law Society Act* and the *Solicitors Act* are statutes *in pari materia* and that they must be read together so as to avoid conflict between their provisions: *Capital Grocers Ltd. v. Registrar of Land Titles*, [1953] 1 DLR 318, 7 WWR (NS) 315 (Sask. CA). Both s. 50 of the *Law Society Act* and s. 1 of the *Solicitors Act* deal with solicitors with what might appear to be incongruous results. Section 50 of the *Law Society Act* appears to permit the respondents to act as solicitors when employed as agents under the *Provincial Offences Act* but s. 1 of the *Solicitors Act* appears to prevent them from being paid for their services. Since the respondents were charged with acting as solicitors, the appellant's argument was that they were in violation of the *Solicitors Act* because it provided for no exceptions and, hence, they were not protected by the exception in s. 50 of the *Law Society Act*.

Two answers were given to this argument in the courts below neither of which, in my respectful opinion, answers Mr. Kellock's argument. Provincial Judge Kerr held that s. 1 of the *Solicitors Act*, to the extent it affected agents, was repealed by implication by the *Provincial Offences Act* which was enacted later. This is not a case where any reliance can be placed on the presumption that a later statute might revoke an earlier one because the provisions for representation by agents in the *Provincial Offences Act* continues the similar provision in the *Criminal Code* which applied to provincial offences. District Court Judge Moore stressed that the charge had been laid under the *Law Society Act* and not the *Solicitors Act* but this does not dispose of the problem created by the necessity of reading the two Acts together. ...

[A lengthy discussion of the statutory histories of the Law Society Act and the Solicitors Act is omitted.]

In reviewing the statutory history certain features stand out. For many years, agents have been permitted to represent parties in several types of legal proceedings. This fact has long been recognized by the Legislature in statutes governing the legal profession by the references to it in parentheses in successive revisions of the *Solicitors Act* and the clear exception made in the *Barristers Act* in 1944. When the sections prohibiting unauthorized practice were transferred to the *Law Society Act* from the *Barristers Act* and the *Solicitors Act* in 1970, this exception for cases "otherwise provided by law" continued to apply to agents acting as barristers and, for the first time, it applied also in specific statutory language to agents acting as solicitors. In addition, the confusing reference to "gain or reward" inserted in the *Solicitors Act* in 1940 was eliminated indicating the Legislature's intent to focus on *the work performed by agents and not whether they were paid.*

The effect of the 1970 revision of the three statutes was to transfer the control of unauthorized practice of the *Law Society Act*. Section 1 of the *Solicitors Act* is merely an ancillary provision. It does not prohibit unauthorized practice. It merely provides penalties additional to those prescribed in s. 50 of the *Law Society Act* by preventing recovery of fees and exposing unauthorized persons to the charge of contempt of court. The section cannot stand by itself. The penalties it provides can only apply to unauthorized practice as defined by s. 50(1) of the *Law Society Act* and as a result do not extend to agents in the position of the respondents whose activities are excepted as being "otherwise provided by law."

This interpretation is fortified by a consideration of s. 1 of the *Solicitors Act* by itself. The Act now deals entirely with solicitor-and-client accounts and it is logical for it to include the prohibition against charges for unauthorized practice. Contempt of court is the other penalty for unauthorized practice contained in s. 1. It is inconceivable that agents acting under the authority of other statutes could be held in contempt of court and this is a further indication that the Legislature intended s. 1 of the *Solicitors Act* to be merely ancillary to s. 50(1) of the *Law Society Act*.

It is ironic that there is lack of clarity in the statutes governing the legal profession and their application to the respondent. I commend for the Legislature's attention the clarification of this legislation and also the status of agents and other paralegals which is now a matter of considerable public discussion.

For the foregoing reasons, I would dismiss the appeals with costs.

Appeal dismissed.

NOTES AND QUESTIONS

1. Do you agree with the result reached by the court in this case? Do you find its reasoning persuasive? Should the court have stated directly that the prohibition against collecting fees in s. 1 of the Solicitors Act was anachronistic? Would it have had to appeal to higher authority such as the Charter to arrive at such a conclusion?

2. There are many issues around paralegals not the least of which is the appropriate boundaries and relations of power between a more established, prestigious profession and one that intrudes on its territory. Similar issues have existed around doctors and midwives, dentists and denturists, accountants and bookkeepers. In this situation, is it appropriate that the established profession should have anything to do with regulating the "intruder," or does the established profession, more than any other, know the issues and how they ought to be addressed, and, therefore, ought to be closely involved? For a series of unadopted recommendations on paralegals, see R. Ianni, Report of the Task Force on Paralegals (1990).

3. Is the toleration of paralegals or even their encouragement by governments primarily about providing another means of access to legal assistance, or is it primarily about governments, ostensibly doing something but, in fact, transferring the burden of the costs of any such services to the public, many of whom might become consumers of government funded services such as legal aid?

4. Do you agree with the claim that the proliferation of paralegal services will result in a two-tier system of justice, with the well-to-do having access to lawyers and the less well-off having access to paralegals?

5. The performance of legal services by persons other than lawyers, and the consequent "deprofessionalization" of the law, is regarded by many as an important step towards the empowerment of oppressed persons. The model for community legal aid

clinics draws on this belief in its incorporation of "community legal workers." In theory (and in some instances in practice) these workers are individuals who are members of the client community that the clinic serves. Either through their work with the clinic, or as a result of earlier experiences, they are persons who have come to know a substantial amount about the law, and its impact on the particular community of which they are a member. These individuals provide direct client service to the community and, in addition, engage in work designed to address the systemic nature of many of the problems faced by the community. These latter efforts largely take the form of community organizing and education. The delivery of legal services by community members helps to ensure that more individuals have access to legal services that are culturally and socially relevant to their experiences. But perhaps more important, both the manner of delivery (by a community member) and the content of what is delivered (organizing and education) may contribute to the empowerment of community members. The empowerment of community members may come about in two related ways: (1) community members come to understand the nature of law, its permeability, and the role that it may play in maintaining the conditions of their oppression; and (2) they become the agents of social change, rather than the objects of the actions of well-intentioned lawyers. See Fernando Rojas, "A Comparison of Change-Oriented Legal Services in Latin America with Legal Services in North America and Europe" (1988), 16 *International Journal of the Sociology of Law* 203, and Carrie Menkel-Meadow, "Now-Professional Advocacy: The 'Paralegalization' of Legal Services to the Poor" (1985), *Clearinghouse Review* 403.

Barbara Whitaker, "Possible Legal Software Ban Raises Free Speech Issue"
The New York Times, February 7, 1999

HOUSTON—It may look like a computer disk, but in the eyes of a federal judge in Texas it behaves too much like a lawyer.

In a ruling last month thought to be the first of its type in the country, Judge Barefoot Sanders of US District Court in Dallas found that Parsons Technology Inc., which publishes Quicken Family Lawyer and Quicken Family Lawyer '99, goes too far in the assistance it provides consumers, resulting in an unauthorized practice of law in the state.

The state's Unauthorized Practice of Law Committee, which sued Parsons, says it will seek to ban the sale of the software in Texas, raising First Amendment concerns. In addition, the case is highlighting arguments about whether the committee is protecting the public from shoddy legal practices or further alienating consumers already priced out of the market for lawyers.

The Quicken software provides more than 100 different legal forms, instructions on how to fill them out and assistance in tailoring the documents to the user's situation.

Parsons, based in Berkeley, Calif., and a unit of Broderbund Software, argued that it had not engaged in the unauthorized practice of law because there had to be some form of contact between publisher and consumer for that to happen. Parsons also said that interfering with the sale of its software would be a violation of the First Amendment right of free speech.

But Sanders found that "Parsons, through QFL, has gone beyond publishing a sample form book with instructions, and has ventured into the unauthorized practice of law." He also found that although there was some restriction on free speech, it was in keeping with the state's interest in protecting "the uninformed and unwary from overly simplistic legal advice."

Mark Ticer, a lawyer for the committee, said he would move to have the company banned from selling Quicken legal software in the state.

Darrell Jordan, who represented Parsons, said he would offer more information and ask the judge to reconsider his position once the injunction was requested. If that failed, he said, he would seek to delay sales limits during appeals.

Software publishers said Texas was alone in its aggressive scrutiny of legal self-help material. But the case is being watched closely. Some software dealers say they steer clear of the state.

The case has also focused attention on whether the Unauthorized Practice of Law Committee is serving the people's interests. The panel, responsible for enforcing the practice-of-law statute, is made up of six lawyers and three nonlawyers, appointed by the Supreme Court of Texas.

"Most of the people who buy this program cannot afford to go to a lawyer," said Jane Winn, an associate professor specializing in the law of electronic commerce at Southern Methodist University in Dallas. "If you take this program away from the people who are using it today, what access do they have to information about their rights?"

Walt Borges, director of Court Watch, a project in Austin that monitors the courts, criticized the committee for promoting a "monopoly of law" and for operating in secret. "Before anybody bans a self-help product they need to be darn sure that this will harm the public," he said.

The committee's secretive operations are already being challenged in the Texas Supreme Court by Nolo Press, which publishes a number of self-help legal manuals.

Ticer defended the committee's right to operate with confidentiality, explaining that the members do their own investigations and could be hampered if their identities were known.

He also countered accusations that the committee was simply trying to protect lawyers' interests in the state. "We don't have an agenda," Ticer said. "We just carry out the statute."

NOTES AND QUESTIONS

1. Does the *Quicken* decision make sense? What arguments are there for and against?

2. If the *Quicken* decision is sound, does it make a difference if the software developer is giving it away free? If the decision is unsound, how far can the developer go? Can the developer offer a customer help line to deal with followup questions users may have?

3. If the *Quicken* decision is sound, does it make any difference if the software was written by a lawyer? By the very best family lawyer in the jurisdiction? Assume that Joe Blow, who is licensed to practise law in the jurisdiction (but knows very little family

law), prepares the software and sells it personally and under his own name. Is this the unauthorized practice of law? Why?

4. What if the software in *Quicken* was produced by a legal publisher and sold only to the legal profession?

5. Is it relevant that lawyers may not exempt themselves from liability for negligence and the *Quicken* software has a broad disclaimer clause? What if in a given jurisdiction there is no mandatory requirement that lawyers carry liability insurance?

6. Assume that "electronic kiosks" are established outside family courts to assist litigants in person to represent themselves, explaining all aspects of the courts' operations, how to complete forms, etc., and explaining the applicable law. Is this the unauthorized practice of law? Does it make a difference if the kiosk is operated by the bar association, the court itself, or by a private entrepreneur?

7. What are the arguments for and against having the legal profession "police" the unauthorized practice of law? In this context, is the judiciary part of the legal profession?

8. What is the rationale for forbidding the unauthorized practice of law—consumer protection? Protection of a monopoly for the legal profession?

9. Do we (the legal profession) want the public to understand the law and how to use it unaided by lawyers?

D. Innovative Reforms

As the courts and legal profession become more sensitive to the difficulties surrounding access to justice, there have been several innovative efforts to combat the problem. One that has been introduced is in the area of class actions where, in certain circumstances, representative plaintiffs can apply to a fund to have certain expenses and disbursements subsidised. This fund is maintained by a tax on the costs of successful plaintiffs (see chapter 5, "Commencement of Proceedings." For an analysis of some of the special funds, see L. Fox, "Costs in Public-Interest Litigation" (1989), 10 *Advocates' Quarterly* 385.

Another innovative suggestion is to allow cost shifting, but to determine its extent by reference to the characteristics of the litigation or litigants. As you read the following extract, recall the models of litigation presented in chapter 2, "The Value of Procedure." How, if at all, are the ideas concerning the "public model" of litigation related to the ideas presented in this section?

Ontario Law Reform Commission, *Report on the Law of Standing*
(Toronto: Queen's Printer, 1989), 137-76 (footnotes omitted)

This Report addressed the circumstances where plaintiffs without a traditional legal interest—a personal, proprietary or pecuniary claim—ought nevertheless be allowed to litigate issues of sufficient importance. (Most such questions revolve around the concept of "standing" which will be addressed in detail in a later chapter.) The Report proposed a liberalized regime for recognizing entitlement to sue and then turned to the issue of costs. ...

In [a previous chapter], we made recommendations to reform the substantive basis of standing in Ontario. As we explained, one of our purposes in making these proposals was to allow a broader range of issues of public importance to be brought before the courts for adjudication. Earlier in this chapter, we concluded that, under the present costs regime in Ontario, many, perhaps even most, plaintiffs will be discouraged from commencing proceedings raising issues of this nature. Without recapitulating that discussion, suffice it to state that, where plaintiffs lack a personal, proprietary, or pecuniary interest in the litigation, or where they possess such an interest, but its value is exceeded by the potential expense of the litigation, they will be effectively deterred. This deterrent effect threatens to frustrate the standing reforms that we have proposed. In the absence of an economic interest in the outcome of the proceedings, any plaintiff, but particularly an individual with limited financial resources, is in a disadvantageous position in relation to a defendant, who is usually a major actor—a government, a large corporation, or trade union. As a result, a person's right of standing, in practice, may be an empty one.

However, not all litigation of issues having a widespread impact will necessarily involve a problem of access. Where a plaintiff has an economic interest in the proceedings of a magnitude that exceeds the potential expense of the proceedings, a disincentive to litigation cannot be said to exist. Rarely will we find this situation in "public interest" litigation.

We are concerned, therefore, about the economic barrier that the existing cost rules will represent for many of those wishing to take advantage of our standing proposals. From this concern arises two interrelated questions. First, in what circumstances is it justifiable to alter the costs rules in order to surmount that barrier? Second, how should the costs rules be changed to achieve that objective? In the balance of this chapter, we shall address these questions. ...

We turn first to discuss the circumstances in which the costs regime should be changed.

Our basic concern that access to the courts should not be effectively undermined suggests a combination of four prerequisites, which together define when a departure from the existing rules is justifiable. We shall discuss three of the criteria at this juncture. We shall later discuss a fourth criterion, which focuses on the characteristics of the defendant, and follows from the particular departure from the costs rules we propose.

The first prerequisite reflects the main rationale for reforming the standing rules: certain issues should not unjustifiably be prevented from being adjudicated. Thus, we recommend that the costs rules should be changed where the proceeding involves issues the importance of which extends beyond the immediate interests of the parties involved. We acknowledge that this is a very general statement of principle. However, in focusing on the larger significance of the issues it does identify what we regard as a crucial factor.

Under certain circumstances, this factor may comprehend an action brought by a person with a traditional legal interest. However, an ordinary action alleging a breach of contract or negligence would not satisfy it, unless it contained significant issues that transcended the litigation itself. The mere impact of proceedings through *stare decisis* should not be sufficient in itself to bring a proceeding within this criterion.

The second prerequisite follows from our fundamental concern about access to the courts. That concern, of course, extends only to those prospective plaintiffs who would be deterred from litigation by the existing costs regime. We are therefore not concerned with plaintiffs whose interest in the proceedings, in nature and degree, constitutes a sufficient counterweight to the disincentives inherent in the existing costs regime, especially the party and party costs rule. Accordingly, the second criterion we recommend is that the person has no person, pecuniary or proprietary interest in the outcome of the proceeding, or, if he has such an interest, it clearly does not justify the proceeding economically.

By including a plaintiff who has a personal, pecuniary, or proprietary interest, but one that does not justify the litigation economically, this criterion would extend favourable costs treatment to persons having traditional legal interests. While our proposals to reform the law of standing are directed primarily at litigants who lack traditional legal interests, we are of the view that our costs reforms should comprehend plaintiffs raising equally important issues, but who remain effectively foreclosed from litigating by a costs barrier. As an example of circumstances in which this criterion might be applied, we suggest the unsuccessful class action brought in *Naken v. General Motors Ltd.*, where the plaintiffs raised important questions about the interpretation of the class action rule, but personally stood to gain only $1,000.

[This case is dealt with in chapter 5, "Commencement of Proceedings."]

The third criterion reflects our concern that the present costs rules will prevent certain important issues from being litigated at all. Accordingly, if the issue has already been adjudicated, there is no reason to assist a person wishing to initiate another action respecting the same issue. For example, where a court has already refused an injunction sought by a canoeist to enjoin activity causing pollution, another canoeist subsequently bringing a similar proceeding raising identical issues should not be able to receive favourable costs treatment. Hence, we recommend that the third criterion should be that the issues have not been previously determined by a court in a proceeding against the same defendant.

[A discussion concerning a public fund that was rejected as a second best solution because of the struggle for funds and administrative burdens is omitted.]

(b) Party and Party Costs

Earlier in this chapter, we concluded that the party and party costs rule will present a formidable deterrent to litigation by persons advancing non-traditional legal interests. While the burden of paying solicitor and client costs may occasionally be alleviated, in whole or in part—for example, if a lawyer were willing to represent the plaintiff on a *pro bono* basis, or if financial assistance were provided from government or other sources—the risk of an order of party and party costs nonetheless would remain. Should the threat of an adverse costs award continue to apply, our standing reforms will have little, if any, effect. The potential costs liability of a plaintiff must therefore be removed. ...

[A discussion of the *Report of the Task Force on Legal Aid* (1974), which took a similar position, is omitted.]

Once there is a preliminary decision that the costs liability of plaintiffs should be removed, whether generally or, as we have proposed, in defined circumstances, the next question is whether defendants should receive the same treatment or should continue to be at risk for party and party costs. The choice, then, is between a so-called "no way rule," analogous to the "American rule" governing attorney fees, or a "one way rule." Under a no way rule, party and party costs cannot be awarded to a successful party simply by reason of the result in the action; costs, however, may be awarded in response to misconduct in the course of the litigation. Under a one way rule, while a plaintiff would be immune from having party and party costs awarded against him only by reason of being unsuccessful in the action, costs may be awarded against an unsuccessful defendant. Indeed, a one way scheme might be structured to *require* that costs be ordered against unsuccessful defendants.

From the perspective of the plaintiff, the one way costs rule is certainly more advantageous, particularly if the rule requires that costs be awarded to her in the event of success. A successful plaintiff, in addition to being generally immune from an adverse costs order, would be responsible for only that part of his solicitor and client costs not indemnified by an award of party and party costs against the defendant. By contrast, under a no way rule, a successful plaintiff would bear the full burden of his lawyer's costs, regardless of the outcome of the proceedings. Thus, for prospective plaintiffs, a considerable disincentive inheres in a no way rule.

In considering the choice between a no way rule and a one way rule, it is important to recall the two functions that the costs follow the event rule is said to serve. Earlier in this chapter, we stated that the most commonly cited purposes are indemnification of successful parties and discouragement of unmeritorious litigation. In the Anglo-Canadian world, these two functions have been so generally accepted that they seem to be sacrosanct. Proposing a change to the party and party costs rule thus places a burden on us to justify compromising these functions.

Turning first to the indemnification function, we suggest that it is useful to begin by asking what precisely is the purpose of indemnifying successful parties. Indemnification is said to "compensate" the successful party for the expense of vindicating his position. The notion of compensation, however, has been understood traditionally to refer to payments to recompense a party for the injury occasioned by the fault of another. Yet, under the two way rule, indemnification follows victory automatically, without regard to whether the unsuccessful party has been "wrong" in bringing or defending the action. Costs are routinely awarded against losing parties, even those who have been entirely reasonable in litigating and who have lost "a close case." Unless failure in the underlying action is itself regarded as a "wrong" for which compensation should be given, in addition to whatever remedy is ordered, it is difficult to ascribe a true compensatory purpose to the rule. Rather, it resembles "a species of strict liability": indemnification follows inexorably from failure, not from attribution of fault.

The second rationale for the rule is that it deters unmeritorious claims and specious defences, and thus acts as a filter for litigation. Few would dispute that the risk of an adverse costs award discourages frivolous claims and defences. Yet, in our view, the threat inherent in the rule is too broad in its effect, for undoubtedly meritorious claims and defences are embraced as well, especially where a party is risk averse. To the extent that the rule deters litigation, regardless of substantive merit, it acts, in our view, as an inappropriate filter.

In its operation, then, the party and party costs rule is a blunt tool, which has an effect extending beyond the purposes that it is claimed to serve. While indemnification of successful parties does perform a true compensatory function in some cases, the virtual inevitability of the practice means that winning parties will receive indemnification even where their adversaries are not at fault. Similarly, when combined with other factors relating to the characteristics of the parties and their stake in the action, the inevitability of that result deters a wide field of proceedings, not just those so lacking in merit that they should not be initiated or brought to trial.

Seen in this light, the party and party costs rule, we suggest, should not be regarded as inviolate, despite its long acceptance as an integral feature of our system of civil justice. In making these observations, however, we must emphasize that we are not concerned about the party and party costs rule generally, but with the effect of its application on the type of litigation that is the main focus of this report, and with whether, and the extent to which, it is justifiable to depart from the rule in this context.

We have concluded that the no way costs rule is not an appropriate solution in this context. We have already explained that a change is warranted where the plaintiff has no personal, pecuniary, or proprietary claim in the proceedings or, if she does, its value does not justify the litigation economically. For such a plaintiff, the no way costs rule offers only the appearance of equality. In reality, regardless of the equal treatment of the parties, as in the case of the party and party costs rule, plaintiff and defendants will be unequally affected by whatever economic incentives are in effect. By definition, the plaintifff has little or nothing to gain personally from the proceedings, but must incur legal expenses to proceed. Whatever deterrence is thus entailed would be increased where the plaintiff also is risk averse. This would tend to be the case if the plaintiff were an individual of modest resources or a person who rarely, if ever, engaged in litigation— a so-called "one shotter."

By contrast, a defendant capable of inflicting a diffuse harm would tend to be a person for whom the costs of defending an action could not be so daunting. Such a defendant often would be a "repeat player," who would be risk neutral to litigation.

Due to the inherent inequality in the positions of plaintiff and defendant in the circumstances with which we are concerned, we have no doubt that a no way rule cannot operate in a balanced fashion. Support for our conclusion can be found in the American experience in the federal courts. As a practical matter, the American rule proved inadequate to the task of facilitating litigation to enforce certain federal statutes. Congress therefore has enacted numerous fee shifting provisions that allowed or required fees to be paid to successful plaintiffs. ...

While it may not be apparent, by proposing a costs immunity, except in the case of improper conduct, we have recommended what may be regarded as an intermediate position. To redress the inherent imbalance between plaintiff and defendant, the Commission could have adopted a form of one way rule that would have required courts to award costs to successful plaintiffs. In addition, a one way rule might have specified that costs must be awarded on a solicitor and client basis. We have left the scale of costs to the court. We considered that, since indemnification on the higher solicitor and client scale generally has been awarded to successful parties only as a response to misconduct by their adversaries, mandatory full indemnification in the context of a one way rule would be unduly harsh and inequitable. As a consequence, even where the stipulated criteria are met, under our proposal the successful plaintiff will remain personally responsible for that part of her solicitor and client costs that is not indemnified by an award of party and party costs, subject to her arrangements with her lawyer.

Notwithstanding our belief that a one way rule is justifiable to redress the imbalance between plaintiff and defendant where the plaintiff has little or no personal economic interest in the proceedings, we are concerned that this rule not prejudice defendants unjustifiably. For this reason, we are of the view that the costs immunity should be further confined to circumstances where the defendant has a clearly superior capacity to bear the costs of the proceeding. This, then, is the fourth prerequisite that we recommend. Where this criterion is met, a defendant will not be seriously affected by either an adverse costs award or the failure to recover party and party costs from a losing plaintiff. Where the defendant is no better able to afford the litigation than the plaintiff, a one way rule, we suggest, would be inequitable.

In determining whether the defendant has a superior capacity to pay litigation costs, we expect that the court would ascertain if, and to what extent, the defendant can absorb the costs or pass them on to others. Where the government is the defendant, costs would be passed on through the vehicle of taxation, and would thus fall on the general taxpaying population. In the case of large corporations, the burden will either be shifted to the consumers or result in diminished profits.

With the introduction of a one way rule, the indemnification function performed by the existing party and party costs rule will, of course, be partially lost. Indeed, this is the essence of the one way rule that we have proposed as a solution to the access problem in the context.

With respect to the function of filtering out specious claims, we have no doubt that this is very important to the administration of justice. We suggest that this objective will be met by the prerequisite that the issues have an importance extending beyond the interests of the parties involved. Such issues would not be frivolous or specious, even though the proceedings might ultimately be unsuccessful. Furthermore, it should be noted that the danger of frivolous or vexatious actions is addressed by the Rules of Civil Procedure.

We realize that it might be argued that reliance on these existing mechanisms and on the requirement that issues be important addresses claims only at one end of the spectrum. The party and party costs rule would discourage not only these claims, but in addition, *bona fide* claims that are not frivolous and vexatious, but ultimately unmeritorious. Since these "better" unmeritorious claims would no longer be discouraged, defendants would have to bear the costs of defending them, a cost that, by definition, could not be shifted in the absence of misconduct.

To this argument, we offer a simple answer: any loss of deterrence, resulting in the litigation of *bona fide*, although ultimately unmeritorious claims, is the justifiable price for allowing the adjudication of meritorious claims that otherwise would be barred.

Before turning to solicitor and client costs, there are two further matters that we wish to address. The first concerns the possibility of awarding costs in favour of an unsuccessful plaintiff. We are aware of certain proposals in favour of a "mandatory" one way rule, which would require that costs be awarded to a plaintiff, regardless of the outcome of the action, thus removing the remaining financial disincentive to potential plaintiffs. Such a rule has been supported by a deterrence rationale, on the premise that it "could promote greater care by potential defendants when engaging in conduct which may offend public rights." Furthermore, it has been suggested that this rule is easier to justify where the defendant is government, and the constitutionality or legality of its actions are in issue.

We have rejected a rule requiring that costs be awarded to plaintiffs as entirely inappropriate. We consider that a one way rule of the nature that we have proposed to be a substantial, and sufficient, departure from the present law, and the proper balance to be struck, in this context.

In rejecting this alternative, we do not wish to be taken to oppose the possibility that costs might be awarded in favour of an unsuccessful plaintiff. Rule 57.01(2) of the Rules of Civil Procedure provides that "[t]he fact that a party is successful in a proceeding or a step in a proceeding does not prevent the court from awarding costs against the party in a proper case." In the past, costs generally were awarded against successful parties only where there has been some misconduct on their part. Since this is a new rule, it seems reasonable to conclude that the reference to "a proper case" does not codify the earlier case law. At present, there is no reason to expect that courts would interpret the rule in a restrictive manner, and consequently it is unnecessary for us to make a specific proposal that the courts should expressly be given this discretion in this context.

Finally, we wish to address the timing of the determination whether a plaintiff is to be immune from an award of party and party costs. If the question is decided at the end of the proceedings, as in ordinary actions, the plaintiff would be left with an uncertainty similar to that inherent in the existing party and party costs rule. While it might be somewhat easier to anticipate whether the proposed criteria for immunity would be met than to predict success on the merits, prospective plaintiffs nevertheless would be unsure whether they would have to pay the defendant's party and party costs, in addition to their own solicitor and client costs, should they lose. For plaintiffs having little or no personal financial interest in the proceedings, the possibility that a court ultimately might find that the requisite criteria have not been satisfied would, in many cases, be sufficient a disincentive to discourage them from proceeding. Without providing an assurance of a general immunity, subject, of course, to costs being awarded in the event of misconduct, the purpose of our basic costs proposal would likely be frustrated.

We believe that the solution to this difficulty is simply to allow a motion to be made at any time in the proceeding for a declaratory order determining whether the plaintiff has an immunity from party and party costs, and we so recommend. ...

If the factual basis of the application is too unsettled to allow the court to decide the motion, the determination could be postponed until later in the proceedings. Requesting the court to make a declaration need not entail an additional, and possibly disruptive, step in the proceedings. Where a defendant brings a motion to challenge a plaintiff's standing, on the hearing of that motion, the plaintiff could request the declaratory order.

[The report then went on to discuss and recommend a form of contingency fees to cover solicitor–client costs.]

V. THE PUBLIC FUNDING OF LITIGATION

A. Institutional Support

Although litigation is largely funded by the litigants, there is a sizable public contribution to the maintenance of the litigation process. The state assumes responsibility for the provision of buildings, judges, and support staff. A small charge is made for the issuing of various documents, but the major portion of these other expenses is assumed by the state. There is a division of responsibility between the federal and provincial governments. In accordance with the Constitution, the federal government funds the federal court system, the Supreme Court of Canada, and the salaries of the provincial superior district and county courts. The provincial governments assumes financial responsibility for the administration and costs of all courts in the province, and for the salaries of lower court judges.

B. Legal Aid

The primary means of public support of certain parties in litigation is legal aid. As you read the following extracts, focus on the question how should society decide who gets legal aid and for what purposes? In answering this question are we led back to the one posed at the beginning of this chapter, What is wrong with allowing people to have as much or as little law (justice) as they are willing to pay for and can afford? If, by contrast, you conclude that there is a basic entitlement to justice, how do we assure that this is obtainable? Also, in a society that seems intent on curbing the role of the state in social affairs, how realistic is it to imagine that there will be a significant appetite to fund legal aid programs adequately?

The two extracts that follow seek to place present legal arrangements in a broad context. The first extract looks to the public policy justifications for providing legal aid and asks whether it is possible to provide a rank-ordering of legal aid needs and expenditures. The second extract introduces the basic structure of legal aid delivery schemes and assesses future challenges.

A Blueprint for Publicly Funded Legal Services
Report of the Ontario Legal Aid Review (Toronto: Queen's Printer, 1997), 67-74
(footnotes omitted)

In order to identify the underlying moral or political justification for the state's obligation to provide legal aid, if indeed it has one, some basic issues of political or democratic theory must be considered. Our purpose in doing so is to inform our understanding of how priority-setting, as a matter of principle, might best be conducted in the legal aid context. It might be assumed that the most fruitful analytical path for achieving this purpose is to identify the normative justifications for the state's obligation to provide legal aid in particular contexts, such as criminal law and family law, and evaluate those justifications with a view to placing them in an order that would suggest, at the level of general principle, that preference should be given to the funding of criminal law or family law legal aid or vice versa.

We have come to the conclusion that such an approach is not fruitful. In coming to this conclusion, we have been much influenced by a thoughtful background paper prepared for the Review by Professor David Dyzenhaus. Indeed, in his view, this approach, which he terms the "box approach," is misguided. In what follows we suggest that the underlying normative foundation for the state's obligation to provide some form of legal aid is to be found in Canadians' shared commitment to the Rule of Law as an essential feature of the Canadian political system. Further, we attempt to demonstrate why the "box approach" to priority-setting is not satisfactory and, more particularly, why a preoccupation with the value of avoiding incarceration, or "negative liberty," will distort priority-setting for legal aid. Finally, we identify the implications of these conclusions for legal aid priority-setting.

(a) Legal Aid and the Rule of Law

The development of democratic societies has been accompanied by the adoption of the notion of the Rule of Law—the replacement of rule by arbitrary measures or by unchecked discretion with rule by law. A well-known statement of the centrality of the concept of the Rule of Law is that of F.A. Hayek, in his essay "Planning and the Rule of Law."

> Nothing distinguishes more clearly conditions in a free country from those in a country under arbitrary government than the observance in the former of the great principles known as the Rule of Law. Stripped of all its technicalities, this means that government in all its actions is bound by rules fixed and announced beforehand—rules which make it possible to foresee with fair certainty how the authority will use its force and powers in given circumstances and to plan one's individual affairs on the basis of this knowledge.

Two features of the concept of the Rule of Law are particularly relevant in the present context. First, it is inherent in the notion of substituting or replacing arbitrary measures with legal rules that the rules can be known. As Hayek says, the rules must be fixed and announced beforehand. Dyzenhaus refers to this as the "publicity" condition of law. Secret law is anathema in a democratic society. The promise of a democratic society that each of its citizens will have equal protection under its laws will be empty if that society fails to meet the publicity condition.

Second, it is implicit in the notion of the Rule of Law that the state's obligation is not one of merely disclosing the law, but rather one of disclosing the law in a fashion which makes it accessible to the individual. Individuals must have access to the law, in the sense that they are enabled to understand their obligations or their rights, as against the state, and to plan their affairs accordingly.

The link between the Rule of Law, then, and an obligation of some kind imposed upon the state to provide assistance to citizens in facilitating their understanding of the law is this: If a state enacts or develops laws which are so complex that many of those who are subject to those laws cannot acquire equal, or perhaps any, understanding of them, such that they can neither understand nor use them, the laws to which they are subject do not meet the publicity condition. There is arguably, therefore, a state obligation of some kind to facilitate meaningful access to its laws. If, for example, our criminal law or social assistance or family law has become very complex, as indeed it has in many areas, the fact that many citizens cannot, without the state's assistance, respond to or cope with that law suggests that the Rule of Law will be undermined if that assistance is not forthcoming.

We do not wish to suggest, however, that the commitment of Canadians to the concept of the Rule of Law leads inescapably to the conclusion that the state has an unlimited obligation to provide, at public expense, lawyers to all citizens who encounter difficulty in obtaining access to any particular law. Rather, our point is a more modest one. In a democratic society committed to the Rule of Law, a publicity condition is inherent in the use of law by the state, and the complexity of that law may, in turn, impose an obligation on the state to facilitate access to the effective use of that law in some fashion. The more complex the law in question, and the greater its impact on individuals who lack the means to acquire help in understanding it, the more intense will be the burdens imposed on the state by the publicity condition. The individual's interest in or entitlement to access to the law thus appears to be inherent in a decision by the state to utilize law to accomplish a particular social or political objective.

While we do not believe that the foregoing principles are controversial, it must be noted that the concept of the Rule of Law is a source of important controversies on questions of political theory and the proper role of law and the state. Hayek, for example, would argue that governments should be reluctant to use law to intervene in the lives of individuals. His premise is the libertarian one: that the space of "negative liberty" (one's liberty to do as one pleases) should be left as large as is consistent with maintaining minimal public order. Intervention beyond that minimum requirement would, in his view, introduce unnecessary uncertainty into the law.

Other theorists argue that the virtue of the Rule of Law is merely instrumental, in the sense that law can be used to implement political values other than that of "negative liberty." Still others would argue that the ideal of the Rule of Law is equality, and attempt to show a necessary connection between the Rule of Law and liberal or democratic political philosophies. As one can imagine, across the broad spectrum of opinion of this kind, one encounters serious debates as to the appropriateness of government regulation of certain activities, the extent to which health care and other social benefits should be seen as entitlements, and so on.

For our purposes, these controversies concerning the ideological content of the notion of the Rule of Law, are, we believe, beside the point. The publicity condition, and the consequent obligation of the state to facilitate meaningful access to the use of law, flow from a decision by the state to use law. These ideological controversies, of course, relate to the question of whether or not the state should use law in the first place. Once that decision has been taken, however, the publicity condition is engaged, and the state is implicated in the problem of ensuring access to the law. This ideological debate is beside the point for our purposes, then, because the legal system in Canada and in Ontario has clearly taken a position that laws—and often very cumbersome ones—will be utilized to implement a broad range of values and programs. Thus, while some may wish to debate whether or not particular uses of law are appropriate, there is no doubt that its widespread use is already entailed in the law of Ontario and Canada and has become part of our social and legal fabric. In short, legal aid must take the legal system as it finds it.

As a matter of principle, then, the underlying rationale for the state's obligation to facilitate access to the law is not restricted to any particular kind of law or type of legal situation. The normative foundations for legal aid do not assist us in making an argument for giving priority to one domain of law over another in terms of access to legal aid resources.

One further implication of some importance can be drawn from the relationship of the Rule of Law, through the publicity condition, to the state's obligation to facilitate access to the law. To the extent that the law is needlessly complex or in some other respect designed in a manner that indirectly or, indeed, directly requires legal advice and assistance, it may be that the legal regime in question has unnecessarily imposed burdens on the state to facilitate access to the law. If, for example, the defective design of a particular statutory scheme makes it necessary that individualized legal problems be handled on a case-by-case basis, the defect in question will have imposed on the parties, and upon the state, a very expensive burden. In some instances, then, the state's obligation to facilitate access might be much better served by removing the defect from the statutory scheme. This is, in our view, an important point, and one which we discuss at some length in chapter 6 of this report.

(b) Beyond "Negative Liberty"

Having set out our conclusion that an examination of the normative foundations of legal aid does not provide a principled basis for giving priority access to legal aid resources to one legal domain over another, we must consider at some length a serious argument to the contrary. Some would suggest that it is easiest to justify imposition of an obligation on the state to fund legal aid in the criminal law context. Two reasons for this suggestion are typically offered.

First, it is suggested that it is in the domain of criminal law that the accused individual is at risk of losing his or her physical liberty, and this factor engages the important value we place on not losing one's freedom, or the "negative liberty" interest. Second, in the context of criminal law, the accused is pitted against the massive resources of the state, and it may be argued that simple obligations of fairness require the state to provide assistance to an accused person facing such an unequal contest. For reasons such as these, it is arguable that the allocation of public resources to legal aid in the criminal law context can be defended on grounds that are unrelated to the publicity condition and the Rule of Law.

It is important that these arguments be examined carefully in the present context as it appears that considerations of this kind lead some to argue either that legal aid for criminal law should trump legal aid in other domains such as family or "poverty law," or that, within the domain of criminal law, the "negative party" interest should trump the need for legal aid resources in cases where no significant risk of incarceration is present. Our response to these suggestions is that, on closer examination, the "negative liberty" test does not seem to be capable of drawing satisfactory distinctions between criminal law and other legal domains, or indeed of establishing a satisfactory priority test within the domain of criminal law itself.

The appeal of the "negative liberty" test or principle may arise from the fact that most observers would agree that it identifies a factual situation in which a compelling case for some form of legal aid is made. What the principle appears to be incapable of doing, however, is successfully identifying contrasting situations in which either no legal aid is appropriate or only some inherently lesser claim to legal aid can be made. Thus, within the domain of criminal law, for example, it is not difficult to imagine cases involving no risk of incarceration in which the claim for legal aid appears stronger than in some kinds of cases involving that risk. Thus, a young adult charged with a first offence who has difficulty communicating and for whom a conviction might result in a loss of employment and other negative consequences that may flow from acquiring a criminal record may appear to make a stronger claim for legal aid than someone who has been convicted several times before, faces an overwhelming and uncomplicated case, is able to communicate and is knowledgeable about the justice system, and risks only a short period of incarceration about which he or she is not particularly troubled.

It is simply incorrect, then, to suggest that in any case where incarceration is a risk because of, for example, a failure to appear, the claim for legal aid resources is inescapably stronger than in any other case where physical liberty is not at risk. This suggests that there are other values or interests at stake in considering the allocation of legal aid resources within the context of criminal law. It may be difficult to articulate the nature of the broader range of interests at issue—Dyzenhaus has suggested that a broader notion of personal autonomy may be illuminating—but the important point for our purposes is that there appears to be a plurality of interests underlying the claim for legal aid in the context of criminal law, and that "negative liberty" cannot serve as a reliable guide to the cases most deserving of legal aid.

Similarly, the "negative liberty" test is not particularly helpful in drawing clear distinctions for priority-setting purposes between criminal law and other legal domains. In the first place, it can be and has been argued that "negative liberty" interests are often at stake in other legal domains. In refugee determinations, for example, the unsuccessful claimants may well face a period of incarceration, or worse, if returned to their jurisdiction of origin. The involuntary civil commitment of a psychiatric patient, although clearly not a criminal law matter, unquestionably engages the "negative liberty" interest. In the family law context, some observers have argued, in effect, that "negative liberty" issues are often at stake. Thus, for example, where an administrative agency threatens to remove a child from the family home because of an allegedly unsafe environment, the situation might be characterized as involving "negative liberty" (at least for the child) and, indeed, as one which places the family in a contest with a powerful agency of the state. Cases of domestic violence where the victim is in need of legal assistance simply to get out of the home or to establish any freedom of movement in the community may also be considered to engage the "negative liberty" interest. In short, the boundaries between the domains based on the "negative liberty" test begin to crumble on closer examination.

More important, perhaps, the kinds of cases in these other domains which would fail a "negative liberty" test are not necessarily less deserving than many criminal law "negative liberty" cases. Where, for example, an unemployed single parent is seeking to enforce legal entitlements to housing or to sources of income, such as workers' compensation, employment insurance, or welfare, the claim for access to legal aid resources may appear stronger than the claim of someone charged for the second time with impaired driving who may face a short period of incarceration if convicted. Indeed, it may well be that an opinion survey of people experiencing poverty would reveal that they rank claims for legal assistance to enforce their entitlement to the basic necessities of life somewhat higher, as a general proposition, than claims they, too, might make for legal aid in criminal law matters.

Further, within other domains, the inability of the "negative liberty" test to function as a sure guide to the most important cases repeats itself. Thus, in the context of family law, while it may well be the case generally that situations of physical abuse can make a greater claim to legal aid resources than those where it is not present, generalizations of this kind tell us very little about the claim of a particular woman in a situation of non-physical abuse. Nor is it difficult to imagine situations in which the health or safety of a spouse or children may be at risk in a case not involving physical abuse where the claim for legal aid resources may appear to be at least as strong as that in some cases involving physical abuse. Custody claims where the current custodial parent poses a grave threat to the emotional health of a vulnerable child offer one illustration of this point.

Focusing on the "negative liberty" interest as a test for the worthiness of claims to legal aid resources, then, leads to a number of difficulties or distortions. First, the "negative liberty" test tantalizingly suggests a clear basis for assigning priority to the need for legal aid resources in criminal law over other areas of law and, within criminal law, for granting priority to cases involving the risk of incarceration. And yet, when the ability of the "negative liberty" test to accomplish these objectives is examined carefully, it appears incapable of providing persuasive grounds for drawing such distinctions.

Second, when a focus on "negative liberty" is extended to other legal domains, it obscures the analysis of priority-setting in those domains. For example, an attempt to set priorities on the basis of the "negative liberty" test appears to obscure the interests at stake in the family law context. Although a case in which a social service agency threatens to remove a child from his or her home may be said to engage the child's "negative liberty" interest, the interests at stake in such a case are not fully, or even best, characterized as related to "negative liberty." Here the invasion of liberty is not designed as punishment, but rather as the product of a decision, however misguided it might be, that removal of the child from the home is, in the agency's view, in the best interests of the child.

Finally, focusing on the "negative liberty" test as a basis for identifying priorities for legal aid runs the risk, especially in the context of capped funding, of creating a legal aid system which favours the interests of men, who are normally those accused of crime, as opposed to those of women, who are more frequently in need of family law or related "poverty law" services than are men. In the recent debates on legal aid in Ontario, many have commented on the patent unfairness that would result if, in the context of domestic violence, legal aid resources were to be made available to the accused male spouse for the assault charge but denied to the victim female spouse pursuing family law remedies in order to deter further the injuries to herself or her children resulting from the abuse.

For all of these reasons, then, we have come to the conclusion that the "negative liberty" interest does not provide a satisfactory basis for a rank-ordering of claims to legal aid resources from one legal domain to the next or, indeed, within particular legal

domains. Although the "negative liberty" interest is, indeed, one of the important normative justifications for providing legal aid, it is only one of several such interests. Focusing on the "negative liberty" interest for priority-setting purposes at the expense of
others will lead, we suggest, to a distorted analysis of the relative weight to be given to
any particular claim for legal aid.

(c) Conclusion

Our conclusion, then, is that an examination of the normative foundations for legal aid
supports the notion that the state has an obligation, varying with the circumstances at
issue, to facilitate access to law. This obligation flows from the condition of publicity,
which is an inherent requirement in the use of law in a society such as ours, which
accepts the fundamental importance of the Rule of Law. Where the law deployed by
the state is complex, and affects important interests of those with limited means, the
publicity condition will require the state to facilitate access to the law. Legal aid is
one, but not the only, device that might be used to meet that obligation. Another, for
example, might be to render the law less complex. An examination of the normative
justifications for legal aid does not, however, appear to provide a basis for a rank-
ordering of claims that might be made by various legal domains, nor, within such
domains, a basis for rank-ordering the claims of particular case types. More specifically, the interest in "negative liberty" does not appear to facilitate such an exercise.
Indeed, we adopt the view that undue reliance on the "negative liberty" interest causes
a number of distortions in the analysis of the relative weight of particular claims for
access to legal aid resources.

　　The interests that support claims to legal aid resources are various, both within
criminal law and in other fields. Analysis at the level of general principle, then, suggests
that priority-setting in legal aid should be premised on the assumption that a rank-
ordering of this kind cannot be sustained. Further, our difficulty in identifying general
principles which will facilitate a rank-ordering of entitlements to legal aid suggests that
priority-setting in the legal aid context needs to be based on the circumstances of
particular cases and the parties to them, should retain an element of flexibility, and
should be subject to revision in the light of experience.

Zemans and Monahan, *From Crisis to Reform: A New Legal Aid Plan for Ontario*
(Toronto: Osgoode Hall Law School, 1996)

Development of Legal Aid in Ontario

A. Legal Aid to 1966: Early Development

Before 1951, legal aid in Ontario was largely voluntary or charitable. Informal legal aid
was provided by members of the bar who would volunteer their services to individuals
who could not afford to pay legal fees. In criminal cases, the Attorney General's department
provided financial assistance through payment of nominal *per diem* fees to volunteer

lawyers. The Attorney General did not, however, pay counsel fees. There was no assistance for civil cases, although an individual lawyer could provide voluntary assistance if he or she chose to do so.

Ontario enacted its first legal aid statute in 1951—the *Law Society Amendment Act, 1951*, which established the province's first statutory legal aid plan. The legislation allowed the Law Society to "establish a plan to provide legal aid to persons in need thereof, to be called 'The Ontario Legal Aid Plan' and for such purposes to make such regulations as are deemed appropriate."

The Ontario *Act* was closely modelled on a similar act promulgated in England in 1949, the *Legal Aid and Advice Act*. Like the British plan, the Ontario Legal Aid Plan was controlled by the Law Society of Upper Canada, not a government agency. Unlike the British plan, however, the Ontario Plan only paid volunteer lawyers for their disbursements and other administrative expenses.

The Ontario Plan covered both civil and criminal proceedings; civil coverage included most civil cases except defamation, breach of promise of marriage, and alienation of affection. Criminal coverage was limited to indictable offences punishable by imprisonment. The Plan did not cover criminal or civil appeals, except where the Provincial Director was of the opinion that there had been a miscarriage of justice. The statute specified that the Plan was to be administered locally by the county and district law associations. Eligibility requirements were based on annual income, number of dependents, and a discretionary "needs" test.

By the early 1960s, it was clear that the volunteer Plan was not satisfying the need for legal services. Plan administrators could simply not find enough lawyers to take on cases. As a result, in 1963, the provincial Attorney General commissioned a review of the 1951 *Act*. A Joint Committee of the Ontario Government and the Law Society of Upper Canada was established to inquire into, and report on, the existing Plan and put forward recommendations for its future. The Committee was composed entirely of lawyers.

The *Report of the Joint Committee on Legal Aid* was tabled in April 1965. The Joint Committee confirmed that the 1951 Plan was unable to meet the demand for legal services. The Committee concluded that the Plan's flaw was that lawyers did not have enough time to provide legal services to the poor on a purely voluntary basis. The Joint Committee also concluded that it was unreasonable to expect lawyers to be responsible for providing legal services to the poor without payment.

Within this framework, the Joint Committee made several policy recommendations which still define the province's legal aid system today:

• The provincial government is constitutionally responsible for legal aid. Legal aid fell under the heading of the administration of justice.

• Legal aid was a right. The Joint Committee reasoned that individuals were only equal before the law if they were assured representation by counsel, irrespective of whether they could afford a private lawyer.

• As a right, legal aid had to be delivered in a uniform manner across the province. The Plan would have to be both funded and administered on a province-wide basis.

• The Plan should be administered by the Law Society and financed by the provincial government.

• Legal aid services should be delivered through private lawyers who would be paid by the Law Society according to a tariff.

• Legal aid should focus on litigation services.

• Services provided to individuals should be determined based on objective criteria, including the seriousness of the matter to the individual, the level of need within the community, and the question of whether equivalent rights existed within the boundaries of the legal aid scheme.

In order to ensure that recipients of legal aid would have their choice of counsel, the Committee proposed that lawyers be reasonably compensated so as to ensure participation by an adequate number of lawyers and to attract senior members of the bar. The Committee concluded that lawyers should be paid the reduced rate of 75 percent of a normal solicitor and client account.

A few of the Joint Committee's recommendations deserve further comment.

First, on the subject of the appropriate governance structure, the Committee adopted, without comment, the "almost unanimous opinion that legal aid should be continued to be administered by the Law Society."

Second, the Joint Committee reviewed two delivery models: the "judicare" model (although it was not described as such), whereby individual clients would be provided with certificates they could take to private lawyers who would provide services and then be paid by the Law Society according to a predetermined tariff, and the "staff" model (described as the "public defender system"), whereby the Law Society or government would establish its own legal offices and employ lawyers directly.

The Joint Committee unreservedly adopted the judicare model, believing that "[it is] wrong in principle that both prosecutor and defender are employed by the same master." Moreover, the Committee concluded that the impersonal and bureaucratic nature of the staff system, "prevented the public defender from exercising the zeal and vigour which should be characteristic of defence counsel in every case."

B. The Legal Aid Act, 1967: Statutory Entrenchment of Judicare and the Right to State-Funded Legal Aid

The provincial government accepted the Joint Committee's major recommendations. The result was the *Legal Aid Act, 1967*. Legal aid was no longer to be a private contribution, but part of the administration of justice and a right for those who could not afford legal assistance individually.

The *Legal Aid Act, 1967* established a statutory right to legal aid and acknowledged the obligation of the government to individuals who could not afford a lawyer. Legal services were to be delivered through the judicare model, using private lawyers as service providers.

The legislation was premised on a desire to make the same legal services available to the poor as were already available to "fee-paying" clients. Legal aid was now established as a government-funded social program for the poor.

The *Act* stated that the Plan was to provide the services of a private lawyer at no charge, or on the basis of a limited contribution, to individual applicants who qualified by virtue of the type of service required and their financial circumstances. Participating lawyers were to be reimbursed according to a prescribed schedule of fees, or tariff.

The *Act* also set out the basic governance and management structure of the Plan, specifying that the Law Society would continue to administer and determine the policy for the Plan. The *Act* and accompanying Regulations also established the Plan's coverage and basic financial eligibility criteria.

C. *The Certificate Program Between 1967 and 1979: Expanding Services and Increasing Costs*

The Plan was embraced by the profession. Approximately one-half of all Ontario lawyers registered their names on legal aid panels to be called if their services were required.

The Plan was also embraced by the public. Both the number of certificates issued by the Plan and the Plan's total costs grew considerably during this period. ...

D. *1971 to 1979: Growth and Integration of Community Legal Aid Clinics*

Despite the growing number of certificates, in the late 1960s and early 1970s many lawyers and social activists concluded that poor people often had much different legal needs than "fee paying" clients. These analysts believed that judicare lawyers were not qualified to address the legal needs of the poor. As a result, a different delivery model was required: the community legal aid clinic. This proposal was based on the American neighbourhood legal clinic model. Operationally, early community clinics were guided by five principles:

1. A strong focus on the legal needs of the poor.
2. Community involvement in decisionmaking.
3. Independence from government and the Law Society-controlled Ontario Legal Aid Plan.
4. A broad definition of "legal services," including law reform, public legal education, and community development.
5. Reliance on staff lawyers and non-lawyers to deliver services.

The early clinics operated very differently from a traditional private legal practice. Clinics focussed on "poverty" law services, emphasizing representation before the many new administrative tribunals which accompanied the development of the welfare state. Areas of practice included workers' compensation, social assistance, children's welfare, immigration, and landlord and tenant matters. Clinics also developed a much broader conception of legal services, including community legal education, law reform, and community development.

The early clinics unique focus was reflected in their governance structure and staffing policies. Clinics were governed by "community boards of directors" and were staffed by a combination of salaried lawyers and salaried "community legal workers" (CLWs). The CLW concept was new to the province. Neither lawyers nor administrative staff, CLWs were primarily community organizers whose main focus was community legal education, law reform, and community development.

The first community legal aid clinic in Ontario was established in 1971. Several other clinics followed. These early clinics were established and funded outside of the existing OLAP management structure. The clinics were funded by a variety of charitable and government grants. As a result, they had a considerable degree of independence. At this time, the clinics were not formally organized into a "clinic system."

As the number of clinics grew, pressure mounted on the provincial government to provide them with funding. As a result, the provincial Attorney General appointed a Task Force on Legal Aid in 1973. The Task Force's mandate was "to review in depth the operation of the Legal Aid Plan in Ontario and determine the parameters of its future direction and development in order to ensure that it has the capacity to meet its objectives in the years ahead." The Task Force was chaired by the Honourable Mr. Justice Osler and consisted of six other members, including non-lawyers.

The report issued by that Task Force, the Osler Report, recommended a "mixed" delivery system for legal aid in the province, in which the existing judicare system would be supplemented by staffed neighbourhood legal clinics funded by the provincial government. The Task Force's conclusions were considered official recognition of the validity of the clinic approach to legal services for the poor.

The provincial government accepted the Osler Report's clinic recommendations. In 1976, a Regulation under the *Legal Aid Act* was introduced which established funding for the existing twenty-two legal aid clinics in the province. To be eligible for funding, a clinic had to be managed by a community-elected board of directors and had to employ both lawyers and community legal workers on a salaried basis.

In 1978, Mr. Justice Samuel Grange conducted another provincial inquiry into legal aid. Its purpose was to examine the relationship between the clinics, OLAP, and the private bar.

Like the Osler Report, the *Report of the Commission on Clinical Funding* (the Grange Report) affirmed the mixed delivery system of legal aid in Ontario. The Report concluded that community clinics played a significant role in Ontario's legal aid system. The Grange Report found that the clientele and legal issues addressed by the certificate program and clinic program were very different. As a result, the Report viewed the relationship between clinics and the private bar as one of cooperation, not competition. The Report thus encouraged the growth of clinics to complement the services provided by the private bar under judicare.

Importantly, the Grange Report concluded that clinics should have "autonomy with respect to policy and administration, subject only to accountability for the public funds advanced and for the legal competence of the services rendered." Policy and administrative autonomy were necessary to ensure community control and preserve the clinics' law reform mandate.

In 1979, the Grange Report's recommendations were incorporated into a Regulation of the *Legal Aid Act* establishing the structure of provincial funding for clinics. The "Clinic Funding Regulation" stated that the Ontario Legal Aid Plan was to fund an "independent community-based clinical delivery system." A clinic was defined as an "independent community organization." The term "independent" was not defined. The Regulation also established the Clinical Funding Committee as a Committee of the Law Society.

E. 1979 to 1990: Systemic Growth

Both the certificate program and the clinic program grew substantially during the 1980s.

Between fiscal years 1980 and 1990, the total cost of OLAP rose almost 500 percent. Despite this increase, as of 1990 neither the Law Society nor the provincial government took steps to reform the fundamental structure and operation of the Plan. The *Legal Aid Act* continued to provide for open-ended funding. Services continued to be provided primarily through a judicare model. The Plan did not introduce significant cost-management measures.

By the end of the decade, the Plan's increasing costs were clearly becoming an important issue for its funders. In the late 1980s, the federal government went so far as to "cap" its contributions to the certificate program. Unfortunately, the Plan's fiscal difficulties were just beginning. Few would have predicted that the cost of the Plan in fiscal year 1995 would be almost double what it was in fiscal year 1990. ...

Models of Service Delivery

• • •

A. Introduction: The Mixed Model

OLAP delivers legal services through three major programs: the certificate program, the community clinic program, and the duty counsel program. Each program is intended to provide distinct services. ...

OLAP is sometimes described as utilizing a "mixed" model because it delivers legal services by means of a variety of service models. ... However, the judicare program has always been the dominant component within OLAP's mixed model.

B. Description of Certificate Program

1. Program Philosophy and Delivery Model

OLAP's certificate program delivers legal services through a "judicare" model. The Canadian Bar Association *Legal Aid Delivery Models* study described the "fundamental elements" of the judicare model as follows:

(1) Private Firms. Judicare employs the services of private firms or practitioners, with a central office undertaking eligibility assessment and referring clients out to the private Bar.

(2) Fee-for-Service. Private lawyers are paid by the legal aid plan on a fee-for-service basis, according to a tariff comparable in structure to that employed by private lawyers. ... The lawyer bills the plan for the services delivered to the approved client.

(3) Bar Involvement in Administration. Judicare plan administration tends to be dominated or controlled by the organized private Bar, through a system of delegated authority, from board on down to area directors.

(4) Traditional Services. Underpinning the judicare model is the notion that "poor people are just like rich people, only without the money." Hence the only function of the

legal aid plan is to ensure payment of services to eligible clients, with clients and lawyers otherwise left to behave as in the paying market.

(5) Individualist Philosophy. Judicare models emphasize equal access to justice for individual clients. Delivery of services by private practitioners theoretically ensures equal access through choice of counsel and absence of the stigma of "legal aid" representation.

The certificate program defines access to justice narrowly. The program is premised on the "assumption that poor people are just like rich people, but without the money, that is, the poor have the same set of legal problems and only require subsidization of the lawyer's fees, due to their inability to pay" and that "[the] principal barrier to access is lack of ability to pay: once the economic barrier has been removed through provision of legal aid, then equality of access has been resolved."

The certificate program has traditionally stressed the fundamental importance of preserving client "choice." The program is premised on a belief that a legal aid client should be able to retain the lawyer of his or her choice, assuming that a lawyer is willing to accept the certificate.

Finally, the certificate program does not determine or evaluate the quality of service being provided pursuant to a certificate. But for the intervention of the Plan as funder, the program is designed to mirror the private bar. As in the private marketplace, the individual client acts on his or her opinion of the quality of service being performed by either switching lawyers or complaining to the Law Society.

2. Eligibility Criteria

The eligibility of any applicant for a legal aid certificate depends on two criteria:

(a) Whether the legal problem for which assistance is sought is covered by the *Act* ("Coverage").

(b) Whether the applicant is financially eligible for assistance ("Financial Eligibility").

3. Coverage

Sections 12 to 15 of the *Legal Aid Act* and sections 40 to 47 of its accompanying Regulation outline the areas of law for which legal aid certificates will or will not be granted, subject to the applicant's financial eligibility.

Briefly stated, the coverage rules in the *Act* are very broad, extending both mandatory and discretionary certificate coverage to a wide range of criminal and civil law proceedings. The *Act* excludes only a small number of proceedings from coverage. ...

4. Financial Eligibility

Section 16 of the *Act* specifies that an applicant's financial position must be considered when determining whether he or she is eligible to receive a legal aid certificate. Depending on financial status, an applicant may be eligible for a free certificate, a partial certificate (requiring a client contribution), or ineligible for a certificate.

The detailed procedures used to assess financial eligibility are the responsibility of the provincial Ministry of Community and Social Services. These procedures are complex and will not be detailed here. Generally speaking, however, OLAP utilizes a "needs" test to determine financial eligibility. OLAP assesses the assets, income, and monthly living expenses of an applicant and/or his or her spouse in order to determine if the person meets the "needs" test threshold. Where the "needs" test identifies disposable income or liquid assets in excess of the allowable amounts, OLAP will request a contribution towards the cost of legal aid.

Subject to asset testing, all recipients of social assistance are automatically eligible for "free" certificates. Applicants whose monthly income exceeds social assistance levels may be eligible for "free" certificates if their monthly income is below specified waiver levels. In 1995, a single adult was eligible for a "free" criminal certificate if his or her income was below $19,656. A couple with one dependant was eligible for a "free" criminal law certificate if their income was below $30,492.

C. Scope and Range of Certificate Services

1. Demand for Certificates/Number of Applications/Certificates Issued

Any discussion of the services provided by the OLAP certificate program must begin with the acknowledgement that OLAP has historically provided a large quantity and a broad range of certificates. In the ten years between 1986 and 1995, the Plan issued over 1.5 million certificates. In this period, certificates were issued for proceedings in virtually every court in the province and for many administrative tribunals, including a wide range of criminal and civil law proceedings. ...

In the last twelve years, the annual number of certificates issued by the Plan has not been stable. Between fiscal years 1985 and 1993, the number of certificates issued grew by more than 250 percent, reaching a peak of over 220,000 certificates in fiscal year 1993. This period was also characterized by increasing applicant approval rates. Since that time, however, the number of certificates issued has contracted by almost two-thirds and the applicant approval rate has declined. In fiscal year 1997, it is projected that the program will issue approximately 80,000 certificates. Should this projection prove accurate, this figure would be the lowest number of certificates issued in twenty-two years. ...

We stated earlier that the increase in demand for certificates and the number of certificates issued was likely the result of several factors outside of the Plan's control, including the recession and changes to both federal and provincial policy. The subsequent decrease in the number of applications for certificates is harder to explain. One potential explanation is that the apparent improvement in the economy has meant that fewer people are eligible for OLAP assistance. The decrease in applications could also be explained by legislative changes. For example, the federal government recently amended the *Immigration Act*, eliminating the need for many immigration certificates. Other potential explanations include the effect of the recently imposed $25 application fee, tighter financial eligibility rules, "pre-screening" of applicants by Area Directors, and the effect of the negative publicity surrounding the Plan's financial crisis.

Most attempts to explain the volatility of legal aid applications and certificate issuance are necessarily speculative. Neither the provincial government nor OLAP have comprehensively studied the demand for legal aid services or the distribution of certificates.

2. Case Mix

The certificate program was originally geared towards providing certificates primarily for criminal proceedings. Over time, the program came to place considerably more emphasis on civil law proceedings, particularly in the area of family law. By the early 1990s, the Plan was issuing certificates for a very broad range of litigation, including immigration proceedings and property and negligence actions. After 1996, however, the mix of the certificate program became weighed heavily in favour of criminal law cases. In the same period, the percentage of family law certificates declined significantly. Table 11, below, illustrates OLAP's changing case mix.

During the period of open-ended funding, it is at least arguable that OLAP's case mix was an accurate reflection of "expressed" legal need. Changes in the case mix could be interpreted as evidence of the volatility of demand for certificates in different areas of law. During this period, the demand-driven nature of the Plan largely determined the case mix. After April 1996, however, this was no longer the case. At that point, the imposition of fixed funding, a certificate priority system, and limits to the number of certificates issued meant that OLAP's case mix became a function of management decisions to emphasize certain services over others. OLAP prioritization system is discussed below.

3. Service Providers

OLAP does not collect detailed information about the private lawyers who accept certificates. OLAP's data is limited to information about the relative seniority of lawyers accepting certificates, the amount private lawyers bill the Plan, and the general participation rate of Ontario lawyers on legal aid panels. Unfortunately, OLAP does not collect information about the proportion of total fees that lawyers derive from certificate work, the proportion of legal aid lawyers who work in large or small firms, or the comparative specialization of those who accept certificates (as opposed to their seniority). Without this information, it is impossible to construct a detailed profile of the certificate program's service providers.

From the data that does exist, it appears that most lawyers accepting certificates are quite experienced. In 1995, 48 percent of all fees paid to lawyers were paid to lawyers who had twelve or more years of seniority. An additional 41 percent of fees were paid to lawyers who had between four and twelve years of experience.

Historically, it appears that most service providers bill the Plan for relatively small amounts. ...

4. Clients

OLAP does not collect comprehensive data about the certificate program's client base. At present, the Plan only records the gender, age, and financial status of certificate applicants.

Table 11 Percentage of OLAP Certificates Issued by Area of Practice
(Case Mix) 1990-1997

Fiscal year	Criminal certificates (% of total)	Civil certificates (% of total)	Breakdown of civil certificates (% of total)		
			Family certificates	Immigration certificates	Other civil certificates
1990	59	41	24	10	7
1991	54	46	26	8	12
1992	51	49	25	10	14
1993	50	50	28	14	8
1994	51	49	28	8	8
1995	51	49	33	6	10
1996	66	34	21	8	5

The Plan does not consistently collect empirical data detailing the experiences of applicants who are refused certificates. As a result, the Plan does not know whether applicants who are refused certificates retain their own counsel, represent themselves, or simply withdraw from legal proceedings (assuming they can). ...

5. Quality

The Plan does not directly or indirectly monitor the quality of work of certificate lawyers. Lawyers providing certificate services must only conform to the same quality standards as those established by the Law society for all Ontario lawyers. ...

Many in the profession believe that the most significant consideration affecting the quality of legal aid services is the inadequacy of the OLAP tariff. Many practitioners argue that the OLAP tariff simply does not provide sufficient compensation to ensure the high-quality representation.

6. Program Priorities and Planning

In November 1995, the Law Society adopted detailed priority rules for each of the Plan's major areas of practice, including criminal, family, immigration/refugee, and other civil litigation. This measure was necessary to coordinate and/or ration the fixed number of certificates the Plan would be able to issue after April 1996.

As a general principle, the prioritization rules are premised on a belief that certificates should be issued on the basis of the relative "seriousness" of the proceeding to an applicant. Thus, the "governing principle guiding the issues [of criminal certificates] is the likelihood of incarceration." In family law, the "governing principle ... is to protect the safety of a spouse or child who is at risk, or to protect an established child/parent bond." The introduction of priority rules has effectively meant that the certificate "case mix" is now a function of planning and management decisions, not client-driven demand.

In practice, OLAP's case mix since the adoption of the priority rules has shifted heavily towards criminal certificates. The percentage of certificates issued for family matters has declined significantly.

D. Description of Clinic Program Operations

1. Program Philosophy and Delivery Model

The community clinic program is based on the American "neighbourhood law offices" model. The *CBA Legal Aid Delivery Models* study described the "principal elements" of the clinic model as follows:

(1) Neighbourhood Offices. Clinics take the form of neighbourhood offices, located within the low-income communities they serve, with services delivered by staff lawyers and community legal workers.

(2) Block Grants. Clinics are funded by plans through block grants, with broadly-phrased terms of service. Staff lawyers and community legal workers are paid on a salaried basis by the clinic.

(3) Community Boards. Clinics are decentralized in nature, made up of a mix in various proportions of the legal professionals and members of the community served.

(4) Distinctive Legal Needs. Most clinics stress the distinctive needs of the defined community served, typically with a heavy emphasis upon those fields of "poverty law" underserved by the other models.

(5) Reform and Interest Advocacy Philosophy. Because the very structure of the clinical model emphasises service to a clearly-defined "community" in fields of law not served by other models, "legal problems" tend to be characterised in different terms, admitting of other than casework or service approaches, leading to a strong orientation towards interest advocacy and law reform in the interests of the defined community.

In contrast to the judicare model, the clinic model is premised on the belief that "poor people are not just like rich people, but without their money." The clinic model stresses substantive social and economic equality between citizens, not just formal equality of access to justice. In this model, legal needs are defined much more broadly than in the judicare model, "emphasising the potential role of legal services in the resolution of disputes between recipients and the machinery of the welfare state, and extending beyond the scope of services to include various methods of changing laws that affect the poor."

There are currently seventy clinics in Ontario, serving over 100 communities. There are two main categories of clinics: general service and specialty clinics. Most clinics (fifty-six) are general service clinics, offering services in core areas of poverty law practice. Specialty clinics specialize in a particular area of law or in the legal needs of a specific client group. Examples of specialty clinics include: the Advocacy Centre for the Elderly, the Advocacy Resource Centre for the Handicapped, Justice for Children and Youth, the Centre for Spanish-Speaking Peoples, the Canadian Environmental Law Association, and university clinics. Three teaching clinics are affiliated with university law schools in the province: the Correctional Law Project (Queen's University), Legal Assistance of Windsor (University of Windsor), and Parkdale Community Legal Services (Osgoode Hall Law School). There are also student-run clinics located within all six Ontario law schools.

2. Eligibility Criteria

Like the certificate program, clinics have both coverage and financial eligibility criteria. In accordance with the community governance model, clinic boards have the authority to establish both types of criteria. Clinic boards must, however, establish these criteria within the confines of the Clinic Funding Regulation, CFC policy, and the terms and conditions of the clinic certificate.

3. Coverage

The Clinic Funding Regulation defines the potential range of clinic coverage very broadly, stating that

> [i]n this Part, "funding" refers to the payment of funds to a clinic to enable the clinic to provide legal services or paralegal services, or both, including activities reasonably designed to encourage access to such services or to further such services and services designed solely to promote the legal welfare of a community, on a basis other than fee for service.

General clinics tend to offer services in four broad areas of law, including:

- [h]ousing law, including rent control and *Landlord and Tenant Act*;
- [i]ncome-maintenance law, including General Welfare Assistance and Family Benefits Assistance;
- [w]orker's compensation law; and
- [e]mployment law, including Unemployment Insurance, employment standards and wrongful dismissal.

Some general clinics also provide limited immigration, criminal, and family law services. Specialty clinics provide services within the area of specialization. The areas of law or specific client groups addressed by specialty clinics include Aboriginals, the elderly, the disabled, environmental law, correctional law, worker's health and safety, children and youth, tenant's rights, and the Chinese and Southeast Asian community.

4. Financial Eligibility

Clinics normally provide general legal information in the form of summary advice to all persons without regard to income.

Client representation is provided to clients who meet financial eligibility guidelines. The clinic certificate specifies that each clinic board must adopt a financial eligibility policy that complies with CFC guidelines. CFC guidelines establish maximum income and asset levels for clients seeking clinic services *other than summary advice and information*.

In practice, clinic financial eligibility rules are not complicated. Most applicants are automatically eligible for clinic services if their primary source of income is either general welfare assistance, family benefits assistance, worker's compensation benefits, or an old age pension. Applicants with other/additional sources of income must comply with the CFC financial eligibility guidelines. Each of the four clinics we studied followed the CFC Guidelines, allowing exceptions in unique cases.

5. Services Provided

Clinics generally provide the following services:

- [s]ummary advice and legal information within clinic areas of practice;
- [r]eferrals to social service and community agencies, lawyers in private practice, and OLAP for certificates;
- [c]lient representation before courts and administrative tribunals, including the Workers' Compensation Appeals Tribunal, the Social Assistance Review Board, the Ontario Human Rights Commission, and the Criminal Injuries Compensation Board;
- [p]ublic legal education, including seminars, workshops, presentations, and the production of pamphlets and videos in many languages;
- [l]aw reform initiatives aimed at protecting and promoting the legal interests of the low-income community, including test-case litigation and appearances before municipal councils, legislative committees, and public commissions and inquiries; and,
- [c]ommunity development projects which assist clients to organize and to form self-help groups focussed on low-income issues, including those affecting injured workers and tenant associations.

Given that each clinic establishes its own priorities and engages in many non-traditional legal activities, it is more difficult to summarize clinic program services than certificate program services. Individual clinics provide specific services—one clinic may emphasize law reform activities, another may emphasize case representation. Even within general categories, clinics may provide a diverse range of services. One clinic may specialize in complex test-case litigation, another in high-volume case representation. As a result, comparative statistical analysis of clinic activities may be misleading.

Our study of four representative clinics in the province suggests that clinics devote most of their resources to traditional legal services in the form of summary advice and case representation. Each of the clinics we surveyed reported that the majority of staff time was devoted to these activities. These estimates ranged from approximately 60 percent at ARCH (the Advocacy Resource Centre for the Handicapped, the only specialty clinic surveyed) to 80 percent at Jane Finch Community Legal Services (a general service clinic). The remaining staff time was devoted to "non-traditional" activities, including community legal education, law reform, and community organizing and development.

6. Summary Advice and Legal Information

Both specialty and general clinics provide summary advice and legal information to persons without regard to financial status. Advice may be given on any aspect of law within the clinic's area of practice. Depending on the clinic, advice may be given over the telephone or in person. ...

7. Client Representation

Clinics provide traditional legal representation before courts and administrative tribunals, including the Workers' Compensation Appeals Tribunal, the Social Assistance Review Board, the Ontario Human Rights Commission, and the Compensation for Victims of Crime Commission. Clinic lawyers also engage in appellate work, both to represent clients directly and as intervenors.

In addition to representing individual litigants, many, if not most, clinics initiated or participated in cases which had significant consequences for their client groups as a whole. Examples include:

• Justice for Children and Youth intervened in the Supreme Court of Canada in the case of *R v. O'Connor*. The Court was considering whether or not defence counsel should have access to private medical/counselling records of witnesses which are in the hands of persons other than the Crown. Justice for Children and Youth, which represents both young accused and young complainants, argued that the Court should require accused persons to meet an evidentiary threshold to substantiate the likely relevance of the records before they can be produced.

• The Toronto Worker's Health & Safety Legal Clinic successfully represented a female bartender in the Ontario Labour Relations Board case *Barmaid's Arms*. The Board ruled in favour of the bartender who had been terminated for refusing to serve an unruly male patron. This was the first time the Board had addressed the issue of violence in the workplace as an occupational hazard.

• South Etobicoke Community Legal Services represented a woman before the Immigration and Refugee Board. The woman had fled her home county of Grenada. The clinic successfully argued that the woman's fourteen-year history of abuse by her common-law spouse constituted persecution according to the Immigration and Refugee Board's Gender Guidelines.

• In *Gail v. Canada (AG)*, the Kinna-aweya Legal Clinic successfully argued before the Federal Court of Appeal that no-fault motor vehicle insurance benefits did not fall within the definition of "income" of the *Unemployment Insurance Act* Regulations.

8. Referrals

Depending on the nature of the inquiry, clinics will often refer persons to social agencies or to private lawyers, including direct referrals to the certificate program. In 1995, clinics referred 68,409 people to other service providers.

9. Public Legal Education

Clinics provide a variety of public legal education materials, including pamphlets, presentations, self-help kits, and seminars. In accordance with the clinic mandate, emphasis is placed on educating those who may not otherwise have access to legal information. Examples include:

• East Toronto Community Legal Services provided a series of five legal education sessions to the residents of its community. The topics were workers' compensation, landlord and tenant law, welfare and family benefits, consumers' rights, and an overview of the Canadian legal system.

• Legal Assistance of Windsor organized a series of eleven public legal education events to discuss welfare reform. These events ranged from appearances on local television to presentations to church groups.

• Scarborough Community Legal Services has conducted regular educational workshops for the residents of Metro Family Residence, Metropolitan Toronto's largest shelter.

Community Legal Education Ontario (CLEO) is a specialty clinic which produces and distributes a wide range of public legal education material on specific legal issues. During 1992-93, CLEO distributed 938,174 pamphlets and other materials.

10. Law Reform

The mandate of community clinics explicitly states that clinics are to undertake law reform activities designed to advance the interests of low-income citizens. Clinics fulfill this mandate partially through test-case litigation. Other activities may include submissions to public decision-making bodies, such as government committees. Recent law reform initiatives are very diverse. Examples include:

• The Director of the Correctional Law Project appeared before the federal Parliamentary Standing Committee on Justice and Legal Affairs to give evidence on Bills C-41 and C-45, concerning proposed legislation on sentencing and corrections.

• Aboriginal Legal Services of Toronto worked with several other native groups and the Ministry of the Solicitor General and Correctional Services to draft a detailed policy which would allow Aboriginal inmates in provincial correctional institutions access to Aboriginal traditional caregivers.

• The Georgina Community Legal Services clinic lobbied the Town of Georgina to institute a "Vital Services" by-law. This by-law would ensure that a tenant's vital services are maintained if their landlords default in payment to service providers.

• The Canadian Environmental Law Association has made submissions to the federal government regarding Bill C-62.

11. Community Organizing and Development

Clinic staff will work with other members of their local community to organize the clinic's target population into groups designed to promote their general and legal welfare. Examples include:

• Community Legal Assistance Sarnia successfully organized a campaign to have the Lambton County Council's Health and Social Services Committee launch a mass mailing to all agencies, schools, churches, and other interested parties within Lambton County asking for delegations on social service issues. As a result of the subsequent public consultations, the County Council agreed to continue to subsidize day-care spaces throughout the year.

• Rural Legal Services (North Frontenac) has been an active member in the Elder Abuse Task Force for the Kingston and Frontenac area. The clinic served as a community legal resource, educating task force members on the legal issues surrounding elder abuse.

• Willowdale Community Legal Services worked with the City of North York to organize two conferences to discuss services for victims of violence.

At least one clinic has a position dedicated to community development. McQuesten clinic has a full-time Community Development Coordinator, whose sole function is to provide community organizing. Parkdale Community Legal Services employs five CLWs whose primary function is community education and development.

12. Clients

Like the certificate program, the community clinic program does not collect comprehensive data about its client base. ...

13. Service Providers

Each clinic is established as a staff legal office, generally made up of three categories of employees: staff lawyers, CLWs, and support staff. Community legal workers are often considered the clinic equivalent of paralegals in a private firm.

Despite the large number and wide variety of clinics, the number of staff in the clinic system is comparatively small. ...

On the whole, individual clinics are fairly small offices, often comparable to small, private law firms. For example, the four clinics we studied had staff complements ranging from eight to eleven full-time personnel. Approximately one-half of Ontario's clinics are smaller still, receiving CFC funding for only three to five positions.

Geographically, clinics are distributed across the province, but not evenly. Some areas of the province appear under-served. Fourteen of the fifteen specialty clinics are located in the Toronto area.

Clinic legal staff are generally quite experienced. Of the lawyers employed in the system, over 45 percent were called to the Bar in 1985 or earlier.

14. Clinic Resource Office

The Clinic Resource Office (CRO) was established in 1991 to provide legal and technical support services to clinic practitioners in the main substantive areas of clinic practice. The CRO provides legal research and training for clinic caseworkers, provides legal resource materials, and assists in information sharing between clinics. As such, the CRO operates as a central support for the entire clinic system. ...

15. Quality Control

Quality control of legal services performed by community legal clinics has three components: (1) CFC and board supervision requirements; (2) the general rules of professional legal conduct; and (3) the clinic complaint procedure.

According to the Clinic Funding Operating Manual, "one of the Clinic Funding Committee's primary goals and responsibilities is to ensure that community legal clinics provide high-quality legal services of importance to low-income communities in an effective and efficient manner." The CFC does not, however, directly supervise or monitor the quality of either traditional or non-traditional activities undertaken in clinics. ...

E. Description of Duty Counsel Operations

OLAP provides three types of duty counsel assistance: the Hotline Service (a twenty-four hour telephone advice service for persons in custody); staff duty counsel (salaried lawyers located in criminal and young offender courts who provide legal advice, conduct bail hearings, and represent clients on guilty pleas); and private bar (*per diem*) duty counsel (who provide civil duty counsel services as well as many of the same functions as staff duty counsel). OLAP also operates a series of duty counsel clinics established in neighbourhood settings across the province.

1. Financial Eligibility

Duty counsel services are provided to any person who has not retained counsel, regardless of income.

2. Scope of Services Provided

In criminal law and young offender law matters, staff and private duty counsel services are generally restricted to matters relating to guilty pleas, bail hearings, providing limited legal advice about legal procedures, and sentencing matters. Duty counsel do not conduct trials. Criminal duty counsel offices are located in the provincial criminal courts.

In civil law matters, staff and private duty counsel services are provided in family courts and psychiatric units in Ontario hospitals. Services are generally restricted to providing legal advice, arranging adjournments, and obtaining consent orders.

Duty counsel clinics offer general legal advice about a broad range of legal issues. Clinics are typically open for a few hours each week at scheduled times. They are often located in community centres, educational institutions, and other public buildings, such as libraries. In fiscal year 1995, OLAP operated thirty-three such clinics.

In fiscal year 1995, duty counsel assisted over 500,000 Ontarians, including 408,097 persons in adult criminal court, 47,404 persons in family court, 4,699 persons in psychiatric institutions, and 40,230 in neighbourhood offices. This figure represents a 15.2 percent increase from the year before and a 43 percent increase from fiscal year 1990.

As part of its 1995 reforms, OLAP proposed expanding the use of duty counsel in both criminal and family courts. As of this writing, the Plan has not released its expanded duty counsel proposal. ...

F. Other OLAP Services

1. Student Legal Aid Societies

OLAP directly funds student legal aid societies at each of Ontario's six law schools. Working under the supervision of review counsel and faculty, these Societies offer legal assistance and public legal education programs. During the 1995 fiscal year, the Societies opened files and provided summary advice to approximately 11,300 people.

2. Research Facility

OLAP's Research Facility conducts research to support the cases of clients receiving legal aid. The Research Facility program includes producing individualized research memoranda for lawyers acting on certificates, research for community legal clinics, and the production of standard memoranda of law available for sale to private practitioners. ...

OLAP in Context: Legal Aid in Canada and Britain

A. Introduction

There is no single standard method of administering and/or delivering legal aid services. Within Canada, each province has developed its own unique plan. Legal aid plans in England and Wales, Australia, and the United States are different again. Ontario's legal aid system has similarities to many of these plans, but also several distinct characteristics.

Six legal aid plans in Canada are administered by an independent statutory organizations. Only three are administered by provincial legal aid societies: New Brunswick, Alberta, and Ontario. Legal aid services in Prince Edward Island are administered directly by the provincial government.

Some plans deliver services through a "judicare" model, whereby services are provided by private practitioners who are paid by the plan on a fee-for-services basis according to a predetermined tariff. Other plans deliver services through a "staff lawyer" model, whereby the plan provides services through salaried staff lawyers who work directly for the plan. (When a staff lawyer model provides criminal services, it is generally referred to as a "public defender" model.) Other models are also used, such as the "neighbourhood law office" model or "contract" model. Several plans, including Ontario, use a "mixed" system, employing several different models to deliver services to clients. No two "mixed" plans are alike, however, as each utilizes a different selection and proportion of models to deliver services.

Two issues cross almost all jurisdictional boundaries. First, almost all of these jurisdictions have had to take steps to reduce costs in the face of rapidly escalating costs and the resulting pressure from governments—who provide the vast majority of legal aid funding—to reduce or limit those costs. Many of these plans have had to make major structural reforms live within newly imposed fiscal limits. Second, most plans have had to address the changing nature of the demand for legal aid services. For example, in almost all jurisdictions, family law cases have a much greater prominence than they did ten or fifteen years ago. Plans have had to adapt to providing these services, often within the context of reduced revenues.

This section will briefly review the administration and delivery of legal aid services in Canadian jurisdictions and in England and Wales. Legal aid in the United States is sufficiently unique that a detailed review of American models would not be productive. Where relevant, we will outline the major reforms in each jurisdiction designed to address these two issues.

This section illustrates that there are many different ways of delivering legal aid services and many different ways of coping with change. We will conclude this section with a brief comparison of legal aid in Ontario with these jurisdictions. Many of the issues and reforms outlined in this section will be discussed in more detail in later chapters.

B. *Comparative Statistics*

Tables 7a and 7b, below, compare some of the key quantitative indicators of legal aid services in Canada in fiscal year 1994. It demonstrates that Ontario's *per capita* spending on legal aid services is more than any other province except British Columbia (comparable post-April 1996 data are not yet available, although we believe it will demonstrate that OLAP's current position relative to other Canadian jurisdictions will be closer to the Canadian average). Tables 7a and 7b also demonstrate that Ontario also relies more heavily on private delivery of services than every other province except Alberta.

C. *Legal Aid in Canada*

1. *Newfoundland*

The legal aid system in Newfoundland is governed by the *Legal Aid Act*. The *Act* establishes an independent seven-member Commission as the body responsible for administering legal aid services in the province. Five members of the Commission are named by the Lieutenant Governor-In-Council. The Deputy Minister of Justice and the Provincial Director serve as *ex officio* members.

Services are delivered through a mixed system of both private and staff lawyers. Approved applicants obtain a certificate that can be presented to a staff lawyer or a private lawyer who belongs to a legal aid panel. As of 1995, staff lawyers took on approximately 86 percent of the total caseloads.

The plan's substantive coverage closely follows the terms of the federal-provincial cost-sharing agreement on criminal and young offenders. The plan covers most family cases. Coverage for other civil legal aid is discretionary, subject to an evaluation of both the likely success of the matter and its cost relative to the anticipated recovery.

2. *Prince Edward Island*

Prince Edward Island has no legislative legal aid program. Rather, the plan is directly administered by the provincial Attorney General.

Services are provided through a salaried public defender office. Private counsel are retained if a staff lawyer has a scheduling conflict, conflict of interest in a particular case, or in a "mandatory choice of counsel" case, as defined by the federal-provincial cost-sharing agreement. Mandatory-choice cases exist where the charge carries a mandatory sentence to life imprisonment upon conviction.

Criminal law legal aid is available to financially eligible individuals charged with those offences described in the federal-provincial cost-sharing agreement. The plan used

Table 7a   Comparative Statistics on Legal Aid in Canada: 1994

	Per capita spending $	Direct legal expenditures		Cost per case	
		Criminal percent	Civil percent	Criminal $	Civil $
Nfld.	8.74	55	45	360	865
PEI	3.81	55	45	228	3275
NB	4.67	57	13	1172	3008
NS	11.97	51	49	520	543
Que.	16.24	35	65	300	400
Ont.	27.71	43	57	1058	1033
Man.	13.48	53	47	455	564
Sask.	8.57	65	35	325	439
Alta.	10.65	70	30	691	948
BC	28.54	46	54	997	1637
CAN	20.67	45	55	664	759

Table 7b   Comparative Statistics on Legal Aid in Canada: 1994

	Direct legal expenditures		Approved application rates /1000 Population		Total legal spending	
	Staff percent	Private percent	Criminal	Civil	Legal services	Central admin.
Nfld.	82	18	11	5	100	0
PEI	83	17	9	1	100	0
NB	0	100	3	0	87	13
NS	75	25	11	10	94	6
Que.	55	45	17	24	92	8
Ont.	12	88	10	13	90	10
Man.	35	65	13	10	89	11
Sask.	93	7	16	6	93	7
Alta.	3	97	10	3	89	11
BC	15	85	12	9	92	8
CAN	25	75	12	13	91	9

to provide coverage for many types of family cases. In the 1991-92 provincial budget, however, family law legal aid applications were restricted to those cases involving domestic violence. Other civil matters are not covered.

3. Nova Scotia

Legal aid in Nova Scotia is governed by the *Legal Aid Act*. The Act establishes the Legal Aid Commission, a seventeen-member independent commission. Fifteen of the seventeen are appointed by the Lieutenant Governor-In-Council on the Attorney General's recommendation. Seven Directors are chosen from nominees presented by the Nova Scotia Barrister's Society.

Legal aid services in Nova Scotia are provided mostly by staff lawyers. Cases are referred to the private bar only in mandatory-choice-of-counsel cases and in cases where staff lawyers have a conflict of interest.

No type of case is expressly excluded from coverage. Cases are, however, prioritized. Criminal law cases have the highest priority, followed by family law cases. Cases in which the applicant is likely to lose his or her home or livelihood, or cannot retain counsel without suffering undue financial hardship, are third priority.

The provincial government has cut the legal aid budget in each of the last two years and is proposing cuts for the next two as well. As a result, the Nova Scotia Legal Aid Commission was recently the subject of an extensive review designed to improve cost efficiency in the program. The published report, *Nova Scotia Review*, recommended greater reliance on staff delivery of services, a reduction in the number of referrals to the private bar, and a clarification of the plan's mandate.

4. New Brunswick

Legal aid in New Brunswick is governed by the terms of the *Legal Aid Act*. The *Act* allows the Law Society of New Brunswick to establish and administer the legal aid plan. The Law Society has established a Legal Aid Committee which oversees the administration of the plan. The Committee is composed of five members of the Law Society. The provincial government also appoints an advisory committee to review legal aid issues. The committee reports to the Minister of Justice and consists of provincial judges, the Deputy Minister of Justice, and two lawyers in private practice.

Legal aid in New Brunswick is delivered exclusively through a judicare model. There is no staff delivery of services. The plan only provides certificates for criminal law cases. Cases covered include proceedings mandated by the federal-provincial agreement and a small number of summary conviction offences where incarceration or the loss of livelihood is likely upon conviction. Civil legal aid was available from 1981 to 1988, when it was abolished. The Law Foundation of New Brunswick provides funding for a limited number of family law cases involving domestic violence or child guardianship.

New Brunswick has historically had a very high average cost per case. As a result, in fiscal years 1994 and 1995 the Law Society introduced a new funding format called the "Global Budgeting Plan." This formula was recommended by the profession as an alternative to the possible introduction of a staff delivery model.

This system calls for holding 40 percent of the fees charged to any particular certificate until the end of the fiscal year. This holdback was designed to ensure that Legal Aid New Brunswick would be able to offer services for the entire year without exceeding its predetermined annual budget. At the end of the year, plan administrators determine what portion, if any, of the 40 percent holdback can be paid out to participating lawyers. In its first year of operation, the Plan ultimately paid out 100 percent of the taxed fees.

5. Quebec

Legal aid in Quebec is governed by the *Legal Services Act*. This *Act* establishes the Commission des services juridiques, a twelve-member independent commission with responsibility for administering legal aid in Quebec. All members of the Commission are appointed by the Lieutenant Governor-In-Council.

The Commission creates and supervises the work of several regional and local legal aid corporations. These regional and local corporations operate the plan within specified administrative areas. Each corporation is overseen by a board of directors appointed by the Commission. The membership of these boards is generally divided equally between the legal profession and residents of the area.

Quebec operates a mixed model of service delivery. Within their specific areas, regional and local corporations provide services through a staff model. The current *Act* specifies, however, that services may be provided to approved applicants by a private lawyer if the applicant specifically requests it, or in the event of a conflict of interest or the need for specific legal expertise. If no request is made, the case will usually be assigned to a staff lawyer. The legal aid program covers almost all areas of law.

The Quebec government has recently introduced several major reforms in order to address cost pressures on the system, including steps apparently designed to restrict client choice by directing legal aid applicants to staff offices in the name of more cost-effective service delivery.

6. Manitoba

Legal aid in Manitoba is governed by the terms of the *Legal Aid Services Society of Manitoba Act*. The *Act* establishes the Legal Aid Services Society, an independent, statutory corporation. The Society's twelve-member Board is appointed by the provincial government. Four of the Board members must be non-lawyers; three must be chosen from a list submitted by the Law Society of Manitoba, one must be a staff lawyer, and one must be a nominee of the federal government.

Legal Aid Manitoba (LAM) uses a mixed-delivery model, employing both private lawyers and nine staff-lawyer offices around the province. The plan also operates two specialty clinics. Approved applicants have the right to choose between private lawyers and staff lawyers. Historically, about 70 percent of applicants have chosen private lawyers.

LAM has been described as "the best example to date of a fully elaborated mixed model of service delivery." LAM projects include the development of a Public Interest Law Centre, the Northern Paralegal Project, the Expanded Eligibility Program, the Portage Legal Services Initiative, other block contracting projects, and the Full Service Duty Counsel Project.

7. Saskatchewan

Legal aid in Saskatchewan is governed by the *Legal Aid Act, 1983*. The *Act* establishes an eleven-member independent statutory commission responsible for the delivery of legal aid services throughout the province.

Legal aid services are provided through a staff delivery system. Legal advice and representation are provided by lawyers and non-lawyers employed by the Commission. Cases are only referred to the private bar in mandatory-choice-of-counsel cases or, occasionally, in cases of a staff lawyer conflict. In conflict cases, the applicant has the option of choosing another staff lawyer or a private lawyer from a panel of lawyers.

Criminal law coverage is provided for all indictable offences. Summary conviction offences and provincial offences are only covered when there is a likelihood of imprisonment or loss of livelihood. All young offender charges are covered. Civil law coverage is restricted to family law matters. Coverage also extends to groups, organizations, or societies, if the majority of their members are eligible applicants and if the matter is within the range of services offered by legal aid.

8. Alberta

Alberta does not have specific legal aid legislation. Rather, the legal aid program is governed by an agreement between the provincial government and the Law Society of Alberta giving the Law Society statutory authority to establish, maintain, and operate a provincial legal aid plan. The Board of Directors of the Law Society is made up of fifteen members, twelve of whom are lawyers. The Board appoints an executive director who is responsible for the administration of the plan.

Services are delivered almost entirely through a judicare model. Clients can choose their own counsel or have one appointed from a panel of participating lawyers if they have not stated a preference.

Criminal law legal aid extends to all matters covered by the federal-provincial agreement. Unlimited coverage is extended to all applicants who are young offenders. Civil coverage is extended when plan officials determine that the case has merit and that the cost of the probable action is reasonable in relation to the remedy sought. The case must also be one in which a reasonable person of modest means would pay for a lawyer. The majority of civil law cases are divorce and related domestic matters.

9. British Columbia

Legal aid in British Columbia is governed by the terms of the *Legal Services Society Act*. This *Act* establishes the Legal Services Society, an independent statutory body responsible for the administration of legal aid in the province. In 1995, the provincial government changed the composition of the Board. There are now fifteen Directors, five appointed by the provincial government, five by the Law Society, two by the Association of Community Law Offices, two from the Native Community Law Offices, and one other community appointee.

Legal aid in British Columbia is delivered through a mixed model. The Society provides services through staff lawyers in eighteen branch offices, through fourteen Community Law Offices, and fifteen Native Community Law Offices. Community Law Offices and Native Community Law Offices are funded by the Legal Services Society and governed by local boards. The Society also provides judicare services in the areas of criminal, family, and immigration law.

Criminal legal aid covers all indictable offences and summary conviction offences in which imprisonment or loss of livelihood is likely upon conviction. Unlimited coverage is extended to all applicants who are young offenders. Civil law coverage is provided for family, immigration, and poverty law matters. The plan also operates an extensive summary information and advice program.

The BC government has recently ordered the BC Legal Services Society to reduce its budget. As a result, the Society has implemented major reforms in an effort to reduce costs and improve service.

The most significant reform was an attempt to substantially increase the proportion of services delivered by staff lawyers. Historically, staff lawyers only delivered poverty law services. The reform plan, however, sought to transfer up to 50 percent of criminal and family law cases to staff counsel.

Tariffs have been cut by approximately 35 percent since 1991, including the imposition of a hold-back.

In 1994, the Legal Services Society implemented its Family Case Management Program. In this program, cases are screened in detail at the intake stage in order to determine coverage. Based upon this initial assessment, cases are either forwarded to a private lawyer or diverted to another agency. The initial retainer is very limited. Lawyers must submit an opinion letter to the Society so that the Society may review the case to determine the need for continuing coverage.

Recent legislation prohibits the Legal Services Society from incurring any deficit without the express written consent of the Attorney General and Minister of Finance.

C. England and Wales

The legal aid system in England and Wales is governed by the *Legal Aid Act, 1988*. Administration for most legal aid services is divided between an independent statutory agency, the Legal Aid Board, and the Lord Chancellor's Department. The Board directly administers civil law legal aid, an extensive summary advice program (known as the "Green Form program"), criminal law legal aid before the Magistrates' Courts, and a criminal law duty solicitor program. The Lord Chancellor's Department administers criminal law legal aid in higher courts. Two other organizations also provide a limited range of legal aid services: Law Centres and Citizens' Advice Bureaus.

All services provided by the Legal Aid Board or the Lord Chancellor's Department are delivered using a judicare model. Law Centres provide summary advice on services through a staff model. Citizens' Advice Bureaus are staffed by volunteers.

The cost of legal aid in England and Wales has been rising dramatically for more than ten years. Between 1983-84 and 1993-94, the cost of legal aid rose more than 500 percent. Between 1990-91 and 1995-96, the cost of legal aid in England and Wales doubled to approximately £1.4 billion.

In response to increased costs, the British government has undertaken a number of legislative reforms, consultations, pilot projects, and policy proposals designed to effectively restructure the entire legal aid system. To date, only a few proposals have been implemented. One commentator notes, however, that "the forces are being massed for truly radical reform."

Past reforms and current proposals include: transferring administration of legal aid from the Law Society to the significantly more business-oriented Legal Aid Board, initiating a program of "franchising" legal aid suppliers as a means of promoting the quality of legal aid work, and undertaking a "Non-Solicitor Agencies Franchising Pilot" project to determine whether independent, non-profit agencies that do not employ solicitors can deliver advice and assistance in the area of "poverty law" to the same standards as solicitors.

The British government has also recently proposed replacing open-ended legal aid funding with capped, predetermined annual budgets, allowing new types of service providers—including non-lawyers, advice agencies, and mediators—to deliver legal aid services and to prioritize legal aid expenditures on the basis of directions from the Lord Chancellor to the Board.

The most significant reform proposed by the British government is a proposal to deliver all civil law legal services through block contracts. These contracts will be let by the Legal Aid Board through thirteen area offices. Area offices will be responsible for drawing up more detailed local plans for letting contracts in their areas.

Of these measures, the contracting proposal is probably the most far-reaching. The British government believes that contracting "will help control total spending and target priority areas, and will enable the Legal Aid Board to insist on efficiency, effectiveness and quality in selecting providers." However, many details of the contracting procedure still need to be determined.

The Lord Chancellor expects to complete the reforms in "at least four or five years."

NOTES AND QUESTIONS

1. What is the rationale for legal aid—effective or formal equality? Is it to put a poor person in the same position as the more comfortable or is it to provide a set of services more sensitive to the different needs of the poor? Does legal aid merely ensure minimal access, but to a system that is tilted against the needs of the poor?

2. The extracts draw a distinction between judicare, where the client brings a legal-aid certificate to a lawyer of his or her choice, and clinics staffed by employed lawyers. What are the arguments for each type of service? Are the clinics an improvement? Is it argued that they are because they offer services not available under traditional legal aid schemes, such as representation before tribunals and general welfare issues. But are they a real solution to the problem of the poor or are they anything more than a band-aid for deeper wounds? A former attorney general of Ontario has said that "the clinics help convince the poor that they have a stake in this society" (The Honourable R. McMurtry, QC, "Notes for a Statement to the Ontario Legislature Standing Committee on the Administration of Justice," December 1, 1982, at 30-31). But do they, or do they simply help to mask the enduring problems of poverty?

3. The hourly rates paid by legal aid may be substantially lower than those which lawyers earn in private practice. Lower fees lead to a situation where only relatively junior lawyers are prepared to act on a certificate. An additional access concern regarding the low fees of legal aid is that lawyers may refuse to act in matters that are particularly complicated. Note that the Rules of Professional Conduct state that "[i]t is in

keeping with the best traditions of the legal profession to reduce or waive a fee in a situation where there is a hardship or poverty, or the client or prospective client would otherwise effectively be deprived of legal advice or representation" (see rule 9, commentary 2). Do you think that this rule goes far enough? Should lawyers be obliged to provide free services, or services at reduced fees? Why or why not? At least two US law schools have instituted a requirement that all students perform a predetermined number of hours of public interest legal services as a prerequisite to graduation. At least part of the rationale is to try to instill in soon-to-be lawyers the "best traditions" of the legal profession referred to in rule 9.

The students' legal aid clinic at the University of Ottawa adopted a policy that, in cases of domestic abuse, only victims (women) would be assisted. This policy was attacked by some members of the Ottawa bar in 1990 and caused an investigation by the Law Society of Upper Canada. The following article discusses the issues raised by these events and the implication for policies regarding legal aid and how such resources are utilized.

R. Carey, "'Useless' (UOSLAS) v. The Bar: The Struggles of the Ottawa Student Clinic To Represent Battered Women"
(1992), 8 *Journal of Law and Social Policy* 55 (footnotes omitted)

• • •

3. The Role of Lawyers in the Clinical Setting

All too often, people think that clinics and fee-for-service lawyers differ *only in the types of cases they handle or the way they are funded.* While these differences, of course, exist, the fundamental difference is the scope of service they are intended to provide. The Regulations give to clinics, and not to fee-for-service lawyers, the mandate to promote "the legal welfare of a community." If clinics do not fulfil this mandate, no one else will. [Emphasis in original.]

In order to understand the role of the lawyer in the clinical setting and the defence bar's objections to the Women's Division, it is necessary to understand at the outset what the local members of the bar considered a lawyer's proper role. They stated that, "the policy violates the most sacred principles on which our justice system is based" and "It's crystal clear to me that they don't understand their role as defence counsel." Clearly, UOSLAS fundamentally disagreed with this assessment. The question is: how did these completely different conceptualizations of what was proper behaviour for the clinic arise?

The legal profession is governed by the Law Society of Upper Canada which publishes a set of guidelines for lawyers' behaviour known as the Rules of Professional Conduct. Arthurs, Welsman and Zemans observe:

The right to define the scope of practice is no less valuable a prerogative in protecting the professional monopoly than is the regulation of entry.

The right to interpret the rules and have one's interpretation accepted as the "right" one, is often representative of a very important power struggle within the profession.

The Rules are extremely vague and open to multiple interpretations, so they are accompanied by commentaries which attempt to explain them. More importantly, the Rules contain enormous gaps. Several commentators have observed that the Rules were created in a particular context, that of traditional practice, and are therefore of little relevance in the clinical setting.

We were accused of breaching several of the rules: Rule 12, Commentary 5—"the lawyer should not exercise the right [to decline employment] merely because a person seeking legal services ... is unpopular or notorious ... or because of the lawyer's private opinion about the guilt of the accused"; Rule 1, Commentary 2—"Dishonourable or questionable conduct"; and Rule 10—"the lawyer ... must represent the client resolutely and honourably. ..." In addition, we were charged with sex discrimination towards the clientele. The only non-discrimination clause included in the Rules is Rule 13, Commentary 5 added as an amendment in February of 1988 in an attempt to make the rules conform to the *Ontario Human Rights Code* and the *Canadian Bill of Rights*. The wording of the rule however, makes it clear that the non-discrimination clause does not apply to clients but rather to other lawyers, employees and articling students. UOSLAS did agree that if the policy constituted sex discrimination, it would be contrary to the *Code* and could not be maintained.

In addition, there were arguments of the bar against the Women's Division along "fundamental justice" terms which seemed to be presented as based in the *Rules*: we had violated the principle of the right to legal counsel and the presumption of innocence. We responded to these arguments by pointing out that no one was going unrepresented, the men were receiving OLAP certificates, and that we were actually extending the right to counsel by offering new legal services to women. This was one of the areas in the dispute where it became obvious that the opponents of the policy actually knew very little about legal aid. As should be clear from the above historical survey, Ontario has always, historically and presently, limited legal aid to a list of prescribed matters. Our response to the presumption of innocence argument was simply to agree with its importance and question what relevance it had to the workings of the Women's Division. The defence bar position was that we had taken on the role of the prosecution:

> We must be vigilant to ensure that the presumption of innocence is not undermined by the adjunct of legal aid and that a social program directed to the assistance of the accused not be transformed into a prosecution agency.

It has been observed that:

> Despite the fact that many private practitioners derive virtually all their income from judicare, the organized profession barely tolerates the salaried legal aid lawyer.

In addition:

> The Canadian legal profession clings strongly to the notion that all its members engage in a common activity, share common attitudes, pursue common interests, and participate equally in the common enterprise of delivering legal services to the public.

It is these attitudes about what it means to be a professional, serving individual needs as a private practitioner and united in a common ideology, that the Women's

Division ran strongly up against. What the defence bar lacked was an understanding of why and how clinic practice differs from what these professional myths may represent.

The community clinics are modelled after the "storefront" law offices which were developed in the United States as a response to President Johnson's so-called "war on poverty." They are premised on the belief that the needs of the poor are not the same as the needs of those who can pay for legal services. The Grange Commission Report recognized that the problems of the poor are structural in nature and systemic in our society. The strategy to be utilized is not the individualized case work of the private lawyer, but rather a combination of activities designed to attack the systemic and structural natures of the problem, as it is assumed that the problems are caused by membership in the group. The regulation describes these strategies and activities as follows:

> … legal services or paralegal services, or both, including activities designed to encourage access to such services or to further such services designed solely to promote the local welfare of a community.

This reasoning regarding the nature of the problem addressed and the strategies to be utilized is equally applicable to the creation of the Women's Division. The problem of violence against women should be seen as a systemic one with roots in our sexist culture, hierarchical intellectual tradition, and misogynist political and social ordering. The difference with the Women's Division's extension of this reasoning to women, was that the women students involved clearly recognized their membership in the group from which the clientele is drawn. The insight of the 1960s that the poor were differently situated in our society due to their poverty can be paralleled to the feminist insight that women are differently situated in our society by reason of their gender.

One of the criticisms of the Women's Division was that the work being done was not legal work at all, but rather "hand holding" more appropriate to a social services agency:

> Helping battered women understand the legal system a little better and holding their hands while they make their way through impersonal and complex court proceedings are laudable initiatives, but it is not the place of legal aid clinics to serve the needs of victims.
>
> There are other organizations and institutions in society to do just that. Legal aid clinics should not be picking up the slack when governments and individuals fail to provide adequate funding to agencies providing services for women.

The defence bar clearly did not understand that clinics are designed and mandated by the regulations to do precisely this kind of community development work, and must be allowed to do this work in order to achieve their purposes.

Mossman and Lightman observe that the creation of clinics meant that:

> There would be a need for "poor peoples" lawyers' who are identified with poor clients and are immune to "conflict of interest" allegations which could result where the same lawyers act for poor clients and against them, depending on the case.

It was in this context that the Women's Division saw the conflict of interest between their work and representing accused charged with violence against the women in their lives. It is also important to acknowledge that the students were attempting to operate in accordance with the Rule of Professional Conduct against conflicts of interest, Rule 5:

The lawyer must not advise or represent both sides of a dispute and … should not act or continue to act in a matter when there is or there is likely to be a conflicting interest.

Initially, the defence bar appeared to have difficulty understanding our conflict concerns because traditional legal practice involves services to individuals, and conflicts arise only on an individual basis. The clinic, by addressing a group need, developed a group conflict of interest policy. The bar reacted because of the designated group—men. Gathercole writes in the poverty law context:

Lawyers cannot accept the fact that the problems of the poor can only be solved through a fundamental restructuring of traditional institutions, not by suing someone in a court of law.

What the feminist law students in the Women's Division were confronted with was the defence bar's resistance to fundamental change which would better the conditions of women.

There were primarily seven criticisms levelled against the policy by the local bar, students and professors who opposed the policy. Two of these arguments were particular to the student opposition and had to do with the structure of student legal aid and its perceived function vis à vis the student body. The remaining five appeared in several newspaper articles and the correspondence with the Law Society Committee appointed to investigate the matter.

First and foremost, the defence bar vehemently believed that the policy was sex discrimination: "It's straight sexual discrimination." "[T]his policy constitutes a denial of equal access to legal assistance for male accused and constitutes discrimination on the basis of sex." Closely associated with this argument was that by targeting our clientele we were misusing public funds: "The publicly-funded Legal Aid program was designed to give legal assistance to *all* on the sole basis of financial need." [Emphasis in original.] This demonstrates the lack of understanding that targeting clientele was exactly what the clinics were designed to do. Characterizing sex discrimination in this fashion reveals an ignorance of discrimination law under the various human rights acts, and of the judicial interpretation of the equality provision of the *Charter of Rights and Freedoms*, section 15. A mere distinction between groups does not constitute inequality. Rather, discrimination is measured by adverse or negative effects on a traditionally marginalized and insular minority. By extending services to women which they were not receiving before, the policy in effect was profoundly anti-discriminatory and in keeping with the affirmative action provision of the *Charter*, section 15(2).

The sex discrimination argument was the initial reaction of opponents to the policy. The bar correctly perceived that the policy represented an attempt to practice "feminist law" and was therefore not only contrary to their vested interests as anti-feminists, but as men.

Secondly, we were accused of being "political" as if that were an inappropriate thing for lawyers to be. As Menkel-Meadow writes: "Going to court is a political act … All of these [legal] acts are assertions or expressions of power or of a right to something." The struggle to redefine the law as innately political has been ongoing in the law school for some time. The debate among students over the policy significantly added to the winning of this struggle, and therefore contributed to the continuing transformation of legal education.

We were attacked on the ground that the policy was adopted in order to prevent us from having to defend unpopular accused, a problem that the Joint Committee had encountered in 1965. An editorial in the *Law Times* interpreted the policy as meaning:

> [L]egal aid [now] means singling out those whose offenses are seen to be most abhorrent and refusing to represent them in court.

A letter from Brian Greenspan to Thomas Bastedo and Marc Somerville claimed:

> The criminal defence counsel has a fundamental obligation in the adversarial process to act on behalf of even the most objectionable accused charged with the most heinous crimes. Criminal lawyers don't defend crimes, hatred, lies or even causes; criminal lawyers defend clients.

What is missing from this line of argument is the fact that UOSLAS is not a firm of criminal lawyers in training. Criminal cases are only a small portion of our total case load. If the argument means that an individual who is training to become a criminal lawyer should be insulated from other legitimate avenues of advocacy, the response must surely be that students have a right to learn as many different areas of the law as possible, and that lawyers have a right to define their own areas of practice. If UOSLAS services were solely confined to criminal matters then the argument might have merit, but then we would not have a Women's Division as it cannot be classified as a "criminal" matter.

There were two additional arguments made by students. It was speculated that the policy would lead to abuses of process as women might "spuriously" ask the clinic for assistance by lying about being assaulted in order to forestall a small claims suit being pursued by a man with the clinic's assistance. The argument is premised on the belief that women are collectively prone to lying, particularly in respect to the violence perpetrated against them by men. It was hardly surprising that the controversy produced comments based on negative and false stereotypes of women, but it was disheartening to hear these remarks from one's classmates.

The second student-produced unique slant on the affair, was published by the *Ottawa Citizen*. Kevin Murphy wrote:

> The impact of feminist perspectives on law reform has been visible and dramatic in the last decade, especially in the criminal justice system. ... The cause of women has also been taken to the highest court in the land. ... This is proof that the feminist perspective is well represented in the Canadian justice system.

This argument, that there is enough feminism in the world, reflects the fact that the school was undergoing an enormous amount of change over a very short period of time and that many students resented feminist legal education being added to the curriculum. The Faculty of Law at the University of Ottawa has made extensive efforts to incorporate alternative perspectives in the curriculum and teaching materials, but there was and is substantial student resistance to feminism within the school. The above argument assumes that feminism is perhaps acceptable as an "add on" to legal education, but reflects a lack of understanding that the feminist legal project is to entirely transform legal thought and practice.

Conclusion

The reaction of some of the members of the local defence bar was described by Dean McRae in a letter to the editor of the *Ottawa Citizen*:

> It is difficult to understand the vehement and at times almost hysterical attack made on this policy.

> One lawyer wrote, "… it is difficult for me to express in civil tones my outrage at the recent decision of the University of Ottawa Student Legal Aid Society." It is my opinion that their continued threats regarding students' future articling prospects was itself a breach of the Rules of Professional Conduct and grounds for a complaint under the *Ontario Human Rights Code*. As a result of their actions, many students felt personally and professionally humiliated.

> Nevertheless, their remarks deserve to be rebutted. They attempted to assert their political ideology by using their legal tools to create arguments concerning the purpose of legal aid and the proper role of a lawyer. None of the students disagreed with the principles of fundamental justice that the defence bar continuously repeated. What was at stake in the debate over the Women's Division was our ability to attempt to put into practice our feminist values and education, and more importantly, our ability to search for "legal remedies to prevent the continuing brutalization of women in our society." These were the real issues involved, and the bar did not address them at all.

NOTE

In 1993, the Law Society of Upper Canada initially turned down approval for a women-only family law clinic as being discriminatory. Unlike the Ottawa clinic's policy on battered women, it was argued that there was no access need that was peculiar to women. Six months later, the Law Society reversed its earlier decision and approved the family law clinic.

VI. RESPONSIBILITY FOR ACCESS

A. The Demographics of the Legal Profession

Insofar as the legal profession is committed to improving the availability to legal services and, therefore to access to justice, it is surely incumbent upon them to ensure that the ranks of the profession are open to all and that they are generally representative of the society that lawyers are intended to serve. In short, a diverse society deserves and is entitled to a diverse legal profession. Without realistic access to lawyers of one's choice, efforts to improve access to justice seem destined to flounder. In reading the following extract, think about the implications of the trend towards fragmentation for questions of access to the legal process.

A. Hutchinson, "Legal Ethics for a Fragmented Society: Between Personal and Professional"
(1998), *Journal of the Legal Profession* (forthcoming)

Whether there ever has been one type of *lawyer* or one kind of *legal practice*, Canada's legal profession at the end of the twentieth century comprises many types of lawyer and many kinds of legal practice. Although the Canadian literature is not as extensive or as thorough as that of the United Kingdom and the United States, there is ample evidence to support the developing view that talk of one legal profession is almost becoming fanciful; there is such a horizontally and vertically differentiated set of people and organisations engaging in different sorts of legal practice that generalisations are as unfounded as they are misleading. The profession is differentiated into megafirms, smaller partnerships, and single practitioners, not to mention government lawyers and the like; there is little shared experience, little interaction between them and each operate in line within different cultures and norms. Indeed, the idea that there is a unified legal profession is not only mythical, but has an insidious bearing on legal ethics. From its elite status at Confederation, the legal profession has become increasingly fragmented, both in terms of diversity (different people and forms of organisation) and stratification (a hierarchical order to such diversity). Unfortunately, there has been a marked tendency for the benefits of diversity to be neutralised by the imposition of stratification: the new and diverse personnel are relegated to the marginalized periphery of the legal profession. While the profession has diversified, the typical lawyer remains male, white, English-speaking, early middle-aged, and Christian: other lawyers who deviate from this norm are greater in number, but still less powerful in prestige and influence.

Legal practice is shaped by many factors, both external and internal to it. In recent decades, the Canadian legal profession has been strongly influenced by a variety of environmental forces over which it has very little control: decreasing state regulation; the juridification of dispute-resolution; the re-structuring of the economy; the extent of globalisation; and the spread of computerisation and information technology. Not surprisingly, these external forces have been mediated through a set of internal filters that affect their impact on the workings of the legal profession. The first thing to note is that there is no longer a Canadian legal profession—there are many different ones, ranging from the solo practice to the large corporate bureaucracy through the small partnerships and government lawyers. The days of the fungible lawyer or legal practice are long gone. There is a wide range of lawyering types who engage in a wide variety of practices. Who does law (men and women, young and old, black and white, etc.), where they do it (office towers, shopping malls, clinics, home basements, government offices, mobile vans, etc.), how they do it (with entrepreneurial flair, part-time, on a shoe-string, as big business, etc.), who they do it for (aboriginal people, rich individuals, international conglomerates, homeless, small businesses, etc.), and what they do it for (subsistence income, personal satisfaction, enormous income, political influence, etc.) has gone through a transformation. However, as well as there being a greater diversification of the legal profession, there has been a marked increase in the stratification. Lawyers are distinguished by not only what they do, but the professional satisfaction, financial reward, public esteem and political influence that they experience.

The size of the Canadian legal profession increased by 430% from 1931 to 1986 and went from 2,710 members in 1986 to 49,680 in 1996. This translated in Ontario into the lawyer/population ratio jumping from 1/1142 in 1960 to 1/574 in 1981. As Tables A and B show, the proportion of different ethnicities, genders, nationalities and religious affiliations has changed significantly: while the percentage of lawyers born in Canada has reduced slightly, the general diversity has improved significantly. As regards the organisation and hierarchy of legal practice, Tables C and D reflect the increasing variety of ways in which lawyers practice law. However, there are certain forms of legal practice that are much more prestigious than others and certain differences have some definite implications for legal ethics. In particular, not only do the elite firms have greater access to the law society bodies that develop the rules and culture of the profession, but the sole practitioner is much more likely to be subject to formal monitoring by the profession. In short, big-time lawyers establish the standards of good lawyering and ensure that small-time lawyers live up to them. A refusal to abandon the assumption of an homogeneous profession, even in the face of a statistically diverse one, will not only be mis-matched to the needs of the public and the profession, but will also exacerbate stratification and hierarchy in the profession.

These changes worked by the external forces operating on the structure and work of the legal profession and its internal re-organisation and economy have exerted a strong influence on the governance of the profession and the status of legal ethics. As well as important changes in the nature of law and legal education, the different kinds of legal practice mean that the effort to impose a unitary and uniform system of governance on the legal profession is coming under increasing pressure; the different constituencies agitate for very different initiatives and regimes of collective supervision. The debates over continuing legal accreditation, articling, diversity, and malpractice insurance pit one part of the profession squarely against another. At its most extreme, this unrest and division of interests will likely precipitate moves to remove or, at least, curtail the legal profession's monopoly. As for legal ethics, the consequences of these external and internal pressures are affecting both the establishment of shared common norms and their enforcement. There are a series of small sub-cultures that have developed and standardised their own standards and expectations for ethical behaviour: small-town family lawyers operate in a different milieu to the metropolitan corporate deal-makers. In this kind of professional climate, it is even more difficult to sustain the idea that there are a common set of Rules and expectations that can both educate and discipline the legal profession in matters of ethical practice.

NOTES AND QUESTIONS

1. As with any survey, the numbers only tell half the story. For instance, although the number of women in the legal profession has had a steady increase over the past decade, there is no real indication that they are taking their place within the elite and powerful sectors of the profession. Women still remain a marked minority in the judiciary, law faculties, etc. Moreover, although women are entering the profession in greater numbers, they are also leaving it in higher proportions than men. See Canadian Bar Association, *Touchstones for Change: Equality, Diversity, and Accountability* (1993).

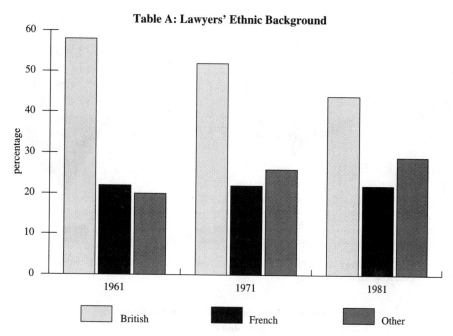

Table A: Lawyers' Ethnic Background

Source: Statistics Canada, *Census of Canada*, decennial pubications.

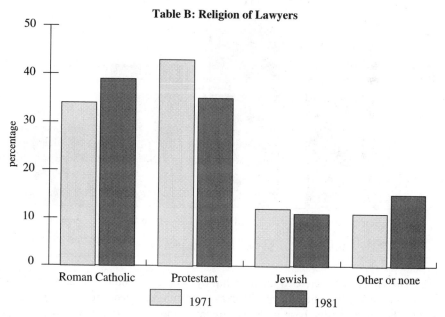

Table B: Religion of Lawyers

Source: Statistics Canada, *Census of Canada*, 1971 and 1981, special tabulations.
Note: There was no question about religion in the 1986 census.

Table C: Industrial Distribution of Lawyers

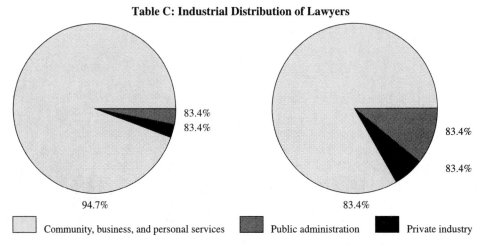

94.7%   83.4%

Community, business, and personal services   Public administration   Private industry

Source: Statistics Canada, *Census of Canada, Occupation by Industry*, decennial publications;
special tabulations for 1986.

**Table D: Distribution of Lawyers in Firms
and Solo Practice**

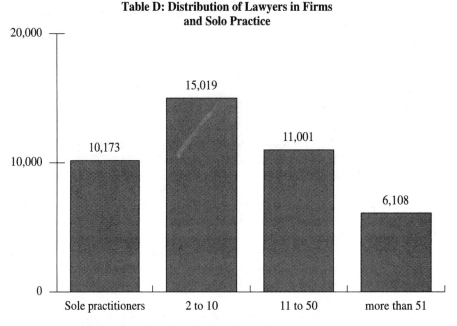

Source: Federation of Law Societies in Canada, 1996 statistics

2. The effect that increased membership by people of colour will have on the legal
profession is very difficult to gauge. Whereas women have at least begun to build qualita-
tively on their quantitative base in the profession, people of colour have yet to achieve a
sufficient foothold. In its preliminary report, the Special Committee on Minority Groups
Assistance Program of the Law Society of Upper Canada recognized underrepresentation.

Even on the most conservative estimates, this discrepancy between the membership of minority groups and their numbers in the legal profession is substantial:

	% of Ontario population or labour force	# of lawyers required to achieve proportionate representation	# of lawyers required to be called each year to maintain proportionate representation
Francophone	6%	1,350	66
Aboriginal People	1.9%	427	21
Visible Minorities	9.6%	1,938	95
Blacks	2.2%*	495	24
Chinese	1.7%*	382	19
Indo-Pakistanis	1.4%*	315	15

* Percentage is of the labour force, not of the population

The committee made a series of recommendations that were intended to address and ameliorate the situation:

1. The Minority Groups Assistance Committee should be made a standing committee charged with the responsibility to carry out these recommendations.

2. The Law Society, in cooperation with the law schools, should develop strategies for attracting law students from among minority groups underrepresented in the legal profession and provide such students with an effective network of support, both financial and otherwise, during law school, the bar admission course, and the first years of practice. Such support could include:

a) bursaries, scholarships, or loans;

b) nomination by law firms or law associations of mentors or advisers to provide guidance and moral support to minority students during the school years;

c) arrangements to assist the placement of students as law clerks and in their articling year; and

d) assistance in securing employment during the first two years following the call to the bar.

3. Means should be found to carry forward to minority groups the message that the Law Society wishes to encourage their enrollment in law schools. Effective dialogue should be established as soon as possible between the Law Society and community leaders to emphasize the significance that the society attaches to involvement in the profession by members of those groups.

4. The Law Society should take a role of leadership in the Ontario legal community, including the law schools, by identifying and coordinating the activities of all programs, organizations, and other resources that are available to support minority students during their studies and early years of practice. In essence, the Law Society should serve as a clearing house for both the problems and the solutions in the areas of minority students' legal studies and practice.

5. Funding for bursaries and scholarships to the amount of $10,000 a year for the next five years available from Butterworths should be used for minority groups.

6. Law associations and individual law firms should be asked to support this program by providing job opportunities and mentors to provide guidance and encouragement.

7. The committee should be provided with a budget of $20,000 to cover any costs the committee may incur in carrying out its mandate.

8. The committee should prepare a three- to five-year financial impact study of the longer-term proposals in the report and make a more detailed analysis of the funding of these proposals by the Law Society and from sources of funding from corporate and other sponsors. The study should report on the cost of establishing an endowment fund and outline the basis on which it would be operated.

9. The Law Society should formally adopt a policy on race relations by which the Law Society and its members will acknowledge the diversity of the community and commit themselves to the equality of treatment and opportunity for all Ontario residents. The policy should reflect the Law Society's present commitment to the provision of services to the public reflecting the particular needs and perspectives of racial minorities.

10. The Law Society should formally adopt an employment equity plan for its own employees that complements the Race Relations Policy and ensures that the Society's employment and promotional practices are consistent with the policy.

11. Appropriate amendments should be made to the Rules of Professional Conduct to require that solicitors abide by the principles of equality of treatment and opportunity to which the Law Society is committed. The Professional Conduct Committee should consider and recommend appropriate changes to rules 1 and 12 in order to achieve that objective.

12. A committee on race relations should be appointed as a standing subcommittee of the Professional Conduct Committee. Its mandate should be to meet as required to continuously monitor the Law Society's procedures, programs, and policies to ensure that they are in harmony with the principles proclaimed in the policy on race relations. Among other things, the committee will constitute a convenient and easily identified "access point" to the Law Society should individuals or groups representing minorities feel that representations should be made to the Law Society on matters or issues that arise from time to time.

13. The Law Society should develop strategies for communicating effectively with minority groups throughout Ontario information on legal services that are available in various languages, and to identify and overcome barriers to the effective delivery of legal services to such groups.

14. The Law Society should prepare a special plan to permit implementation of this report for submission to and approval by the Ontario Human Rights Commission as provided by s. 13 of the Human Rights Code.

Nevertheless, it is likely that the transformative impact of people of colour will be at least as great as that of women. In the United States, the work of Derrick Bell has explored the problems and possibilities for the black challenge to the legal establishment; see *And We Are Not Saved* (1989). In Canada, the work of Patricia A. Monture suggests the kind of large-scale changes that will be necessary to hear and respond to the voice of the First Nations: see "Now That the Door Is Open: First Nations Experience and the Law School Experience" (1990), 15 *Queen's Law Journal* 179.

3. In a similar vein to Mossman, Carrie Menkel-Meadow, "The Comparative Sociology of Women Lawyers" (1986), 24 *Osgoode Hall Law Journal* 397, explores the effect of a feminization of the legal profession and recognizes its transformative potential:

> To the extent that the difference women make is based on their position as outsiders, the discriminated against and dominated, one can imagine a time when parity is achieved that the particular contribution of women to the profession may simply "wither away" as discrimination diminishes and women enter the profession in ever-larger numbers. Those who imagine this time can contemplate an androgynous legal profession, whatever shape that might take. Or, if the differences are of a more complicated origin, some particular contributions of women will continue in forms we probably cannot yet imagine. The hope would be that differences in approach, practice, and substance might serve to broaden the practice of law in such a way that the source of the different contributions would no longer matter—women would make contributions as well as men and the previously disempowered would be empowered so that the source of their disempowerment (gender), might no longer matter. In this view, the feminization of the legal profession is not for feminists only. If feminism's purpose is to help redeem humanism, then the feminization of the legal profession should help redeem the profession from the laws of client domination (both by and for clients), unnecessary and harmful contentiousness, dehumanizing segmentation, stratification, and alienation in the workplace.

B. A Professional Ethic

In matters of regulation, the legal profession engages in much talk about its public responsibility to ensure that the rule of law is upheld and that there is genuine access for all citizens to the legal process so that people can exercise their rights. However, lawyers have tended to be more concerned with the amount and quality of legal services available than with its distribution or general availability. Without access to reasonably priced lawyers, many people will neither know their legal rights nor be able to protect or enforce them. Indeed, a clear part of the compact between the state and the legal profession is that the legal profession can have a monopoly only if it assumes some moral obligation for ensuring that legal representation is reasonably available to all. After all, without such a responsibility, the profession would be a crude cartel that existed simply to limit the supply of legal services, inflate prices, and create market dislocations.

There are three possible ways to approach inequalities in the allocation and distribution of legal services—reduce all barriers to competition among lawyers, including, for example, admission, articling, and compulsory fees; subsidize assistance—for example, legal aid, pro bono, insurance, and tax relief—to those who currently cannot afford legal services; and change the substantive law so that the "have nots" are better protected and favoured—for example, in the areas of rent control and minimum wage. Canadian society has attempted to take initiatives in all three areas, but the overall practical effect manages to be far smaller than the sum of the theoretical parts. Notwithstanding recent efforts at reform, the delivery of legal services is characterised by a strange mix of market discipline and communal regulation. Moreover, the discourse surrounding this contentious topic is also characterised by a similar mix of private and public rhetoric. However, the pattern and logic of the mix is far from consistent or convincing; lawyers tend to favour market discipline for their clients and communal regulation for their own interests. The bottom line is that the costs of legal services continue to be beyond the purse of an increasing number of Canadians. At the same time, the resources of legal aid plans, financed by both government and the legal profession, are being steadily depleted rather than replenished.

Apart from the exhortation "to reduce or waive a fee in cases of hardship or poverty," the Code of Legal Ethics is almost silent about lawyers' duty or willingness to provide services to those who cannot afford legal services (see XI, Legal Ethics, c. 2). While there is much talk about the fair administration of justice and the basic commitment to equal justice for all, lawyers are on their own when it comes to dealing with the less fortunate in society; there is no sense that lawyers as a professional community have any enforceable obligation to serve all sectors of society, rich and poor alike. Indeed, there is only a grudging concession that lawyers "*may* assist in making legal services available by participating in legal aid plans and referral services" (see XIV, Legal Ethics, c. 5). In a code that is partial to the use of "should," this variation in this circumstance is troubling. Moreover, professional rules make it clear that, in the name of free choice, lawyers have a strong right to decline particular employment that is only conditional on the weak duty not to exercise such a right too quickly, not to be too influenced by the unpopularity of the person's cause, and to help rejected clients to find another lawyer (see XIV, Legal Ethics, c. 6).

If the profession is to have any real chance of matching its rhetoric of service to the reality of social need, lawyers must begin to take seriously the obligation to provide their services at reduced rates, to take legal aid clients, and to engage in pro bono work. The following extract raises important questions about the ethical obligations of the legal profession to those who cannot afford legal services.

Andrew Brockett, "New Initiatives in Legal Ethics"
(1993), vol. 6, no. 1 *Westminster Affairs* 16

I plan to describe the Law Society's project to review the *Rules of Professional Conduct*, and to suggest three themes which form part of the context in which the review is taking place.

Over the past couple of years there has been a growing sense among the Benchers of the Law Society that the *Rules of Professional Conduct*, which have been essentially in their preent form since 1978, need to be reviewed. I suggest two reasons for this sense that there is a need to review the *Rules*:

- far-reaching changes in the context in which law is now practised and the increasing complexity of legal practice;
- far-reaching changes in society's ethical values.

An obvious example of the first change would be conflicts of interest in an environment of greater lawyer mobility. As far as the second is concerned, it has been suggested that the present *Rules* date from a time when there was a much broader ethical consensus in the community. Today, the argument runs, some of the ethical values underpinning the

Rules of Professional Conduct are by no means generally shared. If this is true, there may be a need for professional codes of ethics to spell out ethical values which were previously taken for granted.

By the same token, we must not assume that the values which inspired the code of ethics thirty years ago are the appropriate ethical values for the 1990s: the underlying values of the present *Rules* need to be reviewed.

These reasons for undertaking a review of the *Rules* imply that the review will give rise to dynamic ethical debate—which must surely be healthy. They also suggest that there may be a need to spell out the *Rules* in greater detail—to give more specific guidance. Here, there is need to mention one cause for caution.

At a Benchers' Strategic Planning Conference last September entitled "Professionalism in the 90s: Responding to Social and Ethical Change," one of the speakers, Professor Nancy Moore of Rutgers Law School, New Jersey, pointed out that there is a cost to more detailed codification. As codes of ethics move away from a simple statement of ethical principles and begin to take on the characteristics of detailed law, there could well be a consequential loss of ethical aspiration, ethical responsibility and ethical discourse in the profession: to refer to an idea mentioned by Professor Arthurs, a code may lose its didactic effect.

As a consequence of the growing sense that there was a need to review the *Rules of Professional Conduct*, Marc Somerville was asked by the Treasurer of the Law Society last fall to head up the project. A Special Committee of twelve Benchers was appointed at the end of November 1992. ...

Emerging from the Benchers' Strategic Planning Conference on professionalism in the context of social and ethical change were three themes:

- the tension between professional ethics and business imperatives;
- the professional obligation to ensure availability of legal services; and
- competence as a primary ethical obligation.

These will almost certainly influence the review of the *Rules of Professional Conduct* and stimulate ethical debate.

The Tension Between Professional Ethics and Business Imperatives

The September 1992 Conference considered the growing pressures which lead the practice of law to take on the characteristics of a business conducted primarily for profit. This is not a particularly new theme. Mr. Justice Sopinka and Mr. Justice Jennings (then President of the Canadian Bar Association in 1990) have been among those who have spoken about it. I recently discovered the following in the Minutes of Convocation for January 17, 1964:

> Two Judges of the Supreme Court of Ontario have suggested that the Treasurer be asked to give a lecture to the students of Osgoode Hall Law School on the subject "The Practice of Law as a Profession as distinct from a Business."

There are those who argue that the commercialization of the practice of law is a systemic change of enormous significance. Whatever its extent, the trend raises acute questions as to whether professionalism and business imperatives can co-exist. The traditional professional ethic—which surely must inspire all rules of professional conduct—is characterized by a sense of obligation to the community. One way of looking at this is to say that professionals are granted, by the public, a monopoly on the provision of their particular services and the right to regulate or govern themselves. In return, professionals owe a duty to make their expertise available to meet the needs of the public. That public obligation may not always sit comfortably with business demands.

I suggest that the tension between the demands of a business conducted primarily for profit and the public obligations of the legal profession will give rise to much debate as the *Rules* are reviewed. Among other matters, the debate will raise questions as to the ethical responsibilities of large law firms, the role they can play in the ethics of the profession, the effects of the structure of law practice and professional governance on ethics, and questions concerning quality of life, lifestyle and the expectations which firms have of their lawyers.

The Professional Obligation To Ensure Availability of Legal Services

If we return to the social contract theory, we might say that the public grants monopoly rights and self-government to lawyers in return for a recognition by the profession that it has a duty to make its specialist knowledge and abilities available to the public. This tradition is reflected in Commentary 2 to Rule 9 of the *Rules of Professional Conduct*:

> It is in keeping with the best traditions of the legal profession to reduce or waive a fee in a situation where there is hardship or poverty, or the client or prospective client would otherwise effectively be deprived of legal advice or representation.

The Ontario Legal Aid Plan, started by the profession, still administered and to a significant degree financed by the professional, is a practical example of the outworking of this ethical obligation.

At the September 1992 Conference, questions were raised about the implications of the fact that ordinary citizens are increasingly unable to afford the cost of legal services. I suggest this state of affairs will loom large in the ethical debate occasioned by a review of the *Rules of Professional Conduct*. It will affect issues such as fees, whether there should be mandatory *pro bono* obligations, alternative dispute resolution, advertising and hourly billing.

Competence as a Primary Ethical Obligation

We may not be accustomed to thinking of competence as an ethical issue despite the fact that, almost at the head of the *Rules of Professional Conduct*, immediately after the rule on integrity, will be found Rule 2, "Competence and Quality of Service." Much of the Law Society's activity is concerned with competence for entrance to the profession: for instance the Bar Admission Course and its examinations as well as transfer requirements for lawyers from other jurisdictions.

Emerging from the September 1992 Conference is a clarification of the significance of competence. In social contract terms, in return for the monopoly and self-regulation, the profession owes a duty to the public to provide legal services at an appropriate level of competence. More than this, the obligation to the public is to ensure that members of the profession are not only competent when called but continue to be competent to deliver legal services. I suggest this is a theme that will loom large in much of the debate about the *Rules of Professional Conduct*. Consider, for instance, how difficult it is in the increasingly complex environment that is the practice of law today, to be competent as a general practitioner.

The Public Interest

Running through the three themes I have referred to has been a common social contract theory. Of course this is a fiction, but it is one way of illustrating the obligation which lies at the heart of professionalism—the obligation to serve the public interest. In any debate about difficult issues of professional ethics, one crucial question will be: in this situation, what duty does the lawyer owe the public? A closely related question will be: in this situation what would the public perceive to be the correct, ethical solution? If, in response to ethical questions, the solution chosen by the profession, or by the individual lawyer, differs from what the public would consider ethical, we must ask whether we can justify the solution, not in terms of personal or even professional convenience, but in terms of the public interest.

NOTES AND QUESTIONS

1. For some, it is not enough to heap praise on those lawyers who undertake such voluntary work. They argue that this obligation must be built into the basic ethical fabric of professional responsibility. "Access to justice" is a hollow slogan unless there is genuine access to legal services. The legal profession are too quick to trumpet the moral obligation to perform pro bono work, but very slow at fulfilling it. Even when it is done, it is seen as a virtuous act of noblesse oblige rather than a basic responsibility that comes with being a lawyer. The argument is made that, if there is a shortage of affordable lawyers, "it is grossly unfair to conscript the legal profession to fill those needs: if the obligation is one of justice, it is an obligation of society as a whole" (see Fried, "The Lawyer as Friend: The Moral Foundations of the Lawyer–Client Relation," in chapter 3, "The Core Features and Values of the Traditional Model." However, in the light of lawyers' monopoly on a vital social resource, it might seem that it is such hyperbole that is "grossly unfair."

2. Of course, any proposal to require lawyers to do compulsory pro bono work is not without problems. Apart from the ideological argument about infringing lawyers' autonomy, it is seen to devalue the altruistic nature of the work and it is likely to operate in an inequitable way—that is, its burden will be greater for the already economically marginalised practitioner than for partners in large firms. Moreover, it might lead to the wrong kind of work being done and lawyers doing work that they are not trained to do—that is, corporate lawyers representing poor clients for welfare claims. While these objections cannot be ignored, they are insufficient to invalidate the worth of such a proposal—the transformative value of having establishment lawyers appear in provincial

courts ought not to be underestimated. Nonetheless, in response to the traditional concerns, it might be possible, for example, to introduce a coupon scheme whereby clients
are directed to appropriate lawyers and those lawyers who do not receive enough pro
bono coupons will be required to pay into a pro bono fund an equivalent amount to the
hours not done. See D. Luban, "Lawyers and Justice: An Ethical Study" (1988), 277-82,
and Lubet and Stewart, "A 'Public Assets' Theory of Lawyers' Pro Bono Obligations"
(1997), 145 *University of Pennsylvania Law Review* 1245.

C. Access to the Profession

One of the most difficult conflict situations that can arise concerns the circumstances in
which lawyers or their law firms can act against former clients. Rules governing such
situations are not simply specific to a particular transaction, but can have a continuing
impact. For instance, if a lawyer has represented a borrower, he cannot represent a
lender in future dealings with the borrower because he might have confidential information about the borrower's financial position. This duty is triggered not by actual evidence of conflict, but by the possibility of conflict. A particular difficulty is that it is not
always obvious that there might be a conflict; lawyers might not be aware of certain
information that would trigger the awareness of a conflict. However, there is a very
strong duty on lawyers to take all reasonable steps to ensure that there is no possibility
of a conflict arising. Indeed, in most situations that give rise to conflicts of interest,
lawyers will carry a heavy burden of responsibility as compared to their clients.

In many conflict situations, there are a number of competing values in play—
maintaining the integrity of the legal profession and justice system such that clients and
the public at large will have confidence that they operate to the highest levels of professional probity; ensuring that clients can have the widest possible choice and discretion in
selecting lawyers to represent them such that they are not deprived of their chosen
lawyer without very good cause; and facilitating the mobility of the legal profession
such that lawyers are not unduly hampered in their ability to advance their careers or to
practice where and with whom they want. The thrust of these policy arguments in
conflict situations is neither clear nor decisive. While it is crucial to ensure that conflicts
and the resulting dissemination of confidential information does not occur, it is also
important not to place too onerous a restriction on clients in their choice of lawyers or
lawyers in their choice of practice; the injustice and disruption caused by genuine
conflicts do not always outweigh the expense and inconvenience to clients and lawyers,
especially when the action or dealing is well-advanced.

The Canadian legal profession has begun to take much more seriously the problems
that might and do arise in situations where there are conflicting interests between lawyers and their former clients. In particular, there have been numerous cases that have
involved motions to remove the opposing party's lawyers from the record on the ground
that those lawyers had earlier acted for the moving party. Since the late 1960s, two
divergent lines of authority have emerged to deal with these situations. One line developed and applied a narrow "probability of real mischief" test which required that real
conflict and prejudice would almost certainly occur if the lawyer was allowed to continue to take part in transaction or litigation. Another line of authority opted for a

broader test in which it had only to be demonstrated that there was a "possibility of prejudice" or "appearance of impropriety" in order for the lawyer to be removed. Whereas the former led to few lawyers being removed from the record, the latter more readily led to the disqualification of lawyers on the basis of conflict of interest.

A fairly recent Supreme Court of Canada decision has addressed some of these issues. When reading through the judgment, ask yourself whether the court gave enough or appropriate concern to the importance of clients having the widest possible choice and discretion in selecting their lawyer.

Martin v. Gray
[1991] 1 WWR 705 (SC)

Respondent brought an action against appellant for an accounting. Appellant's solicitor was assisted by a junior member of his firm who was actively engaged in the case and was privy to many confidences disclosed by appellant to his solicitor. The junior member later joined the law firm which represents respondent in this action. Appellant made an application to the provincial superior court for a declaration that the law firm was ineligible to continue to act as solicitors of record for respondent. The court granted the application and ordered the firm removed as solicitors of record. The Manitoba Court of Appeal reversed that decision.

SOPINKA J: In resolving this issue, the Court is concerned with at least three competing values. There is first of all the concern to maintain the high standards of the legal profession and the integrity of our system of justice. Furthermore, there is the countervailing value that a litigant should not be deprived of his or her choice of counsel without good cause. Finally, there is the desirability of permitting reasonable mobility in the legal profession. The review of the cases which follows will show that different standards have been adopted from time to time to resolve the issue. This reflects the different emphasis placed at different times and by different judges on the basic values outlined above.

The legal profession has changed with the changes in society. One of the changes that is most evident in large urban centers is the virtual disappearance of the sole practitioner and the tendency to larger and larger firms. This is a product of a number of factors including a response to the demands of large corporate clients whose multi-faceted activities require an all-purpose firm with sufficient numbers in every area of expertise to serve their needs. With increase in size come increasing demands for management of a law firm in accordance with the corporate model. These changes in the composition and management practices of law firms are reflected in changes to ethical practices of the profession. Some of the old practices have been swept aside as anachronistic, perhaps with justification. Advertising to inform the public in a tasteful way of the services provided by a firm and of its fee schedule is but one example.

Merger, partial merger and the movement of lawyers from one firm to another are familiar features of the modern practice of law. They bring with them the thorny problem of conflicts of interest. When one of these events is planned, consideration must be given to the consequences which will flow from loss of clients through conflicts of interest. To facilitate this process some would urge a slackening of the standard with respect to what constitutes a conflict of interest. In my view, to do so at the present time would serve the interest of neither the public nor the profession. The legal profession has historically struggled to maintain the respect of the public. This has been so notwithstanding the high standards that, generally, have been maintained. When the management, size of law firms and many of the practices of the legal profession are indistinguishable from those of business, it is important that the fundamental professional standards be maintained and indeed improved. This is essential if the confidence of the public that the law is a profession is to be preserved and hopefully strengthened. Nothing is more important to the preservation of this relationship than the confidentiality of information passing between a solicitor and his or her client. The legal profession has distinguished itself from other professions by the sanctity with which these communications are treated. The law, too, perhaps unduly, has protected solicitor and client exchanges while denying the same protection to others. This tradition assumes particular importance when a client bares his or her soul in civil or criminal litigation. Clients do this in the justifiable belief that nothing they say will be used against them and to the advantage of the adversary. Loss of this confidence would deliver a serious blow to the integrity of the profession and to the public's confidence in the administration of justice.

An important statement of public policy with respect to the conduct of barrister and solicitor is contained in the professional ethics codes of the governing bodies of the profession. The legal profession is self-governing. In each province there is a governing body usually elected by the lawyers practising in the province. The governing body enacts rules of professional conduct on behalf of those it represents. These rules must be taken as expressing the collective views of the profession as to the appropriate standards to which the profession should adhere.

While there exists no national law society, the Canadian Bar Association, a national society representing lawyers across the country, adopted a Code of Professional Conduct in 1974. The Code has been adopted by the Law Society of Manitoba and by the Law Societies of other provinces. Chapter V, entitled "Impartiality and Conflict of Interest," commences with the following rule:

> The lawyer must not advise or represent both sides of a dispute and, save after adequate disclosure to and with the consent of the client or prospective client concerned, he should not act or continue to act in a matter when there is or there is likely to be a conflicting interest. A conflicting interest is one which would be likely to affect adversely the judgment of the lawyer on behalf of or his loyalty to a client or prospective client or which the lawyer might be prompted to prefer to the interests of a client or prospective client.

The rule is followed by thirteen commentaries. The most relevant of these are Commentaries 11 and 12 which state:

> 11. A lawyer who has acted for a client in a matter should not thereafter act against him (or against persons who were involved in or associated with him in that matter) in the same or any related matter, or place himself in a position where he might be tempted or

appear to be tempted to breach the Rule relating to Confidential Information. It is not, however, improper for the lawyer to act against a former client in a fresh and independent matter wholly unrelated to any work he has previously done for that person.

12. For the sake of clarity the foregoing paragraphs are expressed in terms of the individual lawyer and his client. However, it will be appreciated that the term "client" includes a client of the law firm of which the lawyer is a partner or associate whether or not he handles the client's work.

A code of professional conduct is designed to serve as a guide to lawyers and typically it is enforced in disciplinary proceedings. See, for example, *Law Society of Manitoba v. Giesbrecht* (1983), 24 Man. R (2d) 228 (CA). The courts, which have inherent jurisdiction to remove from the record solicitors who have a conflict of interest, are not bound to apply a code of ethics. Their jurisdiction stems from the fact that lawyers are officers of the court and their conduct in legal proceedings which may affect the administration of justice is subject to this supervisory jurisdiction. Nonetheless, an expression of a professional standard in a code of ethics relating to a matter before the court should be considered an important statement of public policy. The statement in Chapter V should therefore be accepted as the expression by the profession in Canada that it wishes to impose a very high standard on a lawyer who finds himself or herself in a position where confidential information may be used against a former client. The statement reflects the principle that has been accepted by the profession that even an appearance of impropriety should be avoided.

The Law

The law in Canada and in other jurisdictions has adopted one of two basic approaches in determining whether a disqualifying conflict of interest exists: (1) the probability of real mischief, or (2) the possibility of real mischief. The term "mischief" refers to the misuse of confidential information by a lawyer against a former client. The first approach requires proof that the lawyer was actually possessed of confidential information and that there is a probability of its disclosure to the detriment of the client. The second is based on the precept that justice must not only be done but must manifestly be seen to be done. If, therefore, it reasonably appears that disclosure might occur, this test for determining the presence of a disqualifying conflict of interest is satisfied.

[A lengthy discussion of authorities is omitted.]

What then should be the correct approach? Is the "probability of mischief" standard sufficiently high to satisfy the public requirement that there be an appearance of justice? In my opinion, it is not. This is borne out by the judicial statements to which I have referred and to the desire of the legal profession for strict rules of professional conduct as its adoption of the Canadian Code of Professional Conduct demonstrates. The probability of mischief test is very much the same as the standard of proof in a civil case. We act on probabilities. This is the basis of *Rakusen*, [1912] Ch. D 831. I am, however, driven to the conclusion that the public, and indeed lawyers and judges, have found that standard wanting. In dealing with the question of the use of confidential information we are dealing with a matter that is usually not susceptible of proof. As pointed out by Fletcher Moulton LJ in *Rakusen*, "that is a thing which you cannot prove" (at p. 841). I would add "or disprove." If it were otherwise, then no doubt the public would be satisfied upon proof that no prejudice would be occasioned. Since, however, it is not susceptible of proof, the test must be such that the public represented by the reasonably informed person would be satisfied that no use of confidential information would occur. That, in my opinion, is the overriding policy that applies and must inform the court in answering the question: Is there a disqualifying conflict of interest? In this regard, it must be stressed that this conclusion is predicated on the fact that the client does not consent to but is objecting to the retainer which gives rise to the alleged conflict.

Typically, these cases require two questions to be answered: (1) Did the lawyer receive confidential information attributable to a solicitor and client relationship relevant to the matter at hand? (2) Is there a risk that it will be used to the prejudice of the client?

In answering the first question, the Court is confronted with a dilemma. In order to explore the matter in depth may require the very confidential information for which protection is sought to be revealed. This would have the effect of defeating the whole purpose of the application. American courts have solved this dilemma by means of the "substantial relationship" test. Once a "substantial relationship" is shown, there is an irrebuttable presumption that confidential information was imparted to the lawyer. In my opinion, this test is too rigid. There may be cases in which it is established beyond any reasonable doubt that no confidential information relevant to the current matter was disclosed. One example is where the applicant client admits on cross-examination that this is the case. This would not avail in the face of an irrebuttable presumption. In my opinion, once it is shown by the client that there existed a previous relationship which is sufficiently related to the retainer from which it is sought to remove the solicitor, the court should infer that confidential information was imparted unless the solicitor satis-fies the court that no information was imparted which could be relevant. This will be a difficult burden to discharge. Not only must the court's degree of satisfaction be such that it would withstand the scrutiny of the reasonably informed member of the public that no such information passed, but the burden must be discharged without revealing the specifics of the privileged communication. Nonetheless, I am of the opinion that the door should not be shut completely on a solicitor who wishes to discharge this heavy burden.

The second question is whether the confidential information will be misused. A lawyer who has relevant confidential information cannot act against his client or former client. In such a case the disqualification is automatic. No assurances or undertakings not to use the information will avail. The lawyer cannot compartmentalize his or her mind so as to screen out what has been gleaned from the client and what was acquired elsewhere. Furthermore, there would be a danger that the lawyer would avoid use of information acquired legitimately because it might be perceived to have come from the client. This would prevent the lawyer from adequately representing the new client. Moreover, the former client would feel at a disadvantage. Questions put in cross-exami-nation about personal matters, for example, would create the uneasy feeling that they had their genesis in the previous relationship.

The answer is less clear with respect to the partners or associates in the firm. Some courts have applied the concept of imputed knowledge. This assumes that the knowledge of one member of the firm is the knowledge of all. If one lawyer cannot act, no member of the firm can act. This is a rule that has been applied by some law firms as their particular brand of ethics. While this is commendable and is to be encouraged, it is, in my opinion, an assumption which is unrealistic in the era of the mega-firm. Furthermore, if the presumption that the knowledge of one is the knowledge of all is to be applied, it must be applied with respect to both the former firm and the firm which the moving lawyer joins. Thus there is a conflict with respect to every matter handled by the old firm that has a substantial relationship with any matter handled by the new firm irrespective of whether the moving lawyer had any involvement with it. This is the "overkill" which has drawn so much criticism in the United States to which I have referred above.

Moreover, I am not convinced that a reasonable member of the public would necessarily conclude that confidences are likely to be disclosed in every case despite institutional efforts to prevent it. There is, however, a strong inference that lawyers who work together share confidences. In answering this question, the court should therefore draw the inference, unless satisfied on the basis of clear and convincing evidence, that all reasonable measures have been taken to ensure that no disclosure will occur by the "tainted" lawyer to the member or members of the firm who are engaged against the former client. Such reasonable measures would include institutional mechanisms such as Chinese walls and cones of silence. These concepts are not familiar to Canadian courts and indeed do not seem to have been adopted by the governing bodies of the legal profession. It can be expected that the Canadian Bar Association, which took the lead in adopting a Code of Professional Conduct in 1974, will again take the lead to determine whether institutional devices are effective and develop standards for the use of institutional devices which will be uniform throughout Canada. ...

These standards will, in my opinion, strike the appropriate balance among the three interests to which I have referred. In giving precedence to the preservation of the confidentiality of information imparted to a solicitor, the confidence of the public in the integrity of the profession and in the administration of justice will be maintained and strengthened. On the other hand, reflecting the interest of a member of the public to retain counsel of her choice and the interest of the profession in permitting lawyers to move from one firm to another, the standards are sufficiently flexible to permit a solicitor to act against a former client provided that a reasonable member of the public who is in possession of the facts would conclude that no unauthorized disclosure of confidential information had occurred or would occur.

Application to This Case

The answer to the first question in this case presents no problem. It is acknowledged that Kristin Dangerfield actively worked on the very case in respect of which her new firm is acting against her former client. She is therefore in possession of relevant confidential information.

With respect to the second question, there is nothing beyond the sworn statements of Sweatman and Dangerfield that no discussions of the case have occurred and undertaking that none will occur. In my opinion, while, as stated by the courts below, there is no reason not to accept the affidavits of apparently reputable counsel, this is not sufficient to demonstrate that all reasonable measures have been taken to rebut the strong inference of disclosure. Indeed, there is nothing in the affidavits to indicate that any independently verifiable steps were taken by the firm to implement any kind of screening. There is nothing to indicate that when Ms. Dangerfield joined the firm, instructions were issued that there were to be no communications directly or indirectly between Ms. Dangerfield and the four members of the firm working on the case. While these measures would not necessarily have been sufficient, I refer to them in order to illustrate the kinds of independently verifiable steps which, along with other measures, are indispensable if the firm intends to continue to act.

I would therefore allow the appeal with costs to the appellant both here and in the Court of Appeal, set aside the judgment of the Court of Appeal of Manitoba and restore the judgment of Hanssen J.

NOTES AND QUESTIONS

1. Is the test proposed strict enough? Does Sopinka's judgment rest upon a realistic understanding of legal practice? Does he recognize the different context of smaller-scale practice outside of large urban centres? How might lawyers arrange their affairs to get around these conflict problems? What tests might be adopted to gauge whether clients' consent to any pre-emptive arrangement was reasonable and reliable?

2. In his minority opinion, Cory J stated that "where a lawyer who has had a substantial involvement with a client in an ongoing contentious matter joins another law firm which is acting for an opposing party, there is an irrebuttable presumption that the knowledge of such lawyer, including confidential information disclosed to him or her by the former client, has become the knowledge of the new firm. Such an irrebuttable presumption is essential to preserve public confidence in the administration of justice." Is such a strict approach necessary to preserve the integrity of the judicial system and the public confidence in it? Or will the strictness of this approach actually work to produce more problems than it solves?

3. A related issue that has caused concern among the legal profession is the responsibility of lawyers to report alleged breaches of ethical obligations by other lawyers, especially partners and co-workers. In the wake of the so-called Lang, Michener affair, the Law Society of Upper Canada found five partners guilty of professional misconduct for failing to report allegations of impropriety and illegal activity by a former partner. However, they were found not guilty of failing to inform clients of the partner's conduct. The conduct concerned conspiracy and forgery in regard to immigration matters. Should lawyers have a stricter obligation to the profession or their clientele?

Client selection is one of the most important and most neglected issues for lawyers. Indeed, it is arguably the most important decision that any lawyer makes because, once a client is taken on, the lawyer has become committed to a whole host of ethical and moral obligations. They are engaged in a special relationship that lawyers cannot simply abandon as and when they choose. Moreover, all clients are entitled to the same level of competence and commitment from their lawyers. In Canada, lawyers can choose to represent whichever clients they wish. There is no equivalent to the English cab-rank rule that requires barristers to accept any client who seeks their services at a reasonable fee in their area of expertise. While the professional rules are imbued with a general sense that legal services are important and should be made available to everyone, there are no prohibitions on lawyers refusing to represent particular clients or causes. However, while it is arguable that it was the case under most general provincial laws, some provinces have recently declared that lawyers must not make their choice of clients in a way that discriminates on the basis of race or gender, for example. Other than this, lawyers are not formally constrained in their decisions about how to allocate their services and expertise.

The following extract offers an unconventional approach to client selection in that it suggests that lawyers take greater responsibility for the clients and causes that they represent. If more lawyers adopted such an approach, would there be less or more of an access problem?

D. Kennedy, "The Responsibility of Lawyers for the Justice of Their Causes"
(1987), 18 *Texas Technical Law Review* 1157-63

Begin with a vacuous piety: Try your best, oh graduating students of the Washington College of Law, to avoid doing harm with your lawyer skills.

If I asked each of you to swear an oath to try to avoid doing harm with your lawyer skills, I bet most of you would say, "Why object? All right, boss, you're the graduation speaker, sounds harmless, even obvious, to me, I hereby pledge myself to avoid doing harm with my lawyer skills."

But I think this vacuous piety has some controversial bite. It would get many lawyers into trouble. To make the pledge controversial, let me put aside two of its easy meanings. When you represent a client, you should do your best for her, or him. That means: *avoid malpractice*, and who can quarrel with that. Then there's another, slightly more touchy point. I think we would all agree that a lawyer doesn't in most situations have to take on a client. If you think the client is trying to do something terrible, and wants to use your lawyer skills to do harm, you don't have to take the case, unless a court appoints you to take it.

Your right-to-turn-down-a-case goes beyond just not having to do something to help a person with evil intentions. You might not take the case because you didn't want to contribute or even be associated in any way with a client you thought was bad. Your cases are yours to choose on any basis you want.

I know this is a *little* controversial because of the reaction from the establishment bar and editorial writers when students around the country began a boycott of hiring interviews with firms that represent the South African government. A lot of lawyers thought it was outrageous for students to try to influence law firms, or to interfere with the ability of the South African government to get counsel, by threatening not to go to work for those firms.

I want to go a step further than those students. While it's true no one should blame you for refusing to represent a client whose activity your disapprove of, that's not enough. You should feel guilty, and we should disapprove of you, if you go ahead and argue a cause you think will do more harm than good. You shouldn't take the case if you think it would be better for society, or more moral, for the client to lose. You shouldn't take the case if you think the client shouldn't be in court in the first place, for example, because the client should morally have made recompense even though he has a technically good legal defense. You shouldn't take the case if your client is enforcing his legal rights, but is *using* his legal rights in a bad cause.

This is the tough meaning of the vacuous piety that you should avoid doing harm with your lawyer skills. Most lawyers don't agree with it at all. They believe that you are not tarred morally by your clients' underlying intentions, or character, or by the outcome, as long as you don't participate in law breaking yourself. Maybe they make an exception and condemn Mafia lawyers, even when they aren't involved directly in criminal activity. But that's about it. I think you *are* tarred with bad actions of clients that you facilitate in your work as a lawyer.

To the extent this is right, it is wrong to represent an abortion clinic that's trying to lease a new building to expand its operations, if you are pro-life. And it's wrong to represent a landlord who has been intimidated into trying to evict an abortion clinic if you are pro-choice. It's wrong to work against unionization if you believe everyone should have a labor union; and wrong to work for union rights to picket a shopping center if you think unions are generally evil. It's wrong to lobby for the postponement of environmental controls if you think they should be imposed right now; and wrong to do antitrust work against a corporate merger, if you believe mergers are good for the economy.

My position is extreme, and it will certainly apply to you at some point in your lives as lawyers. I suppose that's what graduation speeches are at least sometimes for. I'm saying you should turn down the client even though she isn't trying to get you to do anything illegal, and even though she isn't doing anything illegal herself. She just wants you to argue that the abortion clinic has violated its lease, which you don't believe is the case, or that the merger violates the anti-trust laws. I'm saying that if *you* think the outcome of winning-for-your-client would be on balance a bad thing, socially unfortunate, you should decline to participate, in spite of the fact that the client will pay, and that you wouldn't be doing anything that came close to violating the canons of professional ethics. You'd be in the clear as far as "unethical conduct" is concerned, as it's defined by your profession. But I'm suggesting that you'd be morally in the wrong anyway.

There are lots and lots of objections to what I've just said. I'm going to try to shoot down about twenty of them in rapid succession. First, what about the Porsche? I don't mean mine (I don't have one); I mean the one you might imagine in your future. The short answer is that there's plenty of money to be made out there, for most lawyers most of the time, without becoming a hired gun—that's what we're talking about, the lawyer as a gun for hire regardless of the morals of the client. At least at present, there are tons of morally innocuous, or positively beneficial, or neutral, lawyer work. *Most* lawyer work falls into that category for most people. If sticking to that type of work involves some loss of income, so be it. Maybe you'll win a Porsche in the lottery.

Second, if I don't do it, someone else will. But that doesn't make it right for you to do it. You should avoid doing harm with your lawyer skills even if there is someone else waiting to take your place.

Third, what can be wrong, indeed why isn't it a good thing, to help people enforce their rights? Lawyers should be devoted to legality, but I am proposing that they refuse clients on non-legal grounds—on the grounds that, though within their rights, the clients in question are doing more harm than good.

The simple answer is that law is not coterminous with morality: there is a vast range of behavior that harms people without legal remedy, and when lawyers help people do that harm, they can't escape responsibility for it if it is immoral. Legality is important. It's a good starting point for the discussion. But that your client had a legal right to injure and get away with it doesn't mean that you can have a clear conscience, even if your role was just routinely technical, and it wasn't you who chose the course of action, if the course of action was immoral.

Further, lawyers are often—maybe usually—more than just legal technicians. They shape deals and they make law. They invent new forms of social life, they fill gaps, resolve conflicts and ambiguities. They mold the law, through the process of legal argument, in court, in briefs, in negotiations. It won't do to say, look, I molded the law this way, and this way, and this way. I've made a lot of law. But don't hold me responsible for the actual content of the law I made. That was determined by who happened to be my client at the time. I chose my clients according to their ability to pay. What concern is it of mine if the law they paid me to make goes against my own moral beliefs? I'm just an advocate and I leave the final decision to others.

The trouble with this is that your activity is not neutral, and the better your legal skills, the less neutral you become. Lawyers think up new rules, ideas, arrangements and arguments. Which ones win, which ones judges and juries and legislatures adopt, is a function of who has the legal talent on their side, as well as a function of the justice of the position. If you put your legal talent on the side of outcomes you disapprove of, you make it at least a little more likely that bad outcomes, bad new inventions of your own, will prevail. You bear responsibility when *your* unique way of molding the law, your work product, wins out to the detriment of the community, even if it was not you, but a judge or administrator who "pulled the trigger," so to speak, by actually deciding the case, and even if someone else would have done it if you didn't.

But what would happen to the right to counsel if lawyers were always second-guessing the justice of their clients' causes? And what about Our Adversary System? Isn't it based on the lawyers going all out for their clients, and letting truth emerge through conflict? It's up to the jury or the judge to decide on the justice of the case; it's up to the *lawyer* to present the best possible case for her side, whichever it may be.

These are serious objections, and I'm willing to make some concessions to recognize some counterprinciples to the one I'm arguing for. After all, even on this day of days there are no absolutes.

First, I am *not* saying that you should represent bad clients half-heartedly or incompetently. I'm talking about the choice of clients. Once you sign on, it seems to me you *are* somewhat stuck with being an adversary within the adversary system, unless something unexpected happens that means you have to withdraw. This can pose a lot of delicate problems, if you are really trying not to use your lawyer skills in ways that harm people. But that's not my issue.

Second, people, including your potential clients, have a *right* to counsel, in the sense that the state will provide one if they can't afford one, only in a few situations—in some aspects of the criminal justice system, and in some, though by no means all, family law situations. The only other sense in which they have a right to counsel is that the state will not forbid them to have a lawyer *if* they can find one they can afford. The right to counsel does not mean that clients whose causes hurt the body politic have a right to *your* counsel just because they have the money to pay for it.

I think it's morally fine to be a public defender or a legal services lawyer, in spite of the fact that you will sometimes find yourself representing guilty or immoral people. In those cases, there has been a *social* decision that people should have lawyers even if they can't afford them. I'd go further, and say that if a prospective client can't get a lawyer unless *you* represent them, and if they are likely to be treated unfairly by the system if they don't have a lawyer, then you ought to take the case to prevent the injustice of their being unrepresented.

But what I'm talking about is this: ought you, or ought you *not* to do the paperwork for a real estate developer who is acting legally and completely within his rights in buying up 100 low income apartments housing 400 poor people and converting them to 40 condominiums housing 80 yuppies, when the poor people will have to move into smaller apartments for higher rents and increase the starch content of their children's diets? I say you ought not to do it, and the right to counsel is irrelevant, Let some other lawyer do it, or let the developer do it himself, in the unlikely event that no one else can be bought.

I think the real objection to my proposal is that it contradicts our sense that it's okay to distribute legal services among people according to how much money they can pay. Lawyers want to feel that because society has left the decision about who gets a lawyer, and what lawyer (an incompetent or the best money can buy) to the market, then it's all right for them to forget about it, while selling their own services for what they will command, regardless of the morality of the legal activity.

If you—if most lawyers—took the choice of clients seriously according to the vacuous piety that you should avoid doing harm with your lawyer skills, it seems likely that some clients would have to pay more for less legal service, and other people would get more service for less money. Your moral intuitions would influence the distribution of legal talent, through the market, along with the buying power of clients. Would that be better or worse than the current situation?

I think it would be better. At present, the distribution of legal services is a disgrace: rich people get vastly more than they need or deserve; middle income people can't afford a lawyer in numerous situations in which they are ripped off for relatively small amounts of money, or discriminated against on sexual or racial grounds, or seriously injured. Poor people have virtually no access to legal services, given the abysmal underfunding of the Legal Services Corporation. If lawyers felt morally responsible for their individual contribution to this allocation of legal services, it seems likely to me that they would improve it, though perhaps only marginally. This would hurt, probably, some current excess consumers of lawyer time.

If you applied your moral judgment to the choice of clients not just occasionally but in every case, you might often choose in ways that I disagreed with. Though I think the overall pattern of choices would probably be better than that which emerges from a market where human suffering counts for nothing and dollars for everything, I am in favor of taking client morality into account for its own sake. My proposal is left-wing only in the very general sense of being for liberation and responsibility, even if the consequences may sometimes be conservative.

Discovery

I. INTRODUCTION

In chapter 6, "Pleadings and Disposition Without Trial," we saw that the pleadings in an action serve the dual function of defining the issues that the court will determine at trial and giving notice to each party of the case to be met. The process of *issue-defining* and notice-giving is far from exhausted with the exchange of pleadings; it continues with the discovery stage of the proceedings. Pleading rules only require the party to provide a bare outline of the case that he or she will actually attempt to prove at trial. When the action reaches trial, the party may have abandoned some aspect of the claim or defence initially set up by the pleadings. Particulars provide a good illustration. We have seen that particulars are often overinclusive, and it by no means follows that a party plans to establish all particulars at trial that are contained in the pleading. Similarly, although a party should admit facts that he or she knows to be true, there are many occasions in which a pleading will contain a denial of facts not genuinely in dispute. Thus, although they may be formally correct, the pleadings do not give a very full picture of the claims or defences that will actually be presented at trial, and hardly provide sufficient information to allow for adequate trial preparation or meaningful settlement discussions.

Reduced reliance on pleadings for notice-giving and issue-defining in the United States, and to a lesser extent in Canada, has placed pressure on the discovery process, which can become wideranging, lengthy, and costly.

Notice-giving. Another important function of discovery is to facilitate an exchange of information and evidence between the parties. Discovery allows the parties to a lawsuit to obtain access to documents in the other's possession that are relevant to their claim or defence and to require the other party to attend an oral examination of discovery. This exchange of information stands in tension with the adversary system's emphasis on party presentation and prosecution of claims in civil litigation and presents ethical problems that will be examined in this chapter. Nevertheless, as we will see, full exchange of information is limited by rules of privilege, which allow parties to shield from discovery, *inter alia*, matters that involve attempts to obtain legal advice (the solicitor–client privilege) and documents prepared for litigation (litigation privilege).

Despite the potential cost and the limits posed by privilege, it is important not to lose sight of the fact that discovery can be crucial in some types of cases. Imagine, for example, a products liability case. The plaintiff will usually only know that he or she has been injured. It is only in the discovery process that the plaintiff can learn about the manufacturing process and the risks that the defendant contemplated or ought to have contemplated.

This section will provide a general introduction to the different types of discovery, their purpose and their history.

A. Types of Discovery

1. Discovery of Documents

While oral discovery is often considered to be the most significant pre-trial information-gathering device, rules of court provide for other important methods of discovery. All provinces provide for the compulsory disclosure and production of documents relevant to the case. Documentary discovery is particularly important in complex litigation where reconstruction of the events giving rise to the dispute can only be accomplished through detailed and laborious documentary research. In such cases, documents disclosed on discovery will often be decisive.

After the completion of pleadings, each party is required to prepare a statement listing all documents relevant to the proceedings that the party has or formerly had in his or her possession or control. (See, for example, Ontario rule 30 and Alta. rules 186-199 and 205-209). This document is called variously in various provinces, an "affidavit on production," an "affidavit of documents," or a "list of documents." The opposite party is entitled to inspect and take copies of all documents listed to which the party making discovery takes no objection to producing. As we shall see, rules of privilege protect from production certain types of documents. Such documents must also be listed, and the grounds given for refusal to disclose them, and should there be any dispute as to the validity of the privilege claimed, the matter will be raised on motion to a master or judge to determine the validity of the claim to privilege.

Discovery of documents should be conducted before the oral examination so that counsel conducting the oral discovery is fully prepared to ask the right questions. Often, on oral discovery, the process of document production will continue and questions relating to the documents and the facts disclosed from the documents will be explored in greater depth.

Oral discovery is conducted in an adversarial format. That is, the witness need only answer the questions asked and is not required to volunteer information that the party conducting the examination has overlooked. Discovery of documents operates quite differently—each party is *unilaterally obligated* to disclose all documents that are relevant and (if requested) to produce all such documents that are not privileged. This imposes an important obligation on the party making discovery to ensure that all relevant documents are produced. Why do we make this distinction between oral and documentary discovery? Ought the rules requiring disclosure of all relevant documents be expanded to require disclosure of all relevant facts?

2. Examinations for Discovery

It is through the process of oral examination for discovery that each party can require his or her opponent to provide a much fuller and more complete statement of the basis of the claim or defence. Allegations or denials in a pleading are not made on oath. Pleadings represent initial statements of position, not sworn testimony. On discovery, a party is examined under oath and is sworn to tell the truth. He or she can be forced to specify those aspects of the case pleaded on which he or she actually intends to rely, and to provide sworn answers as to the position he or she takes on all points in issue in litigation. By defining the issues more sharply, discovery enables the parties to concentrate their energies on the matters that are really in dispute.

Oral discovery takes place after the close of pleadings. Rules of court typically provide that a party may initiate oral discovery by serving an appointment or notice, requiring the person to be examined to attend at a specified place and date. In practice, arrangements for discovery are usually made by agreement between the lawyers representing the parties, and the formality of an appointment or notice is not required. The examination itself will not take place in a courtroom but rather in a lawyer's or court reporter's office. The witness is sworn to tell the truth and responds to questions put by counsel for the party on whose behalf the examination is being conducted. The questions and answers are recorded by a court reporter who later prepares a certified transcript of the examination that will be used by the lawyers in preparation for the trial. (As we will see later, this transcript is often referred to at the trial.) Ordinarily, only the witness, counsel for each party, and the court reporter will be present. Questions may be asked to which exception is taken as being improper by opposing counsel who will likely instruct the witness not to answer. After the transcript has been prepared, the party who asked the question to which objection was taken will have to consider whether the information sought is sufficiently important to warrant a formal motion to the court. If it is, a motion will be brought to the appropriate judicial officer who will consider the arguments of the parties with respect to the propriety of the question or objection. Should it be determined that the question should have been answered, the usual order will be for the party subject to examination to reattend so that the question and any questions logically flowing from it may be asked and the answers recorded.

Use of examination for discovery at trial. Examination for discovery would be extremely useful if it did no more than provide each party with an insight into or a preview of the other side's case. While this is probably the most important aspect of the procedure, it does much more. Because the transcript of the examination for discovery may be used at trial in two ways, discovery also is an important evidence-gathering tool. The first way in which evidence can be gathered is by means of *obtaining admissions* that can be used at trial to prove facts that are in dispute. An admission is a statement made by a party before a trial that is adverse to his or her case and can be received at trial as proof of the truth of its contents. Admissions may be obtained otherwise than through oral discovery, but oral discovery remains the most important opportunity to obtain an admission as it will ordinarily be the only pre-trial opportunity whereby one party can force the other to answer questions about sensitive issues in the case.

Another evidentiary device arising from discovery is the use of a *prior inconsistent statement* to impeach the credibility of a witness at trial. The use of a prior inconsistent statement is a familiar technique in cross-examination whereby the credibility of a witness is attacked by demonstrating that the witness has said something different on an earlier occasion from what he or she is now saying at the trial. As the discovery will have canvassed the important issues in the case, it operates to pin a witness down to the version he or she has given at discovery. If the witness varies from that version, he or she will risk having the inconsistency brought to light in cross-examination. The trier of fact may not believe the version given at trial in the light of the prior inconsistent version given on discovery.

The rules of most provinces provide for discovery of non-party witnesses and thereby significantly expand the information gathering possibilities offered by oral discovery. By examining potential witnesses under oath, a party can obtain a much more detailed account of the evidence he or she will be faced with, and may also be able to collect from nonparties information in support of his or her own case.

So far, we have been discussing oral examination for discovery. However, another method of examination for discovery is available in most Canadian jurisdictions—that is, *examination by written questions or interrogatories.* Typically, the two forms of examination are alternatives—that is, a party must choose one method or the other and may not use both, except with leave. (See, for example, Ontario rule 35.) An examination by written questions (interrogatories) is conducted by delivering a list of written questions that must be answered in writing under oath. It is a device that might be useful where the witness is to be examined on some very specific point or where the cost of conducting an oral examination is unwarranted. While it may be considerably cheaper, it is generally considered to be inferior to an oral examination for discovery—the answers received are typically answers that will have been drafted by a lawyer (so you do not get the actual words of the witness) and it is more difficult to ask spontaneous follow-up questions in response to the answers received. Its use in Canada is infrequent.

In England (and indeed in Commonwealth countries outside Canada) the device of oral examination for discovery is unknown. Written interrogatories are provided for under the English rules, but they may only be administered with leave of court and such leave is difficult to obtain. In fact, oral examination for discovery (or deposition procedure as it is known in the United States) is a purely North American phenomenon.

3. Physical Discovery

While examination for discovery (fact discovery) and documentary discovery are by far the most important forms of discovery (and are used on a regular basis), the rules in virtually every common law jurisdiction also provide for two forms of "physical discovery." The more rarely used is *inspection of property* (see Ontario rule 32). This may be useful in certain cases to inspect physical premises, articles, or other things, the state of condition of which is relevant to the action. For example, a plaintiff injured when struck by a car driven by the defendant in which the brakes were faulty, may wish to inspect the brakes to determine whether the allegation that the brakes were defective can be substantiated.

A much more important form of physical discovery is a *medical examination,* which is especially important in personal injury litigation. All provinces permit the defendant in such actions to require that the plaintiff be medically examined on the defendant's behalf (see, for example, Ontario rule 33 and the Courts of Justice Act, s. 118). This provides the defendant with the opportunity to have independent information about the plaintiff's medical condition that would otherwise be unavailable to the defendant. (This procedure is further examined, below.)

4. Continuing Discovery Obligations and Notices To Admit

Examinations for discovery and documentary discovery may take place relatively early in the life of a law suit; in any event, they may occur well before the trial. What happens if a party subsequently acquires information that, because it was unknown to him or her at the time of discovery, was not disclosed to the other side? As we will see below, the law imposes obligations of "continuing discovery" that may require the parties to inform their opponents with regard to subsequently acquired information.

One further procedural device should be referred to, although it is not strictly a discovery device. Modern rules typically provide for a *request to admit* procedure (for example, Ontario rule 51.02 *et seq.*). This procedure permits a party at any time to serve on any other party a request to admit the truth of a fact or the authenticity of a document. Typically, this procedure is used on the eve of trial for the purpose of narrowing the issues or dispensing with the proof of documents. However, it can be used at any time.

B. History and Philosophy of Discovery

Canadian discovery practice has been inspired by American sources, although important differences do exist. In England, oral discovery is unavailable and pre-trial information exchange is restricted to the pleadings, discovery of documents, and written interrogatories. However, as the following extract reveals, modern oral discovery rules are, in a sense, an expansion of a practice that originated in the English Court of Chancery. In reading this material, remember that, although the general philosophy of discovery is the same, rules relating to the scope of discovery may vary from jurisdiction to jurisdiction.

Garry D. Watson and Craig Perkins, Holmested and Watson,
Ontario Civil Procedure
Rule 31, §6, History of Examination for Discovery
(Toronto: Carswell, 1984) (looseleaf)

The early history of examination for discovery is succinctly and ably traced by Clare Choate, *Discovery in Canada* (1978), 1-3. His treatment is worth quoting at length:

> A brief study of the history of earlier discovery methods can be useful as many of our present day practices have their roots in the procedures developed in the early Chancery and Law Courts of England.
>
> Although the right to pre-trial discovery was recognized in Chancery, the Common Law prior to 1854 did not grant any such right, either of evidence or of documents. The medieval law courts relied primarily upon the pleading process to formulate the issues and to afford notice of the scope of the controversy to the parties and to the trier of the facts. Through a lengthy, complex exchange of pleadings it was sought to narrow the dispute to a single issue which, if one of fact, was then tried before a jury.
>
> As the Common Law developed, the pleadings tended to become formalized within a rigid framework of classes of action. The factual allegations were replaced by statements of conclusions of law and fact, sometimes fictitious, and seldom revealing much about the controversy. In addition, newly developed forms of general pleadings made it possible for either party to postpone until trial full disclosure of his case with anticipation of the adversary's strategy being largely guesswork. There were no legal means for determination of the nature of the opponent's case, and, in fact, surprise at the trial formed no valid objection for the surprised party (*Bain v. Whitehaven & Furness Junction Ry.* (1850) 3 HL Cas. 1.). Surprise was no answer even if prior knowledge would have permitted the falsity of the evidence to have been proved. The prevailing argument against the prior availability of such evidence was the fear that perjury might be elicited if a party knew beforehand the exact evidence with which he might have to contend.
>
> During the fifteenth century, the Court of Chancery evolved a procedure for the formulation of issues and the revelation of facts. The plaintiff commenced the suit by serving a bill consisting mainly of a "stating" part, made up of general allegations of the facts underlying the claim, and a "charging" part composed of a detailed statement of

the evidence on which the claim was based. The defendant answered by admitting, denying, or explaining each and every allegation in both parts. Later, in the eighteenth century, the defendant's answers were replaced by responses to written interrogatories which the plaintiff transmitted with the initial bill. A limited discovery of documents was also available by designating the documents desired, their relevancy to the case and the possession of the documents by the opposite party.

A party to an action at law could secure the benefit of these devices by bringing a bill of discovery, alleging that he needed the aid of Chancery to prosecute his claim effectively. The same type of written responses and documents were thus available in law as in equity. Filing a bill in equity only enabled the plaintiff to interrogate the defendant to the bill, and if the defendant wished to interrogate the plaintiff, it was necessary for him to file a cross bill in equity before he could do so ("Developments in the Law—Discovery" (1961) 74 Harvard LR 940).

Eventually, in 1854, a change was made in England enabling a party, without recourse to Chancery, to obtain discovery before trial of documents in the possession or power of the opposite party, and to submit written interrogatories to him "upon any matter as to which discovery might be sought" (Common Law Procedure Act, 1854, 17 & 18 Vict. c. 125). A party was entitled to seek discovery of those facts supportive of his own case, but, at least in theory, was not entitled to seek out those facts on which his opponent depended (*Combe v. London* (1840) 4 Y & C Ex. 139). Thus, after the introduction of the Common Law Procedure Acts and the Judicature Acts, it was no longer necessary to commence suit in the Court of Chancery for the purpose of obtaining discovery as between the parties to an action, for any discovery that formerly could have been obtained in the Court of Chancery could now be obtained in the High Court. Following the introduction of the Judicature Acts, it was no longer necessary to bring an action merely for the purpose of obtaining discovery. "The plaintiff in every action is entitled to discovery as ancillary to the relief which he claims in the action" (*Ind. Coope & Co. v. Emmerson* (1887), 12 App. Cas. 300, at 311).

The Ontario Court of Chancery from 1837 provided for discovery only by means of a Bill of Discovery as in England. In 1849, power was conferred on the Judges to make rules, under which an order was passed providing for the method of discovery by oral examination.

In 1856, Ontario further adopted the provisions of the English Common Law Procedure Act of 1854 relating to discovery by written interrogatories in the Common Law Courts. Thus, from 1856, discovery in the Ontario Court of Chancery was by way of oral examination, while in the Common Law Courts, it was by written interrogatories. It was still possible, though, to resort to a Bill of Discovery in Chancery in aid of an action at law (*Hamilton v. Phipps* (1859), 7 Gr. 483; *James v. Snarr* (1868), 15 Gr. 229). In 1873, the practice of discovery by oral examination, similar to that in the Court of Chancery, was introduced into the Common Law courts, through the Administration of Justice Act of 1873 (*Menzies v. McLeod* (1915), 34 OLR 572).

See also Holmested & Gale, R. 326 §§ 3-8; Williston & Rolls, The Law of Civil Procedure (1970), 745-51; Williams, "Discovery of Civil Litigation: Trial Preparation in Canada" (1980), 58 Can. Bar Rev. 1; Watson, Borins and Williams, Canadian Civil Procedure: Cases and Materials (1977), 9-3 to 9-7.

The examination for discovery system that existed in Ontario down to 1984 was essentially that put in place by the Rules of 1913. The only major amendment made during that period was in 1960. Until that date, the admissions of an officer or servant examined on behalf of a corporation did not bind the corporation. By the Evidence Act, RSO 1960, c. 125, s. 16, such admissions were made binding on the corporation. During the 1970s and early 1980s court decisions tended in the direction of broadening the scope of discovery, but by 1984 numerous restrictions remained, e.g. evidence and the identity of witnesses were not discoverable, and cross-examination was generally not permitted. Moreover, the right to examine for discovery was limited to parties adverse in interest and generally it was not possible to examine non-party witnesses. For a summary of the changes in examination for discovery brought about in 1985 by the Rules of Civil Procedure, see above, 31 § 3.

During the Canada-wide civil procedure reform movement, which began in the late 1960s, significant changes in discovery were made in other provinces which subsequently influenced the drafting of the Ontario Rules of Civil Procedure. In 1972 the new Nova Scotia Rules (adopted in Prince Edward Island in 1977) provided for the examination of non-parties for discovery as of right (see Rule 18.01). In 1977, the new British Columbia Rules provided for the examination of non-parties with leave (see Rule 28), as did the New Brunswick Rules of 1981 (see Rule 32.10). Also, the identity of witnesses was made discoverable (see Nova Scotia and PEI Rule 12.12(2); British Columbia Rule 27(22) and New Brunswick Rule 32.06(2)).

The philosophy of modern discovery is discussed further in the following excerpt, a US work, but one that largely reflects Canadian attitudes towards discovery. Louisell's and Wally's analysis is primarily focused on oral examination for discovery.

Louisell and Wally, *Modern California Discovery*
2d ed. (San Francisco: Bancroft-Whitney, 1972), 1-6 (footnotes omitted)

Uncovering Evidence. The primary purpose of modern discovery procedures is to enable the litigants to obtain a more informed picture of the facts of the case more quickly and at less expense than they could by relying on their own unaided initiative. The basic premise of modern discovery, then, is that fuller disclosure, which may ultimately entail enforced disclosure, will permit each party to present the most complete and favorable case that can be made on his behalf at trial, and will minimize the possibility that ignorance of relevant facts, or the adversary's sudden presentation of unanticipated evidence, will obscure the true state of affairs out of which the controversy arose. ...

[T]he underlying goal of the federal discovery rules and the growing number of modern state discovery schemes is the same: To cause disclosure of relevant information before trial in order to render the judicial process more accurate and fair.

As Justice Peters stated in the landmark case of *Greyhound Corp. v. Superior Court*:

Certainly, it can be said, that the Legislature intended to take the "game" element out of trial preparation while yet retaining the adversary nature of the trial itself. One of the principal purposes of discovery was to do away "with the sporting theory of litigation," namely, surprise at the trial. (... (D)iscovery tends to "make a trial less a game of blindman's buff" and more a fair contest with the basic issues and facts disclosed to the fullest practical extent.)

This theme, that a lawsuit should be an intensive search for truth and not a game to be won by bluff or surprise, has today become commonplace. The widespread acceptance by the bar of the modern federal and state discovery rules attests to the vitality of this philosophy. Furthermore, there is nothing to suggest that the new discovery devices constitute a retreat from the common law's firm conception of litigation as a *competitive adversary* proceeding. The historic notice that a contest between vitally interested partisans is the best mechanism for exposing the truth is consistent with discovery principles.

The rules simply develop discovery, which has its antecedents in English chancery practice, into an efficient technique for fact ascertainment, to take its place in the common law's arsenal along with the advocate's other efficient weapons such as testimony in open court, cross-examination, impeachment, forensic skill, and mastery of legal principles.

In the United States Supreme Court decision in *Hickman v. Taylor* this theme was again emphasized:

[Counsel for plaintiff] bases his claim to [the conversations of defendants' counsel with witnesses] on the view that the Rules were to do away with the old situation where a law suit developed into a "battle of wits between counsel." But a common law trial is and always should be an adversary proceeding. Discovery was hardly intended to enable a learned profession to perform its functions either without wits or on wits borrowed from the adversary.

Encouraging Settlement. In addition to the primary role that comprehensive discovery devices play in facilitating disclosure of information relevant to the litigation, they also serve other functions. Chief among these is the promotion of settlement. Settlement is typically reached when the parties' respective assessments of the value of the case are in substantial agreement. These appraisals are calculations of the maximum worth of the case in the event of recovery, discounted by the likelihood of defeat and of intermediate possibilities. The accuracy of these estimates obviously depends on the factual data available for analysis. Thus, to some extent at least, discovery aids the settlement process by increasing the quantum of information available to the parties. In addition, discovery costs and expenses increase the parties' investment in the case and may make the prospect of total defeat all the more disastrous. This, too, may induce settlement.

Emphasizing Issues. Another function of modern discovery is to isolate issues and facts over which there is no material controversy. In some cases this may lead to a motion for summary judgment. More often, discovery operates like the pretrial conference and obviates the need for costly litigation to establish facts which are not controverted in the lawsuit. Conversely, discovery tends to highlight those claims and defenses for which there is some basis in fact, thus pointing the way for further investigation. ...

Pinning the Witness Down. Discovery presents the opportunity for skilful counsel to compel a witness to commit himself to one version of the facts. In one context this may involve a simple, but nevertheless crucial, admission of lack of knowledge on a given subject. In other situations, the witness may espouse a particular description of an important event or transaction. Of course, the witness may subsequently change his testimony even up to the time of trial. But careful documentation of his testimony at the time of discovery can make subsequent alteration more difficult and embarrassing.

Sizing Up Witnesses and Counsel. Discovery presents the opportunity for observation of the demeanor, attitudes, and responses of a witness and opposing counsel. The former information will dictate how the witness should be handled at trial if he appears. The latter is less important, but may be useful in negotiating a settlement and planning other work connected with the case.

Undesirable Uses of Discovery. It has occasionally been suggested that discovery facilitates perjury by a litigant who "reconstructs" evidence during the discovery proceedings. While this possibility is indeed a fact of life, the very nature of discovery itself tends to minimize such danger. By permitting the broadest and most complete acquisition of information, discovery tends to make perjury difficult to conceal. Further, discovery occurs early in the litigation and is more likely to produce statements that are recorded when they are fresh and unrehearsed or concocted.

NOTE

Robert White, *The Art of Discovery* (Aurora, ON: Canada Law Book, 1990), a Canadian text on discovery, emphasizes technique rather than the law. For a discussion of the law of discovery and a comprehensive digest of Canadian law since 1985, see Holmested and Watson, *Ontario Civil Procedure* (Toronto: Carswell, 1985), rules 30-35.

II. DOCUMENTARY DISCOVERY

A. Affidavit of Documents

Each party is entitled to discovery of documents from every other party in the action as of right: see, for example, Ontario rule 30.

Discovery of documents from parties is a two-step procedure. The first step—disclosure—is the preparation and service of an "affidavit of documents": see Ontario rule 30.03. (In some jurisdictions—for example, British Columbia and the Federal Court of Canada—a party is required in the first instance only to provide an unsworn list of documents; if the other party so wishes it can apply to have this list of documents sworn.) In its affidavit of documents, a party is required to disclose "to the full extent of the party's knowledge, information and belief all documents relating to any matter in issue in the action that are or have been in the party's possession, control or power." The affidavit must list and describe, in separate schedules, all documents relating to any matter and issue in the action (a) that are in the party's possession, control, or power and that the party does not object to producing; (b) that are or were in the party's possession, control, or power and for which the party claims privilege, together with the grounds for the claim; and (c) that were formerly in the party's possession, control, or power, to-gether with a statement of when and how the party lost possession and the documents' present location. The affidavit must also state that the party has never had in his or her possession, control, or power any other document relating to any matter at issue in the action other than that listed in the affidavit. Moreover, at least in some jurisdictions—for example, see Ontario rule 30.03(4)—the party's solicitor must certify that he or she has explained to the deponent the necessity of making full disclosure of all documents relating to any matter in issue in the action.

The second step is the production of documents for inspection. Each party is enti-tled to inspect the documents listed by another party, *other than those documents for which privilege is claimed*—for example, see Ontario rules 30.02 and 30.04. In short, a party has to disclose relevant documents—including privileged documents—but only non-privileged documents have to be produced for inspection. Typically, the obligation under the rules is merely to make the documents available for inspection at the office of the lawyer acting for the party making production. In practice, the parties often ex-change copies of the documents.

Grossman v. Toronto General Hospital
(1983), 146 DLR (3d) 280 (Ont. HC)

REID J: The action arises out of the death of Howard Grossman who is claimed to have been lost while a patient in the Toronto General Hospital ("the Hospital"). It is alleged that his body was discovered after 12 days in an air-duct shaft in the hospital.

The defence entered by the Hospital for itself and its staff amounts to a general traverse. Not even the death was directly admitted.

That document gave a hint of what was in store for plaintiffs. The Hospital's affidavit on production (the affidavit) revealed only one thing the Hospital had no objection to producing: the deceased's hospital record. That was the only entry made in the first part of the first schedule of the form (Form 23) required by the Rules of Practice.

Defendants' position is essentially this: plaintiffs have failed to establish that any documents exist that should be produced other than the deceased's medical record and those now described in paras. 1(a) and (b) of the master's order [requiring production of exhibits filed at a Coroner's Inquest and our investigation report]. When I expressed surprise that a 12-day search for a missing patient in a hospital would not have produced one scrap of paper relevant to the issues in this lawsuit Mrs. Farrer replied that any such piece of paper would be privileged, the Hospital having retained solicitors at a very early point.

That may be so. It may be a proper basis for a claim of privilege for any and all documents other than the one thing produced voluntarily and the others forced out of defendants' hands by reason of the motion before the master (in paras. 1(a) and (b) of Master Sandler's order). However, no one could have told from reading defendants' original affidavit whether or not that claim was justified. The answer made in the second part of the first schedule is a mere boiler-plate calculated to conceal all and any documents from inspection. The result was to deprive opposing counsel of any basis for challenging the privilege claimed. Equally, if a challenge had been made, no court could have decided it, without resorting to ordering production to the court of all the documents referred to in the second part of the first schedule. Since no one could have known from reading the schedule what documents are referred to, that would have been an order made in the dark.

The Rules of Practice are designed to facilitate production, not frustrate it.

Honest differences of opinion might arise over the question whether a given document should or must be produced. If that occurs, the court has power to decide the issue.

It becomes quickly clear to anyone setting out to practice in the courts that "production" is open to serious abuse. The integrity of the system depends upon the willingness of lawyers to require full and fair discovery of their clients. The system is, in a sense, in the hands of the lawyers. The opportunity for stonewalling and improper concealment is there. Some solicitors grasp it. They will make only such production as can be forced from them. That is bad practice. It can work real injustice. It causes delay and expense while the other side struggles to see that which they had a right to see from the first. In such a contest the advantage is to the long purse. The worst consequence is that the strategy is sometimes successful, giving its perpetrators a disreputable advantage. The practice must be condemned. If it were widespread it would undermine the trial system.

Master Sandler has written of the susceptibility of the system to abuse. In *Bow Helicopters v. Textron Canada Ltd. et al.; Rocky Mountain Helicopters Inc. et al., Third Parties* (1981), 23 CPC 212, he said at p. 215:

> I also observe that under our present system of documentary discovery, the choice as to what documents that are in a party's possession are relevant is, in the first instance, left up to the party itself, and my experience and observations have taught me that nowhere is the abuse of our rules of procedure greater than in this area of documentary production and in the failure of each party to fairly and reasonably disclose and produce to the opposite party all relevant documents, and to disclose the existence of all relevant but privileged documents. (This abuse has been recognized and has attempted to be remedied by the Civil Procedure Revision Committee, chaired by the late Walter B. Williston, QC, in draft Rules 31.03(4), 31.06(a), and 31.08 and 31.09 of their Report of June, 1980.)

The duty upon a solicitor is now, and always has been, to make full, fair and prompt discovery. Williston and Rolls, in *The Law Of Civil Procedure* (1970), vol. 2, put it this way, at pp. 892-4:

> A party giving discovery is under a duty to make a careful search for all relevant documents in his possession and to make diligent inquiries about other material documents which may be in the possession of others for him. A solicitor has a duty of careful investigation and supervision and of advising his client as to what documents should be included in the affidavit, because a client cannot be expected to know the whole scope of his obligation without legal assistance. In *Myers v. Elman* [(1940), AC 282] a solicitor was ordered to pay the costs of the proceedings because his managing clerk was guilty of misconduct in the preparation and filing of an incorrect and inadequate affidavit. Lord Atkin said:

> What is the duty of the solicitor? He is at an early stage of the proceedings engaged in putting before the Court on the oath of his client information which may afford evidence at the trial. Obviously he must explain to his client what is the meaning of relevance:and equally obviously he must not necessarily be satisfied by the statement of his client that he has no documents or no more than he chooses to disclose. If he has reasonable ground for supposing that there are others he must investigate the matter; but he need not go beyond taking reasonable steps to ascertain the truth. He is not the ultimate judge, and if he reasonably decides to believe his client, criticism cannot be directed to him. But I may add that the duty is specially incumbent on the solicitor where there is a charge of fraud; for a wilful omission to perform his duty in such a case may well amount to conduct which is aiding and abetting a criminal in concealing his crime, and in preventing restitution.

Lord Wright put the matter even more bluntly:

The order of discovery requires the client to give information in writing and on oath of all documents which are or have been in his corporeal possession or power, whether he is bound to produce them or not. A client cannot be expected to realize the whole scope of that obligation without the aid and advice of his solicitor, who therefore has a peculiar duty in these matters as an officer of the Court carefully to investigate the position and as far as possible see that the order is complied with. A client left to himself could not know what is relevant, nor is he likely to realize that it is his obligation to disclose every relevant document, even a document which would establish, or go far to establish, against him his opponent's case. The solicitor cannot simply allow the client to make whatever affidavit of documents he thinks fits nor can he escape the responsibility of careful investigation or supervision. If the client will not give him the information he is entitled to require or if he insists on swearing an affidavit which the solicitor knows to be imperfect or which he has every reason to think is imperfect, then the solicitor's proper course is to withdraw from the case. He does not discharge his duty in such a case by requesting the client to make a proper affidavit and then filing whatever affidavit the client thinks fit to swear to.

In the same case, there was a discussion of the duty to make further disclosure when subsequent to filing the affidavit other relevant documents were found. Viscount Maugham said:

A solicitor who has innocently put on the file an affidavit by his client which he has subsequently discovered to be certainly false owes it to the Court to put the matter right at the earliest date if he continues to act as solicitor upon the record. The duty of the client is equally plain. I wish to say with emphasis that I reject the notion that it is justifiable in such a case to keep silence and to wait and wait till the plaintiff succeeds, if he can, in obtaining an order for a further and better affidavit. To do so is, in the language of Singleton J, to obstruct the interests of justice, to occasion unnecessary costs, and—even if disclosure is ultimately obtained—to delay the hearing of the action in a case where an early hearing may be of great importance.

Those pronouncements are clear and unequivocal. Anyone familiar with them, or with many others to the same effect, would not require a master's motion to know that the exhibits filed at the coroner's inquest would have to be produced in this case. ...

It has equally always been the case that sufficient information must be given of documents for which privilege is claimed to enable a party opposed in interest to be able to identify them. It is not, however, necessary to go so far as to give an indirect discovery. ...

In *Walsh-Canadian Construction Co. Ltd. v. Churchill Falls (Labrador) Corp. Ltd. (No.* 1) (1979), 9 CPC 229, 23 Nfld. & PEIR. 34, the question of the sufficiency of detail required to be given of documents for which privilege was claimed was dealt with at length in the Newfoundland Supreme Court. In that case the rule of court governing affidavits on production expressly stated that the affidavit "shall specify" which documents the party objects to produce. There is no such reference in our Rules of Practice but the forms, which have the same effect as the rules, require the documents to be "set forth." I see no difference between "set forth" and "specify."

In the course of his learned and exhaustive decision Mr. Justice Goodridge said, at p. 235:

> I do not think it necessary to deal with the matter any further. Upon my reading of these and other cases it appears to me that in discovery proceedings where a party resists the production of documents on the grounds of privilege it should set forth in its affidavit a sufficient statement of facts so that a Judge may say that if the facts are true then as a matter of law the documents are privileged. I would hesitate to expound on that view to any extent. Obviously the party resisting production is not required to give such particulars as will destroy the benefit of the privilege; on the other hand he ought not to be able to avoid production by his own unadorned assertion that the documents are subject to solicitor-and-client privilege.

The sufficiency of the description given to documents must be governed by the circumstances. The rule must be that enough must be given to enable a court to make a *prima facie* decision as to whether the claim for privilege has been established from what appears *on the face of the affidavit.* ...

The rule is, therefore, that a party must candidly describe in an affidavit on production not only documents for which no privilege is claimed but also those for which a privilege is claimed. It is not enough to do the one but not the other.

Litigation is, after all, a search for truth. Its processes are, we all know, imperfect. To permit advantage to be taken of its weaknesses to the point of injustice and unfairness would be wrong. Defendants' strategy in this case must not be tolerated. The appeal must be dismissed.

Plaintiffs ask for costs on a solicitor and his own client scale. That is a punitive award. Yet it was the disposition made by Master Sandler in both orders under appeal. It reveals his view of defendants' course of action.

That course of action may reflect merely excessive concern for the protection of his clients' rights or it may reveal simple stonewalling. My concern that it may be the latter is deepened by the decision of my brother Carruthers in *Fiege v. Cornwall General Hospital et al.* (1980), 30 OR (2d) 691, 117 DLR (3d) 152. I am informed by counsel that the solicitor responsible for the defence in that case up to the point of trial is the solicitor responsible for the conduct of the defence herein. (That is not, I must add,

Mrs. Farrer, whose lot it was to seek to justify someone else's conduct, and who did so with much skill and fortitude.) The failure in *Fiege* to produce an important document was strongly condemned by Carruthers J. He awarded costs on a solicitor and his own client scale against the defendant in that case because of the waste of time and money that resulted. The same may be said of this case. Time has been wasted and money thrown away. There is no merit in defendants' position.

The seriousness of a failure to make proper production is recognized in the rules. Rule 352 states:

> 352(1) If a party fails to comply with any notice or order for production or inspection of documents, he is liable to attachment and is also liable, if a plaintiff, to have his action dismissed, and, if a defendant, to have his defence, if any, struck out.

Attachment of a party is a severe sanction. Defendants' conduct in this case amounts to a deliberate refusal to comply with the notice to produce and is subject to that sanction. But in the absence of any indication that defendants' conduct was other than as advised by their solicitor, the responsibility for it must fall on the solicitor.

The consequences for a solicitor can be severe. In *Myers v. Elman*, [1940] AC 282, [1939] 4 All ER 484 (HL), the solicitor was ordered to pay the costs. If the course of action followed in this case were shown to be widespread, an order to that effect would be appropriate as a general deterrent.

It could be argued that, because this case is a repetition of conduct that has already been deplored, that order should be made here. Although I have some doubt, I am satisfied to treat this case as an example of excessive zeal and to adopt Master Sandler's order. His order shall stand. The costs of the appeal shall be to plaintiffs in any event of the cause as between a solicitor and his own client. However, because this is a repetition of the same error found in *Fiege, supra,* the costs may be taxed forthwith and shall be payable forthwith thereafter.

The further affidavit, or affidavits, shall be delivered forthwith subject, to any extension allowed by Master Sandler.

Appeal dismissed.

NOTES AND QUESTIONS

1. Was the court's costs order appropriate in this case or should the lawyer have been held personally liable? Who of the lawyer and the client is likely to have a more precise sense of what documents need to be disclosed and what should be contained in the affidavit of documents? If a client refuses to follow the lawyer's advice regarding the production of documents, what is the lawyer's responsibility? If a lawyer knows that a client is actually destroying relevant documents, what is his or her responsibility? In *Myers v. Elman*, [1940] AC 282, the leading case at common law about awarding costs against a lawyer personally, the House of Lords held that a solicitor may not assist a client who, to his or her knowledge, has sworn a false affidavit; if a solicitor discovers that his or her client has sworn a false affidavit, the solicitor must decline to act further in the matter. In *Myers*, the solicitor, who knew the client had sworn a false affidavit and did not withdraw, was ordered to pay part of the opposing party's costs.

2. In *Waxman v. Waxman* (1990), 42 CPC (2d) 296 (Ont. Master), the court had to work out the implications of *Grossman*. (You will be in a better position to understand the *Waxman* decision after you have considered the materials on privilege, below.) The defendants claimed privilege in their affidavit of documents for:

> Letters, statements and memoranda passing between the corporations' solicitors and third parties in connection with the litigation herein and in preparation therefor, the earliest of which is dated November 9, 1988.

The plaintiffs moved for an order to require the defendants to produce a further and better affidavit of documents, setting out a detailed list of documents referred to in the paragraph including, with respect to each such document, the name and identity of the "third parties," the dates of communication, and whether any of the communications were expert reports.

Master Sandler granted the motion in part. He held that the rules require that the documents for which privilege is claimed should be described, with the description including the function, role, and status of sender and receiver, and their relationship to the party to the action. However, he held that a party was not required to give particulars that would destroy the benefit of any privilege that might properly have attached to the documents. Under rule 31.06(3), the names and addresses of experts who are retained solely for the purpose of litigation, and whom the party undertakes not to call at trial, need not be disclosed. Moreover, under rule 31.06(2), even the names and addresses of potential witnesses can be kept from disclosure if the court so orders. Consequently, to require the disclosure in the name of every person whose reports or interviews were the subject of a claim for privilege in an affidavit of documents before a ruling on the validity, if such a claim were made, would destroy, in part, the benefit of the privilege that might properly have attached to the document. Accordingly, the defendants were not required to set forth the names or identities of the creators of the documents; the witnesses who gave the statements that formed the substance of the documents; or the names of the experts, investigators, or adjusters who authored any report to whom the solicitors wrote. He further held that in certain circumstances, the use of categories for the listing of certain types of documents might be appropriate, so long as such use was not a stratagem to avoid revealing documents that ought to be revealed.

3. While both the *Grossman* and *Waxman* decisions condemn the use of general, "boilerplate" claims for privilege, such claims are often used in practice. Why? Are lawyers simply flouting the requirements of discovery? The answer is that compliance with the two decisions is expensive. It takes time and money to go through the productions and identify each document for which a claim for privilege is made and describe it individually. Many lawyers avoid this expense for their clients by making a general privilege claim, knowing that if called on to do so by their opponents they will have to describe the documents individually. In cases where both parties are interested in avoiding this expense, and have little interest in the details of the privilege claim, it is still not uncommon to see them making "boilerplate" privilege claims. Of course, in cases where the parties are interested in such details, they will insist on compliance with the *Grossman* and *Waxman* principles. Moreover, parties who know at the time of preparing their affidavits that they will be insisting on compliance by their opponents will themselves comply from the outset.

4. *Solid Waste Reclamation Inc. v. Philip Enterprises Inc.* (1991), 2 OR (3d) 481 (Gen. Div.) involved voluminous documentary discovery. In such cases, counsel are increasingly employing electronic storage and retrieval systems for productions. In *Solid Waste*, the defendants complained that Schedule A of the plaintiff's affidavit was inadequate because it described and numbered many of the documents in bundles rather than individually. Mr. Justice Lane observed

> A modern rule as to identifying documents cannot ignore the computer and its need for a unique identifier for every item to be retrieved. … [P]roper identification demands numbering each document with a unique number. Such a number is far more valuable than a long-winded description of each document including its sender, addressee, date, etc. … . My experience in matters involving thousands of documents is that the initial cost of proper identification of each document with a unique identifier is surprisingly small and is repaid many times over by savings in time during discovery, preparation of witnesses and trial. Whatever the [numbering] system, it must, as a minimum:
>
> (1) enable swift and sure retrieval at trial or discovery;
> (2) enable counsel examining the documents of another party to relate each document to its reference on Schedule A and to satisfy himself that all documents listed are actually in the collection he is examining;
> (3) enable counsel at trial to ascertain swiftly that a document which is tendered to become an exhibit is in fact a document produced in Schedule A;
> (4) be compatible with computer retrieval systems;
> (5) be implemented before copies of the documents are made, so that the copies in the hands of all parties bear the identifier.

To what extent do you think these standards for document identification are realistic and cost efficient?

5. Note again the distinction between the process of oral examination and documentary discovery. The procedure for oral examination is adversarial in the sense that while a party is entitled to have its proper questions answered, the opposing party's obligation is simply to answer the questions asked. It is not permissible for the examining party to ask the party examined, "Tell me everything you know that is relevant to the issues in this action." By contrast, the process of documentary discovery imposes a unilateral obligation upon each party to identify and disclose every document that is or was in their possession and control and to disclose it to the opposing party and then (if requested) to produce to the other side for inspection every such document, other than those for which privilege is claimed.

Can this distinct approach to documentary discovery be reconciled with the basic adversarial nature of our litigation process? The approach taken by US courts is quite different; there is no general obligation of documentary disclosure, and a party's only obligation is to disclose classes of documents demanded by their opponent. Is the Anglo-Canadian approach, in essence grounded on efficiency—that is, is it simply more efficient to require the parties to make disclosure of all documents relevant to the issues in the action rather than having the parties making up lists of classes of documents they wish to have produced? If efficiency is the explanation, should we adopt the same approach with regard to fact discovery?

B. Scope of Documentary Discovery

The scope of documentary discovery is extremely broad. The rules—for example, Ontario rule 30.02—specify the scope. As the following case illustrates, the prima facie rules as to the scope of discovery have been given an expansive interpretation by the case law. However, limits may be imposed by the court because of the costs necessitated by the discovery sought. Has the court correctly identified the relevant competing values and struck the right balance?

Peter Kiewit Sons Co. of Canada Ltd. v. British Columbia Hydro and Power Authority
(1982), 134 DLR (3d) 154 (BC SC)

McEACHERN CJSC: The plaintiffs entered into a contract with the defendant British Columbia Hydro & Power Authority (BC Hydro) for the construction of Segment 5 of a transmission line comprising 189 steel towers between Kingsvale and the Giant Mascot Mine. This project was part of the Mica Creek transmission line.

At the same time BC Hydro had let contracts for other segments of the same transmission line, and for portions of the Kootenay Canal transmission line.

It was a term of the plaintiffs' contract that BC Hydro would furnish the required structural steel for this project on a timely basis at its Kidd Steelyard in Richmond, BC. The plaintiffs contracted with the defendant Columbia Hydro Constructors Ltd. that the latter would furnish all labour required by the plaintiffs for the performance of their contract. The contractors on the other projects mentioned above had similar contractual arrangements for the timely supply of steel and labour for their projects.

The plaintiffs and the contractors on the other projects employed a common trucking contractor, Pe Ben Industries Company Limited (Pe Ben), to take delivery, at the Kidd Steelyard, of any steel the contractors required for transportation to various locations.

The plaintiffs' job did not go well, and one of the principal allegations against BC Hydro is that it did not properly manage the supply of steel. Amongst other things, the plaintiffs say steel was not available as required; that steel intended for one contract was diverted to other jobs with the squeaky contractor getting the steel; and other shortcomings on the part of BC Hydro. The defendant Columbia Hydro Constructors Ltd. is not directly involved in this application.

The foregoing is a brief but sufficient description of the scope of one part of this case.

It is clear that these were major projects requiring much planning and organization. The plaintiffs claim substantial damages on a number of grounds for the failure of the defendants properly to supply steel, designs and labour; and there are also claims in deceit and negligent misstatement. On this application I am concerned only with the question of steel.

In my view, it is appropriate to describe this case as major litigation of a type which is not uncommon in our Courts. I do not suggest that this case is necessarily comparable to *Morrison-Knudsen Co., Inc. et al. v. British Columbia & Power Authority* (1978), 85 DLR (3d) 186, [1978] 4 WWR 193 (CA) (which lasted over 400 days at trial), but the conduct of this case is a very substantial undertaking. It is estimated by counsel to require 20 days for trial.

BC Hydro has furnished about 30,000 documents for inspection by the plaintiffs and, just before the hearing of this motion, BC Hydro tendered a further 12-page inventory of documents it is prepared to make available for inspection.

The plaintiffs now seek an order:

(1) pursuant to Rule 27(10) of the Rules of Court that the Defendant, British Columbia Hydro and Power Authority, produce the documents referred to in the Schedule to this Notice of Motion for inspection and copying by the Plaintiff at such time, place and manner as the Court thinks just.

(2) pursuant to Rule 27(4) of the Rules of Court that the Defendant, British Columbia Hydro and Power Authority, deliver an Affidavit stating whether the documents or class of documents specified or described in the Schedule to this Notice of Motion is or has been in the possession or control of that Defendant and, if not then in the possession or control of the Defendant, when that Defendant parted with it and what has become of it.

Attached to these reasons is the schedule to the notice of motion which sets out what the plaintiffs seek on both branches of its application.

One of the matters in issue between these parties is the extent to which the plaintiffs may require production and inspection of documents relating to this and other contracts which were underway at the same time as the contract in question. The plaintiffs say documents relating to these contracts may contain statements (described, hopefully, by counsel for the plaintiff as "confessions") which may assist the plaintiffs to prove their case or, possibly, impeach the case of the defendants.

BC Hydro says it has now produced all documents relating to the operation of the Kidd Steelyard in connection with this and the other contracts, including Pe Ben's "pullsheets" which record all steel ordered for the project and removed from the Kidd Steelyard. BC Hydro declines to produce all its other "mountains of documents" which relate to various phases of this and other contracts.

BC Hydro says it has complied with the requirements of paras. IV, VI, and VII of the schedule, and will produce bar graphs of progress on all its transmission line contracts, but it objects to a search of everything it has relating to the Mica Creek and Kootenay Canal transmission lines in order to see if anything which may possibly be relevant is resting there. This, I am sure, would be a very extensive undertaking, and no likelihood has been established that anything worthwhile will be found.

The plaintiffs rely on *Compagnie Financiere et Commerciale du Pacifique v. Peruvian Guano Co.* (1882), 11 QBD 55 (CA), which has been followed and applied in numerous cases in this Court for many years. The Rule the Court was there considering required discovery of "a document relating to any matter in question in the action." Our present Rule 26(1) is in practically the same terms.

The *Peruvian Guano* case (as it is usually called) indicates (at pp. 56-7) that the plaintiffs made an affidavit of documents in the usual form, in which they disclosed, *inter alia*, their minute-book. The defendant brought an application for a further affidavit of the following documents, which were described in the minute-book:

... first, drafts of arrangement between the Peruvian Guano Company, and the plaintiff company, referred to in the board minutes of the plaintiff company, dated the 28th of September, 1881; secondly, the letter and two telegrams received by the plaintiffs from Mr. Adam, referred to in the board minutes of the plaintiff company, dated the 2d of November, 1881; thirdly, two further drafts relating to the form of communication to be made, and the letter from M. de Germiny to M. Homeberg, respectively referred to in the board minutes, dated the 3d of November, 1881; fourthly, a letter addressed to Mr. Adam, referred to in the board minutes, dated the 8th of November, 1881; and, fifthly, several letters written from London by Mr. Adam to the plaintiff company, or directors thereof, and the several letters and telegrams sent by the plaintiff company, or directors thereof, to Mr. Adam, as referred to in the board minutes, dated the 16th of November, 1881.

The Master declined to order a further affidavit. Pearson J, sitting in Chambers, made an order as to the first class of documents only. An appeal to the Queen's Bench Division was dismissed, and a further appeal was taken to the Court of Appeal.
Baggailay LJ at pp. 59-60 said:

I assent to the suggestion made by Brett LJ in the course of the argument, that a document, which, it is not unreasonable to suppose, may tend either to advance the case of the party seeking discovery, or to damage the case of his adversary, should be regarded as a document relating to a matter in question in the action. I proceed to apply these tests to the documents in respect of which this appeal is brought. As regards No. 3, the objection taken by the plaintiffs, that it does not appear from the affidavit already sworn that is in the possession or power of the plaintiffs, must I think prevail; but as regards Nos. 2, 4, and 5, I am of opinion that it appears from the minutes that they are in the possession or power of the plaintiffs, and that it is not unreasonable to suppose that they may contain information, directly or indirectly, enabling the defendants to advance their own case or to damage the case of their adversaries.

Brett LJ in the *locus classicus* on this question said at p. 63:

It seems to me that every document relates to the matters in question in the action, which not only would be evidence upon any issue, but also which, it is reasonable to suppose, contains information which *may*—not which *must*—either directly or indirectly enable the party requiring the affidavit either to advance his own case or to damage the case of his adversary. I have put in the words "either directly or indirectly," because, as it seems to me, a document can properly be said to contain information which may enable the party requiring the affidavit either to advance his own case or to damage the case of his adversary, if it is a document which may fairly lead him to a train of inquiry, which may have either of these two consequences ...

It appears from the foregoing that the documents in question in the *Peruvian Guano* case were probably not as extensive as the record of pleadings in this case.

It also appears that a literal reading of Rule 26(1) and the application of the *Peruvian Guano* case leads inexorably to the conclusion that the plaintiffs should succeed on this application.

I hesitate to disturb an authority as ancient and well-established as the *Peruvian Guano* case which has stood unchallenged in Britain and in this Province for 100 years. But Lord Diplock said that all judicial reasoning must be considered "*secundum subjectam materiam*": *Mutual Life & Cilizens'Ass'ce Co. Ltd. et al. v. Evait*, [1971] 1 All ER 150 at p. 161. The Rules of Court are our servants, not our masters.

I respectfully decline to follow the *Peruvian Guano* case, *supra*, or slavishly to apply Rule 26(1) in a case such as this, where thousands or possibly hundreds of thousands of documents of only possible relevance are in question. I do not intend to suggest, however, that the *Peruvian Guano* case does not correctly state the law in most cases. That question does not arise for consideration here.

It does not follow that this motion should be dismissed because, notwithstanding the foregoing, every reasonable effort must be made to enable the plaintiffs to locate any documents which may assist the parties to ascertain the truth. What is not permissible, or reasonable, in my view, is to require a party, in a case as this, to incur enormous expense in what may be a futile search for something which may not exist.

One solution would be to permit the most extensive possible search and inquiry to be made at the plaintiffs' non-recoverable expense; or, alternatively, to require the plaintiffs to post security for the cost of the search, with the cost thereof being assessed ultimately by the Court when the results of both the search and the action are known.

Another suggestion might be to try an issue, if one could be defined, which might resolve this question without the kind of search which the plaintiffs' motion requires. Rule 26(15) provides for such an order. In this connection the plaintiffs' claim is that they did not directly, or by their agent Pe Ben, obtain steel in the manner required by the contract. If that question could be resolved objectively, it might not be necessary to go any further. I suspect, however, that the plaintiffs would wish to have the information they seek on the trial of even a limited issue.

I would give consideration to any reasonable proposal the parties may make regarding the foregoing. If they cannot agree, then, in order to make an effective order, I would direct only that the plaintiffs may apply again for an affidavit, and subsequent inspection, of documents which may be uncovered by a search of greatly reduced scope. To put it differently, the plaintiffs must choose a smaller target within BC Hydro. As is well known, BC Hydro is the largest enterprise in the Province, and the plaintiffs must define a more manageable area for inquiry. In addition, the plaintiffs must establish a *prima facie* case that something relevant will be uncovered before a further affidavit and further inspection will be ordered.

Upon any such further application I would expect a senior responsible officer of BC Hydro to verify on oath the extent of its production to date, the magnitude and estimated expense of the search required to satisfy the further production which is being sought, and such further circumstances as may be necessary to enable the Court to decide whether a further search will be fruitful. In addition, I would expect such deponent to verify, upon grounds which are stated, what his belief is regarding the likelihood of further relevant documents being uncovered.

I hesitate to make pronouncements such as this which carry the risk of being misunderstood. I therefore wish it to be known that what I say in these reasons applies particularly to discovery of documents in cases of this kind. The production of documents made by BC Hydro up to this stage is entirely appropriate, and, notwithstanding anything

I have said, I would have ordered production at least of all the defendant's documents relating to the operation of the Kidd Steelyard—for all contractors. I do not, however, foreclose the right of any party to major litigation to apply at any stage for directions regarding discovery of documents. The time has arrived, in my view, for the Court to become concerned about the cost of litigation subject, of course, to the right of any party to the Court's assistance in the reasonable preparation of his claim or defence.

Order accordingly.

NOTES AND QUESTIONS

1. The court suggested that one option "might be to try an issue, if one could be defined, which might resolve this question without the kind of search which the plaintiffs' motion requires." A number of jurisdictions permit divided discovery of documents and have similar rules regarding oral discovery—for example, see Ontario rule 30.04(8) and New Brunswick rule 31.04(8). Courts have been reluctant to order such procedure but instances certainly exist—for example, *Diamond v. Kaufman* (1985), 1 CPC (2d) 1 (Ont. Master). There, the court ordered divided production and discovery in an action seeking an accounting of the business receipts and disbursements of a computer software business operated by the defendants. Only if the plaintiff had succeeded on the liability issue would the accounting have been necessary, since disclosure of the information could have seriously prejudiced the defendants.

2. In Great Britain, Lord Woolf was recently given the task of recommending reforms of the civil justice system. In his interim and final reports, *Access to Justice* (London: HMSO, 1995 and 1996), he set forth ambitious recommendations for reform. He found that, as in Canada and the United States, there was a general consensus that documentary discovery in more complex litigation can present real problems because of the sheer volume of documents and resulting high costs. Interestingly, he also expressed concern that the breadth of documentary discovery in England (which is no broader than other common law jurisdictions) was having an adverse impact on the ability of English courts to continue to attract important international litigation. (Generally, discovery is unheard of in civil law countries.) As was often the case, Woolf found the answer to his concerns in judicial management and discretion:

> As part of the case management process, the judiciary will have both the means and the responsibility to ensure that discovery is limited to what is really necessary" (Interim Report, at 168, para. 20).

Woolf recommended that the court retain jurisdiction to order full discovery of the kind now presently available, but he anticipated that this will be rare and, generally, discovery will be more limited. Woolf's proposals depend on distinctions that he draws among what are today considered relevant and, hence, producible documents. Documents are divided into four categories: (1) documents that a party relies on to support its case; (2) documents that, to a material extent, adversely affect a party's case or support the other party's case; (3) documents that are relevant to the issues in the proceeding but do not fall into the preceding categories; and (4) documents that are not relevant in and of themselves but might lead to a "train of inquiry" leading to relevant documents. Documents in categories (1) and (2) are to be available as "standard discovery," while the documents in categories (3) and (4) are to be available only as "extra discovery." Normally, in fast-track cases, the parties will be required to give only "standard discovery." In other cases (multi-track cases), discovery will be tailored to the circumstances of the particular case and the procedural judge will decide if and when "extra discovery" will be available.

In making his recommendation Woolf observed:

> The core of the problem is that conscientious lawyers and their clients might feel obliged to troll through all category (3) documents in order to eliminate the possibility of overlooking category (2) documents. To do so would be to defeat the aims of controlled discovery.

He resolved this matter by stating that "initial disclosure should apply to documents of which a party is aware at the time when the obligation to disclose arises." The court and the parties, he says, will have to work out in practice the appropriate balance between what should properly be disclosed under that test and what can legitimately be left for the opponent to canvas on an application for further discovery.

What is your reaction to Woolf's proposed new document discovery regime? Is it worrying to hear Woolf say that a party is not required to "troll through" all of the documents in its possession to find out if category (2) documents exist, because this may open the door to the non-production of damaging documents? Is relieving a party of the obligation to "troll through" all of its documents an open invitation to parties to never "turn up" the smoking gun that favours the opponent's case? Can it be further argued that Woolf's notion, that a party does not have to read through all of its own documents, assumes that documents come prearranged in the four categories that he articulates? Since this is obviously not so, query whether it is in fact wise to relieve a party of the obligation of reading all its own potentially relevant documents?

C. Documentary Discovery from Non-Parties

In most jurisdictions, documentary discovery is available from non-parties (see, for example, Ontario rule 30.10). However, non-parties are not required to produce an affidavit of documents—that is, to make general disclosure of the documents within their possession; however, note Ontario rule 30.02(4) with regard to documents in the possession of a corporation related to a corporate party—but they can, if the court so orders, be required to produce specific documents. As with examination for discovery of non-parties, the rules may specifically place limits on this power to obtain production from non-parties—for example, see Ontario rule 30.10(1). The following case was decided under an earlier version of the Ontario rule.

Woods v. Harris
(1979), 25 OR (2d) 14 (HC)

CORY J (orally): An appeal has been brought from the decision of Master Garfield refusing leave to the defendant to obtain production of documents in the hands of McGraw-Edison.

The plaintiff in the action was injured in a motor vehicle accident in May of 1977. He was off work from May until October of that year. For 33 years he has been employed by McGraw-Edison. Subsequent to the accident, he has apparently taken a position where his hourly rate of pay is $1 less than it was prior to the time of the accident.

The application, as it came before the Master, was broad in the extreme. It sought an order directing McGraw-Edison, its agents, servants and employees to produce to the defendant the employment records made by or on behalf, or obtained by McGraw-Edison during the duration of the employment of the plaintiff Edwin Woods. The application, in my view, is framed so broadly that it ought to be dismissed. That might be enough to deal with the application in itself; however the matter was extremely ably argued by counsel for all parties and, in deference to them, something further should be said.

It was argued that the employment records were relevant and pertinent to the assessment of the damages of the plaintiff. The question of relevancy is a broad one. The social issues which the application raises are significant. The plaintiff, by seeking general damages, including compensation for loss of future employment or reduction in his rate of pay in future employment, must make available as part of his claim certain information. Much of that information might in the ordinary course of events be confidential, and certainly may be confidential as between the plaintiff and his employer. On the other hand, there must be some reasonable limitations to what a person seeking fair and reasonable just compensation from the Courts should be put to by way of such disclosure. Neither a plaintiff seeking just compensation, nor his employer should be subject to needless harassment as a result of the action.

So, too, should there be reasonable limits on what is required of third parties. As yet there is no requirement in our law for production from third parties. There are many factors to be taken into consideration. For example, if the plaintiff were employed by a small company which kept no more than the minimal pay and taxation records, Revenue, Unemployment Insurance and Workmen's Compensation, a requirement to disclose such records would have little or no effect on the plaintiff. Another plaintiff might be employed by a company that, for its own benefit and the benefit of the employee, kept voluminous records that pertain to the attitude, apparent health, marital status, flirtatious interests and many other matters that may be of no relevance or at best marginal relevance, but extremely damaging to the employee. It is no use blandly saying that that information is still confidential in the hands of the defendant. It has by its mere production become to a certain extent public. What the proper balance is to be is difficult to say. Surely we come back to the trite old position that the circumstances of each case will have to determine the matter.

Something was said of the tests to be applied in a situation such as this in *Astral Films Ltd. et al. v. Sherman et al.* (1978), 19 OR (2d) 206 [at 207]:

> In considering an application of this sort, some guidelines should perhaps be considered
> by the Court. The matter must be approached with some caution for it constitutes a form
> of production from a stranger to the action. What then should be the guidelines for
> consideration? Some of those might be: the state of the pleadings at the time of the
> application, the stage the action had reached, whether or not discoveries had been held in
> whole or in part, the apparent *bona fides* of the action, and the basis upon which the

motion is brought (that is to say, what is there to lead the applicant to believe that relevant and pertinent evidence could be obtained that would be significant to the action).

It is necessary to consider only one of those tests to dispose of this application. There is nothing as yet in the examination for discovery that sufficiently narrows and defines the information that is required that would be a basis for a Court granting the order. In all the other cases to which I was referred, some specific information was required or needed from a hospital report, a medical report or a bank record. It may well be that in some or perhaps many cases *some* aspect of the employment record should be produced. What is sought here is far too broad and sweeping. It ought not be allowed or, indeed, encouraged.

In the future the Court will have to consider problems that may arise in situations concerning companies that have been involved in industrial disputes. There the company records may refer to the employer's actions in regard to something that the employer wishes to keep extremely confidential, something that may affect the future of the relationship between employee and employer should it be disclosed or divulged. Clearly, there are problems that will have to be considered in the future. Just as clearly it appears that each case should be approached on the basis of its particular facts and circumstances. Care should be taken not to make too broad and sweeping a generalization with regard to discovery of third parties.

A proper balance will have to be struck between ensuring disclosure by production from third parties of *relevant* information on the one hand, and the prevention of actions that amount to harassment of the plaintiff and his employer, on the other.

Application dismissed.

Ontario (Attorney General) v. Stavro

The Attorney General of Ontario and the Public Trustee (Plaintiffs/Appellants) v. Steve A. Stavro, John Donald Crump and Terence V. Kelly, Executors of the Estate of Harold Edwin Ballard, Deceased, Knob Hill Farms Limited, MLG Ventures Limited, and Maple Leaf Gardens Limited (Defendants/Respondents); Harry Ornest, Ruth Ornest, Cindy Ornest, Laura Ornest, Michael Ornest, Maury Ornest, the Ornest Family Partnership and Jim Devellano (Intervenors)

(1995), 26 OR (3d) 39 (CA)

[The plaintiffs sought declarations pursuant to the Charitable Gifts Act (Ont.) that the executors of the estate of Harold Ballard had acted in breach of their fiduciary duties to the estate as a result of actions leading to the sale of the estate's interest in Maple Leaf Gardens Ltd. (MLG) to MLG Ventures ("Ventures"), a company controlled by Stavro (one of the estate's executors). The plaintiffs also sought an order that the sale was null and void; a declaration that all dividends received by Ventures on the shares of MLG Ltd. were received in trust for the estate, and an order enjoining the defendants from taking steps to amalgamate MLG Ltd. and Ventures, from conducting a shareholders' meeting, or from taking steps to cancel the estate's interest in MLG Ltd. Pursuant to the oppression remedies under the Business Corporations Act (Ont.), the plaintiffs further sought a declaration that the affairs of MLG Ltd. had been carried on in a manner that was oppressive to, unfairly prejudicial to, and unfairly disregarded the interests of, security holders of MLG Ltd., including the estate and beneficiaries of the estate, and an order setting aside the acquisition of the shares of MLG Ltd. by Ventures.

After obtaining an interim injunction, the plaintiffs brought two motions pursuant to rule 30.10(1) of the Ontario Rules of Civil Procedure for production of documents in the possession, control or power of four non-party financial institutions. Two of these non-parties, the Toronto-Dominion Bank and TD Capital Group Limited, opposed production. The motions judge found that the documents were relevant to material issues in the litigation, but he concluded that the plaintiffs had not established that it would be unfair to require them to proceed to trial without the documents or that the documents were vital or crucial to preparation for trial. Consequently the motions were dismissed. The plaintiffs appealed.]

BY THE COURT: The appellants (plaintiffs) appeal from the order of the motion judge dismissing two motions brought pursuant to rule 30.10(1) of the Rules of Civil Procedure seeking production of documents in the possession, control or power of four non-parties to this action. Two of the non-parties did not oppose the motions.

Briefly stated, the action is with respect to issues dealing with the fiduciary duties of the executors in dealing with assets of the estate of Harold E. Ballard, deceased.

The rule provides as follows:

> 30.10 (1) The court may, on motion by a party, order production for inspection of a document that is in the possession, control or power of a person not a party and is not privileged where the court is satisfied that,
> (a) the document is relevant to a material issue in the action; and
> (b) it would be unfair to require the moving party to proceed to trial without having discovery of the document.

The motion judge found that the documents were relevant to material issues in the litigation. He then proceeded to consider whether it would be unfair to require the appellants to proceed to trial without having discovery of those documents. After alluding to a number of factors relevant to that determination, the motion judge turned to the importance of the documents in the litigation. He referred to this consideration as the "most important factor" in the fairness assessment. After reviewing the authorities he said [at 44 ante]:

> [T]he evidence sought must be vital or crucial and such that the moving party cannot adequately prepare its case for trial without access to such documents.

The appellants submit that in holding that the documents must be "vital" or "crucial" to their preparation for trial, the motion judge departed from the test set out in rule 30.10(1).

We agree. The fairness assessment required by rule 30.10(1)(b) is made only after the documents are found to be relevant to a material issue. By requiring that the documents be "vital" or "crucial" before it could be said that it would be unfair to refuse their production, the motion judge combined the separate considerations identified in rule

30.10(1)(a) and (b) into a single test which imposed a higher standard of materiality than that contemplated by the rule. The rule envisions cases where it will be unfair to require a party to proceed to trial without the production of relevant documents even though those documents are not crucial or vital to that party's preparation for trial. By limiting the production of documents to those found to be vital or crucial, the trial judge elevated the materiality standard in rule 30.10(1)(a) and effectively neutered the fairness assessment demanded by rule 30.10(1)(b).

The motion judge did refer to various factors which could be relevant to the inquiry required by rule 30.10(1)(b). He then proceeded, however, to consider the significance of the documents in the litigation to the virtual exclusion of all other factors in determining whether it would be unfair to require the appellants to proceed to trial without production of the documents. In doing so, he erred.

In holding that the motion judge erred, we do not suggest that the importance of the documents in the litigation is not relevant to the fairness assessment required by rule 30.10(1)(b). In *Metropolitan Life Insurance Co. v. Frenette*, [1992] 1 SCR 647, 89 DLR (4th) 653, the defendant sought production of medical records referable to the plaintiff's mental condition before his death. In considering a provision of the *Quebec Code of Civil Procedure*, RSQ, c. C-25, which was said to be analogous to rule 30.10 (p. 690), L'Heureux-Dubé J said at p. 685 (SCR ii):

> Otherwise, judges must exercise their discretion under art. 402 CCP *according to the degree of relevance and importance of the information sought relative to the issue between the parties*. In exercising that discretion, a court must weigh the diverse interests in conflict. (Emphasis added)

Clearly, if a moving party can show that the documents requested are crucial to its preparation for trial, that party has gone a long way to demonstrating that it would be unfair to require the party to proceed to trial without production of those documents. It does not, however, follow that absent a demonstration that the documents are crucial to the litigation, the moving party cannot demonstrate that it would be unfair to require that party to proceed to trial without production of the documents. The importance of the documents requested is a factor, but only one factor to be considered in making the determination required by rule 30.10(1)(b).

The appellants submitted that if we concluded that the motion judge applied the wrong test in denying production that we should vacate that order and require production.

We do not agree. An order requiring production should be made only after a full consideration of all of the relevant factors. The motion judge, who is case managing this complex litigation, is in a much better position than this court to determine whether fairness requires production of all, some or none of the demanded documents at this stage of the litigation. In our view, the policy underlying the case management system is best served by remitting the matter to the motion judge for a determination of the merits.

In making the fairness assessment required by rule 30.10(1)(b), the motion judge must be guided by the policy underlying the discovery regime presently operating in Ontario. That regime provides for full discovery of, and production from parties to the litigation. It also imposes ongoing disclosure obligations on those parties. Save in the circumstances specifically addressed by the rules, non-parties are immune from the potentially intrusive, costly and time-consuming process of discovery and production. By its terms, rule 30.10 assumes that requiring a party to go to trial without the forced production of relevant documents in the hands of non-parties is not *per se* unfair.

The discovery process must also be kept within reasonable bounds. Lengthy, some might say interminable, discoveries are far from rare in the present litigation environment. We are told that discovery of these defendants has already occupied some 18 days and is not yet complete. Unless production from and discovery of non-parties is subject to firm controls and recognized as the exception rather than the rule, the discovery process, like Topsy, will just grow and grow. The effective and efficient resolution of civil lawsuits is not served if the discovery process takes on dimensions more akin to a public inquiry than a specific lawsuit.

The motion judge was properly concerned about the ramifications of a production order in this case. Many litigants, especially those involved in complex commercial cases, find themselves in the position where non-party financial institutions are in possession of documents which are relevant to material issues in the litigation, and which those institutions cannot, or will not, voluntarily produce prior to trial. If this situation alone is enough to compel production during the discovery stage of the process, then production from and discovery of non-parties would become a routine part of the discovery process in complex commercial cases. It may be that it should be part of that process, but that is not the policy reflected in the rules as presently drafted.

In deciding whether to order production in the circumstances of this case, the factors to be considered by the motion judge should include:

- the importance of the documents in the litigation;
- whether production at the discovery stage of the process as opposed to production at trial is necessary to avoid unfairness to the appellant;
- whether the discovery of the defendants with respect to the issues to which the documents are relevant is adequate and if not, whether responsibility for that inadequacy rests with the defendants;
- the position of the non-parties with respect to production;
- the availability of the documents or their informational equivalent from some other source which is accessible to the moving parties;
- the relationship of the non-parties from whom production is sought, to the litigation and the parties to the litigation. Non-parties who have an interest in the subject-matter of the litigation and whose interests are allied with the party opposing production should be more susceptible to a production order than a true "stranger" to the litigation.

In addressing these and any other relevant factors (some of which were identified by the motion judge in his reasons), the motion judge will bear in mind that the appellants bear the burden of showing that it would be unfair to make them proceed to trial without production of the documents.

In our opinion, a consideration of some of these factors will require an examination of the documents as contemplated by rule 30.10(3). That rule provides in part:

> 30.10(3) ... where the court is uncertain of the relevance of or necessity for discovery of the document, the court may inspect the document to determine the issue.

For example, in considering whether it would be unfair to require the appellants to wait until trial to obtain the documents, the number, content and authorship of the documents may be very important. Those facts could be ascertained only from an examination of the documents or perhaps from an examination of an appropriate summary prepared by those in possession of the documents. Similarly, the importance or unimportance of the documents in the litigation may best be determined by an examination of them.

We recognize that this process will be time consuming and will place an additional burden on the motion judge. We are satisfied, however, that in the circumstances of this case and considering the material filed on the motions, that an informed decision requires an examination of the documents. A decision made without reference to the documents runs the very real risk of being either over- or under-inclusive. No doubt, as the case management judge, the motion judge will have a familiarity with the case which will facilitate his review of the documents.

In the result, the appeal is allowed, the order made by the motion judge is set aside, and the matter is remitted to the motion judge for further consideration in accordance with the principles outlined above. The costs of this appeal and of the motion below are left to the motion judge.

Appeal allowed.

NOTES

1. Notice that at the beginning of this case both the short and long "title of proceeding" are given. This is to remind you that, while cases are typically referred to by the short title (referring to just the first plaintiff and first defendant), in modern day litigation there are often numerous parties, particularly multiple defendants.

2. Is the potential complexity of the analysis and the time and expense involved in moving for production from an unwilling non-party likely in most cases to serve to limit such motions to cases in which the evidence is "vital" or "crucial" to preparation for trial?

3. What should be the position of non-party financial institutions? Do they have a responsibility to the public to facilitate the discovery process re legitimate claims? Or should courts be concerned about the potential expense to such institutions of producing documents in litigation in which they have no interest?

4. The following article appeared in *The Globe and Mail*, March 22, 1999:

Stavro misled investors, OSC says
Leafs owner makes deal to settle allegations about Gardens takeover

Steve Stavro, co-owner of the Toronto Maple Leafs and Toronto Raptors, faces allegations that he misled investors during his takeover of Maple Leaf Gardens five years ago. The Ontario Securities Commission alleged yesterday that Mr. Stavro, along with former Gardens director Donald Crump and current director Brian Bellmore, withheld key information from investors when they launched the takeover in March, 1994. The three have proposed an agreement to settle the matter. An OSC panel will decide on March 29 whether to accept the proposal.

"We are pleased to announce that we have agreed with staff of the Ontario Securities Commission on a proposed resolution of a dispute arising from the acquisition of Maple Leaf Gardens," Richard Peddie, president and chief executive officer of Maple Leaf Sports & Entertainment Ltd., said in a press release last night.

The allegations surround key information about Gardens broadcasting revenue that Mr. Stavro allegedly had before launching the takeover. The OSC alleges that Mr. Stavro knew that revenue from broadcasting games was about to soar, which could have increased the value of Gardens stock. The takeover began with a series of private deals in early 1994, based on a price of $34 a share. Those deals gave Mr. Stavro's group 80 per cent of Maple Leaf Gardens shares, which were trading on the Toronto Stock Exchange at the time. The group included the Toronto-Dominion Bank and the Ontario Teachers Pension Plan Board. The group then launched a bid to acquire all remaining shares for the same price. The total price tag was $125-million. At the time, Mr. Stavro was a director of the Gardens and an executor of the estate of Harold Ballard, who died in 1990 and whose estate owned about 60 per cent of the company's shares.

The bid immediately ran into stiff opposition, notably from Ontario's Public Trustee, who acted on behalf of charities in a foundation created by Mr. Ballard. The charities were supposed to receive a cut of any sale of the Gardens. Lawyers for the Public Trustee sued, arguing that the bid was too low. Two other shareholders, Harry Ornest and Jim Devellano, also sued over the price. The case was settled in April, 1996, with Mr. Stavro agreeing to pay $49.50 a share, bringing the total purchase price to about $165-million.

However, documents that surfaced later indicated that TD Bank officials had information in January, 1994, indicating that the shares were worth far more than $34. The bank's assessment was based partly on information from Mr. Stavro's group, indicating that income from broadcast rights was about to increase significantly. At the time, a deal for the rights, involving Molson Breweries, had just been renegotiated, and Mr. Stavro's group allegedly knew that the new deal, set to start in 1995, would be far more lucrative. The rights were worth $4.3-million in 1994-95, according to the OSC documents.

Internal bank memos indicate that in December, 1993, Mr. Stavro told the bank that he expected the broadcast rights to be worth $15-million under the new deal. A handwritten note on one memo, dated Feb. 14, 1994, and filed in court, says the bank may be "perceived to have inside information vis-a-vis potential for television contract." An internal bank memo, dated Jan. 14, 1994, shows that the bank valued Maple Leaf Gardens shares at $48.94 on that date, largely because of the added broadcasting revenue.

If lawyers for the TD Bank and Mr Stavro were aware of the contents of the documents in the TD Bank's possession, was it ethical for them to oppose the application for production from the TD Bank in *Ontario (AG) v. Stavro*?

III. PHYSICAL DISCOVERY

A. Medical Examinations

As already indicated, the rules of the various jurisdictions invariably provide that where the physical and mental condition of a party to a proceeding is in question the court may order a party to undergo a physical or mental examination: see Ontario rule 33 and s. 105 of the Courts of Justice Act. What is the policy behind allowing the courts to order parties to undergo such intrusive examinations even against their will?

Manuel v. Head
(1988), 72 Nfld. & PEIR (2d) 211 (Nfld. TD)

BARRY J: This is an application by the defendant under rule 34 of the Rules of the Supreme Court contained in Schedule D of the Judicature Act (Statutes of Newfoundland 1986) for an order that the first plaintiff be examined by two medical practitioners for the purpose of enabling them to make an assessment of injuries sustained by him in a motor vehicle accident which occurred on June 30, 1984, and of the result of the medical treatment subsequently received. ...

The first plaintiff has alleged in his statement of claim that he sustained serious personal injuries in the automobile accident, above referred to, for which he now claims damages from the defendant. The first plaintiff has already supplied the defendant with medical reports prepared by his own physicians but the defendant alleges that it is necessary to make his own assessment of those injuries to enable him to prepare a proper defence to this action.

Rule 34.01(1) provides for issuance of an order by this court for an examination of a party to an action by a qualified medical practitioner upon application of another party in the same action in the following terms:

> 34.01(1) Where the physical or mental condition of a party is in issue, the court may, at any time on the application of an opposing party or on its own motion, order the party to submit to a physical or mental examination by a qualified medical practitioner.

... The plaintiff alleges that rule 34.01 is unconstitutional because it offends sections 7, 8, and 9 of the Charter by providing means whereby a litigant may be compelled to submit to a medical examination or face the prospect of having his case stayed or dismissed. These provisions are as follows:

> 7. Everyone has the right to life, liberty and security of the person and the right not to be deprived thereof except in accordance with the principles of fundamental justice.
>
> 8. Everyone has the right to be secure against unreasonable search or seizure.
>
> 9. Everyone has the right not to be arbitrarily detained or imprisoned.

In my view, there cannot be a deprivation of liberty within the meaning of s. 7 unless there is a compulsory restriction of movement of one person by another through the exercise by the latter of some measure of authority or control by threat or force. In this case, the order of the court if granted would require the plaintiff to submit his person for a medical examination by two medical practitioners selected by the defendant. While at first sight this measure appears to be an infringement upon the liberty or security of the first plaintiff, yet when put into proper context, it appears in a different light.

The proper context is that of a civil action taken by the first plaintiff against the defendant claiming damages for injuries allegedly caused by the defendant's negligence. The application herein has been made to enable the defendant to defend himself against the first plaintiff's claim. What is involved is a balancing of the first plaintiff's right to sue the defendant for damages and the right of the defendant to inform himself prior to trial by inspection of the damages which the first plaintiff claims from him. There was no obligation upon the first plaintiff to institute action against the defendant seeking damages for the injuries he sustained. However, by doing so, he voluntarily accepted the procedure provided in the Rules of the Supreme Court for the processing of his claim. The question arising upon the application is whether the first plaintiff can invoke the Charter to assist him in avoiding a procedural step which provides that upon application of the defendant the court may order that he be examined by qualified medical practitioners for an assessment of his injuries. The Charter was not designed to take away rights of others in order to convenience persons who themselves are seeking to establish rights before the law. Accordingly, I hold that an order of the court directing the first plaintiff to submit himself to a medical examination would not offend s. 7 of the Charter because it is a necessary step in a proceeding which he himself initiated.

The same reasoning applies to the first plaintiff's allegation that the order requires that he submit to an unreasonable search of his person in violation of his right to the protection from such searches afforded him by s. 8 of the Charter. The search to which he refers is the proposed medical examination which an order under rule 34.01 would direct him to undergo. If the examination can be properly termed a search within the meaning of s. 8 of the Charter, it cannot be held to be unreasonable in view of the fact that it is a necessary part of the procedure involved in the course of his own suit against the defendant. Nor does the proposed order constitute detention within the meaning of s. 9 of the Charter. That section relates to a situation where a person in authority forcefully holds or takes another into custody without his consent. It appears that its scope overlaps that of s. 7 of the Charter to some degree, and for the reasons above set out with reference to that section it is not applicable to a case such as this where the detainment apprehended is merely an order of the court directing the first plaintiff to comply with a necessary procedural requirement in the legal proceeding commenced by the first plaintiff.

If I am wrong in so holding, and the infringements of the Charter alleged or any of them are truly violations of its provisions, I am satisfied that any such infringement is a reasonable limit upon guaranteed freedoms and for the reasons given above, can be demonstrably justified in a free and democratic society in accordance with the provisions of s. 1 of the Charter, which I now quote:

> 1. The Canadian Charter of Rights and Freedoms guarantees the rights and freedoms set out in it subject only to such reasonable limits prescribed by law as can be demonstrably justified in a free and democratic society.

... The purpose of pretrial procedures such as the medical examination of a party is to enable parties to be informed of each other's claims and contentions and of the evidence to be presented at trial in order that they will be prepared to meet the issues involved in particular actions. Such procedures result in narrowing issues, obviating unnecessary evidence and obtaining agreement upon undisputed relevant evidence at trial. These procedures when utilized by parties often lead to settlement of many issues before trial, as well as out-of-court settlements of the claims themselves. The many benefits and advantages which result from pretrial procedures are well-known and generally operate to the benefit of parties to civil actions. In this case the pretrial medical examination sought by the defendant is intended to give him an opportunity to conduct an independent examination of the first plaintiff in order to satisfy himself as to the nature and extent of the injuries complained of.

To recover, the plaintiff must prove his claim not only in respect of the tort involved but also in respect of the damages sustained. Proof of damages involves presentation to the court of creditable evidence to substantiate the nature and extent of the injuries sustained by the first plaintiff as a result of the wrongdoing of the defendant. It is, inter alia, a condition of acceptance of such evidence by the court that upon application the defendant be permitted, where applicable, to examine the objects damaged and to cross-examine the plaintiff's witnesses as to the accuracy of their observations and conclusions respecting such damage.

Rule 30.01 provides for the oral examination of a person intended by a party to be called as a witness in an action at any time before trial, whether such person resides within or without the jurisdiction of the court. Similar provision has been made in rule 32 for the discovery and inspection of documents before trial and in rule 36 for the inspection of real and personal property. While an examination of injuries sustained by a person cannot be equated to an oral examination of a person under rule 30 or the inspection of a damaged motor vehicle under rule 36, nevertheless, a defendant in an action for personal damages has the right to make his own assessment of injuries sustained by the plaintiff to test the accuracy and veracity of allegations of damages made by the plaintiffs. It is alleged that the first plaintiff cannot be ordered to submit to a medical examination because such an order involves a form of restriction upon rights granted him by the Charter, and therefore, the subject of his claim, i.e. his own injuries, should be allowed to escape scrutiny by the defendant. However, the Rules of Court are intended to introduce a procedure which will bring a maximum degree of fairness to parties who are involved in actions before this court. Of the essence of this procedure is the principle that facts in issue be made known by parties relying upon them to other parties and the court. This means that a plaintiff, upon application by the defendant, must make available the subject matter of the damage claimed so that the defendant can inspect the objects about which the issues revolve. To deprive a defendant of an opportunity to make such an examination is to prevent him from exercising his right to inspect the principal object of the plaintiff's claim.

The importance of according such a right to a defendant to a medical examination of the plaintiff to be conducted by a qualified medical practitioner becomes obvious where, as here, he alleges to have sustained very severe injuries for which he claims substantial monetary damages. If an inspection is not allowed, the defendant and the court must accept, without means of testing or verification, the testimony which the plaintiffs will adduce on the nature and the extent of the injuries and the disabilities which ensue therefrom. While the plaintiff is entitled to claim against the defendant the damages he suffered arising out of the alleged wrongful conduct of the defendant, those damages must be proved and assessed in accordance with the Rules of Court. The plaintiff can succeed in his action, only by following the rules of procedure enacted under the authority of the Judicature Act including the rule that he make available for medical inspection the person who sustained the injuries for which damages are claimed, i.e., himself, even though it may be repugnant to him.

In issuing an order for the medical examination of a party under rule 34 the court does not direct that such party be forced or compelled to undergo the examination. The order really means that the defendant is entitled to have the plaintiff's injuries examined by a medical practitioner and that if the plaintiff does not submit to such an examination, he will not be permitted to prove his damages solely upon the evidence of the medical practitioners whom he may choose to call as witnesses. Rule 34.06 states:

> 34.06(1) When a party fails to submit to an examination or deliver a medical report as required by rule 34, the party shall not be liable to contempt but shall, if a plaintiff, be liable to have his or her proceedings dismissed, or, if a defendant, to have his or her defence struck out.

I interpret this as meaning that the court, upon the plaintiff's refusal or failure to comply with an order under s. 36.01, may, not "must," dismiss the plaintiff's action. It appears to me that it is implicit in this rule (34.06) that the plaintiff will not be allowed to adduce the evidence of damages which he alleges to have suffered, where he has refused to undergo a medical examination which has been ordered by the court upon the application of the defendant.

I have referred above to the defendant's application for a medical examination of the plaintiff, but it should be noted that rule 34.01 also permits the court of its own motion to order a medical examination of the plaintiff. The reason for this rule in both instances is to provide a means whereby another assessment of the plaintiff's injuries may be placed before the court so that it will be in a better position to make its own appraisal of the plaintiff's injuries. ...

If all of the above objections were decided in favour of the defendant, I would still have to reject this application because the proposed site of the examination, i.e., Halifax in the Province of Nova Scotia, is clearly very inconvenient to the first plaintiff. There are extensive hospital facilities in this province and many qualified medical practitioners. No evidence has been adduced or offered to show that the site proposed for the examination is the nearest one where the required facilities or the qualified professional personnel are available. In the absence of such evidence, there is no justification for issuance of an order requiring the first plaintiff to go to another province for the requested medical examination. ...

Application dismissed.

NOTES AND QUESTIONS

1. In *Schlagenhauf v. Holder*, 379 US 104 (1964), the court similarly held on fairness grounds that provisions in the US Federal Rules authorizing medical examinations did not violate a litigant's rights to privacy under the Bill of Rights, but stressed that the mental or physical condition of the party to be examined must be "in controversy" and the party asking for the examination show "good cause."

2. How should the court deal with an argument based on s. 7 of the Charter where the order for a medical examination (authorized by the Ontario Courts of Justice Act, ss. 105(2) and (3)) is sought against a party who did not put its own physical or mental

condition in issue and is not making any claim in respect thereof—for example, where a husband brings a divorce proceeding, contests his wife's claim for custody on the ground that she is mentally unfit, and seeks a court ordered medical examination of the wife with a view to establishing her mental instability?

B. Inspection of Property

As noted above, a medical examination is not the only form of physical discovery (though it is the most common). The rules also provide for the inspection of property—for example, see Ontario rule 32.

Callis v. Stop 48 Ltd.
(1990) 50 CPC (2d) 304 (Ont. Ct. Gen. Div.)

POTTS J: The defendants appeal from the June 27, 1990 order of Judge Crossland that gave permission to the plaintiffs to inspect the go-cart involved in an accident. The appeal was heard on September 5, 1990, and at that time I dismissed the appeal, reserving costs to be determined by the trial judge. The following are my reasons. ...

The plaintiffs Tommy Callis and his mother Koula Callis were at a go-cart track at Kirkfield, Ontario, on June 4, 1988. The track was operated by the defendant Stop 48 Ltd., who leased the track from the defendants Giampiero and Daphne Baldini. Tommy paid an admission fee, rode a go-cart and was in an accident. Subsequently, the plaintiffs Tommy and his mother sued the defendants for damages. ...

Rule 32.01(1) of the Ontario *Rules of Civil Procedure* states:

> 32.01(1) The court may make an order for the inspection of real or personal property where it appears to be necessary for the proper determination of an issue in a proceeding.

The defendants submit that the words "necessary for the proper determination of an issue in a proceeding" dominate R. 32: *Nichols v. Toronto Transportation Commission* (1928), 62 OLR 124, 33 OWN 412, 34 CRC 252, [1988] 2 DLR 364 (CA), at 127 [OLR]. By this the defendants seem to suggest that an inspection of the go-cart is not necessary for the determination of an issue in the trial. The plaintiffs respond, however, that the inspection is necessary for a proper determination of one of the principal issues in the action, namely, liability for the accident: *PPG Industries Canada Ltd. v. Tioxide Canada Inc.* (1986), 12 CPC (2d) 158 (Ont. Master), at p. 162. The plaintiffs argue that an inspection should be granted where there is sufficient relevancy between the inspection of the property and a material issue in the action: *Bank of Nova Scotia v. Wu* (1986), 15 CPC (2d) 283 (Ont. Dist. Ct.), at 286. The plaintiffs argue R. 32 should be construed liberally to permit inspections: *Farhi v. Wright* (1987), 26 CPC (2d) 88 (Ont. HC), at p. 91.

The defendants submit that even though the plaintiffs' statement of claim states that the defendants did not properly inspect the brakes on the go-cart or maintain the go-cart in a proper condition, there is no issue with respect to these points. The defendants submit that the examinations for discovery disclose that the go-cart was inspected on the day of the accident and its brakes were working and that the plaintiff did not attempt to use the brakes until he had already lost control of the cart. The defendants submit that the plaintiffs' assertions in the statement of claim are mere bald assertions and are not sufficient grounds to order an inspection: *Lacosse v. Nygard* (1989), 16 WDCP 234 (Ont. HC) [reported 20 MVR (2d) 179]. The plaintiffs, however, respond that they do not agree that the go-cart was inspected on the day of the accident or that its brakes were working. Furthermore, the plaintiffs respond that they wish to look at the go-cart not only to inspect the brakes, but also to look at the overall condition of the go-cart and see how it operates generally. The plaintiffs also argue that *Lacosse* states that the plaintiff is entitled to full disclosure, including inspection, on an issue that is crucial to the action.

The defendants submit that to allow an inspection now, more than two years after the accident, would be extremely prejudicial to the defendants since the defendants have continued to use the go-cart at the track since the accident. Any conclusions drawn from an inspection now will not accurately reflect the condition of the go-cart at the time of the accident. The plaintiffs respond that this sort of prejudice is not a factor to be considered. The plaintiffs state that if there are concerns about the validity of the evidence, this is a factor to be considered at trial when the weight of the evidence is assessed.

I believe the inspection of the go-cart should be allowed to proceed. I agree with the plaintiffs that the inspection is relevant to and necessary for the determination of the issue of liability. *Nichols* and *Lacosse* do not assist the defendants, since these cases concerned the different question of whether the court should permit a re-enactment of the accident. In the case at bar, we are concerned only with the question of whether the plaintiffs should be allowed an inspection. I share some of the defendants' concern that any evidence about the state of repair of the go-cart at the time of the inspection may have little to do with the state of repair of the go-cart at the time of the accident, but this concern can be addressed at trial when the evidence is assigned its probative weight. However, the most important reason for allowing the plaintiffs to inspect the go-cart is that the trial court should be informed of the general operating characteristics of the go-cart. Does the cart have rear-wheel drive and front-wheel steering? Does it have a manual clutch and shift? How are the brakes designed? How are the brakes operated? These and other questions may be crucial to the proper determination of the issue of liability. These questions are independent of the question of the state of repair of the go-cart. A delayed inspection on these general features of the go-cart is not likely to affect the validity of this evidence, thus the defendants will not be prejudiced by the late inspection on these issues. ...

Appeal dismissed

Lagerquist v. Labatts Ltd.
(1978) 19 OR (2d) 586 (HC)

GRIFFITHS J (orally): The plaintiff's claim is for damages for loss of vision in his right eye caused when a bottle of beer brewed, bottled and offered for sale by the defendant exploded and a piece of glass struck the plaintiff, injuring the eye. The plaintiff pleads negligence on the part of the defendant, its servants and relies as well on the doctrine of *res ipsa loquitur*. The allegations of negligence are as follows:

> ... Bottling beer, a carbonated beverage, for sale to the general public in a bottle which it knew or ought to have known was defective and liable to explode.

... The defendant, in its statement of defence, pleaded in para. 5 as follows:

> The Defendant pleads that it took all reasonable steps to ensure the quality of its product, and if a bottle failed, it was not through its negligence.

Mr. Cherniak, counsel for the appellant, conceded in argument that the plaintiff was entitled to an inspection of the manufacturing processes of the defendant, limited to the allegations of negligence, and for that purpose technical advisors of the plaintiff might attend at the plant of the defendant and conduct a visual examination of those processes. He submits, however, that the learned Master erred in ordering that on such inspection the representatives of the plaintiff be permitted to take still and motion pictures of the defendant's manufacturing processes, as provided for in para. 3 of the order.

The learned Master follows the decision of the Senior Master (Rodger) in *Allen v. Carling Breweries Ltd. et al.*, [1972] 2 OR 294, in which in similar circumstances an order of this nature was issued. In his very able argument Mr. Cherniak submits that the Allen case was wrongly decided, and that the authorities relied on therein did not go so far as to justify the order granted. The first decision relied on, in *Walker v. McKinnon Industries Ltd.*, [1948] OWN 537, 8 CPR 129, related only to the right of an inspection, and did not authorize the taking of photographs. The other authority relied upon in *Allen* was *Goldsman v. Sniderman et al.*, [1946] OWN 417 (affirmed on appeal [at 419]), [which] authorized the taking of photographs of premises, the subject of litigation in an occupiers' liability case.

Mr. Cherniak submits that the right to take photographs on an inspection under Rule 372 should be restricted to those cases where the physical make-up of the premises is itself an issue, such as in the occupiers' liability case.

I do not agree. It seems to me that if the plaintiff is entitled to have his representative attend on the defendant's premises to make a visual examination as part of the authorized inspection, there is no logical reason why the representative should not be permitted to take photographs as well for use in Court to supplement his *viva voce* evidence. I fail to see how the taking of photographs or movies of the manufacturing processes of the defendant, for which an order of inspection is appropriate, can cause any additional prejudice to the defendant, particularly when the use of the photographs and movies is limited as it is here by para. 6 of the order.

The appeal is dismissed with costs to the plaintiff in the cause.

NOTES AND QUESTIONS

Destruction of evidence ("spoliation"). What should the court do if a party destroys real evidence? This issue is most likely to arise in the context of products liability litigation. There is considerable US jurisprudence on the subject, often granting summary judgment or precluding expert evidence where spoliation has occurred. The Canadian jurisprudence is sparse. The following is a representative sample.

In *Werner v. Warner Auto-Marine Inc.* (1996), 4 CPC (4th) 110 (Ont. CA), a preservation order had been made under Ontario rule 45 regarding real evidence (certain fuel tanks from a boat). Contrary to the order, the plaintiff carried out destructive tests on the fuel tanks. In response to this, the judge at first instance granted judgment dismissing the plaintiff's action, held the plaintiff's solicitors in contempt, and ordered the plaintiff and his solicitors to pay all the defendants' costs on a solicitor-and-client basis. On appeal, the contempt order was upheld, but the Court of Appeal held that dismissing the action was excessive given that the contempt was a result of the conduct of the plaintiff's solicitors and experts and not of the plaintiff personally. The court regarded the contempt to be a serious one, the result of which was that only the plaintiff had available complete forensic test reports and the real evidence (the fuel tanks) had been destroyed; and in an adversarial process, the rules and orders of the court must be observed and obeyed. However, the appropriate sanction was a prohibition against the plaintiff's use of an expert report arising from the destructive testing, and of any evidence obtained directly or indirectly as a result of the breach of the preservation order.

In *Dawes v. Jajcaj*, [1996] 3 WWR 525 (BC SC), after being told by plaintiff's counsel that a vehicle involved in an accident should not be destroyed, the adjuster for the defendant's insurer retained an accident reconstruction expert (who conducted his investigation) and then she (the adjuster) gave instructions for the disposal of the vehicle. At trial, the plaintiffs submitted that the defence expert report ought to be excluded from evidence, relying upon the principal of "spoliation." The court held, declining to exclude the expert report from evidence, that in order to do so the court must at least be satisfied that the object in issue was intentionally destroyed through bad faith and not as a result of mere negligence on the part of the party or his expert. It was admitted by the plaintiff that the insurance adjuster who ordered the destruction of the vehicle had not acted maliciously or in bad faith and, although she knowingly directed the destruction of the vehicle, the court found that her action was a reflection of her own inexperience.

IV. EXAMINATION FOR DISCOVERY

A. Purposes of Examination for Discovery

Garry D. Watson and Craig Perkins, Holmested and Watson,
Ontario Civil Procedure
Rule 31 §7: Purposes of Examination for Discovery
(Toronto: Carswell, 1984) (looseleaf)

Of all the discovery devices provided by the rules, the most important and powerful is examination for discovery. A key element of examination for discovery is that it permits the proceeding to descend from the mere paper allegation of lawyers to sworn statements by the parties themselves.

The purposes of examination for discovery were conveniently summarized by Trainor J in *Ontario Bean Producers Marketing Bd. v. W.G. Thompson & Sons* (1981), 32 OR (2d) 69, affirmed 35 OR (2d) 711 (Div. Ct.):

(a) to enable the examining party to know the case he has to meet;

(b) to procure admissions to enable one to dispense with formal proof;

(c) to procure admissions which may destroy an opponent's case;

(d) to facilitate settlement, pre-trial procedure and trials;

(e) to eliminate or narrow issues;

(f) to avoid surprise at trial.

Montgomery J in *Malofy v. Andrew Merrilees Ltd.* (1982), 28 CPC 284 (Div. Ct.), after quoting the above, stated "I add to this, to enable payment into Court" (see now rule 49, Offer to Settle). Montgomery J went on to quote Brooke JA in *Perini Ltd. v. Parking Authority of Toronto* (1975), 6 OR (2d) 363 (CA): "These Rules form a scheme to provide procedures through which knowledge of all relevant facts is available to both sides so that each will know his opponent's case and be better able to evaluate his own and so to assist in the early resolution of litigation either by settlement or shorter trials."

Since the answers given by a person on his or her examination for discovery can be used at trial to impeach the witness should the witness give different testimony at trial (see rule 31.11(2)), examination for discovery enables the examining party to pin down the witness by his or her answers on discovery. Examination for discovery also provides an opportunity for counsel to assess the effectiveness and believability of both his or her own client and the opposing party, and to assess the effectiveness of opposing counsel. ...

While intuitively discovery appears to aid the settlement process, such empirical evidence as exists on the relationship between discovery and settlement does not suggest a straight cause and effect relationship. See Glaser, *Pretrial Discovery and the Adversary System* (1968), 91-100; Note, "Discovery: Boon or Burden?" 36 Minn. L Rev. 364 (1952). Glaser, reporting on a major empirical study of discovery in the United States, found that while 96 per cent of all lawyers surveyed in the study felt that discovery promoted settlement, empirical support for such a conclusion was lacking. Cases employing discovery were more likely to reach trial. Discovery did not produce any large statistical increment beyond what lawyers had originally expected would be the settlement prospect for their cases, nor were the settlement rates higher than for cases where no discovery was employed. Not only did the use of discovery correlate inversely with settlement, but so did the intensity of discovery—the greater the time spent in discovery the more likely it was that the case would reach trial. Glaser observed that "the common belief that discovery increases settlement may be due to the fact that a large majority of cases with discovery settle, but this is true simply because most cases settle." It is also interesting to note that in England, where broad-ranging discovery, and particularly examination for discovery, does not exist, a lower percentage of cases proceed to trial than in Canada. (The English figures are in the 2-3 per cent range, whereas the Canadian figures are in the 3-5 per cent range.) It may be that in Canada settlement is often postponed until after discovery, rather than being caused by discovery. If so, presumably discovery does make settlement better informed.

B. Use of Examination for Discovery at Trial

The dynamics of examination for discovery will be easier to understand if we first recall the uses that can be made of the examination at trial. The use that counsel can make of an examination for discovery at trial conditions what they try to achieve in conducting the examination.

There are two basic ways in which an examination for discovery may be used at trial. First, a party may *read into evidence* any part of the examination for discovery of an adverse party (if otherwise admissible)—for example, see Ontario rule 31.11(1). Second, the evidence given on an examination may be used for the *purpose of impeaching* the deponent in the same manner as any previous inconsistent statement—for example, see Ontario rule 31.11(2). (To ensure fairness, where only part of the examination is used in evidence, the trial judge may direct the introduction of any other part that qualifies the part used.) While these uses of examination for discovery are in rules of practice—for example, see Ontario rule 31.11—they in fact flow from well-established rules of the law of evidence. Answers given on an examination for discovery are hearsay (because they are not the evidence of a witness present and testifying at trial and are being tendered for the truth of the assertions contained therein). However, there is a basic exception to the hearsay rule for "admissions made by an opposing party." This is the basis for the "reading in" use of discovery answers. The law of evidence also permits any witness who has given evidence at trial to be impeached by use of a prior inconsistent statement. This can come from any source—for example, a conversation at a cocktail party, a statement made in an affidavit, or a statement made in prior correspondence. It is this principle that permits the "impeachment use" of discovery answers.

The examination of a non-party "witness" may not be read into evidence as an admission, but may be used to impeach the non-party should he or she testify—for example, see Ontario rules 31.11(1) and (2) and 31.10(5).

The two uses of examination for discovery described above condition the conduct of the examination in the following ways. First, counsel will be looking for answers that can be *used as admissions* and hence read in at trial. A simple example may illustrate the importance of admissions. Assume a motor vehicle accident in which the plaintiff alleges that the defendant was negligent in driving at an excessive speed. The plaintiff may have no direct evidence of the speed at which the defendant was travelling. However, on discovery, the plaintiff can require the defendant to state the speed the car was travelling. If the defendant admits to driving too fast, that answer can be used in evidence by the plaintiff (in a way we will explore in greater depth below) to establish that crucial fact. Second, and this may often be difficult to distinguish from the first objective, counsel will be seeking to exhaust the witnesses' recollection and tie the witness down to a story so that, if the witness changes his or her story at trial, the discovery transcript can be used to *impeach the witness*. (Of course, at discovery counsel will also be pursuing objectives which are not so directly related to "trial usage"—for example, trying to understand the opponent's case and what evidence the opponent has to back it up, and searching for evidence that can be used to support counsel's own case.

C. Who May Be Examined for Discovery

1. Parties Generally

On this subject, Ontario rule 31.03 is typical in providing that a party may examine for discovery any other party "adverse in interest." The rule then goes on to make special provisions for corporations (which we will discuss in some detail below) and for other types of parties, such as partnerships, persons under disability, or assignees. The following case explores the meaning of the central phrase "parties adverse in interest."

Menzies v. McLeod
(1915), 34 OLR 572 (SC)

[Motion by the defendant McLeod and two other defendants, next of kin of Margaret Menzies, deceased, to commit the defendant Martha McGuire, for refusal to attend for examination for discovery, at the instance of the applicants, as a "party adverse in interest" to them under rule 327, now rule 31.03(1).

The action was brought by the executor named in an instrument purporting to be the last will of the deceased, to establish it as such; the plaintiff and the defendant McGuire were the principal beneficiaries under that instrument; the applicants, though also beneficiaries under the instrument, would be entitled to larger shares of the estate in the event of an intestacy being declared.]

BOYD C: The object of this action is to establish the will of Margaret Menzies. The judgment will operate *in rem* and conclude the rights of all parties interested. The executor sues alone, and makes the beneficiaries and next of kin defendants. Some of the latter, who are also beneficiaries, contest the validity of the will on the ground of undue influence and incapacity. The will was executed at Daytona, Florida, USA, where, it is alleged, the testatrix, an old and diseased woman, was in the hands of the executor and one of the defendants, Martha McGuire, who was the nurse in waiting on the deceased, and who gets a legacy of $10,000. The estate is a large one, and, after the legacy to the nurse and pecuniary legacies of $1,000 each to eleven next of kin, the residue goes to the executor. The defendant McGuire has entered no defence, and the pleadings against her are closed. It is stated on affidavit that the plaintiff and the defendant McGuire are in the same interest, and are neither of them of the next of kin of the testatrix.

A notice was given by the contestants to McGuire to attend for examination under Rule 327(1) but she made default on the ground that she was not compellable; and to test this question the matter has been argued before me.

Counsel for McGuire relies on a Manitoba decision of Mr. Justice Mathers in 1909, *Fonseca v. Jones*, 19 Man. R 334, in which, declining to regard *Moore v. Boyd* (1881), 8 PR 413, as well decided, he follows English cases and holds that a defendant is not a party adverse in point of interest to another party on the same side of the record within the meaning of the Rule (apparently corresponding to ours) unless there are some rights to be adjusted between them in the action.

This testamentary action discloses really two sets of litigants who are adverse— those who seek to uphold the will and those who seek to invalidate it. No doubt as to which side McGuire is on; if the will stands, she gains $10,000; if it falls, she loses all. She might well have been made a co-plaintiff; her whole interest in the litigation is with the executor and in his success. An actual issue in tangible form spread upon the record is not essential, so long as there is a manifest adverse interest in one defendant as against another defendant. "Adverse interest" is a flexible term, meaning pecuniary interest, or any other substantial interest in the subject-matter of litigation. ...

Having regard to the genesis of the Ontario Rule now in force, Rule 327 and the practice which has obtained, it is not competent to introduce the limitations as to examination of co-defendants which are found in the English practice, under Rules differently framed and expressed. The characteristic English phrase is "opposite party," and ours is "party adverse in interest." The very point of difference is noted by Cotton LJ, in *Molloy v. Kilby* (1880), 15 Ch. D 162, at p. 164: " 'Opposite party or parties,' " he says, "does not mean a party or parties having an adverse interest, but a party or parties between whom and the applicant an issue is joined." The English decisions which Mr. Justice Mathers has followed decide that as between co-defendants one cannot examine the other for discovery unless between the two there be some right to be adjudicated (Lord Esher) or some community of interest (Lindley LJ), or some question in conflict in the action (Lopes LJ). This is the summary of the expressions used in *Shaw v. Smith* (1886), 18 QBD 193, as given by A.L. Smith LJ, in *Spokes v. Grosvenor Hotel Co.*, [1897] 2 QB 124, 127.

Another case under English practice which would conclude the present applicants' right to examine is *Marshall v. Langley*, [1889] WN 222; where the defendant admits the plaintiff's case and puts in no defence and claims no relief, there is no issue raised, and he cannot be treated as an opposite party by a co-defendant who wishes to examine. The last English case is *Birchal v. Birch Crisp & Co.*, [1913] 2 Ch. 375.

I am by no means sure that even under the English limitations there is not something to be adjudicated here between the co-defendants—there is a community of interest in the disposal of the estate, though one claim as against the other is adverse.

In my judgment, *Moore v. Boyd* is to be preferred to *Fonseca v. Jones*. Within the meaning of the Rule, the defendant McGuire is a party to the action adverse in interest to her co-defendants who seek to gain discovery from her as to the execution of the will and the condition of the testatrix. The Court favours an early disclosure of all matters surrounding the execution of an impeached will from those who know, that an opportunity may be given in a proper case to withdraw from hopeless or unnecessary litigation. ...

In all likelihood this nurse knows more about the physical and mental condition of the testatrix than any other available person.

The defendant McGuire should, on due notice of time and place, attend at her own expense and submit to be examined under Rule 327.

NOTES AND QUESTIONS

1. In *Menzies*, would the executor be entitled to examine Nurse McGuire for discovery? Do you think he would need to do so in order to conduct the litigation? Would he be entitled to read in her answers—that is, any admissions she made on discovery—against the next-of-kin at trial? See Ontario rule 31.11(1) (reading in examination of party).

2. Assume that in *Menzies* Nurse McGuire was not a beneficiary and hence was not made a party to the action. Assume also that she "knows more about the physical and mental condition of the testatrix than the other available person." May she be examined for discovery by the next-of-kin? Assume that she is friendly towards the executor, has been extensively interviewed by the executors' solicitors, and has imparted all her

knowledge to the solicitor and the executor. If she may be examined only with leave, should the above interview militate in favour or against the next-of-kin being entitled to examine her for discovery? See Ontario rule 31.10 (discovery of non-parties with leave only where certain conditions satisfied) and below, under the heading "Examination of Non-Parties."

2. Examining a Corporation

Since a corporation is not a natural person and hence cannot be orally examined for discovery, the rules have to regulate who may be examined on behalf of the corporation. Ontario rules 31.03(2) and (3) provide that the examining party may "examine any officer, director or employee on behalf of the corporation, but the court on motion of the corporation before the examination may order the examining party to examine another officer, director or employee," and where such person has been examined, no other such person may be examined without leave of the court. The following cases examine how such rules have been interpreted.

Clarkson Mews Properties Inc. v. Angel Creek Estates Ltd.
(1989), 37 CPC (2d) 104 (Ont. HC)

MASTER DONKIN: The plaintiff brings a motion for two items of relief, one of which has been dealt with. The remaining part of the motion is to substitute Mr. Hrycyna, an officer of the plaintiff, to be examined for discovery in place of Mr. Forgione.

The plaintiff's action is to recover a deposit made in connection with a proposed purchase of real estate. The purchase agreement was entered into by Forgione Investments & Developments Inc., and that company paid a deposit of $200,000 to the defendant Gitalis, who is the real estate agent. The agreement provided that the purchaser had the right to assign to a limited company or individuals. The agreement was in fact assigned to the plaintiff on June 29, 1988. The transaction was to close on July 5, 1988. It failed to close and the contest in the action appears to involve the incidents from about June 30, 1988 to July 5 or 6, 1988. During that time it is alleged that there were requisitions on title and there is a contest as to whether these were proper. A repudiation of the agreement in that period is alleged and contested, and there is a contest as to whether the vendor actually had title in such a way that it could transfer the property on the scheduled date for closing.

Mr. Hrycyna has filed an affidavit in which he says that the plaintiff is a corporation that was set up in order to purchase this property; and when Mr. Forgione had signed the agreement of purchase and sale, he approached Mr. Hrycyna and several other people with respect to participating with him in the purchase. At that point, Mr. Hrycyna swears that he took over as the principal person dealing with this matter and that Mr. Forgione's involvement, other than his monetary involvement, ceased. Mr. Hrycyna looked after the arrangements to set up the corporation and for the purchase. Although he is not able to provide first-hand information on all the issues, he kept himself informed throughout the transaction, and he was the person who provided instructions to the plaintiff's solicitors.

Parts of the affidavit are set out below in full:

> 5. Gus Forgione does not have sufficient knowledge to deal with the examination
> properly. In fact, his attendance may be embarrassing to the plaintiff.
>
> 12. Mr. Forgione was not involved during this time and has absolutely no
> knowledge of any of the issues in the action. His only involvement was in the
> negotiation of the agreement of purchase and sale, which is not an issue in this action.
>
> 13. 1 have discussed with Mr. Forgione the possibility of his being examined for
> discovery. Based on my discussions with him, I verily believe [that] he will not properly
> prepare himself for the examination for discovery and that he will not inform himself of
> all of these issues in the lawsuit. I verily believe that he, in fact, may damage the
> plaintiff's case because of his lack of knowledge and because of his refusal to
> participate fully in this lawsuit.

In *Protter Management Ltd. v. Ont. Housing Corp.* (1975), 8 OR (2d) 445, at 447
(Ont. HC), Pennell J states that:

> I am of opinion that applications must be dealt with upon the circumstances in particular
> cases rather than by a "fixed standard of measurement."

In most of the cases to which counsel have referred me where the court permitted
substitution of a different officer, there was some form of conflict of interest between
the officer selected and the corporation, or at least a divergence of interest. In *Protter
Management v. Ont. Housing Corp.*, supra, the corporation had suspended the officer
who was selected because certain charges had been laid against him in connection with
his employment. In *Kowk v. Kitchener Waterloo Record Ltd.* (1985), 2 CPC (2d) 250
(Ont. Dist. Ct.), there was not only the factor that the person sought to be examined was
not a particularly senior employee but also he had been disciplined by the defendant
corporation for writing a letter about the plaintiff. *In Exhibition Assn. of Saint John (City
& County) v. Cdn. Imperial Bank of Commerce* (1987), 21 CPC (2d) 88, 82 NBR (2d)
337, 208 APR 337, decided by Jones J of the New Brunswick Court of Queen's Bench,
the Court accepts that the officer selected to be examined was in a position of conflict of
interest with the corporation on whose behalf it was sought to examine them.

There are other cases in which the ground for substitution has been that the person
selected is not a responsible officer and does not have knowledge of the matter. That is
not the case in this matter. It is true that Forgione apparently does not have sufficient
knowledge. It is not alleged that he cannot get that knowledge. It is not alleged that he is
not an officer or responsible person. He does have some connection with the transaction,
inasmuch as he entered into the original agreement of purchase and sale on behalf of his
own company and paid the deposit. The real problem as set out in the affidavit is that the
deponent believes that Forgione will not properly prepare himself for examination for
discovery and will not inform himself of all the issues in the lawsuit.

It is trite law that initially the examining party can select the officer or person whom
the plaintiff wishes to examine on behalf of the defendant. It seems to me that it does not
lie in the mouth of the person selected who is a responsible person to simply say that he
refuses to be involved. If that were permitted, examining parties would be frustrated
extremely easily. It is perhaps worth noting that in *Cineplex Odeon Corp. v. Toronto Star*

Newspapers Ltd. (1986), 11 CPC (2d) 291 (Ont. Master), the officer of the defendant being examined refused to answer questions on the basis that they could better be answered by one of the individual defendants, and the corporation undertook to be bound by his answers to those questions. Master Peppiatt decided that that was not a proper course and that the officer who was being examined was bound to obtain the answers from the defendant who knew the answers and to give those answers on discovery on behalf of the corporation. In effect, that case was similar because the officer selected was refusing to obtain the information necessary to allow him to answer properly.

In my view, this part of the motion should be dismissed.

The better part of the argument on this motion was directed to this issue, and, in my view, costs should be to the defendant Angel Creek in the cause. If counsel wish to submit argument on a different disposition of costs, they may request an appointment.

Motion dismissed.

Rainbow Industrial Caterers Limited v. CNR
(1986), 6 BCLR (2d) 268 (SC)

PROUDFOOT J: This is an application pursuant to R. 27(4) of the Supreme Court Rules to substitute R. Gregory in place of J.A. Monaghan as the representative of the corporate defendant to be examined by the plaintiff.

The defendants' arguments are:

1. That Monaghan is in a junior position with the defendant corporation and is not sufficiently informed to be able to answer adequately the questions nor bind the company with his answers.

2. That Gregory is the person responsible for the catering contracts (which give rise to the allegations including allegations of fraud against the company) entered into by the plaintiffs and is fully familiar with all of the terms, etc., of the contracts.

3. That the defendant corporation would be seriously prejudiced if the party to be examined were Monaghan, as he would have to inform himself of all the information which is in the knowledge of Gregory. That process would be costly, inefficient, timeconsuming and totally unsatisfactory.

4. That the plaintiffs would not be prejudiced if Gregory were examined. On the contrary, there would be an imbalance in favour of the plaintiffs if it were Monaghan that was examined.

5. The plaintiffs are examining the person mostly involved, Michael Doroshenko, because he is a defendant, and as Gregory is his supervisor, he would be the most appropriate person to examine. That will result in the plaintiffs having all the information that they require.

The plaintiffs' position is that:

1. It is the plaintiffs' right to select the employee they wish to examine.

2. The interests have to be balanced to achieve justice and the plaintiffs would be prejudiced if they could not examine their choice, Monaghan.

Rule 27(4) reads:

> A person who is or has been a director, officer, employee, agent or external auditor of a party may be examined for discovery, but that party may apply to the court at any time before the examination for an order requiring the examining party to examine instead of that person some other person who is or has been a director, officer, employee, agent or external auditor of the party.

There is ample case authority for the proposition that a plaintiff has that right of choice in the first instance, to select the representative of a corporation which they wish to examine. See *BC Lightweight Aggregate Ltd. v. Can. Cement LaFarge Ltd.* (1978), 7 BCLR 108, 87 DLR (3d) 737 (CA); also *MacMillan Bloedel Ltd. v. Binstead* (1981), 29 BCLR 9, 21 CPC 191 (CA). The question is, should there be, or is there, a qualification of that rule? Should there be permitted in a particular case a substitution of another party for the person selected by the plaintiff. I suggest there might be instances where there can be such an extension of the rule that a qualification is possible, namely, in the interest of achieving a balance so that justice and fairness can be achieved. Macdonald JA in *Landmark Properties Ltd. v. Crown Trust Co.* (1983), 49 BCLR 268, at 269, said:

> I think it is enough to say that in an application such as this made by the appellant to the judge, interests have to be balanced so that justice can be achieved as far as that is possible.

I adopt those words.

There are here some very serious allegations of misrepresentation, recklessness and fraud. I suggest that the defendant could be seriously prejudiced if these allegations cannot be canvassed—through the person having the greatest knowledge, in the most senior position—in reality, the person responsible for the contracts in the first instance. The major issue here will be the question of liability. From the information before me it would seem to me the most informed person would be Gregory. He is the most responsible and his answers would be binding on the corporation. Finally, the plaintiff has put forward no evidence of any prejudice, as far as their position is concerned. On the other hand, there would be a good deal of prejudice to the defendant. The application is granted.

NOTES AND QUESTIONS

1. *Who is an "officer, director or employee"?* The courts have generally taken a flexible and functional approach to interpreting these terms. For example, in *Bell v. Klein (No. 3)*, [1955] 1 DLR 37 (BC CA), in an action in which a corporation was being sued for fraud, it was held that the company's auditors (an independent firm of accountants) were "officers" and could be examined by the plaintiff:

> As one of the chief functions of auditors is to present to shareholders a true account of a company's financial position, I see no reason why auditors should not be examined on

discovery in an action which rightly or wrongly challenges the good faith of directors in the management of company affairs. ... The test to which these decisions point seems to be whether the person sought to be examined can be regarded as an officer or servant in any permissible sense if he is the one person connected with the company best informed of matters which may define or narrow the issues between the parties at the trial.

In *Atherton v. Boycott* (1989), 36 CPC (2d) 250 (Ont. HC), it was held that for the purpose of determining whether an individual is an employee it is not necessary to adhere strictly to the common law principles establishing an employer/employee relationship. The action was one for personal injuries involving an automobile collision in which the plaintiff sued B, a police sergeant, and the owner of the police vehicle, the City of Windsor. The action against B had already been dismissed as being statute-barred. The plaintiff was permitted to examine B as an employee of the defendant City, notwithstanding that B was employed by the Board of Commissioners Police and not by the City, because he fell within the extended meaning of "employee" for the purposes of discovery.

By contrast, in *Joseph Silaschi General Contractor v. City of Kitchener* (1986), 8 CPC (2d) 199 (Ont. HC), in a building dispute case between the contractor and the owner (the City) the court refused to permit the examination of the owner's architect as an "officer or employee" of the City. It was common ground that the architect was a member of an architectural firm, which was a separate entity, and that neither he nor his firm had any connection with the City other than as its representative on the job. (There was no evidence that the architect acted as the City's agent.) While conceding that "officer or employee" could not be defined within rigid limits, but may be amplified or circumscribed by the circumstances of each individual case, the court held that the circumstances of this case did not justify amplification of the word "employee" to embrace a totally different entity, an independent contractor. The court noted that if information was withheld or was unavailable, recourse might be had to rule 31.10, which provides for the discovery of non-parties.

Which is the better approach to this problem—*Bell* and *Atherton* or the *City of Kitchener*? Given the existence of provisions for the examination of non-parties—for example, Ontario rule 31.10—does it matter which approach the court takes?

2. *Former officers and employees.* As we have seen, in Ontario, a party examining a corporation is entitled to only one examination of any "officer, director or employee," unless the court orders otherwise, and no provision is made for the examination of *former* officers or employees.

Among the other provinces there are varying approaches to this question. In British Columbia (rule 27), any person "who is or has been a director, officer, employee, agent or external auditor of a party" may be examined for discovery; but, once such a person has been examined, no other person may be examined except with leave of the court. In Manitoba (rule 31.03(2)) (Saskatchewan rule 223 is similar), any person who is or has been an officer, director or employee of a corporation may be examined, but only one such person may be examined. In Alberta (rule 200), "any officer of a corporate party and any person who is or has been employed by any party to an action" may be examined for discovery, but the court may limit the number of employees or former employees who may be examined. In Nova Scotia (rule 18), discovery is not limited to the parties and "any person" may be examined for discovery.

How do these provisions compare?

Typically, those jurisdictions that permit employees or former employees or officers to be examined for discovery place limits on the use of such examinations against the employer—that is, they may not be used against the employer at all, or only with leave of court.

3. In Ontario, while there is no general right to examine former officers or employees, the courts have on occasion ordered the examination of such persons upon a showing that the officer or employee left the corporation in order to frustrate the opposite party's discovery (*Hamilton Harbour Commissioners v. J.D. Porter Co. Ltd.* (1978), 19 OR (2d) 66 (HC)), or where all the officers and directors of a corporation had resigned and there was reason to doubt that the resignations were bona fide: *Butler v. Dimitrieff* (1988), 66 OR (2d) 707 (Master).

3. Examination of Non-Parties

A basic policy choice facing rule makers is whether to make examination for discovery available against persons other than the parties. In the United States, discovery is not limited to the parties—any person may be examined for discovery (deposed). In Canada, the traditional position has been to restrict the availability of discovery to the parties (though, as we have seen, some provinces have extended this right to include former officers or employees of a party). With the nationwide reform movement of the past few decades, this situation has changed. Nova Scotia, Newfoundland, and PEI adopted the US model and permits the examination, without leave, of "any person." Other provinces have adopted more limited departures from the traditional position. British Columbia permits the examination of non-parties with leave of the court and subject to certain conditions. Ontario, New Brunswick, Manitoba, and Saskatchewan have adopted the same approach; each province has a rule that is virtually identical to Ontario rule 31.10, which permits the court to grant leave for the examination of a non-party, but subject to a stringent test.

What arguments can be made in favour of broadening discovery to non-parties? Are there factors that suggest that traditional restriction to parties is, on balance, preferable? The following case illustrates the courts' interpretation of Ontario rule 31.10.

Carleton Condominium Corporation No. 25 v. Shenkman Corporation Ltd.
(1986), 9 CPC (2d) 233 (Ont. HC)

MASTER DONKIN: This is a motion by a defendant, Dineen Construction Limited, for leave pursuant to R. 31.10 to examine a person who was not a party to this action.

The action involves a claim by the plaintiff, Condominium Corporation, for damages with respect to the construction of a building and for damages for certain repair work undertaken on that building. J.L. Richards & Associates Limited was the consulting engineer with respect to certain aspects of the original construction and was retained to supervise certain repair work after the problems originally arose. The witness whom the moving party seeks to examine is one John Hall McCalla who was at all material times an employee of J.L. Richards & Associates Limited and charged with the responsibility for that firm's involvement in the construction and the repairs. At some period following the relevant time he ceased to be an employee. It is apparent that he would have information relevant to material issues in the action and no counsel has disputed this fact.

The third party, J.L. Richards & Associates Limited, opposes the motion on the basis that the moving party has not satisfied the Court that the moving party has been unable to obtain the information from other persons whom the moving party is entitled to examine for discovery. It is apparent that many questions have been asked of the representative of J.L. Richards & Associates Limited on discovery to which he could not give an immediate answer, but undertakings were given and according to the affidavit of Kevin Murin filed in opposition to the motion those undertakings are in the process of being fulfilled. Many of the undertakings were given in response to requests to make inquiry of Mr. McCalla, and the information which will be provided in response to the undertakings will include the knowledge, information and belief of Mr. McCalla. That being the case I am not satisfied that the moving party has been unable to obtain the information from the person whom it is entitled to examine for discovery on behalf of J.L. Richards & Associates Limited. It is uncontested that Mr. McCalla's position is that he would prefer not to discuss the matter with the solicitors for the other parties.

The question to be decided in this motion is whether the moving party is in fact required to satisfy the Court that the information cannot be obtained from the person whom the moving party is entitled to examine. Counsel for the moving party points out that in this complex action it will be time-consuming to get the answers from a representative of J.L. Richards & Associates Limited by way of questions, undertakings, the response to those undertakings, and possibly further questions arising from the response. It would be in his view far more practical and expeditious to get those answers directly from Mr. McCalla. He cites *Weiszman v. 491 Lawrence Ave. West Ltd.* (1985), 5 CPC (2d) 160 (Ont. HC) as authority for the proposition that the Court should grant leave in such circumstances. In the course of his reasons in that case his Lordship stated [at 163]:

> Unquestionably, it is a balance of convenience. Courts do not wish to unnecessarily or unreasonably ask non-parties to an action to attend for examination for discovery. They are required to attend at trial. But, in my view, when there are material facts suggested by the party seeking the examination for discovery, which are not sufficiently covered in the actual statements provided, then that party ought to have not merely some of the information but all of the information. I asked and was advised that the reasons that the non-parties refused to be interviewed by the defendant was that they had simply said we have given our statement and have nothing more to add. Laymen do not appreciate the niceties of the judicial system. They think their statements are sufficient but that is not necessarily the case. With respect to the lawyer for the plaintiff who questioned the witnesses, and there is no suggestion that he was hiding any information, he may not have asked all the questions that the defendants would like to ask.
>
> As counsel for the defendants put it, are the statements sufficient? He does not really know. He would like to have the same opportunity as the plaintiff has had to find out whether or not these witnesses have any more relevant information. They may not but at least then he would have conducted a complete investigation of the matter prior to going to trial or to negotiating the possibility of settlement.

He further stated:

I should also add that r. 1.04(1) states:

1.04(1) These rules shall be liberally construed to secure the just, most expeditious and least expensive determination of every civil proceeding on its merits.

I think that is very relevant to the interpretation of these rules. As a matter of fairness both parties should have access to the same witnesses in order to promote the most expeditious and least expensive determination of every civil proceeding on its merits. That goes not merely to the determination of issues at trial but to the possibility of resolving the matter before trial by way of settlement. Both parties should have all the information so that either party does not have to go to trial lacking information.

I have examined the documents filed in that case, including the affidavits and the factums filed by both parties before Potts J, and also those filed before Sirois J, who refused leave to appeal on September 12, 1985. That material includes the affidavit of Roger Shoreman who sets out what the issues are in the action and who states at para. 6 that

neither the plaintiff nor the defendant had any knowledge of these two issues. The only information that we have is from the witness' statements on behalf of Mr. Frankin and Mr. Bower.

It was the submission of the moving party in that case that the statements spoken of were not sufficient to provide all the relevant information. From the affidavit material and from the factums it is apparent that the question of whether the information might be obtained from the person whom the moving party was entitled to examine was not addressed and it appears to have been assumed that the information could only be obtained directly from the two witnesses. That case therefore can be distinguished from the present case.

In addition there is the decision in *Rothwell v. Raes* (1986), 13 OAC 60 (Ont. HC). In that case the facts were that the moving party had not shown that it was unable to get the required information directly from the non-party because there was no evidence of requests to that non-party to remedy certain insufficiencies in information he had already given. In the course of his judgment Eberle J states [at 61]:

We are primarily concerned with the provisions of subclause (a) above and with the question of whether or not the comma following the word "discovery," together with the word "or" which follows, have a disjunctive or a conjunctive effect. Must the applicant show both that he has been unable to obtain the information from parties to the action and as well from the person sought to be examined; or is it sufficient to show an inability to obtain the information either from parties to the action or alternatively from the person sought to be examined?

The learned local judge held as follows:

I am not satisfied on the material before me that the moving party has been unable to obtain the information he seeks from the witness as required by Section (sic) 31.10(1)(a).

In so saying, he impliedly held that both parts of the clause in question must be satisfied. I am in entire agreement.

[A]nd further:

> It is evident that the framers of the Rule, while granting a new remedy for the examination for discovery of a non-party, felt it proper to establish a number of conditions which must be satisfied before the new remedy may be resorted to. Otherwise the remedy could easily be subject to abuse. Accordingly, it is consistent with the overall thrust of the Rule to read the two parts of sub-clause (a) as cumulative and not alternative.
>
> In addition, it appears to me that to read sub-clause (a) disjunctively would have the effect of reading out of it one or other of the parts thereof. For example, if on examination for discovery a party were unable to give certain information, the examiner would be able to apply for discovery of the non-party even though the non-party might willingly give the information. That would not be the most expeditious and least expensive way to proceed: see rule 1.04(1). It is likely that in the vast majority of cases the application of rule 31.10 would arise in the manner outlined, i.e., from a failure to get information requested on an examination for discovery of an existing party.
>
> I am satisfied that it is the intent of the Rule as framed that "or" be treated conjunctively and further, that the opposite view would lead to absurd results.

Therefore, since I am not satisfied that the moving party cannot get the information from the representative of J.L. Richards & Associates Limited by way of questions, undertakings and replies to undertakings, the motion is dismissed.

The interpretation of r. 31.10 is probably not yet settled, and costs should be to J.L. Richards & Associates Limited in the cause as between it and Dineen Construction Limited.

Motion dismissed.

NOTES AND QUESTIONS

1. Which is the better approach—that taken by the court in *Weiszman* or that taken in *Carleton Condominium*? Which approach is more faithful to the text and underlying policy of rule 31.10?

2. In general, the Ontario courts have been strict in the interpretation of the requirements of rule 31.10 for the granting of leave, and the reported incidents of courts granting leave have been relatively few. Indeed, there are relatively few reported cases on *requests* for leave to examine non-parties. How might this be explained?

3. In another motion in the Ballard Estate litigation (see the *Stavro* case, above), Ground J considered whether to grant leave to examine a non-party for discovery: *Ontario (Attorney General) v. Stavro* (1995), 44 CPC (3d) 98 (Gen. Div.). He decided as follows:

> This is a motion brought by the defendants in the above action for an order pursuant to subrule 31.10(1) of the Ontario, Rules of Civil Procedure granting leave to examine a non-party, Mr. David R. Peterson.
>
> Mr. Peterson was, at times relevant to issues in this action, Chairman of the Board of the Toronto Raptors Basketball Club Inc. (the "Raptors"). An affidavit of Mr. Peterson filed by the plaintiffs on the motion for an injunction heard August 8, 9 and 10, 1994 referred to discussions between the Raptors and Maple Leaf Gardens Limited

("MLGL") regarding a proposed joint use facility, the interest of the Raptors in acquiring the shares of MLGL held by the Estate of Harold E. Ballard and the price which the Raptors would have been prepared to pay for such shares. In view of the fact that the affidavit was filed at the opening of the hearing of the injunction motion, there was no opportunity to cross-examine Mr. Peterson on his affidavit. The defendants now seek an order pursuant to subrule 31.10(1) to examine for discovery Mr. Peterson as a non-party. ...

It was conceded by counsel for the plaintiffs that the questions of whether the Executors received fair market value for their shares of MLGL and whether a higher price was obtainable elsewhere are material issues in this action. I find that there is good reason to believe that the information which Mr. Peterson has as to discussions between the Raptors and MLGL for a joint use facility, the interest of the Raptors in acquiring the Estate's shares of MLGL and the price which the Raptors [were] prepared to pay is information relevant to such issues and that any threshold test as to degree of relevance has been met.

Subrule 31.10(2) provides as follows:

An order under subrule (1) shall not be made unless the court is satisfied that,

(a) the moving party has been unable to obtain the information from other persons whom the moving party is entitled to examine for discovery, or from the person he or she seeks to examine;

(b) it would be unfair to require the moving party to proceed to trial without having the opportunity of examining the person; and

(c) the examination will not,

(i) unduly delay the commencement of the trial of the action,

(ii) entail unreasonable expense for other parties, or

(iii) result in unfairness to the person the moving party seeks to examine.

Counsel for the plaintiffs conceded that branch (c) of the test for granting leave has been met.

With respect to branch (a) of the test, I am satisfied on the evidence before me that the defendants have been unable to obtain the information from persons whom they are entitled to examine for discovery or from Mr. Peterson.

It remains to consider whether it would be unfair to require the defendants to move to trial without having the opportunity of examining Mr. Peterson.

It is evident from the reasons of Justice Lederman on the injunction motion that he placed considerable reliance upon the information contained in the affidavit of Mr. Peterson in granting the motion. It also appears to me that the evidence of Mr. Peterson as to the nature and the outcome of the discussions with Maple Leaf Gardens on the joint use facility, the extent of the interest of the Raptors in acquiring the Estate's shares of MLGL, as to why no offer was made to the Executors or no competing bid made at the time of the takeover bid and as to the price which the Raptors [were] prepared to pay for the shares and how that price was arrived at is very important evidence on questions which are central to one of the main issues in this action, that is whether the Executors were in breach of their fiduciary duties, and another of the main issues in this action, that is what the fair market value of the shares of MLGL was at the time that the

Executors sold their shares. I conclude, therefore, that it would be most difficult for the defendants to adequately prepare for trial or to determine what evidence or witnesses they must call without having this information. This is particularly so in the circumstances of this case where obviously the plaintiffs have had an opportunity to question Mr. Peterson on all these issues in preparing his affidavit filed by the plaintiffs on the injunction motion. On any test of fairness, it seems to me that the defendants should have a similar opportunity to obtain information from Mr. Peterson prior to trial.

With respect to the submissions of Mr. McRae that the Intervenors be permitted to ask questions on the examination for discovery of Mr. Peterson, the Intervenors are not a moving party on this motion and it appears to me that the order to be made is an order granting the moving party the right to examine a non-party for discovery. As contemplated by subrule 31.10(3), other parties may attend on the discovery and are entitled to a transcript of the discovery but, in my view, are not entitled to ask questions.

Accordingly, an order will issue that the defendants are granted leave to examine for discovery Mr. David R. Peterson pursuant to rule 31.10 of the Rules of Civil Procedure.

How does the analysis in this decision of the fairness issue for granting leave to examine a non-party for discovery compare with the analysis in the decision from the *Stavro* case, excerpted earlier in this chapter, regarding leave to obtain documentary discovery from a non-party?

4. *Letters of request.* Parties to litigation may wish to obtain evidence by examining persons who are outside the province. Where the non-resident to be examined is a party, there is little problem because the court has jurisdiction over a party and can direct where and at whose expense the examination is to be conducted: see, for example, Ontario rule 34.07(1). However, where the non-resident to be examined is a non-party, the situation is more complex because a court in jurisdicition A has no power to force a non-party in jurisdiction B to attend the examination. The party who seeks the examination must ask the court in jurisdiction A to issue "letters rogatory" or "letters of request" addressed to a court in jurisdiction B, seeking the latter court's assistance in securing the attendance of the person to be examined—for example, see Ontario rule 34.07(2)-(7). If the person to be examined will not voluntarily attend, then the examining party will request the jurisdiction B court to issue an order enforcing the letters rogatory. As Mr. Justice Blair noted in *Fecht v. Deloitte & Touche* (1996), 28 OR (3d) 188 (Gen. Div.),

the circumstances in which an Ontario court will grant an order enforcing letters rogatory for purposes of pre-trial discovery of non-parties should not be any rarer, at least, than those in which a similar request might emanate from an Ontario court to a foreign jurisdiction. At the same time, the authorities support the proposition that the enforcement of letters rogatory by an Ontario court will not be limited to those in which an Ontario court would make an order for discovery of non-parties under rule 31.10. ... While I agree ... that the court need not confine the exercise of its discretion, in favour of enforcing letters rogatory where non-parties are the target of the request, to those circumstances in which the requirements of rule 31.10 have been met, I do not believe that those requirements need be disregarded entirely as useful guideposts.

In *Fecht*, the letters rogatory emanated from New York in a class action pending against Northern Telecom based on allegations that the company and some of its directors had made falsely optimistic public statements that artificially raised share prices and caused them later to fall dramatically when the company announced losses. Blair J described the US action, the positions of the parties on the letters rogatory and his conclusions as follows:

> Class actions of this sort are unknown to Canadian law but are not uncommon in the United States, although Congress has recently taken steps to attempt to limit their scope and frequency. They are known pejoratively, by those who oppose them, as "strike suits," apparently because the plaintiffs "strike" immediately upon the downturn of share values and before the makeup or membership of the class they purport to represent can even be known. In some quarters such actions themselves are thought to be "fishing expeditions" in substance, and that characterization plays an important role in the opposition to these letters rogatory by the respondents. ...
>
> Deloitte & Touche and Northern Telecom both vigorously oppose the granting of an order enforcing the letters rogatory. They submit that the US class action is by nature a "fishing expedition" in itself, and that an Ontario court ought not to countenance an extension of the fishing waters into this jurisdiction—"fishing expeditions" being a well-recognized example of the kinds of circumstances in which courts will decline to enforce letters rogatory. They submit, as well, that the court should be very wary about enforcing letters rogatory for purposes of pre-trial discovery rather than for the purpose of providing testimony at trial, and ought particularly to be wary about doing so in a way that will expose Canadian professional firms who simply provide advice to companies that do business in the United States to the very extensive American deposition process. Finally, they raise various technical defences.
>
> The applicants, on the other hand, argue that principles of international comity dictate a liberal approach to requests from foreign tribunals for judicial assistance. They contend that all necessary criteria for the enforcement of letters rogatory, as reflected in the letters rogatory themselves, have been met in the circumstances of this case, and that notwithstanding the pre-trial discovery flavour of the production and examination sought, the evidence gathered will be of great assistance for purposes of trial. In addition, they submit that the court should not embark on an adjudication of the merits of the foreign action, nor should it conduct a review of whether the letters rogatory ought to have been issued. ...
>
> I am not inclined to exercise the court's discretion in the circumstances of this case to order enforcement of the letters rogatory because of the more general principles enunciated in these reasons. In my opinion the record does not justify a finding that the evidence and information sought could not be—or could not have been—otherwise obtained. The transcripts of the depositions to which I was referred do not bear out that Deloitte & Touche was involved in the matters which are at the heart of the US action in any fashion other than the normal connection between independent auditor and client. Without more, I am not prepared to sanction what is in essence the extension of the American pre-trial deposition practice to a non-party providing auditing services in Ontario in the circumstances of this case, particularly in view of the fact that the many senior witnesses from Northern Telecom who have already been deposed were not even asked what information they had provided to Deloitte & Touche and what information had been imparted to them by Deloitte & Touche on the specific areas of questioning now sought to be pursued.

[On appeal, (1997), 32 OR (3d) 417, the Court of Appeal for Ontario upheld Blair J's use of the rule 31.10 requirements as guideposts on an application to examine non-party witnesses for a foreign proceeding. It held, however, that Ontario courts do have the power to narrow a request where this would permit the request to be granted.]

To what extent do you agree with the suggestion that the letters rogatory in this case were part of a "fishing expedition." To what extent could the breadth of the request be explained by the greater emphasis placed on discovery rather than pleadings for notice-giving and issue-defining in litigation in the United States?

D. Scope of Examination for Discovery

The scope of examination for discovery is typically dealt with by the rules—for example, see Ontario rule 31.06—and whether a matter on which a party wishes to examine another party is discoverable is determined by reference to the pleadings (including any particulars). To understand the scope of the permitted questioning it is essential to keep in mind the two broad purposes served by examination for discovery. These are, first, to obtain information about the case of the other party and, second, to secure admissions of fact that can be used as evidence at the trial by the examining party either to advance his or her own case or to weaken or destroy that of his or her opponent. Whether a question on examination for discovery seeks to achieve either or both of these objectives, it is the pleadings that disclose the case of the examining party or the case of the party examined, whichever is relevant. Thus, a question cannot be properly asked on examination for discovery unless it either relates to the pleadings in the sense of seeking an elucidation of the claim or defence raised in the pleadings, or is directed to establishing a fact the existence or non-existence of which is shown by the pleadings to be in issue.

The traditional position (now departed from in several provinces, including Ontario) held that a party being examined need only state the facts on which he or she relies and not the evidence by which they are to be proved. The rule was easy to state but difficult to apply because the distinction between the facts that constitute the case of a party and the evidence to prove them was not always clear. Cases held that in the case of doubt "resolution must be in favour of fact *disclosure*": *Rubinoff v. Newton*, [1967] 1 OR 402. The rationale for the rule restricting discovery to facts and not evidence is discussed and criticized in Williams, "Discovery of Civil Litigation Trial Preparation in Canada" (1980), 58 *Canadian Bar Review* 1.

Several provinces have now expressly abrogated the rule restricting discovery of evidence or of witnesses' names or evidence—for example, see Alberta rule 213(2), BC rule 27(22), NB rule 32.06(2), and Ontario rule 31.06(1).

1. Relation to Pleadings

Czuy v. Mitchell

(1976), 72 DLR (3d) 424 (Alta. SC, App. Div.)

PROWSE JA: This is an appeal by Dr. Mitchell from the order of the Honourable Mr. Justice Greschuk, in Chambers, directing him to reattend and answer questions, which, on the advice of his counsel, he refused to answer on his examination for discovery.

It is alleged in the action that the infant plaintiff, who was born prematurely, suffered the loss of sight in both eyes as a result of the abnormal oxygen level attained in his blood due to treatment administered under the direction of Dr. Mitchell in the defendant hospital.

The questions which were not answered in the examination for discovery fell into three broad categories:

(1) details of the appellant's training and experience in treating and caring for premature babies;

(2) the appellant's knowledge of acceptable standards of treatment and care for premature babies gained from sources other than personal experience; and

(3) the appellant's knowledge, at the material time, of the equipment available in other hospitals in the City of Edmonton for treating and for testing the results of the treatment carried out.

The appellant's counsel admitted that: "... a pediatric specialist, such as Dr. Mitchell, must always meet the objective standard of care exacted from that specialty" and that, consequently, ... questions dealing with the doctor's past medical experience in this area are completely irrelevant," and "... likewise questions relating to his source of knowledge."

The respondents' position was that the above questions were relevant, on the ground that an objective standard of care is not applied if the knowledge, training and experience of the appellant supported the conclusion that he knew, or should have known, that the standard of care applied by an average pediatric specialist was unsafe.

The respondents have framed their case on the premise that the appellant's knowledge and training were such that it is open to a Court to find that he was negligent, even though it might have been open to a Court to find that a less skilful and learned member of the profession, administering the same treatment in the same manner, was not.

In effect, the appellant seeks an order which will impede the respondents in the preparation and presentation of the cause of action alleged in the statement of claim by obtaining a ruling at this time on the standard of care to be applied by the trial Judge in determining liability.

In my view, on an application such as this, a Court should not attempt to resolve the issue of the standard of care to be applied at the trial. The questions are relevant to the cause of action alleged by the respondents, and only in the clearest case should this Court make a ruling which limits a party in the preparation and presentation of the case alleged in the pleadings. On such an application, I am of the opinion that the principle enunciated in this Division in *Cerny v. Canadian Industries Ltd. et al.* (1972), 30 DLR (3d) 462, [1972] 6 WWR 88, should be followed. There, Cairns JA, in delivering the judgment of the Court, stated at p. 468 DLR, p. 95 WWR:

> It is clear from these decisions that a Court should not strike a pleading or part thereof as disclosing no cause of action or as being frivolous or vexatious or as being an abuse of the process of the Court, which in most cases would have the effect of dismissing an action or denying a party a right to defend unless the question is beyond doubt and there is no reasonable cause of action; or a question is raised fit to be tried by a Judge or jury or merely because it is demurrable; or where the matter complained of is only part of the action set up, or where by going to trial the facts could be elicited which would have some effect on the case, or where justice and reason dictate that it should go to trial; or

where a pleading is not clearly vexatious or frivolous which would, if it were allowed to stand, be an abuse of the process of the Court; or where questions of general importance are raised or serious questions of law are in issue unless the matter is entirely clear.

The appellant's application, if successful, would have the effect of striking out the cause of action alleged in the statement of claim, to the extent that it is based on the higher duty alleged by the respondents. Following the *Cerny* case I am of the view that a Court should only make an order having that effect in the clearest case, and where an application to strike out the allegations would be successful.

With respect to the questions in the third category set out above, I am of the view that on an application such as this, a Court should not be called upon to conduct a minute investigation into the relevancy of each question, and that where, as here, the questions are broadly related to the issues raised, they should be answered.

Before concluding, I would make the following comment on the practice of the Court in dealing with applications such as this. The examination was becoming somewhat lengthy, having regard to the issues involved. I say this as it appears that this aspect of the examination may have precipitated some of the objections. In answer to an objection to Q. 607, the respondents' counsel said:

I'm still basically on the generalities pertaining to the type of treatment which was required in certain situations and no doubt will come to the exact type of treatment that was given the child. ... I'm still setting the ground work and will be for some time.

Although generally a Court will not seek to control the manner in which counsel conducts an examination, it will interfere where it appears that the purposes for which they are being held are being abused, such as where the conduct of counsel is abusive, the length of the examination supports the conclusion that it is being conducted as a delaying tactic, or the questions touch and concern matters which are clearly irrelevant. On the other hand, the Court, on the limited material available on such an application, where the relevant documents are not before it, will not conduct a minute examination of each question to determine its relevancy. In my view, a Court, in ruling on such applications, should not unduly restrict an examination by excluding questions broadly related to the issues when it appears that their relevance may well be resolved by other evidence not before the Court on the application.

In the present case, there can be no suggestion that the respondents' counsel was offending any of the above principles. This is a serious claim, and the respondents' counsel obviously had this in mind in preparing for and conducting the rather exhaustive discovery of the appellant.

In conclusion, I would dismiss the appeal, with costs to the respondents. Moir JA concurs with Prowse JA.

HADDAD JA: I agree with the conclusion reached by my brother Prowse. In his reasons, however, there is one aspect which, although touched on, has not been developed, and which is, in my view, pertinent. As the facts have been set out in the reasons written by Mr. Justice Prowse, I will not repeat them.

The point of this appeal, as I see it, is the scope and latitude which ought to be permitted of the questions put to the appellant on his examination for discovery. Mr.

Justice Prowse in his judgment has conveniently separated the questions not answered by Dr. Mitchell into three categories. The basic issue in this action is the standard of care expected of Dr. Mitchell and whether he met that standard. Do the questions which he refused to answer bear on that issue?

The general rule, as I conceive it, which has emerged from the leading authorities is expressed with clarity and simplicity in the headnote of the report of *Rural Municipality of Mount Hope No. 279 v. Findlay*, [1919] 1 WWR 397, as follows:

> The greatest latitude should be allowed to a party who is examining an adverse party for discovery so that the fullest inquiry may be made as to all matters *which can possibly* affect the issues between the parties. (Italics are mine.)

Rule 200 of the Alberta *Supreme Court Rules* permits the oral examination before trial of any party to an action by any party adverse in interest "touching the matters in question" in the action. ...

The words "touching the matters in question" were brought under scrutiny again in an application before Riley J in *Canadian Utilities Ltd. v. Mannix Ltd. et al.* (1959), 27 WWR 508; reversed on other grounds 20 DLR (2d) 654, 29 WWR 289. In that case his Lordship reviewed leading authorities and concluded with this statement at p. 521:

> I am of the opinion that the words "touching the matters in question" and "relating to," quoted *supra*, permit more latitude on discovery than is permitted by the rules of admissibility at trial.
>
> In other words, the above-quoted expressions are, in my opinion, broader in their scope than the expressions "material" and "relevant," and the said expressions do not mean "touching or relating to materially relevant matters as found by the trial judge." While discovery must be kept within reasonable bounds, it is only logical that a certain exploratory latitude be allowed on discovery without being confined by the rather strict rules of evidence at trial.

In a case argued in this Division some 60 years ago *(Medicine Hat Wheat Co. v. Norris Com'n. Co. Ltd.* (1916), 29 DLR 379 at p. 386, 10 WWR 1092 at p. 1099, 10 Alta. LR 19) Beck J spoke of the wide range permitted at discovery with these words:

> An examination for discovery has a wider range than an examination at the trial except that questions are not permissible which go only to impeaching the credit of the party under examination. Questions are relevant which go to the matter really in issue between the parties though strictly speaking an amendment may be necessary to bring them within the issues actually raised by the pleadings.

One of the tests adopted by Courts is that the latitude on discovery is as wide as the scope permitted on cross-examination at trial. In this regard I refer to *St. Regis Timber Co. Ltd. et al. v. Lake Logging Co. Ltd. et al.*, [1947] 3 DLR 56, [1947] 1 WWR 810 (BC CA), and *Carney v. Carney* (1913), 15 DLR 267, 5 WWR 849, 6 Sask. LR 373. In the latter case, at pp. 268-9 DLR, p. 851 WWR, Lamont J stated as follows:

> The object of an examination for discovery is to enable the litigant parties to ascertain if the plaintiff has a good cause of action, or the defendant such a defence as would render

further litigation useless. To effect this purpose, the examination may, so far as the issues raised in the pleadings are concerned, be as searching and thorough as the party's cross-examination of a witness at the trial could be. ... The point to be determined in this appeal, therefore, is, are the questions which the defendant refused to answer relevant to any issue raised in the pleadings, and if so, would he be compelled to answer them on cross-examination at the trial? If he would, he must answer them on his examination for discovery. ...

In my view then, it is the scope of the examination for discovery with which we are concerned in this appeal. Wide latitude is to be permitted. The examination may be searching and exploratory. Questions on discovery are relevant so long as they touch "the matters in question" and fall within the bounds that are reasonable. If the questions asked are relevant to the matters in issue or can possibly affect the issues between the parties—if they are questions which may be permitted on cross-examination—then they must be answered.

Moreover, as stated by Prowse JA, a Court generally will not exercise control over the manner in which counsel conducts an examination for discovery. Certainly a Court will not direct the order in which questions will be asked. There is no obligation on the part of counsel to deal with one category of questions, or to deal with questions involving a particular issue, before moving on to explore other areas. The selection of questions and the sequence in which they are put to a witness will frequently reflect the skill and care employed by counsel.

Clearly, the questions in each of the three categories are, broadly speaking, directed to the issue of standard of care to be expected of Dr. Mitchell as a specialist in his particular field of medicine. The nature of the questions are such that they touch the matters in question. They fall within the broad principles laid down by the Courts. In my view the order made by the learned Chambers Judge, directing that the questions be answered, ought to be sustained.

Accordingly, I would dismiss the appeal with costs.

Appeal dismissed.

NOTES AND QUESTIONS

1. In *Czuy*, Haddad JA says that "[q]uestions on discovery are relevant so long as they touch 'the matters in question' and fall within the bounds that are reasonable." What are the outer bounds? If a question cannot be related to the pleadings, need it be answered? Should the pleadings form the boundaries of what is answerable?

2. In *Milton Farms Ltd. v. Dow Chemical Canada* (1986), 13 CPC (2d) 174 (Sask. QB), an action for damages for breach of warranty and negligence arising from damage sustained to crops after using the defendant's herbicide, the defendant was required to produce complaints received from persons other than the plaintiffs respecting the product, as they were relevant to issues raised by the pleadings—that is, whether the defendant knew or ought to have known that the herbicide might be hazardous, and whether it was in fact hazardous. The defendant was also required to produce a report of

a consultant to a complainant not a party to the action since it might lead to a train of inquiry enabling the plaintiffs to advance their case. The case also raised various questions as to the scope of examination for discovery. How should the court have dealt with the discoverability of the following: (1) The volume of sales of the herbicide? (2) The existence of other claims regarding the herbicide? (3) Evidence of the settlement of such claims? (4) Questions as to the dollar volume of sales of the product? (5) Questions as to an application by the defendant for registration of a different herbicide for sale in the United States?

2. Answering from Knowledge, Information, and Belief

A person examined for discovery is required to answer to the best of his or her "knowledge, information and belief"—for example, see Ontario rule 31.06(1). The nature and extent of this obligation is described in Holmested and Watson, *Ontario Civil Procedure*, 31 § 15[4] as follows:

> [A]n examination for discovery requires the witness to give not only his knowledge but his information and belief": *Rubinoff v. Newton*, [1967] 1 OR 402 (HC). Though not generally permitted at trial, hearsay evidence is permissible on discovery. "As a witness, the party must confine himself to his knowledge: on examination [for discovery] he not only may, but he must give his information": *Van Horn v. Verall* (1911), 3 OWN 439 (HC). On the matter of "belief," the following passage from *Bray on Discovery* p. 128 was quoted, with approval, in *Kirkpatrick v. CPR*, [1926] 3 DLR 542 (Sask. KB):
>
>> As to facts not happening within his own knowledge ... he must answer as to his information and belief and not his information merely without stating any belief either one way or the other; ... as to the act of another which defendant does not certainly know he ought to say he thinks or believes it to be true or does not, and not say only that he has heard. ... He is also bound to state the grounds on which his belief is founded in order that the reality and value of his belief may be tested.
>
> Not only must a party examined give his information, he must inform himself. In *Rubinoff v. Newton*, above, Haines J said: "I can think of no more simple and direct question than, 'On what facts do you rely?' The witness may not know those facts but he must be informed by his counsel. It must be kept in mind that on an examination for discovery a party must qualify himself to give an intelligent statement of his case." A party to an action is bound to inform himself as to the knowledge possessed by his servants, employees and agents: *Bondar v. Usinovitch*, [1918] 1 WWR 557 (Sask.); H & G, R. 342 §§ 35-36. As a general principle there is no obligation on a party to make inquiries of third parties over whom he has no control, in order to inform himself: see *Star Electric Fixtures Ltd. v. Sussex Fire Ins. Co.*, [1936] OWN 654; *Concept 80 Ltd. v. W.A. Const. Co.* (1975), 1 CPC 96 (Ont. HC) (no duty on party to inform himself from independent contractor).

The duty on the party to inform himself or herself is particularly important, and onerous, with regard to persons examined on behalf of a corporation. Such a person is clearly under an obligation to inform himself or herself by making enquiries of the corporation and its officers and servants.

Moreover, the limitations stated above (there is no obligation on a party to make enquiries of third persons over whom he or she has no control in order to inform himself or herself) are disappearing. For example, *Gravlev v. Venturetek Int. Limited* (1979), 15 CPC 18 (Ont. HC) imposed an obligation to make enquiries from former officers and agents: "The test really is that the plaintiff is bound to obtain the information from such former agents or servants unless he can show that it would be unreasonable to require him to do so." To the same effect see *Signcorp Investments Limited v. Cairns Homes Limited* (1988), 24 CPC (2d) 1 (Sask. QB). In *Quintette Co. Limited v. Bow Valley Resource Services Limited* (1988), 29 BCLR (2d) 109 (SC), the corporate defendant's key person in the execution of the project at issue in the litigation had died. The opposing party was left to examine for discovery someone who had no first-hand knowledge of the facts. It was held that since the claim amounted to millions of dollars and in the light of the substantial issues involved, the defendant's representative had a duty to inform himself by making enquiries of independent corporations that had been subcontractors of the defendant. Each of the three corporations was outside of the jurisdiction, two in Alberta and one in France. The defendant had already had three consultations with one of the corporations in Edmonton and two with the French corporation, one in Montreal and one in Paris. Notwithstanding this, the defendant was required to make further inquiries with regard to questions that were clearly relevant to the issues in the action. What would happen if the subcontractors refused to answer the inquiries put to them by the defendant?

3. Continuing Discovery Obligations

Should a party be required to disclose documents or information that come to light after discovery? What should happen where a party later finds that an answer given on oral examination for discovery was inaccurate? What sanctions are available? See, for example, Ontario rules 31.09 (re examination for discovery) and 30.07 to 30.09 (concerning documents).

While the matter is now specifically dealt with by the rules in some jurisdictions— for example, the Ontario rules just referred to—such rules essentially confirm doctrine developed in the case law: see *Ontario Bean Producers' Marketing Board v. W.G. Thompson & Sons Limited* (1982), 35 OR (2d) 711 (Div. Ct.), holding that there is a duty to update an affidavit of documents and a duty to give an undertaking to provide after-required information when requested.

Burke v. Gauthier
(1987), 24 CPC (2d) 281 (Ont. HC)

CAMPBELL J:

The Issue. The case raises this question: should new evidence of a plaintiff's changed physical condition since discovery be admitted in a personal injury action when the new evidence favourable to the plaintiff differs significantly from the answers given on examination for discovery and the plaintiff has given no notice at all of the new evidence?

The Claim. Edward Burke claims damages for personal injuries resulting from a boat collision. Liability is admitted and the only issue is the quantum of damages.

Mr. Burke, a 53-year-old bus driver, is married with nine children. He lives in the isolated village of Killarney, about 75 miles from Sudbury. He is a credible witness and there is no reason to doubt his testimony.

The Accident. On July 1, 1984, Mr. Burke was standing on his 21-foot boat, idling at rest in Killarney Channel. The defendant's 14-foot aluminum boat collided suddenly. It struck so hard that its bow came out of the water and hit the plaintiff in the head, knocking him out and gashing his scalp badly.

The Initial Treatment. Bleeding heavily from the head wound, he was flown by rescue helicopter from Killarney to hospital in Sudbury. He had a laceration of the upper left scalp with heavy bleeding. His scalp was sewn up and he received blood transfusions. His skull was not fractured as the doctors initially suspected. He was reluctant to stay in hospital for any length of time and was released the next day. He had no neurological symptoms but did have a post-concussion syndrome which included headaches.

The Symptoms. His headaches continued as did some neck discomfort. The medical diagnosis was hyperextension injury—of a mild degree to the cervical spine.

He said that he felt rough all through the summer of 1984 and had severe headaches. They gradually improved but he still gets them, sometimes as often as twice a week, and they are sometimes strong. He had significant neck pain, described a year after the accident as moderate and radiating into his shoulder. It hurts particularly if he turns his head to the left. He has a scar from the crown of the head to a point about four inches above the bridge of his nose. The scar is noticeable but not badly disfiguring. He has no sensation in the area of the scar. The lack of sensation, caused by nerve damage from the laceration, is permanent. He finds the scar somewhat embarrassing and has to be careful in winter to guard against frostbite in the area where he has no sensation.

Effect on Earning Potential. He drives a bus with passengers and freight from Killarney to Sudbury and back, loading and unloading the parcels and freight by himself. He has worked since the accident (although he was off for some time during the summer of 1985 with an unrelated ankle injury) and had no trouble passing the regular medical examinations required for his bus driver's licence. He has some difficulty turning his neck but his bus is solid at the back and he used the side mirrors when backing up. The neck pain is worse after driving a lot.

He is worried that his neck might deteriorate and that he might be unable to drive any more, because he would have few other job opportunities. Dr. McMullen testified that x-rays in September 1984, show some degenerative change in the neck. The onset of symptoms was likely caused by the accident. He said it was possible that the plaintiff would become unable to drive because of neck pain brought on by further degenerative change, but that he was all right to drive now and there was no present indication that he would be unable to drive in the future. The evidence does not establish any compensable likelihood of future deterioration that would affect his job. I find no basis for compensation for any possible loss of future earnings or future earning potential.

Overall Prognosis. The plaintiff tendered evidence that his problems became more serious since the examination for discovery in August 1986. The plaintiff did not inform the defendants before trial that his condition or activities had changed.

The defendants objected to that evidence on the ground that they were taken completely by surprise and the plaintiff had taken no steps to inform them before trial of the changed nature of the case.

The plaintiff at the examination for discovery in August 1986, said that he had been able to resume his recreational and sporting activities since the accident, to the same extent as before the accident. His neck bothered him, but he still went fishing. He used his boat less than usually, but he was not thinking of selling it. He had no problems lifting heavy parcels at work.

At trial he tendered evidence that was quite different. He tendered evidence that the pain got worse in the Fall of 1986. After completing his day's work, he could not do much more. He could no longer snowmobile and sold his skidoo. He used to hunt a lot but only went hunting twice the previous year. It affected his bowling, fishing, woodcutting. It was hard to lift things. His wife and friends tendered evidence that he was not the same; he was quieter and "not such a fun loving guy," it was hard to get him to go out, he didn't skidoo or ice fish or dance or cut wood any more.

The plaintiff's answer on discovery that he had no trouble lifting and no diminution of his recreational or sporting activities except that he boated a little bit less, was no longer correct and complete at the time of trial. It had ceased to be correct and complete sometime in the six or nine months before trial.

The case he presented at the examination for discovery was a mild whiplash with no change in personality or lifestyle and no significant work problems. The case he presented at trial was quite different. It involved a loss of recreational activity, trouble lifting, and a change from a fun-loving personality.

Rule 31.09. Rule 31.09(1) puts a duty on the plaintiff to provide the defendant in writing with information that any answer given at the examination for discovery is no longer correct and complete.

Rule 31.09(3) provides that if the plaintiff does not provide the defendant in writing with such information, the information subsequently discovered if favourable to the plaintiff is inadmissible at trial except with leave of the Court.

The purpose of the provision is obvious. The parties prepare for trial on the basis of the evidence given at the discoveries. They assume that the answers given on discovery continue to be correct and complete, unless they are given information to the contrary. They figure out what they have to meet, decide how to prepare their own case, what investigations if any to undertake, what witness to call, what instructions to seek, and what kind of settlement might be reasonable, on the basis of the evidence given at the discoveries. If that evidence changes then there is a different case to meet. If the changes are not brought to the attention of the adverse party before trial he has no time or opportunity to investigate and prepare and consider the need for fresh medical examination and must meet a case different from the one that his opponent has led him to expect.

Unless there is some incentive to the plaintiff to disclose a change in the evidence, there is nothing to discourage trial by ambush and little to promote the objects of discovery which include the encouragement of settlement, the narrowing of issues, and the basic rule of fairness that a party should have reasonable knowledge of the case he must meet.

Rule 31.09, by enacting very explicitly a continuing duty of disclosure or discovery, is obviously designed to give these principles some teeth.

The new evidence in this case goes far beyond mere detail. It goes to the type of personal injury case the defendant has to meet, and it is the very kind of evidence designed to be governed by the rule. It is just about as relevant and material as any evidence can be in a personal injury case.

The difficulty in a personal injury case in deciding whether to grant leave under r. 31.09(3) to lead undisclosed evidence is this: the more significant the change in condition, the greater is the potential prejudice to the defendant in meeting a new case but also and correspondingly greater is the prejudice to the plaintiff in being unable to put favourable evidence before the Court.

In this case the plaintiff was obviously well aware of the change and therefore obviously aware of the new favourable evidence. He gave no reason for failing to provide the defendant with the new evidence favourable to the plaintiff's case. There was no application before trial for an adjournment in order to do so and the plaintiff put forward his case in the face of the rule without giving the defendants any knowledge of the new case they had to meet and no opportunity to investigate the new evidence, or to prepare to meet it or to consider their settlement position.

Had the plaintiff made any attempt to overcome the unfairness to the defendants by even mentioning it before trial or somehow trying to overcome the complete surprise, I might have been inclined to grant leave to introduce the evidence under r. 31.09(3), on terms under r. 53.08 unless the defendants showed some more concrete evidence of specific forms of prejudice.

But the plaintiff decided to move ahead into the teeth of the rule without trying to do anything to overcome the obvious unfairness and prejudice to the defendants at being met in the middle of the trial for the first time with a new case and I therefore see no basis to relieve against the clear consequences of the rule.

The evidence of the change in condition since the examination for discovery will therefore not be admitted.

Damages. On the evidence properly admissible at trial, Mr. Burke suffered a nasty head injury followed by considerable pain for a few months. He felt rough for a few months after the accident. He has some continuing and probably permanent discomfort to his neck. There is a mild permanent disability to his neck which does not affect his present or future earning capacity. He had severe headaches for some months and a temporary suspension of his normal activities for perhaps a year or more but less than two years. He still has some bad headaches.

He has a permanent scar on his head, quite obvious to sight but not badly disfiguring. The loss of sensation around the scar is troublesome for a man so used to being outdoors for long periods in the dead of winter and he has to take precautions against frostbite.

I assess his non-pecuniary damages at $14,000.

The plaintiff shall have judgment for $14,000 plus the subrogated OHIP claim of $1,690.94 plus Dr. Spegiel's account of $525 (US) which is not covered by OHIP, plus $3,200 for boat repairs, plus prejudgment interest.

If the parties cannot agree on the amount of prejudgment interest they may speak to me. The plaintiff shall have his costs unless the parties bring to my attention some reason to the contrary.

Judgment accordingly.

NOTES AND QUESTIONS

1. Was the judgment in this case fair to Mr. Burke? Whose fault was likely the cause of the non-disclosure?

2. Contrast *Burke* with the decision in *Machado v. Berlet* (1986), 15 CPC (2d) 207 (Ont. HC). There, the plaintiff sued the defendants in negligence for personal injuries suffered in a motor vehicle accident. During cross-examination of the plaintiff at trial, the plaintiff denied that he could run, shovel snow, or scrape ice off windshields. As part of the defendants' case, counsel for the defendants sought to introduce surveillance films of the plaintiff doing those activities. The defendants had claimed privilege over the surveillance films and did not disclose them on production of documents. The plaintiff moved to exclude from evidence the surveillance films on the basis of Ontario rule 30.09 (which prohibits privileged documents from being introduced at trial except in certain circumstances). The motion was dismissed, subject to the right of the plaintiff to call reply evidence to explain the impeaching evidence. It was held that the surveillance films were admissible to impeach the testimony of the plaintiff, notwithstanding that the defendants claimed privilege over them. Rule 30.09 reflects a compromise between the obligation to disclose and the right not to disclose privileged documents. In this case, the defendants obviously intended to use the films to impeach the plaintiff's testimony that he was physically incapacitated by reason of the defendant's negligence.

Can the decision in *Machado* be reconciled with the decision in *Burke*?

3. Contrast the result in *Burke* with that in *MacDonald Construction* in chapter 6, "Pleadings and Disposition Without Trial," where the defendants surprised the plaintiff at trial by presenting a different case from that which they had pleaded. There, the court adjourned to permit the defendants to amend their pleadings but ordered the defendants to pay the costs of and occasioned by the amendment including those thrown away for the hearing. Why do you think the court in *Burke* did not adopt the same approach?

V. PRIVILEGE

A. Types and Sources of Privilege

We have seen that in the rules and principles governing modern discovery, there is an unmistakable and unrelenting trend toward more complete pretrial disclosure. Against this pressure is a countervailing one derived from a recognition that there are certain interests that merit special protection and require that certain materials not be disclosed before trial. The law on privilege has traditionally been considered to be part of the law of evidence and is typically discussed at length in texts on that subject. However, in civil cases, the modern, broad discovery rules cause issues of privilege to be raised and resolved typically at the discovery stage, rather than at trial. Since privilege is *the* major limitation on the scope of discovery, in civil cases the law on privilege is to a considerable extent now being developed within a policy framework based on civil procedure policy issues, such as how broad discovery should be, or why the scope of discovery should be limited.

Material that is relevant to the case but that need not be disclosed is said to qualify for a claim to *privilege*. The effect of a rule of privilege is to prevent a party and a court from having relevant information; hence, such rules clearly inhibit the search for the truth in a particular case at hand on the grounds that more important interests are at stake.

McCormick, *Evidence* (1984, 3d ed.), at 171 explains:

> Rules which serve to render accurate ascertainment of the truth more difficult, or in some instances impossible, may seem anomalous in a rational system of fact-finding. Nevertheless, rules of privilege are not without a rationale. Their warrant is the protection of interests and relationships which, rightly or wrongly, are regarded as of sufficient social importance to justify some sacrifice of availability of evidence relevant to the administration of justice.

There are many grounds for privilege that illustrate this point. The right against self-incrimination is an important aspect of criminal and constitutional law. Accused persons may usually be the best source of the truth in a criminal case, yet interests of individual dignity and security are seen to prevail, and the accused person need not testify unless he or she chooses to do so. State privilege permits governments to shield information from disclosure on the theory that the public interest in maintaining certain state secrets should prevail over the interests of private litigants to have their disputes resolved correctly. Detailed study of these and other aspects of privilege must be left to a course in evidence. The focus here will be on those aspects of privilege that are grounded in interests because of the civil litigation process itself.

The general rule is that at a trial or other hearing anybody is subject to being compelled to testify and all relevant questions may be asked and must be answered. However, the law recognizes a variety of "privileges"—that is, that certain persons may not be required to testify—for example, an accused at his or her own criminal trial—or that certain types of information need not be disclosed—for example, solicitor–client communications, matters affecting the public interest (Crown privilege or state secrets), and the identity of police informers. Because the purpose of a privilege not to answer certain questions is, in part, to stop information from being disclosed, the privilege has been logically extended to the discovery process in civil litigation. Hence, privileged documents or privileged information need not be produced or disclosed.

The law does not recognize privilege for "confidential communications" generally—that is, for example, for statements made in confidence to doctors, journalists, priests, or between those involved in business. Consequently, notwithstanding the lofty language as to the sanctity of privilege, it is important to bring a critical eye to this subject and to note who benefits directly and indirectly from it. In civil litigation the important privileges are solicitor–client privilege, litigation privilege, settlement negotiation privilege, and (to a lesser extent) Crown privilege. The solicitor–client, litigation, and settlement negotiation privileges are framed in terms of being the *client's* privilege, but they also have the effect of cloaking a large amount of *lawyer's* work with the protection of privilege. Crown privilege, by definition, protects the Crown (that is, the government). One does not have to be too much of a cynic to realize that those who benefit substantially from the important privileges in civil litigation are also those who are regularly involved in the law-making process: lawyers and the government. Compare "Developments in the Law—Privileged Communications" (1985), 98 *Harvard Law Review* 1450 (attorney–client privilege is a political device for according special protection to a favoured elite). In this context it is worth noting A.A.S. Zuckerman's observation:

> Those who place legal professional privilege on the exalted and unassailable pedestal of fundamental justice may be reminded that there are other professions that provide invaluable services, such as medical practitioners and accountants, who seem to render perfectly good service to both individuals and the public without the benefit of immunity from disclosing what passes between themselves and their clients. "Legal Professional Privilege—the Cost of Absolutism" (1996), 112 LQR 535, at 539.

Daniel R. Fischel, "Lawyers and Confidentiality" (1998), 65 *University of Chicago Law Review* 1, has made the following argument (at 3): "[A] way to ask why encouraging communications with the legal profession is so important is to inquire who benefits from these communications. Stated this way, the question answers itself: confidentiality benefits lawyers because it increases the demand for legal services. The legal profession, not clients or society as a whole, is the primary beneficiary of confidentiality rules." He concludes (at 33): "[T]he attorney–client privilege, and the work product doctrine—benefit lawyers but are of dubious value to clients and society as a whole. Absent some more compelling justification for their existence than has been advanced to date, these doctrines should be abolished."

Below we discuss solicitor-and-client privilege and the litigation privilege (the privilege for documents prepared in anticipation of litigation). Space limitations do not permit a detailed analysis of the privilege regarding settlement discussion, which in any event is reasonably straightforward. With regard to formal offers to settle, made after litigation is commenced and pursuant to rules relating to this subject, the rules of court typically specifically attach privilege to such offers to settle—see, for example, Ontario rules 49.05 and 49.06. However, the common law privilege attached to settlement discussions is broader and not limited to formal offers to settle. The following quotation from the High Court of Australia in *Field v. Commissioner for Railways for New South Wales* (1957), 99 CLR 285, at 291-92, explains the scope and rationale of the common law privilege:

> The law relating to communications without prejudice is of course familiar. As a matter of policy the law has long excluded from evidence admissions by words or conduct made by parties in the course of negotiations to settle litigation. The purpose is to enable parties engaged in an attempt to compromise litigation to communicate with one another freely and without the embarrassment which the liability of their communications to be put in evidence subsequently might impose upon them. The law relieves them of this embarrassment so that their negotiations to avoid litigation or to settle it may go on unhampered. This form of privilege, however, is directed against the admission in evidence of express or implied admissions. It covers admissions by words or conduct.

For example, neither party can use the readiness of the other to negotiate as an implied admission. It is not concerned with objective facts which may be ascertained during the course of negotiations. These may be proved by direct evidence. But it is concerned with the use of the negotiations or what is said in the course of them as evidence by way of admission.

For some centuries almost it has been recognised that parties may properly give definition to the occasion when they are communicating in this manner by the use of the words "without prejudice" and to some extent the area of protection may be enlarged by the tacit acceptance by one side of the use by the other side of these words.

B. Solicitor–Client Privilege

Communications between a solicitor and client for the purpose of giving or receiving legal advice are privileged. The rationale for protecting such communications is well known and generally accepted. If the client does not have the guarantee of confidence, candour will be inhibited and the client will be unable to obtain adequate legal advice. The rationale was well put by Jessel MR in *Anderson v. Bank of British Columbia* (1876), 2 Ch. D 644, at 649:

> The object and meaning of the rule is this: that is, by reason of the complexity and difficulty of our law, litigation can only be properly conducted by professional men; it is absolutely necessary that a man, in order to prosecute his rights or to defend himself from an improper claim, should have recourse to the assistance of professional lawyers, and it being so absolutely necessary, it is equally necessary, to use a vulgar phrase, that he should be able to make a clean breast of it to the gentleman whom he consults with a view to the prosecution of his claim, or substantiating his defence against the claim of others; that he should be able to place unrestricted and unbounded confidence in the professional agent, and that the communications he so makes to him should be kept secret, unless with his consent (for it is his privilege, and not the privilege of the confidential agent), that he should be enabled properly to conduct his litigation. That is the meaning of the rule.

Solicitor–client privilege extends beyond the context of litigation and protects any communication made to a lawyer in a bona fide effort to obtain legal advice. The communication must have been made in confidence—for example, where the communication is oral it would not apply if other people are present, nor does it apply to communications between solicitor and client other than those relating to obtaining legal advice—for example, to social conversations or the giving of business advice. The privilege similarly extends to communications made by the solicitor to the client for the purpose of giving legal advice. The vast majority of cases where the privilege is invoked are straight forward situations where the client is clearly seeking or receiving legal advice. However, there are a number of issues that surround the solicitor–client privilege—for example, exactly when it arises, under what circumstances it may be lost, how it applies when the client is a corporation, and where there are circumstances where it should not be applied. The following cases deal with the last two of these issues.

Upjohn Co. v. United States
449 US 383 (1980)

[In the late 1960s and 1970s, the US public and government were shocked to learn that US multinational corporations were extensively involved in bribing foreign governments and were claiming such payments as a tax deduction. When the general counsel for petitioner pharmaceutical manufacturing corporation (hereafter petitioner) was informed that one of its foreign subsidiaries had made questionable payments to foreign government officials in order to secure government business, an internal investigation of such payments was initiated. As part of this investigation, petitioner's attorneys sent a questionnaire to all foreign managers seeking detailed information concerning such payments, and the responses were returned to the general counsel. The general counsel and outside counsel also interviewed the recipients of the questionnaire and other company officers and employees. Subsequently, based on a report voluntarily submitted by petitioner disclosing the questionable payments, the Internal Revenue Service (IRS) began an investigation to determine the tax consequences of such payments and issued a summons demanding production of, *inter alia*, the questionnaires and the memoranda and notes of the interviews. Petitioner refused to produce the documents on the grounds that they were protected from disclosure by the attorney–client privilege and constituted the work product of attorneys prepared in anticipation of litigation. The Court of Appeals held that, while there was no waiver of privilege, the privilege and the work-product doctrine did not apply. (The "work-product doctrine" is similar to the privilege for documents "prepared in anticipation of litigation," which we will consider in the next section.)]

REHNQUIST J delivered the opinion of the Court: We granted certiorari in this case to address important questions concerning the scope of the attorney–client privilege in the corporate context and the applicability of the work-product doctrine in proceedings to enforce tax summonses. 445 US 925. ...

Federal Rule of Evidence 501 provides that "the privilege of a witness ... shall be governed by the principles of the common law as they may be interpreted by the courts of the United States in light of reason and experience." The attorney–client privilege is the oldest of the privileges for confidential communications known to the common law. (J. Wigmore, Evidence 2290 (McNaughton rev. 1961).) Its purpose is to encourage full and frank communication between attorneys and their clients and thereby promote broader public interests in the observance of law and administration of justice. The privilege recognizes that sound legal advice or advocacy serves public ends and that such advice or advocacy depends upon the lawyer's being fully informed by the client. As we stated last Term in *Trammel v. United States*, 445 US 40, 51 (1980): "The lawyer–client privilege rests on the need for the advocate and counselor to know all that relates to the client's reasons for seeking representation if the professional mission is to be carried out." And in *Fisher v. United States*, 425 US 391, 403 (1976), we recognized the purpose of the privilege to be "to encourage clients to make full disclosure to their attorneys." This rationale for the privilege has long been recognized by the Court, see *Hunt v. Blackburn*, 128 US 464, 470 (1888) (privilege "is founded upon the necessity, in the interest and administration of justice, of the aid of persons having knowledge of the law and skilled in its practice, which assistance can only be safely and readily availed of when free from the consequences or the apprehension of disclosure"). Admittedly complications in the application of the privilege arise when the client is a corporation, which in theory is an artificial creature of the law, and not an individual; but this Court has assumed that the privilege applies when the client is a corporation, *United States v. Louisville & Nashville R Co.*, 236 US 318, 336 (1915), and the Government does not contest the general proposition.

The Court of Appeals, however, considered the application of the privilege in the corporate context to present a "different problem," since the client was an inanimate entity and "only the senior management, guiding and integrating the several operations, ... can be said to possess an identity analogous to the corporation as a whole." (600 F2d, at 1226.) The first case to articulate the so-called "control group test" adopted by the court below, *Philadelphia v. Westinghouse Electric Corp.*, 210 F Supp. 483, 485 (ED Pa.), petition for mandamus and prohibition denied sub nom. *General Electric Co. v. Kirkpatrick*, 312 F2d 742 (CA3 1962), cert. denied, 372 US 943 (1963), reflected a similar conceptual approach:

> Keeping in mind that the question is, Is it the corporation which is seeking the lawyer's advice when the asserted privileged communication is made?, the most satisfactory solution, I think, is that if the employee making the communication, of whatever rank he may be, is in a position to control or even to take a substantial part in a decision about any action which the corporation may take upon the advice of the attorney, ... then, in effect, *he is (or personifies) the corporation* when he makes his disclosure to the lawyer and the privilege would apply. (Emphasis supplied.)

Such a view, we think, overlooks the fact that the privilege exists to protect not only the giving of professional advice to those who can act on it but also the giving of information to the lawyer to enable him to give sound and informed advice. See *Trammel, supra*, at 51; *Fisher, supra*, at 403. The first step in the resolution of any legal problem is ascertaining the factual background and sifting through the facts ... with an eye to the legally relevant. See ABA Code of Professional Responsibility, Ethical Consideration 4-1:

> A lawyer should be fully informed of all the facts of the matter he is handling in order for his client to obtain the full advantage of our legal system. It is for the lawyer in the exercise of his independent professional judgment to separate the relevant and important from the irrelevant and unimportant. The observance of the ethical obligation of a lawyer to hold inviolate the confidences and secrets of his client not only facilitates the full development of facts essential to proper representation of the client but also encourages laymen to seek early legal assistance.

See also *Hickman v. Taylor*, 329 US 495, 511 (1947).

In the case of the individual client, the provider of information and the person who acts on the lawyer's advice are one and the same. In the corporate context, however, it will frequently be employees beyond the control group as defined by the court below— "officers and agents ... responsible for directing [the company's] actions in response to legal advice"—who will possess the information needed by the corporation's lawyers. Middle-level—and indeed lower-level—employees can, by actions within the scope of their employment, embroil the corporation in serious legal difficulties, and it is only natural that these employees would have the relevant information needed by corporate counsel if he is adequately to advise the client with respect to such actual or potential difficulties. ...

The control group test adopted by the court below thus frustrates the very purpose of the privilege by discouraging the communication of relevant information by employees of the client to attorneys seeking to render legal advice to the client corporation. The attorney's advice will also frequently be more significant to noncontrol group members than to those who officially sanction the advice, and the control group test makes it more difficult to convey full and frank legal advice to the employees who will put into effect the client corporation's policy. See, e.g., *Duplan Corp. v. Deering Milliken, Inc.*, 397 F Supp. 1146, 1164 (SC 1974) ("After the lawyer forms his or her opinion, it is of no immediate benefit to the Chairman of the Board or the President. It must be given to the corporate personnel who will apply it").

The narrow scope given the attorney–client privilege by the court below not only makes it difficult for corporate attorneys to formulate sound advice when their client is faced with a specific legal problem but also threatens to limit the valuable efforts of corporate counsel to ensure their client's compliance with the law. In light of the vast and complicated array of regulatory legislation confronting the modern corporation, corporations, unlike most individuals, "constantly go to lawyers to find out how to obey the law" (Burnham, The Attorney–Client Privilege in the Corporate Arena, 24 Bus. Law. 901, 913 (1969)), particularly since compliance with the law in this area is hardly an instinctive matter, see, e.g., *United States v. United States Gypsum Co.*, 438 US 422, 440-441 (1978) ("the behavior proscribed by the [Sherman] Act is often difficult to distinguish from the gray zone of socially acceptable and economically justifiable business conduct"). The test adopted by the court below is difficult to apply in practice, though no abstractly formulated and unvarying "test" will necessarily enable courts to decide questions such as this with mathematical precision. But if the purpose of the attorney–client privilege is to be served, the attorney and client must be able to predict with some degree of certainty whether particular discussions will be protected. An uncertain privilege, or one which purports to be certain but results in widely varying applications by the courts, is little better than no privilege at all. The very terms of the test adopted by the court below suggest the unpredictability of its application. The test restricts the availability of the privilege to those officers who play a "substantial role" in deciding and directing a corporation's legal response. Disparate decisions in cases applying this test illustrate its unpredictability. ...

The communications at issue were made by Upjohn employees to counsel for Upjohn acting as such, at the direction of corporate superiors in order to secure legal advice from counsel. As the Magistrate found, "Mr. Thomas consulted with the Chairman of the Board and outside counsel and thereafter conducted a factual investigation to determine the nature and extent of the questionable payments *and to be in a position to give legal advice to the company with respect to the payments*." (Emphasis supplied.) 78-1 USTC para. 9277, pp. 83,598, 83,599. Information, not available from upper-echelon management, was needed to supply a basis for legal advice concerning compliance with securities and tax laws, foreign laws, currency regulations, duties to shareholders, and potential litigation in each of these areas. The communications concerned matters within the scope of the employees' corporate duties, and the employees themselves were sufficiently aware that they were being questioned in order that the corporation could obtain legal advice. The questionnaire identified Thomas as "the company's General Counsel" and referred in its opening sentence to the ... possible illegality of payments such as the ones on which information was sought. App. 40a. A statement of policy accompanying the questionnaire clearly indicated the legal implications of the investigation. The policy statement was issued "in order that there be no uncertainty in the future as to the policy with respect to the practices which are the subject of this investigation." ... It began "Upjohn will comply with all laws and regulations," and stated that commissions or payments "will not be used as a subterfuge for bribes or illegal payments" and that all payments must be "proper and legal." Any future agreements with foreign distributors or agents were to be approved "by a company attorney" and any questions concerning the policy were to be referred "to the company's General Counsel." Id., at 165a-166a. This statement was issued to Upjohn employees worldwide, so that even those interviewees not receiving a questionnaire were aware of the legal implications of the interviews. Pursuant to explicit instructions from the Chairman of the Board, the communications were considered "highly confidential" when made, id., at 39a, 43a, and have been kept confidential by the company. Consistent with the underlying purposes of the attorney–client privilege, these communications must be protected against compelled disclosure.

The Court of Appeals declined to extend the attorney–client privilege beyond the limits of the control group test for fear that doing so would entail severe burdens on discovery and create a broad "zone of silence" over corporate affairs. Application of the attorney–client privilege to communications such as those involved here, however, puts the adversary in no worse position than if the communications had never taken place. The privilege only protects disclosure of communications; it does not protect disclosure of the underlying facts by those who communicated with the attorney:

> [The] protection of the privilege extends only to *communications* and not to facts. A fact is one thing and a communication concerning that fact is an entirely different thing. The client cannot be compelled to answer the question, "What did you say or write to the attorney?" but may not refuse to disclose any relevant fact within his knowledge merely because he incorporated a statement of such fact into his communication to his attorney. *Philadelphia v. Westinghouse Electric Corp.*, 205 F Supp. 830, 831 (ED Pa. 1962).

See also *Diversified Industries*, 572 F2d, at 611; ... *State ex rel. Dudek v. Circuit Court*, 34 Wis. 2d 559, 580, 150 NW 2d 387, 399 (1967) ("the courts have noted that a party cannot conceal a fact merely by revealing it to his lawyer"). Here the Government was free to question the employees who communicated with Thomas and outside counsel. Upjohn has provided the IRS with a list of such employees, and the IRS has already interviewed some 25 of them. While it would probably be more convenient for the Government to secure the results of petitioner's internal investigation by simply subpoenaing the questionnaires and notes taken by petitioner's attorneys, such considerations of convenience do not overcome the policies served by the attorney–client privilege. As Justice Jackson noted in his concurring opinion in *Hickman v. Taylor*, 329 US, at 516:

"Discovery was hardly intended to enable a learned profession to perform its functions ... on wits borrowed from the adversary." ... [W]e conclude that the narrow "control group test" sanctioned by the Court of Appeals in this case cannot, consistent with "the principles of the common law as ... interpreted in the light of reason and experience," Fed. Rule Evid. 501, govern the development of the law in this area.

Ontario (Ministry of Environment) v. McCarthy Tétrault
(1992) 9 CELR (NS) 12 (Ont. Prov. Div.)

MacDONALD PROV. DIV. J: This is a ruling under s. 160(8) of the *Provincial Offences Act*, RSO 1990, c. P.33 with respect to whether a claim of solicitor–client privilege should be sustained in respect of a number of documents seized pursuant to a search warrant issued under s. 158(1) of the Act. Under the authority of the warrant, the documents were seized from the law firm of McCarthy Tétrault on April 14, 1992. In accordance with the provisions of s. 160(1) and (2) of the Act, the investigators who conducted the search did not examine or make copies of any documents, but rather permitted them to be placed in a sealed envelope which has been filed, unopened, with the clerk of this court. ...

Neil Rickey is an investigator with the Ontario Ministry of the Environment and the informant with respect to the search warrant which was issued in this case. The investigation which he has been conducting concerns alleged spills of wastes at the Lafarge Canada Inc. cement plant at Bath, Ontario. Donald Stafford is the Environmental and Process Quality Manager for Lafarge at the Bath facility. The law firm of McCarthy Tétrault was at all material times retained by Lafarge Canada Inc. to provide legal advice. The solicitor at McCarthy Tétrault who is responsible for advising Lafarge Canada Inc. with respect to environmental law matters is Douglas Thompson. The applicants—Lafarge Canada Inc., Donald Stafford, and McCarthy Tétrault—assert that the documents in issue are protected from seizure by solicitor–client privilege. That claim arises in the following circumstances.

On July 29 and 30, 1991, Mr. Thompson attended a meeting at the Bath facility. Mr. Stafford was present at the meeting, as was the Environmental Director for Lafarge Canada's American parent, and certain other senior managers of the Lafarge group of companies. According to the affidavit which Mr. Thompson filed in support of this application, "the purpose of the meeting was to receive confidential information and provide legal advice concerning the compliance of the Bath facility with applicable environmental statutes, regulations and policies." Mr. Thompson further deposed that during the course of the meeting confidential discussions also took place regarding a potential prosecution in relation to a coal storage settling pond at the Bath facility. The only notes of the meeting were taken by Thompson. He deposed "that the documents for which Lafarge claims privilege are notes and memoranda prepared by me of confidential communications between me and my client, and confidential communications from my client, which were prepared for the purpose of receiving information and providing or recording the provision of ... legal advice" in relation to the facility's compliance with the relevant legal requirements.

Mr. Thompson was cross-examined by Crown counsel on the assertions contained in his affidavit. He was confronted with a reminder notice, circulated by one of the participants prior to the July 29 and 30 meeting, which referred to the meeting as an "environmental audit," and which described Thompson's role as "serving as the recorder and keeper of the information developed." Mr. Thompson firmly insisted that regardless of what was said in that notice, the purpose of the meeting and the role he played was as described in his affidavit.

The claim of privilege made by the applicants is resisted by the Crown on the basis that while Mr. Thompson is a solicitor, and Lafarge Canada Inc. is his client, the purpose of the meeting on July 29 and 30 was not to obtain Mr. Thompson's "legal" advice, and any documents generated for use at this meeting or developed as a result of the meeting were not intended to be confidential. ...

The assertions made by Mr. Thompson in his affidavit and viva voce on this application constitute sworn evidence that all of the circumstances required to establish a solicitor–client privilege were present in relation to the communications between Mr. Thompson and his client concerning the meeting at the Bath facility. As stated above, the position of the Crown, advanced with force and ability by Mr. Berger, is that on the whole of the evidence it has not been shown either that the communications between Mr. Thompson and his client were for the purpose of obtaining legal advice or that they were intended to be confidential.

Underlying the specific dispute in this case concerning the communications between Mr. Thompson and his client is a wider controversy within the field of environmental law, namely the evidentiary status of information and documents generated as part of an exercise known as an "environmental audit." In his cross-examination of Mr. Thompson, Mr. Berger sought to characterize the meeting at Bath as such an exercise; Mr. Thompson vigilantly resisted those efforts; both were plainly alert to the implications which might be argued to flow from classifying the meeting in that way.

In a document entitled *Canadian Environmental Protection Act: Enforcement and Compliance Policy* (Minister of Supply and Services, May 1988), Cat. No. En 40-356/ 1988E), at p. 29, Environment Canada describes environmental audits as follows:

> Environmental audits are internal evaluations by companies and government agencies to verify their compliance with legal requirements as well as their own internal policies and standards. They are conducted by companies, government agencies and others on a voluntary basis, and are carried out by either outside consultants or employees of the company or facility from outside the work unit being audited. Audits can identify compliance problems, weaknesses in management systems, or areas of risk. The findings are documented in a written report.

The elasticity of the term "environmental audit" is well recognized. In "Confidentiality in Environmental Auditing," JELP 1, Paul Edwards states, at pp. 5-6:

> The objectives or purposes of an environmental audit will vary widely. In fundamental terms, the purposes of most audits will be those described by Environment Canada; that is, to verify compliance with legal requirements and with the organization's own policies and standards. Some audits, however, will be for the sole purpose of assessing

legislative compliance. Others may be designed to assist facility management in improving their performance, to assess risks, or to identify potential cost savings. ...

The term "environmental audit" is not a term of art, and somewhat loosely describes a spectrum of activities. Some corporations deliberately avoid using the term audit; others employ it deliberately in order to establish credibility with outside agencies. Other terms that are sometimes used to describe similar activities include: environmental site assessment, evaluation, survey and review.

With respect to the confidentiality of an audit report, Mr. Edwards states, at p. 20:

... [I]n order for the [solicitor–client] privilege to attach, the report must have been created for the purpose of obtaining legal advice or assistance. Whether or not the corporation takes the precaution of asking the consultant to address the report, and all other communications, to the lawyer, can it truly be said that most environmental audits are commissioned for the purpose of seeking legal advice? Even where a legal opinion is given based on the audit report, is not the audit report the document that is of the greatest interest to the client? *There may very well be cases in which the legal opinion really is the client's ultimate objective in having the environmental audit commissioned.* The "audit" in such a case, however, is a substantially different, and less useful, exercise than what is usually thought of an environmental audit. [Emphasis added.]

It is clear that characterizing an exercise as an environmental audit does not, in itself, answer the question of whether the information communicated to a solicitor as part of the exercise is privileged. Thus, the relevant inquiry in the case at bar is not whether the meeting on July 29 and 30 at the Bath facility should or should not be termed an environmental audit, but rather whether the exercise that was conducted at that meeting was truly conducted for the bona fide purpose of obtaining legal advice from Mr. Thompson.

The vigour with which the claim of privilege was challenged in this case was fuelled, at least in part, by a general concern that corporations wishing to conceal their environmental sins from the eyes of regulatory agencies might attempt to adorn environmental audits with the badges of solicitor–client communications in order to assert, disingenuously, that the purpose of the exercise was to obtain legal advice. The concern is not unreasonable. Edwards, supra, notes, at p. 21, that "it is not inconceivable that a court may in certain circumstances be made a little wary of a claim to privilege specifically because of the number of published writings which exhort corporations to have their environmental audits addressed to a lawyer for the express purpose of structuring a claim to privilege."

It is only reasonable that courts be cautious in assessing claims of privilege arising out of environmental self-assessments, however described. The concern must be placed in context, however. Assessing the bona fides of transactions, and the candour and credibility of those who testify about them, is not a novel exercise for the courts. A claim of privilege will not be established by merely asserting it: *R v. Morra*, supra. There must be evidence establishing all the required elements before the claim can be sustained. In most cases, that evidence will consist of the testimony of the solicitor that he or she believes that those elements exist in relation to the communications or documents in issue. The solicitor would be required to swear to a belief that a substantial and bona fide purpose of the communication was to obtain legal advice. Obviously, if the solicitor were aware that the obtaining of legal advice was a mere convenience to attract the protection of the privilege, he or she could not truthfully make that assertion. There is a very high duty on a solicitor who gives evidence to establish a claim of privilege to frankly disclose the existence of any other purpose for which, to the solicitor's knowledge, the communication was made, so that the court can fairly assess the claim. Further, a solicitor's evidence is not determinative of whether a claim of privilege should be sustained. The court is entitled to assess the credibility of that evidence in the same manner as any other evidence. Where the claim is made with respect to documents, as in the case at bar, the court will have the very important advantage of being able to examine the material for which privilege is claimed in order to form an independent opinion as to whether it supports the evidence of the solicitor. These are important practical safeguards, and, in light of them, a court is no more likely to be duped by a claim of privilege in relation to environmental audits than with respect to any other matter.

With respect to the particular circumstances of the case at bar, Mr. Berger submitted that the meeting at the Bath facility was an environmental audit, conducted for internal corporate purposes rather than an assessment of Lafarge's compliance with the law. He submitted that the information developed at such an audit would necessarily be intended to be shared widely, not only within the company but, if the company's written environmental policy is to be taken seriously, with persons outside of the company. He characterized Mr. Thompson's evidence as an ex post facto recasting of the purpose of the meeting in order to shelter the company behind a solicitor–client privilege.

There is little in the record before me to support those submissions. The strongest circumstance in the Crown's favour is the reminder notice sent in advance of the meeting to the apparent participants, including Mr. Thompson. It described the meeting as an environmental audit and Thompson's role as "the keeper and recorder of the information developed," and it made no reference to the obtaining of a legal opinion. However, Mr. Thompson was confronted with that document in cross-examination, and he was adamant that it did not reflect accurately the role which it was clearly understood that he was to play at the meeting. He testified that immediately following the meeting he prepared a written opinion which was circulated only to those who had attended. He testified that this document was contained in the sealed packet, available for the court's perusal.

Mr. Thompson was a credible witness. In addition, I have now had the opportunity of reviewing the document he prepared for his client as well as the related documents which were placed in the sealed envelope. In my opinion, they confirm Mr. Thompson's evidence as to the purpose of the meeting and his role in it. I accept his evidence. Whatever may be the legitimate general concerns of regulatory agencies with respect to the role of solicitors in environmental audits, there is no reason, on the facts of this case, not to take Mr. Thompson's evidence at face value.

As a practical matter, the rejection of the Crown's submission that the purpose of the meeting with Mr. Thompson was other than to obtain legal advice disposes of the Crown's related submission that the communications were not intended to be confidential. I find, based on the affidavit and viva voce evidence of Mr. Thompson that they were so intended. ...

For the foregoing reasons, I find that the claim of solicitor–client privilege, which has been made in relation to documents seized from the law firm of McCarthy Tétrault on April 14, 1992, has been established, and the claim is accordingly sustained.

In order to preserve the confidentiality of the documents while at the same time preserving the status quo pending any appeal from this ruling, I order that the documents remain sealed and in the possession of the clerk of this court pending further order of this court, or any other court having jurisdiction over these proceedings, on application brought by any of the parties.

Application allowed.

NOTES AND QUESTIONS

1. One US commentator has said that the court in *Upjohn* created a new product line for lawyers—confidentiality—without really discussing the issue. Do you agree? What do think of the decisions in *Upjohn* and *McCarthy Tétrault*? How do the situations in these cases differ from the "normal" situation where the privilege is claimed? If you, or a court, believed that the privilege should not apply in these situations how would you explain your decision?

2. *Misuse of privilege.* Geoffrey Hazard ("An Historical Perspective on the Attorney-Client Privilege" (1978), 66 *California Law Review* 1061, at 1062) has suggested that solicitor–client privilege is often a device for covering-up "legally dubious or dirty business." It now appears that the tobacco industry systematically used the device of routing third-party communications, including marketing and other research, through its lawyers in an attempt to attract privilege. See "Release of Tobacco Documents Ordered— Evidence Shows Companies Used Lawyers To Hide Data, State Judge Says," *The Wall Street Journal*, March 9, 1998, reporting that tobacco companies were ordered to produce 39,000 internal documents for which privilege had been claimed. Included were documents concerning research about nicotine addiction and brand preferences of children. Judge Kenneth Fitzpatrick of the Minnesota District Court said "the industry's lawyers misused the attorney–client privilege and deliberately misrepresented documents to hide evidence of crime and fraud from Minnesota's lawyers" in an action by the state to recover health care costs associated with smoking. One example cited by the judge was a study reviewing "apparently problematic research" conducted by "an outside marketing firm for a Canadian affiliate [of BAT Industries plc], Imperial Tobacco Co. The research, according to the review, contained 'multiple references to how very young smokers at first believe they cannot become addicted, only to discover later, to their regret, that they are.'" See also *Minnesota v. Phillip Morris Inc.*, 1998 WL 257214 (Minn. Dist. Ct., March 7, 1998) and 1998 WL 154543 (Minn. Sup. Ct., March 27, 1998).

3. *Solicitor–client privilege for corporate clients in Canadian law.* In Canada there has been broad protection for confidential communications emanating from a corporate employee, regardless of the level of his or her position in the corporate hierarchy, provided the objective was to obtain legal advice. Moreover, as long as the statement was made generally in the course of his or her employment, no specific inquiry need be made of the subject matter to ensure that it fell squarely within the scope of his or her duties.

For the most part, the issue has been treated by Canadian courts as one coming within the agency theory of privilege—that is, any employee can be engaged by the corporate client to pass on information to solicitors for the purpose of receiving legal advice.

4. *Privilege and in-house counsel.* According to Sopinka, Lederman, and Bryant, *The Law of Evidence in Canada* (Toronto: Butterworths, 1992), at 651-52, "Lawyers who are employed by a corporation and therefore have only one client are covered by the privilege provided that they are performing the function of a solicitor. Lawyers, however, whether in house or not, often occupy a dual function and only the portions of the communication made in the capacity of solicitor are protected. ... Thus, the character of the activity carried on by the individual in question must be scrutinized to determine its nature. If the solicitor has information as a result of communications: in his professional capacity as a lawyer, privilege will attach but not otherwise."

C. Litigation Privilege/Lawyer's Brief Rule

1. Nature and Rationale of the Privilege

Robert Sharpe, "Claiming Privilege in the Discovery Process"
in Law Society of Upper Canada, *Special Lectures 1984*, 163-78 (footnotes omitted)

Litigation Privilege Defined

A rule of privilege permits a party to litigation to conceal material that is relevant to the case and, therefore, to prevent the other party and the court from having information which might affect the result. Hence, such rules inhibit in the short run the search for the truth in the particular case, on the grounds that in the long run more important interests would be infringed if the information were revealed. There are many sources of privilege. In the preceding paper, Mr. McDougall has ably discussed Crown privilege and solicitor–client privilege which are governed by the same principles on discovery as at trial. The effect of the successful assertion of a claim of Crown privilege or solicitor–client privilege prevents the information from ever coming to light, whether at discovery or at trial.

Of particular interest at the discovery stage are the rules which are collected under the label "legal professional privilege," sometimes also called "the lawyer's brief rule," or "the litigation privilege." I use the latter label. It is important to distinguish this privilege from other forms of privilege, and the label "litigation privilege" conveniently depicts a distinct area. A definition of this rule, which is often quoted, is that given in the case of *Wheeler v. Le Marchant* (1881), 17 Ch. D 675, at 681, *per* Jessel MR:

> The cases, no doubt, establish that such documents are protected where they have come into existence after litigation commenced or in contemplation, and where they have been made with a view to such litigation, either for the purpose of obtaining advice as to such litigation, or of obtaining evidence to be used in such litigation, or of obtaining information which might lead to the obtaining of such evidence.

This rule protects from disclosure at the discovery stage of an action, investigatory or preparatory work relating to the litigation itself. Because much of this material will actually be used at trial—that is the very reason it is brought into existence—the successful assertion of a claim of litigation privilege will often have only temporary effect. In a pragmatic sense, litigation privilege permits a party to shield from disclosure at the discovery stage material which, if favourable to that party, will be used to that party's advantage at the trial to the surprise of his opponent, and which, if unfavourable, will be buried from sight and never revealed at the trial unless the other side has independent access to it. Because we favour neither surprise at trial nor the suppression of relevant information, there has been an understandable tendency to shrink the scope of privilege.

It is crucially important to distinguish litigation privilege from solicitor–client privilege. There are, I suggest, at least three important differences between the two. First, solicitor–client privilege applies only to confidential communications between the client and his solicitor. Litigation privilege, on the other hand, applies to communications of a non-confidential nature between the solicitor and third parties and even includes material of a non-communicative nature. Secondly, solicitor–client privilege exists any time a client seeks legal advice from his solicitor whether or not litigation is involved. Litigation privilege, on the other hand, applies only in the context of litigation itself. Thirdly, and most important, the rationale for solicitor–client privilege is very different from that which underlies litigation privilege. This difference merits close attention. The interest which underlies the protection accorded communications between a client and a solicitor from disclosure is the interest of all citizens to have full and ready access to legal advice. If an individual cannot confide in a solicitor knowing that what is said will not be revealed, it will be difficult, if not impossible, for that individual to obtain proper candid legal advice.

Litigation privilege, on the other hand, is geared directly to the process of litigation. Its purpose is not explained adequately by the protection afforded lawyer–client communications deemed necessary to allow clients to obtain legal advice, the interest protected by solicitor–client privilege. Its purpose is more particularly related to the needs of the adversarial trial process. Litigation privilege is based upon the need for a protected area to facilitate investigation and preparation of a case for trial by the adversarial advocate. In other words, litigation privilege aims to facilitate a process (namely, the adversary process), while solicitor–client privilege aims to protect a relationship (namely, the confidential relationship between a lawyer and a client).

Rationale for Litigation Privilege

Relating litigation privilege to the needs of the adversary process is necessary to arrive at an understanding of its content and effect. The effect of a rule of privilege is to shut out the truth, but the process which litigation privilege is aimed to protect—the adversary process—among other things, attempts to get at the truth. There are, then, competing interests to be considered when a claim of litigation privilege is asserted: there is a need for a zone of privacy to facilitate adversarial preparation; there is also the need for disclosure to foster fair trial.

Despite the push towards more and more disclosure in pre-trial discovery, the adversarial nature of our process must be kept in mind. We appear to have a firm and unfailing belief in the strength of the adversary system and we continue to rely on self-interest, party-motivation, party-investigation and party-presentation at trial as being the best methods to get at the truth. Our commitment to the adversary system means that despite the unmistakable and unrelenting trend towards more complete and open discovery, we need a more principled and thoughtful approach than simply, "the more discovery the better."

Our belief in the adversary system, however, is not unqualified. More and more, we deprecate its excesses and encourage through our discovery process disclosure and openness, behaviour which is not prompted by self-interest and which seems to be at odds with what motivates the system in the first place. I suggest that the concepts which underlie the rules of litigation privilege attempt to reconcile these competing and, at times, contradictory forces and arguments.

The rationale for litigation privilege has been explained in terms of the "sporting" theory of justice. The least compelling argument to support privilege is that which asserts that an adversary trial depends upon surprise and which argues that disclosure is the enemy rather than the friend of truth. Although the "sporting" theory has a long and respectable history, it is quite clearly out of keeping with the modern view which favours greater pre-trial disclosure, and both case law and the new rules make it clear that the surprise theory has been discarded.

It might be argued, however, that the adversarial incentive to investigate fully would be impaired if litigation privilege did not exist. A party might refrain from conducting a thorough investigation hoping to borrow on the work of his opponent or, perhaps more likely, to refrain from fully investigating those delicate areas where unfavourable information might be uncovered. Counsel might fear pursuing an investigation in a sensitive area if the fruits of such research, favourable or unfavourable, had to be disclosed to the other side. This argument, however, would appear to prove too much. Discovery rules have long forced the disclosure of unfavourable information without destroying the spirit which underlies and motivates the adversary process. The risks of not investigating thoroughly are so great that forcing disclosure of the fruits of the research is unlikely to be inhibiting or destructive of party motivation.

The most convincing rationale for the protection from disclosure of material generated in preparation for litigation is that suggested by the "work product" test. As well, work product analysis best describes the interests actually protected by our rules of litigation privilege, Although the phrase "work product" is only rarely employed by Canadian courts and is not contained in the new rules, I will argue that implicit in the scheme for discovery to be enacted by the new rules is an acceptance of the basic tenets of work product doctrine.

The work product test was enunciated in the leading American decision, *Hickman v. Taylor*. ...

The adversary system depends upon careful and thorough investigation and preparation by the parties through their counsel. The adversarial advocate cannot prepare without the protection afforded by a zone of privacy. Discovery and privilege must strike a delicate balance. Too little disclosure impairs orderly preparation. Counsel cannot come to trial prepared without adequate information about the case the opposing side will present. On the other hand, total disclosure would be demoralizing and would impair orderly preparation. Thorough investigation and careful development of strategy would be discouraged if every thought and observation had to be disclosed. The work product test focuses on the need to protect counsel's observations, thoughts and opinions as the core policy of the protection from disclosure of preparatory work.

NOTES AND QUESTIONS

1. Robert Sharpe argues that it is important to distinguish litigation privilege from solicitor–client privilege. Read again the three important differences he discusses.

The difference is well illustrated by the leading case of *Wheeler v. Le Marchant*, referred to by Sharpe. It concerned an action for specific performance of an agreement by which the defendants were to grant a lease of certain land to the plaintiff. The defendants objected to producing correspondence between their solicitors and an estate agent/surveyor that related to the property that was the subject of the action, but that had come about before the action being contemplated, to enable the solicitors to advise the defendants (as it happened) with regard to another matter. Since the communications were not between a solicitor and client, but between a solicitor and a third party, the solicitor–client privilege was unavailable. Moreover, the litigation privilege was not available—although it was a communication between third parties and their solicitors, the communications were not made in contemplation of this or any other litigation.

Sharpe also notes that the essence of the solicitor–client privilege is the *confidential communication* between the client and solicitor. By contrast the litigation privilege is not based on the confidentiality of a communication—that is, it applies to non-confidential communications. This is well illustrated by the most obvious type of material covered by the litigation privilege—that is, a statement given by a third-party witness to a solicitor. Typically the witness has no intention that the statement given to the solicitor should be confidential. Moreover, as we will see, the litigation privilege is not necessarily limited to material that is communicative in nature.

Despite Sharpe's argument that the solicitor–client and litigation privileges are separate and distinct, analysis of the litigation privilege is often confused by the courts' insistence that there are not two privileges and that the litigation privilege is merely part and parcel of the solicitor–client privilege—for example, see *Hodgkinson v. Simms* (1988), 36 CPC (2d) 24 (BC CA). As to the distinctions between the two privileges, see also Garry D. Watson and Frank Au, "Solicitor–Client Privilege and Litigation Privilege in Civil Litigation" (1998), 77 *Canadian Bar Review* 315.

2. Notwithstanding that the litigation privilege is applied every day in Canada—that is, every time a lawyer or articling student prepares an affidavit of documents—and the privilege is fundamental to our procedural law, clear and articulate statements of the *rationale* for the privilege are rare in Anglo-Canadian case law. It is for this reason that we turn to the landmark US decision in *Hickman v. Taylor*, below, in which the US Supreme Court articulated the rationale for the analogous US "work-product" doctrine.

Hickman v. Taylor
329 US 495 (1947)

MURPHY J: This case presents an important problem under the Federal Rules of Civil Procedure as to the extent to which a party may inquire into oral and written statements of witnesses, or other information secured by an adverse party's counsel in the course of preparation for possible litigation after a claim has arisen. Examination into a person's files and records, including those resulting from the professional activities of an attorney, must be judged with care. It is not without reason that various safeguards have been established to preclude unwarranted excursions into the privacy of a man's work. At the same time, public policy supports reasonable and necessary inquiries. Properly to balance these competing interests is a delicate and difficult task.

On February 7, 1943, the tug *J.M. Taylor* sank while engaged in helping to tow a car float of the Baltimore & Ohio Railroad across the Delaware River at Philadelphia. The accident was apparently unusual in nature, the cause of it still being unknown. Five of the nine crew members were drowned. Three days later the tug owners and the underwriters employed a law firm, of which respondent Fortenbaugh is a member, to defend them against potential suits by representatives of the deceased crew members and to sue the railroad for damages to the tug.

A public hearing was held on March 4, 1943, before the United States Steamboat Inspectors, at which the four survivors were examined. This testimony was recorded and made available to all interested parties. Shortly thereafter, Fortenbaugh privately interviewed the survivors and took statements from them with an eye toward the anticipated litigation; the survivors signed these statements on March 29. Fortenbaugh also interviewed other persons believed to have some information relating to the accident and in some cases he made memoranda of what they told him. At the time when Fortenbaugh secured the statements of the survivors, representatives of two of the deceased crew members had been in communication with him. Ultimately claims were presented by representatives of all five of the deceased; four of the claims, however, were settled without litigation. The fifth claimant, petitioner herein, brought suit in a federal court under the Jones Act on November 26, 1943, naming as defendants the two tug owners, individually and as partners, and the railroad.

One year later, petitioner filed 39 interrogatories directed to the tug owners. The 38th interrogatory read: "State whether any statements of the members of the crews of the tugs *J.M. Taylor* and *Philadelphia* or of any other vessel were taken in connection with the towing of the car float and the sinking of the tug *John M. Taylor*. Attach hereto exact copies of all such statements if in writing, and if oral, set forth in detail the exact provisions of any such oral statements or reports."

Supplemental interrogatories asked whether any oral or written statements, records, reports or other memoranda had been made concerning any matter relative to the towing operation, the sinking of the tug, the salvaging and repair of the tug, and the death of the deceased. If the answer was in the affirmative, the tug owners were then requested to set forth the nature of all such records, reports, statements or other memoranda.

The tug owners, through Fortenbaugh, answered all of the interrogatories except No. 38 and the supplemental ones just described. While admitting that statements of the survivors had been taken, they declined to summarize or set forth the contents. They did so on the ground that such requests called "for privileged matter obtained in the preparation for litigation" and constituted "an attempt to obtain indirectly counsel's private files." It was claimed that answering these requests "would involve practically turning over not only the complete files, but also the telephone records and, almost, the thoughts of counsel." ...

Petitioner has made more than an ordinary request for relevant, non-privileged facts in the possession of his adversaries or their counsel. He has sought discovery as of right of oral and written statements of witnesses whose identity is well known and whose availability to petitioner appears unimpaired. He has sought production of these matters after making the most searching inquiries of his opponents as to the circumstances surrounding the fatal accident, which inquiries were sworn to have been answered to the best of their information and belief. Interrogatories were directed toward all the events prior to, during and subsequent to the sinking of the tug. Full and honest answers to such broad inquiries would necessarily have included all pertinent information gleaned by Fortenbaugh through his interviews with the witnesses. Petitioner makes no suggestion, and we cannot assume, that the tug owners or Fortenbaugh were incomplete or dishonest in the framing of their answers. In addition, petitioner was free to examine the public testimony of the witnesses taken before the United States Steamboat Inspectors. We are thus dealing with an attempt to secure the production of written statements and mental impressions contained in the files and the mind of the attorney Fortenbaugh without any showing of necessity or any indication or claim that denial of such production would unduly prejudice the preparation of petitioner's case or cause him any hardship or injustice. For aught that appears, the essence of what petitioner seeks either has been revealed to him already through the interrogatories or is readily available to him direct from the witnesses for the asking. ...

The District Court, after hearing objections to petitioner's request, commanded Fortenbaugh to produce all written statements of witnesses and to state in substance any facts learned through oral statements of witnesses to him. Fortenbaugh was to submit any memoranda he had made of the oral statements so that the court might determine what portions should be revealed to petitioner. All of this was ordered without any showing by petitioner, or any requirement that he make a proper showing, of the necessity for the production of any of this material or any demonstration that denial of production would cause hardship or injustice. The court simply ordered production on the theory that the facts sought were material and were not privileged as constituting attorney–client communications.

In our opinion, neither Rule 26 nor any other rule dealing with discovery contemplates production under such circumstances. That is not because the subject matter is privileged or irrelevant, as those concepts are used in these rules. [Footnote: The English courts have developed the concept of privilege to include all documents prepared by or for counsel with a view to litigation. "All documents which are called into existence for the purpose—but not necessarily the sole purpose—of assisting the deponent or his legal advisers in any actual or anticipated litigation are privileged from production. ... Thus all proofs, briefs, draft pleadings, etc., are privileged; but not counsel's indorsement on the outside of his brief ... , nor any deposition or notes of evidence given publicly in open Court. ... So are all papers prepared by any agent of the party bona fide for the use of his solicitor for the purposes of the action, whether in fact so used or not. ... Reports by a company's servant, if made in the ordinary course of routine, are not privileged, even though it is desirable that the solicitor should have them and they are subsequently sent to him; but if the solicitor has requested that such documents shall always be prepared for his use and this was one of the reasons why they were prepared, they need not by disclosed." Odgers on Pleading and Practice (12th ed., 1939), at 264.]

Here is simply an attempt, without purported necessity or justification, to secure written statements, private memoranda and personal recollections prepared or formed by an adverse party's counsel in the course of his legal duties. As such, it falls outside the arena of discovery and contravenes the public policy underlying the orderly prosecution and defense of legal claims. Not even the most liberal of discovery theories can justify unwarranted inquiries into the files and the mental impressions of an attorney.

Historically, a lawyer is an officer of the court and is bound to work for the advancement of justice while faithfully protecting the rightful interests of his clients. In performing his various duties, however, it is essential that a lawyer work with a certain degree of privacy free from unnecessary intrusion by opposing parties and their counsel. Proper preparation of a client's case demands that he assemble information, sift what he considers to be the relevant from the irrelevant facts, prepare his legal theories and plan his strategy without undue and needless interference. That is the historical and the necessary way in which lawyers act within the framework of our system of jurisprudence to promote justice and to protect their clients' interests. This work is reflected, of course, in interviews, statements, memoranda, correspondence, briefs, mental impressions, personal beliefs, and countless other tangible and intangible ways—aptly though roughly termed by the Circuit Court of Appeals in this case as the "work product of the lawyer." Were such materials open to opposing counsel on mere demand, much of what is now put down in writing would remain unwritten. An attorney's thoughts, heretofore inviolate, would not be his own. Inefficiency, unfairness and sharp practices would inevitably develop in the giving of legal advice and in the preparation of cases for trial. The effect on the legal profession would be demoralizing. And the interests of the clients and the cause of justice would be poorly served.

We do not mean to say that all written materials obtained or prepared by an adversary's counsel with an eye toward litigation are necessarily free from discovery in all cases. Where relevant and nonprivileged facts remain hidden in an attorney's file and where production of those facts is essential to the preparation of one's case discovery may properly be had. Such written statements and documents might, under certain circumstances, be admissible in evidence or give clues as to the existence or location of relevant facts. Or they might be useful for purposes of impeachment or corroboration. And production might be justified where the witnesses are no longer available or can be reached only with difficulty. Were production of written statements and documents to be precluded under such circumstances, the liberal ideals of the deposition-discovery portions of the Federal Rules of Civil Procedure would be stripped of much of their meaning. But the general policy against invading the privacy of an attorney's course of preparation is so well recognized and so essential to an orderly working of our system of legal procedure that a burden rests on the one who would invade that privacy to establish adequate reasons to justify production through a subpoena or court order. That burden, we believe, is necessarily implicit in the rules as now constituted. ...

But as to oral statements made by witnesses to Fortenbaugh, whether [at present] in the form of his mental impressions or memoranda, we do not believe that any showing of necessity can be made under the circumstances of this case so as to justify production. Under ordinary conditions, forcing an attorney to repeat or write out all that witnesses have told him and to deliver the account to his adversary gives rise to grave dangers of inaccuracy and untrustworthiness. No legitimate purpose is served by such production. The practice forces the attorney to testify as to what he remembers or what he saw fit to write down regarding witnesses' remarks. Such testimony could not qualify as evidence; and to use it for impeachment or corroborative purposes would make the attorney much less an officer of the court and much more an ordinary witness. The standards of the profession would thereby suffer.

Denial of production of this nature does not mean that any material, non-privileged facts can be hidden from the petitioner in this case. He need not be unduly hindered in the preparation of his case, in the discovery of facts or in his anticipation of his opponents' position. Searching interrogatories directed to Fortenbaugh and the tug owners, production of written documents and statements upon a proper showing and direct interviews with the witnesses themselves all serve to reveal the facts in Fortenbaugh's possession to the fullest possible extent consistent with public policy. Petitioner's counsel frankly admits that he wants the oral statements only to help prepare himself to examine witnesses and to make sure that he has overlooked nothing. That is insufficient under the circumstances to permit him an exception to the policy underlying the privacy of Fortenbaugh's professional activities. If there should be a rare situation justifying production of these matters, petitioner's case is not of that type. ...

We therefore affirm the judgment of the Circuit Court of Appeals.

Affirmed.

JACKSON J (concurring): The narrow question in this case concerns only one of thirty-nine interrogatories which defendants and their counsel refused to answer. ...

The interrogatory asked whether statements were taken from the crews of the tugs involved in the accident, or of any other vessel, and demanded "Attach hereto exact copies of all such statements if in writing, and if oral, set forth in detail the exact provisions of any such oral statements or reports." The question is simply whether such a demand is authorized by the rules relating to various aspects of "discovery."

The primary effect of the practice advocated here would be on the legal profession itself. But it too often is overlooked that the lawyer and the law office are indispensible parts of our administration of justice. Law-abiding people can go nowhere else to learn the ever changing and constantly multiplying rules by which they must behave and to obtain redress for their wrongs. The welfare and tone of the legal profession is therefore of prime consequence to society, which would feel the consequences of such a practice as petitioner urges secondarily but certainly. ...

To consider first the most extreme aspect of the requirement in litigation here, we find it calls upon counsel, if he has had any conversations with any of the crews of the vessels in question or of any other, to "set forth in detail the exact provision of any such oral statements or reports." Thus the demand is not for the production of a transcript in existence but calls for the creation of a written statement not in being. But the statement by counsel of what a witness told him is not evidence when written. Plaintiff could not introduce it to prove his case. What, then, is the purpose sought to be served by demanding this of adverse counsel?

Counsel for the petitioner candidly said on argument that he wanted this information to help prepare himself to examine witnesses, to make sure he overlooked nothing. He bases his claim to it in his brief on the view that the Rules were to do away with the old situation where a law suit developed into "a battle of wits between counsel." But a common law trial is and always should be an adversary proceeding. Discovery was hardly intended to enable a learned profession to perform its functions either without wits or on wits borrowed from the adversary.

The real purpose and the probable effect of the practice ordered by the district court would be to put trials on a level even lower than a "battle of wits." I can conceive of no practice more demoralizing to the Bar than to require a lawyer to write out and deliver to his adversary an account of what witnesses have told him. Even if his recollection were perfect, the statement would be his language, permeated with his inferences. Every one who has tried it knows that it is almost impossible so fairly to record the expressions and emphasis of a witness that when he testifies in the environment of the court and under the influence of the leading question there will not be departures in some respects. Whenever the testimony of the witness would differ from the "exact" statement the lawyer had delivered, the lawyer's statement would be whipped out to impeach the witness. Counsel producing his adversary's "inexact" statement could lose nothing by saying, "Here is a contradiction, gentlemen of the jury. I do not know whether it is my adversary or his witness who is not telling the truth, but one is not." Of course, if this practice were adopted, that scene would be repeated over and over again. The lawyer who delivers such statements often would find himself branded a deceiver afraid to take the stand to support his own version of the witness's conversation with him, or else he will have to go on the stand to defend his own credibility—perhaps against that of his chief witness, or possibly even his client.

Every lawyer dislikes to take the witness stand and will do so only for grave reasons. This is partly because it is not his role; he is almost invariably a poor witness. But he steps out of professional character to do it. He regrets it; the profession discourages it. But the practice advocated here is one which would force him to be a witness, not as to what he has seen or done but as to other witnesses' stories, and not because he wants to do so but in self defense.

And what is the lawyer to do who has interviewed one whom be believes to be a biased, lying or hostile witness to get his unfavorable statements and know what to meet? He must record and deliver such statements even though he would not vouch for the credibility of the witness by calling him. Perhaps the other side would not want to call him either, but the attorney is open to the charge of suppressing evidence at the trial if he fails to call such a hostile witness even though he never regarded him as reliable or truthful.

Having been supplied the names of the witnesses, petitioner's lawyer gives no reason why he cannot interview them himself. If an employee-witness refuses to tell his story, he, too, may be examined under the Rules. He may be compelled on discovery, as fully as on the trial, to disclose his version of the facts. But that is his own disclosure; it can be used to impeach him if he contradicts it and such a deposition is not useful to promote an unseemly disagreement between the witness and the counsel in the case. ...

I agree to the affirmance of the judgment of the Circuit Court of Appeals which reversed the district court.

Mr. Justice Frankfurter joins in this opinion.

NOTES AND QUESTIONS

1. What, exactly, is the rationale in *Hickman* for the rule? After recognizing its desirability, the court went on to say, "Where relevant and non-privileged facts remain hidden in an attorney's file and where production of those facts is essential to the preparation of one's case discovery may properly be had." Does the court give a clue to how it would interpret "essential"? Was there something about the facts that militated against such a conclusion being reached in *Hickman*?

2. The court stated elsewhere:

> As additional support for this result, petitioner claims that to prohibit discovery under these circumstances would give a corporate defendant a tremendous advantage in a suit by an individual plaintiff. Thus in a suit by an injured employee against a railroad or in a suit by an insured person against an insurance company the corporate defendant could pull a dark veil of secrecy over all the pertinent facts it can collect after the claim arises merely on the assertion that such facts were gathered by its large staff of attorneys and claim agents. At the same time, the individual plaintiff, who often has direct knowledge of the matter in issue and has no counsel until some time after his claim arises could be compelled to disclose all the intimate details of his case. By endowing with immunity from disclosure all that a lawyer discovers in the course of his duties, it is said, the rights of individual litigants in such cases are drained of vitality and the lawsuit becomes more of a battle of deception than a search for truth.
>
> But framing the problem in terms of assisting individual plaintiffs in their suits against corporate defendants is unsatisfactory.

Do you agree? Is there not something about the particular benefits to larger entities as opposed to individuals that privilege bestows that should be taken into account in determining its ambit?

3. Compare with *Hickman* the following analysis by Jackett P in *Susan Hosiery Limited v. Minister of National Revenue*, [1969] 2 Ex. CR 27, at 33-35, one of the few attempts in Canadian case law to articulate the rationale for the litigation privilege (which President Jackett refers to as the "lawyer's brief" rule).

> As it seems to me, there are really two quite different principles usually referred to as solicitor-and-client privilege, viz:
>
> (a) all communications, verbal or written, of a confidential character, between a client and a legal adviser directly related to the seeking, formulating or giving of legal advice or legal assistance (including the legal adviser's working papers, directly related thereto) are privileged; and

(b) all papers and materials created or obtained specially for the lawyer's "brief" for litigation, whether existing or contemplated, are privileged.

In considering the ambit of these principles, it is well to bear in mind the reasons for them.

In so far as the solicitor–client communications are concerned, the reason for the rule, as I understand it, is that, if a member of the public is to receive the real benefit of legal assistance that the law contemplates that he should, he and his legal adviser must be able to communicate quite freely without the inhibiting influence that would exist if what they said could be used in evidence against him so that bits and pieces of their communications could be taken out of context and used unfairly to his detriment unless their communications were at all times framed so as not only to convey their thoughts to each other but so as not to be capable of being misconstrued by others. The reason for the rule, and the rule itself, extends to the communications for the purpose of getting legal advice, to incidental materials that would tend to reveal such communications, and to the legal advice itself. It is immaterial whether they are verbal or in writing.

Turning to the "lawyer's brief" rule, the reason for the rule is, obviously, that, under our adversary system of litigation, a lawyer's preparation of his client's case must not be inhibited by the possibility that the materials that he prepares can be taken out of his file and presented to the court in a manner other than that contemplated when they were prepared. What would aid in determining the truth when presented in the manner contemplated by the solicitor who directed its preparation might well be used to create a distortion of the truth to the prejudice of the client when presented by someone adverse in interest who did not understand what gave rise to its preparation. If lawyers were entitled to dip into each other's briefs by means of the discovery process, the straightforward preparation of cases for trial would develop into a most unsatisfactory travesty of our present system.

What is important to note about both of these rules is that they do not afford a privilege against the discovery of facts that are or may be relevant to the determination of the facts in issue. What is privileged is the communications or working papers that came into existence by reason of the desire to obtain a legal opinion or legal assistance in the one case and the materials created for the lawyer's brief in the other case. The facts or documents that happen to be reflected in such communications or materials are not privileged from discovery if, otherwise, the party would be bound to give discovery of them. ...

In my view, it follows that, whether we are thinking of a letter to a lawyer for the purpose of obtaining a legal opinion or of a statement of facts in a particular form requested by a lawyer for use in litigation, the letter or statement itself is privileged but the facts contained therein or the documents from which those facts were drawn are not privileged from discovery if, apart from the facts having been reflected in the privileged documents, they would have been subject to discovery. For example, the financial facts of a business would not fall within the privilege merely because they had been set out in a particular way as requested by a solicitor for purposes of litigation, but the statement so prepared would be privileged.

Does this explanation of the litigation privilege differ from that given in *Hickman*? Which is more convincing?

2. Imminence of Litigation and the Purpose for Which a Document Was Prepared

How imminent need the litigation be in order, for example, for a report or a witness statement to be privileged? What is the status of a "dual purpose" document—that is, one made in contemplation of litigation though not solely for the purpose of litigation?

Until 1980, it was generally accepted that privilege could be maintained for a document prepared in anticipation of litigation, even though the document was prepared for a variety of purposes, so long as anticipation of litigation was a "substantial purpose": see, for example, *Blackstone v. Mutual Life Insurance Co. of New York*, [1944] OR 328 (CA). This principle is well illustrated by the case of *Vernon v. North York Board of Education* (1975), 9 OR (2d) 613 (HC). There, the plaintiff sued the defendant for injuries she received from a fall at a public school, claiming that the fall was due to the negligence and breach of duty of the defendant in relation to its obligation to maintain the premises. The vice-principal of the school had made a report of the accident to the school board's area superintendent, with a copy to the defendant's insurance company as required by its policy with the insurer. While acknowledging that it was the general practice of the defendant to make such a report each time an accident occurred and that the report might be used not only by the insurance company for the purpose of determining liability but also by the school board for other purposes, the court upheld privilege. The fact that a report may be used for various purposes was not sufficient for denying privilege, if in fact it was also used for the instruction of counsel.

In 1976, the Australian High Court adopted a requirement that for the privilege to apply, litigation must have been the "sole purpose" for the creation of the document: *Grant v. Downs* (1976), 135 CLR 674. In 1980, the House of Lords in the following case, while declining to go as far as *Grant*, held that anticipation of litigation must be the "dominant purpose" and a substantial purpose would no longer attract the privilege.

Waugh v. British Railways Board
[1980] AC 521 (HL)

LORD WILBERFORCE: My Lords, the appellant's husband was an employee of the British Railways Board. A locomotive which he was driving collided with another so that he was crushed against a tank wagon. He received injuries from which he died. The present action is brought under the Fatal Accident Acts 1846-1959 and this appeal arises out of an interlocutory application for discovery by the board of a report called the "joint inquiry report," made by two officers of the board two days after the accident. This was resisted by the board on the ground of legal professional privilege. The Court of Appeal, Eveleigh LJ and Sir David Cairns, Lord Denning MR dissenting, refused the application.

When an accident occurs on the board's railways, there are three reports which are made: 1. On the day of the accident a brief report of the accident is made to the Railway Inspectorate. 2. Soon afterwards a joint internal report is prepared incorporating statements of witnesses. This too is sent to the Railway Inspectorate. Preparation of this report, it appears, is a matter of practice: it is not required by statute or statutory regulation. 3. In due course a report is made by the Railway Inspectorate for the Department of the Environment.

The document now in question is that numbered 2.

[Lord Wilberforce next examined the evidence concerning the circumstances in which the report was prepared. According to routine practice, the report was prepared for three purposes: (1) to enable the railway to make its report to the Department of the Environment; (2) to assist in establishing the causes of the accident; and (3) "for the purpose of being submitted to the board's solicitor as material upon which he can advise the board upon its legal liability and for the purpose of conducting on behalf of the board any proceedings arising out of such accidents."]

[The following] wording appears at the end of the report:

> For the information of the board's solicitor: This form is to be used by every person reporting an occurrence when litigation by or against the BRB is anticipated. It is to be provided by the person making it to his immediate superior officer and has finally to be sent to the solicitor for the purpose of enabling him to advise the BRB in regard thereto.

Whatever this heading may say, the affidavit makes it clear that the report was prepared for a dual purpose: for what may be called railway operation and safety purposes and for the purpose of obtaining legal advice in anticipation of litigation, the first being more immediate than the second, but both being described as of equal rank or weight. So the question arises whether this is enough to support a claim of privilege, or whether, in order to do so, the second purpose must be the sole purpose, or the dominant or main purpose. If either of the latter is correct, the claim of privilege in this case must fail.

My Lords, before I consider the authorities, I think it desirable to attempt to discern the reason why what is (inaccurately) called legal professional privilege exists. It is sometimes ascribed to the exigencies of the adversary system of litigation under which a litigant is entitled within limits to refuse to disclose the nature of his case until the trial. Thus one side may not ask to see the proofs of the other side's witnesses or the opponent's brief or even know what witnesses will be called: he must wait until the card is played and cannot try to see it in the hand. This argument cannot be denied some validity even where the defendant is a public corporation whose duty it is, so it might be thought, while taking all proper steps to protect its revenues, to place all the facts before the public and to pay proper compensation to those it has injured. A more powerful argument to my mind is that everything should be done in order to encourage anyone who knows the facts to state them fully and candidly—as Sir George Jessel MR said, to bare his breast to his lawyer: *Anderson v. Bank of British Columbia* (1876), 2 Ch. D 644, [at] 699. This he may not do unless he knows that his communication is privileged.

But the preparation of a case for litigation is not the only interest which calls for candour. In accident cases "... the safety of the public may well depend on the candour and completeness of reports made by subordinates whose duty it is to draw attention to defects": *Conway v. Rimmer*, [1968] AC 910, *per* Lord Reid, at p. 941. This however does not by itself justify a claim to privilege since, as Lord Reid continues:

> ... no one has ever suggested that public safety has been endangered by the candour or completeness of such reports having been inhibited by the fact that they may have to be

produced if the interests of the due administration of justice should ever require production at any time.

So one may deduce from this the principle that while privilege may be required in order to induce candour in statements made for the purposes of litigation. It is not required in relation to statements whose purpose is different—for example, to enable a railway to operate safely.

It is clear that the due administration of justice strongly requires disclosure and production of this report: it was contemporary; it contained statements by witnesses on the spot; it would be not merely relevant evidence, but almost certainly the best evidence as to the cause of the accident. If one accepts that this important public interest can be overridden in order that the defendant may properly prepare his case, how close must the connection be between the preparation of the document and the anticipation of litigation? On principle I would think that the purpose of preparing for litigation ought to be either the sole purpose or at least the dominant purpose of it: to carry the protection further into cases where that purpose was secondary or equal with another purpose would seem to be excessive, and unnecessary in the interest of encouraging truthful revelation. At the lowest, such desirability of protection as might exist in such cases is not strong enough to outweigh the need for all relevant documents to be made available. ...

[Lord Wilberforce reviewed the leading English cases, taken to establish that a claim to privilege is made out where "one purpose of preparing the document(s) in question was to enable the defendants' case to be prepared whether or not they were to be used for another substantial purpose." He concluded that "though loyally followed," these cases "do not now enjoy rational acceptance."]

The whole question came to be considered by the High Court of Australia in 1976: *Grant v. Downs*, 135 CLR 674. This case involved reports which had "as one of the material purposes for their preparation" submission to legal advisers in the event of litigation. It was held that privilege could not be claimed. In the joint judgment of Stephen, Mason and Murphy JJ, in which the English cases I have mentioned were discussed and analysed, it was held that "legal professional privilege" must be confined to documents brought into existence for the sole purpose of submission to legal advisers for advice or use in legal proceedings. Jacobs J put the test in the form of a question, at p. 692: "... does the purpose"—in the sense of intention, the intended use—"of supplying the material to the legal adviser account for the existence of the material?" Barwick CJ stated it in terms of "dominant" purpose. This is closely in line with the opinion of Lord Denning MR in the present case that the privilege extends only to material prepared "wholly or mainly for the purpose of preparing [the defendant's] case."

It appears to me that unless the purpose of submission to the legal adviser in view of litigation is at least the dominant purpose for which the relevant document was prepared, the reasons which require privilege to be extended to it cannot apply. On the other hand, to hold that the purpose, as above, must be the sole purpose would, apart from difficulties of proof, in my opinion, be too strict a requirement, and would confine the privilege too narrowly: as to this I agree with Barwick CJ in *Grant v. Downs*, 135 CLR 674, and in substance with Lord Denning MR. While fully respecting the necessity for the Lord

Justices to follow previous decisions of their court, I find myself in the result in agreement with Lord Denning's judgment. I would allow the appeal and order disclosure of the joint report.

LORD SIMON OF GLAISDALE: ... The issue exemplifies a situation which frequently causes difficulties—where the forensic situation is covered by two valid legal principles which point each to a different forensic conclusion. Here, indeed, both principles subserve the same legal end—the administration of justice. The first principle is that the relevant rules of law should be applied to the whole body of relevant evidence—in other words, in principle all relevant evidence should be adduced to the court. The report in question in this appeal undoubtedly contains information relevant to the matters in issue in the litigation here. The first principle thus indicates that it should be disclosed, so that the appellant may make use of it if she wishes.

The second general principle arises out of the adversary (in contradiction to the inquisitorial) system of administration of justice. Society provides an objective code of law and courts where civil contentions can be decided. But it contents itself with so providing a forum and a code (and nowadays some finance for those who could not otherwise get justice). Having done so much, society considers that it can safely leave each party to bring forward the evidence and argument to establish his/her case, detaching the judge from the hurly-burly of contestation and so enabling him to view the rival contentions dispassionately. ... So the adversary system calls for legal representation if it is to operate with such justice as is vouchsafed to humankind.

This system of adversary forensic procedure with legal professional advice and representation demands that communications between lawyer and client should be confidential, since the lawyer is for the purpose of litigation merely the client's alter ego. So too material which is to go into the lawyer's (i.e., the client's) brief or file for litigation. This is the basis for the privilege against disclosure of material collected by or on behalf of a client for the use of his lawyer in pending or anticipated litigation.

Apart from the limited exception of some expert evidence, for which the Rules of the Supreme Court make express provision (Ord. 38, r. 37), a party in civil litigation is not entitled to see the adversary's proofs of what his witnesses will say at the trial; there has been no suggestion that he should be so entitled; and any such development would require the most careful consideration based on widespread consultation. The report in question in this appeal undoubtedly contains material collected by or on behalf of the respondents for the use of their solicitors in anticipated litigation. The second principle thus indicates that the respondents are entitled to claim that it is confidential as between themselves and their solicitors and that they are not bound to disclose it.

Historically, the second principle—that a litigant must bring forward his own evidence to support his case, and cannot call on his adversary to make or aid it—was fundamental to the outlook of the courts of common law. The first principle—that the opponent might be compelled to disclose relevant evidence in his possession—was the doctrine of the Chancery, a court whose conscience would be affronted by forensic success contrary to justice obtained merely through the silent non-cooperation of the defendant (see YB 9 Ed. IV, Trin. 9), and which therefore had some inclination to limited inquisitorial procedures. The conflict between the Chancery and the courts of common law was, here as elsewhere, ultimately resolved by compromise and accommodation.

I can see no intrinsic reason why the one principle rather than the other should prevail in a situation where they are counter-indicative. Neither is absolute: both are subject to numerous exceptions. …

[T]he exception which most nearly touches the issue facing your Lordships was cogently invoked in this very connection by James LJ in *Anderson v. Bank of British Columbia*, 2 Ch. D 644, [at] 656:

> … as you have no right to see your adversary's brief, you have no right to see that which comes into existence merely as the materials for the brief.

The adversary's brief will contain much relevant material; nevertheless, you cannot see it because that would be inconsistent with the adversary forensic process based on legal representation. I would, though, draw attention to the word "merely" in James LJ's dictum.

There is, then, no a priori reason why the one general principle should yield to the other. But in my judgment each party's main contention would virtually result in the total exclusion of the principle relied on by the other. [That relied upon by the defendant] in effect means that reports such as that in the instant case will always be excluded, because it is unlikely that there is not in such circumstances even the subsidiary purpose of informing the legal advisers. On the other hand, to enjoin that privilege can only be claimed if the information of legal advisers is the sole purpose of the report will in effect mean that such reports must always be disclosed, because it is unlikely that in such circumstances there will not be even the subsidiary purpose of ascertaining whether the system of work can be improved. Indeed, in this type of report causation and fault can hardly be kept apart.

Your Lordships will therefore, I apprehend, be seeking some intermediate line which will allow each of the two general principles scope in its proper sphere. Various intermediate formulae as a basis for the privilege have been canvassed in argument before your Lordships, most based on some authority—the obtaining of legal advice was "an appreciable purpose"; "a substantial purpose"; "the substantial purpose"; it was "wholly or mainly" for that purpose; that was its "dominant" purpose; that was its "primary" purpose.

Some of these are in my view too vague. Some give little or no scope to the principle of open litigation with the minimum exclusion of relevant evidence. The one that appeals most to me is "dominant" purpose, as it did to Barwick CJ in *Grant v. Downs*, 135 CLR 674. It allows scope to each of the governing principles. It seems to me less quantitative than "mainly"; and I think it would be easier to apply. …

LORD EDMUND-DAVIES: … Preparation with a view to litigation—pending or anticipated—being … the essential purpose which protects a communication from disclosure in such cases as the present, what in the last resort is the touchstone of the privilege? Is it sufficient that the prospect of litigation be merely one of the several purposes leading to the communication coming into being? And is that sufficient (as Eveleigh LJ in the present case held) despite the fact that there is also "another … and even more important purpose"? Is it enough that the prospect of litigation is a *substantial pur*pose, though there may be others equally substantial? Is an *appreciable* purpose sufficient? Or does it have to be *the main* purpose? Or *one* of its *main* purposes? ...

Ought your Lordships to declare that privilege attaches only to material which (in the words of Lord Denning MR) "comes within the words 'wholly or mainly' for the purpose of litigation"? Or should this House adopt the majority decision of the High Court of Australia in *Grant v. Downs*, 135 CLR 674, that legal professional privilege must be confined to documents brought into existence for the *sole* purpose of submission to legal advisers for advice or for use in legal proceedings? ...

Adopting that approach, I would certainly deny a claim to privilege when litigation was merely one of several purposes of equal or similar importance intended to be served by the material sought to be withheld from disclosure, and a fortiori where it was merely a minor purpose. On the other hand, I consider that it would be going too far to adopt the *"sole* purpose" test applied by the majority in *Grant v. Downs*, which has been adopted in no United Kingdom decision nor, as far as we are aware, elsewhere in the Commonwealth. Its adoption would deny privilege even to material whose outstanding purpose is to serve litigation, simply because another and very minor purpose was also being served. But, inasmuch as the *only* basis of the claim to privilege in such cases as the present one is that the material in question was brought into existence for use in legal proceedings, it is surely right to insist that, before the claim is conceded or upheld, such a purpose must be shown to have played a paramount part. Which phrase or epithet should be selected to designate this is a matter of individual judgment. Lord Denning MR, as we have seen, favoured adoption of the phrase employed in the Law Reform Committee's Sixteenth Report, viz., "material which came into existence ... *wholly or mainly*" for the purpose of litigation (para. 17). "Wholly" I personally would reject for the same reason as I dislike solely," but "mainly" is nearer what I regard as the preferable test. Even so, it lacks the element of clear paramountcy which should, as I think, be the touchstone. After considerable deliberation, I have finally come down in favour of the test propounded by Barwick CJ in *Grant v. Downs*, 135 CLR 674, in the following words, at p. 677:

> Having considered the decisions, the writings and the various aspects of the public
> interest which claim attention, I have come to the conclusion that the court should state
> the relevant principle as follows: a document which was produced or brought into
> existence either with the *dominant* purpose of its author, or of the person or authority
> under whose direction, whether particular or general, it was produced or brought into
> existence, of using it or its contents in order to obtain legal advice or to conduct or aid
> in the conduct of litigation, at the time of its production in reasonable prospect, should
> be privileged and excluded from inspection. (Italics added.)

Dominant purpose, then, in my judgment, should now be declared by this House to be the touchstone. It is less stringent a test than "sole" purpose, for, as Barwick CJ added, 135 CLR 674, [at] 677:

> ... the fact that the person ... had in mind other uses of the document will not preclude
> that document being accorded privilege, if it were produced with the requisite dominant
> purpose.

[Having reviewed the evidence as to the purpose for which the report in question was prepared, His Lordship said that the claims of humanity must surely make the dominant purpose of any report upon an accident (particularly where personal injuries have been sustained) that of discovering what happened and why it happened, so that measures to prevent its recurrence could be discussed and, if possible, devised. And, although Barwick CJ in *Grant v. Downs*, 135 CLR 674, at 677, observed that "the circumstance that the document is a 'routine document' will not be definitive," the "dominant purpose of its production may none the less qualify it for professional privilege."]

The test of dominance will, as I think, be difficult to satisfy when inquiries are instituted and reports produced automatically whenever any mishap occurs, whatever its nature, its gravity, or even its triviality.

My Lords, if, as I hold, *"dominant* purpose" be the right test of privilege from disclosure, it follows that the board's claim to privilege must be disallowed, and the same applies if the *"sole* purpose" test be applied.

[Lords Russell of Killowen and Keith of Kinkel concurred with Lord Wilberforce.]

NOTES AND QUESTIONS

1. *Waugh* and its "dominant purpose" test has now been adopted by all, or virtually all, common law jurisdictions in Canada. Do the following decisions represent appropriate applications of the "dominant purpose" test?

In insurance litigation, adjusters' reports and other documents prepared by them or as a result of their efforts are privileged, because litigation is always a reasonable prospect whenever there is a casualty and hence it is one of the predominant reasons for the creation of the documents: *Sommerville Belkin Industries Ltd. v. Brocklesby Transport* (1985), 5 CPC (2d) 239 (BC SC). In an action on an insurance policy, the court ordered production of adjusters' reports prepared before the insurers' denial of coverage (holding that the dominant purpose for the preparation of these documents was not anticipation of litigation), but refused to order production of similar reports prepared after the insurers' denial of coverage: *Bell v. Pieri* (1985), 12 CCLI 54 (BC SC). In *Turgeon v. Edmonton (City)* (1986), 72 AR 366 (QB), it was held that privilege may be claimed for documents routinely prepared after serious accidents whether or not litigation is being commenced, so long as litigation can be reasonably contemplated. The defendant city had a policy of preparing such reports in the event of a serious accident and it was held that such reports were prepared for the dominant purpose of litigation. Although the fact that the city had a declared policy of requiring employees to prepare reports after accidents to be used in the event of a claim could not itself be determinative of the issue, it was reasonable of the city to contemplate litigation and to instruct its employees accordingly. However, the application of this test to accident reports continues to challenge the courts.

2. Is the *Waugh* test properly applied in the following case? Can the result be justified on other grounds?

Davies v. Harrington
(1980), 115 DLR (3d) 347 (NS CA)

MacDONALD JA: The facts relevant to this appeal are summarized in Chief Justice Cowan's decision as follows [at 200-1]:

On August 19, 1978, a fire occurred on premises of the plaintiff at Kentville, Nova Scotia, and a poultry building owned by the plaintiff was extensively damaged by the fire. The plaintiff's property was insured against fire damage with Kings Mutual Insurance Company, and that company paid an insurance claim filed by the plaintiff. On July 16, 1979, the originating notice (action) in this proceeding was issued on behalf of the plaintiff against the defendant, and the statement of claim alleges that the fire and resulting damage to the poultry building was caused by the negligent operation of the defendant's truck, which was travelling on a public highway adjacent to the premises of the plaintiff, and that, as a result of the negligence of the defendant, the truck left the highway, struck a power pole and thereby set off a chain of electrical events which led to the outbreak of the fire in question.

The proceeding was taken at the instance of the insurance company, in exercise of its rights of subrogation on payment of the plaintiff's insurance claim.

Examinations for discovery were held on January 15, 1980, at which time evidence was given by Earl Leroy Woodman, an adjuster for the insurance company, who gave evidence to the effect that he had retained, on behalf of the insurance company, an electrical engineer named George Baker on August 21, 1978, two days after the fire. Mr. Woodman said that he and George Baker attended at the scene of the fire on August 21, 1978, and that a report was subsequently prepared by George Baker.

The defendant and Co-operative Fire & Casualty Company Limited, the insurers of the defendant's motor vehicle under an automobile insurance policy, state that no demand or claim was made by or on behalf of the plaintiff against the defendant, at any time prior to the filing and service of the originating notice (action) and statement of claim on July 16, 1979. At that time, the premises of the plaintiff had been completely rebuilt, so that no remnants of the fire damage could be seen.

[On oral discovery the general manager of Kings Mutual testified as follows:]

Q. And what was the purpose of engaging Mr. Baker?
A. Well, the only time we engage Mr. Baker is if there's a possibility of subrogation or to take action against another insurance company to recover our loss.
Q. That's the only time when you engage him?
A. Yes.

… Applying the test laid down in *Waugh* it is my view that the dominant purpose for which the report of Mr. Baker was commissioned by the insurance company was to determine whether the fire had an electrical origin. The opinion of Mr. Baker on this point would dictate whether the company sought legal advice as to whether it had a subrogated cause of action against Mr. Harrington. If Mr. Baker's conclusion was completely against the cause of the fire being in any way connected with Harrington's collision with the power pole it is very doubtful whether the company would have forwarded it to their solicitor for advice, there being no practical reason for doing so.

In the result, although I would grant leave to appeal, I would dismiss the appeal with costs to the respondent in any event of the cause [thereby affirming the order below requiring disclosure of the report].

NOTES AND QUESTIONS

1. For a discussion of the *Davies* case and related issues, see Sharpe, "Discovery Privilege and Preliminary Investigative Reports" (1981), 59 *Canadian Bar Review* 830.

2. *Litigation privilege: absolute or qualified?* Recall the following statements of Murphy J in *Hickman v. Taylor*:

> We are thus dealing with an attempt to secure the production of written statements and mental impressions contained in the files and the mind of the attorney Fortenbaugh without any showing of necessity or any indication or claim that denial of such production would unduly prejudice the preparation of petitioner's case or cause him any hardship or injustice. ...
>
> We do not mean to say that all written materials obtained or prepared by an adversary's counsel with an eye toward litigation are necessarily free from discovery in all cases. Where relevant and nonprivileged facts remain hidden in an attorney's file and where production of those facts is essential to the preparation of one's case discovery may properly be had. Such written statements and documents might, under certain circumstances, be admissible in evidence or give clues as to the existence or location of relevant facts. Or they might be useful for purposes of impeachment or corroboration. *And production might be justified where the witnesses are no longer available or can be reached only with difficulty.* (Emphasis added.)

Building on the above statements, the court in *Hickman* established that where "just cause" is shown work-product material is producible—for example, where it cannot be obtained by any other means (because the witness is dead) or only at extraordinary expense (the witness has moved to a distant country). Consequently, the US work-product doctrine is a *qualified* privilege (and, in the final analysis, it is not a rule about whether evidence is discoverable, but how it is to be obtained). By contrast, the commonwealth litigation privilege is stated in absolute, not qualified, terms, and it is no objection to a claim for litigation privilege that the party seeking disclosure cannot obtain the information by any other means. In policy terms which approach, the US or the Commonwealth, makes more sense?

Does the above analysis help to explain what was going on in *Davies*? Commonwealth courts can, if they feel it is justified, achieve the type of result that is possible under the work-product doctrine—that is, disclosure of unique and otherwise unobtainable documents—through manipulation of the dominant-purpose test. In this context recall Lord Wilberforce's statement in *Waugh*:

> It is clear that the due administration of justice strongly requires disclosure and production of this report: it was contemporary; it contained statements by witnesses on

the spot; it would be not merely relevant evidence, but almost certainly the best evidence as to the cause of the accident. If one accepts that this important public interest can be overridden in order that the defendant may properly prepare his case, how close must the connection be between the preparation of the document and the anticipation of litigation? On principle I would think that the purpose of preparing for litigation ought to be either the sole purpose or at least the dominant purpose of it: to carry the protection further into cases where that purpose was secondary or equal with another purpose would seem to be excessive, and unnecessary in the interest of encouraging truthful revelation.

Reconsider the insurance adjuster cases, note 1 following *Waugh*, in the light of this analysis. See also the note below (after the *Yri-York* case) on whether there should be a "good cause" exception to litigation privilege.

3. *Corporate parties and privilege.* The following is an excerpt from *Grant v. Downs* (1976), 135 CLR 674 (Aust. High Ct.), which adopted a "sole" purpose test. The excerpt concentrates on the court's reasons, based on its differentiating between how corporations and other large entities conduct their affairs as opposed to individuals. Is the analysis attractive? How does it relate to the US Supreme Court's observation, on a similar point in *Hickman v. Taylor* and in *Upjohn*, above?

The case involved a claim for the negligent care of the deceased in a psychiatric hospital. The defendant refused to produce certain records on the grounds that one of their purposes was to communicate with legal representatives to solicit advice.

STEPHEN, MASON and MURPHY JJ: There is, we should have thought, much to be said for the view that the existence of the privilege makes it more difficult for the opposing party to test the veracity of the party claiming privilege by removing from the area of documents available for inspection documents which may be inconsistent with that case. To this extent the privilege is an impediment, not an inducement, to frank testimony, and it detracts from the fairness of the trial by denying a party access to relevant documents or at least subjecting him to surprise.

These difficulties are magnified in cases when privilege is claimed by a corporation, whether it be a statutory authority or a company, because the corporation conducts its business through servants, brings into existence voluminous records and institutes systematic standing procedures calling for the preparation of reports and other documents which may serve a variety of purposes, included in which is the submission of documents to a solicitor for the purpose of obtaining legal advice, or for use in existing or anticipated litigation.

With the advent of large corporations, documents necessarily proliferate; the knowledge of servants of the corporation is, in legal theory, the knowledge of the corporation itself but will only become so in fact when communicated to that corporation. It is in the course of converting legal theory into fact that corporations require their servants to furnish to management reports of activities known only, in the first instance, to the servants. Hence, the proliferation of documents.

An individual seeking legal advice cannot be required to disclose the information he communicated to his legal adviser nor the nature of the advice received; nor may the legal adviser disclose it. However, a litigant is, of course, bound to disclose his own knowledge of relevant facts. It would be curious if, because the litigant happens to be a corporation, the rule was for that reason different. Yet it is said that a corporation, necessarily having recourse to documents in the form of reports for the purpose of informing its management of the knowledge of its agents, may claim privilege if one of the purposes of management was to make available such reports to its legal advisers should litigation ensue, the probability or possibility of litigation being anticipated at the time. ...

It is difficult to see why the principle which lies behind legal professional privilege should justify its extension to material obtained by a corporation from its agents with a double purpose. The second purpose, that of arming central management of the corporation with actual knowledge of what its agents have done, is quite unconnected with legal professional privilege; it is but a manifestation of the need of a corporation to acquire in actuality the knowledge that it is always deemed to possess and which lies initially in the minds of its agents. That cannot itself be privileged; quite the contrary. If the party were a natural person or, more accurately, an individual not acting through servants or agents, it would be precisely that knowledge which would be discoverable and the party cannot be better off by being a corporation. The fact that a second purpose may also be being served, a purpose to which the privilege would extend, does not cover with that privilege information which would otherwise be discoverable. ...

All that we have said so far indicates that unless the law confines legal professional privilege to those documents which are brought into existence for the sole purpose of submission to legal advisers for advice or for use in legal proceedings the privilege will travel beyond the underlying rationale to which it is intended to give expression and will confer an advantage and immunity on a corporation which is not enjoyed by the ordinary individual. It is not right that the privilege can attach to documents which, quite apart from the purpose of submission to a solicitor, would have been brought into existence for other purposes in any event, and then without attracting any attendant privilege. It is true that the requirement that documents be brought into existence in anticipation of litigation diminishes to some extent the risk that documents brought into existence for non-privileged purposes will attract the privilege but it certainly does not eliminate that risk. For this and the reasons which we have expressed earlier we consider that the sole purpose test should now be adopted as the criterion of legal professional privilege.

Do you find this reasoning compelling generally for corporate parties? Or is it likely to be suitable only where the corporate party is in a position to frustrate meritorious claim by concealing critical evidence as in this case (and in *Grossman*, above)?

4. Ontario rules 31.06(3)(a) (disclosure of expert opinions on examination for discovery) and 33.04(2) (production of medical reports by a party to be medically examined) refer to expert opinions and reports as not having to be disclosed if they were prepared for contemplated or pending litigation and *"for no other purpose."* Does this suggest that the rule-makers envisaged a "sole purpose" test for the litigation privilege? In general, the language has gone unnoticed by the courts who have regularly applied the "dominant purpose" test: see, however, *Grant v. St. Clair Region Conservation Authority* (1985), 5 CPC (2d) 281 (Ont. Div. Ct.) and *Proctor and Redfern Limited v. Lakehead Region Conservation Authority* (1987), 21 CPC (2d) 163 (Ont. HC).

5. When a claim for privilege succeeds, whether because it has gone unchallenged or because it was upheld, the party can "bury" the evidence. Normally, this is why the privilege is asserted—to suppress unfavourable evidence. However, a party may not use the assertion of privilege to surprise the adversary at trial—by claiming privelege at the discovery stage, but abandoning it at trial and adducing the evidence. See, for example, Ontario rule 30.09. What is the justification for the "impeachment exception" in that rule?

3. "Ingathered" Documents

We have seen that, for litigation privilege to arise, the dominant purpose for the preparation of the document must have been for use in actual or contemplated litigation. Given this, how do we explain cases holding that existing documents (in the hands of third parties) copied for inclusion in a litigation file—"ingathered" documents—attract litigation privilege? Two leading cases so holding are *Hodgkinson v. Simms* (1988), 36 CPC (2d) 24 (BC CA) (where a solicitor exercised knowledge, skill, and industry in collecting photocopies of unprivileged documents from third parties, and the documents become privileged if they were collected for the dominant purpose of advising on or conducting litigation) and *Ottawa-Carleton (Regional Municipality) v. Consumers' Gas Co.* (1990), 74 OR (2D) 637 (Div. Ct.) (where photocopies of public documents—here corporate searches and periodical articles—obtained for the dominant purpose of use in litigation, and the photocopies privileged even though the original documents are not). The following is an extract from the *Consumers' Gas* case:

In *Hodgkinson v. Simms*, supra, McEachern CJBC said at pp. 145-146:

> Considering the purpose for privilege, I see no reason why a collection of copy documents which satisfy all the requirements of *Voth* [*Voth Bros. Construction v. North Vancouver* (1981), 29 BCLR 114, adopting the *Waugh* rule], including literal creation, should not be privileged even though the uncollected originals are not privileged because they do not satisfy the same test.
>
> It is my conclusion that the law has always been, and, in my view, should continue to be, that in circumstances such as these, where a lawyer exercising legal knowledge, skill, judgment and industry has assembled a collection of relevant copy documents for his brief for the purpose of advising on or conducting anticipated or pending litigation he is entitled, indeed required, unless the client consents, to claim privilege for such collection and to refuse production.
>
> I reach this conclusion because of the authorities cited which state the law accurately and authoritatively and because this does no violence to the dominant purpose rule established by *Waugh* and *Voth*, both supra. This conclusion merely extends the application of that rule to copies made for the dominant purpose of litigation. It follows that the copies are privileged if the dominant purpose of their creation as copies satisfies the same test (*Voth*) as would be applied to the original documents of which they are copies. In some cases the copies may be privileged even though the originals are not. ...
>
> Mr. Walsh adds a further argument with which I respectfully agree. He says that what the defendants seek is not just to look at these copy documents but also to

look into counsel's mind to learn what he knows, and what he does not know, and the direction in which he is proceeding in the preparation of his client's case. That, in my view, would be a mischief that should be avoided.

The references by McEachern CJBC, in the passages just quoted, to *Waugh* and *Voth* relate to the rule that has been applied in England and in Canada that for any document, be it an original document or a copy thereof, to be privileged, the dominant purpose for which it was prepared must have been that of submitting it to a solicitor for advice and use in litigation.

It follows that neither an original document nor a copy thereof becomes privileged simply because it gets into the hands of a solicitor. It is only where the original itself was prepared with the necessary dominant purpose or the copy thereof was prepared with the requisite purpose that the original or copy respectively is privileged.

There is no suggestion in any of the cases that an original document, not prepared with the relevant dominant purpose and so not privileged, can become privileged because a copy of such document is prepared and given to a solicitor. In my view, the concern of Craig JA [dissenting] in *Hodgkinson* and expressed in his words already quoted, "I fail to comprehend how original documents which are not privileged ... can become privileged simply because counsel makes photostatic copies of the documents and puts them in his brief" is without foundation.

It was not suggested in *Hodgkinson* nor is it suggested in the case before us that the making of a copy and the giving of it to a solicitor clothes the original document with privilege. What the cases have held is that if the copy has been prepared with the requisite dominant purpose, then the copy, but not the original, is privileged.

The task ... [we are faced with] is often described as the drawing of the proper line between privilege and full disclosure. It might be better described as the duty of the Court to ensure, not just in a particular case, but in the long term and for cases generally, that there be the maximum disclosure that our adversarial system of litigation allows.

I have little doubt if one looks no further than this immediate case, that production of the documents in question would save the defendants enormous expense in preparing their cases, would tend to focus the attention of the defendants and their solicitors on the real issues in the case, would decrease the time needed to prepare for pre-trial and trial and might even increase the chances of settlement. These prospects make it very tempting in a case of this kind to do what is expedient and order production of the documents in question.

In my view, however, any benefit that might flow to the parties and the Court in this case by ordering such production would be gained at the expense of serious interference with our adversarial system of justice and would reduce the likelihood of full and early disclosure in future cases.

The adversarial system is based on the assumption that if each side presents its case in the strongest light the Court will be best able to determine the truth. Counsel must be free to make the fullest investigation and research without risking disclosure of his opinions, strategies and conclusions to opposing counsel. The invasion of the privacy of counsel's trial preparation might well lead to counsel postponing research and other preparation until the eve of or during the trial, so as to avoid early disclosure of harmful information. This result would be counterproductive to the present goal that early and thorough investigation by counsel will encourage an early settlement of the case. Indeed, if counsel knows he must turn over to the other side the fruits of his work, he may be tempted to forego conscientiously investigating his own case in the hope he will obtain disclosure of the research, investigations and thought processes compiled in the trial brief of opposing counsel. See Kevin M. Claremont, "Surveying Work Product" (1983) 68 Cornell LR 760 at pp. 784-788.

I agree in particular with the author's words at p. 788:

> Serving justice by ordering discovery in one case may ultimately hinder it by discouraging attorney preparation in later cases.

In my view, the reasons for maintaining the privilege of a solicitor's trial brief are compelling, and the documents here in question ought to be exempt from production.

I recognize, of course, that through amendments to the Rules some of the solicitor/client privilege that once existed (including some of the privilege that at one time attached to the solicitor's brief) has been removed. For example, names and addresses of witnesses must now be disclosed. The fact only a portion of such privilege has been taken away by the Rules confirms, I believe, that the balance of the privilege is required to preserve the integrity of the adversarial system.

NOTES AND QUESTIONS

1. See also *Ferber v. Gore Mutual Insurance Co.* (1991), 2 WDCP (2d) 565 (Ont. Master) (a fire insurance case, where the defendant's adjuster obtained a memorandum from a police force summarizing evidence of witnesses, and the court held that the document was privileged on the basis of the decision in *Ottawa-Carleton*).

2. *Hunt v. T & N plc* (1993), 15 CPC (3d) 134 (BC CA) is another case involving a claim for litigation privilege for copies of documents "ingathered" by counsel for the purpose of using the copies of documents in pending litigation. *Hunt* involved asbestos litigation, conducted for the plaintiffs by the BC law firm of Ladner, Downs, against a number of asbestos manufacturers who were also defendants in similar US litigation. The South Carolina law firm of Ness, Motley had, since the mid-1970s, been heavily engaged in prosecuting asbestos damage actions. In 1987, that firm was retained by the BC Workers' Compensation Board to prosecute subrogated personal injury accidents in US courts. In the BC litigation, Ness, Motley was working closely with Ladner, Downs to give the BC law firm the benefit of the South Carolina firm's experience in the area. In the course of conducting US asbestos litigation, Ness, Motley assembled copies of a great many documents, including documents from the companies who were now defendants in the BC action. On the basis of the copies of documents they obtained, Ness, Motley had assembled "liability briefs" with respect to various defendants in the US asbestos litigation that included copies of documents obtained from the present defendants.

In the BC litigation, the defendants sought production from the plaintiff of (1) the liability briefs prepared by Ness, Motley, and (2) transcripts of depositions produced in the US asbestos litigation in which Ness, Motley was involved. Ladner, Downs resisted an order for production, relying on the litigation privilege set out in *Hodgkinson v.*

Simms, where McEachern CJBC said that "where a lawyer exercising legal knowledge, skill, judgment and industry has assembled a collection of relevant copy documents for his brief" for litigation purposes, the documents were privileged from production.

On the hearing at first instance, the defendants argued that Ladner, Downs could not show a sufficient degree of skill or selection to satisfy the onus to support the claim for privilege. The judge said he assumed that the degree of skill applied to defining that part of the liability briefs requested by Ladner, Downs "was minimal" and that the BC law firm relied on the US firm to whom Ladner, Downs might have given only very general instructions to select the documents. He then went on to say that while great emphasis was placed on the element of the skill for selection, he was not sure that it was essential to the privilege. He held that the only essential element of the privilege "may be that the decision to obtain the copies was made by a legal advisor for the purposes of litigation in which that advisor was acting," relying on the decision in *Watson v. Cammell Laird & Co.*, [1959] 1 WLR 702 (CA). In the result, the judge dismissed the application for production on the basis that the copies obtained from Ness, Motley were made by the plaintiff's solicitors for the purpose of litigation in which they were acting.

The defendants appealed and the Court of Appeal upheld the claim for privilege. The court stated that the judge at first instance did not hold that on a claim for solicitor's brief privilege it was not necessary to show that some degree of knowledge, skill, judgment, and industry had been exercised. The evidence indicated, the court asserted, that the plaintiff's solicitor, in assembling a collection of relevant copy documents for his brief in this case, must have brought to the task a considerable degree of legal knowledge, skill, judgment, and industry to accomplish that task. (On this point the reasoning in the case is somewhat confusing. It appears that the defendants were seeking the copies of Ness, Motley's liability briefs, which, it was alleged, had been handed over to Ladner, Downs at the latter's request or copied by them. If this is what in fact had occurred, it hardly seems that the request involved Ladner, Downs sifting through thousands of documents and making a selection therefrom, as was implied by the Court of Appeal.)

The Court of Appeal also rejected an argument that the defendants were entitled to production of at least those documents that were, in fact, copies of original documents produced by the defendants in the US litigation. The court stated that the fact that the original documents that had been copied into Ladner, Downs' solicitor's brief were not privileged did not mean that the copies were not privileged. If privilege did not attach to such copies, it would be possible to compel a party to reveal the contents of the solicitor's brief and to permit the adversary to look into counsel's mind to learn what he or she did or did not know and the direction in which he or she was proceeding in the preparation of the client's case. In fact, the defendants were seeking to determine which of the documents copied by Ness, Motley had been included in Ladner, Downs solicitor's brief.

As the Court of Appeal noted in *Hunt*, many have difficulty understanding how the copy of a document can be privileged by inclusion in a solicitor's brief when the original of that document is not privileged. Do you understand?

Does the decision in *Hunt* seem sound? Is it clear that the defendants were seeking to discover Ladner, Downs's strategy and thinking about the case—that is, to examine Ladner, Downs's solicitor's brief? If so, does that justify a finding of privilege? Is it relevant whether Ladner, Downs exercised any skill or judgment in selecting which Ness, Motley documents to copy?

What would be the result if rather than seeking production of these documents from the plaintiff, the defendants sought production of the documents directly from Ness, Motley via production from a third party under a provision such as Ontario rule 30.10?

These cases suggest that the verbal formula typically used to determine whether the litigation privilege is available ("was the document prepared for the dominant purpose of litigation") does not adequately deal with the ingathering of documents. In such cases the original document was not prepared for litigation; rather, the *making or obtaining of the copy* must be for the purpose of litigation. If the copies are ingathered or made for this dominant purpose, then this appears to be sufficient to attract the litigation or solicitor's brief privilege.

3. *More on "ingathered" documents.* In *Ventouris v. Mountain*, [1990] 3 All ER 157, the English Queen's Bench Division took the matter one step further. The court held that privilege attached to the *originals* of documents that had not previously been in the possession of a party to actual or contemplated litigation and that had not come into existence for the purpose of that litigation, but that had been obtained by the solicitor of that party for that purpose. Based on English cases, the court considered it was settled law that privilege attaches to *copies* taken by solicitors of documents held by third parties, where the copying is done for the purpose of actual or contemplated litigation. The court saw no reason to distinguish between copying documents for the purpose of litigation or "ingathering" the originals. On appeal in *Ventouris* ([1991] 1 WLR 619), the Court of Appeal reversed the decision at first instance. Bingham LJ stated: "I can see no reason in principle why a pre-existing document obtained by a solicitor for the purpose of litigation should be privileged from production and inspection. ... I find nothing in anything of the cases which suggests, let alone justifies, such a result. Such a rule would in my view pose a threat to the administration of justice." In response to the statement by the judge at first instance that disclosure would be calculated to diminish or destroy the confidential relationship between solicitor and client, Bingham LJ stated: "I do not ... think it would, any more than if these pre-existing documents had been in the [party's] possession from the beginning, in which case they would admittedly have to be produced." In arriving at its decision the Court of Appeal was undoubtedly influenced by the "dominant purpose" test laid down in *Waugh v. British Railways Board* and concluded that in deciding whether a document should be afforded litigation privilege, the court must look at the purpose for which it was *brought into existence*, rather than look at the purpose for which a document *was obtained*.

In coming to its judgment the court seriously questioned the case law holding that photocopies of unprivileged originals for the purposes of litigation make the copies of the documents privileged. The court also quoted with approval Lord Denning's statements in *Buttes Gas and Oil Co. v. Hammer (No. 3)*, [1981] QB 223:

> But, if the original is not privileged, a copy of it also is not privileged—even though it was made by a solicitor for the purposes of litigation. ... There are some cases which appear to give a privilege to copies in their own account, even when the originals are not privileged ... but those cases are suspect. They were adversely commented on in the Sixteenth Report of the Law Reform Committee on Privilege in Civil Proceedings (1967) *(Cmnd. 3472).*

On these issues, whose views are correct? If copies or "ingathered" originals of unprivileged documents are not privileged, how do we explain this in terms of the rationale underlying the litigation privilege?

4. Do the cases supporting privilege for "ingathered" documents go too far or are they, on close analysis, perfectly consistent with the *Hickman* rationale? In any event, is the result bizarre—that is, pre-litigation documents in the possession of a client are unprivileged and the very heart of documentary productions; on the other hand, pre-litigation documents in the hands of third parties, but obtained by the solicitor for the purposes of litigation, are privileged whether they be the originals or photocopies?

Does *Ventouris* mean that all a solicitor has to do in order to suppress evidence is to "ingather" the originals of any damaging documents in the hands of third parties? The court in *Ventouris* dealt with this objection as follows:

> It might be suggested that, if the privilege extends to original documents (as opposed to copies) obtained by solicitors for the purposes of actual or contemplated litigation, a ready means presents itself for obtaining and then suppressing material adverse evidence. This is not so. Solicitors who obtained documents for the purposes of suppressing them would not be acting in the course of giving necessary legal advice and assistance, but in breach of their duties as officers of the court. Thus no privilege would attach to such documents. Quite apart from this, the source or maker of the document is likely to remain available; and, even if the original owner of the document has given up to the party in question all rights to it, there would be, as I see it, nothing to prevent that person from revealing its contents or indeed what he had done with the document.

Is the court's argument satisfactory?

4. Other Aspects of the Scope of the Privilege

Yri-York Limited v. Commercial Union Assurance Co.
(1987), 70 CPC (2d) 118 (Ont. HC)

CALLAGHAN ACJHC (orally): This is an appeal by the plaintiff from the order of Master Sandler dated March 25, 1987, as a result of which the plaintiff was directed to produce certain statements taken from prospective witnesses in relation to this litigation.

The statements in issue were obtained on the following dates: December 22, 1982, statement from Len Gullins; January 4, 1983, statement from Peter Newberry; May 5, 1983, statements from Frank Power and Brian Buckley; November 9, 1983, statement from Duncan Shearer; May 12, 1983, memorandum from Hazel Carr; and mid-1983, memorandum from John Weber.

On April 18, 1983, the plaintiff filed a proof of loss with the defendant in relation to its claim under a fidelity bond and on October 5 of that year the defendant denied liability.

The statements from Power, Buckley and Shearer were prepared by one Thomas Andrews, a solicitor retained by the plaintiff. The statement of Gullins was a memorandum of an interview prepared by a representative of the plaintiff and forwarded to Mr. Andrews. The memoranda from Carr and Weber were prepared by the witnesses themselves and forwarded to the said solicitor. For the purposes of these proceedings, the statement of Shearer was not in issue as it had been prepared and provided after the denial of liability by the defendant.

In arriving at his decision on this matter, the learned Master stated:

> The plaintiff here must persuade me that these statements were prepared for the dominant purpose of litigation at a time when there was a reasonable expectation or contemplation of litigation and this expectation must be more than a mere possibility and the expectation must be based on an objective test and not a subjective one.
>
> Here, there was nothing emanating from the insurer either by word or deed that would lead the plaintiff or its advisers to the conclusion that litigation was reasonably to be expected before the plaintiff's claim was rejected in October/'83 and this being a fidelity claim, the plaintiff had to prepare a proof of loss and had to be in a position thereafter to negotiate with the insurer to answer queries in order to try and adjust the loss without litigation.

Later on in his reasons, the Master held that there was nothing by way of objective fact from which it was fair to infer the existence of a reasonable anticipation of litigation earlier than October 1983. That, of course, was the date the defendant denied liability.

On the application before the Master, the solicitor for the plaintiff, Mr. Andrews, filed an affidavit which provided in part as follows:

> 10. The purpose of obtaining the statements from these witnesses was primarily in contemplation of litigation. This case involves an insurance claim under a Fidelity Bond. My firm, Borden & Elliot, was retained in September of 1982 several months before the proof of loss was filed in April of 1983 in order to provide legal advise on what appeared to be an exceedingly complex claim which was not at all certain of being immediately accepted and paid by the defendant. From the very beginning it was my opinion that it was very likely this insurance claim would end in litigation. Consequently, Borden & Elliot's advice to our client was not to merely submit an insurance claim but begin collecting evidence from witnesses which would be used in the litigation we fully anticipated. All but two of the disputed documents were prepared after the proof of loss was submitted and the information we obtained from Mr. Newberry in January, 1983 and Mr. Guilins in December, 1982 was of little assistance in preparing our proof of loss.
>
> 11. The reason we anticipated litigation was the nature of the claim in the action. It was not a simple case of embezzlement. Up to the present time there is no evidence that the dishonest employees directly benefited from their acts, other than keeping their jobs. The claim is based on these employees destroying documents and creating erroneous documents which caused a loss to the plaintiff. These employees and the defendant deny any relevant documents were destroyed, and while agreeing the erroneous documents were created, assert that they caused no loss to the plaintiff. I was aware of these defences to our claim from the outset, but fully anticipated that litigation would occur as our instructions from our client were to proceed to litigation if, as expected, the claim was denied.

This affidavit was not cross-examined upon nor was any material filed in contradiction thereto. Mrs. Corey, in a very able argument to me, indicated that I could accept this affidavit as a factual statement and the defendant did not dispute it. The facts relied upon by the plaintiff in the disputed documents were revealed on discovery.

It is clear from the reasons of the Master that, in his opinion, the affidavit of Mr. Andrews simply expressed a fear that litigation was a mere possibility and was, accordingly, insufficient to establish the dominant purpose as required pursuant to that test in these circumstances.

The dominant purpose test, of course, arose from the English case of *Waugh v. British Railways Bd.*, [1980] AC 521, [1979] 2 All ER 1169. ...

It is clear from that decision that in order not to be subject to production, the documents in issue must have been prepared with a view to litigation, which itself must be in reasonable expectation.

The policy behind the rule, as it applies in this context, is clear. Lawyers are not entitled to rely on the preparations of the other side for trial. ...

In this case, counsel for the plaintiff was of the opinion from the outset that the plaintiff's claim would end in litigation. But the matter goes further than that. According to the affidavit of Mr. Andrews, counsel for the plaintiff advised the plaintiff not only to submit its claim to the insurer, the defendant herein, but to begin collecting evidence from witnesses which would be used in the litigation that he fully anticipated. While some Courts have held that such advice constitutes pure speculation, it must be noted that the advice given in the instant case was that given in the context of a claim which was more complex than usual and upon which litigation was, from the inception of the solicitor–client relationship, *bona fide* predictable.

In this case, the plaintiff alleges that Power and Buckley, the third parties, herein, who were its employees at one point in time, destroyed documents and created erroneous documents which caused the loss in issue to the plaintiff. The third parties deny that any such documents were destroyed, but they agree that they did create erroneous documents, and assert, however, that such documents cause no loss to the plaintiff. It can be seen, from these facts, that the claim herein is not the normal embezzlement claim made in respect of a fidelity bond. Nor was the advice given thereon "pure speculation."

If the order of the Master is permitted to stand, the documents prepared by the counsel for the plaintiff in anticipation of this litigation are available to the defendant because, according to the Master's reasoning, they were prepared prior to the denial of October 5, 1983.

In my view, whether the standard is objective or subjective, in relation to the application of the dominant purpose test, the affidavit of Mr. Andrews establishes that the documents were prepared in anticipation of the litigation and, in the absence of any other evidence to the contrary, they should be privileged. In result, therefore, I conclude that the Master erred in the manner in which he applied the dominant purpose test in the circumstances of this case when the only uncontradicted evidence before him established that the documents in issue were prepared in contemplation of litigation. Accordingly, the appeal will be allowed, and the order of the Master set aside.

The plaintiff will have its costs of this application and those incurred before the Master.

Appeal allowed.

NOTES AND QUESTIONS

1. In comparison with the cases we have looked at earlier, does *Yri-York* suggest that the courts treat witness statements and investigative reports differently? Is there any policy reason for treating such statements and reports differently?

2. *Disclosure of facts obtained from a privileged source.* The solicitor–client privilege protects communications and their contents, but on examination for discovery a party cannot refuse to answer a question—for example, how fast were you travelling at the time of the collision?—simply on the ground that she communicated that information to her solicitor. She may not be asked what she told her solicitor, but she cannot claim privilege for facts just because she has related them to her solicitor.

A document covered by litigation privilege does not have to be disclosed as part of documentary discovery. But can a party examined for discovery refuse to disclose relevant information on the ground that the only source of the information sought is the privileged document? No, the courts have held. For example, in *April Investments Limited v. Menat Constructions Limited* (1975), 11 OR (2d) 364 (HC), the plaintiff claimed that the walls of a building on its land had been undermined as a result of the defendant's negligence. The defendant's engineer had inspected the plaintiff's property and provided the defendant with an inspection report. That the engineer's report was a privileged document was not disputed; the defendant objected that it could not be examined on discovery about facts that the defendant knew as a result of the inspection. The court disagreed: "I have no intent to put the privilege attaching to the engineering report to flight but there is a need to preserve the purpose of an examination for discovery. I think there is a distinction between disclosure of privileged information and divulging the facts which are relied upon though the facts may be contained in a privileged document. The tendency of the courts is not to circumscribe the avenues of discovery but to widen them." The court required disclosure with respect to material facts even though they might have come from a privileged document. But, the court added, "nothing in this opinion gives countenance to the view that the defendant must disclose the privileged information in the engineering report." What did the court mean?

On this issue the rule makers have now gone further than court decisions. Would the situation in *April Investments* be addressed differently under the present Ontario rule 31.06? The rule provides:

Expert Opinions

31.06(3) A party may on an examination for discovery obtain disclosure of the findings, opinions and conclusions of an expert engaged by or on behalf of the party being examined that relate to a matter in issue in the action and of the expert's name and address, but the party being examined need not disclose the information, or the name and address of the expert where,

(a) the findings, opinions and conclusions of the expert relating to any matter in issue in the action were made or formed in preparation for contemplated or pending litigation and for no other purpose; and

(b) the party being examined undertakes not to call the expert as a witness at the trial.

3. *Names of witnesses and their evidence.* Changing the law as it existed before 1985, Ontario rule 31.06 provides that a party may not refuse to answer a question on the ground that the information sought is evidence (rule 31.06(1)) and, further, requires that the names and addresses for witnesses must be disclosed (rule 31.06(2)). In combination, do these two sub-rules require parties, on examination for discovery, to give a summary of the evidence that a witness is expected to give? Several cases have held that a party is so required; *Dionisopoulos v. Provias* (1990), 71 OR (2d) 647 (HC); *Blackmore v. SlotAll Limited* (1985), 18 CPC (2d) 181 (Ont. HC), leave to appeal refused 21 CPC (2d) xlvii; and *Leerentoveld v. McCulloch* (1985), 4 CPC (2d) 26 (Ont. Master). However, there is also case law to the contrary: *Wyse v. Ontario Hydro* (1987), 21 CPC (2d) 275 (Ont. Master), and *Williams v. David Brown Gear Industries Inc.* (1986), 14 CPC (2d) 227 (Ont. HC).

Can a requirement that a party provide a summary of the evidence that witnesses will give be reconciled with the rationale underlying the litigation privilege? What did the US Supreme Court say on this issue in *Hickman v. Taylor*? Is a different conclusion on this issue justified, at least in those provinces that have rejected the US approach of permitting unlimited examination for discovery of non-parties? On this issue consider carefully the language of Ontario rule 31.10 (regulating the discovery of non-parties with leave), which prohibits the court from making such an order unless it is satisfied, *inter alia*, that "the moving party has been unable to obtain the information from other persons whom the moving party is entitled to examine for discovery, or from the person he or she seeks to examine." Recall that on close analysis *Hickman v. Taylor* is really a decision not about *whether* you may obtain information but *how* you should obtain it.

4. *Should there be a "good cause" exception to litigation privilege?* Garry D. Watson and Frank Au, "Solicitor–Client Privilege and Litigation Privilege in Civil Litigation" (1998), 77 *Canadian Bar Review* 315, describe the state of litigation privilege in the following terms (footnotes omitted):

> [I]n comparison with solicitor–client privilege, litigation privilege is "truncated." This is so in several ways.
>
> First, and most important, the general principle is that relevant facts contained in a document protected by *litigation privilege* (although not the document itself) are subject to disclosure on examination for discovery, i.e. a party examined for discovery may not refuse to disclose material facts on the ground that the only source of her knowledge of such facts is a document covered by litigation privilege. By contrast, the content of *solicitor–client* communications (e.g. the substance of legal advice received from a lawyer) is not required to be divulged as a rule. [Footnote: But disclosure may be required where solicitor–client privilege is held to have been waived.]
>
> Second, in the case of litigation privilege the courts and rules committees have felt a greater freedom to qualify or "truncate" the privilege for the purpose of maintaining what is perceived to be a reasonable balance between pretrial disclosure and privilege, or on the grounds of fairness. For example, the names and addresses of witnesses are now discoverable under Ontario Rule 31.06(2); and a party examined for discovery may not refuse to answer any questions on the ground that the information sought is "evidence" (Ontario Rule 31. 06(1)). In addition, the Ontario case law now holds that a party may be required to provide a summary of the evidence that a witness is expected to give. Likewise, Ontario Rule 31.06(3) requires the disclosure at examination for

discovery of expert *opinions* unless a party undertakes not to call the expert as a witness at trial (the production of *reports* of trial experts is governed by Ontario Rule 53.03(1)). Also Ontario Rules 33.04 and 33.06 (re court ordered medical examinations) require the production of medical reports formerly covered by the litigation privilege.

This erosion of litigation privilege has been accompanied by the Canadian adoption of the dominant purpose rule, enunciated by the House of Lords in *Waugh v. British Railways Board*, imposing a more onerous test to be met before communications will attract litigation privilege. ...

Since the *Waugh* ruling, Canadian courts have adopted both the dominant purpose test and its underlying rationale. As a result, accident reports which "over a decade ago would not have been disclosed are now routinely ordered to be produced unless the dominant purpose rule with respect to such documents can be satisfied."

The combined operation of the dominant purpose test and the "truncation" of litigation privilege described earlier has circumscribed the privilege within a narrower scope. Moreover, this curtailment has proceeded without any clearly articulated principle, other than fairness or the often vaguely expressed purpose of maintaining a reasonable balance between pretrial disclosure and privilege. By contrast the analogous US "work product doctrine" has been viewed and expressed from its inception, not as a privilege at all but as a *qualified immunity from discovery*. On close analysis the US doctrine is not concerned with *whether* certain information is discoverable, but with *how* it is to be obtained. The court in *Hickman* was concerned that discovery might be abused as a means of conducting trials "on wits borrowed from the adversary," and that parties would not prepare vigorously for fear of having to turn their preparation over to the opponent, with the result that the adversary system would break down. In *Hickman* disclosure of witness statements was refused since there was no "showing of necessity" in that case for the information sought; the party seeking disclosure was free to depose the witnesses under US practice, and that is what the court required the party to do. The court stated, however, that

> [w]here relevant and non-privileged facts remain hidden in an attorney's
> file and where production of those facts is essential to the preparation of
> one's case, discovery may properly be had ... And production might be
> justified where the witnesses are no longer available or can be reached
> only with difficulty.

Under the US doctrine upon such a showing of good cause production may be ordered of virtually any information other than the mental impressions (strategic thinking) of the opposing lawyer.

This raises the question of whether Canadian courts should follow the US lead and openly exercise a discretion to overrule a claim of litigation privilege whenever "good cause" exists. The case law in Ontario, in at least one context, has actually moved beyond the US position by requiring that a summary of witness evidence be provided to the opposite party on examination for discovery, *even without* the showing of good cause. For reasons of economy (i.e. to avoid the expense associated with examining non-parties) the Ontario Rules of Civil Procedure require, as one of the prerequisites to obtaining leave to examine a non-party, that a party seek to obtain from its opponent the evidence of relevant non-parties. Consequently, while the expectation of due diligence operates to protect witness statements from discovery in the United States, the same consideration may not support the protection of witness statements in Ontario. Indeed, if an Ontario court were to rule on the facts of *Hickman* today, the claim of privilege in regard to witness statements would likely be denied.

While the truncation of litigation privilege has already gone far, it may be that litigation privilege should, in other contexts, be qualified when "good cause" (as it is known in the United States) exists, i.e. where a "party is unable without undue hardship to obtain the substantial equivalent of the materials by other means." In this respect, the Nova Scotia case of *Davies v. Harrington* is illustrative. In *Davies*, a fire caused extensive damage to the plaintiff's premises. The insurer of the property retained an engineer to investigate the cause of the fire, and a report was prepared shortly afterwards. The premises was subsequently rebuilt. When a subrogated action was commenced against the defendant (alleging negligent operation of a truck which collided with a power pole, causing the fire in question) nearly a year after the incident, "no remnants of the fire damage could be seen" any longer. The Nova Scotia Court of Appeal held that the engineer's report was not privileged from production, because it was not prepared for the dominant purpose of litigation. As Sharpe observes, this application of the dominant purpose test is open to question, since the evidence suggests that "apart from the prospect of a lawsuit, there was no other reason for obtaining the report." Nonetheless, as Sharpe points out,

> [t]he advantage of production to foster a fair trial is obvious. As the building had been reconstructed prior to the commencement of the action, the defendant had no way of obtaining information he would need to make out a defence. If refused production, he would have to wait until trial, when developing an exculpatory explanation for the fire would be difficult if not impossible.

The *Davies* ruling, and numerous other cases, illustrate how the dominant purpose test can be and is being manipulated to effectively "qualify" litigation privilege, where successful assertion of the privilege would lead to a result perceived to be unjust.

Hence it can be argued that in practice if not in theory the "good cause" exception to litigation privilege does already exist. This being so, a strong case can be made that the courts should exercise their discretionary power more openly. Instead of "regulating" litigation privilege through manipulating the language of "dominant purpose" and "anticipation of litigation," it is preferable that the "good cause" exception be articulated (i.e. where "a party is unable without undue hardship to obtain the substantial equivalent of the materials by other means") and the interests meant to be protected (i.e. truth-finding and trial fairness) be made explicit. Incidentally, this is roughly what the (now almost forgotten) *Report on Evidence* by the Law Reform Commission of Canada recommended. [Footnote: Law Reform Commission of Canada, *Report on Evidence* (Ottawa: Minister of Supply and Services Canada, 1977) at 31, where s. 42 (2) of the proposed Evidence Code reads:

> A person has a privilege against disclosure of information obtained or work produced in contemplation of litigation by him or his lawyer or a

person employed to assist the lawyer, unless, in the case of information, *it is not reasonably available from another source* and its probative value substantially outweighs the disadvantages that would be caused by its disclosure. [Emphasis added.]]

5. *Expert reports and opinions.* Evidence of experts is an increasingly important aspect of civil litigation. Even a "routine" personal injury action may involve complex medical evidence about the nature and prognosis of the plaintiff's injury and condition, evidence respecting the impact of the injury on the plaintiff in the future based on actuarial expertise, or engineering evidence about allegedly defective parts of a motor vehicle. The rules governing the admissibility and use of such evidence are dealt with in courses in evidence. From the procedural perspective, however, such reports present certain issues. In particular, preparations for trial or even settlement discussions in cases involving expert evidence give rise to particular difficulties for the lawyer. He or she must become conversant in the language of the expert and must be able to present the evidence of experts in a manner that will be understood by a judge or jury. The lawyer must also be able to deal with the opponent's expert evidence in a critical way so that its full impact can be assessed and the opposing expert effectively cross-examined. Expert reports are almost always prepared after litigation is contemplated and with the sole or dominant purpose of assisting the lawyer in advising the client and preparing for trial. Thus, such reports are privileged in the absence of any specific rule or statutory exception. Until recently the evidence of the expert did not have to be disclosed and could be sprung at trial where it would be likely to catch the other side by surprise (see below for the modern-day requirements). Moreover, privilege permits parties to shop for opinions in the sense that they need not fear that an unfavourable report will have to be disclosed and they can therefore, quite legitimately, suppress unfavourable expert reports and use only those that tend to support their case.

Is the traditional practice of according such reports privilege conducive to the orderly preparation of a case? What would be the consequences of requiring parties to produce all reports obtained before trial?

Most jurisdictions now require "eve of trial" production of an expert report if a party intends to call the expert as a witness at trial: see, for example, Ontario rule 53.03(1). The converse of such rules is that if the expert is not being called as a witness and the report is otherwise privileged, it need not be produced: see Ontario rule 31.06(3), reproduced above.

Hence a critical determinant for requiring disclosure today is whether the party intends to use the expert as a witness at trial. Is this distinction sound? Should parties be required to disclose all experts' reports, whether or not they intend to call the expert to testify at trial?

6. *Reforming the role of expert witnesses.* In Great Britain, Lord Woolf was recently given the task of recommending reforms of the civil justice system. In his interim and final reports, entitled *Access to Justice* (London: HMSO 1995 and 1996), he was critical of the role being played by expert witnesses. The following extract (from Garry Watson, "From an Adversarial to a Managed System of Litigation: A Comparative Critique of Lord Woolf's Interim Report," in Roger Smith, ed., *Achieving Civil Justice: Appropriate Dispute Resolution for the 1990s* (London: Legal Action Group, 1996), 63) sets forth and appraises Woolf's comments and proposals.

Unhappy with the role currently being played by expert witnesses, Woolf proposes a range of reforms. The calling of expert witnesses is to be subject to the complete control of the court ("all power to the judiciary," again), the court is to have discretion, with or without the agreement of the parties, to appoint an expert to report or give evidence to the court (discretion again) and the court is to be given a wide power to appoint assessors.

Woolf's central complaint here is a current lack of independence and an increased partisanship on the part of experts:

> Expert witnesses used to be genuinely independent experts. Men of
> outstanding eminence in their field. Today they are in practice hired guns:
> there is a new breed of litigation hangers on, whose main expertise is to
> craft reports which will conceal anything that might be to the disadvantage
> of their clients. [Not Woolf's words, but quoted by him (at 183, para 10.).
> Although blunt, the words appear to coincide with his views.]

I believe this is accurate, but only of some experts i.e. those who have gone "into the business" of being court experts e.g. forensic accountants, some engineers. In my experience it does not apply to most doctors who have another professional life. While Woolf makes interesting proposals to curb the partisanship of experts who testify, including removal of privilege from the instructions received from lawyers [in addition, all instructions received by the expert are to be stated in the report, which is to end with the declaration that it includes everything that the expert regards as being relevant, and that he has drawn to the attention of the court any matter that would affect the validity of the opinion (see 188, paras. 27 and 28)], I suggest we may need to go further and remove the privilege surrounding experts who have been consulted but abandoned. What makes experts who are in the "witnessing business" so pliable and partisan is that they are well aware that if their opinion does not (strongly) favour the party consulting them they will be dismissed and the fact that they were ever consulted will never have to be disclosed to the court. Moreover, non-compliant professional witnesses will soon see their business dry up. Entrepreneurship in witnessing ill fits a system that hopes to find the truth!

Whether Woolf's solutions will fix what is a genuine problem is itself problematic. Sweeping aside the objections made to him as to the use of court appointed experts, he optimistically and unabashedly states the "court is perfectly capable of deciding which cases would be appropriate for a court expert and then of appointing an expert with the necessary qualifications and ensuring that he is used effectively." One of the concerns he noted, but swept aside, is the "inability of a court expert to deal with the situation where more than one acceptable view can be held on a particular issue." Anyone who has been through the process of retaining experts soon realizes that this occurs not infrequently, and is hardly the exception, even among experts who are not in the "witnessing business." I suspect that steps to make the whole expert witness process more transparent are more likely to be acceptable to the profession and their clients, and more likely to aid accurate fact finding, than resort to the use of court appointed experts.

What is your reaction to Woolf's proposals and to Watson's critique? In particular, is Watson's suggestion that "we may need to go further and remove the privilege surrounding experts who have been consulted but abandoned" either realistic or desirable?

7. An English reform—disclosure through exchange of witness statements. As we
have already observed, oral examination for discovery is unknown in English procedure
(and written interrogatories may be administered only with leave, which is rarely sought
and rarely given). Traditionally, pleadings and documentary discovery were relied on for
issue definition and information exchange. Recently, the English rules were radically
changed. Now they empower the court to require parties, as a precondition to leading
oral evidence at trial, to provide to opposing parties a written statement of each witness's testimony: O.38, rule 2A. (In essence, the procedure extends to all witnesses the
regime that is currently in place in most Canadian jurisdictions with regard to expert
testimony: see the discussion above.)

The editors of *The Supreme Court Practice* describe the new rule in glowing terms.
They see it as embodying a fundamental innovation in the law and practice relating to
the identity of intended trial witnesses and to the confidentiality of their statements or
"proofs of evidence." Above all, it greatly improves the pre-trial process by providing
the machinery for enabling all the parties to know before the trial precisely what facts
are intended to be proved at the trial, and by whom, and thereby to reduce delay and
costs. The rule is designed to achieve several beneficial objectives, including (1) the
elimination of any element of "surprise" before or at the trial as to the witnesses each
party intends to call or the substance of their evidence (the parties will no longer be able
to surprise or to be exposed to surprise, but will be required to "place their cards on the
table"), and (2) the promotion of fair settlements between the parties.

What do you make of this English innovation? Is it really an effective substitute or
surrogate for examination for discovery? In this context, consider again the purposes of
examination for discovery. Does the English procedure provide the same information as
examination for discovery? Even if it is not a complete surrogate for examination for
discovery, can it be justified, as an alternative to examination for discovery, because it
would be cheaper? Is it functionally different from examination for discovery because it
would come much later in the process and therefore be of less utility in settling cases?
Can the English procedure be justified as an *addition to examination for discovery*, or
would this simply be to add further and unnecessary costs to the litigation?

8. Using witness statements in lieu of oral testimony at trial. In addition to ordering
the exchange of witness statements, it is now the standard practice in England to order
that witness statements be used at trial as testimony in lieu of the witnesses being orally
examined-in-chief. (A similar practice—but only with regard to expert witnesses—is
followed in Canada's Federal Court, and in some tribunals). Witnesses still have to be
available for oral cross-examination, but they no longer give oral testimony-in-chief.

In England, this development has caused problems and has been the subject of
criticism—lawyers now spend an enormous amount of time ironing out and massaging
witness statements with the result that their preparation has had a devastating effect on
costs. The root of the problem appears to be that the use of the exchange of witness
statements has moved beyond being merely a vehicle of mutual disclosure to becoming
evidence at trial in lieu of oral testimony. While this may at first seem efficient (trial
time is no longer consumed by having the witnesses examined-in-chief), it results in
great inefficiency. Lawyers spend a great deal of time polishing witness statements
because they realize that under such a regime the statements become *their whole case.*

Typically, the statements end up being the evidence on which the very outcome of the case (not some mere interlocutory application) will be decided.

A further problem is caused by the enormous front-end loading of costs that results from requiring the *early preparation and exchange* of witness statements. Lord Woolf, who recommends that the existing practice re the exchange and use of witness statements should continue, further recommends that witness summaries should be exchanged in fast track cases within 28 days of the delivery of the defence. But the vast majority of these cases will settle long before the trial date. Requiring such early exchange of witness statements builds up the costs in these cases, which, if "left alone," would settle without such expense.

In Ontario, under the recently introduced Simplified Procedure (see rule 76), examination for discovery is not permitted (rule 76.05) and the parties are required to include in their affidavit of documents a list of potential witnesses. Under the simplified procedure, the parties may opt for a summary trial (although it is consensual and they are not required to opt for this procedure) and if they do so the evidence in chief of witnesses is presented by affadavit.

What do you make of these innovations? Is "canned evidence" (as it is often called) more justified and efficient in simplified procedure cases then in more elaborate cases?

Toronto-Dominion Bank v. Leigh Instruments Ltd. (Trustee of)
(1997) 32 OR (3d) 575 (Gen. Div.)

WINKLER J (orally): This action, at its heart, concerns the strength and enforceability of a series of letters of comfort provided to the plaintiff T-D Bank by the defendant Plessey, in support of a $40.5 million loan extended by the Bank to a Plessey subsidiary, Leigh Instruments Limited. Leigh defaulted on the loan, and the Bank, in seeking to recover on the comfort letters, pleads in its amended amended statement of claim, inter alia, that it relied to its detriment on numerous alleged representations and obligations in the comfort letters.

To this end, the plaintiff pleads, in para. 20, its understanding that the first comfort letter was in the nature of a guarantee, or contractual undertaking, warranty, collateral warranty or representation. These obligations and representations, it further pleads, were of a continuing nature throughout the period of the subsequent comfort letters. The defendants have denied these obligations and representations. It is common ground that the plaintiff, through its pleading, has thereby placed in issue its corporate state of mind in respect to the strength and enforceability of letters of comfort.

Throughout the examinations for discovery, the plaintiff claimed privilege over the knowledge of its legal department regarding comfort letters, and the legal advice proffered by the legal department concerning comfort letters generally and those at issue in this lawsuit.

Pursuant to a ruling of this court made February 20, 1997, the plaintiff has provided a further and better affidavit of documents, listing in Sch. B the documents for which it claims solicitor-and-client privilege. The defendants have challenged the claim of privilege in respect of documents 5, 8, 9 and 10, on the basis that the documents are not capable of attracting a claim of solicitor-and-client privilege, or, in the alternative, that any privilege which may have applied has been waived.

The defendants have requested that I inspect these documents in order to assist in resolving any uncertainty regarding the merits of the claim of privilege. While the plaintiff has urged the court not to inspect the documents, or, in the alternative, not to do so until the submissions of counsel have been completed, no party has challenged my jurisdiction to do so. Accordingly, at the conclusion of submissions from counsel, I received the documents and have reviewed them in arriving at this determination. The defendants have provided me with ... authority in support of the court's jurisdiction to inspect. ...

The defendants assert that the onus of proving that communications are privileged rests with the party claiming the privilege. I agree.

In *Hodgkinson v. Simms* (1988), 55 DLR (4th) 577, at p. 589; 33 BCLR (2d) 129 (CA), McEachern CJBC stated: "There is no doubt the onus of establishing privilege rests with the party claiming or alleging that a document is privileged." See also *Waugh v. British Railways Board*, [1979] 2 All ER 1169, at p. 1181, [1979] 3 WLR 150 (HL); and R.D. Manes and M.P. Silver, Solicitor–Client Privilege in Canadian Law (Toronto: Butterworths, 1993), pp. 23-24.

In support of its claim of privilege, the plaintiff provided the following description of the challenged documents in its affidavit of documents:

January 12, 1988

  5. Newspaper article in the possession of the Legal Department (Solicitor-and-Client Privilege).

Sept. 16, 1988

  8. Head Office Circular from R. Bumstead, Senior Vice-President, General Counsel and Secretary (as a matter of practice distributed to branches, departments, and divisions of the Bank) (Solicitor-and-Client Privilege).

March 16, 1989

  9. Memorandum to Credit Division (handwritten notation "Mr. McDowell"), Corporate Banking (handwritten notation "Mr. Mercier") and SVP's Line Division (handwritten notation "All Division SVP's"), with further notation "Sent—March 28" from Legal Department, with second copy of the same memoranda without handwritten notations and with check mark beside the words "Corporate Banking Division") (Solicitor-and-Client Privilege).

Dec. 1989-Jan. 1990

  10. "Banking Law Update" in the possession of the Legal Department (Solicitor-and-Client Privilege).

Following delivery of the plaintiff's enhanced Sch. B, the defendants cross-examined the affiant, Mr. Colin Taylor, associate vice-president, litigation, to the T-D Bank. His evidence was that all four documents were retained in a general file on comfort letters held in the Bank's legal department. The maintenance of this file was not the responsibility of any one person in the legal department. While members of the department were not free to permanently remove documents from the file, any person was at liberty to add documents as he or she saw fit.

He further testified that each of the challenged documents concerned comfort letters, but that none concerned any specific transaction to which the Bank was a party. Mr. Taylor was also asked whether, during the period of time surrounding the creation of each of the documents, the Bank was involved in any litigation concerning comfort letters. He responded to each question that, to the best of his knowledge, no such litigation was either extant, pending or contemplated. All other questions concerning the content or subject-matter of the documents were objected to by Mr. Campion, including questions about whether they contained policy statements or dealt with the relative strengths and weaknesses of comfort letters. ...

[T]he issue before this court is whether or not documents 5, 8, 9 and 10 are protected by solicitor and client privilege, such that they need not be produced to the defendants.

Solicitor and client privilege has deep roots in the British common law, and is a cornerstone of our legal system. ...

The privilege was described in Wigmore on Evidence, vol. 8 (McNaughton rev., 1961), para. 2292:

> Where legal advice of any kind is sought from a professional legal advisor in his capacity as such, the communications relating to the purpose made in confidence by the client are at his instance permanently protected from disclosures by himself or by the legal advisor, except the privilege be waived.

This statement was adopted by the Supreme Court of Canada in *Descôteaux v. Mierzwinski*, [1982] 1 SCR 860, 141 DLR (3d) 592, and in *Solosky v. [The Queen]*, *supra*. In *Solosky*, the court, in recognizing that the privilege constitutes a substantive right, noted at p. 835 that the privilege was not absolute:

> There are exceptions to the privilege. The privilege does not apply to communications in which legal advice is neither sought nor offered, that is to say, where the lawyer is not contacted in his professional capacity. Also, where the communication is not intended to be confidential, privilege will not attach. ...
>
> [A] communication will be protected by the rubric of solicitor–client privilege if it is made in the context of a solicitor–client relationship, in the course of either requesting or providing legal advice, and if it is intended to remain confidential. Where a lawyer is employed as in-house counsel by a corporation, the privilege will still apply to communications passing between the lawyer and the corporation, as long as they meet the criteria above. ...

In my opinion, each of documents 5, 8, and 10 lack certain essential elements necessary to attract solicitor–client privilege and are perforce producible. But in any event, by pleading its state of mind and thus putting in issue its legal knowledge and advice as to the strength and enforceability of comfort letters, the plaintiff thereby waived its solicitor–client privilege and rendered all four documents producible. My reasons follow.

I will deal with documents 8 and 9 for which solicitor-and-client privilege is claimed first, and will then consider work-product privilege in respect of documents 5 and 10.

Document 8, the "head office circular" from R. Bumstead, senior vice-president, general counsel and secretary, was distributed, as a matter of practice, to all Bank branches and departments. The plaintiff asserts that, on the evidence, the document deals with comfort letter issues, provides legal advice from general counsel, was intended to be confidential and not distributed outside the Bank, and did not deal with a specific transaction involving the plaintiff. As such, they argue, the circular is privileged and ought not be produced.

The defendants challenge this claim on several bases: firstly, they argue that in order for solicitor–client privilege to apply to a communication from an in-house lawyer, that lawyer must have been acting in his capacity as such when the communication was made. The defendants further assert that the document was very widely circulated within the Bank, with no notation on its face that it was to be kept confidential. Hence, this document is not capable of attracting solicitor-and-client privilege. I agree with these submissions.

The law on this point is clear. In order for a communication from an in-house lawyer to attract solicitor–client privilege, it must have been made while he or she was acting in their capacity as such. Lord Denning MR stated the principle in *Alfred Crompton, supra*, at pp. 376-77:

> I have always proceeded on the footing that the communications between the legal advisors and their employer (who is their client) are the subject of legal professional privilege; and I have never known it questioned. There are many cases in the books of actions against railway companies where privilege has been claimed in this way. The validity of it has never been doubted. I speak, of course, of their communications in the capacity of legal advisors. It does sometimes happen that such a legal advisor does work for his employer in another capacity, perhaps of an executive nature. Their communications in that capacity, would not be the subject of legal professional privilege. So the legal advisor must be scrupulous to make the distinction. Being a servant or agent too, he may be under more pressure from his client. So he must be careful to resist it. He must be as independent in the doing of right as any other legal adviser. ...

While document 8 appeared over Mr. Bumstead's signature, his title indicates that he performs in several executive capacities with the Bank, and it is not clear from the evidence that he was acting in his capacity as general counsel when Document 8 was drafted and circulated. Nor was Mr. Taylor able to testify as to who actually drafted the document or whether it had even been drafted by a lawyer. I have had an opportunity to review the document, and in my opinion it is a statement of corporate policy concerning business risks associated with comfort letters and their consequent acceptability to the Bank as security. Indicative of this is the title of the document as "head office circular" as opposed to a memorandum from the legal department. Accordingly, given the nature of the document, I must draw the inference that the document was circulated by Mr. Bumstead in his capacity as a business executive of the Bank. As privilege will not attach to a communication made by in-house legal counsel when acting in another capacity, the plaintiff has not satisfied the first and second parts of the *Solosky* test.

More pointedly, however, the fatal flaw in the assertion of solicitor–client privilege is the absence of confidentiality. This document was widely circulated within the Bank. It was sent to every branch and department, on an international basis. As is set out in *Solosky, supra*, in order to constitute a privileged communication, the parties must have intended that it be kept confidential. Nowhere on the face of the head office circular or in its body is there any warning that the contents are confidential. On cross-examination, with reference to the Bank's 1989 Annual Report, Mr. Taylor acknowledged that a copy of the circular would have been sent to each of the vast number of branches listed there. Thus, in light of all the circumstances surrounding the creation and distribution of this document, including its wide circulation on a global scale to Bank employees, and significantly, absent a confidentiality requirement on the face of the document, I must conclude that this document was not intended to be confidential. Thus it fails the third part of the *Solosky* test and cannot be said to attract the protection of solicitor–client privilege.

Document 9 is a Memorandum to Credit Division, Corporate Banking Division and SVPs (senior vice-presidents) Line Division. As is noted above, it was the evidence of Mr. Taylor that this document contains legal advice on letters of comfort and was prepared by a lawyer in the legal department at the request of Mr. Bumstead.

In applying the three-part *Solosky* test, it appears on the evidence that this document satisfies the first two parts of the test. It was prepared by a lawyer in the legal department, acting in her capacity as such, and at the request of the Bank's general counsel. It was circulated to 13 Bank executives. As well, Mr. Taylor stated that the document contains legal advice on comfort letters. Hence, in my opinion, the memorandum is "a communication between solicitor and client which entails the seeking or giving of legal advice," within the meaning of *Solosky*.

The conclusion with respect to the third branch of the test is less clear. Although the memorandum was circulated to only 13 executives, Mr. Taylor was unable to give evidence as to whether those executives had further circulated the memo throughout their departments. Further, although at least 13 copies of the memorandum were made initially, the Bank is only claiming privilege over two copies, and does not know the location of the other 11. Finally, there is no notation anywhere on the document that it is to be kept confidential. In my view, it is not possible to conclude, simply on the face of the evidence, that the document was intended to be confidential by the parties. In consequence, I have reviewed the document, and have concluded that it was intended to be confidential and that the claim of privilege is properly founded.

Document 5 is a newspaper article from a British publication with some limited circulation in Canada. Document 10 is a newsletter circulated by an Australian firm of solicitors to potential clients, possibly including, but not limited to, other financial institutions. The firm acted as counsel on a leading Australian case concerning the enforceability of comfort letters. Both documents 5 and 10 deal with comfort-letter issues. It is clear that neither of these documents would ordinarily be protected by solicitor–client privilege, since they are not communications between a solicitor and client, were not made for the purpose of seeking or giving legal advice, and were not intended to be kept confidential by the parties. ...

The plaintiff asserts that documents 5 and 10, which are copies of documents not ordinarily privileged, are subject to the lawyer's-brief rule, and as such, ought not to be disclosed. It takes the position that both documents were received by the Bank's legal department and reviewed by a lawyer who retained them and placed them in the general file on comfort letters, to be used for the purpose of giving legal advice. The act of selecting and retaining the documents for the file constitutes, the plaintiff submits, an exercise of the lawyer's professional knowledge and skill and as such, endows the document with work-product privilege. I am unable to accede to this submission.

On the evidence before me, I am not satisfied that these documents properly constitute part of a solicitor's brief. Mr. Taylor stated on cross-examination that the comfort letter file was a general reference file, kept in the legal department for the purpose of giving legal advice on comfort letters. It was not created by any one person, through the exercise of professional knowledge or skill in selecting appropriate documents. Rather, it was a general repository for information on comfort letters. Mr. Taylor testified that no one person was responsible for creating, maintaining or updating the file. Contributions were made to the file on an ad hoc basis, by any member of the legal department who happened to receive material on comfort letters and who decided to place the material in the file. There was no evidence as to who had selected documents 5 and 10 for the file. As such, the documents were not collected in any focused way. This element of randomness defies any characterization as the product of a lawyer's professional knowledge, judgment and skill in selecting and compiling a collection of relevant documents. The mere act of noting that a document bears on the general topic of comfort letters, and deciding to retain the document rather than discard it, cannot be enough to imbue the document with work product privilege. This conclusion alone is enough to dispose of the plaintiff's argument.

In addition, however, the lawyer's work product privilege applies only to files prepared in the context of contemplated or pending litigation. ...

The plaintiff argues that the comfort letter file in this case was compiled and held for the purpose of giving legal advice and that work-product privilege should be extended to encompass it in these circumstances. Mr. Campion asserts that this notion of privilege should not, in the case of in-house legal counsel, be restricted solely to files prepared in contemplation of litigation, and should be held to apply to files created outside the litigation context, for the purpose of giving advice.

The plaintiff has been unable to direct me to any case where the privilege has been so extended. Moreover, I am unable to agree that such an extension is warranted. The purpose of the privilege, as noted above, is to provide protection for a collection of materials carefully selected by a lawyer using legal skill and judgment, in order to prepare for litigation. Such an extension would go beyond the scope of litigation privilege, of which this is a branch. The distinction between solicitor–client privilege and litigation privilege was elucidated by Sopinka, Lederman and Bryant, *The Law of Evidence in Canada* (Markham: Butterworths, 1992), at p. 653:

> Although this extension [of litigation privilege] was spawned out of the traditional solicitor–client privilege, the policy justification for it differed markedly from its progenitor. It had nothing to do with client's freedom to consult privately and openly with their solicitors; rather, it was founded upon our adversary system of litigation by which counsel control fact-presentation before the Court and decide for themselves which evidence and by what manner of proof they will adduce facts to establish their claim or defence, without any obligation to make prior disclosure of the material acquired in preparation of the case.

Accordingly, the lawyer's work-product privilege, as a branch of litigation privilege, is founded upon wholly different principles than solicitor–client privilege, and is intended to achieve a different end. To extend the work-product privilege to files created solely for the purpose of giving advice would be to seriously misapprehend the purpose of the privilege.

In the facts before me, the comfort letter file was of a general reference nature only, and was not prepared in connection with any specific Bank transaction, let alone in contemplation of litigation. The mere fact that a document is in the possession of a solicitor is not enough to make it privileged. In my opinion, documents 5 and 10 do not constitute lawyer's work-product privilege and are thus not privileged.

The defendants have opposed the plaintiff's claim of privilege, in the alternative, on the ground that any privilege which may have attached to the documents in question has been waived by the plaintiff in their pleadings.

The defendants contend that the plaintiff has placed in issue its own corporate state of mind. Specifically, they assert that in paras. 20-23 of the amended amended statement of claim, the plaintiff has pleaded that the Bank understood the Plessey comfort letters to be in the nature of a guarantee or contractual undertaking, warranty, collateral warranty or representation, and that it relied to its detriment on the alleged representations and obligations contained in them. As such, the defendants state that the plaintiff has placed in issue the very matters over which it now claims privilege. The defendants have denied these allegations in their respective statements of defence. Mr. Campion has acknowledged that para. 20 of the statement of claim has placed in issue the plaintiff's state of mind, but takes the position there has been no waiver of privilege. ...

The combined effect of the pleadings, the opening statement of the plaintiff and the evidence is, according to the defendants, that the Bank has placed in issue its state of mind regarding the strength and enforceability of comfort letters. The plaintiff, they assert, has pleaded reliance on the conduct of the defendants, when they knew, or ought reasonably to have known, through the advice of their legal department, that comfort letters were not binding. The consequence, they assert, is that the plaintiff has waived by implication any solicitor–client privilege it may have held over the legal advice or knowledge which gave rise to that state of mind. I agree with those submissions.

Solicitor–client privilege inures to the benefit of the client, in order that the client may participate in full and frank discussion with its solicitor. Any consideration of waiver of privilege must involve balancing the competing interests of full disclosure on the one hand and preservation of solicitor–client confidentiality on the other. Counsel for the plaintiff argued against such a balancing approach, asserting instead that the privilege must remain inviolate. ...

The plaintiff asserts that placing state of mind in issue is not sufficient to waive solicitor–client privilege. Rather, Mr. Campion argues that reliance on legal advice must be specifically pleaded to amount to a waiver. ...

Placing state of mind in issue will not amount to a waiver in every case. The guiding principles must be fairness and consistency. In a case where a party has placed its state of mind in issue, and has given evidence that it received legal advice which, in part, formed the basis of that state of mind, the distinction between state of mind and the legal advice giving rise to it cannot be maintained.

In the present case, ... the plaintiff has placed its state of mind in issue by pleading that it relied upon the defendants' representations and conduct to its detriment, and has led evidence both that it consulted the legal department before doing so, and that it believed the comfort letter to be strong. The defendants Plessey and GEC assert, in paras. 51-52 and

48-49 of their respective statements of defence, that the plaintiff, and its legal department, were at all material times aware that letters of comfort generally, and the Plessey letters in particular, did not constitute guarantees or contractual obligations to repay the indebtedness of Leigh. Here, as in *Rogers, supra,* a "significant legal decision" had been rendered during the material time period. It seems to me that, in all of these circumstances, it would be fundamentally unfair to permit the plaintiff to shield behind a claim of solicitor–client privilege, evidence of the knowledge and advice of the legal department in respect of the strength and enforceability of comfort letters. In the interest of fairness and consistency, any solicitor–client privilege in this respect must be deemed to have been waived.

The plaintiff submits that even if privilege has been waived, it has only been waived with respect to legal advice received in respect of the specific Plessey comfort letters. Mr. Campion asserts that the Bank's state of mind has only been placed in issue in respect of its understanding of the specific letters, and as such, they ought not be forced to disclose legal advice obtained about comfort letters generally. In my opinion, this is an artificial distinction which has no foundation in the facts before me. The four documents in issue here were all created during the period of time in which the Leigh comfort letters were extant. Moreover, the plaintiff has pleaded in para. 23 that the alleged obligations and representations on which it relied were of a continuing nature throughout the period of currency of the letters. Thus, while the documents in issue may deal with comfort letters generally, it cannot be said that they did not influence the state of mind of the Bank in regard to the Leigh letters. Each of the documents was created during the material time. Document 9 was circulated to the very decision makers (Mr. Mercier and Mr. McDowell) who subsequently approved the Leigh corporate credit reviews. As such, it would be unfair to deny the defendants the opportunity to test the alleged state of mind of the plaintiff, whether the state of mind existed as pleaded, and if so, whether it was reasonable in all of the circumstances. The distinction between general and specific legal advice on comfort letters cannot stand. There is a deemed waiver or waiver by implication of the knowledge and advice of the Bank's legal department in respect of the Plessey comfort letters and comfort letters generally. ...

In the present case, the documents at issue concern general letter-of-comfort issues, and may form part of the basis of the Bank's understanding of the strength and enforceability of the letters of comfort in issue in this action. As such, they are arguably relevant both to the state of mind of the Bank placed in issue by the pleadings, and as demonstrating the circumstances surrounding the creation of the contracts between the parties.

For the reasons outlined above, the plaintiff's claim of privilege in respect of documents 5, 8, 9 and 10 listed in Sch. B of their affidavit of documents must fail, and the documents must be produced.

I am obliged to all counsel for their thoughtful and thorough submissions.

Order accordingly.

NOTES AND QUESTIONS

1. The decision in *Toronto-Dominion Bank* on the waiver issue is pretty much "hornbook" law, although some aspects of the law on waiver of privilege (which has

become a "hot topic" recently) are somewhat unsettled: see, generally, Holmested and Watson, *Ontario Civil Procedure*, 30 § 38 "Solicitor-and-Client Privilege—Waiver or Loss of Privilege."

2. What are the ethical responsibilities of a lawyer with regard to asserting and fighting a claim for privilege? Does a lawyer have a duty to make every possible claim of privilege to protect his or her client's interest? Or does a lawyer have a responsibility not to assert specious claims of privilege?

D. Privilege on Grounds of Confidentiality

Traditionally, Canadian courts have been loath to recognize privilege beyond the accepted categories—for example, solicitor-and-client privilege, litigation privilege, without-prejudice communications, or Crown privilege. While solicitor-and-client privilege is based on the confidentiality of the communication, no general privilege has been extended to confidential communications—for example, with doctors or with spiritual advisors. Now this situation is changing:

> [T]he courts have shown, albeit hesitatingly, a more flexible and pragmatic approach to protecting other relationships in certain circumstances. These attempts to expand the doctrine of privilege were bolstered by the Supreme Court of Canada's decision in *Slavutych v. Baker*, [1976] 1 SCR 254, but as yet they have not resulted in the creation of new, identifiable privileges in Canada." (Sopinka, Lederman, and Bryant, *The Law of Evidence in Canada*, 2d ed. (Toronto: Butterworths, 1992), 625.)

In *Slavutych*, the Supreme Court adopted the test propounded by Wigmore that four fundamental conditions must be met before privilege is extended to any communication on the ground of confidentiality. The conditions, quoted in *Slavutych*, at 260, are:

> 1. The communications must originate in a confidence that they will not be disclosed.
> 2. This element of confidentiality must be essential to the full and satisfactory maintenance of the relation between the parties.
> 3. The relation must be one which in the opinion of the community ought to be sedulously fostered.
> 4. The injury that would enure to the relation by the disclosure of the communications must be greater than the benefit thereby gained for the correct disposal of litigation.

Subsequently, in *R v. Gruenke*, [1991] 3 SCR 263, the Supreme Court of Canada (in analyzing statements made by the accused to a spiritual advisor) indicated that the approach it took in *Slavutych* is "the legitimate, principled way to analyze the question which takes into account the particular circumstances of each case" (Sopinka, et al., at 635). In *Gruenke*, Lamer CJC stated:

> This is not to say that the Wigmore criteria are now "carved in stone," but rather that these considerations provide a general framework within which policy considerations and the requirement of fact-finding can be weighed and balanced on the basis of their

relative importance in the particular case before the Court. Nor does this preclude the identification of a new class on a principled basis. (Quoted in Sopinka et al., at 635).

A.M. v. Ryan
[1997] 1 SCR 157

McLACHLIN J: After having been sexually assaulted by the respondent Dr. Ryan, the appellant sought counselling from a psychiatrist. The question on this appeal is whether the psychiatrist's notes and records containing statements the appellant made in the course of treatment are protected from disclosure in a civil suit brought by the appellant against Dr. Ryan. Put in terms of principle, should a defendant's right to relevant material to the end of testing the plaintiff's case outweigh the plaintiff's expectation that communications between her and her psychiatrist will be kept in confidence?

I. The Facts and History of Proceedings

When the appellant was 17 years old, she underwent psychiatric treatment from Dr. Ryan. In the course of treatment, Dr. Ryan had sexual relations with her. He also committed acts of gross indecency in her presence. The appellant asserts that this conduct injured her and has sued Dr. Ryan for damages. Dr. Ryan does not deny that this sexual conduct occurred. He contends, however, that the appellant consented to the acts. He also takes the position that the conduct was not the cause of the injury for which the plaintiff sues.

The appellant alleges that the sexual assault and gross indecency caused her mental distress and anguish, loss of dignity and self-esteem, humiliation and embarrassment, difficulty in forming and maintaining relationships with other persons, lasting psychological and emotional trauma, continuing fear and anxiety, foregone career and educational opportunities, inability to verbalize emotions and recollections of the events, repeated suicide attempts, severe depression and post-traumatic stress disorder. In order to deal with these difficulties as well as other problems, the appellant sought psychiatric treatment from Dr. Parfitt.

The appellant was concerned that communications between her and Dr. Parfitt should remain confidential. Dr. Parfitt assured her that everything possible would be done to ensure that their discussions would remain confidential. At one point, the appellant's concerns led Dr. Parfitt to refrain from taking her usual notes.

The British Columbia Rules of Court permit each party to an action to examine the other for discovery and to obtain discovery of all documents in the possession of the other party that are relevant to the lawsuit and not protected from disclosure by privilege or some other legal exemption. If a party has not voluntarily produced a required document, the court may order that it be produced. The rules also provide for documents to be obtained from third parties. Failing voluntary production, an application for production may be brought under Rule 26(11).

During the examination for discovery of the appellant, counsel for Dr. Ryan requested production of Dr. Parfitt's records and notes. The appellant's counsel advised that they would not be produced without a court order. Accordingly, Dr. Ryan's counsel brought a motion to obtain disclosure. At the hearing before Master Bolton, Dr. Parfitt agreed to release her reports, but claimed privilege in relation to her notes. Counsel for the appellant was present. He supported Dr. Parfitt's objections to production, but did not assert a formal claim to privilege on behalf of the appellant.

The Master found that Dr. Parfitt had no privilege in the documents and ordered that they all be produced to Dr. Ryan. In his view, there is no blanket privilege for communications between patient and physician. The only basis upon which privilege could be asserted would be under the principles approved by this Court for case-by-case privilege, sometimes referred to as the "Wigmore test." The first branch of this test requires that the communications originate in confidence. The Master ruled that this was not the case here, since the appellant had been fearful throughout that the doctor's notes would be disclosed and Dr. Parfitt had assured her only that everything possible would be done to ensure that their discussions were kept private. The Master went on to consider whether the discretion granted by the Rules of Court permitted him to accede to Dr. Parfitt's claim for confidentiality. He found the notes to be relevant. The only remaining question was whether Dr. Parfitt's "embarrassment" at revealing the notes outweighed this probative value. It did not, in the Master's view. Although he acknowledged the legitimate interest of keeping patient–therapist discussions free-ranging and confidential, he held that this was not a factor that he could consider under the law as it stood.

Dr. Parfitt appealed to the Supreme Court of British Columbia. That appeal was dismissed … . Vickers J agreed that the notes were not privileged, not on the ground that they had not been made in confidence as the Master had found, but on the ground that the public interest in the proper administration of justice outweighed confidentiality concerns where the appellant had placed the matters in issue by initiating the suit.

Dr. Parfitt appealed to the British Columbia Court of Appeal. The appeal was allowed in part … . Southin JA began by stating that she was only concerned with Dr. Parfitt's privilege and not the plaintiff's, since the plaintiff had not properly claimed privilege. A physician could only assert privilege if disclosure would harm the physician. Dr. Parfitt had not shown this to be the case. Therefore, no claim for privilege could be made by anyone, and the matter fell to be considered exclusively under the Rules of Court.

Under Rule 26(11), relevant or "material" documents should be produced unless the order is oppressive of the plaintiff or will have such an adverse effect on her that it would be unjust to order production, the Court of Appeal ruled. In applying this test, the court should consider whether the particular invasion of privacy is necessary to the proper administration of justice and, if so, whether terms are appropriate to limit that invasion. On the one hand, a plaintiff should not be "scared away" from suing by fear of disclosure. On the other hand, a defendant should not be deprived of an assessment of the true loss caused by the alleged wrong. There is no perfect balance to be struck, in the court's view.

Southin JA ordered disclosure of Dr. Parfitt's reporting letters and notes recording discussions between her and the appellant. Southin JA did not order disclosure of Dr. Parfitt's personal notes which she uses to make sense of what the patient is telling her. These notes were not disclosed because the appellant assured the court that Dr. Parfitt would not be called at trial and therefore her diagnosis was "of no moment" (p. 19 BCLR). The disclosure ordered was protected by four conditions: that inspection be confined to Dr. Ryan's solicitors and expert witnesses, and that Dr. Ryan himself could not see them; that any person who saw the documents should not disclose their contents to anyone not entitled to inspect them; that the documents could be used only for the purposes of the litigation; and that only one copy of the notes was to be made by Dr. Ryan's solicitors, to be passed on as necessary to Dr. Ryan's expert witnesses.

The appellant objects to this order for limited production and appeals to this Court.

II. The Legislation

British Columbia Supreme Court Rules, Rule 26(11):

> Where a document is in the possession or control of a person who is not a party, the court, on notice to the person and all other parties, may order production and inspection of the document or preparation of a certified copy that may be used instead of the original. An order under Rule 41(16) in respect of an order under this subrule may be made if that order is endorsed with an acknowledgment by the person in possession or control of the document that the person has no objection to the terms of the proposed order.

III. Preliminary Issues

The findings of the courts below raise three preliminary issues. The first is whether the appellant's alleged failure to assert privilege in the records before the Master deprives her of the right to claim it. I respectfully dissent from the Court of Appeal's view that it did. If the appellant had privilege in the documents, it could be lost only by waiver. The appellant's conduct does not support a finding of waiver. ...

A second preliminary issue concerns the relationship between the Rules of Court and the common law rule of privilege. In my view, the present appeal falls to be decided solely on the law of privilege. Where the doctrine of privilege applies, it displaces any residual discretion which might otherwise be thought to inhere in favour of the party claiming privilege. ...

A third preliminary issue concerns the distinction between absolute or blanket privilege, on the one hand, and partial privilege on the other. While the traditional common law categories conceived privilege as an absolute, all-or-nothing proposition, more recent jurisprudence recognizes the appropriateness in many situations of partial privilege. The degree of protection conferred by the privilege may be absolute or partial, depending on what is required to strike the proper balance between the interest in protecting the communication from disclosure and the interest in proper disposition of the litigation. Partial privilege may signify that only some of the documents in a given class must be produced. Documents should be considered individually or by sub-groups on a "case-by-case" basis.

IV. General Principles

The common law principles underlying the recognition of privilege from disclosure are simply stated. They proceed from the fundamental proposition that everyone owes a general duty to give evidence relevant to the matter before the court, so that the truth may be ascertained. To this fundamental duty, the law permits certain exceptions, known as privileges, where it can be shown that they are required by a "public good transcending the normally predominant principle of utilizing all rational means for ascertaining truth": *Trammel v. United States*, 445 US 40 (1980), at p. 50.

While the circumstances giving rise to a privilege were once thought to be fixed by categories defined in previous centuries—categories that do not include communications between a psychiatrist and her patient—it is now accepted that the common law permits privilege in new situations where reason, experience and application of the principles that underlie the traditional privileges so dictate: *Slavutych v. Baker*, [1976] 1 SCR 254; *R v. Gruenke*, [1991] 3 SCR 263, at p. 286. The applicable principles are derived from those set forth in Wigmore on Evidence, vol. 8 (McNaughton rev. 1961), sec. 2285. First, the communication must originate in a confidence. Second, the confidence must be essential to the relationship in which the communication arises. Third, the relationship must be one which should be "sedulously fostered" in the public good. Finally, if all these requirements are met, the court must consider whether the interests served by protecting the communications from disclosure outweigh the interest in getting at the truth and disposing correctly of the litigation.

It follows that the law of privilege may evolve to reflect the social and legal realities of our time. One such reality is the law's increasing concern with the wrongs perpetrated by sexual abuse and the serious effect such abuse has on the health and productivity of the many members of our society it victimizes. Another modern reality is the extension of medical assistance from treatment of its physical effects to treatment of its mental and emotional aftermath through techniques such as psychiatric counselling. Yet another development of recent vintage which may be considered in connection with new claims for privilege is the *Canadian Charter of Rights and Freedoms*, adopted in 1982: *RWDSU v. Dolphin Delivery Ltd.*, [1986] 2 SCR 573, at pp. 592-93; *Dagenais v. Canadian Broadcasting Corp.*, [1994] 3 SCR 835, at pp. 876-77; *Hill v. Church of Scientology of Toronto*, [1995] 2 SCR 1130, at para. 121.

I should pause here to note that in looking to the *Charter*, it is important to bear in mind the distinction drawn by this Court between actually *applying* the *Charter* to the common law, on the one hand, and ensuring that the common law *reflects Charter* values, on the other. As Cory J stated in *Hill, supra*, at paras. 93 and 95:

> … The most that the private litigant can do is argue that the common law is inconsistent with Charter *values*. It is very important to draw this distinction between Charter rights and Charter values. Care must be taken not to expand the application of the Charter beyond that established by s. 32(1), either by creating new causes of action, or by subjecting all court orders to Charter scrutiny. Therefore, in the context of civil litigation involving only private parties, the Charter will "apply" to the common law only to the extent that the common law is found to be inconsistent with Charter values. [Emphasis in original.]

While the facts of *Hill* involved an attempt to mount a *Charter* challenge to the common law rules of defamation, I am of the view that Cory J's comments are equally applicable to the common law of privilege at issue in this case. In view of the purely private nature of the litigation at bar, the *Charter* does not "apply" *per se*. Nevertheless, ensuring that the common law of privilege develops in accordance with "*Charter* values" requires that the existing rules be scrutinized to ensure that they reflect the values the *Charter* enshrines. This does not mean that the rules of privilege can be abrogated entirely and replaced with a new form of discretion governing disclosure. Rather, it means that the basic structure of the common law privilege analysis must remain intact, even if particular rules which are applied within that structure must be modified and updated to reflect emerging social realities.

V. Privilege for Communications Between Psychiatrist and Patient

The first requirement for privilege is that the communications at issue have originated in a confidence that they will not be disclosed. The Master held that this condition was not met because both the appellant and Dr. Parfitt had concerns that notwithstanding their desire for confidentiality, the records might someday be ordered disclosed in the course of litigation. With respect, I do not agree. The communications were made in confidence. The appellant stipulated that they should remain confidential and Dr. Parfitt agreed that she would do everything possible to keep them confidential. The possibility that a court might order them disclosed at some future date over their objections does not change the fact that the communications were made in confidence. With the possible exception of communications falling in the traditional categories, there can never be an absolute guarantee of confidentiality; there is always the possibility that a court may order disclosure. Even for documents within the traditional categories, inadvertent disclosure is always a possibility. If the apprehended possibility of disclosure negated privilege, privilege would seldom if ever be found.

The second requirement—that the element of confidentiality be essential to the full and satisfactory maintenance of the relation between the parties to the communication— is clearly satisfied in the case at bar. It is not disputed that Dr. Parfitt's practice in general and her ability to help the appellant in particular required that she hold her discussions with the appellant in confidence. Dr. Parfitt's evidence establishes that confidentiality is essential to the continued existence and effectiveness of the therapeutic relations between a psychiatrist and a patient seeking treatment for the psychiatric harm resulting from sexual abuse. ...

The appellant too sees confidentiality as essential to her relationship with Dr. Parfitt. She insisted from the first that her communications to Dr. Parfitt be held in confidence, suggesting that this was a condition of her entering and continuing treatment. The fact that she and Dr. Parfitt feared the possibility of court-ordered disclosure at some future date does not negate the fact that confidentiality was essential "to the full and satisfactory maintenance" of their relationship.

The third requirement—that the relation must be one which in the opinion of the community ought to be sedulously fostered—is equally satisfied. Victims of sexual abuse often suffer serious trauma, which, left untreated, may mar their entire lives. It is widely accepted that it is in the interests of the victim and society that such help be obtained. The mental health of the citizenry, no less than its physical health, is a public good of great importance. Just as it is in the interest of the sexual abuse victim to be restored to full and healthy functioning, so is it in the interest of the public that she take her place as a healthy and productive member of society. ...

The fourth requirement is that the interests served by protecting the communications from disclosure outweigh the interest of pursuing the truth and disposing correctly of the litigation. This requires first an assessment of the interests served by protecting the communications from disclosure. These include injury to the appellant's ongoing relationship with Dr. Parfitt and her future treatment. They also include the effect that a finding of no privilege would have on the ability of other persons suffering from similar trauma to obtain needed treatment and of psychiatrists to provide it. The interests served by non-disclosure must extend to any effect on society of the failure of individuals to obtain treatment restoring them to healthy and contributing members of society. Finally, the interests served by protection from disclosure must include the privacy interest of the person claiming privilege and inequalities which may be perpetuated by the absence of protection.

As noted, the common law must develop in a way that reflects emerging *Charter* values. It follows that the factors balanced under the fourth part of the test for privilege should be updated to reflect relevant *Charter* values. One such value is the interest affirmed by s. 8 of the *Charter* of each person in privacy. Another is the right of every person embodied in s. 15 of the *Charter* to equal treatment and benefit of the law. A rule of privilege which fails to protect confidential doctor/patient communications in the context of an action arising out of sexual assault perpetuates the disadvantage felt by victims of sexual assault, often women. The intimate nature of sexual assault heightens the privacy concerns of the victim and may increase, if automatic disclosure is the rule, the difficulty of obtaining redress for the wrong. The victim of a sexual assault is thus placed in a disadvantaged position as compared with the victim of a different wrong. The result may be that the victim of sexual assault does not obtain the equal benefit of the law to which s. 15 of the *Charter* entitles her. She is doubly victimized, initially by the sexual assault and later by the price she must pay to claim redress—redress which in some cases may be part of her program of therapy. These are factors which may properly be considered in determining the interests served by an order for protection from disclosure of confidential patient–psychiatrist communications in sexual assault cases.

These criteria, applied to the case at bar, demonstrate a compelling interest in protecting the communications at issue from disclosure. More, however, is required to establish privilege. For privilege to exist, it must be shown that the benefit that inures from privilege, however great it may seem, in fact outweighs the interest in the correct disposal of the litigation.

At this stage, the court considering an application for privilege must balance one alternative against the other. The exercise is essentially one of common sense and good judgment. This said, it is important to establish the outer limits of acceptability. I for one cannot accept the proposition that "occasional injustice" should be accepted as the price of the privilege. It is true that the traditional categories of privilege, cast as they are in absolute all-or-nothing terms, necessarily run the risk of occasional injustice. But that does not mean that courts, in invoking new privileges, should lightly condone its extension. In the words of Scalia J (dissenting) in *Jaffee v. Redmond*, 116 S Ct. 1923 (1996), at p. 1941:

> It is no small matter to say that, in some cases, our federal courts will be the tools of injustice rather than unearth the truth where it is available to be found. The common law

has identified a few instances where that is tolerable. Perhaps Congress may conclude that it is also tolerable ... . But that conclusion assuredly does not burst upon the mind with such clarity that a judgment in favor of suppressing the truth ought to be pronounced by this honorable Court.

It follows that if the court considering a claim for privilege determines that a particular document or class of documents must be produced to get at the truth and prevent an unjust verdict, it must permit production to the extent required to avoid that result. On the other hand, the need to get at the truth and avoid injustice does not automatically negate the possibility of protection from full disclosure. In some cases, the court may well decide that the truth permits of nothing less than full production. This said, I would venture to say that an order for partial privilege will more often be appropriate in civil cases where, as here, the privacy interest is compelling. Disclosure of a limited number of documents, editing by the court to remove non-essential material, and the imposition of conditions on who may see and copy the documents are techniques which may be used to ensure the highest degree of confidentiality and the least damage to the protected relationship, while guarding against the injustice of cloaking the truth. ...

It must be conceded that a test for privilege which permits the court to occasionally reject an otherwise well-founded claim for privilege in the interests of getting at the truth may not offer patients a guarantee that communications with their psychiatrists will never be disclosed. On the other hand, the assurance that disclosure will be ordered only where clearly necessary and then only to the extent necessary is likely to permit many to avail themselves of psychiatric counselling when certain disclosure might make them hesitate or decline. The facts in this case demonstrate as much. ...

The view that privilege may exist where the interest in protecting the privacy of the records is compelling and the threat to proper disposition of the litigation either is not apparent or can be offset by partial or conditional discovery is consistent with this Court's view in *R v. O'Connor*, [1995] 4 SCR 411. The majority there did not deny that privilege in psychotherapeutic records may exist in appropriate circumstances. Without referring directly to privilege, it developed a test for production of third party therapeutic and other records which balances the competing interests by reference to a number of factors including the right of the accused to full answer and defence and the right of the complainant to privacy. Just as justice requires that the accused in a criminal case be permitted to answer the Crown's case, so justice requires that a defendant in a civil suit be permitted to answer the plaintiff's case. In deciding whether he or she is entitled to production of confidential documents, this requirement must be balanced against the privacy interest of the complainant. This said, the interest in disclosure of a defendant in a civil suit may be less compelling than the parallel interest of an accused charged with a crime. The defendant in a civil suit stands to lose money and repute; the accused in a criminal proceeding stands to lose his or her very liberty. As a consequence, the balance between the interest in disclosure and the complainant's interest in privacy may be struck at a different level in the civil and criminal case; documents produced in a criminal case may not always be producible in a civil case, where the privacy interest of the complainant may more easily outweigh the defendant's interest in production.

My conclusion is that it is open to a judge to conclude that psychiatrist–patient records are privileged in appropriate circumstances. Once the first three requirements are met and a compelling prima facie case for protection is established, the focus will be on the balancing under the fourth head. A document relevant to a defence or claim may be required to be disclosed, notwithstanding the high interest of the plaintiff in keeping it confidential. On the other hand, documents of questionable relevance or which contain information available from other sources may be declared privileged. The result depends on the balance of the competing interests of disclosure and privacy in each case. It must be borne in mind that in most cases, the majority of the communications between a psychiatrist and her patient will have little or no bearing on the case at bar and can safely be excluded from production. Fishing expeditions are not appropriate where there is a compelling privacy interest at stake, even at the discovery stage. Finally, where justice requires that communications be disclosed, the court should consider qualifying the disclosure by imposing limits aimed at permitting the opponent to have the access justice requires while preserving the confidential nature of the documents to the greatest degree possible.

It remains to consider the argument that by commencing the proceedings against the respondent Dr. Ryan, the appellant has forfeited her right to confidentiality. I accept that a litigant must accept such intrusions upon her privacy as are necessary to enable the judge or jury to get to the truth and render a just verdict. But I do not accept that by claiming such damages as the law allows, a litigant grants her opponent a licence to delve into private aspects of her life which need not be probed for the proper disposition of the litigation.

VI. Procedure for Ascertaining Privilege

In order to determine whether privilege should be accorded to a particular document or class of documents and, if so, what conditions should attach, the judge must consider the circumstances of the privilege alleged, the documents, and the case. While it is not essential in a civil case such as this that the judge examine every document, the court may do so if necessary to the inquiry. On the other hand, a judge does not necessarily err by proceeding on affidavit material indicating the nature of the information and its expected relevance without inspecting each document individually. The requirement that the court minutely examine numerous or lengthy documents may prove time-consuming, expensive and delay the resolution of the litigation. Where necessary to the proper determination of the claim for privilege, it must be undertaken. But I would not lay down an absolute rule that as a matter of law, the judge must personally inspect every document at issue in every case. Where the judge is satisfied on reasonable grounds that the interests at stake can properly be balanced without individual examination of each document, failure to do so does not constitute error of law.

VII. Application to This Case

The Court of Appeal declined to order production of Dr. Parfitt's notes to herself on the ground that they were unnecessary given that she would not be called to testify. It ordered the production of notes and records of consultations with the appellant, but under stringent conditions. While the Court of Appeal did not proceed on the basis of privilege, its orders are supported by the principles relating to privilege that I have attempted to set forth.

The interest in preserving the confidentiality of the communications here at issue was, as discussed, compelling. On the other hand, the communications might be expected to bear on the critical issue of the extent to which the respondent Dr. Ryan's conduct caused the difficulties the appellant was experiencing. A court, in a case such as this, might well consider it best to inspect the records individually to the end of weeding out those which were irrelevant to this defence. However, the alternative chosen by the Court of Appeal in this case of refusing to order production of one group of documents and imposing stringent conditions on who could see the others and what use could be made of them cannot be said to be in error. In the end, the only persons to see the documents in question will be the lawyers for the respondent Dr. Ryan and his expert witnesses. Copies will not be made, and disclosure of the contents to other people will not be permitted. In short, the plaintiff's private disclosures to her psychiatrist will be disclosed only to a small group of trustworthy professionals, much in the fashion that confidential medical records may be disclosed in a hospital setting. I am not persuaded that the order of the Court of Appeal should be disturbed.

[Dissenting judgment of L'Heureux-Dubé J omitted.]

QUESTION

Recall that in *Manuel v. Head* (discussed above, on the issue whether mandatory medical examinations violate the Charter) the court placed great weight on the fact that it was the plaintiff who sued and had put his medical condition in issue. In *Ryan*, the court rejected the argument that, by suing Ryan, the plaintiff had lost her right to confidentiality. Are these approaches inconsistent?

VI. IMPLIED/DEEMED UNDERTAKINGS

What is the status of documents that would remain private but for having been produced to other parties as part of discovery? Can a party to whom the documents are produced make them public or use them in another proceeding? Should the party seeking to protect the document from other use or the party seeking to use the document bear the onus of persuading a court that they should be permitted to do so?

Goodman v. Rossi
(1995), 24 OR (3d) 359 (CA)

MORDEN ACJO: This appeal from an order of the Divisional Court is concerned with the question whether a party who obtains a document from the other party under the discovery process in the *Rules of Civil Procedure* is subject to an implied undertaking not to use the document for a purpose other than that of the proceeding in which the document was obtained, except with the consent of the other party or with the leave of the court.

Mr. Justice O'Leary, on behalf of himself and Mr. Justice O'Driscoll in the Divisional Court, concluded that there was no implied undertaking rule in Ontario [(1994), 34 CPC (3d) 18 (Ont. Div. Ct.)]. Mr. Justice Moldaver dissented on this point, holding that there is an implied undertaking in particular terms, which he formulated.

The Facts and the Course of This Proceeding in the Courts Below

The relevant facts are succinctly set forth in the reasons of Mr. Justice O'Leary in the Divisional Court as follows [at 115]:

> The plaintiff, Irene Goodman, was employed as a real estate agent by NRS Royal Realty Inc. The defendant, David J. Rossi, was the president of NRS Royal Realty Inc. Goodman's employment was terminated by her employer. She sued NRS Royal Realty Inc. for wrongful dismissal. Royal Realty produced its documents. One of the documents it produced was a report made by Rossi to the Ministry of Consumer and Commercial Relations. The report was required by s. 21(1) of the *Real Estate and Business Brokers Act*, RSO 1990, c. R.4 and Reg. 986, s. 13(11). The report was made on a form provided by the Ministry. The form is entitled "Notice of Employee Change." The form states in part "Note: A report on the conduct of the above named employee while in your employ should be filed either on the reverse side of this form, or by attaching a separate letter to this form." On the reverse side of the form under the words of the form reading "Employers Report on Employee's conduct while in employ," Rossi wrote the following:
>
> > On November 18th, 1988, I terminated Irene Goodman with cause. Her conduct while in our employ was less than acceptable. Her ethical conduct was questionable in many instances. Fortunately, however, because of close supervision she was made aware of proper ethical conduct which in itself assisted her in keeping out of trouble and offered her the luxury of enhancing her income.
> >
> > Ms. Goodman was a "top earner" and I regret having to report negative behaviour, however, when the public interest is at risk, I feel it my duty to do so.
> >
> > I have never reported anyone negatively before. I wish this were not necessary.

Ms Goodman commenced this action against Mr. Rossi for defamation based on this report. Mr. Rossi, some time after the pleadings were closed, moved for summary judgment dismissing the action and, in the alternative, for an order permanently staying the action on the ground that the claim was based on evidence obtained by the plaintiff in the unjust dismissal action. Ms Goodman brought a cross-motion for an order "giving leave to the plaintiff, *nunc pro tunc*, to commence the pending action for defamation against David J. Rossi."

The two motions were heard by Mr. Justice Borins. He dismissed the defendant's motion and, on the plaintiff's motion, made an order that the plaintiff be granted leave, *nunc pro tunc*, to proceed with the action. In his brief endorsed reasons he said:

I accept that there is a line of authority at first instance in this province which confirms the existence of the implied undertaking in Ontario ... . However, the authorities also recognize a discretion in the court to be exercised in appropriate circumstances to grant leave to a party to make use of information obtained as a result of the discovery process ... . Assuming that the report contains information about the plaintiff which is untrue, in my view the fact that this information is in the possession of the authority to which the plaintiff is required to apply to be licensed as a real estate agent or broker [means] that there is a reasonable risk of prejudice to the plaintiff in terms of her ability to be licensed. She could sustain a real injustice if she were prevented from having the court determine the accuracy of the report written by Mr. Rossi because without this opportunity for the foreseeable future there would be false information in the plaintiff's file at the Ministry which could have a serious effect on her ability to be licensed. Therefore, in my view in the circumstances of this case it is appropriate to grant relief from the undertaking to the plaintiff.

The defendant Rossi appealed, with leave granted by Boland J to the Divisional Court. In her reasons Boland J said:

... I think it is desirable leave be granted to determine the parameters of discretion to be exercised when granting leave to use documents or discovery information obtained in an earlier action.

Before the Divisional Court the issues were expanded beyond what is indicated in these reasons to include the basic question set forth in the opening sentence of O'Leary J's reasons [at 115]:

Is there in Ontario a rule of law that imposes an implied undertaking to the court by a party to whom information or documents are provided in an examination for discovery or through production of documents, that he will not use the information or the documents for any collateral or ulterior purpose, and that any such use is a contempt of court?

As I have said, in O'Leary J's opinion, which was concurred in by O'Driscoll J, there was no such rule. Moldaver J dissented on this question. He held that there was such a rule, which he expressed in the following terms [at 126]:

Where a party has obtained information by means of court compelled production of documents or discovery, which information could not otherwise have been obtained by legitimate means independent of the litigation process, the receiving party impliedly undertakes to the court that the private information so obtained will not be used, vis-à-vis the producing party, for a purpose outside the scope of the litigation for which the disclosure was made, absent consent of the producing party or with leave of the court; any failure to comply with this undertaking shall be a contempt of court.

    This rule shall remain in effect unless and until the private information is revealed in open court.

O'Leary J, on behalf of the majority, then dealt with the case as if Rossi had asked "for an order preventing Goodman from relying on the Notice of Employee Change as the basis for her claim that she was defamed" [at 125]. On this issue, he said [at 125]:

I agree with Borins J as to why such a request must be denied. The ends of justice require that Goodman be allowed to attempt to clear her name with the Ministry of Consumer and Commercial Relations, the authority which determines her fitness to hold a licence to sell real estate. She must be allowed to contest the truthfulness of the report made by Rossi by continuing with her action for defamation.

Moldaver J, at the conclusion of his reasons, came to the same conclusion on this question. He approached the case "as if Ms. Goodman had sought leave of the court to use the information contained within the report to bring a defamation suit against Mr. Rossi." ...

Should This Court Recognize an Implied Undertaking Rule Relating to the Use of Documents Obtained on Discovery?

I say at the outset that, because this is a case concerned with a document obtained on discovery, and not information obtained on examination for discovery, I shall confine this discussion to documents obtained on discovery. It may be that information obtained on examination for discovery does not raise exactly the same issues I shall discuss it briefly later. ...

I have concluded, on the basis of precedent and policy, that a particular version of the implied undertaking rule should be recognized in Ontario and I shall state my reasons for this conclusion in relatively brief compass.

As far as precedent is concerned, it can be discerned that in the latter part of the 19th century in England, courts had recognized a general principle that a party obtaining documents on discovery had an obligation not to make them public or, more specifically, use them otherwise than for the purpose of the proceeding in which they were obtained. ...

Although there were no Ontario decisions on the question in the nineteenth century, I note that when *The Ontario Judicature Act*, 1881 44 Vict. c. 5, was enacted, Rule 222, which was in a schedule to the Act, provided for the production of documents. ... [T]he principle is based on recognition of the general right of privacy which a person has with respect to his or her documents. The discovery process represents an intrusion on this right under the compulsory processes of the court. The necessary corollary is that this intrusion should not be allowed for any purpose other than that of securing justice in the proceeding in which the discovery takes place. ...

To continue with the treatment of the question in Ontario, I refer to W.B. Williston and R.J. Rolls, *The Law of Civil Procedure* (Toronto: Butterworths, 1970), at p. 941:

> There is an implied undertaking by a party to whom documents are produced that he will not use them for a collateral or ulterior purpose; any such use of the documents is a contempt of court.

Alterskye v. Scott, supra, is cited as the authority for this statement.

Finally, in Holmested and Gale's *The Judicature Act of Ontario and Rules of Practice*, vol. 2 (Scarborough, ON: Carswell, 1983), the following appears at p. 1813 [looseleaf] as one of the annotations to Rule 347, the immediate predecessor to the current rules relating to discovery of documents contained in Rule 30:

> Where a party is compelled to produce a document which would otherwise have
> remained confidential he is entitled to insist that it be used for the purposes of that
> action only and is entitled to the protection of the court against any other use.

The English Court of Appeal decision in *Riddick v. Thames Board Mills Ltd.*, [1977] 3
WLR 63, is cited for this proposition.

At p. 1786.36 of Holmested and Gale the following appears:

> Documents disclosed on discovery may only be used in the action in which they are
> disclosed: *Distillers Co. (Biochemicals) v. Times Newspapers Ltd.*, [1975] 1 All ER 41,
> granting an injunction restraining the use of the documents.

The rationale for the implied undertaking rule is compendiously stated in Matthews and
Malek's *Discovery* (1992), at p. 253:

> The primary rationale for the imposition of the implied undertaking is the protection of
> privacy. Discovery is an invasion of the right of the individual to keep his own
> documents to himself. It is a matter of public interest to safeguard that right. The
> purpose of the undertaking is to protect, so far as is consistent with the proper conduct
> of the action, the confidentiality of a party's documents. It is in general wrong that one
> who is compelled by law to produce documents for the purpose of particular
> proceedings should be in peril of having those documents used by the other party for
> some purpose other than the purpose of the particular legal proceedings and, in
> particular, that they should be made available to third parties who might use them to the
> detriment of the party who has produced them on discovery. A further rationale is the
> promotion of full discovery, as without such an undertaking the fear of collateral use
> may in some cases operate as a disincentive to proper discovery. The interests of proper
> administration of justice require that there should be no disincentive to full and frank
> discovery.

As far as the state of the law on this issue at the time of Craig J's decision in *Lac
Minerals* is concerned, I do not, with respect, think that it can be said that this decision
imported the implied undertaking rule wholesale into Ontario or that the decision was
contrary to a generally held opinion of the litigation bar. In this respect Holmes's definition of law as a prediction of what the courts will do, in fact, is apposite. See "The Path
of the Law" (1896-97) 10 Harv. L Rev. 457, at p. 461.

The absence of an Ontario decision on the point does not indicate that the law was
the contrary to that declared in *Lac Minerals*, that is, that a party was free to make any
use that he or she saw fit with documents obtained on discovery. There was no reported
decision to this effect and, to the extent that the question may have been considered
directly, I would think that there would have been an instinctive reaction against such a
use based on the general principles to which I have referred. In this regard, it is instructive to read the views expressed in the Martin Report with respect to the developing
field of discovery in criminal cases, on the importance of privacy interests, and of
preventing the misuse of materials disclosed by the prosecution (Report of the Attorney
General's Advisory Committee on Charge Screening, Disclosure, and Resolution Discussions (Toronto: Ministry of the Attorney General, 1993) (the Hon. G. Arthur Martin,
Chair), at pp. 175 and 179-183).

Further, the legal materials to which I have referred (Taylor and Ewart's *The Judicature Act and Rules, 1881* (1881), Williston and Rolls, *The Law of Civil Procedure* (1970), and Holmested and Gale's *The Judicature Act of Ontario and Rules of Practice* (1983)) all are to the effect that there is an obligation not to make collateral use of documents obtained on discovery and, also, as far as the latter two works are concerned, an implied undertaking to support the enforcement of this obligation. While these works are not, in themselves, law, they reflect the views of eminent and experienced lawyers and should be given careful consideration in determining what a court, in fact, should and would do in deciding the question we are considering.

I have had some concern about recognizing the implied undertaking part of the rule, which, as I have said, affords the basis for the contempt sanction. This concern is based on the fact that the underlying theory, indicated in some of the English cases, is that the undertaking to the court is implied as a condition of obtaining an *order* for discovery of documents (see, e.g., *Alterskye v. Scott, supra*, at p. 470, and Esson JA in *Kyuquot Logging, supra*, at pp. 71-73). Discovery of documents in Ontario since at least 1881 has been virtually automatic. In 1881 a praecipe order, obtained under the rule, triggered the obligation to grant discovery. Since 1913 that compulsion on a party to grant discovery has been imposed directly by a notice under the rules of court without the necessity of a court order. ...

Having considered the matter, I do not think that the absence of an order in our practice stands in the way of recognizing the implied undertaking. The compulsion to disclose and produce imposed by the rule of court is virtually identical to that imposed by an order of the court. In this regard I refer to *Prudential Assurance Co. v. Fountain Page Ltd.*, [1991] 1 WLR 756 (QB), at pp. 764-765, where Hobhouse J said with regard to the implied undertaking:

> This undertaking is implied whether the court expressly requires it or not. The expression of the obligation as an implied undertaking given to the court derives from the historical origin of the principle. *It is now in reality a legal obligation which arises by operation of law by virtue of the circumstances under which the relevant person obtained the documents or information.* However treating it as having the character of an implied undertaking continues to serve a useful purpose in that it confirms that the obligation is one which is owed to the court for the benefit of the parties, not one which is owed simply to the parties; likewise, it is an obligation which the court has the right to control and can modify or release a party from. It is an obligation which arises from legal process and therefore is within the control of the court, gives rise to direct sanctions which the court may impose (viz. contempt of court) and can be relieved or modified by an order of the court. It is thus a formulation of the obligation which has merit and convenience and enables it to be treated flexibly having regard to circumstances of any particular case. ...
>
> The rationale basis for the rule is that where one party compels another, *either by the enforcement of a rule of court or a specific order of the court*, to disclose documents or information whether that other wishes to or not, the party obtaining the disclosure is given this power because the invasion of the other party's rights has to give way to the need to do justice between those parties in the pending litigation between them; it follows from this that the results of such compulsion should likewise be limited to the

purpose for which the order was made, namely, the purposes of that litigation then
before the court between those parties and not for any other litigation or matter or any
collateral purpose: see, for example, per Lord Keith of Kinkel in *Home Office v.
Harman* [1983] 1 AC 280, 308. [Emphasis added.]

I think that there would be a serious gap in the range of possible sanctions for
breach of the obligation not to make improper use of documents disclosed on discovery,
if it were not associated with an implied undertaking to the court and, therefore, capable
of giving rise to a contempt of court order. In many cases, depending on how the issue
arises, other remedies may be more appropriate, such as an injunction, before any
improper use has occurred, or, as in this case, a motion to stay or dismiss a proceeding.
In some cases, however, for example, where the breach has occurred and there is no
other appropriate remedy, contempt proceedings may be the only avenue. It might reasonably be expected that knowledge of the possibility of contempt proceedings would
deter breaches of the implied undertaking from taking place.

With respect to the relevant policy considerations on whether there should be (1) a
general implied undertaking rule, with relief from its application being dealt with in the
form of a motion to the court by the party who has obtained the document on discovery
or the consent of the party from whom the document was obtained, or (2) on the other
hand, a general rule that any use may be made of documents obtained on discovery
unless the party from whom the discovery was obtained obtains an order prohibiting a
particular use, I prefer the first alternative. It is a more logical and efficient rule. Under
it there should be fewer motions to the court than under the second alternative. I shall
not elaborate on this beyond saying that I agree with the reasons of Moldaver J in this
proceeding, the dissenting reasons of Esson JA in *Kyuquot Logging Ltd. v. British Columbia Forest Products Ltd.*, *supra*, and those of the British Columbia Court of Appeal
in *Hunt v. T & N plc*, *supra*. In *Hunt* the court said:

> After much consideration, we prefer the dissenting views of Esson JA in *Kyuquot*,
> mainly because we think it anomalous to recognize a right of privacy and an obligation
> to use discovery documents only in the proceedings in which they are produced, but
> then to require the owner to take steps to prevent a breach of that obligation. As has
> been pointed out in many cases, that party will not always know there is or will be an
> intention not to honour the obligation. It is true that the obligation is enforceable by
> injunction, but quia timet applications should be reserved for unusual cases, and not as
> part of the regular discovery process.

The state of the law on this issue in the rest of Canada is a relevant consideration.
All jurisdictions that have considered it have decided in favour of the implied undertaking rule. ...

At the time of the Divisional Court's judgment, the law in British Columbia, declared in *Kyuquot Logging*, was against the implied undertaking, but *Kyuquot* has since
been overruled by *Hunt*.

Until the decision of the Divisional Court this year in this proceeding, the steady
course of decision in Ontario since *Lac Minerals* in 1985 has accepted the existence of
the implied undertaking rule and, accordingly, whatever may have been the case before

1985, the reasonable expectations of the bar have been that the obligations of the rule are part of the law.

These considerations, uniformity in Canada, and a steady course of decision in this province are factors, in addition to earlier precedent and policy, which support the continued recognition of the rule in Ontario.

In arriving at my general conclusion I have not overlooked the state of the law in the United States, which was a factor in both the majority reasons in *Kyuquot* and the majority reasons of the Divisional Court in this proceeding. In this era of international commerce and litigation it is sensible to consider American law. At the risk of oversimplifying the American position, it appears to be quite contrary to that involved in the implied undertaking. In the United States the general rule is that a party obtaining documents through the discovery process has the right to use them for any purpose unless the other party has obtained a protective order with respect to their use. Protective orders, unless consented to, are granted on relatively narrow or specific grounds. ...

It appears that our discovery law, as articulated in the cases, has proceeded along lines significantly different from that of the United States—such that the adoption of the American position would involve a fundamental shift from, as opposed to a minor adjustment of, our basic principles. I refer, in this respect, to the quotation from *Hunt v. T & N plc*, set forth above. Accordingly, neither principled nor practical considerations suggest to me that we should adopt the United States approach.

It is relevant to an examination of the question before us to consider whether the law on this subject may more properly be legislated by the Civil Rules Committee in the form of additions to the *Rules of Civil Procedure* rather than declared by the courts as cases arise. O'Leary J was of the view that "if the time comes when it appears a rule may be necessary to protect privacy infringed by the discovery process, that rule should be framed by the Rules Committee, not the court."

I think that it is preferable that the rule we are considering be set forth as part of the discovery rules in the *Rules of Civil Procedure* rather than in the case law. This does not mean, however, that I think that the responsible course to take now would be to hold that there is no implied undertaking rule and that there will not be one until the Civil Rules Committee has acted. ...

The advantage of incorporating the law on this subject into the *Rules of Civil Procedure* is that the rules can deal with the subject completely and comprehensively, something that is not really possible or proper within the confines of a single case—and it even can be difficult in a series of cases. A properly drawn rule could meet possible concerns about legislation stultifying the development of the law as new circumstances arise. It could give clear guidance on the nature and scope of the obligation not to make improper use of material obtained on discovery and the exceptions to the rule in the form of relief granted by the court, by conferring discretion on the court, where appropriate, to be exercised having regard to stated factors. See, for example, r. 31.11(7). Further, any identified shortcomings in the rules can be amended more quickly than those in judicial decisions if the field were left to be entirely occupied by case law.

Having indicated my preference that this subject be dealt with by rules, I am, nonetheless, obligated to state my view on the nature and scope of the implied undertaking rule, at least in so far as it relates to this case. The basic question is, what is an "improper" use of documents obtained on discovery? In *Alterskye v. Scott, supra*, at p. 470, there is the much-quoted expression "not to use ... the documents ... for ... any ulterior or collateral" purpose. In *Home Office v. Harman*, [1982] 1 All ER 532 (HL), at p. 536, Lord Diplock said:

> I take the expression "collateral or ulterior purpose" from the judgment of Jenkins J in *Alterskye v. Scott* [1948] 1 All ER 469. I do not use it in a pejorative sense, but merely to indicate some purpose different from that which was the only reason why, under a procedure designed to achieve justice in civil actions, she was accorded the advantage, which she would not otherwise have had, of having in her possession copies of other people's documents.

Lord Keith, at p. 540, treated the obligation as being "not to make use of the documents for any purpose other than the proper conduct of the litigation in the course of which the order [for discovery] was made." ... Still on the scope of the rule, I shall mention other matters which I do not have to decide for the purpose of this case but which the rules-makers would have to consider. The duration of the obligation under the implied undertaking rule is an important question. In *Home Office v. Harman*, supra, the House of Lords held that it continued after the documents in question had been read out in open court during the trial of an action in which the documents had been obtained on discovery. This decision was overruled by r. 14A of O.24 of the *Rules of the Supreme Court 1965* which was added to the rules in 1987. It reads:

> 14A. Any undertaking, whether express or implied, not to use a document for any purposes other than those of the proceedings in which it is disclosed shall cease to apply to such document after it has been read to or by the Court, or referred to, in open Court, unless the Court for special reasons has otherwise ordered on the application of a party or of the person to whom the document belongs.

Moldaver J, in his reasons in this proceeding, would have incorporated this limitation into his common law rule.

Essentially for the reasons of Moldaver J and the dissenting reasons of Lord Scarman in *Home Office v. Harman*, given on behalf of himself and Lord Simon, I incline to the view that the rule should be so limited. It may be noted that r. 14A has an exception not referred to in Moldaver J's proposed rule.

Moldaver J incorporated into his rule two other features that should be considered by the rules-makers: (1) the rule would cover only information that the receiving party could not otherwise have obtained by legitimate means independent of the litigation process, and (2) that the obligation would be in favour of the producing party only, not third parties.

Also, I think that it would be useful to consider whether the obligation should extend to preventing the use of material obtained on discovery from being used for impeachment purposes. It could defeat the impeachment process to require the leave of the court before discovered material could be used for this purpose. See John B. Laskin, "The Implied Undertaking," ... pp. 19-21 [in Canadian Bar Association—Ontario, Continuing Legal Education Program, *Privilege and Confidential Information in Litigation* (Toronto: October 19, 1991)]. See, also, r. 30.09, which enables a privileged document to be used at trial for impeachment without the necessity of obtaining leave.

As far as the scope of the rule is concerned there is also the question of what range of pre-trial disclosures should be covered. Within the area of discovery itself, there is the question whether the rule should cover oral evidence given on examination for discovery. This question does not arise in this case and need not, therefore, be decided. Having said this, I must acknowledge that, having regard to the compulsory nature of oral discovery and its impingement on the right of privacy of a party, it is difficult to see why, as a matter of principle, the rule would not apply to this form of discovery. It has been held that the rule does apply to oral discovery evidence (*Reichmann v. Toronto Life Publishing Co.* (1988), 28 CPC (2d) 11 (Ont. HC)). In the English text, Matthews and Malek, *Discovery* (1992), at p. 312, the opinion is expressed that "[a]lthough there is no reported authority as to whether the implied undertaking on discovery in relation to documents applies to interrogatories, it is submitted that in principle the implied undertaking does extend to interrogatories, as they are a form of discovery, to which answers are given under compulsion and not being provided voluntarily." ...

In *Ray v. Port Arthur, Duluth & Western Railway* (1903), 2 OWR 345 (CA), the examination for discovery of one of the defendants, in another action, was regarded as admissible. This decision was concerned with the method of proof of this evidence. Clearly, it was admissible under the law of evidence as an admission. No issue respecting the improper use of this evidence, having regard to its source, appears to have been raised or considered by the court. ...

In addition, there are existing rules which have some bearing on the matter. Rule 31.11(8) enables the evidence given on an examination for discovery in an action to be read in evidence or used at the trial of a subsequent action between the same parties "involving the same subject matter." Rule 51.06(1), among other matters, enables a party to obtain "such an order as the party may be entitled to on an admission" in the examination for discovery of the other party "in the same or another proceeding."

I mention these factors not to cast any real doubt on the proper applicability of the implied undertaking rule to examination for discovery, but rather to indicate the desirability of having the matter dealt with in a coherent set of rules.

Relief from the Implied Undertaking

It is a necessary and appropriate part of the implied undertaking rule that the court have the power to grant relief from its application. In the present case, Borins J, on the assumption that the implied undertaking rule applied, granted relief from its application so that Ms Goodman would have the opportunity to clear her name with the ministry, which has the authority to license her as a real estate agent or broker.

O'Leary J accepted this reasoning as the basis of *refusing* to make an order preventing Ms Goodman from relying on the notice of employee change as the basis of her action. Moldaver J agreed with O'Leary J's reasons in relieving Ms Goodman from her implied undertaking. O'Leary J said [at 125]:

> The ends of justice require that Goodman be allowed to attempt to clear her name with the Ministry of Consumer and Commercial Relations, the authority which determines her fitness to hold a licence to sell real estate. She must be allowed to contest the truthfulness of the report made by Rossi by continuing with her action for defamation.

I note, at this point, that approaching the question in the context of the law accepted by O'Leary J there would be no restriction on the use of the document unless Mr. Rossi could satisfy the court that there was reason for imposing one. The onus would be on Mr. Rossi. In the context of the law assumed by Borins J for the purpose of addressing the question, and accepted by Moldaver J as being applicable, the onus would be the other way around—the restriction would apply unless Ms Goodman could satisfy the court that it should not apply.

The criteria for granting relief from the implied undertaking rule are an important part of the rule itself. In *Crest Homes plc v. Marks*, [1987] 2 All ER 1074, Lord Oliver said, at p. 108, on behalf of the House of Lords, that the authorities on the question "illustrate no general principle beyond this, that the court will not release or modify the implied undertaking given on discovery save in special circumstances and where the release or modification will not occasion injustice to the person giving discovery."

For the purposes of resolving the case before us I need not deal with this question exhaustively or definitively. Certainly, the accepted grounds for granting relief from the implied undertaking rule should not be so broadly based that the integrity of the rule is routinely infringed. In *Carbone v. De La Rocha* (1993), 13 OR (3d) 355 (Gen. Div.), a defamation action based on documents held to have been produced in the context of discovery in an earlier action, Whalen J refused to grant leave to use the documents as a basis of the claim. His reasons, which include extensive reference to the similar case of *Riddick v. Thames Board Mills Ltd.*, [1977] QB 881 (CA), are a helpful consideration of the "injustice" to the person giving the discovery. He concluded his reasons on this question, at p. 369, as follows:

> The process of this court cannot be or appear to be an instrument of the initiation of litigation not otherwise contemplated or part of the cause of action which disclosed the potentially new claim. To be so would undermine full and frank disclosure by parties. This would be contrary to the public interest and is an abuse of the process of the court.

Of course, there will be cases where the interests of the discovered party sought to be protected by the rule will not be seriously affected, or affected at all, by a collateral use of discovered document, but those of the discovering party would be seriously affected if use could not be made of the documents. This is the kind of case where it would reasonably be thought that the discovered party would give his or her consent to the use of the documents but, failing this, would be a proper case for granting relief.

For the purpose of the present case I am prepared to consider the applicable test as being more liberal than that stated in *Crest Homes*—as one tolerating some injustice to the discovered party if it is outweighed by a greater injustice to the discovering party if he or she could not make use of the discovered documents.

In this case Ms Goodman would not have the alleged defamatory document or be aware of its existence except for its production in the earlier unjust dismissal action. It has not been published in any way and access to it in the ministry file is severely restricted (*Real Estate and Business Brokers Act*, RSO 1990, c. R.4, s. 16). Apart from the publicity which may have been given to it in this action, the filing of the document with the Ministry could not have resulted in any injury to her general reputation.

In this latter regard, the importance of the action to her is said to be to clear her name with the ministry. Insofar as the judgment of a court could accomplish this purpose it would appear that this could equally be accomplished in the unjust dismissal action, if it is found that the alleged basis of her dismissal was unfounded.

Also, there is no reason submitted on behalf of Ms Goodman why she would be unable to challenge the accuracy of the document directly with the ministry should the ministry indicate that it intended to act upon it in any way. I note that we were informed by the parties that some time before the commencement of this action Ms Goodman had, in fact, been registered as a broker under the *Real Estate and Business Brokers Act*.

Returning to Mr. Rossi's position, the action carries with it not only the injustice of being penalized for having made full discovery, but also the risk of prejudice in the form of exerting extraneous pressure with respect to the settlement of the unjust dismissal action.

For these reasons I think that the injustice to Mr. Rossi in allowing the action to proceed significantly outweighs that to Ms Goodman in ordering a stay of it.

Disposition

I would set aside the orders of the Divisional Court and of Borins J. In their place I would grant an order, on the defendant's motion, staying this action, and dismiss the plaintiff's motion for relief from the implied undertaking.

The issues raised are of sufficient novelty and difficulty that I think that it is appropriate to make no order as to costs at any level.

Appeal allowed.

NOTES AND QUESTIONS

1. After this decision, and following the suggestion made by Morden ACJO in *Goodman*, Ontario rule 30.1 was passed. In formulating the rule, the Civil Rules Committee did not limit itself to codifying the case law but took the opportunity to contour and refine the implied undertaking principle. Because (in Ontario) the principle now takes its force from this rule, it seemed appropriate to rename it a "deemed undertaking."

2. Recall *Hunt v. T & N plc*, discussed above, when we were dealing with "ingathered" documents, in which production was sought of documents already produced in US proceedings and of deposition transcripts from those US proceedings. Had the earlier proceedings been in Ontario, rather than the United States, how would the case have played out?

Albert Starr v. Richardson House Limited and George Richardson*

The following is a raw statement of the alleged facts of the case:

The plaintiff, Albert Starr, is 32 years old, married, with one child age 4. He has grade twelve education and up to the time of this incident was employed as a salesman, a job he had held for three years. Before that, he was employed by the same company as a bookkeeper. He lives near Belleville, Ontario where he was born and raised.

He is intelligent—perhaps more intelligent than his grade twelve education and job would suggest. He is of a serious nature but has always been considered by his friends and family as somewhat withdrawn and lethargic. His job as a salesman requires him to travel, to meet people, and to do a certain amount of entertaining. Because of his withdrawn and reserved nature, the job doesn't really suit him, but he doesn't really know what else to do. He is well liked by his employer who recognizes, however, that it was perhaps a mistake to put him into a position where he had a higher profile with the public. In other words, he was a competent bookkeeper although perhaps too bright for the position; in his position as a salesman he is somewhat over his head—not because of any lack of wit or intelligence, but because he finds the personal contact required somewhat difficult. For sometime prior to the incident here, he had been considering a change of job, but had been unable to find any alternate employment.

On the evening of January 18, 1975, Starr drove to the Richardson House, located approximately half a mile from his home. The Richardson House is located in the country approximately two miles from the Belleville city limits. It is accessible only by car. Its main business is that of a beer parlour although there are few rooms in the building.

Starr had been a regular customer at the Richardson House for the last two or three years. He was well known to the manager, George Richardson, who came on duty on the evening of January 18 as manager and tapman at about 7 o'clock. Starr sat by himself at a table approximately 20 feet away from Richardson's position behind the bar where Richardson could observe him at all times. Starr came to the hotel at about 7:30 p.m.

---

* These materials are intended to be used with or without a videotape program, "The Conduct of a Civil Action" (Media Centre, University of Toronto). The videotape is based on the pre-1985 Ontario rules. However, the forms provided here are intended to comply with the new rules.

and left at about 10:30 p.m., during which period he was served at least ten beers and possibly as many as sixteen beers by the two waiters.

On a previous occasion, about six months before this incident, Richardson had had to ask Starr to leave the hotel because he had become intoxicated and somewhat abusive to other patrons. On the evening of January 18, at around 10:25, Richardson became aware that Starr had consumed to excess and that he was becoming somewhat abusive to several other patrons. In particular, he had been troubling a group of younger customers, two men and two women, who were taking exception to some of the remarks that he was addressing to them.

At about 10:25, Richardson went over to Starr and told him that he had better leave. Starr stood up, obviously unsteady, and indicated that he was not ready to go and that he wanted to sit for a while "to steady down." Richardson took him by the arm and escorted him from the beverage room to the door leading out to the parking lot. Richardson asked Starr how he planned to get home and Starr mumbled that since he was too drunk to walk he would have to drive, and that he had no money for a taxi. Richardson waited at the door while Starr struggled to his car. Richardson could see that Starr was intoxicated and that he was having difficulty walking to the car, finding his keys, and getting the car started. Richardson says that the reason he waited until Starr got into the car was to make sure that he would not try to come back into the beverage room.

Starr managed to get the car going and drove out of the hotel parking lot, but within a few hundred yards, the car went off the road and struck a tree. He has no recollection of anything that happened after he got into his car.

In the collision with the tree, Starr sustained a broken wrist which has adequately healed. He also struck his head on the windshield and suffered a minor concussion. He was found shortly after the impact in an unconscious state, taken to the Belleville General Hospital where he was examined, treated, and discharged within two days, his wrist in a cast and apparently having recovered from the bump on the head. He was convicted of impaired driving as a result of the accident, his state of intoxication at the time of driving having been established by the evidence of Richardson in a Provincial Court trial.

Starr returned to work within one week of the incident. From the start he experienced great difficulty in accomplishing his normal work. He was unable to perform his salesman's functions and began to suffer from severe headaches approximately two weeks after the incident. He describes the headaches as involving his whole head and a feeling of pressure, as if his head were in a vice. The headaches made it impossible for him to continue working and after about two-and-a-half weeks of trying to work, he stayed at home, receiving disability benefits for the period allowed by his insurance. He is still experiencing severe headaches although they have become less frequent. However, he has become entirely unable to function and has not been able to return to work. He has no interest in returning to work or in finding another job. At present, his wife, who did not work before this, has obtained a job and is supporting the family. Starr stays at home looking after the child and has become extremely withdrawn and lethargic. He is unwilling to see friends and shows very little interest in life. He finds it difficult to concentrate on any task he undertakes, is irritable, depressed, and tends to weep easily.

He often feels faint and spends prolonged periods in bed, suffers from excessive sweating, and says that he has recurring dreams of being in a car accident.

Starr's general practitioner referred him to a psychiatrist. The psychiatrist examined him on two occasions and has given the opinion that Starr is suffering from a neurosis brought on by the trauma of the accident on January 18. The psychiatrist's opinion is that the neurosis from which Starr is now suffering was definitely triggered by the accident, but he says it was not solely caused by the accident. According to the psychiatrist, Starr was a man with definite emotional and psychological problems prior to the incident, but had been coping with these problems. The psychiatrist says that Starr is now entirely unable to cope as a result of trauma of the collision.

Starr has refused to undergo a course of treatment recommended by the psychiatrist because he is convinced that his problem is of a purely physical nature.

Court file no. *7421/XX*

I don't have this
when file

ONTARIO
SUPERIOR COURT OF JUSTICE

BETWEEN:

Ct. name

ALBERT STARR

PLAINTIFF

Parties

and

RICHARDSON HOUSE LIMITED
and
GEORGE RICHARDSON

DEFENDANTS

STATEMENT OF CLAIM

TO THE DEFENDANTS

*Boiler
Plate
?*

A LEGAL PROCEEDING HAS BEEN COMMENCED AGAINST YOU by the Plaintiff. The claim made against you is set out in the following pages.

IF YOU WISH TO DEFEND THIS PROCEEDING, you or an Ontario lawyer acting for you must prepare a Statement of Defence in Form 18A prescribed by the Rules of Civil Procedure, serve it on the Plaintiff's lawyer or, where the Plaintiff does not have a lawyer, serve it on the Plaintiff, and file it, with proof of service, in this court office, WITHIN TWENTY DAYS after this Statement of Claim is served on you, if you are served in Ontario.

If you are served in another province or territory of Canada or in the United States of America, the period for serving and filing your Statement of Defence is forty days. If you are served outside Canada and the United States of America, the period is sixty days.

Instead of serving and filing a Statement of Defence, you may serve and file a Notice of Intent to Defend in Form 18B prescribed by the Rules of Civil Procedure. This will entitle you to ten more days within which to serve and file your Statement of Defence.

IF YOU FAIL TO DEFEND THIS PROCEEDING, JUDGMENT MAY BE GIVEN AGAINST YOU IN YOUR ABSENCE AND WITHOUT FURTHER NOTICE TO YOU.

If you wish to defend this proceeding but are unable to pay legal fees, legal aid may be available to you by contacting a local Legal Aid office.

IF YOU PAY THE PLAINTIFF'S CLAIM, and $500.00 for costs, within the time for serving and filing your Statement of Defence you may move to have this proceeding dismissed by the Court. If you believe the amount claimed for costs is excessive, you may pay the Plaintiff's claim and $100.00 for costs and have the costs assessed by the Court.

Date September 14, 19XX

Issued by J.J. Jones
   Local registrar
      cf.- registrar office stamp.

To: Richardson House Limited
      264 Careful Drive
      Belleville, Ontario.

Defendants

      George Richardson
      264 Careful Drive
      Belleville, Ontario.

Address of court office: 2 Quinte St.,
                    Belleville, Ontario

CLAIM

1. **THE PLAINTIFF(S) CLAIM(S):**

    (a) special damages in the amount of $24,650.00, and any further special damages incurred up to the time of trial.

    (b) general damages in the amount of $200,000.

    (c) Pre-judgment interest on said amounts.

    (d) the costs of this action.

    (e) such further and other relief as this honourable court may deem just.

2. The plaintiff is a salesman and resides in the City of Belleville in the County of Hastings.

3. The defendant Richardson House Limited is a limited company incorporated under the laws of Ontario and operates a tavern known as the Richardson House in the County of Hastings.

4. The defendant George Richardson is the President and principal shareholder of the Richardson House Limited and is the manager of the Richardson House.

5. On January 18, 19XX, the plaintiff attended at the Richardson House, arriving at about 7 p.m. The plaintiff was served beer by the defendant George Richardson and two waiters employed by defendant Richardson House Limited from the time of his arrival until shortly after 10 p.m.

6. The plaintiff says that he was served beer by the defendant and their servants after he had become intoxicated although the defendant knew or ought to have known that the plaintiff was in a state of intoxication.

7. Shortly after 10 p.m., the plaintiff was evicted from the tavern by the defendant George Richardson. The plaintiff says that at the time the defendant George Richardson evicted him from the tavern, the plaintiff was, to the knowledge of both defendants, in an intoxicated state and incapable of providing for his own safety and security and incapable of driving his automobile.

8. After having been evicted from the tavern, the plaintiff, with the full knowledge of the defendants, proceeded to get into his automobile and attempted to drive the automobile along Highway 14 to his home which is approximately two miles from the defendant's tavern.

9. The plaintiff was unable to properly control the course of his automobile because of his intoxicated state, and the automobile collided with a tree within a few hundred yards of the defendant's tavern.

Material Facts

10. As a result of the collision described in paragraph 9 hereof, the plaintiff sustained serious injury to his body including a fractured right wrist and a severe concussion.

11. As a direct result of the injuries sustained, the plaintiff suffers from a severe depressive neurosis and has been unable to return to work because of this condition.

12. The plaintiff says that in breach of section 56(3) of the Liquor License Act, RSO 1970 c. 250 and section 69 of the Liquor Control Act, RSO 1970 c. 279 and in breach of their common-law duty of care to the plaintiff, the defendants sold and supplied the plaintiff beer when the plaintiff was apparently in an intoxicated condition, and that the injuries sustained by the plaintiff were a direct result of the defendant's wrongful conduct.

13. The plaintiff further says that the defendants were both under a duty in the circumstances to take all reasonable steps to ensure that the plaintiff would not, on account of his intoxicated condition, cause himself harm or so conduct himself as to sustain personal injury.

14. The plaintiff says that the defendants were in negligent breach of their duty of care to him in that they knew or ought to have known that the plaintiff was, due to his intoxicated condition, unable to properly care for his own personal safety in that the defendants failed:

(a) to permit the plaintiff to recover from his intoxication before ordering him from their premises,

(b) to provide a safe means of conveying the plaintiff from their tavern to his place of residence,

(c) to prevent the plaintiff from attempting to drive his automobile.

15. As a result of his injuries, the plaintiff has sustained the following damages:

(a) medical and hospital expenses to date $650,000,

(b) loss of income to date $24,000.00,

(c) general damages—$200,000.00.

The plaintiff(s) propose(s) that this action be tried at: Belleville

Date of issue: 14 September, 19XX   Jones and Jones
                                            Barristers & Solicitors
                                            2 Queen Street
                                            Belleville, Ontario
                                            K1P 3U6
                                            (613) 722-5913
                                            Solicitors for the Plaintiff

ALBERT STARR   **and**   RICHARDSON HOUSE LIMITED and
GEORGE RICHARDSON

PLAINTIFF(S)   DEFENDANT(S)

(Short title of proceeding)

Court file no. 7421/xx

ONTARIO
SUPERIOR COURT OF JUSTICE
Proceeding commenced at Belleville

STATEMENT OF CLAIM

Jones and Jones
Barristers and Solicitors
2 Queen Street
Belleville, Ontario
K1P 3U6
J.J. Jones (613) 722-5913
Fax (613) 722-5914

Court file no. *7421/XX*

ONTARIO
SUPERIOR COURT OF JUSTICE
BETWEEN:

ALBERT STARR

PLAINTIFF

and

RICHARDSON HOUSE LIMITED
and
GEORGE RICHARDSON

DEFENDANTS

STATEMENT OF DEFENCE OF RICHARDSON HOUSE LIMITED and
GEORGE RICHARDSON

1. The defendant admits the allegations contained in paragraphs 2, 3, and 4
of the statement of claim.

2. The defendant denies the allegations contained in paragraphs 1, 5, 6, 7,
8, 11, 12, 13, 14 and 15
of the statement of claim.

3. The defendant has no knowledge in respect of the allegations contained in
paragraph 9
of the statement of claim.

4. The defendants admit that the plaintiff attended their tavern on January 18, 19XX at approximately 7 p.m., and say further that in fact the plaintiff did, of his own volition consume a quantity of beer while in the tavern.

5. The defendants deny that they served beer to the plaintiff after the point at which they knew or ought to have known that the plaintiff was in an intoxicated state. The defendants further deny that the plaintiff was in such a state of intoxication as to be unable to provide for his own safety and security as alleged in the Statement of Claim.

6. The defendants say that in fact the plaintiff became disorderly and unruly while in their tavern and that the plaintiff's conduct fully justified the defendants in evicting the plaintiff from their premises. The defendants plead and rely upon sections 56(5) and (6) of the Liquor License Act RSO 1970 c. 250.

7. In the alternative, the defendants say that if the plaintiff was intoxicated to the extent alleged in the Statement of Claim he came to that state of his own volition, and the defendants deny that they were under any duty of care to the plaintiff in the circumstances pleaded and say that the plaintiff was the author of his own misfortune.

8. In the further alternative, the defendants say that in the circumstances pleaded, the plaintiff was contributorily negligent in driving or attempting to drive while intoxicated and that he drove his car in a negligent manner, and that such negligence was the direct and sole cause of his injuries.

9. The defendants deny that the plaintiff suffers from a depressive neurosis, and in the alternative, if in fact he does suffer from such a condition deny that this condition and the plaintiff's inability to work was in any way caused by the accident or anything done by the defendants.

10. The defendants further say that the damages claimed are excessive and put the plaintiff to the strict proof thereof.

11. The defendants therefore submit that the plaintiff's claim be dismissed with costs.

Date: 3rd day of October, 19XX

Smith and Smith
22 Queen Street
Belleville, Ontario
K1P 3U5
(613) 722-6298

TO: Jones and Jones
2 Queen Street
Belleville, Ontario
K1P 3U6

MEMORANDUM

To: Defence Counsel

From: Articling Student

Subject: Richardson House Limited and George Richardson, ats: Starr

---

At your request, I spoke with Mr. Michael Williams, Albert Starr's employer. He was rather reluctant to talk with me but I did find out a few things about Starr that might be useful. Prior to the accident, Starr had been employed by Williams for about seven years—during the first four years and during the three years immediately before the accident he was a salesman.

Williams says that Starr was an honest and conscientious employee but he always kept very much to himself. He was a first-rate bookkeeper but there was nothing more he could do in that line with the company and Starr decided that he needed more money when his wife became pregnant and decided to stop working so she could look after the child. Williams suggested that he try selling thinking that it might "bring him out of his shell." Starr agreed, and while he did whatever he was asked to do by Williams, he definitely was never a "self-starter." According to Williams, Starr disliked the entertaining and travelling required of a salesman and could never really shake his shyness and withdrawn nature. Williams said that he even had calls from one or two of his better customers suggesting that Starr didn't seem very interested in giving them the service they wanted, and that when he took the matter up with Starr, Starr just shrugged his shoulders. About two months before the accident, Starr came to Williams and asked if there wasn't something else he could do as he "just couldn't take it any longer." Williams told him that he had no other opening and encouraged him to stick it out a little longer. Starr said that he was ready to throw in the towel and asked about the company's group disability benefits. Williams explained what Starr would get and Starr said that he would get his doctor to write the necessary letter and take some time to try and sort himself out.

Williams says that after the accident Starr seemed to be in a daze and just couldn't get going at all. Starr came to him after trying for about a week or two and told him that he was unable to continue. Since Starr stopped working, Williams has seen him on one or two occasions, and Starr has indicated that he is not interested in returning to work.

MEDICAL REPORT

August 14, 19XX

JONES & JONES
Barristers and Solicitors
2 Queen Street
Belleville, Ontario

Re: Albert Starr

Dear Mr. Jones:

I understand that you are acting on behalf of Albert Starr in a law suit and require a report from me as to Starr's psychiatric condition.

Starr was referred to me by Dr. Smithers, his family doctor, and I have seen the patient on two conditions—once in March 19XX and again about two months ago.

During my first meeting with Starr, he emphasized that he could not understand why he had been sent to a psychiatrist because he is convinced that his problems have a physical basis. He repeated this sentiment on the second visit but on both occasions appeared to be doing his best to relate to me and to respond to my questions.

The patient complains of the following symptoms. Shortly after the accident, he began to suffer from severe headaches that he describes as involving his whole head and a feeling of pressure as if his head were in a vice. These headaches continued to be severe for some three to four months after the accident. The patient now experiences them somewhat less frequently and usually after he has been exposed to a stressful situation. He complains of an inability to concentrate, feeling irritable even with his four year old child of whom he is very fond, and a tendency to weep easily. He has experienced a recurring dream of being in a car accident although he apparently has no direct recollection of the actual accident to which he attributes his problems. He also has a tendency to faintness and indicated that he spends prolonged periods in bed.

Generally speaking, on both occasions the patient appeared to be moderately depressed indicated by a pervasive sadness, lethargy, and absence of any emotional modulation in demeanour and conversation.

At our first meeting, I asked him what he did for a living, and he replied that until the accident, he had been a salesman. When asked about what was involved in his work, he indicated plainly that he was "not cut out" to be a salesman, and seemed to be quite uncomfortable about discussing his work at all.

He appears to feel that he is capable of handling a much better job and can't quite understand why he never got himself some other employment. He felt that the customers he had to deal with were unreasonable in their demands and developed a real dread of having to lunch, dine, or have a drink with them although he realizes that they expect this sort of thing. He knows that the customers think him to be a bit strange and that his attitude has cost him sales and income. He mentioned that he had discussed the situation prior to the accident with his wife and employer, and that they had both encouraged him to continue. He obviously feels self-reproach for not having had the initiative that would enable him to support his family.

I inquired of Starr as to his family life before the accident. He appears to have been happily married to a supportive wife, although there had been some quarrelling about his drinking. He is very fond and protective towards his four-year-old daughter.

When asked about the amount of alcohol he consumed, he was obviously uncomfortable. He told me that his father had been an alcoholic and that he wasn't fool enough to repeat that mistake. He also said that he had been mistreated by his father when his father was drunk and that his father had deserted the family when Starr was about thirteen and his brother, the only sibling, about ten. Starr's mother raised the boys and he has rarely heard from his father.

He explained that he refused to have alcohol in his home because he did not want to expose his daughter to it. He says that he has had nothing to drink since the accident but that before he occasionally went out by himself to drink beer. He acknowledges that he cannot hold his drink, and says that he knows enough to watch it. He did give me the impression that he was underestimating the amount of drinking which he did. My assessment of the man's personality leads me to believe that he may well be less than truthful on a number of counts. Part of this is conscious deception; much of it is subconscious. I have, however, taken this tendency into account in forming my opinion as to the man's condition. At both sessions I had with Starr, he appeared to be in a state of moderate to severe depression. As I indicated, he is convinced that his problems are physical and has refused to undergo any sort of psychiatric treatment.

His inability to return to work has aggravated his situation and feeling of self-reproach. His wife is now employed and is the sole source of support for the family.

In my opinion, Starr is a man who had characterological problems prior to the accident, but was, for the most part, adequately coping with his situation in life. In my view, there is no doubt that he is suffering from a post-concussion syndrome and that the symptoms he exhibits were triggered by the accident of January 18, 19XX. Prior to that accident, he was able to compensate for his characterological problems. The effect of the accident has been to decompensate his ability to cope. In my opinion, Starr's symptoms were triggered by his accident in January of 19XX, but the accident must definitely be seen in the context of this man's troubled emotional state, which existed prior to the accident and which contained the potential for and indeed the beginnings of a psychological breakdown. In other words, the trauma of his accident definitely triggered these depressive symptoms, but I could not definitely say that the accident was the sole cause of this man's present condition.

In my view, the patient ought to undergo immediately a course of treatment for this condition. It is extremely difficult to provide a prognosis at the present time. The patient's refusal to accept treatment must, to some degree at least, be seen as a part of the main illness. It is still too early to say whether or not he can be brought round to come to grips with his situation and return to a normal life.

Yours very truly,

PROVINCIAL COURT—CRIMINAL DIVISION

Regina

v.

Albert Starr

Transcript of trial proceedings before his Honour Judge Wilson,
Belleville Ontario, March 14, 19XX

Appearances: Mr. J.J. Hay for the Crown. Accused appearing on his own behalf.

[Note: For the purposes of our exercise, we are only concerned with the evidence given
by Mr. George Richardson on behalf of the crown. Assume that Starr was charged with
impaired driving under s. 237 of the Criminal Code, that he pleaded not guilty, gave no
evidence himself, and that the Crown had no evidence of his blood-alcohol level and
relied solely on the evidence of Richardson to establish Starr's condition and driving.]

Mr. George Richardson, called and sworn

Mr. Hay Q. Mr. Richardson, you are the manager of the Richardson Tavern, located on
Highway 14, two miles north of Belleville?

A. That's correct.

Q. And I believe you were working at the Tavern on the evening of January
18, 19XX?

A. Yes.

Q. Are you acquainted with the accused before the Court, Albert Starr?

A. Yes I am. He has been coming to our tavern for the past 18 months or so.

Q. Do you see Albert Starr in court here today?

A. Yes, that's him right there [indicating the accused].

Q. Was Albert Starr in your tavern on January 18, 19XX?

A. Yes. I remember that he came in at about 6:30 or 7:00 in the evening, said
"Hi" and sat down by himself at a table not too far from where I was
standing behind the bar.

Q. Did he have anything to drink?

A. He sure did. I don't keep a count of what people drink, but Albert had such
a snout-full that he became a bit of a problem.

Q. Did you serve him anything yourself?

A. No, but I operate the tap. The waiters do the serving, but I could see Albert
and he must have had 15 or 20 before we finally had to get him out.

Q. You said 15 or 20. Would that be glasses of draft beer?

A. That's right, standard drafts.

Q. You mentioned that you had some trouble with the accused, could you tell
us about that?

A. Well, this happened once before with Albert. When he gets tanked up, he
can be a bit of a problem. On the night we're talking about, he started after
some kids who were sitting next to him. I think they were University
students from Queens, and Albert was making some pretty crude remarks

about the girls. The two male students were trying to ignore him, but Albert kept after them, and these two guys got a little hot. I could see there might be some trouble, and I really didn't think Albert could handle himself against these two guys sober let alone drunk so I went over and told him he'd better get going home.

Q. What did Starr say or do at that point?

A. Well, he didn't put up too much fuss. He said something about how he was sorry he had started something and that he would settle down if I just left him alone. I told him it would be better for everybody if he got out, and I took him by the arm and he came along with me to the door.

Q. What did he do then?

A. When he got outside, he started fumbling around to find his keys and made it over to his car. I watched him to make sure he wasn't coming back in. He made it over to his car and got in and just kind of sat there for a while. He finally got it going and drove off.

Q. How would you describe Starr's condition when he left and got into the car?

A. Well, as I say, he'd had about 15 or 20 drafts and he was pretty far gone. He was none too steady getting over to the car and had trouble sorting out his keys and getting it going. I'd have to say he was pretty well bombed.

Q. Did you actually see him drive the car?

A. Yes, I waited at the door until he drove out of the lot. I didn't want any more trouble from him.

Q. Thank you, those are all the questions I have.

Court file no. *7421/XX*

ONTARIO
SUPERIOR COURT OF JUSTICE

BETWEEN:

ALBERT STARR

PLAINTIFF

and

RICHARDSON HOUSE LIMITED
and
GEORGE RICHARDSON

DEFENDANTS

AFFIDAVIT OF DOCUMENTS

I, Albert Starr
of the City   of Belleville
in the County   of Hastings
the above named   Plaintiff   in this action, MAKE OATH AND SAY:

1. I have conducted a diligent search of my records and have made appropriate enquiries of others to inform myself in order to make this affidavit. This affidavit discloses, to the full extent of my knowledge, information and belief, all documents relating to any matter in issue in this action that are or have been in my possession, control or power.

2. I have listed in Schedule A those documents that are in my possession, control or power and that I do not object to producing for inspection.

3. I have listed in Schedule B those documents that are or were in my possession, control or power and that I object to producing because I claim they are privileged, and I have stated in Schedule B the grounds for each such claim.

4. I have listed in Schedule C those documents that were formerly in my possession, control or power but are no longer in my possession, control or power, and I have stated in Schedule C when and how I lost possession or control of or power over them and their present location.

5. I have never had in my possession, control or power any document relating to any matter in issue in this action other than those listed in Schedules A, B and C.

Sworn before me at the   City
of   Belleville
in the   County
of   Hastings
on   January 12th,   19XX   _____
                                                    Albert Starr
                                            (Signature of deponent)

M. Teagh
Commissioner for Taking Affidavits, etc.

CERTIFICATE OF SOLICITOR

I CERTIFY that I have explained to the deponent the necessity of making full disclosure of all relevant documents.

Date   January 12, 19XX   _____
                                                    J.J. Jones
                                            (Signature of solicitor)

SCHEDULE A

Documents in my possession, control or power that I do not object to producing for inspection.

1. Police report of the accident in question, Jan. 18, 1975.
2. Schedule of Special Damages, including bills, various dates.

SCHEDULE B

Documents that are or were in my possession, control or power that I object to producing on the grounds of privilege.

1. Correspondence between myself and my solicitor relating to this suit on the ground of solicitor-client privilege.
2. Witness statements obtained by my solicitor on the ground that such documents were prepared in anticipation of and in preparation for this action.
3. Medical reports of my condition obtained by my solicitor on the ground that such documents were prepared in anticipation of and in preparation for this action.

SCHEDULE C

Documents that were formerly in my possession, control or power but are no longer in my possession, control or power.

There are no such documents.

Court file no. *7421/XX*

ONTARIO
SUPERIOR COURT OF JUSTICE

BETWEEN:

ALBERT STARR

PLAINTIFF

and

RICHARDSON HOUSE LIMITED
and
GEORGE RICHARDSON

DEFENDANTS

NOTICE OF EXAMINATION

TO: GEORGE RICHARDSON

YOU ARE REQUIRED TO ATTEND FOR AN EXAMINATION for discovery on your own behalf and on behalf of Richardson House Limited

on Wednesday, 23 January, 19XX, at 10:00 a.m. at the office of A.C. Devenport, 65 Queen Street W., Toronto.

YOU ARE REQUIRED TO BRING WITH YOU and produce at the examination the documents mentioned in subrule 30.04(4) of the Rules of Civil Procedure, and the following documents and things:

All similar documents that have since come into your possession.

Date: January 4, 19XX

Jones and Jones
2 Queen Street
Belleville, Ont.
K1P 3U6
(613) 722-5913
Solicitors for the Plaintiff

TO: Smith and Smith
22 Queen Street
Belleville, Ontario
K1P 3U5
Solicitors for the Defendants.

Excerpts from Richardson's Examination for Discovery Referred to at Trial

1. Q. Did he have anything to drink:
   A. Yes sir, quite a bit.
   Q. What's quite a bit?
   A. Well, I guess.

By Mr. Dunne: Well you know if you remember tell Mr. Stockwood, but you're not here to guess. Give him your best information that you can.

   A. I would guess about 15 or 20.
   Q. That's draft beer. How many ounces in a draft beer glass?
   A. Seven. Regular standard glass.

2. Q. Would you say he was drunk at this time?
   A. Yes sir.
   Q. What did you do?
   A. Well I went over and told him to cool it, and he said he was okay and just let him stay there for a while. And I said no it might be better that he go because I didn't figure he could handle himself with the guys sober, much less when he had a snootful. So I figured it would be best for him if he left.

3. Q. Now, what would be your estimate of his condition when he got in the car?
   A. Tight.
   Q. What does "tight" mean?
   A. Well, I guess it's slang for drunk.
   Q. Bombed?
   A. Yes sir.

4. Q. Do you sometimes let that room in the tavern overnight?
   A. Sometimes.
   Q. Was the room empty on the night of January 18, 19XX?

By Mr. Dunne: If you know. If you don't know.

   A. Well, yes it was.
   Q. Did you think of putting Mr. Starr in that room?
   A. No I didn't.
   Q. Why didn't that occur to you?
   A. Well.

By Mr. Dunne: Answer the question.

   A. Well, it was a kind of a spur of the moment thing because I knew he was married. It was one of those things that popped into my mind. I figured if he stayed there overnight there'd be a hassle with his wife. That's happened before.

Court file no. *7421/XX*

ONTARIO
SUPERIOR COURT OF JUSTICE

BETWEEN:

ALBERT STARR

PLAINTIFF

and

RICHARDSON HOUSE LIMITED
and
GEORGE RICHARDSON

DEFENDANTS

NOTICE OF MOTION

The defendants will make a motion to the court on Thursday, 20th day of February, 19xx at 10.00, or as soon after that time as the motion can be heard, at 327 University Avenue in the City of Toronto.

PROPOSED METHOD OF HEARING: The motion is to be heard (choose appropriate option)

☐ in writing under subrule 37.12.1(1) because it is (insert one of on consent, unopposed or made without notice);

☐ in writing as an opposed motion under subrule 37.12.1(4);

☒ orally.

THE MOTION IS FOR an Order that the Plaintiff Albert Starr give security for the costs of the Defendant and that all proceedings be stayed until such time as security be posted, or for such further Order as may seem appropriate.

THE GROUNDS FOR THE MOTION ARE that the plaintiff now resides out of Ontario within the meaning of Rule 56.

THE FOLLOWING DOCUMENTARY EVIDENCE will be used at the hearing of the motion: Affidavit of George P. Smith, dated February 3, 19xx.

Smith and Smith
22 Queen Street
Belleville, Ont.
K1P 3U5
(613) 722-6298

To: Jones and Jones
2 Queen Street
Belleville, Ontario
K1P 3U6

Court file no. *7421/XX*

ONTARIO
SUPERIOR COURT OF JUSTICE

BETWEEN:

ALBERT STARR

PLAINTIFF

and

RICHARDSON HOUSE LIMITED
and
GEORGE RICHARDSON

DEFENDANTS

AFFIDAVIT OF GEORGE P. SMITH

I, George P. Smith, of the City of Belleville, in the County of Hastings, Solicitor, make oath and say as follows:

1. I am a member of the firm of Smith and Smith, Solicitors for the Defendants and as such have knowledge of the facts hereinafter set out.

2. This action arises out of an incident which occurred on the 18th day of January, 19XX. The Statement of Claim was issued on the 14th day of September, 19XX, and the Statement of Defence was delivered on the 3rd day of October, 19XX.

3. The Plaintiff alleges that he was injured as a result of a motor vehicle accident which occurred while the Plaintiff was driving his own motor vehicle after having been ejected from the Defendant's tavern. As appears from the statement of claim, the plaintiff is alleging the Defendants were negligent in the circumstances, and that their negligence caused the plaintiff to become involved in the said motor vehicle accident.

4. In the Statement of Claim the Plaintiff Albert Starr claims damages in the amount of $224,650.00.

5. Examinations for Discovery were held on the 23rd day of January, 19XX. On his examination, the plaintiff testified that he had moved, with his wife and child, from the City of Belleville to Buffalo, New York, where he is residing with his aunt pending his recovery from the injury he alleges he sustained as a result of the accident described in paragraph 3 hereof.

6. In view of the nature of the injuries allegedly sustained by the said Plaintiff, as pleaded in the Statement of Claim, the Defendant in order to fully present his defence will likely be required to consult and possibly call as witnesses at trial, medical specialists in the fields of neurology and psychiatry. Accordingly, it will be necessary for the Defendant to apply to the Court for an Order requiring the Plaintiff Albert Starr to present himself for a medical examination, before medical practitioners of this Defendant's choosing, the cost of which must be born by this Defendant.

7. I verily believe that much detailed evidence will be adduced at the trial of this action, including medical evidence and evidence with respect to liability, the quantum of damages sustained by the Plaintiff and the extent of his disability.

8. I verily believe that it will likely be necessary on behalf of the Defendant at the trial of this action to arrange for the appearance of the investigating police officer, and two independent witnesses to give viva voce evidence.

9. Further, I verily believe that it may be necessary to obtain an Order directing the production and inspection of all hospital records, x-ray plates, and x-ray reports, in respect of the hospitalization and treatment of the Plaintiff for injuries sustained as a result of the accident in question.

10. I verily believe that the trial of the action will require about three days.

11. Now produced and shown to me and marked as Exhibit "A" to this my Affidavit is a draft Bill of Costs which I verily believe is a proper estimate of the amount of costs that the Defendant would be able to tax if successful in the within action.

SWORN BEFORE ME at the City
of Belleville in the County
of Hastings this 3rd day
of February, 19XX.

    A Commissioner, etc.

Court file no. *7421/XX*

ONTARIO
SUPERIOR COURT OF JUSTICE

BETWEEN:

ALBERT STARR

PLAINTIFF

and

RICHARDSON HOUSE LIMITED
and
GEORGE RICHARDSON

DEFENDANTS

DRAFT BILL OF COSTS OF THE DEFENDANT

Description	Fees	Disbursements
Pleadings	$ 500.00	
Paid to file Notice of Intent to Defend and Statement of Defence		$ 74.00
Motion for security for costs	400.00	
Paid to file motion		75.00
Contested motion for medical examination	200.00	
Paid to file motion		75.00
Contested motion for hospital records	200.00	
Paid to file motion		75.00
Examination for Discovery of the Plaintiff (including counsel and preparation)	1,000.00	
Estimated fees of special examiner		300.00
Examination for Discovery of the Defendant (including counsel fee and preparation)	500.00	
Estimated fees of Special Examiner		150.00
Pre-trial conference	75.00	
Assignment Court	50.00	
Preparation for trial (including correspondence, legal research, brief at trial, summoning witnesses)	2,000.00	
Attendance at trial (estimated three days with jury)	3,600.00	
Expert report fees (two medical reports)		1,600.00
Estimated expert attendance fees		1,000.00
Estimated conduct money and travelling expenses for 3 witnesses in Ontario		159.00
Cost of Summons to Witness		18.00
Judgment	35.00	
Assessment of Costs	50.00	
TOTAL FEES	$8,610.00	
TOTAL DISBURSEMENTS		3,526.00
(GST on taxable disbursements of $3,526.00 and fees of $8,610.00)		849.52
TOTAL FEES AND DISBURSEMENTS		$12,985.52

ASSESSED AND ALLOWED AT $ . . . . THIS DAY . . . . . . OF . . . . , 19XX.

_____
ASSESSMENT OFFICER

Court file no. *7421/XX*

ONTARIO
SUPERIOR COURT OF JUSTICE

BETWEEN:

ALBERT STARR

PLAINTIFF

and

RICHARDSON HOUSE LIMITED
and
GEORGE RICHARDSON

DEFENDANTS

AFFIDAVIT OF WILLIAM BLACKSTONE

I, William Blackstone, of the City of Belleville, in the County of Hastings, student-at-law, MAKE OATH AND SAY, as follows:

1. I am a student-at-law in the offices of Jones & Jones, Solicitors for the Plaintiff herein, and as such have knowledge of the matters herein disposed to.

2. The Plaintiff herein, Albert Starr, has been granted a Legal Aid Certificate from the Ontario Legal Aid Plan with respect to this proceeding.

3. I have reviewed the pleadings and proceedings herein.

4. While the Plaintiff has suffered serious injury, I verily believe that the estimate of three days for trial, made in paragraph 10, of Mr. Smith's Affidavit herein is excessive.

5. I verily believe that the trial of the Plaintiff's action herein should take no more than two days of trial and possibly less time.

6. I have examined a draft Bill of Costs which is Exhibit "A" to the Affidavit of Mr. Smith.

7. With respect to the said draft Bill of Costs, I verily believe that the inclusion of items of $100.00 as costs for contested motion of medical examination and $75.00 for contested motion for production of hospital records unnecessarily inflates the Bill of Costs as it is doubtful in the circumstances of this case that such motions would be contested. I further believe that the item of $100.00 for discovery of documents will not actually arise in a case of this type.

8. I further believe that the item of $4,500.00 for counsel fee at trial and $75.00 for pleadings is excessive in view of all the circumstances referred to herein. In my opinion, a more realistic counsel fee would be $1,500.00 to $2,000.00.

9. I further believe that the disbursement of $300.00 for the attendance of medical specialists at trial may well not be incurred in a case of this type in view of *The Evidence Act* provisions with respect to the admissibility of written medical reports.

10. I am informed by Albert Starr, the plaintiff herein, and verily believe that following the accident that gave rise to this claim to the date hereof he has been unable to return to work and that his only source of income has been disability insurance benefits in the amount of $75.00 per week.

11. To the best of my knowledge, the Plaintiff Albert Starr has no resources, assets, or savings on which he could draw to satisfy an order for security for costs. I verily believe that should this court grant an order requiring the plaintiff to post security for

cost, such an order will likely have the effect of forcing the plaintiff to abandon his claim against the Defendant.

SWORN BEFORE ME at the City
of Belleville in the County
of Hastings this 15th day of
February, 19XX.

A Commissioner, etc.

Rules of Professional Conduct

Most, if not all, jurisdictions have a Code or Rules of Professional Conduct. In some provinces in Canada, the Canadian Bar Association's *Code of Professional Conduct* (1987) has been directly adopted by the body governing the legal profession. In Ontario, the Law Society of Upper Canada has passed its own Rules of Professional Conduct, which are largely based on the CBA's Code but with some significant differences.

At the time this book went to press, the LSUC was in the process of revising its Rules of Professional Conduct. What follows are the proposed draft rules of professional conduct (March 31, 1999) prepared by the LSUC's Task Force on Review of the Rules of Professional Conduct. This draft has been before Convocation (the LSUC's governing body, composed of the Benchers) once, which directed that the draft rules be circulated for comment by the public and the profession. When that has been done, the draft rules (with possible amendments) will be considered by Convocation for enactment, likely in late 1999 or early 2000.

These draft rules are not, on the whole, substantially different from the CBA Code or the existing LSUC Rules of Professional Conduct. They represent the most modern statement of professional conduct standards in the country and will likely be very close to the rules under which students using this book will practise (if they do so in Ontario).

RULE 1: CITATION AND INTERPRETATION

1.01 CITATION

1.01 These rules may be cited as the *Rules of Professional Conduct.*

1.02 DEFINITIONS

1.02 In these rules, unless the context requires otherwise,
"client" includes a client of the law firm of which the lawyer is a partner or associate, whether or not the lawyer handles the client's work,
"conduct unbecoming a barrister or solicitor" means conduct in a lawyer's personal or private capacity that tends to bring discredit upon the legal profession including:

(a) committing a criminal act that reflects adversely on the lawyer's honesty, trustworthiness or fitness as a lawyer;

(b) taking improper advantage of the youth, inexperience, lack of education, unsophistication, ill health, or unbusinesslike habits of another; or

(c) engaging in conduct involving dishonesty.

Commentary

Dishonourable or questionable conduct on the part of a lawyer in either private life or professional practice will reflect adversely upon the integrity of the profession and the administration of justice. If the conduct, whether within or outside the professional sphere, is such that knowledge of it would be likely to impair the client's trust in the lawyer as a professional consultant, the Society may be justified in taking disciplinary action.

Generally speaking, however, the Society will not be concerned with the purely private or extra-professional activities of a lawyer that do not bring into question the lawyer's professional integrity.

"independent legal advice" means a retainer where:

(a) the retained lawyer has no conflicting interest with respect to the client's transaction;

(b) the client's transaction involves doing business with

(i) another lawyer,

(ii) a corporation or other entity in which the other lawyer has an interest other than a corporation or other entity whose securities are publicly traded, or with,

(iii) a client of the other lawyer;

(c) the retained lawyer has advised the client that the client has the right to independent legal representation;

(d) the client has expressly waived the right to independent legal representation and has elected to receive no legal representation or legal representation from the other lawyer;

(e) the retained lawyer has explained the legal aspects of the transaction to the client, who appeared to understand the advice given; and

(f) the retained lawyer informed the client of the availability of qualified advisers in other fields who would be in a position to give an opinion to the client as to the desirability or otherwise of the proposed investment from a business point of view.

Commentary

Where a client elects to waive independent legal representation but rely on independent legal advice only, the retained lawyer has a responsibility that should not be to be lightly assumed or merely perfunctorily discharged.

"independent legal representation" means a retainer where

(a) the retained lawyer has no conflicting interest with respect to the client's transaction; and

(b) the retained lawyer will act in the normal course for the client.

"interprovincial law firm" means a law firm that carries on the practice of law in more than one province or territory of Canada;

"law firm" includes one or more members practising,

(a) in a sole proprietorship,

(b) in a partnership,

(c) in association for the purpose of sharing certain common expenses but who are otherwise independent practitioners,

(d) as a professional law corporation,

(e) in a government, a Crown corporation or any other public body, and

(f) in a corporation or other body;

"lawyer" means a member of the Society, and includes a law student registered in the Society's pre-call training program;

"member" means a member of the Society, and includes a law student registered in the Society's pre-call training program;

"professional misconduct" means conduct in a lawyer's professional capacity that tends to bring discredit upon the legal profession including:

(a) violating or attempting to violate the *Rules of Professional Conduct, the Law Society Act, or the regulations or rules thereto*;

(b) knowingly assisting or inducing another lawyer to violate or attempt to violate the *Rules of Professional Conduct, the Law Society Act, or the regulations or rules thereto*;

(c) misappropriating or dealing dishonestly with a client's money or another's property;

(d) engaging in conduct that is prejudicial to the administration of justice;

(e) stating or implying an ability to influence improperly a government agency or official, or

(f) knowingly assisting a judge or judicial officer in conduct that is a violation of applicable rules of judicial conduct or other law.

"Society" means The Law Society of Upper Canada.

1.03 INTERPRETATION

Standards of the Legal Profession

1.03 (1) These Rules shall be interpreted in a way that recognizes that:

(a) a lawyer should carry on the practice of law and discharge all duties owed to clients, the court, the public and other members of the profession honourably and with integrity;

(b) a lawyer has special responsibilities by virtue of the privileges afforded the legal profession and the important role it plays in a free and democratic society and in the administration of justice, including a special responsibility to recognize the diversity of the Ontario community, to protect the dignity of individuals, and to respect human rights laws in force in Ontario;

(c) a lawyer should uphold the standards and reputation of the legal profession and assist in the advancement of its goals, organizations, and institutions;

(d) the Rules are intended, in part, to express to the profession and to the public the high ethical ideals of the legal profession;

(e) the Rules are intended, in part, to specify the bases on which lawyers may be disciplined; and

(f) rules of professional conduct cannot address every situation, and a lawyer should observe the Rules in the spirit as well as in the letter.

Commentary

Integrity is the fundamental quality of any person who seeks to practise as a member of the legal profession. If a client is in any doubt as to his or her lawyer's trustworthiness, the essential element in the true lawyer–client relationship will be missing. If personal integrity is lacking, the lawyer's usefulness to the client and reputation within the profession will be destroyed regardless of how competent the lawyer may be.

Public confidence in the administration of justice and in the legal profession may be eroded by a lawyer's irresponsible conduct. Accordingly, a lawyer's conduct should reflect credit on the legal profession, inspire the confidence, respect and trust of clients and the community, and avoid even the appearance of impropriety.

General Principles

(2) In these rules, words importing the singular number include more than one person, party, or thing of the same kind and a word interpreted in the singular number has a corresponding meaning when used in the plural.

RULE 2: RELATIONSHIP TO CLIENTS

2.01 COMPETENCE AND QUALITY OF SERVICE

Definitions

2.01(1) In this rule,
"competent lawyer" means a lawyer who has and applies relevant skills, attributes, and values in a manner appropriate to each matter undertaken on behalf of a client including:

(a) knowing general legal principles and procedures, and the substantive law and procedure for the areas of law in which the lawyer practises;

(b) investigating facts, identifying issues, ascertaining client objectives, considering possible options, and developing and advising the client as to appropriate course(s) of action;

Commentary

A lawyer should clearly specify the facts, circumstances and assumptions upon which an opinion is based. Unless the client instructs otherwise, the lawyer should investigate the matter in sufficient detail to be able to express an opinion rather than mere comments with many qualifications. If the circumstances do not justify an exhaustive investigation with consequent expense to the client, the lawyer should so state in the opinion.

A lawyer should be wary of bold and confident assurances to the client, especially when the lawyer's employment may depend upon advising in a particular way.

In addition to opinions on legal questions, the lawyer may be asked for or may be expected to give advice on non-legal matters such as the business, policy or social implications involved in the question, or the course the client should choose. In many instances the lawyer's experience will be such that the lawyer's views on non-legal matters will be of real benefit to the client. The lawyer who expresses views on such matters should, where and to the extent necessary, point out any lack of experience or other qualification in the particular field, and should clearly distinguish legal advice from other advice.

In a multi-discipline practice, a lawyer must be particularly alert to ensure that the client understands that he or she is receiving legal advice from a lawyer supplemented by the services of a non-lawyer. If advice or service is sought from non-lawyer members of the firm, it must be sought and provided independently of and outside the scope of the retainer for the provision of legal services and the advice will be subject to the constraints outlined in the relevant by-laws and regulations governing multi-discipline practices. In particular, the lawyer must ensure that such services of non-lawyers are provided from a separate location from the premises of the multi-discipline practice.

(c) implementing, as each matter requires, the chosen course of action through the application of appropriate skills including:
- (i) legal research,
- (ii) analysis,
- (iii) application of the law to the relevant facts,
- (iv) writing and drafting,
- (v) negotiation,
- (vi) alternative dispute resolution
- (vii) advocacy, and
- (viii) problem solving ability;

Commentary

As a member of the legal profession, a lawyer is held out as knowledgeable, skilled, and capable in the practice of law. Accordingly, the client is entitled to assume that the lawyer has the ability and capacity to deal adequately with legal matters to be undertaken on the client's behalf.

A lawyer who is incompetent does the client a disservice, brings discredit to the profession, and may bring the administration of justice into disrepute. In addition to damaging the lawyer's own reputation and practice, incompetence may also injure the lawyer's associates or dependants.

(d) communicating in a timely and effective manner at all stages of the matter;

Commentary

Whenever it becomes apparent that the client has misunderstood or misconceived the position or what is really involved, the lawyer should explain as well as advise, so that the client is apprised of the true position and fairly advised with respect to the real issues or questions involved.

(e) performing all functions, conscientiously, diligently, and in a timely and cost effective manner;

Commentary

The requirement of conscientious, diligent and efficient service means that a lawyer must make every effort to provide service to the client. If the lawyer can reasonably foresee undue delay in providing advice or services, the client should be so informed.

(f) applying intellectual capacity, judgment, and deliberation to all functions;
(g) complying in letter and in spirit with the *Rules of Professional Conduct*;
(h) recognizing limitations in one's ability to handle a matter, or some aspect of it, and taking steps accordingly to ensure the client is appropriately served;

Commentary

A lawyer should not undertake a matter without honestly feeling competent to handle it, or able to become competent without undue delay, risk or expense to the client. This is an ethical consideration, and is to be distinguished from the standard of care that a court would invoke for purposes of determining negligence.

A lawyer must be alert to recognize any lack of competence for a particular task and the disservice that would be done to the client by undertaking that task. If consulted in such circumstances, the lawyer should either decline to act or obtain the client's instructions to retain, consult or collaborate with a lawyer who is competent in that field. The lawyer may also recognize that competence for a particular task may require seeking advice from or collaborating with experts in scientific, accounting or other non-legal fields, and in such a situation the lawyer should not hesitate to seek the client's instructions to consult experts.

(i) managing one's practice effectively;
(j) pursuing appropriate professional development to maintain and enhance legal knowledge and skills; and
(k) adapting to changing professional requirements, standards, techniques, and practices.

Competence

(2) A lawyer shall perform any legal services undertaken on a client's behalf to the standard of a competent lawyer.

Quality of Service

(3) A lawyer shall serve the client in a conscientious, diligent and efficient manner and shall provide a quality of service at least equal to that which lawyers generally would expect of a competent lawyer in a like situation.

> *Commentary*
>
> This Rule does not require a standard of perfection. A mistake, even though it might be actionable for damages in negligence, would not necessarily constitute a failure to maintain the standard of professional competence described by the Rule.
>
> Incompetent professional practice may give rise to disciplinary action under this Rule.
>
> In addition to this Rule, the Law Society Act provides that the Society may conduct a review of a member's practice for the purposes of determining if the member is meeting standards of professional competence. A review will be conducted in circumstances defined in by-laws. Following a review, a member may be subject to a hearing at which it will be determined whether the member is failing or has failed to meet standards of professional competence.
>
> The Act provides that a member fails to meet standards of professional competence if there are deficiencies in (1) the member's knowledge, skill or judgment, (2) the member's attention to the interests of clients, (3) the records, systems or procedures of the member's practice, or (4) other aspects of the members practice, and the deficiencies give rise to a reasonable apprehension that the quality of service to clients may be adversely affected.

2.02 PARTICULARS OF QUALITY SERVICE

Honesty and Candour

(1) When advising clients, a lawyer shall be honest and candid.

> *Commentary*
>
> The lawyer's duty to the client who seeks legal advice is to give the client a competent opinion based on a sufficient knowledge of the relevant facts, an adequate consideration of the applicable law, and the lawyer's own experience and expertise. The advice must be open and undisguised, and must clearly disclose what the lawyer honestly thinks about the merits and probable results.

Informing Client of Error

(2) When in connection with a matter for which a lawyer is responsible, the lawyer discovers a mistake that is or may be damaging to the client and that cannot be rectified, the lawyer shall:

(a) promptly inform the client of the mistake being careful not to prejudice any rights of indemnity that either of them may have under any insurance, client's protection or indemnity plan, or otherwise; and

(b) recommend that the client obtain legal advice elsewhere as to any rights the client may have arising from the mistake.

Encouraging Compromise or Settlement

(3) A lawyer shall advise and encourage the client to compromise or settle a dispute whenever it is possible to do so on a reasonable basis, and shall discourage the client from commencing useless legal proceedings.

(4) The lawyer shall consider the appropriateness of alternative dispute resolution (ADR) to the resolution of issues in every case and, if appropriate, the lawyer shall inform the client of ADR options and, if so instructed, take steps to pursue those options.

Threatening Criminal Proceedings

(5) A lawyer shall not advise, threaten or bring a criminal or quasi-criminal prosecution in order to secure some civil advantage for the client.

Dishonesty or Fraud by Client

(6) When advising a client, a lawyer shall not knowingly assist in or encourage any dishonesty, fraud, crime or illegal conduct, or instruct the client on how to violate the law and avoid punishment.

Commentary

A lawyer should be on guard against becoming the tool or dupe of an unscrupulous client or persons associated with such a client.

A bona fide test case is not necessarily precluded by rule 2.02 (6) and, so long as no injury to the person or violence is involved, a lawyer may properly advise and represent a client who, in good faith and on reasonable grounds desires to challenge or test a law and the test can most effectively be made by means of a technical breach giving rise to a test case.

Client Under a Disability

(7) When a client's ability to make decisions is impaired because of minority, mental disability or for some other reason, the lawyer shall as far as reasonably possible maintain a normal lawyer and client relationship.

(8) A lawyer may seek the appointment of a guardian or take other protective action when the lawyer reasonably believes that a client's ability to make a decision has become impaired to the degree that the client cannot adequately act in his or her own interest, and is accordingly unable to provide instructions to the lawyer.

Medical-Legal Reports

(9) A lawyer who receives a medical-legal report from a physician or health professional that is accompanied by a proviso that it not be shown to the client shall return the report immediately to the physician or health professional unless the lawyer has received specific instructions to accept the report on this basis.

Commentary

The lawyer can avoid some of the problems anticipated by the Rule by having a full and frank discussion with the physician or health professional, preferably in advance of the preparation of a medical-legal report, which exchange will serve to inform the physician of the lawyer's obligation respecting disclosure of medical-legal reports to the client.

(10) A lawyer who receives a medical-legal report from a physician containing opinions or findings that if disclosed might cause harm or injury to the client shall attempt to dissuade the client from seeing the report but, if the client insists, the lawyer shall produce the report.

(11) Where a client insists on seeing a medical-legal report about which the lawyer has reservations for the reasons noted in subrule (12), the lawyer shall suggest that the client attend at the office of the physician to see the report in order that the client will have the benefit of the expertise of the physician in understanding the significance of the conclusion contained in the medical-legal report.

Title Insurance in Real Estate Conveyancing

(12) A lawyer shall assess all reasonable options to assure title when advising a client about a real estate conveyance and shall advise the client that title insurance is not mandatory and is not the only option available to protect the client's interests in a real estate transaction.

Commentary

A lawyer should advise the client of the options available to protect the client's interests and minimize the client's risks in a real estate transaction. The lawyer should be cognizant of when title insurance may be an appropriate option. Although title insurance is intended to protect the client against title risks, it is not a substitute for a lawyer's services in a real estate transaction.

The lawyer should be knowledgeable about title insurance and discuss the advantages, conditions and limitations of the various options and coverages generally available to the client through title insurance with the client. Before recommending a specific title insurance product, the lawyer should be knowledgeable about the product and take such training as may be necessary in order to acquire the knowledge.

(13) A lawyer shall not receive any compensation, whether directly or indirectly, from a title insurer, agent or intermediary for recommending a specific title insurance product to his or her client.

(14) A lawyer shall disclose that no commission or fee is being furnished by any insurer, agent or intermediary to the lawyer with respect to any title insurance coverage.

Commentary

The fiduciary relationship between lawyer and client requires full disclosure in all financial dealings between them and prohibits the acceptance by the lawyer including the lawyer's law firm, any employee or associate of the firm or any related entity of any hidden fees.

(15) If discussing TitlePlus insurance with the client, a lawyer shall fully disclose the relationship between the legal profession, the Society, and the Lawyers' Professional Indemnity Corporation (LPIC).

2.03 CONFIDENTIALITY

Information Confidential

2.03(1) A lawyer shall hold in strict confidence all information concerning the business and affairs of the client acquired in the course of the professional relationship, and shall not divulge any such information unless expressly or impliedly authorized by the client or required by law to do so.

Commentary

A lawyer cannot render effective professional service to the client unless there is full and unreserved communication between them. At the same time the client must feel completely secure and entitled to proceed on the basis that without any express request or stipulation on the client's part matters disclosed to or discussed with the lawyer will be held secret and confidential.

This rule must be distinguished from the evidentiary rule of lawyer and client privilege with respect to oral or documentary communications passing between the client and the lawyer. The ethical rule is wider and applies without regard to the nature or source of the information or the fact that others may share the knowledge.

A lawyer owes the duty of secrecy to every client without exception, and whether it be a continuing or casual client. The duty survives the professional relationship and continues indefinitely after the lawyer has ceased to act for the client, whether or not differences may have arisen between them.

Generally speaking, the lawyer should not disclose having been consulted or retained by a particular person about a particular matter unless the nature of the matter requires such disclosure.

A lawyer should take care to avoid disclosure to one client of confidential information concerning or received from another client, and should decline employment which might require such disclosure.

A lawyer should avoid indiscreet conversations, even with the lawyer's spouse or family, about a client's affairs and should shun any gossip about such things even though the client is not named or otherwise identified. Likewise, a lawyer should not repeat any gossip or information about the client's business or affairs that is overheard or recounted to the lawyer. Apart altogether from ethical considerations or questions of good taste, indiscreet shop-talk between lawyers, if overheard by third parties able to identify the matter being discussed, could result in prejudice to the client. Moreover, the respect of the listener for lawyers and the legal profession will probably be lessened.

Although the Rule may not apply to facts which are public knowledge, nevertheless the lawyer should guard against participating in or commenting upon speculation concerning the client's affairs or business.

Justified or Permitted Disclosure

(2) Confidential information may be divulged with the express or implied authority of the client.

Commentary

In some situations, the authority of the client to divulge may be implied. For example, some disclosure may be necessary in court proceedings in a pleading or other court document. Further, it is implied that a lawyer may, unless the client directs otherwise, disclose the client's affairs to partners and associates in the law firm and, to the extent necessary, to non-legal staff such as secretaries and filing clerks. But this implied authority to disclose places the lawyer under a duty to impress upon associates, employees and students the importance of non-disclosure (both during their employment and thereafter) and requires the lawyer to take reasonable care to prevent their disclosing or using any information which the lawyer is bound to keep in confidence.

(3) When required by law or by order of a court of competent jurisdiction, a lawyer shall disclose confidential information, but the lawyer shall not disclose more information than is required.

(4) Where a lawyer has reasonable grounds for believing a crime that may cause death or serious bodily harm is likely to be committed, he or she may disclose confidential information, but the lawyer shall not disclose more information than is required.

(5) Where it is alleged that a lawyer or the lawyer's associates or employees are:

(a) guilty of a criminal offence involving a client's affairs;

(b) civilly liable with respect to a matter involving a client's affairs; or

(c) guilty of malpractice or misconduct,

a lawyer may disclose confidential information in order to defend against the allegations, but the lawyer shall not disclose more information than is required.

Literary Works

(6) If a lawyer engages in literary works such as an autobiography, memoirs and the like, the lawyer shall avoid disclosure of confidential information.

Commentary

The fiduciary relationship between lawyer and client forbids the lawyer from using any confidential information covered by the ethical rule for the benefit of the lawyer or a third person, or to the disadvantage of the client.

2.04 AVOIDANCE OF CONFLICTS OF INTEREST

Definition

2.04(1) In this rule,

a "conflict or interest" or a "conflicting interest" means an interest

(a) that would be likely to affect adversely a lawyer's judgment on behalf of, or loyalty to, a client or prospective client, or

(b) that a lawyer might be prompted to prefer to the interests of a client or prospective client.

Commentary

Conflicting interests include but are not limited to the financial interest of a lawyer or an associate of a lawyer, and the duties and loyalties of a lawyer to any other client, including the obligation to communicate information. For example, there would be a conflict of interest if a lawyer, or a family member, or a law partner had a personal financial interest in the client's affairs or in the matter in which the lawyer is requested to act for the client, such as a partnership interest in some joint business venture with the client.

Avoidance of Conflicts of Interest

(2) A lawyer shall not advise or represent both sides of a dispute.

(3) A lawyer shall not act or continue to act in a matter when there is or is likely to be a conflicting interest, unless, after disclosure adequate to make an informed decision, the client or prospective client consents.

Commentary

A client or the client's affairs may be seriously prejudiced unless the lawyer's judgment and freedom of action on the client's behalf are as free as possible from conflict of interest.

As important as it is to the client that the lawyer's judgment and freedom of action on the client's behalf should not be subject to other interests, duties or obligations, in practice this factor may not always be decisive. Instead it may be only one of several factors which the client will weigh when deciding whether or not to give the consent referred to in the rule. Other factors might include, for example, the availability of another lawyer of comparable expertise and experience, the extra cost, delay and inconvenience involved in engaging another lawyer and the latter's unfamiliarity with the client and the client's affairs. In some instances, each clients case may gather strength from joint representation. In the result, the client's interests may sometimes be better served by not engaging another lawyer, for example, when the client and another party to a commercial transaction are continuing clients of the same law firm but are regularly represented by different lawyers in that firm.

Acting Against Client

(4) A lawyer who has acted for a client in a matter shall not thereafter act against the client or against persons who were involved in or associated with the client in that matter:

(a) in the same matter,

(b) in any related matter, or

(c) in any new matter, if the lawyer has obtained from the other retainer relevant confidential information.

Commentary

It is not improper for the lawyer to act against a client in a fresh and independent matter wholly unrelated to any work the lawyer has previously done for that person, and where previously obtained confidential information is irrelevant to that matter.

Joint Retainer

(5) Before a lawyer accepts employment for more than one client in a matter or transaction, the lawyer shall advise the clients:

(a) that the lawyer has been asked to act for both or all of them,

(b) that no information received in connection with the matter from one can be treated as confidential so far as any of the others are concerned, and

(c) that, if a conflict develops which cannot be resolved, the lawyer cannot continue to act for both or all of them and may have to withdraw completely.

Commentary

While this subrule does not require that a lawyer before accepting a joint retainer advise the client to obtain independent legal advice about the joint retainer, in some cases, especially those in which one of the clients is less sophisticated or more vulnerable than the other, it is desirable that the lawyer recommend such advice to ensure that the client's consent to the joint retainer is informed, genuine, and uncoerced.

(6) Where a lawyer has a continuing relationship with a client for whom the lawyer acts regularly, before the lawyer accepts joint employment for that client and another client in a matter or transaction, the lawyer shall advise the other clients of the continuing relationship and recommend that the client obtain independent legal advice about the joint retainer.

Commentary

Although all the parties concerned may consent, a lawyer should avoid acting for more than one client when it is likely that an issue contentious between them will arise or their interests, rights or obligations will diverge as the matter progresses.

(7) Where a lawyer has advised the clients as provided under subrules (5) and (6) and the parties are content that the lawyer act, the lawyer shall obtain their written consent, or record their consent in a separate letter to each.

(8) Save as provided by subrule (9), where clients have consented to a joint retainer and an issue contentious between them or some of them arises, their lawyer, shall:
    (a) not advise them on the contentious issue, and
    (b) shall refer the clients to another lawyer, unless the issue is
        (i) one that involves little or no legal advice, and
        (ii) the clients are sophisticated,
in which case, the clients may settle the contentious issue by direct negotiation in which the lawyer does not participate.

Commentary

The Rule does not prevent a lawyer from arbitrating or settling, or attempting to arbitrate or settle, a dispute between two or more clients or former clients who are sui juris and who wish to submit the dispute to the lawyer.

Where after the clients have consented to a joint retainer, an issue contentious between them or some of them arises, the lawyer is not necessarily precluded from advising them on non-contentious matters.

(9) Where clients consent to a joint retainer and also agree that in the event of a contentious issue arising their lawyer may continue to advise one of the them and a

contentious issue does arise, the lawyer may advise the one client about the contentious matter and shall refer the other or others to another lawyer.

Multi-Discipline Practice

(10) A lawyer in a multi-discipline practice shall ensure that non-lawyer partners and associates observe this rule for the legal practice and for any other business or professional undertaking carried on by them outside the legal practice.

Unrepresented Persons

(11) A lawyer shall not advise an unrepresented person, but shall urge such a person to obtain independent legal representation and, if the unrepresented person does not do so, the lawyer shall take care to see that the unrepresented person is not proceeding under the impression that his or her interests will be protected by the lawyer.

> *Commentary*
>
> When a lawyer is dealing on a client's behalf with an unrepresented person, the lawyer should make it clear that he or she is acting exclusively in the interests of the client and accordingly his or her comments or information may be partisan.
>
> If an unrepresented person requests the lawyer to advise or act in the matter, the lawyer should be governed by the considerations outlined in this rule about joint retainers.

2.05 CONFLICTS FROM TRANSFER BETWEEN LAW FIRMS

Definitions

2.05(1) In this Rule:
"client" includes anyone to whom a member owes a duty of confidentiality, whether or not a solicitor-client relationship exists between them;
"confidential information" means information obtained from a client which is not generally known to the public;

> *Commentary*
>
> In this Rule, "confidential information" refers to information obtained from a client that is not generally known to the public. It should be distinguished from the general ethical duty to hold in strict confidence all information concerning the business and affairs of the client acquired in the course of the professional relationship, which duty applies without regard to the nature or source of the information or to the fact that others may share the knowledge.

"matter" means a case or client file, but does not include general "know-how" and, in the case of a government lawyer, does not include policy advice unless the advice relates to a particular case;

Application of Rule

(2) This Rule applies where a member transfers from one law firm ("former law firm") to another ("new law firm"), and either the transferring member or the new law firm is aware at the time of the transfer or later discovers that,

(a) the new law firm represents a client in a matter which is the same as or related to a matter in respect of which the former law firm represents its client ("former client");

(b) the interests of those clients in that matter conflict; and

(c) the transferring member actually possesses relevant information respecting that matter.

(3) Subrules (4) to (7) do not apply to a member employed by the federal, a provincial or a territorial Attorney General or Department of Justice who, after transferring from one department, ministry or agency to another, continues to be employed by that Attorney General or Department of Justice.

Commentary

The purpose of the Rule is to deal with actual knowledge. Imputed knowledge does not give rise to disqualification.

Lawyers and support staff: This Rule is intended to regulate members of the Society and articled law students who transfer between law firms. It also imposes a general duty on members to exercise due diligence in the supervision of non-lawyer staff, to ensure that they comply with the Rule and with the duty not to disclose, confidences of clients of the member's firm; and confidences of clients of other law firms in which the person has worked.

Government employees and in-house counsel: The definition of "law firm" includes one or more members of the Society practising in a government, a Crown corporation, any other public body and a corporation. Thus, the Rule applies to members transferring to or from government service and into or out of an in-house counsel position, but does not extend to purely internal transfers in which, after transfer, the employer remains the same. [Not yet in effect.]

Law firms with multiple offices: The Rule treats as one "law firm" such entities as the various legal services units of a government, a corporation with separate regional legal departments, an inter-provincial law firm and a legal aid program with many community law offices. The more autonomous that each unit or office is, the easier it should be, in the event of a conflict, for the new firm to obtain the former client's consent or to establish that it is in the public interest that it continue to represent its client in the matter.

Practising in association: The definition of "law firm" (rule 1.02) includes one or more members practising in association for the purpose of sharing certain common expenses but who are otherwise independent practitioners. This recognizes the risk that lawyers practising in association, like partners in a law firm, will share client confidences while discussing their files with one another.

Law Firm Disqualification

(4) Where the transferring member actually possesses relevant information respecting the former client which is confidential and which, if disclosed to a member of the new law firm, may prejudice the former client, the new law firm shall cease its representation of its client in that matter unless,

    (a) the former client consents to the new law firm's continued representation of its client; or

    (b) the new law firm establishes, in accordance with subrule (8), that,

        (i) it is in the interests of justice that its representation of its client in the matter continue, having regard to all relevant circumstances, including,

            (A) the adequacy of the measures taken under (ii),

            (B) the extent of prejudice to any party,

            (C) the good faith of the parties,

            (D) the availability of alternative suitable counsel, and

            (E) issues affecting the national or public interest,

        (ii) it has taken reasonable measures to ensure that no disclosure to any member of the new law firm of the former client's confidential information will occur.

Commentary

The circumstances enumerated in subrule (4)(b)(i) are drafted in broad terms to ensure that all relevant facts will be taken into account. While clauses (B) to (D) are self-explanatory, clause (E) addresses governmental concerns respecting issues of national security, cabinet confidences and obligations incumbent on Attorneys General and their agents in the administration of justice.

Transferring Lawyer Disqualification

(5) Where the transferring member actually possesses relevant information respecting the former client but that information is not confidential information which, if disclosed to a member of the new law firm, may prejudice the former client,

    (a) the member shall execute an affidavit or solemn declaration to that effect, and

    (b) the new law firm shall,

        (i) notify its client and the former client, or if the former client is represented in that matter by a member, notify that member, of the relevant circumstances and its intended action under this Rule, and

        (ii) deliver to the persons referred to in (i) a copy of any affidavit or solemn declaration executed under (a).

(6) A transferring member described in the opening clause of subrule (4) or (5) shall not, unless the former client consents,

(a) participate in any manner in the new law firm's representation of its client in that matter; or

(b) disclose any confidential information respecting the former client.

(7) No member of the new law firm shall, unless the former client consents, discuss with a transferring member described in the opening clause of subrule (4) or (5) the new law firm's representation of its client or the former law firm's representation of the former client in that matter.

Determination of Compliance

(8) Anyone who has an interest in, or who represents a party in, a matter referred to in this Rule may apply to a court of competent jurisdiction for a determination of any aspect of this Rule.

Due Diligence

(9) A member shall exercise due diligence in ensuring that each member and employee of the member's law firm, each non-member partner and associate and each other person whose services the member has retained,

(a) complies with this Rule; and

(b) does not disclose,

(i) confidences of clients of the firm, and

(ii) confidences of clients of another law firm in which the person has worked.

Commentary: Matters To Consider When Interviewing a Potential Transferee

When a law firm considers hiring a lawyer or articled law student ("transferring member") from another law firm, the transferring member and the new law firm need to determine, before transfer, whether any conflicts of interest will be created. Conflicts can arise with respect to clients of the law firm that the transferring member is leaving, and with respect to clients of a firm in which the transferring member worked at some earlier time. During the interview process, the transferring member and the new law firm need to identify, firstly, all cases in which,

(a) the new law firm represents a client in a matter which is the same as or related to a matter in respect of which the former law firm represents its client;

(b) the interests of these clients in that matter conflict; and

(c) the transferring member actually possesses relevant information respecting that matter.

When these three elements exist, the transferring member is personally disqualified from representing the new client, unless the former client consents.

Second, they must determine whether, with respect to each such case, the transferring member actually possesses relevant information respecting the former client which is confidential and which, if disclosed to a member of the new law firm, may prejudice the former client. If this element exists, then the transferring member is disqualified unless the former client consents, and the new law firm is disqualified unless the former client consents or the new law firm establishes that its continued representation is in the public interest.

In determining whether the transferring member possesses confidential information, both the transferring member and the new law firm need to be very careful to ensure that they do not, during the interview process itself, disclose client confidences.

Commentary: Matters To Consider Before Hiring a Potential Transferee

After completing the interview process and before hiring the transferring member, the new law firm should determine whether a conflict exists.

A. WHERE A CONFLICT DOES EXIST

If the new law firm concludes that the transferring member does actually possess relevant information respecting a former client which is confidential and which, if disclosed to a member of the new law firm, may prejudice the former client, then the new law firm will be prohibited, if the transferring member is hired, from continuing to represent its client in the matter unless,

(a) the new law firm obtains the former client's consent to its continued representation of its client in that matter; or

(b) the new law firm complies with subrule (4)(b), and in determining whether continued representation is in the interests of justice, both clients' interests are the paramount consideration.

If the new law firm seeks the former client's consent to the new law firm continuing to act it will, in all likelihood, be required to satisfy the former client that it has taken reasonable measures to ensure that no disclosure to any member of the new law firm of the former client's confidential information will occur. The former client's consent must be obtained before the transferring member is hired.

Alternatively, if the new law firm applies under subrule (8) for a determination that it may continue to act, it bears the onus of establishing the matters referred to in subrule (4)(b). Again, this process must be completed before the transferring person is hired.

B. WHERE NO CONFLICT EXISTS

If the new law firm concludes that the transferring member actually possesses relevant information respecting a former client, but that information is not confidential information which, if disclosed to a member of the new law firm, may prejudice the former client, then,

(a) the transferring member should execute an affidavit or solemn declaration to that effect; and

(b) the new law firm must notify its client and the former client/former law firm "of the relevant circumstances and its intended action under the Rule," and deliver to them a copy of any affidavit or solemn declaration executed by the transferring member.

Although the Rule does not require that the notice be in writing, it would be prudent for the new law firm to confirm these matters in writing. Written notification eliminates any later dispute as to the fact of notification, its timeliness and content.

The new law firm might, for example, seek the former client's consent to the transferring member acting for the new law firm's client in the matter because, absent such consent, the transferring member may not act.

If the former client does not consent to the transferring member acting, it would be prudent for the new law firm to take reasonable measures to ensure that no disclosure to any member of the new law firm of the former client's confidential information will occur. If such measures are taken, it will strengthen the new law firm's position if it is later determined that the transferring member did in fact possess confidential information which, if disclosed, may prejudice the former client.

A transferring member who possesses no such confidential information, by executing an affidavit or solemn declaration and delivering it to the former client, puts the former client on notice. A former client who disputes the allegation of no such confidential information may apply under subrule (8) for a determination of that issue.

C. WHERE THE NEW LAW FIRM IS NOT SURE WHETHER A CONFLICT EXISTS

There may be some cases where the new law firm is not sure whether the transferring member actually possesses confidential information respecting a former client which, if disclosed to a member of the new law firm, may prejudice the former client. In such circumstances, it would be prudent for the new law firm to seek guidance from the Society before hiring the transferring member.

Commentary: Reasonable Measures To Ensure Non-Disclosure of Confidential Information

As noted above, there are two circumstances in which the new law firm should consider the implementation of reasonable measures to ensure that no disclosure to any member of the new law firm of the former client's confidential information will occur:

(a) where the transferring member actually possesses confidential information respecting a former client which, if disclosed to a member of the new law firm, may prejudice the former client; and

(b) where the new law firm is not sure whether the transferring member actually possesses such confidential information, but it wants to strengthen its position if it is later determined that the transferring member did in fact possess such confidential information. It is not possible to offer a set of "reasonable measures" which will be appropriate or adequate in every case. Rather, the new law firm which seeks to implement reasonable measures must exercise professional judgment in determining what steps must be taken "to ensure that no disclosure to any member of the new law firm of the former client's confidential information will occur."

In the case of law firms with multiple offices, the degree of autonomy possessed by each office will be an important factor in determining what constitutes "reasonable measures." For example, the various legal services units of a government, a corporation with separate regional legal departments, an inter-provincial law firm or a legal aid program may be able to argue that, because of its institutional structure, reporting relationships, function, nature of work and geography, relatively fewer "measures" are necessary to ensure the non-disclosure of client confidences.

The guidelines at the end of this Commentary, adapted from the Canadian Bar Association's Task Force report entitled: Conflict of Interest Disqualification: Martin v. Gray and Screening Methods (February 1993), are intended as a checklist of relevant factors to be considered. Adoption of only some of the guidelines may be adequate in some cases, while adoption of them all may not be sufficient in others.

In cases where a transferring lawyer joining a government legal services unit or the legal department of a corporation actually possesses confidential information respecting a former client which, if disclosed to a member of the new "law firm," may prejudice the former client, the interests of the new client (i.e., Her Majesty or the corporation) must continue to be represented. Normally, this will be effected either by instituting satisfactory screening measures or, when necessary, by referring conduct of the matter to outside counsel. As each factual situation will be unique, flexibility will be required in the application of subrule (4)(b), particularly clause (E).

GUIDELINES

1. The screened member should have no involvement in the new law firm's representation of its client.

2. The screened member should not discuss the current matter or any information relating to the representation of the former client (the two may be identical) with anyone else in the new law firm.

3. No member of the new law firm should discuss the current matter or the prior representation with the screened member.

4. The current client matter should be discussed only within the limited group which is working on the matter.

5. The files of the current client, including computer files, should be physically segregated from the new law firm's regular filing system, specifically identified, and accessible only to those lawyers and support staff in the new law firm who are working on the matter or who require access for other specifically identified and approved reasons.

6. No member of the new law firm should show the screened member any documents relating to the current representation.

7. The measures taken by the new law firm to screen the transferring member should be stated in a written policy explained to all lawyers and support staff within the firm, supported by an admonition that violation of the policy will result in sanctions, up to and including dismissal.

8. Affidavits should be provided by the appropriate law firm members, setting out that they have adhered to and will continue to adhere to all elements of the screen.

9. The former client, or if the former client is represented in that matter by a member, that member, should be advised,

(a) that the screened member is now with the new law firm, which represents the current client, and

(b) of the measures adopted by the new law firm to ensure that there will be no disclosure of confidential information.

10. The screened member's office or work station and that of the member's secretary should be located away from the offices or work stations of lawyers and support staff working on the matter.

11. The screened member should use associates and support staff different from those working on the current client matter.

2.06 DOING BUSINESS WITH A CLIENT

Definitions

2.06(1) In this rule,
"related persons" means related persons as defined in the *Income Tax Act (Canada)* and "related person" has a corresponding meaning; and
"syndicated mortgage" means a mortgage having more than one investor.

Investment by Client Where Lawyer Has an Interest

(2) Where a client intends to enter into a transaction with his or her lawyer or with a corporation or other entity in which the lawyer has an interest other than a corporation

or other entity whose securities are publicly traded, the lawyer, before accepting any retainer,

(a) shall disclose and explain the nature of the conflicting interest to the client or, in the case of a potential conflict, how and why it might develop later;

(b) shall recommend independent legal representation and shall insist that the client receive independent legal advice, and

(c) where the client requests the lawyer to act, the lawyer shall obtain the client's written consent or record such consent in a letter to the client.

Commentary

If the lawyer does not choose to make disclosure of the conflicting interest or cannot do so without breaching a confidence, the lawyer must decline the retainer.

The lawyer should not uncritically accept the client's decision to have the lawyer act. It should be borne in mind that, if the lawyer accepts the retainer, the lawyer's first duty will be to the client. If the lawyer has any misgivings about being able to place the client's interests first, the retainer should be declined.

Generally speaking, in disciplinary proceedings under this Rule the burden will rest upon the lawyer of showing good faith and that adequate disclosure was made in the matter and the client's consent was obtained.

If the investment is by way of borrowing from the client, the transaction may fall within the requirements of subrule 2.06 (4).

Certificate of Independent Legal Advice

(3) A lawyer retained to give independent legal advice shall, before any advance of funds has been made by the client,

(a) provide the client with a written certificate that the client has received independent legal advice, and

(b) obtain the client's signature on a copy of the certificate of independent legal advice and send the signed copy to the lawyer with whom the client proposes to transact business.

Borrowing from Clients

(4) A lawyer shall not borrow money from a client unless:

(a) the client is a lending institution, financial institution, insurance company, trust company or any similar corporation whose business includes lending money to members of the public; or

(b) the client is a related person as defined by the *Income Tax Act (Canada)* and the lawyer is able to discharge the onus of proving that the client's interests were fully protected by the nature of the case and by independent legal advice or independent legal representation.

Commentary

The relationship existing between lawyer and client is a fiduciary one, and no conflict between the lawyer's own interest and the lawyer's duty to the client can be permitted to exist.

Professional misconduct by lawyers relating to the misuse of trust funds or the improper obtaining of monies have involved the borrowing of money by lawyers from their clients. Sometimes the monies have been borrowed from the client without security other than the promissory note of the lawyer. Usually the money was borrowed from the client for the purpose of being reinvested by the lawyer for the lawyer's own profit.

Whether a person lending money to a lawyer on that person's own account or investing money in a security in which the lawyer has an interest is to be considered a client within this rule is to be determined having regard to all circumstances. If the circumstances are such that the lender or investor might reasonably feel entitled to look to the lawyer for guidance and advice in respect of the loan or investment, then the lawyer will be considered bound by the same fiduciary obligation that attaches to a lawyer in dealings with a client.

(5) In any transaction in which money is borrowed from a client by a lawyer's spouse or by a corporation, syndicate or partnership in which either the lawyer or the lawyer's spouse has, or both of them together have, directly or indirectly, a substantial interest, the lawyer shall ensure that the client's interests are fully protected by the nature of the case and by independent legal representation.

Lawyers in Mortgage Transactions

(6) A lawyer engaged in the private practice of law in Ontario shall not directly, or indirectly through a corporation, syndicate, partnership, trust or other entity in which the lawyer or a related person has a financial interest, other than an ownership interest of a corporation or other entity offering its securities to the public of less than five per cent (5%) of any class of securities,

(a) hold a syndicated mortgage in trust for investor clients unless each investor client receives;

(i) a complete reporting letter on the transaction;

(ii) a trust declaration signed by the person in whose name the mortgage is registered; and

(iii) a copy of the duplicate registered mortgage;

(b) arrange or recommend the participation of a client as an investor in a syndicated mortgage where the solicitor is an investor unless the solicitor can demonstrate that the client had competent independent legal advice in making the investment or that the client is a knowledgeable investor; or

(c) sell mortgages to, or arrange mortgages for, clients or other persons except in accordance with the skill, competence and integrity usually expected of a lawyer in dealing with clients.

Commentary: Acceptable Mortgage Transactions

A lawyer may engage in the following mortgage transactions in connection with the practice of law:

(a) a lawyer may invest in mortgages personally or on behalf of a related person or a combination thereof;

(b) a lawyer may deal in mortgages in the capacity of an executor, administrator, committee, trustee of a testamentary or inter vivos trust established for purposes other than mortgage investment or pursuant to a power of attorney given for purposes other than exclusively for mortgage investment; and

(c) a lawyer may collect, on behalf of clients, mortgage payments that are made payable in the name of the lawyer pursuant to a written direction to that effect given by the client to the mortgagor provided that such payments are deposited into the lawyer's trust account.

Prohibition Against Acting for Mortgagor and Mortgagee

(7) Subject to subrule (8), a lawyer or two or more lawyers practising in partnership or association shall not act for nor otherwise represent both lender and borrower in a mortgage transaction.

(8) Provided that there is no violation of the provisions of rules 2.04 (Avoidance of Conflicts of Interest), a lawyer may act for or otherwise represent both lender and borrower in a mortgage transaction if:

(a) the lawyer practices in a remote location where there are no other lawyers that either party could conveniently retain for the mortgage transaction;

(b) the lender is selling real property to the borrower and the mortgage represents part of the purchase price;

(c) the lender is a bank listed in Schedule I or II to the *Bank Act* (Canada), a licensed insurer, a registered loan or trust corporation, a subsidiary of any of them, a pension fund, provincial savings office, credit union or a league to which the *Credit Unions and Caisses Populaires Act, 1994* or any other institution that lends money in the ordinary course of its business;

(d) the consideration for the mortgage does not exceed $15,000; or

(e) the lender and borrower are not at "arm's length" as defined in the *Income Tax Act* (Canada).

Disclosure

(9) Where a lawyer sells or arranges mortgages for clients or other persons, the lawyer shall disclose in writing to each client or other person the priority of the mortgage and all other information relevant to the transaction that is known to the lawyer that would be of concern to a proposed investor.

No Advertising

(10) A lawyer shall not promote, by advertising or otherwise, individual or joint investment by clients, or other persons who have money to lend, in any mortgage in

which a financial interest is held by the lawyer, a related person, or a corporation, syndicate, partnership, trust or other entity in which the lawyer or related person has a financial interest, other than an ownership interest of a corporation or other entity offering its securities to the public of less than five per cent (5%) of any class of securities.

Guarantees by a Lawyer

(11) Except as provided by subrule (10), a lawyer shall not guarantee personally any mortgage, or other document securing indebtedness, in which a client is involved as a borrower or lender.

(12) Notwithstanding subrule (9), a lawyer may give a personal guarantee in the following or similar circumstances:

(a) the borrower in the loan transaction is not a client and the lender is a lending institution, financial institution, insurance company, trust company or any similar corporation whose business includes lending money to members of the public and that is providing funds directly or indirectly to the lawyer, the lawyer's spouse, parent or child;

(b) the transaction is for the benefit of a non-profit or charitable institution where the lawyer as a member or supporter of such institution is asked, either individually or together with other members or supporters of the institution, to provide a guarantee; or

(c) the lawyer has entered into a business venture with a client and the lender requires personal guarantees from all participants in the venture as a matter of course and

(i) the lawyer has complied with rules 2.04 (Avoidance of Conflicts of Interest) and 2.06 (Doing Business with a Client), and

(ii) the lender and participants in the venture who are or were clients of the member have received independent legal representation.

2.07 PRESERVATION OF CLIENT'S PROPERTY

Preservation of Client's Property

2.07(1) A lawyer shall care for a client's property as a careful and prudent owner would when dealing with like property and shall observe all relevant rules and law about the preservation of a client's property entrusted to a lawyer.

Commentary

The duties with respect to safekeeping, preserving and accounting for clients' monies and other property are set out in the Regulation made pursuant to the Law Society Act.

The duties here expressed are closely related to those regarding confidential information. The lawyer should keep the clients' papers and other property out of sight as well as out of reach of those not entitled to see them and should, subject to any rights of lien, promptly return them to the client upon request or at the conclusion of the lawyer's mandate.

Notification of Receipt of Property

(2) A lawyer shall promptly notify the client of the receipt of any monies or other property of the client, unless satisfied that the client is aware that they have come into the lawyer's custody.

Identifying Client's Property

(3) A lawyer shall clearly label and identify the client's property and place it in safekeeping distinguishable from the lawyer's own property.

(4) A lawyer shall maintain such records as necessary to identify a client's property that is in the lawyer's custody.

Accounting and Delivery

(5) A lawyer shall account promptly for a client's property that is in the lawyer's custody and shall upon request deliver it to the order of the client.

(6) Where a lawyer is unsure as to the proper person to receive a client's property, the lawyer shall apply to a court of competent jurisdiction for direction.

> *Commentary*
>
> The lawyer should be alert to claim on behalf of clients any privilege in respect of their property seized or attempted to be seized by an external authority. In this regard, the lawyer should be familiar with the nature of the client's privilege and with such relevant statutory provisions as are found in the Income Tax Act (Canada).

2.08 FEES AND DISBURSEMENTS

Reasonable Fees and Disbursements

2.08(1) A lawyer shall not charge or accept any amount for a fee or disbursement unless it is fair and reasonable and has been disclosed in a timely fashion.

(2) A lawyer shall not charge a client interest on an overdue account save as permitted by the *Solicitors Act* or as otherwise permitted by law.

> *Commentary*
>
> What is a fair and reasonable fee will depend upon such factors as:
>
> (a) the time and effort required and spent;
>
> (b) the difficulty and importance of the matter;
>
> (c) whether special skill or service has been required and provided;
>
> (d) the amount involved or the value of the subject matter;
>
> (e) the results obtained;
>
> (f) fees authorized by statute or regulation;
>
> (g) such special circumstances as loss of other employment, uncertainty of reward or urgency.

The fiduciary relationship between lawyer and client requires full disclosure in all financial dealings between them and prohibits the acceptance by the lawyer of any hidden fees. No fee, reward, costs, commission, interest, rebate, agency or forwarding allowance or other compensation whatsoever related to professional employment may be taken by the lawyer from anyone other than the client without full disclosure to and the consent of the client or, where the lawyer's fees are being paid by someone other than the client, such as a legal aid agency, a borrower, or a personal representative, without the consent of such other person or agency.

Breach of this Rule and misunderstandings about fees and financial matters bring the legal profession into disrepute and reflect adversely upon the general administration of justice. A lawyer should try to avoid controversy with a client about fees and should be ready to explain the basis for the charges (especially if the client is unsophisticated or uninformed as to the proper basis and measurements for fees).

A lawyer should give the client a fair estimate of fees and disbursements pointing out any uncertainties involved, so that the client may be able to make an informed decision. This is particularly important concerning fee charges or disbursements which the client might not reasonably be expected to anticipate. When something unusual or unforeseen occurs which may substantially affect the amount of a fee or disbursement the lawyer should forestall misunderstandings or disputes by immediate explanation to the client.

It is in keeping with the best traditions of the legal profession to provide services pro bono and to reduce or waive a fee where there is hardship or poverty, or the client or prospective client would otherwise be deprived of adequate legal advice or representation. A lawyer should provide public interest legal services and support organizations that provide services to persons of limited means.

Champerty and Contingent Fees

(3) A lawyer shall not, except as by law expressly permitted, acquire by purchase or otherwise any interest in the subject matter of litigation being conducted by the lawyer.

(4) A lawyer shall not enter into an arrangement with the client for a contingent fee except in accordance with the provisions of the *Solicitors Act* or in accordance with the *Class Proceedings Act, 1992*.

Statement of Account

(5) In a statement of an account delivered to a client, a lawyer shall clearly and separately detail the amounts charged as fees and as disbursements.

Joint Retainer

(6) Where a lawyer is acting for two or more clients, the lawyer shall divide the fees and disbursements equitably between them, unless there is an agreement by the clients otherwise.

Division of Fees

(7) A lawyer shall not divide a fee with another lawyer who is not a partner or associate unless,

(a) the client consents either expressly or impliedly to the employment of the other lawyer, and

(b) the fees are divided in proportion to the work done and responsibilities assumed.

(8) A lawyer shall not directly or indirectly share, split or divide fees with convey-ancers, notaries public, students, clerks or other persons who bring or refer business to the lawyer's office.

(9) A lawyer shall not give any financial or other reward for referring business to conveyancers, notaries public, students, clerks or other persons who are not lawyers and who bring or refer business to the lawyer's office.

> *Commentary*
>
> An arrangement between a lawyer and a conveyancer to divide fees on applications for probate or administration is improper whether both participate in the work or not.
>
> It is improper for a lawyer, in return for a fee, to permit the lawyer's name to be placed on applications that have been prepared by the conveyancer.
>
> A lawyer may give or accept a referral fee to or from another lawyer with respect to the referral of a client provided that the fee is reasonable and the client is informed and consents.
>
> The rules about division of fees do not prohibit an arrangement respecting the purchase and sale of a law practice when the considera-tion payable includes a percentage of revenues generated from the practice sold.

Exception for Multi-Discipline Partnerships

(10) Subrules (8) and (9) doe not apply to multi-discipline partnerships of lawyer and non-lawyer partners where the partnership agreement provides for the sharing of fees and profits.

Appropriation of Funds

(11) The lawyer shall not appropriate any funds of the client held in trust or other-wise under the lawyer's control for or on account of fees except as permitted by the Regulation made under the *Law Society Act*.

2.09 WITHDRAWAL FROM EMPLOYMENT

Withdrawal from Employment

2.09(1) A lawyer shall not withdraw from employment except for good cause and upon notice to the client appropriate in the circumstances.

> *Commentary*
>
> Although the client has the right to terminate the lawyer–client relationship at will, the lawyer does not enjoy the same freedom of action. Having accepted professional employment, a lawyer should complete the task as ably as possible unless there is justifiable cause for terminating the relationship.
>
> No hard and fast rules can be laid down as to what will constitute reasonable notice before withdrawal. Where the matter is covered by statutory provisions or rules of court, these will govern. In other situations, the governing principle is that the lawyer should protect the client's interests to the best of the lawyer's ability and should not desert the client at a critical stage of a matter or at a time when withdrawal would put the client in a position of disadvantage or peril.

Optional Withdrawal

(2) Subject to the rules about criminal proceedings and the direction of the court, where there has been a serious loss of confidence between the lawyer and the client, the lawyer may withdraw from employment.

> *Commentary*
>
> A lawyer who is deceived by the client will have justifiable cause for withdrawal, and the refusal of the client to accept and act upon the lawyer's advice on a significant point might indicate a loss of confidence justifying withdrawal. However, the lawyer should not use the threat of withdrawal as a device to force a hasty decision by the client on a difficult question.

Non-Payment of Fees

(3) Subject to the rules about criminal proceedings and the direction of the court, where the client fails after reasonable notice to provide funds on account of disbursements or fees, a lawyer may withdraw, unless serious prejudice to the client would result.

Withdrawal from Criminal Proceedings

(4) Where a lawyer has agreed to act in a criminal case and where the interval between a withdrawal and the trial of the case is sufficient to enable the client to obtain another lawyer and to allow such other lawyer adequate time for preparation, the lawyer

who has agreed to act may withdraw because the client has not paid the agreed fee or for other adequate cause provided that the lawyer:

(a) notifies the client, preferably in writing, that the lawyer is withdrawing because the fees have not been paid or for other adequate cause

(b) accounts to the client for any monies received on account of fees and disbursements;

(c) notifies Crown Counsel in writing that the lawyer is no longer acting;

(d) notifies the clerk or registrar of the appropriate court in writing that the lawyer is no longer acting in a case when the lawyer's name appears on the records of the court as acting for the accused.

Commentary

A lawyer who has withdrawn because of conflict with the client should not under any circumstances indicate in the notice addressed to the court or Crown Counsel the cause of the conflict, or make reference to any matter which would violate the privilege that exists between lawyer and client. The notice should merely state that the lawyer is no longer acting and has withdrawn.

(5) Where a lawyer has agreed to act in a criminal case and where the date set for trial is not sufficiently far removed to enable the client to obtain another lawyer or to enable another lawyer to prepare adequately for trial, the lawyer who agreed to act may not withdraw because of non-payment of fees.

(6) Where the lawyer is justified in withdrawing from a criminal case for reasons other than non-payment of fees, and there is not a sufficient interval between a notice to the client of the lawyer's intention to withdraw and the date when the case is to be tried to enable the client to obtain another lawyer and to enable such lawyer to prepare adequately for trial, the first lawyer may withdraw from the case only with the permission of the court before which the case is to be tried.

Commentary

Where circumstances arise which in the opinion of the lawyer require an application to the court for leave to withdraw, the lawyer should promptly inform Crown Counsel and the court of the intention to apply for leave in order to avoid or minimize any inconvenience to the court and witnesses.

Mandatory Withdrawal

(7) Subject to the rules about criminal proceedings and the direction of the court, a lawyer shall withdraw:

(a) if discharged by the client;

(b) if the lawyer is instructed by the client to do something inconsistent with the lawyer's duty to the court and, following explanation, the client persists in such instructions;

(c) if the client is guilty of dishonourable conduct in the proceedings or is taking a position solely to harass or maliciously injure another;

(d) if it becomes clear that the lawyer's continued employment will lead to a breach of these Rules; or

(e) if the lawyer is not competent to handle the matter.

Commentary

When a law firm is dissolved it will usually result in the termination of the lawyer–client relationship as between a particular client and one or more of the lawyers involved. In such cases most clients will prefer to retain the services of the lawyer whom they regarded as being in charge of their business prior to the dissolution. However, the final decision rests with the client, and the lawyers who are no longer retained by that client should act in accordance with the principles here set out, and in particular so as to minimize expense and avoid prejudice to the client.

Manner of Withdrawal

(8) When a lawyer withdraws from employment, the lawyer shall act so as to minimize expense and avoid prejudice to the client and shall do all that can reasonably be done to facilitate the orderly transfer of the matter to the successor lawyer.

(9) Upon discharge or withdrawal, a lawyer shall:

(a) subject to the lawyer's right to a lien, deliver to or to the order of the client all papers and property to which the client is entitled;

(b) give the client all information which may be required in connection with the case or matter;

(c) account for all funds of the client then held or previously dealt with, including the refunding of any remuneration not earned during the employment;

(d) promptly render an account for outstanding fees and disbursements; and

(e) co-operate with the successor lawyer so as to minimize expense and avoid prejudice to the client.

Commentary

The obligation to deliver papers and property is subject to a lawyer's right of lien. In the event of conflicting claims to such papers or property, the lawyer should make every effort to have the claimants settle the dispute.

A lawyer acting for several clients in a case or matter who ceases to act for one or more of them, should co-operate with the successor lawyer or lawyers to the extent required by the Rules, and should seek to avoid any unseemly rivalry, whether real or apparent.

Where upon the discharge or withdrawal of the lawyer the question of a right of lien for unpaid fees and disbursements arises, the lawyer should have due regard to the effect of its enforcement upon the client's position. Generally speaking, the lawyer should not enforce such a lien if the result would be to prejudice materially the client's position in any uncompleted matter.

Duty of Successor Lawyer

(9) Before accepting employment, a successor lawyer shall be satisfied that the former lawyer approves, or has withdrawn or been discharged by the client.

Commentary

It is quite proper for the successor lawyer to urge the client to settle or take reasonable steps towards settling or securing any outstanding account of the former lawyer, especially if the latter withdrew for good cause or was capriciously discharged. But if a trial or hearing is in progress or imminent, or if the client would otherwise be prejudiced, the existence of an outstanding account should not be allowed to interfere with the successor lawyer acting for the client.

RULE 3: THE PRACTICE OF LAW

3.01 MAKING LEGAL SERVICES AVAILABLE

General

3.01(1) Lawyers shall make legal services available to the public in an efficient and convenient way that commands respect and confidence and is compatible with the integrity and independence of the profession.

Commentary

It is essential that a person requiring legal services be able to find, with a minimum of difficulty or delay, a lawyer qualified to provide such services.

The lawyer may assist in making legal services available by participating in the Legal Aid Plan and lawyer referral services, by engaging in programmes of public information, education or advice concerning legal matters, and by being considerate of those who seek advice but are inexperienced in legal matters or cannot readily explain their problems.

Right to Decline Employment: The lawyer has a general right to decline a particular employment (except when assigned as counsel by a court), but it is a right to be exercised prudently, particularly if the probable result would be to make it very difficult for a person to obtain legal advice or representation. Generally, the lawyer should not exercise the right merely because a person seeking legal services or that person's cause is unpopular or notorious, or because powerful interests or allegations of misconduct or malfeasance are involved, or because of the lawyer's private opinion about the guilt of the accused.

A lawyer declining employment should assist in obtaining the services of another lawyer qualified in the particular field and able to act.

Referrals

(2) A lawyer who is consulted by a prospective client but who is unable to act shall assist the client in finding another lawyer who is qualified and able to act.

Commentary

In a relatively small community where lawyers are well-known, a person seeking a lawyer will usually be able to make an informed choice and select a qualified lawyer in whom to have confidence. However, in larger centres these conditions will often not obtain, and as the practice of law becomes increasingly complex and the practice of many individual lawyers becomes restricted to particular fields of law, the reputations of lawyers and their competence or qualification in particular fields may not be sufficiently well-known to enable a person to make an informed choice. Thus, one who has had little or no contact with lawyers or who is a stranger in the community may have difficulty finding a lawyer with the special skill required for a particular task. Telephone directories, legal directories and referral services may help find a lawyer, but not necessarily the right one for the client's need.

When a lawyer offers a client or prospective client assistance in finding another lawyer, the assistance should be given willingly and, except in very special circumstances, without charge.

3.02 LAW FIRM NAME

General

3.02(1) A law firm name may include only the names of persons who, if living, are qualified to practise in Ontario or in any other province or territory of Canada where the law firm carries on its practice, or who, if dead, were qualified to practise in Ontario or in any other province or territory of Canada where the firm carries on its practice.

(2) A law firm name may consist of or include the names of deceased or retired members of the firm.

(3) A lawyer who purchases a practice may, for a reasonable length of time, use the words "Successor to _____" in small print under the lawyer's own name.

Restrictions

(4) The name of a law firm shall not include a trade name, a commercial name, or a figure of speech.

(5) The name of a law firm shall not include the use of phrases such as "John Doe and Associates," or "John Doe and Company" and "John Doe and Partners" unless there

are in fact, respectively, two or more other lawyers associated with John Doe in practice or two or more partners of John Doe in the firm.

(6) When a lawyer retires from a law firm to take up an appointment as a judge or master, or to fill any office incompatible with the practice of law, the lawyer's name shall be deleted from the firm name.

(7) A lawyer or law firm may not acquire and use a firm name unless the name was acquired along with the practice of a deceased or retiring member who conducted a practice under the name.

Limited Liability Partnership

(8) If a law firm practices as a limited liability partnership, the phrase "limited liability partnership" or the letters "LLP" shall be included as the last words or letters in the firm name.

3.03 LETTERHEAD

General

3.03(1) Subject to subrules (2) and (3) and Rule 3.05, a lawyer's letterhead and the signs identifying the office may only include:

(a) the name of the lawyer or law firm;

(b) a list of the members of any law firm including counsel practising with the firm;

(c) the words "barrister-at-law," "barrister and solicitor," "lawyer," "law office," or the plural where applicable;

(d) the words "notary" or "commissioner for oaths" or both, and their plural where applicable;

(e) the words "patent and trade mark agent" in proper cases and its plural where applicable;

(f) the phrase "limited liability partnership" or the letters "LLP" where applicable;

(g) the addresses, telephone numbers and office hours and the languages in which the lawyer or law firm is competent and capable of conducting a practice; and

(h) a logo.

(2) A lawyer or law firm that practises in the industrial property field may show the names of patent and trademark agents registered in Canada who are identified as such but who are not lawyers.

(3) A lawyer or law firm may place after the names on its letterhead degrees from bona fide universities and post secondary institutions including honorary degrees; professional qualifications such as the designations of P Eng., CA, and MD; and recognized civil and military decorations and awards and where the firm is a multi-discipline practice, a list or partners and associates who are non-lawyers identified as such and their designations, if any.

3.04 ADVERTISING

Advertising Services Permitted

3.04(1) Subject to subrule (3), a lawyer or a law firm may advertise their services or fees in any medium including the use of brochures and similar documents provided the advertising:

(a) is not false or misleading; and

(b) is not such as to bring the profession or the administration of justice into disrepute.

Advertising of Fees

(2) Subject to subrule (3), a lawyer or a law firm may advertise fees charged for their services subject to the following conditions:

(a) advertisement of fees for consultation or for specific services shall contain an accurate statement of the services provided for the fee and the circumstances if any in which higher fees may be charged;

(b) if fees are advertised, the fact that disbursements are an additional cost shall be made clear in the advertisement;

(c) advertisements shall not use words or expressions such as "from … ," "minimum" or "… and up" or the like in referring to the fees to be charged;

(d) services covered by advertised fees shall be provided at the advertised rate to all clients who retain the advertising lawyer or law firm during the 30-day period following upon the last publication of the fee unless there are special circumstances which could not reasonably have been foreseen, the burden of proving which rests upon the lawyer.

Restrictions on Advertising

(3) A lawyer shall not:

(a) permit the lawyer's name to appear as solicitor, counsel or Queen's Counsel on any advertising material offering goods (other than securities or legal publications) or services to the public; and

(b) while in private practice permit the lawyer's name to appear on the letterhead of a company as being its solicitor or counsel of a business, or corporation, other than the designation of honorary counsel or honorary lawyer on the letterhead of a non-profit or philanthropic organization that has been approved for such purpose by the standing committee of Convocation responsible for professional conduct.

Commentary

The means by which it is sought to make legal services more readily available to the public must be consistent with the public interest and must not detract from the integrity, independence or effectiveness of the legal profession.

3.05 ADVERTISING NATURE OF PRACTICE

General Practice

3.05(1) A lawyer or law firm may state that the lawyer or law firm is in general practice if such is the case.

Restricted Practice

(2) A lawyer may state that the lawyer is a specialist in a particular area of the law only if the lawyer has been so certified by the Society.

(3) A lawyer may state that the lawyer's practice is restricted to a particular area or areas of the law or may state that the lawyer practises in a certain area or areas of the law if such is the case.

(4) A law firm may state that it practises in certain areas of the law or that it has a restricted practice if such is the case.

(5) A law firm may specify the area or areas of law in which particular members practise or to which they restrict their practice.

Multi-Discipline Practice

(6) A lawyer of a multi-discipline practice may state the services or the nature of the services provided by non-lawyer partners or associates in the practice.

3.06 SEEKING PROFESSIONAL EMPLOYMENT

General

3.06(1) Subject to subrule (2), a lawyer may seek professional employment from a prospective client by any means.

Restrictions

(2) In seeking professional employment, a lawyer shall not use means:
    (a) that are false or misleading;
    (b) that amount to coercion, duress or harassment;
    (c) that take advantage of a person who is vulnerable or who has suffered a traumatic experience and has not yet had a chance to recover; or
    (d) that interfere with an existing relationship between another lawyer and his or her client for the purpose of obtaining the client's retainer, unless the change of retainer is initiated by the client; or,
    (e) that otherwise are such as to bring the profession or the administration of justice into disrepute.

3.07 INTERPROVINCIAL LAW FIRMS

General

3.07(1) Lawyers may enter into agreements with lawyers in other Canadian jurisdictions to form an interprovincial law firm, provided they comply with the requirements of this Rule.

Requirements

(2) A lawyer who is a member of an interprovincial law firm and qualified to practise in Ontario shall comply with all the requirements of the Society.

(3) A lawyer who is a member of an interprovincial law firm and qualified to practise in Ontario shall ensure that the books, records and accounts pertaining to their practice in Ontario are available in Ontario on demand by the Society's auditors or their designated agents.

(4) A lawyer who is a member of an interprovincial law firm and qualified to practise in Ontario shall ensure that his or her partners, associates, or employees who are not qualified to practise in Ontario are not held out as and do not represent themselves as qualified to practise in Ontario.

RULE 4: RELATIONSHIP TO THE ADMINISTRATION OF JUSTICE

4.01 THE LAWYER AS ADVOCATE

Advocacy

4.01(1) When acting as an advocate, a lawyer shall represent the client resolutely and honourably within the limits of the law while treating the tribunal with candour, fairness, courtesy, and respect.

Commentary

This Rule applies to the lawyer as advocate, and therefore extends not only to court proceedings but also to appearances and proceedings before boards, administrative tribunals and other bodies, regardless of their function or the informality of their procedures.

The lawyer has a duty to the client to raise fearlessly every issue, advance every argument, and ask every question, however distasteful, which the lawyer thinks will help the client's case and to endeavour to obtain for the client the benefit of every remedy and defence authorized by law. The lawyer must discharge this duty by fair and honourable means, without illegality and in a manner that is consistent with the lawyer's duty to treat the tribunal with candour, fairness, courtesy and respect and in a way that promotes the parties right to a fair hearing where justice can be done. Maintaining dignity, decorum and courtesy in the courtroom is not an empty formality because unless order is maintained, constitutional and other rights cannot be protected.

Role in Adversary Proceedings: In adversary proceedings the lawyer's function as advocate is openly and necessarily partisan. Accordingly, the lawyer is not obliged (save as required by law or under these Rules and subject to the duties of a prosecutor set out below) to assist an adversary or advance matters derogatory to the client's case.

A lawyer should when, acting as an advocate, refrain from expressing the lawyer's personal opinions as to the merits of a client's case.

When opposing interests are not represented, for example in ex parte or uncontested matters, or in other situations where the full proof and argument inherent in the adversary system cannot obtain, the lawyer must take particular care to be accurate, candid and comprehensive in presenting the client's case so as to ensure that the court is not misled.

Duty as Prosecutor: When engaged as a prosecutor, the lawyer's prime duty is not to seek to convict, but to see that justice is done through a fair trial upon the merits. The prosecutor exercises a public function involving much discretion and power, and must act fairly and dispassionately. The prosecutor should not do anything which might prevent the accused from being represented by counsel or communicating with counsel.

Duty as Defence Counsel: When defending an accused person, a lawyer's duty is to protect the client as far as possible from being convicted except by a tribunal of competent jurisdiction and upon legal evidence sufficient to support a conviction for the offence with which the client is charged. Accordingly, and not withstanding the lawyer's private opinion as to credibility or merits, a lawyer may properly rely upon any evidence or defences including so-called technicalities not known to be false or fraudulent.

Admissions made by the accused to a lawyer may impose strict limitations on the conduct of the defence, and the accused should be made aware of this. For example, if the accused clearly admits to the lawyer the factual and mental elements necessary to constitute the offence, the lawyer, if convinced that the admissions are true and voluntary, may properly take objection to the jurisdiction of the court, or to the form of the indictment, or to the admissibility or sufficiency of the evidence, but must not suggest that some other person committed the offence, or call any evidence which, by reason of the admissions, the lawyer believes to be false. Nor may the lawyer set up an affirmative case inconsistent with such admissions, for example, by calling evidence in support of an alibi intended to show that the accused could not have done, or in fact had not done, the act. Such admissions will also impose a limit upon the extent to which the lawyer may attack the evidence for the prosecution. The lawyer is entitled to test the evidence given by each individual witness for the prosecution and argue that the evidence taken as a whole is insufficient to amount to proof that the accused is guilty of the offence charged, but the lawyer should go no further than that.

The lawyer should never waive or abandon the client's legal rights, for example an available defence under a statute of limitations, without the client's informed consent.

In civil matters it is desirable that the lawyer should avoid and discourage the client from resorting to frivolous or vexatious objections or attempts to gain advantage from slips or oversights not going to the real merits, or tactics which will merely delay or harass the other side. Such practices can readily bring the administration of justice and the legal profession into disrepute.

In civil proceedings, the lawyer has a duty not to mislead the court as to the position of the client in the adversary process. Thus, a lawyer representing a party to litigation who has made or is party to an agreement made before or during the trial whereby a plaintiff is guaranteed recovery by one or more parties notwithstanding the judgment of the court, shall forthwith reveal the existence and particulars of the agreement to the court and to all parties to the proceedings.

(2) When acting as an advocate, a lawyer shall not:

(a) abuse the process of the tribunal by instituting or prosecuting proceedings which, although legal in themselves, are clearly motivated by malice on the part of the client and are brought solely for the purpose of injuring the other party;

(b) knowingly assist or permit the client to do anything which the lawyer considers to be dishonest or dishonourable;

(c) appear before a judicial officer when the lawyer, the lawyer's associates or the client have business or personal relationships with such officer which give rise to or might reasonably appear to give rise to pressure, influence or inducement affecting the impartiality of such officer;

(d) endeavour or allow anyone else to endeavour, directly or indirectly, to influence the decision or action of a tribunal or any of its officials in any case or matter by any means other than open persuasion as an advocate;

(e) knowingly attempt to deceive a tribunal or influence the course of justice by offering false evidence, misstating facts or law, presenting or relying upon a false or deceptive affidavit, suppressing what ought to be disclosed, or otherwise assisting in any fraud, crime or illegal conduct;

(f) knowingly misstate the contents of a document, the testimony of a witness, the substance of an argument or the provisions of a statute or like authority;

(g) knowingly assert as true a fact for which there is no reasonable basis in evidence;

(h) deliberately refrain from informing the tribunal of any pertinent authority which the lawyer considers to be directly on point and which has not been mentioned by an opponent;

(i) dissuade a material witness from giving evidence, or advise such a witness to be absent;

(j) knowingly permit a witness to be presented in a false or misleading way, or to impersonate another;

(k) needlessly abuse, hector, or harass a witness;

(l) when representing an accused or potential accused influence or attempt to influence the complainant or potential complainant with respect to the laying, prosecution or withdrawal of criminal charges;

(m) when representing a complainant or potential complainant advise or threaten the laying of a criminal charge in an attempt to gain a benefit for the complainant;

(n) when representing a complainant or potential complainant advise, seek, or procure the withdrawal of a criminal charge in an attempt to gain a benefit for the complainant; and

(o) needlessly inconvenience a witness.

Disclosure by Prosecutor

(3) When engaged as a prosecutor, a lawyer shall disclose all relevant information to the accused as required by law.

Discovery Obligations

(4) Where the rules of a court or tribunal require the parties to produce documents or attend on examinations for discovery, a lawyer when acting as an advocate

(a) shall explain to his or her client:

(i) the necessity of making full disclosure of all documents relating to any matter in issue; and

(ii) the duty to answer to the best of his or her knowledge, information and belief, any proper question relating to any issue in the action or made discoverable by the *Rules of Civil Procedure* or the rules of the tribunal; and

(b) shall not make frivolous requests for the production of documents or make frivolous demands for information at the examination for discovery.

Disclosure of Error or Omission

(5) A lawyer who has unknowingly done or failed to do something which if done or omitted knowingly would have been in breach of this Rule and who discovers it, shall, subject to Rule 2.02 (Confidentiality), disclose the error or omission and do all that can reasonably be done in the circumstances to rectify it.

Commentary

If the client desires that a course be taken which would involve a breach of this Rule, the lawyer must refuse and do everything reasonably possible to prevent it. If that cannot be done the lawyer should, subject to Rule 2.09 (Withdrawal of Employment), withdraw or seek leave to do so.

Courteousness

(6) A lawyer shall at all times the lawyer be courteous and civil to the court and to those engaged on the other side.

Commentary

Legal contempt of court and the professional obligation outlined here are not identical, and a consistent pattern of rude, provocative or disruptive conduct by the lawyer, even though unpunished as contempt, might well merit discipline.

Undertakings

(7) A lawyer shall strictly and scrupulously carry out an undertaking given to the court or to another lawyer in the course of litigation.

Commentary

Unless clearly qualified, the lawyer's undertaking is a personal promise and responsibility.

Agreement on Guilty Plea

(8) Before a charge is laid or at any time after a charge is laid, a defence lawyer may discuss with the prosecutor the possible disposition of the case unless the client instructs otherwise.

(9) Where following investigation,

(a) a defence lawyer *bona fide* concludes and advises the defendant client that an acquittal of the offence charged is uncertain or unlikely,

(b) the defence lawyer advises the defendant client of the implications and possible consequences of a guilty plea and particularly of the detachment of the court,

(c) the defendant client is prepared to admit the necessary factual elements of the offence charged, and

(d) the client instructs the defence lawyer to enter into an agreement as to a guilty plea,

the defence lawyer may enter into an agreement with the prosecutor about a guilty plea.

Commentary

The public interest in the proper administration of justice should not be sacrificed in the interest of expediency.

4.02 THE LAWYER AS WITNESS

Submission of Affidavit

4.02(1) Subject to any contrary provisions of the law or the discretion of the tribunal before which a lawyer is appearing, a lawyer who appears as advocate shall not submit his or her own affidavit to the tribunal.

Submission of Testimony

(2) Subject to any contrary provisions of the law or the discretion of the tribunal before which a lawyer is appearing, a lawyer who appears as advocate shall not testify before the tribunal save as may be permitted by the *Rules of Civil Procedure* or as to purely formal or uncontroverted matters.

> ### Commentary
>
> A lawyer should not express personal opinions or beliefs, or assert as a fact anything that is properly subject to legal proof, cross-examination or challenge. The lawyer should not in effect appear as an unsworn witness or put the lawyer's own credibility in issue. The lawyer who is a necessary witness should testify and entrust the conduct of the case to another lawyer. There are no restrictions on the advocate's right to cross-examine another lawyer, however, and the lawyer who does appear as a witness should not expect to receive special treatment because of professional status.

Appeals

(3) A lawyer who is a witness in proceedings shall not appear as advocate in any appeal from the decision in those proceedings.

4.03 INTERVIEWING WITNESSES

Interviewing Witnesses

4.03(1) Subject to subrule (2), a lawyer may seek information from any potential witness (whether under subpoena or not) but shall disclose the lawyer's interest and take care not to subvert or suppress any evidence or procure the witness to stay out of the way.

(2) A lawyer shall not approach or deal with a party who is professionally represented by another lawyer save through or with the consent of that party's lawyer.

(3) A lawyer shall not approach or deal with directors, officers, or management personnel of a corporation or other organization that is professionally represented by another lawyer save through or with the consent of that party's lawyer.

> ### Commentary
>
> This rule applies to communications with any person, whether or not a party to a formal adjudicative proceeding, contract or negotiation, who is represented by counsel concerning the matter to which the communication relates. A lawyer may communicate with a represented person, or an employee or agent of such a person, concerning matters outside the representation. Also parties to a matter may communicate directly with each other.
>
> The prohibition on communications with a represented person applies only in circumstances in which the lawyer knows that the person

is in fact represented in the matter to be discussed. This means that the lawyer has actual knowledge of the fact of the representation; but such actual knowledge may be inferred from the circumstances. Such an inference may arise where there is substantial reason to believe that the person with whom communication is sought is represented in the matter to be discussed. Thus, a lawyer cannot evade the requirement of obtaining the consent of counsel by closing eyes to the obvious.

In the case of a corporation or other organization (including for example an association or government department), this rule prohibits communications by a lawyer for another person or entity concerning the matter in question with persons having managerial responsibility on behalf of the organization, and with any other person whose act or omission in connection with that matter may be imputed to the organization for purposes of civil or criminal liability or whose statement may constitute an admission on the part of the organization. If an agent or employee of the organization in represented in the matter by his or her counsel, the consent of that counsel to a communication will be sufficient for purposes of this rule.

A lawyer representing a corporation or other organization may also be retained to represent employees of the corporation or organization. In such circumstances the lawyer must comply with the requirements of rule 2.04 (avoidance of conflicts of interest), and particularly subrules 2.04 (5) through (9). A lawyer must not represent that he or she acts for an employee of a client unless the requirements of rule 2.04 have been complied with, and must not be retained by an employee solely for the purpose of sheltering factual information from another party.

4.04 COMMUNICATION WITH COMPLAINANT

Communication with Complainant

4.04 Where a lawyer is acting for a person who is a defendant in criminal proceedings, the lawyer shall not request nor attempt to persuade the complainant to withdraw the charges.

Commentary

While a lawyer acting for a person who is a defendant in criminal proceedings may communicate with the complainant to obtain factual information, to arrange for restitution or an apology from the defendant, or to settle any civil claims between the defendant and the accused, it is not proper for the lawyer directly or indirectly to request or to attempt to persuade the complainant to withdraw the charges in return for a benefit or for any other purpose. The lawyer, however, may discuss the charges with the Crown and suggest or request that the prosecutor speak with the complainant about the possibility of withdrawal.

4.05 COMMUNICATION WITH WITNESS GIVING EVIDENCE

Communication with Witness Giving Evidence

4.05 The lawyer shall observe the following guidelines respecting communication with witnesses giving evidence:

(a) during examination-in-chief it is proper for the examining lawyer to discuss with the witness any matter that has not been covered in the examination up to that point;

(b) during examination-in-chief by another lawyer of a witness who is unsympathetic to the lawyer's cause the lawyer not conducting the examination-in-chief may discuss the evidence with the witness;

(c) between completion of examination-in-chief and commencement of cross-examination of the lawyer's own witness there ought to be no discussion of the evidence given in chief or relating to any matter introduced or touched upon during the examination-in-chief;

(d) during cross-examination by an opposing lawyer: While the witness is under cross-examination the lawyer ought not to have any conversation with the witness respecting the witness's evidence or any issue in the proceeding;

(e) between completion of cross-examination and commencement of re-examination the lawyer who is going to re-examine the witness ought not to have any discussion respecting evidence that will be dealt with on re-examination;

(f) during cross-examination by the lawyer of a witness unsympathetic to the cross-examiner's cause the lawyer may discuss the witness's evidence with the witness;

(g) during cross-examination by the lawyer of a witness who is sympathetic to that lawyer's cause any conversations ought to be restricted in the same way as communications during examination-in-chief of one's own witness; and

(h) during re-examination of a witness called by an opposing lawyer: If the witness is sympathetic to the lawyer's cause there ought to be no communication relating to the evidence to be given by that witness during re-examination. The lawyer may, however, properly discuss the evidence with a witness who is adverse in interest.

Commentary

If there is any question whether the lawyer's behaviour may be in violation of the Rule, it will often be appropriate to obtain the consent of the opposing lawyer or leave of the court before engaging in conversations that may be considered improper.

4.06 RELATIONS WITH JURORS

Communications Before Trial

4.06(1) When acting as an advocate, a lawyer shall not before the trial of a case communicate with or cause another to communicate with anyone that the lawyer knows to be a member of the jury panel for the trial of the case.

Commentary

A lawyer may investigate a prospective juror to ascertain any basis for challenge, provided that there is no direct or indirect communication with the juror or with any member of the juror's family. But a lawyer should not conduct or cause by financial support or otherwise, another to conduct a vexatious or harassing investigation of either a member of the jury panel or a juror.

Disclosure of Information

(2) When acting as an advocate, a lawyer shall disclose to the judge and opposing counsel any information of which he or she is aware that a juror or perspective juror:

(a) has or may have an interest, direct or indirect, in the outcome of the case;

(b) is acquainted or connected in any manner with any litigant; or

(c) is acquainted or connected in any manner with any person who has appeared or who is expected to appear as a witness;

unless the judge and opposing counsel have previously been made aware of the information.

(3) A lawyer should promptly disclose to the court any information that he or she has about improper conduct by a member of a jury panel or by a juror toward another member of the jury panel, another juror, or to the members of a juror's family.

Communication During Trial

(4) Except as permitted by law, when acting as an advocate, a lawyer shall not during a trial of a case communicate with or cause another to communicate with any member of the jury.

(5) A lawyer who is not connected with a case before the courts shall not communicate with or cause another to communicate with any member of the jury about the case.

Commentary

The restrictions upon communications with a juror or potential juror should also apply to communications with or investigations of members of his or her family.

4.07 THE LAWYER AND THE ADMINISTRATION OF JUSTICE

Encouraging Respect for the Administration of Justice

4.07(1) A lawyer shall encourage public respect for and try to improve the administration of justice.

Commentary

The obligation outlined in the Rule is not restricted to the lawyer's professional activities but is a general responsibility resulting from the lawyer's position in the community. A lawyer's responsibilities are greater than those of a private citizen. A lawyer must not subvert the law by counselling or assisting in activities that are in defiance of it. A lawyer should take care not to weaken or destroy public confidence in legal institutions or authorities by irresponsible allegations. The lawyer in public life should be particularly careful in this regard because the mere fact of being a lawyer will lend weight and credibility to public statements. Yet for the same reason a lawyer should not hesitate to speak out against an injustice.

The admission to and continuance in the practice of law implies on the part of a lawyer a basic commitment to the concept of equal justice for all within an open, ordered and impartial system. However, judicial institutions will not function effectively unless they command the respect of the public, and because of changes in human affairs and imperfections in human institutions, constant efforts must be made to improve the administration of justice and thereby maintain public respect for it.

Criticizing Courts and Tribunals. Although proceedings and decisions of courts and tribunals are properly subject to scrutiny and criticism by all members of the public including lawyers, judges, and members of tribunals are often prohibited by law or custom from defending themselves. Their inability to do so imposes special responsibilities upon lawyers. Firstly, a lawyer should avoid criticism which is petty, intemperate or unsupported by a bona fide belief in its real merit, bearing in mind that in the eyes of the public professional knowledge lends weight to the lawyer's judgments or criticism. Secondly, if a lawyer has been involved in the proceedings, there is the risk that any criticism may be, or may appear to be, partisan rather than objective. Thirdly, where a court or tribunal is the object of unjust criticism, a lawyer, as a participant in the administration of justice, is uniquely able to and should support the court or tribunal, both because its members cannot defend themselves and because the lawyer is thereby contributing to greater public understanding of and therefore respect for the legal system.

A lawyer, by training, opportunity and experience is in a position to observe the workings and discover the strengths and weaknesses of laws, legal institutions and public authorities. A lawyer should, therefore, lead in seeking improvements in the legal system, but any criticisms and proposals should be bona fide and reasoned.

Seeking Legislative or Administrative Changes

(2) A lawyer who seeks legislative or administrative changes shall disclose whose interest is being advanced, whether the lawyer's interest, that of a client, or the public interest.

Commentary

The lawyer may advocate such changes on behalf of a client although not personally agreeing with them, but the lawyer who purports to act in the public interest should espouse only those changes which the lawyer conscientiously believes to be in the public interest.

Security of Court Facilities

(3) A lawyer who has reasonable grounds for believing that a dangerous situation is likely to develop at a court facility shall inform the local police force and give particulars.

Commentary

Where possible the lawyer ought to suggest solutions to the anticipated problem such as: (a) the necessity for further security; and (b) that judgment ought to be reserved.

4.08 LAWYERS AS MEDIATORS

Role of Mediator

4.07 A lawyer who functions as a mediator shall at the outset ensure that the parties to the mediation process understand fully that:

(a) the function being discharged is not part of the traditional practice of law;

(b) the lawyer is not acting as a lawyer for either party but as mediator acts to assist the parties to resolve the matters in issue; and

(c) although communications pertaining to and arising out of the mediation process may be covered by some other common law privilege, they will not be covered by the solicitor-client privilege.

Commentary

In acting in the capacity of a mediator, a lawyer as a general rule should not give legal advice as opposed to legal information to the parties during the mediation process.

As a general rule, neither the lawyer-mediator nor a partner or associate of the lawyer-mediator should render legal representation or give legal advice to either party to the mediation, bearing in mind the provisions of Rule 2.04 and its Commentaries and the common law authorities.

As a general rule a lawyer-mediator should suggest and encourage the parties to seek the advice of separate counsel before and during the mediation process if they have not already done so.

Where in the mediation process the lawyer-mediator prepares a draft contract for the consideration of the respective parties, the lawyer-mediator should expressly advise and encourage them to seek separate independent legal representation concerning the draft contract.

RULE 5: RELATIONSHIP TO ASSOCIATES, STUDENTS, AND EMPLOYEES

5.01 SUPERVISION

Application

5.01(1) In this rule, a non-lawyer does not include a student-at-law.

Direct Supervision Required

(2) A lawyer shall assume complete professional responsibility for all business entrusted to him or her and shall directly supervise staff and assistants to whom particular tasks and functions are delegated.

> *Commentary*
>
> A lawyer who practises alone or operates a branch or part-time office should ensure that all matters requiring a lawyer's professional skill and judgment are dealt with by a lawyer qualified to do the work, and that legal advice is not given by unauthorized persons, whether in the lawyer's name or otherwise.

Permissible Delegation

(3) Where a non-lawyer has received specialized training or education and is capable of doing independent work under the general supervision of a lawyer, a lawyer may delegate work to the non-lawyer.

> *Commentary*
>
> A lawyer may in appropriate circumstances render service with the assistance of non-lawyers of whose competence the lawyer is satisfied. Though legal tasks may be delegated to such persons, the lawyer remains responsible for all services rendered and for all written materials prepared by non-lawyers.
>
> A lawyer may permit a non-lawyer to perform tasks delegated and supervised by a lawyer so long as the lawyer maintains a direct relationship with the client or, if the lawyer is in a community legal clinic funded by a Clinic Funding Committee, so long as the lawyer maintains a direct supervisory relationship with each client's case in accordance with the supervision requirements of the Clinic Funding Committee, and assumes full professional responsibility for the work. A lawyer shall not permit a non-lawyer to perform any of the duties that only lawyers may perform, or do things that lawyers themselves may not do. Generally speaking, and subject to the provisions of any statute, rule or court practice in that regard, the question of what the lawyer may delegate to a non-lawyer turns upon the distinction between any special knowledge of the non-lawyer and the professional and legal judgment of the lawyer which in the public interest must be exercised by the lawyer whenever it is required.

A lawyer may permit a non-lawyer to act only under the supervision of a member of the Society. The extent of supervision will depend on the type of legal matter, including the degree of standardization and repetitiveness of the matter, and the experience of the non-lawyer generally and with regard to the matter in question. The burden rests upon the lawyer who uses a non-lawyer to educate the latter with respect to the duties that may be assigned to the non-lawyer, and then to supervise the manner in which such duties are carried out. A lawyer should review the non-lawyer's work at sufficiently frequent intervals to enable the lawyer to ensure its proper and timely completion.

Permissible Delegation. The following examples, which do not purport to be exhaustive, illustrate situations where it may be appropriate to delegate work to non-lawyers subject to proper supervision.

Real Estate. A lawyer may permit a non-lawyer to attend to all matters of routine administration, and to assist in more complex transactions relating to the sale, purchase, option, lease or mortgaging of land, to draft statements of account and routine documents and correspondence, and to attend to registrations, provided that the lawyer should not delegate to a non-lawyer ultimate responsibility for review of a title search report, or of documents before signing, or the review and signing of a letter of requisition, a title opinion or reporting letter to the client.

Corporate and Commercial. A lawyer may permit a non-lawyer to attend to all matters of routine administration, and to assist in more complex matters and to draft routine documents and correspondence relating to corporate, commercial and securities matters such as drafting corporate minutes and documents pursuant to corporation statutes, security instruments, security registration documents and contracts of all kinds, closing documents and statements of account, and to attend on filings.

Wills, Trusts and Estates. A lawyer may permit a non-lawyer to attend to all matters of routine administration, and to assist in more complex matters, to collect information, draft routine documents and correspondence, prepare income tax returns, calculate such taxes, draft executors' accounts and statements of account, and attend to filings.

Litigation. A lawyer may permit a non-lawyer to attend to all matters of routine administration, and to assist in more complex matters, to collect information, draft routine pleadings, correspondence and other routine documents, research legal questions, prepare memoranda, organize documents, prepare briefs, draft statements of account and attend to filings. Generally speaking, a non-lawyer shall not attend on examinations or in court except in support of a lawyer also in attendance. Permissible exceptions include law clerks appearing on;

(i) routine adjournments in provincial courts;

(ii) appearances before tribunals where statutes or regulations permit non-lawyers to appear, e.g., Small Claims Court, Provincial Courts, Coroners' Inquests, as agent on summary conviction matters where so authorized by the Criminal Code, and administrative tribunals under the Statutory Powers Procedure Act;

(iii) attendance on routine examinations in uncontested matters such as for the purpose of obtaining routine admissions, attendance upon judgment debtor examinations and on watching briefs; however, in no circumstances shall a non-lawyer be permitted to conduct an examination for discovery in a contested matter or a cross-examination of a witness in aid of a motion;

(iv) attendance before a Master on simple ex parte matters or for a consent order;

(v) attendance on assessment of costs.

Improper Delegation

(4) A lawyer shall not permit a non-lawyer to,

(a) accept cases on behalf of the lawyer, except that such persons may receive instructions from established clients if the supervising lawyer is advised before any work commences;

(b) set fees;

(c) give legal opinions;

(d) give or accept undertakings, except with the express authorization of the supervising lawyer;

(e) act finally without reference to the lawyer in matters involving professional legal judgment;

(f) be held out as a lawyer;

Commentary

A lawyer should insure that the non-lawyer is identified as such when communicating orally or in writing with clients, lawyers, public officials or with the public generally whether within or outside the offices of the law firm of employment.

(g) appear in court or actively participate in formal legal proceedings on behalf of a client except as set forth above, or in a support role to the lawyer appearing in such proceedings;

(h) be named in association with the lawyer in any pleading, written argument or other like document submitted to a court;

(i) be remunerated on a sliding scale related to the earnings of the lawyer, except where such person is an employee of the lawyer;

(j) conduct negotiations with third parties, other than routine negotiations where the client consents and the results thereof are approved by the supervising lawyer before action is taken;

(k) take instructions from clients, unless the supervising lawyer has directed the client to the non-lawyer for that purpose;

(l) sign correspondence containing a legal opinion, but the non-lawyer who has been specifically directed to do so by a supervising lawyer may sign correspondence of a routine administrative nature, provided that the fact such person is a non-lawyer is disclosed, and the capacity in which such person signs the correspondence is indicated; and

(m) forward to a client any documents, other than routine documents, unless they have previously been reviewed by the lawyer.

(5) A lawyer shall not permit a non-lawyer to:

(a) provide advice to the client with respect to any insurance, including title insurance without supervision;

(b) present insurance options or information regarding premiums to the client without supervision;

(c) recommend one insurance product over another without supervision; and

(d) give legal opinions regarding the insurance coverage obtained.

Collection Letters

(6) No collection letter shall be sent out over the signature of a lawyer, unless the letter is on the lawyer's letterhead, prepared under the lawyer's supervision and sent from the lawyer's office.

5.02 STUDENTS

Recruitment Procedures

5.02(1) A lawyer shall observe the procedures of the Society about the recruitment of articling students and the engagement of summer students.

Duty as a Principal

(2) A lawyer in the capacity of a principal to a student shall provide the student with meaningful training and exposure to and involvement in work that will provide the student with knowledge and experience of the practical aspects of the law, together with an appreciation of the traditions and ethics of the profession.

Duty of the Articling Student

(3) An articling student shall act in good faith in fulfilling and discharging all the commitments and obligations arising from the articling experience.

5.03 SEXUAL HARASSMENT

Definition

5.03(1) In this rule, sexual harassment is one or a series of incidents involving unwelcome sexual advances, requests for sexual favours, or other verbal or physical conduct of a sexual nature,

(a) when such conduct might reasonably be expected to cause insecurity, discomfort, offence or humiliation to another person or group; or

(b) when submission to such conduct is made implicitly or explicitly a condition for the provision of professional services; or

(c) when submission to such conduct is made implicitly or explicitly a condition of employment; or

(d) when submission to or rejection of such conduct is used as a basis for any employment decision (including, but not limited to, matters of promotion, raise in salary, job security and benefits affecting the employee); or

(e) when such conduct has the purpose or the effect of interfering with a person's work performance or creating an intimidating, hostile or offensive work environment.

Commentary

Types of behaviour which constitute sexual harassment include, but are not limited to,

(a) sexist jokes causing embarrassment or offence, told or carried out after the joker has been advised that they are embarrassing or offensive, or that are by their nature clearly embarrassing or offensive

(b) leering

(c) the display of sexually offensive material

(d) sexually degrading words used to describe a person

(e) derogatory or degrading remarks directed towards members of one sex or one sexual orientation

(f) sexually suggestive or obscene comments or gestures

(g) unwelcome inquiries or comments about a person's sex life

(h) unwelcome sexual flirtations, advances, propositions

(i) persistent unwanted contact or attention after the end of a consensual relationship

(j) requests for sexual favours

(k) unwanted touching

(l) verbal abuse or threats

(m) sexual assault.

Sexual harassment can occur in the form of behaviour by men towards women, between men, between women or by women towards men.

Prohibition on Sexual Harassment

(2) A lawyer shall not, in a professional context, sexually harass a colleague, staff, clients, or other person.

5.04 DISCRIMINATION

Special Responsibility

(1) A lawyer has a special responsibility to respect the requirements of human rights laws in force in Ontario and specifically to honour the obligation not to discrimi-

nate on the grounds of race, ancestry, place of origin, colour, ethnic origin, citizenship, creed, sex, sexual orientation, age, record of offences (as defined in the *Ontario Human Rights Code*), marital status, family status or disability with respect to professional employment of other lawyers, articled students, or any other person or in professional dealings with other members of the profession or any other person.

Commentary

The Society acknowledges the diversity of the community of Ontario in which its members serve and expects members to respect the dignity and worth of all persons and to treat all persons equally without discrimination.

This rule sets out the special role of the profession to recognize and protect the dignity of individuals and the diversity of the community in Ontario.

Rule 5.04 will be interpreted according to the provisions of the Ontario Human Rights Code, and related case law.

Rule 5.04 prohibits discrimination on any of the following grounds: race; place of origin, ethnic origin, creed, sexual orientation, record of offences, family status, ancestry, colour, citizenship, sex, age, marital status, and disability.

The Ontario Human Rights Code defines a number of grounds of discrimination listed in Rule 5.04. For example,

Age is defined as an age that is eighteen years or more, except in subsection 5(i) where age means an age that is eighteen years or more and less than sixty-five years.

The term disability is not used in the Code, but discrimination on the ground of handicap is prohibited. Handicap is broadly defined in s. 10 of the Code to include both physical and mental disabilities.

Family status is defined as the status of being in a parent and child relationship.

Marital status is defined as the status of being married, single, widowed, divorced or separated and includes the status of living with a person of the opposite sex in a conjugal relationship outside marriage.

Record of offences is defined such that a prospective employer may not discriminate on the basis of a pardoned criminal offence (a pardon must have been granted under the Criminal Records Act (Canada) and not revoked), or provincial offences.

The right to equal treatment without discrimination because of sex includes the right to equal treatment without discrimination because a woman is or may become pregnant.

There is no statutory definition of discrimination. Supreme Court of Canada jurisprudence defines discrimination as including:

Differentiation on prohibited grounds. Lawyers who refuse to hire employees of a particular race, sex, creed, sexual orientation, etc. would be differentiating on the basis of prohibited grounds.

Constructive discrimination. An action or policy that is not intended to be discriminatory can result in an adverse effect that is discriminatory. If the application of a seemingly "neutral" rule or policy creates an adverse effect on a group protected by Rule 5.04, there is a duty to accommodate. For example, while a requirement that all articling students have a driver's licence to permit them to travel wherever their job requires may seem reasonable, that requirement effectively excludes from employment persons with disabilities that prevent them from obtaining a licence. In such a case, the law firm would be required to alter or eliminate the requirement in order to accommodate the student unless the necessary accommodation would cause undue hardship.

Human rights law in Ontario includes as discrimination, conduct which, though not intended to discriminate, has an adverse impact on individuals or groups on the basis of the prohibited grounds. The Ontario Human Rights Code requires that the affected individuals or groups must be accommodated unless to do so would cause undue hardship.

A lawyer should take reasonable steps to prevent or stop discrimination by any staff or agent who is subject to the lawyer's direction or control.

Ontario human rights law excepts from discrimination special programs designed to relieve disadvantage for individuals or groups identified on the basis of the grounds noted in the Code.

In addition to prohibiting discrimination, Rule 5.04 prohibits harassment on the ground of race, ancestry, place of origin, colour, ethnic origin, citizenship, creed, sex, sexual orientation, age, record of offences, marital status, family status or handicap. Harassment by superiors, colleagues and co-workers is also prohibited.

Harassment is definedas "engaging in a course of vexatious comment or conduct that is known or ought reasonably to be known to be unwelcome" on the basis of any ground set out in Rule 5.04. This could include, for example, repeatedly subjecting a client or colleague to jokes based on race or creed.

Services

(2) A lawyer shall ensure that no one is denied services or receives inferior service on the basis of the grounds set out in this rule.

Employment Practices

(3) A lawyer shall ensure that his or her employment practices do not offend this rule.

Commentary

Discrimination in employment or in the provision of services not only fails to meet professional standards, it also violates the Ontario Human Rights Code and related equity legislation.

In advertising a job vacancy, an employer may not indicate qualifications by a prohibited ground of discrimination. However, where discrimination on a particular ground is permitted because of an exception under the Human rights Code, such questions may be raised at an interview. For example, an employer may ask whether an applicant has been convicted of a criminal offence for which a pardon has not been granted. An employer may ask applicants not yet called in Ontario about Canadian citizenship or permanent residency. If an employer has an anti-nepotism policy, he or she may inquire about the applicant's possible relationship to another employee as that employee's spouse, child or parent. This is in contrast to questions about applicant's marital status by itself. Since marital status has no relevance to employment within a law firm, questions about marital status should not be asked.

An employer should consider the effect of seemingly "neutral" rules. Some rules, while applied to everyone, can bar entry to the firm or pose additional hardships on employees of one sex, or of a particular creed, ethnicity, marital or family status, or on those who have (or develop) disabilities. For example, a law office may have a written or unwritten dress code. It would be necessary to revise the dress code if it does not already accept that a head covering worn for religious reasons must be considered part of acceptable business attire. The maintenance of a rule with a discriminatory effect breaches Rule 5.04 unless changing or eliminating the rule would cause undue hardship.

If an applicant cannot perform all or part of an essential job requirement because of a personal characteristic listed in the Ontario Human Rights Code, the employer has a duty to accommodate. Only if the applicant cannot do the essential talk with reasonable accommodation may the employer refuse to hire on this basis. A range of appropriate accommodation measures may be considered. An accommodation is considered reasonable unless it would cause undue hardship.

The Supreme Court of Canada has confirmed that what is required is equality of result, not just of form. Differentiation can result in inequality, but so too can the application of the same rule to everyone, without regard for personal characteristics and circumstances. Equality of result requires the accommodation of differences that arise from the personal characteristics cited in Rule 5.04.

The nature of accommodation as well as the extent to which the duty to accommodate might apply in any individual case, are developing areas of human rights law. However, the following principles are well established.

If a rule, requirement or expectation creates difficulty for an individual because of factors related to the personal characteristics noted in Rule 5.04, the following obligations arise:

The rule, requirement or expectation must be examined to determine whether it is "reasonable and bona fide." If the rule, requirement or expectation is not imposed in good faith and is not strongly and logically connected to a business necessity, it cannot be maintained. There must be objectively verifiable evidence linking the rule, requirement or expectation with the operation of the business.

If the rule, requirement or expectation is imposed in good faith and is strongly logically connected to a business necessity, the next step is to consider whether the individual who is disadvantaged by the rule can be accommodated.

The duty to accommodate operates as both a positive obligation and as a limit to obligation. Accommodation must be offered to the point of undue hardship. Some hardship must be tolerated to promote equality; however, if the hardship occasioned by the particular accommodation at issue is "undue," that accommodation need not be made.

RULE 6: RELATIONSHIP TO THE SOCIETY AND OTHER LAWYERS

6.01 RESPONSIBILITY TO THE PROFESSION GENERALLY

General

6.01(1) A lawyer shall assist in maintaining the integrity of the profession.

Meeting Financial Obligations

(2) A lawyer shall meet financial obligations in relation to his or her practice, including prompt payment of the deductible under the Society's Errors and Omissions Insurance Plan when properly called upon to do so.

> *Commentary*
>
> In order to maintain the honour of the Bar, lawyers have a professional duty (quite apart from any legal liability) to meet financial obligations incurred, assumed or undertaken on behalf of clients unless, before incurring such an obligation the lawyer clearly indicates in writing that the obligation is not to be a personal one.

Duty to Report Misconduct

(3) A lawyer shall report to the Society, unless to do so would be unlawful or would involve a breach of solicitor-client privilege:
(a) the misappropriation or misapplication of trust monies;
(b) the abandonment of a law practice;
(c) participation in serious criminal activity related to a lawyer's practice;
(d) the mental instability of a lawyer of such a serious nature that the lawyer's clients are likely to be severely prejudiced; and
(e) any other situation where a lawyer's clients are likely to be severely prejudiced.

Commentary

Unless a lawyer who departs from proper professional conduct is checked at an early stage, loss or damage to clients or others may ensue. Evidence of minor breaches may, on investigation, disclose a more serious situation or may indicate the commencement of a course of conduct that may lead to serious breaches in the future. It is, therefore, proper (unless it be privileged or otherwise unlawful) for a lawyer to report to the Society any instance involving a breach of these Rules. If a lawyer is in any doubt whether a report should be made, the lawyer should consider seeking the advice of the Society directly or indirectly (e.g., through another lawyer). Nothing in this paragraph is meant to interfere with the traditional solicitor-client relationship. In all cases the report must be made bona fide without malice or ulterior motive.

Often instances of improper conduct arise from emotional, mental or family disturbances or substance abuse. Lawyers who suffer from such problems should be encouraged to seek assistance as early as possible. The Society supports the Ontario Bar Assistance Program (OBAP), LINK, and other support groups in their commitment to the provision of confidential counselling. Therefore, lawyers acting in the capacity of counsellors for OBAP and other support groups will not be called by the Society or by any investigation committee to testify at any conduct, capacity or competence hearing without the consent of the lawyer from whom the information was received. Notwithstanding the above, a lawyer/counsellor has an ethical obligation to report to the Society upon learning that the lawyer being assisted is engaging in or may in the future engage in serious misconduct or criminal activity related to the lawyer's practice. The Society cannot countenance such conduct regardless of a lawyer's attempts at rehabilitation.

The Society also recognizes that communications with the ombudsperson appointed to assist in resolving complaints of discrimination or harassment against lawyers must generally remain confidential. Therefore, the ombudsperson will not be called by the Society or by any investigative committee to testify at any conduct, capacity or competence hearing without the consent of the person from whom the information was received. Notwithstanding the above, a lawyer serving as ombudsperson has an ethical obligation to report to the Society upon learning that a lawyer is engaging in or may in the future engage in serious misconduct or criminal activity related to the lawyer's practice.

Encouraging Client to Report Dishonest Conduct

(4) A lawyer shall attempt to persuade a client who has a claim against an apparently dishonest lawyer to report the facts to the Society before pursuing private remedies.

(5) If the client refuses to report his or her claim against an apparently dishonest lawyer to the Society, the lawyer shall inform the client of the policy of the Society's

Compensation Fund and shall obtain instructions in writing to proceed with the client's claim without notice to the Society.

Commentary

A lawyer should inform a client of the provision of the Criminal Code of Canada dealing with the concealment of an indictable offence in return for an agreement to obtain valuable consideration (section 141). In the event the client wishes to pursue a private agreement with the apparently dishonest lawyer, the lawyer shall not continue to act if the agreement constitutes a breach of section 141.

6.02 RESPONSIBILITY TO THE SOCIETY

Communications from the Society

6.02 A lawyer shall reply promptly to any communication from the Society.

6.03 RESPONSIBILITY TO OTHER LAWYERS

Courtesy and Good Faith

6.03(1) A lawyer shall be courteous and act in good faith with other lawyers and lay persons lawfully representing others or themselves.

Commentary

The public interest demands that matters entrusted to a lawyer be dealt with effectively and expeditiously, and fair and courteous dealing on the part of each lawyer engaged in a matter will contribute materially to this end. The lawyer who behaves otherwise does a disservice to the client, and neglect of the Rule will impair the ability of lawyers to perform their function properly.

Any ill feeling which may exist or be engendered between clients, particularly during litigation, should never be allowed to influence lawyers in their conduct and demeanour toward each other or the parties. The presence of personal animosity between lawyers involved in a matter may cause their judgment to be clouded by emotional factors and hinder the proper resolution of the matter. Personal remarks or personally abusive tactics interfere with the orderly administration of justice and have no place in our legal system.

A lawyer should avoid ill-considered or uninformed criticism of the competence, conduct, advice or charges of other lawyers, but should be prepared, when requested, to advise and represent a client in a complaint involving another lawyer.

(2) A lawyer shall accede to reasonable requests concerning trial dates, adjournments, the waiver of procedural formalities and similar matters that do not prejudice the rights of the client.

(3) A lawyer shall avoid sharp practice and shall not take advantage of or act without fair warning upon slips, irregularities or mistakes on the part of other lawyers not going to the merits or involving the sacrifice of a client's rights.

(4) A lawyer shall not use a tape recorder or other device to record a conversation between the lawyer and a client, or another lawyer, even if lawful, without first informing the other person of the intention to do so.

Communications

(5) A lawyer shall not in the course of a professional practice send correspondence or otherwise communicate, to a client, another lawyer or any other person in a manner that is abusive, offensive or otherwise inconsistent with the proper tone of a professional communication from a lawyer.

(6) A lawyer shall answer with reasonable promptness all professional letters and communications from other lawyers that require an answer, and a lawyer shall be punctual in fulfilling all commitments.

(7) A lawyer shall not communicate with or attempt to negotiate or compromise a matter directly with any person who is represented by a lawyer except through or with the consent of that lawyer.

Undertakings

(8) A lawyer shall not give an undertaking that cannot be fulfilled and shall fulfill every undertaking given.

Commentary

Undertakings should be written or confirmed in writing and should be absolutely unambiguous in their terms. If a lawyer giving an undertaking does not intend to accept personal responsibility, this should be stated clearly in the undertaking itself. In the absence of such a statement, the person to whom the undertaking is given is entitled to expect that the lawyer giving it will honour it personally. The use of such words as "on behalf of my client" or "on behalf of the vendor" does not relieve the lawyer giving the undertaking of personal responsibility.

6.04 OUTSIDE INTERESTS AND THE PRACTICE OF LAW

Maintaining Professional Integrity and Judgment

6.04(1) A lawyer who engages in another profession, business, or occupation concurrently with the practice of law shall not allow such outside interest to jeopardize the lawyer's professional integrity, independence, or competence.

(2) A lawyer shall not allow involvement in an outside interest to impair the exercise of the lawyer's independent judgment on behalf of a client.

Commentary

The term "outside interest" covers the widest possible range and includes activities which may overlap or be connected with the practice of law such as, for example, engaging in the mortgage business, acting as a director of a client corporation, or writing on legal subjects, as well as activities not so connected such as, for example, a career in business, politics, broadcasting or the performing arts. In each case the question of whether and to what extent the lawyer may be permitted to engage in the outside interest will be subject to any applicable law or rule of the Society.

Where the outside interest is not related to the legal services being performed for clients, ethical considerations will usually not arise unless the lawyer's conduct might bring the lawyer or the profession into disrepute, or impair the lawyer's competence as, for example, where the outside interest might occupy so much time that clients' interests would suffer because of inattention or lack of preparation.

6.05 THE LAWYER IN PUBLIC OFFICE

Standard of Conduct

6.05(1) A lawyer who holds public office shall in the discharge of official duties adhere to standards of conduct as high as those which these Rules require of a lawyer engaged in the practice of law.

Commentary

The Rule applies to a lawyer who is elected or appointed to a legislative or administrative office at any level of government, regardless of whether or not the lawyer attained such office because of professional qualifications. Because such a lawyer is in the public eye, the legal profession can more readily be brought into disrepute by failure to observe its ethical standards.

Generally speaking, the Society will not be concerned with the way in which a lawyer holding public office carries out official responsibilities, but conduct in office that reflects adversely upon the lawyer's integrity or professional competence may be the subject of disciplinary action.

Conflict of Interest

(2) A lawyer who holds public office shall not allow professional or personal interests to conflict with the proper discharge of official duties.

Commentary

The lawyer holding part-time public office must not accept any private legal business where duty to the client will, or may, conflict with official duties. If some unforeseen conflict arises, the lawyer should terminate the professional relationship, explaining to the client that official duties must prevail. The lawyer who holds a full-time public office will not be faced with this sort of conflict, but must nevertheless guard against allowing independent judgment in the discharge of official duties to be influenced either by the lawyer's own interest, that of some person closely related to or associated with the lawyer, that of former or prospective clients, or of former or prospective partners or associates.

Subject to any special rules applicable to the particular public office, the lawyer holding such office who sees that there is a possibility of a conflict of interest should declare such interest at the earliest opportunity, and not take part in any consideration, discussion or vote with respect to the matter in question.

(3) If there may be a conflict of interest, a lawyer who holds or who held public office shall not represent clients or advise them in contentious cases that the lawyer has been concerned with in an official capacity.

Appearances Before Official Bodies

(4) Subject to the rules of the official body, when a lawyer or any of his or her partners or associates is a member of an official body, the lawyer shall not appear professionally before that body.

Commentary

Subject to the rules of the official body, it would not be improper for a partner or associate to appear professionally before a committee of such body if such partner or associate is not a member of that committee, provided that in respect of matters in which such partner or associate appears, the lawyer does not sit on the committee, take part in the discussions of such committee's recommendations or vote upon them.

Conduct After Leaving Public Office

(5) A lawyer who has left public office shall not act for a client in connection with any matter for which the lawyer had substantial responsibility before leaving public office.

Commentary

It would not be improper for the lawyer to act professionally in such a matter on behalf of the public body in question.

A lawyer who has acquired confidential information by virtue of holding public office should keep such information confidential and not divulge or use it notwithstanding that the lawyer has ceased to hold such office.

6.06 PUBLIC APPEARANCES AND PUBLIC STATEMENTS

Communication with the Public

6.06(1) Provided that there is no infringement of the lawyer's obligations to the client, the profession, the courts, or the administration of justice, a lawyer may communicate information to the media and may make public appearances and statements.

> *Commentary*
>
> Lawyers in their public appearances and public statements should conduct themselves in the same manner as with their clients, their fellow practitioners, the courts, and tribunals. Dealings with the media are simply an extension of the lawyer's conduct in a professional capacity. The mere fact that a lawyer's appearance is outside of a courtroom, a tribunal, or the lawyer's office does not excuse conduct that would otherwise be considered improper.
>
> A lawyer's duty to the client demands that, before making a public statement concerning the client's affairs, the lawyer must first be satisfied that any communication is in the best interests of the client and within the scope of the retainer.
>
> Public communications about a client's affairs should not be used for the purpose of publicizing the lawyer and should be free from any suggestion that a lawyer's real purpose is self-promotion or self-aggrandizement.
>
> Given the variety of cases that can arise in the legal system, particularly so far as civil, criminal, and administrative proceedings are concerned, it is impossible to set down guidelines which would anticipate every possible circumstance. There are going to be circumstances where the lawyer should have no contact with the media and other cases where the lawyer is under a specific duty to contact the media to serve properly the client—the latter situation arising more often in the context of administrative boards and tribunals where a given tribunal is an instrument of government policy and hence is susceptible to public opinion.
>
> A lawyer is often involved in a non-legal setting where contact is made with the media with respect to publicizing such things as fundraising, expansion of hospitals or universities, programs of public institutions or political organizations, or in acting as a spokesman for organizations which, in turn, represent particular racial, religious or other special interest groups. This is a well-established and completely proper role for the lawyer to play, in view of the obvious contribution it makes to the community.
>
> A lawyer is often called upon to comment publicly on the effectiveness of existing statutory or legal remedies, on the effect of particular legislation or decided cases, or to offer an opinion with respect to cases that have been instituted or are about to be instituted. This,

too, is an important role the lawyer can play to assist the public in understanding legal issues.

A lawyer is often involved as advocate for special interest groups whose objective it is to bring about changes in legislation, governmental policy, or even a heightened public awareness about certain issues. This is also an important role that the lawyer can be called upon to play.

Lawyers should be conscious of the fact that when a public appearance is made or a statement is given the lawyer will ordinarily have no control over any editing that may follow or the context in which the appearance or statement may be used, or under what headline it may appear.

Interference with the Right to a Fair Trial or Hearing

(2) A lawyer shall not make a statement to the media about a matter before the court or a tribunal if the lawyer knows or ought to know that the statement will have a substantial likelihood of materially prejudicing a party's right to a fair trial or hearing.

Commentary

It is important to a free and democratic society that the public including the media be informed about cases before courts and tribunals. The administration of justice benefits from public scrutiny. It is also important that a person's, particularly an accused person's, right to a fair trial not be impaired by inappropriate public statements made before the case has concluded. Fair trials are fundamental to a free and democratic society.

The following are examples of extrajudicial statements that are likely to materially prejudice a party's right to a fair trial or hearing:

(a) a statement about the character, credibility, reputation, or criminal record of an accused or witness;

(b) a statement about other pending charges against an accused;

(c) a statement about the existence of any confession, admission, or statement made by an accused or about the accused's failure to make a statement;

(d) a statement about the possibility of a plea of guilty to the offence charged or to a lesser offence;

(e) a statement about the performance or results of any examination or tests or the refusal or failure of an accused to submit to examinations or tests;

(f) opinions concerning the guilt or innocence of the accused, the evidence or the merits of the case; and

(g) unsubstantiated out-of-court criticisms of the competence, conduct, advice, or motivation of a lawyer, police officer, public official, or of the judge involved in the matter.

The following are examples of extrajudicial statements that are not likely to materially prejudice a party's right to a fair trial or hearing:

(a) a statement about the general nature of the claim or charge;

(b) a statement about the fact, time and place of an arrest, the charges, and the date and place of a court appearance;

(c) where the accused has not yet been arrested and a warrant has been issued, any information necessary to aid in apprehension of the accused or to warn the public of any danger posed by the accused but no more information than necessary for these purposes;

(d) a statement about the identity of the investigative agency and the length of the investigation;

(e) a statement about the general nature of the defence including the fact that the accused is presumed innocent and denies the charge or charges;

(f) a statement about the name, age, residence of a person involved except where such information would identify a victim, complainant, or young offender in violation of any judicial or statutory publication ban;

(g) a request for assistance in obtaining evidence and information necessary for the prosecution or the defence; or

(h) information already contained in the public record in the proceedings in question that is not subject to any judicial or statutory publication ban.

6.07 PREVENTING UNAUTHORIZED PRACTICE

Preventing Unauthorized Practice

6.07(1) A lawyer shall assist in preventing the unauthorized practice of law.

Commentary

Statutory provisions against the practice of law by unauthorized persons are for the protection of the public. Unauthorized persons may have technical or personal ability, but they are immune from control, regulation and, in the case of misconduct, from discipline by the Society. Moreover, the client of a lawyer who is authorized to practise has the protection and benefit of the lawyer–client privilege, the lawyer's duty of secrecy, the professional standard of care which the law requires of lawyers, and the authority which the courts exercise over them. Other safeguards include professional liability insurance, rights with respect to the assessment of bills, rules respecting the handling of trust monies, and requirements as to the maintenance of compensation funds.

Disbarred Persons, Suspended Lawyers, and Others

(2) A lawyer shall not, without the express approval of Convocation, retain, occupy office space with, use the services of, partner or associate with or employ in any capacity

having to do with the practice of law any person who, in Ontario or elsewhere, has been disbarred and struck off the Rolls, suspended, undertaken not to practice, or who has been involved in disciplinary action and been permitted to resign as a result thereof, and has not been reinstated or yet been readmitted.

(3) Where a person has been suspended for non-payment of fees or for some reason not involving disciplinary action, the express approval referred to in subrule (2) may also be granted by a committee of Convocation appointed for this purpose.

6.08 RETIRED JUDGES RETURNING TO PRACTICE

Definitions

6.08(1) In this rule, "retired appellate judge" means a lawyer

(a) who was formerly a judge of the Supreme Court of Canada, the Court of Appeal for Ontario or the Federal Court of Canada, Appeal Division,

(b) who has retired, resigned, or been removed from the Bench, and

(c) who has returned to practice.

(2) In this rule, "retired judge" means a lawyer

(a) who was formerly a judge of the Federal Court of Canada, Trial Division, the Tax Court of Canada, the Supreme Court of Ontario, Trial Division, a County or District Court, the Ontario Court of Justice (General Division), or the Superior Court of Justice,

(b) who has retired, resigned, or been removed from the Bench, and

(c) who has returned to practice.

Appearance as Counsel

(3) A retired appellate judge shall not appear as counsel or advocate in any court, or in chambers, or before any administrative board or tribunal without the express approval of Convocation, which approval may only be granted in exceptional circumstances and may be restricted as Convocation sees fit.

(4) A retired judge shall not appear as counsel or advocate,

(a) before the court on which the judge served or any lesser court; and

(b) before any administrative board or tribunal over which the court on which the judge served exercised an appellate or judicial review jurisdiction;

for a period of two years from the date of his or her retirement, resignation or removal without the express approval of Convocation, which approval may only be granted in exceptional circumstances and may be restricted as Convocation sees fit.

6.09 ERRORS AND OMISSIONS

Notice of Claim

6.09(1) A lawyer shall give prompt notice of any circumstance that the lawyer may reasonably expect to give rise to a claim to an insurer or other indemnitor so that the client's protection from that source will not be prejudiced.

Commentary

The introduction of compulsory insurance has imposed additional obligations upon a lawyer, but such obligations must not impair the relationship and duties of the lawyer to the client. The insurer's rights must be preserved. There may well be occasions when a lawyer believes that certain actions or failure to take action have made the lawyer liable for damages to the client when in reality no liability exists. Further, in every case a careful assessment will have to be made of the client's damages arising from the lawyer's negligence. Many factors will have to be taken into account in assessing the client's claim and damages. As soon as a lawyer becomes aware that an error or omission may have occurred which may reasonably be expected to involve liability to the client for professional negligence, the lawyer should take the following steps:

1. Immediately arrange an interview with the client and advise the client forthwith that an error or omission may have occurred which may form the basis of a claim by the client against the lawyer.

2. Advise the client to obtain an opinion from an independent lawyer and that in the circumstances the first lawyer might no longer be able to act for the client.

3. Inform the Lawyers Professional Indemnity Company (LPIC), of the facts of the situation.

4. Co-operate to the fullest extent and as expeditiously as possible with the Society's adjusters in the investigation and eventual settlement of the claim.

5. Make arrangements to pay that portion of the client's claim that is not covered by the insurance forthwith upon completion of the settlement of the client's claim.

Co-operation

(2) Unless the client objects, a lawyer shall assist and co-operate with the insurer or other indemnitor to the extent necessary to enable any claim that is made to be dealt with promptly.

Responding to Client's Claim

(3) If a lawyer is not indemnified for a client's errors and omissions claim, or to the extent that the indemnity may not fully cover the claim, the lawyer shall expeditiously deal with the claim and shall not, under any circumstances, take unfair advantage that would defeat or impair the client's claim.

(4) In cases where liability is clear and the insurer or other indemnitor is prepared to pay its portion of the claim, a lawyer is under a duty to arrange for payment of the balance.

6.10 RESPONSIBILITY IN MULTI-DISCIPLINE PRACTICES

Compliance with These Rules

6.10 A lawyer in a multi-discipline practice shall ensure that non-lawyer partners and associates comply with these Rules and all ethical principles that govern a lawyer in the discharge of his or her professional obligations.

6.11 DISCIPLINE

Disciplinary Authority

6.11(1) A lawyer is subject to the disciplinary authority of the Society regardless of where the lawyer's conduct occurs.

Professional Misconduct

(2) The Society may discipline a lawyer for professional misconduct.

Conduct Unbecoming a Lawyer

(3) The Society may discipline a lawyer for conduct unbecoming a lawyer.